The Great American
SPORTS BOOK

The Great American SPORTS BOOK

A casual but voluminous look at American
spectator sports from the Civil War
to the present time

by

GEORGE GIPE

A DOLPHIN BOOK

DOUBLEDAY & COMPANY, INC.
GARDEN CITY, NEW YORK
1978

PHOTO CREDITS:

Cleveland Indians Baseball Club: No. 93

Frank Leslie's Illustrated Newspaper: Nos. 3, 4, 5, 6, 7, 8, 9, 10, 11, 12, 19, 27, 28, 30

Harper's Weekly: Nos. 13, 16, 17, 21, 29, 33, 34, 36, 37

Library of Congress: Nos. 1, 2, 14, 15, 17, 18, 20, 22, 23, 31, 45, 49, 51, 52, 57, 58, 59, 60, 61, 62, 66, 67

National Police Gazette: Nos. 24, 25, 26, 35, 46, 47, 48, 50, 87

Scientific American: Nos. 39, 40, 41, 42

Tadder Associates: Nos. 104, 121

UPI: Nos. 43, 44, 53, 54, 55, 56, 63, 64, 65, 68, 69, 70, 71, 72, 73, 74, 75, 76, 77, 78, 79, 80, 81, 82, 83, 84, 85, 86, 88, 89, 90, 91, 92, 94, 95, 96, 97, 98, 99, 100, 101, 102, 103, 105, 106, 107, 108, 109, 110, 111, 112, 113, 114, 115, 116, 117, 118, 119, 120, 122, 124, 125, 126, 127, 128, 129, 130, 131, 132, 133, 134, 135

To three sports I could not do without
—Nancy, Geordie, and Larry.

ACKNOWLEDGMENTS

All of the research and writing in this book—with the exception of certain obvious quotes—is the work of the author, who assumes responsibility for any shortcomings, errors, and omissions. The work could not have been completed, however, had it not been for the kindness and expert assistance of many people who donated time and extra effort whenever the author encountered problems. Some of these fine folks include:

Bob Hewes of The Johns Hopkins University, for allowing the use of that school's excellent Milton Eisenhower Library . . . Ms. Bobby Waybright of the Enoch Pratt Free Library, Baltimore, who spent countless hours digging out valuable books . . . Pete Carry and Melissa Ludtke of *Sports Illustrated,* for their encouragement and editorial assistance . . . Sam Lacy of the Baltimore *Afro-American,* who provided access to research in the area of black participation in athletics . . . Larry Ritter, for allowing the author to quote from his superb *The Glory of Their Times* . . . Jim Bready, whose book *The Home Team* is not only the story of a single city's rise to baseball prominence but also is one of the best-researched capsule histories of the national game ever written . . . and Zander Hollander, whose knowledge of basketball, as well as his writings in that field, provided valuable help.

In the area of picture research, special thanks must be given to Charles Purcell for the use of his photographic know-how and to Dan Gallagher of United Press International, whose genial disposition will be a revelation to all who feel New Yorkers are inherently gruff.

Finally, a bow to literary agent *par excellence* Elaine Markson and editor Patrick Filley, who really and truly made it all happen.

Contents

PUBLISHER'S NOTE

The primary purpose of *The Great American Sports Book,* of course, is to provide reading entertainment, but it also fills a historical void. Heretofore, many books have been written about sports in the United States. The overall subject has not been neglected, but unfortunately most of the works have been either encyclopedias dealing with statistics and records; books restricted to a single report or sports figure; or picture books accompanied by lengthy sections of ponderous copy.

The Great American Sports Book, because of its unique format, broad scope, yet attention to detail and human anecdote, is the first history of all American spectator sports that is fun and easy to read. It is neither a book of trivia nor records, although it contains both. Constructed in brief modules, it is simultaneously a book for browsing and serious cover-to-cover reading.

The format of *The Great American Sports Book* consists of eleven sections, each spanning a decade from the end of the Civil War—when spectator sports became possible for the fan with more leisure time and profitable for the promoter—to the present. Contained in each section is one chapter that describes the sports events that made news during a single year of that decade. (The author has chosen years ending with "1" as his subjects.) In addition, each section contains brief rundowns for every year in the decade, listing results of major athletic competitions as well as other sports happenings that happen to be significant, funny, tragic, or outrageous. There are also at least two thematically related chapters per section dealing at length with various aspects of American sports. (Section I, for example, is dedicated to "fixes" and "flaps" in acknowledgment of the fact that while sports may seem orderly, they've often generated considerable player shiftiness and fan controversy.) Finally, a picture segment provides visual illustration of the decade.

Because of this format, *The Great American Sports Book* can be used as both a reference book (Which team won the National League pennant in 1899? Who was middleweight champion in 1927? The answers are there.) and a kind of people's almanac of sports information that can be read in short spurts. And for those with an orderly mind, it should be added that reading the book from the first page to the end will reveal a comprehensive progression of spectator sports in the United States.

The total length of *The Great American Sports Book,* about 325,000 words, insures that most of the truly significant events of all sports during the past century are included. It also allows the author room to include minor but interesting happenings that have never found their way into other books dealing with sports Americana.

The Great American
SPORTS BOOK

CHAPTER 1

In the fall of 1977, an "ABC Monday Night Football" game was interrupted briefly by a news report dealing with terrorists having hijacked an airliner. Frank Gifford, veteran TV sports commentator and former USC-New York Giant golden boy, followed the report with his own comment, "This serves to remind us that what we're seeing tonight is really just a game."

For one of the chief participants in the wedding of electronic entertainment and spectator sports, such an admission was an unexpected expression of philosophical depth. We Americans, after all, had been taught for quite a while to regard the fates of our favorite teams and sports heroes in nothing short of life-and-death terms. "Winning is the only thing," said Vince Lombardi, and we believed. Thus our involvement as spectators, which hardly can be regarded as peripheral, sometimes caused us to write angry letters to editors, adorn our cars with bumper stickers, endure interminable waits and inconveniences, eat food with such dubious quality it would be discarded in another situation, allow the Hyde side of us to overwhelm the Jekyll in broad daylight, causing us to riot, indulge in blasphemy, dig worthless chunks of sod from stadia floors, even occasionally to pray. At the same time, we tended to regard such inanities as nuclear weapons proliferation, national elections, pollution, decaying cities, and a dangerously out-of-control economy with sullen scorn, proud apathy, or apparent ignorance.

Given the opportunity to examine contemporary Americans and their priorities from the perspective of a simpler and safer past, our antecedents might be shocked and dismayed at our preoccupation with and dedication to what they would consider trivia. For them, it was infinitely more important to contemplate eternity with a capital E and the means of spending it at a comfortable temperature than to watch grown men sweat as they punished a piece of inflated leather. Hard work, national honor, and freedom from debt were all ends in themselves, goals much worthier than the struggle to attain the transitory joy of living in the suburbs of some "Titletown, U.S.A."

It would be easy for our antecedents, if they could study us, to regard Americans of the late twentieth century as supine members of a shallow and hedonistic society. And yet the times certainly have changed. Those who came before us never faced such temptation as modern man. Even the most decadent Roman gladiator watcher had to keep his eyes glued to the action lest he miss the kill. No instant replay for him. Early Americans who regarded corn liquor and a buxom farm wench as the ultimate weapons in God's arsenal of earthly temptations simply could not have conceived of the electronic age's contribution to the insidiously fine art of being lavishly entertained at the touch of a button. Thanks largely to television, sports watching has changed from a national diversion into a national pastime. Who can say that if the positions were reversed, that flint-hard Yankee of yesteryear would not fall easily into line as Dyed-in-the-wool Fan No. 1?

If one regards the current American—and in many ways, international—preoccupation with sports as an evil thing, our antecedents can be thankful that, purely by chance, the cup was removed from their reach. Organized sporting events were limited prior to the American Civil War, both the Church and lay establishment frowning on nearly everything that did not point directly to a pious or practical end. Sex, for example, had been invented so that the species could multiply. Reading—the works of approved masters but not necessarily Shakespeare or some of the racier novelists—elevated the spirit and prepared the reader for heaven's grace. Athletic activity, if indulged in as pure exercise, was tolerable. It was not acceptable if it encouraged people to stand about, idly watching, or even worse, to use as a focal point for a wager.

In addition to social attitudes, time worked against our antecedents and sports getting together in a style to which modern Americans are accustomed. Two declared wars, plus at least two undeclared ones, during the first four decades of the new nation's existence diverted both mental and physical energy from the pursuit of anything as recreational in nature as sports-watching.

On a personal level, time was also the enemy of the average man. Early employers tended to be rather like George Washington, who wrote to the overseer of his estate "to request that my people may be at their work as soon as it is light, work till it is dark, and be diligent while they are at it . . ." Added historian Carl Russel Fish: "Few American men had sufficient leisure for much participation in or attendance at games." When Boston workingmen agitated for a ten-hour work day, they were told that "the habits likely to be generated by this indulgence in idleness . . . will be very detrimental to the journeymen individually and very costly to us as a community."

Those opposing shorter hours need not have worried. As late as 1850, the average worker put in nearly seventy hours each and every six-day week, which left few daylight hours for "indulgence in idleness," much less athletic competition or watching. Sunday blue laws, originally inspired by piety, inhibited sports even more on the Sabbath.

There were other factors in addition to those imposed by societal pressure and time. Epidemics of yellow fever and cholera ravaged the nation from the 1790s through the 1850s, spreading death and terror wherever people congregated. Because populations in the crowded cities and along trade routes were hardest hit, those who could only guess at the disease's cause reckoned that quarantine or isolation were safer than any activity that might encourage people to come together in large groups. Agonizingly slow modes of transportation also served as a deterrent to the growth of spectator sports, as did pretelegraphic methods of communication. As a result, few newspapers or periodicals carried much, if any, sports news. A typical example was Horace Greeley's New York *Tribune,* which came into existence on April 10, 1841, and went through twenty-three issues before it grudgingly gave space to its first sports item, the proceedings of a ball game. (The readers must have liked the idea, for a few weeks later, Greeley allotted page-one space for an account of a "ball play game between Bulexe and the Choktaw Indians." The latter team won, incidentally, collecting as a reward the clothing of the defeated team.) In any event, with sports news being the exception rather than the rule, without much promotion of athletic events and the physical means of getting to the scene, it followed that America's early sports watcher was frustrated in all aspects of the game.

There were exceptions to all of these restrictions, of course. Seeking readers for his penny newspaper, the New York *Herald,* James Gordon Bennett, Sr., frequently published accounts of horse races and prizefights, as did Benjamin Day in the *Sun.* Writing in *Spirit of the Times,* William Henry Herbert, using the pen name Frank Forester, became the first writer in America to earn a living writing about horses and hunting.

In fact, horseracing enthusiasts were generally well served during the early nineteenth century, many events drawing huge crowds and generating a great deal of publicity. On May 10, 1842, for example, a match race between Fashion and Boston, won by the former, attracted seventy thousand spectators, including forty United States senators and congressmen, to the Union Race Course on Long Island. A dozen years later, President Millard Fillmore and twenty thousand others traveled to a track in New Orleans, Louisiana, to see the great horse Lexington defeat previously unbeaten Lecomte in a two-heat match race.

With most sports gaining gradual acceptance by the public—boxing was the exception —a major breakthrough seemed imminent during the late 1850s. On April 12, 1859, the first United States billiard match to receive international attention was played at Detroit, Michigan, Michael Phelan defeating John Seeriter for what was called the "world championship." Six months later, the sporting world focused its eyes on, of all places, Hoboken, New Jersey, where a cricket tournament was held between a team of English all-stars and the St. George's Cricket Club of New York City. That summer also saw a pair of amateur firsts, Amherst beating Williams College, 66–32, in the first college baseball game, and Harvard's crew defeating Yale and Brown in the first intercollegiate regatta, rowed over a three-mile course on Lake Quinsigamond, Worcester, Massachusetts. Organized baseball took a giant step on July 20 of the same year when two teams representing New York and Brooklyn charged an admission fee of fifty cents.

In the West, San Francisco became the prewar center of sports activity, organized baseball starting there in February 1860, just three months before the founding of the Olympic Club of San Francisco, the oldest organization in the United States to be dedicated to athletics.

The American Civil War interrupted the growth of public interest in sports but did not halt it. In fact, the conflict is a convenient and accurate "before" and "after" benchmark with which to measure the coming of age of American spectator sports. Before that conflict, going to an athletic event was simply not a regular part of the average person's life; after, it gradually became commonplace.

It is somewhat ironic that this quiet revolution occurred from 1870 to 1900, the late Victorian age, which many modern Americans assume was dull, stuffy, and lacking in innovative spirit. Actually, it was an era of experimentation as well as rapid change in technology and social attitudes. People did strange things then, such as jumping off the Brooklyn

Bridge or pushing a wheelbarrow from coast to coast; women engaged men in athletic competitions, formed baseball teams, and proved they could do stunts hanging from a balloon as well as their male counterparts. Young people even rebelled then. When informed by their elders that bicycle riding was not lady-like, the ladies kept right on doing it. True, there were more timid folks than iconoclasts, but the adventurous spirit was applauded, either aloud or secretly.

Exactly why the revolution occurred at this time is probably a quirk of history. For one thing, it was a period of extended peace in international affairs and comparative quiet at home. With the exception of the 1873 *Virginius* imbroglio, which nearly propelled the United States and Spain into a war for which neither was prepared, and later brushes with Germany and Chile, the United States spent the years from the conclusion of the American Civil War to the brief conflict with Spain in 1898 in improving itself. In 1840, it ranked fifth as an industrial power. By 1888, it was first.

It was an age of invention, producing the electric light, Kodak camera, linotype, portable typewriter, phonograph, and zipper. Its sporting thinkers also dreamed up the Preakness and Kentucky Derby, professional baseball and ladies' day at the ball park, lawn tennis, American-style football, the rain check, ice hockey, boxing with gloves, basketball, the turnstile, polo, target archery, and the first modern Olympic Games. Baseball and football, early daylight outdoor sports, took advantage of technology to play their first games under electric lights at night and indoors.

The development of better transportation systems helped also. As more people left the farm to earn their fortunes in the city, which in turn was swelled by thousands of immigrants, team franchises attached themselves to population centers. As electric streetcars replaced horse-drawn vehicles it became possible to move thousands of people several miles quickly and cheaply. It was hardly a coincidence, then, that early baseball operators found the means to have streetcar lines pass by their parks. Baseball magnates Al Johnson, Frank Robison, and Henry Lucas were all active in the traction business, owning both the franchise and car lines, a profitable double-play combination. When Chris Von der Ahe built a new Sportsmen's Park at St. Louis, he gave the Lindell Railway Company two hundred feet of land next to the park for a loop. The generosity soon paid for itself.

By the 1880s the vicious circle working against spectator sports before the Civil War began to reverse itself. Sensing increased pub-lic interest in the feats of pedestrians, scullers, and baseball teams, the newspapers of the time devoted more space to sports. Most big-city newspapers did not have a special and separate sports page by the 1880s, but they had discarded the practice of treating sports as miscellaneous items that could be dropped in wherever there happened to be space. Among others, the San Francisco *Chronicle,* New York *Herald,* and New York *Times* all had specific areas where the early fan could look and be assured of finding a regular column or two of sports information. By the end of the century, the sports page was standard fare in most up-to-date newspapers.

During this time, technology also produced the bicycle, which involved the average woman in sports for the first time. "It is safe to say," wrote an official of the U. S. Census Bureau in 1900, "that few articles ever used by man created so great a revolution as the bicycle." The gentleman was absolutely right, for the bicycle not only put a small army of vibrant young women on the road with their male counterparts, it also changed the very nature of American womanhood as well as the style of clothing she wore and the way she acted toward men.

Before the 1880s when "wheeling" became popular, the American woman was a uniped. No professor of comparative anatomy would have admitted this in print, but it was nevertheless a fact of life in the United States as well as most other Western nations. Man at this time flaunted his two-leggedness by wearing tight trousers, crossing his legs, and walking with long strides. When he mounted a horse, he casually threw one leg across the animal's back and rode astride his mount.

In contrast, the normal woman was forced to sit bolt upright in her floor-length skirt with her feet together. When she walked, her gait was mincing, rather like that of a trained seal, and when she rode a horse, it was sidesaddle, in a manner that not only diminished her security but also practically wore holes in the poor creature's back. In this way, people of good breeding preserved the myth that woman was a one-legged animal, which solved many problems of a carnal nature.

Accepting this myth was a relatively simple matter—until the bicycle came along. Then a startling fact emerged. It was not—and still is not—possible for a person to ride a bicycle comfortably with one leg. To properly manipulate the pedals the rider must have two separate limbs. Even worse, the limbs must work in such a manner as to emphasize the contours of the upper thigh and hemispheric undulations of the buttocks.

This was more than the dedicated moralists could stand. At first, bans were tried. In

Flushing, New York, a school board resolved that it was immoral for any young lady to ride a bicycle and further noted that if the lady happened to be a teacher, "the practice had a tendency to create immorality among the children of both sexes." Alarmed at the report, Justice of the Peace William Sutton proposed a resolution that banned women teachers from riding their vehicles to and from the schoolroom. Such tactics, of course, served only to make the bicycle more attractive to all women.

Thus thwarted, the opponents of bicycle riding for ladies dreamed up a variety of outfits for the women to wear as a means of disguising the fact that they had two legs instead of one. Baggy Zouave trousers or ingeniously devised split skirts became the order of the day. In February of 1895, the battle was still being fought when Mrs. Frank Sittig announced an exhibition of her new duplex bicycle skirt. On the day of the show, models Eva A. McKean, "the talented young elocutionist," and Vietta Huyler, "the well-known amateur actress," pedaled decorously around a rink in Brooklyn, each wearing a combination skirt-trouser set later adjudged by the New York *Times* to be "An ideal suit for cycling, to which even the most prudish could not object."

Some persons, naturally, would settle for no compromise. In Delaware County, New York, a farmer put up a sign reading, "Any idiot of the new women species found riding or walking on these premises will be arrested." When asked to elaborate on what he meant by "new women species," the farmer defined her as "one of these fools in bloomer costume on a wheel." Even someone as worldly as actress Sarah Bernhardt objected to the bicycle on the grounds that "It brings young people together in conditions unfavorable to strict surveillance."

By the turn of the century, however, the bicycle had done its work. Women were two-legged creatures who were more than ever interested in all sports. Observing this new breed of woman, her grandmother, who grew up before the Civil War, could hardly be blamed if she experienced and expressed a sense of outrage liberally tinged with envy.

The specifics of this two-generation gap explain why this book, which is dedicated to American spectator sports, substantially begins in the 1870s rather than a century earlier. Before the Civil War, observing an athletic contest was the occasional pastime of the elite. Only when technology and opportunity combined did sports watching become a truly democratic institution.

During the decades since that Victorian revolution, Americans have embraced sports closer to our collective breast. Perhaps so closely, as the critics point out, that we have made vicarious success in sports a substitute for success in our personal lives and the life of our country. In the 1920s, the Reverend Dr. John Roach Straton, who was appalled at the nation's growing involvement in athletics, said, "The weaker we become as a people, the more we will point with pride to our 'strong' men. . . ."

Have we indeed come too far? A case can be made for opposing points of view. Americans of World War II who fought for "the right to boo the Dodgers" did not fare too badly in the defense of their national honor. But, of course, that was many years ago. Weakened by the excesses of Sunday afternoon football double-headers, it could well be that modern Americans lack the stamina to accomplish voluntarily what our antecedents did because they had litttle choice. On the other hand, the next crisis may be solved by energetic Americans willing to pay the price for "the right to boo millionaire athletes."

In the meantime, we have Frank Gifford to remind us that it is, after all, only a game. And hopefully this book will prove helpful by reminding us that previous generations of Americans, themselves caught up in the sports mania, frequently acted as strangely and crazily as we do.

Section I
The 1870s

CHAPTER 2—1871

As the new year began, Americans found themselves concerned with a variety of issues and situations. James W. Smith, the unprecedented "colored cadet" at West Point, was a name much in the news as his court-martial trial for "conduct unbecoming an officer and a gentleman" continued. . . . The city of Paris was under siege by a powerful Prussian army but some Americans were considerably more worried by a Communist takeover there. . . . The possible statehood of Colorado and New Mexico was being debated. . . . For entertainment in a sedentary style, many people were reading the best-selling (and even better promoted) novel *Adrift with a Vengeance* by Kinahan Cornwallis.

ICE SKATING

For the sports participant and spectator, there was hardly a wide variety of activity, but at least it appeared that the rivers of the northeastern United States would be covered with ice, which did not happen during the comparatively mild winter of 1869–70. That meant plenty of skating and ice yachting, perhaps many exciting races. While waiting for the Hudson and East rivers to freeze over, crowds in the New York area amused themselves at the commercial ice rinks, many of which had been started following the Civil War craze for ice skating. One of the most popular of these rinks was Brady's in Jersey City, which featured not only a broad expanse of smooth ice but also organized fun on a kinky level. On the evening of January 10, for example, Brady's was crowded with young men and women who had come there not only to skate and "coquette," but also to watch the silly contests devised by the rink management. The first of these featured blindfolded contestants. After being properly masked, six entrants were turned loose, to the delight of the crowd. A gentleman named Weir, described by the newspapers as "the winner of the hurtle race last Thursday," obviously knew what he was doing, for he moved well ahead of the others, reaching the first stake, "followed by his adversaries, who battled with the doors and benches of the rink in fine style amid roars of laughter from the gentlemen and applause from the ladies."

Mr. Weir, as might be expected, won the race and was awarded a silver pitcher for his efforts. The management promised that future events would include a boy's and gentlemen's backward race, a grand pig-chase on ice, a serpentine whirligig, and a serious speed race, the prize for which would be an equally serious "silver allegorical card holder." Just what everyone wanted, no doubt.

OTHER SPORTS ON ICE

In the absence of genuine cold-weather spectator sports, Americans of 1871 adapted warm-weather games to the ice. Before the month of January was over, skaters had played baseball on ice in the northeastern United States, as well as a form of football—really soccer, with fifteen men on a side—cricket, and lacrosse, not to mention a number of well-attended curling matches and exhibitions.

HORSERACING

During that cold month of January 1871, there was plenty of time to at least talk of warm-weather sports. On January 7, the Maryland Jockey Club announced that there would be two major sweepstakes during the fall meet at the brand-new track known as Pimlico, which had opened the previous year. These would be the Central Stakes, a one-mile sprint for two-year-olds, and the Pimlico

Stakes for four-year-olds. "This will undoubtedly prove a valuable stake," one writer predicted, "and as Enquirer, Foster, King-fisher, Preakness, and McCloskey are certain to be entered, the betting-man will be troubled to pick out the winner."

Racing at the Fair:
The final day of the Horse and Cattle Fair of the Bay District Agricultural Association, San Francisco, featured a number of exciting events on August 26. One of the chief attractions was a series of races between the trotters Alexander, May Fly, the well-known Dexter, and Mary Davis. Moving along the mile course in the then-rapid time of 2:31¾, Alexander easily took the first heat. He then returned to win the second in 2:34¼. The fair also featured a novelty race between a D. McCarthy of Stockton and a pacing horse, McCue. The man ran a half mile while the horse was required to cover a full mile. The horse won.

BASEBALL

Around the warm stoves, baseball—already referred to as "the National Game"—was widely discussed, for with the formation of the National Association of Professional Baseball Players, the first play-for-pay league was about to begin. Amateur baseball clubs were losing the services of players left and right, a fact that infuriated many purists, who predicted the game would become the sole province of gamblers, toughs, and seedy, money-grubbing athletes of the worst type. While this new aspect of the game was being debated, many "cranks" discussed which of the new professional teams had the best chance to win the pennant. Most intelligent observers predicted that the Boston Red Stockings would be extremely hard to beat, largely because they had the services of baseball's Wright Brothers, Harry and George, in the outfield and at shortstop, as well as the redoubtable Al Spalding on the mound. But the new Washington Olympics had grabbed five players who were former members of the 1869 Cincinnati Red Stockings, which had barnstormed the nation without a defeat that year. The Philadelphia Athletics, meanwhile, had signed Ferguson Malone as catcher, Levi Meyerle at third base, and Wes Fisler at first. The Mutuals of New York raided nearby Brooklyn for pitcher Bob Ferguson and were planning to use Joe Start at first base. (All of these young men eventually saw action not only in the National Association but also went on to play in the National League's inaugural season five years later.)

No one knew, as of January, exactly how many teams the NA would field. Jim Fisk, the rich speculator, had promised to back a team in Erie, Pennsylvania, but had not been heard from for several weeks. Brooklyn officials were teetering on the fence, no doubt debating whether the new professional league was worth the ten-dollar franchise fee. Cleveland, Fort Wayne, and Rockford, Illinois, were mentioned as possible sites, but the only certain entries were the teams of Philadelphia, New York, Chicago, Boston, Washington, and Troy, who were known as the "Haymakers."

ICE YACHTING

While these discussions continued, interest grew in the Poughkeepsie Ice-boat Association's annual race on the Hudson River. As soon as the upper part of the river was solid, a couple of crews, those of *Zephyr,* owned by J. Buckhout, and *Icicle,* owned by John Roosevelt of Hyde Park, began practicing for the meet. On Friday, January 20, it was decided to race the vessels against an express train out of New York bound for Chicago. With a strong breeze from the southwest behind them, the crews of *Zephyr* and *Icicle* held their craft at a standstill just north of the Poughkeepsie whale dock until the locomotive sounded its whistle. Then "in an instant they were in their boats lying at full length . . . 'down stick' . . . their crafts into the wind."

A sizable crowd that had collected on the shore shouted encouragement to the men on the ice boats. At the same time, passengers on the train braved the winter cold, raising the windows in order to wave and shout at the crewmen pursuing. Joining in the fun, the train's engineer "blew tantalizing whistles as the train thundered through the rock cuts and over bridges, leaving the ice boats gradually way astern . . ."

For a while, it seemed the locomotive would win "in a breeze," but as the wind freshened, the canvas of the ice boats' sails swelled, rigging tightened, and steel runners "commenced humming over the clear, smooth, black ice . . . Then the tillermen of the boats knew they had their ironbound adversary." First *Zephyr* moved past the train, then *Icicle,* both "slipping over the ice at the rate of a mile a minute . . . Never was there a prettier race." After establishing their superiority, the men of the two ice boats veered sideways and waited for the puffing train, which blew one final blast of congratulations as it swung north and west.

Ice Yachting's First Fatality:

On January 20, 1871, while speeding along the ice-encrusted Hudson River, young Jacob Best was stretched full length on the waistboard of his craft when one of his runners struck a crack. Best was shaken loose, right into the path of Ira Whiting's ice boat out of Athens, New York. Best's left breast was caved in by Whiting's bow sprit, causing a death that was at least mercifully quick. "He cried, 'O dear' once, gasped twice, and was a corpse," one account concluded with rather more color than tact.

A month later, spectators came from many miles away to see *Zephyr* and *Icicle* meet in the annual boat race. There were four additional entries, including *Ella, Newsboy, Snowflake,* and *Haze.* Crowds of people lined the area about the pier, and nearby buildings were decorated with flags and bunting to mark the event.

The prize for which the six crews were competing was an eighteen-inch-tall silver wine pitcher designed by Tiffany and Company and valued at two hundred dollars. The course was a "circular" one, in that it was eight miles downriver to a stakeboat and back. On the judge's signal, the ice boats launched themselves into the northeast wind and *Ella* took the lead "with almost the rapidity of lightning." *Newsboy* was right behind, but only briefly. Caught by a "flaw of wind," the craft's nose shot high into the air and she was "whisked like a top," the crewman on the windward runner hurled a hundred yards away, "like a ball from a cannon," as the crowd roared with amusement.

Zephyr, in rapid pursuit, promptly shattered a runner and had to be pulled out of the race, but John Roosevelt's *Icicle* quickly closed the gap and actually passed *Ella* near the stakeboat. Then, just when it seemed *Icicle* would certainly be the winner, the crowd, which had positioned itself near the stakeboat, began to groan or shout. Instead of swinging about, *Icicle* was continuing downstream at top speed! Not until the boat reached the Hamburg buoy was it seen to slow down, veer about, and start up the river. By that time, *Ella* had negotiated the turn at the stakeboat, followed by *Haze, Snowflake,* and *Newsboy* in that order, and all four were heading back toward the finish line.

Apparently *Icicle* was a much faster than average craft, for despite the mistake, she managed to slide past *Newsboy,* then *Snowflake* and *Haze.* But *Ella,* crossing the finish line just thirty-two seconds before *Icicle,* was declared the winner. John Roosevelt protested heartily, explaining that he thought the Hamburg buoy was the turn-around marker. He was politely told to "wait until next year," or diplomatic words to that effect.

BOXING

Early in March, boxing or "prize fighting" briefly became the center of attention when Sam Collyer, a Baltimore lightweight, entered a New York saloon at 8 Centre Street that was noted for housing backers of Billy Edwards, a rival fighter. Collyer and Edwards had tangled twice, with Edward winning both times, but Collyer was convinced he had somehow been cheated out of victory by a lesser man. Buoyed by a few drinks, he waited until Edwards dropped by the saloon, then proceeded to call him a coward, and as one account noted, "many other bad names." For a while, Edwards tried to ignore the abuse; then a rough-and-tumble fight started, the saloon's patrons guarding the doors to make sure no police officers tried to break it up. After several minutes, Collyer was beaten once again. He was ushered out of the tavern, nursing a battered forehead and "a frightful wound in his cheek."

Meanwhile, at Collier's, another saloon not far away, a group of baseball men sat down to determine the rules of the new professional league. Ten cities were represented, but only nine eventually participated in the opening season of the National Association. (Brooklyn declined, but later entered the NA as the Eckfords.)

Professional Baseball's First Franchises:

BOSTON (Red Stockings)
CLEVELAND (Forest Citys)
CHICAGO (White Stockings)
FORT WAYNE (Kekiongas)
NEW YORK (Mutuals)
PHILADELPHIA (Athletics)
ROCKFORD (Forest Citys)
TROY (Haymakers)
WASHINGTON (Olympics)

A month later, as if to dramatize the difference in quality of play between the new professionals and old amateurs, the New York Mutuals took on the much-raided Brooklyn Atlantics, which in its day had been an outstanding amateur nine. On April 24, 1871, however, before a thousand spectators mostly rooting for the amateurs, the Mutuals pounded out forty hits, graciously accepted twenty-two fielding errors by the Atlantics, and went on to win by a score of 48–5. With the inaugural season less than two weeks away, anticipation was high, even in cities such as Cincinnati, which were not directly involved in the venture. "So the prospect is gay for plenty of exciting sport this coming baseball season," one particularly enthusiastic writer concluded.

BASEBALL'S FIRST PROFESSIONAL GAME

It was "gay," indeed, especially when on May 4, the first professional baseball game was played and turned out to be an extremely fine contest. Fortunately for trivia fans, only one game was played that day. Thus a wealth of "firsts" sprang into being during the same two-hour period of the same game, including, of course, the plating of baseball's first professional run, without which there could have been no one-millionth run 104 years later.

The unlikely site of this memorable event was Fort Wayne, Indiana; the team had an even unlikelier name, Kekiongas. Apparently, "Kekionga" was the original Miami Indian name for the tribal village that stood where Fort Wayne does now. During the late 1860s, the leading amateur baseball teams of that city adopted "Kekiongas" as their nickname. In order to get into the National Association, the Fort Wayne team also "adopted" an entire group of players from the powerful semipro Maryland Base Ball Club, which happened to be touring the Midwest during the summer of 1870 and never returned home. After seeing how much talent was contained on the Maryland team, a group of Fort Wayne businessmen suggested that the nine turn fully professional and represent their city. The Marylanders agreed—partly, it has been suggested, because there was no train fare home. At any rate, the transplanted Maryland team was officially the Fort Wayne Kekiongas on May 4, 1871, when the Cleveland Forest Citys came to town for pro ball's first game.

Some Other Teams of the Same Era:
Jersey City Resolutes
Memphis Orientals
Buffalo Niagaras
St. Louis Maroons
Middletown Mansfields
Philadelphia Centennials
Rochester Flour Citys
New Orleans Pelicans
New Orleans Robert E. Lees

The first batter was Cleveland catcher James (Deacon) White, the first pitcher nineteen-year-old Bobby Mathews, the first pitch a ball. White then collected the game's (and pro baseball's) first hit, a double. Gene Kimball lofted a soft liner toward center field but Fort Wayne shortstop Tom Carey grabbed the ball and stepped on second base, doubling White and executing baseball's first unassisted double play.

In the second inning, Cleveland's Art Allison became the first strikeout victim, but on the crucial final swing, Kekionga catcher Bill Lennon committed the first passed ball and Allison reached first base safely.

During the home half of the same inning, however, Lennon achieved the honor of scoring baseball's first run. After smashing a double, he raced home on teammate Joe McDermott's single.

Only one additional run was scored after that, the Kekiongas' 2–0 lead holding up until the bottom half of the ninth, when a sudden downpour caused the game to become the first weather-shortened contest in baseball history. (It had no effect on the outcome, of course, as the Forest Citys had already completed their final time at bat.)

The game, naturally, was baseball's first shutout, and also the lowest-scoring contest in the first four years of the National Association. Everyone agreed that it was a particularly fine game, obviously it being a part of the baseball lover's credo even then that the lower the scoring the better and more interesting the game. That sort of contest did not come along very often, however. A much more representative game was played at Washington a day later between the hometown Olympics and the Boston Red Stockings. The park was jammed with three thousand customers when Harry Wright, Boston captain, won the toss and elected to have the Olympics bat first. Al Spalding then proceeded to walk the first batter, opening the floodgates for a Washington six-run first inning.

Boston scored one run in the bottom of the first, but the Olympics came back with four more in the second to lead, 10–1. Only two of the runs were earned, thanks to George Wright's error on a fly ball.

By the sixth inning, it was Washington 15, Boston 8, but in the bottom of the seventh, Olympic catcher Doug Allison (brother of Cleveland Forest City outfielder Art Allison) split his thumb and had to leave the game. This, according to one reporter, had a "disheartening effect upon the Blues," who had to shift players at three positions to replace Allison. The Red Stockings bounced back to

Whatever Became of Baseball's "First-makers"?

Of the eighteen players who took part in professional baseball's first contest, only a few went on to greater things in the world of sports. Deacon White played until 1890 with a variety of clubs, but premier run-scorer Bill Lennon was out of baseball by 1873. Joe McDermott, credited with that first RBI, also quit the same year. Bobby Mathews went on to pitch for Baltimore, New York, Brooklyn, Cincinnati, Providence, Boston, and Philadelphia before hanging up his glove in 1887. He died in 1898.

score four runs in that inning, making it 15–12.

Showing their grit, the Olympics scored three in the eighth, but so did the Red Stockings. The game went into the bottom of the ninth with the Olympics ahead, 18–15.

Harry Wright, first Boston batter, walked to open the inning, Charlie Gould singled and Harry Schafer doubled, sending two runs home. Al Spalding then singled over second and went to that base as Schafer scored. The game was tied, and Washington fans groaned. A few moments later, Ross Barnes' hit scored the go-ahead run, but according to the rules of the time, play continued until the side was retired. Before Cal McVey grounded out for the game-ending blow, the score was Boston 20, Washington 18.

That, in fact, was a fair sampling of the way the 1871 season started for powerful Boston. During the first week, the Red Stockings played seven games, winning all of them. In the process, they scored a total of 187 runs to 46 for the opposition.

By the time baseball's first runs had scored, the public was caught up in still other sports events. Some pored over telegraphic accounts of the annual British Oxford-Cambridge boat race. Closer to home, there was an important shooting match at Greenville, New Jersey. The participants were John Taylor, an Eastern Seaboard favorite; Fletcher Tueris, described as "the California boy"; and about two hundred unsuspecting pigeons.

PIGEON SHOOTING

There was some concern as to whether the match would take place or not, for Henry Bergh, president of the New York Society for the Prevention of Cruelty to Animals, had made unfavorably threatening noises regarding the sport of pigeon shooting. He did not attend this particular match, however, as he sometimes did, as a form of protest. Instead, he merely reiterated to reporters that his organization was already firmly on record as being opposed to pigeon shooting. Not only was it "cruel and demoralizing," Mr. Bergh said, but also the pigeon was a "heavenly symbol."

Heavenly symbol or not, Taylor and Tueris prepared to bring the birds down by the score. The match, attended by several hundred spectators, began under a clear sky, "shining with all its maiden refulgence," but only a few moments passed before clouds gathered and a pelting rain poured down. (Perhaps Mr. Bergh was right, after all, in calling the pigeon a "heavenly symbol.") That, unfortunately, did not deter the shooters, who "kept right on in their destructive work and sent the feathered victims of their sport into the eternity of such birds." Two hours and forty-eight minutes later, Taylor was declared the winner as a result of having slaughtered eighty of ninety-six pigeons let loose, while Tueris had managed to kill off only seventy-three of ninety-five.

BOXING

At approximately the same time, another form of organized mayhem attracted Americans' attention. Two important prize-fights were announced, one for the heavyweight and one for the lightweight championship. Billy Edwards, unmarked from his saloon encounter with Sam Collyer, was scheduled to fight for the latter crown with Tim Collins. But of even more interest was the heavyweight scrap, for it pitted colorful James (Jim or Jem) Mace—who at forty years of age could still hit but not move very well—against somewhat younger but less colorful Joe Coburn. Late in April, in anticipation of the two bouts, a horde of ex-fighters, promoters, gamblers, and toughs descended on New York City. As one benefit show followed another, the *Herald* saw fit to comment on the popular mania. "New York, perhaps, in its maddest moment of pugilistic bliss, never had a gayer time nor saw a more appropriate assemblage than was gathered last night." Then, noting the amount of money being wagered, it was added that "even the soft depths of the feminine heart were aroused and wagers of dozens of gloves and elegant bouquets, with seats at the opera, were freely offered and taken. New bonnets and glitteringly gilded boxes of bonbons were articles of frequent interchange upon decisions of feminine opinion. . . ."

Adding even more excitement to the events was news that still another celebrated pug, Ned O'Baldwin, had been released from prison at Lawrence, Massachusetts. O'Baldwin, called "the Irish Giant," and a dedicated rowdy who spent an entire lifetime bouncing in and out of prison for fighting in and outside the ring, promptly announced that he could lick either of the heavyweights and would conduct the fight for any amount "from ten cents to ten thousand dollars." On April 30 it was announced that both fights would take place in May, the Mace-Coburn bout in Canada, opposite Buffalo. Canadian officials stated that the fight would be stopped and the participants sent to jail. Such a statement, of course, only added to the air of excitement.

BILLIARDS

While waiting to see if the matches would actually take place, some turned their attentions to the gentler art of billiards. On April 21 at the Crosby Opera House in Chicago, a match for the championship of America was held. About fifteen hundred people, including at least two hundred ladies, attended the affair, which pitted Cyrille Dion, widely recognized as the best player at the time, against Frank Parker. In contrast to some of the matches of that era, the Dion-Parker contest was "one of the most quiet and orderly ever played." Parker started with an early run of 51, but "at the close of the next inning, Parker, by missing an easy shot, left the four balls in a bunch for Dion, who scored 60, slipping up on an easy shot. Parker followed with 75, going to pocket off a count, and secured the lead again. . . ." By the end of the fifty-ninth inning, however, Dion was ahead, 1,214 to 884. At the end of the three-hour, thirty-minute match, after putting together several runs, including one of 183, Dion was declared the winner by a score of 1,501–1,164.

Who was Cyrille Dion?
Born in 1843, Cyrille Dion was a native of Montreal who turned professional billiard player in 1865, winning the championship of Canada shortly afterward. He won the championship of the United States from Maurice Daly, defended against a variety of challengers, but died in October 1878 of "congestion of the lungs" following a three-year cold.

BOXING

Such tame sports, however, were only temporary distractions to those who lusted for the big—that is, 165-pound—heavyweights to begin swinging. For just a moment, on May 4,

it seemed that the fight would be postponed. Already at Buffalo, Joe Coburn received word that his wife had died. Immediately speculation started as to how long the encounter would be delayed by this unfortunate development. Then Coburn sent word that the fight would proceed as scheduled. In one of the more notorious saloons, Jim Coburn, brother of the boxer, said regarding the death: "Well, of course he was kind of put out—it was so very sudden. But then he's game and can stand a darned sight more than that."

Mr. and Mrs. Joe Coburn—A Less Than Idyllic marriage:
Joe Coburn was probably sincerely distraught when his wife was stricken in 1871, but the two had their differences. On November 9, 1870, it was reported that Officer Quinn of the Fifteenth Precinct, New York, saw a woman staggering along the sidewalk on Broadway, bleeding profusely from a wound in her back. She was taken to the station house, treated, and identified as Mrs. Joe Coburn. According to reports, the husband and wife had quarreled and he, being under the influence of drink, had shot her with a pistol. When Joe said the incident was purely accidental and Mrs. Coburn refused to prosecute, the charges were dropped.

Relieved, fight fans of the period settled back to await the newspaper account of the result. Others made their way north to Buffalo so as to be in on the actual event. Preparations for the movement from the American side to the farm of Daniel Wooley, near Fort Dover, Canada, began just before midnight on May 11. At that time, a pair of steam launches left Erie and Buffalo with the fighters and their parties. By eleven o'clock the next morning, fifteen hundred spectators were waiting as referee Dick Hollywood flipped a coin to determine which fighter would be allowed the choice of corners. Jem Mace won and selected the corner that would allow him to have his back to the sun. At eleven fifty-three, the fighters shook hands and prepared for round one of their heavyweight championship bout.

More than an hour later, round one was still in progress and neither fighter had laid a solid glove on the other.

In 1871, of course, there were no three-minute rounds separated by one-minute intervals; instead, the fighters started out at a point in midring (called "scratch") and proceeded to fight until one or the other slipped or was knocked or wrestled to the ground. That constituted a round, the fight ending only when one fighter could no longer continue.

The Mace-Coburn affair of May 1871 was a classic example of how this format could be abused so that a "fight" could become little more than a standing match. The problem seemed to be that, for one reason or another, Joe Coburn wanted to fight in his own corner against the ropes. Mace wanted to fight at center ring. Neither boxer would give in to the other. As soon as referee Hollywood summoned them to "scratch," Coburn would retreat toward his corner, Mace would follow a step or two, and then stop in his tracks. The result was total boredom for the spectators. "At times," one reporter wrote, "the men stood contemplating one another for as much as five minutes at a time without raising their arms."

Sports Reporting 1871
From the telegraphic account of the Collins-Edwards bout, May 1871:
Round 4: *"Sparring, dodging, and dancing for some time, when Tim wiped a dust spot off Billy's arm and partially arrested a puffer on his windbag. After some 'play' and several pretty stops, the Collins boy came home heavily on the whistler and squarely knocked Billy horizontal. Edwards complained of having broken his left hand.*
Round 7: *Timmy, looking fierce, reached the strings of Edward's bosom and right cheek affectionately, and then the left cheek to prevent jealousy. Following Billy into a corner, he fought him down, falling on him.*
Round 8: *Tim got home his Dexter potato crusher on Billy's left cheek. . . .*
Round 14: *Edwards overreached himself in ambitious attempt on Tim's smeller and fell. . . .*
Round 17: *Billy caught it on the right buzzum and blinker. Closed, Billy being visited on the sniffer and Tim on the side of the head. Edwards down.*
Round 18: *Billy's breadbasket again knocked at, then his left breast, then his nose, which wept red tears. . . ."*

Then, at 1:02 P.M., something exciting finally happened. A voice could be heard shouting "Police!" No one paid much atten-

tion. Ringsiders continued to exhort the fighters to fight, but Mace and Coburn continued their charade, glaring at each other. Five more minutes passed. A genuine wave of panic moved through the audience as fifty Canadian troops from the Thirty-ninth Regiment suddenly appeared with Chief Magistrate William Wilson and Norfolk County Sheriff Edmund Deeds. "I order this fight stopped!" Wilson shouted. The participants moved even farther apart. It was all very orderly as Wilson read his official pronouncement, except that a dexterous pickpocket managed to lift the chief magistrate's $175 watch and chain. "It is questionable if ever a proposed fight, either of much or little significance, ever terminated in such a fiasco," one reporter wrote as all bets were declared off and the crowd dispersed.

Thus ended the Mace-Coburn title fight of May 1871, a nonevent that heaped scorn on both men. The lightweight battle between Billy Edwards and Tim Collins, on the other hand, provided considerably more action, although newspapers referred to both bouts that month as "fizzled" affairs. Later in the month, Collins and Edwards fought for ninety-six rounds before darkness was declared the winner after nearly two and a half hours. That fight, too, had been well scouted by the authorities, who followed the participants from one location to another, finally catching up with them on Long Island.

The final result was that on May 27, both Edwards and Collins were arrested and brought to trial in New York City. More than two thousand curious persons crowded the

---

Judge Dowling's Decision (delivered to Tim Collins and Billy Edwards at the Tombs, May 1871):
"This country was open to receive you and assist you if you had behaved yourselves. On the corners of the streets, boys may be heard discussing the great fight between Coburn and that other man, which is disgusting. However, you showed some spirit and courage in fighting, but that big loafer Coburn and that other man were too cowardly to do so, after drawing the eyes of the whole world down upon us. But in order to make an example of you two, and as a proof that prizefighting must stop, the court will knock you out of time, the sentence of the court being that you are to be imprisoned in the penitentiary for one year each and fined $1,000. . . ."

---

hallways and foyer of the Tombs Prison court to hear Judge Joseph Dowling render his verdict, which turned out to be a curious mixture of praise for the fighters, scorn for Mace and Coburn, and firm adherence to the letter of the law.

After the two fights, which did so little to advance the gentlemanly art of self-defense, public interest turned to a variety of other events. James Smith, the "colored cadet" of West Point, was adjudged guilty of the charges brought against him, but President U. S. Grant commuted his sentence from dismissal to suspension. (Even so, the first black cadet, Henry O. Flipper, did not graduate from West Point until 1877.) A congressman from South Carolina named C. C. Bowen shocked the nation by committing bigamy—or more correctly, allowing it to be discovered—and the United States was engaged in a nineteenth-century Corean (the way it was spelled then) war, shelling forts off the coast of that tiny nation in order to prove a point now long forgotten. The New York *Times,* that bastion of literacy, was running a serial entitled "Bertha the Sewing-machine Girl, or Death at the Wheel."

BASEBALL PENNANT RACE

Sports fans of Gotham found themselves grumbling at their professional team, the Mutuals, and even gave them a nickname, "Mutes," presumably out of scorn at the team's mediocre showing. Boston fans also had some cause for alarm, for the meteoric spurt of the Red Stockings soon abated as a three-team race developed among Boston, Philadelphia, and Chicago. Meanwhile, the fate of those athletic innovators known as the Fort Wayne Kekiongas continued along a dismal path. Not being allowed to stop while they were ahead with a record of 1–0, the Kekiongas proceeded sharply downhill, win-

---

The First Black-White Baseball Game?
According to reports printed in the San Francisco Chronicle *of July 23, 1871, the "first time that a colored club engaged in a game with a nine of white players was July 9 in Chicago." About five hundred persons turned out to see the black Uniques take on the white Alerts. "The play was creditable on both sides," it was reported, "and the contest quite exciting and close throughout. The colored boys won the game by one run, the score standing 17–16."*

---

ning only six more games after their impressive opening-day victory. In the process they managed to discover some new methods of losing that have held up until this day. One occurred on June 19, when the Kekiongas were leading Troy, 6–3, in the sixth inning, at which time the ball became ripped. The Haymakers demanded that the Kekiongas furnish a new ball, a request that was refused (quite properly, as the Haymakers were the home team). But for some unaccountable reason, Umpire Isaac Leroy forfeited the game to Troy, 9–0.

That same month, Cyrille Dion and Melvin Foster participated in a championship billiards match "before 2000 men and boys and one lady." Dion won by the impressive score of 1,500–616. A wrestling match for "the championship of the United States and Canada and $2,000" was staged at Titusville, Pennsylvania, Major J. H. McLaughlin throwing Nathan Dorrance; two weeks later, racing fans saw Preakness, the celebrated son of Lexington, lose to New York favorite Longfellow by four lengths at Monmouth.

News from the West Coast:
On August 19, roller skating and bicycle riding were the highlights of the day at the opening of the Occidental Skating Rink, San Francisco. On hand was a Miss Carrie A. Moore, one of the few overt women athletes of the day, who promptly at eight o'clock, tastefully attired in a gown of pink silk trimmed with ermine, glided gracefully onto the floor and executed some "brilliant evolutions" on roller skates for the benefit of the large audience. She then changed into a dress of green silk and returned, this time riding a velocipede. "It was soon evident," one reporter noted, "that she was as much mistress of the velocipede as the casters. . . . She rode sideways and saddlewise with equal ease; stood up in the saddle, rode with both feet off the pedals and both arms lifted in the air; described circles using only one foot; rode slowly and swiftly; picked up a handkerchief from the floor while at full speed; and in short, did everything that it is possible to do on the bicycle. . . ."

PEDESTRIANISM

The pedestrians were also quite active that summer. Thirty-two-year-old Edward Payson Weston, probably the most famous professional walker of the time, started the festivities in mid-June by walking 112 miles in 24 hours and 400 miles in 5 days. In order to keep himself awake, Weston used to whip himself with a riding crop. John Davidson, another pedestrian, tried a variety of methods that summer while demonstrating his ability to walk a hundred miles "almost continuously." As a means of fighting boredom and drowsiness, Davidson walked backward part of the time, and for 8 30-minute periods, carried an anvil weighing 111 pounds. He lost 3¾ minutes on one occasion in order to change his socks and 3½ on another to shave, but he was the undisputed hero of Little Rock when the test was over. A third walker named Cornelius N. Payn attempted to beat Weston's June time a month afterward but became sick to his stomach after walking 45 miles and had to retire.

ROWING

Perhaps the most dramatic sports event of 1871 took place late in August, when a boat-racing crew from England accepted an American invitation to participate in a series of international matches on St. John's Kennebecasis Bay, Montreal's St. Lawrence River, and New York state's Lake Saratoga. With an impressive record of sculling victories behind them, the Tyne Crew—named after the river on which so many famous British races took place—were sure they could win most of the races. Their equipment, notably the forty-two-foot, ninety-pound shell *Queen Victoria*—was excellent. Their manpower, some said, was even better.

James Renforth, a short, flat-featured man of twenty-eight with the physique of a boxer, was the team leader and was generally recognized as the finest oarsman in Great Britain. The son of a Tyne River ferryman, in November 1868 Renforth defeated Harry Kelley, then champion of England, in a man-against-man race on the Thames. It was reported that the athletes rowed so rapidly the referee's steam launch had difficulty keeping pace with them.

A year later, Renforth joined with Kelley to form a four-man crew that took all honors at the Thames River Regatta. And in 1871, despite it being a quarter century before revival of the modern Olympics, the Tyne crew had the rare opportunity to travel and spread their reputation to new lands.

By mid-August, the hotels of St. John, New Brunswick, and nearby villages began to fill in anticipation of the first meet, which pitted the Englishmen against three crews from Halifax, one from St. John, and one from the United States. Despite the discomfort of extreme overcrowding—even the staid Victoria Hotel reportedly had every hallway lined with double rows of cots—a happy carnival atmosphere prevailed. "Large numbers of New York and Boston gamblers and light-fingered men have found their way to New Brunswick," noted the New York *Herald,* "and doubtless trust to reap a rich harvest during the coming week."

The "light-fingered men" may well have done all right, but the gamblers could find only so many partisans willing to bet good money against the favorite English crewmen. Even the natives were impressed at the finely conditioned men, who remained aloof at the Clairmont House prior to racing. The first meet, for a prize of five hundred pounds sterling, was to cover a distance of six miles, starting at Torryburn Cove. After racing three miles to a stakeboat, the crews were to return to the finish line. (Many rowers grumbled at this "circular" course, but it was, after all, the best and perhaps only way to accommodate the sport to the needs of a large group of spectators, who were most interested in the start and the finish.)

Attendance on the day of the race, August 23, could hardly have been better. For the entire three-mile distance, on both sides of the water, people of all sorts gathered, "maidens, young and fair, old women, dignified old ministers of state, astute judges, and learned lawyers . . . black, red, and white, and even the 'heathen Chinee' in a solitary instance." Dressed in resplendent scarlet drawers, pink undershirts, and white stockings, James Renforth, Harry Kelley, and the rest of their crew (James Percy and Robert Chambers) rowed on smooth water to the starting position. Shortly afterward, at the referee's command, the six crews broke from the line to the accompaniment of wild cheers and applause. For two thirds of a mile it was an interesting race between the Tyne and Saint John boats. The latter, pulling off at a rapid forty-two-strokes-per-minute rate, obviously surprised James Renforth, who had set a firm but unsensational thirty-nine-stroke pace at the beginning. After the Saint John boat moved into the lead, the speed of the Tyne boat was seen to quicken as James Renforth ordered a series of spurts designed to narrow the gap. Then, quite suddenly and unexpectedly, "a wild cry rang out from that portion of the shore nearest the scene, and poor Renforth was seen to falter, let his oar slip . . ."

In an instant, the Tyne boat was dead in the water. Onshore, heads turned, people muttered and hissed, not knowing what had happened to cause the Englishmen to "quit."

QUESTION: What about Yale and Harvard? Didn't they have a boat race in 1871?
Unfortunately, no, largely because Yale kept threatening to boycott the boat race unless Harvard agreed to row in a straight line rather than the usual circular course. After a series of letters and meetings, Harvard finally agreed but by then it was too late. Yale stayed home.

Only when the tiny shell arrived at dockside was it discovered that James Renforth, the splendid specimen and pride of England, had suffered an attack of some sort and was near death!

While rumors rushed through the crowd, the Saint John crew rounded the stakeboat and rowed home the winner in 39 minutes, 20% seconds, surprisingly good time for a crew without much competition. James Renforth, despite his own agonized protests that he be left on the grass, was carted all the way back to Clairmont House, where he was subjected to the dubious expertise of five physicians. Their treatment included bleeding the young man, an act that probably contributed to his death an hour later.

The San Francisco Yacht Races:
On September 2, the annual regatta of the San Francisco Yacht Club took place with a race from the clubhouse to the Oakland bar and around Alcatraz Island. Unfortunately, it was very foggy and therefore nearly impossible to see anything. Those who waited around for the conclusion saw Peerless sail in as the winner.

His fellow oarsmen, naturally, were quite shaken as they stood, "faces bedewed with tears," at his bedside. They became even more upset when it was hinted that Renforth had been drugged or poisoned just prior to the race. Substantiating the rumor was Harry Kelley, who claimed the stricken man had shouted words to the effect that, "Something has been given me!" and "It's no fit! I'll tell you about it after!"—a promise he was unable to keep, of course.

An autopsy subsequently revealed no evidence of poison in Renforth's stomach, and his death was attributed officially to "congestion of the lungs." That obviously failed to comfort the Tyne crewmen very much, for when they arrived at Lake Saratoga two weeks later, they seemed disorganized and uninspired. An American boat manned by the Ward Brothers—Joshua, Ellis, Gilbert, and Hank—easily won the main race, and to make matters worse, a New York crew crossed the Tyne boat's bow near the end of the race, throwing the Englishmen completely off stride. A protest to referee John Morrissey, the noted gambler, ex-boxer, and founder of Saratoga Racetrack, brought an expression of sympathy but no rematch. Shortly afterward, it was rumored that Percy and Chambers had nearly come to blows over some minor disagreement.

The disgruntled Tyne crew's next stop was Montreal, where they received still another shock. On the morning of the big race, it was revealed that some Canadian vandals—with *ladies* present, yet!—had broken into the locked boathouse the night before, perforated the airtight compartments of the *Queen Victoria*, and cracked the hull of another Tyne vessel by placing it bottom up and kneeling on it. Thus ended the young English crew's American junket, which promised so much fun and adventure but brought only misery.

America's Most Famous Oarsmen *in 1871 were the four Ward brothers, Hank, Joshua, Ellis, and Gilbert. After winning their first world championship in 1867, they showed America their greatest effort on September 11, 1871, while racing the Tyne crews on Lake Saratoga. At the half-way mark, the Wards were four lengths ahead. They then raised their stroke to forty-two a minute to increase the lead to five lengths, maintaining a good lead until the finish line. The four-mile race was finished in 24:40, fastest time ever recorded for that distance by a four-man crew. The record still stands.*

BASEBALL
By September, interest in the National Association pennant race was red-hot as the lead rotated among three clubs. Then one morning the Rockford team entered Chicago—currently in the lead—to discover that Mrs. O'Leary's cow had reduced a sizable section of the city to ashes, including the ball park area. Forced to play the remainder of their games on the road, the White Stockings became sufficiently demoralized to drop three important games in a row, thus becoming the first team in professional baseball to blow a

pennant lead. All was not lost, however, when they took on the rival Philadelphia Athletics at Williamsburg (Brooklyn)'s Union Grounds. The White Stocking players' appearance did leave something to be desired in that third baseman Ed Pinkham showed up wearing a shirt borrowed from a New York Mutual player; he also wore a pair of Mutual pants but hose belonging to the Red Stockings. Tom Foley, manager and center fielder, wore a shirt emblazoned with "Eckfords." Some Chicago players wore caps, some were bareheaded.

NATIONAL ASSOCIATION STANDINGS
1871

TEAM	W.	L.
Philadelphia Athletics	22	7
Chicago White Stockings	20	9
Boston Red Stockings	22	10
Washington Olympics	16	15
Troy Haymakers	15	15
New York Mutuals	17	18
Cleveland Forest Citys	10	19
Fort Wayne Kekiongas	7	21
Rockford Forest Citys	6	21

Why so few games from May to October? (an average of only thirty per team). The answer is that each club played two sorts of games—those that counted ("for the championship") and exhibitions. For one thing, this saved travel costs. Gradually, sensing that fans were more interested in the games that counted, NA teams increased the average number of "championship" games to forty-eight in 1873, then fifty-eight in 1874.

Fighting such adversity, it would be pleasant to report that the Chicagos triumphed over both their bad luck and the rival Athletics. Unfortunately, pitcher Dick McBride of the A's was having a banner year (20–5) and was definitely in good shape on October 30, putting the White Stockings down by a score

of 4–1. That ended Chicago's hopes and concluded an exciting first season of National Association baseball.

Sports fans of 1871 had little to look forward to after the end of October. With only one professional league, there was no "World Series" to wrap up the season. Nor was there a football season, either professional or collegiate. True, there had been crude "football" contests closely resembling soccer in 1869 and 1870, but because of complaints of roughness, no games were played in 1871. It was truly the football fan's darkest hour.

BOXING

The final day of November did bring forth a much-heralded rematch between Jem Mace and Joe Coburn forty-three miles from New Orleans. Soon after the fight started, however, it began to rain, and the two participants didn't seem very interested in fighting, in any event. After watching the men meander through twelve rounds in three hours, thirty-eight minutes (an average of eighteen minutes per round), referee Rufus Hunt described the boxers as "one afraid and the other afraider." All bets were called off following the twelfth round, which lasted nearly an hour and saw no blows landed. "As an example of scientific defense," one reporter commented, "it was superb. As a fight, it was a disappointing failure." The many excursionists slowly dragged their way back to New Orleans, "wet, cold, and hungry."

A week later, lightweight boxers Tim Collins and Billy Edwards were released from prison, both of them vowing never again to enter the prize ring.

And so the sports fan of 1871 awaited 1872 with more than a few questions on his mind. Would Edwards and Collins adhere to their promise? Would Mace and Coburn ever fight to a decision? Would Ned O'Baldwin stay out of jail? Could the Philadelphia Athletics repeat as baseball's professional champions? Would Harvard and Yale resume their rowing series?

No one could say for sure, but one thing was certain. The year just past had been the best so far in the history of American spectator sports.

CHAPTER 3—FIXES

"Hippodroming," they called it during the nineteenth century. Later it became the "fix"—the deliberate relaxation of effort during an athletic contest so that your opponent will win, or come remarkably close to winning, and you will become richer.

Despite the seeming ease of fixing a game, it is not, and seldom has been, quite as easy as it looks. Measuring human effort and success is an inexact art that cannot always be based on statistics. During the 1919 World Series, for example, shortstop Swede Risberg of the Chicago White Sox made four errors en route to helping the future "Black Sox" throw the series to underdog Cincinnati. But six years later, Roger Peckinpaugh, shortstop for the Washington Senators, made eight errors—two in one game—as his team also dropped the Series. The difference was that Risberg was part of a fix and Peckinpaugh was merely having an extremely poor Series in the field. But at the time who could tell?

Again, in 1951, after young basketballer Junius Kellogg was approached by gamblers who wanted him to help fix the DePaul-Manhattan game, he duly reported the situation but was so nervous during the game that anyone looking around for a likely "bought" player would surely have picked Kellogg. Yet nothing could have been farther from the truth.

It follows that most American athletes have been, and are, quite honest. (In recent years, the escalating pay scales have made honesty a good deal easier.) Nevertheless, more than a century of day-in and day-out sports events has produced, first, the temptation for gamblers to try fixing a game, and, second, the opportunity. Some athletes have given in to the temptation; some have been unjustly accused of doing so. Probably all have thought about it at one time or another.

EARLY BASEBALL

Baseball and betting scandals—despite the generally accepted notion that the 1919 Black Sox were the first such blot on the national game—go back to pre-Civil War days. In the East, for example, it was reported that an 1857 match between the Gothams and Atlantics in New York was the object of so much betting that even the umpire, a Mr. Morrow, had a few dollars down.

On the West Coast, where living was a bit freer, gamblers had a unique way of protecting their bets during a crucial match. Just as a fly ball was about to be caught, the big-money boys would fire their six-shooters in order to disconcert the fielder and make him drop the ball. Obviously some of the more important games were quite noisy affairs.

One early fix took place on September 28, 1865, when the underdog Brooklyn Eckfords stunned the New York Mutuals—both "amateur" clubs—by the score of 28–11. Later it was revealed that Ed Duffy, William Wansley, and Thomas Devyr all conspired to throw the game. There were calls for the three players to be barred forever from the game, but eventually all were reinstated. Ed Duffy even managed to play in twenty-five games for the Chicago White Stockings during the 1871 season of the National Association.

THE LOUISVILLE FOUR

"Gentlemen, what can I do to prove to you I regret my crooked work with the Louisville nine? I have suffered poverty; been obliged to beg; seen my wife and child want for something to eat; been living on charity. And I thought I would come to Utica to this convention as my last hope. I am sorry that I did wrong. I want just one more chance. I think I have repented of my crooked work and don't, for God's sake, refuse to give a man a chance to redeem himself."

The gentlemen at the Utica Convention, an 1879 gathering of baseball officials, absolutely refused to give the author of the speech above a chance to redeem himself. The poor soul delivering it, James Alexander Devlin, was just thirty years old. Born in Philadelphia, he discovered that he had better-than-average ability on a ball field, so he joined the hometown Centennials of the National Association for the 1873 season. In 1874 and 1875 he was with the Chicago White Stockings, then made the switch to the National League as a pitcher for its inaugural season. Having played three years in the National Association, where gambling and fixing games was so prevalent that some ball parks were posted with notices reading NO GAME PLAYED BETWEEN THESE TWO TEAMS IS TO BE TRUSTED, Devlin thought of working a shady deal now and then as a fact of life.

His future would have been brighter had he believed the words of William Hulbert, who founded the new baseball league amid a barrage of statements proclaiming new honesty. The problem for some players was that Hulbert meant what he said. "Ballplayers are to stay clear of anyone known to be tied in with gambling circles," he ordered. "Ladies and children must be allowed to view the competition in a dignified atmosphere."

To implement his new directives, Hulbert banned the sale of all alcoholic beverages in National League parks and did away with betting booths at entrance gates and bookies in the stands. "Such practices," he said, "only detract from the magnificence of our teams."

One of the most magnificent teams at the time was the Louisville Grays, which had finished fifth in an eight-team circuit in 1876 but was making a runaway of the 1877 race. One reason for Louisville's success was Jim Devlin, who won 30 games in 1876 and was on his way to winning 35 the following year. Having built up a 3½-game lead as they moved into their final eastern road trip, the Grays needed to win only half of their 12 remaining games to clinch the pennant. At this point George Hall remembered the words of his brother-in-law, Frank Powell, who had told George he was a fool not to supplement his income by throwing a game here and there. Devlin, meanwhile, also established contact with a gambler named McLeod, who told the pitcher that if he ever wanted to pick up some extra money by fixing a game, he should send a telegram containing the word "sash."

Suspicions began to be aroused during the road trip as Louisville dropped games to Boston and Hartford, especially when it was discovered that the latter team had been the favorite in the Hoboken betting pool for the games. Louisville then traveled to Boston, where they lost another close contest on August 25. By this time, the 3½-game lead had diminished to a single game, and when Cincinnati took another pair, the Grays dropped out of first place.

Soon pieces of the puzzle began to fit together for Louisville Vice President Charles E. Chase. One clue was provided by the number of telegrams received by Al Nichols, who served as a go-between for the players. It seemed illogical that an athlete of Nichols' minor importance should be the recipient of so much important correspondence. A confrontation was arranged on October 4, long after the pennant had been lost to Boston, and the players cracked. On October 30, all four were expelled from major-league baseball. The postscript to the drama occurred when Jim Devlin, after repeated attempts to be allowed back in baseball, if only as a groundskeeper, broke into the Utica convention and begged William Hulbert to reinstate him. Regarding the kneeling figure of the former star pitcher, Hulbert reached into his pocket and withdrew a fifty-dollar bill, which he handed to Devlin. "That is what I think of you personally," he said, "but damn you, you have sold a game, you are dishonest, and this National League will not stand for it."

Notes on the Louisville Four:
George Hall, *a small, handsome outfielder, was actually the first National League home-run king, having hit a grand total of five in 1876. His salary in 1877 was a phenomenal $2,800 and he finished the year with a .323 average.*
Jim Devlin, *who posted a record of sixty-five wins and sixty losses, led the league both years in lost games. He suffered almost constantly from boils and was said to be a chronic sleepwalker.*
Bill Craver, *Louisville's regular shortstop, was thirty-three and had managed three years in the old National Association. He was a classic good-field, no-hit, having an average of .244.*
Al Nichols, *about whom little is known, was the only member of the Louisville Four who was not a regular. His entire big-league career consisted of sixty-three games. He batted .182 lifetime.*

Whatever Happened to the Louisville Four?
George Hall *returned to his hometown, Brooklyn, became an engraver, and was successful at that new profession. He died in 1945, age ninety-six.*
Jim Devlin *attempted to be reinstated in the league, then joined the Philadelphia police force. He soon contracted tuberculosis, dying in 1883, age thirty-four.*
Bill Craver *also became a police officer, in Troy, New York, working until his death in 1901 at age fifty-seven.*
Al Nichols *apparently vanished, although there were reports that he continued to play baseball for a living, most notably with the Franklin club of Brooklyn and Jersey City of the Eastern League in 1886, using the name of Williams.*

Despite this firm—even harsh—action against the players, some felt the scandal had virtually destroyed the national game. "The days of professional baseball are numbered," commented the St. Louis *Globe-Democrat*, "and the hundreds of young men who have depended on the pastime as their means of earning a livelihood will be obliged to change their plans of operation."

That writer, of course, was quite wrong. It would be more than four decades before baseball had to deal with a scandal as big as that created by the Louisville Four.

COURTNEY-HANLAN

In 1878, Charles Courtney and Edward Hanlan were as well known to sports fans of America as Henry Aaron was a century later. Courtney, thirty years old, was tall, lean, and dark-skinned; Hanlan, a twenty-four-year-old Canadian, was blue-eyed and fair, with curly hair and a mustache. Both were at the top of their rowing class. And the 1870s were the days when rowing was nearly as American as baseball and more popular than football. The professionals, who practiced their skill on the lakes and rivers of the United States, often, in the words of a later rower, Robert F. Kelley, "became as famous and well-publicized—and spoiled—as any well-known athlete of today."

Thus, when Hanlan and Courtney agreed to race each other in the fall of 1878, the event attracted as much attention as a World Series contest a half century later. The stakes were high—twenty-five hundred dollars to be put up by each man, plus six thousand dollars from the host city of Montreal. The actual site of the contest was to be Lachine, Quebec, a town of about three thousand population seven miles southwest of Montreal on the St. Lawrence River and the Lachine Canal.

On the day of the race, October 3, the weather was gloomy, but betting was brisk among both the sportsmen and professional gamblers. The odds-on favorite was Hanlan, despite the fact that Courtney was undefeated both as an amateur and a professional. Some gambler watchers took this as a sign that the race might not be quite on the level. "Nonbetting men who are acquainted with the oarsmen," noted the Montreal *Evening Post*, "express surprise that so great and long-continued odds should be offered on the Canadian."

Until two o'clock that afternoon, it was doubtful that the race would even begin, but then the strength of the wind diminished and the judges decided to move ahead. In the meantime crowds of people from hundreds of miles away were pouring into the town and searching for a good spot to watch the race. Having arrived at the water's edge, they were attacked by a sudden thunderstorm, "accompanied by rain, hail, and a fierce squall . . . drenching to the skin the thousands of specta-

tors who by this time were gathered in the grand stand and along the river banks." Soon the sky was bright again and those who had waited were rewarded as Hanlan and Courtney appeared on the river, the young Canadian wearing a red cap and "blue skirt faced with red." Courtney, dressed in blue and white, wore a large blue star on his chest. "Hanlan looked almost boyish in comparison with his antagonist," one reporter noted.

At four fifty-six, both men sprang to their work, Hanlan with a stroke of thirty-one and Courtney pulling thirty-six to the minute. At the end of the first half mile, with 4½ miles to go, Hanlan shot a half length ahead, and Canadians all along the shore broke into cheers. At the three-quarters mark, Hanlan increased his lead to two lengths, but at the mile Courtney, with a beautiful spurt, closed the gap. The first mile was rowed in seven minutes.

During the second mile, as the breeze freshened and the rowers were forced to hug Isle Courcelles in order to find smooth water, Courtney forged ahead. By this time it had started to rain again, but the shower passed as the two men made the 2½-mile turn dead even.

They were still even at the end of the third mile, and the pace during the fourth was furious, the men rowing it in six minutes. Then as they headed into the final mile, Hanlan inched ahead while the older Courtney struggled to pull abreast of him. But near the finish line both rowers headed for a group of small craft that had pulled into the river to watch the race. Hanlan slowed down for a moment, then spurted ahead. Courtney stopped rowing altogether, or at least long enough so that closing the gap on Hanlan was impossible.

The Dramatic Climax
"Here Courtney made a last terrible, telling stroke, crept up inch by inch, and foot by foot, in a way that would have given him the race could he have kept it up to the end. But the strain was too great; he ran his bow to within a length and a half of Hanlan's stern post, but could get it no nearer, and Hanlan swept over the line, winner of the greatest single-scull race ever seen in this country, amid the deafening cheers of the assembled multitudes and the screech of steam whistles."

The race was hardly over when stories began to circulate that Courtney had thrown the match. One gambler told of receiving a telegram from a Montreal associate telling him to "lay low and back the Canadian with his pile, even to his house and store, taking any odds against Courtney." Another piece of correspondence less subtle, said simply: "Back the Canadian. The American is fixed." And while the race was being described via ticker tape at Kelly and Bliss's Exchange in New York City, half a mile from the finish it registered "Courtney ahead," and his American backers were jubilant. At this juncture, a stranger knowingly offered to take any Courtney money in the house at odds of 20–100. More evidence came from studying the betting habits of the professionals, who unanimously backed Hanlan, sometimes at ridiculous odds. But the most damaging statement was made by Edward B. Rankin of the Boston *Herald,* who acted as judge for Courtney and therefore followed his actions from the beginning to the end of the race. "I venture the judgment now that Courtney is the better and more enduring sculler of the two," he said. ". . . He outrowed the Toronto man and only lost the race by ceasing to pull at a critical moment when nearing the goal. Had he continued rowing and hauled out into the course, instead of resting on his oars, the race was his own. It seems incredible that a man of Courtney's intelligence should be so far lost to pride of country and the interest of friends as to lose the race intentionally. . . ."

Charles Courtney's Lament:
"You cannot have—and I pray God you may never have—an idea of what it is to go home to a wife who has cried herself sick over the most damnable charges ever brought against an innocent man. Somebody takes pains to send me marked copies of every newspaper that charges me with this villainy, and before I came home my wife read them and cried over them until she was fairly sick and hysterical . . ."

Reporters attempted to investigate the situation and did succeed in bringing to light certain facts. (It was stated, for example, that Courtney had a thirty-seven-hundred-dollar mortgage on his home and needed money quickly to prevent a foreclosure; in fact, the mortgage was only one thousand dollars and the bank was quite happy.) As for his handling of the race, when he was interviewed, Courtney explained that he was a smooth-water rower and had no idea how to maneuver his shell in the heavy-wake situation near the end of the race. If that reply seems facile,

One Oarsman Who Was Crooked:
Not so well respected as Charles Courtney was John Teemer, who raced during the 1880s in several races against both Courtney and Edward Hanlan. Unfortunately for Teemer, he wrote several letters to his opponents that strongly indicated that he was willing to throw a race if it was convenient. One of the notes, to Edward Hanlan, said in parts: "You don't need to be afraid of me. If you are not in condition I will do anything you ask me to do to make you win the race." (letter dated September 2, 1885)

Despite this incriminating evidence, which was published in newspapers, Teemer never had to answer criminal charges for fixing races in which he was involved.

it nevertheless satisfied most investigators. No one could explain the heavy betting on Hanlan despite Courtney's reputation as the better oarsman, but in the absence of incriminating evidence, most gave Courtney the benefit of the doubt and adjudged him innocent of throwing the race. Even so, the controversy continued to smolder for more than a year, at which time the two men agreed to settle the matter by having a return match. It was set for October 19, 1879, but on the day of the contest, Courtney's handlers checked at the boathouse and discovered that the shell that he planned to use had been neatly sawed in two, ten feet from the bow. No one was officially charged with the vandalism, although theories abounded as to how it had happened.

Meanwhile, a Baseball Item:
In 1882, Richard Higham, an umpire in the National League for two seasons, was suspected of telling gamblers how to bet on games he was officiating. His guilt was established when handwriting experts proved he was the author of several incriminating letters. Higham thus became the first, and to date the last, baseball umpire to be expelled for dishonesty.

It seems that despite his skill, Charles Courtney never had much luck. His biographer, C. V. P. Young, summed it up when he wrote: "The probable explanation for some of the activities of which he was guilty during this period was that he not only became intoxicated with success, as he himself intimated, but was early seized upon by professional gamblers, who took advantage of his inexperience and callowness and used him for their own ends."

WAS LOU DILLON DRUGGED?

There was nothing to indicate that the match race of October 18, 1904, would be much more than exercise for trotter Lou Dillon. Her opponent, Major Delmar, was worthy enough, but Lou Dillon had defeated him the previous year and was a solid 3–1 favorite to repeat. But with the Memphis Gold Cup at stake, eight thousand trotting enthusiasts were on hand at the inauguration of the Memphis Trotting Association meeting. After drawing the pole for the first heat, Major Delmar moved easily ahead of Lou Dillon, never allowing the chestnut mare to come close to challenging.

About Lou Dillon:
Sired in 1898 by Sidney Dillon-Lou Milton, at the Santa Rosa Stock Farm, California, Lou Dillon became the first trotter at Readville, Massachusetts, 1903. Eventually she was purchased by C. K. G. Billings for $12,500. From 1903 to 1906, when she retired, she broke many records for bike sulky and wagon, including a 1:58½ mile in 1903 at Memphis. She died in California in 1925.

The second heat was even more of a walkaway. Lou Dillon performed so poorly, in fact, that a team of veterinarians was summoned to examine her. They said she was suffering from a case of the "thumps" (spasmodic contraction of the diaphragm) and recommended a small dose of belladonna. No one could account for the horse's lack of energy.

Eventually Lou Dillon's loss of the five-thousand-dollar prize—and the first loss of her career—faded into the background, especially after she retired from active racing two years later. But Murray Howe, secretary of the Memphis Trotting Association, could not forget the race and became more determined as the months passed that foul play had rendered Lou Dillon ineffective. "I first became suspicious that something had been done to Lou Dillon while she was warming up for her first heat," he said. "She broke badly, which was the first time I ever saw her break. When the race came off and Mr. Billings climbed into the sulky behind her, she made a good start,

the same kind of a start any horse (if it had only three legs) would have made in the excitement of the getaway. She came back on her driver in the latter part of the race, which was contrary to her usual form, as she is a strong finisher. . . . My suspicions were at once aroused, for I was pretty certain something was the matter with the mare. I determined to make an investigation but took no one into my confidence. I finally obtained proof and corroborating evidence. . . . A small bag of mercury was injected into the mare, not for the purpose of poisoning her or doing her material damage, but in order to divert her attention during the race, and that accounts for her holding back, and evincing a desire to sit in Mr. Billings' lap."

Suit was finally filed in February 1906. It charged that Elmer E. Smathers, owner of Major Delmar, had approached Edward Sanders (the brother of Lou Dillon's trainer, Millard Sanders) through his own trainer, George Spear, with an offer of five thousand dollars to make sure Major Delmar won the match race. At the same time, a deputy sheriff named John Murray entered the apartment of Smathers and repossessed the Gold Cup trophy.

Smathers, of course, was livid. The racing community of Kentucky was both embarrassed and angry at the rash of national publicity brought by the suit. As in many controversies, the case began to be tried out of court. One veterinarian, for example, testified that he had seen Lou Dillon given large doses of ice water, which was the cause of her poor form in the 1904 race. Another attributed the mare's failure to her being rubbed down excessively with alcohol, which "would have the effect of closing the pores and as a natural consequence her blood would become heated." Still others, knowing that the reputation of Murray Howe and the Memphis Trotting Association was good, felt that Smathers must be guilty—otherwise the suit would not have been brought against him.

After being subjected to review by the National Trotting Association, which expelled Edward Sanders and George Spear on the basis of their affidavits filed against Smathers (and in which they admitted their own guilt), the case reached the Tennessee Supreme Court in Memphis in April 1907. The most interesting witness was Millard Sanders, the veteran trainer who had the melancholy job of telling how his brother had tried to get both of them involved in a scheme to fix the race for five thousand dollars. At one point, Sanders testified that his brother said, "Are you going to be a big fool and throw away a chance to make money so easily?"

Millard Sanders, Harness Racing Immortal:
Born in 1858, Millard Sanders was a highly unorthodox but effective trainer. (He was once discharged for driving an owner's horse too fast during a training session.) His most famous horse, of course, was Lou Dillon. Sanders authored one book, The Two-minute Horse, *before passing away in 1928.*

E. E. Smathers, when called to the stand, stoutly maintained his innocence, and the prosecution could produce no evidence that he had taken any action to drug the horse. No one, in fact, could say exactly when Lou Dillon had been drugged, if such were the case, for she seemed in excellent condition until the very beginning of the race.

Eventually the court ruled that Smathers was innocent, and the Gold Cup was returned to him. Edward Sanders and George Spear were forced to seek employment off the trotting tracks. No concrete evidence showed that Lou Dillon's race had been influenced by mercury or any other drug. She simply may have run two of the worst heats of her life, but in view of her excellent record until that time, that seems highly unlikely.

HAL CHASE—A FIXER WHO LEFT QUIETLY

Those who saw Hal Chase play first base with the New York Yankees, Chicago White Sox, Cincinnati Reds, and New York Giants generally marveled at the man's catlike grace and speed. He had excellent hands, good baseball sense, and a whip for an arm. A natural athlete, he was still boyish in appearance in his late thirties. His career spanned a decade and a half, from 1905 to 1919, during which he batted .291 lifetime. His nickname was "Prince Hal."

Yet, for all his speed and agility, Hal Chase was invariably at the top of the list when it came to errors. During his career he averaged more than twenty-six errors per season, and on seven occasions led the league at his position. Because of the nature of the position, first basemen generally make far fewer miscues than other fielders. (In 1917, for example, Honus Wagner had but seven errors all season, and in 1921, Stuffy McInnis of the Red Sox committed just one.) Chase's penchant for letting the ball get away could have been chalked up to a case of bad hands, of course. More than one player has been afflicted with that disorder. Gradually, however, word began to get around the league that Chase occasionally bet on games in which he

was a participant. This so infuriated Frank Chance, who was managing the Yankees in 1913, that he actually accosted a pair of sportswriters on the Sixth Avenue el and said, "I want to tell you fellows what's going on. Did you notice some of the balls that got away from Chase today? They weren't wild throws. They were only made to look that way. He's been doing that right along. He's throwing games on me!"

Hal Chase's Error-laden Career

Year	Team	Errors
1905	New York—A	31*
1906	New York—A	33
1907	New York—A	34
1908	New York—A	22
1909	New York—A	28*
1910	New York—A	28
1911	New York—A	36*
1912	New York—A	27*
1913	New York—Chicago—A	27*
1914	Chicago—A Buffalo—Federal	28
1915	Buffalo—Federal	26*
1916	Cincinnati—N	14
1917	Cincinnati—N	28*
1918	Cincinnati—N	13
1919	New York—N	21

(*) Denotes leading league in errors for first baseman

Some sample average number of errors for other first basemen:

1907—24   1911—17   1917—14

A couple days later, Chase was traded to the Chicago White Sox. The remarks of Chance, naturally, could have been chalked up as the ravings of any manager saddled

How Did Chase Get Away with It?
One sportswriter who observed Chase closely, Fred Lieb, summed up his unique ability to bungle a play and make it seem as if it were the fault of another player. In Baseball as I Have Known It, *Lieb wrote: "His neatest trick (I think) was to arrive at first base for a throw from another infielder just a split second too late. A third baseman, for example, must throw to the bag, whether the first baseman is there or not. . . ."*

with a seventh-place club. But after Chase moved to Chicago and then jumped to Buffalo of the Federal League, the rumors continued. His name seemed always to be linked with suspicious games.

When the Federal League folded and Chase was picked up by Cincinnati, his new manager, Christy Mathewson, made charges to the Cincinnati press and National League President John Heydler to the effect that Prince Hal had thrown some games.

A quiet investigation was started, but when Heydler found he had no evidence that would stand up in court, he dropped it. Chase was traded to the New York Giants. He seemed to be off the hook, but Heydler continued searching for evidence, and in 1919 got a signed affidavit from a Boston gambler along with a photographic copy of a check made out to Chase and endorsed by him. Confronted with the evidence, Manager John McGraw of the Giants and Charles Stoneham, owner-president, informed Chase that he was through with organized baseball. Prince Hal left quietly, most of the American public blithely unaware that anything unusual had taken place.

That, it turned out, was the year the Chicago White Sox dumped the World Series.

1920–26—BASEBALL'S PERILOUS YEARS
"They can't come back. The doors are closed to them for good. The most scandalous chapter in the game's history is closed."
K. M. Landis, January 19, 1934

The story of the Black Sox scandal and the thrown World Series of 1919, which was not "discovered" until a year later, is the most famous fix in American sports history. It is hardly a classic affair of discretion, however. The night before the first game between the White Sox and the underdog Cincinnati Reds, Jack Doyle, owner and operator of an important betting center in New York City, estimated that more than two million dollars had been wagered—nearly all of it on the Reds. "You couldn't miss it . . ." Doyle said. "The thing had an odor. I saw smart guys take even money on the Sox who should have been asking 5–1."

The Series began at Cincinnati where Eddie Cicotte, starting pitcher for the White Sox and one of the bought players, gave up five runs in the fourth inning. The Reds subsequently went on to win by a score of 9–1. The second game followed a similar pattern, the game close until Lefty Williams, another in on the fix, walked three Cincinnati batters, then allowed a three-run triple by light-hitting Larry Kopf (who hit only thirty three-baggers during a ten-year career). In the third game, White Sox pitcher Dickie Kerr, one of the innocent, threw a three-hit shutout at the Reds, but the fourth game went to Cincinnati when Eddie Cicotte chipped in with a couple of errors. Cincinnati led the Series, three games to one, but things were not as desperate as they seemed, for this was the brief era (1919–21) of the best-of-nine World Series. When the Reds went on to win the next game, however, there was cause for panic in Chicago. At that point, the players in on the fix obviously decided to go all out to make it look good, for the next two contests were taken by the Sox, one of them in extra innings, when Gandil singled home Buck Weaver with the deciding run. But the roof fell in during the next game when the Reds scored four times in the first inning and went on to win, 10–5.

Chick Gandil (years later):
"Each year when people start getting excited about the World Series, I find myself wanting to crawl into a cave."

Can You Tell the Fixers from the Innocent Without a Scorecard?

Player	At Bat	Hits	Avg.	Player	At Bat	Hits	Avg.
B. Weaver	34	11	.324	E. Collins	31	7	.226
J. Jackson	32	12	.375	R. Schalk	23	7	.304
C. Gandil	30	7	.233	N. Leibold	18	1	.056
O. Felsch	26	5	.192	B. Lynn	1	0	.000
S. Risberg	25	2	.080	S. Collins	16	4	.255
F. McMullin	2	1	.500				
	149	38	.255		89	19	.213

At left, the six nonpitchers who were in on the fix of 1919. At right, the five nonpitchers who remained clean. Sometimes things are not what they seem.

At three games to five, the Series seemed respectable enough, but Hugh Fullerton, a sportswriter, lost no time in denouncing what had happened. The very day after the Series ended, he hinted broadly in his column that something was amiss. The outcry was not taken up by others, however. Most persons associated with the games insisted that the 1919 collapse of the White Sox was "just one of those things" that occur in sports and could not have been prevented. Disclaimers of some sort or another were issued, and Charles Comiskey even offered a substantial sum of money to anyone who could furnish evidence that the games had been thrown. Even the innocent players, such as catcher Ray Schalk, maintained that they saw nothing wrong with the quality of play in the Series.

Some Early Comments:
"There is always some scandal of some kind following a big sporting event like the World Series. These yarns are manufactured out of whole cloth and grow out of bitterness due to losing wagers. I believe my boys fought the battles of the recent World Series on the level, as they have always done."
Charles Comiskey, owner,
Chicago White Sox
"Because a lot of dirty, long-nosed, thick-lipped, and strong-smelling gamblers butted into the World Series . . . and some of said gamblers got crossed, stories were peddled that there was something wrong with the games. . . ."
The Sporting News, *October 1919*

Eventually, in September 1920, stories started leaking that the previous year's Series had been thrown. Jackson, Cicotte, and Williams signed confessions admitting their part in the scheme, but before the men could be brought to trial, there was a turnover in the Illinois state's attorney's office and all the confessions mysteriously disappeared. When the case entered the courts, the men repudiated their signed statements and the case was dropped.

That the players had been acquitted mattered little to new Baseball Commissioner K. M. Landis. He banned them all from major-league parks, and even went to great lengths to make sure they could not play in minor leagues.

A half century later, he could never have gotten away with such high-handed action. Some ballplayer would have sued the commissioner for conspiring to deprive him of earning a living—and made it stick, too.

1924—THE O'CONNELL SCANDAL
The Black Sox scandal was still quite fresh in everyone's mind when yet another affair erupted. "On the eve of departing to meet the Washington Senators in the World Series," the New York *Times* reported on October 1, 1924, "a blow was struck in the New York Giants' camp when Commissioner Kenesaw Mountain Landis announced that Jimmy O'Connell, outfielder, and Coach Cozy Dolan had been placed on the ineligible list. . . ."

The cause of Landis' ire was a report that O'Connell, of the league-leading Giants, had approached Philadelphia shortstop Heinie Sand and offered him five hundred dollars to "take it easy" during the final series of the season. Sand reported the offer to his manager, Art Fletcher, who relayed the information to National League President Heydler.

A hearing was held during which O'Connell admitted he had followed the instructions of Giant coach Alvin "Cozy" Dolan. He also admitted that three other Giant players—Frank Frisch, Ross Youngs, and George Kelly—knew about the bribe offer. Landis questioned all of the men, then expelled Jimmy O'Connell and Cozy Dolan. It was just three days before the first game of the World Series, but Landis seemed to think that his rapid decision ended the matter. Many, however, were convinced that there was more to the situation than met the eye and wanted to have Landis call off the Series and hold an investigation, by federal authorities if necessary. Landis refused. Ban Johnson, President of the American League and never a fan of the commissioner, protested. It sounded, of course, as if Johnson was glad the shoe was on the other foot, that he hoped the 1924 scandal in the National League would turn out to be as terrible as the 1919 American League one.

Poor Jimmy O'Connell:
Born in Sacramento, California, on February 11, 1901, he was a star member of the University of Santa Clara baseball team. After finishing college, he was purchased by the New York Giants for $75,-000, the second highest price ever paid for a minor league player at that time. (The sale of Willie Kamm from San Francisco to the Chicago White Sox for $100,000 was the record.) In 1923, he played in 87 games with the Giants, batting .250, but in 1924 his average was a more respectable .317.

Baseball men took sides as Johnson announced his intention to boycott the Series. Particularly upset was Clark Griffith, president of the Washington Senators, who had waited decades for the opportunity to play in a World Series and saw no need to call it off. "Johnson is trying to play baseball politics," he said, "and is taking advantage of an unpleasant situation with which he has nothing to do, to put Judge Landis in a bad light."

On the other hand, those who saw a wider scandal tended to side with Johnson. Reporter W. O. Phelan was one. All those who believed that a "green kid" and a "worn-out coach" devised the plot "without full directions from some crooked brain who neatly used them as a catspaw," he wrote, "should hold a meeting in the nearest phone booth, where they would not be crowded." Another writer, who remained unidentified, wrote, "There have been a number of things happen in New York which deserved investigation, but everyone seems to be afraid of McGraw." Landis was accused of having "an astonishing incapacity or unwillingness to probe the case to the bottom."

Eventually, an outside investigation was held by New York District Attorney Joab H. Banton, but it failed to uncover anything noteworthy. Nevertheless, years later *The Sporting News* added a final dash of intrigue to the case when it wrote: "Had Cozy Dolan, backed by the Giants, gone through with [a lawsuit charging Landis with defamation of character], I believe the commissioner would have ripped the game wide open."

1926—COBB AND SPEAKER

Only two years passed before the next bombshell was laid on K. M. Landis' doorstep. From Chicago came the announcement: "New Ball Scandal. Landis is silent." And shortly afterward, on December 21, 1926: "Two of the greatest baseball players in the history of the game, Ty Cobb and Tris Speaker, were named by Commissioner Kenesaw Mountain Landis in an exposé of a scandal that went back to 1919, the year climaxed by the famous crooked World Series between the White Sox and the Reds."

Cobb and Speaker. It seemed impossible. But there it was on the front page. The crux of the story was that the two of them had conspired to fix a game between Detroit and Cleveland played at Detroit on September 25, 1919. Did that also explain why Speaker, only thirty-eight years old and still in good shape, and Cobb, forty but going strong, had both suddenly resigned at the end of the 1926 season?

The confessor, in this case, was a retired pitcher for the Red Sox and Tigers named Hubert (Dutch) Leonard, who happened to meet under the stands with Cobb, Speaker, and Smokey Joe Wood after the first game of the series on September 24. Cleveland had already clinched second place in the American League, but Detroit was in a fight for third with the Yankees and needed help. One bit of conversation led to another and, according to Leonard, it was finally agreed that the Indians would let the Tigers win the game the next day. It then dawned on the players that since they knew which team was going to win, they might as well make a few dollars on it. The men agreed to chip in and place a few bets. "I was to put up fifteen hundred dollars," Leonard said, "Cobb two thousand dollars, Wood and Speaker a thousand dollars each."

The game, played the next day, went off without a hitch. Detroit moved to a 4–0 lead, saw Cleveland nearly close the gap in the top of the fifth, but kept pecking away to win by a score of 9–5. Speaker, if he was in on the conspiracy, covered himself extremely well, going three-for-five, belting a pair of triples, and driving in two runs. In any event, that was Dutch Leonard's story and he produced two letters, one written by Joe Wood, the other by Ty Cobb himself.

The "Infamous" Game of September 25, 1919:

Cleveland	0	0	2	0	1	1	1	0	0	—5
Detroit	2	2	0	0	2	1	0	2	X	—9

The Letters:

"Dear Friend Dutch,

"The only bet West could get up was $600 against $420 (10 to 7). Cobb did not get a cent. . . . We won the $420. I gave West $30, leaving $390 or $130 for each of us. . . . We would have won $1,750 for the $2,500 if we could have placed it. . . ."

Joe Wood

"Dear Dutch:

"Wood and myself are considerably disappointed in our business proposition, as we had $2,000 to put into it and the other side quoted us $1,400, and when we finally assured that much money it was about 2 o'clock and they refused to deal with us. . . . I thought the White Sox should have won the Series but am satisfied they were too confident. . . ."

Ty

When Landis saw the letters, which were obviously authentic, he decided to take a typically firm hand. He immediately called a meeting to interrogate all concerned parties. Landis, hardly a forgiving man, wanted all four men banned from baseball—Wood and Leonard were already finished—but he knew that a scandal as gaudy as the Black Sox affair would not be good for baseball. He therefore suggested that Cobb and Speaker resign immediately "for personal reasons." He even made a straight-faced statement to the press to that effect, adding that since all four men were out of the game, there was hardly any need for a full-scale investigation.

What Landis forgot at that point was that he was dealing with hard-headed Tyrus Raymond Cobb, not genial Joe Jackson of the White Sox. Although Cobb could easily have afforded to retire, he decided he didn't like the commissioner's attitude. He threatened a suit in which he would reveal many interesting things about organized baseball—including fake turnstile-count and book-juggling by major-league owners. Faced with this kind of possible counterattack, Landis knew he had met his match. On January 27, 1927, he backed down, issuing a statement that read in part: "These players had not been, nor are they now, found guilty of fixing a ball game. By no decent system of justice could such a finding be made. Therefore, they were not placed on the ineligible list."

Say It Ain't So, Ty and Tris:
As the scandal progressed, there were increasing signs of support for the two heroes. In Detroit, a corps of schoolboys began a canvass of office buildings in order to obtain fifteen thousand signatures, requesting that the players be allowed an open hearing in which to vindicate themselves.

Will Rogers also wrote: "I want the world to know that I sincerely wish Tris and Ty the same as I have always wished them over an acquaintanceship of fifteen years. . . . If they have been selling out all these years I would have liked to have seen them play when they wasn't selling."

Spoken like a self-respecting cornered rat. (In later years, Cobb stated that the statement had actually been dictated to Landis by attorneys representing Cobb and Speaker.) Both players continued their diamond careers through the 1928 season.

The one question remaining seems to be why Dutch Leonard brought forth the charge and letters that could have incriminated both Cobb and Speaker. The Georgia Peach had an answer to that one. During the 1925 season, Cobb had managed Detroit and Speaker managed Cleveland. Near the end of the year, Cobb sent Leonard to the minor leagues, an act that could have been prevented if Speaker had claimed him on waivers.

There are few things, after all, as wrathful as a left-handed pitcher scorned.

1922—SIKI-CARPENTIER
Few boxers were as colorful as Louis Phal, who took the name Battling Siki when he began to box professionally in 1913, at age fifteen. A Senegalese, Siki was a hero in World War I, destroying a German machine-gun nest almost single-handedly and earning the Croix de Guerre and Medaille Militaire by the time he was seventeen. Although a defender of the traditional French establishment, there was something unusual about his nature—in the parlance of his time, he might have been said to have a "corkscrew brain."

He probably spent less time in the boxing ring fighting than in restaurants, which he loved to visit with his pet lion. When fights started, as they invariably did, Siki pitched right in. Before long, governments on both sides of the Atlantic expressed the view that he simply was not a pleasant person to have around.

Siki could hold his own in the ring with the best, however, and blacks of the 1920s regarded him as their rising young hero. The subject of much racist derision, even from his own manager, Siki lived and fought at a savage pace. Soon he was known as the "Senegalese Windmill" because of his free-swinging tactics and speed in the ring. At 5 feet, 11 inches, and 175 pounds, he was a well-muscled light-heavyweight who could easily

---

Said M. Hetters, Siki's Manager:
"A long time ago I used to think that if one could find an intelligent gorilla and teach him to box one would have the world's champion. Well, that's what I found in Siki. There's much of the monkey about him. He has the gorilla's tricks, the gorilla's skill and manners. Not only does he resemble a highly trained gorilla, but he is just a little bit crazy judged by human standards."

---

have beefed himself into the heavyweight class and challenged Jack Dempsey for the crown. That was his ultimate goal as he entered the ring on the night of September 24, 1922. His opponent was Georges Carpentier, light-heavyweight champion who had failed to dethrone Dempsey the year before.

The French crowd of fifty thousand, equally divided in its loyalty between the fair-haired Carpentier and the fierce Siki, anticipated a classic battle. And in many ways they were not disappointed. Carpentier used his skill at dodging to avoid Siki during the first round, forcing the black man to look clumsy while landing a pair of hard rights of his own. For the next few rounds, the fight continued in that manner, Carpentier in complete command, smiling as if he were enjoying himself immensely. But in the fourth round, Siki carried his attack to the body with devastating effect. A right to the jaw in the sixth sent Carpentier against the posts of his own corner. Siki then landed a chopping left that sent Carpentier to the canvas. As he fell, his legs became entangled in the ropes. He lay writhing on the ring floor, his feet still twisted in the strands as the crowd roared. To everyone's surprise, the referee stepped forward to announce that Georges Carpentier was still the champion, that Battling Siki had been disqualified for tripping!

Siki's Career:
Was known as "spotty." It included seventy-four bouts, of which he won twenty-nine by knockouts, twenty-five by decision. There was one draw, he lost ten times via decision, once by a KO, once by a foul, had six no decisions, and one no contest. Although able to beat the best when he had a mind, Siki often dropped fights to lesser names simply because he wasn't in the mood to participate.

The crowd roared with anger. Intimidated by the uproar, the officials went into a huddle at ringside. They decided that the referee had been in error, that Siki was the new light-heavyweight champion of the world.

That, unfortunately, was not the end of the controversy. Soon afterward, the story began to be circulated that the entire fight had been a fix—that Siki had been bribed to throw the fight, but had double-crossed Carpentier after he got in the ring. As evidence, the referee, Henri Bernstein, testified that he heard Siki say to Carpentier during one of the clinches: "Don't hit so hard. What is the use to hit so

hard when it is all settled?" Another time, during the fourth round, Bernstein asserted he heard Carpentier say: "Will you lie down? Get down!"

The revelations generated a furor, naturally, as the fight looked anything but fake. Even worse, when the French Boxing Federation ordered Siki to appear at a hearing in order to investigate and clear up the charges, Siki refused. Soon the situation, known as *"l'affaire Siki,"* was being debated in the French Chamber of Deputies. Deputy Diagne, himself a Senegalese, defended Siki. He said in part: "Siki refused to carry out instructions which would have caused the public to be fooled and swindled of its money. Suddenly becoming conscious of his own strength while in the ring, he refused to lie down in the fourth round and abandon to Carpentier another victory."

At this point, one wondered if Siki was being charged with dishonesty, honesty, or honesty exercised too late. On December 5, 1922, Siki admitted to Diagne and two witnesses that the fight had been "framed," but that he had changed his mind while in the ring. Fifteen days before the battle, he said, he agreed to lie down in the fourth round. "But inside my heart," he added, "I kept repeating, 'I will knock him dead if I can.'" As to his change of heart, Siki said that, "I entered the ring in a bewildered condition, and began to do as I agreed. . . . I was in a trance throughout the second round discussing within myself whether I should lie down or fight. . . . At the beginning of the third round I had fully decided that I should take another count as agreed . . . but the round had progressed two minutes before Georges hit me hard enough to give me a chance to go down. A right swing then hit me high on the cheek, and I said, 'Here goes.' I dropped to one knee, fully resolved to stay there. . . . Then the howls of the multitude reached my head. . . . 'He's beaten; the Negro is finished.' . . . I made up my mind to fight."

The Agreement, According to Siki:
"I was supposed to take a short count in the first round, then go to the floor again in the second, followed by a nine-second count just before the bell in the third round, come up groggy for the fourth round, then drop with both arms outstretched and be counted out."

Despite the passion of Siki's statement, there were many doubters. One was his own manager, who said he knew of nothing resembling a frame-up. Georges Carpentier, naturally, was mortified and angry. "What credit should one accord this man and what does he hope for in trying to defame me?" he protested. François Deschamps, Carpentier's manager, said, "This charge is infamy."

The next complication came about when the French Boxing Federation studied films of the fight. The actual work in the ring revealed nothing, but the film did show that Deschamps' actions during the fourth round were decidedly strange in that he seemed to spend almost as much time in Siki's corner as his own. What was he doing? Was he protesting a foul blow or the fact Siki wasn't following the prearranged script? To find out, the FBF retained a pair of deaf-mutes, expert lip-readers, to see if they could make out what Deschamps was yelling at Hellers. The interpreters made out several words here and there, but owing to the subject's having his head turned sideways or away from the camera part of the time, nothing conclusive could be obtained. In the meanwhile, the FBF barred Siki from further bouts until the matter was settled. M. Diagne threatened to take the case to court.

Reported the French Newspapers:
"Then comes an amazing sight. François Deschamps, manager of Carpentier, the world's champion, staggering beneath Siki's blows, goes to Siki's corner and visits his manager, Charlie Hellers, in the enemy camp. Onlookers in the front rows were too excited by the fight to notice anything. And presently, having said what he had to say to Hellers with animated gestures not easily explicable in this place, Deschamps returns to his own corner. . . ."

Finally, in January 1923, the FBF issued a statement declaring that all those connected with the alleged frame-up were innocent. Two months later, Siki lost the championship in Dublin to Mike McTigue, never again attaining the form he possessed in the Carpentier fight. He died in December 1925, age twenty-eight, his body found lying in the gutter in front of 350 West 41st Street, New York City. He had been killed by two pistol shots fired from behind. The assailant was never found.

Nor was it ever determined for sure whether or not Louis Phal, alias Battling Siki, had started to take a dive against Georges Carpentier and then changed his mind.

THE BASKETBALL SCANDALS
After more than a half century of relative calm following its invention, basketball embarked on a period of nearly two decades during which a series of betting scandals, point shaving, and outright throwing of games shocked the American public. Strangely, it was not the professionals who were most active in this shady area, but the fuzzy-cheeked college "amateurs."

The first scandal was discovered quite by accident. In January 1945, police in the New York area were watching twenty-nine-year-old Henry Rosen, who was suspected of being a fence for garment thefts. One afternoon, two detectives staking out his home spotted a pair of young men, Bernard Barnett and Larry Pearlstein, entering the suspect's house. Thinking they might be part of Rosen's gang of thieves, the detectives accosted them. Barnett and Pearlstein panicked, revealing how they had received a thousand dollars from Rosen to split among five members, themselves included, of the Brooklyn College basketball team. They also told the police that Rosen—known by the boys as "the mustache"—was to meet them in Boston before the Brooklyn College-Akron game and give them instructions. Plans were in the works for the young players to dump another game, scheduled for February 10, against St. Francis College.

The scandal shocked many people, especially New York Mayor Fiorello LaGuardia, who demanded that the press and public assist him in his efforts to "take these cheap, tinhorn chiselers, these procurers, these punks and thieves, and throw them into jail."

Foiling the Gamblers—by Nat Holman:
In 1945, Nat Holman, the great coach and innovator who was elected to the Basketball Hall of Fame in 1967, was coach of the City College of New York team that was scheduled to meet Brooklyn College in a game one month after the scandal became public. When interviewed about the presence of gamblers, he said he knew of their existence and once, during a game against Syracuse, ordered one of his players, after a foul, to take the ball out of bounds rather than shoot a free throw. On a successful free throw, Holman knew the gamblers would have collected both ends of a bet based on the difference in points.

While most spoke out against the gamblers and susceptible players, only a few, such as Dr. Forrest C. Allen, basketball coach at Kansas, took the viewpoint that the real blame rested with athletic directors, coaches, and faculty members who "have failed utterly to protect college athletics from the stigma of professional gambling."

Others were inclined to play down the situation. Said Harold Olsen, basketball coach at Ohio State: "Just because a couple of kids are stupid enough to accept bribes doesn't mean there's anything wrong with basketball."

In any event, the basketball world was thrown into turmoil. The Akron University Zippers arrived in Boston following a seven-hundred-mile trip only to find that their game with Brooklyn had been canceled. Meanwhile, three additional members of the Brooklyn team confessed to taking money from gamblers, one of whom was president of the Brooklyn College Men's Association, member of the Student Council, and son of "a well-to-do professional man."

Hearings continued through February and into the early spring. No criminal action was brought against the five players, although they were expelled from the college rather abruptly on February 2. Rosen and another gambler, Harvey Stemmer, were indicted and convicted on May 9 by a Kings County jury of conspiracy to cheat and defraud. Judge Louis Goldstein sentenced Stemmer to the state penitentiary for one year and fined him five hundred dollars. A week later, despite a jury recommendation that he be given a lighter sentence because of his record in the Marine Corps, Rosen received the same sentence and fine as Stemmer.

Condemning the Gamblers:
". . . you two defendants brought disgrace and humiliation to these young men and upon one of the leading American amateur sports. . . . Your bribery of these players was a dastardly act of the vilest kind made in order to permit you and your cheating, chiseling, crooked henchmen to reap benefits of bets made with an unsuspecting and innocent public. Nothing concerned you except to fill your pockets with crooked money. . . ."
Judge Louis Goldstein, May 9, 1945

Only one final bit of irony remained in the Brooklyn College basketball scandal of 1945. After player Larry Pearlstein was "expelled" from the college, it was disclosed that he had never registered at the institution as a student.

Four years after the Brooklyn College scandal, another bribing case came to light, this time with a hero. In September 1948, David Shapiro, a twenty-five-year-old basketball player with George Washington University, received a letter from a Joseph Aronowitz stating that he "could make a lot of money."

Later Shapiro met personally with Aronowitz and Philip Klein, who offered him five hundred dollars to one thousand dollars per game if he would make certain his team won or lost by a certain amount of points. Shapiro played along with the gamblers, at the same time contacting New York County District Attorney Frank S. Hogan, who used the young man's co-operation as a means of drawing the gamblers into a trap. After a long series of vacillations by Shapiro, he finally agreed to throw a game if the gamblers would give him a down payment. By this time the number of crooks had increased to four, one of whom suggested that the down payment be given to an outside party. Shapiro's "uncle" turned out to be a detective and the gamblers were arrested en masse on January 4, 1949.

David Shapiro became an immediate hero as the four accused men were indicted and brought to trial. In February they pleaded guilty to charges of attempted bribery and conspiracy. A month later they were sentenced to prison for from 1 to 2½ years.

Two years later, despite an increasing amount of vigilance, bribing scandals seemed to become endemic. One was reported to authorities by Manhattan's six-foot, eight-inch Junius Kellogg, and subsequently two of his teammates and three gamblers were arrested. But investigations continued to turn up evidence of widespread point shaving at CCNY, NYU, LIU, Bradley, Kentucky, and Toledo in addition to Manhattan. Between 1947 and 1950, it turned out, a total of eighty-six games had been fixed by thirty-two players. One of the schools most deeply involved was Kentucky, whose players shaved so many points in the 1949 NIT game against Loyola of Chicago that they ended up losing, 67–56. The National Collegiate Athletic Association forced Kentucky to cancel its entire schedule after these revelations were made known.

Many careers were ruined by the investigations. Ralph Beard and Alex Groza were two Kentucky stars of the era who had graduated and played two seasons with the Indianapolis Olympians of the NBA when their part in the point shaving was brought to light. The league barred the fixers for life. The falling dominos even caused the ruination of an entire professional league. That was the minor American Basketball League, which found itself torn into factions when some of its teams hired Beard, Groza, Sherman White, and Bill Spivey, all of whom were implicated in the basketball scandals. At that point, President

John O'Brien called a meeting to discuss admitting the outlawed players. The ABL, already on shaky footing, apparently could not survive the schism, for on October 23, 1952, the decision was made to disband the entire organization rather than sign the players in question. A month later, Beard, Groza, and Dale Barnstable were banned from participating in sports for three years by a court order.

The Fix à la Hollywood:
By 1951, the basketball bribing scandals were so well known that it was possible to release at least one motion picture based on the problem. Entitled The Basketball Fix, *the movie starred John Ireland as a young and penurious basketball player who needs money in order to marry Vanessa Brown. He accepts bribes from gamblers but is eventually discovered when police become suspicious of his fiancée's expensive engagement ring and trace its purchase to profits earned by the hero's dumping games. "The movie professes to explore the collegiate basketball scandals," one critic wrote, "but merely dribbles adroitly past some interesting questions."*

In 1961, another series of basketball fixing scandals made the headlines, but the number of cases did not involve as many teams or players as a decade before. The disclosures did indicate, however, that it just might be impossible to totally eliminate the temptation to pick up a few dollars by missing a shot here and there.

PRO FOOTBALL'S BIG "FIX"
The gamblers installed the Chicago Bears as ten-point favorites.
The Bears won the game by precisely ten points, 24–14.
One of the players approached by gamblers, left halfback Frank Filchock of the losing New York Giants, threw five passes that were intercepted by the Bears.
Yet the game was not rigged, or at least that was the final decision after the facts were studied at considerable length by pro football officials.
The three names used most in the betting scandal, which broke on the very morning of the professional football championship game of 1946, were Merle Hapes, Filchock, and Alvin J. Paris. The first two were players with the Eastern Division Giants, the latter a twenty-eight-year-old playboy and novelty

salesman, son of Sidney Paris, who had served four years in federal prison on a charge of mail fraud.
Late in 1946, Alvin Paris started courting Hapes and Filchock, taking them to nightclubs and plying them with drinks and women. It was all part of his plan to fix the championship game later in the season, for it was likely the Giants would win in the East and face the Bears. Early in the year the Giants had beaten the Bears, 14–10, but as the championship contest approached, Bear stock rose sharply.
Soon there was an explanation for it. Frank Filchock, only hours before the game was to be played, confessed that he and Hapes had been promised twenty-five hundred dollars each, in addition to a one-thousand-dollar bet to be placed on the Bears, if they would throw the game. Both men, Filchock said, turned down the offers but neither reported them to officials until the last minute.

The Players Involved:
Merle Hapes, *a graduate of the University of Mississippi, played with the Giants for the 1942 season before going into the armed forces during World War II. Thus 1946 was only his second year.*
Frank Filchock, *of Indiana, played with the Pittsburgh Pirates from 1938 to 1941. Near the end of the war, he joined the Washington Redskins for the 1944 season but was traded to the Giants at the end of 1945.*

On the day of the game, a crowd of 58,346 buzzed with speculation that something was amiss. Because he had not contacted the police, even belatedly, Hapes was kept out of the contest, but Filchock was allowed to play. He suffered a broken nose early in the game, but according to one reporter, "played furiously . . . despite the fact that he had been up half the night while the investigation was in progress." After the Bears took a 14–0 lead, Filchock connected with Frank Liebel for a thirty-eight-yard TD pass in the first quarter and came back with a five-yarder to Steve Filipowicz to tie the score.
The issue was settled, however, when Sid Luckman scored his only touchdown of 1946 by running nineteen yards on a quarterback keeper. A field goal by Frank Maznicki increased the final score to Bears 24, Giants 14. That ended the game but not the Hapes-Filchock-Paris imbroglio. Paris was arrested and charged with attempted bribery, a felony

in New York punishable by a one-year-to-five-years' prison sentence and a ten-thousand-dollar fine.

Not long afterward, a familiar name entered the plot—that of Harvey Stemmer, who had already been convicted for bribery and conspiracy in the 1945 Brooklyn College basketball fixing scandal. Two other men, Jerome Zarowitz and David Krakauer, were indicted.

The arrests were made easier by the police wiretapping of Paris' telephone for several days and nights, then moving in when they felt enough evidence of illegal gambling activities had been collected. On January 8, 1947, Paris was found guilty by a grand jury in General Sessions and sentenced on April 7 to a year in prison. He helped his cause considerably by turning state's evidence against his former partners. By September of 1947, he was back on the street, having gotten time off for good behavior.

Stemmer, Zarowitz, and Krakauer were found guilty on March 8, 1947, and sentenced April 2 to indeterminate penitentiary terms for conspiracy.

Merle Hapes and Frank Filchock were suspended "indefinitely" from further play in the National Football League. Hapes quit the game altogether, but Filchock moved to Canada, where he played pro ball with Montreal of the Canadian League for three seasons. He was named "Male Athlete of 1949" for Canada and the following year had his suspension lifted by NFL Commissioner Bert Bell. At the age of thirty-three, he came back to the United States, signing on with the 1950 Baltimore Colts, one of the sorriest teams that ever disgraced a gridiron. In 1949, the Colts won only one game and lost eleven while finishing dead last in the All-America Conference. They were able to equal that mark in their maiden year in the NFL, allowing 462 points while losing eleven of twelve games.

For Frank Filchock, playing with the 1950 Colts was probably more than enough to atone for any sins he had accumulated in the past. He quit at the end of that season.

FIXING THE STEEPLECHASE

All a jockey has to do to fix a race is hold back on the reins a bit. It's as simple as that, or at least that's the popular view. Actually, "pulling" a horse is not always easy and is often quite difficult to disguise.

Since the beginning of organized racing, however, many jockeys have tried to earn a few extra dollars by either betting on themselves and their horses or on the opposition. And despite the growth of racing commissions and other regulatory bodies, the temptation to fix or otherwise influence a race has often proved too strong to resist. Such a case oc-

curred late in 1945 when seven jockeys and a trainer put their heads together and decided to fix the four-thousand-dollar Bryndor Steeplechase on the last day of Pimlico's fall meeting.

The brains behind the project was jockey Howard Cruz, who arranged for bets of from one hundred dollars to seven hundred dollars to be placed on Mamie's Lad, William Owen up. The other jockeys were Francis Passmore, Sidney O'Neill, Vern Haines, Scott Riles, and Douglas Banks. In addition, trainer John Barry and James Byrnes, a jockey agent, were involved or knew about the fix.

Everything seemed fine as the horses started the race, but soon afterward it was apparent that Passmore's mount, Gale Reigh, wanted to run. Before Passmore could do anything about it, she was fifty lengths in front and racing smoothly. Passmore panicked. "I took her out in front and tried to get the wind out of her, but couldn't so I snapped her," he said later. "And I think that a blind man could have seen that I pulled the horse."

Mamie's Lad eventually went on to win, thanks to Passmore's efforts, but the Maryland Racing Commission got wind of the affair and started an investigation. On February 11, 1946, Cruz was arrested. The scandal soon involved others. Headed by George P. Mahoney (who was to run against Spiro T. Agnew for governor of Maryland two decades later), the commission held a quick hearing and dispatched nearly instant justice. All seven of the jockeys were charged with violating the commission's Rule No. 145, dealing with corrupt practices, and ruled off the track for life. Trainer Barry was also ruled off, but Byrnes was given a lighter suspension, one year, because he had just returned from three years' overseas service with the Army.

Later—Two Jockey Heroes:

Lest it be thought that all jockeys have larceny on the mind, it should be pointed out that in 1954, Ted Atkinson and Conn McCreary, after being approached by gamblers, co-operated with federal agents to plan a trap. The focal point was the $133,-600 Flamingo Stakes at Hialeah, which Robert Hugh Lonsford asserted was fixed. To find out which horse was "supposed" to win, Lonsford wrote letters to the two jockeys and placed several telephone calls as well. The FBI agents were able to nab him by disguising themselves as women and staking out a phone booth.

1947—YEAR OF THE FIXED FIGHT

Boxers have been taking dives into the tank since the beginning of that entertainment, so there was little reason for the revelations of 1947 to shock and anger Americans. Perhaps the relative quiet of the war years somewhat anesthetized the population. Or it may have been that Rocky Graziano seemed too lovably dumb to be involved in any illegal activity. Jake LaMotta, of course, was quite another matter.

The headlines shouted "Scandal!" late in January 1947, implicating the colorful Rocky in one-hundred-thousand-dollar fix talk as well as failure to report bribe offers. District Attorney Frank Hogan—already well burdened with sports betting charges as a result of the Brooklyn College basketball scandal and the Hapes-Filchock football imbroglio—made the case against Graziano known shortly after the fighter faked a back injury in order to have a bout with Ruben (Cowboy) Shank canceled.

The most damning bit of evidence against Graziano was that after being offered a hundred thousand dollars to throw the fight, he had said "I'll see you later" to the gambler who visited Stillman's Gym. Later Graziano got a case of cold feet, as he explained it. Although he had not agreed to throw the bout to Shank, he felt that by defeating him he would be double-crossing the gamblers. He therefore invented a sore back as a means of saving his entire hide.

Questioned by Hogan and others, Graziano claimed he did not know the identity of the man who made the bribe offer. Hogan stated that the fighter knew the gamblers' names but was afraid to disclose them. He added that he did not believe the meetings were as casual as Graziano made them appear. After a three-day hearing in February 1947, Graziano was declared "guilty of an act detrimental to the interests of boxing" and deprived of his license. That meant that a March 21 middleweight-title bout between the Rock and Tony Zale would have to be canceled or postponed. That was what the state of New York thought. Later in the month, the National Boxing Association announced that it would not sustain the New York Athletic Commission ruling. The title fight was therefore able to be held during the summer at Chicago. Graziano knocked out Zale in the sixth round to become champion.

The Graziano affair was morally uplifting compared to the dealings of Jake LaMotta that same year. Born on the East Side in 1921, the tough LaMotta quit school at an early age and drifted into boxing as a means of supporting his family. After a brief amateur career, he turned professional in 1941, priding himself thereafter on never having been knocked off his feet.

That did not mean he could not be beaten, however, especially if the price was right. And on November 14, 1947, the price quite obviously was right. LaMotta's opponent was a twenty-two-year-old light-heavyweight from Philadelphia named Billy Fox. A crowd of 18,340 paid more than one hundred thousand dollars for the privilege of seeing the two mix it up for four rounds. Some curiosity may have increased attendance, for it was rumored ahead of time that the bout might not be straight. After a first round during which LaMotta fought in his customary, hard-to-hit style, he suddenly seemed to become an almost stationary target for Fox. "LaMotta's fighting style, or lack of it," wrote James Dawson at the time, "was another strange incident. The husky Bronx Italian . . . fought up to expectations only in the first round."

A brief flurry in the third was followed by

A Fixer Comes to Light:

A decade and a half after his prime (1937-40), a nearly forgotten heavyweight boxer named Harry Thomas shocked the sports world by confessing that several bouts in which he participated were fixed. One was against Max Schmeling at Madison Square Garden on December 13, 1937. Thomas took a dive in the eighth round after discovering that Schmeling was easy to hit and could probably have been easily whipped. "He didn't hurt me any more than my son could," Thomas said.

Another fixed bout in which Thomas participated was against Tony Galento. Thomas told the promoter to have Galento throw punches to the body, "because I know fans can't determine how hurt you are from punches to the body." But Galento insisted on throwing slow rights to the head. "When I'd get up in the clinch," Thomas said later, "I'd tell him, 'For Christ sake hit me in the body.' He'd do the same thing again." After the bout was over, Thomas observed, "I don't think they held another fight in the hall for six months. They had to keep fumigating it."

another retreat as Dawson of the New York *Times* wrote, "He backed across the ring under a right to the head and acted as if his knees were buckling."

The "acting" continued in the fourth and final round, LaMotta allowing the overeager Fox to pummel him at will. But he refused to go down, waiting patiently until Referee Frank Fullan stepped between the boxers at 2:26 to raise Fox's gloved hand.

Once again District Attorney Frank Hogan entered the picture. Having become suspicious when the odds on LaMotta changed from 5–6 early in the week to 5–12 on Fox just prior to the bout, Hogan announced three days after the fight that it was being investigated. The New York State Athletic Commission followed by withholding payment on the purses of the bout—$23,190 for each boxer. A few days later, a statement was issued along with the announcement that LaMotta had been suspended because he "concealed vital facts about his physical condition from this commission, from the doctor employed by the promoter, and even his own manager."

LaMotta on the Alleged Fix:
"All I can say is it's a dirty lie. . . . We know nothing. . . . All I know is I fought the best I knew how and I was in fine shape."

The physical condition cited by the NYBC was a hematoma of the spleen, which LaMotta received a month before the bout. "Such concealment for personal gain this commission holds to be against the best interest of boxing," the statement continued.

Was the hidden injury the answer to LaMotta's seemingly throwing the fight? Such appeared to be the case, for on December 17, 1947, the New York Athletic Commission gave LaMotta not only his share of the proceeds from the fight but its blessing as well. "The results [of the investigation] do not show any evidence that would indicate fraud in the arrangement for or conduct of this match," the commission concluded.

Thirteen years later, Jake LaMotta confessed that he had indeed thrown the fight with Billy Fox.

During the intervening years, LaMotta's career fluctuated between glory and ignominy. In June 1949 he knocked out Marcel Cerdan to take the middleweight championship, but eighteen months later lost on a thirteen-round knockout to Sugar Ray Robinson. LaMotta retired from the ring in 1954. His wife divorced him and in 1957 he pleaded guilty to charges of contributing to the delinquency of a fourteen-year-old girl.

THE LATE 1940S—AN ASSORTMENT OF FIXES

The most scandal-ridden half decade in American spectator sports concluded with a variety of minor betting revelations, none tremendously significant in itself, but the total leading some Americans to conclude that nearly every athlete in the nation was on the take.

WEST COAST FOOTBALL

Late in 1947, members of the Honolulu Warriors, of the Pacific Coast Football League, put their heads together in an off-field huddle. Their scheduled game against the Los Angeles Bulldogs seemed to beckon with opportunity. After reviewing movies of the team, fourteen Warriors agreed that the Bulldogs looked easy, so easy it would be foolish not to bet on the outcome.

Pooling their financial resources, the men gave sixty-seven hundred dollars to a Honolulu gambler with instructions to bet it on the Warriors to lead by at least seven points at halftime and twelve to fourteen at the finish. The scheme worked to perfection—for the first half, which found the Warriors ahead, 7–0. But during the second half the Bulldogs scored six points and, even more important, found their defense. The game ended with the score 7–6.

After the contest, some of the players who bet on the outcome suspected that their partners in crime had let down, perhaps having an alternate bet. A meeting was held and the men talked it over. All were satisfied except one, who reported the betting incident to Keith Molesworth, Warrior coach. Molesworth took the story to the board of directors and then the police.

Careers Cut Short by the Gambling Scandal:
Melvin (Buddy) Abreau, *a halfback from the University of Hawaii, was considered a prospect by the San Francisco 49ers of the All-America Football Conference.*
Jack Keenan, *center, from the University of South Carolina, was a member of the 1944–45 Washington Redskins. As a member of a top minor-league team, he might have been given another try in the big leagues.*
Floyd Rhea, *guard, from the University of Oregon, played with the 1943 Chicago Cardinals, 1944 Brooklyn Dodgers, 1945 Boston Yanks, and 1947 Detroit Lions.*

On December 13, 1947, fourteen players pleaded guilty in District Court to charges of gambling. Their fines ranged from twenty-five dollars to one hundred dollars, but that was only the beginning. Three days later, four of the Warriors were expelled from professional football for life and ten others received indefinite suspensions.

THE HOCKEY HUSTLERS

As a major professional sport in the United States, hockey was hit comparatively late by any sort of betting scandal. First to be implicated was Walter (Babe) Pratt, star defenseman of the Toronto Maple Leafs, winner of the Hart Trophy for the 1943–44 season. On January 29, 1946, the thirty-year-old Pratt was expelled on grounds of wagering on league games. There was no evidence that he had bet against his own team, but he had violated the NHL rules against wagering in general. After a sixteen-day suspension, he was reinstated. At the same time, League President Mervin (Red) Dutton issued a warning that any player found guilty of betting on games would be barred for life.

The new rule was tested during the 1947–48 season. Late in February 1948, NHL President Clarence Campbell began investigating rumors that at least two players had gambled on games in which they were involved. The evidence had been gathered via wiretaps and tips from various underworld characters, but Campbell wasn't picky, especially when he discovered that one of the players had bet against his own team. "Press the investigation," Campbell urged.

All clues seemed to lead to a professional gambler, James Tamer, who obviously was on speaking terms with many players. Wiretaps revealed information that was more than a little incriminating, the most damning concerning a game between the Boston Bruins and Chicago Black Hawks played on February 18. The conversation referred to Jack Crawford,

---

From the Wiretap:
(*Game between Boston Bruins and Chicago Black Hawks—*
February 18, 1948)
TAMER *How are things going tonight?*
VOICE *Don't worry about the game tonight. One of the players is sick and another's baby died and he won't be playing, and I don't intend to do so good. Don't worry. Bet five hundred dollars for me.*

Boston defenseman, whose daughter died on February 18, and Milt Schmidt, Bruin captain, who had a badly damaged knee. Soon police and Campbell were certain the Boston player involved with Tamer was Don Gallinger. Billy Taylor of the New York Rangers was also named as a player who had placed bets on games.

By the end of February, headlines screamed that Detroit gambler Tamer might be just the tip of a huge gambling iceberg involving many other nationwide sports. Tamer, a paroled bank robber, was arrested and sent back to Mississippi State Prison at Jackson while sports fans wondered how many players would follow in his wake. But the list stopped at Taylor and Gallinger. Both were suspended for life on March 9, 1948, although Clarence Campbell issued the somewhat contradictory statement that "nobody fixed anything anywhere."

The most severe penalties given professional hockey players in the history of the game, Gallinger and Taylor's suspensions were not lifted until 1970, when both were middle-aged.

THE NATIONAL GAME AGAIN

Life in the minor leagues can be difficult for a baseball player. The pay is poor, playing conditions are often terrible, and sometimes even the food isn't so good. Small wonder then that more than a few players have given in to the temptation to earn extra pay by influencing what obviously appear as meaningless games.

The Tarnished Playing Career of Bernard DeForge:
Beginning in 1937, Bernard DeForge gradually saw his dream of being a major leaguer fade and die. He started with high hopes with Beatrice of the Sally League, then played with Dayton (Ohio), Durham, Birmingham, Portsmouth (Va.), Montreal, and Natchez. In 1947, as player-manager for Natchez of the Evangeline League, he pitched 147 innings, walking 25 men while winning 12 and losing 4.

Bernard DeForge was a perfect example of the minor-league player who had little to lose by gambling or fixing a few games. In 1948 he was player-manager of the Reidville club in the Carolina League, but having started his career eleven years before, there was little chance for him to make it to the big leagues. On May 10, 1948, DeForge had a meeting at the Hotel Belvedere in Reidville with Ed Weingarten, an official with two other minor-league clubs, and W. C. McWaters, a used-car dealer from Clover, South Carolina.

At that time, "a plan to make a lot of money out of betting on baseball games" was revealed. Four days later, Winston-Salem and Reidville met on the diamond. It was just an ordinary game, except that a large amount of money had been wagered on Winston-Salem. Moreover, the betting angle stated that Winston-Salem would take the contest by three runs or more.

At the end of 7½ innings, however, Winston-Salem was leading, but only by 2–0. Reidville pitcher Tal Abernathy, a twenty-six-year-older who had appeared in a total of five games with the 1942–44 Athletics, was on the mound and doing rather well—obviously too well for manager-bettor Bernard DeForge, who proceeded to remove Abernathy and insert the only pitcher he could trust—himself.

No sooner was he on the mound than DeForge made things happen. He walked four batters, threw a wild pitch, and before too much time had passed, area gamblers had a tidy 5–0 lead.

Pungent aromas from the game soon reached the office of minor-league commissioner George Trautman, who immediately stepped in and pressed charges against DeForge, McWaters, and Weingarten. When it was discovered that DeForge had received an extra three hundred dollars following the game with Winston-Salem, Trautman was satisfied. DeForge was suspended from organized baseball and sentenced to one year in prison for accepting a bribe to throw a game.

McWaters and Weingarten got off scot-free.

GET TO THE OFFICIAL

The first variation for those with fix in mind: If not the player, try the official.

Baseball umpire Richard Higham having succumbed in 1882, gamblers decided to give young Bill Klem a test in 1908. They chose the crucial playoff game that followed the tempestuous race between the New York Giants and the Chicago Cubs. With the entire season hanging on a single game, a man approached umpire Klem as he was walking along Madison Avenue the night before. Exposing a fat wad of bills, the man said, "The Giants mustn't lose tomorrow."

Klem brushed the man aside, but the next day beneath the grandstand, the man appeared again. "Take these, Bill," he said, thrusting the bills in Klem's direction.

"Get out of my way. You stink," Klem shot back.

Several hours later, New York was bathed in sorrow as the Cubs won the playoff. Not until two months later was the sports world informed of the bribe attempt, and then the situation was soft-pedaled. "President Pulliam is very anxious to have it known that the alleged bribery was not done by any person connected with organized baseball," the newspapers reported.

It wasn't true. Investigators discovered that the man who made the offers was none other than "Doc" Cramer, part-time trainer for the New York Giants. He was later barred for life from all National League ball parks.

Because of the nature of basketball and the overwhelming presence of "judgment" calls by referees, it is perhaps more vulnerable than any other sport to a successful fix by officials. In baseball, the umpire can influence the calling of balls and strikes (close calls, that is; no fixer would dare call a pitch in the dirt a strike), as well as balls near the foul line and "foul" or "out" at bases. But if a pitcher throws to a batter who smashes it over the center-field fence, there is very little the dishonest umpire can do to nullify the play. Not without looking suspicious.

But in basketball, the referee has a vast arsenal of judgment weapons. Depending on which team he favors, a couple of players who merge as a basket is scored can generate either a "charging" or a "blocking" foul; "traveling" can be called at any critical time, as can a judicious foul during a rebound melee under the hoop. And a foul call can negate any score the referee wishes.

It was against this background that Missouri Valley Conference officials began to study the record of referee John Fraser in 1956–57. They became suspicious when point-spread changes in nine games, all refereed by Fraser, worked in favor of "smart money" gamblers. After the Wichita-Western Kentucky game of February 13, 1957, a game that attracted a great deal of "smart money" on Western Kentucky (the underdog team), an investigation began. Before long it reached all the way to University of Wichita President Dr. Harry Corbin, who after hearing rumors of gambling went to the FBI. Corbin also contacted the Reverend Paul Reinert, President of St. Louis University. They agreed that John Fraser should be relieved of his duties.

Several weeks later, when the investigation began to turn up unfavorable items in Fraser's past, the referee resigned.

Everything considered, American League umpires Ed Runge and Bill McKinley came out of the situation smelling like a small bouquet of roses.

It was the summer of 1960 and the pennant race was better than usual. That is, the Yan-

A SAMPLER OF REFEREE FRASER'S GAMES:

Date	Teams	Smart Money on	Winner	Note
Dec 8, 1956	Ohio State- St. Louis	Ohio State	Ohio State	23 fouls called on St. Louis, 10 on Ohio State
Dec 27, 1956	Yale-Bradley	Bradley	Bradley	47 fouls called on Yale, 30 on Bradley
Jan 17, 1957	Houston-Bradley	Bradley	Bradley	3 Houston starters fouled out

kees were not making a runaway of things, as they usually did in that era. While seated in a Baltimore bar, Runge and McKinley were approached by a couple of young women and the conversation soon got around to methods of whiling away the rest of the evening. The two arbiters eventually found themselves in a motel near Beltsville, Maryland, with the ladies.

At that point, while unquestionably compromised, the umpires were suddenly confronted by a pair of ex-convicts with a camera. Having gotten their picture story, the men put forth a proposition: The umpires could cough up five thousand dollars for the negative of the picture or arrange to repay the debit by fixing a game or two.

To their credit, Runge and McKinley decided to make a clean breast of their dilemma, however damaging, to American League President Joe Cronin. After the police were notified, it was arranged that Runge and McKinley would pretend to go along with the gamblers.

The day after the motel confrontation, Runge found an envelope containing a picture and a note that had been slipped beneath the door of his Washington hotel room. It contained instructions for meeting a man after that day's game. Runge complied, and subsequently was able to give police information leading to the arrest of the gamblers.

1963—HORNUNG AND KARRAS
"Sure I bet on games—who doesn't?"
                                    Alex Karras
No one believed that after the Hapes-Filchock affair of 1946, professional football players insulated themselves en masse from gamblers and their influence. League rules prohibited players from betting on games, even those in which they were not involved, but obviously there were those who violated the ban. Friendly bets were made—Alex Karras admitted betting on his own club, Detroit, but only for cigarettes as stakes. Still

other wagers for fifty dollars or a hundred dollars, not a great deal of money, were made, leading NFL Treasurer Austin Gunsel to initiate a study of various players' gambling habits and friends. Inevitably the trail led to Detroit defensive tackle Alex Karras, who owned part of a bar that gamblers were supposed to frequent, and Paul Hornung, Green Bay halfback. Hornung, it was discovered, had started placing bets on college and NFL games in 1959, two years after his graduation from Notre Dame. Karras had warmed up with fifty-dollar bets until 1962, when he wagered a hundred dollars on Detroit to beat Green Bay in a decisive game near the end of the season. (Karras lost, as did his team.) Following that defeat, Karras won his money back by betting a hundred dollars on Green Bay, which beat the New York Giants in the championship game.

In January 1963, rumbles were heard to the effect that a U. S. Senate subcommittee was planning an investigation of the links between NFL players and organized gamblers. According to reports, FBI agents visited Karras's bar and questioned his partner, John Butsicaris, about the presence of gamblers there. Edwin J. Anderson, general manager of the Lions, obviously panicked when he heard the reports, for he said, "I don't like the idea of a player owning a part of a bar where he might run into undesirable people." (Why, one might ask, had he not said something before the federal investigation came to light?)

D-day for Karras and Hornung was April 17, 1963, when the NFL commissioner announced that they had been suspended indefinitely for betting on league games and associating with gamblers. Five other Detroit Lion players—John Gordy, Sam Williams, Wayne Walker, Joe Schmidt, and Gary Lowe—were fined two thousand dollars each for betting on the 1962 championship contest. Detroit management was also fined four thousand dollars for failure to report information on gambling and permitting "undesirables" to mingle with players on the sidelines.

What's Wrong with Betting on Yourself?

It's a logical question that was asked by many sports fans in the wake of the Karras-Hornung trouble. NFL spokesmen, of course, were prepared. If it were a well-known fact that a player bet on his own team, they said, what would people think if for some reason he broke the pattern and did not bet one week? Wouldn't it be assumed that the player knew something?

After sitting out the 1963 season, Karras and Hornung were reinstated on March 16, 1964.

1970—DENNY MCLAIN

On September 14, 1968, pitcher Denny McLain of the Detroit Tigers accomplished something only three other men had been able to do since 1920—win thirty games in a single season. At the age of twenty-four, he was sitting on top of the baseball world.

After a good 1969 season, during which he won twenty-four games and lost nine, the McLain luck changed. By 1971, he led the American League in losses with twenty-two, and the next year was his last in the majors. At the age of twenty-eight, he was through.

Heavy moralists might have cited McLain as a classic example of the innocent corrupted by gamblers, for his downfall began in 1970, when his past connections with underworld figures began to be explored.

Although Commissioner Bowie Kuhn took credit for the investigation, the impetus came from the magazine *Sports Illustrated,* which printed a story alleging that McLain missed the end of the 1967 season because gambler friends had made heavy bets on the Boston Red Sox. Thus, *SI* said, McLain claimed to have stubbed his toe and could not pitch.

The story spurred examination of McLain's background, which led in February 1970 to his being suspended by Commissioner Kuhn.

The reason—"1967 bookmaking activities and his associations at that time." McLain's involvement was obviously greater than that of Karras and Hornung in football betting, but for some reason—appropriately, on April Fool's Day—Kuhn announced that the young pitcher's suspension would be for three months. What that amounted to was a slap on the wrist, and a mild one at that. "There are some who wonder if it won't become the equivalent of a three-month paid vacation in Florida," columnist Arthur Daley wrote.

Some Unmemorable Quotes on the McLain Affair:
"The McLain situation is like the difference between attempted murder and successful murder."
    Baseball Commissioner Bowie Kuhn

"My biggest crime is stupidity."
                Denny McLain

After missing spring training and the first 2½ months of the 1970 baseball season, Denny McLain returned to the Detroit mound on July 1. True to their generous nature, the fans forgave him and accorded him a standing ovation. Even Commissioner Kuhn called and wished the young pitcher good luck.

It didn't help. Three Yankee home runs later, McLain departed the game with New York ahead, 5–3. Detroit eventually won the game in extra innings, thus preventing a McLain loss in his 1970 debut. He finished the year at 3–5 and was traded to the lowly Washington Senators for the 1971 season.

Was McLain's downfall caused by gambling? Unlikely, since he obviously was deeply involved before his magnificent season of 1968. What may have hurt his mental state—and pitching concentration—more than anything else was being caught.

1977—DON KING, ABC, AND THE FIGHTS THAT WEREN'T

Boxing on television, which many thought had died during the late 1950s as a result of

---

The Other Thirty-game Winners:
1920—Jim Bagby, Cleveland, won thirty-one games, lost twelve
1931—Lefty Grove, Philadelphia A's won thirty-one games, lost four
1934—Dizzy Dean, St. Louis Cardinals, won thirty games, lost seven

overexposure, staged a comeback during the mid-1970s, thanks largely to a shrewd black promoter named Don King. After bringing together Muhammad Ali and Joe Frazier in a mediocre hype, the "thrilla in Manila," King directed his attention to live television rather than closed-circuit theater showings of championship bouts only. It was King's hope to develop American boxing champions by holding a series of TV tournaments that would make household names of many fighters.

The American Broadcasting Company entered into the $1.5 million venture with King, the first series of bouts being held aboard the aircraft carrier *Lexington* to much fanfare.

Everything went well until the tournament reached the semifinal stage. At that point, a disgruntled heavyweight, Scott LaDoux, charged that the tournament was rigged in favor of those boxers who were handled by associates of King. He also contended that there were kickbacks made by boxers in order to get into the rankings.

That was not all. Investigations proved that several fighters who were signed to appear had their records falsified for *Ring* magazine. One was Ike Fluellen, a junior middleweight of Houston who had not fought for a year prior to the TV tourney. But in the three months just before the tournament was held, Fluellen made a miraculous ascent to No. 3 in the rankings. As more and more evidence came in, ABC became less and less enamored of the unfavorable publicity generated by the atmosphere of fix that surrounded the tournament. The televised series was canceled on April 16, 1977.

The ABC Statement:
"On Friday, April 8, one aspect of this investigation resulted in ABC's obtaining and turning over to the United States Attorney an affidavit from a fighter stating that he had been contacted by a would-be manager who told him he could get him rated in Ring *magazine's top ten United States rankings, although he had not fought in a year and had never been ranked before. . . . ABC has now determined that the records of numerous fighters in the tournament as listed in the 1977* Ring *book are, in fact, inaccurate and contain many fights which apparently never took place."*

Don King was later exonerated in a 327-page report by chief investigator Michael Armstrong, who while finding "a good deal of

unethical behavior," called the tournament's concept "sound and laudable."

It was exactly a century since the Louisville Grays had kicked the National League pennant in Boston's direction. Few could deny that at least sports fixing in America had become more sophisticated with the passage of time.

SOME CELEBRATED "RINGERS"

On September 23, 1977, horse players at Belmont Park saw the oddsmakers take a beating when 57–1 shot Lebón, who had not won in ten months, swept home by four lengths to pay $116 on a $2.00 win ticket. The principal recipient of Lebón's miracle was a forty-three-year-old veterinarian, Mark Gerard, who just happened to purchase $1,300 worth of win tickets and $600 worth of show tickets, enough to earn himself a tidy $80,440.

Was Gerard also the beneficiary of a fix? Belmont officials immediately pieced together a string of clues that indicated that Lebón was not Lebón the winner of $711 in 1976 but another horse named Cinzano, who won seven of eight races at Maronas in Montevideo, Uruguay, prior to being substituted for Lebón for his United States debut.

Some expressed shock and dismay that such a sleazy scam could have been perpetrated on the horse-playing public at a major track. Others knew that such substitutions had been going on nearly as long as organized racing in America.

One of the early practitioners of the "ringer" art was a trainer, William Brannon, who operated during the 1890s with a fast horse named Tanner. "I never saw as good a subject for ringing as Tanner," Brannon said after his deeds at the track were known, "In the first place he was a horse of perfect temper and as docile as the buggy horse of a country doctor. . . . He could carry weight, any going suited him and a stable boy could ride him as well as a Reiff or a Tod Sloan."

In disguising Tanner and other horses for a variety of races, Brannon became quite adept in the art of applying horse makeup. He used ordinary hair dye to change the overall color and was able to snip and paint until he converted a chestnut with white legs into a bay with black points. On one occasion he was able to change a broad blaze in a horse's face to a star.

Brannon's greatest coup took place in September 1891 at Latonia, Kentucky, when Tanner, entered as Polk Badget, romped home an easy winner. Starting as a 25–1 shot, Polk Badget's odds dropped quickly to 8–5, a sure sign that word of the fix had gotten around. Before the race started, thirty bookmakers rubbed the horse's name off their slates. Thus Brannon and his cohorts failed to realize much money on Tanner's victory, but the undetected substitution was counted an unqualified artistic success. Brannon did clean up racing Tanner at Louisville under the alias Little Dan, after which he bleached him chestnut and sold him. Counting his legitimate races, Brannon estimated that Tanner won a total of seventy-five times during his checkered—and multicolored —career.

By 1901, Secretary E. C. Hopper of the American Turf Congress predicted that ringing was a thing of the past. New laws for registering horses and licensing trainers, he said, assured that illegal substitutions would become harder to pull off.

That may have been largely true, but it did not make ringing obsolete. In 1946, Sea Command, the five-year-old son of War Admiral, turned up in disguise as Allpulch, a five-year-old of undistinguished pedigree. Oddly, All-pulch's ascendancy began shortly after Sea Command "retired" from action in the fall of 1945 at Pimlico, where he was claimed for $3,750 and dropped out of sight.

On November 13, Allpulch arrived at Rockingham Park, New Hampshire, winning a mile-and-an-eighth race, paying $26.40 for a $2.00 win ticket. An unknown individual cashed $30,000 worth of $100 tickets placed on the equally unknown horse's nose. Three days later, Allpulch won again, by five lengths at Narragansett. And he continued to win until eight months later, on July 31, 1946, when he was ordered scratched from the fifth race at Rockingham Park by Spencer Drayton, head of the Thoroughbred Racing Protective Bureau.

Between the careers of Tanner and Lebón, of course, many examples of ringing occurred in the racing industry. The main attraction of such a fix seems to be that the principal witness, unless his name happens to be Mister Ed of TV fame, is unable to testify.

CHAPTER 4—FLAPS

One reason given for the increasing popularity of spectator sports is that the games are microcosms of life in which the end result is clear-cut, and victory goes to the player or team that strives harder or is able to apply a greater degree of talent. In real life, the race does not always go to the swiftest; end results are, as often as not, confused or unrecognized; there is no scoreboard or tally sheet spelling out our victories and defeats; except for a few friends or members of the family, cheering sections or fans seldom exist. We accept the victories—nearly always tarnished—and the defeats of life (when we are able to recognize them as such) in an emotional vacuum that becomes more constricted with the passage of time. When we are young, we cheer loudly something that pleases us; when we grow old, a wan smile is sufficient, for we know that all too soon we may see the other side of the coin.

Thus the game remains popular—because it has a definite result which, as Casey Stengel said, you can always look up in the record book. It represents order in a chaotic world, justice in a wasteland of injustice.

Well, sometimes it does. Perhaps we might even extend that to "usually." But many times, because of human nature and human failings, the sports contest ends up being nearly as confused as life itself. An official's decision is questioned, evidence of duplicity is found, a rule is overlooked. Sometimes the controversy is settled—usually it is, just to get it into the record book—but those with an opposite point of view do not always accept the mandate as correct. There are, after all, still a few persons alive, fifty years after the event, who do not believe that Gene Tunney deserved to be heavyweight champion because of the "long count" decision of 1927.

Below, then, a selection of sports contests that created controversy, added frustration and unhappiness—that is, a bit of life's spice—to the otherwise orderly world of athletic competition.

1886—PRINCETON-YALE

In football, they were the giants of their time. Along with Harvard, Yale and Princeton dominated the East (and therefore the nation). There was no official championship to be decided, but of course everyone knew that the winner of the Yale-Princeton football match would be recognized as the best ir the nation.

As Thanksgiving week of 1886 approached, both squads had proved their ability, not only by going through the season undefeated, but also by handling Harvard as well. Princeton had given the Crimson a 12–0 licking; Yale had taken them, 29–4. Those were the only points Yale gave up all year.

Settling the matter of superiority on the football field was not as simple as it sounded, however. Two ancillary questions had to be resolved first: whose field will be used? Who will furnish the referee? Having defeated Yale, 6–5, in 1885, Princeton was the incumbent champion and had no particular desire to play a contest under "adverse conditions"— that is, on unfriendly grounds, perhaps with an unfriendly referee. Thus, when Yale captain Robert N. Corwin demanded that the game be played on Yale's field—in 1885 the game had been played at Princeton—a period of anxious waiting followed. As late as the Tuesday before Thanksgiving, telegrams were flying back and forth between the two schools, both captains toughing it out to the point where many felt no game would be played at all. Captain Savage of Princeton took Yale's refusal to play on Princeton grounds as an act of forfeiture, which meant that Princeton would hold the championship another year. Mass meetings were held at both schools. At this point, Walter Camp, former coach of Yale, set up a meeting in New York's Fifth Avenue Hotel for the purpose of resolving the problem. After two hours of conversation, he convinced the Yale men to agree to play at Princeton, selecting Tracy Harris, a senior at Princeton, to act as referee. Having won these concessions, the men of Princeton even insisted that the game time be changed from two-thirty to one-thirty, which was the time of day at which Princeton normally practiced. This suggestion was turned down. Despite having been forced to capitulate on nearly every issue, Yale held a mass rally that evening and it was generally agreed that Walter Camp had served the old school well, "for it is a matter of faith that what he doesn't know about football isn't worth knowing."

The Records of Yale and Princeton Before Their Meeting, 1886:

Yale	Opponent		Princeton	Opponent	
75	Wesleyan	0	58	Stevens	0
52	Wesleyan	0	61	Stevens	6
96	Technology	0	30	U. of Penn.	0
54	Stevens	0	55	U. of Penn.	9
76	Williams	0	28	U. of Penn.	6
136	Wesleyan	0	12	Harvard	0
82	Crescents	0	76	Wesleyan	6
75	U. of Penn.	0			
29	Harvard	4			

Thursday, November 15, 1886, at 3:30 P.M.—one hour late—the momentous game began. (The delay had been caused by a Princeton plot to renege on the agreement to use Harris as referee by claiming he wasn't in town. He turned up shortly after three o'clock.) From the very outset it was obvious to most of the five thousand witnesses that Yale had the stronger squad, most of the game being played in Princeton territory. (Yale might have had an early touchdown when Princeton Captain Savage fumbled the ball in the end zone and Yale recovered. But Referee Harris said the play did not count because he hadn't seen the ball put in play.)

After that major piece of excitement, the game degenerated into a push-shove-slugfest that, if we can believe journalists of the time, required more ability at street fighting than football. The spectators, of course, loved it, although Yale partisans began to grow anxious that their team score at least once. After a ten-minute break, the second half began with the game still scoreless. It started to rain, turning the field into a muddy pit. Then, suddenly, the break awaited by Yale came. Out of a struggling mass of players, the ball squirted high into the air toward the Princeton goal. It was hotly pursued by a lone Tiger and three Yale men. One of the Yale players captured it as a scream of delight went up from the crowd. Many in the crowd, which had pressed close to the sidelines as the visibility grew poor, rushed onto the field to embrace their heroes. In the confusion, referee Harris decided, after some deliberation, that Yale had indeed scored a touchdown. The score was 4–0.

No attempt was made to kick a goal; in fact, it was raining in such torrents and the sky was so dark that a spontaneous rush from the field in the direction of the railway station began. Before long the grounds were deserted.

The Princeton team was in no mood to accept the weather as an act of God denying them the national championship, however. That very evening a dispatch was sent out declaring that "the game had been decided a draw because it was stopped seventeen minutes before the time limit had expired." That meant, of course, that Princeton would retain the football crown.

Nearly everyone took sides in the ensuing dispute, even Referee Tracy Harris, who said, "All bets are off as far as I am concerned, but I will not take the responsibility of calling this a drawn game."

It remained for the Intercollegiate Football Convention to decide the outcome. Meeting at the Fifth Avenue Hotel two days after the Thanksgiving Day contest, the body—which

A Sample of the Violence:

"Yale's little quarterback, Beecher, who weighs only 130 pounds, slid through the Princeton rushers like an electric eel and went darting forward ten good yards before he was collared and slammed down into the mud as if he were a paving beetle."

"Half a dozen Yale rushers clambered upon Cowan's broad shoulders and the human pile toppled and went down into the triassic stratum of the state of New Jersey with a pathetic squash."

"Ames made a short run, which was concluded by a Yale rusher's sitting on his neck and savagely pulling his hair. . . . A person standing two thirds of the length of the ground away from the players could hear the spat, spat of fists on face constantly."

included Walter Camp, two men from Harvard, two from Princeton, and two from Yale —decided that the 1886 championship belonged to neither team. "No game" was the verdict.

That made no one really happy, of course. There was some talk of getting the two squads together for a later meeting, but this was quashed on November 29 when Yale Captain Corwin said bluntly: "We won the game in Princeton on Thanksgiving Day and we have no cause to play another."

The merits or demerits of the case remained an issue for discussion until the following year when Yale beat both Harvard and Princeton by the score of 12–0. That presumably buried the controversy "into the triassic stratum of the state of New Jersey with a pathetic squash."

1886—DID BRODIE JUMP?

Even today there are those who describe Steve Brodie as one of the world's greatest hoaxsters. For a time he was known as "the first man to jump off the Brooklyn Bridge and live to tell about it." Then, as his reputation for honesty was challenged, he became "the man who *claimed* he was the first."

Chances are Steve Brodie would have been a supplier of colorful copy regardless of the era in which he lived. Born about 1860, he grew up near the New York-Brooklyn waterfront and like many youngsters of the late nineteenth century—when the Battery water was polluted but not yet lethal—he soon learned to swim with the very best. He was such an accomplished swimmer as a teen-ager, in fact, that he was able to rescue a pair of women who fell off an excursion barge. He was also fortunate enough to save a certain Jenny Brett at Coney Island. Miss Brett, an actress, rewarded the lad with a golden locket, which he proudly displayed in his later years. Brodie also became a noted long-distance walker and boxer before he attained his majority.

After opening a Bowery saloon in the 1880s, Brodie was well known as an eccentric character with a rough but generous nature. On rainy days, for example, he used to purchase and distribute umbrellas to the shop girls who hurried by his establishment on their way to work. And on more than one occasion, Brodie insisted on paying the burial expenses of all the unidentified bodies that turned up at the New York City Morgue. If modesty was not one of his overwhelming traits, neither was parsimony.

One thing Brodie enjoyed was a challenge. Thus, when Robert E. Odlum died following a jump from the brand-new Brooklyn Bridge on May 19, 1885, Brodie announced that he

was going to become the first man to make the leap and live to tell about it. On July 23, 1886, with very little advance publicity— which would have alerted the local police— Brodie executed either his genuine leap or a carefully rehearsed canard. (Some said, for example, that a dummy was tossed over the side of the bridge and that Brodie, already in the water, completed the hoax by bobbing his head above the surface on cue.) How many persons actually witnessed the event is not known, although the New York *Times* published an extremely vivid account shortly afterward. "His body inclined a little to the right and his legs were parted," the reporter wrote. "He, however, struck with his feet and then on his side."

Taken to court for a variety of charges, Brodie was sentenced to a brief period in jail, which bothered him very little if at all. After being released, he sold, or rented, himself to a local dime museum for the outstanding price of $250 a week, then returned to his saloon to enjoy the new business generated by his notoriety. When efforts were made to have him repeat the dive, Brodie usually brushed them aside with the line, "I did it oncet." This inevitably led to rumors that Brodie had fabricated the entire story in order to win a bet. A second rumor that made the rounds was that Brodie, a fairly heavy drinker, had worked up his courage for the jump by belting down glass after glass of liquor. It may have been true that he had a drink or two before the event, but Brodie was obviously a daredevil who did not need alcohol to help him perform acts of derring-do.

A Steve Brodie Anecdote:
During the 1890s, when Brodie was introduced to heavyweight champion Jim Corbett's father, the latter said: "So you're the fellow who jumped over the Brooklyn Bridge." "No," Brodie replied, "I jumped off it." To which the elder Corbett replied with some disdain, "Oh. I thought you jumped over it. Any damn fool can jump off it."

In all likelihood, Brodie simply liked to keep people guessing. Not long after the bridge controversy, he turned up at Passaic Falls, New Jersey, where he was seen to leap off the rocks into the water clad only in red underwear. No one raised doubts as to the authenticity of the performance, but in 1889 they did question his claim that he had gone over Niagara Falls in an inflated rubber suit. Even the judge, before whom Brodie appeared on a charge of attempted suicide, didn't believe his claim. But if Brodie confessed that the alleged jump was humbug, the judge said, all charges would be dropped.

Some Who Did Make the Jump, with Witnesses:
Barely more than a month after Brodie jumped off the Brooklyn Bridge, a young man named Larry Donovan performed the trick before a large crowd of friends and curiosity-seekers. A pressman for the Police Gazette, *the twenty-four-year-old Donovan went over the side wearing a red shirt, a pair of dark trousers padded with cotton waste from his employer's press room, and zinc-soled shoes. Although police officers patrolled the bridge at regular intervals, they were unable to stop the young man as he suddenly sprang from an express wagon that came to a halt in the middle of the span. Dropping 143 feet into the water of the East River, Donovan was unharmed except for the $10 fine he incurred for obstructing traffic on the bridge.*

In 1921, a leap from the Brooklyn Bridge was performed for the movie camera by Daniel Carone, an expert swimmer and professional stuntman.

"You mean if I tell you I didn't go over you'll let me go?" Brodie asked.

"Yes."

"Very well. I didn't go over and I'm off," Brodie smiled, starting for the door.

When the judge insisted that Brodie sign an affidavit, however, the Irishman refused, saying he was a good Catholic and couldn't go that far. After several witnesses came forward to say they had seen Brodie make the jump, the judge gave up and let the charges drop.

Nine years later, when rumors were heard that Brodie, not yet forty, had passed away in Chicago, the Bowery went into a state of collective shock. An elaborate funeral was planned, but just as the drama built to a climax, Brodie suddenly appeared. He explained that his "death" had been reported because he had received an overdose of morphine for a pleurisy attack, and the resultant comatose state caused some to assume he was dead.

Three years later, in 1901, Brodie really died, taking the exact details of his career with him. Obviously some were trying to dig information out of him at the very end, for his final words were reported to be something like: "Bridge jumping? Say, you take an old

fool's advice. If you wanter get off the car, just reach up and pull the strap and wait till it stops, see?"

Thus the jury still remains out on the actual accomplishments of Steve Brodie, who seemed to thrive on controversy and deliberate obfuscation. Inevitably, some of the false clues he planted here and there bubble to the surface, as in 1952, when a *New Yorker* article on the history of the Brooklyn Bridge stated that Brodie passed away in 1898, the year of his "morphine overdose."

One has to believe Steve Brodie would have enjoyed that.

THE FORFEITS THAT COST A PENNANT

When Earl Weaver, manager of the pennant-contending Baltimore Orioles, forfeited a game against Toronto on September 15, 1977, because the umpires refused to order removal of a tarpaulin from the Blue Jay bullpen area, the question must have flashed through the minds of some fans: Has a pennant ever been lost because of a forfeited game?

In a word, yes. The incident occurred on Saturday, September 7, 1889, at Washington Park, Brooklyn, where the hometown team and Chris Von der Ahe's St. Louis Browns were battling for the American Association title. More than fifteen thousand were on hand—the largest weekday, nonholiday crowd ever to appear in Brooklyn—to see the game, which was a dandy. At the end of seven innings, the Browns led, 4–2, but as Brooklyn came to bat in the eighth, the skies grew noticeably darker. Charlie Comiskey, first baseman and captain for St. Louis, asked Umpire Goldsmith to call the game. Goldsmith refused.

Some stalling followed until, in a dramatic but unsubtle gesture, President Von der Ahe sent to a grocery store for some candles and had them lit in front of the players' bench. An argument culminated in Comiskey's pulling his men off the field. Goldsmith waited five minutes for them to return, then announced that Brooklyn was the winner, 9–0. The hometown fans promptly celebrated the victory by smashing the windows of the Browns' clubhouse.

The next day, still angry at the forfeiture, Chris Von der Ahe, who was noted for his stubbornness, refused to allow his men to play against Brooklyn at Ridgewood, New York. (Sunday baseball was forbidden in Brooklyn at the time.) His excuse was that he was afraid the police protection would not be adequate.

Umpire Goldsmith, not buying, then awarded Brooklyn the second forfeiture. It might have reached a string of three, except that rainy weather intervened, giving Von der Ahe a bit of time to control his temper. The damage had been done, however. Brooklyn finished the season with a record of 93 wins, 44 losses (.679); St. Louis with 90 wins, 45 losses (.667). Eventually the dispute was brought before the Board of Directors of the American Association and a compromise decision was reached. The first forfeiture was given back to the Browns because it was agreed that the umpire should have called the game while they were leading. The second forfeiture was upheld and the Browns were fined fifteen hundred dollars.

From the New York *Herald*—Spritely Dialogue Between Chris Von der Ahe and Brooklyn President Charles Byrne:

BYRNE *Christ, you're placing me in a very unpleasant position. The crowd to see the game today will be very large, and I can't afford to open the gates unless you say you'll come.*

VON DER AHE *I'll go if you play off yesterday's game on Monday or else let it go to St. Louis. We won it by a score of 4–2.*

BYRNE *Do you think I'm a fool? I stand on the rules of the Association and I'll compel you to do so, too.*

Even one game would have made the difference, however. If the Browns had been able to defeat Brooklyn in the second contest, their record of 91–44 (.674) would have been just a hair better than Brooklyn's 92–45 (.673).

Baseball, they say correctly, is indeed a game of inches.

FRED MERKLE AND SECOND BASE

To baseball fans, Fred Merkle's failure to touch second base on September 23, 1908, is as famous as Moses' stealing from Egypt to the Promised Land a few years earlier.

One should not be too hard on Fred. He was, after all, a nineteen-year-old in only his second season of major-league ball when it happened. Not only that, he got caught at a mistake that was common on the diamond until he transformed it into a classic blunder.

Except for that major error, Merkle had little to do with the New York Giants' losing the 1908 pennant. The team's position was so solid—or at least it seemed that way—on September 14, three weeks before the end of the season, that most sportswriters had conceded the flag to the Giants. During the previous week, the Giants played 7 games, winning six and adding 13 points to their percentage column. They led the Chicago Cubs by only 1½ games and the third-place Pittsburgh Pirates

by 2, however, so it is a bit difficult to explain the optimism that abounded in Gotham. Even more mystifying is that Frank Chance's Chicago Cubs had won in 1906 and 1907. But they were not playing up to their form of those two years, when they won 116 and 107 games, respectively. To repeat in 1908, they would need to win at least 100, it was reasoned, which meant winning 17 out of the last 20 games.

The Giants' Premature Victory:

"With but three weeks before the curtain falls on the baseball season, the Giants' prospects of winning the National League championship were never brighter than at present . . . they are going so strongly . . . that even with his scarcity of good pitchers, Manager McGraw should succeed in landing the pennant."

Giant optimism increased even more by the end of the next week, when they further increased their lead. More important, they were 6 games ahead of the Cubs in the loss column; if the pennant was going to be thrown away, the Giants would have to do it themselves.

This they proceeded to do immediately. On September 21, the Giants lost to Pittsburgh, 2–1, while the Cubs were trouncing the Phillies in a doubleheader. At this point the most dramatic moment of the season arrived— Chicago was the next opponent at the Polo Grounds, a four-game series that would surely decide the pennant winner.

Giant fans moaned in anguish as their favorites dropped both ends of a doubleheader on September 22 and fell into a virtual tie with the Cubs for the league lead. The second game was particularly bitter. Trailing, 2–1, in the seventh inning, the Giants loaded the bases on a single by Mike Donlin and walks to Art Devlin and Al Bridwell. With rookie pitcher Doc Crandall scheduled to bat, McGraw inserted Fred Merkle to pinch-hit. There were two out, and the rookie, who was used only occasionally, swung weakly at three pitches. Merkle had struck out.

But the worst was yet to come. The very next day, Cristy Mathewson took the mound for the Giants against the Cubs' Jack Pfiester, who was hardly the star of the Chicago pitching staff. (Ed Reulbach and Three-finger Brown were on their ways to winning 24 and 29 games, respectively, that year.) The Cubs took a 1–0 lead in the fifth but the home team got a run in the sixth and went into the bottom half of the ninth tied. With two out

"Merkle at the Bat," by the Local Humorist:
Those were the days when a local sportswriter, emulating George Ade or Artemus Ward, frequently described the action in the style of the average fan. Thus W. W. Aulick, as he signed himself, writing of Fred Merkle's dramatic trip to the plate in the seventh with the bases loaded:

"*Come on, Merkle, if they won't let Crandall bat. We trust in you, darlin'.* . . . *Step up there, good man, and play baseball. Pshaw! Why did you hit at that first one? Why did you not wait? It wasn't worth your effort. Pick out a bonny one, Merkle, and then strike for the freedom of your sires, and a little bit more. Not that one, not that, Merkle. Didn't we give you waiting orders? Never mind, there is one chance left. Use it wisely. Get a firm hold on your bat, and slash away over yonder third-base line.* . . . *Or, if you think you can pull it off, a Texas-leaguer will demoralize them. Or you might— Mr. Merkle has struck out, gentlemen.*"

and Moose McCormick on first base, Fred Merkle came to bat and singled, sending McCormick to third. The next batter, Al Bridwell, smashed a hard liner to center field. McCormick ambled home with the winning run, Merkle started for second base as the crowd burst onto the field, but before reaching it, turned to escape the mob by racing for the clubhouse. Cub manager and first baseman Frank Chance, realizing that the run wouldn't count unless Merkle touched second, immediately called for the ball, but Giant pitcher Joe McGinnity grabbed it and threw it back into the crowd. Confusion followed. One version of what happened next was that as the ball disappeared, one of the Cubs threw out another from the ballbag on the bench, and that ball was used to touch second base and force Merkle, by this time almost out of his uniform.

Another version came from second baseman Johnny Evers of the Cubs, who years later claimed that the original ball was retrieved by Joe Tinker—with an assist from Floyd Kroh, who relayed it to Evers. The Umpire, Hank O'Day, had been involved in the same situation just nineteen days before in a game at Pittsburgh. On that occasion, he had allowed the winning run to score even though the

runner had not touched second base. This time he was forced to go by the book. Following Chance's appeal, O'Day announced to the crowd that the run did not count and the game was therefore a tie.

Evers' Version:
"*I can still see the guy who caught McGinnity's throw,*" Evers recalled. "*A tall, stringy middle-aged gent with a brown bowler hat on. Steinfeldt and Floyd Kroh, a young pitcher of ours, raced after him.* . . . *The guy wouldn't let go of the ball. But suddenly Kroh solved the problem. He hit the customer right on top of the stiff hat and drove it down over his eyes. As the gent folded up, the ball fell free.* . . ."

The resin bag hit the fan as soon as O'Day's decision was known. Giant management claimed a 2–1 victory; Cub management claimed a 9–0 forfeit victory because the Giants had left the field with the score tied and failed to complete the game. Upon receiving the umpires' report, National League President Harry Pulliam decided that the game should be counted a tie and replayed at the very end of the season if necessary.

While these matters were being debated, the Giants and Cubs took the field once again and this time the Giants stayed around until the final out was duly registered, defeating the Cubs, 5–4. New Yorkers relaxed, feeling that their Giants were back on the right track, but the very next day the team dropped a doubleheader to Cincinnati as the Cubs beat Brooklyn, 5–1. As the fan who was inclined to worry knew all along, the season ended with the teams tied at 98 victories and 55 defeats. "That" game was then replayed and the Cubs, behind Three-finger Brown, defeated Mathewson and the Giants, 4–2.

Fred Merkle played fourteen more years in the major leagues and lived forty-eight more, never being allowed to forget that he was the "goat who failed to touch second base."

1922—NYU-COLUMBIA
When they met on the gridiron on October 21, 1922, Columbia and New York University were hardly expected to play a game that would arouse much controversy. Columbia was heavily favored, but the contest would not decide a national or even regional championship. Nevertheless, a large crowd was on hand to see if Columbia could remain undefeated.

Playing savagely from the outset, NYU took the lead in the first quarter when Columbia's Ben Roderick attempted to punt deep in his own territory. Berkwit of NYU broke through the line and blocked the ball over the goal line into the end zone. His teammate, Toorock, pursued the ball but could not control it until it bounced past the end line and into the stands. When he came up with the ball at that point, a touchdown was signaled by referee William N. Morice of the University of Pennsylvania.

NYU took the 7–0 lead into the final quarter, fighting off several serious threats until the final minutes when the faster and heavier Columbia line pushed across a touchdown. Roderick's point-after-touchdown was blocked, however, and NYU fans cheered as their team managed to hang onto the one-point margin as the game ended.

The contest was barely over before comments were heard that Referee Morice had made a mistake in awarding NYU a touchdown for what was obviously a safety. Having arrived back at his home in Philadelphia, Morice himself was aware of having made the wrong call, so aware that he issued a statement that in effect reversed his ruling and gave Columbia a 6–2 victory instead of a 7–6 loss.

Referee Morice's Statement:

"In justice to Columbia I feel that I must publicly admit my error and reverse my decision on the play in question, so that the final official score should have been 6–2 in favor of Columbia. I wish to express my very great regret to both teams, to Columbia for having deprived them of a victory at the time, and to New York University for having to reverse my decision at this late date. . . . I feel that I cannot do otherwise."

The action caused a storm of controversy, especially among NYU partisans. "Those who were at the game know we outplayed them, outgamed them, and outfought them," said NYU Coach Tom Thorp, "and now that the game is finished, we won't allow anyone to question it. . . ."

The main point of those attacking Morice's reversal was that a referee's decision, unless it comes at the very end of a game, must be considered final because it influences action following it. NYU fans, quite logically, argued that their team would have played a different sort of game with a 2–0 lead than with a lead of 7–0. Others claimed that an official's authority ended at the final gun, that it was not within his power to declare one team the victor over another after a significant lapse of time.

Sticky as the situation was, it seemed to be the consensus among football officials who were interviewed that Morice "did the right and manly thing" in admitting his error and changing the score of the game.

The net result of the extended controversy is an asterisk in the record books of football. Columbia, going along with the reversal, still lists the game as a 6–2 victory. NYU, refusing to recognize the postgame statement as official, lists the contest as a 7–6 win. To find out who won the game, it obviously depends on whom you ask.

TY COBB'S DISPUTED HIT

During the years 1905–28, while he was active on the playing field, Ty Cobb created a few friends, legions of enemies, and very few people who stood on middle ground. Thus the "disputed hit" controversy of 1922 probably would not have mattered so much if it had revolved about another player. But with Cobb, it was a different matter. Because he fought so viciously for everything he got, those who disliked him were inclined to make nothing easy for him.

In 1922, Cobb was thirty-five but still able to play with the best. He had slowed down on the basepaths from his glory years of 1915–17, when he led the American League with an average of seventy-three stolen bases a season. His batting eye, however, seemed as good as ever, although the presence of George Sisler as a genuine challenger to Cobb's batting skill delighted Ty haters. In 1922, Sisler batted a searing .420 to win the batting championship by a sizable margin.

Just how sizable was the subject of much debate. Ty Cobb had the third-best year at

---

What a Difference One Hit Makes:
The Cobb controversy of 1922: Was it—
211 hits in 526 times at bat for an average of .40114,
or
210 hits in 526 times at bat for an average of .39924?

the plate of his long career, but when the season ended his average was just under .400. Cobb seemed to have fallen just short of matching Ed Delahanty and Jesse Burkett's record of hitting above .400 three times. (Burkett performed the feat in 1895 and 1896 while with the Cleveland Spiders and in 1899 with the St. Louis Cardinals, Delahanty in 1894, 1895, and 1899 with the Phillies.) When it was seen how close Cobb was to the magic figure, it was recalled that one of his "outs" had been quite controversial. On May 15, in a game against the New York Yankees, rain suddenly forced many spectators to seek shelter but was not hard enough to cause a break in the action on the field. Among those who departed for the covered areas was John Kieran of the New York *Times*, who was official scorer of the game.

Shortly afterward, Cobb hit a hard smash at Yankee shortstop Everett (Deacon) Scott, who was handcuffed by the ball and let it squirt into center field. The writer who had remained behind in the better vantage point of the press box, Fred Lieb, called it a hit. Because he was the only one in the press box at the time, Lieb's interpretation went out with the unofficial report of the game.

Later, however, it was revealed that Kieran, from his distant position in the covered grandstand, thought the play was an error by Scott. The later reports of the game, therefore, credited Cobb with only one hit that day instead of two.

Those who felt Cobb deserved to bat .400 pointed out this discrepancy and suggested that American League President Ban Johnson take Lieb's word rather than Kieran's. As it did not seem likely that Johnson would bend to such pressure, the New York *Times* of October 24, 1922, remarked, "It looks as if Cobb will have to be content with a batting average of .398 instead of the .400 which his soul eagerly craves for." (The *Times'* arithmetic was less than perfect.)

After six weeks of debating the issue, however, Ban Johnson overruled the official scorer, giving Cobb a hit on the liner to Scott and raising his average to .401.

Most members of the Baseball Writers' Association were furious—Johnson's action, they said, showed that he had little regard for the writers who served as official scorers or their organization. Even Fred Lieb, then President of the BWA, went on record protesting Johnson's overruling of the official scorer's decision. When the BWA threatened to use its influence to have "their" batting average for Cobb placed in baseball publications rather than that decreed by President Johnson, the controversy grew hotter. Even Cobb spoke up,

angrily charging that the New York scorers had taken away three hits from him late in the season when it seemed he was about to go over .400.

The Baseball Writers' Protest:
"There would be no further need for members of the Baseball Writers' Association serving as official scorers if their scores were relegated to a secondary position whenever they failed to agree with unofficial averages. No member of the New York Chapter of the Baseball Writers' Association begrudges Cobb a .400 batting average, but the use of baseball records will be undermined when records are deliberately tampered with in order to favor any batsman, whether he be a star or a mediocre player."

When Johnson would not yield, the BWA issued an official statement, condemning his action and threatening to "decline to serve as official scorers unless they receive assurance that their scores will be accepted as official and final."

The American League president might have laughed aloud at that last statement, but there is no record he did. (The official scorer at each ball park, a position that was carefully rotated, was paid a handsome fee. Thus it was unlikely the writers would give it up.) Instead, he charged that the writers in many cases were "grossly lacking in efficiency and responsibility," that it was often difficult for the league office to get routine reports from them. The decision would stand, Johnson said in conclusion. Meantime, he added, "it would seem the part of wisdom and prudence for the baseball writers to put their house in order before sending me scurrilous and questionable complaints."

Thus Ty Cobb became only the third major leaguer to bat .400 in three seasons. But he was not the last. Rogers Hornsby, who hit .401 himself in 1922, batted .424 in 1924 and .403 in 1925 to join the charmed circle.

ZEV AND THE CAMERA

Match races are usually dull affairs, but Americans have never given up on them as a means of deciding which of two superhorses is the better.

In 1923, Man o' War having retired earlier, Zev was the top money-winner as a three-year-old, having taken the Kentucky Derby and Belmont Stakes and total prize money of

Inflation and the Three-year-old Horse
Basing a horse's worth on the amount of money it earns can be a tricky business. The value of racing purses did not drastically increase from the 1920s to the 1940s, but after World War II they shot up quite dramatically. Thus a horse winning a dozen races a year in the 1970s might earn four times as much as a horse with a similar record several decades before. A sampling:

Year	Horse	Starts	Wins	Amt. Won	Average/Win
1920	Man o' War	11	11	$166,140	$15,103
1923	Zev	14	12	$272,008	$22,667
1941	Whirlaway	20	13	$272,386	$20,952
1948	Citation	20	19	$709,470	$37,340
1953	Native Dancer	10	9	$513,425	$57,047
1955	Nashua	12	10	$752,550	$75,255
1973	Secretariat	12	9	$860,404	$95,600

$272,008. Late in the year, it was decided to match Zev against In Memoriam, a horse that many felt was just as great or even greater. Forty thousand were in the stands at Churchill Downs on November 17, 1923, for the thirty-thousand-dollar clash of turf stars, and for once in the history of match races, the audience witnessed a classic heart-stopper.

As the horses passed the stands for the first time, In Memoriam was in the lead by two lengths, running easily compared to Zev's short and jerky stride. Jockey Earl Sande managed to keep Zev close through the backstretch and into the turn, at which point the spectators began to yell that the race was over. But they cheered too soon, for Zev slowly crept up in the turn and the two horses moved down the stretch together. Both jockeys went to the whip, their hands rising and falling as the horses matched strides, their necks bending together. Fifty feet from the finish, In Memoriam was a neck behind but seemed to be running stronger and gaining on Zev. When the four bodies crossed the finish line, spectators in the stands were at a loss to tell which horse was the winner.

After a considerable pause, Zev's number went up.

At this point, technology entered the picture in the form of slow-motion film, still a novelty in 1923. (Photo-finish cameras were not used regularly on tracks until 1936.) The next day, motion-picture films shot for Pathé indicated that In Memoriam had won the race by the scantest of margins, a nose.

Those favoring Zev's cause immediately pointed out that the angle at which the films were shot, six feet past the finish line and eight feet in front of the judges' stand, was favorable to the inside horse. In Memoriam was on the rail.

Horsemen viewing the film at a private showing were divided in their opinions as to which horse won the race. Zev therefore remained the winner of one of horse racing's best match races.

Instant replay with stop action could have solved the controversy, of course, but such developments were still in the future. Perhaps it was just as well, for the debate fueled many interesting conversations among turf enthusiasts during the long winter before the start of the 1924 racing season.

SAM RICE'S DEATHBED CONFESSION

For the second time, the Washington Senators were in the World Series. It was 1925, and thirty-seven-year-old Walter Johnson, who had lost two games and won one in relief the year before against the Giants, was determined to perform better against the Pittsburgh Pirates.

In the opening game, he pitched a tidy five-hitter as the Senators won, 4–1. The Pirates came back to win the second contest, 3–2, and were ahead by the same margin at the end of six innings of the third game. At this point, Stanley (Bucky) Harris, the phenomenal twenty-eight-year-old manager-second baseman of the Senators who was having a terrible Series at the plate, tapped a ball in front of the plate that eluded Pirate catcher Earl Smith long enough to become a hit for Harris. (He went two for twenty-six in the Series.) Two singles and a sacrifice fly later, the Senators were ahead, 4–3.

In the eighth inning, the Pirates' first two batters went down meekly before Fred Marberry, Senator pitcher, but Earl Smith then smashed a long drive toward the right-centerfield bleachers. Thirty-five-year-old Sam Rice, who had been moved to right field at the start of the inning so that younger and faster Earl McNeeley could take over center, raced toward the stands, threw up his glove, and seemed to spear it just a split second before disappearing into the crowd. Cy Rigler, the umpire trailing the play, signaled "out," but the Pirates charged after him, protesting that Rice dropped the ball when he hit the bleachers and had been handed the ball by a spectator while out of view.

The debate continued throughout the Series and after. When interviewed, Sam Rice invariably answered in a cryptic manner. "The ump called him out," he said on many occasions, which, of course, was no help to the person seeking the "true" story of Sam's controversial catch. Then, to add a bit of fuel to the decades-old mystery, Rice announced in 1965 that he had written a letter describing the catch and sent it to the Hall of Fame in Cooperstown with the proviso that it be opened only after his death. He survived until October 13, 1974, and a month later the contents of the letter were made public. "I jumped as high as I could . . . and the ball hit the center of pocket in glove (I had a death grip on it). . . ." Sam wrote. "At no time did I lose possession of the ball."

About Sam Rice:
Although elected to the Hall of Fame in 1963, Sam Rice was less well known than many other players of his era. In 1925, he batted .350 while playing in 152 games. Some might have thought that was the high point of his career, but Sam played nine more seasons, not retiring until he was forty-four years old. His lifetime batting average was .322 and he hit 184 triples.

Since deathbed confessions or professions carry added validity, that ended the forty-nine-year-old controversy as to whether Sam Rice had or had not saved the third game of the 1925 World Series with his miraculous catch. Obviously Sam felt there was more fun in keeping the exact details a secret.

THE CONTROVERSIAL JACK DEMPSEY
Perhaps because he had superstar status, Jack Dempsey seemed to create controversy in nearly all his ring encounters. In the beginning, because he was a comparatively small man who packed so much power into short punches, controversy arose because he did not seem big enough to win. (Thus the stories that his gloves were "loaded" for the fight with Jess Willard.) Later, when Dempsey proved how good he was, controversy was generated whenever he lost. Having become

convinced he was virtually unbeatable, the public searched for frauds or excuses when Dempsey was handled, as he was by Gene Tunney on September 23, 1926.

After that bout, which saw Tunney crowned new champion, rumors circulated that someone had put poison in Dempsey's coffee before the fight. The story was laughable, but some, searching for a reason to explain their favorite's poor showing against Tunney, probably believed it, or at least wanted to believe it.

The Poisoned-coffee Mystery
By Charles J. Mabbutt
Writing in the Baltimore News *of December 1, 1926, Charles J. Mabbutt, who was present at the Dempsey training camp prior to the 1926 championship fight, charged that "a poisonous substance introduced into the cream used by our party did the work. . . . On the Saturday preceding the fight, Dempsey, Mike Trent, his bodyguard, Jerry the Greek [Dempsey's trainer], and I had breakfast. . . . After Saturday Dempsey did practically no training and, barring punching the bag for a few rounds Sunday, he discontinued active work of any kind. He was an ill man."*

The story was discounted by everyone close to the champion. "The only poison Jack got was that first right-hand punch of Tunney's to the jaw," said Philadelphia Jack O'Brien, Dempsey's chief second in the fight.

As a warmup for his second bout with Tunney, Dempsey took on Jack Sharkey, a sturdy ex-sailor from Boston, on July 21, 1927. The fight was supposed to go fifteen rounds, but in the seventh, Dempsey landed a blow near the beltline and Sharkey promptly crumpled to the canvas, groaning painfully. He shook his head in feeble protest as Referee Jack O'Sullivan counted him out.

When he was able to get to his feet, Sharkey claimed that he had been fouled by the ex-champion, a view that was held by many in the crowd of eighty thousand that packed Yankee Stadium and paid more than a million dollars to see the fight. Particularly vociferous were those seated along the third-base and left-field sides of the ring. One writer there claimed he saw no less than four low blows thrown by Dempsey during the progress of the fight.

Once again Jack Dempsey was the center of controversy. "I did not foul him," he said when interviewed after the fight. "I hit him with hard rights on the beltline and as his guard dropped brought over a heavy left to the jaw which finished the job. None of the blows were low. I am happy to be a winner again and hope to get another chance for the championship."

The Controversy's Lineup:
The question, "Did Dempsey foul Sharkey?" drew both "yes" and "no" responses from celebrities and members of the press. Among those who expressed their opinion:
YES *Benny Leonard (ex-lightweight champion); Grantland Rice (New York* Herald Tribune*); Damon Runyan (New York* American*).*
NO *Gene Tunney (heavyweight champion); Grantland Rice (New York* Graphic*); Westbrook Pegler (Chicago* Tribune*).*

In view of the fact that Jack Sharkey filed no formal request that he had been fouled, boxing officials were not required to take action. "I have nothing to say other than that the referee who was assigned to the bout rendered the decision as he saw it," said James A. Farley of the New York State Athletic Commission. That ended the controversy officially, although the *Times* remarked, "Not in the history of boxing has there been a bout which caused such widespread discussion, argumentative, approving, disapproving."

The sequel, of course, was just around the corner. Just two months later, on September 22, 1927, Dempsey and Tunney staged their second match, at Soldier Field, Chicago, before 150,000 fans who paid nearly three million dollars to be at one of sport's most controversial events.

From the very beginning, it was apparent that Jack Dempsey no longer possessed the speed, power, and reflexes that enabled him to destroy Jess Willard eight years before. But he still had a punch if he could get in position to throw it. Tunney, boxing in the style of Jim Corbett, managed to score points while keeping away from the ex-champion—until the seventh round. Then Dempsey suddenly lashed a hard left past Tunney's guard. Dempsey followed with a right to the jaw and a left hook. Tunney fell in Dempsey's corner, his hand groping for the ropes as the timekeeper, Paul Beeler, leaped to his feet, watch in hand.

Referee Dave Barry, ready to start the count, saw that Jack Dempsey went to his own corner rather than a neutral one. Barry ordered Dempsey across the ring, delaying the count by four or five seconds. At the count of nine—or approximately fourteen—Gene Tunney got to his feet. His head was clear enough and his legs strong enough to weather the strong rush of Dempsey during the seventh round and the remainder of the fight. At the end of fifteen rounds, Tunney was declared the winner by a unanimous decision. Dempsey and his staff immediately announced their intention to appeal the unpopular decision. "Intentionally or otherwise," Dempsey said in his dressing room, "I was robbed of the championship. . . . Everybody knows I am not a whiner. When Tunney beat me last year, I admitted he was the better man that night. I am not an alibi artist, but I know down in my soul that I knocked Tunney out tonight. . . ."

The Rule That Cost Dempsey the Knockout:
"When a knockout occurs the timekeeper shall immediately arise and announce the seconds audible as they elapse. The referee shall first see that the opponent retires to the farthest corner, and then, turning to the timekeeper, shall pick up the count in unison with the timekeeper, announcing the seconds to the boxer on the floor. Should the boxer on his feet fail to stay in the corner, the referee and timekeeper shall cease counting until he has so retired."

The Illinois State Athletic Commission was deluged with angry telegrams from fans. Twenty-four hours after the fight, Leo Flynn, acting for Jack Dempsey, filed a formal protest, charging that "through a lack of proper co-ordination by the referee and the counting timekeeper . . . Tunney was on the floor from three to six seconds more than the time prescribed by the rules and regulations governing boxing contests. . . ." The petition asked that a formal hearing be held at which Dempsey would be allowed to present his views. The appeal was rejected on the grounds that it was not signed by Jack Dempsey himself. Convinced that the Commission would turn down any petition put before it, Dempsey let the matter drop. In the meantime, Tunney pointed out that he was on the canvas for thirteen or fourteen seconds only because he was allowed that amount of time. "I was getting up at four," he said, "but the men in my corner waved me down, and I took advantage of the extra seconds to get a rest. . . . I am more confident than ever now that I am Dempsey's master. . . . I will be found ready again to defend the title when the proper time comes. I will be ready, too, to meet Dempsey."

A Dramatic Bout for More Than the Participants:
So dramatic was the second Dempsey-Tunney bout, according to the Associated Press, that no less than ten persons died as a direct result of the excitement it caused. Three died of heart attacks while listening to the seventh round on radio; the others died shortly after the fight, including one involved in an argument generated by the decision. Another man was injured when he accidentally stabbed himself with an ice pick while cheering in front of a bulletin board in Los Angeles.

For their pains, Tunney received a bit over $990,000 and Dempsey $425,000, the highest sums ever paid a champion and a challenger. The two men never fought each other again. After beating challenger Tom Heeney, Gene Tunney retired from the ring while at his peak. Dempsey undertook an ill-fated comeback during the early 1930s, but obviously lacked the spark of greatness he once had. Hearing boos for the first time after being unable to knock out third-rate fighters, he too went into a well-deserved retirement.

GAR WOOD'S NASTY PLAN

By the early 1930s powerboat racing was so popular with Americans that four hundred thousand crowded the banks of the Detroit River on September 6, 1931, to witness the battle for the Harmsworth Trophy.

In 1903, Sir Alfred Harmsworth of Great Britain offered the first racing trophy for powerboats. Seventeen years later an American driver, Gar Wood, brought the cup to the United States, where it remained until a daring British challenger named Kaye Don entered the picture. Driving Miss England II with reckless style, the smiling Briton seemed destined to return the trophy to his homeland. On September 6, 1931, he pushed his vessel to an average speed of 89.913 miles per hour, hitting a top speed of 110 miles per hour on the straightaway and leaving Gar Wood in Miss America IX wallowing in his wake.

For Wood, the defeat was the first of his career. It was doubly galling because one additional victory by Kaye Don would recapture the Harmsworth Trophy, but Wood was de-

termined to do his very best. The third boat in the race, Miss America VIII, piloted by George Wood and Vance Smith, seemed hopelessly out of contention, having turned in average speeds four miles an hour slower than that of Miss England II.

Nearly one-half million spectators awaited the final race the next day. Shortly before the race, however, Gar Wood discovered that Miss America IX had a cracked gasoline tank. He requested a forty-five-minute delay in order to have it repaired, but Kaye Don refused. A fiercely competitive man, Wood immediately saw red at what he felt was a lack of sportsmanship on Kaye Don's part. With a leaking fuel tank, Wood could not race six laps, but he could take Kaye Don out of the running. "When Eddie Edenburn, chairman of the race committee, told me Don would not agree to a forty-five-minute delay," Wood said, "I told him . . . I was coming down the river and make a false start purposely. I told him when I did Don likely would follow me."

A premature start for both vessels, of course, would disqualify them and allow Miss America VIII to win the Harmsworth Trophy by default.

The crowd gathered along the riverbanks sensed something was wrong as Gar Wood came roaring down the course on the outside, veering in a bit as he neared the starting line, motors throbbing and exhaust pipes sending out smoke and flame. Accelerating his own vessel nearer the shore was Kaye Don, anxious to get a competitive start, completely unaware of Wood's intention of sacrificing himself. Two seconds apart, the boats thundered toward the line, Wood beating the gun by nine seconds and Don, somehow unable to let himself fall safely behind, beating it by seven. The race was over seven seconds before it even began.

In the roar of the start, neither man heard the starting gun; Kaye Don followed in Wood's wake, twin sprays of water all that the spectators could see of the boats' progress. On the outside a screen of spume indicated that Don, with greater speed on the straightaway, was overhauling the American. Nearing the first buoy, Kaye Don miscalculated, trying to take the turn in the same manner as he had the day before. But now he was not in smooth water. Gar Wood's wake shook Miss England II, then turned her over in a split second. Ten thousand pounds of boat hit the water in a flat arc.

Miraculously, Kaye Don was not only unhurt but also remarkably gracious in defeat. "It's the luck of the game," he said. W. F. Sturm, his manager, added: "Gar Wood evidently knows lots of the tricks in the racing game. No one could race for seventeen years without learning most of them."

Meanwhile, George Wood and Miss America VIII completed three laps of the course as a formality necessary to laying claim to the Harmsworth Trophy.

When the exact details of the race were made known, some Americans and many Britons were shocked and dismayed. Gar Wood's false start was denounced as a deceitful act of poor sportsmanship, but the British kept a stiff upper lip at having lost the race. At first, Wood was inclined to gloat at the success of his ploy, but when he realized just how much animosity he had churned up, he changed his story to the effect that he was not trying to draw Don across the line in a false start, but had been overeager to take the lead. In short, the fiasco had been a "misunderstanding"; rather than an angry bit of unsportsmanlike conduct.

Gar Wood's Conflicting Remarks:

"If Don wanted to play that way with me, all right. I figured I could outsmart him, and you know what happened."
Gar Wood, September 8, 1931

"I don't know how this misunderstanding can be rectified. I've just talked with London over the telephone and they don't seem to understand at all what happened over here. It doesn't seem that any amount of explanation will get it straightened out."
Gar Wood, September 9, 1931

No one believed it.

1940—CORNELL-DARTMOUTH

When Cornell's Big Red team took the field on the afternoon of November 16, 1940, it had not been defeated since the third game of the 1938 season. Eighteen games stretching over a two-year period had produced seventeen victories, a scoreless tie against Pennsylvania the only blot on their splendid football record. The Dartmouth Indians, in contrast, had dropped four games out of the seven played so far in the 1940 season—to Princeton, Yale, Columbia, and Franklin and Marshall. Although heavily favored at odds of 4–1, Cornell was not overconfident; but the weather, which turned the field into a slippery mess, served to narrow the gap between the two teams. The first half of the game was scoreless, neither squad able to mount much of a drive.

Cornell's Streak—1938–40:

1938			
Cornell	21	Penn State	6
Cornell	23	Columbia	7
Cornell	14	Dartmouth	0
Cornell	0	Pennsylvania	0
1939			
Cornell	19	Syracuse	6
Cornell	20	Princeton	7
Cornell	47	Penn State	0
Cornell	23	Ohio State	14
Cornell	13	Columbia	7
Cornell	14	Colgate	12
Cornell	35	Dartmouth	6
Cornell	26	Pennsylvania	0
1940			
Cornell	34	Colgate	0
Cornell	45	Army	0
Cornell	33	Syracuse	6
Cornell	21	Ohio State	7
Cornell	27	Columbia	0
Cornell	21	Yale	0
TOTAL	436		78

In the third period, however, Cornell moved relentlessly toward the goal of the determined Indians. But at the Dartmouth seventeen, a pass thrown by halfback Bill Murphy was intercepted in the end zone by Ray Wolfe. Inspired by the great defensive play, Dartmouth moved upfield, finally settling for a twenty-seven-yard field goal by Bob Krieger. Dartmouth led, 3–0.

Cornell mounted two drives during the final quarter, but each was stopped by an interception. With 2½ minutes remaining, Cornell got the ball for a third time on its own forty-two-yard line. This time fortune seemed to smile on the Big Red team. A pass-interference penalty gave Cornell a first down on Dartmouth's eighteen. Another pass was complete, taking the ball to the six. And there was time enough for a complete series of downs.

Mort Landsberg drove for three yards. Scholl made a yard, then Landsberg edged the ball to the one. With the ball so close, Cornell then committed the unpardonable sin of football—they took too much time and received a penalty of five yards. A pass into the end zone was knocked down by Ray Hall of Dartmouth.

The drive had been halted! But to everyone's amazement, Referee Red Friesell, who had started out toward the twenty-yard line, turned back and placed the ball on the six, indicating fourth down for Cornell. There were three seconds left in the game.

Cornell's Walt Scholl took the snap from center, raced out to his right, spotted Bill Murphy in the end zone, and flipped the ball to him. The extra point was kicked and time ran out, Cornell the victor, 7–3.

Little time elapsed, of course, before it was pointed out that Cornell had remained undefeated only by receiving a gift fifth down on the crucial goal-line series. One explanation of the gift was that another official in the game had signaled both sides offside for the penultimate play in which Hall batted down the pass. That had not occurred, however. The error had been purely that of Red Friesell. He acknowledged that in a public statement, adding that while the football rules "give me no authority to change even an incorrect decision such as the one described . . . I do want to acknowledge my mistake [which was] entirely mine . . . and not shared in or contributed to by any of the three other officials. . . ."

What Down Is It? Update:

Twenty-eight years after the celebrated Cornell-Dartmouth fifth-down controversy, the reverse happened to the Los Angeles Rams in a critical game with the Chicago Bears. It was December 8, 1968, and the Rams were in the midst of a neck-and-neck race with the Baltimore Colts for the Western Division championship of the National Football League. Behind, 17–16, the Rams drove toward the Bears' goal, hoping to get in field-goal range. With first and ten at the Bear thirty-two, Ram quarterback Roman Gabriel threw an incomplete pass to Jack Snow. But the Rams were caught holding and penalized back to the forty-seven. Gabriel then threw three more incomplete passes, at which point Referee Norm Schachter and his crew turned the ball over to Chicago. There were only ten seconds left in the game. When it was discovered that Los Angeles should have had another down, the NFL hit the officials with fines ranging from $250 to $1,650. The score, unfortunately for Los Angeles, remained the same.

The response by Cornell, which was not obligated to abide by the discovery and admission of the official's error, was strange but refreshing. "In view of the conclusion reached by the officials," wired Cornell's Director of Athletics James Lynah to all concerned, including Dartmouth, "that the Cornell touchdown was scored on a fifth down, Cornell relinquishes claim to the victory and extends congratulations to Dartmouth."

The game of November 16, 1940, thus appears in the record books as a 3–0 win for Dartmouth. But in many ways, the game was an even greater victory for Cornell.

1946—RHUBARB AT EBBETS FIELD

Baseball as played at Ebbets Field for the better part of a half century seemed to lend itself to controversy. Some of the many rhubarbs came about because of the Brooklyn Dodgers' rough-and-tumble style of play, general aggressiveness, and desire to win at nearly all cost. Occasionally, however, a controversy arose simply by happenstance.

An example of the latter—rare—type took place on July 20, 1947. The Dodgers were challenging the incumbent champions, the St. Louis Cardinals, in a crucial series. The game was scoreless until the fourth inning when Enos Slaughter, Whitey Kurowski, and Marty Marion combined to produce a pair of runs and a lead that St. Louis took into the top of the ninth.

Then, with two out and no one on base, Ron Northey, Cardinal outfielder who was nicknamed "the round man," hit a towering drive to center field. The ball hit a railing marking the stands, bounded high into the air, and came back on the field. Northey, heading for second base, shot a glance at Umpire Beans Reardon, who twirled his hand and arm in the air, signaling "home run." Northey slowed down and steamed around third to home.

In the meantime, the two other officials, Larry Goetz and Jocko Conlon, realizing that the ball had never entered the center-field seats, yelled that the ball was still in play. Dixie Walker retrieved the ball and relayed it to Eddie Stanky, who threw Northey out at the plate.

Cardinal Manager Eddie Dyer rushed onto the field, declaring that Northey would have made it home if he hadn't slowed down, or at the very least, stopped at third base. When the umpires refused to settle the situation to his satisfaction, he stated that the game was being played under protest.

As luck would have it, the Dodgers came to life in the bottom of the ninth, scoring three runs and sending the crowd of 33,420 home quite happy. Dyer followed through on filing his protest, the necessary paperwork reaching Commissioner Ford Frick's office the next day. The National League boss deliberated a couple of days and then—to nearly everyone's surprise—upheld the St. Louis protest. Basing his decision on statements by the umpires at the game that Northey would have scored had he not slowed down, Frick declared the game "no contest" and ordered it replayed as part of an August doubleheader.

A Previous Similar Situation:

It could have been settled right there as soon as it happened. In a game between Brooklyn and Philadelphia played on July 3, 1942, the Dodgers' Whitlow Wyatt hit a long ball to right field. As he rounded first base, Umpire Tom Dunn gave the home-run signal and Wyatt slowed his pace. The ball bounced off the screen, however, was relayed to the infield, and Wyatt was tagged out. The umpires immediately conferred and made a quick decision as to which base Wyatt could have made had he run instead of jogged. He was then awarded that base and the game continued.

Brooklyn Dodger fans were furious, of course. Manager Burt Shotton charged that the Dodgers had been hurt more than the Cardinals by the game being nullified. Even if Northey's "home run" had counted, he pointed out, the Dodgers had scored three runs in the bottom of the ninth and still had men on base when the game ended.

Fortunately, the game soon faded in importance as the Dodgers moved ahead to win the pennant by five games.

1950—EDDIE STANKY INVOLVED IN ANOTHER

An expert gamesman, Eddie Stanky was involved in many tussles and diamond controversies. One of his most celebrated came in August 1950, which found the Giants, Dodgers, and Philadelphia Phillies "Whiz Kids" battling for the pennant.

In 1948, Stanky had been traded from the Dodgers to the Braves, then to the Giants for the 1950 season. He retained his Brooklyn aggressiveness, which was nurtured by Manager Leo Durocher, also transplanted from Ebbets Field and in the midst of building the sedate Giants into a bunch of scramblers capable of winning their first pennant since 1937. Durocher's philosophy of winning not only allowed controversial situations, it also encouraged them. Thus when Eddie Stanky started planting himself behind second base and waving his arms to distract Phillie batters, it was perfectly all right with Leo.

The goat-getting stunt started on Friday night, August 11. Stanky's primary target was Phillie catcher Andy Seminick, who became incensed and—to Stanky's delight—largely ineffectual as a batter.

Philadelphia Manager Eddie Sawyer immediately protested the arm-waving as "unsportsmanlike and strictly bush-league stuff," but plate umpire Al Barlick was helpless to inflict a penalty because the rules did not mention such a situation. While the problem was being considered by Commissioner Ford Frick, the Phils and Giants took the field for another game. Stanky, meanwhile, had thought of a few new wrinkles overnight and proceeded to execute them in the game.

During the second inning, for example, when Seminick came to bat, "The Brat" waved his arms furiously before Giant pitcher Sheldon Jones was ready to deliver, then made an elaborate show of freezing once Jones went into his pitching motion.

In the fourth inning, Stanky performed the gyrating act so successfully that Seminick flung his bat far onto the diamond. Feeling things were about to get out of control, umpire Lon Warneke thumbed Stanky out of the game for "conduct detrimental to baseball." That brought Leo storming onto the field for a jaw session. He left only after declaring that the Giants were playing the game under protest.

Some Quotes on the Arm-Flapping:

"What's wrong with trying to fool the batter, anyway? Everyone tries to do that one way or another."

Leo Durocher

"I was just out there trying to help win a ball game. If someone pulled that one on me, I'd shake his hand—and try to hit past him."

Eddie Stanky

"I do not want to discourage smart and aggressive play. For years, second and third basemen and also shortstops have been making a dash toward their bases while the batter is up and that is perfectly all right. But there are extremes, and baloney, and this is baloney."

National League Commissioner
Ford Frick

A bit later, when the still-enraged Seminick threw an elbow at Giant second baseman Bill Rigney and was subsequently discharged, the Phillies announced that they were playing the game under protest.

The climax of the afternoon was a ten-minute bench-emptying battle royal, which was stopped only when special police rushed onto the field. As for the game itself, that was won in eleven innings, the Phillies coming out on top, 5–4. Presumably the "kids' day" crowd of 23,741 was both entertained and uplifted by the spectacle.

Two days later, National League Commissioner Ford Frick ruled that Eddie Stanky's arm-waving tactics had to go. While it was not covered in the rule book, he said such actions were "completely against the ethics of sportsmanship."

1951—THE SUGAR RAY FLAP

When he went to Germany in June 1951—just a month before losing his middleweight crown to Randy Turpin—Sugar Ray Robinson had a remarkable record as a boxer. In 125 fights he had been defeated just once. Moreover, he was widely respected the world over as the best fighter, pound for pound, to step into a ring. Thus he was hardly prepared for the outburst that greeted him in Berlin.

The fight of June 24, against a German named Gerhard Hecht, was regarded by Robinson as little more than a tuneup, but the hometown Berliners jammed the Waldbuehne, hoping for an upset.

As he entered the ring, the first world champion to fight in Berlin in twenty-five years, the crowd cheered Robinson. The enthusiasm waned quickly. Midway in the first round, Sugar Ray threw a hard left hook near the beltline that sent Hecht sprawling to the canvas. In the manner of Jack Sharkey trying to convince the crowd that Dempsey had landed a low blow, Hecht writhed in obvious pain, clutching his abdomen. Referee Otto Nispel started the count, then stopped and announced that there would be a pause of one minute to allow Hecht to recuperate from the "low blow." Seconds after the rest period ended, the bell sounded, signaling the end of the round.

The crowd muttered angrily at Robinson during the break, then broke into an angry chorus of abuse as the same thing occurred in the second round. As soon as a blow landed near his waist, Hecht doubled up and collapsed. Cries of "Foul! Foul! Foul!" cascaded throughout the auditorium. Missiles of various

---

A Bit of Dialogue:

ROBINSON (*to Referee Nispel*): *"You know that wasn't a foul."*

NISPEL (*to Fighter Robinson*): *"I have to call it a foul. I want to leave this ring alive."*

---

sorts began descending from the upper tier, causing sportswriters to seek cover. Giving in to the intimidating chorus, Nispel halted the fight and announced that Sugar Ray Robinson had been disqualified for continually landing low blows.

The crowd wasn't satisfied. Fist fights broke out, and American servicemen in the audience, especially blacks, were attacked. Robinson ducked beneath the ring as the local police entered the Waldbuehne in a belated attempt to restore order.

Although the disqualification of Robinson was rescinded the next day, German newspapers attacked the American fighter for landing "low blows," pointing out that Hecht sustained a broken rib and bruised spinal vertebrae. Robinson, they said, had alienated the affections of a crowd that was initially cordial to him by insisting on fouling Hecht after repeated warnings.

The controversy did little for German-American relations. Joe Louis, who had already made plans to fight in Germany, announced that he had canceled the arrangements. Sugar Ray, meanwhile, continued his tour of Europe, although he did not mention Germany when questioned about his itinerary. Instead he went to Belgium, where he fought Cyrille Delannoit, then to Great Britain for his ill-fated battle with Randy Turpin.

After the warmup at the Berlin Waldbuehne, losing the middleweight championship probably seemed almost anticlimactic.

HOCKEY'S THIRTY-FIVE-DOLLAR TOMATO

Professional hockey's long-standing credo, with player and fan alike, has been that violence is not only accepted but also encouraged. Thus it came as a distinct shock to Montreal Canadien fans when their favorite, Joseph Henri Maurice (Rocket) Richard, was banished from the 1955 Stanley Cup playoffs.

The incident leading to his excision, after all, was not really that bad. It had taken place on March 13 at Boston during the third period when Hal Laycoe of the Bruins highsticked Richard. The Rocket, with blood streaming down his cheeks, then struck Laycoe across the shoulders with his stick and pummeled linesman Cliff Thompson with his fists. He was sent to the dressing room, some twelve thousand Boston fans cheering his departure as well as their team's 4–2 victory.

Richard expected a fine or brief suspension to end the incident. Instead National Hockey League Commissioner Clarence Campbell barred the Montreal Canadien star for the remainder of the season. The switchboard at the league office blossomed with color as angry Montreal fans heard that the team would have to face Boston without Richard. But Campbell was adamant. "The time for probation or leniency is past," he said.

Richard—a True Hockey Superstar:
Not only was Richard the most heavily fined player of the 1955 season, he also had talent. During his eighteen-year career, which ended in 1960 when he was nearly forty, Richard played in 978 games and scored 544 goals, not counting playoffs. Twice during his career he went eight consecutive games with at least one goal. He also had seven three-goal games and once scored eight points (5 goals, 3 assists), against Detroit on December 28, 1944. He was elected to the Hockey Hall of Fame in 1961.

Three days later, thousands of demonstrators picketed the Montreal Forum before the Montreal-Detroit Red Wings game. The lobby was packed long before game time and dozens of police officers circulated, but there was no violence until later.

"Later" came with the arrival of Commissioner Campbell, who perhaps should have known better. Midway through the first period, he took a seat at the end of the Forum to the accompaniment of catcalls and various epithets from the crowd. The game was not going well for the Canadiens, the first period ending with Detroit ahead, 4–1. That may have had something to do with the outburst that took place during the intermission.

As soon as the teams skated off the ice, a smoke bomb exploded. Spectators pushed and shoved to get out of the arena, falling over one another in their excitement. The panic spread as Campbell began to make his way to the exit. Programs, peanuts, eggs, fruit, and even a pair of overshoes rained down upon him. At this juncture, twenty-one-year-old André Robinson moved toward Campbell, his hand outstretched as if he were an old friend. When the police allowed him through, Robinson assaulted the commissioner with a tomato.

Outside the main arena, violence spread. Rocks, snow, and bottles were thrown at police officers by angry rioters; corner newsstands were pushed into the street, and trolley lines were torn down; along St. Catherine Street, store windows were smashed, starting a trail of broken glass that continued for fifteen blocks. Cars were overturned as police were helpless to control what was estimated to be a riot of fourteen thousand people.

It continued for seven hours, the worst and most prolonged violence in the city of Montreal since the anticonscription riots of World War II. Finally, after more than a hundred persons were arrested and the game forfeited to Detroit, an uneasy quiet settled over the city.

In the aftermath of the destruction, twenty-seven rioters were ordered to pay fines ranging from twenty-five to one hundred dollars. André Robinson was fined ten dollars and costs on a charge of assaulting the hockey commissioner and twenty-five dollars plus costs for disturbing the peace, a total of thirty-five dollars for throwing a single tomato.

As for the Montreal Canadiens themselves, they were apparently inspired by the whole thing, for they won the Stanley Cup playoffs handily, dispatching the Boston Bruins in five games.

TAKE THE MONEY AND RUN, NO. 1

Unfortunately, not all sports participants—or the officials backing them—are as honest as the men of Cornell who graciously yielded their fifth-down victory in 1940 when the official's error in their behalf was discovered.

There are, sad to relate, some who have valued a win higher than anything else—even when the rules clearly state that they have received that victory via a fluke.

One such case occurred on November 18, 1961, when the University of Notre Dame football team met Syracuse near the end of a season that was less than glittering for both. The Irish had dropped three straight games in midseason to Michigan State, Northwestern, and Navy; Syracuse had lost to Maryland and Penn State. Thus neither squad had anything resembling the Cornell winning streak of 1940 at stake.

Despite the mediocre records, the game was an exciting one that found Syracuse trying to protect a 15–14 lead in the closing minutes of play. Notre Dame was able to move the ball just inside the Orange forty-yard line as time seemed about to run out. Desperately the Irish lined up for what would be a fifty-six-yard field goal, if Joe Perkowski could make it.

The ball was snapped, holder George Sefcik spotted the ball, and Perkowski kicked. It was no good. And just as the ball was about to be kicked, time ran out.

The game was over. Except that Syracuse defender Walt Sweeney had run into George Sefcik on the play. The officials called a personal foul, moved the ball fifteen yards farther downfield, and Perkowski, given a second attempt from forty-one yards away, was able to make the field goal. Notre Dame led, 17–15, and that was the end of the game—a second time.

Shortly afterward, in a joint announcement, the Eastern College Athletic Association and the Big Ten revealed that the officials at the game had made a mistake. Under the then-existing rules, Notre Dame had surrendered the ball as soon as Joe Perkowski kicked it, and with the ball in the air, the game ended at that moment. Thus Notre Dame was not entitled to the extra play, despite the fact a foul had occurred after the ball was in the air.

A week later, on November 29, the National Collegiate Athletic Association, after studying the facts of the case, also ruled that Notre Dame had gotten the field goal on what was in effect an illegal play. At the same time, General Robert Neyland, chairman of the NCAA and athletic director of the University of Tennessee, conceded that there was no official machinery to change the score. If it was to be done, officials at Notre Dame would have to do it.

The problem was then turned over to officials at the celebrated college which for decades had served as the "home team" for Catholics all across the nation. And what was the decision of those running this Church-affiliated school? Was the victory more important than demonstrating a Christian respect for the rules?

You bet. Notre Dame took the decision and ran.

TAKE THE MONEY AND RUN, NO. 2

If the game of golf is, as Stephen Leacock wrote, "a form of moral effort," should a man be penalized for *adding* to his score? Where in golf is justice; and are the gods of the green without mercy?

The crowd's favorite was a forty-five-year-old veteran golfer from Argentina, Roberto de Vicenzo, and a search of the records prior to 1968 reveals that his major tournament win came in 1967, when, after twelve attempts since 1943, he finally won the British Open. Otherwise Roberto de Vicenzo was strictly a journeyman golfer, a gentleman with marginal professional talent but boundless charm.

De Vicenzo's rival in the 1968 Masters golf tournament at Augusta, Georgia, was Robert Goalby, a much-better-than-average golfer who had picked up $77,106 in prize money while on the tournament trail in 1967. His average for ten years on the circuit was nearly $32,000 per year, his total winnings amounting to nearly one third of a million dollars.

Going into the final round of the Masters, Goalby, De Vicenzo, Gary Player, Bert Yancey, and Bruce Devlin were all close to the top. Any of them had a chance, but it was Goalby and De Vicenzo who finally pulled away. On the front nine, Goalby shot a 33

and the Argentine a 31. Playing as well as he ever had in his life, De Vicenzo took the lead by sinking a deuce on the par-3 twelfth and a birdie on the fifteenth. Having learned that it was his birthday, the crowd cheered De Vicenzo as he birdied the seventeenth and sang, "Happy birthday, Roberto, happy birthday to you" at one point during the afternoon. When the final round was completed, De Vicenzo added up his score. His total was 278, one higher than Bob Goalby's 277. Once again De Vicenzo was a runner-up.

A check of the scoreboard, however, showed that in the tension of the close finish, De Vicenzo had given himself a 4 for the seventeenth hole when he actually shot a 3. That meant that the two men were tied, necessitating a playoff round—except that according to the rules of professional tournament play, no alteration was allowed on a scorecard. Having signed the card listing a par-4 for the seventeenth hole instead of the birdie-3 he actually shot, Roberto de Vicenzo was stuck with the higher score. That gave him a 278, enough only for second place.

THE RULE:

3. No Alteration of Scores

No alteration may be made on a card after the competitor has returned it to the Committee.

If the competitor returns a score for any hole lower than actually played, he shall be disqualified.

A score higher than actually played must stand as returned.

De Vicenzo was downcast but accepted the technical defeat gracefully. Less gracious were some of the thirty thousand spectators and millions of television viewers, many of whom sent telegrams to the USGA office in New York or called in person. Most were critical—one man said he would never watch a USGA tournament on TV again—but some offered suggestions as to how the problem could be solved. (One idea was to set up an isolation booth at the end of the course to protect harried golfers from the nerve-wracking attention of well-wishers and broadcasters.) A few persons suggested that Bob Goalby be a good sport and request a playoff round.

Technically, of course, Goalby was the winner. Technically, he was powerless to do anything about the unfortunate error. Actually, he could have requested a playoff and gotten it, had he wanted to take a chance on winning via his own skill rather than by a strict adherence to the letter of the law.

The end result, of course, was that like Notre Dame and many others ahead of him in the line, Bob Goalby took the money and ran.

Roberto de Vicenzo—1968 and After:
Sentiment would dictate that following the Masters fiasco of 1968, Roberto de Vicenzo would emerge triumphant in future tournaments. Sad to relate, he did not, although he continued to play golf professionally. In 1973, at the age of 50, De Vicenzo ended up in 143rd position among the 150 prize-earners of the PGA. His total winnings for the year amounted to $11,242.

THE KENTUCKY DERBY THAT TOOK TWO YEARS TO RUN

The foal of Native Dancer by Noors Image, Dancer's Image was highly touted as a two-year-old thoroughbred, finishing first eight times and placing four times in fifteen starts. The horse was also a crowd-pleaser in that he was a late-closing runner, but the element so necessary to the making of a complete champion—good luck—was missing from his racing career.

During his first start of 1968, for example, he was beaten by Sir Beau in the New Year's Handicap when he stumbled in the stretch. Dancer's Image was plagued also with bad ankles, but he seemed to have overcome that problem when he raced from next to last in a field of fourteen to win the Governor's Gold Cup by three lengths. Owner Peter Fuller joined in the chant of "On to Louisville!" that followed the dramatic comeback.

On May 4, 1968, before a crowd of one hundred thousand at Churchill Downs, Dancer's Image clashed with Forward Pass, the long-time favorite with thoroughbred fans, for ownership of the first jewel of the Triple Crown, the Kentucky Derby. A record $2,350,470 was bet on the race, most of it on the two favorites. And when the two horses crossed the finish line, Dancer's Image was a length and a half ahead.

The joy surrounding the gray colt was short-lived, however. Three days after the victory, the announcement was made that a chemical test showed Dancer's Image had run the Kentucky Derby with Butazolidin, a pain-killing drug, in his system. As a result, the horse was disqualified and the $122,600 first prize awarded to Forward Pass. The disqualification was the first in the history of the ninety-four-race classic.

Butazolidin. Most persons interested in sports had never heard the name. Was it a stimulant—which could be interpreted as an illegal aid to winning the race—or merely a pain-dulling drug similar to aspirin? The sports and medical worlds debated the issue. Some said the drug was merely a mild therapeutic agent; others replied that any drug that could make a horse perform better—that can make an unsound animal become sound for even a short time—was a violation.

Some Professional Opinions:
"Phenylbutazone is used to reduce inflammation—it is neither a stimulant nor a 'pep' drug."

Thomas Campbell,
Geigy Pharmaceuticals

"There are a wide variety of treatments directed toward the healing of inflammation, such as icing, leg washing and diathermy, and phenylbutazone can be used as one of these methods."
Dr. Iain M. Paton, veterinarian

Seven months passed. Then, in December 1968, the Kentucky Racing Commission recognized Dancer's Image as the official record-book winner of the Derby. But the prize money was to remain earmarked for the owners of Forward Pass. The contradictory move satisfied no one, least of all Dancer's owner, Peter Fuller, who announced his intention to appeal the case to the Kentucky Circuit Court. Sportswriters, meanwhile, had branded the ninety-fourth running as "the test-tube Derby."

The next decision by the Kentucky Racing Commission was to instruct its workmen at Churchill Downs to delete all reference to the 1968 Derby winner from all signs—both Forward Pass and Dancer's Image. It was added that Dancer's Image had been installed as the official winner because of the long-established rule in Kentucky that once the official lights on the tote board signaled a winner, there was no way to change the order of finish. But because of the presence of Butazolidin, the prize money could be withheld.

For nearly two years more, the case dragged on. Not until December 11, 1970, was the stain seemingly removed from Dancer's record. On that date Judge Henry Meigs of the Kentucky Circuit Court ruled that the presence of illegal drugging was "wholly lacking in substance and relevant consequence." That did not please the Kentucky Racing Commission, however, which voted to appeal the verdict. Forward Pass was subsequently reinstalled as the official winner.

One Butazolidin User Who Got Away with It:

Nearly a decade before Dancer's Image was disqualified from the Kentucky Derby, the event was taken in 1960 by Venetian Way, a horse with chronically sore legs and ankles. Prior to the race, trainer Vic Sovinsky announced that he intended to use the painkiller Butazolidin on a daily basis. He did, and Venetian Way defeated favored Bally Ache by 3½ lengths.

By that time, Dancer's Image was long retired, bad luck plaguing him the rest of his racing career. Running into traffic problems in the Preakness two weeks after the Derby, he finished third to Forward Pass, but was penalized for impeding Martin's Jog and placed eighth. On May 28, 1968, a few days before the running of the Belmont Stakes, Peter Fuller announced his colt's retirement. The ankle problems had become aggravated to the point where arthritis of the fetlock joint seemed imminent.

The unfortunate colt's later days were rather better. Retiring to stud in the United States, he was taken to Ireland in 1974 and France three years later. His total winnings amounted to $236,636, not a great deal of money considering the fact that Peter Fuller spent approximately $250,000 in his futile attempt to have Dancer's Image recognized as the 1968 Derby winner.

THE 1971 BLOOPER BOWL

It was only natural that in addition to having a total of eleven turnovers, the 1971 Super Bowl game between Baltimore and Dallas also generated a king-sized controversy. It was, after all, the kind of game where nothing came easy.

After two Baltimore errors—a John Unitas pass thrown to Cowboy linebacker Chuck Howley and a fumble by Colt safety Ron Gardin—Dallas stumbled to a 3–0 lead. A bit later, after having a first down and goal to go, the Cowboys managed to work themselves out of touchdown range but were able to kick a field goal and take a 6–0 lead.

Then came the play that everyone talked about. After getting the ball back, Colt quarterback Unitas faded back on third down and threw a pass intended for wide receiver Eddie Hinton. The ball was high over his head, but Hinton leaped high enough to deflect it. Still moving in a low arc, the ball was next seen passing Dallas defensive back Mel Renfro, who seemed to touch it also. Behind him came Colt tight end John Mackey, who reached out and gathered in the pass and raced for a touchdown. When the point attempt was missed, the score was tied, 6–6.

The tragicomedy of errors continued until well into the final period, at which point Baltimore's field-goal kicker, Jim O'Brien, booted a thirty-two-yard three-pointer to give the Colts a 16–13 victory. "Esthetically, it wasn't very good football," wrote Tex Maule in *Sports Illustrated*, "but it was far from boring. Mistakes create excitement and there were at least eleven big ones in this game. It was the first truly exciting Super Bowl."

The excitement lasted after the game when Dallas defender Mel Renfro denied that he had touched the ball on Baltimore's Unitas-to-Hinton-to-perhaps-Renfro-to-Mackey touchdown play. "Somebody touched the ball," Renfro said. "I don't think I did."

If Renfro was correct, if only Hinton and Mackey touched the ball, the play was an illegal one, since two offensive men cannot handle the ball consecutively unless a lateral is involved. The touchdown should not have counted.

Game film that was processed and shown the next day, however, showed clearly that Renfro had deflected the ball, its path changing markedly when the Cowboy defender reached upward. "I might have touched it with my fingernail," Renfro acknowledged when the film's evidence was made available.

That ended the Blooper Bowl controversy of 1971, a situation that might never have been solved without the magic of multiple-camera photography. For those who derided the game as a sloppy mélange of errors, at least the filmwork was outstanding.

1972—FEAR AND LOATHING AT THE OLYMPICS

The United States Olympic basketball team in 1972 was looked upon as virtually unbeatable. On August 29, the United States won its fifty-eighth straight basketball game in the Olympics by defeating Cuba, 67–48. By September 7, the streak rose to sixty-three. But next on the agenda was the Soviet Union and a challenge that was not only physical but also political.

The scene was Munich, West Germany, the date September 10, just a few days after the 1972 summer Olympics were turned into a battlefield by Arab terrorists. The decisive game between the Soviet and American squads was postponed because of the tragedy, not beginning until eleven-thirty in the evening, which was six-thirty Eastern Standard Time in the United States.

From the very beginning, it was apparent that winning No. 64 would not be easy. Led by Aleksander Belov, a muscular six-foot, eight-inch forward, the U.S.S.R. moved to a 38–28 lead with ten minutes left in the game. With a bit more than six minutes remaining, the Soviets led by eight points.

The Teams:

UNITED STATES—*had won every game in Olympics since the sport was inaugurated in the 1936 Games. The defense in 1972 allowed opponents an average of only 43 points.*

U.S.S.R.—*Practiced together for a year, then toured the United States, where it won 8 or 9 contests. Prior to Olympics, played 739 games together compared to 7 by the U.S. team, which was composed primarily of collegians.*

Changing tactics, the American squad applied a full-court press and closed the gap to 44–42. Going into the final minute, the Soviets still clung to their lead, but Doug Collins managed to grab a loose ball at midcourt and drove for the basket with six seconds remaining. He was also fouled while shooting. The United States led, 50–49, with only three seconds left.

The Soviets put the ball in play under their own basket, but when an inbounds pass was deflected, time ran out. The United States players began jumping up and down, excitedly congratulating each other on winning the Olympic gold medal.

Meanwhile, at midcourt, Robert Jones, secretary general of the International Amateur Basketball Federation, decided that the Soviets had called time before putting the ball in play, that there still remained three seconds in the game. The ruling so enraged United States coach Hank Iba that he had to be forcibly restrained by his players.

After order was restored and the court cleared of spectators, a Soviet player threw a desperation pass that traveled the length of the court before reaching Aleksander Belov, who was guarded by Kevin Joyce and James Forbes. All three men went up, but Belov grabbed the ball and made the shot. The Soviet Union led, 51–50, as the clock ran out a second time.

A protest was immediately filed. "I don't think it's possible to have made that play in three seconds," Hank Iba shouted. "There's no damn way he can get that shot off in time."

Two hours after the game ended, as players and spectators lingered in the dressing room and tunnels, officials announced that the protest had been refused.

At the awards ceremony held the next day, the Soviet Union was there, as was Cuba, which finished third. The United States was not.

Thus the frustration of defeat overpowered the alleged Olympic spirit of fair play and goodwill.

1977—YEAR OF THE "NONFUMBLES"

Rarely had so few been maligned by so many. The few were National Football League officials, whose only job was to compete with a variety of television cameras equipped with slow motion; the many consisted of fans, players, coaches, and armchair quarterbacks blessed with hindsight and instant replay. It was an uneven contest. By Super Bowl time 1978, NFL officials had taken sufficient abuse to last a decade.

The escalation of anger began after a December 18, 1977, game between the Baltimore Colts and New England Patriots at Baltimore. The Pats, already eliminated from either the Eastern Division title or wild-card berth, were angry at both the Colts and fate, which had dealt them a cruel hand the week before when a Baltimore loss to the Detroit Lions threw New England out of the running. (A detailed explanation of the NFL ruling would require another chapter.) In any event, the Patriots roared into Baltimore and were leading 24–3 in the third quarter.

At that point quarterback Bert Jones rallied the Colts, who scored three touchdowns. An extra point was missed, however, and New England retained a slim 24–23 lead. Baltimore also maintained the initiative, getting the ball back and driving once again toward the New England goal. With a first down and goal to go, it seemed certain that Baltimore would get the go-ahead touchdown or at least a field goal. That turned out to be the dramatic moment when Bert Jones fumbled. New England recovered and pranced happily, having stopped the Colt drive. Presumably, both fans and players in Miami—the city that would benefit from Baltimore's loss—also exulted.

But the exultation was short-lived. An official anxious to protect Jones from injury had blown a quick whistle, despite being in a position of limited visibility. Order was restored and the Colts were given the ball, second down and goal to go. With such a break under their belts, the Colts smashed across the score, stopped New England after the kickoff, and won, 30–24.

Instant replay, exhibited countlessly the following week, revealed that the official had been wrong. Bert Jones had indeed fumbled.

There ensued an outpouring of wrath equaling lesser injustices such as the Sacco-Vanzetti and Alfred Dreyfus cases. Pilots in Miami spelled out messages in the sky, reviling the NFL; letters and telegrams poured into the league office; TV commentators pontificated. And the result remained Baltimore 30, New England 24.

Two weeks later, after Baltimore had been eliminated by the Oakland Raiders, the Oakland-Denver playoff to determine which team would meet Dallas in the Super Bowl was enlivened by a similar play. With the Broncos leading, 7–3, in the third period, Denver running back Rob Lytle was hit near the Oakland goal and fumbled. The Raiders recovered on their own seventeen and prepared to see if the offensive team could put them ahead. But once again the zebra's whistle turned the course of the game. Officials called the play dead despite being in poor position to rule on it. And once again TV's instant replay showed they were in error. To Oakland's dismay, the ball was returned to the Broncos, who scored and eventually won, 20–17.

By mid-January 1978, nearly as much attention had been given to the possibility of official error "ruining" the big contest as to normal pre-Super Bowl publicity. Fortunately, the men in stripes called a near-perfect game, partly redeeming themselves when instant replay showed that a controversial call on a Butch Johnson TD pass for Dallas had been absolutely correct. But the feeling remained that "something had to be done" in order to eliminate or minimize the possibility of future fluffs on the part of the only-too-human officials.

A few weak voices protested that the NFL season and Super Bowl were, after all, just games rather than life-and-death struggles. But with the winning players receiving $32,000 each and TV commercials selling for up to $325,000 a minute, no one seemed to be listening to that argument.

CHAPTER 5 — 1871–80

1871

Winners: Baseball: Professional baseball is started in America with formation of National Association. Philadelphia wins first season pennant with 22–7 record. . . . *Belmont Stakes:* Harry Bassett . . . *Boxing:* Jem Mace and Joe Coburn fight two inconclusive battles for heavyweight "championship." After second fight Coburn retires from ring. . . .
Other Happenings: Organizations formed: National Rifle Association . . . New York Canoe Club . . . Rowing Association of American Colleges . . . Chicago Athletic Association . . . *Careers started:* Twenty-year-old Adrian Constantine (Cap) Anson opens the baseball season at third base for the Rockford Forest Cities. He continues as active player until 1897, retires with career batting average of .333, and is one of only seven men elected to Baseball Hall of Fame who play in National Association. . . . Twenty-year-old Al Spalding begins career with Boston Red Stockings, records 207–56 mark in NA, then wins 47 and loses 12 with Chicago of National League. . . . The Wright Brothers, George and Harry, begin their careers with Boston Red Stockings, are both elected to Hall of Fame. . . . In billiards, three-ball game is introduced. . . . Champion harness race horse Goldsmith Maid, undefeated in 1871, appears at St. Joseph, Missouri, and town goes wild. . . . The Davidson County and Middle Tennessee Colored Agricultural and Mechanical Association holds its first fair and plays baseball games. . . . October 12–23, America's Cup competition is held, the *Columbia* and *Sappho,* both United States ships, winning two races to a single win for Great Britain's *Livonia.*

George Rooke challenges Tom Chandler, but the latter ignores him, and Rooke claims title. . . . Lightweight Joe Collyer of England, touring United States, defeats Billy Edwards of America and Arthur Chambers of England. Collyer soon retires. . . . *Football:* Yale has a football team and plays one game, defeating Columbia, 3 goals to 0, soccer rules. Princeton plays one game with Rutgers, winning, 4 goals to 1. Stevens also fields a team. . . .
Other Happenings: In billiards, Cyrille Dion wins undisputed four-ball championship. . . . *Founded:* Young Men's Gymnastic and Athletic Club of New Orleans; National Association of Amateur Oarsmen . . . John Hatfield throws baseball 400 feet, 7½ inches at the Union Baseball Grounds, Brooklyn. The record holds up for thirty-eight years. . . . Baseball "legalizes" the curve ball. . . . The first eight-oared shell race is held in the United States, between *Undine* and *Crescent* on November 28. *Undine* is the victor. . . . A British cricket team, headed by William G. Grace, tours the United States. . . . Goldsmith Maid, champion trotter, is undefeated in 1872. . . . In wrestling, Major J. H. McLaughlin proclaims himself champion and issues challenge to other wrestlers. . . . Match race is arranged between Harry Bassett, winner of 1871 Belmont Stakes, and Longfellow, a horse many think is the greatest of all time. But Longfellow is disabled and loses the race. . . . J. B. Johnson attempts to swim the English Channel but fails. . . . Boxing, still illegal, is watched closely by police, who arrest pugilists Ned O'Baldwin and Jem Mace at Baltimore. . . . Mace heads for Europe, O'Baldwin for Philadelphia in the confusion that follows.

1872

Winners: Baseball: The Boston Red Stockings, with a record of 39–8, win second National Association season, trailed by Philadelphia Athletics, Lord Baltimores, and New York Mutuals. . . . *Belmont Stakes:* Joe Daniels . . . *Boxing:* In middleweight class,

1873

Winners: Baseball: Boston Red Stockings repeat as champions of National Association, winning 43 games, losing only 16. . . . *Preakness* (first): Survivor. *Belmont Stakes:* Springbok . . . *Boxing:* Jem Mace, forty-two, retires. Mike McCoole and Tom Allen fight near St. Louis on September 23, Allen winning in seven rounds. He proclaims himself "world champion" of heavyweights. . . . *Football:* Columbia, Rutgers, Princeton, and Yale all play seasons of from one to three games, but when Cornell players attempt to travel to Cleveland for the purpose of playing a thirty-man squad from Michigan, President White of Cornell turns thumbs down on the proposal, saying, "I will not permit thirty men to travel four hundred miles merely to agitate a bag of wind."

Other Happenings: Trotting's "Grand Circuit" officially opens at Buffalo Driving Park and racing begins at the New Orleans Fair Grounds. . . . In December, Major Walter Clopton Wingfield introduces guests at lawn party to new game he has invented called *sphairistike,* which turns out to be tennis. . . . *Founded:* San Francisco Yacht Club; Intercollegiate Football Association . . . New baseball rule prohibits players from catching the ball in their hats. . . . Baseball is introduced into Japan by Horace Wilson, an American teacher in Tokyo. . . . On April 25, the first rifle tournament is held at Creedmore, Long Island. . . . On November 4, the first club organized in North America for the playing of golf is organized in the office of John S. Sidney of Montreal. The club is soon renamed the Royal Montreal Golf Club. . . . Prizefighter Ned O'Baldwin, still running from police, is arrested at Steubenville, Ohio, and sentenced to jail term for participating in illegal fights. . . . On September 6, a novel swimming match takes place on the Harlem River, ten young women racing a mile for a silk dress valued at $175, Miss Delilah Goboess of Philadelphia winning by covering the distance in forty minutes. . . . *First run:* on May 14, the California Derby at Oakland Trotting Park. Filly Camilla Urso wins and retires undefeated.

1874

Winners: Baseball: The Boston Red Stockings win their third consecutive National Association pennant, winning 52 games, losing 18. Closest rival is New York Mutuals at 42–23. . . . *Preakness:* Culpepper. *Belmont Stakes:* Saxon. . . . *Boxing:* In middleweight division, Mike Donovan defeats George Rooke, claims crown of still-unrecognized weight classification. . . . *Football:* On May 14, Harvard plays McGill University in first college game in which football-style goal posts are used and admission charged. Harvard wins, 3 goals to 0. The next day, a second

contest is played according to rugby rules, ending in a 0–0 tie. . . . Columbia plays most football games during year, six, but loses five of them. Yale has undefeated three-game season. . . .

Other Happenings: Horseracing begins at Saratoga. . . . The first Withers Stakes is run at Belmont Park, the winner is Dublin. . . . Led by Harry Wright, members of the Boston and Philadelphia baseball clubs play fifteen games in England and Ireland, July 30–August 27 . . . but baseball is also played in England several months earlier, on February 27, pitcher Al Spalding of Boston hurling for one team. . . . On July 3, the Guelph (Ontario) Maple Leafs baseball team beat the Ku Klux Klan club of Oneida, New York, 13–4, in an amateur tournament. . . . Yale-Harvard varsity boat race of three miles is won by Harvard when Yale boat collides with Harvard and does not finish. . . . Mary Ewing Outerbridge of Staten Island introduces tennis to the United States. . . . Big event of the year is July 16 nine-team boat race on Lake Saratoga, but race is postponed twice because of choppy water. More than twenty-five thousand spectators finally watch Columbia win as Yale and Harvard, true to tradition, exchange foul charges. . . . Charges are brought against John Radcliff of the Philadelphias, National Association, for throwing baseball games. He is "expelled," but turns up in 1875 with another team in league.

1875

Winners: Baseball: In fifth and final year of National Association existence, Boston Red Stockings win fourth consecutive pennant, taking 71 of 79 games. . . . *Kentucky Derby* (first): Aristides, ridden by Oliver Lewis, black jockey. *Preakness:* Tom Ochiltree. *Belmont Stakes:* Calvin . . . *Football:* Yale and Harvard meet for first time, play rugby rules, and Harvard wins, 4 goals to 0.

Other Happenings: On July 28, Joe Borden of Philadelphia pitches first recorded no-hitter in professional baseball. . . . An unpadded catching glove is introduced by Charles G. Waite. . . . Matthew Webb becomes the first swimmer to conquer the English Channel, performing the feat in 21 hours, 45 minutes. . . . First Kentucky Oaks is run at Churchill Downs, Vinaigrette winning the race for three-year-old fillies. . . . Top hitter in National Association is Boston's Ross Barnes, who hits .355. . . . Boston club makes slight profit of $2,261.07 but most other clubs in league are near bankruptcy. . . . First reorded 1–0 game in professional baseball history occurs on May 12 when Chicago defeats t. Louis. . . . Famous racehorse Lexington's keleton is sent to National Museum in Washington. . . . Most unfortunate fatal accident 1 sports world during 1875 involves Washington Donaldson, veteran balloonist, whose vehicle falls in lake. . . . After being undefeated rom 1871 to 1874, trotter Goldsmith Maid is eaten in a four-heat race at Rochester by ula, August 14. But at year's end, Goldsmith Maid remains undisputed champion. . . . In eptember, yacht *America* creates excitement y sailing 240 miles in 16 hours. . . . Hugh Donohue, champion pedestrian, walks 1,100 miles in 1,100 quarter hours. . . . Association ngle sculls champion, 1½ miles, is Charles . Courtney. . . . Harvard again beats Yale 1 annual 3-mile varsity boat race, covering istance in 17 minutes, 5 seconds. . . . Most hameless showman of the year is Captain aul "Billy" Boyton, who tours world promoting rubber swimsuit, crossing English Channel hree months before Webb. . . . First published: *The Kentucky Live Stock Record.*

meet, held July 20–21, is won by Princeton. Horace H. Lee of Pennsylvania becomes first American amateur to run hundred-yard dash in ten seconds. . . . August 11–12, renewal of America's Cup competition is held, *Madeleine* of the United States winning two races to none for Canada's *Countess of Dufferin.* . . . Display of bicycles at Centennial exhibit in Philadelphia provides stimulus to sales of new vehicles throughout nation. . . . Pedestrian-watchers get a shock when young Mary Marshall, a mere woman, beats a man, Peter Van Ness, in best-of-three walking matches in New York. . . . Football comes to the University of Pennsylvania, which loses pair of matches against Princeton, but is able to defeat a team of Philadelphia stars. . . . Prizefighting gets a black eye when James Weeden kills Billy Walker in a fight near Pennsville, Pennsylvania. In November, two months after fight, Weeden is convicted of manslaughter and sent to prison. . . . Baseball owners consider appeals to reduce admission to games from fifty cents to a quarter, finally decide to continue the higher price. . . . In billiards, Jacob Schaefer, Sr., later a great national champion, enters his first tournament and finishes last.

1876

Winners: Baseball: National League begins s first season as an eight-club loop. Chicago Vhite Stockings, paced by pitcher Al Spalling's forty-six wins, takes initial pennant, with t. Louis and Hartford in second and third pots. . . . *Kentucky Derby:* Vagrant. *'reakness:* Shirley. *Belmont Stakes:* Algerine . . *Boxing:* Joe Goss of England challenges om Allen and they fight for heavyweight are-knuckle championship on September 7 ear Covington, Kentucky. When Goss starts vinning easily, Allen begins to foul and is lisqualified in twenty-seventh round. . . . *'ootball:* Yale beats Harvard, Princeton, nd Columbia to emerge as logical choice as national champion. . . .

Other Happenings: First National League aseball game is played on April 22, Joe Borden of hometown Boston pitching 5–4 win ver Philadelphia. . . . Three days later, Al Spalding of Chicago pitches first NL shutout, –0 over Louisville. . . . First no-hitter in ew circuit comes on July 15 when George Bradley leads St. Louis to 2–0 win over Hartford. . . . During season, Deacon White bats n runs in twelve consecutive games, but NL's irst batting champion is teammate Ross Barnes, who hits ball at .404 clip. . . . Franchises in 1876 National League cost one hundred dollars each. . . . First Intercollegiate Association of Amateur Athletes of America

1877

Winners: Baseball: Boston—known as the Red Caps—wins pennant in second season of new National League. Tommy Bond leads Boston and rest of league's pitchers with forty wins, seventeen losses. . . . *Kentucky Derby:* Baden Baden. *Preakness:* Cloverbrook. *Belmont Stakes:* Cloverbrook . . . *Boxing:* James Weeden, serving term for manslaughter of Billy Walker, dies in prison. . . . *Football:* Yale, with three victories, no losses, and one tie, has best record among eastern football powers.

Other Happenings: Goldsmith Maid runs last race, wins it, and retires, age twenty. . . . Baseball rules call for home plate to be moved from behind diamond to spot even with third and first base, where it remains to present time. . . . Biggest scandal of year in sports is that of Louisville baseball team, which has four players involved in game-throwing. . . . George McManus, manager of St. Louis, is also named as possible crook. . . . Most baseball players earn from eight hundred to three thousand dollars for their year's work. . . . Football rules permit fifteen players on a side—nine men on line, one quarterback, two halfbacks, one three-quarterback, and two fullbacks. . . . Sport of paper-chasing is born when group of New York runners decide to adapt British "hare and hounds" cross-country race to local use. . . . In September, Frederick Cavill follows Matt Webb in attempt to swim the English Channel and comes within fifty yards of the British shoreline in twelve hours, fifteen minutes. But he fails to land when watching boatmen refuse to send a vessel to guide him through the shallow waters. . . . Eliza Bennett, meanwhile, succeeds in crossing the Hudson River in August. . . . Baseball rules require canvas-covered bases, fifteen inches on a side. . . . Owners also pass rule that states that club can deduct thirty dollars of a player's annual salary toward the expense of his uniform. . . . Harvard wins four-mile varsity boat race against Yale, completing course in twenty-four minutes, thirty-six seconds. . . . Wrestling matches between men and bears are staged in New York City. . . . First published: The *American Bicycling Journal*, in Boston.

1878

Winners: Baseball: Boston Red Caps repeat as National League pennant-winners, winning forty-one of sixty games. Tommy Bond, ace pitcher, wins all but one of the victories, takes all nineteen losses. . . . *Kentucky Derby:* Day Star. *Preakness:* Duke of Magenta. *Belmont Stakes:* Duke of Magenta . . . *Football:* Princeton finishes season with six wins, no losses, looks best in eastern football world.

Other Happenings: College football comes to Brown University, which loses only game of season to Amherst. . . . First pocket billiards tournament is won by Cyrille Dion. First three-cushion tournament is won by Leon Magnus. . . . Baseball uses turnstiles for first time. . . . The University of Wisconsin is the first educational institution in the United States to send a baseball team to Japan. . . . Captain A. H. Bogardus, America's premier trap-shooter, hits 5,000 glass balls in 500 minutes. . . . Maud S, champion trotter, runs mile in 2 minutes, 17½ seconds, and is bought by W. H. Vanderbilt. . . . Woman pedestrian Ada Anderson proves endurance of her sex by packing them into New York's Mozart Hall as she walks 1,000 miles in 1,000 quarter hours. . . . Her success touches off rash of "lady walker" matches. . . . Football rule change requires that players discard tights and wear canvas jackets and pants. . . . Founded: Pacific Yacht Club; Boston Cycling Club; Cricketer's Association of the United States . . . Fad of bear-wrestling comes to natural conclusion on April 14 when Jean Francis Borne is squeezed by bear named Lena until

he dies of internal injuries. . . . Long-dis tance walking (with a handicap) is carried t its inane extremity when R. Lyman Potte walks from New York to San Francisco push ing a wheelbarrow. . . . He arrives on Wes Coast on October 15, followed by a larg crowd. . . . Top hitter of National league i Paul Hines of Providence, who leads with av erage of .358 and 4 home runs. . . . U. S Patent No. 200,358—a baseball catcher' mask—is issued on February 12 to Frederic Thayer. . . .

1879

Winners: Baseball: In the National League it is brother against brother for the pennant— George Wright of Providence vs. Harr Wright of Boston. George and Providence wi with a record of 59 wins, 25 losses. Boston' mark is 54–30. . . . *Kentucky Derby:* Lor Murphy. *Preakness:* Harold. *Belmont Stakes* Spendthrift . . . *Boxing:* In lightweight divi sion, Arthur Chambers fights John Clark i Chippewa Falls, Canada, March 27, with bar knuckles, 133 pounds. Chambers wins on fou in 33 rounds and is regarded as cham pion. . . . *Football:* Among United State college teams, Princeton seems to be the best winning 4 games, losing 0, and tying 1. . . .

Other Happenings: Founded: The Nationa Association of Archers, on January 23 a Crawfordville, Indiana. Eight clubs make u the membership. August 12–14, the NA holds its first grand meeting, at which 2 women and 69 men compete. Will H. Thomp son wins, scoring 172 hits for a total of 62 points. . . . The Childs Cup is inaugurate by George W. Childs of Pennsylvania, bein awarded to the best 4-oared crew among Co lumbia, Pennsylvania, and Princeton. (Occa sionally, Navy and Cornell participate but ar not eligible for the prize.) The Cup is won b Pennsylvania. . . . Football is started at th University of Michigan. . . . Founded: Na tional Association of Amateur Athletes o America (later NCAA). . . . In baseball Boston owner Arthur Soden devises reserv clause as means of binding players to one clu and reducing salaries. . . . Average salary o Boston team in 1879 is $1,430 per man. . . Speed-walking or pedestrianism is big indoo sport and Madame Ada Anderson amazes th United States by walking 2,700 miles in 2,70 quarter hours. . . . Founded: United State Amateur Lacrosse Association, followin growth of popularity as the result of a tourna ment at Gilmore's Gardens, New York, i 1877. . . . Shooting contests are also popula and one of America's greatest shots is Captain A. H. Bogardus. In January, he breaks 3,000 glass balls catapulted into the air, without a miss. The next day he dispatches 6,000 out of 6,013. . . . 1879 Astley Belt competition at New York is regarded as one of biggest sporting events in the United States until that time. Edward P. Weston, the pedestrian who won the belt by defeating a variety of British and American walkers earlier in the year, is unable to repeat as champion. Charles Rowell of Great Britain wins the prize. . . . At a meeting held in Buffalo on September 29, baseball owners agree to hold five players per club off the market and refuse to negotiate with "reserved" players of other teams. . . . Football comes to the U. S. Naval Academy, the men of Annapolis playing a single contest with the Baltimore Athletic Club. It ends in a 0—0 tie. . . . National League home-run leader is Charley Jones of Boston, with 9.

1880

Winners: Baseball: The fifth season of the National League does not produce much in the way of excitement. Cap Anson's Chicago White Stockings win 67 games and lose only 17. Far behind is Providence, with a mark of 52—32. . . . *Kentucky Derby:* Fonso. *Preakness:* Grenada. *Belmont Stakes:* Grenada . . . *Boxing:* On June 21, America's Paddy Ryan knocks out Joe Goss of England in eighty-seventh round near Colliers Station, West Virginia, thus becoming the first American to hold undisputed bare-knuckle championship of the world. . . . *Football:* Princeton and Yale, both with records of 4—0—1, seem to be best college teams in nation.

Other Happenings: Columbia oarsmen win Childs Cup, and Yale defeats Harvard in annual 4-mile boat race, rowing the course in a slow 24 minutes, 27 seconds. . . . The O'Leary Belt, prize given for fastest speed-walker, is won by Frank Hart, a black man. . . . Founded: The League of American Wheelmen, dedicated to bettering conditions for American bicyclists. . . . Also founded: American Canoe Association, on August 3 at Lake George, New York. . . . On June 12, organized baseball's first recorded perfect game is pitched. The hurler is John Lee Richmond, 23, a left-hander just about to graduate from Brown University. His team is Worcester, the opposition Cleveland, and according to the rules of the game at the time, Richmond must deliver the ball underhand—and where the batter wants it. Despite these disadvantages, Richmond allows only three balls to get past the infield. All are caught. In the fifth inning, Worcester scores a run, thanks largely to Cleveland rookie second baseman Fred Dunlap's making a pair of errors on a potential double-play ball. That's all Richmond needs to record a 1—0 perfect game. Six years later, he retires from organized baseball with a career total of 75 wins and 100 losses. . . . The length of college football field is reduced from 140 to 110 yards. . . . William Muldoon and Charles Whistler, popular wrestlers of the day, come to grips with each other for 9 hours, 35 minutes without a fall. . . . On March 31, H. Leussing, a strongman of Cincinnati, lifts 1,384 pounds. . . . Clay birds as substitutes for live pigeons are invented by George Ligowsky and first used on September 7 at a Cincinnati shooting match. . . . The number of men on a football team is reduced from 15 to 11. . . . Baseball officials reduce number of "balls" necessary for a walk from 9 to 8. . . . Also, a base runner is declared out if he is struck by a batted ball. . . . Jim O'Rourke and Harry Stovey tie for home-run leadership of National League with 6. . . . Besides Richmond, no-hitters are pitched by Monte Ward of Providence (also a perfect game), Larry Corcoran of Chicago, and Jim "Pud" Galvin of Buffalo.

Section II
The 1880s

CHAPTER 6 — 1881

The price of ham was $.11 a pound; quail sold for $1.25 a dozen; turkey cost $.15 a pound; wild ducks cost $1.00 each; for $.25 you could buy a six-pound striped bass right out of the water. On the other hand, eggs sold for $.70 cents a dozen, and strawberries, raised in hothouses, were $10 a quart, which was far more than an average American earned in a week. But the new year of 1881 brought forth many expressions of faith in the good life here. America had elected a new President—a Republican, naturally—named James A. Garfield, and he was busily immersed in selecting a new Cabinet from among the party loyal. Meanwhile, the Apache Indian chief Victorio continued to cause trouble in New Mexico even as Sitting Bull crossed the northern border into Canada. Desperate to get the "Ignoble murderer of General Custer" back, U. S. Army leaders promised him a pardon if he surrendered. Incredibly, Sitting Bull believed they would keep their word and did so. The next thing he saw was the inside of a prison cell.

While all this was going on, Americans were reading Lew Wallace's novel *Ben Hur,* Margaret Sidney's *Five Little Peppers and How They Grew,* Mary Brine's *Madge the Violet Girl and Other Poems,* or praising the late Thomas Carlyle, the great writer-philosopher whom everybody had heard of but very few read.

As the new year began, sports enthusiasts discussed the baseball season just past, which had produced numerous individual thrills but not much of a championship race. In fact, the Chicago White Stockings, led by Cap Anson, seemed nearly unbeatable. It was also a year for the pitcher. With home plate and the pitcher's mound separated by a distance of just forty-five feet, four no-hitters—two of them perfect games—had been pitched in

1880. Even then, there were those advocates of offensive baseball who wanted to take the advantage away from the hurlers, but the same basic rules of play would govern 1881 as the year before. Meanwhile, baseball buffs or "kranks" waited for the National League meeting in Buffalo, scheduled for March, in the hope it would produce some interesting changes.

How They Finished in 1880:		
	W.	L.
Chicago	67	17
Providence	52	32
Cleveland	47	37
Troy	41	42
Worchester	40	43
Boston	40	44
Buffalo	24	58
Cincinnati	21	59

BILLIARDS

Indoor sports flourished in January, especially billiards, which saw the emergence of two brother teams—Jacob and Leslie Schaefer and George and Albert Frey. The public was especially taken with blond Albert Frey, dubbed "the Boy Expert," and Jacob Schaefer, known as "the Wizard." The press at the time was inclined to wax rhapsodic when describing the feats of these two, as on January 2 when Frey concluded a match with Frank Smith by sending "the numbered spheres flying into the pockets . . . with a stroke of dazzling certainty." As for Jacob Schaefer, he "whisked the fourth game from the table with lightning-like rapidity, making many dazzling shots. The fifth game followed in its wake, and the balls whirled in the pockets so quickly and so prettily that there was general laughter as well as applause."

PEDESTRIANISM

Public interest was still high in pedestrianism and the turnout was good for the 1881 race for the O'Leary Belt at New York's American Institute Building on January 23. Compared to the "old days" of the 1870s when the walker-runners rested on benches when they were off the track, the accommodations of 1881 were sumptuous. Each of the racers was provided with a ten-foot-by-five-foot wooden cell, "which resembles in elegance and finish the boxes called at the seaside bathing apartments. The furniture comprises a wooden frame known as a bed, on which are spread a mattress, blanket, and pillow; a washstand, small mirror, a chair, and a gas stove . . . the cells are robbed somewhat of their naked appearance by tasty decorations and painted furniture."

The "scene of agony," as it was described, further consisted of an eighth-mile track of clay, mixed with tanbark and sprinkled with sawdust, the whole forming a spongy surface three inches thick. Seats for spectators lined the north and south walls of the building, "those on the north side being reserved for gentlemen accompanied by ladies."

None of the really big names of pedestrianism—Weston, O'Leary, Charles Rowell, or Frank Hart—had entered the competition, but the audience didn't seem to mind very much. Sleek bookmakers moved through the crowd, establishing Daniel Burns of Elmira, New York, as a 6–1 favorite, and Frederick Krohne, known as "the awkward Prussian," 15–1. But it was an unknown, John Hughes, who moved into the lead, and he established such a brisk pace that fans began to wonder if the black pedestrian Frank Hart's 1880 record (See "Breaking the Color Barrier") would be broken after only one year. Those who were searching for a new "white hope" of the track openly rooted for Hughes to succeed. At the end of the first 48 hours, Hughes, having accumulated 229 miles, was 4 miles ahead of Hart's record.

WRESTLING

While the go-as-you-please race continued, a grueling wrestling match took place at New York's Terrace Garden Theater between William Muldoon, who claimed he was "the champion," and a challenger named Clarence Whistler, who claimed to be only "the wonder of the West." Two thousand spectators jammed the building to watch Muldoon, a New York police officer deemed to be on the skids, pit his shoving, bull-like style against the agile, perfectly proportioned Whistler.

The match began shortly before 9 P.M. on January 26, 1881, few of the spectators suspecting they would be there until it was nearly time for breakfast. Such were the rules of Greco-Roman wrestling that dull periods were almost inevitable. This happened at the very beginning when "Whistler got Muldoon down on the carpet, and crawled over and around him like a cat in vain efforts to turn him on his back. This lasted twenty minutes, and then the same scene was repeated, but Muldoon was on the top this time." By midnight, Whistler had taken the offensive, locking his hands behind Muldoon's back and boring his head against the policeman's neck and chin. "This made the champion irritable," noted the New York Times, "and the men had some ugly slaps and thrusts." Once, while boring his head against Muldoon's neck, Whistler slipped to all fours. Muldoon clapped him in a necklock "and hugged him as though he would choke him to death. A terrific struggle ensued for a minute, the entire audience rising to its feet. At last Whistler broke his opponent's hold, and the spectators cheered wildly."

They were jeering an hour later when the battle settled down into a sweaty standoff. Finally becoming frustrated at Muldoon's penchant for lying on his stomach, Whistler began boring his head into the back of Muldoon's neck, thereby grinding his face into the stage. He then slipped his forearm under the policeman's right arm and, "digging his toes or knees against the carpet, pried him along the stage, like a tortoise, moving him two or three feet at a time. For fully half an hour this game was continued."

Concerning "Greco-Roman" Wrestling:
The Greco-Roman style belies its name by having little similarity to classical wrestling. It was developed in France about 1860 and in America a decade or so later, and persists in modified form as an Olympic sport. In order to score a fall, a wrestler had to throw his opponent so that his two shoulders touched the floor simultaneously. Neither tripping nor any holds below the waist were allowed.

Inevitably, the spectators grew as weary of this as the wrestlers, and the theater soon reverberated with cries of "Get up, Billy, and do something!" and "I want my dollar back!" and "Let him up and see if he can stand!" By two-thirty, the men had been at it for nearly six hours, at which point a significant portion of the audience repaired to the theater bar-room. When they returned a half hour later, the two wrestlers were on their feet, heads locked together like a pair of rams. It continued that way until nearly four o'clock, when suddenly the gas border lights of the stage went off. Instantly the stage was filled with people. Confusion reigned as the referee explained that the proprietor had ordered the lights turned off. With coats thrown over their shoulders, Muldoon and Whistler kept screaming that they wanted "no draw." A group of diehard enthusiasts even tried taking a collection to pay for the extra gas, but the proprietor was adamant. The crowd slowly trudged out of the theater, "swearing and growling."

PEDESTRIANISM

Some of them no doubt turned up at the American Institute arena to see the conclusion of the pedestrian match, which had narrowed down to seven participants out of thirty. John Hughes, footsore, moving "as if every step was taken on a red-hot track," still held the lead, and even better from the promoter's point of view, still had a chance to beat Frank Hart's record of 565 miles in six days. As a result, by five o'clock on the evening of the sixth day—the 137th hour—more than four thousand spectators jammed the building with more coming every minute. "The place more nearly resembled Bedlam than anything else that can be imagined," wrote one reporter, "beer glasses were clinking at the counters, and the booths were doing a lively business. The large painting of a steam-boat could hardly be discerned across the building, so thick was the smoke." (This despite a strong official ban on smoking.)

At five forty-three, when Hughes equaled Frank Hart's score, the spectators broke into deafening applause. The weary runner added one more mile to beat the best international time—Charles Rowell's 566 miles at Agricultural Hall, London—then tacked on another mile for good measure before retiring.

ROWING

The month of February was enlivened by an international race of another kind. The scene was London's Thames River, the participants Edward Hanlan, champion sculler of Toronto, and Elias C. Laycock of Sydney, Australia. A frequent racer on the rivers and lakes of North America, Hanlan was a favorite with rowing enthusiasts in the United States as well as Canada. As a result, telegraphic news was eagerly awaited on the progress of the race, which began at the Star and Garter, at Putney, and concluded at Mortlake, 4½ miles away.

Rowing in California:

July of 1881 featured a great rowing race on the West Coast, more than five hundred enthusiasts jamming the Mission Day Wharf, San Francisco, to see the beginning of the three-mile single scull race between Dennis Griffin and Louis White, members of the Pioneer Boat Club. With a bet of five hundred dollars on a side, considerable comment was made on the fact that both young men had lost their amateur standing. Had the distance been only a mile or mile and a half, the race might have been closer, but Griffin pulled away just after the halfway mark and "won in a walk."

Because of his recent victories—in 1879 he beat William Elliott on the Tyne and in 1880 Edward Trickett on the Thames—Hanlan was the odds-on favorite at 3–1. For the then-considerable price of two pounds sterling, a nineteenth-century "closed circuit" view of the race could be purchased. It entitled the spectator to a seat on one of three steamers accompanying the athletes.

A fast starter, Hanlan moved into the lead, then crossed to the middle of the river, treating Laycock to his wash. He completed the first mile in four minutes, forty-eight seconds, Laycock in four minutes, fifty-nine seconds. When Laycock spurted in an effort to close the margin, Hanlan "responded immediately with some dozen powerful strokes, and held his opponent until the spurt was exhausted. At the soap works, Hanlan, in response to the cheers of the crowd, ducked his head and laughed." At the top of Corney Beach, with the race nearly over and Hanlan leading by four lengths, the betting odds rose to 50–1, with no takers. Struggling mightily, Laycock could not manage to close the gap, which caused the London *Sportsman* to write, with perhaps just a dash of sour grapes, "We have never seen Laycock sculling worse than now. He wastes too much work in the air." Having been officially declared champion, Edward Hanlan returned to America and a triumphant welcome.

By the time he arrived, numerous significant events had taken place in the world. President Garfield had been inaugurated, and Czar Alexander II of Russia assassinated by revolutionaries who used as their weapon a glass bomb filled with nitroglycerine. Peru and Chile were at war, and the search for the North Pole had been slowed down by the strange disappearance of the vessel *Jeannette*.

Some things do remain the same, however, which is probably why, in the midst of all this change and ferment, baseball's leaders were able to sit down in March 1881 and decide to do practically nothing.

BASEBALL

Actually, they did take one significant backward step by increasing the pitching distance from forty-five to fifty feet. Some attention was also given to what should happen in the event of rain during league games. "It was resolved that when play is interrupted by rain," the moguls stated, "neither money nor tickets should be refunded." (In a year when nearly every baseball team managed to show a profit, that was a curiously niggling rule.) Secretary Nick Young, of Washington, was presented with "an expensive fishing rod." Otherwise, the status quo remained supreme.

Another Baseball Opening:
On April 3, 1881, the beginning of organized baseball on the West Coast featured games between the California and Mystic clubs of the new California Baseball League. Played at Oakland Park, Oakland, the game, according to one reporter, "was a poor one, without any redeeming qualification." No doubt he was a California club fan, for the Mystics romped to an easy 9–1 victory.

BOXING

On April 1, Morris Grant, Charles Cooley, "both gentlemen of color," fought for a prize of five hundred dollars. Using small gloves rather than bare knuckles, the two fighters battled for six rounds and twenty minutes.

The two participants were veterans, in Morris Grant's case decidedly so, for he admitted to being born in North Carolina in 1837. "His last encounter," noted the New York *Herald,* "was at Harry Hill's about a year ago, with a black man known as 'Dangerous Jack,' which ended in a draw." Charles Cooley, thirty-six, weighed in at 195 pounds, and therefore had an advantage in weight as well as age. Nevertheless, it soon became obvious to the crowd of approximately three hundred that Grant possessed greater skill.

In the very first round, Grant delivered a blow to Cooley's stomach and took a return shot to the ribs, and for a while it seemed the heavier man had the better of it. But by the third round it was clear who the winner would be. "It was apparent Cooley had tired of the job he had engaged in," the *Herald* reported, "for after delivering his right on

Grant's ribs he dropped to his knees purposely, expecting a blow from Grant and in this way win the fight [*sic*]. But this game did not take with the referee."

In the fourth round, Cooley seemed almost to panic as Grant attacked his face and stomach. Taking a hard right to the body, Cooley went down, automatically ending the round. He did the same in round five, and was bleeding by the sixth when Grant really turned on the offensive. "This continued for a minute all over the ring, until Grant gave Cooley one on the neck . . . he went down, and when time was called Cooley declined to come to the scratch again. . . . Grant was declared the winner, amid the boisterous cheers of all present."

ROWING

One of the high points of May 1881 was the rousing sendoff given Cornell University's champion oarsmen, who were on their way to conquer Europe. Or at least that's what the script called for. Leaving Ithaca to the echoes of a cheering crowd, the crew stopped at Troy and all the other railroad points, where they were greeted by bands and banners. Rowing enthusiasts throughout the East were firmly convinced that Cornell would cover America with glory overseas. By the process of elimination, everything fell into place. In 1878, America's top crew was Princeton, but Columbia had beaten Princeton. And then Cornell had outraced Columbia on Lake George, earning a bid to Europe in the bargain.

Upon arriving at New York, however, the crew members were horrified to read a dispatch that stated that because Cornell had not properly proved each man's amateur status, the crew had been declared ineligible. A flurry of panic ensued as officials representing the university contacted British officials, dispatched wires of their own and waited impatiently for replies that never came. Finally, a difficult decision was made. Dispatching a telegram to London that read, "We sail today for England and expect to enter the Henley Regatta," the men of Cornell boarded a steamship bound for Europe. Americans could not help wondering what would happen to their heroes when they arrived abroad, but there was nothing to do but wait.

In the meantime, the weather grew warmer and the baseball season moved into high gear. The Chicago *Tribune* broke a story dealing with a bribe offer made to "James E. Clapp, captain and catcher of the Cleveland base-ball nine . . . whereby the nine was to win or lose games. . . ." Actually, Clapp's real name was John, not James, but nothing really significant came out of the revelation. It did serve to draw some attention to the new pennant race, then less than twenty games old, however, al-

A Nineteenth-century Standings Chart—May 30, 1881. Reading It Is Probably Very Good for the Neck Muscles:

Clubs	Chicago	Worcester	Buffalo	Cleveland	Boston	Providence	Detroit	Troy	Games Won	Games Played	Games to Play
Chicago (White Stockings)		2	0	3	3	2	0	2	12	18	66
Worcester (No Names)	1		1	0	0	0	3	5	10	17	67
Buffalo (Bisons)	0	2		0	1	1	5	1	10	18	66
Cleveland (Spiders)	3	3	0		0	1	0	2	9	18	67
Boston (Red Caps)	0	0	2	3		3	0	0	8	17	66
Providence (Grays)	1	0	2	2	2		1	0	8	17	66
Detroit (Wolverines)	0	0	1	0	3	2		2	8	18	66
Troy (Trojans)	1	0	2	1	0	0	1		5	17	67
Games Lost	6	7	8	9	9	9	10	12	70		

On the other hand, once you learn how to read it, it tells you a lot more than a twentieth-century standings chart. Even better, if you hold the paper a certain way, your cellar club could be in first place.

though most baseball men were noticeably nervous about betting scandals after what the game had been through during the 1870s.

BICYCLING

Those Bostonians who were not interested in watching the home-town Red Caps lose to Chicago for the third straight year could, of course, turn to other sporting pursuits. That city became the mecca for "wheelmen" or bicyclists during the first week of June 1881, when riders from all over the East gathered there for the first meet sponsored by the American League of Bicyclers. At the time, it was important for wheelmen to get together with their contemporaries, as bicyclers of the 1880s were not always held in exalted positions. Some communities would not allow them to use public roads or ride in the parks; some antagonistic citizens even tossed pointed objects on the roads when bicyclers appeared. And of course it was always great fun for youngsters to toss a stick through the spokes of a wheel and then stand back to watch the resultant abrasions. Horses were particularly bothered by the new vehicles, or so it seemed, and the riders themselves were frequently the subject of satiric editorialists. Thus practitioners of the sport found both physical and emotional protection in numbers. Getting together also provided the opportunity to race, and the Boston meeting of 1881 was no exception. Beacon Park, thanks to city officials who saw no harm in the cyclists, was the scene of four major speed events. The first was a quarter-mile dash, which was won by Lewis Frye of the Marlboro, Massachusetts, club; there followed a half-mile race, also won by Frye, in a time of forty-two seconds. The third event was a mile dash, featuring a pileup when C. S. Nauss of the Waltham Club ran into Joe Lafon of the Manhattan Club. Frye, also unable to stop, added his body and machine to the ensemble. The event was won by William Woodside of Waltham, amid applause for the battered trio, which picked themselves up and continued to the finish line. The only serious casualties were Lafon's machine ("twisted and jammed so as to be useless") and one of Nauss' treadles. The final race, over a two-mile course, was also won by Woodside.

Editorial on Bicyclists—
September 9, 1881:
"Undoubtedly the bicyclist is a curious object. His calves are elaborately displayed, and are, in most cases, as grossly improbable as those of the ballet. His flannel clothes, which sometimes emulate the zebraic beauty of the Sing Sing convicts, and at others approach the simplicity of the most delicate undergarments, may perhaps bring a blush to the cheek of a young person. . . . It has been alleged that the bicycle itself frightens horses. This hardly needs to be refuted. . . . It is the bicyclist who inspires the horse with terror. . . ."

ROWING

Early in June, word reached the United States that the Cornell rowing crew had arrived safely in Great Britain, but that the team would not be allowed to row for the Visitor's Cup at Henley. The reason given was that this competition was open only to college crews and Cornell was a university. That, as it turned out, was just the beginning of the nightmare trip. Accepting an offer to row in the Stewards' Cup instead, the American crew lost dismally. But according to J. G. Allen, one of the oarsmen, there were extenuating circumstances. "The Henley course is notoriously an unfair course on account of the bend in the river, and we had the worst position, on the outside, which was made still worse by a headwind," he explained later. "To show you how unfortunate our position in this race was I need only say that out of seventeen races rowed on that day but one was won by a crew having the outside. The course to be rowed over, owing to the bend in the river, is longer, and the current is worse. That is why I call Henley an unfair course."

Most American rowing enthusiasts took the loss hard. Included were many editors, who tended to regard the latest fiasco as a national tragedy. "We have sent five crews over to England to row against Englishmen," one wrote, "and the result has not been, to put it mildly, very satisfactory. The Atalantas simply made themselves ridiculous; the Harvards showed themselves to be entirely unfit to cope with their opponents; . . . of the Cornell crew it is only too evident that they would have been wiser had they staid at home. . . . This does not mean that the American is in any way inferior to the Englishman, but it does mean that crews selected from a single college or from a small club in a country where rowing is comparatively a novelty cannot row as well as crews selected from large universities where rowing has been practiced for generations. . . . Let us accept the fact that rowing is not and cannot be made an American sport, and urge young men to waste no more time and energy in it."

That may have provided a blueprint for the prevention of long-range disappointment, but it did not solve the immediate problem: Cornell was obligated to run still more races in England and Austria. Would the crew embarrass America even more?

Before the question could be answered, a major distraction was provided. On July 2, President James A. Garfield was approached in a Washington, D.C., train station by Charles Guiteau, a disgruntled office-seeker. With lightning speed, Guiteau pulled a revolver from his pocket and fired several times.

Garfield fell to the floor but was still alive. Physicians were summoned and an operation performed that removed some, but not all, of the metal from Garfield's body.

A nation poised to celebrate the Fourth of July was stunned. In Norwich, New York, a seventy-nine-year-old man named James Legrand was so affected by the news as to be adjudged legally insane by a team of doctors. City councils all across the country suspended celebrations planned for Independence Day. The exception seemed to be Newport, Rhode Island, which issued a report that "In view of the later encouraging reports from Washington, the celebration tomorrow will proceed, but will be abandoned should the President die."

Soon, however, it became obvious that the wait might be a long one. One piece of bullet had become lodged in Garfield's body, but the team of physicians was not sure where it was. Meanwhile, the President seemed to improve, which turned out to be a perfect stimulus for doing nothing. Hourly pulse counts were published; minor operations to release pus were performed; optimistic bulletins continued to assure the public that Garfield was improving; and all the while the Chief Executive continued to die by inches.

Archery on the Beach:
. . . was the attraction of early July at Alameda, California. Both women and men, belonging to the Merry Foresters Club, were on hand for the competition. The ladies' prize, a handsome card-case, was won by a Miss E. Patrick, but not everyone was pleased with the shooting. Decourcey Duff of Great Britain, a foreign visitor in attendance, no doubt irritated more than a few of the local archers by exclaiming, "You should see what we do in England, by Jove."

CAT-BOAT RACING

During that steaming hot summer, while the President seemed to be on the verge of recovery, the nation slowly returned its interest to recreation. On July 14, the natives of Long Island were treated to a cat-boat race starting from Echo Bay, fifteen miles down the Sound and back. Ranging in length from thirteen to twenty-four feet, the boats got away in good shape, without fouls, although several barely escaped collision. The little fleet then pointed itself toward the buoy off Execution Light just as the weather turned dark. As the boats rounded the buoy, a thunderstorm, accompanied by vivid flashes of lightning, started. The spectators and judges of the race promptly retired to the piazza of the Hudson Park hotel, from which the conclusion of the race could be seen through the trees.

One of the spectators who remained outside was Stephen Stouter, a park policeman, who opted for the protection of a tree instead. It turned out to be a poor decision for, according to the New York *Times,* "All at once, while the crowd on the piazza was intently gazing at a yacht just about to cross the home line, the air seemed to bristle with the sharp cracking of electricity, and the pine tree under which the policeman was standing was struck on its highest branch, the bark ripped off to the roots, and Stouter knocked to the ground. It all happened in a second. Several men at once ran out from the piazza, which was about a hundred feet from the tree, and picked up Stouter, who had only been stunned. He seemed for some time afterward dazed and stupefied, and said he felt a peculiar tingling on the bottoms of his feet."

HORSERACING

It was, after all, that kind of a summer, with three steps being taken forward and four back. On the same day that Stephen Stouter was struck by lightning, a record was established at Pittsburgh. The record-setter was a seven-year-old trotter named Maud S. Preparations for her speed trial were quite elaborate for the period. After the track had been scraped and rolled by a team of horses, a twelve-foot space just wide enough for a sulky to have full play was smoothed and checked for excess water. Then, as the crowd cheered in anticipation, jockey Bair moved the mare in a flying start past the starting wire. As she reached the first turn, Maud S.'s stride began to lengthen, her feet falling in rapidly accelerating speed. At the quarter post, her time was 00:33. That pace was maintained throughout the mile run, except for a slight burst toward the end, which brought the mare's time to a record-breaking 2:10½. The demonstration that followed was spontaneous. "People rushed from the grandstands and crowded down to the fence to get a better look at the queen, and to give vent to their exuberant satisfaction with her performance. . . . Then Mr. Ryers, one of the judges, had time to announce to the crowd that Maud S. had trotted the heat in 2:10½, beating her own record of 2:10¾ and making the fastest mile ever trotted in the world. At his proposal three cheers were given for Maud S. with unanimity and heartiness."

That Pittsburgh meet, however, did not end on such a high note. The next day, a ten-year-old stallion named Bonesetter started to weave

and stagger in the backstretch. Ten feet from the finish line, his rider tried to steady him, but the horse lurched ahead with sufficient force to finish fifth before expiring against the fence. Seeing that the horse was dead, officials of the track suggested that Bonesetter be removed to the infield and be given a ceremonial burial and a monument erected. Later, it was discovered that the horse had been ill for a couple of weeks "but it was thought he was sufficiently recovered to go. . . ."

ROWING

The bad news continued as word reached America's shores that the Cornell rowing crew had lost more races in England and Vienna. In fact, they had not won a single race of any consequence. What had happened? The answer came soon enough with the hardly triumphant return of the oarsmen. "We have been sold out," they said simply, explaining much of their failure.

Sold out by whom? In reply, J. G. Allen pointed out that one member of the crew, J. N. D. Shinkel, a twenty-three-year-old senior from Rochelle, Illinois, was the culprit. As evidence, it was noted pointedly that Shinkel had not accompanied the rest of the team off the boat.

America wanted to know what had happened, and Allen was quick to supply an explanation. His evidence was mostly circumstantial, but for those seeking a readily believable excuse for American failures, it was enough. While in England, Allen said, Shinkel had started acting "queerly," continually arguing and trying to manage the crew in his own way. "He injured us in this way but we never thought of his betraying us until the affair at Vienna," Allen said. "The course was a mile and a half up the Danube . . . and we were four lengths ahead of the Donauhort crew and rowing easily, when Shinkel suddenly rowed a half-dozen strokes faster than the time and leaped forward with his head upon his hand. I threw water upon him and asked him what was the matter. He said that he had a pain in his chest and could row no more. In the meantime the German crew pushed ahead, and we allowed our boat to drift down to the boat-house." Here Shinkel was given a physical examination and nothing found. He had improved sufficiently to attend a party given that evening, even "drinking wine as freely, if not more so, than any of his companions."

That pricked Allen's curiosity to the point where a constant watch was put on Shinkel. It was soon discovered that he had a habit of meeting several "sporting men" who had bet against the American crew, and that, while he claimed to have no money, he was seen arranging a bank draft sent home to America. A search of Shinkel's room turned up a diamond ring valued at approximately seventy-five dollars, and it was also noticed that he had taken to sleeping with a vest on.

Finally, it was decided to confront Shinkel with the evidence. The young man shrugged off the accusations, even suggested that the others search his trunk if they wished. But when someone asked if his clothes could be searched, Shinkel became angry and refused to allow anything to be examined. When last seen, he was still in London. "He will never get back," Allen said in conclusion, "unless he buys his ticket with some of the money paid to him as the price of our defeat."

That may have satisfied some of his countrymen, but many rowing enthusiasts in America must have cringed with embarrassment and anger as the London *Standard* gloatingly repeated the Viennese reaction that "The American oarsmen's defeat being a complete surprise, the jubilation here is all the greater."

BALLOONING

Defeat seemed to be everywhere, including the air. On September 8, at Boston, a Professor G. A. Rogers entered the gondola of his balloon with a friend, but after rising forty or fifty feet, the vehicle began to descend rapidly. As it neared the ground, the friend wisely leaped out, but Rogers hesitated just long enough for the balloon to rise again. Arriving over Long Beach, he made preparations to throw out the grappler and catch something, bringing himself to earth. But the basket oscillated so violently in the strong winds that Rogers was forced to sit in the very bottom, his feet braced against the sides. At that point, the huge bag started to rip, emitting gas in large volumes, sending the vehicle plunging toward the earth. Just before striking the ground, however, some ropes of the balloon caught a telephone pole, causing it to wrap itself around the pole and break the force of the fall. That was all that saved the professor's life.

Eleven days later, life ended for the President of the United States. After ten weeks of generally favorable bulletins, minor "relapses" followed inevitably by reports of "rallying" and "improved condition," it came almost as a complete shock to realize that Mr. Garfield had, in fact, expired. Brushing aside any possibility that they acted with anything less than complete competence, the team of attending physicians blandly chalked up the death as an act of God that could hardly have been avoided regardless of what they had done.

Americans generally believed—and grieved

the loss of a man whose position, rather than his own ability, entitled him to the utmost respect. "Garfield! Ours Yesterday—God's Today" was the sentiment of a banner draped across Harrigan and Hart's Theater immediately following the President's death. Most sports events were quickly canceled, even when it meant embarrassment for the management. At the Polo Grounds, for example, where hundreds of fans were queued up to watch a game between the Metropolitans and Philadelphia Athletics, an announcement was made that the game would not be played. The same was true of a cricket match between New York and Philadelphia teams, as well as an international yacht race between the Scottish cutter *Madge* and the American sloop *Schemer*. All National League games were canceled.

Despite the Death of a President:
Sporting activity continued about as usual in California, the annual state fair opening at Sacramento right on schedule. Horse races were held, the most exciting being a 1½-mile dash, won by Jim Brown. And as the newspapers continued to line their columns with strips of black, the sporting activity went on, including a hotly contested bicycle race between H. C. Eggers of San Francisco and Russell Flint of Sacramento. A third participant named H. C. Finckler was not highly regarded and was given a 95-yard start. But Flint broke a pedal and Finckler turned out to be faster than anyone expected, winning the mile race in 3 minutes, 26½ seconds to Eggers' 3 minutes, 29½ seconds.

HORSERACING

The nation survived, of course. It even survived Garfield's successor, Chester A. Arthur, and before many weeks had passed, American love—perhaps need—for sports had surfaced once again. Confident that a catastrophe, if not a tragedy, had been avoided, interest revived, especially when word came from Rochester, New York, that not one, but two, female riders were touring the country with a highly innovative attraction. That was a twenty-mile race between Bell Cook of California and Emma Jewett of Minnesota, a pair of women riders who regularly wore down as many as sixteen horses a race in their efforts to beat one another. When they arrived at Rochester after three races, interest in the women was at its peak. As a result, more than twenty thousand persons elbowed their way into the western New York fairgrounds for what they sensed would be a sensational spectator event. According to the papers of the period, they were not disappointed. "The contest was one of the most exciting ever seen on the Driving Park," wrote one reporter. "Some of the horses were sent two miles without a stop, and others only one, the riders making the change from saddle to saddle with wonderful rapidity. Cook, who is the lighter, made one of her changes in seven seconds."

When the women competed at Rochester's Driving Park on September 29, Bell Cook was the favorite, largely because she had defeated Emma Jewett on three previous occasions. The bookmakers, who seemed to be everywhere there was a reasonable contest and a chance to make some money on it, installed Cook at 3–1.

For the first mile, the women raced neck-and-neck. Then, at the first change of horses, Cook gained a length and steadily increased the lead until she was a quarter mile ahead at the end of the fifth miles. At this point, Emma Jewett mounted one of her best horses and was able to close the gap. The women were even once again as they swung into the seventh mile. Charmed by the unusual contest and impressed by the women's ability to quickly leap from saddle to saddle, the crowd applauded enthusiastically.

For a mile the two riders galloped dead even. First one, then the other edged to the front for the next three miles, but neither could take a strong advantage. Not until the twelfth mile, when one of Bell Cook's mounts quit in the backstretch, was the tie broken. Emma Jewett plunged ahead, quickly gaining a three-quarter-mile lead while Cook was obliged to limp along until a new horse could be brought to her. Desperate to regain the lead, she rode recklessly, and the crowd, sensing an exciting finish, urged her on. By the nineteenth mile the gap had been diminished, but Cook was still a half mile to the rear. She didn't give up, however, having saved her best horse for the final mile. Racing to where her husband held the reins for her, Bell Cook leaped from the saddle of her perspiring mount and grasped the new set of reins. Too anxious for her own good, she failed to get a good grip and the horse bolted, jumped the fence near the judge's stand, and went into the crowd. As he leaped the barrier, one hind leg caught on a picket and the horse fell heavily upon his side. Having thrown herself clear at the last moment, Bell Cook was unharmed except for minor scratches and a pain in her back. She stood up and reassured the crowd, which applauded her in return. Emma Jewett, meanwhile, moved briskly around the track to her first victory in the series. Her time for the twenty miles was forty-five minutes, five seconds.

As the year moved into its final quarter, much attention was given to a pair of court trials. The first, naturally, was that of Charles Guiteau for the murder of President Garfield. Having been seen by more than a dozen witnesses, Guiteau's only defense was that of pleading insanity, but most Americans were inclined to dismiss that notion. Recalling the assassination of the Russian Czar earlier in the year, more than one citizen advocated the same treatment for Guiteau as that meted out to the revolutionaries who were convicted of murdering Alexander II (they were strangled in sacks). Guiteau's defense attorneys did the best they could under the circumstances, but from the very beginning it seemed the verdict in the case was a foregone conclusion.

The second trial dealt with a certain Lieutenant Henry O. Flipper, who had gained a measure of notoriety and respect in 1877 by being the first black man to graduate from West Point. After receiving his commission, Flipper was assigned to the 10th Cavalry in the West and promptly faded from public attention for the rest of the decade. In 1881, however, his name reappeared when the U. S. Army started court-martial proceedings against him for misappropriation of funds and conduct unbecoming an officer in making false statements to cover up shortages. Some said that Flipper was being persecuted; others maintained he should be tried like any other officer who was suspected of wrongdoing.

LACROSSE

With the passing of baseball for another year, one sports highlight of October 1881 was a game of lacrosse played between the Shamrock Lacrosse Club, holders of the Canadian championship, and the New York Lacrosse Club, which claimed the U.S. title. About three thousand spectators came to the Polo Grounds on October 22 to see what was billed as the "championship of America."

After a forty-five-minute delay, the contest finally started, with New York winning the toss and choosing to attack the eastern goal so that the sun would be in the Canadians' eyes. The advantage was slight, for in a quarter-hour the Shamrocks scored the first goal, then another soon afterward to make the score 2–0. The hometown crowd cheered heartily when the New Yorkers came back to score a goal after eight minutes to make the contest closer. But after twenty-three more minutes, the Canadians came back to score the third, and deciding, goal, winning, 3–1. Unlike lacrosse games of the twentieth century, the 1881 contest was halted every time one team scored a goal. A ten-minute rest period ensued, followed by another scrimmage until another goal was scored. By prearrangement, the team which scored three goals first was declared the winner.

The Press on Lacrosse's "Super Bowl":
"The New Yorkers were defeated but by no means disgraced. They played up with great pluck and energy, but they were matched against some of the finest players in the world, who were vastly their superiors in experience and in all the fine points of the game. The 'passing' and 'dodging' shown by the Shamrocks was marvelous as an exhibition of magnificent play and was a lesson to the home team, by which they will doubtless profit in the future."
—New York Herald, *October 23, 1881*

FOOTBALL

Meanwhile, the college football season opened with major games between Yale and Michigan and Harvard and Pennsylvania, powerhouses of the East and Midwest. Still in its infancy, the game was no rival for the "national game" of baseball, a fact attested to by the crowds of six hundred and two hundred, respectively, that attended the two contests. The sparse attendance was partially explained by threatening weather, and, perhaps, by the feeling that the games were basically mismatches. Harvard, it was noted, "was made up of heavy-weights, the average being 160 pounds, while that of their adversaries reached only 145 pounds." It was hardly a matter of scoring at will, but Harvard did put across three touchdowns and two field goals, while holding Penn to nothing. The same sort of contest developed between Yale and Michigan, the boys from New Haven outweighing their opponents by a significant amount. The score in this contest was two goals for Yale, none for Michigan.

An even soggier but much more satisfying contest was played on November 12 when Yale and Harvard came together in the rain and mud at New Haven. Although the drizzle of a week before had turned into a downpour, more than fifteen hundred spectators braved the weather to urge on their favorites.

Devoid of passing, even of touchdowns or field goals, the game was decided as a result of Harvard's having committed four "safety-touchdowns" (that is, four times Harvard players were tackled behind their own goal line) to Yale's none. But there was a great

deal of action, at least for that era, and at least one exciting play that didn't count. After Harvard's third safety, the ball was kicked back to Yale. "After the punt," it was reported, "Hull [of Yale] was on the ball. . . . Yale won ground by inches. This was very exciting, and the ball was carried almost on the goal line. Amid wild cheers Storrs carried the ball over the line. The Harvards claimed a foul, and the referee allowed it. Yale was disgusted." The punter for Yale during this game, incidentally, was named Walter Camp.

Officiating at the time was obviously less than totally competent, for the Columbia-Princeton game, played a week later, was marred by a curious decision. Not long after the opening kickoff, Princeton obtained possession of the ball and started to move. A player named Haxell took the ball, or "sphere," as the 1880s journalists called it, and "dashing through Columbia's forwards, planted it behind the latter's goal line. It was seemingly a touchdown, and a cheer went up from the Princeton boys in the stand. The referee did not allow it, however, as he did not see it made."

Eventually Princeton did score—after thirty-eight minutes of playing time—and the field-goal attempt was made by Harlan, but "on account of the treacherous sod he failed to score the coveted point." In the second half, Princeton scored another touchdown to chalk up a fairly easy win.

BOXING

The day after that particular combat, *aficionados* of the pugilistic art began to gather near Cleveland for a featherweight boxing match between George Holden and Frank White. The bout, of course, was illegal, but promoters were hoping to cross into Canada if American authorities would not allow the fight to take place on American soil. Rumors flew back and forth, the smart money placing Erie, Pennsylvania, as the most likely site of the battle, and Simcoe, Ontario, as the second most likely. Just in case anyone crossed into Canada, the sheriff of Port Dover ordered two companies of volunteers supplied with ammunition and fifty pairs of handcuffs.

On November 15, both Holden and White arrived at Buffalo. They were greeted at dinner by a Pennsylvania sheriff who warned them to stay out of his state. Even as he spoke, persons determined to see the fight continued to pour into Erie and charter boats for Canadian ports if the promoters decided to leave the United States.

Finally, intimidated by authorities of New York, Pennsylvania, and Canada, the fighters boarded a westbound Lake Shore train for Ohio. A ring was pitched about two miles east

1. By the outset of the 1870s, baseball was well established in the United States as the "national game" and promoters had even taken to exporting it. Following the 1874 National Association season, the pennant-winning Boston Red Stockings and Philadelphia Athletics, who finished third, toured England, playing on Lord's Cricket Grounds before sizable audiences. Boston won 8 of 14 matches.

2. Rivaling baseball for popularity was rowing, which featured many athletes who were nationally known. Edward Hanlan of Canada (r.), was a fair-haired popular hero, while Charles Courtney (l.) was regarded as a bit of a villain. The two had their most famous match in 1878. Hanlan won but the result was clouded by rumors that Courtney had accepted a bribe to lose the race. (See "Fixes.")

3. Another popular hero of rowing was James Renforth of England, who came to America in 1871 with the intention of showing European superiority in the sport. Unfortunately, Renforth passed out during the middle of a critical race and was pronounced dead soon afterward. Rumors flew about that he had been poisoned, but it seems more likely he died of apoplexy or a heart attack. (See "1871.")

4. Another rowing match among young women was part of the tenth annual Empire City Rowing Club regatta, held on the Harlem River, New York, September 25, 1871. (See "1871.")

5. Another highly popular spectator sport of the 1870s was pedestrianism or speed walking, which started as an outdoor attraction but soon came indoors, where the money was. America's first pedestrian to attain fame was Edward Payson Weston (1839–1929), who thrilled sports fans of 1870 by walking 100 miles in 22 hours. (See "Doing It Until It Hurts.")

6. Pedestrianism was one of the first sports in America in which blacks participated with whites. Frank Hart of Haiti and Boston finished well behind the leaders in the 1879 Astley Belt competition, a 6-day race covering 500 miles at Madison Square Garden, but by the next year he was a top money-earner and one of America's first respected black athletes. (See "Breaking the Color Barrier.")

7. Sports were popular even during the coldest winters. When the lakes and rivers of the Eastern Seaboard became frozen, teams participated in curling or baseball on ice. (See "1871.") The groups of curlers seen here are using the lake in Central Park, New York, in 1872.

8. For the well-to-do, ice yachting was an exciting sport, especially when the wind was right and a race could be arranged between an express train and some ice yachts. On January 20, 1871, John Roosevelt's *Icicle*, with 1,070 square feet of canvas, was more than fast enough to defeat the *Chicago Express* on the Hudson River. (See "1871.")

9. During the 1870s, archery attained popularity with both men and women, leading to the formation in 1879 of the National Archery Association. The first annual meeting and competition was held that year at Chicago's White Stocking Park. The winner was Will H. Thompson.

10. Following formation of the National Rifle Association in 1871, Americans regularly participated in international matches against top foreign competition. Creedmoor, Long Island, was the scene of many early matches, with crowds of as many as 100,000 in attendance. In September 1876, the Irish team, with 1,528 points, barely defeated the Australians, with 1,527. The U.S. team came in third with 1,487, the Scottish last with 1,443.

11. Already a well-worn tradition of two decades by 1871, the third America's Cup yacht race series pitted *Columbia* and *Sappho* of the United States against Great Britain's *Livonia*. The American entries each won two races to *Livonia's* one. (See "1871.")

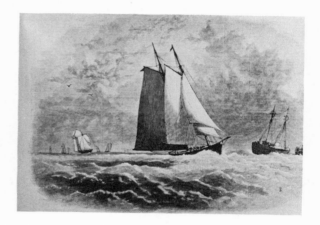

12. Not all sports competitions inaugurated in the 1870s retained their popularity to the present time. One nearly forgotten spectator attraction was known as "paper chasing" or "hares and hounds," which was little more than cross-country running mixed with littering. Note decorative bunnies on jackets of runners and one man's dropping paper "trail" in this 1879 chase held by the Westchester Hare and Hounds Club. (See "Sports That Never Made It.")

13. Some early sportsmen had strange ideas and inventions they hoped to promote, one of the more colorful being Captain Paul Boyton. Boyton's vehicle was an inflatable rubber dress, in which he crossed the English Channel before Matthew Webb swam it and traversed many rivers of the world, including the Mississippi. Boyton usually towed a small raft filled with supplies and shaded his face and eyes from the sun with a canopy attached to the dress. (See "Technology Rears Its Leg.")

14. Baseball continued to grow in popularity during the 1880s, which featured the first "World Series" between the National League and the American Association. (See "Other Leagues.") Nearly always in the thick of the pennant fights of the decade were the N.L. Chicago White Stockings, seen here in a group portrait following back-to-back victories in 1885 and 1886. Of more than average interest are foster members Billy Sunday (back row, left), who went on to become a famous evangelist; Ned Williamson (back row, third from left), who smashed 27 home runs in 1884, a record until Babe Ruth broke it 35 years later; King Kelly (middle row, left), whose base-running derring-do inspired the song "Slide, Kelly, Slide"; and Cap Anson (front row, middle), who played from 1871 to 1897, finishing his N.L. career with a lifetime batting average of .333. Anson was also a leader in preventing blacks from joining organized baseball. (See "Breaking the Color Barrier.")

15. Baseball of the 1880s was such a well-established sport that cartoonist H. C. Megerle was able to get a little humor out of baseball terminology. In one, he turned a pitcher on the mound into a pitcher to hold liquid. That the mug resembles a beer stein is probably not accidental, for many ballplayers of the 1880s were notorious tipplers.

16. In 1886 the New York baseball fan had two teams to root for (not counting Brooklyn). In the National League, the Giants, who finished third, played in the magnificent Polo Grounds. The scene depicts a dramatic moment in the home opener against Boston.

17. Advertisement of 1887 listed home games of New York Giants and depicted Polo Grounds as haven for the rich, if we can judge by the high silk hats and victorias parked in the outfield areas.

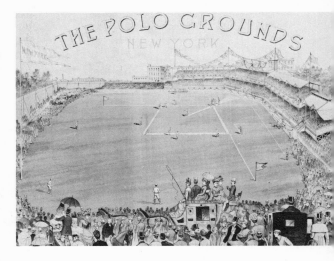

18. American-style football gradually grew in popularity during the 1880s, although many regarded it as a barbaric sport not worthy of attention. Scene from Cornell-Rochester game of October 19, 1889, seems to resemble a group boxing exhibition.

19. Despite widespread prejudice against football because of its roughness, football attracted the attention of young women as well as men. The annual Yale-Princeton match, such as this one of Thanksgiving Day 1881, invariably drew large crowds. (See "1881.")

20. Lawn tennis, brought to the United States in the 1870s, became more popular during the 1880s. The scene shows a "first national lawn-tennis tournament" played at New Brighton, Staten Island, in 1880, although first official championship, won by Richard D. Sears, was not held until a year later.

21. Tennis became one of the first outdoor sports to go inside. It was tried on a mass scale on November 26, 1881, at the 7th Regiment Armory, New York City, 12 courts being put into use for women enthusiasts and their male partners. Only one light became a casualty. (See "1881.")

22. Roller skating at a Washington, D.C., rink in 1880, four years before introduction of the first ball-bearing skate. The sport had a long period of popularity immediately following the Civil War but went into a 50-year decline until the 1930s.

23. In 1885, an advertisement showing the top fighters of the day was issued by, appropriately, the Liston Beef Company. Besides a young John L. Sullivan, the honor roll includes long washed-up Joe Coburn (see "1871"); the first Jack Dempsey, Andy Burke, who in 1893 would participate in the world's longest fight (see "Doing It Till It Hurts"; and Tug Wilson, who attained distinction by going four rounds with Sullivan during Sullivan's prime. (See "A Century of Upsets.")

of Conneaut, on the border, and three rounds fought before an Ohio constable appeared with orders to desist. The fighters and crowd responded by running a short distance into Pennsylvania in order to continue the bout, but the Ohio lawman followed them. After catching a freight train for Erie, White and Holden ran into Sheriff Stiles of Ashtabula County, Ohio, who had preceded them by taking a faster passenger train. "Much chagrined at the turn of affairs," the fighters were escorted back to Ohio, where they were tried, found guilty, and fined twelve hundred dollars each. Neither man having that amount of money, they were thrown into seven-by-nine-foot cells.

FOOTBALL

The featherweight fiasco prompted at least one editorialist to direct his ire not only at the fight game, but also at the growing violence of college football. "The pleasure with which decent people learned the other day of the arrest of two notorious prizefighters was marred by the recollection of the utter failure of our local police to interfere with a disgraceful football fight between two mobs of old offenders, well known as the Yale and Columbia 'gangs,' " he wrote. "The fight took place in the presence of a large crowd of spectators, and from first to last not a single policeman made the slightest effort to stop it." Comparing the new tackle football with the old-style game, which was more similar to soccer, he added, "A foot-ball match is precisely like a free fight between two mobs of unarmed street thieves over some article of value which each one is desirous of stealing. . . . If they must fight, and if the authorities are too timid or too feeble to interfere, let them fight with rifles, like civilized beings. They can throw up entrenchments from which they can fire at one another, and storming parties, carrying the ball with them, can charge on the enemy with fixed bayonets. Such fights would be much less disgusting than the present savage fights with fists and feet, and they would possess the additional advantage that the ranks of the 'roughs' would be nicely thinned out at every contest. . . ."

Such attacks on the organized mayhem known as college football of the 1880s had little effect, naturally, although the championship contest played by Yale and Princeton four days after the above editorial appeared was quite a gentlemanly affair. "It was the opinion of old football men present," noted the New York *Herald,* "that if the teams had not been so much afraid of each other a better game might have been witnessed." Ten thousand fans saw the game end in a scoreless tie.

With the conclusion of the football and baseball seasons—Chicago's White Stockings again ran away with the National League race —the year ended with a revived interest in indoor sports. Jacob Schaefer continued to win regularly at billiards while "the Boy Expert," Albert Frey, faded into comparative obscurity. Wrestlers William Muldoon, along with the likes of Theobald Bauer and Joe Acton, entertained audiences in smoke-filled arenas and theaters for the rest of the year and decade.

A Long and Distinguished Career: *Although he died at age fifty-five, Jacob Schaefer was tops in billiards for nearly four decades. Beginning in 1873, when he was eighteen, he played a series of fifty-seven matches with fellow artist George Slosson, "winning" by the narrowest of margins (29–28). Schaefer died in 1910, leaving behind a son with the same name and ability for billiard lovers of the twentieth century.*

Baseball also made news in a smoke-filled room late in 1881. The occasion was a convention at Cincinnati, which was held for the purpose of starting a second baseball league. Representatives from New York, Boston, St. Louis, Pittsburgh, Cincinnati, Brooklyn, and Philadelphia were present. Of those major cities, only Boston had a major-league team. Cincinnati had been in the National League from 1876 through 1880, St. Louis in 1876 and 1877, Philadelphia and New York in 1876 only. Pittsburgh and Brooklyn had never had a team in the league. Eventually St. Louis, Pittsburgh, Cincinnati, and Philadelphia, along with Baltimore and Louisville, banded to form the new American Association.

With spectator sports in early-winter doldrums, renewed interest in the trials of Charles Guiteau and Lieutenant Flipper was inevitable. The defense attorneys of both men worked hard, but though no decision had been rendered in either case by the end of the year, even the bookmakers weren't taking odds on Guiteau's chances. Flipper's chances for acquittal seemed much better, although the evidence continued to mount against him; on December 9, final arguments were heard in the case and a holiday recess taken.

As they looked back over the year, sports enthusiasts—despite some notable defeats for America—had reason to be thankful for the athletic thrills provided by 1881. For the first time, a large midwestern school, Michigan, had come East to play schools such as Yale and Harvard; a second baseball league seemed to be a definite possibility; advocates of less traditional sports such as lawn tennis could be happy about the formation of the United States Lawn Tennis Association and Richard D. Sears' winning the first men's singles championship on August 31; Dartmouth students could be grateful for their school's first year of college football; even blacks could take some comfort and pride in the fact that pedestrians Frank Hart and William Pegram raced on better-than-even terms with white athletes. For fifty million Americans with a bit more leisure time on their hands, the prospects for enjoying and participating in sports seemed bright.

And what about Guiteau and Flipper, by the way? Guiteau, of course, was found guilty and executed in 1882. Flipper, also adjudged guilty, appealed his case to President Chester Arthur in May 1882, but the new Chief Exec-

utive saw fit not to intervene. On June 20, 1882, an order issued by the War Department said curtly, "By direction of the Secretary of War, the sentence in the case of Second Lieutenant Henry O. Flipper, 10th Cavalry, will take effect June 30, 1882, from which date he will cease to be an officer of the Army."

That could have been that—except that Henry Flipper had the last laugh on just about everyone living in 1881. After leaving the Army, he worked as a special agent for the Department of Justice, then put in four years as a resident engineer for a mining company before serving as translator and interpreter of Spanish for the subcommittee of the Senate Committee of Foreign Relations investigating Mexican Affairs, from 1919 to 1921. Not until 1940 did the former slave and first graduate of West Point pass away, just two weeks shy of his eighty-fourth birthday.

CHAPTER 7—SPORTS AND THE PRESIDENTS

"When I was a small boy growing up in Kansas, a friend of mine and I went fishing and as we sat there in the warmth of a summer afternoon on a riverbank we talked about what we wanted to do when we grew up. I told him that I wanted to be a real major-league baseball player, a genuine professional like Honus Wagner. My friend said that he'd like to be President of the United States. Neither of us got our wish."

Dwight D. Eisenhower

Because the nearly two-score men who have served as United States President have come from varying backgrounds, their interest in sports and ability to participate do not follow a particular pattern. Some, such as James K. Polk and Martin Van Buren, were unathletically inclined; others, such as James Garfield, whose favorite trick was to write Latin with one hand while writing Greek with the other, were just not interested in sports. Still others—Andrew Jackson, Abraham Lincoln, John F. Kennedy, Teddy Roosevelt— were robust figures who enjoyed participating in athletics even more than watching. But the majority of those who rose to the nation's highest office—partly, no doubt, because it was good politics—showed at least a healthy interest in sports and usually made it a point to be on hand for the more important athletic events.

Below, a modest history of United States Presidents and their favorite athletic pursuits:

GEORGE WASHINGTON, a physically vigorous, uncommonly fine rider who enjoyed all manner of athletic games, had a great deal of prejudice to overcome when he took office; for prior to the Revolution, the First Continental Congress of 1774 passed a resolution calling for the colonies to "discountenance and discourage every Species of Extravagance and Dissipation, especially all horse racing, and all kinds of gaming, Cock Fighting, Exhibitions of Shows, Plays, and other expensive Diversions and entertainments."

President Washington, it turned out, was not put off by the prejudice against sports and games. A frequent visitor to Annapolis, Maryland, which had a long tradition of horseracing predating the Revolution, Washington enjoyed the company of betting men and breeders. During the 1760s, a group of horse fanciers formed an exclusive Jockey Club in Annapolis, transforming the racing season into a major social occasion for the Chesapeake tidewater, complete with balls, dinners, and performances at the theater. In 1771, the Annapolis races attracted the best horses of the area, including Alexander Spotwood's Apollo and Colonel Edward Lloyd's mare Nancy Bywell. Major George Washington obviously enjoyed Annapolis, often called the "Athens of America," but while he frequently attended the races there he was not addicted to them.

If Washington had a sporting addiction, it was not watching horses in action, but riding. He loved few things as well as a stirring fox hunt, continuing to ride to the hounds after he took office, despite the feeling of some that a fall would be catastrophic to the new nation. Washington also enjoyed cockfighting, hunting, and fishing, his journal containing many references to outdoor trips and recreation. "Went a ducking between breakfast and dinner and killd a Mallard and 5 Bald Faces," he wrote once. Another, less successful, trip produced the line: "Fishing for sturgeon but catchd none."

Presidential Name-alike
George Washington, born June 7, 1907, played major-league baseball for a total of ninety-one games with the Chicago White Sox in 1935–36. An outfielder, Washington hit nine home runs, twenty-four doubles, three triples, and batted a lifetime .268.

During the Revolutionary War years, Washington often played billiards with the Marquis de Lafayette and managed to sneak in at least one game of wicket during the dreary winter spent at Valley Forge. After retiring from the presidency, he gave up fox hunting, but continued to ride until a few days before his death.

JOHN ADAMS, the second President of the United States, was identified with baseball rather than any more traditional sports of the time. A short, chubby man, he is credited with "frolicking with the bat and ball" in Boston, presumably playing a variation of English rounders, which evolved into America's national game a century later. Aside from that, Adams' sports activity was limited compared to that of George Washington. He was, however, the first U. S. President to play a form of baseball.

Presidential Name-alike
John Adams, of Notre Dame, played tackle for the Washington Redskins from 1945 to 1949. In addition, a back, also named John Adams, was with the Chicago Bears from 1959 to 1962 and the 1963 Los Angeles Rams. And John ("Bert") Adams was a catcher for the Cleveland Indians and Philadelphia Phillies from 1910 to 1919.

THOMAS JEFFERSON, who once swam across a quarter-mile-wide millpond thirteen times in a row, also enjoyed chess because of its intellectual quality. He felt that man's degeneration started when he tamed the horse, and thus gave up riding in favor of walking as a means of daily exercise.

JAMES MADISON, who never weighed more than a hundred pounds and was once described as "a withered little-apple-john," was a sickly child who enjoyed walks in the woods. For the rest of his life he remained a naturalist and bird-watcher.

JOHN QUINCY ADAMS, the son of John Adams, was a plumpish man whose favorite athletic activity was swimming. Living in the new capital city when it was still largely rural, he used to enjoy slipping into the Potomac early in the morning and taking a dip *au naturel*. On one occasion, an enterprising woman reporter named Anne Royall sat down on his clothes and refused to move until he granted her an exclusive interview.

ANDREW JACKSON, perhaps the most *macho* of all United States Presidents, was a fighting outdoorsman in every sense of the word. A cool and expert shot, he fought and won duels with regularity, enlisted in the Army at age fourteen, was an ardent cockfighter and horsebreeder. "He worked a horse to the limit of endurance," one of Jackson's biographers wrote, "but somehow implanted in the animal a will to win, a circumstance that epitomizes the character and elucidates the singular attainments of Andrew Jackson."

Jackson's favorite horse was named Truxton, a huge bay stallion that won many races for the general and President. One of his most famous victories was against Ploughboy, in 1806, which Truxton won despite going lame before the race. Friends urged Jackson to cancel the contest—which was to be the best of two three-mile heats—but Jackson refused, and to everyone's surprise, he won his bet.

Presidential Name-alikes:
John Tyler, an outfielder with the 1934–35 Boston Braves, played in just 16 games but batted a quite respectable .321, hitting two home runs.

Zack Taylor (1898–1974) spent sixteen years behind the plate with the Brooklyn Dodgers, Boston Braves, Chicago Cubs, New York Yankees, and Dodgers once again for his final year, 1935. His best year was 1925, when he batted .310 in 109 games. Ironically, the Dodgers then traded him to the Braves.

James Buchanan, a pitcher, spent just one year in the major leagues, winning five and losing ten for the last-place St. Louis Browns of 1905. Like the one-term President of the same name, he then vanished into a probably deserved obscurity.

ABRAHAM LINCOLN, America's sixteenth President, was an imposing figure of a man at 6 feet, 4 inches and a well-muscled 180 pounds. Early in life, Lincoln developed great wrestling skills and soon earned an awesome reputation after defeating a local streetfighter named Jack Armstrong. The bout took place while Lincoln was employed as a clerk at New Salem, Illinois. Bill Clary, a saloonkeeper, arranged the match by offering Lincoln ten dollars if he could throw Armstrong.

People came from fifty miles away to see the fight, and betting was brisk, most of the money being placed on the shorter but more powerfully built Armstrong. But once the fight started, it was no contest. "Lincoln lifted him by the throat," wrote Carl Sandburg, "shook him like a rag, and then slammed him to a hard fall." Armstrong shook his head and said, "He's the best feller that ever broke into the settlement."

Not long afterward, Lincoln went off to the Black Hawk War and while at Beardstown, Illinois, met his match in a wrestler named Lorenzo D. Thompson. Captain Abe, said the men in Lincoln's company, could beat any man in the Army, a boast that was soon challenged by backers of Thompson. "Lincoln's friends bet money, hats, whiskey, knives, blankets, and tomahawks," Sandburg wrote. "On the day of the match, as the two wrestlers tussled in their first feel-outs of each other, Lincoln turned to his friends and said, 'Boys, this is the most powerful man I ever had hold of.' For a while Lincoln held him off; then Thompson got the 'crotch hoist' on him, and he went under, fairly thrown." The next fall, Lincoln went down but dragged Thompson with him. Lincoln could have called it a draw but instead he said, "Boys, give up your bets. If this man hasn't throwed me fairly, he could."

Apparently Lincoln suffered little physical degeneration from that time until he died at age fifty-six, for when physicians undressed him as he lay dying on the night of April 14–15, 1865, they were amazed at how perfect his physique was. Charles Sabin Taft, one of the attending doctors, reported that there was hardly an ounce of visible fat on Lincoln's entire frame; another doctor, Charles Augustus Leale, stated that the President could have been the model for Michelangelo's *Moses* so well proportioned were his powerful muscles.

ANDREW JOHNSON, the unfortunate individual who followed Lincoln to the White House, had no great interest in organized sports, but it was during his tenure of office that baseball gained a measure of respectability by being played on the "White House lot." The Philadelphia Athletics were first to perform, soon followed by superb amateur clubs of New York, the Nationals and Atlantics.

It was during the summer of 1865 that these matches were held, and they delighted natives and reporters of the capital city. "Never before in the annals of the game has there been a season marked with so many contests illustrative of the uncertainty of the game of baseball as this," one commentator noted on August 30. "The signal victory obtained by the Athletics over the Nationals on Monday led everyone to suppose that the champion Atlantics would almost annihilate them, but . . . a better contested game and a finer display of skill in a match, on both sides . . . we have not witnessed this season. . . ."

The Exciting Match Between the Nationals and Atlantics, August 29, 1865:										
Nationals	2	2	6	0	7	0	1	0	1—19
Atlantics	1	3	5	3	0	0	8	13	0—33

Although the players on both sides were alleged amateurs, many of the athletes performing that day in Washington turned professional when the National Association was formed in 1871. These included John Galvin, Fred Crane, Harry Berthrong, and the winning pitcher for the Atlantics, Al Pratt, who skillfully scattered "only" nineteen runs. "After the game was over," the account concluded, "the parties adjourned to the National Hotel where their hospitable hosts had prepared a sumptuous feast for them, and the remainder of the evening was spent in social enjoyment. On Wednesday the Atlantics were to have called upon the President and then take cars for New York. . . ."

ULYSSES S. GRANT's sporting passion was horsemanship in all its phases. From breaking wild ponies to jumping thoroughbreds, he was, by all accounts, quite expert. As a young boy, he even performed acrobatic feats on horseback, and was the first to volunteer when the circus came to town and the ringmaster challenged members of the audience to see if they could break a certain pony. Grant invariably succeeded, even on the occasion when one ringmaster suddenly threw a monkey across his shoulders to disconcert him.

While at West Point, Grant was no great shakes as a student, but was the best horseman in his class. "It was as good as a circus to see Grant ride," a classmate wrote. "There was a dark bay horse that was so fractious that it was about to be condemned. Grant selected it for his horse. He bridled, mounted, and rode it every day. . . . The whole class would stand around admiring his wonderful command of the beast. . . ."

Before graduating, Grant established a West Point high-jump mark of nearly six feet, a record that lasted more than a quarter century. In the U. S. Army, he distinguished himself at the Battle of Monterrey in the Mexican War by clinging to the side of a horse and riding it—in the style of many a latter-day movie hero—through the heavy fire of his enemy in order to reach an ammunition wagon.

Following the Civil War, Grant seemed self-conscious as President, but regained much of his old assurance when he was able to seat himself behind a team of fine horses and high-step them along M Street. While in the White House, he rebuilt the stables and added horses so that he had the choice of more than a dozen. He also enjoyed watching youngsters play baseball near the White House and frequently acted as umpire or took a turn at bat.

GROVER CLEVELAND, a slow-moving 240-pounder who arrived on the scene before golf became a popular sport, used two of his better characteristics—patience and good eyesight—to enjoy hunting and fishing. In fact, he was frequently criticized by the press because of the long trips he took with gun and rod.

Cleveland was seldom satisfied to fish for just a couple of hours; his idea of a trip was at least two days, and a good catch of fish might run into the hundreds. One such grand affair took place on July 27–28, 1888, near the end of Cleveland's first term as President. For the jaunt, which took place off Fire Island, Long Island, Joseph Stickney's steam launch *Susquehanna* carried the President and his personal secretary, Postmaster General Don M. Dickinson, and a large group of friends. A pair of fishing smacks accompanied the ship, each fitted out with a supply of chumming bait and appropriate fishing gear.

Dressed in a blue serge suit and gray flannel shirt, Cleveland used his favorite bamboo rod, and according to Captain Cushing of the *Susquehanna,* "had his usual good luck," catching more than his share of the twenty-four blue fish that were taken the first morning. One of the President's was a five-pounder. By dusk, fifty-seven more fish had been hauled in, at which time Cleveland adjourned the sport in favor of dinner.

A more publicity-minded man might have taken the opportunity to mingle with natives of the region, but Cleveland was on the water to fish, and that was all he did. Rising early the next morning, he and his party pulled in ninety-eight more blue fish during twelve solid hours of fishing. The first hour was most productive, according to Smith M. Weed, one of the guests, who attested that Cleveland himself pulled in a fish every three minutes.

When the day was over, Cleveland headed back to New York and Washington, completely happy. "As far as my attachment to outdoor sports may be considered a fault," he said once, "I am utterly incorrigible and shameless."

The worst part of the trip, apparently, was combating the rumor—no doubt started by Republicans—that the President had been unable to land a single fish and in his frustration had purchased his entire cargo of nearly two hundred from a passing fisherman.

BENJAMIN HARRISON, twenty-third President of the United States and grandson of William Henry Harrison, was another outdoorsman. But in contrast to Grover Cleveland, Harrison loved hunting much more than fishing. He was apparently an excellent shot.

Presidential Name-alike:
During the 1901 season, a Ben Harrison played in one game for the Washington American League baseball club. An outfielder, he came to bat three times, walked once, and failed to get a hit the other two times. In the same year, former President Benjamin Harrison died.

WILLIAM MCKINLEY was the first U. S. President to develop an affection for golf. Though taken for granted in later years, participating in some form of recreational activity was not always looked upon with favor then. In 1899, a lady wrote to the editor of the Boston *Herald* hoping he would be able to quell the rumor that President McKinley "had been seen playing golf." Her tone seemed to indicate that there was something eccentric if not downright un-American in a Chief Executive of such a great nation wandering around an oversized lawn behind a small white pellet.

Presidential Name-alike:
During the 1971 professional football season, the Buffalo Bills carried a linebacker-end named William McKinley. His alma mater was Arizona.

THEODORE ROOSEVELT liked to think that he was capable of performing well at any sports activity—and he probably was. At Harvard, he starred on the boxing team, and loved to wrestle, run, hike, and hunt. Political opponents referred to him as "that damned cowboy" because he had worked on a ranch and was such an excellent horseman. His tennis game, he admitted, was "not so good," but he was a deadly shot with a rifle, and according to aide Ike Hoover, used to hop from his desk at the White House and run several laps around the Washington Monument when he felt himself getting lethargic.

But T.R. was hardly a fanatic about sports, even compared to his contemporaries. Many of them felt the uncontrolled violence of football was all right, that it provided a good groundwork for a man's becoming a leader in war or the business world. Roosevelt, despite having a son on the Harvard football squad who was regularly bruised and cut during scrimmages, did not feel that the purpose of sport was to maim or render an opponent insensible. Rather, he believed in reform that would leave the physical contact but discourage roughness. And he was the first U. S. President to involve his office in the quest for cleaning up those sports that produced injury and death, particularly college football as it was played at the turn of the century.

"Having ended the war in the Far East, grappled with the railroad rate question and made his position clear, and prepared for the tour of the South," one paper reported in October 1905, "President Roosevelt today took up another question of vital interest to the American people. He started a campaign for reform in football."

The first five seasons of the new century having been extremely rough ones on the football field, Roosevelt called a White House conference, inviting men such as Walter Camp of Yale and Glenn Warner of Cornell, along with a handful of college and university administrators. The men decided that the game needed to be opened up in order to neutralize the deadly effectiveness of the mass play, hurtling, and dragging ball-carriers. One solution was to permit the forward pass and prohibit hurtling and practically all mass formations. After the edicts were announced, some of the old violations continued for several years (see 1911), but Roosevelt's interest in cleaning up the game provided much-needed leadership in that area.

WILLIAM HOWARD TAFT, America's heaviest President, was not much of an athlete, but he did enjoy golf and encouraged organized sports every chance he got. As a golfer, Taft in 1910 became involved in a minor controversy over the legality of the Schenectady or center-shaft putter. Taft favored the innovation but apparently officials

Taft's Reply:
"My Dear Mr. Travis:
"I have yours of Dec. 7. I think the restriction imposed by St. Andrew's is too narrow. I think putting with a Schenectady putter is sportsmanlike, and gives no undue advantage.
"Sincerely yours,
"William H. Taft."

at St. Andrew's, Scotland, disagreed. The issue was discussed at length between American and British golfers until Walter Travis finally wrote a long letter to the President, asking his opinion on the matter. Taft responded, thus becoming the first U. S. President to declare himself on the subject of golfing rules legislation.

That same year, 1910, Taft also became the first American President to formally endorse baseball as the "national game" by throwing out the first ball of a new season. The big day for Taft was April 14, and it also turned out to be an enjoyable day for the Senators, who won by a score of 3–0 over Connie Mack's Philadelphia Athletics. Twenty-two-year-old Walter Johnson was the starting pitcher for Washington, opposing thirty-four-year-old Eddie Plank. The attendance, 12,226, "broke all records" for the small ball park, and if it had not been for Frank Baker's single, Johnson would have pitched a no-hitter. President Taft, loving every minute of the experience, stayed until the final out. He might have enjoyed the game less had he known that from that point the 1910 season would be all downhill for the Senators, who finished seventh in the eight-team league.

"The game of baseball is a clean straight game, and it summons to its presence everybody who enjoys clean, straight athletics."

W. H. Taft (*1910*)

WOODROW WILSON, although thin and handicapped by poor eyesight most of his life, had a keen interest in athletics. When he was a seventeen-year-old freshman at Davidson College (North Carolina), he played center field on the baseball team but seemed to lack the drive necessary to be a really fine player. Said a teammate, Robert Glenn: "Tommy Wilson would be a good player if he wasn't so damned lazy." Others have suggested that Wilson, who was christened Thomas Woodrow and called "Tommy," was restricted more by delicate health than laziness. In any event, the first year at college was too much for young Wilson, who was forced to return home and rest for a year. But because he never lost interest in the game he was elected president of the Princeton Baseball Association during his senior year (1879) at that school.

While at Princeton, Wilson took up golf but was not a particularly good player, frequently shooting over 100. He never broke 90, but when he approached that magic figure he was always delighted.

President Wilson on Wilson the Golfer: *"My right eye is like a horse's. I can see straight out with it but not sideways. As a result I cannot take a full swing, because my nose gets in the way and cuts off my view of the ball. That is the reason I use such a short swing."*

A willing spectator whenever he could find the time, Wilson became the first American President to attend a World Series game when he traveled to Philadelphia in 1915.

WARREN G. HARDING was also a baseball enthusiast, not only playing the game in his youth but also later purchasing a minorleague franchise in Marion, Ohio. During his brief term as President (1921–23), he did a lot of golfing, and on one occasion—April 24, 1923—shook the hand of Babe Ruth, who then went onto the field and hit a home run against the Washington Senators.

CALVIN COOLIDGE, America's thirtieth President, was not enthusiastic about much other than big business, but he did manage to show up at several sporting events in an official capacity. One such occasion was on October 4, 1924, when the Washington Senators somehow beat the Yankees for the American League pennant and ended up in the World Series. Coolidge became the first President to throw out the ball, for game No. 1, which was pitched by Walter Johnson, then thirty-six but eager to appear in his first World Series. Coolidge also presented Washington Manager Bucky Harris with a silver trophy and told the players they had "made the national capital more truly the center of worthy and honorable national aspirations."

Not long afterward, when the Senators tied the game at 3–3 in the ninth inning, Coolidge stood and applauded with the rest of the fans. A flying newspaper thrown by a celebrant struck the President's hat, nearly knocking it off, but as he always did, Coolidge remained cool.

HERBERT HOOVER is perhaps best known in sports as the butt of a joke by Babe Ruth. In 1930, when the slugger was holding out for more money, someone suggested that the nation was in the midst of a severe depression and, besides, Ruth was already making more money than President Hoover. "What the hell has Hoover to do with it?" Ruth was reported to have said. "Besides, I had a better year than he did."

As an undergraduate at Stanford (Class of 1895), Herbert Hoover was associated with the football team as manager, a position in which he revealed ability to organize, cajole, and scrounge. His biggest moment came in 1892, when John Whittemore of Stanford decided to take on the University of California, a faster and much larger squad. Hoover was selected to arrange the contest, procure uniforms, and handle the collection of receipts and any other duties that might be necessary.

Just seventeen at the time, Hoover plunged into the task with alacrity. His first job was to talk a sporting-goods dealer into giving the team uniforms on credit. He then rented a baseball grounds for $250 and ordered tickets printed for five thousand spectators.

On the day of the game, twice that many persons crowded into the park, which caused Hoover to send assistants looking for pots and pans and washbasins—anything that would hold coins. All seemed to be going well until game time, when it was suddenly realized that the two teams had everything except a football. Forced to improvise again, Hoover agreed to the suggestion that a punching-bag bladder be put into the skin of an old ball, creating an object that was flattened at the poles but usable. When the clever Whittemore saw the condition of the football, he chose to kick off, hoping that California would find the object hard to handle. That was exactly what happened several plays later. Inspired, Stanford executed a clever reverse play for a touchdown and eventually won the game by a score of 14–10.

Hoover, who had spent most of the time counting coins and stuffing them into cloth bags, realized after the game that he had been too busy to see it.

FRANKLIN D. ROOSEVELT, before he contracted polio, was an ardent sailor and occasional golfer. While at Harvard, he was elected editor of the undergraduate newspaper, *Crimson,* for which he wrote editorials urging the football team on to victory. After the age of thirty-nine, when he became paralyzed from the waist down, Roosevelt enjoyed swimming because it gave him a feeling of physical lightness and provided much-needed exercise.

HARRY S. TRUMAN was sickly as a child and never developed a great love for any particular sports activity. Instead, he got all the exercise he needed by walking. As a spectator, he seemed to enjoy horseracing most. "I've gotten a great deal of pleasure out of horseracing ever since my father began taking me when I was five," he said in 1960, seven years after leaving office. "Why didn't I go to the races when I was President? I had no time."

Presidential Name-alike:
No one knows why Harry Truman, who was born in 1866 at Utica, New York, changed his name to Harry Raymond before breaking into organized baseball with the Louisville club of the American Association. Perhaps it was because not everyone looked upon baseball players in those days as entirely respectable characters. In any event, Harry Raymond (nee Truman) began playing in 1888 as a third baseman-outfielder. After hitting .211, .239, .259, and .203 for four seasons, he was traded to Pittsburgh in 1892, then to Washington, where he appeared in four games, hitting .067. As a pitcher, he started one game for Louisville and despite giving up eight hits and 11 bases on balls, won it. He died in 1925.

DWIGHT D. EISENHOWER in his youth was a gifted athlete, playing left halfback on the West Point football team until he damaged his knee while tackling the legendary Jim Thorpe. After that he devoted himself to less violent sports, but remained a typical American enthusiast of most organized athletics. Most persons remember him as a dedicated golfer who used to play nearly every Sunday on the Gettysburg golf course near his home. What most people did not know was that until 1960, the year before Ike left office, playing golf on Sunday in Pennsylvania was a violation of a 1794 law that nobody had bothered to repeal.

Eisenhower on Sports:
"There are three that I like all for the same reason—golf, fishing, and shooting— because they take you into the fields. . . . They induce you to take at any one time two or three hours, where you are thinking of the bird or that ball or the wily trout. Now, to my mind, it is a very healthful, beneficial kind of thing, and I do it whenever I get a chance, as you well know."

JOHN F. KENNEDY, the youngest man elected to the presidency (although Teddy Roosevelt was one year younger when he succeeded to the office following McKinley's assassination), was the perfect embodiment of the good amateur athlete who enjoyed participating in sports rather than merely watching.

Soon after he took office, Kennedy gave the job a sport image by playing touch football. (As a student at Harvard, he had given much of his time to all forms of athletics until he seriously injured his back while playing football.) Some of the well-publicized contests took place on the White House lawn; on other occasions, the Kennedys were seen hiking or jogging. As a result, his presidency seemed to be one of constant movement, energy, and decisiveness.

Baltimore Colt Tackle Art Donovan on the Kennedy Games:
"They even had John Unitas over there to play in one of their touch games. But they wouldn't take me. I was shanty Irish."

Several times during his brief tenure in office, Kennedy wrote articles in which he tried to impress Americans with the need to give up "spectating," as he termed it, and participate in more vigorous sports activity and exercise. "His bad back gave him a clear mandate to relax and take it easy, to spectate for the rest of his life," reported *Sports Illustrated* the week after Kennedy was shot and killed. "Instead he played in his pain and showed the Soft American the way of a man with guts."

Presidential Name-alike:
The name being a fairly common one, it is not surprising that organized baseball had a pair of John Kennedys in its ranks. The first played in just five games for the 1957 Philadelphia Phillies, batting twice without a hit. The second, more famous John Kennedy played a total of twelve years (1962–67; 1969–74) for the Washington Senators, Los Angeles Dodgers, Yankees, Seattle Pilots, Milwaukee Brewers, and Boston Red Sox. An infielder, his career average was .225.

RICHARD M. NIXON was exactly the opposite of Kennedy. An athletic nonentity at college, Nixon tried out for the Whittier (California) team for four years, played only on the freshman squad (when only eleven men turned out), and was used as "cannon fodder" during weekly scrimmages with the varsity.

Nixon's coach, Wallace Newman, characterized the man who would become President as "an athlete with a lot of spunk and drive" —which usually means no talent. "He didn't have all the physical equipment, but he was all enthusiastic and played hard."

"One reason he didn't put me in," Nixon himself said on one occasion, "was because I didn't know the plays. I knew all the enemy's plays, though. I practiced them all week."

Next to being President, Richard Nixon several times said that his fondest wish was to be a sportswriter. At first glance the ambition seems modest enough, albeit a bit strange. Upon closer examination of the Nixon character, however, the choice seems a logical one. Sportswriters are frequently frustrated players, they have ample opportunity to see a variety of games free, and, given a chance to become set in their views, most tend to look upon every aspect of life as a kind of neat athletic contest, complete with good guy, bad guy, final score, instant replay, and self-containment.

As he became older, Richard Nixon seemed to develop this attitude about life and politics, domestic and foreign: If we can successfully apply the discipline of winning sports to the problems that confront a nation, we can WIN. At the height of the Vietnam War, columnist Russell Baker wrote: "In the metaphor of war as sport, President Nixon assumes the role of coach. The United States becomes a team. The Yanks, perhaps. No. The Americans. The United States Americans . . . There hasn't been a team like the Americans since Frank Merriwell attended Yale. . . ."

Beset by problems (opposing teams) that refused to be defeated, Richard Nixon, like many ordinary persons seeking order in any form, retreated into the role of superspectator. On a typical Saturday afternoon in the fall, he was likely to hop aboard his presidential jet and fly a thousand miles to see a football game. One such occasion was on December 6, 1969, Nixon's first year in office, the attraction a critical game between Arkansas and Texas at Fayetteville, Arkansas, for a sort of mythical national championship. Armed with a plaque for the winner, Nixon settled down to enjoy the game, which was a thriller, won by Texas, 15–14. The President thereupon presented the team with the trophy declaring them the No. 1 team in the nation and hopped aboard his jet, satisfied with a job well done.

But then as later, Richard Nixon had a knack for annoying some of the people a lot of the time. Hardly had he made the presentation of his plaque than Joe Paterno, coach of Penn State, declared that the President had no right to make such a judgment, especially in the light of Penn State's undefeated record over a three-year period.

Nixon quickly backtracked, sending off a telegram of congratulations to Paterno and his team. That bit of controversy did not cure the President of becoming more and more involved in the politics of sports, however. By 1970, his habit of appearing in the locker rooms of winning teams, either in person or by telephone, had become part of the American football ritual. Occasionally—although he bestowed no more national rankings on teams —he threw out a quote in praise of some squad or other, usually couching the language in the very best sportswriterese. Most of all, he loved the actual experience of calling the players and chatting with them—hearing the reverential tone of their voices?—as he did following the 1970 Super Bowl. On that occasion, the lucky recipient of the call was winning quarterback Lenny Dawson of the Kansas City Chiefs. The cost of the six-minute call was $2.68.

Some Nixon Bouquets:
"One of the greatest Trojan teams of all times."
"What makes Texas a great team is its ability to come from behind."
"The youth of the world looks up to pro players for courage."

But Nixon's affinity for the long-distance phone call was not limited to events of Super Bowl caliber. Sometimes he went rather far afield, as he did on July 9, 1971, when he called Susan Mara, daughter of the New York Giants' owner, Wellington Mara, in order to congratulate her family on the birth of its tenth child. (The President suggested that one more would be enough for a football team.) Not long afterward, Nixon was out on the White House lawn, greeting a group of sixteen Seattle cyclists who had traveled 3,617 miles cross-country in fifty-eight days. Then he was off to the locker room of the Washington Redskins, paying them a surprise visit just prior to their playoff game against the San Francisco 49ers. When the Skins lost, Richard Nixon stood by them. A few minutes after they went down to defeat on the West Coast, the phone rang, and there was the voice of Fan No. 1. "All of Washington is proud of you," he said. "Don't look back."

Nixon Talks with the Players:
Referring to a sprinkling of boos that Washington fans had given the Redskins the previous week, Nixon said: "I've heard a few myself in my lifetime."

For the next Super Bowl, Nixon became even more involved, sending in a play for the Miami Dolphins to use against the Dallas Cowboys. Two weeks before the scheduled contest, coach Don Shula received a phone call from the President, who alerted Shula to the fact that the Cowboys were a good football team and suggested that a down-and-out pattern run by Paul Warfield would be a sure-fire long gainer against the Texans. This was not the first time Nixon had sent in a play. Before the playoff loss to the San Francisco 49ers, the President suggested that the Redskins run a flanker reverse to Roy Jefferson. Late in the second quarter, Washington Coach George Allen sent in the play, with the situation second down, six yards to go for the Redskins on the 49er eight-yard line. After the President's play had been run, it was third down, nineteen yards to go from the twenty-one.

Despite the President's blemished record as a play-caller, Coach Don Shula's Miami Dolphins had been in the 1971 Super Bowl (played on January 16, 1972) only seven plays before Paul Warfield darted downfield on his down-and-in pattern recommended by Nixon. Lee Roy Jordan, Cowboy linebacker, raced across to help Mel Renfro, who had not been fooled by the quick Warfield's fake. Griese wisely overthrew his flanker and the play gained nothing.

The Dolphins, befriended by Nixon, lost that Super Bowl, but that did not deter the President from armchair participation in sports. After doing his best to make sure the 1972 baseball strike did not interfere with the season, Nixon offered advice to Charles Finley, owner of the Oakland A's, when a dispute developed between him and the talented (24–8) pitcher Vida Blue. "He has too much talent," the President told members of the press. "Maybe Finley ought to pay."

A couple of months later, the sports-minded Nixon announced the members of his baseball all-time all-star team, a task he approached with great trepidation, enlisting the help of David Eisenhower before entrusting himself with such an awesome undertaking. In order to get as many players into the selection as possible—Nixon was ever the politician—he and David picked one team from each league for the years 1925–45, another from each league for 1945–70, and then threw in some reserves to make certain no one was left out. His total list included eighty-three players. Unless one happened to think Frank Malzone was a better third baseman (AL, 1945–70) than Brooks Robinson, it was hard to find anything to quarrel with in the presidential selections—which, of course, was the object of the whole thing.

By the end of 1972, after becoming involved in the Watergate affair—a down-and-out pattern in the realm of politics—Nixon seemed to have worn out his welcome in the various locker rooms, at least around the nation's capital. On December 3, 1972, Wash-

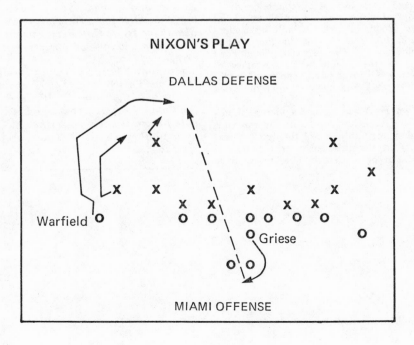

NIXON'S PLAY

DALLAS DEFENSE

Warfield

Griese

MIAMI OFFENSE

ington quarterback Billy Kilmer, hardly a roaring liberal, commented to the press that Nixon was hurting the Redskins' progress. "He calls all the time," Kilmer said. "He told some guy from Cleveland he met in New York that Cleveland had a good team, but they had quarterback problems. Then Cleveland gets all psyched up and they're much harder to beat."

Soon it all became academic, for Nixon found himself trapped by the Watergate tapes he had ordered and found it harder and harder to venture outdoors into crowds. He feared, of all things, boos, a fact that was admitted by one White House staff member who explained why Nixon had decided to watch the Rose Bowl of 1974 at home rather than come to Pasadena.

In August 1974, Richard M. Nixon, America's No. 1 spectator, surrendered to the evidence that was mounting as a result of his own taped comments regarding Watergate. He stepped down, the victim of, of all things, a form of instant replay.

There is a certain ironic neatness in that.

GERALD FORD, the man who succeeded Nixon to office, was probably the best athlete to occupy the White House. The center and captain of Michigan's football team, he played in the College All-Star game and turned down offers from professional teams. He also enjoyed skiing and was a strong swimmer. But so inept was Ford as a person with charisma that he somehow destroyed his own image as an athlete by stumbling down the ramps at airports and slipping at official occasions. Soon, in fact, he built up such a reputation for lack of co-ordination that a joke going around Washington depicted Ford sprawled on the ground while Secretary of State Henry Kissinger said, "You know I told you not to walk and chew gum at the same time."

And yet Ford was simply a victim of circumstances. Well into his sixties, he was trim and athletic, certainly one of the best physical specimens in the presidency since Abraham Lincoln. But he was never able to convince the American people that he was anything more than a mental and physical klutz.

JIMMY CARTER, America's thirty-ninth President, ran cross-country while at the Naval Academy, played tennis and softball, and also had a liking for auto racing. One White House aide, Caroline Shields, added that as a softball pitcher, the President "has a mean pitch." What she did not say was that Jimmy Carter, the man from the South whom many said had no chance when he entered the primaries in early 1976, was breaking a long-standing presidential sports profile, that of the golf-swinging Chief Executive.

Presidential Name-alike:

Lightweight boxer Jimmy Carter of the Bronx was the presidential name-alike who accomplished most in his particular field of endeavor. During his fighting career, Carter fought 120 times, won 31 by knockouts, 49 by decision, had 9 draws, lost 28 by decision, and was knocked out 8 times. On May 25, 1951, he knocked out Ike Williams in the fourteenth round to win the world lightweight championship, but nearly a year later, on May 14, 1952, he was outpointed by Lauro Salas of Monterrey, Mexico. Five months later, Carter regained the title from Salas, then knocked out challengers Tommy Collins, George Araujo, and Armand Savoie while retaining the title for nearly two years. On March 5, 1954, Carter was again an ex-champion, losing on points to Paddy DeMarco, but he regained the crown eight months later by KOing DeMarco at the Cow Palace, near San Francisco. He again lost the title to Wallace (Bud) Smith on June 29, 1955, and was never able to win it back. Nevertheless, Carter's accomplishments as a fighter were considerable.

CHAPTER 8—SPORTS AND THE LANGUAGE

"Crack! went Ray's heavy oak stick," reported the 1891 sportswriter, "Gastright raised his hands in an instant to stop the powerful impetus of the ball, which was whistling to centre field, and it broke through his grasp by the sheer force of velocity. . . ."

That is, the poor fellow dropped it.

". . . He may not be the bearded brute who crushed the Orchid Man of France, Carpentier . . . but he still looks good enough to take the English palooka. He still is a shuffler and a roarer, but, boy, that danger kick is always around. One can't dope the big brawl from watching him paste over his ham sparring partners; they just powder-puff him. . . ."

That is, Dempsey is still a very good fighter.

Faced with the need to fill ever-increasing amounts of space for a public more addicted to sports news, those reporting the athletic events of the past century have developed embellishment and convolution to fine arts. Some of the jargon has just evolved; some of it has been invented by a specific individual bent on turning a colorful phrase. In a way, the sports phraseology of any period is similar to popular music. For a while it is on everyone's lips. Then most of it becomes faint, quaint, obscure. Succeeding generations smile indulgently at an old-timer's using a bit of slang-cant from the past. Historians and writers listen carefully, hoping that someday they will have the opportunity to use the jargon as background for an era.

Not everyone approves of sports jargon, naturally. Purists have been complaining for the better part of a century in America, and on at least one occasion, the outcry was sufficient to generate a vote on whether or not slang should be used in daily sports columns. The balloting, conducted by a Chicago newspaper in 1913, produced 3,390 votes: 2,004 against the use of slang, 1,926 in favor. In the prephoto-finish era, the purists won by a nose.

Sports jargon, like slang of any other sort, is divided into three groups. There is, first of all, a vast body of phraseology that quickly goes out of style, never to return. Who today, for example, refers to a "dunch shot" (a heavy or soggy shot in golf) while on the links? What baseball fan refers to a spectacular catch as an "à la carte"? These phrases, along with countless others, have simply passed out of usage by contemporary fans and writers.

Some Boxing Jargon That Is No Longer with Us:

Bacteria	Fight fans
Bearcat	Excellent fighter
Bugs	Fight fans
Cold packer	Knockout blow
Curb broker	Pseudo fight expert
Derbied boys	Gamblers
Ethel	A boxer afraid of being hit
To gum	Wrestle in clinches
Gummed Card	Poor array of fighters
Maulies	Fists
Red tape	Training period
Ring worms	Those with ringside seats
Roarer	Fighter who boxes with mouth open
Wooden shoe	German or Dutch fighter

Because it is the most complex game and is played most often in America, baseball inevitably has produced the greatest body of jargon. Some of it is now obscure, but a surprising number of words and phrases have survived from the nineteenth century. Pitchers still "warm up" in the "bullpen," perfecting their "hooks" or "smoke" until the moment when they get the chance to "whiff" a few "lumbermen." Of course, they know full well that if they throw a "cripple," or "hang a curve," they'll end up "wearing the horns" and the batter will have a "round-tripper." Better to toss a few "dusters" and make them "hit the dirt" so they won't get "good wood." Then again, some days nothing goes right. A "chucker's" ball can have a good "hop" on it and the batter may still "hang a rope" or get lucky with a "Texas Leaguer" or "Baltimore chop" that just barely becomes a "bingle."

The second type of sports jargon, that which is associated with the particular game but has no other meaning (Baltimore chop, for example), is quite common but specialized. People who do not play the game or watch it are apt to be confused by some of the terminology. Fans, of course, accept the colorful words as a part of the game, perhaps only faintly aware that they have absorbed and use an arcane language.

Some Baseball Jargon Already Obscure or
Well on the Way:

Plugger	a fan, rooter
Mackerel	curve ball
Pay station	Home plate
Dog kennel	Dugout
Unbutton one's shirt	Swing hard
Groundhog	Groundkeeper
Murphy money	Expense money
Peg the bases	Throw to baseman
Fizzle	A stupid play
Can of corn	Fly ball
Skyscraper	Fly ball
Orchard	Outfield
Japanese liner	Soft liner that just drops safely

Occasionally a piece of sports jargon will
make good and step into the third group,
which consists of words and phrases that may
be used by those with no knowledge of the
game whatever. An example might be the
phrase "pinch-hit," which in baseball means
the substitution of one batter—usually a better
or more appropriate one—for the scheduled
man at the plate. The phrase is used today by
most people in situations that have nothing to
do with baseball—that is, when an emergency
arises and someone needs a substitute to carry
on the job. In the same manner, "in there

pitching" describes a person who is determined; to have "struck out" is to have failed
miserably (the only solution being to "punt");
one "roots" for another in a variety of nonsports situations. Slowly but surely, such terminology works its way into the language of
ordinary life, giving life and color to the
speech patterns of our particular society. At
some date thousands of years in the future,
historians may be unable to trace the origins
of some words and phrases, of course, but that
is not contemporary society's problem. If
they're not satisfied to take what the defense
gives them, they'll just have to eat the ball.

QUOTES

Being a random collection of quotes and mis-
quotes by celebrities, players, literary figures,
and radio and TV announcers on a variety of
sports:

BASEBALL

"Baseball has the great advantage over cricket
of being ended sooner. . . . It combines the
best features of that primitive form of cricket
known as Tip and Run with those of lawn
tennis, Puss-in-the-corner, and Handel's *Messiah*."

George Bernard Shaw

"Catching a fly ball is a pleasure but knowing
what to do with it after you catch it is a business."

Tommy Henrich

LOVE STORY—Sports Jargon Style:
*She was a knockout. As soon as I spied
her, I was on the ropes, punch-drunk,
ready to go down for the count. Right off
the bat I felt we'd make a good twosome,
but I knew she was out of my league, a
triple-threat heavyweight woman with me
a second-stringer at best, a bush-league
benchwarmer who couldn't caddie for the
superjock type of guy who probably made
a hit with her. Why, compared to them,
I'd be lucky to even get to first base, much
less score.*

*Still, there had to be a way to have my
innings, even if I had to start from
scratch. But with my track record with
women, it's par for the course for me to
start out with two strikes against me. It
would be a long shot, but I decided to
throw the bomb, let her know how I felt*

*straight from the shoulder, hoping I could
hit the bull's-eye by making a grandstand
play. Of course, she might decide I was a
real foul ball, that it was out of bounds
and way off base for an eight-ball like me
to come out of left field and think I could
have a turn at bat. What a low blow that
would be, especially if I seemed to be in
the running only to be thrown a curve and
fumble the ball in the stretch.*

*If that happened, if I got caught in a
squeeze play or shut out before going the
limit, I'd just have to take it on the chin,
go into a huddle with myself, and try
another tack, that's all. I mean, taking a
lacing and being an also-ran is no reason
to be teed off. What is bad is standing on
the sidelines being stymied by the situation. At least if you tackle the job and go
down swinging, you have no kick coming.*

"In the long history of organized baseball I stand unparalleled for putting Christianity into practice. . . . Last season I gave up an all-time major-league record of forty-one home runs. No one has ever been so good to opposing batsmen. And to prove I was not prejudiced, I served up home run balls to Negroes, Italians, Jews, Catholics alike. Race, creed, nationality made no difference to me. . . ."
Robin Roberts

"An ardent supporter of the hometown team should go to a game prepared to take offense, no matter what happens."
Robert Benchley

"I never heard the crowd boo or hiss a homer, and I have heard plenty of boos after a strikeout."
Babe Ruth

"Baseball is a kind of collective chess with arms and legs in full play under sunlight."
Jacques Barzun

"Every great hitter works on the theory that the pitcher is more afraid of him than he is of the pitcher."
Ty Cobb

"When a man asks you to come and see baseball played twice it sets you asking yourself why you went to see it played once."
George Bernard Shaw

"I never blame myself when I'm not hitting. I just blame the bat and if it keeps up I change bats. . . . After all, if I know it isn't my fault that I'm not hitting, how can I get mad at myself?"
Yogi Berra

"Baseball is almost the only orderly thing in a very unorderly world. If you get three strikes, even the best lawyer in the world can't get you off."
Bill Veeck

"Baseball is a circus, and as is the case in many a circus, the clowns and the sideshows frequently are more interesting than the big stuff in the main tent."
W. O. McGeehan

"The ballplayer who loses his head, who can't keep cool, is worse than no ballplayer at all."
Lou Gehrig

"Brooks Robinson is not a fast man, but his arms and legs move very quickly."
Curt Gowdy

"Gentlemen, swinging a bat is a great tonic, a fine exercise. It strengthens the diaphragm. Besides, you may hit the ball."
Billy Southworth

"When we are getting some hits we aren't getting them when we have somebody on the bases. It's very aggravating. But maybe it's better to see them left there than not getting on at all. If they keep getting on you got to figure one of these days they'll be getting home. Or it could be one of these years, you know."
Casey Stengel

"Knowing all about baseball is just about as profitable as being a good whittler."
Kin Hubbard

"Willie Mays won't start today because the Mets' regular outfielder, Rusty Slob, will be playing. Wait, that's Rusty Staub!"
Curt Gowdy

"Baseball gives you every chance to be great. Then it puts every pressure on you to prove that you haven't got what it takes. It never takes away the chance, and it never eases up on the pressure."
Joe Garagiola

"A baseball fan has the digestive apparatus of a billy goat. He can—and does—devour any set of diamond statistics with insatiable appetite and then nuzzles hungrily for more."
Arthur Daley

"And at the game's end, it's National League, 6, American League, 4. That score again is American League, 6, National League, 4."
Curt Gowdy

"Most males who don't care about big-league baseball conceal their indifference as carefully as they would conceal a laughable physical deficiency."
Russell Maloney

"They still can't steal first base."
Phil Rizzuto

"Any manager who can't get along with a .400 hitter is crazy."
Joe McCarthy

"The secret of my success was clean living and a fast-moving outfield."
Lefty Gomez

"Get your seat in the shade/Buy some cool lemonade/Tell her each player's name/And all the points of the game/And all of her life she'll be thankful to you."
George M. Cohan

"Baseball belongs to the extensive genius of civilized athletic competitions stemming from the primitive play-urge to whack a fragment of rock about the place with a club."
Encyclopaedia Britannica

"Every boy likes baseball, and if he doesn't he's not a boy."
Zane Grey

"All winter long I am one for whom the bell is tolling/I can arouse no interest in basketball, indoor fly-casting or bowling/The sports pages are strictly no soap/And until the cry of 'play ball' I simply mope."

Ogden Nash

"Folks, this is perfect weather for today's game. Not a breath of air."

Curt Gowdy

"Shouting on the ball field never helped anyone except where it was one player calling to another to take the catch."

Gil Hodges

"What is both surprising and delightful is that the spectators are allowed, and even expected, to join in the vocal part of the game. I do not see why this feature should not be introduced into cricket. There is no reason why the field should not try to put the batsman off his stroke at the critical moment by neatly timed disparagements of his wife's fidelity and his mother's respectability."

George Bernard Shaw

"There is only one sport that appeals to them all/When you size up the dope on the case/There is only one sport and its name is baseball/Others follow; it sets the pace."

The Sporting News, 1912

"If you're playing baseball and thinking about managing, you're crazy. You'd be better off thinking about being an owner."

Casey Stengel

"A ballplayer's got to be kept hungry to become a big-leaguer. That's why no boy from a rich family ever made the big leagues."

Joe DiMaggio

"One reason I have always loved baseball so much is that it has been not merely the 'great national game,' but really a part of the whole weather of our lives, of the thing that is our own, of the whole fabric, the million memories of America."

Thomas Wolfe

"Baseball is immensely exciting to watch and reaches at moments an ecstasy of speed and accuracy."

John Drinkwater

"The two great American sports are a good deal alike—politics and baseball. They're both played by professionals, the teams are run by fellows that couldn't throw a baseball or stuff a ballot box to save their lives and are interested only in counting up the gate receipts, and here we are sitting out in the sun on the bleaching boards, paying our good money for the sport, hot and uncomfortable but happy, enjoying every good play, hooting every bad one, knowing nothing about the inside play and not caring, but all joining in the cry of 'Kill the umpire!' They're both grand games."

Finley Peter Dunne

"Luis Tiant comes from everywhere except between his legs."

Curt Gowdy

FOOTBALL

"Football is a sensible game—but it is surrounded by crazy people."

Lou Little

"Football season is the only time of year when girls whistle at men in sweaters."

Robert Q. Lewis

"The only qualifications for a lineman are to be big and dumb. To be a back, you only have to be dumb."

Knute Rockne

"a develische pastime . . . and hereof groweth envy, rancour and malice, and sometimes brawling, murther, homicide, and great effusion of blood."

Stubbes' *Anatomie of Abuses* (1583)

"Unless he grows up to be President or defendant in an important murder trial, the college football player is likely to receive far more extensive and searching newspaper publicity in his undergraduate days than at any other period in his life."

Heywood Broun

"Football has become so complicated, the student will find it a recreation to go to classes."

T. S. Eliot

"Joe Paternity . . . Paterno's fine defensive line from Pencil State University . . . I mean, Penn State University, has played well."

Bud Wilkinson

"Often an All-American is made by a long run, a weak defense, and a poet in the press box."

Bob Zuppke

"I won't mention the name of this particular team we were playing, but at halftime we came in, pulled off our socks and began putting iodine on the teeth marks on our legs. Coach Bob Zuppke said, 'I'll tell you one thing: If we ever play this team again, it'll be on a Friday.'"

Red Grange

"To give you a better idea of how the teams shape up against each other, we'll be throwing up statistics like these all during the game."

Curt Gowdy

"That football is one of those sports to which the human race clings because it satisfies a human elemental need, seems to be evidenced by the fact that it was played forty centuries ago in China, that the Greeks and Romans were playing it at the dawn of history, that the Irish played it two thousand years ago, that the Esquimaux and many other primitive peoples all played games resembling it."

Wainwright Evans

"I do not see the relationship of these highly industrialized affairs on Saturday afternoons to higher learning in America."

Robert Hutchins

"All that the spectator gets out of a game now is the fresh air, the comical articles in his program, the sight of twenty-two young men rushing about in mysterious formations, and whatever he brought along in his flask."

Robert Benchley

"Battle, murder, sudden death, and many other things are done amply well in films. Football is different. Though it injure the heart, increase the blood pressure, and shorten life, only the reality will do."

Heywood Broun

"And now, football fans, it's time for the kiss-off."

Don Meredith

"Am I so round with you as you with me/That like a football you do spurn me thus?"

William Shakespeare

"To get bruised ribs and dislocated shoulders in practice flights out of second- and third-story windows I should understand: an accomplishment of that kind might be useful in time of fire; but to what end does all the bruising of football tend?"

Max O'Rell

"The bonds uniting old football men are strong enough to conquer any other association. When recounting bygone games, telling over again of magnificent runs, the beautiful drop, how the game was lost and won, enthusiasm grows strong, the time slips by, and true football lore obliterates for the time all antagonisms and rivalry."

Walter Camp

"If a boy wants to play football and for any reason you keep him from it, you will probably find that his character—or his temper, at least—will not improve."

Eleanor Roosevelt

"Every student during undergraduate days should experience a losing football season."

John A. Hannah

"I have to keep playing so people over forty will have somebody to root for on Sunday afternoon."

George Blanda

GOLF

"Rail splitting produced an immortal President in Abraham Lincoln; but golf, with twenty-nine million courses, hasn't produced even a good A-No. 1 congressman."

Will Rogers

"Isn't it a lot of fun to get out on the old golf course again and lie in the sun?"

Bob Hope

"A really fat man is no good at the game of golf because if he tees the ball where he can hit it, he can't see it; and if he puts the ball where he can see it, he can't hit it."

Anonymous

"Give me my golf clubs, the fresh air, and a beautiful partner, and you can keep my golf clubs and the fresh air."

Jack Benny

"Playing the game I have learned the meaning of humility. It has given me an understanding of the futility of human effort."

Abba Eban

"Golf: the Scottish game of swinging, swatting, sweating, and swearing."

Willie Collier, Sr.

"Next to the idiotic, the dull, unimaginative mind is the best for golf."

Sir Walter Simpson

"Golf is the only game where the worst player gets the best of it. He obtains more out of it as regards both exercise and enjoyment, for the good player gets worried over the slightest mistake, whereas the poor player makes too many mistakes to worry over them."

David Lloyd George

"Golf is the only sport I know of in which a player pays for every mistake. A man can muff a serve in tennis, miss a strike in baseball, or throw an incomplete pass in football and still have another chance to square himself. But in golf every swing counts against you."

Lloyd Mangrum

"If all the golf clubs were used properly every rug in the world would be beaten twice a month."

Seth Parker

"Many people strike at the ball as though they anticipated it striking back. In one way or another it usually does, with repercussions so devastating you'd think the player had stepped on a land mine."

Milton Gross

"It is almost impossible to remember how tragic a place the world is when one is playing golf."

Robert Lynd

"The average golfer doesn't play golf. He attacks it."

Jack Burke

"It took me seventeen years to get three thousand hits in baseball. I did it in one afternoon on the golf course."

Henry Aaron

"Show me a man who is a good loser and I'll show you a man who is playing golf with his boss."

Nebraska *Smoke-eater*

"After three sets of clubs and ten years of lessons, I'm finally getting some fun out of golf. I quit."

Orben's *Current Comedy*

"Every bad stroke we bad players make we make in hope. It is never so bad but it might have been worse; it is never so bad but we are confident of doing better next time. And if the next stroke is good, what happiness fills our soul. How eagerly we tell ourselves that in a little while all our strokes will be as good."

A. A. Milne

"It is nothing new or original to say that golf is played one stroke at a time. But it took me many years to realize it."

Bobby Jones

"Golf is an expensive way of playing marbles."

G. K. Chesterton

"I'm playing like Tarzan—and scoring like Jane."

Chi Chi Rodriguez

"Golf is a funny game. If there is any larceny in a man golf will bring it out."

Paul Gallico

"The least thing upset him on the links. He missed short putts because of the uproar of the butterflies in the adjoining meadows."

P. G. Wodehouse

"The sport isn't like any other where a player can take out all that is eating him on an opponent. In golf it's strictly you against your clubs."

Bob Rosburg

"The only shots you can be dead sure of are those you've had already."

Alexander H. Revell

"The golf links lie so near the mill/That almost every day/The laboring children can look out/And watch the men at play."

Sarah Norcliffe Cleghorn

TENNIS

"I don't go to tennis matches—it's too hard on my shirt collars."

Herb Shriner

"Mixed doubles are always starting divorces—if you play with your wife, you fight with her; if you play with somebody else, she fights with you."

Sidney B. Wood

"W. C. Fields had a court at his home and would play tennis for hours, holding a racket in one hand, a martini in the other; probably serving the olive.

Fred Allen

"Writing free verse is like playing tennis with the net down."

Robert Frost

"Four out of five points are won on your opponent's errors. So just hit that ball back over the net."

Billy Talbert

HORSERACING

"No horse can go as fast as the money you put on it."

Earl Wilson

"The last nag I bet on escaped from a bottle of glue."

Jack Benny

"It is difference of opinion that makes horse-races."

Mark Twain

"I wouldn't bet on a horse unless he came up to my house and told me to himself."

Eubie Blake

MISCELLANEOUS

"In recognition of the high salaries being paid sports figures, a new award should be established—for the player who holds out for the highest salary contract each year. It would be called, 'The Heistman Trophy.' "

Bill Edwards

"Since the invention of kite skiing on water, a person can go fly a kite and jump in the lake at the same time."

Ross Glover

"It's a hot night at the Garden, folks, and at ringside I see several ladies in gownless evening straps."

Jimmy Powers

"Politics is like roller skating. You go partly where you want to go, and partly where the damned things take you."

Henry Fountain Ashurst

"The athlete approaches the end of his playing days the way old people approach death. But the athlete differs from an old person in that he must continue living. Behind all the years of practice and all the hours of glory waits that inexorable terror of living without the game."

Bill Bradley

"The first thing I do every morning is read the sports page. I read it before I do the front page because at least on the sports page you have a 50-50 chance of being right."

Gerald R. Ford

CHAPTER 9—SPORTS AND THE MOVIES

And now, sport and movie fans of America, here is the moment you've been waiting for—the introduction of the players making up the all-time, all-star Hollywood baseball team:

In center field: Anthony Perkins
Left field: Burt Lancaster
Right field: William Bendix
First base: Gary Cooper
Second base: Frank Lovejoy
Shortstop: Dean White
Third base: Stuart Randall
Catcher: Paul Winfield
Pitchers: Dan Dailey, Jimmy Stewart, Richard Crenna, Ronald Reagan, Lou Gossett

The lineup, of course, is a formidable one, or would be if the actual baseball immortals portrayed by the actors could have been put on the field at the exact moment of each's prime. The lineup also becomes a reasonably challenging trivia quiz for motion-picture sports buffs. Nearly everyone instantly recognizes Gary Cooper as the screen version of Lou Gehrig in *Pride of the Yankees,* of course, but who in the name of heaven did Dean White portray? The answer is the star shortstop of the Chicago White Sox from 1930 to 1950, Luke (Old Aches and Pains) Appling.

Luke Appling? A fine player, but was there a film biography made about him? Well, there really wasn't, but he turned up in *The Stratton Story* as a teammate of Monty Stratton (Jimmy Stewart) and was played by a Hollywood actor, Dean White. In the same fashion, Frank Lovejoy breaks into the lineup as Rogers Hornsby in *The Winning Team,* Stuart Randall as Frankie Frisch in *The Pride of St. Louis,* and Richard Crenna as Dizzy Dean's brother Paul in the same film. The easy entries in the lineup, of course, include Tony Perkins as Jimmy Piersall in *Fear Strikes Out,* Burt Lancaster as *Jim Thorpe,*

All-American (who also played the outfield for the New York Giants), Cooper as Gehrig, William Bendix as Babe Ruth in *The Babe Ruth Story,* Paul Winfield as Roy Campanella in *It's Good to Be Alive,* Ronald Reagan as Grover Cleveland Alexander in *The Winning Team,* Dan Dailey as Dizzy Dean in *Pride of St. Louis,* and Lou Gossett as Satchel Paige in the most recent film biography of a sports hero.

Of course, Hollywood could have fielded a team of ringers if it had wanted. Jackie Robinson, star second baseman of the Brooklyn Dodgers, played himself in *The Jackie Robinson Story;* Gene Bearden, Bill Dickey, and Jimmy Dykes were in *The Stratton Story,* Mickey Mantle and Roger Maris portrayed themselves in *Safe at Home,* Babe Ruth was Babe Ruth for the Lou Gehrig epic, and Yankee second baseman Mark Koenig was himself in both the Gehrig and the Ruth biographies.

The trivia quiz continuing, sports and movie fans might well ask: Could Errol Flynn in his prime have beaten Coley Wallace? What would be the outcome of a Greg McClure-James Earl Jones match? And despite the weight difference, could Cameron Mitchell have taken Paul Newman? Even more mind-bending: What would have happened if Greg McClure had gotten in the ring with Ward Bond? (Bond played John L. Sullivan opposite Flynn's *Gentleman Jim.*)

Because athletes have been regarded and treated as larger-than-life figures, they have been used by the movies as both participant and biographical subject. What is surprising, however, is how seldom organized athletics have been the focal point or background of motion pictures, especially considering America's love for spectator sports. A survey of some 20,000 films dating from the late 1920s to mid-1970s revealed that only about

---

The Matchups:

Errol Flynn	*James J. Corbett* in Gentleman Jim (*1942*)
Coley Wallace	*Joe Louis* in The Joe Louis Story (*1953*)
Greg McClure	*John L. Sullivan* in The Great John L. (*1945*)
James Earl Jones	*Jack Johnson (Jack Jefferson)* in The Great White Hope (*1970*)
Cameron Mitchell	*Barney Ross* in Monkey on My Back (*1957*)
Paul Newman	*Rocky Graziano* in Somebody Up There Likes Me (*1956*)

350 movies—less than 2 per cent of the total —dealt with sports. (This includes *Rhubarb,* the 1951 opus dealing with a cat that inherits a baseball team and helps them to win the pennant by becoming their mascot. It also includes several musical films in which ice-skating star Sonja Henie displays her post-Olympics form.) It is also surprising that although popular mythology tells us that basketball and baseball are the most-attended spectator sports in the United States, neither of them ranks particularly high as far as being the subject of sports movies. In fact, horseracing is the top drawing card on the field of action. It is also second at the movie box office, if frequency of use as a sporting background is a valid basis for judgment.

Where They Rank—Seven American Spectator Sports:

Attendance	As Movie Subjects
1. Horseracing	1. Boxing
2. Auto racing	2. Horseracing
3. Football	3. Football
4. Baseball	4. Auto racing
5. Basketball	5. Baseball
6. Hockey	6. Hockey
7. Boxing	7. Basketball

One reason for baseball, football, and basketball's relatively low positions as movie subjects may lie in the fact that it is difficult to stage contests and make them look convincing. In contrast, even early horseracing films got by on closeups with a process screen behind the subjects, mixed with a variety of wide shots. Boxing, by being confined to such a comparatively small area, was also easily filmed. The first film of a sporting event, in fact, was made by Thomas Edison at his West Orange, New Jersey, laboratory on June 14, 1894. The two participants were Mike Leonard, a rather well-known fighter, and Jack Cushing, a lesser figure in the boxing world. In order that all the action might be taken in by the stationary camera, Edison had the men fight in a ring twelve feet square. The scenario called for Leonard to carry Cushing a sufficient number of rounds to make the filming profitable, then knock his man out if possible. Leonard did exactly that, sparring until the sixth round, when he put Cushing down for good. The film was separated into rounds and shown at a Kinetoscope parlor at 83 Nassau Street, New York City, two months later. Customers, faced with the choice of paying ten cents a round for the entire fight or seeing the knockout, generally saved their money and watched only the sixth round.

Said Boxing's First Movie Winner After the Battle:

"I hit him when I liked and where I liked. I'd hit him oftener, only Mr. Edison treated me right and I didn't want to be too quick for his machine. I generally hit 'im in the face, because I felt sorry for his family and thought I would select the only place that couldn't be disfigured."

Mike Leonard, postfight interview,
June 14, 1894

While this financially unsuccessful revolution was taking place, three American athletes were in the process of preparing for a momentous evening—Monday, September 3, 1894. If any one day can mark the beginning of the era that saw athletes graduate from the field of battle to the field of entertainment (assuming there is a difference), this was the moment. For on that single evening, three of the country's most famous athletes shared opening nights in three different plays. Not as bit players, it should be added, but as stars with many lines and, in one case, music to be sung.

There was, first of all, ex-heavyweight champion John L. Sullivan. His opening-night vehicle at Jacobs Third Avenue Theater in New York was entitled *A True American.* Written by veteran playwright Edmund A. Price, the show concerned an archvillain's attempt to gain possession of another man's wealth. "A comedy in three acts," the New York *Herald* described it, "although tragedies seemed ever imminent. The plot is thin and on hackneyed lines, but the dialogue is often bright and the incidental specialty business is excellent." That business, of course, consisted of Sullivan's boxing onstage, for he had been deftly cast as "John D. Newman, alias Desmond," a comic-heroic figure whose punches and punch lines kept the audience excited and amused.

The Critic on John L. Sullivan:

"Mr. Sullivan was manly and spoke his lines distinctly and with good effect."

At the very moment Sullivan was strutting his part, James J. Corbett opened at the American Theater in what the New York *Times* called "the pugilistic drama," *Gentleman Jack,* a play by Charles T. Vincent and William A. Brady that was on its second go-around. A few weeks after Corbett dethroned

Sullivan on September 7, 1892, *Gentleman Jack* had a trial run at the Temple Opera House in Elizabeth, New Jersey. Apparently it was not a smash hit, for it was soon withdrawn and extensively rewritten for the gala New York opening of September 3, 1894.

Everything went better on that occasion. Corbett was greeted by an enthusiastic crowd that obviously enjoyed the play despite its labyrinthine plot. Corbett was cast—also deftly— as Jack Royden, who was alternately a college athlete, bank clerk, and lover before becoming heavyweight champion of the world. Along the way, the audience was treated to scenes depicting a college campus, banking office, athletic club, and as a grand realistic climax, the roof of Madison Square Garden. Both the play and Corbett were well received by the large opening-night crowd.

The Critic on James J. Corbett:
"He has improved decidedly as a comedian and if anyone in the cast is awkward or stage frightened, it is not he."

Meanwhile, at Brooklyn's Bijou Theater, Steve Brodie opened in a four-act melodrama entitled *On the Bowery*. Brodie, a boxer, street fighter, tavern owner, swimmer, and first man to jump off the Brooklyn Bridge and survive (although some doubted this claim), was undoubtedly the most colorful character of the three athletes making simultaneous assaults on art that evening. The *Times* reported that Brodie's appearance in *On the Bowery* was his theatrical debut. Actually, he had made a cameo appearance in a show entitled *Money Mad* two years before at Niblo's Gardens. On that occasion, he had leaped from a stage bridge into a stage river. Playwright R. N. Stephens, noting the young man's ruffianly charm, immediately fashioned a play for Brodie to have as his very own.

In the opening scene of *On the Bowery,* for example, Brodie bursts through the swinging doors of a saloon just in time to teach a lesson to a tough who was "tumping his steady." Having demonstrated his pugilistic ability, Brodie then had the opportunity to sing. The Brooklyn audience loved every moment of it, but the true test came a week later when the play was moved to New York's 14th Street Theater amid a barrage of publicity. "The sensation of the hour!" one advertisement trumpeted. *"On the Bowery—a mirror of the most striking and amusing phases of New York life . . . the Bowery at night . . . the wonderful Brooklyn Bridge scene."* More sophisticated New Yorkers might have been expected to

sneer at the crude melodrama and hammy technique of Brodie, but if they felt any revulsion, it was not evident. Perhaps the presence of an entire gallery filled with Brodie's tough-looking friends from across the river helped his cause. In any event, at the conclusion of Steve's song, the show stopped dead while a quartet of ushers showered him for ten minutes with a variety of flowers—wreaths shaped like the Brooklyn Bridge, an anchor, a horseshoe, and more than twenty set pieces. Because the playing area was so small, the play then had to be stopped again so a gang of stagehands could cart the flowers away.

The Critics on Steve Brodie:
"Brodie sang 'The Bowery Girl' in a round but slightly husky voice which came out of one corner of his mouth. . . . Neither Brodie nor the play can be taken seriously, the former because it has no originality . . . the latter because the people who go to see him do so because he was foolhardy and lived to reap the benefits. . . ."
"No tragedian or comedian has of recent years been drowned in such a storm of applause and no prima donna swamped in such a sea of flowers as was our Steve Brodie last night."

Such an auspicious beginning led more and more athletes into the entertainment field. Jim Corbett made films for Thomas Edison, who in turn produced *Casey at the Bat,* a brief baseball film of 1899. Fourteen years later, Frank (Home Run) Baker became the first famous athlete to perform in a feature with a plot, a film entitled *The Short Stop's Double.* After World War I, when the film industry expanded enormously, sports movies were released at regular intervals, many of them with top stars and big-name directors. But nearly all of them were poison at the box office. No one can say for sure why this happened. Probably it was because in nearly every case the film was ludicrously phony.

As early as 1920, critics recognized that movies featuring sports celebrities were apt to be turkeys; thus, when one came along that was better than the average, it was greeted with surprised praise. Such a picture was Babe Ruth's first, a product of the silent era entitled *Headin' Home.* The Babe was a young man of but twenty-five when it was produced and shown, but he had just rocketed to stardom as a home-run hitter and was smart enough to demand fifty thousand dollars for his part in the picture, which, incidentally, featured captions by Arthur "Bugs" Baer, a writer who had tried his hand at professional sports when a young man.

The Critic on *Headin' Home:*
"Whenever a celebrity of the sports world or divorce court appears in pictures, the public, as a rule, doesn't expect much in the way of story or acting, and usually doesn't get as much as it expects, chiefly because the celebrity takes himself or herself and the picture seriously and attempts to be heroic. It is, therefore, of moment to record that Babe Ruth and Headin' Home do not deal, except occasionally and briefly, in the regulation movie stuff. They try for comedy, not heroics, and score not infrequently."

The plot of *Headin' Home* poked fun at the hero, a country bumpkin who apparently could not hit a home run unless he was angry. (His first such clout was hit through a church window five blocks from the playing field.) The story skipped around a bit, but in an entertaining way told the story of the bumpkin's rise to fame and return to his hometown, unaffected by the notoriety.

During the 1920s, most of the top sports celebrities dabbled with movies or talked about doing so—Jack Dempsey, Red Grange, Jess Willard, Suzanne Lenglen, Bill Tilden, Benny Leonard, Battling Siki. The most successful was Grange, whose *One Minute to Play,* filmed for $100,000 at Pomona College, grossed $750,000. That so surprised the moguls of the industry that when Grange was subsequently hired to appear in a picture about auto racing, they lost their perspective and dropped the Galloping Ghost to second billing when he demanded a share of the gross. If they had taken advantage of Grange's popularity, they, as well as he, might have profited immeasurably.

One of the first athletes to be praised for his acting ability in talking movies was Max Baer, who appeared in *The Prizefighter and the Lady* in 1933 with Myrna Loy, Walter Huston, Jack Dempsey, and Primo Carnera, the latter two playing themselves. At the time, Baer was still quite active in the ring, having defeated Max Schmeling in June 1932. (Carnera had beaten Jack Sharkey for the crown in June 1933 and would lose it a year later to Baer.) Thus critics and public expected all the fighters in the picture to be stiffs as far as acting went, but Baer handed them a surprise.

The story of *The Prizefighter and the Lady* dealt with a nightclub singer, Belle (Myrna Loy), who falls in love with a fighter named Steve Morgan (Baer). When Baer temporarily falls for a younger woman (Muriel Evans), Belle returns to her first love (Otto Kruger) but is won back when Morgan proves himself in the ring against Carnera. Jack Dempsey, having retired and turned to officiating by that time, was appropriately cast as the referee.

The Critic on Baer:
"Mr. Baer is easily the outstanding thespianic graduate of the squared ring. He does not speak in the husky tones associated with most prizefighters, even those who have played before the footlights and the camera. His voice is clear and pleasing and it causes one to wonder whether his success as a player will not interfere with his fighting."

Following the tradition established by Corbett, Sullivan, and Brodie, boxers early established themselves as leaders in making the switch from ring to theater or film. Not all were successful. Benny Leonard, although an outstanding champion, was reportedly the recipient of the first rotten egg ever tossed at the prestigious Palace Theater on Broadway. Others, try though they might, could not break the public's image of them as inarticulate clods. "In every role, I'm supposed to talk as if I have a mouthful of ravioli," said Lou Nova, after appearing in a score of movies, road shows, and TV plays. "My father was a concert pianist, my father-in-law was a botany professor, and I've been to college. But I've also been a pug, and they never let you forget that. So I must learn the mush talk. When *The Millionaire* opened on the road, I made with the 'dese-dem-dose' and do you know what the critics wrote about me? They wrote, 'Lou Nova plays himself.'"

Anecdote:
LADY JOURNALIST (to Chalky Wright, a fighter who reportedly loved classical music): *What is your opinion of Bach?*
CHALKY WRIGHT: *A very clever boy. He can't miss.*

During the thirty-five years between *The Pittsburgh Kid* (1942) and *The Greatest* (1977), pictures in which Billy Conn and

Muhammad Ali played themselves, boxers were more likely to be seen as thugs than as fighters in the squared ring. In *On the Waterfront,* for example, a trio of ex-pugs turned up as important extras—Abe Simon, Tami Mauriello (most famous for losing in a single round to Joe Louis), and Tony Galento, whose big moment came when he threw a tomato at Karl Malden (Father Barry). As thugs, the fighters generally acquitted themselves well. They could have handled themselves well in the ring also, no doubt, but somewhere along the line Hollywood decided it was more difficult to teach a boxer to act than it was to teach an actor to box. So the heroes of the fight movies were professional actors, often with laughable results.

The actor who appeared most frequently as a boxer in Hollywood B movies was Wayne Morris, who turned up as *The Battling Bellhop* in 1936, as the kid in *The Kid Comes Back* (1938), and in *The Big Punch* (1948). Unfortunately, Wayne Morris did not have the build of a boxer and handled himself awkwardly in the ring. But he seemed powerful and smooth as silk compared to Robert Montgomery in *Here Comes Mr. Jordan* (1941). With his narrow shoulders and soft midsection, Montgomery's fight scenes must have brought a smile to every boxer, not to mention a large section of the nonfighting audience.

Generally speaking, it might be said that despite their acting failures, boxers have been kinder to Hollywood than Hollywood has been to the fight game. The fictionalized accounts have been hampered by poor scripts, stilted direction, and the inevitable side effects of low budgeting. Of the seventy-five boxing films produced from about 1930 to 1975, only three or four are commendable in the handling of fight sequences as well as overall entertainment values. (*Here Comes Mr. Jordan,* for example, is a pleasant and amusing film until the fight sequences begin. Then it becomes pure hoke.) *The Harder They Fall*

(1956), based on Budd Schulberg's novel and starring Humphrey Bogart, Max Baer, and Jersey Joe Walcott, is a fine film despite some moralizing. *The Champion* (1949), with Kirk Douglas as the believable fighter struggling to get to the top of the heap, well deserves the Academy Award it won that year for best editing as well as its citation as one of the year's ten best pictures. Likewise, *Body and Soul* (1947), with John Garfield, is a rare classic in the field. Finally, two films of the seventies, *Fat City* (1972) with Stacy Keach, and *Rocky* (1976), starring Sylvester Stallone, seem to indicate that in the hands of talented people, the fictional fight movie does not have to be as stylized as a B Western of the 1930s.

Dabbling in popular biography, it was inevitable that Hollywood try its hand at depicting the lives of America's great pugilists. One of the lavish early attempts was *Gentleman Jim* (1942), in which Errol Flynn was cast—none too badly, as it turned out—as the handsome and elusive James J. Corbett, a fighter who was so deft in avoiding punches that he amazed professional boxers when he was well into his fifties. Directed by Raoul Walsh with a screenplay by Vincent Lawrence and Horace McCoy, *Gentleman Jim* is limited in biographical scope in that it follows Corbett's career only until he wins the heavyweight title from the boisterous John L. Sullivan (Ward Bond). One would have liked to have seen the screen version of Corbett's bout with Bob Fitzsimmons in 1897, but Lawrence and McCoy were apparently interested in leaving Corbett and Flynn at the apex of glory. Despite a depiction of Corbett's family life that seems spurious, the movie holds up well nearly four decades after it was produced.

Three years later, Hollywood gave equal time to John L. Sullivan, United Artists producing *The Great John L.* as one of the first offerings of the newly launched Bing Crosby Productions. Starring Greg McClure in the title role, the script by James Edward Grant

---

Some Hollywood Stars Who Played Boxers:

Kirk Douglas	Buster Crabbe	Robert Taylor
John Garfield	Victor McLaglen	Stacy Keach
Richard Conte	William Holden	Robert Montgomery
Curly ("Three Stooges")	Scott Brady	Lew Ayres
Jeff Chandler	Stuart Erwin	Bruce Cabot
Richard Dix	Richard Arlen	Paul Newman
John Payne	Mickey Rooney	Anthony Quinn
Cameron Mitchell	Tom Neal	Dick Powell
Don (Red) Barry	Robert Blake	Tony Curtis
William Lundigan	Frankie Darro	Eddie Albert
Lee Tracy	Audie Murphy	Jack Oakie

The Critic on *Gentleman Jim:*
"*. . . Not only the story of a great and colorful ring personality but a vividly illustrated album of a once outlawed sport at which the spectator was wont to keep one eye on the gladiators, the other peeled for the raiding police. . . . If the original battle [between Sullivan and Corbett] was as good as that served up by the Warners, then it surely must have been a corker. . . .*"

devotes considerable attention to Sullivan's love for "Black Velvet" (a mixture of champagne and stout) as well as his penchant for womanizing. Thus it is a less glamorous portrayal of the fighter's life than that of *Gentleman Jim*, which ought to make the film more interesting but somehow succeeds only in making it more pedestrian. There is considerable moralizing, J. M. Kerrigan (Father O'Malley) warning at one point that "each man has a personal demon he must wrestle with and defeat," all of which produces lots of hand-wringing but little dramatic action. Greg McClure, a fine physical specimen, looks very much the fighter, although if old prints and photographs are accurate, Ward Bond of *Gentleman Jim* had a chunky physique much closer to that of the real Sullivan.

The Critic on *The Great John L.:*
"*A curious mixture of excitement and tedious drama . . . overlong and occasionally boring.*"

In 1953, Hollywood marked the second anniversary of Joe Louis's being KO'd by Rocky Marciano by producing *The Joe Louis Story*, with a new actor, Coley Wallace, in the title role. Unfortunately, the real Joe Louis story, that of a generally quiet and methodical man, did not lend itself to dramatization. The result is a dull movie, the best parts of which are film clips of Louis's actual fights with Jim Braddock, Max Baer, and Max Schmeling.

Shortly after *The Harder They Fall* was released, the other side of the coin appeared in MGM's *Somebody Up There Likes Me*, starring Paul Newman as Rocky Graziano. Whereas the first film depicted the fight game as rotten, the latter indicated that the prize ring was a good place for an antisocial type to vent his spleen and gain for himself not only widespread attention but also public respect.

Playing the young Graziano in a slouching, rolling, smirking Marlon Brando style, Paul Newman is alternately tough, funny, despicable, and pathetic. Pier Angeli is the love interest, inserted, one supposes, as evidence of the old Hollywood adage that while it is important to have somebody up there who likes you, it is also good box office to have someone down here feel the same.

The Critic on *Somebody Up There Likes Me:*
"*. . . the picture is edited to give it a tremendous crispness and pace. The representation of the big fight of Graziano and Tony Zale is one of the whoppingest slugfests we've ever seen on the screen.*"

Somebody Up There Likes Me having succeeded, Hollywood turned in 1957 to another fistic biography, this time becoming even more daring by telling the story of fighter-champion-drug addict Barney Ross. (In December 1955, Otto Preminger's *The Man with the Golden Arm*, depicting the evils of heroin, had paved the way.) Entitled *Monkey on My Back*, the film stars Cameron Mitchell as Ross, who reigned as welterweight champion from 1935 to 1938 before becoming a war hero and eventually a drug addict. The film created immediate controversy between Edward Small, its producer, and the Production Code representatives, who objected to a scene in which Ross, desperate for a fix, slugs a pusher, and hiding in an alley to avoid police, injects the drug into his arm with a hypodermic needle. Later the hero is shown wrestling with the horrors of withdrawal from heroin. Critics generally agreed that the episodes dealing with drugs were relatively tame and that Mitchell's portrayal of the addict, "with the exception of occasional back twitching, devoid of flamboyance." Others went even further, calling Mitchell "superb." Few described the overall picture as much better

Another "Hype"?
When Monkey on My Back *appeared, it was accompanied by a damage suit for five million dollars, Barney Ross charging that the film "hurt his reputation."*

than average, however. The 1970s featured a couple of film biographies of black fighters who had much in common. *The Great White Hope*, based on Howard Sackler's prize-winning play of the 1968–69 season, depicted the life of Jack Jefferson, a thinly disguised version of Jack Johnson, the powerful and lightning-fast heavyweight who became the first black champion by defeating Tommy Burns in 1908. Thereafter Jefferson (James Earl Jones) manages to succeed in the white society until brought down not by white challengers in the ring, but by white women. Despite generally believable performances by Jones and Jane Alexander, the film seldom realized the excitement even a loose treatment of Jack Johnson's life promises. But when he saw the play in 1968, Muhammad Ali, then fighting a charge of draft evasion, said, "You just change the time, date, and the details, and it's about me." In 1977, Ali's screen biography, *The Greatest*, revealed some of the parallels between the life of Ali and Johnson, while giving the fighter a chance to demonstrate not only his skill in the ring but also his natural abilities as an actor.

Digression—Another Athlete Sues:
Barney Ross was not the first athlete to sue Hollywood for an alleged outrage against his reputation. In 1933, Brooklyn-born matador Sidney Franklin brought a three-hundred-thousand-dollar suit against Columbia Pictures for releasing a film about him entitled Throwing the Bull. *At the beginning of the movie, a narrator said, "Now folks, meet Sidney Franklin, the greatest bullthrower—I mean bullfighter—ever born under the sunny skies of Brooklyn." Franklin asserted that the term "bullthrower" was an insult to his art and a reflection upon his veracity and reputation.*

In March 1935, New York Supreme Court Justice John F. Carew agreed with Franklin—but only seven thousand dollars' worth. In addition, an injunction was issued against further distribution of the movie.

HORSERACING
The second most popular sports movie in America, that with a horseracing background, was more popular during the 1930s and 1940s than more recently. Looking back on the list of titles of that era, one is most likely to think of the slow-burn race-track types such as James Gleason (*Hot Tip*, 1935) or William Gargan, who starred in several hoof operas such as *Harrigan's Kid* (1943) and *Breezing Home* (1937). Or the vision of a young horse-

lover is conjured up—Lon McAllister, for example, currying his charges in *The Boy from Indiana* or *Home in Indiana*. And who can forget the love of Elizabeth Taylor for her horse as she somehow found a way to win the Derby in *National Velvet* (1945)?

Sample Dialogue—*Breezing Home:*
WENDY BARRIE (After hearing trainer remark on how thoroughbred horse is nature's noblest creation): *Don't ever change, Steve. Don't ever stop thinking that.*

The year 1949 brought two decades of racing movies to a fitting climax with the release of two horse biographies. One, *The Great Dan Patch*, immortalized America's most famous harness racer, Dan Patch, the only world champion never to lose a race. By the time he retired in 1909, he had earned more than three million dollars and held nine world records. (The horse, appropriately enough, was named after the great American daredevil who thrilled audiences while Andrew Jackson was President by leaping over falls into churning rapids.) During his later years on the track, Dan Patch raced only against his own records, there being no competition. He died in 1916, but three decades later was still sufficiently remembered to be the subject for a movie. Filmed in color, the film starred—in addition to a horse impersonating the hero—Dennis O'Keefe, son of Dan Patch's owner, and Gail Russell as the girl who secretly loves him. The story, according to most critics, was not only spurious but also inconsequential.

The Critic on *The Great Dan Patch:*
"*There is nothing prettier in the animal kingdom than a fine fast pacer or trotter in action. But—and there is so often a 'but' in Hollywood films—The Great Dan Patch is burdened with a corny romance, written, acted, and directed at a slow walk.*"

Simultaneously, *The Story of Seabiscuit* broke from the cinematic starting gate, Lon McAllister up, with Shirley Temple rooting the great horse on to victory. Mixing black-and-white newsreel footage with the rest of the movie's color produced a somewhat unpleasant effect, but the presence of Barry Fitzgerald as a whimsical trainer kept the biography from becoming totally pedestrian. "This picture is one of the best race-track studies ever made when Seabiscuit is on the screen," one critic noted, then added, ". . . the human actors, with one bright exception, run out of the money."

FOOTBALL EPICS

Because football has been one of the most difficult sports to stage for movies, the most successful pigskin pix have been comedies. The 1930s saw a great number of these, one of the most notable being a low-budget musical about a small Texas college that received an invitation—by mistake—to play Yale. (The college hastily assembles a team and manages to win.) The hastily assembled movie, *Pigskin Parade,* also became a hit, perhaps because of the singing of fourteen-year-old Judy Garland, who starred along with Jack Oakie, Betty Grable, and Stuart Erwin. Aside from this spate of college pictures with football action, not much attention was given to football as a "serious" sport. Even when the "immortal" Knute Rockne died in 1931, no one rushed headlong into production of the inevitable film biography. In fact, nearly a decade passed before Hollywood felt up to tackling a football movie that was not supposed to generate laughter.

In order to execute *Knute Rockne, All-American,* Warner Brothers enlisted the services of Pat O'Brien (who had already gained experience as a coach by leading Calvert College to victory in the 1933 movie *College Coach*) as the hero. Johnny Sheffield, later to swing through the jungle as Tarzan's "boy," was signed to play "Rock" as a lad of seven; Ronald Reagan, also experienced at college athletics, was recruited to play the great runner George Gipp. In short, no expense was spared to make the tribute to Knute Rockne the very best.

When it was completed in October 1940, *Knute Rockne, All-American* was premiered before nearly ten thousand persons at four theaters in South Bend, Indiana. The stars of the movie were there, helping to guarantee the picture's success. It did succeed, then and later, eventually becoming one of the earliest football films that can still be viewed with a minimum of embarrassment. Some liberties were taken, of course. Players who were in the

dressing room when Rockne delivered his speech about "the Gipper," imploring his boys to return to the field and overcome Army's lead, deny that the coach ever said the line, "make just one for the Gipper." According to Jack Chevigny, who later scored a touchdown in the second half, Rockne's speech was much shorter and more subdued than in the movie. No matter. Most critics were inclined to be generous, taking a view similar to that of the New York *Times'* Bosley Crowther, who wrote, "As a memorial to a fine and inspiring molder of character in young men, this picture ranks high. But like the Carnegie Foundation has done on previous occasions, we are inclined to question its overemphasis of the pigskin sport."

Other producers of football films at about the same time were not quite so fortunate. In 1941, when Columbia Pictures tried to cash in on the fame of Michigan running back Tom Harmon by releasing a potboiler entitled *Harmon of Michigan,* most of the critics saw it for what it was: a throwback to the old days of low-budget formula shows. One of them wrote, "Though Tom Harmon, as some zealots have held, may be the greatest American since Abraham Lincoln, and a pigskin scrimmage can sometimes make rapid entertainment, this film is about as lethargic as a benchwarmer's pulse. Stout men heave against each other, and now and then the leather oval darts across the open field, but for the most part, *Harmon of Michigan* never gets off its own five-yard line."

Even worse was the reception given Glenn Davis and Felix (Doc) Blanchard, the two young men who dominated football action for Army during the war years. Their collegiate playing days over, the dynamic duo decided to cash in with an autobiographical epic called *Spirit of West Point.* Independently produced by John W. Rogers and Harry Joe Brown from a screenplay by Tom Reed, the two-hundred-thousand-dollar paste-up of newsreel footage and minimum dialogue by the principals was released in late 1947 to less than thunderous applause. Tom Harmon, incidentally, played himself in the movie, thus

---

Some Hollywood Stars Who Lugged the Pigskin:

Nelson Eddy	Tony Curtis	Richard Arlen
Bruce Cabot	Jack Oakie	Victor Mature
Fred MacMurray	The Marx Brothers	Jimmy Stewart
The Three Stooges	Charlton Heston	Joe E. Brown
Wayne Morris	John Derek	Tom Brown
Robert Montgomery	Lew Ayres	Robert Cummings
Burt Reynolds	Robert Sterling	Eddie Quillan

continuing his record of appearing only in turkeys. Glenn Davis played not only himself, but also the part of his twin brother, Ralph. It didn't help.

The Critic on *Spirit of West Point:*
"Messrs. Davis and Blanchard—Mr. Inside and Mr. Outside—are no threats when it comes to acting before the camera, and the supporting cast is no great help. . . . Strictly a teen-agers' drama . . ."

Somewhat better was 1953s *Crazylegs*, the story, naturally, of Elroy (Crazylegs) Hirsch, passing-catching end for the Chicago Rockets and Los Angeles Rams. Although hampered by a screenplay that devotes considerable attention to other people in Hirsch's life, such as his ailing father, devoted wife (Joan Vohs), and gruff high-school coach (Lloyd Nolan, of course), the movie successfully tells the story of a man born in humble circumstances who serves his country during the war and returns to become a star football player only to be hit on the head and lose his co-ordination. But the ending is happy when he rises above the handicap and goes on to become the scoring leader of the National Football League in 1951. Hirsch's acting surprised many critics by being of an extremely high quality. He later appeared in other nonsports films, such as *Unchained* (1955).

Although it continued to grow as a spectator sport during the late 1950s and 1960s, football nearly disappeared from feature films during that period. One example that received more attention than it deserved was *John Goldfarb, Please Come Home,* a 1965 comedy in which a pilot known as "Wrongway" and a magazine photographer-writer dubbed "Iceberg" land in a desert kingdom where the pilot is forced to coach a native football team to defeat Notre Dame. Trapped in this inane plot were Shirley MacLaine, Peter Ustinov, Richard Crenna, Jim Backus, and Scott Brady. The movie probably would have died a natural death had it not been for a legal hassle involving the use of the name Notre Dame, the threat of court injunctions, and other problems. As a result, *John Goldfarb, Please Come Home* enjoyed moderate success at the box office.

Another product of the sixties was *Number One,* in which Charlton Heston plays a forty-year-old quarterback who must decide whether to play one more season before retiring. The playing sequences, while not extensive, are the best parts of the film, which tends to ramble and get bogged down in long talky sequences and pregnant pauses.

During the 1970s the quality improved. *The Longest Yard,* featuring Burt Reynolds and a number of professional players as prison inmates who have their chance to destroy authority on the football field, is the best of the fiction. *Brian's Song,* the story of Chicago Bear running back Brian Piccolo's losing fight with cancer, not only wins the award for nonfiction but also displays the best integration of filmed sequences and stock footage of any sports biography.

Some Movies That Sound as if They Might Be Sports Movies but Are Not:

Passport to Pimlico *is not a racing film, but the story of a suburb of London whose residents tear up their ration cards.*

Star Packer *is not a biography of a famous Green Bay football player, but the story of a western marshal who "packs" a star.*

Triple Play *is not a baseball yarn, but three short playlets.*

Neck and Neck *has nothing to do with horseracing but is a 1931 situation comedy with Walter Brennan and Vera Reynolds.*

Tip on a Dead Jockey *is not about the track, but a pilot who gets involved with an international smuggling ring.*

Destination: Miami *does not deal with a football team's attempts to win a bid to the Orange Bowl. It's a gangster film.*

The Catcher *has no connection with baseball, but concerns efforts of the Seattle police to track down fugitives.*

Some other titles to beware of:

The Fan	The Lineup	The Naked Runner
The 49ers	The Mad Bomber	Night Games
Hit and Run	The Miami Story	Tinker
The Raiders	The Violent Patriot	Mr. Inside, Mr. Outside
Run Home Slow	The Texas Rangers	The Last Run

BASEBALL

"The Late Show" runs that 1949 movie perhaps once a year, usually at the beginning of the baseball season. Entitled *It Happens Every Spring,* the film stars Ray Milland, freshened up from his lost weekend, as a college professor who invents a compound that causes balls to curve away from bats. A dedicated fan, Milland volunteers his services to the St. Louis team, wins thirty games during the regular season, and also pitches the conclusive World Series game. He then retires, thanks to a conveniently broken arm. The story is charming and the special effects well executed for the time, but considering America's love for baseball, it seems strange that *It Happens Every Spring* should have been practically the only movie dealing with this sport that could be viewed without embarrassment until *Bang the Drum Slowly* (1973). Yet there is little doubt that America's filmmakers have done poorly by the national game. One almost suspects deliberate sabotage.

Between *The Short Stop's Double* and *Pride of the Yankees* (1942), the diamond pickings are indeed meager. There's Joe E. Brown cavorting as *Alibi Ike* and *Elmer the Great,* Robert Young investigating *Death on the Diamond, The Babe Comes Home,* and not much else. But when Lou Gehrig died at a tragically early age in 1941, the film industry, notably Sam Goldwyn, decided to produce a memorial to the Iron Man that would be tasteful, well done, and, hopefully, profitable.

Selected for the title role was Gary Cooper, perfect casting in that Gehrig himself was modest, homespun, inclined to saying "yup" or "nope" in most situations. No great shakes as an athlete, Cooper seems awkward in the field or at bat, but in the final scene, in which he calls himself "the luckiest man on the face of the earth" even as he feels the crippling paralysis about to claim him, his performance is moving. The movie is also noteworthy in that several Yankee ballplayers are visible, especially catcher Bill Dickey, who slugs a guy.

The Critic on *Pride of the Yankees:*
"*As a baseball picture . . . [it] is not anything to raise the blood pressure. But as a simple, moving story with an ironic heart-tug at the end, it serves as a fitting memorial to the real Lou. . . .*"

The next time baseball tried to immortalize one of its team members, however, disaster descended. By 1947, Babe Ruth, stricken with cancer of the throat, knew he was finished. Others knew it as well, and efforts were made to put together a movie biography to honor the Babe. William Bendix, a likable, chunky actor who projected the aura of Ruth if he did not resemble him physically, was selected for the part, and a screenplay was written by Bob Considine. By July 1948 the project was finished in time for Babe Ruth to struggle out of Memorial Hospital and attend the première at the Astor Theater, New York City. Insulated by a police cordon from a cheering crowd of more than a thousand, Ruth walked slowly into the theater, supported on both arms, seemingly too weary to do anything but smile wanly and painfully. Considering the low quality of the picture, one can only hope that Ruth was in no condition to be offended by the movie, which was a total disaster at the box office as well as with critics. Subsequently, *The Babe Ruth Story* was given credit—or discredit—for applying the kiss of death to sports films for quite some time afterward, but this is not true.

The Critics on *The Babe Ruth Story:*
"*. . . Here, in the treatment of a subject which has the makings for a warm, appealing film, we see a typical debasement of human qualities in the muck of the cliché . . . Ruth, played by William Bendix, is made to seem just a big, mawkish clown. . . .*"
"*Regardless of advertised coaching, Mr. Bendix still swings like a rusty gate, and the atmosphere of a big-league ball park is as remote from this picture as that of a church. . . . A tedious and tasteless sick-bed ordeal, with sound-track sobs and angel voices, ends the show.*"

The very next year, in fact, *The Stratton Story* was released, telling the story of Chicago White Sox pitcher Monty Stratton, who lost his leg in a 1938 hunting accident. Van Johnson was originally selected to play the title role, but he eventually yielded to Jimmy Stewart. Directed by Sam Wood—who also directed *Pride of the Yankees*—*The Stratton Story* was more generously received by both audience and critics than the deplorable Ruth biography, Stewart giving the best performance of his postwar acting career.

In 1950, *The Jackie Robinson Story* not only kept the bio-baseball film rolling but also was a landmark in that it dealt with America's first major-league black baseball player of the twentieth century. Robinson followed the examples of Glenn Davis and Doc Blanchard by playing himself, but turned out to be a much better actor. Ruby Dee and Louise Beavers, as Jackie's sweetheart and mother, performed capably. The film's major drawback seemed to be the handling of the scenes on the field, most of which were shot on a studio stage.

The Critics on *The Jackie Robinson Story:*

"Mr. Robinson, doing the rare thing of playing himself in the picture's leading role, displays a calm assurance and composure that might be envied by many a Hollywood star."

"The scenes of baseball action . . . look as staged and phony as a wrestling match."

The year 1952 saw a pair of baseball epics added to the list of biographies. (*Rhubarb* the cat had stolen everyone's thunder in 1951.) *The Pride of St. Louis* appeared first, telling the story of Jay Hanna (Dizzy) Dean, Cardinal pitcher who won 102 games in four seasons before suffering a freak accident during the 1937 All-Star game. There was a decided twist to this film, however. The majority of sports bios conclude with the hero somehow engineering a victory against an opponent on the playing field. Dizzy Dean's climactic struggle came after he retired and went into broadcasting. When they heard his assault on the American language, English teachers banded together to try to force Dean off the air on the grounds that he was polluting the spoken word and setting a horrendous example for youngsters. When informed that his syntax offended the educators, Dean replied: "Sin tax? Are them jokers down in Washington puttin' a tax on that, too?" As played by Dan Dailey, the movie Dean was boisterously appropriate and his battle with the forces of correct usage at the end of the film an amusing and touching conclusion.

A Few Dizzy Deanisms:

"He slud into third."

"That boy looks mighty hitterish to me."

"They was really scrummin' that ball over today." *And after he used the line, "The trouble with them boys is they ain't got enough spart," on being asked to explain the definition of "spart":*

"Spart is pretty much the same as fight or pep or gumption. Like *The Spart of St. Louis,* that plane Lindbergh flowed to Europe in."

At the same time, the resurrected George Gipp of *Knute Rockne, All-American,* Ronald Reagan, came out of athletic retirement to play the part of Grover Cleveland Alexander, major-league pitcher from 1911 to 1930 and hero of the 1926 World Series. Entitled *The Winning Team,* the film is a genial whitewash of Alexander's love for liquor, attributing his occasional "fainting spells"—which resembled hangovers—to his having been struck on the head by a baseball early in his career. Credit for the seemingly washed-up hurler's comeback in the 1926 Series is given to the inspiration of his wife, played by Doris Day. Having died in 1950, the real Grover Cleveland Alexander was not available for comment. During the 1960s, baseball like football, tended to disappear from the movie screen, no doubt aided by the appearance in 1962 of a film so bad as to preclude any producer laying a glove on sports for some time. That movie was *Safe at Home,* which Columbia Pictures released following Roger Maris' and Mickey Mantle's torrid home-run race of 1961 and Maris' setting of a new record-*cum*-asterisk.

Other Sports Bio Films of the 1950s:

1951—Jim Thorpe, All-American
Burt Lancaster, well-cast as Jim Thorpe, Olympic track-and-field star as well as baseball and football player.

1951—Follow the Sun
The story of golfer Ben Hogan's automobile accident and subsequent comeback. With Glenn Ford.

1954—Go, Man, Go!
Collective biography of the Harlem Globetrotters, starring the Globetrotters, Sidney Poitier, Dane Clark.

1954—The Bob Mathias Story
Mathias plays himself in the story of his two Olympic decathlon victories.

1957—Fear Strikes Out
Story of baseball's Jim Piersall and his bout with mental illness. With Anthony Perkins.

"Mickey Mantle and Roger Maris came up to bat in unfamiliar surroundings yesterday and went down swinging," noted one critic after the grand opening of *Safe at Home.* (It was part of a double bill that included *Don't Knock the Twist,* starring Chubby Checker.) He then added: "Since Maris and Mantle have lost ball games before, they will probably survive."

Columbia, having released 1,705 movies before *Safe at Home,* should have known better, one supposes, except that producer Tom Naud managed to convince the studio hierarchy that the M & M boys of 1961 would be hot items at the box office. The story deals with a youngster who brags about his friendship with the Yankees and then is forced to deliver Maris and Mantle to his Little League banquet. And Tom Naud wondered why customers didn't storm the box offices.

Perhaps it was because people merely wanted a change, but the 1960s saw a decided trend away from the traditional sports movie. Baseball and football were out; auto racing was in, very big. Even horseracing and boxing had faded; in their places were films about skiing, surfing, martial arts, and sky diving. Biography was also out. Fiction gave more latitude for good story-telling. Two outstanding films of the decade included *The Hustler* (1961), with Paul Newman as a traveling pool shark who meets his equal in Jackie Gleason, then regains his self-respect by beating him in a return match. A year later, there

----

All-time Sports Money-makers:
Until Rocky (1976) *was released, no sports film had earned more than four million dollars in grosses, that honor belonging to* Evel Knievel (1971), *with George Hamilton in the starring role. According to* Variety (January 3, 1973), *that movie was listed as All-time Top Domestic Box Office Grosser No. 569.*

----

was the brooding import, *Loneliness of the Long-distance Runner,* which sensitively portrayed the rebellion of a young man in reform school being used because of his athletic talents.

The 1970s saw some interest in basketball as a background for movies, although the vehicles that were released were almost uniformly bad. *Drive, He said* (1971), although directed by Jack Nicholson with Bruce Dern and Karen Black as stars, is a tedious piece of campus claptrap; *Maurie* (1973), which deals with professional basketballer Maurice Stokes' paralysis and friendship with white teammate Jack Twyman, could have been a reverse-polarity version of *Brian's Song.* It was, alas, ruined by a stilted script and direction by Daniel Mann that has all the subtlety of leprosy. A third film, *Mixed Company,* dealing with a basketball coach (Joseph Bologna) whose wife insists on integrating the family by adopting a black, an Indian, and an oriental child, is the type of cloying sentiment that can cause permanent brain damage if watched too extensively.

Not that sentiment and sports cannot mix—if done well. In fact, the 1970s seemed to prove that if you build your story around a character who has cancer, start your title with the letter B, and treat the whole thing with tender loving care, you can't miss. Viz:

1971—Brian's Song
1973—Bang the Drum Slowly
1975—Babe

CHAPTER 10—1881–90

1881

Winners: Baseball: Cap Anson's Chicago White Stockings again have a fairly easy time, winning the National League pennant by nine games over Providence. . . . *Kentucky Derby:* Hindoo. *Preakness:* Saunterer. *Belmont Stakes:* Saunterer . . . *Boxing:* In September negotiations begin for a title fight between heavyweights Paddy Ryan and John L. Sullivan. . . . Thirty-four-year-old Mike Donovan is still recognized as middleweight champion but is reported ready to retire. . . . *Football:* Michigan comes East to challenge strong teams, but loses to Harvard, Princeton, and Yale. Princeton wins seven games, ties two, Yale takes five and ties one and claims national championship on basis of better record.

Other Happenings: Founded: United States Lawn Tennis Association, May 21 . . . Dartmouth joins ranks of colleges taking up football, playing a two-game season with Amherst. . . . Baseball rule changes include reducing number of "balls" for a walk from eight to seven, and pitching distance is moved back to fifty feet, both rules that benefit the batter. . . . Most National League clubs, after a trying period, are out of the red, but on September 12 only twelve paying customers show up for the final game of the season between Chicago and Troy. A driving rainstorm does not help attendance. . . . Princeton wins Childs Cup, and Columbia's coxwain drowns shortly before an important race. . . . On September 10, the first major-league grand-slam home run is hit by twenty-four-year-old Roger Connor, first baseman for Troy. It leads to an 8–7 victory over Worcester. Connor hits only one other home run in 1881 but finishes an eighteen-year career in 1897 with a total of 136. . . . August 1: first national tennis championship is held at Newport, Rhode Island. Winner is Richard D. Sears, with W. E. Glyn the runner-up. Men's doubles are also played and won by team of F. W. Taylor and Clarence M. Clark. . . . College football rules committee declares that in the event of a tie, two additional periods, each of fifteen minutes, will be played. . . . English champion walker Charles Rowell again beats America's unofficial champion, Edward P. Weston, but many pedestrian-watchers declare that black Frank Hart and John Ennis are better representatives of the United States. . . . Weston, now over forty, seems to have no inclination to retire. . . . On November 9–10 the third America's Cup yacht race is held, the United States represented by J. Busk's *Mischief*, Canada by A. Cuthbert's *Atalanta*. *Mischief* wins the match, two races to none.

1882

Winners: Baseball: Chicago White Stockings have more competition in 1882 from Providence and Boston, but still manage to win third consecutive pennant. The National League suddenly finds itself with competition, however, the American Association having fielded teams in Cincinnati, Philadelphia, Louisville, Pittsburgh, St. Louis, and Baltimore. Offering Sunday baseball and beer in the parks, the AA has a reasonably successful year, Cincinnati winning the first pennant with a record of 55–25. . . . *Kentucky Derby:* Apollo. *Preakness:* Vanguard. *Belmont Stakes:* Forester . . . *Boxing:* On February 7, at Mississippi City, Mississippi, John L. Sullivan knocks out Paddy Ryan in nine rounds to become the recognized heavyweight bare-knuckle champion. . . . Mike Donovan announces his retirement from the middleweight championship, but continues to fight until 1891. . . . *Football:* Harvard has an excellent season, winning seven games and losing only one, but that loss is to Yale, which wins eight games with no losses and can logically claim the championship. . . .

Other Happenings: Minnesota joins the ranks of college football teams, playing a two-game season with Hamline. . . . At YWCA in Boston the first athletic games for women are held. . . . Founded: United States Intercollegiate Lacrosse Association, with teams representing Harvard, Princeton, and Columbia; Yale and NYU are admitted in 1883. . . . Founded: National Croquet Association . . . Started: St. Louis Derby . . . On September 6, members of the Boston Bicycle Club make their first trip of more than 100 miles. The course is actually 102½ miles long and is negotiated in twelve hours, six minutes riding time. . . . In January, the Nansen Ski Club is formed at Berlin, New Hampshire. . . . In vital football game between Yale and Princeton on November 30, James Haxall of Princeton kicks a sixty-five-yard placement. . . . Richard Higham, National League umpire, is found to have bet on outcome of baseball games and is removed. . . . Black pedestrian Frank Hart wins race at Boston, then loses at Madison Square Garden. . . . Baseball season closes with an aborted "World Series" between the pennant winners of the two rival leagues. Chicago and Cincinnati split two games, but then executive problems develop. Denny McKnight, president of the American Association, threatens to expel Cincinnati, and the first "World Series" expires before a winner can be decided. . . . No-hitters are pitched in both baseball leagues—by Larry Corcoran of Chicago (his second) and Tom Lovett of Brooklyn in the National League; by Tony Mullane and Guy Hecker, both of Louisville, in the American Association. . . . Bookmakers are allowed at Churchill Downs for the first time. They establish Runnymeade, who runs second, as 4–5 favorite, and set winner Apollo at 10–1. . . . On September 25, the first major-league doubleheader is held between Providence and Worcester. . . . The Williamsburg Athletic Club sponsors a twenty-four-hour race at the American Institute arena in New York to see how long a man can walk in one day. James Saunders covers 120 miles and collects a hundred-dollar cash prize.

1883

Winners: Baseball: In National League, Boston finally overcomes the Chicago domination, winning pennant by four games. In American Association's second season, Philadelphia and St. Louis engage in an exciting race, which sees the former win by a single game. . . . *Kentucky Derby:* Leonatus. *Preakness:* Jacobus. *Belmont Stakes:* George Kinney . . . *Boxing:* John L. Sullivan becomes a fighting champion, taking on Charlie Mitchell at the old Madison Square Garden, knocking the Englishman through the ropes in the second round and onto the boards in the third. Next on the list is Herbert Slade, a tall New Zealander, whom Sullivan also disposes of in three rounds. . . . *Football:* Yale, with a record of 8–0–0, outscoring the opposition 482–2, is generally recognized as champion.

Other Happenings: Founded: The New York Fencing Club . . . First intercollegiate tennis match is held June 7–8 at Trinity College, Hartford, Connecticut. Joseph Sill Clark of Philadelphia, representing Harvard, wins the singles. . . . On September 6, Chicago (NL) scores 23 runs, 18 in a single inning, against pitcher George "Stump" Weidman before he is removed from the game. Final score is Chicago 26, Detroit 6. . . . Hugh H. Baxter of New York AC becomes first to polevault over eleven feet, clearing bar set at eleven feet, one-half inch. . . . Parole becomes leading American money-winner among race horses by reaching $82,815. . . . Mrs. M. C. Howell wins her first archery title. Between 1883 and 1907, she wins the national championship for women seventeen times. . . . Baseball home-run champion of National League is William "Buck" Ewing of the New York Giants, who hits ten, the most he ever hits in a season during an eighteen-year career. In the American Association, Harry Stovey of Philadelphia hits fourteen. . . . No-hitters are pitched by Charles "Old Hoss" Radbourn of Providence (NL) on July 25 and Hugh Daily, the one-armed pitcher of Cleveland (NL) on September 13. . . . Summer of 1883 is perhaps first time in American history when even the most skeptical are convinced that baseball is truly the national game. In Philadelphia the game is played by two teams of handicapped railroad workers, one team composed of those with missing arms and the other of those with missing legs. The game goes five innings and is won by the one-arms, 34–11. . . . Orientals also play the game ("Lee Yaw eyed bat suspiciously and handled it very much as if it had been a flat-iron," one newspaperman writes), and so do women. Philadelphia is the scene of a contest between blondes and brunettes. . . . In the major leagues, meanwhile, infielder Arthur Irwin perfects the first fielder's mitt, while the bosses in the front office, more concerned with cash than comfort, agree to extend the "reserve clause" to the point where each club can protect eleven players from the evil of individual or collective bargaining. . . . Tragedy occurs during the summer when Matt Webb, first to swim the English Channel, is drowned while trying to swim the rapids at Niagara Falls. . . . On June 16, the first baseball "ladies' day" is staged by the New York Giants, both escorted and unescorted women being allowed into the park free.

1884

Winners: Baseball: For the first time in its history, the United States has three major leagues, the third being the Union Association, which lasts but a single season. Providence wins in the National League, New York (the Metropolitans or original Mets) takes the pennant in the AA, and St. Louis, with a remarkable record of 94–19, wins the UA flag. Altogether, there are thirty-four major-league teams, the highest in baseball history. There is even a World Series at the end of the season, Providence defeating the Mets in the best-of-five playoff, three games to none. But the owners cannot take the losses, and the UA quickly goes under. . . . *Kentucky Derby:* Buchanan. *Preakness:* Knight of Ellerslie. *Belmont Stakes:* Panique . . . *Boxing:* John L. Sullivan agrees to a rematch with Charlie Mitchell in June, but when he arrives at ringside, it is apparent that Sullivan has been drinking and is in no condition to stand up, much less defend his crown. (Instead of knee breeches, Sullivan is dressed in a tuxedo, which provides a clue to many.) Five months later, in another appearance against John Laflin, Sullivan is overweight and out of condition. But after Laflin punches the champion around a bit, Sullivan becomes so angry he wins on a third-round knockout. . . . In middleweight class, battle for championship takes place between Jack Dempsey, "The Nonpareil," and George Fulljames. On August 30, using heavy gloves instead of bare knuckles, Dempsey knocks out Fulljames in the twenty-second round. . . . *Football:* College champion selected by Helms Athletic Foundation: Yale (9–0–0).

Other Happenings: In billiards, 14.2 balkline is introduced, and in the first tournament, George Slosson wins and is declared champion. . . . Founded: United States Skating Association . . . The American Derby is first run at Washington Park, Chicago. The winner is Modesty, ridden by Isaac Murphy, black jockey who also rides Kentucky Derby winner Buchanan. . . . Fight against the anti-Sunday-baseball movement gains some momentum, with Sabbath games being played at Chicago, St. Louis, Cincinnati, Indianapolis, Louisville, Milwaukee, Dubuque, and Kansas City. . . . Scoring system in football is changed so that a safety is worth one point; a touchdown, two; a goal from touchdown, four; and a goal from the field, five. . . . On November 4, Wyllys Terry of Yale runs 115 yards from scrimmage to score against Wesleyan. Final score is 46–0. . . . On August 2, Maud S., a ten-year-old mare, is first to trot a mile in less than 2 minutes, 10 seconds (2:09¼). . . . Formed: International League, minor-league baseball circuit that flourishes for decades . . . First running of Suburban Handicap at Belmont Park is won by General Munroe, a six-year-old. . . . First ski tournament is held by Norwegian Americans in Minnesota. . . . John A. Hillerich devises the first Louisville Slugger baseball

bats. . . . Pitching rules altered so that hurler can use any windup so long as he faces batter at the beginning of it. . . . It is a great year for major-league pitchers. In National League, Larry Corcoran hurls his third no-hitter and Jim "Pud" Galvin his second; American Association produces four—by Al Atkisson of Philadelphia, Ed Morris of Columbus, Frank Mountain of Columbus, and Sam Kimber of Brooklyn, who has game called in the eleventh because of darkness. Union Association produces no-hit games by Dick Burns of Cincinnati and Ed Cushman of Milwaukee. . . . Robert Gordon of New York donates a trophy to promote curling competition between the United States and Canada. First competition is held in 1884, the United States winning over Canada, 36–28, at Montreal. . . . Number of balls necessary for a free ticket to first base is reduced to six. . . . Bicyclist Thomas Stevens announces that he intends to pedal around the world (oceans excepted) on his high-wheeler and promptly departs. . . . Sampling of football expenses, 1884: Receipts from Yale-Harvard football game, $650. Cost of Yale trip from New Haven, Connecticut, to Hanover, New Hampshire, $217. Training expenses for Yale squad for entire year, $25.

1885

Winners: Baseball: The Chicago White Stockings return to the top of the National League, edging New York by two games, and Charlie Comiskey's St. Louis Browns make a runaway of the AA race. At season's end, the Browns and White Stockings meet in a postseason playoff, but it is indecisive, each team winning three games and one game ending in a tie. . . . *Kentucky Derby:* Joe Cotton. *Preakness:* Tecumseh. *Belmont Stakes:* Tyrant . . . *Boxing:* Heavyweight bare-knuckle champion John L. Sullivan gives a return match to aging Paddy Ryan and is in the process of defeating him easily when New York police break up the show (still technically illegal). Several months later, Sullivan goes to Cincinnati for a bout with Dominick McCaffery, which ends with Sullivan's decision that he doesn't feel like fighting anymore after seven rounds. The fight is later awarded to the champion. . . . *Football:* College champion selected by Helms Athletic Foundation: Princeton (9–0–0), which outscores opposition, 637–25.

Other Happenings: Formed: Southern League, baseball, consisting of teams in Alabama, Georgia, and Tennessee. . . . Football is abolished at Harvard, officials at the school deciding by a vote of 25–4 that the sport is too violent. No games are played in 1885, but the sport returns the following year. . . . Founded: The National Association for the Advancement of Physical Education; the New York State Intercollegiate Athletic Association; the International Training School of the YMCA, Springfield, Massachusetts . . . On September 23, Goldsmith Maid, age twenty-eight, dies of pneumonia. During her long career, she made 426 appearances on the track and won 350 of them. Undefeated in 1871, 1872, 1873, and 1874, her total winnings amounted to $364,200. . . . In gymnastics, some new devices are first used: parallel bars, horizontal bars, Indian club swinging. . . . A hockey league is formed in Canada, made up of teams representing the Royal Military College, Queen's University, the Kingston Hockey Club, and Kingston Athletics. . . . On January 20, the ice yacht *Scud,* owned by Commodore James B. Weaver, races along the Shrewsbury River in New Jersey at a speed of 107 miles per hour. . . . Baseball rules permit using bat that has one flattened side. . . . First black team known as Cuban Giants starts play, men receiving ten to twelve dollars per week. . . . No-hitters are pitched in National League by John Clarkson of Chicago and Charlie Ferguson of Philadelphia. . . . Leading home-run hitter in National League is Abner Dalrymple of White Stockings; in American Association, Harry Stovey of A's—Dalrymple has eleven, Stovey thirteen. . . . When Buffalo club of NL folds at end of season, Detroit has eyes on four players—Dan Brouthers, Jack Rowe, Deacon White, and Hardy Richardson. When it develops that these players cannot be gotten separately, Detroit then purchases the entire Buffalo roster. . . . America's Cup yacht race is held after four years. On September 14–16, U.S. yacht *Puritan* defeats Great Britain's *Genesta,* two races to none.

1886

Winners: Baseball: Despite the Detroit Wolverines' having bought and kept a half-dozen good players from defunct Buffalo, the best they can do is make the pennant race uncomfortable for the Chicago White Sox, who win by 2½ games. In the American Association, the St. Louis Browns again find it easy going. They cap the season by defeating Anson's White Stockings in a best-of-7 playoff, 4 games to 2. . . . *Kentucky Derby:* Ben Ali. *Preakness:* The Bard. *Belmont Stakes:* Inspector B. . . . *Boxing:* John L. Sullivan again fights Paddy Ryan and knocks him out in San Francisco, the fight being watched by a twenty-year-old named James J. Corbett. . . .

Jack McAuliffe, lightweight, knocks out Billy Frazier in twenty-one rounds at Boston and claims the division championship. . . . *Football:* College champion selected by Helms Athletic Foundation: Yale (9–0–1), which defeats all opponents and leads Princeton in game called because of rain and darkness that is eventually ruled a tie.

Other Happenings: High football scores of season include Yale's 136–0 demolition of Wesleyan and Harvard's defeat of Exeter, 158–0. . . . There are eight hundred tracks in the nation at which harness races are run, but the Chicago Reform Alliance succeeds in closing down tracks in that area. . . . Great Britain and the United States stage an international polo match for the Westchester Cup. Played at Newport, Rhode Island, the contests are easily won by England, 10–4, 10–2. . . . On January 19, the Aurora Ski Club is formed at Red Wing, Minnesota. . . . Miss Woodford is leading money-earner of flat-racing horses, having won $118,270. . . . In baseball's first big-money deal, Chicago sends slugging Michael Joseph "King" Kelly to Boston for ten thousand dollars, despite his leading the league in 1886 with a .388 average. . . . Base rule change allows captain of home team to decide which team goes to bat first. Number of balls required for pass to first base increased to seven. . . . "Kilroy is here," they say in Baltimore, referring to the amazing twenty-year-old rookie pitcher with the Orioles of the American Association. Working with a team that comes in dead last, Kilroy manages to win 29 games, lose 34, and pitch a no-hitter against Toledo on October 6. He also strikes out 513 men, a phenomenal feat even considering the fact that the pitching distance is only 50 feet. Other no-hitters are pitched in the AA by Al Atkisson of the A's and Bill "Adonis" Terry of Brooklyn. . . . Another America's Cup yacht race is run September 9–11, General J. Paine's U.S. entry, *Mayflower,* defeating Britain's *Galatea,* two races to none. . . . It is the year of Brooklyn Bridge jumpers, Steve Brodie and Larry Donovan being the most celebrated of the daredevils. Brodie performs the leap as a publicity stunt but Donovan obviously decides he likes it and makes a near-occupation of leaping à la Sam Patch into various bodies of water in the United States and Great Britain.

1887

Winners: Baseball: Detroit Wolverines win first pennant in National League, then take on St. Louis Browns, winners in AA, in post-season barnstorming tour that becomes the longest World Series on record. The teams play fifteen games in practically every city of both leagues, the Wolverines winning ten and the Browns five. Public interest in the drawn-out affair is almost nonexistent, total attendance amounting to only 51,455. . . . *Kentucky Derby:* Montrose. *Preakness:* Dunbine. *Belmont Stakes:* Hanover . . . *Boxing:* John L. Sullivan goes to England to defend his crown (successfully) against Jem Smith and Charlie Mitchell, while Richard K. Fox of the *National Police Gazette* proclaims Jake Kilrain champion and presents him with an ornate "championship" belt. Sullivan's contempt for the pretender's belt is obvious when he says, "I wouldn't put it around the neck of a Gah-damn dog." In featherweight class, Ike Weir, the "Belfast Spider," is rated champion, but when he is challenged by an American, Harry Gilmore, he declines. . . . Tom Kelly, weighing 105 pounds, claims bantamweight title. . . . *Football:* College champion selected by Helms Athletic Foundation: Yale (9–0–0).

Other Happenings: Ellen F. Hansell wins United States outdoor tennis championship. . . . It is a rough year on the gridiron for Wesleyan University, Middletown, Connecticut. After losing an early game to Yale by a score of 106–0, the margin of defeat against Harvard is 110–0. . . . Football comes to Penn State, Cornell, and Notre Dame, which plays one game, losing to Michigan, 8–0. . . . Founded: the American Trotting Association . . . First run: The Brooklyn Handicap at Aqueduct, for three-year-old and over flat-racers. Winner is Dry Monopole. . . . Evidence that more and more Americans are participating in sports can be seen at Brooklyn's Prospect Park, where there are 416 tennis clubs composed of 6,000 players. During the year, more than 450 amateur baseball games are played on the Parade Grounds. . . . On February 8, the Aurora Ski Club holds its first classic, and Mikkel Hemmestvedt jumps thirty-seven feet. . . . Gus Guerrero runs ninety-three miles without stopping, near Easton, Pennsylvania. . . . First Dwyer Handicap—promoted by Philip and Michael Dwyer, former meat dealers who turn horsemen—is won by Hanover, winner of Belmont Stakes. . . . New baseball rule allows batter four strikes before he is out and five balls for free base. For one year only, bases on balls are counted as hit and charged as time at bat. Under this rule, James "Tip" O'Neill of St. Louis Browns bats .435 (if his fifty passes are not counted, his average is .375). . . . Professor Paul Boyton negotiates the Hudson River in his rubber dress, having failed to sell the product to foreign navies as a safety device. . . . For the third year in a

row, an America's Cup yacht competition is held, and the result is the same: The U.S. representative, *Volunteer,* defeats *Thistle,* the British entry, two races to none, September 17–30. . . . Matt Kilroy leads American Association pitchers with record of 47–20, and John Clarkson (38–21) of Chicago is tops in the NL, but no no-hitters are pitched. . . . Thomas Stevens, having traversed the world on his bicycle, gets a warm reception at San Francisco in January.

1888

Winners: Baseball: Charlie Comiskey's St. Louis Browns win once again in the American Association, their fourth consecutive pennant. In the National League, the New York Giants beat out the White Stockings, then defeat the Browns in postseason play, six games to four. The series is enlivened by Browns' owner Chris Von der Ahe hiring a special train on which there is so much partying the team is in no condition to play. Von der Ahe is not upset, however, terming the fifty-thousand-dollar binge "lots of fun and a good investment." . . . *Kentucky Derby:* Macbeth II. *Preakness:* Refund. *Belmont Stakes:* Six Dixon . . . *Boxing:* John L. Sullivan defeats Charlie Mitchell and returns home in triumph, but Sullivan drinks too much and ends up with a combination of typhoid fever, liver trouble, and a mysterious itch. . . . In bantamweight division, Tom Kelly and black George Dixon fight a nine-round draw. . . . *Football:* College champion selected by Helms Athletic Foundation: Yale (13–0–0), which outscores opposition, 700–0.

Other Happenings: During 1888 football season, Yale plays three games against Wesleyan, the aggregate score being Yale 227, Wesleyan 0. . . . Harvard also has good season, losing only to Princeton, 18–6. (Harvard and Yale do not meet, but Princeton drops only game to Elis, 10–0). . . . Football is also inaugurated at Duke and North Carolina. Duke plays only one game, whipping NC, 16–0. North Carolina plays another contest, losing 6–4 to Wake Forest. . . . John G. Reid, a Scot in Yonkers, New York, demonstrates the game of golf to some friends on February 22, then holds meeting on November 14 at which the St. Andrew's Golf Club of Yonkers is founded. . . . The gentlemen formulating baseball's rules change their minds again, deciding that a base on balls will no longer count as a hit or time at bat. They also reduce the number of strikes for a strikeout to three. . . . In minor-league happenings, the

Texas League is founded. . . . Also in the great Southwest, the first rodeo at which admission is charged is held on July 4 at Prescott, Arizona Territory. . . . In November James Oldreive attempts to walk on the Hudson River using a set of long flat shoes. He succeeds in traveling a few miles but gives up after a day or two. . . . Jack Williams, meanwhile, does succeed in swimming from Alton, Illinois, to St. Louis, a twenty-five-mile distance, with his hands and feet tied. . . . There are no no-hitters pitched in the National League, but the AA has four—by Bill Terry of Brooklyn (his second), Henry Porter of Kansas City, and Ed Seward and Gus Weyhing, both of Philadelphia. . . . In curling, the second Gordon International Medal competition is held, following a three-year hiatus, at Montreal, with Canada defeating the United States team, 68–28. . . . Charlie Ferguson, a twenty-five-year-old pitcher-outfielder for the Philadelphia Phillies, dies on April 29 of typhoid fever. . . . Tim Keefe, of New York Giants, pitches nineteen consecutive wins en route to his league-leading 35–12 record. . . . Football comes to USC, the Trojans winning a pair of games vs. the Alliance Athletic Club, 16–0 and 4–0. . . . Crouching start is first used by Yale track star Charles Sherrill at the Rockaway Hunt Club games, Cedarhurst, Long Island, May 12: Actor DeWolf Hopper first recites *Casey at the Bat*, beginning a long association with Ernest Thayer's poem.

1889

Winners: Baseball: The first Brooklyn-New York confrontation occurs when Brooklyn wins in the American Association and the New York Giants finish atop the National. The postseason playoff series consists of nine games, and in the first of them, played on October 18, the "seventh-inning stretch" is born. Brooklyn wins that game, but the Giants take the "World Series," six games to three. . . . *Kentucky Derby:* Spokane. *Preakness:* Buddhist. *Belmont Stakes:* Eric . . . *Boxing:* The much-anticipated Sullivan-Kilrain battle for the heavyweight championship takes place on July 8 in Richburg, Mississippi, Sullivan stopping Kilrain in seventy-five rounds. It is the last bare-knuckle fight of consequence in the United States. . . . In the middleweight division, George LeBlanche knocks out Jack Dempsey with a "pivot punch," but is never acknowledged as champion because of the supposedly illegal blow. . . . Featherweight "champion"

Ike Weir visits the United States and fights Frank Murphy of England, the bout ending in a draw after eighty rounds. . . . *Football:* College champion selected by Helms Athletic Foundation: Princeton (10–0–0).

Other Happenings: During 1889 season, enthusiastic baseball fans at Brooklyn number 350,000, a record high. But storm clouds appear on the horizon when the "Manifesto of Brotherhood of Baseball Players" is published on November 4. It means that players intend to form their own league as means of enjoying increased profits and freedom. The raiding of major-league rosters to supply Brotherhood clubs begins immediately. Al Spalding, meanwhile, takes a world tour with a baseball team of all-stars. . . . On June 19, William Ellsworth "Dummy" Hoy, a Washington outfielder who is deaf and dumb, throws out three runners at the plate in a single game. But Indianapolis beats Washington, 8–3. . . . On June 23, Louisville beats St. Louis of the AA to end a twenty-six-game losing streak, record for ineptitude in the major leagues. . . . Hanover is top-earning horse among flat-racers, having won $118,872. . . . Axtell, a champion trotting horse, is sold for $105,000. . . . The first professional tennis contest is held in the United States on August 29 at Newport, Rhode Island, an Irish pro named George Kerr beating Thomas Pettit, 6–3, 6–1, 6–1. They then travel to Springfield, where Pettit wins on September 21, 6–4, 2–6, 6–3, 6–4. The rubber match takes place at Brookline four days later, Kerr winning, 6–3, 3–6, 6–4. . . . In other racing quarters, Churchill Downs reduces the minimum parimutuel ticket from $5.00 to $2.00, and the first Realization Stakes for three-year-olds is run at Belmont, Salvator winning. . . . Football comes to Syracuse (which loses to Rochester, 36–0) and Iowa (which loses to Grinnell College, 24–0). . . . On July 8 the new Polo Grounds are opened, the baseball Giants celebrating with a 7–5 victory over Pittsburgh. . . . John Reid and Miss Carrie Low defeat Mrs. Reid and John Upham in golf's first mixed foursome. The match takes place on March 30 at Yonkers, New York. . . . Baseball fans see no no-hitters in 1889. . . . Jake Kilrain's timekeeper at championship bare-knuckle fight with Sullivan is none other than "Bat" Masterson.

1890

Winners: Baseball: Three major leagues in operation once again, the third known as the Players' League, which has drawn heavily from rosters of both the NL and the AA. King Kelly's Boston club wins in the Players', Brooklyn in the National, and Louisville in the American Association. The postseason series ends indecisively, each team taking three games, with one game tied. All three circuits lose money. "Not in the twenty years' history of professional club organizations," laments A. G. Spalding, "was there recorded such an exceptional season of financial disaster and general demoralization as characterized the professional season of 1890." . . . *Kentucky Derby:* Riley. *Preakness and Belmont Stakes:* For the only time in the history of the Triple Crown, the Preakness and Belmont Stakes are run on the same day at the same park. Because of a disagreement, the Maryland Jockey Club quits Pimlico, and the Preakness is held for more than a decade at Norris Park and Gravesend. On June 9, 1890, the second race is the Preakness Handicap, which is won by Montague. The fourth race is the Belmont and is taken by Burlington. . . . *Boxing:* Featherweight Billy Murphy arrives from Australia, defeats Ike Weir in San Francisco on January 13 to become champion, then outgrows class and retires. . . . George Dixon, an American black, defeats Nunce Wallace of England in London and claims the title. . . . *Football:* College champion selected by Helms Athletic Foundation: Harvard (11–0–0), which outscores opposition, 555–12.

Other Happenings: Yale football team appears wearing extra-long hair, a first on gridiron. . . . Virginia tops Randolph-Macon, 136–0. . . . Football comes to Army, which plays a single game and loses to Navy, 24–0. . . . Also joining the ranks of colleges with football teams: Pittsburgh, Colgate, Vanderbilt, Missouri, Washington, Ohio State, Kansas, Illinois, and Northwestern. . . . On May 8, Wee Willie McGill establishes a major-league record by pitching Cleveland to a 14–5 victory over Buffalo of the Players'

League. Willie is just sixteen years old. He retires at twenty-three, with a career mark of seventy-one wins and seventy-four losses. . . . On February 27, boxers Danny Needham and Patsy Kerrigan fight a hundred rounds—six hours, thirty-nine minutes—at San Francisco before bout is declared a draw. . . . Founded: United States Polo Association . . . Big-college football game brings together undefeated Harvard and Yale, Harvard eking out 12–6 victory. . . . Amos Rusie, nineteen-year-old second-year pitcher with New York Giants, leads major leagues in both strikeouts (345) and bases on balls (289). . . . John Weyhing, younger brother of star pitcher Gus Weyhing, dies at age twenty after two brief stints with Cincinnati and Columbus. . . . Bill Hallman, Philadelphia Phillie infielder, jumps to Players' League and brings suit against old club, charging that reserve clause is violation of individual rights, but court rules that Hallman and others legally sold themselves for life to baseball clubs. . . . Newport opens first golf course, and Denver holds a "cowboy tournament" or rodeo. . . . Track star John H. Owens runs the first sub ten-second 100-yard dash at Washington, D.C. Representing the Detroit Athletic Club, he is timed in 9.8 seconds. Another star runner of the time, Luther Cary, finishes second. . . . No no-hitters are pitched in first—and only—season of Players' League, but there is one in American Association—by Ledell Titcomb of Rochester. At the age of twenty-five, Ledell is washed up in the major leagues, however, retiring with a career mark of 30–29. Many other players fall by the wayside with the demise of the Players' League and, one year later, the folding of the AA. . . . Oyster Burns of Brooklyn bats in runs in twelve consecutive games. . . . Oliver S. Campbell, winner of the United States tennis singles championship, is the youngest to hold the title, at nineteen years, six months, and nine days.

Section III
The 1890s

CHAPTER 11—1891

As the first year of the decade later known as the "Gay Nineties" began, the United States was beginning to feel strong enough to take on the world. The American Indians had been all but officially eradicated at the massacre at Wounded Knee Creek two days before the year started; trouble was brewing in the Behring (as it was then spelled) Sea over sealing rights, the principals being Russia, Great Britain, Japan, and the United States; elaborate plans were being made for the American tour of the great actress Sarah Bernhardt, who was planning to immerse the culture-hungry nation in the mediocrity of such tear-jerking plays as *Fedora, Theodora,* and Sardou's *Cleopatra;* and an instructor at the Springfield, Massachusetts, YMCA was struggling with the problem of developing a new sport that could be played indoors during cold weather. (The problem was that Y members were becoming bored with noncompetitive sports or calisthenics, and membership was declining.)

BASKETBALL
Dr. James A. Naismith's response was to erect a couple of peach baskets at either end of the gymnasium, toss a soccer ball at his squad of eighteen players, and explain that the object was to put the ball in the basket. Thus began one of the few sports to have a crystal-clear origin.

BASEBALL
There seemed to be no lack of spectator sports for Americans, the year before being the first since 1884 when there were three baseball major leagues. The third was the "Players' League," which had been formed as an alternative to the monopolistic American Association and National League. (See "Leagues That Didn't Make It.") After giving both older organizations a good run for their money in 1890, the Players' League made headlines on the first day of 1891 by announcing that plans were being made to organize a circuit of clubs representing Philadelphia, Brooklyn, New York, Boston, Cleveland, Columbus, St. Louis, and Cincinnati to play Sunday baseball at twenty-five cents a game. The double promise of violating the Sabbath on a wholesale basis and at a wholesale price no doubt caused considerable anguish in the hearts of rival-league moguls.

LACROSSE
The first major sports event of the new year turned out to be the generally unfamiliar lacrosse. Normally an outdoor sport, of course, an exhibition at Madison Square Garden on a reduced playing area proved so popular that a tournament was arranged. The teams selected to participate were the Montreal team, "champions of Canada," the Caughnawaga Indian team, "professional champions of Canada," the Staten Island Athletic Club, the Druid Hill Lacrosse team of Baltimore, a team from Brooklyn, and representatives of the Manhattan Athletic Club. On January 9, the first exhibition was held before approximately six hundred paying customers, "including the band," and pronounced a qualified success. It was conceded, first of all, that most members of the audience were "Canadians who wanted to see their favorite game played under a roof in a glare of electric lights." The New York *Times* added that "to watch it for two or three hours in a place where the light prevents effectiveness of play to a large extent is tiresome," but the crowd seemed to have a delightful time. High point of the evening was a snowshoe race, three times around the Garden, by a quartet of Indians named Thorontentha, Ositakete, Tekari-

hoken, and Shohounasi. After that, the Indian team was defeated by Montreal, 3–1, and by a picked group of United States players, 5–1. "The Indians play a rough and earnest game," one reporter noted, "but throw and pass poorly."

ICE SKATING

In Holland, Joe Donoghue, the amateur skating champion of Canada and the United States, was engaged in a series of international races. On January 8, word was received that Donoghue had won both the mile race (in 3 minutes, ⅘ second) and the five-mile run (in 16 minutes, 2⅕ seconds). Immediately a fund was started on both sides of the northern border to purchase a suitable medal for Donoghue, who arrived back in America on January 24. A rousing reception awaited him at Newburg, New York. "For blocks the streets were thronged from curb to curb," one reporter wrote, "colored fires made the sky as bright as day, rockets cleaved the air, bands played, and the people yelled themselves hoarse as the modest-looking youth of twenty who left here a few weeks ago to conquer Europe on steel passed through the streets in a carriage, en route from the station of the West Shore Road to the rooms of the Whittier Athletic Club, under whose auspices the reception was carried on." At the club, Donoghue was treated to the inevitable speeches by local politicians and sports figures, shook more than a thousand hands, and enjoyed a magnificent banquet at the Orange Lake Club. In return, he gave them the prize punch bowl he had received at Amsterdam.

BASEBALL

Midway through the month of January, baseball was again in the news when a convention was arranged between owners of the National League and the American Association. It was generally agreed that, despite the Sunday baseball plans announced earlier, the Brotherhood or Players' League was dead, but there was still considerable animosity between the two established circuits. The purpose of the convention was to draw up a peace treaty among dissident elements, a matter of considerable interest. As a result, the exterior of the Fifth Avenue Hotel in New York was cluttered with a variety of types awaiting word from the convention delegates inside.

Late on the evening of January 13, A. G. Spalding emerged to report that nothing had transpired, but word leaked out that in order to assure the death of the Players' League, a proposal had been made to absorb the Boston, Philadelphia, and Chicago clubs into the American Association. It was also suggested that Toledo be kicked out of the Association to make room for the new teams, a situation that promised trouble. An interesting commentary on money values of the time can be found in the assertion of H. V. Ketcham, president of the Toledo club, that "the Association offered me seven thousand dollars to withdraw, but I would not accept the offer. Last season I lost twice that sum, and I propose to take a chance at making up my losses next season. I don't want money; I simply want to retain my franchise in the Association, and if there is any justice in the courts, Toledo will have a club in the Association." General Brinker, a representative of Rochester, another club reported to be on shaky ground, tried to make a fight of it, although he was less determined than Brinker. It was rumored also that Boston officials were unhappy at the suggestion that the Players' League franchise from Boston be absorbed rather than scrapped. For the next few days, charges and countercharges filled the newspapers, signifying not very much.

Need It Be Told That:
The "little" franchises of Toledo, Rochester, and Syracuse were sacrificed on the altar of expediency? By the summer of 1891, all were gone, along with Buffalo from the Players' League. Such was the price of making sure the Players' League remained dead.

WEIGHTLIFTING

Refreshing indeed, compared to all the official bombast, was news of a genuine strong man then just beginning to make headlines in America. His name was Louis Cyr, a twenty-seven-year-old native of Quebec who had set just about every record in weightlifting by 1891. On January 26, 1891, he received a championship belt at Queen's Hall, Montreal, a gift of appreciative citizens. Concerning his career, he indicated, "My first lift was in this way: There was a load of bricks—over a ton, I guess—stuck in a hole in the road and the horse couldn't pull it out. I was only seventeen, but was a big fellow, weighed 240 pounds, and I got underneath the cart and lifted it off the ground and got it out. Then I tried to see what I could do, and have never had any difficulty in lifting 2,500 pounds since then. My mother was very strong. She could always carry a barrel of flour upstairs to the second flat. She weighed 265 pounds. My father weighed 220, but could not lift more than other men." A teetotaler and nonsmoker, Cyr presented the perfect image of cleanliness for American youth of the 1890s, although he did create a bit of controversy by wearing his blond hair abnormally long. Such an affectation was not to emulate Samson, Cyr explained, adding, "It's attractive when exhibiting."

Louis Cyr's Dimensions and Other Feats:
Height: 5 feet, 10½ inches
Weight: 318 pounds
Chest: 60 inches

Once pushed a freight car up an inclined railroad track.

Lifted a platform containing 18 men—a total of 4,300 pounds.

Lifted 588 pounds off the floor—with one finger.

HORSERACING

About a month later, on February 19, the largest crowd ever seen at a horse sale assembled at Lexington, Kentucky, for a horse auction, and the largest amount ever paid for a horse was negotiated. A cold rain fell throughout the day, but it did not deter twenty-five hundred persons from attending, including the agent for John D. Rockefeller, America's most celebrated racing enthusiast. When Anteeo, a twelve-year-old trotter sired by Electioneer, went on the block, Rockefeller's agent and George C. Morgan of Chicago sent the bidding to $55,000, the largest price ever paid for a horse at auction. By contrast, fifty head sold for a total of $135,167, an average of $2,703 per horse. Rockefeller may have thought he was getting a bargain, but Anteeo's best days were behind him.

PEDESTRIANISM

March was enlightened by the exploit of a San Francisco woman named Zoe Gayton—who also called herself Zoreka Gaytoni Lopeazaro—a pedestrian who left the West Coast in August 1890 with the intention of reaching New York within 226 days for a wager of $2,000. On March 20, 1891, she arrived at Castleton, New York, well within the time limits imposed on her. The Poughkeepsie *Eagle* reported that she was suffering "somewhat from neuralgic pains in the head, and thought it best to remain at Castleton overnight." A week later, 213 days after leaving San Francisco, she arrived at New York's Grand Central Station, where she took a cab to the office of Richard K. Fox, publisher of the *National Police Gazette*. Described as "a

rather short woman of about thirty-six, of stout build," she was dressed in a long brown ulster and felt hat. In addition to the $2,000, Miss Gayton announced that she was certain of winning another $9,000 or $10,000 in side bets. She had started from San Francisco in a bloomer costume, "but that gave out, and she had to wear the ordinary skirt, which was very inconvenient when the wind was blowing."

According to the lady, when no other shelter could be found at night, she slept in a hut made out of railroad ties. Once, while in Nevada, $70 had been stolen from beneath her pillow, and near Battle Mountain she had been forced to go without food for three or four days "because none could be obtained from the section houses or Chinamen along the road." Despite these hardships, she averaged eighteen miles a day over extremely rough terrain. After resting and collecting her bets, Miss Gayton added that she was really an actress who had made her debut on the stage as a ballet girl in a Broadway museum. As for returning to San Francisco, she said, that was no problem. She would form a theatrical troupe and work her way back.

HORSERACING

The spring and fall of 1891 were enlivened by one of the strangest race-track capers in the history of American sports. It all began when Philip Dwyer, president of the Brooklyn Jockey Club, decided to up the ante for providing track information from his Gravesend course at the tip of Sheepshead Bay, Coney Island, to the various poolsellers (or bookies) in Manhattan. Off-track betting, of course, was illegal, but Dwyer and the Western Union Telegraph Company had worked out a mutually lucrative agreement whereby telegraphers stationed themselves at Gravesend, sending back odds, weights, jockey selection—whatever data were needed—to receivers at the bookie joints in New York City. For this favor, the bookies reimbursed Western Union's dummy organization, the Ditmas Company, and Dwyer also received the tidy sum of a thousand dollars per day.

Problems developed when Dwyer decided he wanted four thousand dollars a day, ostensibly because the New York *Times* and other crusaders had mounted a heavy propaganda campaign against the off-track betting system. The *Times* described the Manhattan poolrooms in deliciously grim detail, excoriating Peter DeLacy, the "king of the poolsellers," as a debauched Svengali leading America's youth down the path of sin. DeLacy was no such thing, of course. He was simply giving the public what it wanted eight decades before OTB became legal in New York. But as a businessman, DeLacy tended to be hard-headed. When informed of Dwyer's financial demands, he quickly conferred with the other leading poolsellers and told Dwyer to cut the telegraph wire if he wanted. The poolsellers would find ways and means of collecting the betting information on their own.

The battle that followed delighted most of the nation's readers who were able to follow it in the papers. It also provided a first-class side show for those patrons of Gravesend race course who eagerly went to the track to see what would develop. "If Phil Dwyer bars Western Union's operators from the track," Peter DeLacy warned, "we'll send in messengers to bring out news of each race."

The Wages of Sin, 1891

With typical nineties fervor, the New York Times *described the clientele of Peter DeLacy's poolroom, breaking them down into five categories. They were (1) "The office-boy type," who were presumably new to this life. The* Times *asked: "Are they stealing anything else but time? Where do they get the money to bet?" (2) The "tough boy," who was older than (1) but shabbier and more disreputable-looking. According to the* Times, *the tough boys seldom bet, but peddled tips to suckers, demanding a share when they won. (3) The clerk, who usually bet $2.00 or $5.00 a race. "How does he stand his losses?" the* Times *asked. "Information on this point can be found in the annual report of the Society for the Prevention of Crime under the head of 'thefts, embezzlements, and defalcations.'" (4) The ordinary workingman, described most poignantly as those who "wait with an anxiety that is actually painful until the race is called. . . . [They] leave after losing and return under the influence of liquor. (5) The "broken-down sports," or those "looking for a lead-pipe cinch."*

Philip Dwyer promptly cut the wire, sending the poolsellers and their henchmen into action. Their first retaliation was to rent an old hotel across from the track, where men stationed in the cupola could pick up a fine view of the course with a spyglass. Wires were run into the hotel and information telegraphed back to Manhattan with a minimum of delay. To provide detailed facts on scratches and weights, etc., DeLacy's men shuttled messages from the track to the hotel

with what seemed to Philip Dwyer maddening efficiency.

Dwyer retaliated by hiring more than one hundred Pinkerton cops, whose sole duty was to stop the runners, but eventually the runners became other than athletic-looking men. Old ladies and children began carrying the mail for the poolsellers, a situation that so infuriated Dwyer that he ordered his Pinkertons to close the gates at Gravesend as the first race started. The New York *World,* which opposed Dwyer's holy campaign to teach DeLacy a lesson, countered with blistering headlines. "Track a Prison," the paper reported, "thousands penned up on Brooklyn race course. Pinkerton sluggers club inoffensive citizens." The New York *Herald* described Dwyer as "King Phillip the First" and his cops as "chuckle-heads."

That did not open the gates, but DeLacy's men countered by devising a variety of other ploys. One group of toughs inside the park carried placards denoting horses in each race; as the official results were posted, they galloped across the paddock in the order of finish. Invariably the Pinkertons galloped after them, causing the crowd to roar with delight. The poolsellers also filled the park with hollow wooden balls, each capable of being filled with a message and thrown over the fence to a waiting confederate. Robert A. Pinkerton and his men duly stationed themselves, like center fielders, near the edge of the track, ready to pounce on any and all missiles headed their way.

The *Sun,* which was allied with the *Times* against the poolsellers, demanded that New York's police force, which was said to be collecting up to five hundred dollars a day protection money from each of the sixty illegal OTB establishments, make some arrests and thus force the bookies to fight a two-front war. The police complied, although some suggested it was halfhearted. On May 18, about a dozen arrests were made, including that of Charles Carlin at Sandy McDougall's place, Henry Kylie in Newton Allen's establishment, and James O'Brien in Barney Michael's parlor at 112 West 33rd Street. But the biggest fish was Thomas Wynn, who worked at Peter DeLacy's 33 Park Row office. Meanwhile, at the track, serious consideration was given to posting the wrong numbers on the board, thus confusing the poolsellers and perhaps making them pay large amounts on losing horses. At the last moment, the plan was discarded because it was reasoned more confusion might result inside the track than outside.

The spring meet finally ended, the Gravesend track in a state of siege, and both sides claimed victory. The *Times* described the long waits at the poolsellers' offices and grumbling of their patrons; Peter DeLacy acknowledged some delays but claimed that the bookies' pluck and cleverness had succeeded in getting nearly all the necessary information out of the track. The next test would come in the fall, both sides agreed, and the public waited eagerly to see what they had up their sleeves.

BASEBALL

In the meantime, a new baseball season had started, which was always an occasion for rejoicing after a long winter without later sports such as ice hockey or basketball. The fans of Washington, D.C., were especially excited in 1891, for they were getting not only a new team but also a new ball park. Located at Seventh Avenue and the boundary, no sod had been laid in either the infield or the outfield by Opening Day, but no one was particularly upset. President Harrison, along with members of the Cabinet and district commissioners, was expected to attend. Wilfred "Kid" Carsey, a twenty-year-old pitcher who had never made a major-league appearance before, was listed as the starter for Washington, but his lack of experience was just another example of the new beginning. "In honor of the occasion the Bostons, who will be the opposing club, will pitch Haddock, who is a former Washington player," wrote the Baltimore *Sun*. Well, the "Bostons" may have wanted to honor the occasion, but they apparently knew what they were doing, for George Haddock had a record of 34–11 in 1891, following that with a 29–13 year in 1892.

Washington's Record, 1871–89:

League	W.	L.	Year
National Association	16	15	1871
National Association	2	7	1872
National Association	8	31	1873
National Association	4	23	1875
American Association	12	51	1884
Union Association	47	65	1884
National League	28	92	1886
National League	46	76	1887
National League	48	86	1888
National League	41	83	1889
	252	529	

Despite the handicaps attending a new team, it was a festive day on April 13 when Umpire Jones yelled "Play ball!" in the presence of four thousand Washingtonians, who nearly filled the cozy ball park. As the Nationals walked onto the field, dressed in white uniforms with maroon stockings and trimmings, a roar of approval greeted them. Washington batted first, shortstop Gil Hatfield accepting a base on balls. He promptly stole second, and the crowd cheered heartily. But from that moment on, it was all downhill for Washington's new team. Ed Beecher, Fred Dunlap, and Joe Visner left Hatfield stranded. In the Boston half of the inning, Washington did receive one break of sorts when Dan Brouthers hit a long smash to center field. It struck a friendly oak tree and bounded back onto the playing area, forcing Brouthers to stop at third, where he remained. But luck ran out for the Nationals in the third when Boston scored on an error by Dunlap, two stolen bases, and a single. By the seventh, Boston led, 6–0, and young Carsey was in constant trouble. He "worked hard from start to finish," the papers noted, "but his curves were easily solved by Boston." The final score was 6–0. The 1891 Nationals staggered through the year to a 43–92 record—using four managers along the way—and Kid Carsey contributed fourteen wins and thirty-seven losses to the season.

Baltimore also had a new park that year, and the Opening Day festivities were, if anything, even more colorful. In fact, they assumed the nature of near-riot as more people than the park would hold attempted to elbow their way into the stands. "Quickness of access was the first consideration and comfort the last," wrote the *Sun*. "Men with plug hats, straw hats, and brimless hats; broadcloth coats, and coats of many kinds, representing all classes of society, packed into the cars until even the conductors were satisfied. . . . The horses had a hard time of it. Pant and tug as they might, frequent stops had to be made on account of the heavy loads they were obliged to draw. . . ." Enthusiastic young women were present in abundance, and shortly after the first customer—his name, William Williams, was taken down and preserved for posterity—entered, it was agreed almost by acclamation that the ten-thousand-seat park was magnificent.

Opposition was furnished, ironically, by the St. Louis Browns (who became the Baltimore Orioles sixty-three years later), and the end result was considerably happier for the hometown fans than Opening Day in Washington. John J. "Sadie" McMahon, twenty-three, a veteran of two seasons, was the starting pitcher for Baltimore, John "Happy Jack" Stivetts for the Browns. Charles Comiskey, playing first base for St. Louis, contributed a hit and scored "on a clever slide," but the hometown Orioles delighted their fans with an

8–4 victory. McMahon went on to lead the league with thirty-four wins that year, but Stivetts wasn't far behind, with a record of 33–22.

In the National League, Cap Anson's Chicago White Stockings opened up a lead but no one was discounting Boston or even the New York Giants, who played well at the beginning of the season.

HORSERACING

Horseracing fans turned their attention on May 13 to the running of the Kentucky Derby at Louisville, the seventeenth renewal of a race that had become a classic as early as 1891. But the event that year was severely criticized as a "farcical race throughout." Chief reasons for the carping of the press seemed to lie with the fact that the field was small—only four horses—and none of the mounts was a "quality" horse. Despite these drawbacks, the usual Derby crowd arrived at Churchill Downs, augmented by delegates of the state Democratic Convention, Scottish-American Convention, and Elks, who happened to be in town. "But there was no enthusiasm," according to the New York *Times,* because "there was nothing to get enthusiastic over."

Still, a race was run, with Balgowan breaking into the lead early. A mile later, Kingman was given his head and quickly passed High Tariff, Hart Wallace, and Balgowan to win by a length. "How very poor a race it was is shown by the fact that the time was 2:52¼," said the *Times.* "Spokane won the Derby of 1889 in 2:34½." The paper then went on to disparage the winner: "Kingman never did much as a two-year-old, winning only four of the sixteen races in which he ran, and being unplaced in three of his defeats. His victories were in purse runs at that, the lot he defeated being very commonplace. . . . The slow time of yesterday's race does not make him out anything more than an ordinary colt. . . ."

A couple of days later, some racegoers back East might have settled for a dull event—instead of the derailment of their Manhattan Beach train. The sixteen-car local had left Gravesend Track shortly after four o'clock and was in the vicinity of Parkville when the accident occurred. Apparently the rails had spread, a fairly common failing, but this was small consolation to the many bruised and injured. The cars were crowded and panic took hold of the passengers, many attempting to jump through the windows when it became obvious there was trouble. This, of course, only complicated an already nervous situation.

Then, as if the horses at Churchill Downs had somehow heard the Derby criticism and conspired to do something about it, Louisville fans were treated to "a race probably without parallel in the history of racing." That description is overstated, naturally, but the second race of May 16, 1891, did pack more than its share of thrills. Thirteen horses started, the favorite being Ed Leonard, carrying ninety-nine pounds. Until the horses arrived at the stretch, Ed Leonard seemed to be a sure winner, but when he was halfway down the stretch Comedy caught him and the pair battled so closely that the judges declared the race a dead heat.

After the third race, Ed Leonard and Comedy returned to the track for a runoff. Again they moved around the track neck-to-neck and once again they crossed the finish line so close together the judges called it a dead heat. Their time for this mile run was 1:45¼, only a quarter-second slower than their time for the second race.

The horses were allowed to rest until the final race, then repeated the two-horse race. This time Ed Leonard moved slightly ahead and remained in the lead, crossing the finish line with a time of 1:45½.

The entire year of 1891, in fact, was one of the greatest years for racing in American history, with more than $200 million being wagered at the combined tracks. The Belmont Stakes alone brought in $750,000, an astronomical figure for that time.

There was also a race on the high seas in May of 1891 as the United States flexed its muscles for the benefit of Latin America. Civil war had broken out in Chile early in the year, and a rebel steamer, the *Itata,* made its way to California for the purpose of obtaining arms. United States authorities, fearing possible complications, detained the ship at San Diego, but on May 6 the crew overpowered the guard and steamed out of the harbor. Americans were incensed as U.S. ships followed. The rebel ship would have to be overtaken and her crew punished. But day followed day without word that the *Itata* had been found.

BOXING

While awaiting the outcome of that international event, which ended a few weeks later when the ship reached Chile and surrendered to United States vessels, Americans discussed the heavyweight prizefighters. In May, the up-and-coming Jim Corbett had fought a sixty-one-round draw at San Francisco with black Peter Jackson, in what was considered the first important interracial fight. Actually, heavyweight Jake Kilrain, who had very nearly beaten John L. Sullivan, had fought and defeated George Godfrey, "the colored champion," two months earlier in the same city, San Francisco.

On June 16, Jake Kilrain's opponent was Australian heavyweight Frank Slavin; the scene, Hoboken, New Jersey; and the outcome, "one of the most brutal prizefight contests that has been seen in the vicinity of New York for many years." The newspapers called it a "disgrace to the community that countenanced it," which no doubt explained the contest's popularity.

Slavin, regarded as a comer, presented an interesting proposition to Kilrain, who was regarded as a fighter on the way down: Kilrain would receive five thousand dollars if he could avoid being knocked out for ten three-minute rounds, twenty-five hundred dollars if he failed. Thus the difference between Kilrain's pride and getting his brains scrambled was established at twenty-five hundred dollars.

The battle took place in a large frame building in the mud flats. An organization known as the Granite Association had assured that the authorities would not interfere with the fight. In fact, it turned out that the police were the most enthusiastic onlookers. "A more disreputable gang was never seen around a prize ring," wrote one reporter. "Fully five thousand uglies hung around the outside unable to gain admission. . . . Among the faces noticed were those of Tony Pastor . . . Umpire John Kelly, Maurice Barrymore . . . and Police Captain Reilly."

Because of the confusion, the participants did not get into the ring until 11:10 P.M. Kilrain, as it quickly turned out, was the favorite with the crowd, but the betting was 5–3 that Slavin would dispose of him within the specified ten rounds. William Muldoon the wrestler was Kilrain's second.

During the first round, Kilrain carried the fight to Slavin, hitting him several times about the head with great force. Slavin concentrated his attack to the body, specifically the region around Kilrain's heart. The crowd thought Jake was getting the better of it as the first round ended, but those closer to the action, and also the more knowledgeable, knew that Slavin was doing more damage.

In the middle of the second round, Slavin applied the pressure. He "gave Kilrain a couple of crushing body blows that seemed to turn his stomach. Before he had a chance to recover, Slavin dealt him a terrible left-hander on the neck and followed it up instantly with one squarely in the face. Kilrain fell to the floor like a dead man. His nose was broken, his jaw cut, and the blood was streaming down over his body. Everyone thought that the fight was over, but, urged on by his seconds, Kilrain staggered to his feet and was saved from more punishment by the ringing of the bell on that round."

During the next three rounds, Slavin pummeled Kilrain from one side of the ring to the other, knocking him down again and again. But every time Jake somehow managed to get to his feet, return a couple of clumsy blows, and hold on. The sixth, seventh, and eighth rounds developed a pattern, Kilrain hugging Slavin as long as he could, then using his powers of endurance to avoid being knocked out.

Sensing that Jake had a chance to win the five-thousand-dollar prize if not the fight, the crowd cheered as he stumbled out for the ninth round. Slavin approached, more determined than ever to finish Kilrain, raining blows that forced him into a corner. "There he dealt him a terrific heart blow and followed it up with a punch on the side of the head that knocked his antagonist down and split his ear. He lay on his back for a second or two, and then struggled to his feet again. He was hardly up before Slavin rushed toward his tottering form, gave him a swinging right-hander on the side of the head, and knocked him to the floor again. It was the knockout blow. Kilrain had been down for fourteen seconds when the bell was rung and the night given to Slavin."

As soon as Slavin's hand was raised in victory, the police quickly moved toward the ring and hustled Kilrain's rooters out of the building before they could find something to protest or fight about. "The evicted ones took possession of every beer saloon along the road to the ferries," a reporter wrote in conclusion, "and made Hoboken a place for decent people to avoid until a late hour in the morning."

TENNIS

From the gross to the genteel, one had to move only a few miles to Chestnut Hill, Pennsylvania, where lawn tennis, only a decade and a half old in America, was being practiced by members of both sexes. On June 26, a great crowd assembled at the Wissahickon Inn for the championship round of the Ladies' National Tournament. The finalists were Miss Mabel Cahill, challenger, and Miss E. C. Roosevelt, holder of the crown in 1891. Every stroke, according to the papers, "was liberally applauded," although both women tended to rely on their staying powers in the backcourt. "The lobbing," one sportswriter-critic said, "was beautiful and the sideline planing true and swift. Miss Roosevelt's backhand strokes were always accurate, and every now and then Miss Cahill would get in a forehanded 'Lawford' stroke that would have done credit to Hobart himself. . . . Every point was fought to the end with wonderful tenacity. . . ." The final result was a victory for Mabel Cahill by a margin of 6–4, 6–1, 4–6, 6–3.

TRACK AND FIELD

Another "respectable" sport engaging the attention of spectators and athletes was track and field. By 1891, the sport had amassed a considerable body of statistics proving that athletes were getting better every year. For some reason this amazed even those involved, such as runner Lon Myers, who established several records as an amateur before turning professional. "The boys keep on improving all the time," Myers said in an 1891 interview, "It's a hard matter to explain this, but it is nevertheless true. Some years ago, a man who could do 0:10¾ for 100 yards was considered a flier, but every club has one or more men who can beat that now. To-day we have two men who can, with fair conditions, beat 10 seconds. Both Owens and Cary accomplished that feat in the championships at Washington last summer. . . . In the long-distance races the boys have shown the most improvement. Last summer A. B. George ran the mile 12 seconds faster than he did the previous year. He comes from a family of runners and is a good one. . . . A man has got to keep working all the time in order to hold his end up. You can't afford to lay off for a season or two and then face some of the men of to-day. If you do, you are likely to run unplaced."

Track-and-field Events	Record 1883	Record 1890
100-yard run	:10¼	:09⅘
220-yard run	:22⅘	:22⅕
440-yard run	:52⅛	:50
880-yard run	2:04⅖	1:59⅕
One-mile run	4:36⅘	4:24⅘
Five-mile run	26:47⅖	25:37⅘
Long jump	21'7½"	23'3⅛"
High Jump	5'8½"	5'10"
Pole vault	11'0½"	10'6"
16-lb. hammer throw	93'11"	130'8"
56-lb. weight throw	25'1¾"	32'10"
Putting the shot	43'0"	43'9"

The reporter who interviewed Myers added that, "Year after year athletes break records, and naturally the question suggests itself. When is this recordmaking going to stop?" Nearly a century later, it is still a valid question.

BASEBALL

By July of 1891, baseball had recaptured the attention of many Americans, thanks to an interesting three-way race in the National League, Chicago, Boston, and New York taking turns knocking each other off as the weather grew hotter. (There were temporary diversions, of course. On July 3, Brazilian journalist Dr. Silva Jardin created quite a stir when he bent over the crater of Mount Vesuvius and fell in; on July 7 four men were electrocuted at Sing Sing, the largest group execution via the chair to that time; and on the thirteenth, at Washington, Ohio, a team of society girls challenged a team of men to a game of baseball. The men, gallantly playing left-handed, won by a score of 22–15.) By midsummer, many players were tired of riding the hot trains from city to city. On the other hand, the season was only 130 games long and no contests were played at night. So the daily grind continued, delightful for the fans as the race tightened, a joy when they were able to see the kind of game pitched by Amos Rusie on July 31.

Miles Traveled by 1891 Clubs: (a sampling)	
Boston	10,678
Brooklyn	8,795
Philadelphia	9,455
Cleveland	8,883
Chicago	11,220
Cincinnati	10,109
Pittsburgh	9,003
New York	9,052

Earlier that month, the twenty-year-old Giant hurler had injured his hand and was taken out of the rotation. When the Brooklyn Bridegrooms arrived on Friday the thirty-first, however, he asked to be sent in. Captain Buck Ewing agreed. Facing Rusie on the mound was Bill "Adonis" Terry, who had won twenty-six games in 1890 but was having his troubles in 1891.

The way Rusie pitched, it need not have mattered what kind of year Terry was having. In the words of one inspired reporter, "He [Rusie] sent the balls over the plate with rare speed, and he curved the sphere in a manner startling to behold." In the very first inning, Rusie's teammates staked him to a 1–0 lead when George Gore walked, was forced at second by Mike Tiernan, who in turn moved to second when Terry walked Charley Bassett. Jim O'Rourke bunted safely to load the bases. Bassett then scored on a sacrifice bunt by Roger Connor.

For five innings, it was an exciting match as neither team scored and Brooklyn continued to beat Rusie's pitches into the dirt or pop the balls to catcher Dick Buckley. (Despite his "rare speed," Rusie struck out only four batters in nine innings.) Only one man was able to hit the ball out of the infield, and that was a routine fly to Gore in center.

A Short Glossary of Nineteenth-century Baseball Jargon:

Hippodrome	To throw a game
Air ball	A fly ball
Chicagoed	Shut out
Muffin match	Game with many errors
A Wide	A called ball
Stroke	Base hit
The square	Home plate
Striker	Batter
Crack	Expert

When the Giants scored two runs in the sixth inning and three more in the seventh, it became a matter of waiting to see if Amos Rusie could retire the Bridegrooms without a hit. When the final out was made, the young man had his no-hitter, although it was far from a perfect game. He walked seven and another got on base via an error. But the game was the only no-hitter of the season.

Four days later, interest was understandably high as Rusie took the mound again. He pitched New York to another win, but couldn't duplicate the no-hit performance. The score was 9–4, Rusie yielding seven hits.

After that glorious moment, New York's pitching became unsettled, and it seemed that Boston and Chicago were about to slip away from the Giants. In desperation, Manager Jim Mutrie obtained thirty-five-year-old Bob Barr and inserted him in the lineup on August 13 against Cincinnati. Barr gave up a run in the first inning, then struck out the side in the second. But the very next inning, he was struck on the head by a ball thrown by a policeman in the grandstand and knocked unconscious. Reported the New Yorks *Times* with some pique: "The officer in the absence of a victim to club was probably anxious to show his strength. He threw the ball with all his might and it caught Barr behind the ear. He dropped like a log and did not recover his

National League—the First Three Clubs on August 13, 1891:

	W.	L.	G./Bh.
Chicago	55	38	—
Boston	52	38	1½
New York	49	36	2

senses for over five minutes." Apparently Barr never recovered his pitching skills after that, for he was 0–4 with the Giants in 1891, his last season in the major leagues. With only two solid pitchers, Rusie and John Ewing, New York's prospects were difficult to view with optimism.

The month of August 1891 was marked by the deaths of two famous people, the first being James Russell Lowell, editor, poet, abolitionist, and former U.S. ambassador to Spain. The other departed was Japanese wrestler Matsada Korgaree Sorakichi, who had built quite a following among Orientals in the United States since he came to America in 1883. Two years later, Sorakichi had defied convention by marrying an American woman named Ella Lodge, a Quaker. Their marriage was a stormy one, Sorakichi being taken to court numerous times on the charge of assaulting his wife with intent to kill. Moralists of the period insinuated that the rocky road was a sign from God that race-mixing just wasn't in good taste.

In between marital crises, Sorakichi found time to come to grips with some of the West's best wrestlers, including Carl Abs, "the German Giant"; James Quigley, champion of the New York Police Department; Duncan Ross of Cleveland; Ernest Roeber, "the Adonis of the Bowery"; and Evan Lewis, who was the first to use the appellation "Strangler Lewis," largely as a result of the tactics he used on Sorakichi in their 1886 bout. Lewis won that contest, breaking the Japanese wrestler's leg for good measure. After that, Lewis moved from city to city, finally succumbing to tuberculosis at the age of thirty-two.

HORSERACING

Early in September, at Independence, Iowa, two world harness-racing records were broken on the same day. Allerton, owned by C. W. Williams, trotted the mile in 2:10, making him the fastest-trotting stallion in the world. (The time equaled that of the famous gelding Jay Eye See and was only a quarter-second slower than the best time by Maud S., the famous mare.) Meanwhile, Direct, a black pacing stallion, covered a mile in 2:06, the fastest time by any trotter or pacer.

September also brought horse-racing fans Act II of the Philip Dwyer-Peter DeLacy confrontation at Gravesend race track. During the summer, Dwyer had escalated the war by constructing a 65-foot fence at the track, completely obscuring the view from the hotel nearby. But just one day before the September 15 opening, Peter DeLacy's men swung into action. Groups of carpenters suddenly moved into the hotel, bringing with them sections of wood already partially nailed into the shape of platforms and extensions. Within hours, a tower 42 feet above the cupola was in place, complete with four telegraph wires and six operators.

Dwyer countered by increasing the height of the fence, but the bookies added ever new and inventive methods of signaling race information to the poolroom telegraphers. One woman fanned a baby in code; others moved handkerchiefs in significant ways; still others twirled their mustaches or smuggled pigeons into the park. Pinkerton men raced from one customer to another, trying to determine who was an innocent patron and who was a tool of the bookies. One of the more spectacular events was the erection of two poles, the taller 120 feet, from which solo telegraphers sent down whatever information they could spot inside the park. A touch of class was added by one operator's pulling a miniature American flag from his pocket and nailing it to the top of his station as the crowd marveled at his nerve.

Peter DeLacy's Code:
In order to speed up telegraphic information on bets, Peter DeLacy invented a crude code that assigned words for every conceivable situation. A $1.00 bet, for example, was "bacon." A $7.00 bet was "banana." A bet on the nose was given the code word "gab"; a "place" bet, "gammon." Even the jockeys had their own words, the famous Ed "Snapper" Garrison being known as "Pension," and John Lambley as "pestilence." The various horses were given numbers from 1 to 100 in the daily paper and assigned code words ranging from "Fabian" to "Flapper" (No. 99) and "Flaning" (No. 100).

Thus a sample betting request might read: "Lancet Balcony Gander Image Fable," meaning, "At Sheepshead Bay Track, put $5 on a third-place finish in the second race on horse No. 2."

Despite all this activity, it soon became apparent that Philip Dwyer's persistence was slowly paying off. Delays at the poolsellers' halls became commonplace and there was frequent misinformation. One telegrapher, for example, had his horses engaged in a stretch run that lasted two minutes; other establishments posted signs explaining that the management could not be responsible for incorrect information. Finally, Dwyer's Pinkertons countered the high-altitude telegraphers by raising their own series of poles within the

park, each equipped with a flapping sail designed to obscure vision.

But the most ingenious scheme of all came midway during the fall meet, when suddenly for a period of several days, nearly every bit of data concerning odds and weights and winners flowed effortlessly from park to poolroom. "By some mysterious means," the *World* wrote, "whether by necromancy, juggling, or what, the 'pool rooms' yesterday seemed in their normal condition. Betting was in full swing on all the events at Brooklyn. Jockeys, with the exception of the first race, were listed. No one seemed to know how the information from Brooklyn had been obtained."

Eventually the scheme was discovered, but not before the poolsellers thoroughly embarrassed the Pinkerton forces. The means of sending information was inside the tall silk hat of a barouche driver, who every day would sit with his carriage on the infield grass while the young people he brought to the park picnicked nearby. What was not known for several days was that the driver, one C. S. Pearsall, was also a telegrapher and that his hat contained a light bulb attached to a battery concealed in the carriage. By leaning his hat forward, Pearsall was able to flash code messages through a hole in the top to DeLacy's men stationed on poles or in trees outside the park.

The fall meeting came to end with Robert Pinkerton arresting Pearsall (and receiving a blow to the head by a parasol-wielding woman, it was said) as the crowd threatened the law officers with cries of "Lynch 'em!" No one was seriously hurt, fortunately, and the fall meet ended with both sides claiming victory.

Whatever Happened to Dwyer and DeLacy?
Philip Dwyer continued to prosper until his death in 1917, racing a string of horses until New York Governor Charles Evans Hughes banned horseracing after the end of the 1910 season. Peter DeLacy carried his conviction (that if betting was legal at the track, it should be legal off) into the courts, attempting to have the race courses closed after 1893, when his own pool rooms were shut down. Nevertheless, he prospered until his death in 1915, when he reportedly left an estate of one million dollars to his heirs.

FOOTBALL
With the coming of cooler weather, football fans of the period began to hope they would

be able to see a renewal of the first service academy game, which had been played between Army and Navy in 1890. That contest had not been intended to inaugurate a long series. As a matter of fact, as the fall of 1891 approached, there was considerable doubt that the two schools would be able to get together on the gridiron for a second time. Neither academy placed a great deal of emphasis on athletics other than the intramural variety, and because comparatively few members of the American population had been in the armed forces prior to 1891, there was less rooting interest than in later years. But red-hot football fans, of whom there were many, were eager to see any new rivalry continued. In addition, the West Point cadets were anxious to avenge their 24–0 drubbing of the previous year. Scheduling practices were so casual during the 1890s, however, that few dared predict as late as October whether or not the two "trade schools" would have a game the following month.

GOLF

While waiting for the final disposition of this situation, the New York *Times* devoted nearly a full column to explaining the mechanics and rules of a new "outdoor pastime which appears to be gaining favor in this country." The players, according to the article, "are called 'golfers,'" and the game's central objects, "a white, hard rubber ball 1¼ inches in diameter . . . and a number of golf clubs . . . An American boy would describe any of the golf clubs as a 'rattling shinny stick.' . . . Play is started from the grounds at the head of the links. The game consists in putting the ball into . . . a number of tin basins called goals, about 4½ inches in diameter around which a space about 6 feet in diameter, called a putting green, is leveled off. . . . In England and Scotland, where the game is very popular, it is the practice to have a small boy, called a 'caddie,' to follow each player and carry his or her golf clubs, handing out the particular club required when the ball is located and the next strike is to be made." As for the course itself, it was explained that natural obstructions such as a "clump of bushes, piles of stones or logs," or even "a railroad" were desirable. For those interested in taking up the sport, all three of the golf clubs in the vicinity of New York City—Yonkers, Meadowbrook, and Shinnecock Hills—were cited.

BASEBALL

The exciting pennant race in the National League, meanwhile, had turned into a morass of anger, threatened lawsuits, and charges of thrown games. Chicago, which had led throughout most of the season, was finally overtaken by Boston late in September. The Boston Beaneaters, as they were known in 1891, came to New York for a five-game series that would be decisive for both Chicago and Boston, the Giants having faded quickly after the high point of Amos Rusie's no-hitter. But the White Stockings were hoping New York had enough left to help them.

To the chagrin of Chicago Manager Cap Anson and Owner James A. Hart, the Giants not only completely folded during the series, but also declined to play some of their best men. Amos Rusie, for example, was excused from the entire series and didn't pitch once; Roger Connor missed three of the games because of an injury, but instead of replacing him with .347-hitting Buck Ewing, who was available, Manager Mutrie inserted Lew Whistler, a .245 hitter. In addition, regular second baseman Danny Richardson was removed for the final two games without explanation. "Were I under indictment for murder," said James Hart, "with the circumstantial evidence against me as strong as it appears against the New York club, I should expect to be hanged." With that, Hart announced his intention of investigating the matter, through the Supreme Court if necessary.

League officials established an investigating committee in a hurry as baseball fans in all three cities seemed about to rise up in anger. Conducted by E. B. Tallcott and J. W. Spalding, the investigation consisted mainly of a presentation of excuses rather than a systematic examination of the underlying reasons. The absence of Amos Rusie, for example, was explained away by the pitcher's statement that he wanted to go home, felt he had had a good year, and asked to leave after hurling both ends of a doubleheader on September 26 against the Brooklyn Bridegrooms. Why owner John B. Day allowed his best pitcher to disappear prior to a crucial series was left uncovered. The remaining explanations dealt mainly with injuries. On the basis of the report, New York players and officials were exonerated of "throwing" charges. It was an unpleasant ending to an otherwise entertaining season.

National League Season, 1891; Final Results—First Three Clubs:			
	W.	L.	G./Bh.
Boston	87	51	—
Chicago	82	53	3½
New York	71	61	13

The brief interval between the ending of 1891 baseball and the full swing of the football season was enlivened by still another international incident between the United States and Chile. On the afternoon of October 16, 120 seamen from the U.S.S. *Baltimore,* then in Valparaiso Harbor, got drunk in the True Blue Saloon and started a riot when a Chilean spat in an American's face. Two sailors were killed in the brawl and seventeen injured. Rather than trying to break up the melee, the local police pitched in on the side of the Chilean rioters.

Americans were outraged as the days dragged by without an official apology from Chile or even an expression of regret. Young Theodore Roosevelt promised to lead a cavalry charge against the Chileans if he was given permission, and a Kentucky congressman predicted that a million men would answer the call to arms if President Harrison declared war. Eventually the war talk simmered down as diplomatic notes started to be passed back and forth, but many Americans remained on fire to "go South and show them what we're made of."

FOOTBALL

The spirit of derring-do may have infected the Yale football team of 1891, for rarely has a squad gone through an entire season with such complete command of the opposition. It began on September 30, when Yale defeated Wesleyan by the kindly score of 28–0; following that warming-up exercise, twelve more games were played with a variety of teams with the result being the same in every case. Admittedly, some of the opposition was hardly championship caliber, but Pennsylvania, Harvard, and Princeton had fairly good teams. Incredibly, Yale's scoreless record was not the first time in its football history that such a feat had been accomplished. The trick had been performed in 1888 as well, but that team was adjudged inferior to the 1891 squad,

which was led by pulling guard "Pudge" Heffelfinger, the first lineman to become famous in the game of football.

The season was financially profitable as well. For the "big" game of the year, the grand finale with Princeton, attendance reached a high of forty thousand. Each school earned seventeen thousand dollars, a princely sum then that would seem like chicken feed a few decades later.

Army and Navy, following their inaugural game of 1890, met again on the football field, the second game of the series taking place at Annapolis on November 28. Apparently feeling was high, for five Navy men and four members of the Army squad had to be carried off the field before it was over. "A broken rib, a gashed scalp or two, a sprained knee here and there, with occasionally a missing portion of an ear, were distinguishing features of the day's sport," one reporter commented lightheartedly.

Neither team had prepared for the game by meeting top-class opposition. Navy had warmed up by beating the Kendall College deaf-mute team of Washington, but the game had been halted at the end of the first half because one of the teams had to catch a bus. Army had tackled the likes of Stevens Institute. Despite a glaring lack of experience, both teams had enthusiasm and determination.

Army outweighed Navy by 175 to 170 and the average age of the West Pointers was 22 to Navy's 19. The straight-ahead V formation was the standard play at that time, and within five minutes of the opening kickoff, Army had moved to the Navy goal. A plunge into the end zone made the score, 4–0; a kicked goal added two more points to make it Army 6, Navy 0.

Not long afterward, Army regained the ball and tried a trick play. Center S. P. Adams passed the ball to the halfback P. W. Davidson, who spun in the direction of the other halfback, E. J. Timberlake. Somehow Davidson managed to smuggle it "into Timberlake's arms without being detected, running straight ahead in the meantime clasping an imaginary ball in his arms with half of the Navy team striving to down him. While this was going on, the nimble Timberlake spurted sixty good yards of three feet each, and the Army again went crazy."

The opportunity was lost on a fumbled snap from center and before long Navy was on the Army one-yard line. Because any man on the team was entitled to carry the ball, Navy gave it to M. E. Trench, a guard who was the heaviest man on the field, and he plunged over the goal line. The score was tied following the kick, 6–6.

Yale's Football Record, 1891				
September 30	Yale	28	Wesleyan	0
October 3	Yale	26	Crescents	0
October 7	Yale	36	Trinity	0
October 10	Yale	46	Williams	0
October 14	Yale	28	Stagg's Team	0
October 24	Yale	36	Orange Athletics	0
October 31	Yale	38	Lehigh	0
November 3	Yale	70	Crescents	0
November 7	Yale	76	Wesleyan	0
November 12	Yale	27	Amherst	0
November 14	Yale	48	Pennsylvania	0
November 21	Yale	10	Harvard	0
November 26	Yale	19	Princeton	0
Total:	Yale	488	OPPOSITION	0

Army scored again, then took the ball from Navy. Again the crisscross trick was worked to perfection, inspiring both a long run and a piece of purple prose from a writer covering the game. "Davidson," he wrote, "advanced over the ground like a shot from a gun. Bagley [Navy's quarterback] alone stood between him and the goal. Would Bagley stop him? He would. Down into the bowels of the earth went Bagley, Davidson, and the ball. . . ."

It was a gallant effort, but it did not prevent Army's winning by a score of 32–16. The series was tied.

The football season over, sports enthusiasts looking about for something to watch found meager pickings. One enterprising promoter staged an international tug-of-war tournament at Madison Square Garden in December, but as one paper noted, "it was not a tremendous success, for it was decidedly monotonous to the two thousand or so spectators present." That comment was made on December 22. By the next evening, the crowd had diminished to fifteen hundred. By the twenty-seventh, when the event closed, even the promoters admitted it was "a flat failure." McNeil and Sanderson, the two gentlemen sponsoring the event, blamed the failure partly on the number of free tickets given away by policemen at the gate, partly on "the fact that New Yorkers do not realize the quality of such an exhibition." Regardless of the reason, watching a team of men attempting to pull seven feet of rope from another team just never caught on.

One worthwhile event did take place on December 20, 1891, but one had to go to Sohmer Park in Montreal to see it. There, before a crowd of ten thousand, Louis Cyr, the strongman, was fitted with a special harness, which was attached to four draft horses, two to his right and two to his left. With his feet planted wide apart, Cyr gave the word and the teams pulled in opposite directions. The rules of the contest stated that if Cyr's arms were dislodged from his chest or he lost his footing, he would lose. The horses, urged on by grooms, slipped and slid but failed to budge Cyr an inch in either direction. Even taking into account the fact that the teams were pulling against each other, it was a remarkable feat of strength, and a fitting close to the year.

As for Chilean-American relations, it need hardly be added that the smaller nation began the new year of 1892 with an appropriately abject apology, for these were the "good old days" when the Great White Fleet was about to give the rest of the Western Hemisphere a dose of *Pax Americana,* whether they liked it or not.

CHAPTER 12—OTHER LEAGUES

In 1871, when the National Association of Professional Baseball Players sold its franchises for ten dollars each, it was not easy to find nine takers. And for a while afterward, as gambling took hold and the first league folded only to be reborn as the National League, which is still playing today, baseball and spectator sports in general were considered bad business investments.

By 1880, that situation had changed to a large degree. Businessmen regarded baseball as a good way to make money. Land was cheap, as was the cost of constructing a suitable arena. The players themselves were not greatly overpaid, and the game did seem to be catching on as the national pastime. Trolley lines were being built everywhere, connecting neighborhoods and communities dozens of miles apart. And along the route ball clubs sprang up. Soon, even at admission prices of fifty and twenty-five cents, baseball became a speculator's dream. The number of minor-league teams grew and so did the clamor for admission to the major league. But then as now, the men who ruled the roost were not particularly eager to let others into the business. After starting the new National League with teams representing cities such as Harrisburg, Louisville, and later Indianapolis and Milwaukee, the league seemed to settle down during the period 1879–82, only two franchises being changed.

In order to protect their assets, the National League owners in 1880 passed the first reserve clause, which in effect bound players to their clubs for life—unless the owners wanted to release them. This not only eliminated the possibility of collective bargaining and thus kept players' salaries low, it also made it more difficult for new teams to build by signing up stars from established clubs.

THE AMERICAN ASSOCIATION: BORN, 1882; DIED, 1891.

Discontent among players with the reserve clause and discontent among fans in cities ignored by the National League combined to make the climate favorable for the establishment of a second league in 1882. New York had not had a club in the major league since 1876. Nor had Philadelphia. Cincinnati, a hot baseball town, had been replaced in the National League by Detroit following the 1880 season. St. Louis had been shunned since 1877, as had Louisville and Baltimore. When attempts to rejoin failed, a Colonel Harris of Cincinnati succeeded in persuading a coterie of businessmen to pledge money for a new circuit.

By late 1881, backing for the new league began to appear. A constitution was drawn up that was similar in many respects to that of the National League, but innovative in others. Chief among the differences were the American Association's determination to charge twenty-five cents for admission rather than fifty cents; to play ball, where allowed, on Sundays; to permit the sale of alcohol in the parks; and to pay umpires a regular salary rather than fees. (The decision on alcoholic beverages, by the way, was arrived at because of the high percentage of beer manufacturers backing the clubs.)

As the spring of 1882 approached, the inevitable trade war started. Two of the first players to be involved were John (Dasher) Troy and Sam Wise, a pair of infielders who had played in a total of twelve games for Detroit the previous year. Troy and Wise signed with the AA's Philadelphia and Cincinnati clubs, respectively, but were then persuaded to return to the National League before playing a single game in the enemy's uniforms. The

---

Some Sample Salaries of the Period (Average per Man)

Boston (10 men) 1878	$1730
Boston (10 men) 1879	$1430
Boston (10 men) 1880	$1377.50
Providence (16 men) 1882	$1278.51
Providence (15 men) 1883	$1446.66

National League Cities, 1882		American Association Cities, 1882	
Chicago	Cleveland	Cincinnati	Pittsburgh
Providence	Detroit	Philadelphia	St. Louis
Boston	Troy	Louisville	Baltimore
Buffalo	Worcester		

incidents served to anger owners on both sides of the fence. National Leaguers waved the threat of a blacklist while AA members warned that they would take matters to the courts if necessary.

Soon it became evident that the AA would be no pushover for the old National League. Negotiations had fallen through for the fielding of a New York team, but even so, the six cities in the AA had a half million more population than the eight cities in the NL.

The first year turned out to be a victory for the AA, even the Cleveland *Leader* admitting that five cities of the rival circuit outdrew Cleveland, which sported the top attendance in the older league. In addition, the American Association developed several pleasing ballplayers who thrilled the fans and became household names the same as Cap Anson, Harry and George Wright, Jim O'Rourke, Pud Galvin, and King Kelly of the National League. The combination of Sunday baseball at lower prices and liquor at the ball park was obviously hard to beat, for it was not long before rumors of peace talk were heard. In the meantime, negotiations continued for the entry of New York into the American Association, which was brought about in time for the new league's second season. By that time, an "arrangement" had been hammered out in which the National League agreed to recognize the AA and the two leagues work on a co-operative basis. There were complaints on

both sides, naturally. Some said the AA had "eaten humble pie" and given in to the National League when it was not necessary. Hard-liners on the opposite side felt that the AA would fold after its second year. But at least one newspaper praised the settlement as being the beginning of a new epoch in baseball history. In that two leagues in any sport —or one league with two divisions—has always provided more franchises and fan interest, it seems this view of the situation was accurate.

The American Association lasted ten years, being dominated by the St. Louis Browns most of that time, and fans of the 1880s were able to see several postseason attractions that were in effect the first "World Series." In 1882, Cincinnati (AA) and Chicago (NL) played two games, each team winning one contest. After the next season, the Philadelphia Athletics of the AA were scheduled to play Boston of the NL, but they did so poorly in several October exhibition games against other clubs that the Series was canceled. But in 1884, a three-out-of-five Series was played, and for the next six seasons after that, postseason Series of varying lengths were held. One of the most bizarre was a traveling World Series played in 1887 between the St. Louis Browns and Detroit Wolverines. It took in eleven cities, Detroit winning the eighth and decisive game on October 21 in Baltimore. Despite the fact that the teams had

---

Some American Association Players Who Went on to Stardom:

CHARLIE COMISKEY *Played eight seasons for St. Louis in the AA, five more with other major-league clubs, managed for a dozen years, and was elected to the Baseball Hall of Fame in 1939.*

TONY MULLANE *Known as "the Apollo of the Box" because of his natty dressing, Mullane won 30 games, lost 24 for the Louisville club in Cincinnati (all AA) before finishing his career in the National League, 1890–94. His lifetime record was 285 wins, 215 defeats.*

JOHN (BID) MCPHEE *Was a premier second baseman for 18 years, 1882–99, with only two teams, Cincinnati in the AA and Cincinnati in the NL. He accumulated 2,291 hits in 8,324 times at bat for a .275 lifetime batting average.*

PETE BROWNING *Nicknamed "the Gladiator," Browning spent 13 years in the major leagues, most of them with Louisville of the AA. In 1887 (the year a base on balls was credited as a hit) he batted .402 but did not lead the league. (That honor went to Tip O'Neill.) In 1882, he did lead the AA with an average of .382. His lifetime average was .343.*

The First Seven World Series:

Year	American Assoc.	National League	Games	Winner
1884	New York "Mets"	Providence	3	Providence
1885	St Louis	Chicago	7	Undecided
1886	St Louis	Chicago	6	St Louis
1887	St Louis	Detroit	15	Detroit
1888	St Louis	New York Giants	10	New York
1889	Brooklyn	New York Giants	9	New York
1890	Louisville	Brooklyn	7	Undecided

In 1885, during the seventh game, Charlie Comiskey took his St. Louis teams off the field when he did not like an umpire's decision. At the time, St. Louis led in the Series, three wins to two losses and one tie. The umpire forfeited the seventh game to Chicago.

In 1890, each team won three games and one ended in a tie.

played only nine games, the rest of the Series was continued until all fifteen contests had been played (and the admission money collected). Notwithstanding its good start, the American Association lasted only until the early 1890s. After surviving an onslaught by another league, the Union Association, the AA and NL almost met their collective match in 1890 when the ballplayers themselves formed the Players' League. From that three-way conflict only the National League survived.

THE UNION ASSOCIATION: BORN, 1884; DIED, 1884

The newspapers had the gist of the information right although some of the details were faulty. "A new base-ball association, to be known as the Union League of Base-Ball Clubs is to be organized," the papers noted on September 9, 1883. "The parties interested here have been working the scheme quietly since the beginning of the present season, and representatives are expected to be present from Richmond, Virginia, Washington, Baltimore, Wilmington, Philadelphia, Trenton, New York, Brooklyn, Albany, Troy, Boston, and Hartford, Connecticut. Only eight clubs will be admitted."

The battle had been drawn, thanks to a St. Louis millionaire named Henry V. Lucas, whose ambition was to challenge Chris Van der Ahe's American Association team in his hometown and bring down the reserve clause. (The AA had conveniently forgotten about the objection to the rule after attaining respectability.) And so on September 12, 1883, Lucas and a group of businessmen met at Pittsburgh to form the "Union Association of Base-Ball Clubs." Amid the legal language of the constitution and bylaws adopted, one paragraph stood out:

"Resolved, that, while we recognize the va-lidity of all contracts made by the League and American Association, we cannot recognize any agreement whereby any number of ball-players may be reserved for any club for any time beyond the terms of their contracts with such club."

Members of the baseball establishment derided the new entrepreneurs as "dead-beats," "played-out bummers," and quickly gave the new league the nickname "Onions." Forgetting that the American Association had been financed by brewers to a large extent, the same charge was leveled at the Union Association membership. Blacklists were promptly instituted and raiding began, despite promises on both sides that the situation would be handled in a gentlemanly and legal manner. One of the more colorful jumpers was Tony Mullane, who had attained a 35–15 pitching record with St. Louis (AA) the year before. "The Count of Macaroni," as he was sometimes called in addition to other nicknames, Mullane turned down Von der Ahe's offer of

Some Who Crossed the Line:
Among those players who jumped from the National League and American Association were Jack Glasscock, Larry Corcoran, Hugh (One-arm) Daily, George Schaffer, Emil Gross, Fred Dunlap, Charlie Broidy, Jim McCormick, Charlie Sweeney, Tommy Bond, Jack Gleason, William Taylor, Davy Rowe, Sam Crane, George Bradley, and Tony Mullane. The list totaled about forty. Bond, Corcoran, Mullane, and Taylor subsequently returned to their original leagues as Dasher Troy and Sam Wise had done two years before.

nineteen hundred dollars to remain with the Browns in November 1883, signing with the rival St. Louis Unions for twenty-five hundred dollars. But before the season started, Mullane jumped back to the AA Toledo club.

When he made his debut in St. Louis early in May, wearing a Toledo uniform, it was only natural that fans favoring both the AA and the Union Association should display their wrath on the young, brilliant, but fickle pitcher. When Mullane came to bat, he was hissed and jeered violently. He responded by doffing his cap, bowing, and then struck out.

In many respects, the season of 1884 was one of the most remarkable in the history of American baseball. Before it was over, no less than thirty-four cities had participated (some only briefly, it is true) in major-league baseball. It was the year when Ed Williamson of the Chicago Nationals hit twenty-seven home runs, a record that stood for thirty-five years until broken by Babe Ruth in 1919; it was the year in which two black players, Fleet and Weldon Walker, played as a brother team for Toledo; when a man with an amazingly durable arm, Old Hoss Radbourne, won sixty games and lost only twelve to lead Providence to a pennant; and it was the season of baseball's first "official" World Series.

It was also the year when a team set a record for starting off with a bang that has never been equaled. The St. Louis Unions were a very good team in a very mediocre league, no doubt about it. Only two of their players failed to find a place with major-league teams when the Union Association disbanded. Until that fateful day, they proceeded to make a shambles of the pennant race. For a while, it seemed that Baltimore and Boston might make a race of it, but the St. Louis squad then engaged Boston in a series at St. Louis that made a mockery of the standings. On May 21, they took their nineteenth game without a defeat, although the contest was not without its unpleasant side. A slow drizzle fell early, and after five innings, with St. Louis ahead, 5–2, both teams wanted Umpire Holland to call it. When he refused, Tommy Bond, who was pitching for Boston, became angry and proceeded to toss the ball gently at the batters instead of throwing it. The batters, in turn,

pounded the stuffings out of Bond, scoring seven runs in three innings to win, 12–3. The next day St. Louis won its twentieth straight, by a score of 16–4. On May 24, 1884, a crowd of five thousand saw the streak come to an end, Boston winning, 8–1.

Despite such artistic accomplishments on the part of one team, the Union Association was soon in trouble. Six weeks after Opening Day, Altoona became the first franchise to fold. Kansas City took its place, but in August Chicago quit along with Philadelphia. St. Paul and Wilmington joined the league, the latter being subsequently replaced by Milwaukee. The league truly resembled a revolving door by the end of summer.

With franchises being moved around and St. Louis dominating the game on the playing field, those who might have backed the Union Association soon lost interest. No one knew how much Lucas or the league lost. Lucas himself admitted having dropped $17,000 by the end of the year. Estimates of the UA's total losses ranged from $50,000 to $250,000. In any event, the players soon realized that they were on a sinking ship, and many tried to woo their way back into the AA or NL. Most of the better ones succeeded, for then as now, baseball owners have never let principle stand in the way of getting a good player.

As for the "pennant race" of that one year, St. Louis finished with a record of 91 wins and 16 losses. Cincinnati, second with a very respectable mark of 68–35, was nevertheless 21 games out of first place. When it was all over, no one regretted it, least of all members of the American Association, which had suffered more than the National League. Just the year before, it had expanded to a twelve-club circuit, and the added competition for players and increased salaries put even more pressure on the weaker franchises. Six weeks before the end of the season, Washington had to be replaced by Richmond.

It was, on the whole, an interesting but disastrous year, especially for those fans of Washington, who found themselves in the terrible predicament of having not one, but two miserable teams.

THE PLAYERS' LEAGUE: BORN, 1890; DIED, 1890

The brief and sad history of the Baseball Players' Brotherhood and the league of 1890 is the story of a good idea torn to pieces by the forces of greed. To be sure, the players themselves were more than a little greedy. But for the most part, they were discontented primarily with measures such as the blacklist, reserve clause, arbitrary fines, and overall inability to bargain.

The Union Association Standings: May 12, 1884					
Team	Won	Lost	Team	Won	Lost
St Louis	12	0	Chicago	3	4
Baltimore	10	3	Washington	2	12
Boston	10	3	Philadelphia	2	12
Cincinnati	9	4	Altoona	1	11

The Categories:

A—$2,500 per season. (*Top-quality ball-player who also co-operated with management in all respects.*)

B—$2,250 per season. (*Very high-quality ballplayer with perhaps a tendency to drink or carouse.*)

C—$2,000 per season. (*Somewhat above-average player who co-operated or top-quality player who tended to be a club-house lawyer.*)

D—$1,750 per season. (*Marginal player with maximum co-operative spirit. Or maximum-ability player with minimum degree of co-operation.*)

E—$1,500 per season. (*New player or veteran on the way out.*)

(NOTE: *The "job descriptions" were never spelled out as precisely as above but they seemed to work out in more or less this way, the overriding consideration being a player's co-operativeness.*)

It was the overwhelming greed of the owners, on the other hand, that nearly destroyed baseball as it was ready to enter the third decade as America's premier professional spectator sport. And the greediest, and most stubborn, owner of all was St. Louis' Chris Von der Ahe. Not satisfied with having dominated the AA during the 1880s, Von der Ahe came to the conclusion in the fall of 1888 that the players were making too much money. "The Brooklyn club," he said, "will pay Caruthers $5,000, Lovett $4,000, Foutz $3,500," he exclaimed in amazement, adding that for a pennant-winning team, his own salaries for the year had averaged only a bit more than $3,000 per man (including Charles "Silver" King, his star pitcher, whose record in 1888 was 45–12).

Not long afterward, the other owners fell into line. It was, after all, easy to agree with Von der Ahe, especially if some system could be established whereby there were salary scales that rewarded the better players while still holding salaries down as a whole. Finally a classification plan was put into effect that separated players according to their ability, "habits, earnestness, and special qualifications," meaning ability to go along with the whims of management, do a superb job on the field, and lead clean private lives.

The classification plan, which could hardly be kept from the players, infuriated them, but there was little they could do but play out the 1889 season. In fact, John Montgomery Ward, who had played baseball at Penn State and had a law degree, advised his fellow players to go along with the system that year. No sense, he said, pulling a strike that would be organized hastily and tend to alienate the fans and press more than necessary. Instead the year was spent talking with the owners, trying to get them to understand just what the players disliked about the system.

One gets the impression that the owners nodded and somehow managed to sleep with their eyes open, for they did not budge a single inch. The fact is that they seriously doubted that the players would cut themselves off from their main source of income; nor did they believe they would hold together as a group once a few of them received offers well above the maximum.

So no attempt was made to alter the classification system or find a more equitable alternative to the reserve clause. Faced with owner recalcitrance, the players met at the Fifth Avenue Hotel, New York, on November 4, 1889. It was rumored that they planned to strike, but actually the men had a more daring plan in mind. They would organize their own league, one in which all shared the profits and shared in the governing responsibilities. Eight Brotherhood cities were named in which enlightened "capitalists" had put up twenty

The Players' League—1890

City	Manager	Previous Club
Boston Beaneaters	King Kelly	Boston (NL)
Brooklyn Wonders	Monte Ward	New York (NL) (1884)
New York Giants	Buck Ewing	New York (NL)
Chicago Pirates	Charlie Comiskey	St. Louis (AA)
Philadelphia Quakers	Ben Hilt	None
Pittsburgh Burghers	Ned Hanlon	Pittsburgh (NL)
Cleveland Spiders	Jay Faatz	Cleveland (NL)
Buffalo Bisons	Jack Rowe	Pittsburgh (NL)

thousand dollars each to get the project under way. Despite this, as well as the fact that the new league would include most of the better players in the NL and the AA, the press was skeptical. "The scheme is like all other co-operative schemes that overlook the necessity of business ability in a business enterprise," the New York *Times* wrote. ". . . The prima donna who undertakes to manage her own company, or the star actor who hires or buys his own theater, or the author who becomes his own publisher, commonly comes to grief, and we fear this will be the fate of the ball players if they put their scheme into execution."

But there was no backing out. In fact, the players deliberately arranged the schedule of the new league so that there was a maximum number of conflicts, and except for Buffalo, every city selected had a team already in either the National League or the American Association. It would be, as some newspapers warned, truly a war to the death. Von der Ahe, true to his own stubborn nature, added that it would be a holy war, capital against labor, anarchy against law and order, etc.

The Players Were Confident:

As shown in this November 4, 1889, exchange between Al Spalding, representing the establishment, and Fred (Dandelion) Pfeffer, twenty-nine-year-old Brotherhood advocate:

SPALDING *"You fellows don't know how to run a league. It takes brains as well as money to run baseball."*

PFEFFER *"That's so, Mr. Spalding. But the brains of your organization have always been among the players. When backwoodsmen and old fossils can make money in baseball, there is a bright prospect in store for us."*

During the winter of 1889–90, the players met frequently and planned ways to prevent defections back to the established leagues. The owners, meanwhile, tried their best to lure back some of the ringleaders with higher salary offers, but were largely ineffective. Just how unsuccessful they were can be shown by glancing at the roster of the 1889 Pittsburgh Nationals (then known as the Alleghenys) as compared to that of the same franchise in 1890 (then known as the Innocents) after being raided by the Players' League. In 1889, the Alleghenys were hardly a great team, but they did manage to win 61 games while losing 71. Then, during the winter, seven of eight

starters left along with three of four pitchers. Forced to fill ten vital positions, Pittsburgh signed untried rookies, managed to get hold of a few veterans with a small amount of time left in them, and generally looked to the sandlots. Those viewing the 1890 outfit characterized it as "a crowd of stiffs," with only "four ballplayers in the lot."

Not surprisingly, the 1890 Pittsburgh team was disastrously poor. It won only 23 games all season, dropping 113. In some ways, it was amazing that they managed to complete the schedule, for the players that were selected to fill the spots of the 1889 team were largely untalented. So bad was the situation that Billy Sunday, a weak-hitting utilityman in 1889, was forced into playing 86 games (second highest of his career) before being traded to Philadelphia. Of the regular eight starters of 1889, only Doggie Miller remained during the war of 1890. As for the pitchers, Pud Galvin, a 23-game winner, and Gerry Staley, who won 21 in 1889, both left, leaving only Bill Sowders and a group of, to use the polite term, "stiffs."

The battle for attendance was won by the Players' League, although not by a great margin. All three leagues lied about the number of people who came to see their games, but one thing is certain: Less people came to see the three leagues combined in 1890 than came to games played by the two leagues the year before. Why? A writer named Caspar W. Whitney of the *Fortnightly Review* wrote not long afterward that "the people were . . . bored with newspaper recrimination and tiresome warfare. . . . It went from bad to worse until, in the last year or so, the better class of American sportsmen appear to have lost all interest in professional baseball; in fact, professional sports in the United States is dead."

If that view turned out to be premature, it was true that only two teams in the Brotherhood—Boston and Chicago—made money, and the National League was reported to have dropped between $200,000 and $300,000. Hard-hit by raiding from both sides, the less affluent American Association had sufficient strength to last only one more season, expiring in 1891.

The "peace" that ensued was a joyful victory for the capitalists who had scorned the players' efforts to share the fruits of their labor. The New York *Times* gloated that the rebellious players "could have made very much more money and have had a very much better time by subjecting themselves to the tyranny of the league than by rising up against it. . . ."

Who Killed Baseball?

(A piece of free verse written shortly after the 1890 season summarized the view of the press, which, by and large, co-operated with National League owners by giving the Players' League less than full coverage.)

Who Killed Baseball?

Who killed baseball? "I," said John Ward: "Of my own accord, I killed baseball."

Who saw it die? "We," said the slaves; "From our own made graves, we saw it die."

Who'll make its shroud? "I," said Buck Ewing, "I'll do it well, I'll do the sewing, I'll make its shroud."

(Six more questions and answers using the names of six other Players' League representatives)

And now all the cranks have forgotten the game
And the ex-slave perceives that D. Mud is his name.

THE U.S. LEAGUE: BORN, 1912; DIED, 1913
The majority of baseball historians do not consider the U.S. League a genuine threat to the established American League and National League of the early twentieth century. This view is correct, but because it started with the avowed intention of becoming the third major circuit and played some games, the U.S. League should be mentioned as the fourth attempt to move into baseball's big time. (The fifth attempt, actually, considering the successful American League, which changed its name from Western League in 1901.)

William Abbott Witman of Reading, Pennsylvania, was the first president of the U.S. League, and his motto was, "There can be no such thing as too much good baseball." Early in 1912, without a great deal of planning and less financial backing than previous efforts to break into the majors, the U.S. League was born. Part of the haste was caused by rumors that still another league, known as the Columbian, was about to form. On January 20, 1912, a meeting was held at the Hotel Imperial in New York to announce that all was going well and that a field for the New York nine had been secured at 145th Street and the Harlem River. The other franchises included Brooklyn, Reading, Cincinnati, Pittsburgh, Richmond, and Washington. It was reported that groups from Chicago, Baltimore, Louisville, Cleveland, Buffalo, and Philadelphia were also interested.

At first, the established leagues, through their spokesmen, were inclined to look benevolently upon the newcomers. "The two leagues [Columbian and U.S.] are not outlaws," said August Herrmann, chairman of the National Baseball Commission, "they are independent bodies within their rights and not trespassing on ours."

One day later, Thomas J. Lynch, president of the National League, took it upon himself to retract what Herrmann said. "You can take it from me," he charged, "these new leagues are outlaws and know they will get no recognition from us."

Despite the chilly atmosphere, Witman and his backers continued to make plans for a May opening. By March, Cleveland had been taken in as the eighth team, and it was confidently predicted that parks would be ready for all teams in time to start the 126-game season. The managers of several teams were announced and the names included at least three former major-leaguers. An air of excitement was added by the disclosure that both New York area franchises of the new league planned Sunday ball games. A few years before, Brooklyn tried playing National League games on the Sabbath but had been stopped by the police.

Big-league Stars Managing U.S. League Teams:
Washington—George Browne, outfielder (1901–11)
Cleveland—Jack O'Connor, catcher (1887–1910)
Pittsburgh—Deacon Phillippe, pitcher (1899–1911)

Later in March, however, the U.S. League seemed about to die before playing a single game. New York franchise holder Charlie White announced that he was resigning because plans for securing a playing area in Manhattan had fallen through. Panic followed. Then it was discovered that no schedule had been drawn up. Panic turned to despair. But early in April, when it was announced that the New York club had leased the Bronx Oval for five months, hopes for the new circuit were revived. Brooklyn, meanwhile, dropped out of the league but Chicago entered.

On May 1, 1912, teams representing New York and Reading played the first U.S.

League game at the Bronx Oval, 163rd Street and Southern Boulevard, before a crowd of about 2,500. The New York players were "nattily attired in cream-colored uniforms, trimmed with narrow black braid, black stockings with white stripes, and black caps. . . . The Reading players wore uniforms of bluish gray with black trimmings." As for the game itself, it was marked by wildness on the part of the pitchers, but when the batters swung they usually connected. The result was a wild contest in which Reading jumped to a four-run lead, then went to pieces in the field, allowing New York to tie the game at 7–7. After ten innings the score was still tied, 10–10, at which time Umpire Henry Tone called the game because of darkness.

A Clue to the U.S. League's Unimportance:
By this time in United States history, the President threw out the first ball of the new baseball season (in 1912, still William Howard Taft, the man who inaugurated the habit).

The man who threw out the first ball of the 1912 U.S. League opener was James A. Delehey, clerk of the New York Supreme Court, Special Term, Part IV. Music was provided by a band from the Catholic Protectory of New York.

Two days later, a second contest was held at Bronx Oval, Reading winning this time by a score of 13–8. Only about 250 fans attended. And by the end of the month the league was in severe trouble. Cleveland's franchise folded, was hastily replaced by St. Louis in the standings, and New York's team was put up for sale. Its backers blamed the weather, which forced numerous postponements, and poor play, which sent the team to the bottom of the U.S. League standings.

By June 1, it was rumored that William Witman was about to file for bankruptcy. In the meantime, some games had been called off in Cincinnati because of lack of attendance, and Richmond dropped out of the league, its players complaining they had not been paid. And on June 4, 1912, the bank account of John J. Ryan, owner of the Cincinnati franchise, was garnisheed when fourteen players filed separate suits for twelve hundred dollars in back salary. A hastily called conference in early June, attended by only six club representatives, failed to resolve any of the major financial problems, although there was some brave talk about continuing to play with new franchises. On the field, one or two games a day were reported at the bottom of the sports pages, then a game every other day, and then, finally, no more contests for the year 1912.

The following spring, however, the U.S. League tried again, opening on May 10, 1913, at Morris Park in Newark. But the weather was unexpectedly chilly and only about a hundred persons saw the game, "if the band and ground attachés were counted in." Even the modest guarantee of fifty dollars for the visiting New York team (winners, 3–1) could not be raised. The next day, when the weather improved slightly but the crowd did not, the game was forfeited to Newark. (Sensing the lack of interest in Newark, the New Yorkers had caught a train to New Brunswick in order to play an exhibition game and earn a few dollars.)

The U.S. League—A League of Losers:
Regrettably, the U.S. League did not turn out to be the training ground of a baseball great such as Babe Ruth, who might have saved the league from total ignominity by the very presence of his name. To a large degree, the players were old-timers such as Charlie Malay, thirty-three, who had played one season (1905) at second base with the Brooklyn Nationals. Then there was Joe (Gummy) Wall, thirty-nine, who played a total of forty games in 1901–2 with two National League clubs, and Matt Broderick, thirty-six, who came to bat three times for the 1903 Brooklyn Su-

perbas. (He failed to hit.) After the U.S. League failed, these men retired permanently from the game as active players.

The league also had some "promising" young players, but none went on to great heights. Frank Bruggy, catcher, later played from 1921–25 with three major-league teams; Del Young played in the Federal League and with the 1919 Cincinnati Reds; and outfielder Hack Eibel signed on with Cleveland for the remainder of 1912. He also was on the roster of the 1920 Boston Red Sox. Other than that, the U.S. League died with hardly a ripple in the pool.

But the saddest story of the 1913 season belonged to Baltimore, which joined the league during the winter. On May 11, the Baltimores won their opener at Lynchburg, Virginia, 7–4. The following day, they pounded out a 10–8 victory, then won a thirteen-inning slugfest, 13–10, a total of thirty-seven hits enlivening the action. Leading the league, the jubilant Baltimore players prepared to return to Maryland for a home opener before expectant fans as well as an enthusiastic press that had reported "These Locals Can Win!" in a happy headline following the triple win.

That very night, of course, the U.S. League folded for good.

THE FEDERAL LEAGUE: BORN, 1913, DIED, 1915

The notion that a third major league was needed refused to die. Even as the U.S. League players returned to their homes or tried to find a spot for themselves in the minor leagues, plans were being made to convert the stillborn Columbian League into a rival circuit. John T. Powers of Chicago, who as first president of the Wisconsin-Illinois League had been elected head of the Columbian League in January 1912, was the man who got the ball rolling.

After picking out a new name—Federal—for the organization, Powers found backing in Chicago, St. Louis, Cleveland, Pittsburgh, Indianapolis, and Cincinnati and announced that the new league would start operations. Organized baseball, in response, yawned. During the summer of 1913, the Federal League was treated with the same respect given a minor circuit; Western Union often neglected to carry scores of the game, and newspapers dumped them at the bottom of long columns describing American League and National League action. But once the new owners

began raiding the rosters of major-league clubs during the winter of 1913–14, it became obvious they meant business. Unlike their counterparts in the U.S. League, the Federal men managed to attract big names to their organization, such as Joe Tinker, the superb shortstop who had been part of the Tinker–Evers–Chance double-play combination for so many years. After eleven years with the Cubs and one with Cincinnati, Tinker was sold to Brooklyn. He was not pleased with the prospect of working for Charles Ebbets, hardly one of the most generous and pleasant club owners, so he began looking around. Ebbets finally offered Tinker a bonus to sign but he wanted the shortstop to be presented with the check at the annual National League meeting in February 1914. "That's circus stuff," Tinker snarled. He eventually signed with Chicago of the "Feds."

One of the next to go was Mordecai Peter Centennial (Three-finger) Brown, who had one of the best records of any active pitcher at that time. Although thirty-seven years of age, Brown still had thirty-three major-league victories left in his arm. After Bill Killifer, Philadelphia Phillie catcher, made a quick trip to the Chicago Feds in January 1914, then back home again, rumors began to fly. On the very same day that Killifer was reported to have jumped, for instance, reports were circulated concerning pitchers King Cole (Pittsburgh Pirates), Ad Brennan (Phillies), and Gene Packard (Reds). Cole was enticed back to the National League but Brennan and Packard signed with the Feds. Otto Knabe, the veteran second baseman who had jumped from the Pirates to Baltimore of the Federal League, boasted that no less than nine genuine major-league players would be in the starting lineup when that team took the field in April 1914. Actually, Knabe underestimated the power of

---

The Baltimore Terrapins, 1914—a Successfully "Stolen" Team:

Of the twenty-eight men who would play with the 1914 Terrapins, eighteen were former major-leaguers. They included:

Name	Position	Former Club	Name	Position	Former Club
Bill Bailey	Pitcher	St. Louis(A)	Benny (Earache) Meyer	OF	Brooklyn(N)
Mickey Doolan	SS	Philadelphia(N)	Hack Simmons	2B-OF	New York(A)
Vern Duncan	OF	Philadelphia(N)	Frank Smith	P	Cincinnati(N)
Fred Jacklitsch	C	Philadelphia(N)	George Suggs	P	Cincinnati(N)
Enos Kirkpatrick	IF	Brooklyn(N)	Harry Swacina	1B	Pittsburgh(N)
Otto Knabe	Mgr-2B	Pittsburgh(N)	Jimmy Walsh	IF	Pittsburgh(N)
Fred Kommers	OF	Pittsburgh(N)	Irvin (Kaiser) Wilhelm	P	Brooklyn(N)
Jack Quinn	P	Boston(N)	Guy Zinn	OF	Boston(N)

After Opening Day 1914, two additional former major-leaguers, Johnny Bates (OF, Cincinnati) and Felix Chouinard (OF, Chicago White Sox) joined the team.

---

the new league to attract players from the old, for when the Federal Terrapins raced onto the field of their new park on Opening Day, there were sixteen men on the squad who had played in either the National League or the American League. Of these, fourteen were from National League clubs, Knabe's experience in that league obviously having helped him acquire the men he wanted. If Baltimore fans regarded the team as tarnished goods, they didn't show it—more than twenty-eight thousand of them jammed the park on Opening Day to watch the Terrapins take on the Buffalo Blues in the first Federal League game in history.

On the mound for the Terrapins was twenty-nine-year-old Jack Quinn, a Pennsylvania Pole whose real name was Picus. Having acquired a record of forty-four wins, thirty-six losses in five seasons with the New York Higlanders and Boston Braves, largely on the strength of an excellent spitball, Quinn proceeded to delight the hometown crowd by handling the Blues in fine fashion. Baltimore exulted in the 3–2 victory, the first of twenty-six wins earned that season by Quinn, who went on to become the next-to-last spitballer in the major leagues. (He retired in 1933, followed only by Burleigh Grimes one year later.)

No one can say for sure how the quality of play in the Federal League compared to the American League and the National League. Probably the teams were of high-minor-league caliber; on the other hand, by raiding the majors of more than fifty good players, it is conceivable the Federal League brought the quality of play in those two circuits down a notch or two. In any event, the pattern of economics in 1914–15 followed other attempts to found third leagues: All suffered. At the end of the first season, the New York *Times* estimated that only half of the sixteen teams in the "majors" made money. Federal League losses were placed at $176,000. The Indianapolis Hoosiers, winners of the first year's pennant, promptly folded.

From August, 1914, until the end of the year, there was almost continuous talk of im-

Meanwhile, Across the Street:
Baltimore had two teams that year, 1914, the other belonging to the International League. When the fans took the Terrapins to their heart following the invasion of the Federal League, Jack Dunn's Orioles suffered greatly, despite being an excellent club. The first week in July, the Orioles were 5½ games in front of the rest of the International League, and owner Dunn was twenty-eight thousand dollars behind as a result of lagging attendance. Less than two hundred people showed up for the pitching debut of nineteen-year-old George Herman Ruth. (He hurled a six-hit shutout.)

pending peace negotiations. Then, in December, following the breaking up of a talk between Charles Weeghman of the Federal League and Garry Herrmann of the Cincinnati Reds, *Sporting Life* headlined, "Feds Terminate All Peace Negotiations," and the war for players continued anew.

The second season of the Federal League began with a great deal of fanfare—parades, concerts, high-powered promotions featuring free tickets and souvenirs—as well as strengthened player lists. True, Indianapolis was no longer around but it was expected that the move to Newark was merely a prelude to invading the big city itself. And the Baltimore Terrapins had been able to entice Chief Charles Albert Bender, the American League's leading percentage pitcher of 1914 (17–3) from the Philadelphia Athletics.

But the high hopes of 1915 never materialized, for the league or Baltimore fans. The Chippewa Indian was able to win only four games, losing sixteen, while the public muttered about firewater. Despite draping their usherettes in red, white, and blue sashes, Newark officials saw attendance sag day after day. The admission price in some Federal League parks dropped to as low as ten cents,

---

The End of the Federal League—1915:
Final Standings

Team	W.	L.	Team	W.	L.
Chicago Whales	86	66	Newark Peppers	80	72
St. Louis Terriers	87	67	Buffalo Blues	74	78
Pittsburgh Rebels	86	67	Brooklyn Tip-Tops*	70	82
Kansas City Packers	81	72	Baltimore Terrapins	47	107

* The backers of Brooklyn's club were the Ward Brothers, makers of Tip-Top Bread.

and on one occasion, Brooklyn simply opened the gates and let everyone in free. Nothing seemed to help, not even an extremely good pennant race, which saw Chicago edge St. Louis by a single percentage point. In fact, only sixteen games separated first and seventh place, after which came another twenty-four-game interval and the Baltimore Terrapins, waiting to be boiled by their angry fans.

After the second season, the losses of the three leagues were again the subject of much speculation. It was estimated that each had dropped as much as two hundred thousand dollars. Most of the Federal League owners could afford their portion of that, however; they also had a strong suit pending in court before Judge Kenesaw Mountain Landis, urging nullification of the reserve clause as an illegal monopoly and restraint on business.

Thus it was all the more surprising when suddenly the Federal League owners agreed to disband. They were offered excellent terms, even being paid for their players, but no one knows exactly why the capitulation came so rapidly. Some said it was because they had been hard hit by the death of prominent members; that as inexperienced baseball operators, they were weary of the struggle; that the depression of 1914 and the onset of World War I caused attendance to diminish. Whatever the exact cause, the Federal League was dead.

THE AMERICAN FOOTBALL LEAGUE (PART ONE): BORN, 1926; DIED, 1926
Professional football in the United States was just seven years old when the first serious challenge was offered to the single major league, the National Football League.

Conceived in July 1919 at Canton, Ohio, when four teams signed up to participate in the first pro football league, the NFL was originally known as the American Professional Football Association. Franchises were sold for twenty-five dollars apiece to representatives from Akron, Canton, Columbus, Dayton, and Rochester. The first round of games was played that year, although there was no set schedule, and frequently players jumped from one team to another in order to grab themselves an extra payday. The Canton Bulldogs claimed the championship, beating Massillon, 3–0, at the end of the season when Jim Thorpe kicked a field goal.

In 1920 the new league added more teams, upped the franchise price to one hundred dollars, and in 1922 changed the name to the National Football League. By 1925, the NFL received a top box-office attraction when Red Grange, the most celebrated collegiate football player of the time, decided to turn pro-

fessional. When he joined the Chicago Bears in November 1925, more than thirty-five thousand fans jammed Wrigley Field to watch his debut. (The game ended in a scoreless tie, however, when the Chicago Cardinal punter, Paddy Driscoll, refused to kick the ball anywhere near Grange.)

After the 1925 season was over, promoter Charles C. (Cash and Carry) Pyle obviously saw green whenever he thought of Grange, for he sought him out and proposed that a new league be built around the Galloping Ghost. Grange was to be the star of the New York entry, naturally, and other franchises were to be set up in Boston, Brooklyn, Chicago, Cleveland, Newark, Philadelphia, Rock Island, and Los Angeles, a team that would play no home games because of that city's considerable distance from the other entries.

In March 1926, formal announcement was made of the new American Football League's birth, the job of first president being awarded to William H. (Big Bill) Edwards, former deputy of street cleaning for New York City, chief of waste disposal for the city of Newark, and U.S. collector of Internal Revenue. Having swept all before him in his previous positions, Mr. Edwards envisioned a great future for the new circuit. "I have accepted the presidency because I want to help preserve high-class football as it is played at the colleges," he said.

The quality of play was probably not much better than that of the better colleges, but when Red Grange was on the field it didn't make much difference. On October 3, 1926, more than five thousand fans turned out at Rock Island, Illinois, to see the hometown Independents try to stop the Galloping Ghost. Even on a muddy field they were helpless. Grange scored after receiving a fifteen-yard pass from quarterback George Pease, then in the third period turned the end for twenty yards and another TD. The result was an easy 26–0 win for New York.

It continued that way for a while, large crowds assembling for Red Grange, especially at New York, where thirty thousand and more came to see his appearances. One particularly interesting game was the "first battle of the boroughs" between New York and the Brooklyn Horsemen, on November 7, 1926. Brooklyn, having won only one game of three, was primed for an upset, and might have pulled it off had not Elmer Layden been out of action. As it was, Stuhldreher by himself was not bad. "He hurled passes accurately," one reporter wrote, "caught them dexterously, and every now and then broke away to long gains, but his efforts were offset and surpassed by Eddie Tryon, the former Colgate star, and the one and only Red Grange, both of whom wore the red jerseys of New York."

Brooklyn's AFL Team Really Were the "Horsemen"

On the Brooklyn roster in 1926 were two of the famous "Four Horsemen" of Notre Dame, who led the Irish to a record of twenty-seven wins, two losses, and one tie from 1922 to January 1, 1925. Jim Crowley and Don Miller had played the 1925 season with the professional Providence Steamrollers of the NFL. In 1926, when the new Brooklyn entry in the AFL was able to sign Harry Stuhldreher and Elmer Layden, the team was referred to as "Horsemen."

Before the first quarter was over, the Yankees had scored two TDs and were on their way to a third. "Eddie Tryon, snatching passes out of the air promiscuously, paved the way and scored the first two," it was noted. A bit later, however, Eddie's promiscuity got him in trouble, one of the Horsemen racking him up after he intercepted a pass and sending him out of the game.

With Grange ripping off yardage almost at will, "shaking off tacklers with snaky hips," it was difficult for Brooklyn to get back in the game. They did manage to make the final score a respectable 21–13, which sent New Yorkers home happy, and may have convinced some that the new league was off to a roaring start. In fact, the other franchises were in severe economic trouble, a fact borne out by Cleveland's quitting after playing only five games.

The National Football League, meanwhile, was not doing all that well, franchises moving in and out of the circuit in the manner of a revolving door. Nevertheless, in the time-tested manner of the "in" party, officials of the Frankford Yellow Jackets, winners of the league championship, refused to play a challenge postseason game with the AFL champion Philadelphia Quakers, despite the fact that such a game could have produced a great deal of revenue. The New York Giants, who finished the season in seventh position with a record of 8–4–0, were less disdainful. They agreed to meet the Quakers on December 12, 1926, in what could be called the first postseason "Super Bowl" in American professional football.

Only five thousand persons braved the snowy weather to attend the game at the Polo Grounds. Perhaps because of wet field, neither team could move the ball well during the first half. Jack McBride managed to kick a field goal for the Giants but that was the extent of the scoring. In the second half, however, New York moved the length of the field following the kickoff, took the ball away from the benevolent Quakers, and added another TD. From there on, it was a rout, the Giants proving their superiority by a score of 31–0.

Pro Football's First "Super Bowl"

Philadelphia Quakers (AFL)	0	0	0	0	0
New York Giants (NFL)	3	0	14	14	31

On the field, the season may have been a fine one for the Giants, but the team lost fifty thousand dollars at the box office. Brooklyn also lost money with its NFL entry, but in the AFL, financial anemia was even more widespread. Only the Philadelphia Quakers, Chicago Bulls, and New York Yankees completed

---

The Standings on November 8, 1926—a Plethora of Teams:

American Football League	W.	L.	T.	National Football League	W.	L.	T.		W.	L.	T.
Team				Team				Team			
Philadelphia Quakers	4	1	0	Chicago	7	0	1	Kansas City	3	3	0
New York Yankees	6	2	0	Frankford	8	1	1	Dayton	1	2	0
Cleveland Panthers	3	2	0	Pottsville	6	1	0	Brooklyn	2	5	0
Chicago Bulls	3	3	2	Green Bay	5	1	2	Hartford	2	5	0
Los Angeles Wildcats	4	4	1	Duluth	4	1	2	Milwaukee	2	6	0
Boston Bulldogs	2	3	0	Los Angeles	3	1	1	Akron	1	4	2
Rock Island Independents	2	4	1	Providence	4	3	0	Racine	1	4	0
Brooklyn Horsemen	1	3	0	Detroit	4	3	1	Canton	1	5	2
Newark Bears	0	3	2	New York	4	3	1	Columbus	1	6	0
				Cardinals	5	4	0	Louisville	0	3	0
				Buffalo	3	3	1	Hammond	0	3	0

the schedule, a fact of ebbing life that led to the new league's demise well before the second season could be planned, much less played. The NFL, of course, was only too happy to welcome back Red Grange and other stars of the upstart league who had proved their ability on the field.

AMERICA'S "PROFESSIONAL GOLF LEAGUE":
BORN, 1930; DIED, 1930

On May 28, 1930, the announcement came from Chicago that an embryonic professional golf league had been formed, with teams in Cleveland, St. Louis, Detroit, and Chicago. "To avoid the semblance of commercialization," it was explained, "the first games will be played for charity, receipts from the Hawthorne Club meet going to the Michigan Society for Crippled Children."

Unfortunately for golf buffs, the league never really got off the tee.

THE AMERICAN FOOTBALL LEAGUE (PART
TWO): BORN, 1936; DIED, 1937

A decade after the demise of the first AFL, a second attempt was made to form a rival league to compete with the established NFL. Dr. Harry A. March, president and organizer of the new circuit, announced on April 11, 1936, that franchises had been awarded to teams in Boston, Providence, New York, Jersey City, Syracuse, Cleveland, Pittsburgh, and Philadelphia.

That statement was not definitive, of course. As the spring and summer passed, the exact setup of the new AFL changed frequently. The raiding of NFL rosters continued, however, with the New York Yanks being the most proficient thieves. One of the greatest steals engineered by them was the wooing of 1933 scoring leader Ken Strong from the Giants. In addition, end Les Borden and back Stu Clancy were signed. The prize catches of the Cleveland Rams were Damon Wetzel, back and coach plucked from the Chicago Bears, and the signing of All-American Center Gomer Jones of Ohio State. The Pittsburgh Americans raided the Pirates, who finished third in the Eastern Division of the 1935 NFL race, signing end Ben Smith and guard Loran Ribble. Ironically, the Boston Shamrocks, who finished first in the 1936 AFL season with a record of 8–3–0, signed very few NFL players.

When the first game of the regular season was held in New York on September 27, 1936, a crowd of sixty-five hundred was on hand at Randalls Island Stadium to see the Yanks tackle the Syracuse Braves. (The Syracuse team would not complete the season.) It may not have been up to the standard of NFL play, but the fans seemed to enjoy it. New

York, led by Strong, Charlie Siegel, Al Rose, and Irv (King Kong) Klein, survived a late rally by the Braves to win, 13–6.

Three days later, the Yanks traveled to Boston for a night game with the rugged Boston Shamrocks, whose top player was a young man from Providence named Albert (Hank) Soar, who was destined not only to star on the football field but also to become a highly respected major-league baseball umpire a decade and a half later. Despite the threat of rain, more than five thousand Boston fans turned out to watch their heroes defeat the New Yorkers, 7–0.

By the end of October, the new league was showing both weaknesses and strengths. The Boston Shamrocks, winners of four straight games, played before crowds of ten thousand; the Syracuse Braves, having lost five straight contests, folded and were replaced in the standings by Rochester.

An interborough battle between the New York Yanks and Brooklyn Tigers drew only four thousand fans at Randalls Island Stadium, but when the Yanks moved over to Yankee Stadium for a night game with Pittsburgh on October 21, 1936, more than twenty-six thousand fans were there to cheer the team on. Part of the enthusiasm may have been caused by the fact that the game was the first night football contest to be played at Yankee Stadium. If the times had been better, it seems possible that the AFL's second attempt to achieve parity with the NFL might have succeeded. But the nation was in a highly selective mood as far as spending money was concerned. After the 1936 season, it was decided to try to broaden the base of the AFL by expanding westward to Cincinnati and Los Angeles. (The teams were nicknamed the Bengals and the Bulldogs, respectively.) But the 1937 season turned out to be a financial disaster, partly because Los Angeles won all eight games, while Rochester, the closest rival,

---

A Product of the AFL (Part Two) Who Went on to Better Things:
A rookie from Ohio State named Sidney Gillman played end with the second-place Cleveland Rams during the 1936 season. That turned out to be his only year as an active professional player. But in 1955 Gillman returned to the NFL as head coach of the Los Angeles Rams. In 1960, he jumped to the AFL (Part Four) to become the first coach of the Los Angeles Chargers, then moved to San Diego with the franchise the following year.

had a record of 3–3. Owner Bill Scully of the Boston Shamrocks admitted losing twenty thousand dollars during the season, and his situation was probably better than that of backers in other cities. As a result, the AFL degenerated into an obvious minor league after 1937, the contests being played in small parks by teams whose names have long since been forgotten except by those few who happened to see them play—the Cincinnati Blades, the St. Louis Gunners, the Louisville Tanks, the Nashville Rebels, the Dayton Rosies, and the Chicago Indians.

THE AMERICAN FOOTBALL LEAGUE (PART THREE): BORN, 1940; DIED, 1941

On Bastille Day 1940, the announcement was read in most newspapers as to what had transpired at Chicago the day before. The American Football League was going to try again. Prominently mentioned in connection with the New York entry was—once again— former Princeton star and expert on waste disposal Big Bill Edwards. Joseph Carr, Jr., son of the late NFL President, was also present as a potential backer for the Columbus team.

Franchises were eventually awarded for the 1940 season to Columbus, New York, Milwaukee, Buffalo, and Cincinnati, and preparations made for the coming season. Many players were secured from the rosters of minor-league teams, but once again the temptation of luring away veterans from the NFL proved too strong for the AFL owners to resist. The Bears of Boston were the most prolific raiders, securing seven players from the established league; the New York Yankees were second, with a total of five. But the Columbus Bullies made

the best steal by plucking quarterback Jay Arnold from the Eagle roster. A three-year veteran from Texas, Arnold helped Columbus win eight of ten games and take the 1940 title with a record of 8–1–1.

In 1941, Arnold was enticed back to the NFL Pittsburgh Steelers, but the Columbus Bullies continued to roll through the new league's second season under the leadership of John Le Bay, from West Virginia Wesleyan. The Boston Bears were no longer around, but otherwise the AFL seemed healthy and eager for battle. In fact, the AFL completely stole the spotlight from its senior rival in October 1941, when it was announced that John Kimbrough, star back for Texas A&M, and Tom Harmon, the miracle man from Michigan, would appear with the Yankees in a game against the powerful Columbus Bullies.

More than twenty-five thousand fans turned out to watch the pair's debut, the press buildup having predicted great things of the men despite their having participated in only a couple of practice sessions. But as Coach Jack McBride said: "Kimbrough and Harmon in the same backfield form a real quarterback's delight. Those fellows, when they get into shape, should be a revelation." They were hardly a revelation that afternoon, however, Harmon throwing a pair of interceptions and both showing only flashes of their running ability. Near the end of the game, some fans were shouting "We want Hutchinson!" (New York's regular running back). The game itself, in addition, was a dull affair, which saw Columbus score a touchdown in the second period and the Yanks tie it in the third. That was the way the contest ended.

How the Raiding Went, 1940:

Big losers in the inevitable raiding war that followed announcement that the AFL would try again in 1940 was the Brooklyn Dodger team, but it didn't seem to hurt them on the playing field. Other results of the war:

NFL Team	No. Players Lost to AFL	Position/1939	Position/1940
Brooklyn	(7) Carl Kaplanoff, Joe Ratica, Alec Shellogg, Paul Humphrey, Ed Merlin, George Lenc, Les Lane	3rd East 4–6–1	2nd East 8–3–0
Pittsburgh	(4) Ernie Wheeler, Carl Littlefield, Ed Karpowich, Joe Williams	5th East 1–9–1	4th East 2–7–2
Chicago Cardinals	(2) Joel Mason, Frank Patrick	5th West 1–10–0	5th West 2–7–2
Cleveland	(2) Bill McRaven, Ralph Niehaus	4th West 5–5–1	4th West 4–6–1

Philadelphia, Washington, Detroit, Green Bay, and New York lost one member each. The Chicago Bears did not suffer a single roster loss.

The Dynamic Duo's Statistics—October 19, 1941:

	Rushes	Yards	Avg.	Passes	Comp.	Int.	TD Rush
John Kimbrough	8	27	3.4	3	1	0	0
Tom Harmon	10	37	3.7	5	0	2	1

Two weeks later Tom Harmon was gone, having decided that his job with a Detroit radio station was more important than running for the Yankees, and John Kimbrough found the Milwaukee Chiefs' line just as hard to penetrate as that of Columbus. Even worse, only 11,753 fans bothered to turn out.

Meanwhile, the Bullies of Columbus clinched at least a tie for their second straight AFL championship by knocking off the Buffalo Tigers, 24–7, the same weekend. The schedule ended in late November with high hopes that the 1942 season would be better. But the entrance of the United States into World War II on December 8, 1941, ended any speculation as to the future of the young football league. With players being drafted every day, it soon became evident that only the established leagues would be able to function, and perhaps they would have to adopt limited schedules. On September 2, 1942, formal announcement was made by William B. Cox, president of the American Football League, that no games would be played until the war ended. "We do not have time to go into the football business this fall," he said, and then added bravely, no doubt for the benefit of those poor stockholders who had backed the league through two lackluster seasons, "I want to stress that there is no financial problem involved. Each team definitely has enough finances to continue."

American Football League—1941
Final Standings

	W.	L.	T.
Columbus Bullies	5	1	2
New York Yankees	5	2	1
Milwaukee Chiefs	4	3	1
Buffalo Tigers	2	6	0
Cincinnati Bengals	1	5	2

Translated, what he really meant was that the war had come along just in time.

THE POSTWAR BOOM—TWO LEAGUES THAT
DID NOT FAIL

It could have been that the time was just right. An army of Americans returning to a brave new world of peace, a home in the suburbs, and universal plumbing facilities may have been ready for innovation in the world of spectator sports. Certainly there was more room for expansion than before the war; certainly there were more dollars to be spent; and with a full supply of strong young athletes from the armed services and colleges available, it seemed almost foolish not to try to buck the establishment.

Baseball, a prime target for expansion, was ruled out from the very beginning of the peaceful era, however. Some enterprising American group might well have started a third league to rival the entrenched pair, except that the Mexicans blew the whistle first. During the first three years following World War II, money from south of the border enticed more and more American ballplayers to the new Mexican League. Recriminations, threats, and court suits followed. Not since the days of the Federal League three decades before had the ranks of the national game's rosters been so threatened. While the ferment continued, baseball in the United States was impervious to domestic attack, but football and basketball felt the pressure for expansion.

Some Names from the Mexican League Controversy:
The following left—and despite the threats of baseball's moguls that they would never play another game in the good old U.S. of A., returned:
Mickey Owen—*Brooklyn Dodger catcher who had gained a measure of reverse notoriety by dropping the third strike that led to the Dodgers' 1941 World Series loss to the Yankees.*
Luis Olmo—*A nearly forgotten name now, Olmo batted .303, .258, and .313 for the Dodgers in 1943, 1944, and 1945, respectively.*
Danny Gardella—*New York Giants outfielder. Later claimed he was allowed to return only because he dropped suit against baseball.*
Max Lanier—*St. Louis Cardinal pitcher who won forty-five games during war years 1942–44.*

THE BASKETBALL ASSOCIATION OF AMERICA

For a decade the National Basketball League enjoyed the unique position as America's premier professional basketball circuit. The name was first used in 1898, when a league with that title was formed in Philadelphia. Years of reorganization followed until 1937, when the NBL began play with teams in a variety of smaller midwestern cities. Despite having no franchises in major population centers, the NBL from 1937 to 1946 was relatively unchallenged as the major league of United States basketball.

In the summer of 1946, however, a group of men who owned some of the nation's largest sports arenas decided the time was right to bring basketball to the major cities. Led by Walter Brown, president of the Boston Garden, and Al Sutphin, owner of the Cleveland Arena, a group met in New York City to organize what came to be known as the Basketball Association of America. Maurice Podoloff, a New Haven, Connecticut, lawyer, was elected president, and franchises were awarded to backers in New York, Boston, Providence, Philadelphia, Washington, Toronto, Detroit, Cleveland, St. Louis, Chicago, and Pittsburgh.

The battle for supremacy in professional basketball began with efforts of both leagues to sign George Mikan, the six-ten giant from DePaul who was considered a top attraction. Minneapolis of the older NBL won that initial battle, but a year later the BAA had sufficient strength to pick up four of the NBL franchises, including Minneapolis. With Mikan in the rival camp, the older league was soon ready to talk peace. In December 1949, a merger agreement was announced. The new league was called the National Basketball Association, and Maurice Podoloff was installed as first president. For the first time since the American League challenged the National in baseball, the outsiders had won.

THE ALL-AMERICA FOOTBALL CONFERENCE

When the Yanks came home again following World War II, football was more popular than ever. Thanks to the enormous popularity of the gridiron battles between the powerful service academies, the public was ready to accept professionalism and the excellence that went with it. When it was organized in 1946, the new All-America Football Conference had two things going for it—rich owners such as Ben Lindheimer of the Los Angeles Dons, and a plethora of fine players such as Otto Graham, quarterback of the Cleveland Browns.

During the four years of its existence, the AAFC generated excitement on the field and at the box office. Cleveland, which won forty-seven games and lost but four while winning four straight AAFC titles, was an enormous

success on the field and off; Baltimore, which joined the league during its second season, soon proved a strong professional football town; and San Francisco illustrated that Los Angeles was not the only major city on the West Coast. But both sides were adamant in their determination to win the battle at the turnstiles. The battle eventually became focused at Los Angeles during 1949; when the NFL Rams won the Western Division championship while the Dons finished with a dismal 4–8 record, the senior circuit seemed to have won. Just before the curtain rang down on the 1949 season, however, a peace agreement was reached whereby a thirteen-team league called the National-American Football League was to be the final result. (The title was never used, of course.) What it meant was a merger, with ten of the NFL teams—the entire complement—joining the Cleveland Browns, San Francisco 49ers, and Baltimore Colts from the AAFC.

Some Heroes of the AAFC:

Marion Motley—(*Cleveland*) *Great rusher from Nevada gained 3,024 yards in 489 attempts (6.2-yard average) in four years. Elected to Pro Football Hall of Fame in 1968.*

Mac Speedie—(*Cleveland*) *Receiver from Utah caught 211 passes for 3,554 yards (16.8-yard average) in four years.*

Otto Graham—(*Cleveland*) *Quarterback from Northwestern led league with a 55.8 per cent completion average. Elected to Pro Football Hall of Fame in 1965.*

Ben Agajanian—(*Los Angeles*) *Placekicker from New Mexico started with Pittsburgh Steelers in 1945, eventually played twenty years of pro ball with eleven teams.*

Lou Groza—(*Cleveland*) *A tackle-kicker, Groza (product of Ohio State) scored 259 points in four seasons. Elected to Pro Football Hall of Fame in 1974.*

Y. A. Tittle—(*Baltimore*) *A college hero from LSU who was thrown into action his first year with the pros. Tittle played seventeen years and was good enough to lead all passers in his sixteenth year. Hall of Fame, 1971.*

In 1950, the first year of the new alignment, Cleveland surprised more than a few football "experts" by rolling to a 10–2 mark in the consolidated league, then defeating the Los Angeles Rams in a thrilling 30–28 victory in the championship game.

THE WORLD PROFESSIONAL TENNIS LEAGUE:
BORN, 1947; DIED, 1947

Not every sports venture following World
War II was a success.

Tennis, quite popular in the United States
since the days of Big Bill Tilden, no doubt
seemed a likely vehicle for exploitation during
the late 1940s. And so it was that Vincent
Richards became commissioner of the World
Professional Tennis League in March of 1947.
With a list of players that included Bobby
Riggs, Don Budge, Frank Kovacs, Fred Perry,
Welby Van Horn, Wayne Sabin, George Lott,
John Nogrady, and Jack Lossi, the success of
a pro tennis venture seemed assured. The first
event of the new organization was a ten-
thousand-dollar tournament at Philadelphia.
"Our aim is not only to promote the interests
of the men at the top," said Tony Owen, president of the new league, "but to see that the
players of the lower flight benefit financially
to a greater extent than they have in the
past."

It failed to work out that way. Nine months
later, the WPTL disbanded, Commissioner
Richards reporting meekly, "Unfortunately,
there are not enough top-notch pros to give
the public the brand of competition it deserves."

What he did not say was that the main attraction of the new league, Bobby Riggs, often
failed to play in scheduled tournaments when
a better offer for a personal tour came along.

THE NATIONAL BOWLING LEAGUE: BORN,
1961; DIED, 1962

Why not bowling as a professional spectator
sport?

Primarily, in pretelevision days, because it
was difficult to arrange enough seating so that
those who were willing to pay their way in
could have a good view of the action. Bowling
alleys are not built as arenas, there being only
enough seats, in most cases, to accommodate
patrons waiting for the bowlers to finish.

As early as the 1930s, talk of a professional
bowling league was heard by Louis Petersen, a
Chicago promoter of the sport. It was discarded as a pipe dream when Petersen, with
scattered support, urged city proprietors' associations to construct special bowling arenas so
that a traveling major league could perform
and be watched comfortably by a sizable audience. But by 1957 the dream seemed less fantastic when Matt Niesen, another Chicago
sportsman, began promoting bowling as a
sport that could pit one city against another in
the manner of football or baseball.

It took four years before the experiment got
off the drawing boards, but in October 1961
the operations of the National Bowling
League began. Teams had been established in

Kansas City, Los Angeles, Fort Worth, Min-
neapolis-St. Paul, Detroit, Fresno, Dallas, Totowa (New Jersey), Omaha, and San Antonio.

The first match was held on October 12,
1961, at Dallas, where the hometown Broncos
took on the Totowa (called New York because it sounded more impressive in Texas)
Gladiators. The contest, held in what was
called the Bronco Bowl, was witnessed by
about two thousand persons, who paid from
one dollar to three dollars' admission. J.
Curtis Sanford, owner of the Bronco team, expected the arena to be filled but nevertheless
pronounced the debut successful.

Carmen Salvino started the festivities by
beating Jake Charter, 205–167, putting hometown Dallas ahead. Then Red Alkins of
Dallas whipped Vince Lucci by a score of
201–194 and Dallas was never headed. The
final score of the head-to-head series of
matches was 22–2.

Less than a week later, on October 17, the
Totowa team was home in New Jersey, where
it made its home debut against the Kansas
City Stars. It was the East's first taste of professional bowling, but only five hundred spectators paid their way into the twenty-five-
hundred-seat Gladiator Bowl, located on
Route 46 in northern New Jersey. Kansas City
made matters even worse by defeating the
home team, 17–8.

The league struggled bravely until near the
end of 1961, when Omaha and San Antonio
folded. Dick Charles, NBL commissioner, pronounced the rest of the league "quite sound"
and reported that the eight remaining teams
would carry on in fine fashion. But less than a
week later, Kansas City also withdrew from
the loop after performing before less than a
hundred fans in a home match that turned
out to be the final one for San Antonio.

Despite these losses, the league continued
playing through the winter of 1961–62. A
best-of-five playoff series between the Detroit
Thunderbirds and Twin Cities Skippers, held
in May 1962, proved to be the swan song of
the league. About a thousand fans attended
the third game, which saw Detroit become the
first and only champions of the National
Bowling League. On July 9, Edwin Tobo-
lowsky, acting commissioner, announced that
the experiment was over.

THE AMERICAN FOOTBALL LEAGUE (PART
FOUR): FINALLY MAKING IT

And so it came about on its fourth try that
the organization known as the American Football League finally made it.

The reasons for its success seemed to be evident from the very beginning. In 1959, the
National Football League drew 3,140,409 paying customers, the eighth consecutive rec-

ord attendance. The audience, businessmen agreed, was there, plenty for another league. Television was also there to help spread the word, make the new teams instantly familiar not only in their hometown by also across the nation. For its fourth attempt, the AFL had something else it had never had before—good leadership and lots of money, men such as Lamar Hunt, owner of the Dallas franchise, and K. S. (Bud) Adams, Jr., Texas oilman. (It also had a few bad apples, such as Harry Wismer, onetime sportscaster who mishandled the New York Titans into near-oblivion.)

The initial battlegrounds were Los Angeles, where the AFL Chargers would try to buck the established Rams; New York, Titans vs. Giants; and Dallas, which had become the NFL's thirteenth franchise that season of 1960—some said to embarrass Lamar Hunt and literally run him out of Texas.

In September 1960, the new league played the first games of its schedule. Attendance was disappointing, and the play, while often exciting, was ragged. But it was generally agreed that play would improve, especially when members of the defensive teams grew used to working together.

The first game in AFL history was played in Boston, where 21,597 turned out to see the favorite Patriots tackle the Denver Broncos. In anticipation of another Boston massacre, the field was decked out in red, white, and blue, and a horseman depicting Paul Revere pranced up and down the sidelines. But the Broncos pulled an upset, winning by a score of 13–10. At Los Angeles, only 17,724 were on hand to see the hometown Chargers win a thriller, 23–20, Ben Agajanian kicking a last-seconds field goal. New York, with bad weather, drew only 9,700 paid customers to the Polo Grounds, where the Titans beat Buffalo, 27–3, on the passing of Al Dorow. At San Francisco, the Oakland Raider-Houston Oiler game, won by Houston, 37–22, attracted only 12,703 fans. AFL Commissioner Joe Foss was undismayed, however. "Of course it wasn't exceptional attendance," he said, "but it really wasn't too bad. We recognize it's going to be a long pull, but we're here to stay."

It may have sounded like whistling in the dark, but Foss was right. For more than three years the AFL's future was in doubt—until January 1964, when the National Broadcasting Company and the league signed a five-year contract that would pay the eight clubs $36 million. That, it turned out, was sufficient to get the AFL over the financial hump. Soon merger talk started, and in June 1966 a consolidation was agreed upon, with the first Super Bowl being set for January 1967. After four decades, the AFL had made it.

THE AMERICAN BASKETBALL LEAGUE: BORN, 1961; DIED, 1962

When pear-shaped promoter Abe Saperstein, owner of the renowned Harlem Globetrotters, was turned down by the NBA, he decided to do the only thing possible: establish an entire new league to rival the older one.

In October 1961, the schedule of the new American Basketball League was drawn up. Those who understood travel budgets drew a sharp breath, for Saperstein's ambitious project called for eight teams from Washington, D.C., to Honolulu, Hawaii, to play eighty games. Some of the franchises had weak financing, but the charismatic Saperstein seemed to be the league's biggest asset. He urged innovative changes, such as the rule that a basket scored from farther than twenty-five feet out be awarded three points instead of two—the basketball equivalent of a home run, which would encourage a wide-open game. Saperstein also put forth a plan in which all eight clubs would share equally in the travel costs. And while the ABL did not have many players who could compete with the established league, there was a nucleus of stars who had jumped. There was also Saperstein's Harlem Globetrotters, a crowd-pleasing attraction that could be used as a pregame warmup to entice fans past the turnstiles.

What Saperstein apparently did not realize was that even the NBA could not have survived had it not been for a profitable TV contract. The new ABL was trying to make it primarily by paid attendance, a difficult undertaking, especially in Los Angeles, where the Jets played in the shadow of the Lakers and Elgin Baylor. Reportedly, the Jets could not fill the house with a competitive audience even by giving away free passes. Even the Kansas City franchise ran into immediate trouble, despite winning eighteen of its first twenty-three games and being free of strong competition. Needing to attract only three thousand fans per game and break even, the Steers averaged only fifteen hundred. The San Francisco Saints, strongest organization in the new league, averaged about thirty-five hundred fans a game as the first season progressed.

Desperately trying to create a glimmer of light in the ABL darkness, promoter Saperstein made an asset of the league's failure to compete by noting that "our league is giving employment to the little men in basketball—which is something the pro sport hasn't done before." Those words of encouragement did not help the Washington franchise, which folded before the end of the season, moving to Long Island. Los Angeles was the next casualty.

Death watchers found much to observe in

The American Basketball League and Its Top Stars:
Eastern Division
Chicago Majors: *Coach: Andy Phillip, ex-NBA coach*
Cleveland Pipers: *Dick Barnett, Larry Siegfried, ex-NBA players*
Pittsburgh Rens: *Jim Palmer, Connie Hawkins, ex-NBA players*
Washington Tapers: *Tony Jackson, Cal Ramsey, ex-NBA players*
Western Division
Hawaii Chiefs: *Red Rocha, ex-NBA coach, Frank Burgess, ex-NBA player*
Kansas City Steers: *Coach: Jack McMahon, ex-NBA player*
Los Angeles Jets: *Bill Sharman (player-coach), Bill Spivey, Hal Lear, George Yardley, ex-NBA players*
San Francisco Saints: *Mike Farmer, Ken Sears, ex-NBA players*

---

the operation of the new league. It was noted, for example, that the Los Angeles Jets used air travel for most of their trips, but upon arriving in the Midwest, switched discreetly to private automobiles as a means of cutting

---

Want to Set Up a Losing League? Here's the Title to Choose:

The title given a prospective major league that has failed uniformly during the twentieth century has been "Continental." It was first tried in 1921 when a group of businessmen led by Herman (Andy) Lawson went through the process of establishing a Continental Baseball League that never got off the ground. During the late 1950s, Branch Rickey and William Shea revived the idea of a third baseball league —called Continental—which so frightened the powers of the American and National Leagues that they quickly voted in favor of expansion. That, of course, killed the Continental. In 1966, the title was again used for a third professional football league to rival the AFL and the NFL. It never succeeded in attaining major-league status. Thus the phrase dating back to colonial times, "not worth a continental," has held up concerning successful sports leagues.

costs. Teams traveling to Honolulu, in order to save money, would play the Hawaii Chiefs four or five nights in a row before flying back to the mainland. With that kind of handwriting on the economic wall, it was nothing short of amazing that the ABL lasted two seasons. On December 31, 1962, Saperstein finally threw in the towel. Not a single club operated in the black, losses totaling $1 million the first season and $250,000 the next. Perhaps the biggest loser, in addition to Saperstein, who staked his reputation on the new league, was Paul Cohen of New York. Cohen owned not one, but a pair of franchises that folded: the Washington Tapers and the Pittsburgh Rens.

THE 1970S—LEAGUES GALORE

The decade of the 1970s saw an explosion of sports franchises in the United States. Some died slow deaths, some bombed completely, and some managed to hang on despite growing pains. Into the latter category must go soccer, the sport with a strong nucleus of backers who felt the time was right to bring the world's favorite outdoor sport to America. The time, unfortunately, was not quite right. Soccer proved dull on television (and had no easy method for breaking so that commercials could be inserted). Franchises folded from one end of the country to the other, but were replaced by others. The sport did not become the instant success its backers predicted; yet it did establish a foothold during the 1970s that seemed solid enough to carry it into the next decade.

The decade also saw the beginnings of the American Basketball Association, World Team Tennis, the World Hockey Association, and the beginning and end of World Team Boxing and the World Football League. During the summer of 1974, the height of this period of athletic overkill, 44 cities (or combinations of cities) had a total of 146 franchises representing 10 leagues (not counting World Team Boxing and a proposed women's basketball circuit).

Prime mover of the expansion mania was Gary Davidson, who helped found the ABA, World Team Boxing, and the World Football League. The latter began operations during the late summer of 1974, fortuitously at the height of a strike of National Football League players. At first the new league seemed highly successful, and on July 24, the Birmingham Americans defeated the Memphis Southmen before a hometown crowd announced as 61,319, a WFL record. The WFL also managed to sign several stars from the older league—Paul Warfield, Larry Csonka, and Jim Kiick for a total price of three million dollars. And innovations were introduced on the playing field as well, such as moving the kickoff back to the thirty-yard line in order to prevent the ball being kicked through the end zone instead of to a return man. But the WFL soon ran into problems, including that of a credibility gap, when it was discovered that attendance figures were being padded by adding free-pass holders in with those who had paid their way to the games. Failure to obtain a national television contract also hurt the league's chances for survival. After the first championship game—won by the Birmingham Americans, 22–21, over the Florida Blazers—WFL officials admitted that most of the teams were in financial hot water. Many players were owed back salary—so many, in fact, that when Tommy Reamon was asked what he intended to do with the league prize of $3,333.33 presented to three outstanding players at the end of the first season, he replied, "I'll let you know when I see it."

Despite these problems, the WFL staggered into a second season with most of the clubs under new management (and some renamed). But on September 2, 1975, the Chicago franchise disbanded after only five games. The rest of the league continued to operate until October 22, when the WFL officially disbanded. A grand total of about $20 million had been lost in the attempt to found what really amounted to a third football league.

If there is any lesson to be learned from more than a century of establishing sports leagues in the United States, seeing some of them prosper and some fail, it might be that it is easier to set up a second league in any sport than either a first or a third one. Americans, for some reason or other, prefer the even number.

Who Now Remembers the—?
Birmingham Americans (Vulcans)
Charlotte Hornets
Chicago Fire (Winds)
Detroit Wheels
Florida Blazers
Hawaiians
Houston Texans
Jacksonville Sharks (Express)
Memphis Southmen
Philadelphia Bell
Portland Storm (Thunder)
San Antonio Wings
Shreveport Steamer
Southern California Sun

CHAPTER 13—OTHER RULES

Americans love to tinker with things. Thus it is hardly accidental that the games and spectator sports that have been accepted as "most American" have evolved, with many rule changes, during the past eight to ten decades until in many respects they hardly resemble the original contest. (The main exception seems to be lacrosse, a game of such basic simplicity—like soccer—that it defies alteration.)

Well into the twentieth century, the tinkering process continued, often to the dismay of traditionalists who believed that well enough should be left alone. Changes were made, however, although it can be safely said that the vast majority of ideas suggested as means of speeding up the game or increasing the scoring or equalizing the battle between offense and defense were quickly laid to rest,

most of the time without the benefit of a fair trial.

Some of the proposed rule changes are merely bizarre. Others could probably work, if given the opportunity. A few, put forth soon after the sport settled down into the basic game we know today, were pushed aside and then resurrected at a later date. The limitations and possibilities of television as a spectator tool no doubt helped bring about many changes and discouraged others.

BASEBALL

When first played, baseball involved wooden posts instead of bases; allowed the fielder to "plug" (hit) the batter with the ball for an out; and the game continued until one

Evolution of Baseball Rules During the 1880s:

Year	No. of Balls for a Base on Balls	No. of Strikes for an Out	Pitching Distance	Other
1880	8	3*	45 ft.	*Batter received extra strike via "good ball" warning
1881	8	3	50 ft.	
1882	7	3	50 ft.	
1883	7	3	50 ft.	Foul ball caught on bounce no longer an out
1884	6	3	50 ft.	
1885	6	3	50 ft.	Pitcher could use any motion besides underarm or sidearm; batters could use bat with one flat side
1886	7	3	50 ft.	
1887	5	4	50 ft.	Base on balls counts as hit
1888	5	3	50 ft.	Base on balls not counted as hit
1889	4	3	50 ft.	
1893	4	3	60 ft., 6 in.	Flat-sided bats banned

24. Accidents sometimes happen to participants in sports, of course. Certainly one of the most unusual was reported in 1889. The victim was a young man with the habit of playing baseball while carrying shotgun cartridges in his pocket. When a wild pitch struck the cartridges, his pants exploded. (See "Being a Player Isn't Always Easy.")

25. Controversy over heavyweight championship was created in 1887 when *National Police Gazette* publisher Richard K. Fox decided the title belonged with Jake Kilrain rather than John L. Sullivan. Accordingly, Fox presented Kilrain with a gaudy championship belt at the Monumental Theater in Baltimore. (Sullivan responded: "I wouldn't put it on a dog.") In 1889, the two fighters met in the last bare-knuckle fight of importance, Sullivan severely battering the game Kilrain into submission.

26. Women continued to try their hand at various sports during the 1880s, and one of the most successful was Rose Coghlan, who took on men at the fine art of pigeon shooting. (See "Breaking the Sex Barrier.")

27. Lacrosse enthusiasts had big moment when a match for the championship of America was held at the Polo Grounds on October 22, 1881, between the Shamrock Club of Montreal and the New York Lacrosse Club. The Shamrocks won before a crowd of about 3,000. Note that "goal" is nothing more than pole that must be touched by player holding ball. (See "1881.")

28. Fencing was also popular as a spectator sport during the 1880s, this match held in 1887 at Cosmopolitan Hall, New York, between the American Regis Senas and Louis Tronchet of Paris. Tronchet won, 3 matches to 2.

29. Unusual sports events were tried during the 1880s, including races between bicyclists and ice skaters, both traveling over the frozen Schuylkill River near Philadelphia. Surprisingly, in this event and others on the Delaware from Philadelphia to Trenton, it was the cyclists who won going away.

30. Another interesting "mixed media" race of the time took place on May 24, 1881, when a woman cyclist named Elsa von Blumen raced the trotter Hattie R. Using the handicap provided her very well, Elsa won 2 out of 3 races. (See "Can a _____ Beat a _____?")

31. Horseracing continued to grow in popularity during the 1880s, new tracks springing up all over the nation. A new stakes race of 1888, the Futurity, was run at Sheepshead Bay, New York, and has been run every year since that time. Inaugural race was won by Proctor Knott, ridden by black jockey "Pike" Barnes. Another black jockey, Tony Hamilton, brought Salvator home second. Along with Isaac Murphy, Barnes and Hamilton were just a few of the blacks who handled themselves extremely well as riders. (See "Breaking the Color Barrier.")

32. The 1890s started big as far as baseball was concerned, three major leagues functioning in 1890, the year of the players' revolt (see "Other Leagues"). But by 1891 the Players' League had folded and the American Association was in its final season. For the remainder of the decade the National League contained an unwieldy number of clubs. Drawing depicts late-summer action of 1891 National League season.

33. Football during the 1890s continued to grow rougher and rougher, with the "flying wedge" and other mass formations contributing to mounting injury tolls. John Heisman, who played football at Pennsylvania from 1889 through 1891 (after two seasons at Brown), wrote, "Once a game started a player could not leave unless he actually was hurt, or at least pleaded injury. . . . We had no helmets or pads of any kind. . . . Hair was the only head protection we knew. . . ." Contemporary artist conceived of typical football games as something very close to war, with bandaged player calling for medic to come to aid of unconscious teammate.

34. Badminton, which officially started in the United States in 1878 with the formation of the Badminton Club of the City of New York, was sufficiently popular by the nineties to be played by many well-dressed ladies and gentlemen. Artist of 1891 depicted society get-together in New York City.

35. During the last decade of the nineteenth century, Louis Cyr of Canada, Eugene Sandow of Germany, and George Hackenschmidt of Russia did much to popularize the sport of weight lifting. Drawing of 1891 shows Cyr at work but does not depict one of his favorite feats—that of lifting 535 pounds from the floor with one finger, the weight attached to a chain and ring. (See "1891.")

36. Following the development during the 1880s of indoor swimming tanks, water polo came to be played under a system of haphazard rules. Not until 1897 did Harold Reeder, a devotee of the game in America, set up formal rules designed to take most of the rough tactics out of water polo. Artist depicts 1891 action, before official rules were adopted.

37. Gravesend Race Track at Sheepshead Bay, New York, was the scene of major controversy in 1891 when Philip Dwyer, president of the Brooklyn Jockey Club, discontinued use of a telegraph line from the course to New York bookie palaces. Desperate to get information on the races to their betting customers, the pool sellers tried everything from hand signals to releasing carrier pigeons. (See "1891.")

38. "Fight of the Century" was held on September 7, 1892, at New Orleans, John L. Sullivan defending his heavyweight title against underdog James J. Corbett. Contemporary engraving shows the champ landing a hard left to the challenger's jaw, but in the end it was Gentleman Jim who landed a left "audible throughout the house" in the twenty-first round that put Sullivan down for good.

39. With growing interest in sports, inventors of the 1890s turned out a variety of gear that was supposed to improve the player's game or even create a new sport. One invention of 1894 was a bent rifle for the marksman who was right-shouldered but left-eyed. (See "Technology Rears Its Leg.")

40. Another brainstorm of 1892 was Curran's swimming equipment, which supposedly allowed the swimmer to generate more hand- and leg-power. The life-belt obviously was provided just in case it didn't work. (See "Technology Rears Its Leg.")

41. In 1897, a Professor Hinton created a stir by inventing a "baseball cannon" designed to save wear and tear on pitcher's arms. It came complete with several means of changing speeds as well as a raised lip at the end of the device that would cause a curve ball. The only problem was that Hinton's early version of "Iron Mike" didn't work very well. (See "Technology Rears Its Leg.")

42. The year 1894 produced the Centrifugal Bowling Alley, a new indoor game. For some reason it never caught on. (See "Sports That Never Made it.")

43. One sport that did make it from scratch was basketball, the brainchild of Dr. James Naismith, an instructor at the International YMCA Training School at Springfield, Massachusetts. Searching about for a game that could be played in a gymnasium, Naismith used a peach basket and a soccer ball to fashion the new sport.

side or the other reached a score of twenty-one. When the first intercollegiate baseball game was played on July 1, 1859, between Williams College and Amherst, there were thirteen players on each side. Later the number was reduced to ten and then nine.

Other early rules allowed a batter to be called out on a ball, even a foul one, that was caught after a single bounce. In recompense, the batter was allowed to call for either a high pitch or a low one and was not required to swing if he did not receive what he requested. (If a good pitch crossed the plate according to the batter's demands and he failed to swing, the umpire shouted "good ball," which meant that the batter should swing at the next one or have it counted a strike.) This rule was used until 1881, when umpires counted every good pitch, swung at or not, as strikes. Pitchers were further hampered by being required to throw sidearm or underhand, but were helped by a relatively short pitching distance. During the 1880s the rules were changed every year as fans and players complained about the dominance of either the defense or the offense.

If baseball can be assigned a magic date, that year would be 1893. By then it was possible to get a free ticket to first base on four balls and strike out a batter on three strikes from a pitching distance of sixty feet, six inches (the last half foot courtesy of a surveyor who misread the blueprints). The game had evolved to a semblance of modern baseball.

Nevertheless, the game was subjected to a variety of suggested changes by both laymen and professionals during the decades following.

BOB UNGLAUB'S ARC

In the early years of the twentieth century, the game of baseball favored the pitcher. No longer was he required to throw in an underarm or sidearm fashion, and the ball was relatively "dead." In 1903, it was ruled that the pitcher's mound could not be more than fifteen inches above the levels of the base lines and home plates, but some felt the batter needed even more help.

A unique suggestion came from Bob Unglaub, whose best years were those with the Boston Red Sox, from 1904 to 1908. Unglaub felt that heavy hitters were being neutralized by outfielders who simply stationed themselves against the fences and let the batters slam away, merely trotting in a few paces to turn a long smash into an easy flyout. Unglaub proposed that an arc eighty yards from home plate be drawn through the outfield, beyond which no fielder could move until the ball was hit. Thus a smash to the fence would become an exciting race between outfielder and ball. The fans would be happier, Unglaub claimed, and so would batters with power. Predictably, his idea was never put into use.

CONNIE MACK—BACK TO FOUR STRIKES

In 1910, Connie Mack's solution to the problem of getting more hitting in baseball was to suggest that the batter be given four strikes instead of three. He also proposed that the rule calling a foul ball a strike be eliminated, thus allowing batters to deliberately foul off pitches in an effort to upset and tire the pitcher.

An English Critic on American Baseball: *In 1919, even the English noticed that the typical American pitcher, playing his interminable game of tag with a base runner, was slowing down the game. Describing a baseball contest in* The London Field, *he wrote: "The American pitcher, in a match against Canada, was so deliberate in his methods as to be the subject of wonder not unmixed with admiration. . . . If a man was at first base [he] raised his hands as if about to throw, dropped them, and twiddeled the ball several times in his glove, swung his arms in a windmill fashion, and, finally, when one had almost given him up in despair, threw the ball toward the batter. . . . Several times he began his duties by holding the ball at arm's length and standing motionless for some seconds. . . . Once or twice he altered his mind, signaled to the catcher, met him half way, had a consultation. . . . Yet baseball enthusiasts did not seem to recognize that there was anything slow about these things."*

THE YELLOW-BALL PROPOSAL

During the 1920s, when baseball became enormously popular and bleachers filled with thousands of fans wearing white shirts, it was suggested that changing the color of the baseball from white to yellow might help the batters.

On August 28, 1928, an experimental yellow baseball was first used by a professional team during a doubleheader between Milwaukee and Louisville of the American Association. Although the games went off without mishap, proving that the yellow balls could be seen easily and were less likely to discolor, major-league officials did not fall over each other in an effort to convert National and American League balls from white to yellow.

During the early 1970s, Charles O. Finley also proposed that yellow baseballs be used, but perhaps because the Oakland owner was regarded as something of a maverick, the idea was killed at that time.

THE DESIGNATED HITTER

Although the use of a designated hitter—adopted permanently and officially by the American League at its December 1975 meeting—came as something of a shock to baseball traditionalists, the idea was then nearly a half century old, having been suggested first by National League President John A. Heydler in December 1928.

Heydler, correctly, looked upon the plan as a means of saving time and providing more action, and during the annual meeting of the league at the Waldorf-Astoria he trotted out all the good reasons why it made sense to adopt the rule. "With the exception of two or three," he said, "practically all pitchers are weak hitters and weaker base runners. When they come to bat they literally put a drag on the game. No one expects them to do anything, and they simply suspend the action of the play. . . . With the adoption of this rule we could do away with the necessity of seeing a pitcher who may be pitching very well for four or five innings removed to make way for a pinch hitter because his team is in need of a run. . . ."

Because the proposal generally made sense despite removing some "strategy" from the game, Heydler's designated-hitter plan ran into considerable opposition, although he received a great deal of lip service from the various club owners. The plan, called "ten-men baseball" (which suggests a much more radical alteration than it really embodies), was tabled, although some owners suggested that a couple of teams try the plan during spring training. Heydler, angry at not having the proposal accepted wholeheartedly, snapped,

---

Heydler on Baseball's Resistance to Change:

"I remember that there was a tremendous uproar when an order went out that the pitcher must keep his foot on the rubber. The pitchers had been starting their deliveries away round to one side of the pitching rubber, giving a cross-fire effect to every pitch. Pitchers said they could not pitch if they had to stand on the rubber, and one would have thought that the game would be just about ruined. . . ."

"Until it becomes an approved practice there is nothing to be gained by having a few clubs experiment with it in the South. . . . It will prove nothing and only serve to deprive pitchers of a chance to get some actual batting practice in competition, something they sorely need."

And so baseball, that bastion of tradition, waited a few more years—forty-seven—before giving the Heydler plan a real try. But only in one league. There was no need, after all, to go completely overboard.

EJECTION FOR INNINGS

A suggestion made in 1930 by Judge Emil Fuchs, president of the Boston Braves, was that players or managers who have incurred the wrath of an umpire be ejected from the game for a number of innings, rather than the entire game. After he had served his penalty, he would be able to return, in the manner of a hockey player.

THREE BALLS AND TWO STRIKES

In order to prove that baseball could be speeded up, the college squads of Penn State and Dickinson played a game on May 14, 1932, in which batters were called out on two strikes and received a pass on three balls. The innovation, which was suggested by Physical Education Director Hugo Bezdek of Penn State, seemed to work very well. Penn State won the game, 5–3, and the contest lasted an hour and twenty-five minutes.

SPEEDING UP THE GAME

On June 23, 1956, a Kansas City sportswriter named Dick Wade decided to find out exactly how much "action" occurred in a typical baseball game. The decision was generated by considerable outcry at the time that baseball games were running too long as the result of managers and pitchers dawdling. Wade's *modus operandi* was to start his stopwatch every time "real action" took place during the contest between the Kansas City Athletics and the Washington Senators and stop it when nothing was happening. He counted the time required for a pitch to travel from the pitcher's hand to home plate—about one second—but not the time consumed by the catcher's return throw to the mound. The watch was allowed to run on all hit balls until the batter was either out or safe at the base.

Baseball Slowing Down?

Average Time of Games in Major Leagues:

1913	1 hour, 58 minutes
1954	2 hours, 25 minutes
1955	2 hours, 31 minutes

The total "action" during the two-hour, thirty-eight-minute game (which was 8½ innings in length) worked out to nine minutes, fifty-five seconds.

The "wasted" time was spent primarily by the pitchers. Dean Stone of Washington used an average of fourteen seconds between pitches, while Camilo Pasqual, a genuine "dirt-kicker and pants-tugger," utilized seventeen seconds between each throw. Pedro Ramos, on the other hand, used only eight seconds between pitches. Changing pitchers consumed seven minutes for two occasions.

Batters such as José Valdivielso, who took regular eleven-second strolls out of the batter's box between pitches, also added to the ennui. A catcher's throw back to the mound took two seconds; that of an umpire, three.

Kansas City won, 15–6. The twenty-one runs crossing the plate no doubt added both to the "action" and total time of the game.

No major proposals followed Dick Wade's research.

FOUR STRIKES REVIVED

Because so many Americans like baseball, it follows that suggestions for improving the game would come from all walks of life, in addition to the diehard fan, player, or coach. In 1957, U. S. Representative Kenneth B. Keating came out for the offense, stating that "the thing that makes an exciting game is people running around the bases, double plays and home runs, lots of action." In order to bring this about, Mr. Keating harked back to Connie Mack's 1910 proposal, suggesting that giving the batter four strikes instead of three would give him a better chance to connect.

What Mack and Keating did not say was that giving the batter—and pitcher—an extra strike might waste more time than it saved. The pitcher would probably be so intimidated by the situation that he would try harder than ever to nip the corners of the plate, in the process fondling the resin bag and stepping on and off the rubber even longer than before.

All in all, adding another pitch to the game must be considered one of the worst solutions for the alleged boredom of baseball.

LETTING THE PLAYERS BACK

Thirty years after National League President John Heydler made a daring proposal, American League President Will Harridge suggested that baseball might be more exciting if Rule 3.03 were changed so that: (1) A player removed from the game for other than a rules infraction be allowed to return after one inning's absence. This would include pitchers removed for pinch hitters. (2) A player sent into the game as a pinch hitter could remain in the game or be used as a pinch hitter a second time, provided one inning elapsed between his appearances.

The idea was not actually the brainchild of President Harridge, it turned out, but was conceived by Lew Fonseca, a player from 1921 to 1933 who in 1958 was motion-picture director for the American and National Leagues. "With this change baseball will become a more suspenseful spectator activity," Fonseca said in defending the rules change proposal. "Imagine Ted Williams leaving the game with Boston a run or so ahead, then when the score is tied he returns with a man on base. Of course it'll create suspense."

Others cared little for the plan. "I think it's a terrible idea," said New York manager Casey Stengel. "If they want to legislate against something, why don't they legislate against the curve ball?" Added Cleveland General Manager Frank Lane: "It's a horrible idea. For one thing it would make the games much longer than they are now."

Thus Lew Fonseca's plan to let players wander in and out of the game died a quick death. He never even had time to explain why a manager would take Ted Williams out of the game with Boston only a run or so ahead.

PITCHLESS PASSES

One early suggestion to the ever-lengthening baseball games was that time could be saved by eliminating the dullest play in baseball— the intentional pass. Simply have the pitcher wave the batter to first, some said, and get on with the game.

In January 1959, members of the Class AA Texas League committee got together and passed a ruling that would allow this time-saving event to happen. In a trice, Baseball Commissioner Ford Frick was on the telephone, warning Texas League President Dick Butler that such a drastic change could not be implemented, that it simply was not legal according to baseball's rules.

TRADITION TRIUMPHANT AGAIN

Two years after the sanctity of the intentional pass had been defended by Commissioner Frick, the Pacific Coast League attempted to allow the substitution of a pinch hitter without removing the pitcher from the game. The change was to be instituted during the 1961 season, but at the last moment professional baseball's Playing Rules Committee voted, 8–1, against allowing the experiment.

THE VEECK SOLUTION

Baseball's bad boy, Bill Veeck, also joined the ranks of those who felt the national game had developed hardening of the arteries during the 1950s and 1960s. His solution was not to institute rule changes, but to eliminate some traditions and enforce those rules already on the books. For example, Veeck said that it was not necessary for infielders to throw the ball around the bases after a putout; nor did he believe a reliefer needed eight warmup pitches. To help enforce the rule that stated that a pitcher was required to get his throw off in twenty seconds, Veeck had a clock, called a "pitchometer," installed in the Comiskey Park scoreboard that was supposed to tick off the time in full view of the audience as the pitcher performed his usual ablutions on the mound. Veeck left Chicago, however, before the rule could be enforced.

THE ULTIMATE SOLUTION

Perhaps the most daring and innovative proposed rule change for baseball was made in 1974 by a Maryland writer named George Udel, who put his thoughts down on paper after watching the Baltimore Orioles and New York Yankees play a game that summer. His proposal went like this:

"As a youngster I played baseball and still have a somewhat twisted finger to illustrate my general ineptness, but my being a no-field, no-hit (but otherwise quite acceptable) player did not embitter me toward the game. I have always felt that baseball was fun to play, but watching it as entertainment is about as exciting as watching a Liberty Ship rust.

"This revelation came as somewhat of a shock to me. Not that I was unaware of vague grumblings of dissent. I recall hearing that Bill Veeck as in Wreck once tried to eliminate pitcher dawdling a few years back, but I knew nothing would come of it and of course nothing did. I also knew, from personal experience, that baseball on TV is a bore.

"What disturbed me was finding out, after being away from the game for a year or two, that baseball at the park is also a stiff. Let me tell you what we got for our money. With variations, you have seen it many times yourself, I'm sure, but it bears repeating, especially in view of the startling proposals I have to offer. First of all, we saw pitcher Dave McNally play catch with Elrod Hendricks and Mel Stottlemyre play catch with Thurman Munson, which constituted the bulk of the action. In addition, we saw several dozen foul balls, an intentional pass, a seven-minute rhubarb, a great deal of nose-picking, sweat-wiping, armpit-scratching, pants-hiking, cap-removing, muscle-stretching, cap-replacing, time-calling, and a teensy bit of action. At the end of seven innings and nearly 2½ hours, with the score Baltimore 3, New York 2, my eleven-year-old bored son and I called it a day.

"An unusually dull game? I don't really think so. The reason I say this is that after three or four innings of gradually encroaching boredom, I began to analyze baseball to see if there were ways of speeding up the old game. Naturally, I saw the usual things—the intentional walk, most colossal piece of dullness in any sport, and the pitcher's attempt to pick off a runner, which is easily the most tedious nonaction in any organized sport. The foul ball, repeated several times, can also be pretty boring. But those are minor things. Along about the sixth inning, it suddenly struck me what was the dullest thing in baseball!

"It is this: The dullest thing in baseball is the sight of all those men jogging back and forth between the dugouts and their positions at the end of each half inning.

"This led me to a daring hypothesis. Instead of having nine innings of three outs per side, why not have three innings of nine outs per side?

"I mean, why nine innings? Who said so? Does it matter? More important, does anyone realize that nine innings, or eighteen half innings, is rather like an eighteen-act play with seventeen intermissions? Let's face it, intermissions are dull. When times were slower, plays were written in five acts, then reduced to four and then three. Today most plays have but one intermission. So why can't we reduce the number of intermissions in baseball?

"Doing so would have several major advantages (I'll get to the minor disadvantages in a moment), the greatest of which lies in the answer to this question: When is baseball most exciting?

"When a batter hits a home run? Not likely. Most people agree that baseball is most exciting when there are men on base, less than two out, and anything happens. A fly ball or a grounder can score a man from third base. Or that runner can be thrown out. Exciting. Failure to execute perfectly can result in all hands being safe. Exciting. A runner caught in a rundown can cause the defensive team to hesitate long enough for a teammate to score. Exciting. Even a base on balls with men on has a modicum of interest.

"But the nine-inning, three-out rule under which we are now pinioned assures that comparatively few men get on base during an inning, and those who do are left stranded. After one or two outs have been made, it is nearly impossible to have any sustained excitement. (I am aware of the old saw that states that anything is possible until the last out is made, but the odds are horrendously against that saw becoming reality.) Faced with empty bases and two outs, most batters try for the long ball and further reduce the chance of anything getting started.

"If, on the other hand, each team had nine outs per half inning, it would be much more likely to play hit-and-run baseball, try to squeeze in a run, and employ other stratagems that would add to the drama of the game by putting men on base and increasing their opportunity for scoring. All would not score, of course, but at least the odds would favor something happening rather than nothing happening, as is now the case.

"Furthermore, the action would be cumulative, as in football. Each inning would build to something, rather than being over after eleven pitches, and patrons' attention would be less likely to wander. After each half inning, there would be a three-to-five minute intermission to recoup the TV commercials lost by not having intermissions every ten minutes, as well as to allow fans at the park to purchase a two-dollar hotdog and dollar Coke. In the event of a tie, the teams could play standard three-out half innings until the deciding run is scored.

The Udel Solution—a Sample-inning Broadcast:

"The next batter here in the third and final inning, ladies and gentlemen, is Bill Johnson. In the first inning, Johnson doubled and struck out. In the second, he flied to right, walked, and scored. The score stands now at 6–6, the Dodgers have four outs, and the bases are loaded. Here comes the first pitch to Johnson. He hits a sharp ground ball to second. Miller takes it, throws to Jackson, who relays to first. Double play! There are six outs now, but on the play Wilson scored and Howard moved to third base. The Dodgers lead, 7–6. . . ."

"Now I don't say this will eliminate all the boredom of baseball, but it will make the sweat-wiping more tolerable.

"Aside from tampering with tradition, the disadvantages of the system would be minimal. The television networks would not care for it, I suppose, primarily because they would have fewer commercial possibilities. But if we increased the intermission time, they could double- or triple-spot. (As a matter of fact, I really wouldn't mind if an intra-inning break were called at the discretion of the umpire in order to give the pitcher a breather and the sponsor a chance to sell some beer. The important thing is to avoid all those men trotting back and forth.)

"I am aware that this would change the complexion of the game some. (Nine innings of three outs is not the same as three innings of nine outs, either for the participant or the statistician.) But we would still compute earned-run average, for those who insist that being able to define ERA is equivalent to having a Christian burial. And the pitcher who threw a no-hitter would still have to face twenty-seven men to earn his way into the Hall of Fame.

"Pitchers might complain about the new system, naturally, at least until they worked themselves into the shape athletes are supposed to be in. I do not deny that it would be more difficult to face nine, fifteen, or even twenty men an inning, but I'm sure those brave men with the rubber arms will be able to manage. Isn't the purpose of baseball, like horseracing, to improve the breed? And what breed was ever improved by sitting down every ten minutes?

"Traditionalists, naturally, will balk at the proposal. Their concern with preserving the game as it is, was, and ever shall be, no doubt stems from some unwritten pact with future generations of baseball buffs. They ask, 'What will history think of us in the year we rolled out the big asterisk and broke faith with both the past and the future?'

"Well, I happen to think history will forgive us. If they don't, I guess they'll just have to sue."

Mr. Udel's modest proposal for revolutionizing baseball was published in the Baltimore *Sun* under an assumed name. He had little desire, after all, to expose his family to the fury of aroused traditionalists, should they be momentarily diverted from their campaign against colored bases long enough to notice and digest the importance of his proposal.

BASKETBALL

When Dr. James Naismith invented the game of basketball—he wisely turned down the suggestion that it be called "Naismith Ball"—in 1891, he envisioned the new sport as one that could be played by any number of people on a side. The original rules, all thirteen of them, made no provision for dribbling and stated that if any team made three consecutive fouls, it counted as a goal for the opposition.

Early basketball games tended to be low-scoring. When a pair of squads representing the Central and Armory Hill branches of the YMCA met in February 1892, for example, the contest ended in a 2–2 tie. A month later the same two teams battled to a scoreless tie. Eventually the number of players was reduced to five a side and play speeded up. After a team scored, however, the action slowed to a crawl as the ball was brought back to center court and a jump ball used to determine which side gained control. That was the situation in basketball until the 1937–38 season, a milestone date when the center tap was eliminated and the ball given to the scored-on team.

Like baseball, basketball has been the subject of occasional rule changes, as well as many suggestions that were never put into the books. Unlike baseball's tradition-bound leaders, those deciding the fate of basketball have been rather more inclined to adopt rules to speed up the game.

THE HALF-POINT SOLUTION

In 1921, it was pointed out by some of those interested in basketball that the penalty shot was reduced to a meaningless gesture if the shooter did not have the ability to make it. By contrast, it was added, the penalty in other sports such as football or horseracing was absolute.

The transgressor paid, and that was that. Something in America's Puritan past was irritated by the fact that the guilty in basketball were occasionally to go unpunished for their "crime."

The remedy suggested for this moral oversight was that one-half point be added to the score of those against whom the foul was committed, thus eliminating the penalty throw. Fortunately for newspaper typesetters, the proposal was never adopted.

THREE POINTS FOR A GOAL

In 1933, as later, there were many coaches and fans who felt that basketball was dominated by officials' calls, an inordinate number of games being decided by the foul shot. In that year, the solution of Coach H. C. Carlson of the University of Pittsburgh was to propose that the value of a field goal be increased from two to three points. This, he said, would serve to restore the proper importance of the successful play by a team, as opposed to the accident of being fouled.

The idea of making certain baskets worth three points instead of two was revived when the American Basketball Association was founded in 1967. In order to challenge the strongly entrenched NBA, it was felt that the ABA needed a gimmick or two with which to entice the fans. One new rule put into use was the three-point basket, which counted when a player hit from beyond an arc roughly twenty-five feet from the hoop. The three-pointer may have helped some good long-shooters, but it produced no revolutionary effect. When the ABA and NBA merged following the 1975–76 season, the three-point basket was eliminated.

THE CENTER-TAP CONTROVERSY

Criticism against the slowness created by the center tap began during the 1920s and continued to grow along with interest in the game itself. One of those most interested in bringing about a change was Nat Holman, a highly respected coach and member of the original Boston Celtics. On April 2, 1933, Holman was able to demonstrate his alternative to the center tap during a game held at the Young Men's Hebrew Association at Ninety-second Street, New York City. A packed house, including many basketball officials, was on hand. The teams consisted of players representing the YMHA vs. a squad of stars from St. John's University and CCNY.

A Slow Game of 1930:
Perhaps the dullest basketball game, from the point of view of scoring, was played on March 7, 1930, between Georgetown of Chicago and Homer. After scoring on a foul shot in the first period, Georgetown proceeded to stall. Realizing they were only a point behind, the Homer players made little attempt to break up the delaying tactics until the final three minutes of play. By then, however, it was too late. Georgetown won, 1–0.

Holman's solution to the center tap was to give the ball to the scored-on team at half court. The officials who were invited to see the game, which was won by the YMHA, 28–25, were noncommittal.

Despite the success of Holman's experiment, nothing was done for five years, and even after the decision was made to eliminate the center tap, many opposed the new rule. On January 21, 1938, for example, Dr. Marcus Hobart, physician for the Northwestern University basketball team, stated that experiments had shown that eliminating the center jump (and subsequent period of relaxation) stimulated players' hearts to a dangerous degree. He claimed that the normal beat of 60 to 90 per minute was increased in many cases to as high as 144.

Once fans were exposed to the new excitement of the game and raising of their own pulse rates, however, the center tap in basketball went the way of the minuet.

RAISING THE BASKETS

When Dr. Naismith laid out his first basketball court in 1891, the balcony railing of his gymnasium just happened to be ten feet from the floor. He therefore hung his peach baskets at that altitude, which is where they have remained ever since.

Not everyone has been happy about this, however, particularly those who feel the ten-foot height gives a marked advantage to those players who are merely tall, rather than tall and skillful. As early as 1932, Forrest (Phog) Allen, coach at Kansas, promoted the idea of raised baskets. "The muscles of the eyes accommodate easily to changes in height," he argued. "Once this accommodation is made it is just as easy to shoot at a twelve-foot basket as it is at a ten-foot one."

Allen staged several experimental games while at Kansas, but in 1954 the National Basketball Association went even further by actually playing a game with twelve-foot baskets that counted in the standings. The participants in the game of March 7 were Minneapolis and Milwaukee. The Lakers had difficulty hitting the twelve-foot hoops and were outscored from the field, 26–22, but overcame the deficit at the foul line by making twenty-one free throws to win, 65–63. Perhaps the lower score of the experimental game deterred league officials from playing additional contests with higher baskets, for no more were scheduled after the single game of 1954.

Other Scores of the Same Evening:
Contrasted to the Minneapolis-Milwaukee score of 65–63 were the following results of March 7, 1954:
  Rochester 91, New York 88
  Syracuse 103, Baltimore 77
  Boston 86, Fort Wayne 80
Which meant that each side playing with conventional ten-foot hoops scored 87 points compared to the 64-point average in the twelve-foot game.

Thirteen years later, interest in twelve-foot baskets resurfaced when Tennessee Coach Ray Mears co-operated with *Sports Illustrated* to stage an intrasquad game with elevated hoops. Dividing the first-stringers evenly between the Orange and the White teams, Mears assigned seven-foot Tom Boerwinkle to the Oranges and six-ten Bobby Croft to the Whites. A crowd of fifty-one hundred was on hand for the game, which featured the two squads missing their first seventeen shots at the basket. "Poor shooting was not surprising," wrote *SI*'s Mervin Hyman, "because none of the players had had enough time to become familiar with the new dimensions, but all agreed that they could achieve former accuracy with practice."

The final score of the game was Whites 43, Oranges 36. The unhappiest player was Boerwinkle, who complained, "There is just no way to get a tip-in. I hope twelve-foot baskets never come about."

THE TWENTY-FOUR-SECOND CLOCK

The lowest score in modern professional basketball was registered on November 22, 1950, when the Detroit Pistons beat the Minneapolis Lakers, 19–18.

Visions of such "freezing" tactics obviously frightened NBA officials, for they soon set to looking for ways to guarantee a certain amount of scoring. The result, first employed in 1954, was the twenty-four-second rule, which required a team to shoot within twenty-four seconds of gaining possession of the ball or turn it over to the opposing team.

The innovation proved successful, streamlining the professional game even further.

FOOTBALL

During the first decades of its existence, American college football changed considerably from soccer and rugby, reaching milestones in 1880 when a crude scrimmage line was used, in 1882 when the idea of "downs" originated, and in 1883, when numerical scoring was introduced. Subsequent changes occurred with the legalization of the forward pass and increase in value of the touchdown, thus placing more emphasis on pushing the ball across the goal rather than kicking it through the uprights. By 1912, when the number of downs was set at four and the kickoff moved from the fifty- to the forty-yard line, football very nearly resembled the game that is played today.

Tinkering continued, however, resulting in occasional changes in the rules and methods of scoring.

RUNNING WITH A FUMBLE

One of the rules surviving the evolution of football from rugby was that permitting a player to pick up an opponent's fumble and run with the ball. By 1921, however, the highly influential Fielding "Hurry-up" Yost was already on record as being against the rule, feeling that the ball should be whistled dead at the point of recovery. "It is doubtful if Mr. Yost's suggestion will meet with the favor of the sport-loving public," one reporter wrote, "who are always looking for these unexpected thrills at big games."

Mr. Yost happened to be on the football rules committee, however, and continued to push for the rule change, which finally came about in 1929.

Some Great Fumble Recoveries Resulting in Touchdowns:

Most dramatic—*In 1911, Princeton end Sam White grabbed a Yale fumble on his own 40-yard line and rambled 60 yards for the touchdown that enabled his team to win, 6–3.*

Longest—*In 1901, Sanford B. Hunt of Cornell picked up a fumble by the Carlisle Indians and raced 105 yards for a touchdown.*

Professional football took the opposite point of view. NFL officials obviously felt that the run with recovered fumble was an exciting play, retaining it in their rule book.

THE VITAL POINT(S) AFTER—PART ONE

In the early days of football, the point after touchdown was actually more important than the TD itself, the rules of 1883 providing only two points for a touchdown, but four points for the kick after goal. Later the rule was adopted that following a touchdown, the scored-on team lined up on the goal line while the scoring team kicked from placement at the ten-yard line. Members of the defensive team were not allowed to rush the kicker or in any other way try to impede the ball's progress.

Critics of this method charged that the point-after try was too mechanical. In 1922, therefore, a new rule was instituted whereby the ball was put on the five-yard line after a touchdown. From that point, the offense could add the extra point by run or kick and the defense had the opportunity to influence the outcome.

THE 160-PLAY GAME

One of the more interesting experiments in football was carried out on November 7, 1925, when Brown and Boston University took the field at Providence, Rhode Island, to play a game composed not of four fifteen-minute quarters, but of four periods, each composed of 40 plays.

The game grew out of the research of Harry R. Coffin of Harvard, who tabulated the results of various college games at the time. After showing that there was an average of 166 plays per game, he suggested that the stopwatch be eliminated in favor of a flat rate of 160 plays per game.

Why? Mr. Coffin claimed that the new system would (1) eliminate the frantic use of the forward pass near the end of a game, when a team has the opportunity to win but very little time and no means, other than an incomplete pass, of stopping the clock; (2) eliminate controversy as to whether or not the clock should be kept running; and (3) increase the interest of spectators.

Somehow Brown and Boston University were talked into playing a game under the new system, but unfortunately for Mr. Coffin and those who advocated his plan, the game was hardly a fair test. For one thing, Brown scored on the third play of the game and by halftime held a 21–0 lead. And for the final 20 plays of the game, Boston watched frantically as Brown controlled the ball, grinding out just enough yardage to keep the slow-moving drive alive. The final score was Brown 42, Boston University 6. "Whether the system proved successful or not is open to argument," one writer noted, "for the game was so drab, the football displayed so poor, that only an earthquake, blizzard, or a typhoon would have raised the spectators from their lethargy."

The 160-play system definitely added to the drabness, however, for later in the game, without the urgency of the clock to propel them, Boston's players tended to waste time between plays. By the third period, the game had consumed so much time that by mutual agreement both the third and fourth quarters were reduced from 40 to 35 plays each. That was the end of Coffin's football follies.

COUNTING FIRST DOWNS AS POINTS

Although counting first downs as points in football is roughly the equivalent of counting

Some Games Using the Warner System:							Actual	Warner
Game	Teams	Tds.	FG.	XP.		1st D.	Score	Score
1947 NFL	Chicago Cardinals	4	0	4		11	28	35
Championship	Philadelphia Eagles	3	0	3		22	21	40
1958 NFL	Baltimore Colts	3	1	2		27	23	48
Championship	New York Giants	2	1	2		10	17	25
Super Bowl	Oakland Raiders	4	2	2		21	32	51
XI	Minnesota Vikings	2	0	2		20	14	32

singles and doubles in baseball as partial runs, no less a person than Glenn "Pop" Warner in 1928 advocated that a first down add one point to a team's score. His reasoning was that rewarding a ball-control team would tend to upgrade the overall quality of football, encouraging coaches to abandon long pass plays in favor of a solid and consistent attack. Warner's scoring system would count touchdowns as six points and field goals as three, but would eliminate the point-after attempt. In later years, the system might have been appreciated by Woody Hayes of Ohio State or Vince Lombardi during his ball-control days with the Green Bay Packers, but little credence was given to it at the time. By switching the emphasis from touchdowns scored from any point on the field to grind-it-out single points, the system could have revolutionized football. But fans and coaches of the late 1920s and early 1930s had already decided they liked the game the way it was.

THE VITAL POINT(S) AFTER—PART TWO

Less than a decade after the extra-point dilemma seemed to have been solved, Chuck Collins, football coach at the University of North Carolina, suggested that teams have a choice following a touchdown. Collins proposed that after a TD the ball be placed on the ten-yard line, where the scoring team would have four more downs to add two additional points by running or passing the ball across the goal line. Or, if it decided on a kick, it could earn one point.

Collins' rationale, that such a system would tend to eliminate tie games, was valid, but the time was not ripe for such a rule change.

A LEGAL FIFTH DOWN

In 1933, Ed Thorp, chairman of the Eastern Association of Intercollegiate Football Officials' rules committee, along with Al Farrier of Dartmouth and W. R. Crowley of Bowdoin, made an interesting recommendation at a meeting of the EAIFO. They had studied the game carefully, they said, and had discovered that a better balance between offense and defense might be brought about if the football field were divided into three zones. In two of the zones, the team with the ball would have five downs to gain ten yards instead of the traditional four. The three men had arrived at the decision because (1) a team within its own twenty-yard line often tended to kick on second or third down in order to avoid a blocked punt, and (2) teams often had trouble gaining ten yards once they moved deep into their opponent's territory. By giving the offensive team an extra down deep in its own territory and as it neared the opposing goal, it was argued, a drive might have a

better chance of getting started and end successfully. The result, Thorp said, would be less punting and more scoring.

The proposal generated interesting discussion but no action.

The Zone System:

Offensive Team Has Ball On	Name of Zone	Number of Downs
OWN 0–20 Yard Line	Frigid	5
OWN 20–Opponent 20	Temperate	4
Opponent 20–goal	Torrid	5

HAVING THE SECOND HALF BEGIN WHERE THE FIRST HALF ENDED

In 1939, there was considerable discussion given to the possibility of resuming play at the beginning of the second half at the point where the first half ended, the proponents arguing that often a team made an excellent drive only to have time run out. Those against the suggestion stated that the point of the intermission was not only to rest but also to have the opportunity to start, to borrow a boxing term, from "scratch."

A compromise proposal was that the team in whose territory the first half ended would kick off from the yard-line to which the ball had been advanced. Thus the team that had worked the ball into its opponent's territory would not lose possession.

Proponents could not muster sufficient enthusiasm, however, and once again no action was taken.

COLORED HELMETS

In 1949 the National Football League passed a ruling that, provided they all wore the same color, eligible pass receivers of a team would be permitted to wear helmets that were different from those of their ineligible teammates.

The rule was generally ignored in the NFL, but when the World Football League came along in 1974, its eligible receivers were clothed in everything from different-colored helmets to different-colored pants.

THE TWO-POINT CONVERSION

It came as a shock to most college coaches in January 1958 when the National Collegiate Athletic Association football rules committee followed the lead of the retiring chairman, Herbert O. "Fritz" Crisler, who proposed that teams have the option of trying to run or pass for two points after a touchdown or kick a single-point conversion. "It will add drama to what has been the dullest, most stupid play in the game," Crisler said. "It is a progressive step which will make football more interesting for the spectators."

Generally speaking, the majority of college coaches were appalled. They also incorrectly predicted that coaches would always go for the two points from the three-yard line rather than try for the safe kick. The very opposite turned out to be the case, most college coaches opting for the single point if they had a fair kicker. That way, the other coach was saddled with the need to make a decision.

In 1960, when the American Football League came into existence, the two-point conversion was adopted for the professionals. But when the AFL and NFL merged, the option—and subsequent potential for agonizing over a wrong decision—was eliminated. Commissioner Pete Rozelle obviously reasoned that NFL coaches had enough troubles without having to worry about losing games by the margin of an extra point.

CHAPTER 14—1891–1900

1891

Winners: Baseball: Boston wins in both the National League and American Association, but there is no postseason series. Sapped by financial losses, the AA expires quietly at end of season. . . . *Kentucky Derby:* Kingman, last of three Derby winners ridden by black jockey Isaac Murphy. *Preakness:* Not raced. *Belmont Stakes:* Foxford . . . *Boxing:* In middleweight division, Bob Fitzsimmons stops Jack Dempsey "The Nonpareil" in thirteen rounds at New Orleans. . . . *Football:* College champion selected by Helms Athletic Foundation: Yale (13–0–0).

Other Happenings: Belmont Stakes brings in $750,000 and total betting across nation for year amounts to $200 million. . . . Rising young heavyweight James J. Corbett and Peter Jackson, black, fight to sixty-one-round draw. . . . Ski tournament is held January 16 at Ishpeming, Michigan. . . . First Metropolitan Handicap is run at Belmont, Tristan, a six-year-old, winning. . . . John McGraw, eighteen, plays first game with Baltimore Orioles of the American Association. He boots a grounder in the field and strikes out with the bases loaded, but manages to do well enough to be asked back for 1892. . . . The Jockey Club of New York is founded by Leonard Jerome with 1,250 "annual members" and 50 life members, February 16. . . . The Shinnecock Hills Golf Club, first for women, is also organized. . . . An international tug-of-war tournament is held at Madison Square Garden the week before Christmas. . . . A new baseball rule allows player substitution any time during game. Previously, player cannot be put in game after second inning. . . . Will Smalley, third baseman for Cleveland and Washington, 1890–91, dies of cancer on October 11, age twenty. . . . Jim Fogarty, manager of Philadelphia club in Players' League, dies of consumption at twenty-seven. . . . Amos Rusie of Giants pitches no-hitter in National League— vs. Brooklyn, July 31—and Ted Breitenstein, of St. Louis in AA, becomes first pitcher to hurl no-hitter in his first major-league start, beating Louisville, 8–0, on October 4. . . . Mike Tiernan of New York Giants wins National League home-run title by hitting seventeen, one more than Harry Stovey of Boston. Duke Farrell of American Association Boston club leads that circuit with twelve.

1892

Winners: Baseball: For the first time in a decade, the National League has a monopoly in baseball. It also has twelve teams and a problem as to what to do to sustain interest through a 150-game season. It "solves" the problem by playing a split season, the winner of the first half playing the winner of the second half. Fortunately, different teams win, Boston taking the first-half honors, Cleveland the second. Boston wins the postseason series as well, taking 5 games in a row after a tie. . . . *Kentucky Derby:* Azra. *Preakness:* Not run. *Belmont Stakes:* Patron . . . *Boxing:* "Battle of the Century" brings together John L. Sullivan, thirty-three, and James J. Corbett, twenty-six, which is won in twenty-one rounds by Corbett on September 7 at New Orleans. Sullivan's comment: "I fought once too often." . . . In the welterweight division, "Mysterious Billy" Smith defeats Danny Needham in fourteen rounds and claims title. . . . *Football:* College champion selected by Helms Athletic Foundation: Yale (13–0–0).

Other Happenings: To inaugurate first twelve-team National League, Amos Rusie of Giants beats Tim Keefe of the Phils, 5–4, on April 12. . . . Cincinnati Reds celebrate first Sunday baseball game on April 17 by beating St. Louis, 5–1, as Biddy McPhee hits home run (and during 143 more games, he hits three more). . . . On June 6, Willie Keeler makes pro debut as a left-handed shortstop with Binghamton in Eastern League. He gets one hit, makes one error. . . . The same day, President Benjamin Harrison watches Cincinnati beat Washington, 7–4, in eleven innings. It is the first visit by a U. S. President to a National League ball park. . . . On June 10, Wilbert Robinson goes seven-for-seven and bats in eleven runs as Orioles trounce St. Louis, 25–7. . . . The month of February is enlivened by a seventy-seven-round, five-hour, eight-minute fight at Nameoki, Illinois, the longest under Marquis of Queensberry rules to end in a knockout. The winner is Harry Sharpe; the loser, Frank Crosby. . . . Professional football begins as Pudge Heffelfinger accepts five hundred dollars for helping Allegheny Athletic Association defeat rival Pittsburgh, 6–0. . . . Black-college football also begins when Livingstone College and Biddle (later Johnson C. Smith) University play Thanksgiving Day game at Salisbury, North Carolina. Biddle wins, 4–0. . . . Football begins at Stanford, the team playing four games in the spring and five in the fall. . . . Also, Auburn and Georgia Tech start first seasons. . . . On October 15, Charlie Jones of Cincinnati becomes second pitcher in major-league baseball to hurl a no-hitter in his first start. The 7–1 victory over Pittsburgh is Charlie's entire record for 1892, coming so late in the season, but great things are predicted for the twenty-two-year-old rookie. . . . Other no-hitters are credited to John Stivetts of Boston and Alex Sanders of Louisville. . . . Best mile run of year is made by G. W. Orton (4:27⅜). . . . On August 29, Billy "Pop" Shriver of Chicago becomes the first baseball player to catch a ball dropped from the top of the Washington Monument. . . . On January 20, students at the International YMCA Training School in Springfield, Massachusetts, play a basketball game, the first using Dr. Naismith's new rules.

1893

Winners: Baseball: National League remains unwieldy twelve-club circuit as Boston wins pennant, Washington finishes last. Owners cannot decide on what to do at close of season, so do nothing. . . . *Kentucky Derby:* Lookout. *Preakness:* Not raced. *Belmont Stakes:* Comanche . . . *Boxing:* Having won heavyweight title, James J. Corbett continues to pursue his career as an actor. . . . Kid Lavigne claims lightweight title, and most fight experts agree he is best in division. . . . *Football:* College champion selected by Helms Athletic Foundation: Princeton (11–0–0).
Other Happenings: The University of Pennsylvania holds its first series of relay races. The first contest is between teams from Penn. The second is among Penn and Princeton runners, the latter winning the mile relay in 3 minutes, 34 seconds. . . . On April 6, longest fight with gloves is held at San Francisco between Andy Bowen and Jack Burke, the two fighting to a "no contest" decision for 110

rounds (seven hours, ten minutes). . . . Sunday baseball is played in Chicago for the first time and football comes to Tulane, Texas, Mississippi, Oregon State, and LSU. . . . Hockey on ice is introduced to the United States at Yale and Johns Hopkins universities. Stanley Cup, the oldest trophy competed for by professional athletes in North America, is donated by Frederick Arthur, Lord Stanley of Preston and son of the Earl of Derby. The trophy, worth about fifty dollars in 1893 money, is to be presented to amateur hockey champion of Canada but in 1910 it is taken over by professional National Hockey Association. . . . First winner of trophy in 1893 is Montreal Amateur Athletic Association. . . . On August 16, the first no-hitter pitched at new distance of sixty feet, six inches is that of William Hawke of Baltimore, who defeats Washington, 6–0. . . . Another baseball rule change makes round bats mandatory. . . . On August 27 Washington and St. Louis play a twelve-inning scoreless tie, then play fourteen more innings the next day for a grand total of twenty-six scoreless innings. Washington finally scores a run and wins in the fifteenth inning of the second game. . . . Domino wins nine races and $170,790 as an undefeated two-year-old. . . . First Kentucky Futurity for three-year-old trotters is run and won by Oro Wilkes in 2 minutes, 14½ seconds. Oro Wilkes is leading money-winning trotter of 1893 with earnings of $13,425. Leading pacer, May Marshall, wins $9,200. . . . Baseball holds popularity contest. Winners are Buck Ewing, former New York Giant with Cleveland Spiders; Ned Williamson; Cap Anson, in his eighteenth season with Chicago, and King Kelly, the colorful slugger finishing his baseball career with the New York Giants. . . . A scandal develops when it is discovered that seven members of the University of Michigan football team are not students at the school. . . . A. A. Zimmerman becomes first internationally known American amateur bicyclist by winning one-mile and ten-mile sprints. . . . America's Cup yacht race of October 7–13 shows superiority of United States' *Vigilant,* which wins three races to none for England's *Valkyrie.* . . . Charlie Jones, sensational rookie of 1892 who pitched no-hitter in first major-league start, wins one game, loses four, and is finished in major-league baseball.

1894

Winners: Baseball: The Baltimore Orioles, with Willie Keeler, John McGraw, Hugh Jennings, Wilbert Robinson, and Dan Brouthers, win pennant in National League, then play second-place club, New York, for "championship" and first Temple Cup. New York embarrasses the Orioles by taking the series, four games to none. . . . *Kentucky Derby:* Chant. *Preakness:* Assignee. *Belmont Stakes:* Henry of Navarre . . . *Boxing:* Heavyweight champion Jim Corbett, his ego wounded by insults from challenger Charlie Mitchell, successfully defends his crown on January 25 at the Duval Athletic Club, Jacksonville, Florida. . . . In welterweight division, Tommy Ryan defeats "Mysterious Billy" Smith in twenty rounds at Minneapolis. . . . George Dixon outgrows bantamweight division and retires, but continues to fight as featherweight. On September 25, Jimmy Barry and Casper Leon battle for vacant title, Barry knocking out Leon in twenty-eight rounds. . . . *Golf:* First *USGA Open* is held and won by Willie Dunn. . . . *Hockey:* 1893–94 Stanley Cup winner: Montreal Amateur Athletic Association . . . *Football:* College champion selected by Helms Athletic Foundation: Yale (16–0–0).

Other Happenings: Football comes to Oregon, Texas A&M, and Tuskegee. . . . The first intercollegiate fencing tournament is held at New York City's Racquet and Tennis Club on May 5. Harvard defeats Columbia, 5–4. . . . Stanley Cup championship match between Montreal AAA and Ottawa Capitols draws five thousand fans. . . . In American football, the "flying wedge" is outlawed and game playing time reduced from ninety to seventy-one minutes. . . . Jack Johnson, age sixteen, takes part in "battle royal" ring fights, which usually involve groups of blacks fighting against each other until only one survives. . . . Founded: United States Golf Association, on December 22 . . . In his debut with Louisville on June 30, later Hall of Famer Fred Clarke hits a home run and four singles. He finishes season with .275 batting average but later retires after twenty-one seasons with .330 career average. . . . No no-hitters are pitched in National League. . . . Beatrice Von Dressden, a daring woman balloonist, is killed in October when she falls from the basket of her vehicle during Buffalo Fair. . . . The University of Chicago becomes the first college to play a full basketball schedule of games, defeating the Chicago YMCA training school, 19–11, in the first contest. Season record is six wins, one loss. . . . On May 30, Bobby Lowe becomes first major leaguer to hit four home runs in a single game. The Boston second baseman ends the season with seventeen, but loses home-run title to teammate Hugh Duffy, who hits eighteen. . . . On August 1, George Samuelson and Frank Harbo complete their task of crossing the three thousand miles of the Atlantic

Ocean in a rowboat. The trip started on June 6. . . . In sensational match race held on September 15, Domino and Henry of Navarre finish in a dead heat after a mile and an eighth. . . . First midwestern football team to play on the West Coast is the University of Chicago, which defeats Stanford, 24–4, on Christmas Day. For three games, Washington Senators use left-handed second baseman, Ernest "Kid" Mohler, nineteen, who goes on to become top base stealer in minor leagues until 1914.

1895

Winners: Baseball: The Baltimore Orioles again win pennant in National League and once again lose Temple Cup series to second place Cleveland Spiders, four games to one. . . . *Kentucky Derby:* Halma. *Preakness:* Belmar. *Belmont Stakes:* Belmar . . . *Boxing:* Jim Corbett announces retirement in November but hardly anyone believes it. Top challenger Bob Fitzsimmons fights and defeats Con Riordan, who dies following bout. . . . *Golf:* USGA Men's Open: Horace Rawlins . . . *Hockey:* 1894–95 Stanley Cup champion: Montreal Victorias . . . *Football:* College champion selected by Helms Athletic Foundation: Pennsylvania (14–0–0).

Other Happenings: Mrs. C. S. Brown wins first USGA Women's Amateur Open golf championship at Meadowbrook course, Westbury, New York. . . . Football comes to Mississippi State, but not very happily, the first game being a 21–0 loss to Southwest Baptist University. . . . The American Bowling Congress holds first convention on September 9 at Beethoven Hall, New York City. . . . Van Cortlandt Park golf course, New York, is opened to the public. . . . First auto race held in United States, sponsored by H. H. Kohlsaat, publisher of the Chicago *Times-Herald,* is won by Charles Duryea, who drives part of the way through a blinding snowstorm. . . . Not counting the pro career of Pudge Heffelfinger, the official beginning of professional football is linked to September 3 game at Latrobe, Pennsylvania. Quarterback John Brallier, who is paid ten dollars, leads Latrobe to a 12–0 victory over Jeannette (Pa.) Athletic Club. . . . The first USGA Amateur Golf Championship for men is won by Charles B. MacDonald. . . . Volleyball is invented by William G. Morgan, physical director of the YMCA at Holyoke, Massachusetts. His original name for the new game is "Minonette." . . . Domino becomes top money-winner among flat race horses, amassing $193,650. . . . First Kentucky Oaks for three-year-old fillies is run at Churchill Downs, won by Vinaigrette. . . . In first international track meet in United States, New York AC defeats London AC on September 21. . . . Michael F. Sweeney, champion high-jumper, leaps 6 feet, 5⅝ inches. . . . Bernie Wefers also equals world record for 100-yard dash by racing it in 9.8 seconds. In a total of eleven events, Americans finish first eleven times, have six seconds and two thirds. . . . At the Penn Relays, the United States team beats the London Athletic Club runners. . . . Founded on January 11: the Western (Big 9) Conference for collegiate football. The charter members are Chicago, Illinois, Michigan, Minnesota, Northwestern, Purdue, and Wisconsin. Indiana and Iowa join in 1899. (Chicago drops out in 1939 and Ohio State joins in 1912.) . . . Jack Dempsey "The Nonpareil," generally recognized as champion middleweight boxer during later 1880s, dies of tuberculosis at Portland, Oregon, age thirty-three. . . . Singles tennis champions for 1895 are Fred H. Hovey and Juliette P. Atkinson. . . . On September 7, America's Cup race begins, ends on the twelfth with the *Defender* (United States) having defeated Britain's *Valkyrie II*, three races to none.

1896

Winners: Baseball: Baltimore Orioles win third National League pennant in a row, then break the Temple Cup jinx by defeating second-place Cleveland, four games to none. . . . *Kentucky Derby:* Ben Brush. *Preakness:* Margrave. *Belmont Stakes:* Hastings . . . *Boxing:* James J. Jeffries, twenty-one, begins his boxing career while Corbett and Fitzsimmons talk about having a heavyweight championship bout. Kid McCoy becomes welterweight champ by knocking out Tommy Ryan in fifteen rounds at Maspeth, Long Island. . . . Kid Lavigne takes over lightweight title by dispatching Dick Burge in seventeen rounds at London. . . . *Golf: USGA Men's Open:* James Foulis . . . *Hockey:* 1895–96 Stanley Cup winner: Winnipeg Victorias (February); Montreal Victorias (December) . . . *Football:* College champion selected by Helms Athletic Foundation: Princeton (10–0–1).

Other Happenings: College football comes to Clemson College, a three-game season ending with wins over Furman and Wofford after a loss to South Carolina. . . . On Thanksgiving Day 1896, 5,000 games involving 120,000 players are seen. . . . On January 26, 1,200 spectators see basketball game between

Yale and the Central YMCA of Brooklyn. Yale wins, 8–7. . . . On September 7, Baltimore defeats Louisville in a baseball triple-header, 4–3, 9–1, 12–1. . . . Kentucky Derby winner Ben Brush is ridden by Willie Simms, a black jockey who is one of first to shorten stirrups and ride "monkey on a stick" style. . . . In baseball, Ed Delahanty hits four home runs in a single game and receives four boxes of chewing gum as a prize. . . . Touring Australian cricket team is defeated by Philadelphia club, 282–222. . . . Beatrix Hoyt wins first of three consecutive USGA Women's Amateur golf championships, defeating Miss N. C. Sargent at the Essex County Club. Manchester, Massachusetts. . . . Formed: the first United States ice hockey league. The amateur group, organized in New York City, consists of four teams. . . . Tim Keefe, former major-league pitcher, 1880–93, resigns as National League umpire, expressing disgust at fans and players' lack of respect. . . . No no-hitters are pitched in National League as Cy Young, with 29–16 record for Cleveland, finishes third in pitching honors behind Kid Nichols of Boston (30–15) and Lefty Frank Killen of Pittsburgh (30–18). . . . First six-day bicycle race for women starts on January 6 at New York's Madison Square Garden. . . . On January 16, basketball game with five players on a side, the first, takes place at Iowa City, Iowa, between the University of Iowa and University of Chicago. Chicago wins, 15–12. . . . An intercollegiate basketball game between women's teams is staged at the San Francisco Armory on April 4, Stanford defeating California, 2–1, before a crowd of seven hundred women.

1897

Winners: Baseball: Baltimore Orioles finish second in National League race to Boston but turn tables by winning the fourth and final Temple Cup Series, four games to one. . . . *Kentucky Derby:* Typhoon II. *Preakness:* Paul Kauvar. *Belmont Stakes:* Scottish Chieftain . . . *Boxing:* Heavyweight champion Jim Corbett is knocked out by Bob Fitzsimmons in fourteen rounds at Carson City, Nevada, March 17. Kid McCoy, Jack O'Brien, and Tommy Ryan all claim middleweight title. . . . When McCoy and Ryan step up from welterweight to middleweight, Mysterious Billy Smith claims welterweight title. On October 4, Solly Smith wins twenty-round decision from George Dixon to take featherweight title. . . . Jimmy Barry knocks out Walter Croot in London to become bantamweight champion. . . . *Golf: USGA Men's*

Open: Joe Lloyd . . . *Hockey:* 1896–97 Stanley Cup winner: Montreal Victorias . . . *Football:* College champion selected by Helms Athletic Foundation: Pennsylvania (16–0–0).

Other Happenings: Founded: Golf Association of Philadelphia . . . First Boston Marathon is run, J. J. McDermott of New York winning in two hours, fifty-five minutes, ten seconds. . . . Five-man basketball game (down from 7) played at New Haven, Connecticut, Yale beating Pennsylvania, 32–10, on March 20. . . . First fencer to win three titles (foil, epee, saber) in a year is Charles Bothner, New York Athletic Club, who accomplishes feat on May 1. . . . First pacer to cover mile in less than 2 minutes is Star Pointer, who is clocked in 1:59¼ at Readville, Massachusetts, on August 28. . . . On October 3, Cap Anson closes out twenty-seven-year baseball career, hitting two home runs. At forty-six, he is oldest to hit major-league home run. . . . Chicago Nationals, meanwhile, score in every inning in June 29 game vs. Louisville, setting major-league record for runs with 36–7 win. . . . Basketball, growing quickly, is played by fifty-seven athletic clubs around the nation. Harold Reeder, member of New York's Knickerbocker Athletic Club, puts together rules for new game of water polo. . . . Football scoring is changed so that touchdown is worth five points, goal after TD one point, and field goal five points. . . . College football comes to Hardin-Simmons. . . . Australian baseball team tours United States and embarrasses Americans by winning all ten games it plays against local clubs. . . . Cy Young throws his first no-hitter, beating Cincinnati, 6–0, on September 18. Year is enlivened by Wee Willie Keeler's hitting them where they ain't in forty-four consecutive games. . . . On July 31, more excitement is occasioned when pitcher Brickyard Kennedy of Brooklyn, protesting decision, throws ball at umpire Hank O'Day, allowing winning run to score. . . . In billiards, green chalk is introduced by William Spinks of Chicago. . . . Cruiser *Detroit's* baseball team wins tournament to become "champions of Uncle Sam's Navy." . . . Bicyclist M. Cordang rides for twenty-four hours at average speed of 25.7 mph. . . . Six-day bicycle races at Madison Square Garden are condemned and described as "brutal."

tucky Derby: Plaudit. *Preakness:* Sly Fox. *Belmont Stakes:* Bowling Brook . . . *Boxing:* Tommy Ryan is recognized as middleweight champion when he wins eighteen-round decision over George Green at San Francisco, February 25. . . . Dave Sullivan knocks out Solly Smith in five rounds to become featherweight champ, then is kayoed in ten rounds six weeks later by George Dixon. . . . *Golf:* USGA *Men's Open:* Fred Herd . . . *Hockey:* 1897–98 Stanley Cup champion: Montreal Victorias . . . *Football:* College champion selected by Helms Athletic Foundation: Harvard (11–0–0).

Other Happenings: On January 1, bicyclist Teddy Edwards begins to ride a hundred miles per day and keeps it up until September 7, covering a total distance of twenty-five thousand miles, the earth's circumference. . . . On July 9, U.S. cyclist W. W. Hamilton travels a record twenty-five miles, six hundred yards in an hour. . . . On April 21, Bill Duggleby makes pitching debut with the Philadelphia Phillies and hits bases-loaded home run in first major-league time at bat. The pitcher throwing the gopher ball is Cy Seymour of the New York Giants, who later becomes an outfielder and batting champion, finishing major-league career in 1913 with a .303 average. . . . On March 25 the International Shooting Association meets at the Fifth Avenue Hotel in New York and forms body composed of riflemen from Columbia, Princeton, Yale, Harvard, and Cornell. First meet is held on May 7. . . . Best kick of 1898 football season is sixty-two-yard goal by Pat O'Dea of Wisconsin in 47–0 rout of Northwestern. . . . Intercollegiate hockey is born on January 19 when Brown beats Harvard, 6–0, at Boston's Franklin Park rink. . . . Professional basketball starts with formation of National Basketball League, with teams in Philadelphia, New York City, Brooklyn, and southern New Jersey. . . . The New England League is also founded, its players being paid $150 to $225 a month. . . . Baseball increases number of games in season from 140 to 154. . . . Major-league no-hitters are pitched by Jim Hughes of Baltimore, Frank Donohue of Philadelphia, Walter Thornton of Chicago, and by Ted Breitenstein of Cincinnati. . . . Beatrix Hoyt wins third consecutive USGA Women's Amateur title by defeating Maude Wetmore at Ardsley-on-Hudson.

1898

Winners: Baseball: Still a twelve-club circuit, the National League does not bother with a postseason series after Boston edges the Baltimore Orioles for the pennant. . . . *Ken-*

1899

Winners: Baseball: The National League, a benevolent monopoly, features a modest pennant race between the Brooklyn Superbas,

Boston Beaneaters, and Philadelphia Phillies. There being no World Series of any sort, everyone goes home after Brooklyn wins by eight games. . . . *Kentucky Derby:* Manuel. *Preakness:* Half Time. *Belmont Stakes:* Jean Bereaud . . . *Boxing:* The two-year reign of heavyweight champion Bob Fitzsimmons comes to an end on June 9 at Coney Island when Jim Jeffries KOs Bob in the eleventh round. There is no official light-heavyweight division as yet, but Tommy Ryan rules the middleweights and Kid McCoy the welterweights. On July 3, Frank Erne wins the lightweight crown from Kid Lavigne via a twenty-round decision. . . . *Golf: USGA Men's Open:* Willie Smith . . . *Hockey:* 1898–99 Stanley Cup is won by Montreal Shamrocks. . . . *Football:* College champion selected by Helms Athletic Foundation: Harvard (10–0–1).

Other Happenings: University of Chicago comes East and becomes the first "western" football team to defeat a strong eastern squad by winning game with Cornell, 17–6. . . . College football is introduced at Baylor. . . . Yale's basketball team goes to Chicago for a series of exhibitions. . . . Founded: the Southern California Golf Association . . . On April 18, John McGraw, age twenty-six, makes his debut as manager of the Baltimore Orioles in the National League. He scores a 5–3 victory over the Giants, the team he will manage from 1902 to 1932. . . . In the world of bicycling, America's most popular sport, Charles "Mile a Minute" Murphy speeds a mile in just 57⅘ seconds on January 3. A railroad train just ahead of him creates a convenient vacuum for his record run. . . . The first motion picture of a real (nonstaged) fight is made during the Jim Jeffries-Tom Sharkey heavyweight fight at Coney Island on November 3. The twenty-five-round battle is won by Jeffries. . . . No-hit games are pitched in National League by Deacon Phillippe of Louisville (May 25, vs. New York) and Vic Willis of Boston (August 7, vs. Washington). . . . In football, Army beats Navy, 17–5, and Princeton wins a thriller over Yale, 11–10, when Poe's last-minute kick splits the uprights. . . . America's Cup competition of October 16–20 ends when U.S. vessel *Columbia* defeats British entry—first by Sir Thomas Lipton—*Shamrock I*, three races to none. . . . In November, newspapers make first mention of young billiard-playing boy named Willie Hoppe. . . . First telegraph billiards match is played between Wayman McCreery of St. Louis and Martin Mullin of Cleveland, fourteen-inch balkline. McCreery wins, 500–471. . . . James Gibbs, an engineer and founder of Amateur Athletic Union, invents new game by stretching a string across table and hitting rubber ball over string to family member. Game is at first called Ping-Pong, then changed to more respectable-sounding table tennis. . . . On December 12, United States patent number 638,920—for a golf tee—goes to George Grant.

1900

Winners: Baseball: The National League's decade as America's only major baseball circuit comes to a conclusion as Brooklyn wins its second consecutive pennant, edging Pittsburgh by 4½ games. . . . *Kentucky Derby:* Lieutenant Gibson. *Preakness:* Hindus. *Belmont Stakes:* Ildrim . . . *Boxing:* In the welterweight division, Rube Ferns wins the crown on a foul delivered in the twenty-first round by Billy Smith, then loses the title on October 16 to Matty Matthews. Featherweight Terry McGovern wins the championship on January 9 by knocking out George Dixon. . . . *Golf: USGA Men's Open:* Harry Vardon . . . *Hockey:* Montreal Shamrocks repeat to win the 1899–1900 Stanley Cup. . . . *Football:* College champion selected by Helms Athletic Foundation: Yale (12–0–0).

Other Happenings: Connor, an eleven-year-old pacer, wins $9,875, and Cresceus takes $13,250 to lead harness racers for the year. . . . Dwight Filley Davis offers a prize cup for intentional tennis competition and the Davis Cup is born. The first competition is held at Brookline, Massachusetts, in early August. The United States wins the first three matches and two more are rained out. The United States is declared the winner. The team consists of three Harvard men: Malcolm Davis Whitman, Dwight Filley Davis, and Holcombe Ward. . . . In January, Marty Bergen, twenty-nine-year-old catcher for the Boston Beaneaters of the National Baseball League, goes berserk, killing his family and then taking his own life. . . . John B. "Brewery Jack" Taylor, a pitcher for the Cincinnati Reds, also dies, of Bright's disease. . . . On July 12, Frank Hahn of Cincinnati pitches a 4–0 no-hitter against the Philadelphia Phillies. . . . Football fans are used to high-scoring contests, so when word arrives that Dickinson has defeated Haverford, 227–0, no one doubts that a new record has been achieved. The high score, however, turns out to be a telegrapher's error, the real margin of victory being a more modest 27–0. The triple-digit score goes into many records books, though, and remains there for years. . . . In spring,

Wilbert Robinson and John McGraw, both baseball stars and co-owners of the Diamond Bowling Alleys in Baltimore, introduce the game known as duck pins. John Ditmar, a Baltimore wood turner, produces the first set of ten-inch pins. . . . In a nontitle fight, Bob Fitzsimmons, 172 pounds, knocks out Ed Dunkhorst, 312 pounds, in Brooklyn.

Section IV
The 1900s

CHAPTER 15 — 1901

"Now a word as to the Orient Motor-Cycles," proclaimed the newspaper advertisement of the new century's first year, "they hold the often contested automobile road record from Philadelphia to Atlantic City, and in winning it maintained an average speed of 28 miles an hour for almost two and a half hours. . . . As to the expense, under ordinary conditions one of these machines can be operated on a quarter-cent a mile. We have several times run a Quadricycle with two people from Philadelphia to Atlantic City on less than a gallon of gasoline—less than 10 cents for 60 miles. Last Summer a commercial traveler in New England, instead of going to see his customers by rail, used an Orient Tricycle and covered 2,000 miles of rough road for less than $15."

Everyone seemed to be predicting great things for America as the century began. In Washington, Census Commissioner Robert P. Porter said that the population of the United States would reach three hundred million by the year 2001. President William McKinley, a dignified father-image who was said to be the most popular man in America, prepared to become the first President to succeed himself in office since U. S. Grant. Actuaries predicted that Americans of the twentieth century would live longer; industrialists predicted they would enjoy better products—if only organized labor would be reasonable in its demands. It was a land of opportunity and forgiveness, a nation where even a convicted bank-robber and cutthroat such as Frank James could be discharged from prison and immediately run for the Missouri Legislature.

In sports, the big news was that after nearly a decade of having but one major baseball league, the new American League was ready to challenge the old National. International competition added new excitement to specta-tor sports. In 1896 the first modern Olympics had been inaugurated at Athens, Greece. Following the 1900 Olympic Games at Paris, it was reported that the city of Chicago would put in the strongest bid for the 1904 Games. (They were eventually held in St. Louis.) The Davis Cup, started in 1900, provided interest for tennis enthusiasts. Auto racing, ice hockey, golf, college football, and bicycling challenged the decades-old supremacy of baseball, rowing, and pedestrianism as favorite American spectator sports.

BOXING

Of all the popular sports, boxing seemed to be at an all-time low, despite Gentleman Jim Corbett's bringing a measure of glamor to what was once the exclusive province of street fighters and broken-nosed semiliterates. Even Vice President Theodore Roosevelt, an advocate of nearly every sport, criticized boxing on January 9, 1901. "Boxing," he said, "might have been going on in New York right now if the men who had charge of the clubs had handled it with credit. They made a mistake by not stopping contests when they became brutal, or when it was manifest to all that one of the contestants had no possible chance of winning."

In a bit over a year, at least four men had died in the squared circle, two of them at New York's Greenwood Athletic Club. America had been treated also to what one newspaperman called "the fiercest fight ever seen in this country" at the Coney Island Athletic Club on August 3, 1899. The participants were Jim Jeffries and Tom Sharkey, Jeffries winning on points at the end of the twenty-fifth round. Before that, he pounded Sharkey from one side of the ring to the other. "The bout," Roosevelt said, "should have been stopped at the end of the twenty-third round, as it became brutal after that, and Sharkey had no chance." Then, turning his attention to the more recent battle between Corbett and Norman Selby, alias Kid McCoy, which ended in a fifth-round knockout for Corbett, Roosevelt added that the fight "was a sell-out. There are only a few honest fighters." With that, the man with the toothy smile departed for Meeker, Colorado, where a long-awaited hunting expedition ended with Roosevelt being chased up a tree by wolves and held prisoner for four hours.

HOCKEY

Those who were inclined to worry about the growing tendency toward roughness in sports pointed to a January 1901 hockey match at the Clermont Avenue rink in Brooklyn between the New York Athletic Club and Brooklyn Skating Club. "All former exhibitions of ruffianly methods were eclipsed last night," one reporter wrote. The incident in question took place when Cobb, a forward for New York, struck Brooklyn's Murray on the hand with his stick "with a force that fractured several small bones and sent Murray into the surgeon's care." After having his hand bandaged, Murray returned to action. He was hardly on the ice when words were exchanged between him and the New Yorkers. No one knows exactly what was said; the next action, however, was plainly clear: Murray raised his stick and brought it down with full force on Cobb's head. Bleeding from a long scalp wound, Cobb fell to the ice. Hissing and shouting, spectators poured onto the playing area, determined to tear Murray to shreds if they could get near him.

Cobb later went home under his own power, his head bearing eighteen stitches as a result of the incident. In the dressing room later, Murray said that he had not tried to avenge the blow on his hand, but had reacted to a sneering remark from Cobb. New York, weakened by Cobb's loss, dropped the game, 6–2.

BILLIARDS

There were gentler moments in the 1901 world of sports. One occurred at the billiard parlor of Maurice Daly, where "a new star in the billiard world," and even more amazing, a woman, was on exhibition. Her name was May Kaarlus, and her presence guaranteed a large crowd of both professionals and amateurs. May's specialty was the trick shot, and being ambidextrous, she constantly amazed the crowd as well as her opponent, Maurice Daly himself. The format was simplicity itself. Miss Kaarlus would perform a shot or series of shots and Daly would attempt to duplicate the feat. He seldom succeeded, for "the shots made included many seemingly impossible counts, the most spectacular of which were her 'push draw,' a massé known as 'May's own,' and some brilliant follows. As a windup she kept eight balls going in procession, hardly a foot apart . . . then, with sixteen balls, played in the same manner, from many cushions gathered the sixteen in a compact bunch in one corner of the table."

A week later, to celebrate ladies' night at the Hanover Club, Brooklyn, May Kaarlus added several finishing touches to her dazzling display. On this occasion, Arthur Townsend, club champion, was given the task of repeating her shots, faring not much better than Maurice Daly. May executed a total of fifty-five different plays—draws, follows, two- and more cushion caroms, force draws, and one spectacular trick shot in which "the ball was made to jump from the cushion fully three feet back over the table, Miss Kaarlus catching it like a baseball, throwing it down the table and then shooting the other ball after it. . . . Mr. Townsend failed to make the ball jump more than a few inches. . . ." Of the fifty-five shots, Townsend was able to equal the young woman on but eleven occasions. Even more amazing is the fact that May Kaarlus was only fifteen years old.

February of 1901 found Americans mourning the recent death of Queen Victoria of Great Britain, victims of the Pacific mail steamer *Rio De Janeiro,* which struck a rock in San Francisco Harbor, and the five killed when the *Chicago Limited* became derailed near Greenville, Pennsylvania. Spectator sports attractions were at a minimum, unless one counted the systematic dismantling of Kansas saloons by women of the WCTU. In that respect, February was a banner month for ax-wielding reformers.

BOXING

March 1901 was ushered in by news of an attraction that usually drew good crowds—an interracial fight. The site was Germania Hall in Baltimore, the participants Harry Lyons, "colored," and Jack Hamilton, a journeyman boxer from Troy, New York. Hamilton weighed in at 135 pounds, Lyons at 129. Interestingly, the fight was held on the stage at the club, which sloped several degrees to the south. The men had never fought each other; therefore they spent considerable time in the beginning examining each other's style. Lyons, the quicker of the two, managed to land many more blows than Hamilton, who was handicapped by less reach as well as by heavy feet. Nevertheless, the fight was a very interesting one, even during the slow start. By the third round, however, Lyons was in such command that he was characterized as moving around

Hamilton "like a squirrel around a nut. He hit and jabbed as he pleased and Hamilton appeared to be defenseless." In the eighth round, Hamilton absorbed a great deal of punishment, but did not appear distressed, giving Lyons several good shots in return. By the seventeenth round, it was obvious that Lyons didn't pack a strong enough punch to dispatch Hamilton with one blow, and the heavier man seemed to be able to take as many of Lyons' flurries as the black could manage. The eighteenth round began with Lyons landing a left to the jaw and a vicious uppercut with his right. Hamilton came back with a "punch so strong that the people yelled: 'Good boy, Jack.'" Unfortunately for Hamilton, the blow struck mostly air, but as one reporter noted, it showed "that Hamilton was still in the running and that the crowd comprehended that . . . [he] was ready to hand out a blow at any time."

A "Funny" Interracial Fight

Later in 1901, another interracial contest took place at Germania Hall that confirmed what white people had always known about blacks:

"The preliminary fights were fast and furnished the spectators with many opportunities to give vent to their pent-up enthusiasm. The first pair was 'Kid' Green, colored, and Harry Boxley, white. Boxley gave a practical demonstration of the old saying, 'to hurt a negro kick him on the shin.' After beating Green with his gloves on every part of his anatomy from waist up, without making any perceptible impression, Boxley suddenly hit a bit low as Green lifted his left leg, his shoe accidentally striking Green's shin. The colored boy's mouth flew open, his eyes bulged, and in a few seconds, he was out of the ring, giving up the fight without a murmur or protest."

Baltimore Sun, *November 9, 1901*

In the nineteenth round, Hamilton actually landed several blows, most of them short lefts. Lyons took most of them on his gloves or shoulders. The fight continued that way until the end of the twenty-fourth round, when Lyons was declared the winner on points.

BASEBALL

March brought confirmation that the new American League was serious in its intent to challenge the National. Because of the pres-

ence of competition, of course, many of the better ballplayers had either jumped to the new league for more money or insisted on getting more from their own clubs. The situation distressed the owners as well as a modicum of newsmen. "If more National League players jump, the salary bills will be increased proportionately," wrote the Chicago *Journal*. "As it is, the eight clubs are down for salaries amounting to $203,000. At $.25, that means that 812,000 people must see the American League games to even pay the players, to say nothing of the cost of the new grounds, traveling expenses, pay of umpires, price of balls, home plates, and benches, pay of secretaries, groundskeepers, and employees, adverting, and a hundred minor bills. Can the new league get away with it? On the cold figures, it looks as if they would have trouble in the effort." As usual, the majority of sportswriters at the time favored the establishment rather than the players or new operators.

Some "Rich" Ballplayers, 1901	
Napoleon Lajoie (Philadelphia, AL)	$3,500
Herm McFarland (Chicago, AL)	$2,800
Win Mercer (Washington, AL)	$3,000
Lave Cross (Philadelphia, AL)	$3,000
Joe McGinnity (Baltimore, AL)	$2,500

But it promised to be an interesting season. Boston, of the fledgling American League, had a new stadium on Huntington Avenue, which officially opened on March 7. In Chicago, the season promised excitement because so many playing dates clashed, the city—like Boston and Philadelphia—having teams in each circuit. The American League schedule was supposed to be 140 games in length, but actually no team played more than 136.

MOTORCYCLING

The first year of the new century was a significant one for motorcyclists. George Hendee, the father of American motorcycles, was busily at work developing his model known as The Indian, barely in time to beat the first Harley Davidson by the Davidson brothers of Milwaukee. In March 1901, a young speedster named Frank Clark made what he claimed was the first "century (a hundred miles without rest) on a motorcycle. Accompanied by members of the Century Cycling Club (bicycles) of Maryland, he left the organization's headquarters at 513 West Baltimore Street shortly after seven o'clock on the morning of March 17. The wind was strong and thus conditions were unfavorable. During the course of his eight-hour journey, Clark stopped four times to renew cylinder oil in the engine and three times to add gasoline. Then, as he neared the ninety-eighth mile, he punctured a tire at Belvidere and Park Heights Avenue. The chance to break eight hours for the trip was threatened, but Clark hurriedly repaired the break and covered the final two miles in five minutes. Actual riding time, less maintenance delays, was six hours.

HORSERACING

Meanwhile, horseracing fans, particularly those interested in seeing records fall, "waxed enthusiastic" at the announcement of one of the biggest harness events of all time. The race was to match Cresceus, Charley Herr, and Boralma, three champion trotters, for a top prize of thirty thousand dollars. The site of 1901's "dream race" would be the track at Readville, Massachusetts, the date mid-September. The object, besides pitting the top trotters in a best-of-five-heats competition, was to see if any of the horses could break two minutes over a mile course.

PIGEON SHOOTING

In April there was a recurrence of the great pigeon controversy, which dated all the way back to the 1870s when SPCA gadfly and sometimes playwright Henry Bergh tried to put official clamps on pigeon shooting. Although clay pigeons and glass balls had been substituted for live birds on occasion during the latter part of the century, some gunners thought there was nothing like the real thing. Killing real birds, however, could produce a lot of casualties, especially during a shoot such as the Grand American Handicap of April 1–5, 1901. The greater the number of pigeons shot, the more likely the chances of community protests, as the participants of this meet rediscovered. To have an ample supply of living targets, more than twenty thousand birds were delivered to Interstate Park "to be butchered," in the words of one writer, "to make a trapshooter's holiday." The critic was hardly exaggerating, for during the first eight-hour shoot, more than twenty-nine hundred pigeons were killed or wounded. "In the majority of kills," the writer continued, "the bird falls dead, a bag of riddled skin and broken bones. . . . In many instances, however . . . the flying target receives only the outer pellets of the 'pattern' instead of the more penetrating and deadly centre . . . and it may fall maimed in the boundary marked to constitute a count

for the shooter or out of it. In the one case it is roughly snatched up by a boy employed to retrieve the birds that go to make up the scores, in the other it is allowed to linger and suffer until the official butchery is over and the 'round-up' of the 'cripples' is in order."

Such purple prose, along with actual horror at the killing taking place, caused a great deal of community protest. Most of it was simply brushed aside. The Grand American Handicap was a considerable attraction for tourists, an economic boon. And so the shooting continued. But so did the pressure from angry citizen groups, aided by indignant journalists.

The next batch of dead birds exceeded three thousand. "Women Watch the Butchery," one paper headlined. "Maimed winged targets allowed to suffer in full view of sportsmen and spectators. . . ."

The 222 entries were not particularly bothered by the criticism. Undeterred even by a bill prohibiting pigeon shooting that was sent to the New York Legislature, they continued to fire as fast as their weapons allowed.

BOXING

Boxing also survived its critics. In April 1901 Rube Ferns became the new welterweight champion of the world by defeating Matty Matthews via a knockout in ten rounds at Toronto. Meanwhile, soon-to-be lightweight champion Joe Gans took on Martin Flaherty of Lowell, Massachusetts, in still another interracial contest. Because there was so much interest in the bout, the stage on which the bout was held was also occupied by a sheriff, deputy marshal, police captain, chief engineer of the fire department, clerk of the court, and a "prominent capitalist." In a lower proscenium box, the newspapers reported, "were six negroes clad in the sportiest of dress and wearing much jewelry." Also in the audience —in the third row, to be exact—was a young woman dressed as a man in order to witness the bout. The fight, unfortunately, was hardly a crowd-pleaser. Gans was suffering from a cold, and Flaherty "looked as if he could have taken off a few pounds and been in better condition." During a preliminary conversation the fighters agreed to fight straight Marquis of Queensberry rules, which allowed hitting with the forearm.

The first couple of rounds were miss-and-clinch affairs, with referee Cadwallader getting nearly as much exercise as the participants by separating them. At one point he had to pry Flaherty away by grabbing him under the chin. This excited the crowd—"some spectators thought the officer was choking Flaherty and said so in plain, if not refined, English." After another clinch was broken, Gans lashed out with a quick right hand to Fla-

The Lady at Ringside—A daring story
A pretty and rather modest-looking young woman, who dressed as a man, went to see the Gans-Flaherty prizefight last night was locked up later at the Western Police Station on the charge of masquerading in male attire. In a voice almost inaudible, she said her name was Elizabeth Moore, and that she was twenty-four years old. . . . Beside her was a young man whom she declared was her husband, and who, she said, had gotten for her the clothing in which she was dressed. . . . Afterward he left the station and about midnight returned with $105, which he deposited as collateral. . . . The young woman . . . had by her trim figure and girlish face attracted general notice from those near her. . . . Captain Cadwallader was attracted by the curly wig. . . . She had arisen from her seat at the sound of the gong and hurried from the theater. . . . She sought refuge in a dining room in the vicinity and Captain Cadwallader came up with her just as she started to go into Kelly's Hotel. . . . On the way to the station the young woman told Captain Cadwallader that she had wished for a long time to see a fight. . . . The police are inclined to believe that she did not give her correct name. She told them she lived on Calvert Street, near Read. But does she?"
—*Baltimore Sun, April 2, 1901*

herty's jaw, sending him to the floor. Flaherty got up without a count. By the fourth round Gans decided to end the farce quickly. After landing a series of left jabs he faked with the left and sent Flaherty sprawling with a solid right. Once again, Flaherty got to his feet, "but he appeared to have no real fight left in him."

Gans bided his time for a while, then hit his opponent with another hard right, at which juncture "Martin went down and then assumed a sitting posture. He shook his head and did not appear to know where he was. He tried to get up but before he could do so 'Colonel' Haley threw up the sponge. Flaherty then got up and walked to his corner. Time of the round, two minutes and twenty seconds."

The crowd wasn't happy. Cries of "Fake!" and "April fool!" rained down from the gallery. Taking offense, Gans' manager, Al Herford, yelled to the crowd that if any of them wanted to go into Martin Flaherty's six-by-eight-foot dressing room and accuse him of taking a fall, he would arrange it. A few of the more incensed customers attempted to crawl onto the stage, but employees of the theater shoved them back into the aisles.

Despite such lapses into semibarbaric behavior, the spring of 1901 was a happy one for most Americans. President McKinley, following his second inauguration, toured the nation from coast to coast, his speeches filled with assurances that the best in technology was just around the corner. To prove how right the popular President was, a Northwestern fast mail train sped from Chicago to St. Paul at ninety miles an hour. John P. Holland, inventor of the first practical submarine, told an audience that in the near future submarines would supplant travel by surface, especially for short journeys. And as the living embodiment of the vast number of good things Americans would enjoy in the future, there was the Pan-American Exposition in Buffalo, opening May 1, which included dazzling displays of the latest developments in agriculture, electricity, forestry, and transportation, along with a scenic railway, "Venice in America" exhibition, and a world of cascading fountains and historical montages. Although he was needed in Washington during most of the summer, President McKinley promised to visit the exposition early in September.

BASEBALL

As mid-April approached, fans in thirteen major-league cities prepared for the opening games of their sixteen teams. The grand opening of the new American League, intended to be a historic event, was spoiled by bad weather throughout most of the East. In fact, only one game was played, at Chicago, between the hometown White Sox and Cleveland, known that year as the Bronchos (the correct spelling). For Chicago, Roy "Boy Wonder" Patterson was the pitcher, starting the first game in his first year in the major leagues; on the mound for Cleveland was veteran Bill Hoffer, starting what would be his final season in baseball. One hour and a half later, the American League's initial game was over, Chicago victorious by a score of 8–2. Attendance was listed as eight thousand. For the record, then, the first winning pitcher in the new league was Roy Patterson (who went on to log a 20–16 season); the first loser was Hoffer (who finished at 3–7); the first double play was made by Chicago, Dave Brian to Frank Shugart to Frank Isbell.

For the even then long-suffering fans of Washington, the new century marked still another new start in baseball. After piling up an unenviable record starting in 1871 with whatever league would have them, the Senators found eight years of stability in the bottom half of the National League before losing the franchise for the 1900 season. But that was all past. The new year started off in fine fashion. After putting together back-to-back wins on the road, the American League Senators inaugurated the 1901 season at home before ten thousand fans, who filled every seat in the new ball park at New York Avenue and Fourteenth Street. Also present was Admiral Dewey, the hero of Manila, who "attired in a black frock coat and glossy silk tie," looked more like a banker than the fearless seaman who had damned the torpedos and moved full speed ahead.

Washington's National League Record, 1892–99:

	W.	L.	Pos.
1892	58	93	10
1893	40	89	12
1894	45	87	10
1895	43	85	8
1896	58	73	6
1897	61	71	7
1898	51	101	10
1899	54	98	7
Total	410	697	
Avg.	51	87	9

The admiral received a solid round of cheers and was then promptly forgotten as a young man named William (Doughnut Bill) Carrick proceeded to pitch a masterful game. Alternating a good fast ball with a better-than-average "bender" and "drop," Carrick held the Baltimore Oriole batsmen in check while the Senators went on to score a 5–2 victory. The Washington papers were ecstatic. "It is something new to see a Washington team in the lead in the pennant race," one reporter wrote, "and new to see it defeat Baltimore, and the local rooters enjoyed the sensation immensely, especially their revenge over Baltimore for many a good drubbing in former years."

Of course, the new position atop the league didn't last long (the team finished sixth, with a record of 61–73), but for a time the frustrating past could be forgotten.

It was not a very good summer to be a baseball umpire, despite league rulings that the arbiters were to be obeyed with a minimum of temper tantrums. Taking the ruling seriously, umpires of 1901 on more than a few

What a Baseball Club Cost—1901:

During the summer of 1901, articles continued to appear outlining what terrible escalating costs the baseball owners faced because of the presence of two leagues. Outfielder Jimmy Sheckard was cited as an example of the rampant greed of ballplayers, his salary having gone from $1,200 in 1899 to $1,800 in 1900 and $3,000 in 1901. Typical expenses for each club also included:

Rental for grounds	$3,000
Ticket sellers, park force	$1,500
Salaries of officials	$12,000
Salaries of players	$25,000
Traveling expenses ($.02 per mile)	$2,520
Sleeping-car fare	$1,080
Bus fare	$500
Balls	$1,000
Hotels	$4,000
League and umpire expenses	$3,000
Taxes, miscellaneous	$7,000
Total	$60,600

occasions actually forfeited games because of protests, an act that went out of fashion later in the twentieth century. One notable scuffle occurred on May 13, at the Polo Grounds. Umpire Hank O'Day was in command when Brooklyn came to bat in their half of the ninth inning, with New York leading by 7–6. With one out, Jimmy Sheckard singled, reaching second on a balk by Giant pitcher Luther (Dummy) Taylor. After Joe Kelley struck out, Willie Keeler singled, and a base on balls to Tom Daly loaded the bases. Dahlen lined a clean hit to left, which was fielded cleanly by Kip Selbach, who threw to third baseman Sammy Strang. Meanwhile, it seemed that both Keeler and Sheckard would score. But a split second before Keeler crossed the plate, Strang tagged Tom Daly for the third out. When informed that the score was merely tied at 7–7, instead of Brooklyn leading 8–7, the Superbas (as the Dodgers were known then) rushed O'Day, throwing their gloves to the ground and "kicking" furiously. After absorbing as much abuse as he could, O'Day awarded the game to New York by a score of 9–0.

This did not mean umpires always had control of the games. Less than two weeks later, Andrew Freedman, president of the New York Giants and one of the worst enemies of umpires in general, decided that he was not going to allow the scheduled umpire, Billy Nash, to call the game. In explaining the action of refusing Nash permission to enter the park, Freedman said that he did not propose to accept "incompetent" umpires "whose decisions create disorder on the grounds." The game was umpired by two players instead, catcher Chief Zimmer of Pittsburgh, and Giant catcher John Warner.

HORSERACING

Two days later, racing fans gathered at Morris Park for the thirty-fifth running of the Belmont Stakes, a rather unique event in that only three horses were entered. These included the powerful Commando, "esteemed by shrewd judges to be the best in America," The Parader, and All Green. Everyone seemed to agree that Commando would win the race; the question was whether he could set a new record for the Belmont Stakes. Fair weather attracted many persons to the park, especially those of notable rank and fortune. The result was a colorful display of expensive costumes and four-in-hands, black brakes, and coaches, while here and there motor carriages buzzed and whirred about the clubhouse. Bigwigs representing Tammany Hall choked the betting ring to the point where placing a wager was a dangerous undertaking.

The start of the major event was made directly in front of the grandstand, from which "a great roar went up from the crowd as the horses went away, and continued with a babel of attending it until the finish was reached." Entering the stretch, Commando led The Parader by a length, but was striding easily compared to the desperate pace of The Parader. When the two horses crossed the finish line, Commando was 1½ lengths in front and had established a new Belmont record of 2:21, ½ second better than Ildrim.

GOLF

Although more and more people were enjoying spectator sports in America that summer of 1901, there was still a considerable amount of moral residue left over from the Victorian era. On June 2, for example, the Reverend John Havemeyer of the Central Methodist Church, Yonkers, used his pulpit as a means of attacking all forms of amusement on the Sabbath. He also included using trolleys and steam roads, saying that patronage of these roads by church people encouraged the owners to keep their employees working on Sunday, thereby violating the laws of God and man. The attack was not a new one. Three weeks before, a group of New York ministers got together to demand an end to Sunday baseball. The police commissioners responded by

ordering an end to all recreation on the Sabbath, including golf.

When several wealthy parishioners who were also golf players threatened to leave their churches, two of the ministers who had signed the petition recalled their signatures and explained in a local newspaper that they hadn't really signed what they had meant, or meant what they had signed, or words to that effect.

But Havemeyer and others were determined that the police should stick to their guns and arrest lawbreakers. Accordingly, on June 2, 1901, an example was made of a lawyer named Benjamin Adams. While hitting his golf balls around the Saegkill Golf Club course, he was accosted by officers and charged with violating the Sunday amusement laws. The arrest created an immediate furor, even in the church of the Reverend Havemeyer, where a man stood up and demanded that the minister tell him where it stated in the Bible that amusements should not be practiced on the Sabbath. Havemeyer replied disdainfully that the church was not the place to discuss such matters.

A Lawyer's Argument in Favor of Sunday Golf:
"To keep the Sunday as these good people wish us to keep it would be to put us in the boots of the small boy who sat on his mother's knee and was told that if he was good all the time he would surely go to Heaven. 'But what is Heaven?' asked the little chap. 'Why, Heaven, darling, is a place where it is always Sunday,' the fond mother answered. 'I guess—I guess I'd rather go to the other place, then,' the boy decided."
Attorney Joseph F. Daly for the defense of Sunday golf player Benjamin Adams, June 6, 1901

The trial of Benjamin Adams was held on June 7, and was brightened at the very beginning when one of the six selected jurors showed up wearing a golf costume. He was excused.

There followed some wrangling, which dealt with the use of "private" grounds vs. "public" grounds, but in the end Judge Kellogg left a number of questions unanswered so that the jury could render a quick decision. The courtroom was crowded with visitors who were interested in the outcome, which was given after forty-five minutes of deliberation. "We, the jury," the foreman announced, "find the defendant, Adams, not guilty, and we recommend that the existing law in regard to the observation of the Sabbath on the first day of the week be repealed or so amended as not to interfere with the innocent amusement of the citizens of this state on that day." The crowd cheered, shook hands with each other, and congratulated the gentlemen of the jury. It was obviously a highly popular decision. Two days later, golf courses and baseball fields were crowded with people while local constables stood by and watched.

Sermon Samplings on the Golf Decision—
June 9, 1901:
"The acquittal of Benjamin Adams in a farce of the worst kind. . . ."
                                Rev. Dr. J. E. Price
"The local authorities are straining at the gnat golf and swallowing the camel saloon, allowing the saloon to run openly . . . that they might turn their attention to the minor offenses called Sunday sports, which do less harm in a cycle of time than the saloons and other vicious resorts do in an hour."
      Father Brady, St. Joseph's Church
"The great and prosperous nations of the earth are those who, as a nation, observe Sunday as a sacred day. These are the nations which, according to the Bible promise, are going up to the high places of the earth."
        Rev. Robert Stuart MacArthur
        Calvary Baptist Church

SWIMMING

Later in the month of June, twenty-seven-year-old William J. Glover, a copper mill worker, announced his intention of swimming across the largest American estuary, the Chesapeake Bay. The task was undertaken, one must suppose, because it had never been accomplished prior to this time. Accompanied by his sixty-two-year-old father and brother Edward, Glover boarded a steamer at Baltimore bound for the eastern shore on Monday, June 24. The small team took an "ordinary bateau" and a parcel of food, along with a supply of paraffin and oil to provide a protective coating for the swimmer.

Glover, according to his own admission, was not in the best of training for such a grueling mission. During the entire year, for example, he had been in the water only three times, never for longer than an hour. After spending the night at Tolchester on the eastern shore,

the three men started the journey. The elder Glover rowed for the entire trip while Edward and another man occupied the rear seat of the boat, a life line attached to their belts.

The party set out at 4:20 A.M. A bit more than an hour later, young Glover discovered that the paraffin and oil had peeled off. In the middle of the Chesapeake, he caught a flood tide but met an ebb tide not long afterward. He swam on his stomach most of the way, occasionally moving over on his back so that he could rest his neck. Soon the party began to approach familiar landmarks in the Baltimore area, and as they did so, people gathered on the shore or at railings of steamers to shout at them. It was nearly eight-thirty in the evening when the exhausted Glover finally reached the wharf at River View, having covered slightly more than twenty-three miles in sixteen hours, ten minutes. Five thousand persons were on hand to meet him—despite the fact that neither the time nor the distance swum entitled the young man to a world's record. After giving him a big ovation, the crowd watched appreciatively as Glover was awarded the mayoralty of Canton, a nondescript section of Baltimore.

BASEBALL

Back at the baseball wars, July found Washingtonians in an angry mood. For starters, the Senators had slowly reverted to form, so that by the tenth of the month they were in fifth place, with a record of 26–28. Then came umpire Jack Sheridan's decision in a game against Baltimore, which seemed to release whatever frustration had been held in check until that time.

The situation was all the more irritating because it seemed that the Senators had broken out of their dismal playing style to win a game in the final minutes. With the score 1–0 against them in the ninth inning, Washington came to life. After Dale Gear flied out, Clarence (Pop) Foster hit a long fly to center field, which was misplayed by Jim Jackson as he tripped over a mound of dirt, turning the second out of the inning into a double. Joe Quinn hit a grounder to Jimmy Williams at second base, and Williams promptly committed another error. Bill Coughlin's grounder to shortstop Bill Keister was very efficiently gathered in. Unfortunately, he then threw it well over the head of first baseman Warren Hart as Senator runners flashed around the bases. Thinking the game had been won, hordes of people poured out of the bleachers. One of them grabbed the ball before Hart could reach it, and threw it over the fence.

At that point, umpire Jack Sheridan was faced with a crucial decision: Allow the runs to be counted on the logical assumption that

Hart could never have thrown the ball home in time to catch the winning runner—or infuriate the hometown fans by declaring a "block ball" and sending the last two runners back to their bases? Sheridan chose the latter course of action, and the score reverted to 1–1. The next two Senator batters went down easily, and Baltimore scored two runs in the tenth inning to win, 3–1. Immediately shouts of "Robber!" "Soak him!" and "Kill Sheridan!" rained down on the field. Sheridan and Alfred Mannassau, the other umpire, were forced to take refuge in a lemonade and peanut stand until they could be rescued by Washington police.

Other Highlights of the Season:

May 9: *American League pitcher Earl Moore of Cleveland pitched nine innings of no-hit ball against Chicago, but finally lost in the tenth by a score of 4–2.*

August 7: *In the eighth inning of a game between Cleveland and Milwaukee, Hugh Duffy, following a controversial decision on a foul ball, slugged umpire Alfred Mannassau.*

August 29: *Walter Scott (Steve) Brodie, after singling, became so interested in whether the next batter, Roger Bresnahan, would make it to third base that he stopped and watched, being tagged in the process.*

YACHT RACING

Besides baseball, the sport of international yacht racing generated considerable excitement during the summer of 1901. After having failed to win the America's Cup with the first vessel he called *Shamrock*, famous British sportsman and tea merchant Sir Thomas Lipton was back for another try with an even grander ship, known as *Shamrock II.* Opposing him was the American yacht *Columbia,* with the races scheduled for August 31 to September 3. Inaugurated in 1851, when Queen Victoria watched a schooner named *America* win a sixty-mile race around the Isle of Wight, the fifty-year-old race was the oldest international sporting competition. Queen Victoria had passed away and Sir Thomas Lipton was eager to win back the trophy in what he considered a particularly symbolic year.

HORSERACING

While Americans waited for the new challenger to cross the Atlantic, attention was turned to the trotting tracks, particularly that

at Columbus, Ohio, where the champion trotter Cresceus was the main attraction. Late in July, Cresceus broke The Abbot's 1900 record time for the mile, 2:03¼, by ½ second. That event took place at Cleveland. From there, Cresceus was taken to the Columbus Driving Park, where plans were announced that he would race against his own record time of 2:02¾. Twelve thousand people showed up to witness the event, all eager to see the great horse in motion, but few expecting him to be able to beat his own best time so soon.

One problem was that it was an extremely windy day, with the breeze's strongest force turned against the stretch runner. Because of the high wind, the race was postponed from three o'clock to six, but the velocity did not diminish a great deal during the interval. It was decided to go ahead with the race, however, for a lot of money had been wagered. The betting started at the rate of twenty-five dollars for time against seventeen dollars for Cresceus. The odds grew heavier as the wind failed to die down, eventually reaching twenty-five to eight dollars against the stallion's being able to beat his record time.

"Gamely facing the breeze, the champion started on his journey, moving with apparent ease and at his greatest speed," one description of the race began. "The half-mile pole was passed in 59¾ seconds, a record never before attained. . . . The three-quarter pole was reached in 1:30¼. . . . Then came the final trial, for as Cresceus turned into the stretch, the strong wind struck him full in the face and held him back by force. For the fraction of a second he seemed to falter, but his driver's voice encouraged him, and on he came. With splendid courage he plunged in toward the finish with unweakened stride, and in spite of weariness and the buffeting of the breeze, he flashed under the wire a winner against time. . . ."

Cresceus's new record, one mile in 2:02¼, was widely hailed as a breakthrough in racing history, in addition to an event that thrilled twelve thousand people. "It has taken more than a generation to reduce the mile time of a trotter by 17½ seconds, from the 2:19¾ of Flora Temple to the 2:02¼ of Cresceus," one wise old editor wrote. "It does not seem likely that the trotter that is to reach the 2-minute goal has yet appeared. It is quite possible that he or she has not yet been foaled."

The horse destined to break the two-minute mark had been foaled quite a while before. Cresceus's record held up only two years, being broken by Lou Dillon's 1:58½ in 1903.

TRACK AND FIELD

Early in August another record was set, although subsequent histories of track-and-field events generally fail to mention a Ute Indian named Candiras De Foya running the hundred-yard dash in nine seconds flat during the athletic contests held at Colorado Springs, Colorado. Newspapers hearing of this event were understandably hesitant to proclaim it a new world's record, for it cut four-fifths of a second off the amateur time until then, three-fifths of a second from the professional mark. "In the announcement of the feat by De Foya," one paper hedged, "no mention is made of the conditions under which the athlete ran, or whether or not the games were sanctioned by the Amateur Athletic Union, and were held in a manner that would give the runner the record officially." Then, getting to the meat of the situation, it was added, "Whatever the circumstances, however, and whether or not De Foya's performance shall be admitted to the official record of athletic feats, if the Indian really ran over a measured hundred yards' course in nine seconds his achievement is one of the most remarkable ever made by an athlete."

Hundred-yard Dash Record Holders—
1901
Professional: *Edward Donovan: 09⅗*
Natick, Massachusetts, September 2, 1895
Amateur: *09⅘, held jointly by:*
Bernard Wefers
John Owen, Jr.
John Crum
J. H. Mayberry
Arthur Duffy
W. T. McPherson (Australia)

As September 1901 approached, interest was high in the coming yacht races, the pennant fights in both leagues, and a variety of smaller events. At that moment, however, something else happened to put the concern for athletics into proper perspective. While at the Pan-American Exposition in Buffalo, President William McKinley was shot by Leon Czolgosz, an American-born anarchist. Wrapping his revolver in a large white handkerchief, Czolgosz somehow avoided the gaze of more than fifty Secret Service agents, waited for the line in front of him to decrease, even explained the handkerchief to an agent as a "hurt hand," and then fired two shots into the President from a distance of three feet. Eight days later, after a succession of optimistic bulletins, McKinley died. Those who had suffered through the Garfield assassination of 1881 must have been truly imbued with a feeling of *déjà vu*.

The sports world was affected in various ways. One would have thought, for example, that the baseball leagues had not heard of the tragic event, as all games were played. The news of McKinley's being shot was announced during a game in Cleveland by umpire Tom Connolly, but the contest continued. The following day, all scheduled games were played in both leagues. Not until Thursday, September 19, was officially proclaimed a day of mourning did baseball cease.

Other sports seemed to react quicker. Horseracing tracks at Harlem, near Chicago, Fort Erie, near Buffalo, and Delmar, near St. Louis, immediately closed. A championship golf match at Atlantic City was postponed, as were the international cricket matches at Philadelphia and the Atlantic Cup race. At Sheepshead Bay, racing continued but no music was played. Even an auto endurance contest at Rochester, which was in the last of its six-day format, came to a halt.

YACHT RACING

By the end of the month, a certain degree of normalcy returned. On September 26, an attempt was made to run the first of the America's Cup races, but an eighteen-knot breeze early that morning died completely in a few hours and the race was canceled. Two days later, aided by some clever jockeying at the start, *Columbia* beat *Shamrock II* by a narrow one-minute, twenty-second margin. The victory touched off a wild display of rejoicing by those in the assembled pleasure fleet that had moved off Sandy Hook, New Jersey, for a better view of the race. In London, of course, reaction was more subdued. There, crowds gathered to watch the bulletin boards, colored bombs, and flashlights that told which yacht was ahead. When it was announced that *Shamrock* was leading at the outer mark, those gathered at the Crystal and Alexandra palaces and on the Thames embankment became increasingly cheerful. As the successive green illuminations continued, the crowds broke into cheers. But shortly after the turn, a red signal flare indicated that the American ship had taken the lead. Immediately a hush settled over the audience, except for the occasional shriek of an American. When it was learned that *Columbia* was the winner, groans and hisses preceded the gradual breaking up of the crowd.

Subsequent races between *Columbia* and *Shamrock II* were distinctly anticlimactic, *Columbia* retaining the America's Cup for the United States. By the end of the year, Sir Thomas Lipton had put the vessel on the auction block and was busily at work on a new design that would defeat the Americans. (By 1930, twenty-nine years and five million dollars later, he was still searching for the magic success formula.)

FOOTBALL

Shortly afterward, the 1901 football season began in earnest, and it soon became obvious that Michigan was the most powerful team in the nation. On October 26, the University of Buffalo made the journey to Ann Arbor after beating Columbia, a fair eastern team, by the score of 5–0. The men of Buffalo may have expected some trouble from the Wolverines, but no one could have foreseen what would happen to them. Jumping ahead quickly, Michigan simply buried Buffalo, 128–0. "Mason of the Buffalo team narrowly missed a goal from a place kick from the twenty-five-yard line," one reporter noted. "This was the only time in the course of the game that Buffalo was anywhere near a score. The lack of training of the visiting eleven was plainly apparent, especially in the second half, when a man was laid out after almost every rush. Coach Brown of the Buffalo team said after the game: 'Michigan can defeat any team in the East.'"

The remark was a fine piece of unintentional understatement. Michigan subsequently dismantled Beloit by a score of 89–0 on a field that was so wet it had to be filled in with sawdust, then beat Iowa on November 28 by the score of 50–0. The season ended with Michigan having run up a total of 501 points to 0 for the opposition. In that context, it seems remarkable that several enterprising sportsmen of the West Coast decided to inaugurate a new event called the Rose Bowl game, the first contestants to be Stanford and Michigan. The contest was another runaway for Michigan, 49–0, which so discouraged the Westerners that it was not until 1916 that the second Rose Bowl was held.

BOXING

One other major sports event took place in 1901, a championship heavyweight match between champion Jim Jeffries and the Akron Giant, Gus Ruhlin. Held in San Francisco, the fight was the second between the two men, the first having taken place in the same city four years previously. That had turned out to be a twenty-round draw, not without its moments of controversy, which included Ruhlin's hitting Jeffries after the bell. Since that time, when both men were contending for the crown held by Bob Fitzsimmons, a great deal

had happened. Jeffries had defeated Joe Goddard, Peter Jackson, Tom Sharkey, and Bob Armstrong, then knocked out Fitzsimmons in eleven rounds to win the title. Ruhlin's career, including losses to Fitzsimmons and a win over Sharkey, was at best checkered. But because Ruhlin seemed to be one of the best challengers at the time, the fight was staged and publicized as an important event.

The crowd was in the mood for a good fight, cheering expectantly when the men entered the arena. Jeffries, wearing a red sweater, sat in his corner chewing gum furiously. At nine twenty-seven the fight began, but the first round was tame. The second and third rounds were marked by Ruhlin's appealing to the referee concerning Jeffries' "fouling" him. The crowd was less than happy.

Ruhlin	The Statistics	Jeffries
28	age	26
209	weight	214
6'1¾"	height	6'1½"
76¾"	reach	77½"
43½"	chest expanded	46"
35"	waist	34"

In the fourth, Jeffries started to land some solid punches and just before the bell sent Ruhlin to the floor. Saved by the bell, Gus "wore a distressed expression" when he came out for the fifth round. Jeffries landed a right hook to the jaw and a short left to the ribs, then a right to the neck. Ruhlin retreated steadily. After forcing Ruhlin to the ropes, Jeffries managed to land several punches that dropped the challenger for a five-count. After that, according to accounts, Ruhlin just stopped fighting, allowing Jeffries to finish him off in that round. This touched off a wave of anger from the crowd, who "cheered the champion while they denounced Ruhlin as a quitter and a faker."

Thus ended the main heavyweight attraction of the year. It must have seemed a fitting conclusion to a year that began with high hopes for humanity but ended with the uneasy feeling that perhaps the new century might not be the utopia the optimists predicted it would be.

CHAPTER 16—TECHNOLOGY REARS ITS LEG

Americans pride themselves on being an innovative people, and the United States Patent Office has more than four million examples of individual brainpower at work. Unfortunately, most of the patents filed since the USPO opened its doors did not work except on paper. Either that or they were obviously so much trouble for so little benefit—a cumbersome spoon with a lid arrangement, for example, to protect the mustache from soup stains —that nobody bothered to build a prototype.

Sports were not exempted from the inventors, of course. Studying the game or activity, they imagined literally thousands of ways, over the course of a century, to make sports safer, faster, improve training techniques, even mechanize the officials. And so they went off by themselves and drew their plans, convinced that fame and fortune awaited them. Obviously that did not happen, but often enough their efforts were amusing or bizarre, and a few, for whatever it was worth, actually worked.

One reason given by inventors for expending so much effort is that their product will benefit the human race by making the sporting activity safer.

CAPTAIN PAUL BOYTON'S MAGIC DRESS

Had he lived a century later, Peter Paul (Billy) Boyton undoubtedly would have found a position with a manufacturer of automobile seat belts, devising new and better ways to coerce motorists into buckling up for safety or face frightening consequences.

No doubt about it, Boyton had a crusading spirit when it came to water safety. After serving in the Union Navy during the American Civil War, young Boyton helped organize a life-saving brigade at Atlantic City, New Jersey, where people were taking to the surf in great numbers for the first time in American history. Largely ignorant of how to handle themselves in the water, many bathers—even experienced swimmers—were drowned.

A variety of solutions was proposed and tried, including the laying of tow ropes, buoys, and damlike barriers in the water, but many drownings were still reported. Some, taking the narrow view, blamed the rising death rate on the fact that people were learning how to swim. "The day Americans forget how to swim," wrote the New York *Times* on September 1, 1880, "they will cease to drown in appreciable quantities. Let us, in the interest of humanity, hasten that day by every means in our power."

Paul Boyton's solution was that every swimmer—or potential swimmer, such as passengers on vessels that might founder—be made to wear a special life-saving dress invented in 1869 by a C. S. Merriman. Made of India rubber, the outfit consisted of pantaloons and a tunic, the whole thing furnished with five tubes that could be "inflated at will." The dress, Boyton said, "can be donned in less time than it takes to put on a pair of gloves . . . will sustain for an indefinite time . . . and keep the wearer perfectly dry."

There was, of course, a small catch in Paul Boyton's philosophy. Surfers, then as now, did not go to the beach in order to paddle about in a "perfectly dry" state wrapped in several pounds of India rubber. But that thought, if it occurred to him, did not deter Boyton from setting out to demonstrate the dress's effectiveness. In October 1874 he boarded the *Queen,* bound for England, stating his intention to jump overboard when the ship was two hundred miles from Sandy Hook, New Jersey, and return to America. In order to make his trip easier, Boyton had fashioned a special paddle and provisions buoy that contained food, flares, signal flags, some tools, and fishing gear. But when the *Queen*'s captain heard of Boyton's scheme, he refused to allow him near the railing.

But Boyton could not be watched every minute. Ten days later, when the captain's guard was down and the ship seven miles south of Baltimore, Ireland, Boyton slipped over the side in his rubber dress and paddled ashore at Skibbereen. He immediately found himself an international hero, and just as quickly took advantage of the situation. Slowly working his way eastward, he gave exhibitions—including one trip across Dublin Bay—until April 5, 1875, when he performed before Queen Victoria.

"Surely never did human being," wrote the London *Daily News,* "present himself in such a costume as the India rubber suit in which Captain Boyton made his bow to the Queen on the quarterdeck of the royal yacht."

By this time, Boyton had embellished his outfit by adding a sail fastened to his feet and neck. Lying on his back in the water, sporting an American flag at his ankle, "he ran back before the wind to the royal yacht at a prodigious rate. Then he returned to the inexhaustible buoy and took out a carrier pigeon, which he dispatched to show one of the uses to which the apparatus may be applied." Later, Boyton discharged several rockets, caught a fish, and lay back to read the morning newspapers. Queen Victoria was so impressed she bought a set for the royal yacht.

This triumph was promptly followed by an assault on the English Channel. Accompanied by the steamer *Rambler,* Boyton paddled out of Dover Harbor on the morning of April 10, 1875, blithely puffing a cigar. But by nightfall, high winds and crosscurrents forced him to abandon the project six miles from Cape Griz Nez.

Later in May, moving in the opposite direction, Boyton was more successful, paddling from Boulogne to Folkestone in just under twenty-four hours. Two members of Parliament, the prefect of the department of Calais, and numerous scientific and naval persons were on hand to greet him. A proposal was even made to name the exact landing spot Boyton Point, but nothing came of it. Some persons, of course, derided the American and his ludicrous outfit, maintaining—correctly— that the English Channel still remained to be crossed by a legitimate swimmer. Paul Boyton didn't mind the criticism. He seemed to be accomplishing his mission—that is, publicizing the Merriman invention.

For the next four years, Boyton's life was one exhibition after another as he tackled the rivers of the world. In October 1875 he floated down the Rhine; in January 1876 he maneuvered through cakes of ice down the Mississippi; in April he returned to Europe to promote the dress for the British Coast Guard. Wherever he went, large crowds were on hand. Encouraged by their enthusiasm, Boyton took to blowing a bugle as he floated along.

There were, of course, moments of trial and tribulation. In November 1877, for example, while descending the Somme, Boyton was fired at by a duck hunter and wounded in the foot. On the Seine he was nearly crushed between a coal scow and an arch of the Bercy Bridge. Another time, while dozing down the Danube, he was suddenly awakened by the blade of a giant millwheel striking him above the right eye. His cries for help finally attracted the attention of a miller, who lifted Boyton out of the water but promptly threw him back when he saw the bloody face. While negotiating the Straits of Messina shortly afterward, the slap of a large fish's tail broke one of Boyton's ribs.

Even worse, no one really seemed interested in buying the rubber swimming device, except as a novelty item. When Boyton suggested that all bathers should be required to wear them, writers invariably pooh-poohed the notion. "No doubt a bather thus equipped would be safe unless his India-rubber armor should be perforated by a shark's tooth or by a broken bottle shied at him by a small boy who objects to newfangled costumes," the New York *Times* editorialized. "To guard against these dangers, a bathing-dress of sheet-iron, with water-tight compartments, would be preferable to one of India-rubber." The satirical remarks were the kiss of death for Boyton's hope to start a gigantic industry manufacturing the dresses for hundreds of thousands of bathers and travelers. Nevertheless, he continued to float hither and yon, occasionally appearing with Barnum's Circus or at Coney Island, where he exhibited a trained-seal act and was credited with inventing the thrill ride known as "Shoot the Chute." He died in 1924, aged seventy-six.

SAFETY IN THE BOXING RING

Shortly after the death of George Flores in a 1951 fight at Madison Square Garden, some attention was given to improving safety conditions, adding padding to the floor of the ring. The results proved negligible, but several years later, a tree surgeon named Ralph Dougherty suddenly saw the answer to the problem. He was having a glass of milk at the the time, he recounted later, and "I looked at the bottle cap on the table and it hit me. Boxing should have a round ring. Anything to cut down injuries."

The completely round ring never came about, but on May 13, 1967, an octagonal ring was tested at the West Orange (New Jersey) Armory. The theory was that fighters pinned in corners were subjected to brutal punishment—ergo, eliminate corners. Among those who were interested enough to watch the demonstration were officials from the Amateur Athletic Union and Emile Griffith, former welterweight champion who had killed Benny (Kid) Paret in a 1962 bout.

Eleven amateur bouts were held and the crowd of twenty-six hundred seemed to enjoy them, although no one could say for certain if the conformation of the ring would actually cut down on injuries. Most agreed that shiftier fighters would fare better in the cornerless area, but others said that fists did the damage rather than the shape of the ring. Still others were apathetic, as was one of the winning fighters, George Thomas, who said, "I don't care if I fight in a triangle."

IN THE NAME OF COMFORT AND CONVENIENCE

Since inventors turned their attention to devising improved sporting equipment, another reason given for their efforts has been to make things easier for the participant. Why, after all, should athletic pursuits be any more difficult than absolutely necessary? With this in mind, Professor Charles Howard Hinton of Princeton in 1897 perfected his revolutionary new "pitching cannon," a device to hurl a baseball mechanically and thus save pitchers' arms for the game itself. A well-known mathematician, Professor Hinton was most interested in the problem of devising a machine capable of throwing a curve ball, that form of delivery being a subject of much conjecture during the 1890s. (Some people, in fact, still maintained even then that the "curve" was merely an illusion.)

In March 1897, Hinton felt he had mastered the puzzle, reporting to a group of three hundred Princeton men that the cannon barrel had two holes bored into it, into which rods had been inserted. "The baseball, after leaving the muzzle of the gun," he said, "strikes first one rod and then the second, and by the contact is given a complete rotary motion, which produces the desired curve."

In June, the cannon was put into action on the Princeton baseball field, a number of reporters and sportsmen being in attendance. Activated by an electrical spark, the gun used good old-fashioned gunpowder to send the ball out the tube and in the direction of the batter. Despite the problems inherent in such an operation, *Scientific American*'s reporter stated that all went well. "The tension was varied," he wrote, "and drop and curve balls were discharged by the gun with ease." Later, however, it was admitted that there were some problems. "The ball comes too suddenly," he added. "There is nothing to compensate for the motion of the pitcher's arm." As a solution, it was suggested that either a system of warning signals or some means of self-activation by the batter be used. In any event, the device never caught on. The 1898 issue of *Reaches Guide,* the bible of baseball, said simply, "Professor Hinton's pitching cannon was given further trial . . . but not much is thought of its practicability by players."

Mechanical pitchers continued to be "perfected" during the early years of the twentieth century, the next major effort after Professor Hinton's device being the work of one Alexander MacMillan, who was also associated with Princeton University. MacMillan's pitching device was placed on display in 1914, the young man charging the public one cent per offering to try the thing. The device was similar in design to mechanical pitchers later set up in amusement parks, its chief drawback to professionals being, according to one reporter, the fact that "it is not calculated to throw curves, although the speed, the height and the time of the ball can be regulated in such a way as to fool the batter just as the human pitcher tries to do."

Occasionally, players themselves got into the inventing act, one of the first being George Henry (Dode) Paskert, an outfielder for Cincinnati and Philadelphia during the early years of the century. On December 31, 1916, Paskert was at Cincinnati, trying to interest Reds' General Manager Herrmann in purchasing his mechanical pitcher, which was activated by means of electrical current. Apparently Herrmann was not interested, nor was anyone else.

Another player who dabbled in invention was Hugh Mulcahy, who pitched for the Philadelphia Phillies and Pittsburgh Pirates during a nine-year stretch. By way of being distinctive, Mulcahy was probably one of the few pitchers with such a long time in the major leagues who never had a winning season. He usually received plenty of starting assignments—during the period 1937–40, for example, he was 8–18, 10–20, 9–16, and 13–22—but his teammates could never seem to get him runs. After a while the philosophical Mulcahy picked up the nickname "losing pitcher," because it appeared ahead of his real name in the box score so often.

Mulcahy's two best years were 1936 and 1947, when he logged records of 1–1 and 0–0. Later, he became a coach and in 1953 patented a mechanical catcher that was supposed to retrieve balls and automatically return them to pitchers (live pitchers, not mechanical devices) during batting practice.

In that Mulcahy's invention was never put into wide use, it could deservedly be called a "losing catcher."

Eventually, of course, mechanical pitchers were perfected, the most famous being "Iron Mike." Most major-league teams, however, still prefer batting-practice serves delivered by a live person, the chief throwers being coaches or regular pitchers trying to iron out a few kinks in their delivery.

THE MECHANICAL PINBOY

Until the 1940s, bowling balls were regularly returned by pinboys, who also set up the pins for the next round. But as early as 1903 inventors were tinkering with methods of doing away with human pinsetters and ball returners.

At Tempelhof, a suburb of Berlin, an automatic alley was put into operation that year, using a device that consisted of a set of wires and pulleys. "At the end of the alley," it was explained, "a box is erected through the bottom of which the pins are suspended, so that their bottom edges hang about 1¼ inches over the board floor of the alley. The pins are suspended in the box in such a manner that they can oscillate freely. . . . The device for returning the balls is very simple. A ball of medium force, which has traversed the pin, drops into a groove that is inclined to the right. Through this groove the ball enters a small shaft. At the bottom of the latter is an iron tongue, which is raised up by a pull on the lever . . . throwing the ball out and into the sloping return chute in which it rolls back to the players. . . . No pinboys are required and the possibility of carelessness on their parts is done away with. After each throw all the pins can be brought into their correct position ready for the next throw, by a single pull at the lever."

Aside from the fact that the bowler had to wait until the pins stopped swaying in the breeze following their being "set up" for the next round, the main drawback of the 1903 device was that pins hanging in the air do not move about the same way as free pins sitting on the alley. But it was a good enough try.

FOR THE MARKSMAN

During the later years of the nineteenth century, when pigeons were killed by the millions, it was necessary for the marksman to be as comfortable as possible. One device fashioned for him in 1905 was an under-the-arm supporter, which was strapped to the person and came automatically into position when the rifleman lifted his arm. The outer end of the device was a curved plate, which could be raised or lowered to any angle. The inventor, a William S. Dunham of Sharpsville, Pennsylvania, recommended that the plate be set at ninety degrees for pistol shooting. To release himself from the support, the person had only to raise his arm higher than the desired position, allowing the pawl to disengage itself and slide back to a folded position. Because the principle is basically the same as folding lawn chairs of a later era, it is quite obviously suspect.

A second aid to riflemen, concocted in 1894, brought up the possibility that a certain percentage of right-handed marksmen are left-eyed. To overcome this dilemma, a special curved stock rifle allowed the user to exercise the control of his right hand and arm and to sight with the left eye. No mention was made of the possibility that a marksman could be left-handed and right-eyed.

IN THE NAME OF BETTER TRAINING

Over the years a number of sports inventions have been devised in order to better prepare the participant for battle. Usually

Uphill Skiing, Anyone?

The year 1953 added the invention of Stanley Van Voorhees of West Los Angeles (U. S. Patent No. 2,625,229). A power-driven ski was envisioned as the perfect answer to long lines at the chair lift or rope tow. Van Voorhees' skis could be fitted with a pair of motor-driven endless belts with bristles pointed toward the rear in order to give better traction. In addition, the skier had to carry a gasoline engine on his back with a flexible drive shaft going to each ski. Thus the problem of long lines would be eliminated as the skier moved quickly uphill against the normal traffic flow. What would happen if the skier hit a mogul and fell forward with the gasoline engine strapped to him is left to the reader's imagination (as was what one did with all the gear at the top of the slope).

these training aids were used in advance of the sports contest but occasionally the device was simple enough to take along. Into this latter category falls the 1972 bowling shoe awarded Patent No. 3,641,687. The invention of Douglas L. Reeder, Jr., and William M. Hibbard, the shoe had a sighting line on top of the toe; the bowler was supposed to point the line at the pin or pins he wanted to hit, then swing his arm directly parallel to the line.

FOR THE GOLFER

More inventions involve golf than any other sport, perhaps because it is an individual game in which concentration is needed in massive doses. Most duffers feel—or perhaps hope—that they are separated from the great golfers by a thin line. Crossing that line may be possible if only the duffer can learn a few additional skills—how to keep the head down, the arm straight, etc. And if a mechanical device can teach the golfer that skill, why hesitate to use it? And thus it is that hope springs eternal in the average golfer and those who invent methods of improving his game.

THE GOLFER'S MAGIC GLASSES

In 1972, Charles W. Conrose, Sr., of Webster, New York, took out Patent No. 3,436,151, a pair of golfer's glasses with lines scratched on the lenses to enable him to line up putts. According to Mr. Conrose, the glasses could also be used and adapted for baseball pitchers, the lenses being marked with a rectangle indicating the strike zone of a batter.

THE APPLAUDING GOLF CLUB

In 1942, a golf club was invented by George Carney of Duluth, Minnesota, that automatically applauded the golfer when he started his swing correctly. The club had a small roller set into the metal plate on its bottom. The end of the roller was toothed, bearing against the end of a small spring brass plate. When the roller turned, the teeth caused the plate to vibrate and make a rapid, harsh buzz. This was the "applause," emitted when the club was dragged along the ground for about sixteen inches before the backswing, which, the inventor said, would automatically cause the golfer to go into the correct pivot so ardently sought by the duffer. When the golfer did not drag his club the necessary distance, he received no applause and thus knew he was executing the movement incorrectly.

THE ANTIFALSE-MOVE MACHINE

Even more elaborate than the applauding golf club was the 1953 invention of George M. Troutman Jenks of St. Petersburg, Florida. In an effort to teach the golfer the value of making every swing a precise movement, the inventor specified that various parts of the body were to be "secured" into the correct positions —that is, the feet were strapped to a set of foot plates, the head fitted with a cap and chin guard, a belt trussed about the golfer's waist and linked by rods at three positions, and the club held by a boomlike arrangement linked to the mechanism. By some process of complex planning, the machine moved everything in sequence, swinging the club and golfer's hips, keeping his head in the correct position, pivoting his knees and shoulders in a correct and smooth motion. By being forced to repeat the process over and over, it was presumed the swing would become second nature.

ANOTHER STROKE MACHINE

A decade before Jenks' complex iron-and-leather maiden was proposed, a more modest invention to teach the correct swing was patented by William Beil and Floyd Farley of Oklahoma City. Their machine was composed of an arm sticking downward and outward to the golfer, holding a club just below the grip. The golfer was supposed to grasp the club and pull it back in his normal swing. If the method he used was "incorrect," the machine would not let the club move. When the golfer learned the correct swing, the machine graciously released the club.

GOLF BLINKERS

In 1916, C. T. Ramsay of Liverpool, England, patented an optical device that acted as blinkers, the sight of the player being restricted to a small area around the ball. Thus, it was reasoned, he would be compelled to keep his eye on the ball.

FINDING LOST BALLS

During the course of a century, golfers have lost innumerable balls, and it was only a matter of time until inventors applied their talents to creating golf balls that could not be lost. In 1937, Sir John Simon, British Home Secretary and inventor, developed a golf ball with a mechanism inside it rather like that of a Mills bomb or hand grenade. Instead of pulling the pin, the golfer pressed a button before driving the ball, which on coming to rest emitted a loud squeaking sound at ten-second intervals until the owner pressed the button a second time.

Other inventors tried rather less sophisticated methods as means of producing unlosable golf balls. In 1928, Samuel J. Bens of New York patented a ball that would discharge a visible cloud of ammonium chloride vapor when the ball came to rest. Another proposal was to apply a pyrotechnical composition sold for Fourth of July celebrations called "spit devil." When the ball was hit, the "spit devil" would cause an initial explosion followed by a series of crackling explosions when it landed. Mr. Bens also suggested that balls be coated with various aromas so that the golfer—or a trained dog—could locate them with his nose. Still another suggestion along this line was that golf balls be treated with chemicals that would attract butterflies or other insects. Presumably all the golfer would have to do then was look for the nearest winged mob. How he was to concentrate on his swing with the insects milling about was not explained.

After World War II, inventions to render golf balls unlosable became increasingly complex. In June 1950, the B. F. Goodrich Company unveiled an experimental "talking golf ball" at Akron's Portage Country Club, complete with male and female celebrities driving the new product off carefully sculptured tees. According to Goodrich technicians, the "talking golf ball" contained one-fiftieth gram of radioactive material under its rubber cover, which was sufficient to generate a reaction when approached by a Geiger counter. Unfortunately, the amount of radioactive substance that could be used without endangering the golfer's life was so small that a Geiger counter had to be within three or four feet of the lost ball to be effective. Most golfers with normal vision would be able to discover the ball with the naked eye at that range. Not surprisingly, Goodrich's invention never got off the ground.

The same fate befell a 1955 ball equipped with a complete transmitter, oscillator, and miniature batteries. Its radio frequency was supposedly strong enough to be picked up by a portable receiver carried in the golfer's pocket.

Practically the only successful development in twentieth-century golf balls, as far as being more readily found, was the type designed to float on water. Otherwise the object exists as an eternal reminder of the consequences that follow man's inability to follow the straight-and-narrow.

RENÉ LACOSTE—NETMAN AND INVENTOR

"In defeating Big Bill Tilden last August," the Associated Press reported on November 9, 1927, "René Lacoste had a mechanical accomplice—a machine of his own invention—the French star disclosed today."

The announcement hardly surprised some people who had seen either the United States, Australia, or Great Britain win every Davis Cup until that time. France was hardly a tennis power and no one thought Lacoste could defeat Bill Tilden's vicious backhand. But in 1927 everything was different. The United States was leading, 2–1, when Tilden and Lacoste took the court at the Germantown Cricket Club in Philadelphia. Tilden seemed in good shape, hitting the ball hard and true. But invariably it came right back, just as if he were hitting balls against the side of a wall. Gradually Tilden weakened, and Lacoste won by scores of 6–3, 4–6, 6–3, 6–2. American domination of the Davis Cup was ended. Surely Lacoste had used some secret weapon.

In November he revealed that he had. For six months he worked to perfect a mechanical

tennis ball machine which, turned by a crank, sent balls in rapid succession at one of four unpredictable angles. The player in training literally had no moment to relax. Up to a thousand balls would be fired his way before the device had to be reloaded. Thus, according to Lacoste, he developed the stamina and precision to withstand the best Bill Tilden had to offer.

BASKETBALL

When is it desirable to always miss the basket? When practicing the art of grabbing rebounds, naturally.

In 1973, Ken Hayden of Avon, Ohio, himself a basketball player, devised a gadget to make certain no ball would go through the nets during a rebound practice session. Called "Reboundome," Hayden's invention was a sort of plastic lid that fit over the hoop like the cover on a soup pot. In order to generate unpredictable bounces, the plastic was molded with lumps and bumps of various sizes. Coaches at several colleges and universities immediately expressed interest in the device.

Less successful was U. S. Patent No. 3,629,869, granted to Virgil L. Sweet, a basketball coach at Valparaiso (Indiana) High School. In order to teach a player to dribble without looking down at the ball, Sweet invented a pair of glasses with a special set of shields. The shields, made in a U shape, prevent the player from seeing when he looks down but allow him to see straight ahead.

According to Mr. Sweet, the glasses were flexible enough to be used by players from grammar school through college.

THE MAGIC BASEBALL CURVER

During the latter part of the nineteenth century a device was sold that supposedly ena-

---

From *Reaches Guide* for 1898:
"The Magic Baseball Curver!!
Patent Pending
This is the third season I have sold this little mechanical wonder, but having made a very valuable and effective improvement in its construction, it is now far superior to what it was. In its original form it had one weak point, but this I have overcome and it is now absolutely perfect. It is neatly constructed on scientific principles and is truly a marvel of simplicity. With it any average pitcher can soon pitch better 'curves' than the best professional in existence. The pitcher who uses one of

these 'curvers' has the opposing team completely at his mercy and the batsmen wonder where those AWFUL curves come from. With the old-style 'curver' 17 men have been struck out in a single game, but with the new model that record can easily be beaten. Although it is worth twice as much as it was, I offer it this season at the same prices, viz., one 'curver,' by mail, postpaid, for 25 cents in cash or 30 cents in stamps, two for 40 cents in cash or 45 cents in stamps, three for 50 cents in cash or 55 cents in stamps. Beware of worthless imitations. The is the only genuine 'curver.'"

bled the buyer to throw a curve ball as soon as he put the thing on. One end of the "magic baseball curver" fit over the index finger and the other end was held in the palm of the hand. Although no one ever demonstrated that the gimmick worked, it was supposedly endorsed by professionals.

The Bat with a Hole in It

In 1977, a baseball fan and inventor named Joe Martino, of Brooklyn, made a special training bat with a hole in the ordinarily "fat" part. The idea, to swing and have the ball pass through the hole, would supposedly indicate to the batter that he had made perfect contact.

THE SEARCH FOR A MECHANICAL OFFICIAL

It is hardly a secret that players, fans, and coaches have at some time or another been infuriated by the calls of referees, umpires, and officials, who, like themselves, are only human. If an official makes a call favorable to the host team, he is a "homer"; if he makes the opposite decision, he is deliberately favoring the visitors to prove that he cannot be intimidated by partisan crowds. Sometimes, it is charged, he is completely out of position to see the play. Or he may be simply blind—physically or with his own arrogance or preconception as to who's going to win. Actually, officials in all sports have an extremely good record as far as accuracy goes, and even without benefit of instant-replay devices have shown themselves to be amazingly perceptive. But because occasional errors have been made—or are thought to have been made—officials have been targeted for replacement by inventors of mechanical scoring devices.

SOME BOXING DEVICES

One of the first geniuses to come on the scene was a Joseph Donovan of Chicago, who in 1895 patented a jacket that was not only designed to absorb some of the shock of the blows and thus increase safety, but also to register the number of blows landed. The jacket was outfitted with electrical connections over the pit of the stomach, the heart, and the ribs, and the headpiece had similar "strike points" on the nose, jaw, and cheeks. On the back of the gladiator was a bell, which rang as the fighters hit each other, and twin registers implanted in the jacket revealed how many blows had been landed.

A mere sixty-one years later, along came Willie P. Roberson of Winston-Salem, North Carolina, with still another method of scoring punches. Instead of strapping the fighter in a heavy jacket, Roberson suggested, via Patent No. 2,767,920, that the onus for scoring could be in sets of registering boxing gloves. Consisting of an air-filled bladder, the glove contained a pneumatic tube leading to a counter embedded in the wrist section. When a fighter landed a heavy blow, the counter would ring it up, and obviously the man with the higher score at the end of the fight would be declared the winner. The device, Mr. Roberson explained, could be adjusted to rule out very light blows, registering only those with great force behind them.

Some critics of officials, of course, do not want to replace them completely with the help of new inventions, but only make their judgments less recondite. Nothing infuriates fight fans so much as watching their man land a veritable whirlwind of blows against his opponent—and then be told at the end of ten rounds that their favorite lost by a considerable margin. To soften the blow for fans, Michael J. Mesi and Raymond G. Davis of Portland, Oregon, invented a boxing scoreboard (U. S. Patent No. 2,669,389) in 1954 that was designed to provide up-to-the-round information as the fight progressed. Noting that boxing was the only American spectator sport in which the onlookers had no official information as to the "score" until the match was concluded, Mesi and Davis designed their scoreboard so that both judges and referee could flash their scores for each round by touching a button. Besides keeping fans posted, they said, another purpose would be to "disclose to the spectators . . . any chronic variance of some particular official so that incompetent officials will be revealed and replaced. . . ."

FOOTBALL

Football is equally burdened with judgment calls, the most outstanding being whether or not a close field-goal attempt is good or not. On December 3, 1939, the Washington Redskins and New York Giants met in a game to decide which Eastern Division club would play Green Bay for the NFL championship. Late in the contest, with the Giants ahead, 9–7, Washington drove within field-goal range and made the kick, only to have it called bad by the referee, Bill Halloran. A great deal of controversy was generated by the call, enough to stimulate work on an electric eye designed to rule on field goals. Oddly, the work was started by a director of the Detroit Lions, Leo Fitzpatrick, who also happened to be vice president of a radio station. "Our engineers believe they can perfect an electric machine that will record the kick immediately," he said. "The eye has been proved effective at race tracks, and I can see no reason why it can't be used in football."

The reasoning had some merit, but of course nothing was done in this regard. Following Green Bay's playoff victory over the Baltimore Colts in 1965 by the margin of a field goal that films showed was bad, some persons revived the electric-eye principle. NFL officials decided it would be cheaper to add several feet of pipe to the uprights.

BASEBALL

As might be expected, baseball proved especially attractive to inventors because of its need for officials to make from three hundred to five hundred judgment calls per game. In 1938, a mechanical umpire to call balls and strikes was patented by John Oram of Dallas, Texas. It consisted of two lights, a pair of photoelectric cells, some reflecting mirrors, and an electrical circuit. Instead of being stationed behind the batter, as might be expected, the robot was placed near first base. One of its lights was mounted overhead, directing a vertical beam of light the same width as home plate through a slot in front of the plate, where it was picked up by a mirror and reflected onto a photoelectric plate. The second light sent a horizontal beam across the plate to another battery of mirrors. Thus— theoretically—a "strike zone" was formed, the ball generating an electrical impulse when it entered the area. Despite the fact that it was all very complicated, it probably didn't work.

At approximately the same time, another would-be inventor wrote to the editor of the New York *Times* lauding the photoelectric strike zone idea and further suggesting that "some magnetic metal could be put in the bases and in the spikes of the base runners' shoes and in the ball, so that when contact is made the base runner could be ruled safe or out by a mechanized signal." As if anticipating that the letter might draw some criticism, the writer, R.M.S., added: "Remember, they laughed at and criticized Orville Wright in 1910." (Unfortunately, R.M.S. did not explain why they laughed at Orville seven years *after* the Wright brothers made their first successful flight.)

After the war, the search for an infallible official continued. In 1949 a Washington in-ventor named Allen K. Nelson was granted U. S. Patent No. 2,461,836, for an electrical foul indicator. Situated at the farthest point of the outfield at the foul lines, Nelson's apparatus consisted of a post and set of crossarms from which a series of free-swinging rods were suspended. Half the rods were over foul territory, the other half over fair. The point soon becomes obvious: A ball striking the rods in fair ground caused a green light to flash on the post, while, of course, a ball hitting the rods in foul ground caused a red glow.

The world never saw Allen K. Nelson's invention in action. Nor did it witness the glorious debut of Lloyd and Nellie Holiday's 1953 invention (U. S. Patent No. 2,647,032) that suggested that balls and strikes be decided by a pair of cameras, one set up behind the batter, the other behind the pitcher (hopefully, a good-fielding camera). "When both agree it's a strike, a light shows on the bulletin board," the Holidays explained. They did not say what happened if one lens system liked the pitch and the other did not.

Two more decades passed. Then in 1974, eleven-year-old Tom Perryman of Dallas, Texas, one of the top science pupils at Greenhill School, tried his hand at the problem by designing a machine that moved on tracks in a half circle behind the batter and the catcher. It was movable so that it could face both left- and right-handed swingers and came complete with a blower to dust off the plate. But after conferring with his father, Dr. Ray Perryman, young Tom decided to eliminate the machine and use instead an energized crystal beneath home plate that would decide balls and strikes by computing the time it took sound waves to leave the crystal, strike the ball, and echo back to re-energize the crystal. The individual strike zone, Tom said, could be predetermined according to a batter's size and then programmed into the computer, which would recall it as soon as that batter stepped to the plate.

Despite the sophistication of Tom Perryman's mechanical umpire, it seems unlikely that American sports will ever outgrow its need for the human element in officials. It is, after all, vastly more satisfying to scream "Kill the umpire!" than it would be to yell "Unplug it!"

CHAPTER 17—DOING IT INDOORS AND AT NIGHT

If there is one time-tested rule in the history of spectator sports, it is the one that tells us how the growth of a popular event is invariably matched by the opportunistic shrewdness —dare we call it greed?—of entrepreneurs and promoters and owners. It was noted soon after the Civil War, for example, that given an exciting contest, or even a mediocre one under certain circumstances, people were usually eager to attend. The main problem then became how to make the product available at the best place at the best time. Most men worked ten- or twelve-hour days from dawn to dusk, and women seldom ventured forth unescorted.

Thus scheduling events during daylight hours left untapped all those potentially lucrative hours after dark. (Sunday was a different—that is, moral—problem.)

In addition to the limitations imposed by natural light and contemporary mores, some sporting events such as bicycling, rowing, and swimming took place at spots far removed from population centers, such as country roads or lakes. Promoters realized to their chagrin that it was difficult to charge admission—and collect it—at such locations without an army of scouts to ward off freeloaders. It was also difficult to focus the action of these events into one easily seen area, then as now a prerequisite to spectator satisfaction.

For these reasons, entrepreneurs soon began to explore the possibilities of adding lights, enlarging, or building new arenas so that existing sports could be moved indoors or played during evening hours.

THE FIRST ARTIFICIALLY ILLUMINATED ATHLETIC EVENT IN AMERICA

It was August 31, 1859, and Jean Francis Gravelet, a slight, blue-eyed Frenchman who used the name "Blondin" because of his long flowing hair, was about to make his first tightrope crossing of Niagara Falls at night.

Just thirty-five, Blondin had already crossed the body of boiling water several times since June 30, when he made his debut as a ropewalker at that particular spot before a crowd of several thousand. On July 4, he had crossed with a sack over his head as an encore, then repeated the trip with a wheelbarrow on July 15. On August 17, he walked the twelve hundred-foot strand of rope with his manager on his shoulders.

There seemed to be nothing left but the grand spectacle of a night performance, with its attendant dangers. But as this was before the era of massed floodlighting at the Falls, Blondin was obliged to have locomotive headlights drawn up at either end of the sagging rope. In order to be certain the audience saw him, Blondin secured colored lights on the ends of his balancing pole.

Thousands were on hand for the illuminated event, which reached a climax when Blondin reached the middle of the crossing. At that moment, the lights on his pole suddenly disappeared, and the audience gasped, assuming that the young man was headed toward the rapids nearly two hundred feet below. But such was not the case. The lights had gone out, but Blondin continued to walk to the other side. The first illuminated athletic event in the United States was a rousing success.

ILLUMINATED GOLF

Golfers being more than normally fanatic about their game from the very beginning of its existence, it was perhaps inevitable that the players try to find a way of indulging their passion beyond the limitations of the sunlit day.

One method of playing golf at night was to treat the balls with a phosphorescent material so that they could be followed during the flight path and located once they came to a stop. Such a method was devised as early as 1871, when a late-evening match was played at the St. Andrew's course in Edinburgh.

The match was the idea of a Professor P. G. Tait, who explained the concept to fellow members of the British Association at the annual meeting. The men immediately went out on the course and played a round with the chemically treated balls. With the exception of Professor Crum Brown, whose hand caught on fire as a result of prolonged contact with the phosphorescent material, all went well.

A bit more than a half century later, on October 28, 1924, a major attraction took place in the United States at Briarcliff Manor, New York, where more than a thousand persons gathered to see golf played at night.

Light was supplied by a four hundred million-candlepower searchlight, the largest of its kind in the world, along with other electric illuminations. Sponsored by the Illuminating Engineers Society, then holding its eighteenth annual convention, the star of the show was Gene Sarazen, America's most famous golfer.

Assisting Sarazen was a one million-candlepower searchlight mounted at the first tee of the Briarcliff Lodge course, aimed down the fairway to the green, 246 yards away. The larger light was placed on a truck in a roadway 200 feet to the side, 50 feet from the tee. In addition, the trees on both sides of the fairway had been decorated with lamps and reflectors so that as one reporter put it, "the ensemble was like a stage setting, and peculiarly beautiful."

Curious and perhaps alarmed, the residents of Ossining, Mount Kisco, and the Sleepy Hollow Valley turned out to see what was happening. Soon there was a cluster of people at every vantage point. Sarazen then stepped into the blazing radiance of the first tee. He proceeded to drive about a dozen balls down the fairway "like a silver bullet." They could be seen easily. Two were lost in the rough beyond the lights but the promoters were satisfied that the "first advertised attempt to shoot a golf ball at night" was a success.

The next evening, before a crowd of about ten thousand, Sarazen duplicated the performance and even scored a hole-in-one, electrifying the spectators on the electrified course. "The ball was plainly visible throughout its flight from the tee to the hole," the papers noted.

And Even Indoor Golf:
As early as January 1911, serious consideration had been given to finding a way to play golf indoors—real golf, not the miniature variety. Tom Wells, a New York professional, was the chief advocate of an indoor system where ten thousand square feet of floor space could be used as the arena. The players, using this system, would drive their balls as hard as if they were outdoors, but the balls would be caught by huge canvas pockets and the likely distance awarded the golfer according to the pocket reached. The "hole" would then be completed by utilizing a small putting green. The system was quite popular for a while and even allowed for the playing of some intercity matches by telegraph, but never took firm hold.

Sarazen's 1924 promotional experiment, of course, involved but a single hole. In order to make nighttime golf a possibility for untold numbers of players, it was necessary to study the problem of illuminating a vast area. This inevitably followed, the first professional night tourney being held at Eastwood Hills, Kansas City, Kansas, in August of 1930. Nine holes were festooned with banks of lights as Harold McSpaden, who carded 35–33, led the field of more than sixty golfers. There were occasional problems, as might be expected, especially when caddies could not locate balls that had been driven deeply into the rough. Some golfers also found the artificial light harsh and distracting. But the innovation was pronounced a success. Not until 1963, however, was the first public course with night lighting opened, at Sewell, New Jersey.

Would the Glowing Ball Revolutionize Golf?
Speculated one editor: "If this innovation is adopted an entirely new and much-needed line of golf stories will go the rounds. We shall hear of the unlucky man who was just on the point of winning his match when his ball went dark, and his opponent would not allow him to renew the phosphorus. . . ."

There were some persons, naturally, who felt that illuminating an entire course, or even half of it, was not only expensive but also foolhardy. Harking back to Professor Tait without realizing it, they suggested that golf could be played quite well at night if only the balls were lit. And so it was that on a November night in 1927, a long streak of phosphorescence—like a slow-moving tracer bullet—unraveled from the first tee at New York's Van Cortlandt Park course. When people gathered to see what was happening, they found a man unwrapping tin foil from golf balls that glowed with a curious green-yellow light. One by one he drove them off the tee. Each rolled to a stop and sat shining in the fairway like a giant glowworm.

The luminous ball-belter was Millard J. Bloomer, who had been experimenting with the new-style golf ball for several months. "I believe we will have all-night golf in a short time due to the luminous ball," he predicted confidently. The composition used to coat the balls, he explained, was a secret formula devised by a chemist at Columbia University, and each ball, once unwrapped, would retain its illumination for from eight to ten minutes. "We may succeed later in finding a practicable substance that will produce a more permanent glow," added Bloomer, "like that of the radium composition used in watches." The illuminated golf ball never made a hit with the players, although night driving ranges eventually became a standard part of the American landscape.

TENNIS—INDOORS AND UNDER THE LIGHTS

As early as 1881—less than a decade after being introduced to Americans—tennis had become popular enough for at least one club to announce that a special indoor facility was being built. On May 4, New Yorkers learned that members of the Tennis Building Association had filed incorporation papers in order to erect a tennis building at the corner of Forty-first Street and Seventh Avenue.

The plan of the structure called for three floors—the bottom to be used as private stables for club members and their friends; the second floor for dressing and bathing facilities as well as accommodations for coachmen and their families; and a third floor for the courts. These would be illuminated by day through a system of skylights and by night by electricity.

Even more revolutionary, the club, newspapers said, "is intended for the use of ladies as well as gentlemen."

While awaiting the construction of their new facility, tennis enthusiasts of New York were able to convince municipal authorities to allow them to use the Seventh Regiment Armory drill hall, which became the scene of a mass indoor tennis rally on the night of November 26, 1881. "The spectacle," *Harper's Weekly* reported, "was a novel and brilliant one. . . . Ten of the courts were occupied by players in every variety of costume . . . and a few ladies were courageous enough to take part in the games, which were watched with evident interest by a large company of visitors in the galleries."

There were problems, of course. One of the wires used to suspend a string of electric lights was defective, so that a large portion of the arena was in darkness. In addition, the balls were painted the same color as the floor, making it difficult for the players to judge the bounce. But all in all, the evening was a great success, a carnival atmosphere prevailing until the shockingly late hour—for young Victorian ladies—of 10:30 P.M.

BASEBALL

Having been hailed as the "national game" around the time of the Civil War, it was inevitable that baseball be the subject of much speculation and work in order to make it available to enthusiasts during all seasons and at all times of the night and day.

Accordingly, as soon as the electric light made its appearance, it was tested on the baseball diamond. The first illuminated night game took place between two amateur teams at Nantasket Beach, Massachusetts, in 1880, but the play was ragged and marred by errors because of the poor quality of the early lights.

Another pioneer night game took place three years later, on June 2, 1883, at Fort Wayne, Indiana. The two teams, the Quincey Professionals and M. E. College, played before a crowd of two thousand. According to the Fort Wayne *Journal Gazette*, seventeen lights of four thousand candlepower each were used during the seven-inning game, which was won by Quincey, 19–11. The test was judged successful.

Despite the experiment's auspicious beginning, playing baseball at night under the lights was neglected during the rest of the nineteenth century. Much more attention was given to adapting the game to indoor arenas, so that athletes could continue to play during the colder months. According to contemporary accounts, the first indoor baseball game was played on Thanksgiving Day 1887, at the Farragut Club of Chicago, an athletic association for young men. Several of the club's members were boxing when, in a spirit of fun, one of them pulled off a glove and threw it toward another man at the other end of the room. A third man, who happened to be holding a broom at the time, swung it at the flying glove and the game of indoor baseball was born.

The story may be pure fancy, but if it is not, the man claiming the title "Father of Indoor Baseball" was George W. Hancock. On that occasion at Chicago, according to the story, he ordered the wrestling mats turned sideways to form a diamond and called for a suitable bat and ball to be brought forth so that a game of baseball could be played on the spot. Two days later, after tinkering with the problems attendant to playing baseball indoors, the first "regulation" contest was played. The final score was 41–40.

Regardless of the exact details of the game's beginning, indoor baseball was popular enough to attract more than two thousand Philadelphians to an 1888 match held in the main building on the State Fair grounds between teams north and south of Market Street. The building, three hundred feet long and a hundred feet wide, was crammed not only with interested spectators but also with baseball celebrities such as Kid Gleason, John Coleman, Jack O'Brien, and Jerry McCormick, all of whom were curious to see how their livelihood could be played under roof.

The teams themselves had a sprinkling of professionals, including outfielder Ed O'Brien and Jack Clements of the Phillies, Tom Burns of Chicago, Jimmy Freel of Newark, and Curt Welch of the Athletics. The downtown team won by a score of 6–1.

By 1890, indoor baseball had graduated to Madison Square Garden, a situation made possible not only by the game's popularity but also by improvements in artificial lighting. The indoor variety never became popular with the professionals, but it caught on with military and amateur groups to the extent that by 1900 an indoor league with more than a dozen teams played regularly at Madison Square Garden from November to March. Purists, of course, maintained that coming indoors was a gross bastardization. Baseball, they pointed out, was a game to be played in the warm sun. The only exception was the World Series, which even in the early years of the twentieth century, with a shorter season, was often played in near-freezing weather for profit if not fun.

A Comment on Indoor Baseball:
"A few years ago such a thing would have been utterly impossible," Harper's *remarked. "Base-ball by gaslight or candlelight might send a few patients to the hospital, but it could never be a recreation for anybody, or a pleasure to either players or spectators . . . this is a fast age, and it could hardly be safe to say for certain that during the next ten or twenty years yacht races may not be sailed under glass and before a grandstand. Certainly base-ball has been tamed."*

Baseball finally got around to tinkering with night illumination in 1909. In February of that year, the Cincinnati National League club announced, "The first game of baseball at night will be played in this city, Sunday, April 11. Teams from the Cincinnati National and Chicago American clubs will play the match, and representatives from both leagues will be present to see if the idea is feasible."

It was to be nothing more than an exhibition, to be sure, but it was an important one. In order to provide the correct amount of light, the park was encircled with 100-foot steel towers, each holding a pair of powerful carbon lamps. According to *Scientific American*, three of these lamps were found nearly sufficient to illuminate the playing area, but to be absolutely certain everything went off well, a total of 14 lamps were used. Three-phase current was supplied by a 250-horsepower, 60-cycle dynamo, operating at 345 revolutions per minute. According to accounts, the lamps

had been designed by George F. Cahill, who also invented "an ingenious baseball pitching machine."

By April 11, however, problems forced the postponement of the game until June 18. In addition, President Garry Herrmann of Cincinnati obviously got a case of cold feet about experimenting with his own players and decided not to risk their safety under the lights. Thus the game was played by teams representing the Elk Lodge of Cincinnati and the Elk Lodge of Newport, Kentucky. More than three thousand persons, including members of the Cincinnati and Philadelphia squads, watched the amateurs cavort without mishap.

"The players had no difficulty keeping their eyes on the ball," one reporter noted. "All of them seemed to perform as well as if it had been bright daylight. Long flies, balls that went high in the air as fouls, grounders, the pitchers' swiftest curves and slants were easily handled." Errors, it was noted, came about more because of the Elk Lodge players' lack of experience rather than lack of light. The scheme was pronounced a success, although several big-league players who watched expressed the opinion that there would have to be considerable improvement in lighting techniques "before championship games may be played."

And Just One Month Later:
On July 8, 1909, a regular game between two teams in the Central League was played under the lights at Grand Rapids, Michigan. Grand Rapids beat Zanesville, 11–10, in a contest that was unmarred by problems.

Another long hiatus followed, until June 24, 1927, when teams from Lynn and Salem of the New England League played a game that was then called "the first professional baseball game ever played under artificial light." The contest was actually arranged at the insistence of General Electric Engineers at Lynn, Massachusetts, more to test new equipment than to promote the cause of night baseball. The field was surrounded and illuminated by seventy-two projectors giving an estimated total of twenty-six million candlepower. In addition, four floodlights with another half-million candlepower "lighted up the ceiling . . . of the field . . . so that outfielders had no trouble with high flies."

Approximately eight thousand fans attended the game, which was marked by several spectacular running catches, a pair of double plays, and a diving catch of a hard liner for the final out. Goose Goslin, Washington Senator outfielder, was one of the most enthusiastic onlookers. "I didn't believe they could do it," he said. "It's just as good ball as they could play by daylight."

Assuming Goslin's remark wasn't a slap at the New England League's normal style of play, one may conclude that he approved of the lighting.

Despite the obvious success of night illumination by the end of the 1920s, major-league baseball continued to favor the daylight game. But in the minor leagues and especially on the Pacific Coast, night baseball grew to have stronger and stronger appeal. One of the pioneers was the Shreveport club of the Texas League, which played several games under the lights and distributed ballots to see whether its fans approved of the innovation. They heartily approved, and baseball at night became a weekly attraction. At Los Angeles during the summer of 1930, baseball attendance of women increased by 50 per cent at night, and San Francisco reported that patronage for the "owl games" tripled that of daylight contests. On the other hand, Pacific Coast League players complained that the night contests upset their eating and sleeping routine, caused eyestrain, and filled the field with shadows that made easy plays difficult. Some minor-league players even anticipated early retirement, seeing the handwriting on the wall when they could no longer see the stitching on the ball. One such person was veteran catcher "Beans" Miner, who obtained his release from the Peoria club of the Three-I League when it became apparent that most of Peoria's games would be played at night. "I can't see 'em back of the plate," he complained just before being shipped to Nashville of the Southern Association in July 1930.

Nevertheless, Some Expressed Amused Disapproval of Night Baseball:

"The bases are filled . . . the score is tied in the fifteenth inning . . . Babe Ruth is at bat . . . it is three o'clock in the morning. Suddenly the arena is plunged into darkness. . . . A hush falls over the assemblage as the announcement booms through the grandstand: 'Game called on account of blown fuses.'"

Irving Gutterman, 1930

That same month, night baseball took major steps into the eastern establishment areas when games were played for the first time at Dexter Park, Woodhaven (New York), and Jersey City, New Jersey. The former was played on July 23, 1930, between the Springfield team of Long Island City and the Brooklyn Bushwicks; the latter on July 24 between Jersey City and Newark of the International League. Seated in the stands was Colonel Jacob Ruppert, Yankee owner, who issued the guarded statement afterward, "I imagine night baseball will prove a great benefit to the minor leagues, and if it becomes definitely popular in the minors I don't see why someday it should not become part of major-league baseball."

The very next season saw the first major-league teams meet under the lights, but true to baseball's approaching innovation on tiptoe, the contest was merely an exhibition. The scene was Houston, Texas, where the New York Giants met the Chicago White Sox on March 21, 1931. Artistically the game was a success—lighting was perfect and the Giants' Fred Lindstrom made a superb running catch—but twenty-five hundred fans shivered in the cold wind that swept across the adjacent prairie. Chicago won the game by scoring five runs in the top of the tenth inning to go ahead, 11–6.

Four seasons later, the major leagues finally got around to playing an official contest under the lights. More than twenty thousand fans made the scene at Cincinnati to see the Reds take on the lowly Philadelphia Phillies. A floodlight inaugural ceremony featured President Franklin D. Roosevelt pressing a button at the White House that turned on 363 1,000-kilowatt lights mounted on eight giant towers. Ford Frick, president of the National League, and Will Harridge, president of the American League, were in the ball park to witness the contest, which was errorless, although Phillie outfielders dropped a pair of fly balls that were scored as hits. Not everyone was ecstatic about the experience. "Night baseball is all right," said Phillie Manager Jimmy Wilson, "if the fans want it. But I'd rather play in the daytime." The Phillies lost the low-hitting contest, 2–1.

Trivia from the First Major-league Night Game (May 24, 1935):

First time to score under the lights—*Cincinnati*

First RBI—*by Ival Goodman, Cincinnati outfielder (in first inning, ground ball scoring Billy Myers from third)*

Winning pitcher—*Paul Derringer, Cincinnati*

Losing Pitcher—*Joe Bowman, Philadelphia*

Complaints still abounded from baseball's purists, but more and more night games began to work their way into the schedule. A notable milestone was reached on June 15, 1938, when in the first night game ever played at Ebbets Field, Brooklyn, Cincinnati's Johnny Vander Meer became the first pitcher to throw back-to-back no-hitters by blanking the Dodgers, 6–0. That put night baseball into the record books with a bang. And for those who might have charged that the limited visibility of night baseball cheapened Vander Meer's feat, Cookie Lavagetto said: "The lights were new to us then. But Vander Meer was good enough that game to pitch a no-hitter under any conditions."

Twelve years later, baseball took another giant step into the darkness when the first night Opening Game was held. The date was April 18, 1950; the scene, St. Louis, Missouri, where a crowd of twenty thousand saw the hometown Cardinals win by a score of 4–2. A year later, the American League saw an Opening Game at night, the Washington Senators defeating the Athletics, 6–1, at Philadelphia.

Then, on October 14, 1971, thanks largely to the needs of commercial television, baseball held its first night World Series contest. More than twenty-one million TV sets were tuned in to watch the Pittsburgh Pirates defeat Baltimore, 4–0. It was an even greater defeat for those who still maintained that the "national game" was bastardizing itself by forsaking God's good sun for the dollars of darkness.

FOOTBALL

Immediately following the announcement of plans to play the University of Chicago-University of Michigan football game indoors, there were more than a few complaints and satirical jabs. "Such a hothouse idea!" some said. "Completely contrary to the spirit of the game," moaned others. A real football rooter, it was pointed out, "prefers to tramp around in the snow or mud and yell himself into a croupy condition rather than be confined to a hard-bottomed chair and breathe a torpid atmosphere."

On the other side of the controversy, advocates of the revolutionary idea predicted that the first indoor game—or what was considered the first—would be "the most perfect arrangement for seeing a football game that has ever been devised. . . . It will pass into history as the best and most thoroughly viewed conflict waged on a college gridiron."

Thus were the philosophical battle lines drawn, not in twentieth-century Houston, where the Astrodome bothered some purists, but in Chicago in 1896. The scene of the "first" indoor football game was the Chicago Coliseum, a cavernous structure on Sixty-third Street with a seating capacity of about twenty thousand. Because Chicago's weather often turned foul by November, city officials decided to try using the Coliseum for the highly popular Thanksgiving Day contest. Press reaction was generally enthusiastic, although some writers tended to regard the innovative step as a mere novelty. A note of satire crept into some accounts, as when the Chicago *Tribune* remarked, "As far as the audience is concerned, it might be grand opera or a Shakespearean drama. . . . The boxes are placed near the scene of the conflict just as they are nearest the stage in a theater." More on that unusual aspect of the situation later.

A Previous Indoor Football Game:
Was played at New York's Madison Square Garden following the close of the regular 1891 season. The teams were Yale Consolidated (which had five Yale players on it, including Pudge Heffelfinger) vs. Springfield (Massachusetts) YMCA. Yale won, 16–10, Pudge scoring once near the end of the first half.
A Previous Game Under Lights:
Was played on September 29, 1892, at the Mansfield Fair, Mansfield, Pennsylvania, between Wyoming Seminary of Kingston, Pennsylvania, and Mansfield Teachers College. Twenty lights of two thousand candlepower each were used to illuminate a seventy-minute half. Neither team scored.

Purists charged that there would be great difficulties for signal callers, that "the place will reverberate . . . until it will be impossible to think, much less to talk." Even as workmen began hauling in tons of earth and sand for the playing surface, the lighting was discussed. Although the Coliseum's side walls were punctuated by numerous glass interstices, lighting conditions tended to range all the way from excellent to atrocious. During the summer months, for example, incoming light was often so bright that opaque dressings had to be placed over the windows to reduce glare. With the dressings in place on a dull day, however, the arena resembled a tomb.

Another controversial point dealt with the possible effects confinement would have on the athletes. Outdoor advocates contended that "the pressures of an immense crowd . . . will pollute the atmosphere even in a structure of such massive proportions . . . the players will be enervated and unable to play with snap and vigor. . . ."

As for the possibility that a punt might hit a girder projecting from the ceiling, no one seemed to know what to recommend. This knotty problem was soon lost amid the pregame ballyhoo attending the arrival of the Michigan players, who were depicted as behemoths in that they outweighed underdog Chicago by an average of 175 pounds to 170. Despite this appalling mismatch, the game was looked forward to as a truly "scientific test of the comparative merits of two distinct systems of play." Michigan, according to contemporary analysts, slugged out yardage along the ground; Chicago, led by ace punter Clarence Herschberger, depended on a strong kicking game to put opponents in a hole.

Aided by a miserable downpour—the event's promoters could not have programmed the weather much better—attendance was excellent on the day of the game. "Herschberger sent the leather down to the Michigan goal line," jargoned the *Inter-Ocean*. "A great shout went up as the Peoria lad's toe touched the ball." The first indoor football game was under way.

An Assenting Voice:
"Since its inception, the Coliseum has held a variety of sounds. Its iron girders have broken the war whoops of Buffalo Bill's Indians. Its arched roof has hurled back the echo of the oratory of William Jennings Bryan. Its walls have rattled with the roar of campaign applause. But there was never heard in that building the loudest, most unique and picturesque noise in the universe—the college yell!"
        Chicago Inter-Ocean

By no stretch of the imagination can the contest be described as a classic, although the first half featured one play that seems straight out of a Marx Brothers movie. Backed against its own goal line, Michigan attempted to punt the ball, but a Chicago player broke through and knocked the ball clear out of the end zone into the seats drawn up, theater-style, to the very edge of the playing area. "Both teams dashed after it," one reporter wrote, "and the unfortunate spectators fell over chairs to get out of the way. Halfway up a Michigan man discovered it. He fell on the ball in the aisle, making a safety touchdown, and Chicago had scored two points."

After getting the ball back, Chicago's Herschberger drop-kicked a field goal from forty-five yards out to bring the score to 7–0,

field goals being worth five points in that era. Considering the slow style of play, such a lead seemed insurmountable, but Michigan, a team well populated with professionals, some of whom did not even attend that school, gave it the old college try. Three times they drove within Chicago's ten-yard line only to fumble or lose the ball on downs. In the meantime, the sky outside continued to darken. By the second half, it was not only impossible for the fans to see the players, it also was difficult for the players to see the ball. "The fullbacks . . . were forced to wait until it struck the ground to locate it," reported the *Inter-Ocean*.

Ironically, at this juncture the Michigan team put together a good drive. "It was too dark to see how," one reporter wrote, "but Michigan advanced the ball fifteen yards. Somebody went around the left end for five more . . . then a touchdown." Unfortunately for the Wolverines of 1896, a touchdown and extra point then added up to but six points. Chicago was still ahead.

Eventually the darkness became so oppressive that a halt was called in order to connect some arc lights suspended from the bottom of the gallery. During the pause, according to the *Tribune*, "a novel sight was witnessed. . . . Someone struck a match to light a cigar. Someone else thought it was done as a joke to secure a little illumination and lighted another match. Then others took it up and in a minute hundreds of matches were blazing around the entire field."

Shortly afterward, Michigan failed once again to score, and the home team emerged triumphant. Attempts to analyze the success or failure of the indoor experiment proved inconclusive. A Michigan trainer was interviewed but proved understandably surly. "The ground was soft and should have been underlaid with clay," he complained. "Instead it was a sandy loam, mixed with fine shavings. The only place to play a football game is outdoors on the sod. The air in there was bad. The ground should have been firmer. The cleats did not hold."

Even the Chicago newspapers, which could not be accused of a sour-grapes attitude, gave the experiment mixed reviews. "There was none of the sunshine," one noted, "none of the sparkling snow, and none of the coaching parties which made last year's game spectacular. It was the close score and enthusiasm and immense crowd . . . Had the day outside been more pleasant, the idea of football indoors must have been pronounced a failure." Total gate receipts for the contest amounted to ten thousand dollars.

Early in the twentieth century, an indoor football tournament was held at Madison Square Garden that featured professional teams composed of former college stars. The squads, which included the New York Knickerbockers, the Philadelphia Athletics, the Watertown (New York) Red and Blacks, Syracuse, and the New York Athletic Club, were quite enormous for their time. "The New York team has a heavier line than any used this season," a reporter wrote on December 29, 1902. "It averages 206 pounds. Every man on the team has been at some time a star player on one of the big American college elevens and four of them were varsity captains."

The team from Syracuse was indeed a powerhouse, having such players as Glenn S. Warner and his brother Bill, Hawley and Bemus Pierce of Carlisle, and Phil Draper, former miracle-man back at Williams College. A pro football doubleheader started the proceedings on December 29, the main contest being that between the two heavyweight teams, Syracuse and New York.

The Career of "Pop" Warner:
Was already in full swing by 1902. A 1896 graduate of Cornell, he coached at Georgia, 1895–96; Cornell, 1897–98; Carlisle, 1899–1903 (where he brought the team into first prominence by beating Columbia by 42 points and Pennsylvania, 16–5); and at various schools until his retirement in 1945.

The wooden flooring of the Garden had been taken up and a gridiron, thirty-five yards wide and seventy yards long, laid out on the earthen surface, "which proved to be rather too sticky and holding for fast work," one critic noted. Nevertheless, it was an excellent opportunity for thirty-five hundred early pro football enthusiasts to see top players in action. That action began when Glenn Warner kicked off. New York put the ball in play at its ten-yard line, but neither team could advance the ball very far toward the opposite goal. Glenn Warner, it must be admitted, did not exactly cover himself with glory on the occasion, missing three field-goal attempts early in the game. The first half ended in a scoreless tie.

The second half began with New York kicking off to Syracuse, which moved steadily down the field on runs by Draper and Hawley Pierce. At the two-yard line, the entire Syracuse squad pushed their right halfback, Bottger, across the end line for a touchdown. (The rules of the time allowed a runner to be helped by his teammates, sometimes even dragged.) At this point, an unusual situation occurred. The New Yorkers pointed out that

one of the umpires had called them offside. Rather than have the touchdown count, they insisted that they be penalized half the distance to the goal and run the play over. The officials denied this rather bizarre petition and Syracuse led, 5–0. Glenn Warner then missed the try for extra point. After an exchange of kicks, Phil Draper executed the best play of the game, a thirty-yard run that would have been a touchdown except for a splendid tackle by Kennedy of New York. No additional scoring occurred, and Syracuse had won the first round.

Having disposed of the New York Athletic Club, the boys from Syracuse rolled over the Knickerbockers two days later by the score of 36–0. One of the game's highlights was a pass from Warner to Draper that covered the entire length of the field but was called back because it had been caught out of bounds. With the Syracuse team ahead by 24–0 at the end of the first half, an interesting element of mercy entered the tournament: By mutual agreement it was decided to reduce the length of the second half from twenty to ten minutes. Syracuse won the first indoor professional football tournament two nights later.

A second tournament was held in 1903. A team from Franklin, Pennsylvania, which had lured away many players from other teams with higher salaries, easily won. According to Dr. Harry March in *Pro Football's Ups and Downs*, Frank Hinkey, former Yale end, and Big Bill Edwards officiated the night football games in evening dress—white gloves, tails, top hats, and patent-leather shoes. As the tournament proceeded, it became difficult for some of the free-spirited players to avoid the temptation of befouling those immaculate officials. And so on the final night of the tournament they entertained the crowd by attacking Frank Hinkey en masse.

Getting the Officials—a Genial Trick, 1903:
"In the very last play of the Franklin-Watertown game, with the contest safely in the bag, the Franklin backfield huddled and agreed to run over Frank Hinkey, dress suit and all. They did, soiling him effectively and emphatically. He took it good-naturedly and the Franklin management paid his cleaning and pressing bill."

Pro football played indoors went into a decline after that, although the reasons are unclear in that the tournaments were well attended. No doubt the popularity of college football had something to do with it; or it may have been that football was entering a period of growing roughness that worked against all forms of the sport. The next indoor contest seems to be that of December 18, 1932, which brought the season to an exciting and unusual climax. Following the final game of the season, which saw the Chicago Bears defeat Green Bay in the snow at Wrigley Field to bring on a postseason playoff between the Bears and the Portsmouth Spartans, George Halas decided to move the game indoors. He chose Chicago Stadium, a three-tiered, cavernous structure capable of holding about 12,000 customers, as the site of the playoff. A layer of dirt, left over from a circus, was conveniently in place, but the dimensions of the building were hardly suited for football. As a result, the crucial contest was played on a field only eighty yards long, with all boundary lines cheek-by-jowl with the stands.

Despite the artistic limitations, a crowd of 11,198 turned out to see the game, which was scoreless for three periods. The Chicago Bears were then a mixture of experience and youth, the latter supplied by second-year quarterback Keith Molesworth and third-year running backs Bronislaw "Bronco" Nagurski and Richard Nesbitt, the former by Red Grange, then in the twilight of his career. But there was enough left in old No. 77 to eke out a victory.

By Contrast, the Portsmouth Spartans Were a Bunch of No-names:
Most pro football fans of later eras recognize the names Nagurski, Grange, Molesworth, and others of the Chicago Bear Lineup. But only the true aficionado recalls the Portsmouth backfield of quarterback Leroy (Ace) Gutowsky, Glenn Presnell, John Cavosie, and Roy Lumpkin. And yet this less-distinguished backfield managed to finish the season with a record of six wins, two losses, and four ties.

After Nesbitt intercepted a pass by Gutowsky at the Spartan seven-yard line, Nagurski made six yards, then was stopped for no gain twice. On fourth down, Nagurski faked into the line, backed up two steps, and threw a pass to Grange, who took it in the end zone for a touchdown. Coach George Clark of Portsmouth charged onto the field, screaming that Nagurski's pass had violated the rule, then in existence, that stated that a forward pass could not be thrown legally unless the passer was at least five yards behind the line of scrimmage. The officials did not allow the

protest, although Clark's charge, seen from a later perspective, seems reasonable. A safety was added just before the end of the game when Mule Wilson of the Spartans, ready to punt, fumbled Clare Randolph's snap from center, the ball rolling out of the end zone to bring the score to Chicago 9, Portsmouth 0. Thus ended the first indoor playoff in National Football League history.

College football, meanwhile, also explored the possibilities of playing indoors when it was announced on January 10, 1930, that Atlantic City, New Jersey, would be the site of the "first indoor football game ever to be played" when Washington and Jefferson met Lafayette on October 25 in the Atlantic City Auditorium. Compared to the facilities offered the 1932 Chicago Bears and Portsmouth Spartans, those at Atlantic City were lavish. The playing field, of regulation size and made of 6 inches of turf, was covered by a roof 135 feet high, adequate for even the highest punts, it was said. Seating capacity was nearly forty thousand, but the game attracted a crowd of only twenty-five thousand. Washington and Jefferson won by a score of 7–0.

At the Same Time:
On July 30, 1930, night auto racing was advertised at the Ocean Speedway, Daytona Beach, Florida. The races were run over a half-mile course lighted from the promenade and marked off by illuminated barrels.

Thirty-four years later, Atlantic City was the site of the sixth annual Liberty Bowl game, which was played indoors at Convention Hall and even then was considered something of an innovation. After playing five Liberty Bowls in the cold of Philadelphia's Municipal Stadium with little profit, the Liberty Bowl Company, headed by Bill Dudley, decided to bring the 1964 contest inside. The decision turned out to be a good one as there were no mishaps and the crowd was comfortable in the sixty-degree temperature. The two colleges earned about sixty-thousand dollars each from the game, which was won, 32–6, by Utah over West Virginia. Star of the winners was Roy Jefferson, who had already been selected by the National Football League Pittsburgh Steelers and the AFL San Diego Chargers.

TRACK AND FIELD

One of the first sports to come indoors was track and field, which utilized the new Empire City Skating Rink on Third Avenue, between

Sixty-third and Sixty-fourth streets, in New York City. "The first semi-annual games of the New York Athletic Club," it was reported on November 12, 1868, "were witnessed by a large concourse of people. The rink is a magnificent structure, with arches having the largest clear span in America. . . . Dodworth's Band was present and rendered choice music at intervals during the evening." Also on hand were members of the various athletic clubs from the New York and Philadelphia areas. J. E. Russell, a noted pedestrian, drew loud applause by walking a mile in 7 minutes, 57½ seconds. He was followed by an exhibition of French velocipedes, "two of which were driven rapidly around amid the plaudits of the audience." As for the athletes, they competed in due course and were also applauded, although their times in the various races seem slow by later standards. (The 75-yard dash, for example, was won by William Curtis of the New York Athletic Club in 9 seconds flat.) The opening of indoor track and field was considered a great success by those present and, of course, the indoor meet became a standard attraction in years following.

Statistics on the Old Sixty-third Street Rink:

An impressive building for its time, the Empire City Skating Rink was 350 feet long, 170 feet wide, and 70 feet high, with a ground floor and raised platform for spectators. Approximately ten thousand persons could be admitted. During its history, the rink was used not only for athletic games but also for various pedestrian contests, which were so popular after the Civil War.

HARNESS RACING

Because it was one of the most popular American spectator sports of the nineteenth century—by 1886 there were eight hundred tracks around the nation—it was only natural that early attempts be made to make night racing a reality.

One of the first illuminated cards was in 1888 at Fostoria, Ohio, with the light being furnished by stand pipes or flambeaux of natural gas. A large crowd of people from all parts of Ohio showed up for the novelty, which was judged a complete success.

The major question that was answered was whether or not the horses would be "spooked" by the artificial illumination. Not only did they run well, but also it was noticed that

they trotted or paced three or four seconds faster than during the afternoon. The answer, of course, could have been the fact that temperatures at night were generally cooler.

Despite the successful experiment, night racing was not seriously tried again until 1929, when a five-night meet began at the Fort Miami Track in Toledo, Ohio, on June 25. Attendance immediately doubled, although some traditionalists continued to maintain that the horse would not put forth his best effort during the evening, that he ran best only "on a bright, sunny day when the air is clear, pure and bright and the 'smile of nature' dwells upon the scene."

The stock market crash of 1929 hit the tracks hard and delayed experiments with night harness racing until 1940, when the lights were turned on to stay at Roosevelt Raceway in New York. Horsemen at first boycotted the new venture—on the afternoon of the first night card there were not sufficient horses to fill an evening of racing—but eventually the "gimmick" became a fact of life.

HOCKEY

Bringing ice hockey indoors depended more on technology rather than space problems, as the main consideration was how to manufacture ice and keep it from melting. Some of the earliest experiments with artificial ice-making were carried out in England. In 1876, scientists there mixed glycerin and water, chilled it with ether, and sent it through copper tubing covered by water. Old Madison Square Garden, with a surface area of six thousand square feet, became the first indoor ice arena in the United States to use artificial ice, in 1879.

In later years, experiments continued, using brine as a refrigerant, and in 1897 St. Nicholas Arena opened and was used by a four-team hockey league. Artificial ice rinks were not used in Canada until 1911, when they appeared in Vancouver and Victoria.

Professional hockey was still in its infancy in the United States—Boston, the first American entrant in the National Hockey League, had been awarded a franchise in November 1924—when promoter George "Tex" Rickard decided to move the sport into Madison Square Garden in 1925. Early the previous year, he had announced that a new and faster method of installing artificial ice had been developed. "A hockey surface can be provided within six hours and can be removed in a similar space of time," he said, adding that "the mechanical arrangements will in no way interfere with the use of the Garden as a swimming pool in the summer months."

The first game using the new system at the Garden was scheduled for Tuesday, December

15, 1925, between the New York Americans and Montreal Canadiens.

Pregame publicity made the event seem truly monumental. Two bands—the Governor General's Royal Footguard Regimental Band from Ottawa and that of the U. S. Military Academy—were on hand along with a group of musicians from Paul Whiteman's orchestra. Festoons of red, white, and blue bunting hung from the fronts of the boxes, which were occupied by the cream of society and the upper crust of New York politics. Except for the vendors moving among the spectators with their apples, oranges, and souvenir hockey sticks—as well as the occasional appearance of a matron wearing galoshes over her evening slippers—the scene could have taken place in a foyer at the opera.

The game began with some interesting rough-and-tumble play that culminated in a goal for New York. The team was called for being offside, however, and the cheers turned to groans as the score was rolled back to 0–0. A second assault by the Americans was blunted when Captain Billy Burch's shot hit the side of the net. Then, with poetic justice befitting the gala occasion, New York wingman Shorty Green maneuvered through the Canadiens' defense and slapped the puck past goalie Rheaume. The home team led by 1–0 as the first period drew to a close.

Montreal came back to score a pair of goals in the second period and another in the third to spoil that gaudy Garden opener, but most of the audience were undisturbed. The inauguration had been a success and indoor hockey was big-league in Gotham.

The following season, after a year of relative calm, promoter Tex Rickard ran into a bit of trouble when T. P. Gorman, secretary of the New York hockey club, filed suit because the temperature of seventy degrees maintained by Rickard was too high for good hockey. Gorman claimed that temperatures above sixty degrees depleted the players' physical powers and slowed the game. Rickard explained that a lower temperature would "imperil the health" of the patrons.

Eventually the controversy was straightened out, but it is an interesting example—a rarity, indeed—of a sports promoter being sued for placing too much consideration on the needs and comfort of the fans.

THE ULTIMATE WEAPON

The ultimate weapon against the traditional method of playing sports outdoors under nature's sun was born in 1960. On August 20 of that year, plans for a dome-covered, all-weather stadium at Houston, Texas, were announced by the Harris County Board of Park Commissioners. The original price sounded expensive at the time—$15 million—but later developments in the area of skyrocketing inflation soon made the cost seem quite reasonable. The Houston revelation of 1960 was not the first time a similar project had been predicted. It was, however, the first time such a grandiose scheme was actually completed.

Nearly five years after the announcement and $31.6 million later, Houston's Astrodome—the world's largest air-conditioned room—opened on April 19, 1965. The attraction was a series of exhibition baseball games between hometown Houston and American League teams.

President and Mrs. Lyndon B. Johnson were among the Opening Day crowd of 47,876, but the throwing of the historic first ball was performed by Texas Governor John Connally. Mickey Mantle, leading off for the Yankees, collected the first major-league hit in the stadium, a line single to center field. In the sixth inning, he also hit the first home run and scored the first run. Houston won the game, 2–1, in twelve innings.

All was not peaches and cream, however, for it soon leaked out that the Astrodome had a few faults—4,596 of them, to be exact. This was the number of small plastic panes through which the sunlight penetrated—or more specifically, glared. The problem was discovered during pregame workouts, when Houston outfielders began to misjudge fly balls hit at them by as much as 30 feet. They lost the balls, they explained, against the background of battleship-gray steel girders and transparent lucite panels that made the roof into a giant jigsaw puzzle.

As soon as the problem became apparent, more than 1,000 solutions were offered. Charles O. Finley, owner of the Kansas City Athletics, sent six dozen orange balls by air

---

National Hockey League Standings After Garden Opener of December 15, 1925:

	W.	L.		W.	L.
Ottawa Senators	5	1	Toronto St. Patricks	2	3
Montreal Maroons	4	2	Montreal Canadiens	2	4
Pittsburgh Pirates	4	2	Boston Bruins	2	6
New York Americans	2	3			

express. (They weren't used.) Sunglasses in a variety of shades were ordered from an optical company. Scientists and engineers prowled the outfield, peering upward. Someone wondered aloud if Houston was on the verge of being the first major-league city to call a game "because of sunlight."

The players themselves were bemused and amused. Baltimore Oriole pitcher Robin Roberts, betraying a typical pitcher's point of view, remarked, "That dome is going to get a lot of lousy outfielders off the hook." Teammate Boog Powell, never considered a top outfielder under even the best conditions, said after a few minutes of practice, "It's tough out there. I tell you one thing: I'm going to wear a helmet in the field."

The second game in Astrodome history, and the first amid the sunlight's red glare, was eventually played but was not an artistic success. Six errors were recorded, half of them attributable to the skylight problem. In addition, there were at least three "near misses," which didn't show in the box score. In the fifth inning, for example, Oriole catcher John Orsino hit a fly ball toward Astro left fielder Mike White. White ran over, looked up into the glare, flinched, and watched the ball drop to the Tifway Bermuda grass surface. Houston won the game, 11–8, but few were happy with the way the new facility worked.

Eventually the problems of skylight and playing surface were resolved and Houston's Astrodome, while not the "eighth wonder of the world" in the less-than-inspired words of Billy Graham, became a highly respectable stadium. The fact that it worked so well no doubt led other cities, notably Detroit—that is, Pontiac—and New Orleans to explore the possibility of building more domed facilities.

With the coming of the 1970s, the corner had been turned—to use a sports phrase—and the outdoor-to-indoor revolution decided if not completed. For better or for worse, sporting men with sufficient money or the ability to float bond issues would never need to fool with Mother Nature again.

CHAPTER 18—1901–10

1901

Winners: Baseball: The baseball season of 1901 provides action by two leagues but no World Series, the National League stubbornly refusing to recognize the upstart American League. In the National, Pittsburgh is the champion, while Chicago wins the AL race by four games. . . . *Kentucky Derby:* His Eminence. *Preakness:* The Parader. *Belmont Stakes:* Commando . . . *Boxing:* In the welterweight division, Rube Ferns regains his crown from Matty Matthews in May, but then loses to Joe Walcott in December. Featherweight Abe Attell, who later becomes famous as one of the go-betweens of the 1919 baseball "Black Sox" scandal, decisions George Dixon while Young Corbett knocks out Terry McGovern. Meanwhile, bantamweight Harry Harris becomes the new champion of his division by winning a fifteen-round decision from Pedlar Palmer in London. . . . *Golf: USGA Men's Open:* Willie Anderson . . . *Hockey:* 1900–1 Stanley Cup winner: Winnipeg Victorias . . . *Football:* College champion selected by Helms Athletic Foundation: Michigan (11–0–0).

Other Happenings: On October 19, Alberto Santos-Dumont startles the world by circling the Eiffel Tower in his balloon, proving that the hitherto erratic airship can be steered. . . . American League plays its first game on April 24: Chicago 8, Cleveland 2. Three other contests were rained out. . . . On August 21, Umpire Tom Connolly declares a game forfeited to Detroit when Baltimore pitcher Iron Man McGinnity steps on his feet and spits in his face. . . . Most one-sided contest in new league occurs on September 15, Detroit defeating Cleveland by a score of 21–0. . . . Pitcher Earl Moore of Cleveland hurls first no-hitter in American League on May 9, but loses the game in the tenth inning to Chicago, 4–2. . . . Christy Mathewson throws no-hitter for Giants against St. Louis, 5–0, on July 15. . . . Most remarkable comeback of American League takes place on April 25 when Detroit, losing 13–4 going into the bottom of the ninth, scores 10 to win, 14–13. First baseman Pop Dillon has 4 doubles for the Tigers. . . . In college football, Willie

Heston begins his fabulous career at Michigan, scoring the first of his 93 touchdowns and 465 points. . . . Another high scorer in 1901 is Russell Bowie of hockey's Montreal Victorias, who scores 24 goals in 7 games, 7 of them in a single contest against the Amateur Athletic Association team. . . . American Bowling Congress, which has only 200 officially registered members, holds its first national tournament in Chicago, 41 5-man teams competing for total prize money of $1,592. . . . *Columbia,* U.S. entry in America's Cup competition, wins 3 races to 0 for Sir Thomas Lipton's *Shamrock II.* . . . Horseracing is banned in city and county of San Francisco, the last race being run at the Ingleside Race Track on March 16.

1902

Winners: Baseball: In National League, Pittsburgh walks away with pennant, leading by 27½ games with 103–36 record. Connie Mack's Philadelphia A's take American League pennant but no World Series is held . . . *Kentucky Derby:* Alan-a-Dale. *Preakness:* Old England. *Belmont Stakes:* Masterman . . . *Boxing:* The only crown to have a new champion during 1902 is that of lightweight division, Joe Gans knocking out Frank Erne in the first round at Fort Erie, Canada (interracial bouts are still frowned upon in many parts of the United States). . . . *Golf: USGA Men's Open:* Lawrence Auchterlonie . . . *Hockey:* 1901–2 Stanley Cup winner: Montreal Amateur Athletic Association . . . *Football:* College champion selected by Helms Athletic Foundation: Michigan, which repeats the same record (11–0–0) as previous season . . . First *Rose Bowl* is played at Pasadena, California, touchdowns and field goals each counting 5 points. Michigan defeats Stanford so badly (49–0) that game is discontinued until 1916.

Other Happenings: On June 15 in Texas League baseball game Corsicana beats Texarkana, 51–3, a score so high that some telegraphers assume it is an error and report final score as 5–3. Nineteen-year-old Jay Austin

"Nig" Clarke hits 8 home runs in game. By 1905 he is with the American League Cleveland Naps. . . . On July 4, a motorcycle race of 245 miles (Boston to New York City) is held. Only 13 finish of 31 who actually leave starting line. . . . Boxer Kid McPartland retires at age of 27, having won 62 of 92 bouts since 1894. . . . Jimmy Callahan of Chicago White Sox pitches only no-hitter in major leagues, beating Detroit, 3–0, on September 20. . . . Michigan's football team, with a record of 11 wins and 0 losses, outscores the opposition, 644–12. . . . Arthur Duffey of Boston runs 100 yards in 9.6 seconds at Berkeley Oval, New York, a mark that stands until 1905, when officials decide that Duffey had "professionalized" himself prior to 1902. Record then reverts to John H. Owen's 1890 record of 9.8 seconds. . . . Harvard sets mile-relay record by running it in 3:21.2, beating the 3:23.2 established in 1897 by another quartet of Harvard men. . . . Popularity of indoor tennis or Ping Pong starting to spread in the United States. . . . The home-run champ of the National League is Tom Leach of Pittsburgh, with 6. Ralph Seybold in the American wins with 16, a record for the junior circuit that will last until 1919. . . . United States wins Davis Cup competition, 3–2, over British Empire. Contests are played at Crescent Athletic Club, Brooklyn.

1903

Winners: Baseball: First World Series of twentieth century is held between Boston of American League and Pittsburgh of National. It seems to be a runaway for the establishment when the Pirates take a 3–1 lead in games, but Boston roars back to take 4 games in a row to win the best-of-9 Series. . . . *Kentucky Derby:* Judge Himes. *Preakness:* Flocarline. *Belmont Stakes:* Africander . . . *Boxing:* New Classification for boxers comes into existence when Lou Houseman, a boxing promoter and writer, suggests that gap between heavyweights and 158-pound limit then put on middleweights (since raised to 160) be filled with 175-pound limit known as light-heavyweight. As manager of Jack Root, a fighter too small for the heavies and too big for the middleweights, Houseman has a vested interest, but the idea is a good one and is accepted. On April 22, Jack Root outpoints Kid McCoy to lay claim to the new title. On July 4, however, Root is knocked out by George Gardner in 12 rounds, who is in turn outpointed by Bob Fitz-

simmons on November 4. . . . In bantamweight division, Frankie Neil knocks out Harry Forbes, who had beaten Andy Tokell earlier in the year to establish clear claim to the title. . . . *Golf: USGA Men's Open:* Willie Anderson . . . *Hockey:* Winner of 1902–3 Stanley Cup: Ottawa Silver Seven . . . *Football:* College champion selected by Helms Athletic Foundation: Princeton (11–0–0).

Other Happenings: Just one week after pitching and winning a doubleheader on August 8, Iron Man Joe McGinnity of the New York Giants beats Brooklyn, 6–1, 4–3. He also steals second base in one of the games and ends the year with 31 wins. . . . In the first World Series game between the AL and the NL, Deacon Phillippe of Pittsburgh beats Cy Young of Boston, 7–3. . . . Lou Dillon becomes the first trotter to smash the 2-minute barrier, racing a mile in 1:58½ at Readville, Massachusetts. . . . On May 30, a motorcycle hill-climbing contest is held and is won by G. H. Curtiss. . . . George A. Wyman, meanwhile, is partway across the country on his 3½-horsepower, single-cylinder, belt-drive motorcycle, having left San Francisco for New York on May 16. He completes the transcontinental journey on July 6. . . . Harvard, going first-class in the football world, constructs the first all-concrete stadium and 40,000 show up for the first game in it on November 14. Dartmouth spoils the show by beating the home team, 11–0. . . . In the Midwest, Michigan (11–0–1) scores 565 points to 6 for the opposition, the only points given up those to Minnesota (14–0–1), which outscores the enemy, 661–12. . . . Professional hockey begins in the United States with the establishment of the International Hockey League in northern Michigan. The Portage Lakers win 24 of 26 games in 1903. . . . The Harmsworth Trophy, symbol of excellence in motorboating, is originated. . . . In a Stanley Cup game between Ottawa and Portage, the puck slips through a hole in the ice and cannot be retrieved. . . . Also lost is baseball star Ed Delahanty, who on July 2 falls off a bridge near Niagara Falls and is drowned. He is just 35. . . . The major leagues' only no-hitter of '03 is pitched by Chick Fraser of the Phillies, a 10–0 whitewash of Chicago on September 18. . . . Sir Thomas Lipton makes third attempt to capture America's Cup, but his *Shamrock III* loses, 3–0, to U.S. *Reliance*. . . . Berna "Barney" Oldfield, auto racer, becomes first man to travel a mile a minute in an automobile. . . . Jamaica Race Track on Long Island opens, with notables such as Lillian Russell and Diamond Jim Brady in attendance.

1904

Winners: Baseball: Boston repeats in the American League and the New York Giants make a runaway of the National League race but Manager John McGraw refuses to play against the "upstarts." The players and fans petition in vain and no World Series is held. . . . *Kentucky Derby:* Elwood. *Preakness:* Bryn Mawr. *Belmont Stakes:* Delhi . . . *Boxing:* On April 30, Kid Dixie wins on a foul in twenty rounds from welterweight champion Joe Walcott, but few experts recognize him as the new titleholder. They later fight a twenty-round draw, which further confuses the issue. . . . The featherweight division is also confused as the result of both Terry McGovern and Young Corbett's having moved into the lightweight class. Abe Attell and Tommy Sullivan fight for the title at St. Louis in October, Sullivan winning on a foul in five rounds. . . . In bantamweight class, Joe Bowker of England outpoints Frankie Neil, then promptly outgrows the division. . . . *Golf: USGA Men's Open:* Willie Anderson . . . *Hockey:* Ottawa Silver Seven take 1903–4 Stanley Cup, their second in a row. . . . *Football:* College champion selected by Helms Athletic Foundation: Pennsylvania (12–0–0).

Other Happenings: On April 26, young Tyrus Raymond Cobb, 17, makes baseball debut with Augusta in South Atlantic League. He doubles and hits home run in 8–7 loss to Columbus. . . . The first Gold Cup for motorboat racing is awarded to C. C. Riotte, who roars along at 23.6 miles per hour. . . . On October 8, the Vanderbilt Cup for auto racing is held at Hicksville, Long Island, George Heath in his Panchard speeding the 30-mile course at 52.2 mph to win. . . . On February 21, the National Ski Association is formed at Ishpeming, Michigan, with 17 charter members. . . . Minnesota's football team, with a 13–0 record, overpowers the opposition, 725–12; Michigan, at 10–0 and a point spread of 567–22, is not far behind. . . . F. J. Robson and Morris Wood speed skate an indoor mile in 2:41.2. . . . T. Walters, meanwhile, ski jumps 82 feet. . . . In other winter sports, Lester Patrick of the Brandon Wheat Kings becomes the first defenseman in hockey to score a goal when he performs the trick against the Ottawa Silver Seven. . . . On May 5, Cy Young of Boston pitches a perfect game, 1–0, vs. the Philadelphia A's. The no-hitter is followed in the National League by Bob Wicker's 9 hitless innings against the New York Giants (Wicker allows a hit in the tenth but the Cubs win for him in 12), and Jess Tannehill, a teammate of Young, pitching a 6–0 no-hitter against the White Sox on August 17. . . . On February 1, 39-year-old Dan Mahoney, formerly catcher with Cincinnati and Washington of the National League, commits suicide by swallowing carbolic acid. The incident is duly reported in *Reach's Baseball Guide* for 1905.

1905

Winners: Baseball: The second World Series between the new American League and old National is finally played, and New York Giant pitcher Christy Mathewson emerges as the obvious hero. He wins three of the four games necessary to subdue the Philadelphia A's, who manage only one victory. . . . *Kentucky Derby:* Agile. *Preakness:* Cairngorm. *Belmont Stakes:* Tanya . . . *Boxing:* After retirement of James J. Jeffries, Marvin Hart and Jack Root battle for the empty throne. Hart wins on twelve-round KO. . . . In light-heavyweight division, "Philadelphia" Jack O'Brien (later manager of Jack Dempsey) knocks out Bob Fitzsimmons in thirteen at San Francisco. Bantamweight champion Joe Bowker having outgrown the division, Digger Stanley and Jimmy Walsh claim title. They meet on October 20 in Chelsea, Massachusetts, Walsh winning a fifteen-round decision. . . . *Golf: USGA Men's Open:* Willie Anderson (third consecutive year). . . . *Hockey:* Winner of 1904–5 Stanley Cup for third season in a row: Ottawa Silver Seven . . . *Football:* College champion selected by Helms Athletic Foundation: Chicago (11–0–0).

Other Happenings: Chicago's being selected as top college team in football is based on November 23 game when they take on powerful Michigan, which has silenced ten opponents by an aggregate score of 495–0. But Chicago uses safety to eke out 2–0 victory. . . . On April 26, Chicago Cubs outfielder Jack McCarthy throws out three runners at the plate, but Pittsburgh wins, 2–1. . . . On August 4, the winning battery for the New York Yankees (Highlanders) consists of pitcher Jim Newton and catcher Mike Powers, both medical doctors. . . . Founded: the Intercollegiate Soccer Association, which consists of Columbia, Cornell, Harvard, Haverford, and Pennsylvania . . . Also founded: the Intercollegiate Wrestling Association, which draws one thousand persons to its first tournament on April 7 at the University of Pennsylvania.

Yale wins, followed by Columbia, Princeton, and Pennsylvania. . . . President Roosevelt says that football must be made safer for young men to play, which seems reasonable in view of the large number of fatalities during first half decade of the century. . . . On August 30 Ty Cobb makes his major-league debut with Detroit, getting a double off New York's Jack Chesbro. The Tigers win, 5–3. . . . Dan Patch paces a mile in 1:55¾, but leading money-winner in his class is Bolivar, with $10,220 for 1905. . . . Cleveland builds an indoor ice rink . . . 1904–5 season is first in which hockey pros paint red line on ice, the debut of this innovation coming in game between Winnipeg and Ottawa. Hockey season produces thrill when Montreal Westmount goalie Brophy scores. . . . Major leagues furnish quartet of thrillers for fans who relish no-hitters. Mathewson of the Giants silences the Chicago Cubs, 1–0, on June 13; in the American League, Weldon Henley of the A's no-hits St. Louis, 6–0, on July 22; Frank Smith of the White Sox blanks Detroit, 15–0, on September 6; and Bill Dinneen of Boston turns the tables on Chicago, 2–0, on September 27, dealing the White Sox' pennant hopes a death blow. . . . Commando, winner of the 1901 Belmont Stakes, dies of lockjaw in March. . . . Direct, a champion pacer on the harness circuit, dies two days later. . . . Columbia University, reflecting public sentiment against organized athletics, in December bans all sports except rowing. . . . Barney Oldfield, already a celebrated auto driver, crashes in August but soon returns to the track. . . . American ski-jumping records are set when Julius Kulstadt jumps 92½ feet at Ishpeming, Michigan, and Gustave Bye leaps 106 at Red Wing, Minnesota. . . . For the second time since its inception in 1875, only three horses run in the Kentucky Derby.

1906

Winners: Baseball: First World Series to be held in one city features Chicago White Sox vs. Chicago Cubs. The "Tinker to Evers to Chance" combination of the Cubs is more celebrated, but the White Sox win the Series, four games to two. . . . *Kentucky Derby:* Sir Huon. *Preakness:* Whimsical. *Belmont Stakes:* Burgomaster . . . *Boxing:* The brief reign of heavyweight champion Marvin Hart comes to an end when he runs into five-foot, seven-inch Tommy Burns, who wins a twenty-round decision. In the welterweight division, Honey Mellody wins a fifteen-round decision from Joe Walcott to become new champion. . . . *Golf:*

USGA Men's Open: Alex Smith . . . *Hockey:* Winner of 1905–6 Stanley Cup: Montreal Wanderers . . . *Football:* College champion selected by Helms Athletic Foundation: Princeton (9–0–1, having been forced to settle for a 0–0 tie with Yale).

Other Happenings: In the National League, there are three no-hitters—by John Lush of Philadelphia, Mal Eason of Brooklyn, and Harry McIntyre, also of the Superbas, who loses in tenth inning. The only near-no-hitter in the American League is pitched by Rube Waddell of the A's. It takes place on May 17, the spoiling hit being a bunt single by Detroit's Ty Cobb. . . . On July 22, Bob Ewing of the Cincinnati Reds beats the Phillies without the aid of a single assist from his teammates. . . . In football, the forward pass is encouraged—to open up the game and cut down on injuries from mass plays—and one of the first teams to use it is Wesleyan of Connecticut. In the first game of the season, Moore of Wesleyan throws to Van Tassel, but Yale wins, 21–0. . . . Daniel J. Kelly is credited with running the 100-yard dash in 9.6 seconds, a world record, but shortly after pacer Dan Patch races a mile at Hamline, Missouri, in 1:55, officials disqualify the horse because there are "too many pacemakers." Dan Patch's record mile of September 8 is, in fact, made with the help of three additional horses—one pacesetter in front of Patch, a second to the side, and a third that picks up the pace in the stretch. . . . In flat racing, meanwhile, Jockey Walter Miller rides 388 winners during the year, a record until this time. . . . Wrestler Frank Gotch, considered by many unbeatable, meets his match when challenger Freddie Beall hurls him against a ring post and knocks Gotch unconscious. . . . For the first time, basketball baskets are opened at the bottom so that the ball drops automatically to the floor and does not have to be retrieved. Backboards, although initially unpopular with fans because they obstruct the view, are also put into use. . . . The Davis Cup in tennis goes back to Great Britain, the U.S. team losing, 5–0, at Wimbledon. . . . The first golf club is established in Russia. . . . F. A. Rodgers runs a mile in 4:22.8, and pole vaulter A. C. Gilbert clears 10 feet, 9 inches. . . . Willie Hoppe, young billiard player, wins the world championship in Paris.

1907

Winners: Baseball: Detroit baseball fans have their first chance to celebrate since 1887, when the old Wolverines won in the National

League. The first World Series game ends in a twelve-inning tie, 3–3, and after that it is all downhill for the Cobb-led Tigers, who fall in four games to Frank Chance's Chicago Cubs. . . . *Kentucky Derby:* Pink Star. *Preakness:* Don Enrique. *Belmont Stakes:* Peter Pan . . . *Boxing:* Heavyweight champion Tommy Burns wins a twenty-round decision over Jack O'Brien, but makes no claim to O'Brien's light-heavyweight title. Mike "Twin" Sullivan defeats Honey Mellody in twenty rounds at Los Angeles to win welterweight crown. Bantamweight title is vacated by Jimmy Walsh and Digger Stanley, claimed by Johnny Coulon. . . . *Golf: USGA Men's Open:* Alex Ross . . . *Hockey:* 1906–7 Stanley Cup taken by Kenora Thistles (January), then by Montreal Wanderers in March. . . . *Football:* College champion selected by Helms Athletic Foundation: Yale (9–0–1).

Other Happenings: The once-powerful University of Minnesota football team has fallen on bad days since 1904, when it outscored the opposition, 618–12, and won all 13 games on its schedule. By contrast, 1907 squad is able to score only 55 points all season (5 games), 44 of the points on 4-point field goals by George Capron. Chicago and Carlisle beat the Gophers, who are also tied by Wisconsin. . . . John A. Miskey of Philadelphia becomes the first United States singles champion in squash. . . . Jimmie Lee, a black jockey, rides all the winners at Churchill Downs on June 5, and Walter Miller brings home 334 winners for the year. . . . Ole Feiring makes a ski jump of 112 feet. . . . On October 21, the first American balloon race is held at St. Louis. . . . Baseball no-hitters are pitched by Frank Pfeffer of Boston Nationals, beating Cincinnati, 6–0, on May 8, and Nick Maddox of Pittsburgh, who downs Brooklyn, 2–1, on September 20. . . . Also in the baseball news: Two players, both 34 years old, pass away within hours of each other, bringing grief to Boston fans. One is Patrick Henry "Cozy" Dolan, an outfielder with the Boston Braves, who dies of typhoid fever on March 29; the other is Boston Red Sox Manager Charles "Chick" Stahl, who commits suicide on March 28 (the team finished last in 1906). . . . Frank Chance, manager of Cubs, says in September that "wetball" pitchers are becoming extinct. . . . John L. Sullivan, former heavyweight champion, visits Cardinal Gibbons of Baltimore and tells him about his fights. . . . Major Taylor, great black bicyclist, announces his decision to retire from competitive racing in September. . . . Margaret and Harriet Curtis, sisters, meet for the USGA Women's Amateur golf title at the Midlothian Country Club, Blue Island, Illi-

nois. Margaret wins, 7 and 6. . . . Kid McCoy, 34, still active in the ring, becomes a used-car dealer. . . . Charles M. Daniels, king of American swimmers, sets records in the 100-yard free-style, 220-yard free style, and 440-yard free-style. . . . Amateur tennis champions in the United States are Bill Larned and Evelyn Sears. . . . On January 1, Charles W. Oldreive sets out to establish a distance record for walking on water. Using a set of custom-designed wooden shoes, he plods down the Mississippi from Cincinnati to New Orleans, a distance of 1,600 miles, in a bit less than 40 days. His shoes are 4 feet, 5 inches long and made of cedar. Walking only during the daylight hours, he is followed in a boat by those who have made bets on him and his wife. On one occasion, he slips and turns upside down in the water, but his wife comes to the rescue.

1908

Winners: Baseball: The Chicago Cubs and Detroit Tigers stage a repeat of the 1907 World Series, which varies only in that the Tigers win a single game instead of being blanked. . . . *Kentucky Derby:* Stone Street. *Preakness:* Royal Tourist. *Belmont Stakes:* Colin . . . *Boxing:* On December 26 at Sydney, Australia, Jack Johnson, 30, becomes the first black heavyweight champion by knocking out Tommy Burns in 14 rounds. Stanley Ketchel claims middleweight crown, as does Jack "Twin" Sullivan. They meet on February 22, Ketchel winning on a 20-round knockout. Seven months later, Ketchel is himself KO'd by Billy Papke in San Francisco, but in November the championship again goes to Ketchel when he gains revenge with an 11-round KO of Papke. Lightweight champion Joe Gans, 34, nearing the end of his career, loses the title on a 17-round KO by Battling Nelson, and featherweight titleholder Tommy Sullivan is knocked out by Abe Attell. . . . *Golf: USGA Men's Open:* Fred McLeod . . . *Hockey:* 1907–8 Stanley Cup winner: Montreal Wanderers . . . *Football:* College champion selected by Helms Athletic Foundation: Pennsylvania (11–0–1).

Other Happenings: On September 26, pitcher Ed Reulbach of Chicago Cubs shuts out Brooklyn in both ends of a doubleheader, 5–0 and 3–0. . . . No-hitters include those by Cy Young of Boston, Robert Rhoades and Addie Joss of Cleveland, and Frank Smith of Chicago, all in American League. In National, Nap Rucker of Brooklyn blanks Boston. . . . On December 5, the first football team with numbered players makes its appearance on a field. The numbers do not help Pittsburgh, however, which loses to Washington and Jefferson, 14–0. . . . The first steel ski jump is installed in the United States at Chippewa Falls, Wisconsin, in November. It is 98 feet high, including the concrete foundation. . . . In baseball parks across the nation, the term "hot dog" is first applied to a frankfurter in a roll, as a result of cartoonist T. A. Dorgan's depicting the sausage as a dachshund. . . . On October 10, Oberlin's George C. Gray makes a 109-yard run from scrimmage against Cornell. . . . Jockey Vincent Powers rides 324 winners during the year. . . . Professional hockey league is founded in Canada; it is the Ontario Professional League, consisting of teams representing Toronto, Berlin, Brantford, and Guelph. . . . In a game played June 9, every player in the Cleveland Indian batting order makes a hit and scores a run during the fifth inning. The final score is Cleveland 15, Red Sox 6. . . . Sam Crawford leads American League in home runs with 7, and Tim Jordan of Brooklyn, who hits only 32 round-trippers during an 8-year career, leads the National with 12. . . . Local sheriff almost halts Kentucky Derby, citing presence of bookmakers on the course, but compromise with reality is made at last moment.

1909

Winners: Baseball: The Detroit Tigers capture their third consecutive American League pennant, but once again end up losers in the World Series. This time they are the victims of Honus Wagner and the Pittsburgh Pirates. Wagner bats .333 and steals 6 bases. The Tigers lose the Series, 4 games to 3. . . . *Kentucky Derby:* Wintergreen. *Preakness:* Effendi. *Belmont Stakes:* Joe Madden . . . *Boxing:* No changes are brought about in any boxing division, the reigning champs continuing to be—heavyweight: Jack Johnson; light-heavyweight: Jack O'Brien; middleweight: Stanley Ketchel; welterweight: Mike "Twin" Sullivan; lightweight: Battling Nelson; featherweight: Abe Attell; bantamweight: Johnny Coulon. . . . *Golf: USGA Men's Open:* George Sargent . . . *Hockey:* 1908–9 Stanley Cup winner: Ottawa Senators . . . *Football:* College champion selected by Helms Athletic Foundation: Yale (10–0–0), which outscores the opposition, 209–0.

Other Happenings: Showdown of the football season comes on November 20 at Cambridge, Massachusetts, when Yale and Harvard, both undefeated, meet. Yale wins,

8–0. . . . Leon Ames of New York Giants opens the 1909 season with 9 innings of hitless pitching against the Brooklyn Superbas, but with an out in the tenth, the Superbas break the spell and go on to win in 13 innings, 3–0. . . . Robert Guggenheim offers a $2,000 prize for the winner—or survivor—of a transcontinental auto race, New York to Seattle. It is won by Bert W. Scott and C. James Smith, who drive a Ford. . . . In Davis Cup competition, Australia defeats the United States, 5–0, at Sydney. . . . Football officials vote to reduce the value of a field goal from 4 to 3 points. . . . First official horseshoe-pitching contest is held in United States at Bronson, Kansas; winner is Frank Jackson. . . . Ralph Rose tosses the 16-pound shot a record 51 feet, and Edward P. Weston, 70, walks 3,895 miles from New York to San Francisco in 105 days. . . . Dirigible race at St. Louis on October 4 is won by veteran aeronaut Lincoln Beachey, who also likes to disguise himself as woman while flying. . . . Tragic incident on baseball diamond involves Dr. Mike Powers, catcher for the Philadelphia A's who is seized by violent pains during Opening Game of season. He continues the game but collapses afterward and is taken to a hospital, where doctors report he is suffering from "strangulation of the intestines." On April 26, Powers dies, the official cause being listed as gangrene poisoning. . . . Death also comes to Harry Pulliam, former president of the National League who, some say, is so disturbed by the vicissitudes of his office that, when voted out, he commits suicide. . . . Last game of 1909 World Series is played in freezing weather. . . . Army and Navy football teams do not meet because of public outrage over deaths on the gridiron.

1910

Winners: Baseball: Having slumped for the past four seasons, the Philadelphia A's win the American League pennant by 14½ games, then continue to dominate all opposition by defeating the Chicago Cubs, 4 games to 1, in the World Series. . . . *Kentucky Derby:* Donau. *Preakness:* Layminster. *Belmont Stakes:* Sweep . . . *Boxing:* Middleweight championship becomes vacant when Stanley Ketchel is shot and killed by Walter Dipley (real name, Hurtz), the husband of a woman with whom Ketchel was thought to be trifling. When Wilson Mizner, a friend of Ketchel, hears of the shooting, he says: "Start counting now, because he'll get up at nine." In welterweight division, Mike Sullivan moves up to middleweight class, and Jimmy Clabby and Jimmy Gardner claim throne. Clabby is recognized as new champ when he defeats the Dixie Kid in a 10-round decision. Another top fighter dies prematurely when Joe Gans, 35, succumbs in Baltimore of tuberculosis. Battling Nelson, who defeated Gans in 1908, loses a 40-round bout with Ad Wolgast at Port Richmond, California. In bantamweight division, Johnny Coulon establishes his claim to the title by defeating Jim Kendrick in 19 rounds at New Orleans. . . . *Golf: USGA Men's Open:* Alex Smith . . . *Hockey:* 1909–10 Stanley Cup winner: Montreal Wanderers . . . *Football:* College champion selected by Helms Athletic Foundation: Harvard (8–0–1).

Other Happenings: In an unusual statistical freak, on August 18, Brooklyn and Pittsburgh play to an 8–8 tie—a game in which each team has 38 at-bats, 13 hits, 12 assists, 2 errors, 5 strikeouts, 3 walks, 1 hit batsman, and 1 passed ball. . . . The first juvenile baseball league is started at Waynesburg, Pennsylvania, admission $.10. . . . On April 20, Addie Joss of Indians pitches the second no-hitter of his career, a 1–0 win over the Chicago White Sox. . . . Sheldon Lejeune, a player whose entire major-league career consists of only 24 games, on October 9 beats John Hatfield's 38-year record of throwing a baseball 400 feet, 7½ inches. Lejeune's throw measures 426 feet, 9½ inches. . . . Top star of U.S. women's amateur golf is Dorothy Campbell, who wins her second USGA tournament in a row, defeating Mrs. Ronald H. Barlow, 3 and 2. . . . Besides Joss, other no-hitters are thrown by Chief Bender of the A's and Tom Hughes of the New York Highlanders. Hughes, unfortunately, loses the game in the eleventh inning, 5–0. . . . J. C. "Bud" Mars, an early stunt flier, escapes serious injury on June 2 when his plane falls on an automobile. . . . In July Cy Young wins his five hundredth game, but the season is a disappointing one for him (7–10). . . . Most anticipated sports event of year takes place on July 4 at Reno, Nevada, when 35-year-old James J. Jeffries comes out of retirement to answer the need for a "Great White Hope" to upset Jack Johnson. Jeffries lasts 15 rounds. . . . On March 23, the first trial races are held at the first U.S. automobile board track speedway at the Los Angeles Motordrome.

Section V
The 1910s

CHAPTER 19 — 1911

The United States' heaviest President, 325-pound William Howard Taft, was just about halfway through his single term as the year began and already he had left his physical mark on the nation in that a special bathtub had to be built and moved into the White House. Taft's game was golf.

The nation, along with the rest of the world, feared that war was coming, but it was nearly impossible to stay depressed long in an era of such undeniable gaiety. Master showman George M. Cohan's latest hit was *Get Rich Quick Wallingford;* Victor Herbert offered *Naughty Marietta* for the student of more serious musical comedy; and Lew Fields was starring in *The Hen-pecks.* Slightly more garish amusement could be found at theaters such as the New York Hippodrome, which opened the year with *The Great American Ballet of Niagara* ("superb scenic series, twelve hundred people on the stage") as well as a girlie show that boasted "no parallel in pulchritude or prodigality of production."

It was the era when stunt flying was considered a spectator sport, with awards and trophies being offered for the pilot who could fly highest, longest, or in the most convoluted fashion. In nearly every major city across the nation, grandstands were hastily erected and torn down to accommodate those who wanted to see their favorite fliers in action.

STUNT FLYING
Sometimes, of course, there were accidents. The new year of 1911 started with twin reports, in fact, of aviators perishing before great crowds of people. The first casualty occurred at Los Angeles, where Archibald Hoxsey, holder of the world-record altitude mark of 11,474 feet, went aloft in an attempt to beat that figure. He encountered bad winds, however, and when only 500 feet from the ground a burst of turbulence turned his plane over and sent it plunging to the ground. Hoxsey was crushed beneath the engine and died immediately. Meanwhile, at New Orleans, John B. Moisant, who had won the ten-thousand-dollar Ryan purse in October 1910 by flying around the Statue of Liberty, took off in an effort to set a new endurance record that would bring the highly coveted Michelin Cup to the United States. Moisant chose a Bleriot monoplane as his vehicle because it was larger and could hold more fuel. In addition, the ship had been fitted with an extra thirty-five-gallon gasoline tank fastened directly beneath the regular oil tank. Some said this was a major cause of the accident because the extra weight lowered the plane's center of gravity, making it more difficult to control.

The Moisant-Hoxsey accidents of December 31, 1910, were not isolated events. Here, for example, is what happened during the rest of that month:
December 3: *Lt. Cammarata of the Italian Army, in a Farman biplane, lost control of the machine. Two were killed.*
December 22: *Cecil Grace of the United States disappeared while flying a Wright biplane across the English Channel.*
December 25: *D. Piccollo killed in an Antoinette machine at São Paulo, Brazil.*
December 28: *Alexander Laffont fell 200 feet and died, along with M. Paulia, the plane's designer.*
December 30: *Lieutenant Caumont of the French Army Aviation Corps fell 60 feet from a new monoplane at Versailles and died.*

In any event, when a sudden gust of wind struck Moisant's ship, he could not right it, and the plane pitched to earth, wildly out of control. Moisant was thrown free, his arms crossed over his breast. When he was about 30 feet from the ground, "the spectators saw his body turn over and fall head downward into the mud of the marsh." A civil engineer named O. M. Sutter was first to reach the pilot, who died moments later as a result of a broken neck. The remainder of the aero meet was called off.

BOXING

A week later in Los Angeles, racing driver Barney Oldfield issued a statement that brought a certain measure of comfort to those who were still mourning Jim Jeffries' losing the heavyweight title fight to the first black champion, Jack Johnson. That event, which had taken place at Reno, Nevada, on July 4, 1910, had created an ever-widening whirlpool of controversy. Moving pictures taken of the battle were still being held by courts in many parts of the world on the grounds that seeing a mixed match—especially one in which the black man was the victor—had the potential of inflaming angry emotions. The assertion was probably true in part, for Johnson's easy win had infuriated and embarrassed many whites, including some who weren't boxing fans. Barney Oldfield's statement, then, no doubt came as a pleasant shock to those who still could not accept the Jeffries defeat. The gist of the racing driver's headline-making story was that Jeffries had been "poisoned" before the fight. The exact details as to how this had been accomplished were not fully supplied. Oldfield did say that members of the former champion's training staff were innocent. Eventually the story was laid to rest as days passed without the presentation of solid evidence. The search for a "White Hope" to recapture the title continued apace, with few prospects on the horizon as the year began.

FOOTBALL

Another controversial story, which appeared on January 29, 1911, dealt with the rapidly growing game of football. The sport had survived the injury-ridden 1890s when the "Flying Wedge" created havoc and was finally outlawed, but many were still concerned about the amount of physical damage brought about by the game. One of the most prestigious antifootball writers of the period was a New York physician, Dr. Morris Joseph Clurman, whose *magnum opus* of 1911 was an article for the *Medical Record* entitled, "The American Game of Football: Is It a Factor for Good or for Evil?" Dr. Clurman's answer was that it was an unqualified vote for evil. "No

elaborate comment is required upon a sport that permits of the possibility of a player's rib being broken and forced through the heart," he wrote. "According to all our statistics it is safe to say that at the close of the next football season we shall again have about 20 deaths and nearly 150 reported injuries of a serious nature. To all serious-minded people it should be a frightful thought that the finger of Fate to-day marks these unknown 20 of our young men as a sacrifice upon the altar of the 1911 football season!"

Football Deaths and Injuries, 1905–10

Year	Deaths	Injured
1905	26	N/A
1906	11	103
1907	11	97
1908	13	84
1909	33	73
1910	19	400

The main problems associated with football, according to Dr. Clurman, were running, blocking, and tackling. Other than that, the game was all right. Except for "(1) the disadvantages in scholarship that the players suffer who devote so much of their energies and time to football; (2) the psychological aspects of an enthusiasm among spectators of a football game that is so extraordinary as to be not far removed from a true form of hysteria; (3) the great temptations that arise in the course of the game for the use of unnecessary roughness and the employment of surreptitious and easily overlooked foul play; (4) the exaggerated ideas of importance that college players who should be students first, last, and all the time, unconsciously assume when they are so publicly praised for their work on the gridiron; (5) the false valuation of college standards that prospective students and others get from football reports of the daily press." One would have to say that Dr. Clurman was not football's No. 1 fan of 1911.

Dr. Clurman was not alone, as it turned out. In February, the *Daily Maroon* published by the University of Chicago, issued an article entitled "Our Opposition to Athletics," which echoed the New York physician's comments and criticisms. "One per cent of the student body specializes in athletics, supposedly representing the student body," the article charged, "while the other 99 per cent sit on the bleachers and give vent to primitive shrieks." Recruiting techniques and the need to practice long hours were also criticized. Clearly a significant portion of Americans felt that there was an undue emphasis being placed on sports,

Meanwhile, in the World of Flying, Some Notable News Flashes of 1911:

BIPLANE STRIKES COW

Los Angeles, California, May 29—Bry Wiliams, who is trying for a license as a pilot, struck a cow while sailing a biplane yesterday, and was hurled to the ground by the shock, while the machine was driven a distance of two miles without a pilot. . . . Williams tumbled from his seat but was unhurt. The machine was finally halted by a haystack.

AERO CLUB BARS HER OUT

New York, New York, January 29—The Aero Club of America has decided not to admit women to membership. Miss Charlotte Granville, an English sportswoman now in this city, received a letter yesterday from C. F. Campbell Wood, secretary of the Aero Club, denying her application for membership. Miss Granville is a member of the Royal Aero Club of England, the Aero Club of France, and several other similar organizations. She has made more than fifty flights. "How perfectly stupid!" was the comment of Miss Granville.

FIRST COLLISION IN AIR

Paris, January 10—What is said to have been the first real collision in the air occurred between two aeronauts last Saturday at Issy-les-Moulineaux. Neither of the two aviators was hurt, but both machines were smashed. The operators were comparative novices. M. Cei, who had just got a pilot's license from the French Aero Club, had been twice round the aerodome on his biplane and was coming to ground when a monoplane rising into the air just behind him dashed into the back of the biplane. . . . At first it was feared that one or both of the aviators must be killed. But the two men crawled simultaneously from under the wrecks and sat up, looking at one another and laughing. "We have made a new kind of record," said M. Cei.

---

especially football, but no one offered much in the way of reform other than outright abolition.

Some suggestions that the rules be changed did come out of a meeting of college football coaches held that February. It was not suggested that blocking and tackling be eliminated in favor of a daintier method of aiding or stopping the ball carrier, but some coaches still did not approve of the forward pass. According to opinions expressed at the meeting, Harvard and Princeton favored the new aerial weapon, while Yale and Dartmouth were against it. The secretary of the committee, Mr. B. K. Hall, pointed out that as many teams were not able to advance the ball ten yards in three downs, the number of downs should be increased to the point where a team would have five chances to make fifteen yards. This would encourage teams to run more often rather than pass, Hall said. Nothing came of that proposal until 1912, when a compromise was adopted allowing each team four downs to make ten yards.

TRACK AND FIELD

In March of 1911, the exploits of America's track-and-field stars stole the sports headlines, thanks largely to a pair of world records being set on the same day. That day was March 4 and the scene of the first was Buffalo, New York, where Cornell's 4-man relay team beat that of the University of Pennsylvania. Previously, the 4-mile intercollegiate record was 18 minutes, 10⅖ seconds, an average of 4½ minutes per mile. Paced by J. P. Jones, who finished his mile in 4:22, the Cornell squad of T. S. Berna, L. Finch, H. N. Putnam, and Jones completed the race in 17 minutes, 43⅗ seconds. Later in the year, Jones set a new intercollegiate mile record with a time of 4 minutes, 15⅖ seconds.

Track-and-field Leaders—1911

60-yard dash: *J. Wasson, Notre Dame, 6⅖ seconds*

125-yard dash: *Gwynn Henry, Celtic Park, Long Island, 12⅕ seconds*

5,000 meters: *Louis Scott, South Paterson AC, 15 minutes, 23⅕ seconds*

Two-mile (indoor) walking: *J. H. Goulding, Canada, 13 minutes, 45⅕ seconds.*

56-pound weight throw for distance: *M. J. McGrath, Montreal, Canada, 40 feet, 6⅜ inches.*

It came as no surprise to most track-and-field enthusiasts of 1911 that still another record should be established by George V. Bonhag, for he was regarded as the best long-distance runner in the nation. When Bonhag took the floor on March 4, the record for 3,000 meters was 8 minutes, 54 seconds, which had been made by the Swedish runner John Svanberg several years before. Bonhag, who represented the Irish-American Athletic Club, was opposed by Tom Collins, M.D., Huysman, and Mike Ryan, all of the Winged Fist AC. At the pistol, Bonhag moved quickly into the lead, with Ryan to his immediate rear, followed by Huysman. The mile mark was reached in 4:38, at which point "the rest of the field began to feel the effects of the fast pace and slowly fell back. . . ." Bonhag's time for 1½ miles was 7:05: his final mark for the 3,000 meters was 8 minutes, 52⅖ seconds.

HORSERACING

New Yorkers whose game was horseracing faced the year 1911 with sad faces. The year before, reform Governor Charles Evans Hughes rammed a bill through the New York Legislature that outlawed all race-track betting. The defense of horseracing's being for "the improvement of the breed," rather than gambling, was then put to the test. Every track closed, there obviously not being enough customers interested in watching the races without the added amusement of a wager. Those directly involved in the racing industry, in addition to the regular bettors, cried economic woe. It was true that more than 40,000 persons earned legitimate livings as a result of horseracing. These included about 5,000 employed on breeding farms, 15,000 stable hands and trainers, and about 300 licensed bookmakers. The exact amount of financial loss varied from track to track, of course, but it was generally agreed that Saratoga would be hardest hit, that small city basing its entire economy on a brief summer racing season. "The breeding farms in Kentucky have also undergone a great change," noted one prognosticator." . . . unless a market can be found for the product by the opening of racing in some other section of the country, which does not seem likely, as the agitation at present is killing the game. . . ."

BOXING

March of 1911 brought a small amount of hope to those looking for a white challenger capable of defeating Jack Johnson. Urged on by various athletic clubs across the nation, which advertised "white hope" meetings, more and more young men stepped into the ring to see if they could measure up to the job. (They knew, naturally, that a great deal of money awaited the man who won.) The entry from Sapulpa, Oklahoma, was Carl Morris, who stepped down from the cab of a locomotive immediately following the Johnson-Jeffries bout to become a prizefighter. Like most of the other white hopes, Morris was large in physique but slow, with none of the catlike instincts of Johnson. But when Morris climbed into the ring with an equally inept fighter, he sometimes appeared quite impressive. On March 28, 1891, Morris took on Mike Schreck of Cincinnati in Sapulpa. The fighters were greeted by a noisy audience of cowboys, with here and there a scattering of Indians. (Morris was part Cherokee.) Several hundred railroad workers, all of whom claimed to be close friends of the former engineer, were also on hand. They brought with them a bell from an engine that Morris ran during his last trip on the railroad. It was hung near the press box and rung whenever the local favorite landed a good series of blows.

Baseball News Flash—1911

CY YOUNG QUITS BASEBALL

Hot Springs, Arkansas, March 15—Famous pitcher finds he is too old and fat to be useful in game longer.

On this particular day, the air was filled with gong sounds. "There was never a moment after the first round was a minute old that the result was in doubt," one reporter wrote, "Morris completely outclassed his opponent. . . . He showed in this fight that he

---

Financial Loss as the Result of Governor Hughes' Race-track Ban	
Salaries of officials, employees, clerks, stable help	$6,000,000
Loss in admission fees to track	$6,000,000
Money spent by customers in adjacent stores, hotels, etc.	$11,000,000
Annual sale of yearlings	$2,000,000
Feed for horses	$750,000
Railroad fares	$350,000
	$26,100,000

could battle with both hands. Heretofore, his work with his left hand had been slow."

Or perhaps it was merely that Mike Schreck was even slower. During the fight he managed to land less than half a dozen solid blows, all the while taking fearful punishment from Morris. After the sixth round was a minute old, Morris landed a hard right hook to Schreck's jaw that sent him to the canvas for the count. Those with a strong penchant for irrational optimism could say that the hunt for America's white hope was over.

BASEBALL

With the arrival of spring, the American tradition of baseball began. The season was only a couple of games old, however, when a pair of tragic events diverted attention from the game itself. The first of these occurred the night after Christy Mathewson had been driven from the box at the Polo Grounds by a fusillade of fifteen Philadelphia Phillies' hits. That gave the Giants their second loss in a row to open the season, but that wasn't the worst. Shortly after midnight, Patrolman McGann of the West 152nd Street police station heard an explosion. Running to the Polo Grounds nearby, he saw that the ball park was on fire. He and several other officers tried to check the blaze with hand grenades, but were unsuccessful. When firemen arrived, a brisk wind from the southeast had driven the fire over the entire lower timbers of the grandstand. Flames reached a hundred feet into the air, soon spreading the fire to storage yards of the Ninth and Sixth Avenue elevated railway lines. Two hours later, the blaze was pronounced under control, but by then nothing remained except the left-field bleachers and the clubhouse backing on Eighth Avenue. The railway building was also destroyed, along with a number of cars.

Manager John McGraw, who raced to the scene as soon as he was told about the fire, suggested that the explosion had started in some peanut shells, great masses of which had accumulated beneath the grandstands. Additional light was added by pitcher Arthur "Bugs" Raymond, who said he had discovered a small fire feeding on dried peanut shells before that day's game. He had notified groundkeepers, he said, and the fire had been extinguished.

Fortunately for the Giants, no one had been killed; and when New York Highlander President Frank Farrell stepped forward and suggested that the Giants and the American League team share ball parks, it turned out that not a single game was lost. The fire's total damage came to about a quarter of a million dollars, including the losses sustained by the railway company. Not so fortunately, little interest was expressed in rebuilding the park with steel or concrete. Wood construction was cheaper and faster, and for the moment, that was all the Giant management wanted. Immediate plans were therefore made to begin a new set of wooden stands.

Even the Brooklyn Dodgers (Then Still Called "Superbas") Came to the Rescue: *Telegram to New York Giants: "Words fail me to adequately express my feelings for your great loss. I am confident you will rise, phoenix-like, above it all. It goes without saying that Washington Park is at your disposal."*

Charles H. Ebbets

One day later, word reached baseball fans throughout the nation that Addie Joss, a superb right-handed pitcher for Cleveland, had died. Cause of death was listed as tubercular meningitis. Only 31 years old, Joss had a record of 160 victories (including no-hitters in 1908 and 1910) and 97 losses.

Other Ball-park Fires of the Period:

1894: Boston: *Stands caught fire during the third inning of a game, starting in pile of rubbish. Stands were completely destroyed along with some nearby buildings. Loss: one million dollars.*

1894: Chicago: *During sixth inning of game with Cincinnati, blaze broke out in fifty-cent seats, and in the stampede that followed, forty persons were injured.*

1894: Philadelphia: *A plumber's stove set* *fire to the stands in the morning while the players were at practice. Stands were empty, but entire park was wiped out. Loss: eighty thousand dollars.*

1908: St. Louis: *Grandstands caught fire in second inning of a game with Chicago.*

1909: Toronto: *Park of team on Hanlan's Island completely destroyed.*

1911: Washington: *All grandstands destroyed except small section of bleachers. Rebuilt in time for season opener.*

AUTO RACING

The arrival of spring also brought out America's motorcyle and auto enthusiasts. "With the most spectacular burst of speed that has ever been witnessed on historic Daytona Beach," one reporter wrote, "Bob Burman, driving the powerful 200-horsepower 'Blitzen' Benz, covered a mile to-day in the remarkable time of 25.40 seconds, lowering his own world's record of 26.12 seconds, made yesterday in the same car." That computed to about 140 miles an hour. The driver also lowered the world kilometer record of 16.27 seconds to 15.88 seconds and drove 2 miles in 51.28 seconds, shattering Barney Oldfield's 55.87-second record of the year before. But no one expressed any great amount of shock or amazement when these times were announced. Too many records had been shattered during the first decade of the new century to surprise anyone. The year 1911 also promised to be the biggest in the history of motorcycling, advocates of which were rapidly replacing bicyclists on the nation's roads. During the winter of 1910–11, more than 2,500 riders were enrolled by the comparatively new Federation of American Motorcyclists.

Compared to 1896:

On Memorial Day 1896, the second "horseless carriage" race in America, known as "The Cosmopolitan Race," was held, with a grand prize to be given for speed. The announcement touched off protests because it "encouraged foolhardy drivers to risk their own lives and those of the public . . . by tearing over the roads and back again at speeds of 12 miles an hour."

The sound of engines continued to fill the air, although sometimes with a new twist, as when America's first woman pilot made her appearance that spring of 1911. The public took to Harriet Quimby immediately. She was attractive, decisive, daring, and projected the air of knowing exactly what she was doing and where she was headed—in life and above the ground. Slender and athletic-looking, she dressed in aviation jacket and trousers of wool-backed satin, leather puttees, heavy goggles, and a debonair flying cap. Determined to become America's first woman to win a pilot's license, she worked hard and long, not always with great success. On one of her early flights, for example, she totally wrecked a Bleriot-type monoplane near Hempstead, New York. While turning with the engine running at full speed the wheels of the running gear were wrenched off, causing immediate shearing of the forks and wings. "The plucky girl," one account noted, "retained her seat, shut off the power, and jumped from the machine." Such triumphs over bad luck convinced the public that it was only a matter of time before the young woman attained her goal.

Harriet Quimby on Flying:

"Do I like flying? Well, I'm out here at four o'clock every morning. That ought to be answer enough. I took up the sport just because I thought I should enjoy the sensation, and I haven't regretted it. Motoring is all right, but after seeing monoplanes in the air, I couldn't resist the desire to try the air lanes, where there are neither speed laws nor traffic policemen, and where one needn't go all the way around Central Park to get across Times Square. . . ."

Yale University, meanwhile, made history of sorts by becoming the first major college in America to sponsor an aviation meet. Held on May 19, 1911 (between flashes of lightning and occasional rain), the affair featured stunt flying by Lincoln Beachey and J. A. D. McCurdy.

More "traditional" sports were witnessed that spring, although the Fordham Marathon of May 6 ended in a fashion that can be described only as bizarre. Beginning at the university, it was proposed that the contest end at New York's City Hall, where appropriate awards could be made to the winners. Julian Beaty, secretary of Borough President McAneny, gave his approval, suggesting that the twenty-five or so who finished the race avail themselves of City Hall's sanitary facilities if they wished. That final courtesy provoked a near-riot in the building, for as it turned out, not twenty-five but five hundred young, perspiring men completed the marathon. Halfnude men swarmed through the building, using the corridors and chambers as dressing rooms, disfiguring the costly mahogany desks in the Board of Estimate Room and the Aldermanic Chamber. Expensive carpets were injured, and a delegation of women schoolteachers who had been attending a meeting in connection with the Board of Education was put to rout. Nearly fifteen hundred men took possession of the building and used it as they would a public bath. The antics of the Fordham Marathon runners belied later assertions that the turn-of-the-century years was an age of bashful courtesy. Each of the actual runners, accompanied by two attendants, did just about as he pleased. Some leaped on the fifteen-thousand-dollar Board of Estimate table and used it as a rubbing table, splashing strong liniment on the polished wood. Liniment was also smeared over desks and on walls, and rubbed into carpets. In various stages of undress, the runners tore from room to room, hoping to find some business to interrupt. After sending the lady teachers scurrying, hands over eyes, out of the building, some of the young men broke into another room where a serious discussion of the new charter was taking place. Then, rushing into the office of Weights and Measures Commissioner J. J. Walsh, they scattered water everywhere, overturned desks and tables, whooping and yelling every step of the way. When the marathon runners were finally forced out of the building, it took a force of cleaners two hours just to set things upright and cart away the scattered lemon and orange rinds, empty bottles, and soggy towels.

Was It a Hoax? A Walking Feat

On May 7, 1911, a 28-year-old man who identified himself as Julius Rath of St. Louis arrived in New York clad in a khaki suit liberally decorated with ribbons and badges. He said that he had started out on January 1, 1897, determined to walk 500,000 miles by 1915 in order to win a $30,000 bet. He had already accomplished 475,000 of those miles, he said, pointing proudly to letters and testimonials from many cities of the world. Once, he added, he had been attacked by African savages. Another time in Mexico he was shot in the leg, which caused him to spend four months in the hospital. A stickler for details, he claimed to have worn out 433 pairs of shoes during the 19 times he had circumnavigated the globe.

Americans shook their heads and wondered if young Mr. Rath was telling the truth.

AUTO RACING

"Highly tuned and mechanically as perfect as the skill of the modern motor car maker can produce," one reporter wrote on May 28, 1911, "forty-four of the fastest racing cars ever assembled are at the Indianapolis Motor Speedway awaiting the 500-mile international sweepstake race. . . ."

The first running of the Indianapolis 500 carried a purse of $25,000—$10,000 for the winner—and was eagerly awaited by motor enthusiasts across the nation. The world's most celebrated drivers entered—David Bruce-Brown, Bob Burman, Ralph DePalma, Arthur Chevrolet, and Ray Harroun were among the total of 44. Officials estimated that at 75 miles per hour, the contest would take seven hours. More than 80,000 were in attendance when the cars started, and a high pitch of excitement was maintained throughout the entire afternoon, which was marred—or highlighted—by a succession of accidents and near-collisions. The most serious accident came when the race was only 30 miles old, in the backstretch, when one of the front wheels of Arthur Greiner's Amplex flew off. The car twisted and hopped about the track, hurling S. P. Dickson, Greiner's "mechanician," against a fence 20 feet away and killing him immediately. Greiner was also thrown out of the vehicle but escaped with a fractured arm. Some additional casualties included Davis Lewis, Harry Knight, John Glover, Bob Evans, and John Wood.

The crowd, much too large to be controlled by a company of militia and several hundred policemen, became unruly at times. When Dickson was thrown against the fence, thousands pressed tightly about the body and refused to move until soldiers clubbed a pathway for the surgeons. "The throng went wild with excitement after the first accident," a reporter wrote, "and rushed back and forth over the field when the other accidents were reported. . . . In the stands the men and women were on their feet for hours, cheering their favorites and exclaiming with apprehension when cars escaped each other or ran off the inner edge of the track."

When the race was half over, Louis Disbrow's Pope-Hartford threw a tire at the entrance to the home stretch and swerved in front of another car, which turned upside

---

Winners—First Indianapolis 500		
Name	Car	Prize
R. Harroun	Marmon	$10,000
R. Mulford	Lozier	$5,000
D. Bruce-Brown	Fiat	$3,000
S. Wishart	Mercedes	$2,000
R. DePalma	Simplex	$1,500
C. Mertz	National	$1,000
W. H. Turner	Amplex	$800
H. Cobe	Jackson	$700
F. Belcher	Knox	$500
H. Hughes	Mercer	$500

down while tearing the wheels off Disbrow's vehicle. At about this point, a woman in the stands fainted, starting a small chain reaction of hysteria in her immediate vicinity. Wholesale panic was avoided in this instance, but not shortly afterward, when Burman's Mercedes threw a tire high into the air over a retaining wall, causing a stampede among the spectators.

The finish of the race provided genuine excitement in that the three leaders were seldom more than 30 seconds apart. When Mulford lost considerable time on a tire change, Ray Harroun was able to move ahead and win by a narrow margin. Nearly everyone agreed that the inaugural test of men and machines had been a smashing success.

POLO

Equally successful, although vastly more genteel, was the international polo match between the United States and Great Britain that was played on June 1, 1911, at Westbury, New York. More than 10,000 persons assembled to watch the game, including former President Roosevelt and scores of wealthy persons in great gleaming automobiles. The fifth such competition since 1886, the teams played 8 periods of 7½ minutes each, and before the contest was 2 minutes old, America's H. P. Whitney scored. The audience of country-club ladies and gentlemen cheered as lustily as they dared; then groaned a minute later when Great Britain's Lieutenant A. N. Edwards tied the score. During the second and fifth periods, Edwards added three more goals to give the visitors a decided advantage, the third and fourth periods being scoreless. Then Milburn and Waterbury of the United States tied the score going into the seventh. The crowd settled back to watch the exciting conclusion.

There were several falls during the match, the most sensational being that of America's Monte Waterbury in the fourth period, which occurred when his mount stumbled. Waterbury was thrown to the turf in the midst of a melee of prancing hoofs, but escaped injury. Locating his pony, he remounted and raced off to the cheers of the crowd.

Earlier International Polo Matches
1886: At Newport, Rhode Island. Won by England.
1900: At Hurlingham, United Kingdom. Won by England.
1902: At Hurlingham, United Kingdom. Won by England.
1909: At Hurlingham, United Kingdom. Won by United States.

The match contained not only thrills but also examples of British fair play. One such instance occurred between two periods when the American four did not hear the whistle signaling start of play and were more than a hundred yards away when the referee dropped the ball. "A gasp went up from the stands as it became evident that the Englishmen had only to sweep the ball, uncontested, to another goal. The gasp changed to a cheer, however, when one of the Englishmen was seen to ride slowly forward, reach down, and touching the ball gently with his stick send it rolling back to the feet of the referee. Until their opponents were as ready as themselves the Englishmen would take no part in the game." Such a bit of stiff-upper-lip courtesy may have cost England the match, for America took the lead in the seventh period and held on to win. Several days later, the United States team clinched the series, retaining the Westchester cup.

STUNT FLYING

Aviators were back in the news in June, sometimes generating stories of derring-do, sometimes humor. One of the lighter instances took place at Garden City, New York, where instructor William Houpert was preparing to take to the air with Harriet Quimby. After testing the Moisant monoplane, Houpert decided the tailpiece was too heavy and landed in order to adjust it. After changing the angle of the tailpiece, he returned to the front of the plane, grasped the propeller blades, and gave them a whirl. Apparently he had not shut down the gas and spark as far as he imagined, however, for as soon as he moved the propeller blades, the machine lurched forward at a great rate. Leaping out of the way, Houpert grasped the plane's fuselage, hoping to get into the driver's seat and take over the controls. In the meantime, his assistants raced across the field to his assistance.

As the plane bucked over the ground it continued to gain momentum, so that by the time Houpert's mechanics were halfway to the spot, plane and leader were whirling about at thirty miles per hour. Houpert, shaken loose from the fuselage, was now lying on his back, hanging tenaciously to the rear of the ship. One assistant grabbed at a wing, but the plane shook him off as it did others who tried to handle it. Houpert's weight finally caused the rudder to buckle, causing the ship to spin in a circle. "Round and round it went, the faithful mechanicians leaping at it as it passed, only to be knocked down, run over, and left to arise, each time more painfully but with unshaken resolve to catch it on the next lap. From behind trees and at other vantage points Miss Quimby and several others watched the strange spectacle, wondering how long the

The End of the Birdman:

Eccentric and withdrawn, Lincoln Beachey hated the crowds who turned out to watch his death-defying stunts, even though they provided him with up to a thousand dollars a week in 1911. "They want my blood," he declared, "and they'd tear me and my plane apart if they got the chance." To show his disgust, Beachey often buzzed crowds so low that many were forced to duck for cover. On May 12, 1913, Beachey announced his retirement, stating that the deaths of several other fliers rested heavily on his conscience. "I'll no longer stand accused of leading others to death," he said. But six months later, he was back in the air, trying to become the first American to loop the loop. He was successful. Nearly two years later, on March 14, 1915, Beachey roared skyward on Beachey Day at the Panama-Pacific International Exposition in San Francisco. After a graceful loop, he began his famous "dive of death." But this time it was for real. The force of the three-thousand-foot plunge tore the wings from his plane and Lincoln Beachey disappeared into the cold waters of San Francisco Bay.

gasoline would last. . . ." Finally, a few minutes later, the plane dipped into a low spot of the field and one of the propeller blades snapped. The engine continued to roar but had lost sufficient pulling power to enable the men to hold the plane in place while one of them clambered aboard and turned the infernal machine off.

A more competent exhibition of the aviator's art took place on June 27, 1911, before an immense crowd of 150,000 assembled at Niagara Falls. Ignoring the advice of friends, who warned him that the swirling air currents over the Horseshoe Falls would be too tricky for him to handle, aeronaut Lincoln Beachey took off from a baseball diamond on the American side, about a mile from the Falls and to the north. Climbing steadily, moving always in the direction of the main cataract, he swung the ship in a great circle when he arrived at two thousand feet, then plunged downward in the direction of the great Horseshoe Falls. Passing over the Falls, he continued down the river. "The crowds held their breath as he dived into the gorge," one eyewitness reported, "and after he had passed under the bridge and was skimming along less than fifteen feet from the tumbling water, the odds that he wouldn't get out were lowered."

Beachey waited until his ship was nearly enveloped by the spray of the whirlpool rapids, then pushed the controls upward, missing the top of the gorge by a few feet. He landed on the Canadian side a minute later. Acknowledging the tremendous ovation, he announced that he would repeat the flight the following day.

BASEBALL

By July 1911, both baseball pennant races were in full swing, Connie Mack's Philadelphia Athletics starting to apply the finishing touches to what would be a runaway (101–50) season. Frank Chance's Chicago Cubs, winners in 1910, were having a much more difficult time with the New York Giants. Aside from the pennant races, fans found much to interest them in both on- and off-the-field developments in the "national game." By midsummer the pitchers started to get into shape, resulting in at least three first-class games for those fans who enjoyed watching strong hurlers overpower the hitters. The first took place on July 22 in Brooklyn. Pitching for the hometown team was Nap Rucker, a twenty-six-year-old left-hander; for Cincinnati, Frank Smith was on the mound, and as it turned out, both men were in exceptionally sharp form. For three full innings, no batter on either club was able to get a hit. Brooklyn's first baseman, Jake Daubert, managed to get a scratch hit off Smith, "the noted piano mover," in the fourth, but was left on base. There followed three more complete innings of no-hit pitching until the seventh, when Brooklyn scored a single run as the result of a walk to Daubert and Eddie Zimmerman's hit. Nap Rucker took that lead and his no-hitter into the final inning. Veteran catcher Larry McLean was the lead-off batter for Cincinnati, but the string continued as Rucker retired him easily. Tom Downey, sent in to pinch-hit for Smith, also failed to connect solidly. Nap Rucker was a single out away from the Hall of Fame as Bob Bescher walked to the plate, "his broad grin working overtime." Wasting no time, Bescher lashed out and sent the ball on a line over second base. Brooklyn second baseman Johnny Hummel threw himself toward the bag, stretched out his glove, and felt the ball strike it. But he couldn't hold on. Bescher's "gold dust" single had spoiled Nap Rucker's no-hitter.

Later that month, Boston Red Sox pitcher Joe Wood turned out to be luckier than Rucker, as did Ed Walsh of the White Sox on

August 27. Both won no-hitters by the identical score of 5–0.

Pitching continued to make sports headlines when a bidding war between the Chicago White Sox and Pittsburgh Pirates started over the services of a certain Marty O'Toole, a 22-year-old sensation who had a brief tryout with Cincinnati in 1908 before moving to St. Paul. While there, he struck out 17 Milwaukee batters, equaling Rube Waddell's major-league record and convincing most of the owners that he was big-league material. As the bidding for his services rose, one team after another dropped out until only Barney Dreyfuss of the Pirates and Mike Cantillon of the White Sox remained. Eventually Dreyfuss "won" the bidding war, which gave him and the Pirates the honor of having paid the highest price for a player in the history of organized baseball, $22,500. For that astronomical figure the Pirates received 25 victories and 35 losses from O'Toole over a 3½-year period. By 1914, O'Toole was out of the major leagues, his lifetime pitching record a nondescript 27–36.

Baseball News Flash, 1911. Ward Wins His Libel Suit

"The jury which has been hearing the libel-slander suit brought by John M. Ward against Ban B. Johnson, president of the American League, in the United States Circuit Court, returned a verdict for the complainant yesterday afternoon, taxing Johnson $1,000 for calling Ward a "trickster."

(Ward, an active player from 1878–1894, was an early organizer for the player's union, and in 1911 was appointed a member of a national commission to arbitrate baseball disputes.)

BOXING

The great "White Hopes" were back in August, including a new aspirant named Al Palzer. On August 3, Palzer, a plodding free-swinger in the style of Carl Morris, took on Tom Kennedy, a former amateur heavyweight champion who had also entered the race to dethrone Jack Johnson. The fight convinced most of the astute watchers that neither man could do the job. Palzer won as a result of a solid left hook that rendered Kennedy incapable of answering the call for the beginning of the tenth round; Kennedy, on the other hand, made a good showing because of his gameness. Even optimists concluded that gameness would not be enough to bring the

heavyweight crown back into the Caucasian sphere.

Not long afterward, Carl Morris himself disappointed even his most enthusiastic admirers by standing up for ten rounds against Jim Flynn, "the Pueblo fireman," and doing little but absorb punishment. When the bout ended the right side of Morris's face was battered almost out of shape, his right eye was closed, and one long bruise extended from his temple to his lower jaw. From the second round to the end, Morris bled profusely, "as if an artery had been severed." Even the referee's shirt and the floor of the ring had changed from white to crimson by the time the fight was over. Reporters, themselves white and perhaps angry at Morris for letting them down, spared the young man nothing in describing the dreadful loss. "Morris last night was fat," one wrote. "Rolls of flesh stood out on his stomach every time he bent over in the clinches and loose fat danced on his back every time Flynn landed a hard blow to the body. His face puffed easily from punches, he was slow on his feet, and lack of condition was apparent in every move. He takes rank with Ed Dunkhorst, Mike Schreck, and so-called fighters of that caliber, rather than the real fighters who can be put into regular fighting trim. As an opponent for Johnson it would be a shame to think what the black champion would do to him."

The fortunes of Jack Johnson, meanwhile, may have seemed high but were rapidly moving from apex to nadir. During the summer of 1911, Johnson accepted the offer of a fight with Bombardier Wells of Great Britain and left immediately for England. The fight was set for October 2 in the Empress Hall, Earl's Court, and there was a lively interest in the outcome despite the fact that Wells seemed inexperienced compared to Johnson. But at least in England Johnson was not detested by a majority of the population. In fact, according to the London *Times,* "During his visits to this country, Johnson has always tried to fall in with the English sportman's ways of thinking. He has avoided the braggadocio of many transatlantic boxers, refrained from taking himself *au grand serieux* (as J. L. Sullivan did when he said to an interviewer 'Heaven has made me champion of the world'), and never made the mistake of belittling his unsuccessful opponents." With such favorable press backing, it seemed safe to assume that Johnson would receive an honest chance to display his talents and earn some money in the bargain.

Not quite. No sooner had the bout been scheduled than a variety of objections to it sprang to life. H. J. Shakespeare, of the Baptist Union of Great Britain and Ireland, attacked it on the grounds, "This is not a mere trial of skill, to be decided on points, but it has contrived to gather into itself every motive of race, publicity, and occasion which will convert it into a violent, gory, determined pounding of two men into a mass of blood and wounds. It focuses and intensifies brutality in its extreme forms for the combatants and the spectators. . . . Whatever the issue might be, again white and black will be pitted against each other in anger, revenge, and murder, especially in those lands like America in which the negro is the gravest of all problems."

The debate reached a white-hot temperature, at which point a memorial was made to the Home Secretary, a certain Winston Churchill, late in September. After examining the charges, Churchill issued an order that the fight be stopped on the grounds that it was a breach of the peace. Jack Johnson was incensed. "I am going on with my training, expecting the fight to come off," he said. "If they stop this fight, England cannot claim again she is the nation that allows fair play. They say I am just after money. Well, I'm just doing my work, and can any man be blamed for getting the best price he can? I know this, that Jack Johnson has spent more money in London than he ever got out of it."

Later, in court, Johnson acquitted himself well. Addressing the police superintendent, he asked,

"How do you know that Jack Johnson and Mr. Wells, should they box on October 2, will break the peace?"

"I don't say they will."

"Have you ever seen a championship contest?"

"No."

Despite the bout's being barred on flimsy evidence, the ruling was allowed to stand. Johnson departed with the statement that he would never again fight in any land where the British flag flew.

BASEBALL

Johnson had no real intentions of retiring, of course; even forty-four-year-old Cy Young had gone back on his March decision, returning to the mound for one final fling with Cleveland. After compiling a 3–4 record by midseason, he was traded to the Boston Nationals, where he finished his career with an overall 7–9 mark for the season. With those kinds of statistics, it seems safe to say that Young had no influence on the pennant races in either league. The World Series of 1911 saw the Philadelphia A's and New York Giants meet for the second time in the young fall classic (New York made a runaway of the 1905 series, four games to one), and fans of both cities were understandably excited.

Ticket speculation on such a grand scale as to require a post-Series investigation added to the hysteria.

The series began in "normal" fashion—the National League having won four of the six meetings and the last three in a row—with New York, behind Mathewson, defeating Philadelphia. The teams then moved to Philadelphia on October 16, where the A's tied it, thanks to a two-run home run in the sixth inning by Frank Baker. The next day, in New York, the A's went ahead when Baker hit another homer, this in the top of the ninth to send the game into overtime. (Baker had hit only nine round-trippers during the season. His best year was 1913, when he managed twelve.)

Several days of rainy weather followed, but when the teams once again took the field, Philadelphia was still hot. This time they gave up a two-run lead before winning, 4–2. New Yorkers who were inclined to panic began their postmortem ceremonies a day in advance.

The Giants bounced back on the twenty-fifth. A run behind going into the bottom of the ninth, the team rallied to tie the game; then with Larry Doyle on third base, Fred Merkle hit a long fly ball near the right-field foul line. Danny Murphy of the A's took it after a long run. As Doyle raced home, Murphy threw to the plate, too late to catch Doyle, who slid in with the winning run. Later, however, Bill Klem, umpire at the plate that day, said that Doyle missed tagging home by a good six inches and that he would have allowed the protest if the A's had lodged it. That, of course, would have ignited a pleasant ceremony on the Polo Grounds field, which was jammed with celebrants seconds after Doyle scored. Doyle, incidentally, said Klem was in error about his missing the plate, but Manager John McGraw was supposed to have noticed the mistake and spoken to Klem about it.

It all turned out to be academic twenty-four hours later. Returning to Philadelphia, the Giants were surprised to see Chief Bender on the mound—he had won the fourth game just two days before and was supposed to need more rest. He pitched well enough to win, however, and the Giants' ragged play eventually turned the game into a rout for the A's. With the score tied, 1–1, going into the bottom of the fourth inning, the New Yorkers started doing everything wrong, which included allowing a Philadelphia batter to go completely around the bases on a bunt. The game leaped out of the realm of respectability in the seventh when the Athletics scored seven times. The final score was an embarrassing 13–2.

Danny Murphy the Goat? It Could Have
Been, Except . . .
*Fred Merkle, one of baseball's earliest and
most famous "goats," was the hero of this
game, but of course no one remembers
that. What is also forgotten is that Danny
Murphy could have been the goat of the
whole Series. According to those at the
game, Merkle's fly ball was in foul territory when Murphy caught it. If he had
had the forethought not to catch it, Doyle
couldn't have scored. The rub, naturally, is
that the A's won the Series. No matter
how poorly you play, it's impossible to be
a "goat" if your team wins. Conversely,
no matter how well you play otherwise,
it's impossible to be other than a "goat"
if you commit one mistake that leads to
the team's ultimate defeat.*

FOOTBALL

A freak play also was instrumental in helping Princeton become the nation's top college
football team only a few weeks later. On November 11 it took the field against Dartmouth, which was not expected to furnish exceptional competition but turned out to be
very tough indeed. For three periods neither
team could score. Ten thousand spectators
were preparing themselves for a 0–0 ball
game when Princeton's Hobey Baker fell on a
loose ball at the Dartmouth thirty-five-yard
line. Two bucks at the line gained only four
yards, making it third—last—down and six to
go. Princeton kicker DeWitt ran onto the field
and took his position on the forty-five-yard
line preparatory to kicking a field goal. The
ball was centered to him and DeWitt drop-
kicked it . . . . on target but obviously too low.
Just before going under the crossbar, however,

the line shot struck a Dartmouth player on
the back, and the ball spun higher in the air,
plunged to the ground, and bounced through
the uprights. The Dartmouth players assumed
the field-goal try was no good, that the ball
was theirs as the result of a touchback.

Eight minutes passed while Referee Lang-
ford consulted his rule book. Then he indicated the kick was good! Subjected to a fury
of questioning, he reported, correctly, that the
football rule book of the time did not mention
what to do if the ball struck an opposing
player or ground but made it through the uprights. It stated only that if the ball passed between the goal posts, the kick was good; if it
did not pass between them, it was no good.
Princeton was awarded the game by a score of
3–0 and soon afterward the rule book was
supplied with additional information.

And so the year 1911 came to an unusual
conclusion. It had been a total washout for
New York horseplayers, but fans of most other
spectator sports were supplied with ample
thrills and heroes. In lawn tennis and golf,
women such as Hazel Hotchkiss, Eleanora
Sears, and Margaret Curtiss attracted large
followings, as did Harriet Quimby in the air.
Regrettably, the latter young woman had only
six months to live as the year 1911 ended. In
July 1912, while flying with a passenger
named W. A. P. Willard, she crashed into
Dorchester Bay near Boston.

Those searching for a white hope to take
the heavyweight championship from Jack
Johnson also counted 1911 as a year of disappointment. Not only did Carl Morris end the
year in disgrace, so too did Al Palzer by losing
to light-hitting Tom Kennedy in a dull fight
that destroyed Palzer's credibility as a genuine
challenger. Palzer, incidentally, died only a
few years later, in 1917, when his father shot
him during a domestic quarrel with Al's
mother. Apparently he was not only a mediocre fighter, but also not a very good referee in
the bargain.

CHAPTER 20—DOING IT THE HARD WAY

For some, the mere acts of walking, running, swimming, bowling, or otherwise competing athletically has not been enough. The compulsion to do it the hard way, by imposing an arbitrary handicap, proved too much to resist for a small percentage of American athletes almost from the very beginning. And so we have been given the mixed blessing of a century of blindfolded golfers, handcuffed swimmers, and pedestrians trundling along behind an anvil or wheelbarrow. Sometimes the public has been enchanted with such forms of sporting lunacy; on other occasions the promoter was left with a bad case of flat feat.

SWIMMING

"Professor" Marquis Bibbero's brief period of fame came during the spring and summer of 1882, following a discussion between Richard K. Fox, publisher of the *National Police Gazette*, and a Washington La Brie. Fox, who loved a good wager, said he thought it would be possible for a good swimmer to make it across the East River with his feet bound at the ankles and his arms tied behind his back. La Brie, a betting man himself, thought otherwise. A bit of haggling followed, the two men finally settling on a bet of $250, with Fox's man to have three tries at making the crossing. This would reduce the possibility that an adverse tide, bad weather, or freak encounter with one of the many vessels plying that waterway would prevent the swimmer from accomplishing the task.

Fox selected Marquis Bibbero, a strong swimmer who happened to be in New York at the time and was willing to attempt the trick for a piece of the action and resultant publicity. The newspapers were alerted and the public prepared to enjoy a feat of "rare novelty."

Bibbero's first attempt, on Wednesday, May 31, 1882, began in the saloon of William McCoy near the Fulton Ferry dock at South Street. While others drank champagne, Bibbero prepared himself for the swim by smearing his body with a mixture of porpoise oil and lard. "He explained that this delightful mixture would enable his body to retain its heat and prevent the sharks from biting him," one reporter wrote.

Just before one o'clock, Bibbero hopped aboard a small boat with Fox, several well-known sporting gentlemen of the time, and a fellow daredevil-swimmer named Robert Donaldson, who had been assigned the task of following Bibbero across the river in a small boat. (Donaldson's proclaimed specialty was jumping from high places into bodies of water, à la Sam Patch, and he had already announced that he had his eyes on the still-incomplete Brooklyn Bridge.)

As the boat pushed away from the pier, a cry of encouragement went up from the crowded docks and riggings of nearby ships. When Bibbero "divested himself of his coat and pantaloons," a moment later, it could be seen that he was dressed in colorful tights and that his hands were already bound with stout cord.

Once in the water, Bibbero began to propel himself, as one writer described it, "like a porpoise, with his knees." Making good headway —or kneeway—despite his handicap he soon reached the middle of the river. At that point, however, a strong current began sweeping him quickly southward in the direction of Governors Island. Bibbero battled it fiercely for a while, but as he neared the Battery after being in the water about an hour, he gave up, raising his hands to signal for help. Donaldson promptly leaped into the river and cut the professor loose. The first attempt had been a failure—except as a news and sports event. "During the time he was in the water, the crowds on both sides of the river continued to increase," reported the New York *Times*. Then, as if it were bad taste to inadvertently promote such an event, it was quickly added, "Few seemed to know, however, that a manfish was swimming for a wager. It was generally supposed that a convict had escaped from Blackwell's Island."

Three weeks later, Bibbero made his second attempt, despite cloudy weather, which turned to rain later in the day. Little consideration was given to canceling the event, apparently, even though less people watched than the first time around. Those who took the trouble were rewarded by the sight of a professor dressed to kill, for when Bibbero emerged from McCoy's saloon, it could be seen that he wore an elegant pair of alligator shoes, a tightly knit shirt, and blue trunks. Accompanied by Patsy

Owens, who was obviously the resident ichthyologist and shark catcher of Peck Slip, and Donaldson, Bibbero reversed his previous procedure by swimming from the Brooklyn side in the direction of New York. After smearing himself from head to foot, this time with goose grease and turpentine, and being transported in a small boat to Brooklyn, he leaped overboard and slithered toward his objective, his feet moving, according to the New York *Sun,* with the "motions of a dog-fish's tail."

The tide was moving out with a fury that might have deterred an ordinary swimmer, and those who saw Bibbero when he appeared several yards ahead of the rowboat freely expressed the opinion that he was indeed a very bold man. "He wriggled like an eel," reported the *Times,* "and shot ahead with astonishing rapidity."

But for the second time, Bibbero fell victim to the tide, and after a long struggle he again signaled to Donaldson. Afterward, he said, that while sitting in his tights in the boat, he had become chilled during the crossing and lost much of his strength.

For his third and final attempt to prove his mettle and win some money for Fox, Bibbero waited until July 3. In the meantime, public attention grew. The weather on the climactic day was clear, and the tide was not running. But the better conditions brought a new threat —increased river traffic by excursion vessels. After a dramatic dive into the water on the Brooklyn side, Bibbero was under way.

A quarter hour later, as Bibbero's powerful thrusts brought him abreast of the Roosevelt Street pier in New York, the hazard of ferryboat traffic began to be felt. "Passing steamers churned up the water and sent waves over Bibbero," the *Sun* wrote, "but he apparently was not affected in the least by rough water. When the ferryboat *Garden City* came along, it was alternately head and heels up with Bibbero, but he once more got his bearings and continued on manfully for the shore."

After being in the water only twenty minutes, Bibbero was within ten yards of the pier, at which point Referee Charles Sherer became alarmed at the tangle of river craft and ordered the professor pulled aboard. The decision generated a certain amount of controversy as to whether the swimmer had fulfilled his obligation, but La Brie graciously conceded the bet to Fox. Saloon owner McCoy, having picked up eighteen hundred dollars in side bets, gave Bibbero a hundred dollars for his trouble.

For several years immediately afterward, strong swimmers felt compelled to prove their capability by performing in the constricted manner first displayed by Marquis Bibbero.

On July 27, 1885, Dennis F. Butler, a swimming teacher at the Battery Bath, duplicated the feat on the East River despite harassment by conscientious police officers and near-envelopment by water traffic. Three years later, a Maltese sailor named Jack Williams, trussed hand and foot, swam twenty-five miles from Alton, Illinois, down the Mississippi River to St. Louis.

Buster Elionsky was only nineteen-years old in 1913 but weighed 265 pounds when he took up swimming the hard way. Having heard, no doubt, of Bibbero and his followers, Elionsky, a New London life-saving "commodore," decided to swim from the Battery to Coney Island, about twelve miles, with his hands and feet tied. Dropping into the water on October 5, 1913, he immediately encountered an unfavorable tide, which threatened to carry him up the East River. For a while, he battled back, propelling himself down Buttermilk Channel to a point just opposite Brooklyn's City Hall. He then gave up.

But not for long. He was back in November, this time with an entirely new stunt. Not only were Elionsky's hands and feet bound, he also had been fitted with a huge dutch collar so that he could tow a boat and several passengers behind him—a total weight of a thousand pounds. After waiting for two hours so that the tide would be heading toward the ocean, he toppled over the side at 12:49 A.M. on November 3, to the cheers of a sizable crowd.

The heavy tide proved almost as much a burden as a help, carrying the boat off course. At one point, an eddy carried him and the craft under a dock, but Elionsky managed to swim to midstream and continue south. Swimming almost entirely underwater so as to offset the wind, he moved along the west shore of Governors Island, then cut across toward the Brooklyn shore. When he reached Bay Ridge, approximately two thirds of the way to Coney Island, he pulled ashore, exhausted and bleeding from the collar's effect on his shoulders and neck. Although he did not make the predicted distance, Elionsky seemed satisfied with the success of his mission.

Three years later, Buster and his seventeen-year-old sister Ida were back in the news. Starting from the foot of Fifty-ninth Street, the two plunged into the water. This time, however, it was Ida's show. In order to demonstrate her strength and ability, she was doing all the swimming, the 265-pound Buster having been lashed to her back as pure dead weight.

All went well until the pair reached Charlton Street, at which point a twenty-five-foot launch carrying newsmen and photographers went out of control and rammed a barge. Although no one was hurt, some panic followed, and the Elionskys were promptly forgotten.

Handicap swimming went into a modest decline until revived in the 1920s by Lotty Moore Schoemmell, at that time holder of twenty-two world's swimming records as well as being the mother of two children. On October 4, 1928, Mrs. Schoemmell announced her intention of swimming from the Statue of Liberty to the Battery, approximately two miles, with arms and legs tied.

The next day, promptly at 11:45 A.M., she started the first such trip ever undertaken by a woman. For nearly two thirds of a mile she had to contend with a strong back current before she reached the channel and got the benefit of the flood tide. Then she began to pick up speed. An hour after she started, she was helped out of the water near Pier 7.

In the crowd of several thousand awaiting her at the Battery was twelve-year-old Harold Schoemmell, who kissed his mother time and again while photographs were taken.

Nearly a half century after Mrs. Schoemmell and ninety-two years after Marquis Bibbero, Jack LaLanne, physical culturist and American TV celebrity, celebrated his sixtieth birthday by swimming from Alcatraz Island to Fisherman's Wharf in San Francisco, a distance of two miles, with his legs and hands similarly bound. The date was October 4, 1974, and the feat was nothing unusual for the man who spent years smiling and talking while performing rigorous exercises on television. "I just wanted to prove that I practice what I preach," he replied in response to a question asking what he intended to prove by performing such a stunt.

BASKETBALL

Although there is little demand for such talent in a regular game, John T. Sebastian on May 18, 1972, made sixty-three consecutive free throws while blindfolded. The event took place at Maine Township High School East, Park Ridge, Illinois.

CHIN-UPS

It is estimated that only one of about 100,000 people can chin a bar with one hand. In 1878, an Englishman named Cutler completed twelve one-handed chin-ups, a record for its time.

Another record was set in 1914 when eighteen-year-old Francis Lewis of Beatrice, Nebraska, achieved seven straight chin-ups using only the middle finger of his left hand.

In 1918, along came thirty-six-year-old ninety-five-pound Lillian Leitzel, an acrobat and aerialist with Ringling Brothers and Barnum and Bailey productions. When she insisted that she could beat the world's record for one-armed chin-ups, the other gymnasts at Hermann's Gym, in Philadelphia, challenged her to prove it.

Leaping to the bar, Miss Leitzel executed twenty-seven one-armed chin-ups in a row. She then switched to her left arm and performed nineteen more, beating both ways the record set by Cutler in 1878.

PUSH-UPS

On September 12, 1974, twenty-eight-year-old Henry Marshall of San Antonio, Texas, performed 124 push-ups using only his right arm, then did 103 with his left arm.

James Ullrich on March 11, 1974, performed 140 fingertip push-ups in one minute, twenty seconds.

RUNNING

It is difficult enough for the average person to run 100 yards in less than 15 seconds, much less backward or in a huge sack reaching to the neck.

On May 1, 1929, in New York's 106th Regiment Armory, Johnny Finn negotiated 100 yards enmeshed in a sack, breaking the tape in just 14.4 seconds.

Bill Robinson, a professional tap dancer who lived from 1878 to 1949 and was one of the few persons to upstage Shirley Temple on camera, once raced 100 yards in 13.5 seconds —backward.

WALKING

Because pedestrianism was one of America's earliest spectator sports, it was one of the first to develop variations as a means of entertaining the customers. By the 1870s, many walkers were doing it backward or with the handicap of carrying an anvil, but the ultimate in walking weirdness was undoubtedly Leon Pierre Federmeyer. "Some of the walkers are queer specimens of humanity," wrote the New York *Times* in 1879, "but he is the queerest of all."

They were probably right. Dressed in a floppy tunic that made him resemble, as one reporter put it, "either a stuffed doll or a ghost on a spree," his unkempt hair trailing behind him, the twin American and French flags just forward of his legs rippling in the breeze created by his industry, Federmeyer was indeed an unusual-looking athlete.

He was also the self-proclaimed "wheelbarrow-pushing champion of the world," which meant that he had walked while pushing a wheelbarrow farther and faster than any other man alive. If the title was not one sought after by the greatest athletes of the period, Federmeyer did not seem particularly upset. The sobriquet set him apart from the rest of humanity and gave him the opportunity to earn a few dollars, which was apparently all that mattered.

Why anyone should feel the impulse to push a wheelbarrow beyond the limits of a construction site is a somewhat moot point. The phenomenon seems less bizarre when one remembers that people who attended pedestrian events during the 1870s were looking for oddities, such as the man who walked a considerable distance carrying a regulation musket or an anvil, as did John Davidson of Little Rock.

Against this background an obscure gentleman named R. Lyman Potter announced in early 1878 that he intended to push a wheelbarrow across the entire continent—from Albany, New York, to San Francisco. Attended by well-wishers and hecklers at every large community along the way, Potter arrived at his destination in mid-October and promptly issued a challenge that for fifteen hundred dollars he could win a similar race headed in the opposite direction.

At this juncture Leon Federmeyer, a forty-one-year-old Frenchman who had been in the United States only three years, stepped forward, wheelbarrow in hands. Accompanied by J. T. Fuller, a gentleman who offered to serve as referee, the participants left Woodward's Garden, San Francisco, on the afternoon of December 8, 1878. Federmeyer's vehicle, which weighed a total of 133 pounds when loaded with bedclothes, food, and tent, was adorned with American and French flags on either wheel. From the trailing edge of the wheelbarrow, Federmeyer had fashioned a homemade fan that turned as the wheels moved, theoretically cooling the pusher.

The fan was hardly needed, as it turned out, for by the time the men arrived at Carlin, Nevada, the temperature had dropped to sixteen degrees below zero, and food was in short supply. Fuller, who had brought along his rifle, shot at the numerous antelopes that crossed their path but missed every time. Lyman Potter reacted to the situation by taking a brief "respite" at Battle Mountain while Federmeyer and Fuller pushed onward—directly into a violent snowstorm. Both would have frozen to death except that like heroes in a dime novel of that period, they happened to stumble across a log cabin appropriately inhabited by an old Swede.

By April 1879, Federmeyer and his friendly referee companion arrived at Kansas City, with still no word from Lyman Potter. Proceeding at a more leisurely pace over somewhat better roads, winner Federmeyer

dragged into New York City on July 24, 1879, wearing a straw hat that, according to the *Times,* was "so thoroughly perforated with holes that it might have been used for a sieve." The rest of his outfit was similarly disheveled.

Rumors having preceded him that Lyman Potter was still marooned somewhere in Kansas, Federmeyer was able to claim the "wheelbarrow-pushing championship" of the world, but found collecting the winner's purse considerably more difficult. He was also dismayed to learn that many people did not believe he had actually crossed the entire continent with the wheelbarrow. Federmeyer therefore decided to try to earn some money and silence his critics at the same time by giving a six-day walking exhibition at the American Institute Ice Rink on Sixty-third Street. During that period, he promised to travel five hundred miles, pushing his wheelbarrow the whole way, or forfeit a prize of five hundred dollars offered him by a group of French admirers.

The event began just after midnight, August 11, 1879. Federmeyer, dressed in a red flannel shirt reaching nearly to his knees, and blue pantaloons, covered the first mile—six laps—with quiet efficiency. In fact, most persons were surprised at the speed he was able to attain. "The barrow," noted one reporter with obvious surprise, "rather than retarding, seems to help him along." The New York *Herald* added that "while the motion of his feet and limbs are not graceful, it was indicative of vigor and strength."

At the end of the first twenty-four-hour period, Federmeyer had covered 101½ miles, a considerable distance by any standards. Unfortunately, that turned out to be the high-water mark of the galloping Gaul's career, both artistically and financially. After an initial burst of curiosity-seekers dropped by, attendance was poor, and Federmeyer could not maintain the pace of his first day. After walking 83½ miles on the second day, his right ankle became swollen and his pace erratic. His appearance, never exactly suave from the very beginning, deteriorated even more, and the newspapers began to lay on the heavy sarcasm. "Any spectator who didn't take him for a scissors-grinder," one reporter wrote, "would certainly take him for a hand-organ man taking the place of his own monkey."

In desperation, the rink management tried to pump some life into the exhibition, especially after Federmeyer took to lying "almost helpless on his cot in his room." On the fourth day some other pedestrians were brought in to fill the void—one, named Sebastian Cabot, set out to cover 50 miles without stopping but was summoned back to his regular job by a "ruthless employer." Federmeyer somehow

44. With the start of the new century, the "national game," baseball, saw the birth of a new league and once again a postseason series to determine the champion of the United States. In 1903, Pittsburgh of the National League was favored to defeat Boston of the upstart Americans, but the fans who jammed Boston's Huntington Avenue Baseball Grounds (presently the site of Northeastern University) wanted to be shown. In the first game they were, the Pirates winning, 7–3, but the Red Sox came back to take the first World Series of the century, 5 games to 3.

44a. Joe Tinker (left) and Johnny Evers (right) of the shortstop–second base–first base double-play combination of Tinker to Evers to Chance. As the nucleus of a Chicago Cubs team that was light on hitting but strong on defense, Tinker and Evers led the way to three consecutive pennants, 1906–8, the final two culminating in World Series victories.

44b. Fred Merkle, who as a 19-year-old utilityman with the New York Giants failed to touch second base in a critical game against the Cubs, thus forcing a playoff contest that the Giants lost. (See "Flaps.") Merkle retained the "goat" image along with another Giant, Fred Snodgrass, who combined with Merkle in the 1912 World Series to hand the Boston Red Sox the decisive seventh game. Snodgrass started it by dropping a fly ball and Merkle then let Tris Speaker's pop foul get away.

45. The face of John F. (Jack) Sheridan, who umpired in the National League during the 1890s, then switched to the American League, 1901–14.

46. "Major" Taylor, probably the most respected black athlete in America at the turn of the century. His specialty was short-distance sprints and during his prime he was considered nearly unbeatable in the two-mile bicycle race. (See "Breaking the Color Barrier.")

47. Most celebrated fighter during early years of the century was Jim Jeffries, who knocked out heavyweight champion Bob Fitzsimmons in 11 rounds on June 9, 1899, and held title six years before retiring. Unfortunately, Jeffries did not make his retirement stick, answering the call for a "great white hope" five years later and losing to Jack Johnson.

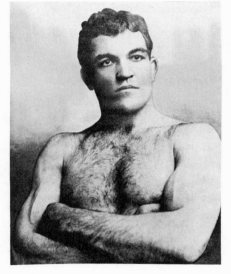

48. Sixteen-year-old May Daarlus, who surprised and delighted billiard enthusiasts by performing a variety of trick shots beyond the capabilities of most male experts. (See "1901.")

49. Women were getting more and more involved in sports activity as the new century began, thanks largely to the influence of the bicycle and opportunities that beckoned once that pastime was mastered. Fencing, of course, could be taken up on the grounds that it taught young ladies grace and body control. Picture was taken in April 1904.

50. Those who permitted young women of the early twentieth century to indulge in bicycling or fencing were not so tolerant of those who wanted to participate in male contact sports such as football. Scene of young women playing football took place at Detroit in 1901.

51. A startling new piece of equipment on the sports scene early in the twentieth century was the automobile. In 1908, much excitement was generated by marathon New York to Paris race across the United States, Siberia, and Europe. (See "Doing It Till It Hurts.")

52. Inventors continued to dabble away in their efforts to construct better sports equipment, this one known as an "aeroplane swimming device." Conceived by a Pittsburgh inventor, it turned out to be neither fish nor fowl.

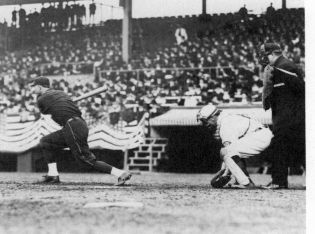

53. Baseball was more popular than ever in second decade of the twentieth century, a situation that led speculators to form a third league for the first time since 1890. The Federals played in 1914 and 1915, gave established Nationals and Americans a good run for their money, then capitulated on the eve of World War I. Action here is during opening game of the 1915 season, Joe Agler of Buffalo getting the first hit against the Brooklyn Feds, whose owner tried to stick them with the nickname "Tip-Tops." (See "Other Leagues.")

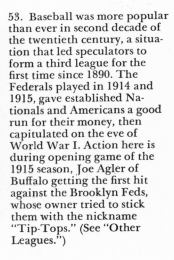

54. Decade came to an end as 1919 Chicago White Sox, prohibitive favorites to defeat Cincinnati in World Series, suddenly turned into misfits. (See "Fixes.") Eddie Cicotte (left), with record of 29–7 during regular season, lost two games of Series, and Claude (Lefty) Williams (center) dropped three. A third pitcher, Dickie Derr, who was not involved in the scandal, won a pair of games as Cincinnati won, 5 games to 3. Not until 1920 did bribe offers become public. Cicotte and Williams were banned from organized baseball the following year.

55. One of America's first golf heroes was Francis Ouimet, who was given slight chance to win the U.S. Open in 1913. But Ouimet defeated British stars Ted Ray and Harry Vardon and suddenly became a national celebrity. He was only 20 years old at the time of the upset.

56. Jim Thorpe dispelled the notion that Indian athletes were somehow inferior to whites when he led Carlisle to series of football victories over prominent eastern schools, then ran away with honors in 1912 Olympic Games. Though later stripped of his Olympic medals, Thorpe retained his reputation as a superathlete, even after he joined the New York baseball Giants and failed consistently to hit a good curve ball. (See "Breaking the Color Barrier.")

57. Another athlete who broke the color barrier with a vengeance was Jack Johnson, the extraordinary heavyweight champion many still consider the best of all time. Johnson combined quickness with crushing power to beat Tommy Burns in 14 rounds, then battered Jim Jeffries when the ex-champ tried to make a comeback. Johnson held the title for nearly seven years before losing to Jess Willard in 1915.

58. The New York Female Giants entertained curious audiences during the second decade of the twentieth century, turning out in bloomers for their games. Pictured in 1913 action, Miss McCullum catches a high pitch as Miss Ryan ducks.

59. Basketball at Vassar College, May 1913. Note absence of backboard.

60. Occasionally, enthusiasts attempted to adapt favorite sports to another medium, such as auto polo, boxing on ice, etc. This scene depicts a game of water baseball, which was popular to the turn of the century, especially in indoor pools. (See "Sports That Never Made It.")

61. Inventors kept on inventing, of course, and one product from 1911 was the aero sled. Mr. Cyril, the inventor, glares at us from the front seat.

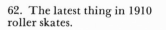

62. The latest thing in 1910 roller skates.

managed to get back on the track after this, but was able to cover only 407 miles by 10:30 P.M., Saturday, August 16, at which point the rink's gas was turned off "as a forcible hint to the few in the audience to leave the hall." The *Herald* concluded that the exhibition was "disastrous not only to the managers but to those who hoped to gain a record in this field of exertion."

In even worse financial straits, Federmeyer decided to enter the Astley Belt competition the following month. This was an international go-as-you-please (walk or run or jog, but without wheelbarrow, anvil, or other gimmickry) contest for a large purse and considerable prestige. The problem for Federmeyer was that among the entrants were the world's best walkers and runners, including Great Britain's Charles Rowell and America's Edward P. Weston, the incumbent belt-holder. Although Federmeyer was given little chance to win from the very outset, he did manage to cover 348 miles in five days (compared to the leader's 457 miles) before dropping by the wayside on the final day. Even so, it must have been apparent to all that Federmeyer's heart just wasn't in it, for at the conclusion one reporter noted archly, "Federmeyer should either improve decidedly before he tries this kind of work again or drop it."

The unhappy Frenchman obviously did the latter, vanishing into obscurity after that. Gone with him was any explanation as to why he moved slower without his wheelbarrow than with it.

Another unusual walker of the period was Robert J. Russell, whose specialty was covering long distances underwater. In 1878, Russell made a bet with several sporting men that he could walk eight miles in five hours, clad in a diving suit. A purse of five hundred dollars was held and the contest started on July 24, 1878.

The scene was Rikers Island, near Hell Gate, New York, where a one-sixth-mile course had been laid out in water that was only six feet deep at the beginning of the test and twelve feet at the end, owing to the tide. Russell's suit resembled an old-fashioned armor coat of mail, to which was attached a helmet with a rubber tube and shoes weighing twenty-five pounds each. Above him was a rowboat with a referee and friends, who made sure the tube did not become tangled and deprive Russell of air.

Dropping into the shallow pool at 11:30

A.M., Russell plodded along the muddy bottom for thirty-five minutes, at which point he accomplished his first mile. He did his second mile in even faster time, thirty minutes, then obviously became tired, turning in the next two miles at an average time of forty-six minutes each. He gained speed after that, finishing the eight-mile walk in four hours, thirty-seven minutes.

When he emerged triumphant, he was interviewed by a *Herald* reporter, to whom he said proudly, "This thing was never attempted before. . . . Many people thought it could not be done, but I believe I have set that question at rest."

No doubt. The only question remaining was: Why?

BOWLING

In order to demonstrate the effectiveness of "spot" bowling, in 1933 a professional bowler named Bill Knox had a special screen built at the Olney Alleys in Philadelphia and instructed two pinboys to hold it a foot above the foul line so that Knox could not see the pins.

Bowling only with the aid of the spots at the edge of the lane, Knox made twelve strikes in a row for a perfect game of 300.

Fifteen years later, at Dunbar, West Virginia, another bowler named Al Wells had a curtain stretched across the lane in a similar fashion and also rolled a 300 game. It was the first perfect game at that establishment as well as the first perfect game ever rolled by Wells.

GOLF

Golfers, despite their reputation as staid old codgers, have always had a penchant for experimentation on the courses. In 1929, for example, one golfer bet he could defeat another using a baseball bat instead of regular clubs.

The players, Tillar Cavet, a Tucson baseball player, and A. B. Chase, an "average golfer" of the same city, were supposedly of about equal ability. At the end of nine holes, the two were even. Chase took the eleventh to go 1-up, but Cavet came back to win the thirteenth and fourteenth. Chase evened things up again on the fifteenth.

The next hole, however, was won by the man with the baseball bat, and that was the way it remained until the end. Winning by a score of 1-up, Cavet had a total of 90 strokes for the round.

CHAPTER 21—DOING IT TILL IT HURTS

For some athletes, doing it well hasn't been enough. Having perfected their particular skills to the limit of their ability, the next step was obvious: Would it not be interesting and challenging to see how long a sports activity could be performed before the athlete gave in to exhaustion? Surely this would benefit science by defining the limits of human endurance (they said in the beginning). Even more to the point: Would the act of doing it till it hurts bring them the attention and financial rewards they sought?

Sometimes it did. On other occasions the contest of endurance carried over to the spectator, creating mass ennui. Regardless of the end result as a spectator event, however, the "breed," as horseracing enthusiasts might have described it, has been considerably improved during the century-plus in which Americans have attempted to run or swim or otherwise athletically extend themselves. The late-twentieth-century athlete is a better beast than his nineteenth-century counterpart. An improved standard of living, improved nutrition—any of a number of reasons may be cited as the cause. Or it may be simply because the sports showman of the past gave him a rich legacy of targets to aim at and eventually destroy with his own ability.

THE "PEDS"

The modern—that is, since 1776—American mania for doing it longer and harder and more often got its impetus from the British pedestrians of the late eighteenth and early nineteenth centuries. In 1764, a 30-year-old lawyer named Foster Powell walked from London to Bath, a seaside resort 50 miles away, in seven hours, a speed of about seven miles an hour. Twelve years later, he walked from London to York and back—396 miles—in 140 hours. Although this averages out to but 66 miles a day, Powell was acclaimed as an endurance champion, partly because the roads at the time were hard to traverse, and partly because his feat was an original one.

Captain Allardyce Barclay of Ury, Scotland, became a rich man in 1809 by betting that he could walk 1,000 miles in 1,000 hours, a trick that was matched in 1850 by Richard Manks. Americans, meanwhile, heard of the records, but it was not until the eve of the Civil War that a man came along who would destroy all British records in the area of long-distance walking.

AMERICA'S FIRST GREAT ENDURANCE WALKER

Born in 1839, Edward Payson Weston's first celebrated long-distance walk came early in 1861, when to pay off an election wager (he had bet against Abraham Lincoln) he agreed to walk from Boston to Washington, D.C., in 10 days. He covered the 450 miles over rutty and potholed roads quite easily, arriving at the Capitol on March 4, 1861, a bit too late to see Lincoln sworn in, but not too weary to

---

SOME "IRON MEN" OF PROFESSIONAL SPORTS AND THEIR RECORDS:

Baseball (American League): *Lou Gehrig, New York Yankees, played in 2,130 consecutive games from June 1, 1925, to April 30, 1939.*

Baseball (National League): *Billy Williams, Chicago Cubs, played in 1,117 consecutive games from September 22, 1963, to September 22, 1970.*

Boxing: *Most career fights credited to Abraham Hollanderski, also known as "Abe the Newsboy," who appeared in 1,309 bouts from 1905 to 1918. He also wrestled an additional 387 times.*

Basketball: *National Basketball Association record of 844 consecutive games was established by Johnny Kerr of Syracuse, from October 31, 1954, to November 4, 1965.*

Football: *Defensive end Jim Marshall of Minnesota Vikings, still active at end of 1977 season, had played in 252 consecutive games by that time.*

Ice Hockey: *Going into the 1977–78 season, Garry Unger of the St. Louis Blues had appeared in 723 consecutive games in nine seasons.*

Horseracing: *Jockey Johnny Longden, whose career spanned the years 1926 to 1966, rode a total of 32,407 races. Willie Shoemaker, still active at the end of 1977, had ridden 30,939 times.*

But There Were Some Detractors:
While granting that Weston possessed abundant "pluck and endurance," the New York Times *editorialized that it could not see the purpose for the jaunt other than providing "an opportunity for betting to professional gamblers, who would just as soon have bet on two raindrops running down a pane of glass, or on the length of two straws drawn from a wheat stack, and the gratification of a few curiosity-hunting sight-seers."*

attend the inauguration ball that evening. For his trouble, Weston received a bag of peanuts, according to terms of the wager, but because he became an instant celebrity at the same time, he never had to walk for peanuts again.

After the war, Weston became a reporter for the New York *Herald,* but was more often out walking than in the office. In 1867, finding himself in need of funds—a condition that was to plague him nearly all his life—he accepted a wager of $10,000 to walk from Portland, Maine, to Chicago, a distance of about 1,300 miles, within 26 days. That meant he had to average approximately 50 miles a day, which was child's play for Weston. Leaving Portland at noon on October 29, he progressed steadily through small towns and large, always greeted by crowds of friendly people—although here and there an irritating prankster turned up. Weston apparently did not mind. Moving briskly over the rough roads, riding crop in hand, he enjoyed meet-

ing the well-wishers and children who turned out along the route. When he arrived in Chicago late in November, he was the toast of the town.

After being saluted by civic leaders, he was taken to the Opera House, where he delivered a lecture on long-distance walking and its virtues to the mind and body.

The following summer, Weston suffered his first disappointment when a promoter talked him into exhibiting his talents on a circular track near New York. The goal of the attraction was to see if Weston could walk 100 miles in a 24-hour period, a magic figure that pedestrians of that era regarded as something akin to a 4-minute mile. Weston failed to achieve the mark, however, complaining that "the circular, monotonous round . . . made me sick to the stomach and rendered me as weak as a child."

In 1871, Weston succeeded in covering 112 miles in a single day at the American Institute track in New York, but his next goal—to travel 500 miles in 6 days—eluded him for 3 years. In May of 1874, his followers felt he was closing in on the mark, for they jammed the arena to watch Weston, dressed in black velvet jacket and knee breeches, begin the track's first circuit accompanied by *Herald* publisher James Gordon Bennett. At the end of the first day Weston had completed 115 miles, but his feet became so sore by the third day that a desperate measure was taken, namely to pour "some spirit . . . into his shoes to stimulate the sluggish circulation of blood." Predictably, this caused the inner sole of Weston's shoe to bind and blister his feet. Although he did not accomplish his goal, he did earn $5,000 after expenses.

Some Other Famous Pedestrians of the Era:
Undoubtedly the best was Daniel O'Leary *(1842–1933), who was born in Cork, Ireland, and came to the United States in 1861. In 1875, O'Leary beat Weston and became America's foremost representative on the track. When he died at the age of 90, it was said he could walk a mile in 9 minutes and that he had logged 300,000 miles during his lifetime.*
Hugh Donahue, *of Springfield, Massachusetts, attained instant fame in 1875 when he walked 1,100 miles in 1,100 hours at Mystic Park, Brighton, Massachusetts. At the time, the feat was regarded as "reckless." Newspapers told of Donohue's hair turning gray on the track and predicted*

death, adding that whenever the walker took a brief rest, it was necessary to use ammonia and "severe castigation with whips" in order to awaken him. Nevertheless, on July 21, 1875, Donahue completed his task.
William H. Dutcher, *of Poughkeepsie, flourished during the late 1870s, once walking 110 hours without a break. In December 1875 he walked 150 miles in 36 hours at New Britain, Connecticut, and then, to prove he was still fresh, performed some gymnastics.*
Frank Hart, *one of America's first black athletes, also walked and ran against Weston and other pedestrians of this period. His career is discussed at length in "Breaking the Color Barrier."*

Four months later, Weston was back on the track, but was done in this time by an inflamed right foot. In October 1874 he was forced to halt once again after becoming giddy, and some began to wonder if he would ever attain his goal. Complaining of the New York smoke and ruffianism, Weston's answer was to take his act to an arena in Newark, where he promptly beat the mark with 20 minutes to spare. Even so, near the end he experienced considerable paranoia, accusing those who had bet against him of planning to throw pepper at him or drop "chemical preparations" on the track to harm his feet. A warrant was even sworn out against the prizefighter Joe Coburn (see "1871" for this fighter's additional exploits), who supposedly wanted to see Weston lose and had dropped by to make sure his bet was safe. When the record was broken, Edward Weston's wife and children appeared at the track, happy embraces were exchanged, and Weston—who never walked on Sunday—announced to reporters that he intended to take only a few hours' rest in order to be ready for church services.

THE EARLY BOXERS

Unlike later boxers fighting within the fixed-time limitations of 3-minute rounds, prizefighters of the early and middle nineteenth century had to be prepared to battle from a minute to 3 hours. Rounds ended when a man was thrown or knocked to the ground, at which point he had 30 seconds to return to "scratch." But there was no limit to the number of rounds that could be fought, unless one side threw in the towel or the referee decided to end the match.

Under these rules, the greatest number of recorded rounds was 278, when Jack Jones beat Patsy Tunney in Cheshire, England. The 4½-hour marathon took place in 1825.

AMERICA: O'NEIL—OREM

In the United States, on January 2, 1865, a more modest 185 rounds were fought when 138-pound Con Orem, a 29-year-old professional fighter, took on 34-year-old Hugh O'Neil, a veteran barroom brawler and miner.

The site was Virginia City, a boisterous gold camp in Montana Territory, and interest was high in the fight largely because it pitted an excellent little man against a good big man. At 190 pounds, O'Neil was a legitimate heavyweight of the period fighting a man of welterweight size.

Entrepreneur J. A. Nelson, who staged the battle at his own Leviathan Hall, also refereed. For two rounds the sparring was dull, but in the third, O'Neil landed a hard left hand just below Orem's shoulder, knocking the smaller man cleanly off his feet.

By the fiftieth round, as both fighters battered each other but were unable to land a knockout blow, the two men were in bad shape. O'Neil, the victim of Orem's faster reflexes and professional experience, had a bloody nose and swollen eye. But he was able to use his greater weight in the clinches to advantage, continually throwing Orem to the floor with savage force.

Round 119 was probably the best of the fight. Both men seemed determined to end it, trading blows in midring until they knocked each other off their feet at the same time. Seconds dragged the men to their corners and were able to send them back to scratch, but the fighters were so drained of energy that each was powerless to take advantage of the other man's grogginess. For 60 rounds the two fought in a semidaze, Orem weakening probably more than the heavier O'Neil. Rounds 180, 181, 182, and 183 ended with O'Neil pounding Orem almost at will. Then, in round 184, after landing desperation rights to O'Neil's nose, he simply slipped to the ground. When Orem became little more than a

---

Some Other Marathon Fights of the Period:
The little-known lightweight Billy Kelly fought Johnny Grady on May 7, 1866, a 118-round battle that lasted 3 hours, 10 minutes, and was declared a draw. A year and a half later, Kelly entered the ring against veteran Sam Collyer, who used his greater experience to batter Kelly unmercifully for 111 rounds. After seeing their favorite knocked down or thrown for the last 30 rounds, Kelly's seconds threw in the towel.

On March 27, 1879, at Chippewa Falls, Canada, Arthur Chambers and Johnny Clark battled for the lightweight title, Chambers winning after 136 rounds.

The longest recorded fight with gloves and 3-minute rounds took place in New Orleans on April 6–7, 1893, between Andy Bowen and Jack Burke. The fight was declared a draw after 110 rounds and 7 hours, 19 minutes, when both men were unable to continue.

punching bag for O'Neil in round 185, Nelson stepped in and declared the battle a draw. The verdict, as might be expected, was not a popular one.

LURE OF THE CHANNEL

The earliest endurance attraction for swimmers was "La Manche" (the sleeve), as the French call the 20.6-mile-wide English Channel. Since the early nineteenth century, men have tried to navigate the body of water on a bedstead, in a bathtub, in a canoe, kayak, and on a bale of hay. In 1963, one David Trapp made the journey in 7 hours, 45 minutes on an amphibious farm tractor.

The man who tried it on a bundle of straw, an English seaman named Hoskins, got all the way across on December 20, 1962, but his feat did not count with swimmers, of course. Neither did the May 1875 crossing of Professor Paul "Billy" Boyton, an American who was using the event as a means of demonstrating an inflatable swimming suit (see "Technology Rears Its Leg"). Twenty-seven-year-old Matthew Webb, the son of a successful surgeon who had taught himself to swim at the age of nine, came along three months after Boyton, buoyed by nothing but dreams of glory and the offer of fifty pounds from a newspaper entitled *Land and Water.*

By the time Webb finished training, however, wealthy members of the London Stock Exchange had agreed to donate several hundred pounds more if the young man were successful. Less happy results attended the selection of a best route, nearly every "expert" in the area having his own pet theory. The problem, naturally, was a severe tidal change, which could carry the swimmer parallel to the shoreline while little actual headway would be made. Webb decided to proceed from the Admiralty Pier at Dover, and land at Cape Griz-Nez, the closest point in France.

After one failure—which could have been contrived—during which he was carried almost due east by the tide, Webb dove from the steps of the pier and at the end of three hours, had covered almost 5½ miles. By that time, the flood tide was running up the Channel in an easterly direction; Webb was far enough out, however, so that a repeat of the earlier failure was avoided. The water was flat and a reporter from *Land and Water* took the opportunity to join Webb for ten minutes.

Progress continued at a steady one-mile-per-hour pace as darkness came on, but just as the tidal current was starting to reverse itself, about 9:00 P.M., Webb was stung by a jellyfish. He returned to the following boat and drank down several large swallows of brandy. Avoiding the patch of water in which he had encountered the jellyfish, he then swam strongly, making his best progress of the trip (three miles between 10:30 P.M. and 1:00 A.M.) beneath a moon in a cloudless sky. An hour later, after being visited by a paddle steamer and ogled by the passengers and crew, the first signs of fatigue began to show. At 3:00 A.M. Webb rolled over on his back and floated for five minutes, took some beef tea, then proceeded as quickly as possible, knowing that a tide change catching him too far from land could make the job of landing most difficult. By dawn, Webb's stroke rate had slowed from twenty-three to fifteen and he seemed irritated at the short, choppy waves off the coast of France. Drifting eastward, he moved away from Cape Griz-Nez toward Calais. By eight o'clock on the morning of August 25, 1875, it was obvious that Webb was exhausted, his progress during the next hour was barely one-half mile, and there was talk of aborting the attempt. But the young Shropshireman somehow managed to find hidden energy that allowed him to struggle ashore at 10:41 A.M. Feted and applauded, he continued to delight swimming enthusiasts and sports fans in general for another eight years, dying with his trunks on at age thirty-five.

THE 100-MILE SKATING MATCH

It was not exactly the World Series of long-distance ice skating; no official champion was recognized in 1881, but John Ennis, a champion pedestrian, had acquitted himself well as a skater in Chicago two years before, and

---

Other English Channel High-water Marks:
First to swim the Channel in both directions: E. H. Temme (*1927, 1934*)
First to swim in both directions during same year: William Barnie (*1951*)
First woman to swim the Channel: Gertrude Ederle (*1926*)
First American to swim the Channel: Henry Sullivan (*1923*)

First to swim the Channel underwater: Fred Baldasare (*1962*)
First to swim the Channel round trip in one session: Antonio Abertondo (*1961*)
Fastest time, round trip: Cindy Nicholas, *a 19-year-old Canadian woman, who made it back and forth in a total time of 19 hours, 55 minutes* (*1977*)
Fastest time, one way: Penny Dean (*1978*), *7 hours, 42 minutes*

Rudolph Goetz had done equally well in Milwaukee at about the same time. Thus a periodical of sports named *Spirit of the Times* offered a prize of $200 as well as a championship belt to the man who could finish first in a special 100-mile match race. The scene of the race was the Manhattan Polo Grounds rink, 110th Street between Fifth and Sixth avenues.

Their Previous Marks:
John Ennis: *100 miles in 11 hours, 37 minutes, 45 seconds; January 7, 1879, Chicago.*
Rudolph Goetz: *50 miles in 4 hours, 23 minutes, 43½ seconds; February 7, 1879, Milwaukee.*

The conditions would have horrified those of later days who insisted that times could not be declared official unless everything were perfect. Part of the ice at the rink had melted and then refrozen, creating alternate potholes of crusty ice and slush. In order to avoid these dangerous areas, the referee, W. B. Curtis, along with other officials present, decided to string ropes that would change the length of each lap from one-fifth mile to one-seventh mile. The problem was that everything was guesswork, especially when a snowstorm arrived during the race, necessitating the racers' swinging wide of or inside gangs of maintenance men with brooms.

Those who attended did not seem to mind very much. The 9th Regiment band enlivened matters by playing popular airs, and when it became dark, the few spectators who remained had the eerie pleasure of seeing one of America's first electrically illuminated sports events, thanks to several large reflecting lamps that were turned on.

John Ennis took an early lead, skating the first 10 miles in a bit less than 50 minutes, despite falling at the seventh mile and cutting his left wrist. Goetz, ahead at first, soon lost his lead and was even heard to express his wish to give up the race. But his supporters urged him to continue, even though he was 2 miles behind at the 20-mile mark. Later John Ennis jammed his thumb in another fall, and at the completion of 85 miles suddenly sat down on the ice. "Immediately all was excitement," one reporter wrote, "and the rumor went around that Ennis had broken down. However, he had only broken a shoestring." Leaping to his feet once again, Ennis finished his 100 miles shortly after Goetz completed 93. In the spirit of the times, Ennis "ran at once over to Goetz, shook hands with him heartily, and told him how much it pleased

him to contend with such a gritty, plucky fellow."

A 100-Mile Skating Postscript:
A dozen years after John Ennis made his 100 miles (or slightly less) in 10 hours, 56 minutes, 42½ seconds, another "100-mile championship of America" was held at Cove Pond near Stamford, Connecticut, on January 23, 1893. The winner, Joe Donoghue, 18, completed the distance in 7 hours, 11 minutes, 38.2 seconds.

STEVENS AROUND THE WORLD
For whatever it is worth, Thomas Stevens in 1884–86 became the first person to ride a bicycle "around the world," that being everyplace there was land. In all, Stevens—who also traveled across Russia on a horse—pumped his high-wheeler more than 13,500 miles in the process, taking his vehicle across lands then traveled by no Americans.

Because he was the first, of course, Stevens left in a burst of glory, and soon his countrymen were reading of his exploits in *Outing,* a sporting magazine, as well as the daily newspapers. Leaving his native San Francisco in April, he reached Boston in August, secured the financial backing of Colonel A. A. Pope, a prominent bicycle manufacturer, and then sailed for Europe.

Traveling across Europe was pleasant for Stevens; the roads were generally better than in the United States, and there was no lack of mechanics able to help him when his five-foot wheel broke down, as it frequently did. Asia was another matter. While in Persia, for example, he became caught in a blizzard. "Arrayed in a summer suit with sun helmet, cycling stockings and gear," he wrote, "I had to ford through snow drifts, when the cold was sufficient to form icicles on eyelashes and transform the mustache into a cake of ice."

In China, he ran into not only muddy roads but also a particularly severe outburst of anti-foreignism. One night he was forced to huddle in a bamboo grove, clutching his bicycle while angry mobs searched for him. Sanitary conditions were poor in many spots, and police in Afghanistan arrested him at one point for violating a ban against all foreign visitors. The "imprisonment" turned out to be quite genial, Stevens being provided with good food and a pleasant sendoff after the minor scuffle.

When Stevens arrived at San Francisco in January 1887, he discovered that he was quite famous and that a craze for cycling had swept the entire United States.

Some Other Cyclists' Deeds at This Time: *Riding continuously for 24 hours, H. L. Cortis in 1883 established the first bicycle record by covering 200 miles, 300 yards during that time.*

In September 1883, G. M. Hendrie of Springfield, Massachusetts, and W. G. Rowe engaged in a road race that was billed as "for the national championship." Hendrie, by winning, became the first national champion.

THE SIX-DAY BICYCLE RACES

Four years after Thomas Stevens popularized the bicycle, Americans eagerly awaited the beginning of the first six-day race at Madison Square Garden. Cyclists had been going round and round London's Agricultural Hall as early as 1879, but the Yankee version had had to wait until enough persons became "wheel cranks" to guarantee financial success. In 1891 that moment arrived. It was truly an international occasion, contestants coming from all over Europe to compete with America's favorites. Bets were made and the crowd cheered as a band played "Rule Britannia" for the British entrants, "St. Patrick's Day" for the Irish, *"Wacht am Rhein"* for the Germans, "Scots Wha Hae" for the pair of Scots, and "Yankee Doodle" for the half-dozen Americans.

According to the rules, each man was an entity unto himself. He could ride or rest as he pleased, but could not be relieved by a partner (this rule was later changed). Under these conditions, the first American six-day race at Madison Square Garden was more a true test of endurance than later contests.

It began with William Lamb of England taking an early lead. Not long afterward, the first bit of excitement occurred when Alfred Robb, also of England, took a nasty fall and was forced to retire. Then O'Flanaghan "began to show signs of distress early in the day, and so did Wood, the Englishman with the ponderous legs. Each dismounted and took frequent rests. It was evident, too, that Lumsden was not right. He has the reputation of being a good stayer, but he jumped off the machine several times to take a rest. . . ."

Compared to later six-day races, which featured collisions and angry flare-ups, the 1891 event was comparatively tame. Detroit-born William "Plugger" Martin, riding an old-style bicycle with the high front wheel, soon took the lead and fought off challenges by Charles Ashinger for the rest of the week. Not far behind was Albert Shock of Germany, who was described as "by far the ugliest rider in

the race, but . . . a wheelman of the 'git that' order." One minor embarrassment did take place on the third day of the race, when a deputy sheriff appeared with a writ of attachment for the vehicle belonging to J. S. Prince, an American rider who apparently had some heavy debts. Manager T. W. Eck somehow managed to smooth things over before the law officer was able to confiscate Prince's cycle as payment.

Meanwhile, moving along at a speed of approximately 12½ miles an hour, Martin completed his one-thousandth mile on the fourth day of the event, finally logging a total of 1,466 miles, 6 laps, to defeat Ashinger. For his victory, Martin received more than $1,200

The next year, Ashinger, riding a high-wheeler, won the event, but in 1893, Albert Shock won astride the new-style "safety" bicycle, with equal-sized wheels. That was the end of the Thomas Stevens type of vehicle in major competition.

The End of the One-man System: *Came in 1898, when Charlie Miller, with 2,093.4 miles, set such a blistering pace that he nearly wrecked the men behind him trying to keep close to him (some, in fact, ended up in the hospital following collapses from exhaustion). The promoters of six-day endurance races, facing public censure of the event, then changed the rules so that teams of two men raced instead of single entrants.*

HOOPER AND THE HUDSON

Long-distance swimmers continued to fascinate Americans during the decades following Matthew Webb's conquest of the English Channel. Because of its length as well as its proximity to New York City, the Hudson River soon became a favorite highway for daring young men and women trying to display their talents. One young Englishman undertaking the journey from Troy to New York City, a distance of 165 miles, was James Hooper, who set out in early September 1897.

For the first 20 hours of his trip, Hooper remained in the water without a rest, accomplishing 37 miles with the help of a moderate current. Arriving at Castleton, he seemed in good shape, but at New Baltimore he was in such an exhausted condition he had to be lifted bodily from the water. Some thought he would fail to complete the trip and thus lose the wager of $500 he had at stake, but Hooper was soon revived by a rubdown and announced that he was ready to continue. Eleven days after leaving Troy, he arrived at the Audubon Yacht Clubhouse, 125 Street and North River, New York City. The next day, after swimming from there to Pier 1, the Battery, his mission was accomplished. When he left Troy, Hooper weighed 161 pounds; his weight was 128½ pounds at the Battery.

AMERICA'S MARATHON

Endurance running in the United States did not begin with the first Boston Marathon of 1897, but that event, inaugurated one year after the revived international Olympic Games, soon became the most famous and prestigious race in America. The distance from the Hopkinton, Massachusetts, starting line to the Lenox Hotel finish is exactly 26 miles, 385 yards, a "standard" length that was established in 1908. The winner of the first event was J. J. McDermott of New York City, who completed the circuit in 2 hours, 55 minutes, 10 seconds, which turned out to be the slowest winning time in the history of the Boston Marathon. Successfully received, the race was held every year until 1918, when it was canceled because of World War I. The following year it was revived and continued uninterrupted—even through World War II— until the present day. Traditionally, the Boston Marathon has been held on the third Tuesday of April, but there have been exceptions, as in 1968, when the event was run on Patriot's Day, a Friday. One of the beauties of the marathon is that older runners stand a better-than-even chance of winning. Certainly the most remarkable runner over the years was Clarence DeMar, of Melrose, Massachusetts, who competed in the 1909 Boston Marathon against the advice of his physician, who predicted he would die of heart failure. Two years later, DeMar set a new BM record, won the event a total of seven times—his last in 1930 at age 42—and outlived the doctor as well. In 1951, DeMar started and completed the one-thousandth road race of his career.

Boston Marathon Highlights:
1911—Clarence DeMar runs event in 2:21:39.6, lowering winning time by more than 7 minutes.
1921—Frank Zuna sets new mark of 2:18:57.6.
1922—Clarence DeMar lowers time to 2:18:10, a record that stands for 34 years.
1956—Aniti Viskari, Finland, sets new mark of 2:14:14.
1969—Yoshiaki Unetani, Japan, lowers time to 2:13:39.
1970—Ron Hill, England, lowers time still further to 2:10:30.

THE LADY CYCLISTS

With the growing popularity of cycling during the 1890s—one of the few sports in which women were reluctantly "allowed" to participate—it was inevitable that both men and women would attempt to set new endurance records. The "century" run became a popular term (cycling nonstop for 100 miles), and cycling enthusiasts inevitably asked each other how many centuries they had to their credit. And when the century became old hat, cyclists simply started putting them together in the manner of a young man named Miller, who pedaled 2100 miles in six days during the winter of 1898–99.

Some Other Marks of Note, Circa 1899:
On September 16, 1897, M. Cordang of Holland rode his bicycle nonstop for 24 hours, covering a distance of 616 miles, an average of 25.7 miles per hour.
From January 1 to September 7, 1898, E. S. (Teddy) Edwards rode a century a day, thus covering the distance around the earth's equator, 25,000 miles.

When the young women entered the endurance derbies, there was a certain amount of understandable resistance, but for the most part they were applauded for their pluck and determination.

During the last two years of the nineteenth century, three young women attracted a great deal of attention in the eastern United States by engaging in a modest series of century-run contests. The first to start the wheel rolling was Miss Irene Brush, of Brooklyn, who rode 400 miles in 48 hours. Miss Jane C. Yatman, also of Brooklyn, then rolled off 500 miles in 58 hours, and Jane Lindsay rode 600 in 72.

In September 1899, the rivalry continued. "On the smooth macadam roads of Long Island a little woman on a bicycle flitted hither and thither," reported the New York *Times,* ". . . bent on accomplishing a task which the average woman, or the average man, for that matter, would no more undertake than she or he would attempt to fly. The little woman on the wheel was Miss Jane C. Yatman. . . . The task which she has set for herself this time is that of riding 700 miles in 84 hours or less."

The 125-pound woman, paced by men and women who shared her enthusiasm for cycling, rolled off her first century in about 9½ hours, took a rest, then continued the assault on Jane Lindsay's record run. Moving along at speeds as high as 14 miles per hour and as low as 10 miles per hour, she stuck to her task, even during the final hundred miles, which was run during a drenching rainstorm. Then, wet, shivering, but happy, she paused at West's Hotel before a crowd of cheering friends and admirers, having covered 700 miles in 81 hours, 5 minutes. During the 3½-day experience, she rested less than 2 hours. All women's endurance records were broken, the newspapers noted happily.

What Does One Eat During an 81-hour Bicycle Ride?

Miss Yatman's fare was as follows:
4 chickens (in broth)
2 pounds oatmeal
24 eggs
½ gallon cold tea
1 gallon milk
24 ounces beef extract
½ gallon coffee
1 quart cream
1 pony brandy
Presumably the ingredients were well stirred by the time the event was over.

Naturally, Jane Lindsay was not about to stand for that. Less than a month elapsed before she announced that she would scale the next obstacle—namely, eight centuries. Repairing to West's Hotel at Valley Stream, Long Island, where she was greeted by a wall plaque commemorating rival Yatman's feat of September 1899, Jane Lindsay started on her task.

Obviously a headstrong, quixotic type, Jane Lindsay started the contest wearing a modest skirt, but when she found that it interfered with her pedaling, she switched to a sweater and an old pair of her husband's trousers. Riding a good deal at night, she outfitted her bicycle with an acetylene lamp so arranged that she could turn it in any direction she liked. According to the New York *Tribune*, one of her primary joys during the nearly four days she was "awheel" was turning the glaring light into the eyes of passing farmers when they least expected it.

Her impressions during the ride varied considerably. At first she reported that the country seemed very gay and "beautiful in its autumn tints," but as she progressed, everything started to appear black to her. At times, she said, she was very dizzy and felt as though she would fall off her bicycle. By the end of the third century, she suffered from severe pains in her wrists and knees, and when rain came, changing the dirt road into a slippery quagmire that threatened to throw her at every turning, her miseries increased. But she refused to quit or even slow down. Regularly,

she pulled to the side of the road, had some liquid refreshment, changed her linen, was vigorously rubbed down, and proceeded. Finally, after 91 hours, 48 minutes, she finished the 800-mile journey. She then returned to the hotel, where she tore down the Yatman plaque, ate a porterhouse steak and a huge piece of pie, and fell into a deep and rewarding sleep.

Why Did She Do It?

"Why did not her friends prevent her from making such a ride?" asked one wheelman of another at Valley Stream yesterday. "Oh!" replied the other, who pretended to know what he was talking about. "She is redheaded, and you could not have stopped her with an ax."
New York Tribune, *October 19, 1899*

NEW YORK TO PARIS

The odds were against a majority, or even a handful, of the starters finishing the race, for in 1908 the automobile was looked upon as much too undependable to travel very far. The idea of an endurance race from New York, across the United States, Russia, Europe, and to Paris was so inconceivable that some bets were made that not a single car would finish.

The total land distance of the race would be 14,000 miles, most of it on roadbeds that were unpaved at best and primitive at worst.

America's entry was a 4-cylinder, 60-horse-power Thomas Flyer driven by Montague Roberts, with George Schuster as mechanic. Others included three French cars, one Italian, and a German Protos. The group departed Times Square on February 13, 1908, to the cheers of a sizable audience. The itinerary called for crossing the continent to San Francisco, where the cars would be shipped by boat to Valdez, Alaska. After motoring to Nome, the contestants were expected to cross the Bering Sea by whatever means possible (including driving on the ice), thence across Siberia's wastes to Paris.

It was not long before the first dropout occurred, the French Sizaire-Naudin, a 15-horsepower, 1-cylinder model, petering out in upstate New York. The American Thomas took a quick lead, heading West to Chicago through a snowstorm, but driver Roberts soon tired of the race, turning over the car to mechanic Schuster at Cheyenne. By the time he arrived at San Francisco, Schuster was 12 days ahead of the other four cars, the French Moto-Bloc having stalled in Iowa mud, and the German Protos developing mechanical problems in Idaho.

While Schuster and the Thomas followed the prearranged schedule, by boat to Alaska, the others sailed directly for Vladivostok, thereby incurring 15-day penalties. (The German Protos added another 15 days by being shipped from Idaho to the West Coast via flatcar.) Finding the Alaskan roads impassable, Schuster caught a boat for Japan, crossed to Vladivostok, and pulled even with the others on May 22, 1908. But because of the penalties, he had a 15-day advantage on the Italian Zust, the French De Dion, and 30-day advantage over the German Protos. When the French and Italian cars dropped out, it became a two-car race.

The conditions were worthy of a Mack Sennett comedy, the cars having to plow through swamps and even follow the tracks of the Trans-Siberian Railway. On one occasion, Schuster drove into a tunnel only to hear the whistle of an oncoming train. He had barely time to back out and down an embankment before the engine roared past.

After stripping its gears for the third time, the American entry fell behind at Moscow, but when the Protos rolled into Paris on July 26, it was only four days ahead of the Thomas and Schuster. That meant that the U.S. car had won by 26 days. Two of the six cars had actually finished the grueling trip, thereby proving to all but a few diehards that even the primitive cars of that era could be pushed farther than most men could imagine.

The Statistics of 1908:

By traveling 14,000 miles in approximately 5½ months, the two cars in the 1908 endurance race averaged 84 miles a day, or about 3.5 miles an hour.

THE SWIMMERS AGAIN

During the summer of 1911, endurance swimming experienced a revival, thanks perhaps to the efforts of Englishman William T. Burgess's continuous assault on the English Channel. Since 1904, Burgess had averaged two attempts each year, but it was not until 1911 that he swam the Channel on his fourteenth attempt, thus becoming only the second person to accomplish the feat in 36 years.

Americans at home had no lack of targets. One was the enticing 20-mile expanse of water from Sandy Hook, New Jersey, to New York, or vice versa. Like the English Channel, the area was swept by strong tides, which often forced the swimmer to move in a tiring zigzag course, or even worse, be dragged away from land, finding it impossible to accomplish the task. Nevertheless, one endurance swimmer who felt he could turn the trick was

Charles Durburow of Philadelphia, who held several swimming records. Going from the Battery, New York, to Sandy Hook had never been accomplished, and for that very reason Durburow decided to try it.

Another Who Tried the Sandy Hook–New York Swim:

Was 22-year-old Agnes Beckwith, an English woman who astounded the world by being the first of her sex to swim a significant length of the Thames in 1875. On June 30, 1883, having arrived in America on a tour, she jumped into the water off Sandy Hook, bound for Coney Island and accompanied by the steam launch Bonnie Doon.

For a while all went well. Swimming at 24 strokes per minute, Agnes made steady progress for 2½ hours before running into a thunderstorm. The seas became so high she could hardly move, but she continued to struggle for more than 2 hours before being taken from the water against her will. At that point, she had covered more than three quarters of the distance.

Unfortunately, Durburow's timing did him in. He hoped to take advantage of a strong ebb tide to carry him the second half of the distance, but he mistimed the current and was caught on a vicious flood tide instead. After battling in the water 1½ miles from his goal, he was forced to give up.

Three weeks later, a 17-year-old swimmer named Rose Pitonof announced her intention of going from the pier at Twenty-sixth Street, Manhattan, to the Steeplechase Pier, Coney Island, a distance of about 17 miles. Having warmed up by swimming from Charlestown, Massachusetts, to Boston Light—a distance never conquered by a woman—the native of Dorchester, Massachusetts, approached her task with confidence. At 9:20 A.M. on August 13, 1911, she dove into the water, and swimming smoothly with the benefit of a correctly timed tide, neared Coney Island 8 hours later. Having heard of the young woman's plan, a capacity crowd awaited her. "From the time she first made her appearance around Norton's Point," one reporter wrote, "thousands gathered along the shore to watch her progress and cheer her on to victory, and all bathing was suspended for practically the last hour of her swim. At Steeplechase Park the crowd swarmed on and around the pier to such an extent that the attendants were totally unable to hold the people in check, and it required ten minutes from the time the girl walked along the sandy beach at the end of her long swim until she was in her dressing room, less than 200 feet away."

Endurance Note from Abroad—1913:
"London, August 30—Tom Burrows, the Australian all-around athlete and champion club-swinger, collapsed at the Earl's Court exhibition tonight in an attempt to swing 3½-pound clubs 100 hours continuously. He succeeded in keeping the clubs in motion for 97 hours and 35 minutes, and then dropped over.

"Last April Burrows swung a pair of 3-pound, 6-ounce Indian clubs for more than 100 hours, but later became delirious."

ALSO IN 1913—CHINNING AD NAUSEAM

It was in a Brockton, Massachusetts, theater that Anton Lewis, a professional strongman, grabbed a high bar and proceeded to chin himself 78 times without stopping. According to experts, 20 chin-ups is an excellent performance by an athlete.

ENDURANCE BOWLING

At about the time of World War I, bowling enthusiasts conceived the idea of staging endurance contests, one of the early games taking place at Fulling's Hall, Brooklyn, in March 1914. Seven teams of two men each rolled for 12 hours continuously, the winning pair of players scoring 3,792 pins.

In January 1915, at Sioux City, Iowa, bowler Darrell Hamlet began rolling balls at 9:00 A.M. one Sunday and continued to bowl for 36 hours without a pause. During that time he was able to roll 194 games, his top score coming in game No. 153, when he scored a total of 256. A week later, at Elk Point, South Dakota, Hamlet returned to the lanes, this time combining endurance with speed. The object—to see how rapidly 100 games could be rolled. Working with smooth precision, Hamlet managed to average 183 pins a game during the 9 hours, 56 minutes he required. He thus broke the 1908 record for 100 games, held jointly by Frank Griffith and J. F. Upson, who, rolling at Hartford, Connecticut, required 13 hours to complete 100 games.

COAST-TO-COAST MOTORCYCLING

Soon after the turn of the century, when motorcycles came into use, their drivers decided to see how long and far they could go. Accordingly, the first known endurance run was made by George Hendee of Springfield, Massachusetts, on July 4, 1902, when he sputtered all the way from New York City to Boston. A second run, of 250 miles, was made from New York to Waltham, Massachusetts, in 16 hours, 30 minutes.

After this, along came the most famous early motorcyclist, Erwin G. (Cannonball) Baker, who specialized in breaking his own records. On May 3, 1914, Baker left San Diego, California, in an effort to break the fastest time for crossing the United States by a motor-driven vehicle. Driving the entire distance—3,500 miles—by himself, Baker arrived at the West Forty-second Street ferry, New York City, on May 14, thus establishing a record-breaking time of 11 days, 11 hours, 18 minutes. Eventually Baker lowered that mark to 8 days, 21 hours, 16 minutes.

Baker also established records for most

Bowling Endurance Update:
Records are made to be broken, of course, but in 1960 bowler Don Newport relegated the marathon efforts of Darrell Hamlet and others to the scrap heap by rolling 1,000 games during a four-day period. Those who kept statistics of the Fort Lauderdale event reported that Newport lifted the ball 18,647 times, knocked down 123,205 pins, bowled a high game of 212, and a low of 1 pin.

In 1961 Frank Mazzei bowled steadily for 110 hours, 30 minutes at Roslindale, Massachusetts, claiming a new marathon record. A 24-year-old ex-Navy man, Mazzei

bowled with both right and left hands, staying awake 6 days and nights while knocking down a total of 120,209 pins. He made 115 strikes, 2,903 spares, averaging 119 pins per game. Mazzei also lost 20 pounds during the marathon, his waist size shrinking from 40 inches to 36 inches. His feet, however, swelled from a size 10½ to 13.

Fourteen years later, 46-year-old Richard Dewey of Omaha, Nebraska, bowled 1,472 consecutive games in 114½ hours, June 5–10, 1975. His average score was 126 pins.

miles covered during 24 hours in January 1916, when he raced 930 miles in a single day (an average of 38.75 miles per hour), thereby shattering the mark of 775 miles set by H. H. Collier at Canningtown, England, on May 5, 1909.

The Previous Records—May 1914:
Crossing United States by automobile: 15 days, 10 hours
Crossing United States by motorcycle: 20 days, 9 hours, 1 minute

---

PARADE OF GOOSE EGGS

Baseball players, generally speaking, have little desire—compared to swimmers or runners or gymnasts, for example—to show how long they can participate at their specialty. The object is to score enough runs to win while getting the opposition out as expeditiously as possible. Thus a marathon in baseball is considered, except for the pitchers, a sign of futility, ineptness, dullness.

Unlike other sports—except a football Super Bowl, perhaps—baseball allows a contest to continue forever if need be, and there have been more than a few games in the history of the sport when it must have seemed, to both participant and spectator, that forever had arrived.

During the early years of the century, the American League record for length was established on September 1, 1906, when the Red Sox needed 24 innings to beat the White Sox, 4–1. In the National League, the early record was 22 innings, set on August 22, 1917, Brooklyn defeating Pittsburgh in that marathon contest, 6–5.

Those overlong games, however, were before the Brooklyn Dodgers and Boston Braves met on May 1, 1920. After 4 scoreless innings, the Dodgers pushed across a single run, which was matched in the Boston sixth when Walton Cruise tripled and Tony Boeckel singled. Rabbit Maranville followed with a double, but Boeckel was tagged out at the plate when he tried to score from first base.

After that, pitchers Leon Cadore of Brooklyn and Joe Oeschger of the Braves took command of the situation—a bit too well. A total of 20 more innings passed without a score until Umpire McCormick decided to call it a day at the end of 26 innings. According to baseball legend, there was at least one protest, from Brooklyn shortstop Ivy Olson. "Come on, just one more inning," he said to McCormick, "so we can say we played the equivalent of three full games in a day."

That was not the end of the marathon, at least not for Brooklyn. Having participated in the longest major-league game of all time, the Dodgers returned to their native grounds for a Sunday game with the Philadelphia Phillies while Boston took the day off. As luck would have it, the lowly Phillies turned out to be tough that day. Led by former Dodger Casey Stengel, who got a pair of hits and made a sensational one-handed catch of a liner, Philadelphia jumped to a 3–0 lead in the top of the seventh inning. The Dodgers got back two in the bottom half, then scored the tying run in the ninth on Zack Wheat's home run. The game went to the thirteenth inning before the Phillies pushed across what proved to be the winning run on Jack Miller's sacrifice fly.

Thirty-nine innings in two days is plenty, but that still was not the end of the Dodger martyrdom. Back to Boston they went, where the script seemed suspiciously similar to that of two days before. On the mound for Brooklyn was Sherry Smith; for Boston, Dana Fillingim. Both went along for four innings without allowing a run. In the Brooklyn fifth, Smith singled, took third base on a hit by Ivy Olson, and scored on Jimmy Johnston's single. Boston returned with a single run in the fifth inning, and the marathon of May 1 started all over again.

Once again both starting pitchers were superb. Not until the nineteenth inning, when an outfielder named John L. Sullivan singled, moved to third on Walter Holke's safety to right, then scored on a hit by Tony Boeckel, did Boston break the tie. Brooklyn's marathon —58 innings in a bit more than two days— came to an end. Having played the equivalent of 6½ games during that time, the Dodgers had a total of no wins and two losses to show for their trouble.

Marathon Baseball Update:
Since 1920, there have been numerous overtime games in the major leagues, of course. Some of these include:
On June 24, 1962, the New York Yankees and Detroit Tigers battled for 22 innings before New York won, 9–7. The game took 7 hours to play.
On May 31, 1964, the New York Mets and San Francisco Giants played a 23-inning game, won by the Giants, 8–6, that required 7 hours, 23 minutes to play. (It was the second game of a double-header.)
On September 12, 1974, the New York Mets and St. Louis Cardinals played a night game that lasted 25 innings, the Cardinals winning, 4–3.

BACK TO THE WATER

The 1920s, which saw a wealth of great swimmers in Johnny Weissmuller, Norman Ross, Sybil Bauer, Duke Kahanamoku, Gertrude Ederle, Lottie Schoemmel, and Millie Gade, was another era of long-distance events. After Millie Gade (later Millie Gade Corson) swam from Albany to New York, a distance of 153 miles, in a bit over six days, and Gertrude Ederle conquered the English Channel, millionaire businessman William Wrigley, Jr., decided the time was ripe to stage a highly publicized marathon event in the United States.

It turned out that Wrigley owned a large island off the coast of Southern California, Santa Catalina, which was situated 22 miles from the mainland. Promotion began late in the fall of 1926 for the "World's Greatest Sporting Contest for One of the Greatest Prizes Ever Hung Up," otherwise known as the Wrigley Marathon. First prize was $25,000, plus $15,000 for the first woman to finish, it being decided beforehand that a woman's winning the whole bundle would be highly unlikely. So successful was the advance publicity that more than 1,000 persons entered. The number was quickly reduced to a more manageable figure when the true facts of swimming such a distance in 52° temperatures were revealed. Even so, the best swimmers of the nation—except Weissmuller and Ederle—signed up, including Henry Sullivan and Charles Toth, the first American men to conquer the English Channel; 240-pound Norman Ross, a strong swimmer considered the favorite; and Lottie Schoemmel, a New York lifeguard who trained by swimming around Manhattan Island in 14 hours, 11 minutes.

Fear of the low water temperatures (the contest was held in January) prompted some of the swimmers to take all manner of precautions. Lottie Schoemmel, for example, put her faith in 15 pounds of bear grease as insulation against the cold; another contestant, Philip Moore, had encased himself in a half-dozen long-john undershirts, each heavily greased, three pairs of heavy winter drawers tied at the ankles with ropes, and topped off the whole costume with an inch-thick coating of rendered beef suet. When the gun sounded for the beginning of the race, he sank like a stone. Seven minutes after the Wrigley Marathon started, he was fished from the water, barely alive.

Most of the other swimmers were hardly more fortunate. Lottie Schoemmel succumbed to leg cramps before sunset and by midnight no more than 12 of the 102 original entrants were in the water. The favorite, Norman Ross, made a poor decision early in the race by heading for the northern end of the island and was victimized by an offshore tide within a few miles of Point Vicente.

It remained for a complete unknown, a 17-year-old Canadian named George Young, to win the first Catalina swim. Having driven partway to California on a third-hand motorcycle that broke down in Arizona, Young had hitchhiked to the starting line, but said later he had no doubts that he would win. Shortly after he struggled from the water at 3:08 A.M. on January 16, 1927, he was another instant hero of the 1920s.

Whatever Happened to George Young?

A trusting soul, George succumbed to the lure of California agentry, hiring a "business manager" immediately after winning the Wrigley Marathon (the agent thereupon extracted his 40 per cent of the winnings). In 1931, Young returned to the water to win another marathon sponsored by Wrigley, this a 21-mile swim at Toronto. In 1947, after a long period of relative obscurity, George Young tried making a comeback at the age of 37. He failed, then took a job with the Department of Parks and Recreation at Niagara Falls. He died in 1972.

Lottie Schoemmel, meanwhile, undaunted by the failure of her bear grease, looked to other goals. In March 1928 she took herself to the Deauville Pool at Miami Beach in order to beat the world's indoor endurance swimming record of 31 hours, set in 1881 by Edith Johnson of England. She succeeded, too, lasting 32 hours and adding another record to a list of 27 marks she claimed to have.

MEANWHILE, ANOTHER WOMAN

There were few sports at which Eleonora Sears did not excel. An expert horsewoman, she also played tennis, golf, and was a strong long-distance walker. Four times she was the women's national doubles champion, twice a finalist in the national tennis singles, and she also found time to be president of the National Women's Squash Racquet Association. By 1928, Miss Sears was well into her forties but she had not given up long-distance walking.

Her mission on April 23 of that year was to see how rapidly she could travel the 74 miles between Newport, Rhode Island, and Boston. Dressed in a black woolen skirt and jacket, thin woolen stockings with short socks pulled over them, heavy shoes that were cut low, and a sports hat of white felt, she set out, displaying the brisk stride that could carry her the length of a mile in 12 or 13 minutes if she so desired. On this occasion, accompanied by three Harvard seniors who took turns serving as pacers, Miss Sears started from the Casino in Newport at exactly 4:00 A.M. Seventeen hours, 15 minutes later, undeterred by a downpour of cold rain, she ended the walk before her home at 122 Beacon Street, Boston. At 4.29 miles per hour, she had averaged a mile every 13.9 minutes.

Eleonora Sears' Previous Jaunts:
1912—*Walked from Burlingame to Del Monte, California, 109 miles, averaging 3 miles per hour.*
1925—*Walked from Providence to Boston, 47 miles, in 10½ hours.*
1926—*Walked from Providence to Boston, 47 miles, in 9 minutes, 53 seconds.*

SKIING—1929
Could a skier make 25 miles a day for 20 days? That was the question facing Canadians Kennelm Hulme and Jack Forbes in late January 1929. Some friends were willing to wager that it could not be done, offering $250 to the two men if they could ski from Timmins, Ontario, to Toronto in that time.

On January 29, the two men left Timmins, and by arriving at Toronto on February 17, collected their winnings with a day to spare.

TENNIS
On January 7, 1936, women's tennis champion Helen Wills Moody and Howard Kinsey, a former Davis Cup player, volleyed a ball 2,001 times without a miss. The marathon took 1 hour, 18 minutes. Both participants said they experienced eye weariness after about 1,100 shots but that it gradually wore off. The volleying may have continued indefinitely except that Mr. Kinsey had to teach a lesson.

THE GREATEST SITTER OF THEM ALL
Sitting on a flagpole may not require a great deal of athletic co-ordination, but it does require endurance and strength, and was undoubtedly an American spectator sport of the 1920s and 1930s. The greatest of them all was Alvin "Shipwreck" Kelly, who following a career as shipbuilder, steeplejack, and prizefighter, took up the art of endurance flagpole sitting.

Kelly didn't invent the gimmick, flagpole (or column) sitting going all the way back to the days of St. Simeon Stylites and St. Anthony, both of whom retreated vertically upward as a means of demonstrating their reli-

gious fervor. What Shipwreck Kelly did was popularize the art, and for more than a decade he reigned as the king of American pole-sitters. Unlike others, Kelly's appurtenances were spare—no tents or platforms for him. His perch was usually nothing broader than 13 inches. To maintain his balance, he fashioned thumbholes in the side of the pole, and he even learned the technique of sleeping with his little fingers between his teeth, so that that the slightest movement to one side or the other would cause a twinge of pain and awaken him.

A Pre-Kelly Sitter:
In the early twentieth century, Shipwreck Kelly was preceded by 27-year-old Henry Vogel, who on July 29, 1906, clad in gray flannel underwear, clambered to the top of a 30-foot flagpole at 140 Ridge Street, New York City. According to one account, the mentally as well as physically unbalanced Vogel's only words were "nevermore, nevermore." Finally a police officer named Clark conceived the idea that if everyone stopped looking at Vogel, he would come down. He chased the crowd away and made sure that all curtains were drawn in the neighborhood. After that, Vogel did descend and was taken to the psychopathic ward at Bellevue Hospital.

Shipwreck's first major ascent was in 1924, when he sat above a Los Angeles movie theater for 13 hours, 13 minutes. He was an instant success, other theaters and hotels and amusement parks beckoning for his services. The sky was literally the limit.

Scorning superstition, Kelly often used No. 13 in his feats. In 1927, for example, he perched atop a hotel in St. Louis for 7 days, 13 hours, 13 minutes, 13 stories above the ground. He then moved to the St. Francis Hotel in Newark, staying aloft for 13 days, thereby beating his own record. For that episode he received $6,000. In December 1929 he appeared atop the Paramount Hotel in New York for 13 days, 13 hours, 13 minutes, but ironically only 13 copies of a pamphlet he had prepared about himself were sold to the crowd below.

The year after this triumph, Kelly announced that he intended to beat the endurance record of the flying Hunter brothers, who had flown nonstop for 23 days at Chicago. Ascending a pole at the Boardwalk and Steel Pier in Atlantic City in June 1930, Kelly broke the record by July 13. "Kelly sent down word that he was feeling fine and had no intention of coming down," one reporter wrote. "At least not until Saturday, when he will have been aloft 28 days. He is of the opinion that a 28-day record will be unbeatable for a long time. . . ."

By this time, Kelly was receiving 100 letters a day, indicating that the public loved him and wanted more. So Kelly gave them more, remaining aloft even longer. Three thunderstorms and one hailstorm later, he had remained on the pole 1,177 hours—nearly 50 days. He then decided to call it quits.

Shipwreck Kelly's Lifetime Statistics:
Total time aloft—20,613 hours (more than 2 years, 4 months)
including—57 hours of snow
—1,400 hours of sleet and rain
—210 hours of below-zero temperature
Off the pole, he also survived 5 sea disasters, 2 airplane accidents, 3 automobile wrecks, and 1 train wreck.

Shortly before descending, however, the fastidious Kelly, in the words of one reporter, "had a complete tonsorial overhauling this morning when one of the prettiest of lady barbers went aloft and for an hour and a half gave him everything from a haircut to a manicure, including the liberal application of many aromatic scents known to her profession. The bill was $4.25 and Kelly, generous to a fault, gave the girl a $5.00 bill and gallantly waved aside her proffer of change."

That was literally the high point of Shipwreck Kelly's career. Haunted by imitators who used his name—he was once served papers for a nonpayment suit sworn out against one of the bogus Kellys—and finding money considerably tighter during the Depression than during the glittering 1920s, the real

Endurance Golf—Part One:
June 27, 1930—Playing continuously from 4:30 A.M. until late afternoon, Leo De Korn completed 144 holes of golf on the Purchase (N.Y.) Country Club Course. He used 925 strokes and averaged 5 minutes per hole.
July 27, 1931—At Boonville, New York, Jack Milburn played 280 holes between 3:30 A.M., and 8:25 P.M., a marathon record for a single day.

Shipwreck Kelly was reduced to performing brief stints atop a Wild West saloon in a shabby section of New York. He even tried copyrighting his name in order to cut down the competition, but such a tactic proved virtually useless. "I once had seventeen other Shipwreck Kellys arrested," he complained. "But what's the use? There's always more."

THE SUMMER OF 1930—WHEN ENDURANCE REIGNED

It Started in Hackensack.

The title for a B movie or camp musical? Possibly. But until something better comes along, the town of Hackensack, New Jersey, will be remembered most as the place where America's endurance madness of 1930 began.

No one can say for certain how or why a significant portion of the population went slightly balmy that summer while the rest stood by shouting encouragement. Certainly the mania was a natural culmination of the 1920s' craving for doing things longer and farther. During that decade the first Americans conquered the English Channel; a pair of "bunion derbies" saw runners plod from one coast to the other; Shipwreck Kelly's endurance flagpole sitting drew large crowds; even stunt-flying pilots turned their attention to the problems of midair fueling so they could break the record for nonstop flying.

The Hunter brothers' remaining aloft for 553 hours could have been the trigger for that midsummer madness. Exhausted and well oiled from a leaking engine, they descended at Chicago on July 4, 1930, as thousands cheered. Two days later, a quartet of Hackensack boys, led by Jimmy Dooley, announced that they intended to beat the existing record for keeping a bicycle in continuous motion—5 days, set by four Indiana boys in 1929. Riding in 6-hour shifts, young Dooley and his friends established a new mark on Friday, July 11, at 7:00 P.M., but it had been too easy. They decided to see how long they could continue.

A modest chain reaction of competing cyclists quickly pedaled to action. In New Brunswick and Little Ferry, towns adjoining Hackensack, teams were formed and started out after the record. Even at that stage the cyclists received an inordinate amount of publicity and respect from the press and public. Merchants in the general area of the bicycle marathons offered loving cups and medals to the boys who could pedal longest; grocers contributed food, and in several instances the authorities went out of their way to make sure the riders had no interference from police or motorists.

By July 14, the Hackensack quartet had covered 168 hours, but the New Brunswick team had been forced out by a loosened nut on their bicycle. Their loss was hardly felt, for by that time new teams from Newark and Jersey City had gotten under way—the latter with the official blessing of the safety commissioner, who gave the starting signal. These teams were followed by entries from Union City and Evansville, Indiana, the mania breaking state boundaries for the first time.

Also for the first time, a bit of resistance to the cyclists appeared. At Newark, the team led by Gustav Klink was told to desist because they had become "a public nuisance, a menace to life and property, and a hindrance to traffic." When another Newark team was ordered off the square bounding St. John's Lutheran Church, they merely pedaled to another location and continued the marathon. The Hackensack boys, meanwhile, passed their 220th hour in the saddle, despite a "slight wabble" in their vehicle's rear wheel.

On Wednesday, July 16, the endurance contests not only showed no signs of diminishing, but even developed some bizarre side effects. In an effort to put Jimmy Dooley out of the race, an unidentified youngster—"a jealous rival," newspapers speculated—leaped from behind a clump of bushes and threw a baseball at his head. In response, the Hackensack Police announced that from that moment on, Dooley and his team would have official protection. In neighboring Jersey City, the cops went even farther, donating 2,400 feet of departmental rope as a means of holding back the crowds.

By the time the Hackensack team began its twelfth day, more than 2,000 persons gathered to watch them and listen to a band concert given in their honor. Cities and towns all over the United States had their own groups, each pedaling furiously, waiting for the Hackensack boys to falter so the endurance record could pass to them. The mania also spread to other sports activities. Nonstop seesawing, scooter-bike racing, and swinging started. In Kansas, Bill Kearny climbed a tree and remained there; others followed his example, included a black fellow who hoisted a barrel into a tree and crawled inside. Meanwhile, in Newark, neighbors angry at the police for forcing them to lose their bicycling team franchise sent a petition to Chief Harris, demanding that he allow the boys to return to the square at St. John's Church. Chief Harris, obviously a determined advocate of law and order, refused to let the team pedal in his district.

As the endurance mania headed into its second week, there were some dropouts. At North Tarrytown, a tree sitter named Martin De Bree, 12, succumbed to a swarm of mosquitos; others gave in to the heat or the threats of groups such as the Provincial Children's Aid Society of Niagara Falls. At Harrisburg, Pennsylvania, the police simply lost their tempers, literally shaking one tree sitter loose from his perch.

Even as reports of dropouts appeared, however, new endurance advocates took their places. Nonstop kite flying and roller skating were added to the list of pastimes. At National Park, New Jersey, a 33-year-old mother, Mrs. Edna Knight, joined the tree-sitting contest, taking a galvanized tub into the tree after her—to bathe in, she explained to curious neighbors. The Hackensack quartet pedaled into its fifth day even as official resistance grew. "These contests," said Judge Joseph Ziegler of the Essex County Juvenile Court in Newark, voicing the strongest complaint against the mania, "are pure nonsense. . . . The parents may be charged with neglect, with exploitation of the children for monetary gain. . . ." Added George Bigelow, Massachusetts health commissioner: "These activities are comparable to eating soup with a blotter, notable only for the fact that to date no sensible person has tried to indulge in them."

As if to punctuate these acid remarks, the rains came, drenching the weary riders and threatening tree sitters with lightning bolts. At Biloxi, Mississippi, 11-year-old Bill Moss fell from a hickory limb 35 feet from the ground and fractured his shoulder. Another casualty was 4-year-old John Auchu of Niagara Falls, who was hit on the face by a tree sitter's falling milk bottle. The heavy rains forced some participants out of competition, but others were hardened by adversity. Eddie O'Toole of New Brunswick, for example, continued to pedal his bicycle through a tornado that destroyed one house and tore the roofs from several others. When the boy refused to yield to his father's entreaties, the elder O'Toole got out the family car and rode beside young Eddie in order to break the wind's force. Meanwhile, new contests started: At Rockaway Beach, two young ladies decided to see how long they could float; at Bloomfield, New Jersey, eight boys began to toss a baseball back and forth, the idea being to keep it in motion as long as possible; on July 26, two teen-agers staggered into Atlantic City from Camden, a distance of 60 miles, claiming the record for pushing a baby carriage; and in Chicago, a 40-year-old black woman announced that she intended to stand motionless on a street corner until she had a record of some kind or other. She was quickly dislodged by police.

On July 23, the first signs of the endurance mania's waning began to show. Their bicycle literally falling to pieces under them, the Hackensack boys decided to call it quits. With 386 hours to their credit, they claimed the record, but another squad from Lodi Street in Hackensack had 200 and was still moving.

A few two days later, the baseball-tossing contest ended after 130 hours when two team members retired because of lack of public interest. A pigeon ended a kite-flying competition by colliding with the leading entrant, and a skunk compelled one tree sitter at Lexington, Kentucky, to make a forced landing. But new participants thrust themselves on the scene as old ones bowed out. At Richmond, Virginia, two high-school students began a game of nonstop tennis even as a Captain Jack Evans of Atlantic City announced that he would lie in a coffin until he had a record. "He reclines in a ventilated coffin and takes his meals in it," one reporter wrote, "but nobody seems to care." The month of July 1930 ended as the Lodi Street team of Hackensack passed the record for continuous bicycle riding and increased the number of consecutive hours to 450. Most officials, however, decided they had had enough. Police throughout New Jersey began to break up cycling events even as the Children's Aid Society took both parents and youngsters to court. At New Brunswick, following a rash of milk-bottle stealing and flower trampling, Jeremiah Donovan, parks commissioner, officially withdrew his support. And when Judge Ziegler found four bicyclists and their young manager guilty of "incorrigibility" and their parents guilty of neglect, the crusher had been applied. The endurance riders disappeared from the streets; tree sitters deserted their perches; even Captain Jack Evans resurrected himself from his coffin.

A month of endurance madness had passed. But for those who had participated—especially the four cyclists who left New York in July and found themselves stranded in Florida two months later—life would never be quite the same.

THE END OF THE 1930S

Life was less frivolous as the Depression took its economic toll, and with less money to be spent, promoters found it more difficult to entice the public away from the great escape machine, the movies. Some, of course, continued to try, and one was Robert Ripley, the compiler of "Believe It or Not" books and syndicated features. In 1934, Ripley ran a contest to encourage daredevils and athletes to attempt unusual feats, and one who applied was Walter Nilsson, a vaudeville star who volunteered to travel from coast to coast on a unicycle.

Seated atop the 8½-foot-tall contraption, Nilsson began his 3,306-mile jaunt at New York. The trip turned out to be a painful one, but 117 days later, the actor pedaled into San Francisco, winning Ripley's award for "The Most Unbelievable Feat of the Year."

ENDURANCE GOLF—PART TWO:

J. Smith Ferebee's 1938 feat started when, as a typical golf fanatic with atypically strong walking powers, he played 72 holes during a single day in 1938. When friends dared him to perform the trick again, Ferebee replied that not only could he play 72 holes a day, he could play 144 and also break 95 for each round.

The bet soon escalated to the point where Ferebee and Fred Tuerk, a friend who co-owned a plantation with Ferebee, staked the entire piece of property on the golfer's ability to play 600 holes in four days. The kicker was that the rounds would have to be played in eight different cities from coast to coast.

Ferebee's pilgrimage began at the Lakeside Country Club, Los Angeles, on September 25, 1938, where he quickly played 84 holes, then caught a plane for Phoenix, where he played his second round of 81 at the Encanta course. The next day, at dawn, he was at Kansas City, where he logged 72 holes and pulled a tendon in his leg. Limping the rest of the way, Ferebee traveled next to St. Louis, then Milwaukee and Chicago. With three days completed, he had played 453 holes of golf, putting him slightly ahead of the number he needed (450) at that juncture. But his leg was in terrible shape, blisters having developed, and his pace was visibly slowing. After adding 72 holes at Philadelphia's North Hills Country Club, Ferebee landed at Mitchell Field, New York, at 1:30 P.M. for the final effort. Struggling slowly, it was 8:00 P.M. before the final round could be started, but the natives of Westbury were not about to let Ferebee lose his bet because of darkness. A fire truck was driven onto the course, lighting every green and fairway; gallery members carried flashlights and used flares to mark the spot where each ball had fallen. At 10:30 P.M. on September 28, 1938, J. Smith sank his final putt and won his bet.

BASKETBALL FOUL SHOOTING

One of the first celebrated free-throw shooters was Harold "Bunny" Levitt, whose great moment of glory came on April 6, 1935, at the Madison Street Armory, Chicago. At 7:00 P.M. he moved to the foul line and using his underhanded, two-hand grip, deftly twirled 499 consecutive shots through the cords without a miss. On shot No. 500 Levitt miscalculated, but then proceeded to shoot 371 more without missing. By that time it was well after midnight and most of the crowd had disappeared, so Levitt agreed to stop. Later he joined the Harlem Globetrotters, who offered a prize of $1,000 to anyone who could beat Levitt in a contest of 100 throws. No one collected the money, however, for the best challenger made 86 while the worst Levitt ever did was 96.

Marathon Free-throw Update:
On February 28, 1975, Ted St. Martin tossed 1,704 straight free throws without a miss.

Unfortunately, during Levitt's career, as well as now, basketball had nothing comparable to baseball's "designated hitter" rule, for shooting fouls is the only way he could have made it as a player, being only five feet, four inches tall.

HOLDING ONE'S BREATH

As a spectator sport, holding the breath while underwater isn't exactly the most exciting event, but it is a valid test of an athlete's lung-power. On July 4, 1958, Dr. Robert W. Keast, 36, of San Rafael, California, decided to see how long he could stay underwater without breathing. He prepared himself by inhaling pure oxygen for a half hour before entering the water. In addition, he attached 40 pounds of lead to his body so that he would not have to expend any effort remaining under the surface. He also wore a skin-diver's mask so that he would not have to hold his nose.

Once on the bottom of the Burlingame Country Club pool, Keast remained perfectly still while a friend at poolside relayed the number of minutes via a system of underwater hand signals. When Keast passed the previous endurance record of 11 minutes, 40 seconds, he was nearly ready to burst but he hung on to establish a new mark of 13 minutes, 35 seconds. When he was able to talk again, he said, "I disliked the experience very much. I'll never do it again."

Eight months later, on March 15, 1959, another Californian, named Robert Foster, dropped into the pool of the Bermuda Palms Hotel in San Rafael and remained underwater for 13 minutes, 42.5 seconds, just enough to emerge as a new record-holder.

GYMNASTICS

Most athletes pride themselves on the strength of their abdominal muscles if they can do a few hundred sit-ups without stopping. On November 29, 1965, a 17-year-old high school student at Rome, Georgia, named Dale Cummings started to do sit-ups at 11:00 A.M. By the time he had performed several hundred of the exercise, schoolmates, athletic coaches, and newsman were on hand. They watched, fascinated, as young Cummings continued to perform sit-ups all through the day and into the evening.

While Cummings did a sit-up every 3 seconds, interest continued to grow. An all-night radio station broadcast regular reports on his progress; those in the Berry Academy gymnasium played musical records to keep Cummings in good spirits. And not until he had completed 14,118 sit-ups in 12 hours did he stop.

Six years later, on September 13, 1971, a 30-year-old Marine Corps captain, Wayne Rollings, beat Cummings' record before a number of witnesses by doing 17,000 sit-ups in 7 hours, 27 minutes. This averaged out to 38 sit-ups per minute, less than 2 seconds each.

The next entrant in the sit-up marathon was Richard John Knecht, age 8, who performed 25,222 sit-ups in 11 hours, 14 minutes at the Idaho Falls High School gymnasium on December 23, 1972. The average was 37.4 per minute.

On June 23, 1969, William D. Reed of the University of Pennsylvania chinned the bar (pull-ups) 106 times from a dead hang.

Steven Welsher of Long Beach, California, performed 15,025 side-straddle hops (jumping jacks) on July 27, 1974. The feat required 3 hours, 32 minutes.

A push-up record was established in 1965 when 16-year-old Charles Linster of Wilmette, Illinois performed 6,006 of them without stop-

---

Hockey's Longest Game:
During the 1933 Stanley Cup playoffs between the Boston Bruins and Toronto Maple Leafs, the teams played the regulation three periods with no score. They then continued to skate for an additional 1 hour, 44 minutes, 46 seconds before the Leafs scored a goal in the sixth overtime period.

Incredibly, that record lasted only three years. In the first game of the 1936 playoffs between Detroit and the Montreal

Maroons, the teams played scoreless hockey for a full regulation game. Both goalies made fantastic saves as the contest went through five complete overtime periods. The sixth overtime period was nearly over when Mud Bruneteau, a rookie from the minor leagues, took a pass from Hec Kilrea, firing the puck past Montreal goalie Chabot. The time was 16 minutes, 30 seconds of the sixth extra period. The teams had played a total of 2 hours, 56 minutes, 30 seconds. It was 2:20 A.M.

ping. Done at the rate of a push-up every 2⅓ seconds, the accomplishment took 3 hours, 54 minutes.

FOOTBALL

Before the National Football League rule change requiring regular-season games, if tied at the end of the fourth quarter, to go into overtime, there had been only four "sudden death" games in American professional football history, all of them in playoff contests.

The first took place on December 28, 1958, when the Baltimore Colts and New York Giants tangled for the championship of the NFL. The Colts swept to a 14–3 lead at halftime, but lost their cool following a third-quarter drive that stalled on the Giants' 5-yard line. Three plays later, Charlie Conerly found Kyle Rote with a pass and Rote carried all the way to the Colt 25 before fumbling. As luck would have it, the ball was recovered by Giant running back Alex Webster, who took it all the way to the Colt 1-yard line. The Giants scored, then added another TD to take a 17–14 lead early in the fourth period.

Running into a fired-up Giant defense, the Colts could not manage a decent drive until only 2 minutes remained in the game. Then John Unitas completed 4 of 7 passes, the last 3 passes to Raymond Berry for gains of 25, 15, and 22 yards to the Giant 13. Steve Myhra kicked a field goal from the 20-yard line to tie the game and sent it into overtime.

New York received the kickoff but could gain only 9 yards in three plays, despite the Colts having lost standout defensive end Gino Marchetti. Taking over on the Colt 20, Unitas continued to mix his plays well, throwing to Raymond Berry when he needed yardage in clutch situations. On the thirteenth play of the drive, running back Alan Ameche rambled through an enormous hole to score. The game was over at 8:15 of the sudden-death period.

1958

Baltimore Colts	0	14	0	3	6—23
New York Giants	3	0	7	7	0—17

The second overtime contest in pro football history took place when the Dallas Texans (soon to be transplanted to Kansas City) met the Houston Oilers for the 1962 championship of the three-year-old American Football League.

At halftime, Dallas seemed to have the situation well in hand, leading by a score of 17–0. But in the third period, Houston quarterback George Blanda threw a 15-yard strike to Willard Dewveall, and Charlie Tolar ran a yard for another score. When Blanda added a 31-yard field goal in the final period, the game went into overtime.

The fifth period passed with neither team getting within range, but after 12 minutes of the second overtime period, Tom Brooker of Dallas kicked a 25-yard field goal to give the Texans the championship.

1962

Dallas Texans	3	14	0	0	0	3—20
Houston Oilers	0	0	7	10	0	0—17

Professional football's third overtime marathon, in 1965, also featured the Baltimore Colts, this time playing with "instant quarterback" Tom Matte. The game was for the Western Conference championship; the site was Green Bay, where the temperature was 32° at kickoff.

Earlier, the Colts had lost both regular quarterback John Unitas and backup Gary Cuozzo, forcing coach Don Shula to send running back Tom Matte into the game with plays taped to his wrist. With the Baltimore attack handicapped, the defense rose to the occasion. After Green Bay received the kickoff, Anderson fumbled on the opening play, and Colt linebacker Don Shinnick scooped up the ball and ran it for a touchdown.

Green Bay tried to get the equalizer, but the weather penalized both teams. On the next series, Paul Hornung fumbled, and the ball was recovered by Lenny Lyles of the Colts. But on the very next play, Lenny Moore bobbled the ball, and Green Bay had it right back.

At halftime, the Colts led, 10–0, having added a field goal by Lou Michaels, but the third quarter was only 5 minutes old when Colt punter Tom Gilburg received a high pass from center, and Baltimore was forced to turn over the ball on its own 35. Zeke Bratkowski passed to Carroll Dale for 33 yards and Hornung ran for the score that brought the Packers to 10–7.

The Colt defense continued to play inspired ball, but with 9:03 left, Green Bay got the ball on its own 28-yard line. A determined Packer drive, aided by a questionable facemask penalty against the Colts, brought the ball to the Baltimore 20. Tom Moore gained 2 yards, Jim Taylor ran for 3, and a Bratkowski pass fell incomplete. With fourth-and-5 the situation, kicker Don Chandler entered the game and from the 22-yard line shanked a field-goal attempt that seemed to skim wide of the left upright. Chandler hung his head and started back to the sideline. But the officials called the kick good. The game was tied at 10–10 and went into sudden-death overtime.

If the Chandler kick was questionable, there was nothing spurious about the Packer fifth-quarter drive. After Lou Michaels missed a desperation field-goal attempt from 47 yards out, the Packers moved methodically from their 20 to the Colt 18. Chandler then kicked a 25-yarder that gave Green Bay the Western Conference title, 13–10.

Although league officials refused to comment on film of the Chandler kick, which clearly showed the ball veering wide of the upright, they did acknowledge, however reluctantly, that the Baltimore protest had some merit by extending the uprights nearly into the stratosphere for the 1966 season.

1965

| Baltimore Colts | 7 | 3 | 0 | 0 | 0—10 |
| Green Bay Packers | 0 | 0 | 7 | 3 | 3—13 |

The fourth overtime contest was also a divisional playoff one, this time involving the Kansas City Chiefs and the Miami Dolphins. Played on Christmas Day 1971, at Kansas City, the game to decide the championship of the American Football Conference of the National Football League caused many holiday dinners to be postponed from late afternoon to early evening. The scoring began with Jan Stenerud of the Chiefs booting a 24-yard field goal, followed by a 7-yard scoring pass from Len Dawson to Ed Podolak. At the end of the first quarter Kansas City led, 10–0.

Miami came back to tie the score before halftime, however, and during the third and fourth quarters the lead was taken twice by Kansas City and the game was tied twice by the Dolphins. With 1:36 left in regulation time, Miami kicked off to the Chiefs' Ed Podolak, who returned the ball 78 yards to the Dolphin 22-yard line. But from there the usually reliable Stenerud missed a 31-yard field-goal attempt and the game went into overtime.

The fifth period was scoreless, thanks once again to Stenerud missing a field goal that would have won the game for the Chiefs, but in the sixth period the Dolphins methodically moved the ball toward the Kansas City goal. The highlights of the drive was a 29-yard run by Larry Csonka that put the ball on the Chiefs' 36. Three running plays netted

Miami only 6 yards, at which point a balding, 5-foot, 7-inch former soccer player named Garo Yepremian entered the game to kick the winning goal from the 37. The game, which left 50,374 Chief fans standing in numbed anguish, was the longest—82 minutes, 40 seconds —in the history of American professional football.

1971

| Miami Dolphins | 0 | 10 | 7 | 7 | 0 | 3—27 |
| Kansas City Chiefs | 10 | 0 | 7 | 7 | 0 | 0—24 |

In keeping with their pattern of participating in every other overtime championship game, the Baltimore Colts were around for the third longest game in NFL history, which was played at Baltimore on December 24, 1977. This time the opposition was furnished by the NFC Western Conference champion Oakland Raiders, the Colts having earned the AFC championship the week before on a controversial call. (See "Flaps.")

Smarting from the criticism that they had backed into the playoffs, the Colts, led by quarterback Bert Jones, played the Raiders extremely tough throughout the regulation four periods. Oakland seemed to be running roughshod over the Colts, but when the Colts needed a big play to stay in the game, they got it. In the second period, Bruce Laird intercepted a pass intended for Mark Van Eeghan and raced 61 yards for a score. In the third quarter, Marshall Johnson ran 87 yards with a kickoff to give the Colts a 17–14 lead. The Raiders stormed right back, blocking a David Lee punt and capitalizing on the break to take a 21–17 lead into the final period. At the end of 60 minutes' play, however, the score was tied at 31–31.

The Colts won the toss but could not move the ball against the stubborn Raider defense. Yet Baltimore's defense was nearly as good and the first overtime period passed without a score. Finally, 43 seconds into the second overtime period, Ken Stabler tossed a 10-yard TD pass to Dave Casper for the tie breaker. "It's a shame in these kinds of games there has to be a loser," Oakland Coach John Madden said graciously. The Baltimore fans, cheering their losers heartily, agreed.

1977

| Oakland Raiders | 7 | 0 | 14 | 10 | 0 | 6—37 |
| Baltimore Colts | 0 | 10 | 7 | 14 | 0 | 0—31 |

ENDURANCE GOLF—PART THREE:

During the early 1970s, Raymond Lasater became the new champion of endurance golf by playing 1,053 consecutive holes in 49 hours, 18 minutes. His average per 18-hole round was 91. When he trudged wearily off the Hunter's Point course at Lebanon, Tennessee, on June 22, 1972, Lasater said, "I don't plan to do it again."

One year later, he not only did it again but also bettered his record by playing 1,530 holes in 62 hours, 20 minutes, on June 19–21, 1973. On this occasion he used a motorized golf cart for transportation and luminous balls.

1975—ANOTHER YEAR OF ENDURANCE

Archery—June 21–22, Greentown, Ohio. Shooting continuously for 24 hours, Stan Kiehl and Greg Shumaker scored 45,454 during 42 Portsmouth rounds (60 arrows at a distance of 20 yards with a 2-inch-diameter 10 ring).
Basketball—October 10–13, Southington School, Southington, Ohio. Using 2 teams of 5 players each, with no substitutions, a marathon match continued for 60 hours.
Bowling—June 5–10, Omaha, Nebraska. Using both hands, 46-year-old Richard Dewey bowled 1,472 nonstop games in 114½ hours, averaging 126 pins per game.

Ice Skating—January 1–5, Ice Dome Rink, Indianapolis, Indiana. Mark Losure and Steve Roberts skated continuously for 100 hours.
Pool—March 21–29, Los Angeles. Longest recorded game for four players continued for period of 200 hours.
Roller Skating—March 11–19, Skatehaven, Montgomery, Alabama. Tammy Wilson and John Fowler skated nonstop for 178 hours.
Soccer—April 25–26, Toccoa Falls, Georgia. Teams with 11 men on a side played continuously for 37 hours, a mark that was equaled by teams from Tenney High School, Methuen, Massachusetts, June 7–8, 1975.
Table Tennis—August 30–September 2, Long Beach, California. Longest singles match: 96 hours, between Greg Clarke and Pat Goodman.
Tennis—May 10–11, Beltsville, Maryland. Sandy Goss and Rita Santarpia played continuously for 30 hours, 30 minutes.

Author's Note:
It is hoped that the reader will recognize that the author, having gotten into the endurance spirit, has made this the longest chapter in the book.

CHAPTER 22—1911–20

1911

Winners: Baseball: For the second time in the brief history of the World Series, the opponents are the New York Giants and the Philadelphia Athletics. This time the result is different, the A's avenging their 1905 defeat by taking the Giants, 4 games to 2. . . . *Kentucky Derby:* Meridian. *Preakness:* Watervale. *Belmont Stakes:* Not run in 1911 or 1912, horseracing having been banned in New York . . . *Indy 500:* First of the series is won by Ray Harroun, whose Marmon Wasp averages 74.59 miles per hour. . . . *Boxing:* Following death of Ketchel, middleweight title is claimed by Mike Gibbons, Eddie McGoorty, and former champion Billy Papke. . . . Jimmy Clabby also vacates welterweight championship to move into middleweight class. . . . *Golf: USGA Men's Open:* John J. McDermott . . . *Hockey:* 1910–11 Stanley Cup winner: Ottawa Senators . . . *Football:* College champion selected by Helms Athletic Foundation: Princeton (8–0–2).

Other Happenings: Big football game of year takes place on November 11, Harvard meeting the Carlisle Indian School, led by Jim Thorpe. The contest is a thriller for the partisan crowd at Cambridge, Carlisle winning by a narrow 18–15 margin. . . . April 8–10, the first tournament sponsored by the National Squash Association is held in New York City. Dr. Alfred Stillman defeats J. W. Prentiss, 15–5, 17–15. . . . The Pacific Coast Hockey League is formed. . . . Jem Mace, saloon owner and old-time boxer who fought two nondecisions with Joe Coburn in 1871, dies at the age of 80. His last years were spent trying to get a pension. . . . At Montcrief Park in Jacksonville, Florida, a 500-yard race is run among two men, a pair of racehorses, two mules, and an automobile. The winner is C. E. Dowling, followed by R. E. Kennedy, then Ben Double, one of the horses. The auto finishes out of the money, taking too long to accelerate. . . . Leaving New York City on July 30, Ralph Tompkins, a one-legged youth of Poughkeepsie, reaches Chicago on October 2, averaging about 15 miles a day. "The thing people forget," he says, "is that by swinging in my crutches, I take bigger steps than the average person and therefore can make better time." . . . Cut down in the primes of their careers: Addie Joss, 31, star pitcher of the Cleveland Indians, and Simon Nicholls, 28, shortstop and captain for Baltimore of the Eastern League . . . Second person to make descent over Niagara Falls and live to tell about it is an Englishman named Bobby Leach, who breaks both kneecaps and suffers a brain concussion. Not long afterward, while in New Zealand, he slips on an orange peel, breaks his leg, contracts gangrene, and dies. . . . On May 13, New York Giants score 10 runs against the St. Louis Cardinals before a man is retired, most in National League history.

1912

Winners: Baseball: Going into the World Series, the New York Giants seem to have the edge in pitching, with Rube Marquard (26–11) and Christy Mathewson (23–12) forming the nucleus of an excellent staff. But the Boston Red Sox have 22-year-old Smoky Joe Wood (34–5), who wins 3 games. The Sox win in 7 games. . . . *Kentucky Derby:* Worth. *Preakness:* Colonel Halloway. *Belmont Stakes:* Not run in 1911 and 1912, horseracing having been banned in New York . . . *Indy 500:* Joe Dawson . . . *Boxing:* In lightweight division, Willie Ritchie wins on foul from Ad Wolgast in 16 rounds at San Francisco, and featherweight Johnny Kilbane outpoints Abe Attell in 20 rounds, also at San Francisco. . . . *Golf: USGA Men's Open:* John J. McDermott . . . *Hockey:* Quebec Bulldogs win 1911–12 Stanley Cup. . . . *Football:* College champion selected by Helms Athletic Foundation: Harvard (9–0–0).

Other Happenings: On April 20, Fenway Park is opened in Boston. The Red Sox celebrate by beating New York, 7–6, in 11 innings. . . . In a rousing game on June 20, the Boston Braves score 10 runs and the Giants 7 in the ninth inning. The Giants win, 21–12. . . . Eddie Collins steals 6 bases in a single game against the Tigers on September 11, the A's winning, 9–7. . . . Eleven days later, Collins again swipes 6, vs. St.

Louis. . . . The World Series turns out to be a famous one, featuring Fred Snodgrass' dropping an easy fly that—along with Christy Mathewson's error in judgment on a pop-up—allow the Red Sox to win. But Snodgrass lives the rest of his life with the "goat" tag. . . . Jim Thorpe leads Carlisle to a 12–1–1 record in football while scoring 198 points. . . . On October 27, Martin Erehart of Indiana returns a punt 112 yards against Iowa, but Iowa wins, 13–6 (this is one of last of 100-plus football plays, as the field is reduced in 1912 from 110 yards in length to 100—goal line to goal line). . . . Value of touchdown is increased from 5 to 6 points and teams are given 4 downs instead of 3 to make 10 yards. . . . Changes are also made in hockey, the National Hockey Association, forerunner of the National Hockey League, reducing the number of players in the game from 7 to 6. . . . For the first time, hockey players wear numbers on their sweaters. . . . On June 17, the first mutuel ticket to pay more than $1,000 is cashed at Latonia, Ohio. Only four tickets are sold on 900–1 shot Wishing Ring, which pays $1,885.50, $744.40, and $172.40. . . . Major-league no-hitters: Jeff Tesreau of Giants vs. Phillies (September 6); George Mullin of Detroit vs. St. Louis (July 4); Earl Hamilton of White Sox vs. Red Sox (August 30). . . . Also, Rube Marquard of Giants wins 20 consecutive games. . . . On May 25, Lincoln Beachey, aeronaut, dresses himself in women's clothes and flies to height of 5,000 feet. . . . Balloonist F. Goodal, the next day, crashes into Palisades Amusement Park grandstand. . . . Other summer incidents include balloonist and acrobat F. Owens being dragged across three New Jersey towns while strapped to his trapeze, and parachutist Thibedeau dropping into the Cleveland reservoir and drowning. . . . Many young women at American colleges take up the latest athletic fad: wall scaling. . . . In January Charlie Ebbets announces plans to build a new stadium for the Brooklyn Trolley-Dodgers. . . . On November 9, Pop Warner, coach of Carlisle Indian School, first uses his double-wingback formation to demoralize an Army team, 27–6. Star of Carlisle is Jim Thorpe. Comparatively unknown halfback of Army is Dwight Eisenhower.

1913

Winners: Baseball: For the third time the World Series involves the New York Giants and Philadelphia A's. (It is also the last time.) Led by Frank "Home Run" Baker, the A's win the rubber Series, 4 games to 1. . . . *Kentucky Derby:* Donerail. *Preakness:* Buskin. *Belmont Stakes:* Prince Eugene wins as racing returns to New York. . . . *Indy 500:* Jules Goux . . . *Boxing:* In middleweight division, Frank Klaus takes crown from Billy Papke on a foul, 15 rounds, then is knocked out by George Chip, 5 rounds, just 9 months later. . . . *Golf: USGA Men's Open:* Francis Ouimet beats Harry Vardon and Ted Ray in playoff to score what many sports experts call one of the greatest upsets of the twentieth century. . . . *Hockey:* 1912–13 Stanley Cup winner: Quebec Bulldogs . . . *Football:* College champion selected by Helms Athletic Foundation: Harvard (9–0–0).

Other Happenings: On April 9, Ebbets Field opens and 10,000 are on hand to see the first Dodger game in the new park. Nap Rucker holds the Phillies to a single run, but that's more than enough for Tom Seaton, who goes on to lead the league with 27 wins. The Phils win, 1–0. . . . Football fans get a thrill when highly favored Army plugs a hole in its schedule with a breather against Notre Dame and gets clobbered, 35–13. This is the celebrated "forward pass" game in which Knute Rockne and Gus Dorais dazzle the Cadets with aerials. . . . Also on the gridiron, the University of Chicago puts numbers on its players in a game with Wisconsin and wins, 19–0. . . . Al Spiegel leads Washington and Jefferson to a 9–0 season by scoring 127 points. . . . On March 10, William Knox of Philadelphia becomes the first to score a perfect 300 in an American Bowling Congress tournament. . . . Founded: United States Football (Soccer) Association. First champion, for 1913–14 season, is Brooklyn Field Club. . . . Duke Kahanamoku, later star of silver screen, on July 5 swims 100-yard freestyle in 54.6 seconds. . . . The United States wins Davis Cup, 3–2, defeating British team at Wimbledon. . . . In unusual baseball training development, the coach of Kalamazoo College's team announces that because his players lost the 1912 Michigan Intercollegiate Athletic Association championship by shying away from fast balls, each man's inside foot would be shackled to the plate during batting practice in 1913. . . . Standout performances in major-league baseball include Walter Johnson's pitching 56 consecutive scoreless innings and Christy Mathewson's going 68 innings in a row without issuing a base on balls. . . . The year 1913 begins with revelation that Jim Thorpe "professionalized" himself and thereby made himself ineligible for 1912 Olympics by playing semipro baseball while at college. Thorpe returns his trophies and signs to play with New York Giants. . . . Federal League (formerly U. S. League) becomes a threat to organized baseball when announcement is made that third major circuit will operate in 1914. . . . Frank L. Kramer begins his thirteenth consecutive year as United States professional bicycle sprint champion. . . . Fred Perrine, American League umpire, 1909–12, turns up in hospital insane ward.

1914

Winners: Baseball: The Boston Braves make their first appearance in a World Series as a result of a "miraculous" spurt from last place in July to first place in August and eventually win the pennant by a margin of 10½ games. Facing the Braves in the Series are the powerful Philadelphia A's, but the Braves, in sports parlance, have impetus going for them and sweep the Mackmen in 4 games. . . . *Kentucky Derby:* Old Rosebud. *Preakness:* Holiday. *Belmont Stakes:* Luke McLuke . . . *Indy 500:* Rene Thomas . . . *Boxing:* Middleweight Al McCoy knocks out George Chip in first round to become new champ, and lightweight Freddie Welsh wins decision from Willie Ritchie. Bantamweight crown is also transferred from Johnny Coulon to Kid Williams, who knocks out the champion in third round at Vernon, California. . . . *Golf: USGA Men's Open:* Walter Hagen . . . *Hockey:* 1913–14 Stanley Cup champion: Toronto Blueshirts . . . *Football:* College champion selected by Helms Athletic Foundation: Army (9–0–0).

Other Happenings: On April 13, Federal Baseball League plays its first game in Baltimore's Terrapin Park. Contest is both artistic and financial success, more than 28,000 fans turning out. Two months later, after serving a brief apprenticeship with the International League Baltimore Orioles across the street from the Terrapins, Babe Ruth makes his major-league debut. On July 11, he pitches the Boston Red Sox to a 4–3 victory over Cleveland, but, ironically, is removed in the seventh inning for a pinch-hitter. . . . Founded on May 16: the Grand League of the American Horseshoe Pitchers, at Kansas City, Kansas . . . Powerhouse on the college gridiron is the Missouri School of Mines, which goes undefeated in 8 games and outscores opposition, 540–0. John Imlay scores 180 of the team's points. . . . Jockey John McTaggart rides 157 winners during the year. . . . Dodge City, Kansas, celebrates the Fourth of July by staging a 300-mile motorcycle race on a 2-mile dirt track. Of the 36 who start, 18 finish, the winner being Glen R. "Slivers" Boyd, who

covers the course in 4 hours, 24 minutes, an average of 67.92 miles per hour. . . . On March 20, a figure-skating tournament is held at the Arena Ice Rink, New Haven, Connecticut. Teresa Weld and Norman Scott are declared the winners. . . . No-hitters are pitched by Jim Scott, Chicago White Sox (who loses in tenth inning), Joe Benz, also of the White Sox, and George Davis of the Boston Braves. . . . One innovation of new Federal League is the publication of players' batting averages vs. both right-handed and left-handed pitchers. Benny Kauff, of Indianapolis, who wins overall batting title with an average of .370, hits .422 against righties and .352 vs. lefties (Kauff is a left-handed batter). . . . In the spring, Charles Victory Faust, good-luck charm of the New York Giants, turns up in the insane ward of a hospital in Portland, Oregon. . . . After regular season, New York Giants and Chicago White Sox make a barnstorming tour of the world. While in Egypt they become the first teams to play baseball in the shadow of the Pyramids. John McGraw caps the trip by receiving the Pope's blessing. . . . To help finance 1916 Olympic Games, Chicago children collect and donate 41 pounds of pennies. . . . California Legislature outlaws professional boxing.

1915

Winners: Baseball: The Boston Red Sox and Detroit Tigers both win 100 games, but the Red Sox earn their way into the World Series by a 2½-game margin. National League Phillies are paced by superb pitching of Grover Cleveland Alexander (31–10), but in Series Boston's pitching is even better. Only 13 runs are scored by both clubs in first 4 games, 3 of which are won by the Red Sox. Boston takes fall classic in 5 games. . . . *Kentucky Derby:* Regret, the only filly ever to win the Derby. *Preakness:* Rhine Maiden. *Belmont Stakes:* The Finn . . . *Indy 500:* Ralph DePalma . . . *Boxing:* Heavyweight battle between Jack Johnson and Jess Willard, the white hope, takes place on April 5 at Havana, Cuba. Johnson, 37, loses on a 26-round knockout. Later he claims he threw the fight, but most experts believe the KO is legitimate. Most significant action of the middleweight division is official setting of weight limit at 160 pounds. Welterweight crown is taken by Ted Lewis, who wins a 12-round decision from Jack Britton. . . . *Golf: USGA Men's Open:* Jerome Travers . . . *Hockey:* 1914–15 Stanley Cup winner: Vancouver Millionaires . . . *Football:* College champion selected by Helms Athletic Foundation: Cornell (9–0–0).

Other Happenings: The spring of 1915 is enlivened by aviatrix Ruth Law's dropping a grapefruit on former major-league catcher Gabby Street, who previously caught baseball dropped from top of 555-foot-high Washington Monument. Miss Law does not intend to drop grapefruit, but forgets ball and selects grapefruit at last minute. Casey Stengel, then a Brooklyn Dodger outfielder, describes the event: "The missile caromed off the edge of the mitt and hit him right in the chest," he says. "And he spun around and then fell over, like in a Western picture where you see an Indian that's out on the hill and they shoot him and he goes around in a circle and falls dead." . . . On May 6, Babe Ruth of Red Sox hits first major-league home run, off Jack Warhop of the Yankees. . . . On June 17, George Zabel enters baseball game as relief pitcher with 2 out in the first inning. He pitches 18⅓ innings for the Cubs, who beat Dodgers, 4–3, in 19 innings. Zip Zabel's relief effort is longest ever pitched. . . . In the Central Association, meanwhile, Wilmington and Keokuck battle for 22 innings without a run being scored. The game is finally called because of darkness. . . . Norman Taber, U.S. runner, races a mile in the record time of 4:12.6. . . . Founded: the Pacific Coast Conference, composed of college football teams from Washington, Oregon, Oregon State, and California . . . On October 23, the town of Kellerton, Iowa, hosts the first official horseshoe pitching tournament in the United States. The winner is Frank Jackson. . . . Marke Payne of Dakota Wesleyan drop-kicks a 63-yard field goal against Northern Normal. . . . Two no-hit games are pitched in National League, by the Giants' Rube Marquard on April 15 and by the Cubs' Jimmy Lavender on August 31. . . . Davis Cup tennis competition is suspended because of World War I. . . . Despite stalemate in the trenches, there is still hope that 1916 Olympics will be held, especially in Germany. Philadelphia leads U.S. cities in bidding for games. . . . In April, intercity badminton matches are held between New York and Boston. . . . Tim Hurst, colorful umpire who worked in both American and National League, dies on June 4. . . . Joe Tinker's Chicago Whales win second and final season championship of Federal League, challenge AL and NL champs to playoff; the offer is ignored. . . . Honus Wagner, in his nineteenth year, hits his No. 100th home run of his career. When he retires as a player two years later, he has 101. . . . Portland, Oregon, becomes first American city to be eligible for Stanley Cup by joining Pacific Coast Hockey League. . . . Great

Britain and Canada cancel major golf tournaments because of war.

1916

Winners: Baseball: Wilbert Robinson leads the Brooklyn Dodgers out of a 15-year wilderness and puts the team into its first World Series, against the Boston Red Sox. But the Dodgers drop the first 2 games and can never get back, Boston taking the Series, 4 games to 1. . . . *Kentucky Derby:* George Smith. *Preakness:* Damrosch. *Belmont Stakes:* Friar Rock . . . *Indy 500:* Dario Resta . . . *Boxing:* Following Jack O'Brien's retirement in 1912, light-heavyweight division is dominated by unofficial champion Jack Dillon. On October 24, 1916, Battling Levinsky claims the title when he outpoints Dillon in a 12-round bout. . . . *Golf: USGA Men's Open:* Charles Evans, Jr. . . . *PGA:* In first annual tournament, James M. Barnes is winner. . . . *Hockey:* 1915–16 Stanley Cup champion: Montreal Canadiens . . . *Football: Rose Bowl* is resumed after 14 years, Washington State beating Brown, 14–0.

Other Happenings: On June 26, Cleveland Indians appear in game with numbers on their sleeves, first time in baseball. . . . George Sisler, pitcher, wins the final game of his career (5 wins, 6 losses) by defeating Walter Johnson and Senators, 1–0, on September 17. He then becomes full-time first baseman, bats over .400 twice. . . . One week later, Marty Kavanagh of Cleveland smashes first pinch-hit grand-slam home run in major-league history. The ball rolls through a hole in the fence, enabling Indians to win, 5–3. . . . American League President Ban Johnson offers his solution to the problem of hit batsmen, apparently with a straight face: Give a batter hit on the head two bases instead of just one, he says. . . . October 9: In longest World Series game on record, Babe Ruth pitches 14-inning victory, allowing only a single run. . . . College season features two of three highest scores in football history: Georgia Tech 222, Cumberland (Tennessee) 0; and St. Viator Indiana) 205, Lane College (Chicago) 0. In Lane-St. Viator game, Leo Schlick of St. Viator scores 12 touchdowns and kicks 28 of 29 extra points for total of 100 points. . . . But Ivan H. Grove of Henry-Kendall is college scoring leader for year with 196 points. . . . Jockey Frank Robinson rides 178 winners during year. . . . In the major baseball leagues, Connie Mack's once-proud Athletics lose 20 games in a row and end season in AL cellar. . . . New York Giants do not lose from September 7 to September 30, taking 26 games in a row—but still manage to finish season in fourth place. . . . No-hitters are pitched in National League by Tom Hughes of Braves, in American by George Foster of Red Sox, Hub Leonard, also of Boston, and Joe Bush of A's. . . . In July, the greatest pacer of his day, Dan Patch, dies, having registered 30 2-minute miles and never having lost a race. His owner, M. W. Savage, dies of a heart ailment the day after Dan Patch succumbs. . . . Seattle becomes second American city to join professional Pacific Coast Hockey League. . . . The first transcontinental trip by women on a motorcycle begins when Adelina and Augusta Van Buren leave New York on July 5. They arrive, safe and well, at San Diego on September 12.

1917

Winners: Baseball: The Chicago White Sox, with much the same cast of characters who will throw the 1919 Series, win the American League pennant and handle the New York Giants, 4 games to 2, in the World Series. . . . *Kentucky Derby:* Omar Khayyam. *Preakness:* Kalitan. *Belmont Stakes:* Hourless . . . *Indy 500:* Race not held because of war. . . . *Boxing:* November 14—middleweight Mike O'Dowd knocks out Al McCoy in 6 rounds to become new champ. Benny Leonard becomes lightweight champion, beginning a reign of 8 years, by knocking out Freddie Welsh in 9 rounds. Pete Herman wins bantamweight crown by beating Kid Williams in 20 rounds at New Orleans. . . . *Golf: USGA Men's Open:* No tournament because of war . . . *PGA:* No tournament because of war . . . *Hockey:* National Hockey League is founded, 1917. Seattle Metropolitans win 1916–17 Stanley Cup by defeating Montreal Canadiens in playoffs, March 21, 24, 27. . . . *Football: Rose Bowl:* Oregon 14, Pennsylvania 0. . . . Because of war, some major colleges discontinue football—Arizona State, George Washington, Georgia, North Carolina, Tennessee, and Virginia during 1917.

Other Happenings: On May 2, Fred Toney of Cincinnati and Hippo Vaughn of Chicago Cubs pitch first double no-hit game in history. Toney lasts 10 innings to defeat Vaughn, who yields hit after 9⅓ innings. . . . On June 23, Babe Ruth starts for Boston, walks first batter, then gets into an argument with umpire Clarence "Brick" Owens, who ejects him from the game. Ernie Shore enters the game and after the runner is caught stealing, goes on to

pitch a perfect game, retiring every Washington Senator batter to win, 4–0. . . . Other no-hitters in American League, which has a banner year, are credited to Eddie Cicotte of the White Sox, George Mogridge of the Yankees, Ernie Koob of the Browns (who finishes the year with a 6–14 record), and Bob Groom, also of the Browns. The last two games come on successive days, May 5–6, both against the White Sox. . . . Batters, meanwhile, have the opportunity to earn extra money by hitting the various "Bull Durham" signs located in the ball parks. In 1917 the reward per hit is $50, and a total of 14 prizes is awarded in the National League. Only the signs in Boston and Cincinnati are missed. . . . Hank Gowdy, catcher for Boston Braves, is first major leaguer to enlist in armed forces. . . . Jockey Willie Crump rides 151 winners, Willie Ingram leads the nation by scoring 162 points for Navy's football team, and Henry Hall ski jumps an American record of 203 feet. . . . At outset of war, U. S. Government closes down the Carlisle Indian School, and it does not reopen. . . . On September 5, Hawaiian prince Duke Kahanamoku swims 100 yards in 53 seconds. . . . A. L. Monteverde, nearly 50 years old, runs from Milwaukee to Chicago, 96⅔ miles, in 14 hours, 50 minutes. . . . Most celebrated stillactive athlete to die during year is 22-year-old Les Darcy, Australian middleweight who comes to America to box, among others, Al McCoy. The cause of Darcy's death is pneumonia. . . . As baseball teams go to spring training, American League President Ban Johnson offers $500 prize to team that is best drilled. Some teams practice manual of arms with baseball bats, to accompaniment of audible grumbling. . . . On March 17, first bowling tournament for women under the auspices of the Women's International Bowling Congress is held in St. Louis, Missouri.

1918

Winners: Baseball: Panic sets in on the home front to the extent that some fear that America's involvement in World War I means the elimination of organized baseball and the World Series. A compromise is worked out, however, the teams playing a 125-game season and a Series that begins on September 5. Babe Ruth and submarine-balling Carl Mays are the pitching stars as the Boston Red Sox defeat the Chicago Cubs, 4 games to 2. . . . *Kentucky Derby:* Exterminator. *Preakness:* War Cloud and Jack Hare, Jr. (the field being too large for one running, it is decided to run the 1918 Preakness in two separate heats; for some reason, the deciding race between War Cloud and Jack Hare, Jr., is never run). *Belmont Stakes:* Johren . . . *Indy 500:* Race not held because of war. . . . *Boxing:* Like many other aspects of American life, all boxing titles remain "frozen" during war year of 1918. . . . *Golf: USGA Men's Open:* No tournament because of war . . . *PGA:* No tournament because of war . . . *Hockey:* Winner of 1917–18 Stanley Cup in first year of new National Hockey League: Toronto Arenas . . . *Football:* The *Rose Bowl* goes patriotic, pitting the Mare Island Marines against the Army's Camp Lewis. Mare Island wins, 19–7.

Other Happenings: Joining the ranks of those major colleges eliminating football in 1917 are many more for 1918, including: Alabama, Arizona, Boston University, Colgate, Cornell, Detroit, LSU, Marshall, Missouri, Montana State, New Mexico State, Stanford, Texas Western, Utah, Utah State, Washington, Washington State, West Virginia, William & Mary, Wyoming, and Yale. . . . Willie Hoppe runs the exhibition record of 25 points at 3-cushion play against Charles Peterson. . . . Jockey Frank Robinson rides 185 winners. . . . Joe Malone of Quebec City is top National Hockey League scorer with 44 goals in 20 games. . . . On June 3, Hub Leonard of Boston pitches only no-hit game in American League, and majors, defeating Detroit, 5–0. . . . Hobey Baker, great amateur hockey player, is one of World War I casualties; a combat pilot, he is killed in a plane crash. Other athletes among the missing include Eddie Grant, former third baseman with Cleveland, Phillies, Reds, and Giants, who is killed in the Argonne Forest, and Alex Burr, a minor leaguer who played briefly with the Yankees. . . . In February, Knute Rockne is appointed athletic director at Notre Dame. . . . Major-league baseball owners chip in to help the war effort by raising admission prices (the rationale is that by not having to handle pennies, they will free ticket sellers for war work). . . . Fight fans are saddened to hear of the death of John L. Sullivan in February. . . . American League season concludes with Babe Ruth and Clarence Walker of the A's tied for home-run leadership with 11. . . . American Army and Navy men perform a series of baseball exhibitions for King George of Great Britain during the summer. . . . The American Association quits for the duration and, getting into the spirit of performing nonessential work in a hurry, the Giants defeat the Brooklyn Dodgers on August 30 in just 56 minutes.

1919

Winners: Baseball: Having made the world safe for democracy—temporarily—the United States returns to baseball with a vengeance. One change increases the World Series to a best-of-9 playoff. Ironically, the new utopia created by war's sacrifice begins with a World Series that is so obviously fixed that even baseball's highest officials see it. For the record, the Cincinnati Reds, underdogs, crush the surprisingly docile Chicago White Sox, 5 games to 3. . . . *Kentucky Derby:* Sir Barton. *Preakness:* Sir Barton. *Belmont Stakes:* Sir Barton (first Triple Crown winner) . . . *Indy 500:* Howdy Wilcox (88.05 mph) . . . *Boxing:* Not being able to avoid defending his heavyweight crown much longer, Jess Willard finally creeps into the ring with Jack Dempsey, sits down in his corner in the third round, takes the $100,000 guarantee, and runs. On March 17, Jack Britton knocks out Ted Lewis in 9 rounds to become welterweight champion. . . . *Golf: USGA Men's Open:* Walter Hagen . . . *PGA:* James M. Barnes . . . *Hockey:* 1918–19 Stanley Cup winner: no one. For the first and only time in the history of the NHL, a Stanley Cup champion is not declared. After the fifth game of the playoffs between Seattle and Montreal, it is decided to cancel the series because of the raging influenza epidemic, which decimates Canadien ranks. Bad Joe Hall dies in a hospital several days later and the playoff is never completed. . . . *Football:* Not knowing that the war would end quite so suddenly, the *Rose Bowl* committee selects Great Lakes Navy and Mare Island Marines as participants in the postseason classic. Great Lakes wins, 17–0.

Other Happenings: On September 28, the Giants beat their own "short work" record of 1918 by doing away with the Phillies, 6–1, in just 51 minutes. . . . Not only are the Chicago White Sox a bit venal, on November 23, the original Mr. Clean of American college football, George Gipp of Notre Dame, plays as a professional and collects $200. . . . Henry Kendall College outscores the opposition on the gridiron, 592–27, and Ira Rodgers of West Virginia is the national scoring leader with 147 points. . . . Biggest upset of the year is reserved for race horse named Upset, who upsets Man o' War on August 13 at Saratoga, winning the Sanford Memorial Stakes and spoiling the great horse's record. . . . On January 1, pitcher Fred Toney is convicted of violating the Mann White Slave Act and sentenced to 4 months in jail. . . . Babe Ruth hits 29 home runs, breaking Ned Wiliamson's 1884 record of 27. . . . Major-league no-hitters are pitched by Hod Eller of the Cincinnati Reds and Ray Caldwell of the Boston Red Sox. . . . In September an announcement is made that a professional football club known as the New York Giants will be formed. . . . Pitcher Slim Sallee, having his best year with the Cincinnati Reds, dispatches the Brooklyn Dodgers in a game on just 65 pitches.

1920

Winners: Baseball: In one of the most interesting World Series since its inception, the Cleveland Indians meet the Brooklyn Dodgers. Unusual plays abound—pitcher Jim Bagby of the Indians smashes the first home run ever by a pitcher in the Series, while teammate Elmer Smith hits the first World Series grand-slam homer. Bill Wambsganss, Cleveland second baseman, performs the first Series unassisted triple play, in game No. 5, and Dodger pitcher Clarence Mitchell reaches the nadir of futility by hitting into a triple play and then a double play. The Indians win, 5 games to 2. . . . *Kentucky Derby:* Paul Jones. *Preakness:* Man o' War. *Belmont Stakes:* Man o' War . . . *Indy 500:* Gaston Chevrolet . . . *Boxing:* On October 12, French light-heavyweight Georges Carpentier knocks out Battling Levinsky to take crown, then looks to fight with Dempsey. In middleweight division, Johnny Wilson wins a 12-round decision over Mike O'Dowd to become new champ. Crowd at ringside is not happy with verdict of judges, however. . . . Bantamweight Joe Lynch wins title from Pete Herman via a 15-round decision. . . . *Golf: USGA Men's Open:* Ted Ray. *PGA:* Jock Hutchison . . . *Hockey:* 1919–20 Stanley Cup winner: Ottawa Senators . . . *Football: Rose Bowl:* Harvard 7, Oregon 6 . . . *Basketball:* College champion selected by Helms Athletic Foundation: Pennsylvania (22–1).

Other Happenings: On October 2, in the only baseball tripleheader of the twentieth century, Cincinnati beats Pittsburgh twice, then has the third game called because of darkness. . . . On February 22, the first dog race using a mechanical rabbit is run at Emeryville, California. . . . Football is broadcast on radio on November 25, WTAW, College Station, Texas, carrying the game between Texas and Texas A&M. Texas wins, 7–3. . . . WWJ, Detroit, carries prize fight on September 6, Jack Dempsey vs. Billy Miske. The new champion wins by a knockout in the third round. . . . James Leech of VMI leads nation's scorers on gridiron with 210 points, and Henry-Kendall College continues to smother the opposition—in 1920 by 622–21. . . . Jockey James Rutwell rides 152 winners during the year. . . . The first horseshoe-pitching tournament for women is held at Asbury Park, New Jersey. Miss Marjorie Voorhees is winner. . . . In National League, Brooklyn and Boston play the majors' longest game, a 26-inning, 1–1 tie. Both starting pitchers, Leon Cadore for Brooklyn and Joe Oeschger for the Braves, are there at the end. . . . Walter Johnson of Senators pitches only no-hitter in major leagues, blanking the Red Sox on July 1, 1–0. . . . Sports casualty of the year is Notre Dame's George Gipp, 1920 All-American, who dies on December 14, of pneumonia. . . . On October 12, Man o' War becomes top money-winning race horse by beating Sir Barton in match race at Kenilworth Park. It is Man o' War's last race. . . . On September 17, a meeting is held in Canton, Ohio, at which the National Football League, known initially as the American Professional Football Association, is formed. . . . Sir Thomas Lipton returns for another go at America's Cup but his vessel, *Shamrock IV,* loses a close series of races, 3–2, to the U.S. entry, *Resolute.* . . . Man o' War is not entered in Kentucky Derby because his owner thinks 1¼ miles in May is too far for a 3-year-old to run. . . . Founded on February 12: the National Negro Baseball League.

Section VI
The 1920s

CHAPTER 23 — 1921

The word "league" was on many people's lips as the new year began. President Woodrow Wilson had spent his final year in office lobbying for the United States to join the League of Nations, and George Herman (Andy) Lawson announced on the first of January that 1921 would bring Americans a third baseball league, the Continental, to compete with the existing circuits. Not many people agreed that there was a need for another baseball league; fewer still thought the League of Nations was worthwhile.

There was unfinished business from 1919 and 1920 to be taken care of, the new year starting with conspiracy charges being leveled at the eight "Black Sox" players charged with throwing the World Series of 1919. On September 28, 1920, indictments had been brought against the men but several important witnesses still remained to be found before the trial could proceed.

Warren G. Harding, the man who looked like he ought to be President, announced that he would be the first man to be driven by motorcar, rather than carriage, to the inauguration. It was, some said, his first and last really good decision.

In anticipation of that innovation, Americans spent their second New Year's Eve without the support of strong drink, Prohibition having been enacted in 1919. They discovered that enforced sobriety did not get much better with repetition, but the crowds were generally sober. Occasionally, local authorities admitted, there were glimpses of obviously "soaked" violators amid the silent celebrants. As to what they were drinking and how they obtained it—well, it was most likely a bottle of pre-1919 whiskey that had been tucked away rather than illegally manufactured spirits.

MOTORCYCLING

At the stroke of midnight, at least one organized athletic event started, the Crotona Motorcycle Club of the Bronx laying claim to the first officially sanctioned event of 1921. During the hours before midnight, a large group of riders began to assemble at Fordham Square, for the 150-mile endurance race to Poughkeepsie was truly a democratic affair. Everyone was eligible, including champion endurance riders, hill climbers, factory riders, even a smattering of motorcyclists who had first spun wheels in France as Army dispatch riders. A prolonged cheer sent the men northward.

TENNIS

More significant from an athletic point of view, news arrived to happy Americans that the Davis Cup tennis sweep by the U.S. team was complete. On January 1, William T. Tilden II of Philadelphia and William M. Johnson of San Francisco applied the finishing touches to the Australian team at Auckland, New Zealand, by defeating Gerald L. Patterson and Norman L. Brookes in the men's singles events ending the tournament. The United States won the cup by a score of 5–0.

As the day began, every seat was taken as William Johnson and Norman Brookes moved onto the court for the first match. Volleying superbly, Brookes continued to break Johnson's game, and after a "keenly contested battle," took the first set, 7–5. After that, the younger American forced the action, winning the next three sets, 7–5, 6–3 and 6–3. Bill Tilden started off in the same manner, seeming listless compared to the brilliant play shown by his opponent. "From cuts to drives and from volleys to smashes he scarcely missed anything," a reporter wrote of Patterson. But after taking the first set by a score of 7–5, Patterson visibly slackened the pace and Tilden's game steadied. The American took the second set, 6–2, then with the third set tied at 2–2, Patterson began to show signs of extreme fatigue, missing strokes he had made bril-

Tennis's Top Twenty—1921 (United States)

Men

1—*William T. Tilden II, Philadelphia*
2—*William M. Johnson, San Francisco*
3—*Richard N. Williams II, Boston*
4—*Ishlyo Kumagas, New York*
5—*Willis E. Davis, San Francisco*
6—*Clarence J. Griffin, San Francisco*
7—*Watson M. Washborn, New York*
8—*Charles S. Garland, Pittsburgh*
9—*Nathaniel E. Niles, Boston*
10—*Wallace F. Johnson, Philadelphia*

Women

1—*Mrs. Molla B. Mallory, New York*
2—*Miss Marion Zinderstein, West Newton, Massachusetts*
3—*Miss Eleanor Tennant, Los Angeles*
4—*Miss Helen Baker, San Francisco*
5—*Miss Eleanor Goss, New York*
6—*Mrs. Edward Raymond, Hartsdale, New York*
7—*Miss Marie Wagner, Yonkers, New York*
8—*Miss Helene Polink, New York*
9—*Miss Edith Sigourney, Boston*
10—*Miss Margaret Grove, New York*

liantly earlier in the contest. Tilden went on to take the third and fourth sets, 6–3 and 6–3.

BOXING

Boxing was also much in the news at the beginning of the new year, lightweight champion Benny Leonard becoming the first to stage a title defense. The battle, held at Madison Square Garden on January 14, was unique in that it was attended by a variety of high society people, many dressed in evening clothes for the occasion. There was a catch, naturally. Women going to boxing matches were still frowned upon, but the Leonard-Ritchie Mitchell fight had been given society's blessing in that it was sponsored by the American Committee for Devastated France. Before the evening was over, more than eighty thousand dollars had been raised for America's World War I ally.

The fight crowd that night was unlike any preceding it. When the doors of the arena were thrown open, a wave of austere men in drab business suits began to fill the four galleries and much of the level area around the ring. Next appeared a group of women in bright evening dress—program vendors selling their wares for war-torn France. They were greeted with cheers followed by sharp injunctions to "buy them programs," and hisses for those who declined.

The heroine of the affair, Mrs. Anne Morgan, leader of the charity drive for France, then swirled imperiously into her box on the Twenty-seventh Street side of the arena. She too received prolonged applause, as did former New York Governor Al Smith and other stalwart figures of the social and financial world. Veteran ring announcer Joe Humphreys, clad in tails—which seemed to shock the galleryites and regulars, some of whom shouted sarcastic comments to him—introduced the fighters, and one of the most

crowd-pleasing bouts ever held in the Garden began.

Ritchie Mitchell of Milwaukee was regarded as a promising young fighter but few gave him much of a chance against Leonard, the "boxing master" from New York's East Side. As the bout started, however, almost as many eyes were on the society women as the fighters, for there was a great deal of curiosity as to whether the ladies would react with revulsion or delight at the spectacle of near-naked men hammering away at each other.

The first round brought a rapid end to concern about the ladies. Leonard started in his usual cautious manner, his hair carefully slicked down as if he were out for a night on the town rather than in the ring. Less than a minute after the bout started, however, he suddenly saw an opening and threw a quick left hook to Mitchell's exposed jaw. Mitchell fell to the canvas and took an eight count. When he arose, Leonard immediately pursued the attack by throwing a shower of lefts and rights, completely dazzling his opponent. A right to the ear sent Mitchell down for a second time.

As soon as he staggered to his feet, the challenger ran into another series of blows and for the third time in less than two minutes was on the canvas. The count of nine was barely heard over the shouting. Leonard kept after Mitchell but was obviously arm-weary and unable to apply the final blow. Recovering quickly, Mitchell suddenly lashed out a left hook and for the first time since he had won the lightweight championship at age twenty-one, Leonard left his feet. A stunned crowd watched as he managed to get up and dance away for the remainder of the round.

The second round was a continuation of the first, the big blow being a solid right by Mitchell that shook Leonard from head to toe. The champion fell into a clinch, from which Mitchell could not free himself in time to follow up the advantage. And near the end of the round Leonard had recovered sufficiently to stagger Mitchell with a hard right to the jaw.

The next three rounds were a series of give-and-take that brought nearly continuous cheering from the audience of raucous regulars and bemused socialites. In the sixth, Leonard followed a short sparring session with a right that sent Mitchell sprawling. Taking a nine count, he arose, took a left and right, went down a second time for another nine count, got up, and retreated into a neutral corner where Leonard showered him with blows before Referee Haukop declared the fight over. "The fight, from beginning to end," one reporter enthused, "will live long in memory."

Other boxing news that month revolved about the coming Dempsey-Carpentier heavyweight title fight, which had become an on-again, off-again affair. On January 14, 1921, news that the National Boxing Association had placed a fifteen-dollar maximum ticket price threw the promoters into a state of shock. George "Tex" Rickard, who had promised Dempsey three hundred thousand dollars and Carpentier two hundred thousand dollars for just getting into the ring, argued that unless the ceiling were raised, it wouldn't be possible to stage big bouts in the future. He was crying wolf, of course. Eventually he made an enormous profit, but because citizens of the United States and France, where Carpentier had won just about every title available, were enthusiastic about the match, Rickard was not above injecting a bit of suspense into the buildup, perhaps raising the ante in the bargain.

Boxing news also emanated from Boston, where the Massachusetts commission, at the request of the American Legion, issued a ban against boxers wearing trunks decorated with stars and stripes or other emblems similar to the American flag. They also requested that prizefighters refrain from making religious signs while in the ring.

WRESTLING

In addition, 1921 saw the emergence of a new wrestling champion named Ed "Strangler" Lewis. These were the days when wrestling was a genuine sport rather than a well-rehearsed exhibition of ham acting. Nevertheless, Lewis had a great deal of ham in him, realizing that gate receipts went up in direct proportion to the amount of hatred audiences felt for colorful ring villains. In 1920, Lewis—his real name was Robert Friedrich—met wrestling champion Ed Strecker at the 71st Regiment Armory in New York, winning as the result of his deadly headlock, a hold

from which no opponent could seem to escape. This, naturally, earned Lewis the title "Strangler" (there was also a nineteenth-century wrestler with that name) as well as the enmity of crowds all across the nation.

The month of January 1921 was a busy one for the new champion, Lewis. First he took on Earl Caddock, a perfectly proportioned 188-pound Iowan who was very popular with wrestling audiences everywhere. Lewis, at 228 pounds, was not only heavier but also considerably stronger. The outcome, then, was obvious from the outset, but the crowd gave Caddock every bit of vocal support it could muster. For more than ninety minutes the two traded holds, and at one point, when Caddock got Lewis in a powerful toehold, it seemed that the miracle was about to happen. Referee George Bothner—formerly a wrestling champion himself—stepped in and "asked Lewis if he wished to concede the fall to escape the pain, but the Kentuckian grimly shook his head negatively and finally knocked Caddock from him."

Caddock, who was obviously more slippery than most, committed the mistake of allowing Lewis to fasten his patented headlock for one minute, forty-five seconds, at which point Caddock worked his way free but was considerably weakened by the effort. Not long after that, Lewis wore his opponent down to the point where he threw him bodily to the canvas and won the fall. As Caddock lay motionless on the floor of the ring, the crowd exploded with anger against Lewis, who had to be escorted to his dressing room by police officers. The following week, Lewis defended his title at Rochester against a Texan named Dick Daviscourt. The match lasted one hour, twenty minutes, ending with Daviscourt being carried out of the ring with a dislocated vertebra. Five days after that, the unpopular champion was again escorted from the ring, this time at Kansas City, following the application of a deadly headlock on Gustav Sulzo. When Sulzo lay on the canvas, apparently unconscious, an angry crowd rushed forward to surround the ring, but police arrived in time to prevent injury—which more than likely would have befallen the first person foolhardy enough to take on Lewis.

Strangler Lewis's Lifetime Statistics: *6,200 matches, defeated only 33 times Total earnings: $4 million*

HORSERACING

On January 29, 1921, the horse called the greatest racer of all time, Man o' War, made

Man O' War's Record:

1919—2-year-old:

Date	Track	Event	Finish
June 6	Belmont	Purse Race	1st
June 9	Belmont	Keene Memorial Stakes	1st
June 21	Jamaica	Youthful Stakes	1st
June 23	Aqueduct	Hudson Stakes	1st
July 5	Aqueduct	Tremont Stakes	1st
Aug. 2	Saratoga	U. S. Hotel Stakes	1st
Aug. 13	Saratoga	Sanford Memorial Stakes	2nd (by ½ length)
Aug. 23	Saratoga	Grand Union Hotel Stakes	1st
Aug. 30	Saratoga	Hopeful Stakes	1st
Sept. 13	Belmont	Futurity Stakes	1st

1920—3-year-old:

Date	Track	Event	Finish
May 18	Pimlico	Preakness Stakes	1st
May 29	Belmont	Withers Stakes	1st
June 12	Belmont	Belmont Stakes	1st
June 22	Jamaica	Stuyvesant Handicap	1st
July 10	Aqueduct	Dwyer Stakes	1st
Aug. 7	Saratoga	Miller Stakes	1st
Aug. 21	Saratoga	Travers Stakes	1st
Sept. 4	Belmont	Lawrence Realization Stakes	1st
Sept. 11	Belmont	Jockey Club Stakes	1st
Sept. 18	Havre de Grace	Potomac Handicap	1st
Oct. 12	Kenilworth Park	Kenilworth Park Gold Cup	1st

his final public appearance before a large crowd at the Kentucky Jockey Club track at Lexington. Galloping up and down the homestretch twice, the huge chestnut stallion seemed as spry as ever, but the decision had been made to retire "Big Red" to stud. The jockey for this proud and melancholy event was a workout rider named Clyde Gordon, who had helped train the horse from the time he was a yearling.

The next day, announcement was made that the New York Yankees, "who have been living with their stepbrothers, the Giants, for so long a time that the hospitality of the latter appeared slightly frayed in spots a year or so ago," planned to build a new facility. The site, occupied in 1921 by the Hebrew Orphan Asylum, was bounded on the north and south by 138th and 136th streets, respectively, just off Broadway. The cost, it was disclosed, would be "heavy . . . in the neighborhood of two million dollars. It may run a little under this figure but not much." Only twenty minutes from Times Square, the new stadium was to be built of steel and concrete and have a size sufficient to "surpass in seating capacity any stands ever erected for a baseball park. In fact, it is said only the Yale Bowl will surpass the new stadium in this respect among all stands built for purposes of sporting spectacles."

WRESTLING

In February, Ed Lewis was back in the headlines, largely as a result of promoter Jack Curley's announcement that he would promote no more bouts in which the headlock was permitted. Billy Sandow, Lewis's manager, responded in a conciliatory tone. "Jack Curley has done so much for the game," he said, "that we will be the last ones to handicap him with any selfish motives. If Jack feels that the game would suffer through the headlock we can get along without it. His fairness to us is unquestionable, and we will abide by his ruling." With that, Ed "Strangler" Lewis continued to grind opponents' heads and necks into gross caricatures of themselves.

BASEBALL

Interest in the trial of the Black Sox was re-

The 1921 Yankees' "Expensive" New Facility
Compared to Later Stadia:

Houston: Astrodome	$31.6 million
Pittsburgh: Three Rivers Stadium	$55 million
Pontiac: Metropolitan Stadium	$55.7 million
Seattle: Kingdome	$60 million
New Orleans: Superdome	$163 million

The Eight Black Sox—Comparison of their records in 1917 World Series performances (clean) with that of 1919 (thrown):

Player		Position	A.B.	H.	B.A.	W.	L.
Eddie Cicotte	(1917)	Pitcher				1	1
	(1919)	Pitcher				1	2
Claud Williams	(1917)	Pitcher				0	0
	(1919)	Pitcher				0	3
Oscar Felsch	(1917)	Outfield	22	6	.272		
	(1919)	Outfield	26	5	.192		
Charles Gandil	(1917)	First base	23	6	.261		
	(1919)	First base	30	7	.233		
Joe Jackson	(1917)	Outfield	23	7	.304		
	(1919)	Outfield	32	12	.375		
Fred McMullin	(1917)	Infield	24	3	.125		
	(1919)	Infield	2	1	.500		
Charles Risberg	(1917)	Infield	2	1	.500		
	(1919)	Infield	25	2	.080		
George Weaver	(1917)	Infield	21	7	.333		
	(1919)	Infield	34	11	.324		

vived when the opening court session was set for March 14. Judge William E. Dever also ordered the state's attorney to start extradition proceedings against any defendants who skipped town in order to avoid being brought to trial.

In fact, the decision had already been rendered. Arriving in Chicago on the day before the trial, White Sox owner Charles Comiskey disposed of any notion that the players might be allowed to play ball again, even if they were acquitted. "Those players," he said, "are on my ineligible list. There is absolutely no chance for them to play on my team again unless they can clear themselves to my satisfaction of the charges made against them by three of their teammates."

As Opening Day of 1921 approached, thirty-four-year-old Frank "Home Run" Baker, who had retired in 1919, announced that he was making a comeback. The Yankees, who owned his contract, readily agreed—providing the new strongman of baseball, Commissioner K. M. Landis, would allow Baker to return after in effect declaring himself a free agent for the 1920 season.

When a delay in their trial was announced, the eight players known as the Black Sox decided to capitalize on their notoriety by scheduling an exhibition game in Chicago with a team known as the Aristo Giants. When word of the coming contest at Murley Park reached the directors of the Chicago Baseball League, an emergency meeting was called for the purpose of banning the game and protecting the innocent from being soiled by the outlaws. Word was sent out to members of the Aristo Giant squad that any players who engaged the Black Sox in a game would be outlawed themselves from organized ball. The Commonwealth Edison Company, which owned the park in which the contest had been scheduled, also panicked, quickly notifying the manager of the Giants that the grounds would not be available for the eight players under indictment. If that were not enough, the Umpires' Protective League then ordered its men to refrain from working games of this nature. Not unexpectedly, the game between the Black Sox and the Aristo Giants was canceled.

Opening Day, meanwhile, was a big success as more than 160,000 fans paid their way into the ball parks, breaking two attendance records and causing officials to proclaim "the comeback of baseball." A noticeable sigh of relief accompanied the successful debut of the game's first season since the Black Sox disclosures, a sigh that often found expression in purple prose. In fact, many officials and ordinary lovers of baseball had expressed concern that Americans might have lost faith in the sanctity of the national game as a result of the fix charges. They need not have worried, of course, as Americans, then as later, loved nothing better than expressing forgiveness to persons or even national institutions.

Sportswriter Purple Prose—1921:
"The baseball season of 1921 burst into being full-panoplied, like Minerva emerging from the cracked brow of Jove, yesterday afternoon at the Polo Grounds. . . ."

The baseball season barely started, interest continued in a variety of other sports, although not with the same amount of sustained intensity. Western athletes seemed to be making considerable inroads on the accomplishments of Easterners. In swimming, Honolulu's Judy Langer was recognized as the best in her class, especially the 100- and the 440-yard free-style. Even more impressive were the running records being broken by Charles W. Paddock of the University of Southern California. Already the holder of the Olympic 100-meter record and national 220-yard championship, in April Paddock broke four existing records and tied two, including the 100-yard dash (9⅗ seconds) and the 220-yard dash 21⅕ seconds). All of this was accomplished, incidentally, at the same meet. (The 100-yard time of 9.6 seconds was first made by Dan Kelly in 1906 at Spokane, Washington, and equaled in 1914 by Howard P. Drew.)

Charles Paddock's Records—1921:
100 meters—10⅖ sec. (New Record)
200 meters—21⅕ sec. (New Record)
300 meters—33⅘ sec. (New Record)
300 yards —30⅕ sec. (New Record)

What, by the way, was happening to the new Continental Baseball League, scheduled to open its first season on May 20? The question was not exactly a burning one, but a certain number of people were mildly curious, especially if they lived in Chicago, Winnipeg, Boston, Philadelphia, New York, Buffalo, Cleveland, or Providence, the eight cities with franchises. Commissioner Lawson replied that everything was proceeding as scheduled, or similarly vague words to that effect.

Baseball nostalgia was created when word arrived from Decatur, Illinois, that Joe McGinnity, known as "Iron Man," had celebrated his fiftieth birthday by pitching four innings for a team known as the Staley Yanigans (or "rookies") against the state regulars. McGinnity, whose major-league career spanned the years 1899–1908, gave up two hits and no runs.

Nostalgia on a different level reared its head several days later as officials opened all stops in order to track down everyone connected with the 1919 World Series scandal. George Gorman, assistant state's attorney for the prosecution, was concerned that a couple of important witnesses had fled the country. These were Abe Attell, former world's featherweight champion, and Joseph "Sport" Sullivan, a well-known gambler. Without the testimony of these men, it was feared the case against the Black Sox would crumble. Meanwhile, Hal Chase, a former baseball player, was arrested in San Jose, California, and ordered sent to Chicago in order to testify. Ban Johnson, president of the American League, perhaps summarized the feeling of most sports fans when he said, "I believe that all the guilty ones, players and gamblers, will be dealt with severely. A term of imprisonment would not surprise me at all."

The activity on the playing field during all this legal maneuvering was sufficient to keep most fans interested. In 1920, the Cleveland franchise had won its first pennant of any sort, then defeated the Brooklyn Dodgers in the best-of-nine World Series, 5 games to 2. Led by Tris Speaker, the Indians were anxious to prove that 1920 had been no freak of nature, and they moved into a quick lead, followed closely by the New York Yankees. New York had finished third in 1920 as pitcher-slugger Babe Ruth hit 54 home runs, a figure so high many fans could barely comprehend it—unless they had seen the spindly-legged, barrel-chested Ruth in action. Breaking quickly from the starting gate in 1921, Ruth had eight round-trippers by May 7, when he smashed the longest home run ever hit at Washington off Walter Johnson. Somewhat surprisingly, the city of New York soon noticed that a friendly intramural rivalry had developed between Ruth and Giant first baseman George Kelly. In 1920, Kelly hit only 11 home runs in 155 games with the Giants, but as the 1921 season progressed, it was noted that he was only one home run behind Ruth. The National League record for round-trippers in a single season at that time was a modest 27, set by Chicago's Ned Williamson in 1884. Since then, only Washington's Buck Freeman had come close, by hitting 25 in 1899. Thus, as 1921 statisticians pointed out, it might be possible for the home-run records in both leagues to be wiped out in the same season—by players representing New York clubs! Both players, of course, generated a faithful following urging them in the direction of that goal.

WRESTLING

In May there was a temporary but happy diversion from the baseball races as Stanislaus Zbyszko, a veteran Polish wrestler, took on the still unpopular Strangler Lewis for the world's championship at New York's 22nd Regiment Armory. "The bout," one reporter wrote, "was one of the fastest, most furiously contested wrestling tests ever seen in this city." Even better from most fans' standpoint, Lewis was defeated. True to his image, Strangler started the bout by leaping at Zbyszko with his arm poised, ready to grasp the Pole's neck and shake until he was ready to drop. But Zbyszko hunched his shoulders in such a way that not only did Lewis miss the hold, he also landed flat on his back on the mat, stunned. Without a moment's hesitation, Zbyszko rushed at the fallen Lewis and quickly encircled his neck, pinning his shoulders to the canvas at the same time.

Suddenly the match was over. Lewis had been dethroned. The crowd was spellbound for a moment; then "there came a volcanic roar which swept over the big armory. Also came one of the wildest scenes ever enacted at a local wrestling bout. Men and women, carried away in the prevailing spirit of excitement, rushed and crushed each other in their eagerness to gain the ringside and there clamber upon the platform to congratulate the winner."

BOXING

By this time Americans were preparing for the great heavyweight championship battle between Jack Dempsey and Georges Carpentier, for all financial and moral obstacles had been swept aside and work started on a huge octagonal stadium capable of seating 90,000 people. Situated on a lot near Jersey City—it was called Boyle's Thirty Acres in honor of a paper manufacturer—the arena was actually the world's largest collection of cheap temporary seats. Work began on the $250,000 structure on April 28, 1921, and continued for two months, at which time the last nail was driven and the hulk declared "a testimonial to the daring of Rickard." In a way, this is absolutely true. The arena, hastily thrown together, could just barely support the anticipated weight and no one had the slightest idea what would happen if that weight began shifting or moving in unusual ways. Such considerations were swept aside in the preflight ballyhoo, which continued for more than two months. The public seemed about evenly divided in preference for the two men, although few realized how small Carpentier was compared to Dempsey, and Tex Rickard, not wishing to destroy the Frenchman's image, did little to inform them. In fact, at 170 pounds, Carpentier was not only giving away a strong edge in talent and ferocity but 25 pounds as well.

One ingenious method of keeping Carpentier from public view was to set up a private training camp on an estate at Manhasset, Long Island, complete with barbed-wire entanglements and state troopers patrolling as guards. Ostensibly, these precautions were taken to prevent the discovery of Carpentier's "secret punch." Newsmen who climbed trees with spyglasses or disguised themselves as society folk and gained entrance reported seeing no such punch, however, and of course there was no such thing.

Going along with the prefight con act,

Dempsey himself expressed concern over the fact that because he did not understand French, it might be possible for Carpentier and his seconds to take advantage of him during the fight "by passing out forbidden advice." Exactly what this "forbidden advice" might be was not disclosed. In an effort to combat it, however, Dempsey stated his intention of learning French before July 2, the date of the fight. Reference was made also to the "hypnotic eye" employed by Carpentier, another red herring, as well as the fact that Dempsey had tried to evade the draft in 1917–18. (That charge had been disproved, but much of the public, including many veterans' groups, refused to accept Dempsey's innocence.) At any rate, the natural charm of Carpentier, added to Dempsey's being cast as a semivillain, guaranteed the box-office success of that battle.

BASEBALL

While waiting for the fight to take place, those interested in baseball took time to speculate on the growing epidemic of home runs in both major leagues. In 1920, it was pointed out, the American League produced a total of 369 home runs and the National 261. Both of these figures, it was noted, "were so far beyond the normal totals for home runs that they occasioned considerable comment. . . . A livelier ball is the only answer that fits the case. It is true that the restrictions which were imposed upon pitchers, starting with the 1920 season [primarily abolition of the spitball and other unorthodox deliveries] and still in force, have made hitting easier, but even this does not explain the great advance in home-run hitting. The fact that many players who seldom hit for the circuit have branched out as long-distance sluggers is not explained satisfactorily by changes in pitching rules." Thus began a controversy that was to last for decades. Baseball manufacturers, when interviewed, officially denied tampering with or adding anything new to the post-1919 balls. They did admit to using a better grade of Australian wool. "That may be the answer," one writer concluded. "At any rate the ball is livelier than in the past and home runs are blooming where they never bloomed before."

Records of another sort were being challenged in the highest minor league, the International, where a gawky, twenty-one-year-old left-handed pitcher named Robert Grove (often misspelled Groves) was leading the Baltimore Orioles in an assault on professional baseball's undefeated game streak. Early in June, Grove and the Orioles won game No. 20, bringing the team's log to a scorching 35–10. Six more victories followed and the Orioles were just a single game from tying,

Home-run Hitting, 1910–60 (8-club Leagues, 154-game Season)

Year	League	Total H.R.	Avg. per Club
1910	National	214	27
1910	American	145	18
1915	National	225	28
1915	American	160	20
1920	National	261	33
1920	American	369	46
1925	National	634	79
1925	American	533	67
1935	National	662	83
1935	American	663	83
1950	National	1100	138
1950	American	973	122
1960	National	1042	130
1960	American	1086	136
1970 (12-club Leagues, 162-game Season)			
1970	National	1683	140
1970	American	1746	146
Adjusted to 154 games			
	National	1599	133
	American	1659	138

two games from beating, the record when they took the field for a doubleheader with Buffalo. Two hours later, they had won game No. 27, but the nightcap was a disaster. Buffalo jumped all over the Oriole pitchers for a 19–8 victory.

Undefeated Record, 1921
Major Leagues: 1916, New York Giants: 26 games (27 if one tie game is counted)
All Professional: 1902, Corsica, Texas League, 27 games

With the major-league season one third completed, New Yorkers began to hope that for the first time in the history of the modern World Series, teams from their city would represent both leagues (the only other intracity series had been in 1906, involving the Chicago White Sox and Cubs). Tied at the top of the National League were Pittsburgh and the New York Giants; at the top of the American were Cleveland and the Yankees. Thus the stage was definitely set for an early showdown when Cleveland arrived in New York on June 10 for a two-game confrontation with the Yankees. Twenty thousand persons stormed the Polo Grounds for the first contest, which featured the Yankees' underhander Carl Mays (26–11 in 1920) against Cleveland ace Jim Bagby (31–12 the previous year).

Cleveland jumped to an early 1–0 lead, but the Yankees tied it in the third when Babe Ruth hit his seventeenth homer of the year into the upper deck. Then, after falling behind, 3–1, the home team scored five times in the seventh and eighth innings to take the field for the ninth with a 6–3 edge.

The trouble started immediately when Roger Peckinpaugh scooped up Bill Wambsganss' grounder and hurled it far over first baseman Wally Pipp's outstretched glove. Tris Speaker followed with a double and Elmer Smith singled. Bob Shawkey came in to relieve Mays, but the onslaught continued, Larry Gardner, rookie Luke Sewell, and Jack Graney hitting safely to tie the game. In the tenth, neither team scored, but Larry Gardner led off the eleventh with a home run, and another run was added on a single by Sewell, an infield out, and Pinch Thomas's double. Cleveland won the game, 8–6.

BOXING
Then it was nearly time for the celebrated heavyweight championship fight. Tex Rickard's gamble had paid off: It appeared that the contest would be the first million-dollar prizefight in the history of the sport. Of that million-plus figure, the shrewd promoter would earn between three hundred thousand and four hundred thousand dollars after taxes, twice as much as the two fighters combined. But then, as Rickard was quick to point out, he was the one who made the ini-

tial financial outlay and took the lion's share of risks.

Betting on the fight was heavy, estimates indicating that upward of six hundred thousand dollars had been put up in the New York area alone. The odds varied from 4–1 down to 2–1 on the champion. At the last moment, a group of reformers attempted to use a court order as a means of stopping the fight, but the grand jury in Jersey City was not convinced. The reformers, however, did have the law on their side. According to New Jersey law, no prizefight could be held unless it was merely an exhibition. This meant that no decision could be rendered, nor could the bout last longer than twelve rounds. Intimidated by public opinion favoring the bout, the jury turned its head and threw out the injunction request.

Much more attention was given to making certain the fight would be an orderly affair. Rickard spent money from his own pocket to supplement the one thousand plainclothesmen and police officers assigned to the scene, and orders were issued that no planes would be allowed to fly over the arena. (Apparently there were those who were merely curious as well as those who saw the mass of people as an excellent target for advertising leaflets. The thought of several hundred thousand pieces of paper descending on his pet project during the middle of an exciting round must have haunted Rickard.)

Even more attention was given to getting the word out as to how the fight was progressing. Planes were hired to fly both news accounts and pictures of the event to all parts of the nation, and cable systems were devised in order to reach foreign countries. In Times Square, a wireless telephone was put into operation so that an announcer at ringside could send messages that would be displayed immediately in downtown New York, Boston, Philadelphia, and Syracuse. Written commentary would be supplemented by voice descriptions over giant amplifiers. "It will be the first time such close communication has ever been established between a great sporting event and the man in the street," one reporter noted. "The three horns will carry at least one hundred feet from the building, so that thousands will be within range of their powerful tones."

To make certain the battle would be preserved for posterity—and make a lot of extra money, besides—five motion-picture cameras were installed in the arena, two of which took nothing but slow-motion film, a decidedly new innovation.

On the morning of July 2, limousines, private railway cars, and ordinary trolleys started to disgorge an army of spectators that included not only ordinary fight fans but also princes, counts, ministers, ambassadors, baronets, countesses, and more than five thousand women. "Did you ever see so many millionaires?" Tex Rickard was supposed to have said over and over as he admired the quantity and quality of audience swarming into the house that Tex built. When Georges Carpentier arrived, the "Marseillaise" burst forth from a band, and the audience erupted into prolonged cheers. At that point, the huge structure began to sway noticeably and a few fans even cried out in alarm. Their voices were not heard, fortunately, and those down front, closer to the ground, apparently did not notice the upheaval quite as much.

Game Called on Account of Fight
On July 2, 1921, a scheduled baseball double-header between Newark and Jersey City of the International League was called off because none of the players showed up. As a matter of fact, no fans showed up. Everybody, it seemed, had gone to the Dempsey-Carpentier fight.

A Trend That Said Carpentier Would Win Against Dempsey:
Perhaps it was merely a desire to generate some interest, but shortly before the fight it was noted that an alarming number of favorites in recent years had lost. The bouts were carefully selected to prove that point, but here is the "evidence" that Carpentier would win:

Year	Participants	Favorite	Winner
1892	Sullivan-Corbett	Sullivan	Corbett
1897	Corbett-Fitzsimmons	Corbett	Fitzsimmons
1899	Fitzsimmons-Jeffries	Fitzsimmons	Jeffries
1910	Johnson-Jeffries	Jeffries	Johnson
1915	Johnson-Willard	Johnson	Willard
1919	Willard-Dempsey	Willard	Dempsey
1921	Dempsey-Carpentier	Dempsey	?

Jack Dempsey arrived soon afterward, being greeted by a round of genuine applause mixed with occasional cries of "slacker!" and "bum!"

Having been urged by Tex Rickard to take it easy on Carpentier, ("If you kill this Frenchman, you'll kill boxing!") as well as advised by Jack Kearns, his manager, to box rather than rush, Dempsey did not charge straight ahead as he usually did. As a result, he looked awkward compared to the dazzling Carpentier. Several jabs bounced off Dempsey's face, including one that stung his right eye. The champion, angered, countered with a left to the body and a straight right to Carpentier's nose.

The second round was Carpentier's high-water mark. Instead of jabbing and feinting, he came out slugging, landing a hard right to Dempsey's jaw that sent him reeling backward. The crowd leaped to its feet, roaring to Carpentier to rush in and follow up his advantage. To his credit, Carpentier gave it a good try. Pinning Dempsey against the ropes, he threw punch after punch. Dempsey slipped some and blocked others, but enough landed so that it could truly be said that Dempsey was saved by the bell.

In Times Square, the audience gathered outside the bulletin board near the loudspeakers was nearly as excited as those in New Jersey. One particularly outspoken Frenchman entertained as well as infuriated those around him. "When the second round was conceded by the bulletins to Carpentier," a reporter wrote, "the Frenchman danced with glee and turned with an 'I told you so' expression to those about him. . . ."

The situation changed shortly after that. Springing at Carpentier at the sound of the gong, Dempsey reverted to his old form of charging bull, taking punishment but giving more. Retreating, Carpentier took shots to the eye and nose, his face became blotchy from the force of the blows; then blood spurted from his mouth. He, too, was saved by the bell, but not for long. In the fourth round, Dempsey continued to pursue, finally caught Carpentier, and sent him to the canvas. In Times Square, the horns squawked, "Carpentier down for the count of nine. . . ." In New Jersey, Dempsey stalked his foe, nearly helpless on wobbly legs. Another flurry of solid lefts and rights landed. On the radio, announcer J. Andrew White yelled: "The Frenchman is counting. . . . Carpentier makes no effort to rise. . . . The fight is over! Jack Dempsey remains heavyweight champion of the world!"

In Times Square there was bedlam. "Men threw their hats in the air, turned and shook hands with each other, patted each other on the back. Whatever feeling there might have been for Carpentier seemed to have been drowned by that growling roar of triumph. The world loves a winner."

Not everyone, of course, loved the fight. The Reverend John Roach Straton, of Manhattan's Calvary Baptist Church, immediately attacked the spectacle in his Sunday sermon the next day. "The most shocking thing to me," he said, "was the number of women who witnessed such a degrading spectacle, and even little girls in short dresses. These little girls came into the arena during a bloody preliminary contest and solicited funds for a hospital. They saw half-naked men pummeling each other in a brutal combat. . . . The International Reform Bureau, of which I am a member, is going to wage a vigorous campaign to stop prizefighting in the United States."

There's Always a Hoaxster

Geneva, Switzerland, July 3—A "pirate" newspaper that appeared for the first and last time last night under the title Les Nouvelles Sportives *published a long and vivid account of how Carpentier defeated Dempsey by a knockout blow within thirty seconds after the fighters entered the ring. The newspaper was eagerly purchased by rejoicing crowds in the cafes and hotels. When reliable newspapers appeared an hour later announcing Dempsey's victory, the majority refused to believe the news.*

The fight, an extremely profitable venture in that it generated gross receipts of $1.6 million and plenty of profit for everyone—including the United States Government, which grabbed about $600,000 worth of taxes—was followed by the inevitable next question: Who will be Dempsey's next opponent?

Jack Johnson had an answer to that. Just released from prison at Leavenworth, Kansas, following conviction of violating the Mann Act, Johnson issued a challenge: "I weigh 220 pounds and am in the best shape in my life," he declared. "The public wants Dempsey whipped and they know I'm the man to do it."

Dempsey's reply was swift and perhaps too much to the point. He would not fight Johnson "or any other Negro fighter. I will meet anyone else that Kearns picks for me," he said.

The summer of 1921 continued, creating new heroes and heroines of the sports world. There was, for example, golfer Jim Barnes' winning the twenty-first National Open Golf

Tourney at Washington, D.C., his first major victory in more than a decade. (President Harding proudly shook his hand.) . . . There was a young swimmer named Eugene Bolden, twice winner of the National AAU Ten-mile Championship, winning the event for a third time but being disqualified because he wore only an elastic supporter instead of a regulation swimsuit. (He had discarded the suit in the water when it became uncomfortable, he said.) . . . There was Suzanne Lenglen's promise to come to the United States and entertain the nation with what she hoped would be her best style of tennis. (She came but got sick and left in a huff.) . . . There was Maurice Archdeacon, nicknamed "Flash," a baseball player from Rochester who circled the base paths in 13⅗ seconds, beating Hans Lobert's 13⅖ seconds of October 9, 1910. (Archdeacon's major-league career was brief, 1923–25, and for all his speed he stole only thirteen bases during that time.) . . . There was Henry Sullivan, the swimmer from Lowell, Massachusetts, trying for the fourth and fifth times since 1913 to swim the English Channel. (He failed again.) . . . There was Elmer Smith, Cleveland right fielder, establishing a major-league record by hitting seven consecutive extra-base hits, for a total of twenty-two bases. (Cleveland traded him the next year.) . . . There was British speedboat driver Colonel Arthur Tate's challenging Gar Wood with his best vessel. (It sank.) . . . There was young Claude Noel, a pitcher for the Marshfield team of the Wisconsin Valley Baseball League, hurling two no-hitters within a four-day period and signing a big-league contract with the St. Louis Browns. (He never pitched an inning in the majors.) . . . And there was the conclusion of the Black Sox trial, which should have proven to all Americans the penalty of cheating when a jury returned a "guilty" verdict and recommended long prison sentences.

But that was not the way it turned out. Early in August, the eight players were acquitted, mostly because there was a distinct lack of hard evidence. The verdict of the courts mattered little to Commissioner Landis, however, as he proceeded to bar the players from the major leagues and went out of his way to hound them for decades thereafter. Minor-league officials jumped on the bandwagon, refusing to employ the players, who had been legally adjudged innocent. Most Americans agreed that this brand of free-lance justice was justified.

As summer turned to fall, the dream of New Yorkers to have an all-Manhattan World Series seemed closer to reality. As Babe Ruth passed his own record fifty-four home runs in a season, the Yankees gained on the Cleveland

Indians, then passed them. Total vengeance was exacted in September when the "Hugmen," as the Yankees were nicknamed in honor of their manager, Miller Huggins, defeated the Indians by a score of 21–7. The Giants, meanwhile, despite the failure of George Kelly to set a new National League record for homers—he hit only twenty-three after a brilliant start—gradually edged in front of Pittsburgh. And by the end of September it was official: The Yankees and Giants would fight it out during the best-of-nine World Series. New York, of course, was in a frenzy as the long-awaited conflict began. Giant fans were thrown into an immediate panic when Carl Mays shut out their favorites in the first game and Waite Hoyt did the same in the second. John McGraw, at least on the surface, remained calm. "I think we will go into Sunday's game with the Series tied," he said. He then added a few clichés that have held up quite well over passing decades. "Of course, when a team isn't hitting it looks bad . . . when a club can't hit it can't hope to win ball games. . . . Don't forget that a lot of people had us counted out of the National League race when we were 7½ games behind the Pirates, but we came through. . . . That's the kind of fighting ball club the Giants are. They are never licked until they have taken the full count."

News Item on the Series: Brother vs. Brother
The 1921 Series was only the second in which brothers played on opposite sides. (In 1920, Wheeler "Doc" Johnston of Cleveland faced his brother Jimmy Johnston of Brooklyn.) The brothers of 1921 were Bob Meusel of the Yankees and Emil Meusel of the Giants.

McGraw's prediction came true. In the very next game, the Giants rediscovered the art of hitting, drove across eight runs in one inning, and won going away, 13–5. The next day it was more artistic, a 4–2 victory, and the Series was even. The fifth game was highlighted by Babe Ruth's beating out a bunt to start a rally that led to Yankee victory No. 3, but the Giants tied it in the sixth game with an 8–5 win.

By this time, the public was visibly tired of the "fall classic," a fact that was not unnoticed by Commissioner Landis. Nine games, he said, was probably too much to sustain the average fan's interest. It would be better to reduce the World Series to a best-of-seven Series, as it had been from 1905 through 1918, at which point the owners' greed got the best of them.

That didn't solve the immediate problem, of course, which was left to the Giants. They disposed of the Yankees in the next two games, 2–1 and 1–0, to win it all. George Kelly, climaxing his swan dive after a highly successful spring, struck out ten times in the Series to equal the futility record set by Pittsburgh's Bill Abstein in the 1909 classic. Giant fans could hardly have cared less, for they had been forced to endure four consecutive World Series defeats since the McGrawmen won in 1905, and any kind of victory was sweet.

FOOTBALL

Attention was immediately switched to the college football season, already in full swing by the time the World Series ended. Thrills in abundance were available to Cornell rooters when the Big Red took on Western Reserve on October 15 at Ithaca. Cornell was favored to win the game, but no one was prepared for what happened on that fall afternoon. Capitalizing on spectacular runs by halfbacks Eddie Kaw and Red Gould, Cornell moved to a quick lead, then settled back and waited for Western Reserve to make mistakes. One came on the interception of a pass that was run back for a touchdown. It seemed that no matter what Western Reserve did, it eventually turned sour. During the third period, a pretty pass completion netted the men from Cleveland their only first down of the game, but on the very next play the runner was smothered and the drive halted. Displaying a sense of pity, the Cornell coach sent in the second and third teams, but nothing helped. "It was hardly football," one reporter wrote. "The constant sprinting of the Red backs reminded one more of a track meet."

The Score by Periods:

					Total
Cornell	21	34	21	34	110
Western Reserve	0	0	0	0	0

The threat of a national railroad strike caused football enthusiasts some concern that October. Of particular interest was the upcoming game between Harvard and Centre College of Danville, Kentucky. Harvard, undefeated in twenty-three games since 1916 (there were no contests during the war years of 1917 and 1918), would be engaging a team that many said was the best in the nation. Those advocates, however, were from the western portion of the country, which meant that their opinions were not necessarily valid. It would be academic, of course, if there were no means of transporting the teams from one area to another.

The strike did not affect football, as it turned out, which enabled Centre College to make the trip to Cambridge, Massachusetts, for the game on October 29. More than forty-five thousand fans were in the stands to see which of the teams could live up to its highly vaunted reputation.

Somehow, both clubs accomplished that goal. The first half was a scoreless tie characterized by hard hitting and stubborn defenses. Shortly after the second-half kickoff, Centre College took possession of the ball on its own forty-five-yard line. After a tripping penalty was called on Harvard, Centre picked up a first down on the Crimson thirty-three. The men of Harvard were not unnerved by this development. During the first half, Centre had driven to the Harvard thirty-two but had been stopped cold. On this occasion, however, Centre College quarterback Bo McMillin kept the ball himself and broke through a large hole with hardly a hand being laid on him. Suddenly there were only two men between McMillin and the goal line. McMillin raced as hard as he could for the corner of the end zone; then, as he was about to be hit, he stopped short and pivoted for the chalk marker. He was hit, but too late. Centre College led, 6–0.

When the Centre kicker missed the extra point (or "try for goal"), Harvard took heart. After another Centre College drive stalled, the Crimson took over on their own seven-yard line. Slowly the ball was moved up the field, the highlight being an eighteen-yard run that placed the ball on Centre College's forty-four. On third down, Harvard was faced with the need to gain seven yards. Quarterback Buell faded back and lofted the ball to Churchill. The pass was complete but before Churchill could cross the goal line he was smashed to the ground by McMillin and Roberts. Still, Harvard had possession on the Centre College three-yard line.

On the next play, however, Harvard was offside. The penalty was enough to spell the difference between victory and defeat. Centre College held and Harvard's undefeated streak was snapped at twenty-three.

The next week, a small crowd at the Polo Grounds had a taste of professional football when Jim Thorpe's Cleveland Tigers took on Charlie Brickley's Giants. The newspapers were decidedly lukewarm about the pro sport, however, seeming to think that it was beneath an athlete to perform after he had graduated from college. "The game was lopsided and had little to excite even the most rabid of rooters," one commentator wrote. "It was an orderly but nonpartisan gathering which contented itself with quietly watching the game over the tops of its well-buttoned overcoats, emerging now and then to laugh at the grotesqueness of some former star vainly trying to hit the line or run the ends as in days of yore." Thorpe's team won by a score of 17–0.

Two days before, professional football had been attacked in an editorial of the *Yale Daily News,* which stated that while college football had certain gentlemanly standards, pro ball had no such humane guidelines. "The growth of professional football," the editor added, "has not, fortunately, been rapid. Most college men recognize the risk of its degeneration and refuse to take it up. The exceptions that go into the football business are rewarded by the loss of respect of their colleges."

With that reservation, it was generally agreed that 1921 had been a banner year for sports in the United States. Many individual and team records had been made; the World Series had drawn more people and gate receipts than any previously; radio station WJZ, Newark, had become the first to broadcast play-by-play accounts of the World Series. But if there was any doubt as to the American's affinity for sports, one had to look only at the July 3, 1921, edition of a large metropolitan newspaper such as the New York *Times.*

On that date, two news items were carried that seemed of major importance. One, dealing with President Harding's signing a peace decree officially ending World War I, was assigned to a tiny single column to the far left of the page. The other, announcing Jack Dempsey's defeat of Georges Carpentier, consumed five columns of the front page in addition to a three-level headline.

It is well known that spectator sports such as baseball, basketball, soccer, football, ice hockey, golf, and tennis became favorites in various parts of the world during the second half of the nineteenth century, solidified their positions early in the twentieth, and now have huge international followings. These games, of course, were neither the first nor the last to be tested before an audience. As the "winners" for the hearts of spectators, they are remembered. But what of the "losers," the sports that flourished briefly and then passed into obscurity? What were they like and why did they fade away? Was it some arcane process of natural selection that did them in, or merely quirks of fate?

Below, a random selection of losing sports that were invented from scratch, evolved of necessity, or just happened along. The reader is free to judge if fate has been cruel or mercifully kind in relegating each to oblivion.

PAPERCHASING (HARES AND HOUNDS)

To the young men who inaugurated paperchasing in America, the sport must have seemed as delightfully wicked as streaking a century later. Hot-eyed runners pounding down city streets, leaping hedges, fording brooks, and leaving trails of shredded paper wherever they went constituted the sort of foolishness certain to raise eyebrows among the more sober citizens of the late 1870s and early 1880s. And when dozens of equally frantic pursuers came on the heels of the paper droppers, it seems safe to assume that the cry, "the younger generation is going to hell," was heard as often then as it is today.

The idea of paperchasing was started in England and first popped up in America during the fall of 1877. A group of young and athletic businessmen gathered around the forward cabin stove of the *Sylvan Dell,* one of the many Harlem River steamers that carried people to and from their New York jobs, were facing the prospect of another dull winter. Walter S. Vosburgh suggested that the men adopt the new outdoor game to amuse themselves during the cold weather. A few moments later the Westchester Hare and Hounds Club was formed.

Although the sport was simple enough, Vosburgh wrote to England for a book of instructions. Shortly after it arrived the first meeting

of the club was held, and Christmas Day 1877 was set as the date for the first paper chase. By the end of the decade, groups of young men all along the Eastern Seaboard were participating in the game.

Any number could play. Two, usually, were designated "hares," and the rest were "hounds." The hares, who were given a head start of from five to ten minutes, attempted to beat the hounds to a predetermined spot by any course they so desired. Their only obligation was to drop bits of the "scent," colored pieces of paper, along the route. It was a fine elemental competition, but there was one problem: The hares always won.

Nevertheless, the game was popular. Harvard students were particularly fond of paperchasing, which was demonstrated on December 6, 1879, when three hundred assembled in front of Matthews' establishment to cheer on forty hounds pursuing the hares, Manning and Thatcher (both Class of '82), through the streets of Cambridge. After dashing across Harvard Square into Church Street, Manning and Thatcher scaled an eight-foot fence and raced down Palmer Street. The chase continued past the James Russell Lowell home and the Brighton abattoir, then up Carey Street in Brookline. The first casualties were several hounds who became stuck in the mud. The rest charged to the top of the hill, where they found only an empty sack (the hares had run out of scent and gone for more). By the time the hares returned, most of the hounds had quit in disgust and left for Cambridge.

A week later the match was rerun. The route on this occasion went past Henry Wadsworth Longfellow's home—apparently it was not easy to go anywhere in the Greater Boston area without passing the residence of some famous poet— and the hares won with two minutes to spare.

During the heyday of paperchasing, foul weather hardly deterred the participants. When the ground was covered with snow, as it was for the 1880 Westchester Thanksgiving meet, the hares merely changed the color of their scent to red, green, and blue. At eleven o'clock that morning, hares Vosburgh and Frank Banham arrived at Schraeder's Hotel dressed identically in black trousers and blue jackets. The hounds, clad in crimson jackets and dark blue trousers, ceremoniously broke

Occasionally There Were Mishaps:
"While crossing the Bronx by means of a fallen tree Peter Donohue, one of the hounds, lost his balance and fell into the icy cold water. He extricated himself as quickly as possible and returned home dripping wet and shivering with cold. The hares, after leading the trail to Yonkers, doubled on it and ultimately found themselves, after a long and wet tramp through woods and underbrush in Tremont. They had lost themselves. Turning about, they got back near Yonkers again, when they met a milkman, by whom they were directed the way homeward. They reported having seen the hounds only once. . . . As the New York Hares and Hounds Club were also having a chase in the vicinity of Mount Vernon the two trails got mixed and the two clubs got to following alternately each other's trails. As a consequence, the hounds reached home ahead of the hares, something that never happens in a regular chase. . . ."*

From The Westchester Hare and
Hounds Chase of November 1881

---

into a chorus of yelps and baying upon seeing the quarry.

At the firing of a pistol, Vosburgh and Banham took off along White Plains Road. A newspaper reporter perched in the top of a tall tree saw them split up—or "throw off," in the parlance of paperchasing—as soon as they were out of sight of the hounds. Banham then pulled off the ploy of the day when he came to the top of a rocky precipice twenty feet high. Grasping the rock with his hands, he made a track as if he had let himself slide over the edge. Instead, he drew himself back carefully, retraced his old footprints in the snow, and started off in a new direction. When the hounds arrived on the scene, they took the bait and scrambled en masse down the cliff face.

covered with thin ice that cracked beneath each step and ended by covering a dozen miles in forty-five minutes. The hounds pursued across the swamp and finished cold, wet, and nearly a half hour behind the hares.

One year later, with Banham on the opposite side as master of the hounds, the result was different. The race took place in the vicinity of Bayonne, New Jersey, where it seemed the entire juvenile population took off after the hares. After following the tracks of the Jersey Central Railroad for several hundred yards, the hares, confident of victory, pinned a sign to a fence and started back toward Bayonne. The note read: "Dear Hounds. Good-bye. We are on our journey home. The smell of the dinner has acted exhilaratingly on our gait."

Frequently There Were Mishaps:
"In one instance the eager master of the hounds was ensnared into a brook six feet deep, from which he was rescued in a dripping and half-frozen condition. At another time the chase led through a swamp a quarter of a mile long."

From The New York Hare and
Hounds Chase of November 1881

Later it was thought that the hounds were resorting to trickery when several were seen lifting objects from their back pockets to their faces. One reporter assumed they were peering through spyglasses in order to spot the hares. Then he discovered that the objects were "not telescopes, but something better suited to the festive character of the day."

The hounds probably needed a nip or two by the time Vosburgh and Banham were through with them. They crossed a swamp

In Fact, It Seemed There Was Always a Mishap:
"The hounds followed the trail to Mount Vernon, where they lost it owing to some boys having picked up the paper. . . . Once across the Bronx, the trail was found and followed to a farmhouse, where four of the nine hounds ran riot and the rest went on. After running after a mile, two of those left behind came up, leaving two still behind, eating mince pie and drinking milk. . . ."

From The Westchester Hare and
Hounds Chase of November 1881

Shortly afterward, however, they were dismayed to see Banham less than a hundred yards behind. After tagging W. I. K. Kendrick, Banham took off after Harry Drake. An exciting two-man chase concluded with the hounds' first victory.

The high-water mark of paperchasing had been reached. The growing popularity of less chaotic cross-country running no doubt contributed to the demise of the sport, and by the 1890s it had been relegated to a child's game that survives as hares and hounds and its variations.

Perhaps that is just as well. Considering the amount of litter the twentieth century has produced, any modern hares would have an extremely difficult time leaving a recognizable scent.

ROLLER POLO

During the 1870s, several wealthy young socialites at Newport, Rhode Island, bored with the ending of each polo season, looked about for a substitute for their favorite sport. This happened to be the beginning of America's roller-skate craze of the late nineteenth century, so it was almost inevitable that a version of polo on skates was developed. This also allowed the game to be moved indoors on a playing area eighty feet long by forty feet wide.

Some Roller Polo Teams:
Providence Grays
Salem Witches
Waterbury Blues
Newport Trojans
New Bedford Whalers

From Newport, roller polo soon spread to Ivy League athletes and then to professional sports promoters, who formed the New England League and helped spread the pro game as far west as Muncie, Indiana. By the turn of the century the sport was quite the rage, a promotional advertisement claiming it would "arouse the sluggish blood, make the businessman forget his troubles, and afford much food for heated argument the following day. It will undoubtedly become the national indoor sport."

The rules of roller polo were simple enough. At the beginning of play, a hard rubber ball was dropped into a neutral zone in the center of the playing area. Immediately, opposing forwards skated from their cages to capture the ball, at which point the game proceeded in the manner of ice or field hockey. Each player used a stick four feet long to advance the ball; the game consisted of four twelve-minute periods.

Inevitably roller polo created several outstanding players, the most famous being Wild Bill Buggan (1889–1971), who terrorized the opposition during the first two decades of the twentieth century. Duggan established two records: quickest goal scored (three seconds after the dropped ball and whistle), and most rushes (twenty-four) per game. It seems likely these two marks will stand forever.

BATTLE BALL

The best thing about battle ball was its catchy title. When it was first played, in 1895, it was touted as a sport capable of "quite replacing tennis as a competitive game." Its inventor, Dr. Dudley A. Sargent of Harvard, described battle ball as a combination of bowling, baseball, cricket, football, handball, and tennis. (He did not mention weight lifting.) The main advantage of battle ball was that it could be played by a large number of players in a small area and was a natural gymnasium game. Anticipating that the sport would catch on with young women, Dr. Sargent added that despite its title, battle ball was a "dignified" game, in his words, "antagonistic without allowing any opportunity for injury from personal contact or collision."

Played on a fifty-by-twenty-five-foot court, battle ball could tolerate as many as twenty players on a side. At each end of the court was a goal line on which sat three pairs of Indian clubs. Seven feet above the line was a cord stretched from posts at the corner. A leather ball weighing a hefty two pounds completed the equipment.

Battle Ball—the Space-saving Game
Dr. Sargent proudly pointed out that battle ball required only 120 square feet per player. In contrast, he noted that tennis required 2,500 square feet per player; football, 6,764; baseball, 10,000. Dr. Sargent did not say how he arrived at his figures, but it is easy to see that he fudged just a bit. An 1895 football field, for example, was slightly longer and wider than a later version, but the 6,764 figure would be accurate—for 11 men. Likewise, a baseball park with 300-foot foul lines would have an area of 90,000 square feet, or 10,000 for each of 9 men. But baseball isn't played by 9 men or football by 11. The games use two teams of 9 and 11 men, respectively. Even so, the professor was correct in pointing out that battle ball was a space-saver.

Apparently the object of the game was to prevent unemployment among CPAs, for there were many complex ways to score. If, for example, a player threw the ball over the enemy's goal and hit an Indian club, his team received five points. If the ball missed the clubs as it rolled across the goal line, the throwing player's side received ten points. (One was rewarded for missing rather than hitting, curiously.) If the ball flew over the pins but under the cord, the throwers were awarded three points. Balls heaved over the cord cost the heavers one point and loss of ball. It was recommended that a referee be employed to call fouls, but apparently there was only one infraction for the official to watch for: stepping across the center line, which could lead to that most vile of all Victorian transgressions, body contact. Crossing the center line cost the errant player's team two points. "The entire separation of the opposing sides, excluding all roughness . . . make it more suitable than basketball for women," wrote the New York *Times*. Despite this recommendation, battle ball never really caught on.

ROYAL

A couple of years later, a brief flurry of interest greeted royal, a game devised for bicyclists. One would think that a contest involving moving vehicles would be relatively simple, but as described in *Current Literature* in 1897, royal appears to have been almost as complex as battle ball. The object, to drive a "play wheel" (a 4½-inch-wide pneumatic tire mounted on a 28-inch bicycle rim) through the opponent's goal while riding a bicycle, seems basic enough. But the playing area called for a center alleyway of cables that, according to *Current Literature,* formed "two upright sides, between which the play wheel rolls, and is driven backward or forward by the riders. . . . Players ride in single file and always circle to the left. The teams are constantly meeting and passing each other in opposite directions on opposite sides of the alleyway. The game requires much skill in riding and is very exciting." Especially, no doubt, for the poor soul charged with picking up the play wheel every time it flopped on its side.

CAPTUS AND OVAL POOL

Following the popularity of billiards, several late-nineteenth- and early-twentieth-century sportsmen-inventors tried their hand at devising variations of pool or pocket billiards. One 1884 game, called captus by its inventor, George Calder of Mill Creek, Utah, was played on a platform eighteen inches high, eight feet wide, and twenty feet long. The cue resembled a toilet plunger with an extremely long handle, its end a concave head capable of manipulating a six-inch ball. The object of the game was to pocket the balls, but the greater number of caroms before pocketing the better, each earning the player extra points. In order to eliminate the possibility of luck becoming a factor, Calder specified that each attempt would have to be preceded by the player's "calling" his shot. The game of captus, of course, never caught on, but does seem to have somewhat survived in the form of shuffleboard.

In 1907, J. J. Pearson, an English architect, worked out a design for an oval billiard table (called the "arc-oval" table) in order to add more science to traditional billiards. "Among the many recognized geometrical figures," *Scientific American* added by way of explanation, "none approaches in versatility of angle problems those of a curved formation."

The arc-oval table had other advantages. Because of the lack of corners, the balls were more accessible, and consequently "one does not have to assume difficult attitudes to make a stroke. . . . For the equipment of the private house it possesses distinct advantages, and owing to the absence of the awkward right-angular corner, lends itself particularly to the encouragement of billiard play by ladies." The player who happened to be bored with traditional billiards was likely to be enchanted by the arc-oval table, for instead of rebounding in a "normal" manner, the balls often followed a whizzing course around the circumference of the cushion at great velocity.

CAR VS. BULL

At least the 1901 innovation of Henri Deutsch was simple. The première of that entrepreneur's new sport took place on a Sunday afternoon in September at Bayonne, France, a town whose residents love bullfighting nearly as much as their Spanish neighbors. The precise site was the local Plaza de Toros, where a capacity crowd of six thousand gathered to watch the first combat between a bull and a motorized matador.

As Deutsch promised in his prefight advertising, the entrance of the *caballero de plaza,* Ledesma, was like none other in the history of El Cid's ancient and noble art. Instead of arriving astride a horse, Ledesma waved to the crowd from the seat of a twelve-horsepower Peugeot. Occasionally a word passed between the bullfighter and another man in the car. This was M. Chevrin. As Deutsch's chauffeur, he had been named to drive Ledesma into battle.

No one could doubt that the audience was interested. A silence settled over the arena as the bull and Ledesma stared at each other for a long moment. Then the Peugeot lurched forward. In response, the bull moved with great speed—away from the car. In the succinct description of the *Times* of London, the animal "turned tail and ran."

Maneuvering furiously, Chevrin followed the terrified *toro* as closely as he dared, for he was concerned that the bull might change its mind, turn suddenly, and charge the light machine. (Light armor-plating had been laid across the front and sides of the vehicle, but it was almost of a ceremonial nature. A strong charge by the bull could have overturned the car quite easily.) But the animal was determined—he wanted absolutely nothing to do with the sputtering Peugeot. When Chevrin turned one way, the bull turned the other. It became a contest of agility as the car and the bull, trailed by a disorganized horde of picadors on horseback, swerved from one side of the arena to the other. Hoofbeats mingled with the roar of engine as clouds of dust rolled up from the floor of the stadium. The crowd was neither stimulated nor amused. M. Deutsch presumably took the money and ran.

Other Attempts at Unusual Bullfighting: *M. Deutsch was neither the first nor the last to bring together a vehicle and a bull. In 1897, matador Manuel Garcia, then nearing the end of his career, decided to fight a bull from a bicycle. A large crowd attended the event, which began with Garcia having good success against the baffled bull. But when the bicycle hit a small stone and threw the rider to the ground, the bull saw its chance and took it. Charging, he lifted both the bicycle and Garcia, clinging to his vehicle, over the balustrade and into the first row of seats.*

In 1932, the city of Madrid, Spain, experimented with a matador who fought from the seat of a motorcycle. The novelty was not a notable success.

CENTRIFUGAL BOWLING

During the 1890s, bowling grew in popularity, it being deemed a game that was not only dignified (the ladies could play while wearing full skirts and corsets), but beneficial. "The exertion required to project the balls involves nearly all of the muscular system of the thorax," *Scientific American* wrote. "The arms, lungs, heart, back, and loins all respond to the movement, and the play is at once healthful and invigorating."

The main problem, it seemed, was that bowling was not generally accessible to the public; there were few commercial alleys, and most private homes were too small. As one writer noted, "A first-class single bowling alley costs $250, and requires a flooring 85 feet long and six feet wide. The practice of bowling at home in ordinary dwellings is, therefore, out of the question."

To circumvent this problem, a now-forgotten inventor dreamed up the centrifugal bowling alley in 1894, which forced the ball to travel a spiral pathway, rather like a loop-the-loop, before striking the pins a dozen or so feet from the bowler. The device came in two models—one with the pins directly opposite the bowler, the other with the pins at his or her side, the ball traveling 180 degrees before striking the target. The advantage of the second style was that the balls could be retrieved and pins reset with less strain on the bowler's loins and other vital parts. History records no great rush to buy either centrifugal bowling model.

SPORTS ON THE ROCKS

With the coming of winter, Americans tried to adapt some of their favorite warm-weather sports to a climate in which the basic medium was ice. Ice boating, an obvious adaptation of sailing, became quite popular in the northeastern United States about the time of the Civil War. Some of the boats constructed especially for ice boating were quite extravagant and were capable of speeds of a mile a minute. Winters were enlivened by ice-boat races on the Hudson River, and the sport thrived and survived into the twentieth century.

Less logical than ice boating was ice baseball, which came into vogue a decade or so after the game's general acceptance as the national sport. Following the Civil War, rules for ice baseball were formulated, and team play started with a fair amount of regularity. Most of the early players were amateurs, members of the top-notch summer teams of that era such as the Atlantics, Excelsiors, Mutuals, and Eckfords.

The rules of ice baseball were the same as those of traditional baseball except where logic dictated otherwise. Players were permitted to overrun the "bases," for example, and sliding was held to a minimum. The bases themselves were large squares etched into the ice rather than upright posts or bags, which could have destroyed the flying skater who collided with them.

One early game of ice baseball took place on January 12, 1867, at the Satellite Skating Park in Brooklyn between the Eckfords—"the well-known ex-champions"—and the Fulton Market club. Both teams were purportedly amateurs, although at least one player, shortstop Josh Snyder of the Fultons, went on to play professionally with the 1872 Brooklyn Eckfords of the National Association (he batted .171 in nine games). "The game itself was not expected to be remarkably scientific," the New York *Herald* noted, "but it nevertheless was well played and thoroughly enjoyed. The downfalls were not as numerous as were expected, but considerable fun was created by the maneuvers of the stiff-jointed but good-natured veteran in his efforts to 'hold' the bases by falling on them." Added the *Times:* "It being the first appearance of these clubs in a game on the ice, the *contretemps* were numerous and laughable beyond imagining. The ground and lofty tumbling of some of the players in their efforts to take balls on the fly, or while making a base, caused considerable merriment to the spectators, and was not the least enjoyable part of the affair. As a general thing the most skilled skaters had the best of it, while the poor ones —no matter how good ballplayers they might be—were at a discount." The game differed even more from later baseball contests in that each team had ten men, the extra person appearing in the lineup followed by the letters "r.s." He was a kind of roving shortstop who played in back of second base, backing up both the regular shortstop and the second baseman.

An Early Ice Baseball Contest:

Fulton	2	8	9	7	6—32
Eckfords	5	12	4	5	0—26

Time of game—2 hours, 20 minutes

While the game of January 12 was enjoyed as entertainment, it was agreed that another contest four days later, between the Empire and Eagle clubs, was considerably more artistic. It featured a double play, a sensational catch of a line drive by Dunlap of the Eagles, and a come-from-behind victory by the Empire club, which scored four runs in the top of the fifth inning to win, 15–13. The crowd in attendance included many young ladies as well as a "fine band of music." Nat Hicks, who caught for the Eagles, later went on to play four seasons in the National Association.

Four years later, ice baseball was almost completely in the hands of young men who were about to turn fully professional. In a game played at the Capitoline Grounds, Brooklyn, the Atlantics showed up with a team composed of Joe Start, Bob Ferguson,

George Hall, and Charlie Smith, all of whom would join the National Association later in the year. Only two pros showed up to represent the Mutuals, John Hatfield and Marty Swandell, so they were compelled to "enlist" a squad from local skaters. The resulting game—umpired by Tom York of the Troy Haymakers—was a fiasco, won in six innings by the Atlantics, 36–6. But the crowd had a good time watching the players struggle with the mechanics of playing baseball on ice skates, a game that never caught on. Players continued to revive the idea, however, or reinvent it at periodic intervals. In 1920, for example, baseball on ice was acclaimed as the latest sports fad in the Cleveland area, a league having been formed with six industrial teams and a following of twenty thousand.

Cleveland sports fans that year also staged several boxing matches on ice at Rockefeller Park. Apparently this was as much fun to watch as ice baseball, even though the fighters were heavily dressed in sweaters, which lessened the force of the blows. "Aside from having to dodge the blows," a reporter noted, "contestants experienced much trouble in keeping their feet when they missed blows."

In 1932, even basketball on ice skates was tried by two teams at the University of Illinois, captained by baseball pitchers Walt Hazzard and Joe Bartulis. Hazzard's team won.

SPORTS ON HORSEBACK

With the exception of polo, horse racing, and especially in the state of Maryland, jousting, comparatively few sports take place on horseback. That does not mean, of course, that attempts have not been made to adapt familiar games to the mounted variety.

Football on horseback was one of the first sports to undergo this form of adulteration, a game being played at Dickel's Riding Academy, New York, in April 1901. The rules of mounted football called for there to be only four players per side; tackling was allowed— that is, a player could attempt to pull another off his horse, but could use only one arm in doing so. "The man tackled, when unhorsed, loses the ball if he fails to retain possession of the reins," one writer explained, "and it is with difficulty that he remounts, as the other horsemen interfere with him as much as possible."

Scoring occurred when the rider with the ball was able to advance sufficiently to touch a piece of cloth used as a goal. In the game of April 9, no one was hurt during the two fifteen-minute halves, although "Marshall Clapp, one of the players, had a particularly hard time of it in the second half. His sweater was torn in two, and he was carried along the side of the building hanging to his horse, from which he was finally thrown, the hoof of the horse just missing his head." To make matters worse, Clapp's team lost by three goals to one.

Boxing on Horseback:
Ever practical, it was the Germans who conceived the idea of staging boxing matches on horseback in 1912—not as a major sporting event but as a training for war. Paradoxically, it was an American, Joe Edwards, of the Anglo-American Boxing Club in Berlin, who invented the game, but the Germans demonstrated most enthusiasm for it. "The new sport will be valuable for the soldier on horseback in time of war," it was explained, "as when he loses his weapons he will have to fall back on his natural means of defense."

During the early part of the twentieth century, some Americans also adapted basketball so that it could be played on horseback. Rule changes included moving the foul line to a point thirty feet from the basket—to compensate for the additional height of the mounted players—eliminating dribbling, and playing with a ball that was stuffed instead of inflated in order to make it easier to catch and handle. Predictably, scoring was light in mounted basketball. In a game played on February 24, 1929, between Battery D and Battery F of the 104th Field Artillery, New York, Battery F won by a score of 9–4. The third period of the hotly contested game featured a collision between Horton of Battery F and Van Iseghan of the losers, the former fracturing his left leg and the latter sustaining a possible spine fracture.

AUTO POLO
By 1913, when the first pangs of automobile mania were being felt in America, someone thought of playing polo with the riders in cars rather than on horseback. The result was a series of contests played and watched by a small army of dedicated fans and even, on occasion, viewed by movie photographers. Such an event took place on July 18, 1913, at the Garden City Polodrome between one team representing the Auto Polo Association and another calling itself the "Aero Team." Fred Campbell of the former group soon became one of the most celebrated auto poloists of the period, leading his team to one victory after another.

The auto polo team of 1913 consisted of two cars, one forward and one back, each with a driver and a player wielding a mallet.

Spectators, instead of taking seats, simply drove their own cars to the edge of the playing area, parked, and watched. Others got out and stood on the sidelines, despite the danger of spinning cars and distinct lack of safety precautions.

BASKETBALL ON ROLLER SKATES
"The recent revival of roller skating," wrote a reporter in 1906, "has resulted in the introduction of many novel and interesting athletic sports on skates, among them being pushball, broomball, gymkhana, medley races, and basketball."

Though still in its infancy, basketball was already popular enough to bastardize in 1906. In fact, applications had been received for franchises in a new roller-skate basketball league, more than fifty clubs reportedly asking permission to join the Madison Square Garden circuit.

For a brief period, enthusiasm was so high that advocates of roller-skate basketball predicted it would take the place of the traditional version. The game proved to be a passing phenomenon, however, with few games being played and no grandiose league formed.

WATER BASEBALL
Early in the twentieth century, several groups adapted baseball to the limitations of an indoor pool. The "New York game" used large cork buoys as bases and required that all players be stationed in the pool. The batter stood in thigh-deep water awaiting the delivery of the pitcher, who was in water up to his waist. The infield players, meanwhile, were submerged to their necks and the outfielders in deep water.

In contrast, the "Philadelphia game" of about 1915 required that a platform be anchored in the center of the tank, on which the pitcher would stand and throw the ball, "thus relieving the strain of treading water during the entire time that the twirler is required to stand in deep water." Fielders were allowed to stand on the edge of the pool. "In this way they have a better chance to catch fly balls and can even jump and catch a fly ball before it hits the surface of the water."

Another difference in the two styles of water baseball pertained to base running. According to the Philadelphia rules, a base runner had to stay on the surface the entire time. By New York rules, a runner could take his choice. Both versions of the game served their purpose—to improve the swimmers' skills. Neither had pretensions of becoming a "new national sport" or even a game that would involve more players than those in the immediate vicinity. Nevertheless, it could have happened, but didn't.

A Pair of Incidents in Water Baseball:
"Another base runner was not so accurate in following the baseline under water, and reappeared after leaving third directly in front of the pitcher, who had the ball, and promptly tagged him out, adding a ducking for good measure."
New York, June 15, 1913
"The left fielder saw that a fly ball which was hit in his direction would fall short and land on the water. He took a long dive, caught the ball in the air, and disappeared beneath the surface with the sphere still clutched in his hands. The 'runner' who was on third at the time got home before the fielder could come to the surface and make the throw."
Philadelphia, September 9, 1915

AERIAL GOLF
One of the most bizarre adaptations of a sport was aerial golf, which was first played in 1928 at the Old Westbury Golf Club, Long Island. Each team had two players, one on the ground and the second in an airplane.

To begin the match of May 27, 1928, M. M. Merrill and Arthur Caperton, the aerial halves of their teams, took off from Curtiss Field in two planes with cargoes of golf balls. Flying about fifty feet above the ground, the men attempted to drop a ball as near as possible to the cups of nine holes. After they had completed this part of the match, their partners on the ground played the balls from the dropped locations. Merrill, it turned out, was an excellent shot from the air. All of his nine balls landed on the greens, and it was a simple matter for partner William Hammond to hole out. Caperton, on the other hand, tended to be erratic, depositing three of his nine chances in the rough. As a result, the Merrill-Hammond team defeated Caperton and William Winston, 3 up.

Two months later, the new sport caught on to the extent that U. S. Congressman Fiorello LaGuardia participated in a match at the Dunwoodie golf course in Yonkers. LaGuar-dia's partner in the air was pilot J. P. Maloney, who demonstrated sufficiently good aim to help the congressman record a 1-up victory over three other teams.

In 1930, aerial golf actually spread to England, where a match was played on February 20 at a course in Sonning, Berkshire. That was the high point of the game, however, which was admittedly not much more than an oddity bred by the decade that gave the world marathon flagpole sitting and goldfish ingestion as alternatives to conventional sports watching.

ALMOST ANYTHING GOES
Inventing "new" sports or adulterating old ones went into a bit of a decline during the 1930s and the World War II period. It was, after all, a serious time, and probably the old standby spectator sports seemed quite good enough. Not until the advent of television, which brought new leisure and accessibility to sports events, was there any imaginative effort in the area of developing alternatives to basketball, baseball, football, and boxing. Then, particularly on Saturday afternoon, viewers found themselves watching epics such as the National Invitational Wrist Wrestling Championships, the Demolition Derby, and other equally obscure events.

But the Saturday afternoon dredging up of time-filling sports was nothing compared to the accomplishments of the television series "Almost Anything Goes," which appeared for a brief time during the mid-1970s. The very purpose of "AAG" was to invent athletic events as a background for competition between small-town sports squads. A sample contest might require the participant to hurl a basketball into a hoop while balancing himself on a swaying rope bridge over water; another put the contestants inside a giant wheel, which they were to move via a combination of good co-ordination and musclepower. It was all good fun, of course, and no one expected the individual sports competitions to evolve into America's athletic rage of the twenty-first century.

On the other hand, that may be what they said when Henry Chadwick first described baseball.

CHAPTER 25 — BAD HYPES

The history of American sports watching has been degraded on a few—well, perhaps more than a few—occasions when promoters thought they could interest the public in an athletic contest that was less than superb. Either that or they extended a good thing far past the law of diminishing returns. The results of such shortsightedness sometimes paid off for the quick-buck entrepreneur who was agile enough to take the admissions money and run. On other occasions, the public shrewdly stayed away or expressed its displeasure in a variety of ways, most of them high-pitched and cacophonous.

When does an innovative gamble cross the line to become just another bad hype? No one can be exactly sure; all we can be sure of is the fact that the U.S. sports watcher has been subjected to many dogs and turkeys promoted under the guise of genuine sports.

1880—BULLFIGHTING IN NEW YORK

It was the summer of 1880 when the garish announcements first appeared. They promised excitement to the lucky spectators, who were advised they could anticipate *toreadores* "among the most celebrated and applauded in all the Spanish cities," capable of escaping death or mutilation only as a result of "their great skill and intelligence." Many New Yorkers, never having witnessed a bullfight in their city before, were enchanted with the idea as put forth by promoter Angel Fernandez. One exception was Henry Bergh, a leading force with the local SPCA, who promptly announced that his organization would not allow a typical Spanish *corrida de toros* to take place. Fernandez responded that there would be no cruelty to the animals. Instead of stabbing the bulls with lance and *banderilla,* the *matadores* would affix gummed ribbon rosettes to their foreheads. Thus the combat would be skillful but extremely "agreeable to the ladies," and presumably to Mr. Bergh as well.

The site of Fernandez' attraction was a rented piece of ground at 116th Street and Sixth (now Lenox) Avenue—"up among the shanties"—where a circular board wall approximately a hundred feet in diameter was constructed as the arena. Outside the main circle were two additional fences, five feet apart, between which the bulls could be led.

The corridor was also designed to serve as a buffer between the combatants and the spectators. General admission for the latter was $1.50 for adults, $.75 for children under eight years of age—fairly steep prices by 1880 standards.

The week before the first battle was to take place, it became evident that Señor Fernandez' bulls would not be among those bred for their ferocity in Spain and Mexico, but products of a local stockyard. The "ferocious beasts" promised by Fernandez, procured at bargain rates from a New York slaughterhouse, turned out to be a dozen Texas steers that had been "packed in cars for some days and were pretty well worn out," as the *Times* put it.

New York sports fans apparently did not mind this lapse of authenticity, for on the day of the first *corrida,* July 31, 1880, all the elevated trains on the West Side Road were jammed. Outside the makeshift arena the crush included private equipages driven by liveried servants, as well as common hacks, and long lines of ticket seekers. Henry Bergh, with a dozen denizens of the SPCA, was also in attendance and quite willing to be interviewed. "There seems to be an appetite among men for anything that savors of cruelty," he told a New York *Herald* reporter. "If this sport should become popular here we should soon be reduced to the level of Spanish character and nothing would satisfy the public but blood." So much for Spanish-American relations in 1880.

Bergh need not have worried about any excess of blood, however. Soon it became obvious that Angel Fernandez' promotional ability had exceeded his product. Shortly after five o'clock, eight Spaniards entered the arena in costumes that were described as "gorgeous and graceful as the holiday attire of a sunflower." But closer examination of the brave young bullfighters revealed that they were a shabby lot who might have been recruited off the streets of any small Spanish town. And when the first steer entered the ring shortly afterward, it became apparent that the men knew little of bullfighting, and the spectacle degenerated even further.

When steer No. 1, a large black-and-white fellow, found his way into the arena, the Spaniards waved their capes in the manner

Said the *Times* of the Toreadores:
*"They were as bad a looking set of men
as ever picked a pocket, and looked as if,
while they would fight a steer for a dollar
and a half, they would cut a throat for a
quarter. . . . No one of them had been
shaved, apparently, since the death of
the late Pope."* (For the record, Pope
Pius IX died in 1878.)

---

expected of them. But when the animal made
a sudden movement toward one of them, the
Spaniard suddenly wheeled, raced furiously
for the fence, and hurtled himself over it.
"The fence was very conveniently arranged
for this purpose," the *Times* reporter noted.
"It was about six feet high, and about two
feet above the ground was nailed a wide cleat
to enable the 'fighter' to jump over quickly.
Anybody but a blind man could get over this
fence in something less than two seconds."

It soon became apparent to the crowd that
Fernandez' magnificent bullfighters—all of
them—had few skills besides fence jumping.
Although the steers had been outfitted with
leather pads, rather like boxing gloves, on the
tips of their horns, even the slightest movement toward the Spaniards in the ring caused
instant panic and flight. One large yellow
steer that obviously meant business was particularly devastating. "There were eight gorgeous
Spaniards in the ring when the Texican entered," one reporter wrote. "In just twenty
seconds by the watch the steer had the ring to
himself and the Spaniards were on the other
side of the fence."

The crowd began to hoot and hiss about
this time and some even shouted lines such as
"Put Bergh in there!" Laughter turned to
derision and then back to laughter, but soon it
became obvious that the audience, knowing it
had been taken, was growing ever angrier.

In an effort to put some life into the show,
one brave bullfighter actually worked himself
close enough to a steer to stick some rosettes
on its forehead, but the attempt had so infuriated the animal that it jumped the fence
three times before the Spaniard could succeed, and so exhausted itself that it became
hung up with two legs on either side. Another
steer caught a cloak on its horns and ripped it
in half. One piece fell down over the animal's
eyes, causing it to race around blindly, eventually charging head-first into the boards. This
amused the audience temporarily but caused
Henry Bergh to grow restive. When he glared
at the spectacle, some wondered if he were
about to call the police and bring the fiasco to
a rapid conclusion. Before that happened,
however, the crowd began to drift off of its
own accord, many booing or muttering angrily
as they left the arena. The event, quite naturally, was not considered an artistic success.
"Driving a frightened steer into a ring," editorialized the *Herald* the next day, "and then
daubing him all over with bunches of ribbons
fastened to adhesive plasters is not an exhila-
rating sight, even when the two-legged performers prance about in tinsel dresses."

By mid-August Fernandez was hopelessly in
debt, owing large sums of money to his
"fighters," an interpreter, and the owner of
the boardinghouse who had foolishly extended
credit to the promoter and his company. Fernandez' gate receipts for the first match, the
only financially successful one, were soon attached as a result of two judgments filed
against him. Another bout was postponed because of rain, but that probably would not
have helped very much, as attendance was
sparse. Charges and countercharges in the
courts soon overshadowed all other aspects of
New York bullfighting except the fact that
Fernandez left town, bankrupt.

Four years later, at an Independence Day
fair, a bullfight held in Dodge City, Kansas,
was hailed by newspapers there as the first
such entertainment ever seen in the entire

The "Bulls" Had the Last Laugh:
*In an effort to recoup some of his losses,
Fernandez sold the steers used in his bull-
fights to an East Side butcher. While being loaded onto a large cattle truck that
was to take them to a Forty-fifth Street
abattoir, however, three of them managed
to escape. After wallowing in the goose
ponds at Seventh Avenue and 117th
Street, they wandered into Central Park
and splashed about in the lake. Their next
stop was the Twenty-third Precinct, which*
*they visited just long enough to precipitate
in a Keystone Kops chase across town.
Two of the three steers were finally driven
into enclosures at Eighty-fourth and
Eighty-ninth streets early the next morning but they broke away again, one destroying about three hundred feet of
fencing that it tossed about in sport. Both
were eventually shot and trucked off to
become sirloins. History does not record
the fate of the third "bull."*

United States. Given the quality of Señor Angel Fernandez' exhibitions, they probably were right.

1888—THE GREAT TRICYCLE REGATTA

"Just after twelve o'clock tonight, when Monday is five minutes old," promised the New York *Sun* of October 7, 1888, "three strokes will be hit upon a gong and twelve brawny men will start to row around the track in Madison Square Garden. There won't be any water and there won't be any boats."

The Contestants of the Great Tricycle Regatta:

The names of the champions of 1888 are all but forgotten today, but they glittered brightly during their time. There was, for example, Jacob Gaudaur, a Canadian known affectionately as the "black Brunswicker" because of his swarthy complexion; George Bubear, champion sculler of England; William O'Connor, a strong candidate for the American title; John McKay, champion of Nova Scotia; Irish champion John Largan; and Albert Hamm, whom the Sun *characterized as "something of a jolly wanderer, but when he is in good condition he is a hard fellow to beat." Prize money of ten thousand dollars added inducement to the glory of winning the first indoor rowing contest in America.*

The striking of a gong, the *Sun* might have noted but did not, was symbolic of the event's dreary nature. But in 1888 the debut of "rowing without water" was regarded as a great step toward bringing together a dozen super-scullers—all under one roof instead of on a faraway lake or river. It was a promoter's dream, one that had been thought about for years but never implemented because of the lack of a machine that could be powered by a rower's arms rather than the legs and feet. That problem was apparently solved with the invention of the rowing tricycle or roadsculler, and the great sports hype of 1888 was on.

The roadsculler seemed to work perfectly. Constructed of light iron with a single twenty-inch-diameter wheel in front and two forty-inch wheels in the rear, the vehicle was equipped with a system of grooved pulleys, axles, and great lengths of one-eighth-inch wire cables. Though intricate, the machine could move along at speeds of more than fifteen miles an hour when the operator pulled

the handle toward his chest in the manner of an oarsman.

No one derided the idea of bringing rowing indoors. Oarsmen of the 1880s were national heroes, and the possibility of seeing a dozen of the most celebrated stars, close up, in one magnificent six-day race must have been more than the enthusiast of the day could bear. The site for the contest was a one-eighth-mile track twenty-one feet wide. Composed of four lanes, the three inside ones were designated for normal racing, the outside one for passing or "spurting." Confidence—at least that of the official variety—was high in the dependability of the new rowing machine, but arrangements had been made as to what action should be taken if they happened to break down. "There is some danger in the race," the *Times* conceded, "for the pulley wire will break and collisions may occur. If a man is dismounted, he may continue the lap afoot and have it counted and find another machine awaiting him at the goal."

Despite the possibility that a race of scullers could turn into a race of angry walkers, the crowds were enticed to the Garden. Celebrities such as Robert Ingersoll and General William T. Sherman were in the opening-night audience along with several thousand others as the first of the contestants, Peter Conley, jogged onto the track "gay in a pink shirt." Irish champ Largan drew cheers with his green outfit, the 13th Regimental band struck up a lively tune, and the twelve racers were off in a flurry of well-muscled arms, bobbing heads, and turning wheels.

The *Sun*'s Opening Sentence Was Nearly as Complex as the Roadsculler:

"The twelve oarsmen set off upon the first six hours of their sixty amid the glare of thirty-five electric arc lights and some hundreds of gas jets, the blare of seventy-five musicians, each trying to outblow the other, and the cheers of something more than seventy-five hundred spectators, among whom were included some hundreds of women whose bright costumes illuminated the boxes all around the track, and the battery of whose eyes made even the electric lights dim, and the music and huzzas were terrific for those of the oarsmen who had susceptible hearts beneath the gay and scanty gauze shirts which covered their manly forms."

Everything worked perfectly. For five minutes.

Fred Plaisted's machine was the first to develop mechanical difficulties. This happened at twelve-ten. Five minutes later, William East's vehicle conked out; then so many oarsmen ran into difficulties that "two men were kept busy in dragging off the damaged steeds while the oarsmen completed their laps on foot." The first real smash-up occurred not long afterward when John Teemer's vehicle jammed and sent him sprawling in front of the scorer's box. "Ross' machine was on top of him in an instant," the *Sun* reported, "and Gaudaur's on top of them both." Although no one was injured, the prospect of solid contact obviously appealed to the audience, especially when City Coroner Messemer, who was getting ready to leave the premises, took his seat with the remark, "I guess I'll stay."

To their discredit, some of the customers even tried to help the chaos along. At one-twenty, John Largan took a nasty fall when a stick thrown from the stands became caught in the gears of his vehicle. Somehow, the day's rowing was completed and one newspaper even remarked, "It looks as if the new sport introduced at Madison Square Garden has been stamped with popular approval."

Less optimistic and approving were the contestants themselves. With the exception of Jacob Gaudaur, whose machine functioned perfectly, allowing him to pile up a substantial lead, nearly all of the racers had complaints. Largan, it was reported, was greatly annoyed "by the tendency of his wires to slip without gripping the wheels so that pull hard as he would he could not attain great speed." William East had so many spills that he withdrew from the race after only seven miles, seven laps. Hamm's steering gear once gave way just as he was rounding a curve and "he ran plump into the front bench. Gaudaur was right behind him, and the machines and men were all in a tangle in a quarter of a second." Hamm lost considerable time as a result of the mishap, but the lucky Canadian got off with nothing more than a broken spoke.

At the end of two days' racing, Gaudaur led with 172 miles, but crowd interest was decreasing as a result of the lack of competition and many breakdowns, both mechanical and physical. Teemer, for example, awoke on the third day with blisters "as large as copper pennies" on his hands, and O'Connor, in the words of one reporter, was "crippled elsewhere"—perhaps an indication that the sliding seats were malfunctioning as well.

The grim marathon continued despite the mishaps. And the mishaps continued. On the third day a vendor started a charcoal fire in a portable furnace and left it unattended. It emitted a huge cloud of suffocating smoke into which Plaisted and Largan plunged and almost disappeared from view. When they finally worked their way out of the mist, both were sick to their stomachs, Largan so violently that he was unable to row for a quarter hour. The next day, as Teemer and O'Connor continued to boycott the event, frustration reached a climax when a fight broke out on the sidelines. A free-for-all followed, and when the race was finally concluded, no one dared say that the winner, Gaudaur, was the best rower in the world. So many mishaps had taken place that any man whose tricycle held up would have won the prize. Perhaps the only thing that was certain as a result of the disastrous event was that sometimes rowing on land can be almost as difficult as walking on water.

One Who Went on to Greater Things:
Of the men who took part in the 1888 tricycle regatta, Fred Plaisted lived the longest and died with greatest honors. Born in 1851, he won his first race at age 17 and continued to row with the best of them for the next three quarters of a century. (He was not uniformly fortunate, however. Once he went to China to race for an expensive-sounding purse, only to find after his victory that it amounted to only ten dollars.) On his eighty-ninth birthday Plaisted raced the much-younger Olympic sculler John B. Kelley and beat him. Plaisted died in 1946, age ninety-five.

1894–97: THE TEMPLE CUP

In a one-league monopoly, such as that enjoyed by the National League of baseball during the 1890s, the excitement and postseason receipts of a "World Series" were lacking. The league's thinkers, therefore, put their heads together to come up with a capper for the seasons following those of 1891, when the American Association finally went broke after a decade.

The first idea, actually carried out in 1892, was to play two half seasons and climax the year with a playoff series between the two winners. (No provision was made in the event the same team won both miniseasons.) Fortunately, two different teams, Boston and Cleveland, won, and Boston went on to trounce Cleveland in the playoff. (The Baltimore Orioles, by finishing last twice that season, achieved a distinction attained neither before nor since.)

The next year no series was played. Then

William C. Temple of Pittsburgh came to the rescue by offering an ornate thirty-inch-high cup worth about eight hundred dollars to the winner of a seven-game postseason series between the first-place and second-place teams. If anyone noticed that the first-place team really had little to gain and the second-place club little to lose, he kept strangely silent. And thus, in the absence of a better idea, the Temple Cup series was born.

From the very outset, the nonclassic received just about the respect it deserved. The Baltimore Orioles, considerably improved since 1892, won the 1894 pennant, their first in any kind of competition. The team members returned to a hometown parade with two hundred floats and two hundred thousand spectators, were treated to a sumptuous banquet, and then fell flat on their faces in the initial Temple Cup series.

Beneficiaries of the Oriole flop were the New York Giants, who swept the series in straight games, the last by a score of 16–3. The Orioles returned home, consoling themselves by saying that they were the true champions and the Temple Cup meaningless.

The next year, Baltimore repeated as pennant winners. The New York Giants finished ninth in a twelve-club race, the runner-up spot going to the Cleveland Spiders. Led by scrappy first baseman Pat Tebeau, Cleveland was detemined to prove that the previous 132 games had not been an accurate barometer of the two teams' skills. Stung by a year of being taunted as paper champions, the Orioles departed for Cleveland after a modest celebration of their pennant victory.

Again, disaster. Led by their rabid fans, the Spiders defeated the Orioles, 5–4, in a game that featured a fan's flinging his coat in Baltimore left fielder Joe Kelley's face in order to prevent a cutoff throw. There were also occasional barrages of potatoes and stones from the crowd, which the Baltimore newspapers described as "thugs and toughs whose conduct would disgrace a decently conducted dog fight."

But there was no denying the skill of thirty-five-game-winner Cy Young and twenty-six-game-winner George Cuppy, who simply leveled the Orioles in the series. The Clevelands, winners of the second Temple Cup, somehow managed to get out of Baltimore alive—although not without a police escort—and promptly spent the winter extolling the virtues of the series. Discontent was evident in Baltimore, however, where the Herald, making no attempt to disguise its sour-grapes attitude, wrote, "The Temple Cup is not a good thing for baseball inasmuch as it detracts largely from the laurels of the pennant winners if they lose the trophy."

Attendance for the series reflected this editorial discontent. In both Cleveland and Baltimore, crowds were light. The following year, which saw both teams repeat their positions in the standings, was even worse from a financial standpoint. Receipts for 1896 came to only sixty-eight hundred dollars, compared to twenty-one thousand for 1894. Less than four thousand fans showed up for the first game in Baltimore, which prompted the Herald to ask: "What is the matter with Baltimore rooters?"

Whatever it was, it was also infecting Cleveland fans. Only two thousand of them turned out for the fourth and final game of the series, which was actually won by first-place Baltimore. Sensing public apathy, officials at the annual baseball meeting of 1896 proposed dumping the nonclassic, but James A. Hart of Chicago blocked the move.

If more evidence was needed that the Temple Cup series was a loser, the year 1897 supplied it. From midsummer on, Baltimore and Boston battled for the pennant; then, almost as if the season had been carefully scripted in advance, the two teams arrived in Baltimore for a crucial three-game series. Boston took the first game, 6–4, but the Orioles came back to win the second. Union Park, with ten thousand seats, was then stormed by nearly thirty thousand fans. It was the largest crowd to attend any baseball game prior to 1900.

Boston won the crucial game, 19–10, and interest in baseball for the year promptly died. "The Temple Cup is still to be won," remarked the Baltimore Herald, "but generally speaking, the exponents of professional baseball went into retirement last week."

It was all too true. Attendance for the Temple Cup series in both cities was meager, and the Beaneaters stumbled through the playoff almost as lethargically as the Orioles had in 1894. After Boston won the opener, 13–12, Baltimore won four straight—six, counting a pair of exhibitions in Worcester and Springfield in an effort to raise money—and the final game at Baltimore was so bad that some newspapers accused the Boston players of deliberately trying to end their own misery by giving the Orioles runs.

A month later, at the 1897 National League meeting, the Temple Cup series was abolished by unanimous vote.

1928—THE BUNION DERBY

Promoter C. C. Pyle—often known as "Cash and Carry"—was a con artist who might have brought a blush to the cheeks of even the opportunist P. T. Barnum. More than a little dishonest and extremely eager to make a buck, Pyle decided to see if he could cash in on the marathon mania sweeping the country in the 1920s by inaugurating a running contest that would rival William Wrigley, Jr.'s, successful Catalina endurance swim.

There were two major differences in the schemes, however. One was that Pyle did not have sufficient funds to finance his project. He solved that by charging each entrant a hundred dollars for the privilege of participating in the race. The second major difference was that instead of cluttering a narrow waterway with swimmers for one evening, Pyle opted to clutter the nation's highways with runners for a period of two or three months.

Officially it was called the first Transcontinental Race. Unofficially, it was the "Bunion Derby." The prize offered to the lucky and skillful runner able to cover the thirty-four hundred miles from Los Angeles to New York first was twenty-five thousand dollars. Second-place money was ten thousand dollars. Pyle, of course, did not have the money, but as an unscrupulous promoter and manipulator of people, he was confident he could find ways of dealing with that minor problem after the race started. Ever optimistic, Pyle expected a thousand runners to enter the race, but as it turned out, there were not that many crazy people in America. Less than two hundred showed up on March 4, 1928, when Red Grange gave the starting signal from the muddy turf of Los Angeles' Ascot Speedway.

How Would He Get the Money? Pyle's Reply:

"We'll run through thousands of towns, cities and villages. Spectators by the thousands will be attracted to those places to see the race pass through. That will mean money for the towns, especially where the race halts overnight. It will help the sale of everything from mousetraps to grand pianos. Each town will be assessed so much for the advertising, or we won't run through it. We'll run through a rival town. . . . Then we'll sell a million programs, easy. You can't tell the runners without a program. I'll get a hundred thousand dollars for the advertising in that. I'll have a traveling vaudeville show with the race. Admission will not be free. I'll make money on that, too. In fact, it's the easiest thing I've ever seen."

It also turned out that a significant percentage of the runners were less hardy than Pyle imagined. On the very first lap—a mere six-

teen-mile jog from Los Angeles to Puente—76 of the original 199 fell victim to the steaming pavements. Worse for Pyle, disappointing crowds turned out, and Oklahoma City's Chamber of Commerce backed out of the five-thousand-dollar guarantee promised the promoter. In Chicago the U. S. No. 66 Highway Association informed Pyle that it had changed its mind about shelling out its promised funds, largely because the Bunion Derby had strayed too often and too far from the highway to merit paying the fee. Rumors began to be heard that Pyle was in debt for nearly two hundred thousand dollars.

Things thereupon went from worse to terrible. Red Grange, Pyle's partner in a previous scheme designed to tackle the National Football League, got off the merry-go-round in Chicago, and the runners started complaining about sanitary conditions. Pyle's initials changed from "Cash and Carry" to "Corn and Callus." But a mildly interesting stretch run between racers John Salo and Andy Payne helped stimulate some interest in the conclusion of the event.

Despite this minor resurgence, the newspapers of the East were less than enthusiastic when the small group of survivors approached New York. The Newark *Evening News* described the runners as "emaciated, unshorn scarecrows," while the New York *Herald Tribune* dismissed the race as "the aching dog caravan." New York's *Evening Sun* was less polite, calling the event "the flop of the century" and "a tinhorn side show."

Andrew Payne, nineteen, somehow managed to win the race, accepted the first prize of twenty-five thousand dollars, and then staggered into a concrete pillar and fell unconscious. Pyle prided himself on having paid off his winners, despite losing between seventy-five thousand and one hundred thousand dollars.

The following year an encore was staged, this time from New York to California, but it turned out to be an even worse event than in 1928. Peter Gavuzzi, a strong runner from England, proceeded to make a farce of the contest by piling up a lead of six hours. Faced with rapidly diminishing attendance, Pyle strong-armed Gavuzzi into frittering away his lead as a means of building interest in the race. The naïve Englishman agreed, only to find out that Pyle had manipulated things so that Johnny Salo, a popular favorite, could actually win the race. Pyle then proceeded to cheat Gavuzzi out of the ten-thousand-dollar prize money for second place, giving him a promissory note that the young man never collected, although he once made an effort to catch up with the wily promoter. As many another creditor had discovered, that was not so easy a matter. The 1929 event, a second financial disaster, was the end of the cross-country derby promotions. To the very end, however, Pyle continued to act out the role of master showman by maintaining that he had given the public not merely a new sporting event but also history's most notable experiment in chiropody.

Whatever Happened to—?
Johnny Salo—*Not long after winning the 1929 Bunion Derby, he was struck on the head and killed by a foul ball at a sandlot baseball game.*
Peter Gavuzzi—*Continued to run until World War II, then took a job with a Paris newspaper and returned to England.*
C. C. Pyle—*Besides avoiding creditors, he spent the next ten years in radio, leasing transcribed programs. He died of a heart attack in 1939 at age fifty-five.*

BOBBY RIGGS' BARNSTORMING CAPER
Never one to shy away from the opportunity to promote an unusual event into a few dollars, tennis star Bobby Riggs conceived the idea in 1950 of reviving the old barnstorming baseball tours of the 1920s.

Riggs had already made a handsome profit by promoting an exhibition tour of tennis matches featuring Jack Kramer and Pancho Gonzales and was all set to launch the controversially sexy Gussie Moran. That, apparently, was not enough for the intrepid hustler, who felt the American public, and neighboring Canadians, would be delighted to see a thirty-two-game traveling extravaganza featuring American League All-Stars vs. National League All-Stars.

After huddling with partner John Jachym, Riggs ventured forth to sign as many bonafide living baseball legends as his pocketbook would allow. At first he ran into trouble. Ted Williams, Joe DiMaggio, Stan Musial, Roy Campanella, and Vern Stephens, all of whom were important to Riggs, begged off for one reason or another. Campanella, Stephens, and Musial complained of injuries; DiMaggio was tied down by television commitments; and Ted Williams, displaying his independent spirit once again, simply stated that he preferred to go fishing after the hard season.

Despite these setbacks, Riggs and Jachym were able to sign two quite acceptable eighteen-man squads for the tournament. That seemed to assure the venture's success, and prospects seemed even brighter when the group assembled at Montreal for the first game. At that time the sun was shining, the air was cool, and ticket sales were moving well. But several hours later, the picture changed dramatically as the sun disappeared behind threatening clouds, which soon began to dump torrents of rain. Refunding the money that had been collected, Riggs and company were forced to leave Montreal without having made a cent.

Some of the Stars:

National League	American League
Gil Hodges	Al Rosen
Ralph Kiner	Early Wynn
Alvin Dark	Dizzy Trout
Larry Jansen	Sherman Lollar
Howie Pollet	Jerry Coleman
Ted Kluszewski	Mike Garcia
Duke Snider	Ned Garver
Don Newcombe	Gus Zernial
Red Schoendienst	Dom DiMaggio

The bad weather continued all the way to Syracuse, the skies clearing only much later in the day, when it was too late to sell many tickets. The first game was played before a crowd of barely three thousand.

Returning to Toronto, where advance sales were good, the troupe once again encountered rain, and the game had to be postponed. By this time Bobby Riggs must have had an inkling that the venture was doomed, but he proceeded to Chicago's Comiskey Park for the next contest. Previous losses may have forced a cutback on promotional spending; or it could have been simply that Americans were weary of baseball for 1950 or had no desire to see the meaningless game. In either case, the proof of the moldy pudding was in the stands. In a ballpark designed to hold more than forty-six thousand customers, barely three thousand were on hand for the game. The next stop, Cincinnati, added some more evidence that people just weren't interested in Bobby's hype. The weather was fine, just right for baseball, but instead of coming in droves to see the All-Stars, the sports lovers of Cincinnati packed the stadium for a nearby college football game. Riggs and company drew thirty-five hundred.

"I know there's somebody up there—I can hear them," said Virgil Trucks shortly before game time as he tried counting the house. *"But I'll be darned if I can see them."*

It was even worse at Pittsburgh. On a Sunday afternoon blessed with beautiful weather, slightly more than twenty-six hundred folks bothered to make the trip to Forbes Field. In fairness, it should be added that a newspaper strike certainly did not help Bobby's chances of promoting the ball game. But more and more it was becoming evident that baseball barnstorming was a phenomenon whose day had ended. Yet the baseball-hungry crowds in Canada had seemed on the verge of turning out, and would have turned out had the weather been better. With that thought, Bobby Riggs determined to return to Canada for his lost gold. Juggling the schedule so that there would be time to fly back to Toronto and Montreal, Riggs learned at the last minute that someone had neglected to obtain permission to land in Canada. That meant the troupe would have to travel across the line via bus, an indignity the high-salaried players had not been forced to suffer since their minor-league days. Most of them bore up well, although there was considerable acid commentary during the trip.

At Pittsburgh the Players Turned Satirical:

"Kiner could attract more people than that by whistling for a cab on any Pittsburgh street corner."

Duke Snider

"After watching the last-place Pirates for six months, you can't blame the Pittsburgh fans for being fed up with baseball."

Early Wynn

By the time the bus ambled into Toronto, however, thick fog had descended and nearly obscured Maple Leaf Stadium. A crowd of about 7,000 waited outside for tickets, which was encouraging enough to make Riggs delay the game until the fog lifted. Long pregame introductions made were in order to stall, but still the fog remained. From behind home plate it was nearly impossible to see much beyond second base.

Rather than refund the ticket money once again, Pittsburgh catcher Clyde McCullough put forth a novel suggestion: Anything hit to the outfield would be a ground-rule double.

An announcement was made that fans could take their choice between having their money refunded and watching a game between All-Star teams handicapped slightly by playing in a blanket of fog. It was hoped, of course, that the fans would be willing to put up with the inconvenience for the privilege of seeing the Americans in action.

Faced with that choice, the Canadians promptly made a headlong rush for the refund counters.

The only fragment of hope after the second Toronto fiasco lay in the southern United States, where ticket sales were also brisk. But as the disgruntled group of exhibitionists headed for Miami, a hurricane struck Florida, reducing the attendance at a game played in its aftermath to a mere three thousand.

That was the final blow. After having played thirteen contests to a combined audience of thirty-two thousand intimates—an average of slightly less than twenty-five hundred—the barnstormers disbanded. Riggs and Jachym lost about sixty-six thousand dollars. They had a great deal of bad luck, to be sure, but it seems unlikely that huge crowds would have foresaken television for their offering under even the best conditions.

THE CHICAGO ALL-STAR GAMES

The annual contest between college football All-Stars and the reigning NFL professional champion did not start out as a cynically contrived hype, of course. In the beginning, the game for Chicago *Tribune* charities, the idea of newspaperman Arch Ward, seemed like a reasonable opportunity to bring together a pair of teams of approximately equal strength. During the first five years of the game, 1934–38, the college All-Stars won twice, the professionals once, and two games ended in ties. During the next thirty-seven meetings, however, the college boys were able to win only seven times. Even worse, after 1963, they were never to win again. No one in his right mind even gave them a chance. But the tradition continued year after year until it had long outlived its usefulness. By the late 1960s, a good idea had been transformed into just another dreary chore, uninteresting to watch and a burden for player and fan alike.

What destroyed the original freshness of the concept? For one thing, the growing prowess of professional football. Back in 1934, there was not a great deal of difference between a top pro team and a select squad of the nation's best college football players. But as the defenses became more and more sophisticated, it became obvious that the short training period was simply not long enough to put the collegians on a competitive basis. In all likelihood, after the start of the 1960s, it seems fair to say that the All-Stars would have needed a year or more of experience to get them ready for their annual tangle with the best pro team.

Worse, the defending champions found themselves in the position of not wanting to be the first in a long while to suffer defeat at

Decline of the Chicago All-Star Game, 1934–76

```
-O-XXOOOOXOOXXOOXOOOOXOOXOOOOXOOOOOOOOOONOO        Log
1  11      1   11   1       1   1      1            1      -  Tie game
9  99      9   99   9       9   9      9            9      O  Win by pros
3  33      4   44   5       5   5      6            7      X  Win by collegians
4  78      3   67   0       5   8      3            4      N  Game canceled
                                                              (player strike)
```

After its last win in 1963, the All-Stars were outscored by the pros, 304–118, in the last 12 games (average score, 25–10). But the problem wasn't that the games were lopsided. The biggest wins were in 1949 and 1966, when the Philadelphia Eagles and Green Bay Packers won by the score of 38–0. The worst thing about the later games was that it was akin to watching a cat stalk a mouse in a cage. One knew the mouse had no logical chance of actually winning. The best to hope for was seeing him get in a good lick or two before going down to defeat.

the hands of the collegians. And so the pros took the game seriously, bearing down until the score indicated there was little danger of losing.

After a time, even the "honor" of being selected to play with the college All-Stars became tarnished. Young men taken from the camps of the teams they hoped to make discovered that the time training with the All-Stars was simply experience down the drain. Often they returned to their parent clubs only to find that they had lost the coaches' eyes in favor of another rookie not saddled with the loss of time at Chicago. Thus the contest gradually came to be a source of discontent with nearly every element connected with it.

There were, of course, some exciting moments during the four decades of games. The 1958 contest, won by the collegians, featured a one-man show by flanker Bobby Mitchell, who scored on eighty-four- and eighteen-yard passes from quarterback Jim Ninowski. Jim Pace of Michigan also caught a pass from King Hill of Rice and scooted fifty-seven yards to the Detroit Lions' three-yard line, setting up a nineteen-yard field goal by Bobby Joe Conrad of Texas A&M. There was also the chilling moment in the 1959 contest, won by Baltimore, 29–0, when Colt linebacker Bill Pellington clotheslined Don Brown of Houston so viciously that it was feared for a moment the young All-Star would die on the field. But after the All-Stars' final victory, when Green Bay plainly was not up to the game, the annual contest became a mechanical bore.

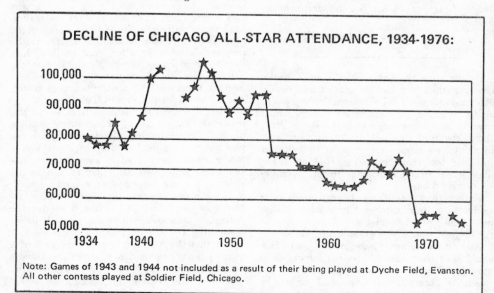

DECLINE OF CHICAGO ALL-STAR ATTENDANCE, 1934-1976:

Note: Games of 1943 and 1944 not included as a result of their being played at Dyche Field, Evanston. All other contests played at Soldier Field, Chicago.

Finally, in 1976, the dreariest contest of all was held before a crowd of 52,895, the second-smallest attendance in the series. After Pittsburgh took a 24–0 lead with 1.22 left in the third period and a violent thunderstorm flooded the field, it was agreed to suspend play. It was also announced that that was the end of the entire series, a worthy idea destroyed by predictability but carried by habit to the point where it became just another bad hype.

HARNESS RACING'S FIASCO

The annual Cane Pace for three-year-olds at Yonkers Raceway is a highly prestigious race in that it is the first leg of pacing's Triple Crown, which also includes the Messenger Stake and the Little Brown Jug. As such, it hardly needed any artificial incentives for the 1959 running at Roosevelt Raceway.

Background on the Cane Pace:
In 1950, William H. Cane became President of Yonkers Raceway and remained with the park until his death six years later. Born in Jersey City, it was Cane who built "Boyle's Thirty Acres" with 80,000 seats for the celebrated Dempsey-Carpentier fight. His home-bred pacer, Good Time, was top money winner with $318,712 until 1958.

Obviously the track officials felt differently, for in an effort to ensure an all-time betting record, they allowed no less than fifteen entrants to move onto the half-mile oval. That meant that a normal start would have to be replaced by a double-tiered one in which eight horses started in the first row and seven in the second. Because there is not enough room for fifteen horses and sulkies to maneuver on a half-mile track, the 1959 running almost assured that the race would not go to the best horse, but the luckiest. It also raised the problem of accidents, for there is real danger in racing in such close quarters. Stanley Dancer, one of the drivers, said after looking over the vast field, "I've just become the father of a nice baby boy and I'd like to spend some time with him before I get killed in a race." Added Joe O'Brien, "I'd say this is not a horserace. There's Adios Oregon out in fifteen post position in the second tier. A lot of people think he's the best horse in the race. Well, they'll never find out tonight. He doesn't have a chance to show his real ability."

The other drivers made sardonic comments about "riding into the valley of death" as the race began. It was, as predicted, a mad scramble from start to finish and, also as predicted, Adios Oregon had no chance to work his way through the maze to exhibit his true form. The winner was Adios Butler, driven by an expert, Clint Hodgins, who managed to use the confusion to his advantage.

That there were no accidents was a fortunate bit of luck. But experts maintained that the attempt to put all the good horses of the time onto the track at one time was a dangerous way of hyping a race that needed no hype at all.

THE INDOOR BICYCLE RACE REVIVAL

For more than four decades, the six-day bicycle race was a standard form of athletic entertainment in America. But by the 1930s it was apparent that the medium was in decline. After the race of 1939, it seemed that the sun had set on six-day bicycling.

There were some, however, who felt the sport should be revived, and they kept the vigil for more than two decades. Then, in July of 1961, the announcement was made that a new version of the six-day bicycle race would be held in Madison Square Garden. Prime mover of the revival was a New York attorney and restaurateur, Dave Paully, who provided financial backing. A long-time bike buff, Jimmy Proscia, helped organize the race according to old-time standards.

Fifteen two-man teams were named as participants in the race, which was slated to start on September 22, 1961. In the meantime, Paully and his associates turned their attention to the task of laying down the track, or "pine saucer," on which the entrants would go round and round. When questioned about the construction, one of the men in charge blandly stated that blueprints were not necessary. Nevertheless, blueprints were obtained, but when they arrived, they were promptly misread. Planks of the big saucer were placed counterclockwise in spots that were supposed to be clockwise—and, of course, vice versa. The mistakes went unnoticed until the afternoon before the race, when the track was brought up from the basement at Madison Square Garden prior to assembly. Then it was noticed that if the track was not changed, the safety of the riders would be endangered.

With ticket holders already on the way for the beginning of the first great six-day bike race in a generation, everyone—including the cyclists themselves—pitched in to reverse the pitch of the track. More than sixty carpenters hammered feverishly as the Garden began to fill with spectators. Before long, eight thousand were on hand, many no doubt wondering if they had misread the date on their tickets or stumbled onto a carpentry seminar by accident.

Some persons drifted away, but most accepted the mixup philosophically. A brass band played, hot dogs and soda pop were purchased, and Dagmar, the buxom television star, did her best to divert attention from the mass disarray by telling jokes. Meanwhile, as they paid the carpenters $9.50 an hour plus time and a half after midnight, David Paully and his associates were getting poorer by the minute. Some of the riders began to grow restive and irritated. Dominique Forlini of France said, "It's amazing how they could get things so fouled up."

After midnight, the crowd of onlookers thinned considerably. Most got their money back and went home. A few stayed around until shortly before three o'clock Saturday morning, when the reconstruction work was finally completed.

Once started, the six-day race—although somewhat shortened—went off smoothly enough. Seven of the teams whirled round and round until the bitter end 141 hours later, covering a distance of 2,359.2 miles in the process and delighting the hard-core fans who stopped by to witness the event. The final day of racing brought in a crowd of 14,200, who yelled continuously as the team of Oscar Plattner and Armin Von Buren of Switzerland pedaled home first. The race was judged an artistic success. First prize was a $1,500 silver trophy standing 4½ feet high.

Financially, the event was disastrous in that Paully and associates lost more than $30,000. Nevertheless, the 54-year-old promoter was determined to stage more bicycling events in the future. "Next time," he said, "I'll read the blueprints myself."

THE "RUNNER-UP" BOWL

By 1960, moguls of the National Football League realized they were riding a crest of popularity. Helped by the "greatest game ever played," the overtime title contest between the Baltimore Colts and the New York Giants, televised professional football was in the midst of a violent upsurge in public approval. The TV watchers obviously wanted more, and the TV sponsors were willing to pay for more.

The problem was: How would it be possible to give them more? The league had been expanded in 1960 to admit Dallas and in 1961 to accommodate Minnesota. The twelve-game schedule, which had existed for three decades, had been extended to fourteen games, thereby enriching the take. Was there anything besides the title game and Pro Bowl exhibition that could be added as a money-maker?

At this point—history does not record who first thought of the concept—someone suggested that a playoff be held between those teams that had finished the regular season in second place in the Western and Eastern conferences. Miami's Orange Bowl was selected as the site for this meeting, which certainly resembled the old baseball Temple Cup in that it decided very little. Would the winner of the Playoff Bowl be permitted to call itself the second-best team in the entire league? Or merely the third, behind the winner and the loser in the title game? Even more important, did it matter at all?

It did matter, of course, in that the game was designed to bring in more dollars and did succeed moderately well in that department. From an artistic point of view, the games were not much more than glorified postseason scrimmages. An indication of the respect, or lack of it, given them by the players can be found in the record of Green Bay in these postseason nonclassics. During the 1960s, Packer teams were usually most proficient in games that counted, yet Green Bay dropped both its Playoff Bowl games in rather lackluster fashion. Some teams, such as the 1965 Baltimore Colts, used the game to experiment in the same way new tricks might be tried in exhibition games. During the contest with Dallas, for example, the Colts gave the ball frequently to a rookie running back who responded by earning considerable yardage. That turned out to be his high point as a runner, however. His name was Mike Curtis, and the leading ground-gainer of the 1965 (played January 16, 1966) Playoff Bowl later

Can We Ever Forget Those Playoff Bowl Games? Well, Probably.

Following the Season	Teams and Results
1960	Detroit 17, Cleveland 16
1961	Detroit 38, Philadelphia 10
1962	Detroit 17, Pittsburgh 10
1963	Cleveland 40, Green Bay 23
1964	St. Louis 24, Green Bay 17
1965	Baltimore 35, Dallas 3

went on to become one of pro football's top linebackers.

Following the merger of the NFL and the AFL and the subsequent agreement to play the first Super Bowl, the Playoff Bowl was quietly dropped. For all but those who like to watch pro football under any conditions, it was probably just as well.

THE SECOND ALL-STAR BASEBALL GAME

In devising artificial money-makers of dubious value, organized baseball was not far behind football. The first All-Star Game, played on July 6, 1933, at Chicago in conjunction with the Century of Progress World's Fair, was founded on good concept—that the money be used to provide pensions for the players. Of course, the game was meaningless, even in determining the relative strength of the two leagues (anything, the axiom goes, can happen in a short series), but the opportunity to see the best players on the diamond at the same time was certainly appealing.

Except for the war year 1944, the annual All-Star baseball game was an event that was looked forward to by both avid and casual fan. Artistically, the series seemed blessed in that by the end of the first quarter century, 1958, the games were nearly even, at fifteen wins for the American League and ten for the National.

Then the players got greedy. If one All-Star game added so many dollars to the pension fund, would not two add twice as many? Not overly familiar with the law of diminishing returns, the players pushed through a proposal that a second game be held, beginning in the summer of 1959.

The plan was put into effect, and the first year saw each league take one contest. In 1960 the National League won both games, and the following year, during the second contest, viewers were treated to the first All-Star game tie, as a torrential downpour forced cancellation. By this time there was considerable controversy as to the merits and demerits of the two-game system. In August 1961, player representatives of the two leagues took a vote and, somewhat predictably, emerged in favor of continuing the double dip. Bob Friend of the Pittsburgh Pirates, speaking for the players, asserted that the fans enjoyed and wanted two games instead of merely one. As evidence, he pointed out that the second contests outdrew the first, 125,318 to 110,011, thereby proving that the fans wanted another game. In response, *Sports Illustrated* remarked that "Friend and his playmates would be willing to play a third, or even a fourth All-Star game, but the fans, upon whose con-

What Bob Friend Didn't Say:
Bending the statistics just a bit to his advantage, Bob Friend was correct in pointing out that the second games produced more fans. What he did not say was that the first games of the series drew 110,011 to ball parks with seating capacities of only 108,741. Thus the first games produced houses with 101 per cent capacity. By contrast, the second games drew 125,318 fans to parks with seating capacities of 195,857, a pull of only 64 per cent capacity.

tinuing loyalty the pension fund ultimately depends, evidently feel that two games are one too many. So do we."

Not giving in easily, the players continued the experiment through 1962 (each team won a game), then discontinued the two-game series. Thus ended one of the few times when the fans had been raped by the players rather than by the owners.

THE "WORLD HEAVYWEIGHT MARTIAL ARTS CHAMPIONSHIP BOUT"
"This match is really serious."
Muhammad Ali, June 24, 1976

"I am approaching this bout in dead seriousness."

Antonio Inoki

Certainly. Of course. And strangely enough, some persons actually believed that the Ali-Inoki boxer-vs.-wrestler battle was something more than a money-maker devised especially for the television networks and the supergullible.

Certainly the prices were serious enough—a thousand dollars for some ringside seats to watch a pair of very athletically talented businessmen grapple their way to a few million dollars. Estimates of the take varied between six million and twelve million dollars.

Angelo Dundee, Ali's trainer, kept the promotional fires going by telling how seriously the boxing champion was training for the bout. Inoki, on the other hand, worked out in secret, presumably perfecting his karate chops, drop kicks, and elbow stomps, as well as devising methods of "strengthening his chin," if such can be done, in order to protect himself from Ali's fists.

Came the day of the fight, June 26, 1976, and the thirty-four-year-old American and thirty-three-year-old Japanese farmer's son

*"I'm so fast that last night I turned off
the light switch in my hotel room and was
in bed before the room was dark."*
                    —Muhammad Ali

moved to the Martial Arts Hall in Tokyo for
their moment of truth.

The truth—like the confessions of a nineteenth-century librarian—turned out to be
rather dull. Ali landed only two punches, both
left jabs, during the fifteen rounds. Inoki's
strategy seemed to be to kick Ali's legs from
under him while keeping his chin out of the
way of the champion's punches. And so the
fight degenerated into a predictable pattern—
Inoki lashing out with his feet while lying on
his back and Ali dancing backward. At the
end, the fans in attendance were so bored
with it all that they tossed trash into the ring.
Once or twice Ali stumbled or was felled momentarily, which drew cheers from the crowd,
but such moments of exquisite anguish were
few and far between. Referee Lebell scored
the bout at 71 to Ali and 71 for Inoki, using a
system whereby the winner of each round was
to receive 5 points and the loser from 1 to 4.
Judge Ko Toyamo scored it 74 for Ali and 72
for Inoki; Kokichi Endo 74 for Ali and 76 for
Inoki.

"I wouldn't have done this fight," said Ali
afterward, "if I'da known he was going to do
that."

Certainly. Of course. And if you get the
chance, Ali, you might tell it to P. T. Barnum.

CHAPTER 26—CAN A ———— BEAT A ————?

Since the very beginning of organized sports entertainment, some promoters and spectators have enjoyed mixing the media. In Roman times, it was, "Can a bear beat a lion?" in the *venatio,* an event that featured wild animals; or perhaps "Can a *mirmillo* [gladiator armed with shield, helmet, and sword] beat a *retiarius* [whose only weapons were a net and trident]?"

With the passing of the Roman Empire, the legalized killing subsided, but the desire to mix media remained. Opportunity was limited, however, until the nineteenth century, when technology provided a wealth of new equipment—velocipedes, bicycles, balloons, and all manner of steam- and gasoline-driven vehicles.

To some, these contests were symbolic of the old and reliable vs. the newfangled and threatening. Thus many cheered when Peter Cooper's engine named Tom Thumb developed mechanical troubles and finished second to a train pulled by a horse. But while the race may have been a struggle between the technological and natural worlds, no one doubted that it was also a very real sporting event.

The nineteenth century, the dawn of spectator sports, also provided an element so necessary to races and contests between machines and men of varying capabilities: uncertainty. No one could define the limits of human speed and endurance. Roads were often poor or impassable, and mechanical devices had a way of malfunctioning with maddening consistency. Thus the contest was not always to the swiftest. And so promoters continued to think of new matchups, or in many cases, the matchups just happened.

Mixing the media continued into the twentieth century, although the contestants soon ceased to be various forms of mechanical equipment, which soon became consistently predictable. Instead, the hybrid matches pitted the skills of the most unpredictable energy package yet devised: the human being.

————HORSE————BICYCLE?

Although late-nineteenth-century bicycles were slow, heavy, and awkward-handling compared to later standards, people were justifiably impressed with what they could do. Except when on a train or a horse galloping near the

limits of its speed, man had never moved across the ground as rapidly as 20 miles per hour before the 1880s. The bicycle provided not only the opportunity to speed along at 20, 30, or even 40 mph, but the propulsion was actually generated by the rider himself. The idea of city streets clogged with bicyclists moving along at such breakneck velocities frightened more than one writer of the period; thus a wave of feeling against the "scorcher," or fast-moving wheelman, existed for some time. But under controlled conditions, on a track, closed-off road, or in an arena, speed cycling was tolerated by some, enjoyed by many.

Testing the speed and endurance of bicycles against that of horses was first done on a grand scale at New York's Madison Square Garden in June 1886. The six-day race featured Charles M. Anderson of California, a champion long-distance equestrian, with a team of twenty horses. Against him were William Woodside of Ireland, and John Brooks of Pennsylvania, two champion wheelmen of the period. The rules were simple: Racing would continue for twelve hours each day, from 1:00 P.M. to 1:00 A.M. Anderson could switch horses as often as he liked. The two cyclists could spell each other as frequently as they liked.

Cappa's 7th Regiment band sent the men, animal, and machine off to a musically exciting start, Brooks on his cycle and Anderson astride a bay gelding named Blue Front. They started evenly but the bicyclist was soon ahead, building up the lead slowly until at the end of the first hour Brooks had a two-mile advantage—16 miles, 7 laps to 14 miles, 7 laps. At the end of the hour, Woodside took Brooks' place. Meanwhile, Anderson continued to move along steadily if not sensationally. "Much interest was taken in him when he changed horses," one reporter wrote. "The speed with which he dismounted from one horse and mounted another was simply wonderful. Once when his horse stumbled against the woodwork Anderson was thrown. It was at first supposed that he was badly hurt but he was quickly on his feet, and within a second on his horse's back."

By five o'clock, when a large portion of the Garden crowd scattered for dinner, Brooks and Woodside led, 65 miles to 61 for Ander-

An Earlier Bicycle-horse Race—with Women the Main Participants:

Five years before the Madison Square Garden event, Rochester, New York, was the scene of a trial of speed between Miss Elsa Von Blumen on a bicycle and the trotting mare Hattie R. Handicapped by the high-wheel vehicle, Miss Von Blumen was allowed to pedal only one mile while the horse was required to trot a mile and one half.

Pushing her vehicle furiously, Elsa won two of three heats, each by a matter of seconds. Her best time, however, came in the first heat, which she lost. She covered the mile in 4 minutes, 56 seconds; Hattie R., obviously pretty slow for a trotter, made the mile and a half in 4.55.

son. At that point the equestrian stopped, wolfed down a dozen eggs and a pint of sherry, then continued the race. (During his next hour, perhaps as a result of the heavy meal, he logged only 8 miles on his score.) Meanwhile, spurred on by the band playing airs from *The Mikado,* the bicycle team generated an 18-mile lead by the end of the first day's competition, 184 miles, 4 laps to 166 miles, 7 laps.

On the basis of that first day, some were willing to give up on Anderson, but by the end of the next 12-hour racing period, the lead of Woodside and Brooks had been shaved to a bit more than 16 miles, 354.5 to 338. Even more disconcerting for the wheelmen and their followers was the fact that Brooks had been able to collect a free five miles at the beginning of the day while Anderson was seized with cramps.

The close race, of course, was good for business. During the evening, more than 5,000 spectators were on hand. The next evening, while Anderson cut the bicyclists' lead even more, attendance continued to improve. The fifth day of the meet started with the wheelmen leading, 658–646, and it was at this juncture that equestrian Anderson made his most concerted effort to move ahead. Before a cheering crowd, he cut the lead in half by ten o'clock. Woodside, considerably winded, yielded the track to Brooks, who proceeded to cover the next mile in 3:20, the fastest logged to that point. Anderson countered by mounting his best horse. "The appearance of the thoroughbred Jo Nay," the papers noted, "evoked loud applause, and when he was on the track the contest became exciting. When

Brooks had completed his 758th mile he received a handsome bouquet. . . . Brooks, who has never ridden in long-distance matches before, looks fagged out and drives his wheel around with labor. It is thought that if Anderson's horses are fresh to-day he will have an excellent chance of winning the match." The penultimate day ended with the wheelmen ahead, 803–795.

During the afternoon of the final day, when it was heard that Anderson had narrowed the cyclists' lead to less than 4 miles, the Garden started to fill with a large crowd anticipating a whirlwind finish. "Anderson's admirers believed that he would be able to overhaul his opponents before midnight," it was reported, "at which hour the race would be concluded." No racing, of course, was allowed on the Sabbath, which explains the early finish time.

The crowd was not disappointed. Although thoroughly exhausted, the cyclists realized that they had to hold on only a few more hours. They pedaled desperately. Anderson, in a grand gesture, flung aside his cap and urged his horses on with plaintive cries and authoritative shouts. As first one rider surged to the front and then the other, a continuous uproar arose from the audience, for it was obvious that they were about evenly divided in their partisanship. Smoke filled the arena as burning eyes tried to make out the number of laps covered by each team on the chalkboard at the end of the oval track.

Horse-bicycle Update:

More recently, Mike Cavanaugh of Northbrook, Illinois, took on Worthy Bret at Chicago on November 13, 1973. The one-mile contest between trotter and bicyclist, billed as the "great match race," was close until the final turn when the horse surged into the lead and went on to win.

Then, at 11:30 P.M., it was suddenly over. Finding that he could not cut the wheelmen's lead any farther than 4 miles, Anderson decided to spare his horses the agony of running the final futile half hour. To cheers from both those who were for him and those against him, he strode off the racing surface and sat down. The final mileage count was 957–953 in favor of the men on metal.

———HORSE———CATAMARAN?

It was late June 1883 when Ezra Daggett and Frederick Hughes, two sporting men of New York, began their friendly argument as to the relative merits of sea vs. land travel. Daggett owned a powerful horse named Boston, Hughes a twin-hulled sailing boat named *Jessie*. Both were proud of their charges, it turned out, and both were prepared to wager five hundred dollars on the outcome of a ninety-mile race from New York City to Stony Creek, Connecticut. "Hughes was on the way to New London," Daggett explained later. "He told me he was going to stop at Stony Creek, and I said I would start with my horse and be there before he was. He said that I couldn't do it and we agreed to have a trial."

On June 30, the race began. *Jessie* slid from the dock at the foot of Twenty-fourth Street, East River, at the same time Daggett trotted out of the stable at Madison Avenue and Twenty-seventh Street. The wind, Daggett noticed with dismay and Hughes with considerable pleasure, was out of the southwest. Knowing he would have to hurry, Daggett urged Boston forward at a steady six-miles-an-hour gait. The pace attracted the attention of villagers along the way, as horses were seldom moved along the highway at such speeds unless there was an emergency, or the driver was slightly out of his head. In any event, word soon reached the ears of ever-vigilant SPCA officials that a horse was being driven to death.

When Daggett and Boston pulled into New Haven, just a few miles west of Stony Creek, the news was not good. He discovered that the catamaran had passed there an hour before. It was also hinted that a warrant for Daggett's arrest might be in the hands of several constables. Undeterred, Daggett pressed on until he arrived at Tomlinson Bridge, where a cold breeze swept off the harbor, causing Boston to shiver. Daggett led him to a hotel a quarter mile away, where he was met by Dr. C. A. Adams of the Connecticut Humane Society. After examining the horse, Adams said it was not fit to continue. By this time a Constable Lanfair arrived. Lanfair said that Hughes and *Jessie* had already won the race and that Daggett was liable for arrest if he continued.

Daggett had Boston rubbed down, allowed him to rest a couple of hours, and then moved on to Stony Creek, paying his wager and complaining about the favorable wind Hughes received. When he arrived at dockside the next morning, however, he was greeted by police officers with formal writs and thrown into jail. Daggett was indignant. "I haven't shown any cruelty to animals," he complained. The run didn't hurt him in the least. I have often taken drives of fifty and seventy-five miles with him and thought nothing of it, and on this trip I stopped several times on the way and gave him food and rest. Why, I have driven him fifty miles in six hours time and again."

"If I was you," said Chief of Police Webster, to whom Daggett issued his complaint, "I wouldn't tell that part of the story."

"Oh fudge," Daggett is reported to have said in rebuttal. "That statement couldn't do me any harm before any sensible man who understood the horse. It is an extraordinarily long-winded horse."

Two days later, Judge Denning of the Connecticut Criminal Court agreed. Daggett was dismissed of the charges of causing the horse to be "overworked, overdriven, and cruelly treated."

Ezra Daggett was not completely happy following this development. Losing the race still bothered him. As soon as he could locate Hughes, he challenged him to a rematch. In the meantime, Hughes had sold *Jessie* and bought a better boat, called *Cyclone*. Daggett insisted on a second race, however, and finally Hughes agreed. By this time, word had gotten around, and a third contestant stepped forward, a bicyclist, challenging them both. But the bicyclist couldn't locate a backer willing to put up five hundred dollars for him and was forced to drop out of the race.

Word had also gotten around to Henry Bergh, the New York SPCA's most crusading member. Determined to stop the contest before it started, Bergh recruited a team of men to make certain Boston was kept under twenty-four-hour surveillance. Informants told him that Boston was being kept at a stable on Twenty-fourth Street and that the race would start from that point. Armed with a description of the horse, four of Henry Bergh's men stood in a cold, drenching rain for hours until rumors reached them that the race had already started. At this point, a grinning stable-boy appeared in the doorway with a horse and threw off its blanket, revealing "to the astonishment and dismay of the discomfited officers" that the animal was not Boston "but a horse that had acted as his representative for the occasion."

Daggett and Boston had actually begun the race at four-thirty in the morning, the rider wearing a rubber coat and oilskin hat pulled down over his eyes, the better to protect him from the elements as well as possible identification. He proceeded up Central Avenue at a twelve-miles-per-hour gait, determined this time that a steady jog would not be enough to win. Soon the speed was increased until "the big-boned gelding was leaving a mile behind him every three minutes."

Ninety minutes after leaving Manhattan, Boston and Daggett arrived at New Rochelle. The rain had nearly stopped by this time and the road was less heavy. Stamford was reached at eight-fifteen, when a short rest of forty-five minutes was given the horse. He was also given a shot of diluted brandy and rubbed down. Bridgeport, the next stop, was entered shortly before noon, the horse showing no ill effects of the long drive through rain and mud. In fact, after resting the animal for another hour, Daggett chirped and Boston "responded by dropping into a spanking gait," which was maintained until the team arrived at New Haven. At two forty-five in the afternoon, the gelding rattled across Tomlinson's Bridge just east of New Haven, then trotted into Stony Creek at four thirty-four, having covered the estimated ninety miles in a bit over twelve hours. The crowd of fifty or so cheering townspeople standing in front of Frank's Hotel told Daggett he had won the race.

As for Frederick Hughes, it was just not his day. A stiff east wind was blowing when he eased *Cyclone* into the East River and pointed her prow toward Hell Gate. A party of New York sporting men were on board to help him celebrate the victory that never came. Instead, he bucked head winds for nearly twelve hours, then gave up the race just off Bridgeport.

Ezra Daggett, claiming ultimate victory, offered to bet two thousand dollars his horse could beat Hughes' boat two times out of three. Anticipating another arrest for cruelty, he armed himself with a number of affidavits showing that the animal was in perfect condition after the drive, then started home by boat. By the time he arrived at New Haven, he obviously thought better of inciting the humane societies further, for he announced that he and Boston were retiring. "I only indulged this time," he said, "to even up on the former race."

It was reported that Frederick Hughes had the last laugh, however, paying the five-hundred-dollar bet in trade dollars.

———ICE SKATER———BICYCLIST?

Not surprisingly, there have been only a few ice skater-bicycle races, not many cyclists being foolhardy enough to venture onto the slippery ice to test their speed against skaters. Those early bicyclists who ventured forth, however, did very well.

One early series of contests took place on the Schuylkill and Delaware rivers during the winter of 1881. "Unless the surface is slightly roughened, the wheel is apt to slip sideways when a sharp turn is made," *Harper's Weekly* warned, ". . . and some of the most experienced and skillful masters of the art have declared after a fall or two . . . that they will not risk another attempt."

Despite the problems, the matches of 1881 were all won by the cyclists. "Only the best skaters could keep up with them," *Harper's* concluded.

———MEAT EATER———VEGETARIAN?

Meat vs. potatoes. It could be summed up that simply. If not a burning issue, at the very least it came close to being overdone.

The question, to be specific, was whether a purely meat or vegetable diet was better for an athlete. Late in the nineteenth century, when both vegetarianism and organized sports began to grow in popularity abroad and in America, it seemed only natural to put the two together. Meat—the decayed flesh of living animals— was bad for the system, said the highly vocal vegetarians. A bland vegetable diet, replied the meat eaters, left the constitution weak and lacking in endurance.

The battle lines were drawn in 1897 when H. Light, captain of London's Vegetarian Cycling Club, expressed the view that "a man is in better condition when he is on vegetable food." As evidence, Light pointed to a cyclist named S. A. Whorlow, whose racing career had been a complete disaster—until he switched from meat eating to vegetarianism. Then he "carried everything before him, and the following year won the North London Club's fifty-mile road race, another vegetarian member being second, and both handsomely breaking the record for the distance."

There were other examples, not sufficient in numbers to convince men of the opposite position, but enough to elicit a certain amount of anger. For a while the issue was debated; then the inevitable head-to-head, or stomach-to-stomach, match was proposed. "The relative powers of endurance between vegetarians and those persons who follow a meat diet will be tested next Saturday by a walking race from Newark to Philadelphia," reported the New York *Times* of October 28, 1907. Carrying the banner of the vegetarians was Henry W. Miller and H. P. Sweeney; for the meat eaters there was Howard Smith and Charles E. Knell.

The start was made from the corner of Market and Broad streets, Newark, the entrants dressed comfortably in jerseys, light coats, and hobnailed boots. Both teams were to check in at Trenton that night, but as neither group showed up, the test must be judged inconclusive.

A similar test was made in 1911 by two brothers, Warren and Jesse Buffum of Harvard, who left Los Angeles in July bound for New York. Warren ate only vegetables during the cross-country journey, and Jesse ate a normal diet of basically carnivorous fare. When they arrived at their destination six months later, Warren was definitely in better physical shape. In addition, it was noted that Jesse had "worried" quite a bit, "became exhausted, and was compelled to board a train when still three hundred miles from his goal."

It seemed to be a clear-cut triumph for vegetarianism, until advocates of the opposite view pointed out that Warren had been the stronger and heavier at the beginning of the race. In any event, skeptics added, the "race" had really taken too long to test the brothers' powers of endurance.

Still, the vegetarians were persistent. In 1914, when Harvard's football captain was stricken with appendicitis, it was immediately pointed out that meat had been the cause. Dr. Richard C. Newton, president of the New Jersey State Board of Health (and at least a closet vegetarian, one suspects), wrote, "Dr. Nicholas Senn was told by the hospital surgeons in Africa that they had never seen a case of appendicitis in a vegetable-eating African. This immunity to the disease is also alleged of the Brahmins in India, who are strict vegetarians. . . . The idea that meat eating may cause appendicitis is so prevalent that it would seem to have some foundation in fact."

Other races were held, of course. In 1927, it was between two young men of Lexington, Kentucky, who chose a ten-mile foot race as the means of telling which diet was better. Forest Cleveland, twenty-one, was the vegetarian; his opponent, twenty-one-year-old James Walter, it was reported, "partakes of meat freely and is also fond of desserts." Walter won the race, but only by about ten seconds. This led one editorial writer to remark, "Such an outcome would seem to indicate that what is one man's meat is another man's vegetable. . . . It would be pleasant if everybody found, like these two, that what he likes is good for him. On the other hand, one need not believe with puritanical self-denial that all that looks appetizing must be indigestible."

Then in 1931 there was the "duel between beefsteak and banana," which took place at Copenhagen, Denmark, before more than twenty thousand onlookers. This time it was a bicycle race between a pair of middle-aged diet enthusiasts as the climax of an argument that aroused all Scandinavia. The meat eater was Axel Randrup, chairman of the Copenhagen Butchers' Guild, who extrolled the virtues of meat for athletes. He was immediately challenged by Frederich Nadsen, a vegetarian.

The whole route of the resultant contest between Copenhagen and Rosklide, a distance of about forty miles, was lined with spectators. A neck-and-neck struggle ensued, Randrup winning by a bare couple of seconds. Ten eminent Danish physicians then examined the two racers and declared the contest a dead heat from the point of view of their energy expended vs. energy remaining.

The next year, a physician from the Mayo Foundation Graduate School at Omaha placed himself on the side of the meat eaters.

"The roughage diet is all right," said Dr. Walter C. Alvarez, "for people who have the digestion of an ostrich. Let the cow eat the greens and give the children milk, cream, and butter."

Undeterred, one vegetarian named Barbara Moore set out to "exemplify stalwart feminism and the merits of vegetarianism" just before Christmas 1946. A 56-year-old dietician, Dr. Moore's plan was to walk from Edinburgh, Scotland, to London, a distance of 373 miles, in one week. That amounted to more than 50 miles per day, but "head high and jaw outthrust," she plodded ahead. Armed with lots of oranges, apples, dates, and nuts, Dr. Moore was cheered along much of the route by people who walked alongside her. Congratulatory telegrams awaited her when she arrived at her destination.

Unfortunately, her destination turned out to be a London hospital, which she reached on the point of collapse. Blistered and weary, she refused the hospital's traditional Christmas turkey and plum pudding. "If somebody challenged me to walk around the world, I think I would take it on," she said bravely.

Thus ended more than a half century of food faddism applied to athletic ability. True, nothing much was decided, but at least it provided some diversion as well as food for thought.

———TRAIN———AIRPLANE?

By the turn of the century, travel by train was the speediest on earth, and with the exception of the larger ocean liners, the most luxurious. Holding a strong hand, railroad officials discouraged races and never admitted their trains had taken part in one. Still, there were occasional engineers who couldn't resist the temptation to kick the engine ahead a few notches when challenged by an ice yacht or a low-flying monoplane.

That was the situation on May 16, 1911, when Earle L. Ovington, a young aviator soon to represent the United States in an international flying contest in England, took off from Belmont Park aerodrome for a few practice turns. After reaching an altitude of one thousand feet, he headed for Garden City, where he made a graceful slide down to within one hundred feet of an airfield there, tipping his wings and generally showing off for the people on the ground. He then headed for Mineola flying field. There he "cut the figure eight twice, making dips and curves with little apparent effort."

On his way back to Belmont Park, Ovington followed the line of railroad tracks. When he spotted an express train approaching, he curved his monoplane around, waited until he was on even terms with it, and then opened the throttle. The engineer of the train put on more steam, and before long both vehicles were hurtling along at seventy miles per hour.

Having experienced the surge forward and seen the low-flying aircraft, most of the train's passengers crowded against the windows to get a better view. Ovington responded by waving and pushing his ship gradually but steadily ahead. By the time he veered off in the direction of Belmont Park the plane was a half mile ahead of the train.

A similar race took place on February 12, 1912, between a New York Central engine and Clinton O. Hadley, an aviator who started the day by performing tricks and racing with automobiles adapted to move along the ice-covered Hudson River. A crowd in excess of ten thousand turned out near Tarrytown, many of the natives wrapped in heavy coats and furs or huddled about stoves. There were two moving-picture houses in the town, which were usually crowded, but during the Hadley exhibitions the theater clientele consisted mainly of "gentlemanly ushers." As one old-timer remarked, "something for nothing or a fire are the only things that will attract a crowd in Tarrytown."

Hadley's first attraction was a five-mile straightaway race against the cars. Fred Koenig, in a Mercedes, made a good run for a while, then whirled into a snowbank and couldn't move. It was an hour before he was freed. Hadley circled about until he spotted the train near Helen Gould's estate, heading north. Recognizing it as the Lake Shore Limited, he dropped to about five hundred feet and stayed even with it for several miles until they approached a sharp curve. At that point Hadley roared ahead, acknowledged the engineer's friendly whistle with a wave, and headed back to the Tarrytown station.

The next day, Hadley announced that he intended to take on the fastest train in the East, the *Twentieth Century Limited* but just as he started his plane a section of the carburetor broke off, caught in the propeller, and smashed it.

————TRAIN————MOTORBOAT?

It remained for America's most famous powerboat driver, Garfield A. Wood, to take on the *Twentieth Century Limited* about a dozen years later. A wealthy New York and Detroit sportsman, Gar Wood's first long-distance race with a train took place in April 1921. Wood, in his 900-horsepower cruiser *Gar II, Jr.,* roared out of Miami Harbor at midnight on April 25, just as the Atlantic Coast Line's fastest train, the *Havana Special,* departed Miami Station. On the powerboat was C. F. Chapman, editor of *Boating* magazine, who had deemed the contest interesting enough to document.

Wood's itinerary called for an average speed of 30 miles per hour in the open sea for 41 hours, which would enable him to beat the *Havana Special* by about three hours. Seven hundred gallons of gasoline were loaded as a hundred of Wood's friends gathered on the dock to wish him well.

The first reports came from Savannah, stating that despite some rough weather, Wood was leading the train by approximately 11 miles. Southport, South Carolina, was reached at 1:15 P.M., 13 hours after leaving Miami. While taking on gasoline there, Wood noted that he was well ahead of the schedule he had set for himself. But the following night, when several hundred people gathered at the Columbia Yacht Club's West 86th Street landing, nothing was heard from the ship, which was supposed to be leading. In the meantime, word arrived that the *Havana Special* had pulled in shortly after 10:00 P.M., right on schedule. The crowd drifted off, considerably disappointed and concerned.

The next morning, Wood arrived at New York with the explanation that his cruiser had broken a shaft, which had necessitated a stop at Sandy Hook for repairs. Refusing to accept the fact that he had finished second, Wood stated that the actual running time, less maintenance, was less for the motorboat than the train. He had covered the distance in 47 hours, 23 minutes; the *Havana Special* in 47 hours, 44 minutes.

After concentrating on defeating other powerboats for the next few years, Wood decided in 1925 to race the *Twentieth Century Limited* from Albany to New York, a distance of approximately 150 miles. The train's usual time was 3 hours, 13 minutes. Before Wood could bring off the race, however, another pilot named George Mead, in the *Teaser,* left New York with the intention of beating this time. With him was Charles F. Chapman as official observer. Moving along at 2,100 revolutions per minute over an extremely smooth river, Mead pulled into Albany 2 hours, 40 minutes later, an average of 56 miles per hour. Yet even at Mead's moment of glory there were dissenters. "To say that the *Teaser* beat the *Twentieth Century* is highly inaccurate," one editor wrote, "as the boat can carry no other cargo and only the men in its own small crew, the contribution it makes to the practical problems of transportation can be set down as about zero."

That criticism, of course, missed the point. Americans were not the least bit interested in the practical problems of transportation. What interested them was the contest. There was so much enthusiasm, in fact, that when Gar Wood announced that he was determined to race the train despite Mead's effort, radio stations along the route made plans to cover the event. A 50-watt aircraft telephone and telegraph transmitter was installed in a twin-engined S-29-A plane. WGY, Schenectady, established three relay points from which to pick up and hurry along the plane's reports so that they could be retransmitted by wire to New York.

Wood, meanwhile, drove a pair of boats to Albany, *Baby Gar IV* and *Baby Gar V*. Railroad officials did their best to ignore the air of excitement, although it was announced that no alteration would be made in the *Twentieth Century Limited*'s schedule. That meant that the regular five-minute delay to change engines at Harmon, New York, 32 miles from Grand Central Terminal, would be part of the run.

The race was truly one of the major spectator happenings of 1925. Powerboats came from miles around, turning the river into a shimmering mass of crisscrossed wakes; Governor Al Smith's son Walter arrived and asked for a tour of the vessels; a half-dozen small airplanes, in addition to the radio transport, waited for the race to begin.

At 6:52 A.M. on May 26, 1925, orange-and-white streamers trailing from her rear platform, the *Twentieth Century Limited* moved across the New York Central Bridge at Albany. From the docks below all eyes were on the bridge. When the streamers were spotted, someone yelled, "Gas!" and the two crews tumbled into the speedboats. The engines exploded with twin roars, lines were cast off, the crowd cheered. Less than a minute later, the two ships were moving down the river at the head of two furrows of flying spray.

All along the route crowds collected at the water's edge to get a good view of the powerboats and airplanes that circled overhead. At one point, there was considerable excitement

when Gar Wood, realizing that *V* was making better time than *IV*, which he was driving, decided to switch boats in midriver. He signaled to his brother George to bring the ships alongside each other, slowing their speeds from about 50 miles per hour to 40. "It required expert maneuvering to keep them close together," one reporter wrote, "with both craft whirling along in clouds of spray, their bounding bows thumping the water, Gar Wood and Charles M. Chapman climbed over from the *IV* to the *V*, while George Wood and a newspaperman, R. R. Batson, came to the *IV*."

Not long afterward, the crews had to switch once again, for the *V* developed mechanical difficulties in the form of a broken camshaft housing and had to be withdrawn from the race.

Some of the railroad crew, unlike the top officials of the company who remained aloof, took the race quite seriously and wanted to pour on the speed. The *Twentieth Century Limited* had arrived early at Albany, however, and orders were to proceed to New York at less than full speed so as to arrive "on schedule." The train with such a fine reputation for speed, then, dragged along the tracks at nothing better than three-quarter power.

New Yorkers started watching the sky shortly before ten o'clock, knowing that the first indication of Wood's approach would be the convoy of airplanes above the craft. A large crowd gathered on the driveway and park paths of the Columbia Yacht Club, surging inside the exclusive grounds before an attaché could be sent to lock the gate. At 9:47 A.M., Wood passed 125th Street and, letting the engine out, boiled into the club entrance just 3 minutes later. His time—2 hours, 58 minutes—was slower than that of the *Teaser*, but fast enough to defeat the *Twentieth Century Limited*.

The Speed of Things for a Mile, As of 1931:

Running Man	4 minutes, 10⅖ seconds (Paavo Nurmi, 1923)
Running Horse	1 minute, 34⅘ seconds (Roamer, Saratoga, New York, 1918)
Swimmer	21 minutes, 27 seconds (Clarence "Buster" Crabbe, Long Beach, California, July 1930)
Motorboat	36.5 seconds (98.76 mph) (Major Henry Segrave, 1930)
Airplane	12.9 seconds (278.48 mph) (Warrant Officer Bonnett, France, 1930)
Bicyclist	1 minute, 4⅕ seconds (Menus Bedell, 1917) Motor-paced against time)
Motorcycle	24 seconds (150.5 mph) (Joe Wright, 1930)
Ice Skater (1,500 meters)	2 minutes, 18.8 seconds (Clas Thunberg, 1928)
Harness Trotter	1 minute, 56¾ seconds (Peter Manning, 1922)
Harness Pacer	1 minute, 55¼ seconds (Dan Patch, 1905)
Sculler	5 minutes (James Paddon, 1924)
Automobile	14.6 seconds (246.086 mph) (Sir Malcolm Campbell, 1931)

Cornelius Jordan, engineer of the train, was not happy about being forced to drag his heels along the route. Given a special engine, he said, along with the right-of-way, he was willing to bet he could beat any boat Wood could put on the river. Three weeks before, as a matter of fact, Jordan had left Albany 32 minutes late and pulled into Harmon 2 minutes early. The company's thanks for arriving early, he noted sardonically, was a 10-day suspension.

By the 1920s, technology had improved to the point where there was little point in racing different machines against one another. But if there was less interest in pitting a motorboat against a train, sports fans continued to be curious about hybrid contests involving human skills and endurance. During the golden age of boxing and wrestling, for instance, they asked:

―――――BOXER―――――WRESTLER?

In the early 1920s in America, there were two names synonymous with perfection in boxing and wrestling. Heavyweight champ Jack Dempsey seemed capable of demolishing taller and heavier men with a single punch; in the ranks of then-legitimate wrestling, the reigning king was Ed "Strangler" Lewis, owner of the famous headlock that rendered opponents insensible with frightening regularity. During the promotion-minded decade, it was inevitable that the two champions of the most violent sports get into the same ring.

The idea was not exactly a novel one. Several good boxers and wrestlers had tangled, one of the more famous matches taking place in Reno, Nevada, where Farmer Burns, a retired wrestler, easily pinned a better-than-average middleweight boxer, Billy Papke. A year later, in 1922, "Strong Boy" Price, a wrestler from Eldorado, Kansas, took on "Sailor" Adams, a boxer from Joplin, Missouri. As the hometown Joplinites cheered, Adams sent Price to the canvas four times, but each time the wrestler regained his feet and continued to stalk the boxer. Eventually Price pinned Adams in the sixth round. But if the odds seemed to favor the wrestler, boxing fans were quick to point out that a champion with a truly potent punch could win in a flash. As evidence they cited a match in 1913 at Paris, when the champion, Jack Johnson, lost his temper while wrestling with a Liberian named Spoul and knocked him out with a stiff punch to the stomach.

In any event, it seemed that Dempsey vs. Lewis would be an ideal attraction that would draw a record crowd. A year earlier, Dempsey had knocked out Georges Carpentier, solidifying his title and creating a competitive vac-

uum. Lewis had also done well. Both drew well wherever they appeared. It was natural that the public would support a no-holds-barred match.

The challenge came from Billy Sandow, Lewis's manager, in March 1922. Stating that he had deposited five thousand with a Nashville sporting editor as a guarantee "anywhere in the United States at a date that may be selected later," Sandow proposed a time limit of twenty minutes, with Dempsey being allowed to fight with bare fists or wrestle while Lewis would be restricted to wrestling. Jack Kearns, Dempsey's manager, contacted at the New York Hippodrome, jumped at the challenge, offering to post a side bet of ten thousand with the sporting editor of the New York Times that Dempsey could KO Lewis within the twenty-minute period.

That seemed to settle the issue, except that Kearns and Dempsey promptly left for Europe for a series of exhibitions. Lewis continued his exhibition tour of the United States, defending his title against local wrestlers. The public waited. By December, the betting had increased to twenty-five thousand, and a sports editor for the Chicago Tribune, Walter Eckersall, predating the Ali-Marciano computer battle of a half century later, described a fictitious bout in which Lewis emerged victorious after a bloody thirty-eight minutes. His script called for Dempsey landing a solid blow, but only after he had been weakened by repeated falls.

The Strategy:
"I've done a lot of wrestling as part of my preliminary training and I think I've got the old toehold and headlock down close to perfection. If I can win the first fall from him, I'll begin to use my fists. But I've got a funny little hunch that maybe I can dump him without rapping him on the chin."

Jack Dempsey
"I can throw myself, feet forward, at least fifteen feet. In doing so, I believe I could break the leg of a man like Dempsey. . . . I could cover up long enough to get hold of him, and once I got hold, he would not have a chance in a thousand that he might hit me with a punch hard enough to knock me out. . . .

Ed "Strangler" Lewis

Rumors continued to fly for months afterward, the inevitable checks being written and deposited until the public finally began to

Boxer-Wrestler Update (1976):
More than half a century after the Dempsey-Lewis battle was first mentioned, interest in staging boxer-wrestler matches produced a pair of bouts within hours of each other. In the more famous one, an out-of-condition Muhammad Ali fought to a draw with Japanese champion wrestler Antonio Inoki at Tokyo. Inoki's main weapon was lying on his back and kicking outward at Ali with his feet.

The second bout took place at Shea Stadium, New York City, the participants being Chuck Wepner and 7-foot, 4-inch wrestler André the Giant. In the first round, the crowd of 32,897 roared as Wepner landed a jab that drew only a smile from André. Sparring continued until the third round when André suddenly became tired of the whole business and tossed Wepner out of the ring. The boxer could not return within twenty seconds.

---

sense that the entire thing was a bit of promotional hokum that would never develop. What surely would have strengthened this viewpoint was the knowledge that Jack Kearns had an earlier fling at the wrestling racket and had once taken a bath when one of his fighters had been upset in a bout that was supposed to be an easy victory. Having no desire to see Lewis pull a double cross on Dempsey, Kearns no doubt milked talk of the fight for all its promotional value, then quietly let the idea die.

————MAN————HORSE?

The remarkable performance of Jesse Owens in the 1936 Olympic Games generated interest in the possibility that a sprinter capable of a lightning-fast start could defeat a race horse over a short distance. Owens wasted little time capitalizing on the possibilities of such a race. His first professional appearance as a runner took place on December 26, 1936, before a crowd of three thousand at Tropical Stadium, Havana, Cuba. The audience, assembled for a football game, was just as interested in the halftime show, which featured Owens racing against a chestnut gelding named Julio McCaw.

There was one catch, however: Julio McCaw started 40 yards behind Owens. At the starting gun, Owens increased his lead but midway through the race the horse began cutting down the gap with every stride. At the end of the 100 yards, Owens was 20 yards in front. "Since I haven't competed for such a long time . . . I'm satisfied with my showing," said the triple Olympic winner. "I would be willing to run a horse without a handicap, provided the animal selected wasn't particularly fast."

The event spawned both imitation and controversy. In 1937, another sprinter, named Forrest "Spec" Towns, took on a cavalry horse in a 120-yard hurdle race at Chattanooga. The contestants covered the same distance, but Towns' hurdles were low and those of Tommy Roberts, the horse, were high.

As in the Owens-Julio McCaw race, the track was wet, but Towns moved away to a quick lead before Private John Henry could get Tommy Roberts into a good stride. By the time they reached the 100-yard mark, rider and horse were closing fast on Towns. At the finish line, both parties crossed in a blur. The judges finally decided that Towns had won by a nose, a fair decision in view of the fact that Tommy Roberts had knocked down two of his hurdles along the way.

Most observers agreed that a man, especially a lightning-fast starter such as Owens, could defeat a horse in a short race, but the question arose as to how long man's superiority would last. In 1932, it was pointed out, Equipoise had run a mile in 1:34.4 (or 5.35 seconds for each 100 yards of distance). Had Jesse Owens and Equipoise raced a mile together, even at Owens' breakneck speed of 9.4 seconds for the 100-yard dash the man would have finished 325 lengths behind.

Those who insisted man was the stronger animal pointed out that while he undoubtedly would lose a mile race, man would win an endurance contest. This, too, was contested, the horsemen noting that on November 12, 1853, the trotter Conqueror, pulling a sulky, negotiated 100 miles in 8 hours, 55 minutes, 53 seconds.

————ARCHER————HANDGUNNER?

The swashbuckling Robin Hood movies of the past invariably included a scene in which some expert archer split the arrow of his opponent at 500 yards. Although most of the audience dismissed such feats as poetic license, the truth is that a top archer can be extremely accurate, sometimes accurate enough to challenge a pistol champion.

One such test took place on January 24, 1927, between General I. Thord-Gray, president of the Metropolitan Archery Association, and fourteen men firing pistols. The scene was the 9th Regiment Armory on Fourteenth Street, New York City.

Standing 80 yards from the target, Thord-Gray shot his arrow 70 times, missing the target twice but scoring consistently well on the remaining 68 attempts. Situated 75 yards from their targets, the pistol men were less accurate. They hit the bull's-eye more times than the archer, but were not as close on their other shots. As a result, Thord-Gray was declared the winner by 37 points.

Another contest, arranged by the Isaac Walton League, was held on March 6, 1937, at Utica, New York. Shooting the bow and arrow was Grant Merriman, a local archer; Lieutenant Dennis Janiekwicz of the Utica Police opposed him with a .38-caliber revolver. Out of a possible 300 points, Janiekwicz scored 267 points: Merriman, 242.

In 1964, another contest was held following statements, "Bows are more accurate than pistols," which were made by several of the archers from the Golden Arrow Indoor Archery Lanes, San Mateo County, California. The challenge was taken up by pistol shooters in the area, and the match held at the public range at Coyote Point.

Team captain for the archers was John Gary, singer and one of the top bowmen in California. But his five-man team was defeated by the pistol shooters, 1448-44X–1301-16X.

Finally, on July 18, 1965, at Chappaqua, New York, a match was held between two teams of eight men each, one armed with .45-caliber revolvers, the other with crossbows. The pistolmen scored a narrow 1,927–1,898 victory, but as one of the archers pointed out, four of the bowmen outscored their opponents and four lost. Therefore the match should be considered a draw.

————ARCHER————GOLFER?

The sport of archery golf has had many advocates, but certainly the most energetic during the 1960s and 1970s was George Mann of Silver Spring, Maryland, an amateur archer who also happened to be director of the U. S. Information Service at the American Embassy in Israel in 1964.

At that time, he had taken up the habit of going around a golf course with a bow and arrow, seeing how many "strokes" it could take him to put the arrow in a 4¼-inch target stationed near the cup. It was not only good exercise but also in some ways more challenging than ordinary target shooting. Eventually Mann realized that an archer could "hole out" in about the same number of strokes as a good golfer. It was inevitable after this discovery that a match be arranged between Mann and Charlie Mandelstam, professional golfer at the Caesarea Club, Israel.

Mann drew up a list of rules for archery golf, which stated that the archer must use the same bow regardless of where he happens to be on the course, and that he cannot use artificial sighting devices. "I found the hardest part of the game was in properly judging distances," Mann said. "Out on the course, the green usually looks closer than it is, and I tended to undershoot on approaches."

The archer-golfer match took place on September 3, 1964. Mandelstam won the first hole and Mann the second, and so it went for eight holes. Starting the ninth and final hole, the match was all even, both in holes won and overall number of shots. The two men reached the edge of the last green in two shots each and nearly "holed out" with their third shots. When both made their fourth shot, the contest was declared a draw.

The hybrid sport never caught on in a sensational manner, but George Mann continued to promote it and found that audiences enjoyed the matches whenever they were played. A more recent match took place on June 21, 1975, at Martinham Golf Course, near St. Michaels, Maryland. On this occasion Mann's opponent was Tom Smack, the Martinham professional, who fell behind immediately by scoring a par on the 333-yard first hole while Mann hit the bull's-eye for a birdie 3. On the second hole Smack again settled for par while Mann overshot his target and had to take a bogie 5. The match stayed even until the sixth hole, on which Mann scored a 3 to his opponent's 5. The archer dropped a stroke on the next hole but won the eighth hole and the match. Final scores were 33 for Smack and 31 for George Mann.

CHAPTER 27—1921–30

1921

Winners: Baseball: New Yorkers celebrate the first World Series between the Yankees and Giants (the first of six before the Giants move to San Francisco). Babe Ruth, who has hit 54 and 59 home runs since being converted to a full-time outfielder for the Yankees, seems to be the difference between the teams. But he manages to hit only one home run and the Giants defeat the Yanks, 5 games to 3. It is the last of the extended World Series. . . . *Kentucky Derby:* Behave Yourself. *Preakness:* Broomspun. *Belmont Stakes:* Grey Lag . . . *Indy 500:* Tommy Milton . . . *Boxing:* The only change of champions occurs in bantamweight division when Pete Herman regains his crown by winning a 15-round decision over Joe Lynch. But Herman's new reign lasts only two months, Johnny Buff defeating him via a decision in September. . . . *Golf: USGA Men's Open:* James M. Barnes. *PGA:* Walter Hagen . . . *Hockey:* 1920–21 Stanley Cup goes to Ottawa Senators for second year in a row. . . . *Football: Rose Bowl:* California 28, Ohio State 0 . . . *National Football League* (APFA): Chicago Staleys (10–1–1). . . . *Basketball:* College champion selected by Helms Athletic Foundation: Pennsylvania (21–2).

Other Happenings: On August 5, first radio broadcast of major league baseball game is made by KDKA, Pittsburgh. The Pirates beat the Phillies, 8–5, as described by Harold Arlin. . . . World Series of 1921 is also broadcast, the first to be sent over the airwaves. . . . Jockey Chick Lang rides 135 winners, and young Johnny Weismuller swims 100 yards in 52.6 seconds. . . . On July 4, motorcyclist Ralph Hepburn churns 300 miles on a dirt track at Dodge City, Kansas, in 3 hours, 30 minutes, 3 seconds, an average speed of about 86 mph. . . . In college basketball, Pennsylvania, coached by Edward McNichol, finishes season with 21–2 record, best in nation. . . . Professional bicycle racer Frank L. Kramer, having won his first major event before the turn of the century, makes a comeback in 1921 and wins the pro track sprint championship. . . . In collegiate baseball, when Syracuse University manager Cy Thurston hears that Goucher College in Baltimore has one of the best college teams in the nation, he sends off an invitation for the two schools to meet. Then he discovers that Goucher is one of Maryland's finest colleges for women. . . . Playwright George Bernard Shaw, showing his utter lack of knowledge of boxing, picks Frenchman Georges Carpentier to beat Jack Dempsey in title fight. . . . Jack Johnson, having been convicted of violating the Mann White Slave Act, is sent to Leavenworth Prison. . . . Wrestler Strangler Lewis, who loses only 33 matches of more than 6,200, has a temporary setback when he is defeated in May by Stanislaus Zbyszko. . . . There are no no-hitters pitched in major leagues, but Walter Johnson does pass Cy Young's record 2,804 strikeouts by fanning 143 men during the 1921 season and bringing his total to 2,834. . . . Charles W. Paddock runs 100-yard dash in 9.6 seconds. . . . In Rose Bowl game, viewers estimate that pass thrown by Brick Muller of California travels 70 yards. . . .

1922

Winners: Baseball: The New York Yankees and the Giants stage a rerun of their subway World Series of 1922, this time with a revised format of best-of-7 games. Babe Ruth is held to a pathetic .118 average with no home runs, but the Yankees are in command from beginning to end. One lowlight of the Series, which the Yanks take in 4 games plus a tie, comes in the second contest, which is called "on account of darkness" with the sun still high in the sky. Commissioner Landis is so infuriated he donates the game's receipts to charity. . . . *Kentucky Derby:* Morvich. *Preakness:* Pillory. *Belmont Stakes:* Pillory . . . *Indy 500:* Jimmy Murphy . . . *Boxing:* The years 1921 and 1922 are bad ones for Georges Carpentier. After losing challenge for heavyweight title vs. Dempsey, he drops light-heavyweight title to the Senegalese Battling Siki in a sixth-round knockout. . . . Welterweight champion Jack Britton also loses his crown, to Mickey Walker, and Johnny Buff, bantamweight king less than a year, is knocked out in 14 rounds by former champ Joe Lynch. . . . *Golf: USGA Men's Open:* Gene Sarazen. *PGA:* Gene Sarazan . . . *Hockey:* 1921–22 Stanley Cup winner: Toronto St. Patricks . . . *Football: Rose Bowl:* California 0, Washington & Jefferson 0 . . . *National Football League:* Canton Bulldogs (10-0-2) . . . *Basketball:* College champion selected by Helms Athletic Foundation: Kansas (16–2).

Other Happenings: On May 29, U. S. Supreme Court rules that organized baseball is a sport, not a business, and hardly anyone laughs. . . . On August 25, Chicago Cubs build up 25–6 lead over Phils in fourth inning, have to hang on to win 26–23 thriller. . . . First international golf match is held at Southampton, New York, August 28–29. United States beats Great Britain, 8–4, to win the first Walker Cup. . . . The year also features the first USGA-sponsored Amateur Public Links championship. The event draws 140 entries and is won by Edmund R. Held of St. Louis. . . . On October 28, first coast-to-coast football broadcast is made by radio station WEAF, New York. Fans hear Princeton beat Chicago, 21–18, at Stagg Field, Chicago. . . . During the baseball season, the St. Louis Cardinals and Chicago Cubs make a trade involving outfielder Cliff Heathcoat. In the morning game of a Memorial Day doubleheader, Heathcoat plays left field for the Cards; following the midday trade he plays the second game against his former teammates. . . . Knute Rockne tells a credulous public that athletics can cure "the male effeminate." Referring to the "male lizard who wears complexion dope . . . the sissie who wears the corsets or pinch-back coat," the Rock recommends a strong dose of football to set him straight. . . . In a football game between Ohio State and Chicago, Nick Workmen of Ohio State kicks a punt measuring 100 yards with roll. But Chicago wins the game, 14–9. . . . On April 30, Charlie Robertson of the Chicago White Sox pitches a perfect game against Detroit, 2–0. It is Robertson's second year in the major leagues and he finishes at 14–15. In six more seasons, he never has a winning record. . . . Jesse Barnes of the New York Giants also pitches a no-hitter, against the Phillies on May 7. . . . Sybil Bauer swims the 100-yard backstroke in 1 minute, 17.6 seconds. . . . Joie Ray, champion runner since 1915, races a mile in 4 minutes, 17 seconds. . . . In May, Ty Cobb is suspended for treading on an umpire's shoes. The same week, Babe Ruth is banished for throwing dirt in an arbiter's face and attacking a fan in the stands. . . . Motorcyclist Cannonball Baker goes from New York to Los Angeles on 40 gallons of gas. . . . In September Whitey Witt, Yankee outfielder, is knocked unconscious by a pop bottle thrown from stands. American League President Ban Johnson offers a reward for information leading to the identity of the bottle thrower, and actually pays reward when a fan testifies that Witt stepped on bottle that was already on field, thereby knocking himself out. . . . Champion bicyclist Frank Kramer retires again. . . .

1923

Winners: Baseball: Each team having won a World Series against the other, the New York Yankees and the Giants play a rubber match. This time Babe Ruth has a good Series, smashing two home runs in the second game and another in the sixth and final contest of the Series, which the Yanks take, 4 games to 2. . . . *Kentucky Derby:* Zev. *Preakness:* Vigil. *Belmont Stakes:* Zev . . . *Indy 500:* Tommy Milton . . . *Boxing:* Mike McTigue becomes light-heavyweight champion by winning 20-round decision over Battling Siki at Dublin, Ireland. Johnny Wilson loses middleweight crown, to Harry Greb, and Johnny Kilbane, featherweight champion since 1912, finally turns over title to Eugene Criqui on a sixth-round KO. A month and a half later, Criqui loses 15-round decision to Johnny Dundee. . . . *Golf: USGA Men's Open:* Bobby Jones. *PGA:* Gene Sarazen . . . *Hockey:* Winner of 1922–23 Stanley Cup: Ottawa Senators . . . *Football: Rose Bowl:* USC 14, Penn State 3 . . . *National Football League:* Canton Bulldogs (11–0–1) . . . *Basketball:* College champion selected by Helms Athletic Foundation: Kansas (17–1).

Other Happenings: Jim Thorpe begins 1923 season as player-coach with NFL Oorang Indians (Marion, Ohio), but the franchise folds with a 1–10 record and Thorpe joins the Toledo Maroons. . . . In the eleventh round of a scheduled 12-round fight between welterweight champion Mickey Walker and challenger Cowboy Padgett on July 2, both fighters fall out of the ring at the same time, landing on the press table. Padgett breaks two ribs. Walker, unhurt, wins the fight. . . . Two months later, on September 5, Canadian flyweight champion Gene LaRue throws a hard left to the jaw of challenger Kid Pancho. Pancho throws a punch at the exact moment. Both boxers connect, both fall to the canvas, and both are counted out by the referee. . . . Knute Rockne announces that every Notre Dame player will be required to take dancing lessons—"to develop a sense of rhythm essential in the timing of shift plays." . . . The first game of baseball is played at New York's brand-new Yankee Stadium on April 18. More than 72,000 turn out to see Ruth homer and beat the Red Sox. . . . On September 27, a rookie for Yankees, Lou Gehrig, hits his first home run off Bill Piercy of the Red Sox. . . . November football game features the use of rubber pants by players, designed by Glenn "Pop" Warner to lessen discomfort and prevent mud buildup. West Virginia tries them in the mud against St. Louis University and wins, 49–0. . . . John Levi of Haskell begins two-year reign as college football scoring champion, tallying 24 touchdowns in 1923. . . . Robert Newton of the University of Florida kicks 57-yard field goal (from placement) in leading team to 16–7 victory over Wake Forest. . . . The Philadelphia A's lose 20 in a row, tying their own record for futility in 1916. . . . World Series of 1923 is first to gross one million dollars. . . . Two no-hitters are pitched in majors, both in AL—by Sam Jones of Yankees and Howard Ehmke of Boston Red Sox. Both come against inept Philadelphia A's (September 4 and 7). . . . On October 20, Zev succeeds Man o' War as top money-winning horse by beating Papyrus in match race at Belmont Park.

1924

Winners: Baseball: Walter Johnson leads the American League with a mark of 23–7 and the Washington Senators barely edge the Yankees for the pennant. The New York Giants finish 1½ games ahead of the Brooklyn Dodgers for their fourth consecutive National League pennant. Giant outfielder Ross Youngs spoils Walter Johnson's first World Series game after an 18-year pitching career, singling in the twelfth to win the first game for New York. But the Senators come back to take the Series, 4 games to 3. . . . *Kentucky Derby:* Black Gold. *Preakness:* Nellie Morse. *Belmont Stakes:* Mad Play . . . *Indy 500:* L. L. Corum-Joe Boyer . . . *Boxing:* Heavyweight champion Jack Dempsey is challenged to a title bout by Muhammad Ali, who offers to wager $100,000 that he can KO the champ. Dempsey ignores the challenge. (The full name of the challenger, incidentally, is Prince Muhammad Ali Ibrahim of Egypt, who possesses some of his later namesake's promotional ability. "The prince has developed a right-hand blow he calls the 'Pyramid punch,'" his manager tells newsmen. "This blow lands with the force of a falling Pyramid and knocks a rival stiffer than a Sphinx.")

. . . In the lightweight division, Benny Leonard retires undefeated at the age of 28. . . . Abe Goldstein becomes bantamweight champion on March 21, outpointing Joe Lynch. Nine months later, Eddie "Cannonball" Martin wins a 15-round decision from Goldstein. . . . *Golf: USGA Men's Open:* Cyril Walker. *PGA:* Walter Hagen . . . *Hockey:* 1923–24 Stanley Cup winner: Montreal Canadiens . . . *Football: Rose Bowl:* Washington 14, Navy 14 . . . *National Football League:* Cleveland Bulldogs (7–1–1) have best percentage of 18-club league. . . . *Basketball:* College champion selected by Helms Athletic Foundation: North Carolina (25–0).

Other Happenings: First bowler to roll back-to-back 300 games is Frank Carauna of Buffalo, March 5, who adds five strikes at beginning of 247-pin third game. . . . The Boston Bruins obtain a franchise in the National Hockey League, becoming first American team. . . . Jockey Ivan Parke rides 205 winners during the year. . . . As evidence that college football is becoming more and more popular, it is noted that Stanford University makes cheerleading a regular-curriculum subject. Topics of some lectures include "bleacher psychology," "correct use of the voice," and "what a coach expects of the yell-leader." . . . The French Boxing Federation takes an important step by issuing an official ban against boxers kissing each other at the end of a bout. . . . Baseball fans bemoan the tragic death of Jake Daubert, first baseman and captain of the Cincinnati Reds. Operated on for appendicitis in early October, he dies of complications on the ninth. World Series crowd of 37,000 pays homage to him. . . . Baseball season is spiced by Jess Haines' no-hitter of July 17, a 3–0 victory for the St. Louis Cardinals over the Dodgers. . . . Jim Bottomley, also of the Cards, bats in 12 runs during a 9-inning game. . . . United States tennis squad beats Australia, 5–0, in Davis Cup play at Germantown Cricket Club, Philadelphia. . . . Bill Tilden, U.S. singles champion, 1920–24, withdraws from 1924 Olympics because of ban placed on players' writing about athletic contests. . . . Ed "Strangler" Lewis locks his manager in a hotel room and marries Bessie McNear in March. . . . Professional boxing, outlawed in California in 1914, is made legal there once again. . . . Ty Cobb, manager of Detroit Tigers, bans golf for his players and is rumored to be confiscating clubs. . . . In Dublin, Ireland, less than 20 people attend an exhibition game between the Chicago White Sox and New York Giants. The local papers say it is because the game is played while church is on.

1925

Winners: Baseball: Washington Senators repeat as American League champs but lose World Series in 7 games to Pittsburgh Pirates. Senator shortstop Roger Peckinpaugh, who makes only 28 errors during the entire 1925 season, commits 8 miscues in Series. . . . *Kentucky Derby:* Flying Ebony. *Preakness:* Coventry. *Belmont Stakes:* American Flag . . . *Indy 500:* Pete DePaolo (101.13 mph), first to average better than 100 mph. . . . *Boxing:* On May 3, Paul Berlenbach outpoints Mike McTigue to become new light-heavyweight champion. . . . Jimmy Goodrich is proclaimed champion as the result of elimination tournament to find successor to retired lightweight champion Benny Leonard. But on December 7, Goodrich loses the crown to Rocky Kansas in a 15-round decision. . . . In featherweight division, Johnny Dundee outgrows championship, which is filled when Louis "Kid" Caplan knocks out Danny Kramer. . . . Cannonball Martin loses decision to Charles "Phil" Rosenberg, who becomes new bantamweight champion. . . . *Golf: USGA Men's Open:* Willie Macfarlane. *PGA:* Walter Hagen . . . *Hockey:* 1924–25 Stanley Cup champion: Victoria Cougars . . . *Football: Rose Bowl:* Notre Dame 27, Stanford 10 . . . *National Football League:* Chicago Cardinals (11–2) finish atop a league of 20 clubs. . . . *Basketball:* College champion selected by Helms Athletic Foundation: Princeton (21–2).

Other Happenings: On June 1, Lou Gehrig of Yankees bats for Pee Wee Wanninger in the eighth inning. Gehrig appears in next 2,129 games until 1939. . . . June 15: Cleveland leads Philadelphia A's, 15–4, in last half of 8th inning, but when game is over, Philadelphia wins it, 17–15. . . . First East-West Shrine football game is played on December 26, the West All-Stars defeating the East, 6–0. . . . American Professional Basketball League is formed with teams in 9 cities. Players are paid up to $1,500 a month for a 6-month season. League is not recognized as major professional circuit, however. . . . Charles Flourney of Tulane leads college football players in scoring with 19 touchdowns. . . . Only no-hitter in major leagues is pitched by Dazzy Vance of Brooklyn Dodgers, the Phils absorbing the 10–0 defeat. . . . Sudden death comes to Louis Phal (Battling Siki) on December 14, when he is shot in the back at age 28. . . . Pancho Villa, flyweight, also dies at age 24 of blood poisoning following a tooth extraction. . . . Paavo Nurmi, Finnish runner with 4:10.4 mile to his credit, announces plans to visit the United States. . . . In May Ty Cobb gets one thousandth extra-base hit,

in twenty-first season. . . . United States Patent No. 1,559,390—for water skies—is issued to Fred Waller. . . . Notre Dame's celebrated "Four Horsemen" play together for the last time in 1925 Rose Bowl.

1926

Winners: Baseball: The New York Yankees are back in the World Series, but the St. Louis Cardinals, led by Rogers Hornsby and Pete Alexander, seem to be hungrier. Despite four homers by Babe Ruth, the Cards win, 4 games to 3. . . . *Kentucky Derby:* Bubbling Over. *Preakness:* Display. *Belmont Stakes:* Crusader . . . *Indy 500:* Frank Lockhart . . . *Boxing:* After touring Europe and signing autographs and tinkering with the stage and movies, heavyweight champion Jack Dempsey finally steps into the ring with a genuine challenger. Gene Tunney emerges as new champion on a 10-round decision, September 23, Philadelphia. . . . Paul Berlenbach also loses his light-heavyweight crown, Jack Delaney winning a 15-round decision. Harry Greb, one-eyed middleweight champion, loses on a decision to Tiger Flowers, first black to win in that division. But Flowers' reign lasts only 10 months, Mickey Walker becoming new middleweight champ on December 3. . . . Walker's impetus for challenging Flowers is result of losing welterweight crown on May 20 to Pete Latzo. There is action in lightweight class also, Sammy Mandell winning decision over Rocky Kansas. . . . *Golf: USGA Men's Open:* Bobby Jones. *PGA:* Walter Hagen . . . *Hockey:* 1925–26 Stanley Cup winner: Montreal Maroons . . . *Football: Rose Bowl:* Alabama 20, Washington 19 . . . *National Football League:* The Frankford Yellowjackets (14–1–1) are first in circuit of 22 teams. . . . *Basketball:* College champion selected by Helms Athletic Foundation: Syracuse (19–1).

Other Happenings: Army-Navy football game produces extra anticipation because of excellent team records as well as presence of stars such as halfback Tom Hamilton for the Middies and Red Cagle for Army. Game, a thriller, ends in 21–21 tie. . . . On May 1, Satchel Paige, 19, makes pitching debut for Chattanooga in Negro Southern League. He hurls 5–4 victory over Birmingham. . . . On October 6, Babe Ruth becomes first player to hit three home runs in a single World Series game. . . . Boxing fans are saddened to hear of death of Harry Greb. After being hurt in an automobile accident, he is operated on because bone between bridge of nose and base of skull is fractured. The 32-year-old Greb dies on the table, however. . . . The Milwaukee Badgers of the National Football League are fined $500 for using four high-school players in game. Player age limit of NFL in 1926 is 18. . . . In college football, Brown defeats Yale, 7–0, without the benefit of a single substitution. . . . First running of the Hamble-tonian, for 3-year-old trotters, is won by Guy McKinney in 2:04¾. . . . The 1926 baseball season is enlivened by Brooklyn's Babe Herman tripling into a double play. With men on second and third, Herman drives a long fly to right-center field. Both runners hesitate, thinking the ball might be caught; all the while, Herman races madly around the bases. The ball drops for a hit but when it is relayed to the infield all three Dodgers are in the vicinity of third base. Herman makes it safely but others are tagged out. . . . Ted Tyons of Chicago White Sox pitches only no-hitter in major leagues, a 6–0 drubbing of Boston on August 21. . . . Alabama is first southern football team to play in Rose Bowl. Johnny Mack Brown, star for winners, begins promising movie career that ends in B Westerns. . . . On July 22, Babe Ruth catches a baseball dropped from an airplane 250 feet above Mitchell Field, New York, flying at a speed of 100 miles per hour. . . . Ernie Nevers, former Stanford football star and later NFL back with Duluth and the Chicago Cardinals, on August 4 pitches his second complete game for the St. Louis Browns, defeating the A's, 3–1. His lifetime record for 3 seasons is 6 wins, 12 losses.

1927

Winners: Baseball: The superefficient New York Yankees of 1927 climax their magnificent (110–44) season by demolishing the Pittsburgh Pirates, 4 games to 0, in the World Series. Babe Ruth adds 2 homers to his record-setting 60 for the regular season. . . . *Kentucky Derby:* Whiskery. *Preakness:* Bostonian. *Belmont Stakes:* Chance Shot . . . *Indy 500:* George Souders . . . *Boxing:* Gene Tunney successfully defends his title against Dempsey in the disputed "long count" decision. Jack Delaney, new light-heavyweight champion, resigns title to fight as heavyweight, and vacant title is claimed by Mike McTigue. Tommy Loughran also claims title and earns it by winning 15-round decision from McTigue. In welterweight division, Joe Dundee outpoints Pete Latzo. Kid Kaplan, featherweight champion, retires when he cannot make the weight and crown goes to Benny

Bass, who wins decision over Red Chapman. . . . *Golf: USGA Men's Open:* Tommy Armour. *PGA:* Walter Hagen (fourth year in row) . . . *Hockey:* 1926–27 Stanley Cup champion: Ottawa Senators . . . *Football: Rose Bowl:* Stanford 7, Alabama 7. . . . *National Football League:* New York Giants (11–1–1) . . . Second: Green Bay Packers (7–2–1) . . . *Basketball:* College champion selected by Helms Athletic Foundation: Notre Dame (19–1).

Other Happenings: On May 30 and 31, unassisted triple plays are made in major leagues. The first is by Jim Cooney of Chicago Cubs, the second by Johnny Neun, Detroit Tiger first baseman. . . . New York Football Giants give up only 13 points during entire season. . . . Boston bruin star Eddie Shore accrues 165 minutes of penalties in the course of only 44 games. . . . On April 5, Johnny Weismuller swims 100 yards in 51 seconds. The feat is performed in a 25-yard-long tank at Ann Arbor, Michigan. . . . "The Curse of Muldoon" is born at the end of the 1926–27 NHL hockey season. When Chicago Black Hawk coach Pete Muldoon is fired, he predicts, "This team will never finish first." The Black Hawks do not finish first for more than 40 years, but they do win Stanley Cup playoffs in 1934, 1938, and 1961. . . . Still-active athletes who die suddenly in 1927 are Tiger Flowers, middleweight boxer who dies following an operation; baseball player Ross Youngs, 30, of the New York Giants, who dies of Bright's disease; and swimmer Sybil Bauer, 23. . . . In January, promoter Abe Saperstein takes a step that will delight millions of sports fans by forming the Harlem Globetrotters. . . . Football goal posts are set at rear of end zone, and teams allowed 30 seconds to put ball in play. . . . Jimmy Doolittle turns "upside down" for first time as aerial barnstormer. . . . After winning Davis Cup competition, 1920–26, the United States is defeated by France, 3–2, the matches being played at the Germantown Cricket Club, Philadelphia. . . . Notre Dame's "Fighting Irish" football team wear green jerseys for first time on November 12, vs. Army, discarding blue jersey worn since 1887. . . . On July 18, Ty Cobb makes four-thousandth career hit, the first player to do so.

1928

Winners: Baseball: New York Yankees of 1928 win 101 games, but it is barely enough to get them past the surging Philadelphia A's into the World Series. Once in the fall classic, however, the Yankees have no trouble with the St. Louis Cardinals, defeating them in 4 games. . . . *Kentucky Derby:* Reigh Count. *Preakness:* Victorian. *Belmont Stakes:* Vito . . . *Indy 500:* Louis Meyer . . . *Boxing:* After knocking out Tom Heeney on July 26, Gene Tunney announces his retirement. In featherweight division, Benny Bass loses decision to Tony Canzoneri, who in turn loses decision to André Routis of France. . . . Bantamweight championship is divided between Bud Taylor (National Boxing Association choice) and several other boxers following Phil Rosenberg's inability to make weight. . . . *Golf: USGA Men's Open:* Johnny Farrell. *PGA:* Leo Diegel . . . *Hockey:* 1927–28 Stanley Cup winner: New York Rangers (first American team to win NHL playoffs) . . . *Football: Rose Bowl:* Stanford 7, Pittsburgh 6 . . . *National Football League:* Providence Steamrollers (8–1–2) . . . *Basketball:* College champion selected by Helms Athletic Foundation: Pittsburgh (21–0).

Other Happenings: For the second time in his career, Babe Ruth hits three home runs in a single World Series game—the fourth and deciding contest against the Cardinals. . . . Ken Strong of NYU scores 21 touchdowns during season. He leads all collegiate scorers with 153 points. . . . New York Giants sign W. T. Lai, Chinese infielder, but he does not make it to major leagues. . . . Army concludes season of 1928 not with Navy, as in previous years, but with Stanford. Stanford wins, 26–0. Navy replaces Army with Princeton and wins, 9–0. . . . 1928–29 National Hockey League season is known as "the year of the shutout." The man who turns in a record number of them is goalie George Hainsworth of the Montreal Canadiens who, during the course of a 44-game schedule, blanks the opposition 22 times. . . . France again defeats the United States in Davis Cup competition, 4–1. . . . On August 28, a yellow baseball is used by a professional team for the first time during a doubleheader between Louisville and Milwaukee of the American Association. . . . On January 19, the first U.S. women's squash racquets singles championship is won by Eleonora Sears at the Round Hill Club, Greenwich, Connecticut. . . . Hockey fans get thrill on April 7 when 45-year-old Lester Patrick is forced to take the ice as a goalie because of injury to regular, Lorne Chabot. Patrick succeeds in saving game for his New York Rangers, who defeat Montreal Maroons. . . . polo, Tommy Hitchcock leads United States to 13–7 victory over Argentina on October polo championship of the Americas.

1929

Winners: Baseball: Philadelphia A's finish 18 games ahead of New York Yankees in American League and carry that superiority into the World Series against the Chicago Cubs. Four different pitchers win a game each (Rommel, Earnshaw, Ehmke, and Walberg) as A's take Series in 5 games. . . . *Kentucky Derby:* Clyde Van Dusen. *Preakness:* Dr. Freeland. *Belmont Stakes:* Blue Larkspur . . . *Indy 500:* Ray Keech . . . *Boxing:* After Jack Sharkey beats William L. "Young" Stribling and Max Schmeling stops Johnny Risko and Paulino Uzcudun, Sharkey and Schmeling emerge as logical contenders for heavyweight crown. In light-heavyweight division, Tommy Loughran resigns to enter heavyweight class. Lou Scozza, Jimmy Slattery, and Maxie Rosenbloom are contenders. Jackie Fields defeats Joe Dundee on foul to win welterweight title. Christopher "Battling" Battalino wins featherweight title by defeating André Routis in a 10-round decision. Al Brown claims bantam-weight championship but is not recognized as titleholder until 1931. . . . *Golf: USGA Men's Open:* Bobby Jones. *PGA:* Leo Diegel . . . *Hockey:* 1928–29 Stanley Cup winner: Boston Bruins . . . *Football: Rose Bowl:* Georgia Tech 8, California 7 . . . *National Football League:* Green Bay Packers (12–0–1). Second: New York Giants (13–1–1) . . . *Basketball:* College champion selected by Helms Athletic Foundation: Montana State (35–2).

Other Happenings: Only no-hitter in major leagues is pitched by Carl Hubbell of New York Giants, 11–0 over Phillies on May 8. . . . The Chicago Cardinals of the National Football League are the first pro team to go to training camp away from home. They select Coldwater, Michigan. . . . Notre Dame-USC contest draws 112,912 spectators to Soldier Field, Chicago. Frank Carideo, quarterback for the Irish, leads Notre Dame to 13–12 victory. . . . On November 28, Ernie Nevers of Chicago Cardinals makes 6 touchdowns and kicks 4 extra points to score all points in 40–6 win over Bears. . . . On May 6, A. L. Monteverde, 60, leaves City Hall, New York City, for San Francisco. He runs the 3,412 miles in 79 days, 10 hours, 10 minutes, arriving on July 24. . . . World Series highlight is produced in fourth game when Philadelphia A's score 10 runs in seventh inning to overcome 8–0 deficit. . . . In one of more daring sports robberies of the year, thieves make off with the fifth green of the North Hills Golf Course at Douglaston, Long Island. Three hundred square feet of its new sod are dug up during the night and simply carted away. . . . Dick Norment, a 19-year-old pitcher for Lumberton, North Carolina, High School, pitches a no-hit, no-run game despite having only one arm and one leg. . . . Discovered in October: The "Salem Trade School," which has fielded a football team for six years and collected receipts for its games, does not exist; the team is merely group of players who share profits and are always in demand because they invariably lose. . . . During a game at Oshkosh, Wisconsin, basketball player Frank Andresko escapes with a torn jersey when the ball explodes into fragments just as he receives a pass. . . . A baseball game at Hazelton, Pennsylvania, features a ball bouncing off the Triple Cities center fielder's head for a home run, allowing Hazelton to win, 10–9. . . . For second year in a row, Navy is missing from Army's football schedule. Final game of West Point season is with Stanford, which wins, 34–13. Navy defeats Dartmouth, 13–6, in Navy's season finale. . . . On March 9, Eric Krenz becomes the first man to throw the discus farther than 160 feet, reaching 163 feet, 8¾ inches at Palo Alto, California.

1930

Winners: Baseball: Connie Mack's Philadelphia A's win their second World Series in a row, defeating the St. Louis Cardinals, 4 games to 2. . . . *Kentucky Derby:* Gallant Fox. *Preakness:* Gallant Fox. *Belmont Stakes:* Gallant Fox . . . *Indy 500:* Billy Arnold . . . *Boxing:* Gene Tunney having retired, Max Schmeling and Jack Sharkey meet to decide who will be the next heavyweight champion. Schmeling becomes the first in the division to win the title on a foul, Sharkey delivering the low blow in fourth. . . . Jimmy Slattery defeats Lou Scozza for light-heavyweight crown, then loses it to Maxie Rosenbloom. Jack Thompson takes welterweight title by beating Jackie Fields, then loses it four months later to Tommy Freeman. The lightweights are also active, Al Singer knocking out Sammy Mandell in the first round to become champ, then lasting only a round himself in a title bout four months later against Tony Canzoneri. . . . *Golf: USGA Men's Open:* Bobby Jones. *PGA:* Tommy Armour . . . It is the year when Bobby Jones wins not only the U. S. Open but also the U. S.

Amateur, British Open, and British Amateur. . . . *Hockey:* 1929—30 Stanley Cup winner: Montreal Canadiens. . . . *Football: Rose Bowl:* USC 47, Pittsburgh 14 . . . *National Football League:* Green Bay Packers win with season record of 10–3–1. Second are New York Giants, 13–4–0. . . . *Basketball:* College champion selected by Helms Athletic Foundation: Pittsburgh (23–2).

Other Happenings: Most sensational rookie of baseball season is Wally Berger of Boston Braves, who hits 38 home runs in first year. He never comes closer than 34 thereafter. . . . Big football contest of the year takes place on November 22, when Rockne-led Notre Dame hands previously undefeated Northwestern a 14–0 loss. . . . On May 26, Joe Sewell of Cleveland Indians who strikes out only three times all year, is fanned twice by Pat Caraway of the Chicago White Sox. Caraway finishes year with mark of 10–10. . . . On July 25, Philadelphia A's execute triple steal in first inning and again in fourth against Indians. It is the only time two triple steals are made in one game by same club. . . . Football has a landmark of sorts when first game is broadcast by radio to England. The score is Harvard 13, Yale 0. . . . Jockey Joe Sylvester has great day at Ravenna, Ohio, on October 18, riding seven winners. In third race, he finishes third. . . . In November, miniature golfer catches hand in hole. . . . In May, Vincent Wong, first Chinese bullfighter, makes his debut. . . . National AAU basketball champion team for men is Henry Clothiers, Wichita, Kansas; for women, Sunoco Oilers of Dallas. . . . On September 6, Gallant Fox becomes top money-winning racehorse by winning Lawrence Realization Stakes at Belmont. . . . America's Cup yacht race pits *Enterprise* of the United States against Sir Thomas Lipton's *Shamrock V*, and once again the United States wins. . . . On January 24, Primo Carnera makes his boxing debut in America, knocking out Big Boy Peterson in 1 minute, 10 seconds of the first round as 20,000 watch. . . . Stella Walsh, a 17-year-old girl from Cleveland, sets her second world record in a week by running the 220-yard dash in 26⅖ seconds. She then comes back on March 12 to break her own record at the Knights of Columbus games, New York, running the 220 in 29⅒. . . . First national open miniature golf tournament is held in Chattanooga, J. F. Scott winning the men's title and Mrs. J. E. Rankin the women's.

Section VII
The 1930s

CHAPTER 28 — 1931

The Great Depression was nearing its peak as the year 1931 began, but that did not stop 70,000 fans from making the seventeenth Rose Bowl a financial success. It was the first important athletic contest of the year, once again pitting the theoretically best football teams of the East and the West. (In 1930, Notre Dame under Knute Rockne had a record of 10–0, scoring 265 points to its opponents' 74, and was generally regarded as the nation's No. 1 team.) For the East, Alabama was made the underdog against the Washington State Cougars. "The general belief is that the two elevens, probably as great as any in the nation defensively," one prognosticator wrote, "will blossom out with a passing attack in an effort to win."

FOOTBALL

Since 1916, when the series was resumed after Michigan's 49–0 defeat of Stanford in 1902, the eastern representatives had not performed very well at Pasadena. Alabama was regarded as a strong opponent, however, if only for the reason that Coach Wallace Wade had announced his retirement from that university in favor of Duke, and the players were determined to give the likable man a good sendoff. On the other hand, rumors circulated that the Alabama squad was having difficulty rounding itself into shape for the game.

Even as the teams prepared to take the field, college football came under attack at the twenty-fifth annual convention of the NCAA, where several noted educators, including Dr. James R. Angell of Yale, commented unfavorably on the overemphasis colleges were placing on the game. "I believe that any system which by its very nature encourages proselyting among boy athletes in the secondary schools is pernicious," he said. "I do not believe there is any obligation on the part of the college to furnish the general public nor even the alumni with substitutes for the circus, the prize fight, and the gladiatorial combat."

Added Dr. Charles W. Kennedy of Princeton: "I earnestly hope that the colleges of our country. . . . will deflate intercollegiate football and restore it to its natural place in the life of the undergraduates. Should they fail to do so, I predict that it will be done for them by the forces of undergraduate and public opinion."

Chief among the learned gentlemen's

Did the Gentleman from Princeton Read His Own School's Financial Report?
According to the statement prepared by the Princeton University Athletic Association for fiscal year 1930, football was the only sport to show a profit, and, in fact, wiped out the deficits generated by all other sports.

Deficits:			Profit:	Football	$259,574.61
	Track	$28,312.42			
	Crew	23,696.07			
	Baseball	17,447.72			
	Basketball	9,835.24			
	Hockey	8,128.78			
	Others	37,529.11			
		$124,949.34			

---

suggested improvements were the reduction of the football season to six games per school, and an adjustment of the coach's duties so as to make him "a teacher, a counselor, and a friend, but not a ringmaster."

Meanwhile, on the field football was doing quite well, drawing cheers of excitement as Washington State and Alabama battled through a scoreless first period. Then, led by All-American guard Fred Sington, Alabama took the ball on its own forty-yard line. Two short gains were nullified by an offside penalty, but on the next play Alabama left end Jimmy Moore took a handoff from the quarterback and started to his right as if it were a reverse. Then, stopping suddenly, he lofted the ball far down the field to halfback Flash Suther, "whose twinkling toes had carried him over the green turf beyond the Washington defense." Catching the ball on the Washington State thirty-six, Suther scampered into the end zone untouched.

Minutes later, Alabama intercepted a pass on the Cougar thirty-seven-yard line, Jimmy Moore again passed to the one-yard stripe, and quarterback Campbell squeezed over on the next play. A third touchdown was added almost immediately when Campbell ran forty-three yards in an attempt to gain six inches needed for a first down. When Alabama kicked a field goal in the third period to go ahead 24–0, the game was out of reach of Washington State, but the West Coast representatives refused to stop fighting. In ten plays, the Cougars drove the ball seventy-six yards to the Alabama one-yard line, but a fumble there was recovered by Fred Sington. There was no further scoring as Alabama emptied the bench and Washington State threw desperate passes during the final period.

TENNIS

Those concerned that Americans were allowing amateur sports to be dominated by a growing spirit of professionalism received another blow early in January 1931 when it was announced that the top tennis player in the United States, William T. Tilden II, was turning pro. The decision was made, Tilden said, when a contract to make movies for Metro-Goldwyn-Mayer was deemed a violation of the United States Lawn Tennis Association contract. Forced to make a choice between an amateur status that was often hypocritical and lucrative professionalism, Tilden selected the latter. The signing came just ten years after Tilden won his first Davis Cup matches at Auckland, New Zealand.

BOXING

The god of professionalism gaveth but it also tooketh away. The loser just days after Tilden became eligible for all manner of professional rewards was Max Schmeling, the young German heavyweight boxer who had come to America following Gene Tunney's retirement in 1928. Two years later, Schmeling met Jack Sharkey before a crowd of nearly eighty thousand in New York, but the fight wound up in wild disorder when Sharkey delivered a low blow at the end of the fourth round. The referee and one judge did not see the punch. Harold Barnes, the second judge, declared he saw it and the heavyweight championship was awarded to Schmeling. A week later, the New York Athletic Commission voted the German official champion, with only William Muldoon, the wrestler of a half-century before, casting a negative vote. But by January 1931, when Schmeling refused to sign for another fight with Sharkey, the Commission changed its mind. Withdrawing title recognition from Schmeling, it went on record as stating that Sharkey was the outstanding contender for the vacant championship. While they were at it, the Commission members also stripped Edward "Mickey" Walker of his middleweight crown "for violation of all rules and regulations affecting championships." Walker, not able to make the 160-pound limit five years after winning the title, had also refused to defend his title against a selected candidate.

Reaction to the Walker decision was minor, but Max Schmeling criticized James J. Farley of the Commission as unfair and anti-German. "Mr. Farley, good friend of Jack Sharkey," Schmeling said when interviewed at Garmisch, Germany, "never could reconcile himself to a non-American holding the title and naturally wants to set all the wheels in motion to hoist his friend Sharkey onto the throne."

While waiting for the heavyweight situation to straighten itself out, some fight fans could glimpse a figure of past glory in the ring, but not as a boxer. Three years after announcing his retirement, Jack Dempsey had returned to the ring as a referee. Ironically, his second bout in that capacity was marred by a timing imbroglio nearly as bizarre as the famous "long count" that had given Gene Tunney a victory over Dempsey in 1927. The stakes in the fight of January 17, 1931, of course, were not nearly as high as those of four years before. Nor were the participants—Max Baer and Tom Heeney of New Zealand—as well known as Dempsey and Tunney. But the crowd of eight thousand who witnessed the fight seemed to protest just as loudly as those partisans watching the "long count" battle.

The fight between Baer and Heeney was scheduled for ten rounds, but both men were strong hitters, and it was suspected that the

Basketball News Flash, 1931:
Monticello, Arkansas, January 10:
"The girls' basketball team of the Magnolia
A. and M. School played the Jonesboro
Baptist girls last night and won, 143–1.
Miss Louise Hicks scored 69 points and
Miss Ruby Selph ran her a close second
with 53 to her credit. The Magnolia girls
have played five games this season, amass-
ing a total of 455 points. The total score
of their opponents is 29."

---

bout would not go the limit. In the third round, Baer moved in on Heeney, assaulting him with a volley of lefts and rights to the head and body, gradually forcing him across the ring. Heeney, more as a result of Baer's rush than his blows, slipped through the ring ropes in his own corner, falling heavily but surely across the edge of the apron. He was assisted back into the ring by the upward push of three writers into whose laps he threatened to fall. Referee Dempsey, meanwhile, picked up the count—he thought—and tolled off eight seconds while Heeney rested on one knee.

At the count of eight, however, Arthur Donovan at ringside brought down his gavel as official knockdown timekeeper, indicating that Heeney had been counted out. Everyone, including Heeney, Dempsey, and the crowd, was stunned. A deafening roar flooded the arena as Heeney protested—to no avail, of course. Donovan informed the men that the count had started from the exact moment when Heeney had been deposited on the ring apron and that ten seconds had transpired between that moment and Jack Dempsey's count of eight. Baer was declared the winner. Thus Jack Dempsey, the victim of a long count given an opponent, deprived another fighter of a chance to win by giving him too much time.

January of 1931 was a happy time for golfers with radios, for Bobby Jones became one of the first professional athletes to have his own regular program on the relatively new medium. Predictably, his format was the "golf tips" variety, and soon became quite popular along with similar shows such as "Sport Chat" with Jack Filman, concerts by the Marine Band, lectures on chiropractics, and musical serenades by the Edna White Trumpet Quartet.

BASEBALL

Even in January, baseball was on many sports fans' minds, one of the chief topics being the effect of the "jackrabbit" ball on hitting habits and statistics during the past decade. After a careful study of the 1920s ball's resiliency, National League President John A. Heydler announced at the winter meeting that the chief difference in the pre-jackrabbit ball and that currently in use was the cover. In order to reduce the number of balls flying over fences in 1931, a new ball with slightly heavier cover and raised instead of countersunk stitching would be put into play. The total weight and size of the ball, according to the manufacturer, would remain the same. The raised stitching, it was pointed out, would allow pitchers to get a better grip on the ball and throw a greater variety of good-breaking stuff.

AUTO RACING

On February 5, 1931, front-page news was made when Captain Malcolm Campbell directed his 1,450-horsepower Bluebird car over a wet and misty racecourse at Daytona Beach, Florida. After a 5½-mile flying start, Campbell made his first run, heading from north to south, over the mile in 14.60 seconds for a speed of 246.575 miles per hour. Then, turning north, he made his second mile run in somewhat slower time, 14.70 seconds. The average two-way time of 14.65 seconds, or 245.733 miles an hour, gave him the world's record for speed on land.

It was not accomplished without danger. On his second run, the mist nearly betrayed Campbell by obscuring a red bull's-eye hung low over the course to guide him. "I failed to see the bull's-eye until I was within 200 yards of it," Campbell said, "and when I finally picked it up I found I had headed off the course toward the dunes. I barely had time to straighten the Bluebird out into the trap and down the measured mile. . . ."

Campbell's record exceeded by 14.37 miles per hour the run of 231.36 established in 1929 by Sir Henry Seagrave, who was later killed in a motorboat accident on Lake Windermere. Even with the setting of a new record, however, Campbell was disappointed. "I should have liked to have proven that my car will do 260," he said, "but the wet sand cut my speed."

At this point, Malcolm Campbell probably felt the temptation to sit back and wait for a movie offer to reach him, for it was the era when sports heroes, regardless of their talent or lack of it, were being continually tested for the silver screen. Johnny Mack Brown, star of the 1926 Rose Bowl game that saw Alabama beat Washington by a single point, was already established as a cowboy star. Jack Dempsey had dabbled with both vaudeville and the movies during his reign as heavyweight champion, as had lightweight Benny

Leonard. Latest in the long line of athletes-turned-star was Babe Ruth—who had already demonstrated atrocious ability in front of the camera—and Notre Dame Coach Knute Rockne. On February 10, 1931, the names of these two men were mentioned in a column stating that they had signed contracts for two-reelers with Universal Studios, Rockne would leave for Hollywood on February 14 to supervise his series, which dealt with famous football plays. "Plans for Ruth's return to the movies are indefinite," it was reported, "but it is probable he will not start until after the coming baseball season."

BULLFIGHTING

It was even rumored that Sidney Franklin, an American turned bullfighter, would find his way into the movies. Not, of course, if his fortunes got much worse than in February 1931. A Brooklyn boy, Franklin had followed the example of H. B. Lee, another American who achieved a measure of fame as a matador two decades before. After a flurry of success, Sidney Franklin ran into trouble at Nuevo Laredo, Mexico, where he was gored through the right leg, fainted, and had to be carried from the arena. After the next fight, however, he insisted on being allowed to return to the scheduled format, which called for him to fight two more bulls. He did so, receiving an ovation from the Mexicans, who called him "very brave" and "bold." As this was not too long after Valentino's film hit *Blood and Sand,* it was suggested that Sidney Franklin might be the next great bullfighter of talking movies.

Hollywood and America were enthusiastic regarding heroes and heroines who were at the top of the heap, but sometimes neglectful of those who had outlived their primes. A case in point emerged in early March 1931, when it was learned that Jim Thorpe, generally acclaimed during his time as the nation's greatest football player and perhaps the world's best athlete, was working as a pick-and-shovel laborer at the rate of four dollars a day. He was discovered among a motley crew of diggers excavating for the Los Angeles County Hospital. After work, he explained, he returned to a small cottage where his wife and two children waited for him. The article intimated that Thorpe, like many American Indians, had trouble handling firewater. "I guess it's an old story," he replied when asked how he had arrived at his present state, "I liked to be a good fellow with the boys. But I'll come out of this, and I'll do some saving when I do." It was added that Thorpe hoped to find a coaching position at Mississippi A. and M. or Dickinson College at Carlisle, Pennsylvania.

TENNIS

But others were doing better. Bill Tilden followed his professional signing by filling Madison Square Garden for his debut against Karel Kozeluh of Czechoslovakia. "Here was the perfect foil," one newspaper enthused, "the man of flamboyant attack against the man of the Gibraltaresque defense, brilliance and daring of shotmaking against machinelike faultlessness in the methodical returning of the ball. In other words . . . the speed, daring, and artifice of one of the cleverest manipulators of the attack against the more prosaic virtues of Kozeluh's steady hand and granite legs."

Before the thirteen thousand who returned to the Garden for professional tennis, Tilden put on quite a show. Kozeluh won the opening game of the first set, and that turned out to be the only time he led during the contest. Utilizing his cannonball service to perfection, Tilden took three games in a row. Kozeluh, playing entirely in the neighborhood of his base line, tried to draw Tilden out of position by angling his shots to the corners. When that failed, he attempted to lure Tilden to the net and lob the ball over his head. Tilden responded with a series of brilliant overhead smashes. During the third set, Kozeluh played some of his best tennis, but his improvement only served to inspire Tilden, his spinning soft shots smothered at the net whenever Big Bill felt he needed a point. The final score was a sweep for Tilden, 6–4, 6–2, 6–4.

March 1931 also brought news that eighteen-year-old Sonja Henie, who had dominated figure skating since 1927, would turn professional following the 1932 Olympics. The world of amateur athletics seemed to be crumbling, or at least losing much of its sophisticated veneer and respect.

Another Norwegian had something to say about those who railed against the growing tendency toward professionalism in all sports and college football in particular. That was Knute Kenneth Rockne, a solid folk hero by 1931 who was doing nothing more than looking forward to Notre Dame's spring football practice—which was criticized by many as one of the examples of rampant commercialism and overemphasis on winning. Rockne was not upset by the charges, however. "If a coach or an educator doesn't favor spring practice," he said in early March 1931, "I want to hear him tell why. I think the other way and I'm always ready to tell why. I think this does a lot of good. An argument never makes me sore. Getting into an argument is one way of proving that you're still alive."

At that moment, Knute Rockne had just three weeks of life remaining to him.

Horses Winning More Than $200,000 (as of March 23, 1931)			Coronach	Eng.	$247,370
			Amounts	Australia	$241,487
Gallant Fox	U.S.	$340,665	Rock Sand	Eng.	$238,900
Zev	U.S.	$313,639	Phar Lap	Australia	$234,310
Isinglass	Eng.	$291,275	Sarazen	U.S.	$225,000
Donovan	Eng.	$277,215	Bayardo	Eng.	$223,665
Blue Larkspur	U.S.	$272,070	Gloaming	Australia	$215,500
Sun Beau	U.S.	$271,469	Sardanapale	France	$211,505
Display	U.S.	$256,526	Lemberg	Eng.	$204,795
Victorian	U.S.	$253,425	Crusader	U.S.	$203,261
Exterminator	U.S.	$252,596	Flying Fox	Eng.	$203,200
Man o' War	U.S.	$249,465	Mike Hall	U.S.	$201,095

POWERBOAT RACING

Record breaking continued to move at an ever-increasing pace. Sir Henry Segrave's motorboat mark for a statute mile was challenged on March 20 by America's premier racer, Gar Wood, in his *Miss America IX*. In order to make certain the mark would be official if he broke it, Wood had Odis A. Porter, American Automobile Association timer and representative of the American Power Boat Association, install electrical timing equipment similar to that used in automobile speed trials at Daytona Beach. One end of the measured mile was in front of Wood's home on Indian Creek, near Miami Beach, the other one mile south from that point. Only a handful of spectators were on hand when Wood moved his craft to a bridge north of the starting point so that he would have a clear run of better than three miles. But among the sparse crowd were six official observers, which was what Wood wanted.

Powered by a pair of 12-cylinder motors, *Miss America IX* turned at the bridge and was soon cutting a swath of silver spray as she bore down on the starting line. No mechanical difficulties developed, the first run south being accomplished in 35.53 seconds or 101.351 miles per hour. Two additional runs were made, both beating Segrave's record of 98.76 mph but neither equaling the speed of Wood's first dash down the creek. Nevertheless, an average speed of 100.6 mph was maintained, bringing with it a new mark for powerboats. "With 2,000 more horsepower than the 2,200 in *Miss America IX*," Wood said, obviously thinking of future plans, "I can get 20 miles an hour more speed without difficulty. The whole thing is merely a matter of getting engines to do the work."

HORSERACING

With the slightly warmer weather, interest began to grow in outdoor sports other than boatracing. One event looked forward to by horseracing enthusiasts took place at Agua Caliente, Mexico, where Sun Beau, ranked sixth on the all-time list of money winners, was making a bid to take over the first position by winning the $117,000 ($100,000 for first place) Agua Caliente Handicap. The big bay six-year-old was established a 3–5 favorite at post time, but the crowd waiting to see the race had to wait until the twelfth race—then six minutes more as Caruso caused a delay at the starting gate by bucking. When the horses got away, Sun Beau was far to the rear, but by the halfway mark had closed the gap and taken the lead. The crowd of 25,000, which included luminaries such as William G. McAdoo, former Secretary of the Treasury, Paulino Uzcudun, prizefighter, and veteran autoracer Barney Oldfield, broke into cheers, suspecting that Sun Beau would have a romp to the finish.

Neither they nor Sun Beau had reckoned on a seven-year-old named Mike Hall, which had come out of retirement for the race. Ninth at the halfway mark, Mike Hall had won more than $100,000 during his career, but had done very little in 1930. His last start following his comeback had been on March 15, 1931, when he ran sixth to Choctaw, one of the horses well ahead of him at the three-quarter pole. But by the beginning of the stretch, Jockey O'Donnell urged his mount into third position, a length behind Choctaw and a length and a half behind Sun Beau. At that point, Sun Beau faded quickly. The stretch run became a battle between Choctaw and Mike Hall that was so frantic that Mike Hall established a new track record for the mile and a quarter of 2:03, finishing a neck ahead of Choctaw. Sun Beau could do no better than fifth. By winning, Mike Hall edged into the charmed list of those horses having won more than $200,000, an impressive figure in 1931.

BASEBALL

Another impressive piece of news came from Chattanooga, Tennessee, where manager Joe Engel announced that a seventeen-year-old girl named Jackie Mitchell would sign a contract to pitch for the Lookouts of the Southern Association. "So far as could be learned," the papers noted, "Miss Mitchell was the first woman to enter professional baseball." A few days later, Engel received a telegram from the Memphis Chicks offering him two male players for the left-handed woman pitcher. "Joe once traded a shortstop for a turkey," one reporter noted sardonically, "but parting with his only girl left-hander is another matter." He refused to do it.

One reason he refused, no doubt, was that an exhibition game had been arranged between the Chattanooga club and the New York Yankees, then engaged in spring training down South. As Engel was shrewd enough to suspect, a battle of the sexes between Miss Mitchell and Ruth-Gehrig-Lazzeri would bring in the customers like nothing else. The newspapers, predictably, played the novelty to the hilt. When the contest was rained out, it was immediately rescheduled for the next day and the media void filled with background information and interviews. Miss Mitchell, it turned out, was named Virne Beatrice Mitchell, the daughter of a local optician who believed she possessed major-league talent. "Her best asset is control," he said. "I've seen her strike out the side on nine pitched balls, every one over the middle of the plate."

Slim and five feet, eight inches tall, Miss Mitchell professed to being disappointed at not facing the Babe for another twenty-four hours. "Yes, I think I can strike him out," she said while practicing throwing in her backyard. "Of course, I haven't had much chance to get my arm ready for baseball. I've been home only a week after our basketball trip—the Mitchelettes, you know—to Dallas. I haven't pitched a game since last season." As for her long-term goals, she said, "I don't expect to become a World Series hero. To tell the truth, all I want is to stay in professional baseball long enough to get money to buy a roadster." The young woman also claimed that she had been taught to throw a baseball by none other than Dazzy Vance, "when he lived next door to us in Memphis about ten years ago."

Babe Ruth, interviewed on the same day, expressed a certain amount of concern at the situation, although one can never be sure how much was feigned. "I don't know what's going to happen if they let women in baseball," he said. "Of course, they will never make good. Why? Because they are too delicate. It would kill them to play ball every day."

The next day, a crowd of about four thousand filled the tiny ballpark at Chattanooga to see what would happen. After Clyde Barfoot, a thirty-nine-year-old former major-league pitcher with the Browns and Tigers, issued a double to Earle Combs and a single to Lyn Lary, Ruth strode to the plate and Jackie Mitchell to the mound. The crowd cheered wildly. On the first pitch, Ruth swung lustily and missed. He did the same on the second, then stood with his bat on his shoulder for the third, registering disgust when the umpire called him out. Lou Gehrig stepped into the batter's box, swung three times without connecting, and walked back to the dugout. Tony Lazzeri missed a bunt attempt, then stood in the box as four wide pitches sailed by. As he trotted down the first-base line, Jackie Mitchell was taken out of the game "amid cheers," and the Lookouts went on to lose by a probably respectable score of 14–4. Jackie Mitchell's debut had been a success, although one suspected even then that her value was a promotional rather than real one. "Perhaps Miss Jackie hasn't quite enough on the ball yet to bewilder Ruth and Gehrig in a serious game," one editor noted, "but there are no such sluggers in the Southern Association, and she may win laurels this season which cannot be ascribed to mere gallantry. The prospect grows gloomier for misogynists."

FOOTBALL

Then, on April 1, 1931, the sports story of the year—which took place off the field—hit the front page of every major newspaper in the country. The night before, Knute Rockne dined at a Chicago hotel with two friends, after which he climbed into a taxicab preparatory to flying to Los Angeles, where he planned to appear in a football film and hold a sales promotion meeting for local Studebaker salesmen. As Rockne got into the cab, his friend Albert Fuller said, "Soft landings, Coach." To which Rockne replied, "Yes, but you mean happy landings."

Several hours later, in a hazy drizzle that afforded poor visibility, a trimotored Fokker of Trans-Continental & Western Airways took off from Kansas City with Rockne and seven others aboard. The plane was due at Wichita at 10:25 A.M. but was forty-five minutes late because of a poor mail connection. Flying above the clouds, the transport maintained radio communications with Kansas City until it approached Cassoday, just southwest of Bazaar, Kansas. Witnesses near that small town heard the drone of the motors above the clouds, then heard a sputter and saw the plane flash down through the cloud bank with a trail of smoke behind it. A wing could be seen swirling away from the craft, which buried itself in the pasture of S. H. Baker. Clarence McCracken, a farmhand, helped Baker remove the bodies from the plane and locate the four that had been thrown clear. All eight—six passengers and two pilots—were dead. Rockne, who was reported to have died holding a rosary clutched in his hands, was forty-two.

Rockne's Record at Notre Dame:

Year	Won	Lost	Tied	Pts.	Opp. Pts.
1918	3	1	2	133	39
1919	9	0	0	229	47
1920	9	0	0	251	44
1921	10	1	0	375	41
1922	8	1	1	222	27
1923	9	1	0	275	37
1924	10	0	0	285	54
1925	7	2	1	200	64
1926	9	1	0	210	38
1927	7	1	1	158	57
1928	5	4	0	99	107
1929	9	0	0	145	38
1930	10	0	0	265	74
	105	12	5	2,847	667

The death of America's most celebrated coach and father figure touched off a wave of mourning and nearly continuous tributes long after the funeral procession had carried the man to his final resting place.

POWERBOAT RACING

Life and sports continued, of course, particularly in the area of record-breaking accomplishments. On the morning of April 2, at Parana de las Palmas, Argentina, British powerboat racer Kaye Don towed his *Miss England II* to the head of a measured mile course in the swollen waters of the Parana River. There, along with two mechanics, he put on a life preserver, started the engines of the powerful craft, and took her thundering downstream in a cloud of smoke in four practice runs. A pair of Argentine gunboats at opposite ends of the course were his steering markers. When Don returned for the record run, however, conditions were not quite as good as they might have been, but the British racer was in no mood to disappoint the large crowd that had gathered along the shore to see if his boat could set a new mile record. At two o'clock he turned *Miss England II* downriver, seeming to shoot by the crowd like a shell from a big gun. Less than thirty-five seconds after he shot past the starting marker, Kaye Don had a new power-

boat record for the mile—103.4 miles per hour. How long it would last was another matter. It had taken him less than two weeks to eclipse the mark set by Gar Wood at Miami Beach.

TRACK AND FIELD

Another success story was recorded on April 20, when half a million persons lined the road from Hopkinton to Boston in anticipation of the thirty-fourth running of the Boston Marathon. The participants included Clarence H. DeMar of Melrose, Massachusetts, who won the event in 1930, 1928, 1927, 1924, 1923, 1922, and 1911, and as a result of that amazing record was clearly the man to beat. Strong contention was supplied by John C. Miles of Hamilton, Ontario, who had captured the prize in 1926 and 1929. By contrast, thirty-nine-year-old James P. Henigan of Medford, Massachusetts, had little going for him but determination. He had run in the classic ten times, finished twice, but had managed to arrive in eighth position in 1930. Clarence DeMar was clearly the favorite as the field of 203 started the race under a hot sun that beat on their backs from beginning to end.

The heat may have helped Henigan, for he had no trouble in the early stages, beating off a lengthy challenge by David Kononen of Toronto, slipping in front just outside of Natick, where he picked up speed and increased his lead. From Coolidge Street in Brookline to the Exeter Street clubhouse of the Boston Athletic Association, where the finish line is located, Henigan strolled, beating John Ward, Jr., of New York by 2½ minutes. DeMar finished fifth, Miles tenth. In nearly twenty years of competitive running, the prize was the most prestigious ever captured by Jimmy Henigan. But neither he, Miles, nor DeMar ever won another Boston Marathon.

BASEBALL

Baseball took the spotlight soon after that, the favorites being Connie Mack's Philadelphia Athletics, going for the team's third straight American League pennant, and the St. Louis Cardinals, defeated in the 1930 World Series by the A's, four games to two. From the very beginning, both teams showed they meant business, Mack's A's getting the jump on Joe McCarthy's Yankees even as the Cardinals moved ahead of McGraw's Giants. But the front-running teams had to take a temporary back seat on April 29, when Cleveland's Wes Ferrell became the first pitcher of the new season to pitch a no-hitter. He also hit a home run and a double in leading his team to a 9–0 win over the St. Louis Browns. It was the first no-hitter in either league since

May 8, 1929, when the Giants' Carl Hubbell beat Pittsburgh, 11–0. In gaining his victory, Ferrell struck out eight, allowed three walks, and did not permit any runner to reach second base. He also had to contend with the atrocious support of infielder Bill Hunnefield, who committed three errors behind him during the game. (Early in May, Hunnefield was dealt to the Boston Braves, then later in the season returned to the New York Giants. He was out of major-league baseball by the end of the 1931 season.)

A Connie Mack Prediction, 1931:
On April 27, veteran manager Connie Mack made the prediction that in the not-too-distant future, baseball would be played on the tops of skyscrapers, perhaps outfitted with waterproof domes to remove the weather hazard. He also said that those who ran the game would always keep prices down. Baseball "has kept faith with the public," he said, "maintaining its old admission price for nearly thirty years while other forms of entertainment have doubled and tripled in price. And it probably never will change."

HORSERACING
Early May brought racing fans to Pimlico for the running of the $50,000 Preakness Stakes. Experts predicted that Mrs. Payne Whitney's Twenty Grand and C. V. Whitney's Equipoise were the horses to beat, although the latter was coming off an illness suffered while at Havre de Grace. The Baltimore weather was ideal for the race, thousands of persons from all sections of the state arriving at the track by 11:30 A.M. Eight special betting booths for the Preakness only were placed at one end of the plaza, another at the rear of the clubhouse porch. The first $2.00 ticket was purchased by a gentleman named Jack Horner of Baltimore, the first $10 bet placed by Peter Small of Toronto. By noon the park was jammed, not only with notables such as Vice President Charles Curtis and Maryland Governor Ritchie but also a number of pickpockets, who relieved patrons of sums up to $400 per purse, wallet, or pocket.

The race was an exceedingly close one, all seven entrants entering the stretch in a near-dead heat. Straightening out for the run down the backstretch, Mate, with George Ellis up, took the outside, and Twenty Grand the rail. Equipoise appeared to run "under sufferance," as one reporter noted. At the wire, Mate managed to pull away from Twenty Grand, upsetting the odds and tying the Preakness record of 1:59, set by Coventry in 1925.

A week later, at Louisville, it was Twenty Grand's turn to establish a new track record for the Kentucky Derby and exact revenge for the second-place finish at Baltimore. "The rataplan of Twenty Grand's hoofbeats which came to Mate as only a faint tattoo in the Preakness," one writer exuded, "swelled to a roaring drumbeat today at Churchill Downs. . . ." The new track record, 2:01⅘, was nearly six seconds faster than Gallant Fox's 1930 victory.

Equipoise, which was forced out of the race by lameness, won none of the Triple Crown races that year (Twenty Grand won the Belmont Stakes), but did earn a healthy $338,610 during a career that included 29 wins out of 51 starts.

Sports on Television—1931:
"London, June 3—Remarkably clear television pictures of the English Derby were transmitted over a second of the British Broadcasting Corporation's circuit today by the Baird Television Company. Scenes of the 'telecast' included the parade of the horses before the start of the race and the crowds at the winning post during the race. The experiment was hailed as a great success as the first attempt made in Great Britain or elsewhere to obtain television transmission of a typical public event held in the open air where artificial lighting was impossible. Because of electrical interference scenes at times looked as if they were being viewed through a snow-storm, but the inventors claim they have a process by which this interference can soon be overcome."

AUTO RACING
May of 1931 did generate one record that may never be broken. The scene was Indianapolis, where the usual field of top drivers gathered for the nineteenth running of the Indy 500. Among the entrants was a man named Clessie Cummins of Columbus, Indiana, who had converted a diesel marine engine to automotive use and signed up for the race—not to win but to prove the durability of diesel operation. "I have the sturdiest, most reliable engine," Cummins told reporters before the race, "and we'll prove it by making the distance without stopping."

The idea of traveling all 200 laps of the

grueling race without a single pit stop had never occurred to automotive engineers and drivers, who dared not carry all that excess weight, which was also highly explosive. But a diesel had never raced in the 500 before, either. After using his influence with Eddie Rickenbacker so that the rules at Indy would be bent to allow a diesel to be entered, Cummins hired veteran driver Dave Evans for the project. Just before the race began, Evans looked at the track, which was still slippery from a recent rain, and said to Cummins, "Whatever you do, don't let them cremate me."

Despite the dangerous track, the 1931 Indy 500 was relatively free of accidents and injury. It was won by Louis Schneider in a Bowes Seal Fast, with an average speed of 96.629 miles per hour. Ambling along in thirteenth place, at 86.17 miles per hour, was Dave Evans in the first Indianapolis diesel, the first and probably last vehicle in the racing classic to cover the entire 500 miles without a stop.

BOXING

During the late spring and early summer, boxing returned to the public eye. First to win public attention were the amateurs, American Golden Glovers taking on a team of touring Frenchmen at Soldier Field, Chicago. More than forty thousand fans turned out to watch the eight fights, five of which were won by the American team. Because pro-France feeling was still high in the United States only a dozen years after the end of World War I, the newspapers were inclined to be generous rather than gloat over the international victory. "America won," one reporter wrote, "but the crowd can never forget the gallant assault the French lads, four thousand miles from home, made to wrest boxing honors from superior opponents. Some of the invaders were badly beaten, but they never quit. Their ability was not equal to the task but their courage was undaunted."

The feeling generated when an Italian team visited New York a few weeks later was considerably less genteel, however, perhaps because Mussolini's Fascist regime in the homeland created small armies of partisans in the United States. More than eight thousand customers were settled in Madison Square Garden on the evening of June 3 when Edelweiss Rodriguez of Italy and Louis Salica, New York Metropolitan flyweight champion, squared off. The bout turned out to be a nip-and-tuck affair, so close that at the end of three rounds the judges could not decide on a winner. They then asked the fighters to box an additional round, after which Salica's hand was raised in triumph.

At that, bedlam broke loose. "Roars of disapproval, mingled with hisses and boos, burst like a tempest from the galleries. In an instant the air was full of flying missiles. A hunting knife with a two-inch blade flashed across the arena. It ricocheted off the canvas of the ring, just missed Mrs. Charles Francis Coe, wife of the writer, and dropped with a thud among a group at the ringside. A penknife hurled from the Ninth Avenue side glanced off the head of another woman. Pennies, nickels, and other small coins rained into the ring . . . popcorn boxes and caps from soft-drink bottles descended in a shower . . . in the most riotous demonstration the Garden has ever seen. . . ."

The United States won by a score of 5–2.

A month later, Max Schmeling entered the ring at Cleveland Stadium to fight W. L. (Young) Stribling for the heavyweight championship, the state of New York notwithstanding. Both men were nearly identical as far as height, weight, reach, and age were concerned, but Stribling, deemed faster and more clever by the experts, was installed as the 7–5 favorite. By the standards of the 1920s, the bout was hardly impressive in that it drew only about 35,000 customers and receipts of $375,000, but it did please the diehard boxing fan as well as demonstrate that Max Schmeling was deserving of the title until someone better came along.

Throughout the fight, Schmeling fought his usual style, boring in fearlessly, taking his

Major Fights of the Period			
Participants	Place Held	Attendance	Receipts
Dempsey-Tunney (1927)	Chicago	145,000	$2,658,680
Dempsey-Tunney (1926)	Philadelphia	130,000	$1,880,000
Willard-Firpo	Jersey City	100,000	$700,000
Dempsey-Carpentier	Jersey City	90,000	$1,626,580
Dempsey-Firpo	Polo Grounds, N.Y.	90,000	$1,188,822
Dempsey-Sharkey	Yankee Stadium, N.Y.	80,000	$1,083,529
Schmeling-Sharkey	Yankee Stadium, N.Y.	79,222	$749,934

rival's hooks and jabs while waiting for an opening. In the first round, he found one opening and managed to connect with a right cross, short to the jaw, that caused Stribling's knees to sag as he clinched. For the next five rounds, the fighters sparred cautiously until Schmeling obviously decided he had taken the best Stribling had to offer without damage and started boring in recklessly. In the tenth Schmeling drilled home a right to the jaw that had Stribling reeling at the bell, but couldn't finish him. From that point on, it was a matter of not who would win but whether Stribling could stay on his feet until the end.

As the men came out and shook hands for the fifteenth round, it seemed that Stribling would manage to avoid a knockout. He landed an uppercut to Schmeling's jaw but took a hard right to the body in return. Moments later, another right by the champion sent Stribling down for a count of nine. When he rose, he was rushed into a corner by Schmeling and was in a helpless condition, taking punch after punch, when Referee George Blake stepped in to separate the men and declare the German the winner by a TKO. Only fourteen seconds remained in the final round.

Sun Beau's Revenge:
On July 25 in Chicago, Sun Beau got his revenge by winning the Arlington Cup, finishing two lengths ahead of Mike Hall, and sending his winnings to $302,794.

TRACK AND FIELD

The world of spectator sports was treated to several new faces in 1931, and probably the most exciting belonged to that of a young woman from Texas. "A new feminine athletic marvel catapulted herself to the forefront as an American Olympic possibility at Pershing

Field in Jersey City yesterday," Arthur Daley wrote in the New York *Times* on July 25, 1931, "when 19-year-old Mildred (Babe) Didrikson of Dallas broke the world's record for the 80-meter high hurtles, shattered the American mark for the baseball throw and topped off her activities with a victory in the running broad jump."

Miss Didrikson, who obtained her nickname "Babe" after hitting five home runs in a baseball game, was in her first season of running the high hurdles, yet she displayed remarkable finesse in flying over the 80-meter course in 12 seconds flat, .2 second better than the world's mark for women. Dressed in a flaming orange running suit, Babe then threw a regulation National League baseball a distance of 296 feet.

TENNIS

Another new face was that of a gangly, sandy-haired youth of 19 named Ellsworth Vines, a native of Pasadena, California, who came East with a tennis racket to make a name for himself. In 1930, he had not fared very well, losing to Bryan Grant and G. Lyttleton Rogers, defeats that caused him to remark, "I guess I'm just a false alarm."

Later, however, Vines defeated Wilmer Allison, the fourth-ranking player of the country, and John Doeg, the national champion, to win the Longwood Bowl. "It goes without saying," wrote Allison Danzig on August 3, 1931, "that it would hardly be possible to keep Vines out of the Davis Cup picture next year if he is available. . . . The fact is that, with the exception of Tilden, no player in tennis hits with the terrific speed that does Vines. Although his spare frame of 6 feet, 2½ inches carries only 150 pounds of weight, his drives travel with the velocity of a bullet."

In August, American women were active in tennis, staging an international match with Great Britain at Forest Hills, New York. The

---

Some Sports Suggestions of 1931 Whose Time Had Not Yet Come:
Golf: *Augusta, Georgia, March 9:*
"Insisting that the introduction of modern science in the ancient game of golf has wrought developments at least equal to those through which undertakers have evolved into morticians and ditch diggers into excavators, Ernest Ryall, professional at the Forest Hills-Ricker course here, moves that golf teachers change their name. He suggests 'golfologist.'"
Hockey: *Kitchener, Ontario, February 24:*

"Irvin Erb, Ontario Hockey Association manager, has come forward with a suggestion designed to aid long-suffering hockey referees. Instead of having the officials on the ice, as at present, Erb would enclose them in a glass, soundproof cage along the sidelines, where they would be safe from the stormy protests of the crowd, which sometimes take the form of showers of coins, peanuts, chairs, and bottles. The cage would be equipped with loudspeakers."

Americans were favored, especially when the semifinals pitted Miss Helen Jacobs of Berkeley, California, against a relative unknown, Mrs. Eileen Bennett Whittingstall. More than three thousand spectators were on hand as the match started in a predictable manner. Although allowing the Englishwoman to take a brief lead, Miss Jacobs bore down to win the first set, 6–3. Mrs. Whittingstall won the second by the same score and took the lead in the third and final set. The woman from California was too much of a veteran to panic, however. She battled back to tie the set at 3–3, but lost her service in the seventh game and went into the tenth game behind, 4–5. Mrs. Whittingstall took the count to within a point from victory. But Jacobs managed to tie the score, throwing the gallery into near-pandemonium. When she won the game, bringing the count to 5–5, a prolonged cheer held up the match. And by winning the next game to move ahead, 6–5, Helen Jacobs seemed to have pulled off one of the best comebacks ever seen at Forest Hills.

Mrs. Whittingstall showed her coolness at this point. Attacking furiously, she forced Jacobs to make one mistake after another, finally winning the deciding set 8–6. Unfortunately for Mrs. Whittingstall, her glory lasted only a few hours until she was eliminated in the finals by America's premier woman of tennis, Helen Wills Moody.

BASEBALL

Unless one happened to be a Philadelphia Athletics' fan, the baseball season of 1931 was not much more than a formality. For the Yankees, Babe Ruth and Lou Gehrig hit a total of ninety-two home runs between them, nearly doubling that of the A's two top sluggers, Foxx and Simmons. But nothing seemed to help. Philadelphia won seventeen games straight early in the year, then came back with a thirteen-game streak during the summer. And whenever an important game needed to be won, there was Lefty Grove on the mound to do the job. Putting together a personal sixteen-game winning streak, Grove finally lost in late August, just a few days after Babe Ruth hit his six-hundredth lifetime homer and Gehrig played in his one-thousandth consecutive game. On September 18, Grove's record stood at 30–3. He was to win one and lose one during the final days of the season, becoming the only left-hander to win thirty games in the American League.

FOOTBALL

Even before the A's and Cardinals began the World Series of 1931, professional football had opened its season at the Polo Grounds. Before a crowd of five thousand, the New York Giants, led by former Army star Christian (Red) Cagle, bombed the Hominy Indians of Oklahoma by a score of 53–0. The college season also started with a thrilling game, although experts predicted that the University of Southern California's opener against St. Mary's College of California was nothing more than a limbering-up exercise. In the first period, USC immediately drove for three first downs that put the ball on St. Mary's one-foot line, from which point Shaver bucked for the TD and Johnny Baker kicked the extra point.

The Trojans opened the second period with a twenty-seven-yard run, a 20-yard pass play, and a reverse that took them to the St. Mary's fourteen-yard line. But the Gaels stiffened and the first half ended with USC ahead, 7–0. USC kicked off to St. Mary's to open the third period, Bud Toscani returning the ball twenty-four yards to his own forty-two-yard line. A pass caught the Trojans napping, Toscani running forty-four yards for the score. The placement was blocked, but the small-college players came right back with another long pass to go ahead, 13–7. Incredibly, that was how the score stood at the end, the Galloping Gaels having pulled a major upset at the very outset of a new season.

Halftime Ceremony, 1931:
It happened again and again during the football season, but few had the temerity to suggest that it was becoming a bit overdone. On September 26 at Los Angeles, the "Tribute to Knute Rockne" was delivered by screen actor Conrad Nagle, after which the seventy-five thousand fans stood in silence while a bugler played taps.

Back East, 150,000 applications for World Series tickets created havoc in the Athletics' front office while newsmen looked for fresh ways of describing the battle between Connie Mack's steady crew and Gabby Street's fiery scrappers led by Pepper Martin and Jim Bottomley. While the writers turned out reams of copy, the final games of the schedule were played even though they were meaningless as far as the standings might be concerned. These games did give managers and owners the opportunity to test youngsters, as Connie Mack did on September 25 when he started 18-year-old Lew Krausse on the mound. A former star at Media, (Pennsylvania) High School, young Krausse gave up just four hits to the Boston Red Sox, earning his first major-league victory by a score of 7–1. Admittedly, the Sox, mired in sixth place and going nowhere, may not have provided top competition, but Mack had reason to be optimistic. Lew Krausse, Sr., did not fulfill his bright promise as a pitcher, however, departing the game after the 1932 season with a lifetime record of 5 wins and 1 defeat.

Like Father, Like Son?
Thirty-two years after his father broke in with the A's as an 18-year-old high school star, Lew Krausse, Jr., also 18, pitched his first major-league game for the A's (of Kansas City). That was the beginning of a career spanning 12 years with six different clubs, Lew, Jr.'s lifetime record being 68 games won, 91 lost.

The World Series of 1931 once again proved the axiom that in a short series the team that gets the most breaks usually wins. Even so, the baseball classic that fall was an extremely exciting one for a change (the last World Series to go the full seven games was in 1926). The Athletics took the first game, and the Cardinals the second. Then the A's bowed to the base-running of Pepper Martin and the pitching of Burleigh Grimes, who was good—or wet—enough to beat even Grove in the third game. Behind George Earnshaw, the A's evened the series at two apiece, then lost the advantage by dropping the fifth—and last at Philadelphia—by a score of 5–1. Grove came back strong to win the sixth game at St. Louis, evening the Series once again.

The final game looked like a shoo-in for the Cardinals as George Watkins hit a two-run homer in the third and the A's couldn't seem to buy a hit off Grimes. Going into the top of the ninth, the score was 4–0 in favor of the Cardinals and the natives were on the verge of mass celebration. Al Simmons led off with a walk, however, and those inclined to worry began their fidgeting. Jimmy Foxx followed with a high pop-up that was caught next to the grandstand by Ace Wilson. Bing Miller's grounder promised a double play and victory for St. Louis, but after Simmons was forced at second, Frankie Frisch threw low to first. The A's were still alive, even more so when Grimes gave up another walk to Jimmy Dykes. Dib Williams drove a liner that just cleared the glove of Cardinal third baseman Andy High. Sharp fielding, however, prevented Bing Miller from coming home.

With the bases loaded, substitute outfielder Roger Cramer looped a single to center and the score was 4–2, Cardinals. Burleigh Grimes was taken out of the game, being replaced by Wild Bill Hallahan. Pitching to Max Bishop,

Hallahan ran the count to 3–2 before Bishop drove a fly ball for the final put-out. The town went wild.

FOOTBALL

With the return of attention to football, much interest was generated as to the fate of Notre Dame under new coach Hunk Anderson. The team was too well drilled to fall apart completely. It had not lost since the final game of the 1928 season, building a winning streak of nineteen games before the '31 season started. Rolling right along, the Irish (or "Ramblers," as they were often called then) ran the streak to twenty-five games on November 7, then to twenty-six a week later. Only two obstacles remained, USC and Army, to a third consecutive season without defeat.

The USC game took place at South Bend before a crowd of fifty-two thousand, including celebrities such as New York Mayor Mickey Walker, Mayor Cermak of Chicago, and Edsel Ford, all avid Notre Dame supporters. Led by Marchy Schwartz's slashing runs, the Irish drove for one TD in the second period and another in the third to lead 14–0 going into the final period. That seemed an insurmountable challenge to any team, much less a USC squad that had played as lackadaisically as in their earlier game with St. Mary's College. But somehow the Trojans pulled their game together in the last quarter, alternating laterals with strong blocking in the line that opened large holes for running back Gaius Shaver. After being turned back after an advance to the Notre Dame ten-yard line, USC regained possession of the ball and drove downfield again. This time the "irrepressible, hard-running" Shaver took the ball into the end zone. Not long afterward, Shaver again found the end zone, carrying an Irish defender on his back across the line. But place kicker Johnny Baker missed one of his extra-point attempts and Notre Dame still led, 14–13.

Meanwhile, a Pro Football First:
On November 8, 1931, the NFL saw its first "Ladies' Day" at the Polo Grounds, as football's leaders emulated baseball in order to raise attendance. The Giants beat the Portsmouth Yellow Jackets, 13–0.

With four minutes left to play, USC got the ball deep in its own territory and began still another drive toward the Notre Dame goal line. Two passes for a total gain of seventy-three yards plus the gift of a five-yard penalty put the ball on the Irish twelve-yard line.

Notre Dame's rooters pleaded for the line to hold, and for two successive plays, USC was unable to advance the ball. On third down, the Trojans shifted into kicking formation, Johnny Baker standing on the twenty-three-yard line for the placement. USC quarterback Orville Mohler had called the play on third down because he knew the Irish, suspecting a fake kick and pass play, would not rush as hard as on fourth down. Thus, when the ball was centered to Mohler, he had all the time in the world to spot it for Johnny Baker. The kick was good and USC destroyed Notre Dame's winning streak with a thrilling 16–14 victory.

The next week, perhaps demoralized by the upset, Notre Dame traveled to New York and lost to an inferior Army team, 12–0.

Professional football carried the sports addict into December, although the National Football League consisted of but one division, eliminating the possibility of a playoff series of any sort. (That situation was rectified two years later, when the league split into two divisions.) In any event, there was hardly much of a race that month, Green Bay pulling away to clinch first place as early as November 28. All that remained was the excitement of three teams being fined a thousand dollars each for using players who had not graduated from college (the miscreants were Green Bay, the Chicago Bears, and Portsmouth, Ohio), as well as concern over which franchises would survive into the 1932 season.

NFL Standings—November 22, 1931

	W.	L.	T.
Green Bay	10	1	0
Portsmouth	10	3	0
Chicago Bears	6	3	0
Chicago Cardinals	4	3	0
Providence	4	3	2
New York	5	5	0
Stapleton	3	6	1
Cleveland	2	7	0
Brooklyn	2	10	0
Philadelphia	1	6	1

Criticism of football as a brutal sport continued to mount during the year, especially after young Richard Brinsley Sheriden, an end at West Point, died following a severe spinal injury sustained while making a tackle in a game versus Yale. An alarming report issued following the 1931 season indicated that football-related fatalities had increased dramatically. In commenting on the number of accidents, the report noted that, "this season was free of freak accidents such as took place two years ago when a grandmother was playing with her grandchildren and received a broken leg. However, two coaches, Little of Columbia and Hanson of Syracuse, were carried on the injured list. The Columbia coach received a neck injury that was quite serious and the Syracuse mentor was cut and bruised in a practice session."

FOOTBALL FATALITIES, 1906–31:

1906	11	1913	5	1925	20
1907	11	1914	13	1926	9
1908	13	1915	15	1927	17
1909	12	1917	12	1928	18
1911	11	1921	12	1929	12
1912	13	1923	18	1930	13
		1931	40		

(No records kept in omitted years)

Criticism of football followed publication of the report, naturally. One of the most prominent and outspoken critics was Dr. Beverly R. Tucker, a Richmond neurologist, who petitioned President Herbert Hoover to appoint a commission that would study ways of reducing the football mortality rate. The flurry of interest in Tucker's petition soon died down, of course, and little was heard of it as the year came to a close. Some attention was given to eliminating the kickoff play, which even then was recognized as perhaps the most violent of the game, but coaches and players across the nation were lukewarm to suggestions that the ball be given to a team on its 20-yard line. And so the petition that football become a less violent game faded into obscurity. The sports-minded public had other things to think about, such as whether Connie Mack should break up his Philadelphia Athletics "for the good of the game," or whether Notre Dame might have beaten USC if the immortal Knute Rockne had not taken his tragic dive into the Kansas countryside.

And since 1931:
Although no drastic changes were made following the 1931 season to reduce the violence of football, record-keeping continued to show that approximately 18 players a year died from 1932 through 1977. The total figure, 839, included 75 professionals and semi-pros, 527 high school players, 73 college athletes, and 164 sandlotters.

CHAPTER 29—BREAKING THE COLOR BARRIER

The barriers against black participants in American spectator sports, like those of a social nature, were not erected overnight shortly after the Civil War. No legislation or reverse gentlemen's agreement stated that blacks were to be excluded from participation, but it was generally understood that a color line existed. Nevertheless, some blacks did break into professional athletics during the latter part of the nineteenth century.

FRANK HART

One of the first was Frank Hart, a gifted, flamboyant athlete who in some ways anticipated Muhammad Ali's gift for showmanship. Arrogant at times, Hart knew what he could do and he usually managed to do it, often in a way that seemed effortless. He "moved like a machine," one reporter noted in 1880. Not everyone liked the coffee-colored Haytien," as he was frequently called, but most men were forced to respect his ability.

Perhaps the name Frank Hart has fallen into obscurity because the athletic sport in which he excelled is no longer as popular as it used to be. The "go as you please" race, which usually lasted 6 days, was quite a spectacle during the 1870s and 1880s. The entrants, as the title implies, were allowed to move at whatever pace they desired—walk, run, sprint, jog. Compared to modern football or baseball, it was a seemingly disorganized event. A scoreboard at one end of the arena told which athlete had covered the most laps, but at any given moment one or more of the contestants might be in his tent, sleeping, while the others moved about the track.

"Black Dan," as Frank Hart was known, made his appearance on the tracks of America when pedestrianism as a spectator sport was still quite young. His first race took place in 1879 and immediately there was trouble. "The others objected to me and asked [Fred Englehardt, his manager] if he was going to let me run," Hart recalled later. "He answered 'yes' and told those who did not like that to get out. They didn't get out and I won the race."

After running at Boston—where a spectator tried to fling pepper into his eyes—Hart was entered in the prestigious Astley Belt competition in New York City. If Daniel O'Leary wanted to obtain maximum publicity for his young black charge, this was the event that could do it. The entire United States was interested in the outcome of the race, partly because Edward P. Weston, an American, was the defending champion. Frank Hart didn't win the 1879 Astley Belt competition, but he did make a strong showing. And, of course, the press noticed him immediately. The New York *Herald* described his gait: "Swinging his arms in an airy fashion . . . he carried his head high, with a quill toothpick between his lips. . . ." When the band stationed in the arena broke into Hart's favorite number, "Baby Mine," he invariably flung himself ahead even faster, taking the toothpick from his mouth and placing it behind one ear.

Although he finished fourth, Frank Hart made sure that everyone knew he was in the race. Singling out Englishman Charles Rowell as a likely candidate for spoofing, Hart did exactly as he did. When Rowell sprinted, so

---

How "Black Dan" Got His Nickname:
When America's premier pedestrian, Daniel O'Leary, began to approach the age of forty, he began looking around for young men who could be trained to take his place. In 1879, he was told about twenty-two-year-old Frank Hart, then a grocer living in Boston. Hart, it was said, had great speed and endurance. When O'Leary found out the rumors were true, he suggested that Hart accept his backing and enter some of the larger races. Hart's

answer was characteristically uncompromising. He demanded only one thing, "that I be allowed to win where I could . . . You know, some of these gentlemen in sporting business sometimes keep their men back to make money and other things, but I don't want that. I must go straight and win or I'll go back to groceries." When O'Leary agreed, the two men entered into partnership and Frank Hart became known as "Black Dan."

did Hart. When he walked, Hart walked alongside. Occasionally, he raced far ahead of Rowell, paused casually to have a drink of water, then waited impatiently for the Englishman to catch up. Unfortunately, Rowell had built a commanding lead early in the race, so there was little chance for Hart to win, but by the time the event was over, New York blacks loved the young Haitian so much they presented him with a magnificent floral design.

Shortly afterward, Frank Hart won his first major race, the Rose Belt, during which he covered 540.1 miles in six days, beating veteran Fred Krone by 4 miles. Thus the stage was set for a spirited rematch in April 1880, when both men entered the O'Leary Belt competition at Madison Square Garden. The prize, for its time, was a considerable ten thousand dollars, and public interest was at fever pitch by midnight, April 5, when more than four thousand fans jammed the arena. "Not in the history of walking-matches," noted the *Herald*, "has such a crowd gathered in the capacious building. . . ." Frank Hart was apparently confident. "I'll break dem white fallas' hearts, I will—you hear me!" he was reported to have said. And then he proceeded to do just that.

The 1880 O'Leary Belt race was unique in that three blacks were entered. In addition to Hart, there was William Pegram and Edward Williams, both of whom were strong runners. "The three negroes made a great show of sombre color on the track," one reporter wrote, "but they kept well up with the others and demonstrated their constitutional right to walk in public, without regard to any previous condition whatever."

At the end of the first 24 hours, Frank Hart led John Dobler of Chicago, 131 miles to 129. Within sight was "Blower" Brown's six-day record total of 553 miles, which would earn the man who surpassed it an extra $1,000. By the second day, there were so many people in the Garden that the floor and every available bench were lined with bodies. Rancid smoke filled the vast cavern but the pace continued to quicken. Celebrities such as General Tom Thumb and Commodore Nutt, midgets from Barnum's Circus, dropped by. Pickpockets and con artists had a field day, as did the concessionaires, who sold nickel cigars for the bargain price of $.15. In the meantime, Hart and Dobler continued within 2 miles of each other.

Not until the fifth day did Frank Hart manage to open a comfortable lead, beginning the final 24 hours with 492 miles to Dobler's 473. Now he was certain not only of winning but also of beating "Blower" Brown's record. Celebrants lined the outside of Hart's tent, tossing flowers at their hero as he passed one milestone after another. When he reached 500

miles, Hart "was greeted by a burst of applause which awoke the sleepers. . . ." When he passed Brown's 553-mile record, he stopped at his tent, reached inside, and "grasped a broom to which a flag was attached and ran the next lap as nimbly as a deer." And as he moved along, prizes continued to pile up outside his tent—a red, white, and expensive blue sash "from a lady," a pair of expensive walking shoes, and a loaf of French bread ornamented with flowers.

When he finally stopped running, with a total of 565 miles and a new "go as you please" record for 6 days, Frank Hart received the best prize of all—a total of $16,784, including the losers' entrance fees, several smaller awards, and a share of the gate receipts. It seems likely this is the largest purse ever won by a black athlete for a single event until that time.

Most whites were not upset by Hart's victory (as they would be by boxer Jack Johnson's victories three decades later), although some objected to his smiling "arrogance" and were eager for someone to come along who could beat Hart. But no one outran him consistently, at least not for a while. Hart won major races in 1881 and 1882 and continued to perform well until the 1890s, when 6-day bicycle events gradually replaced the sport that gave a black man his first opportunity to beat whites at their own game.

How the Other Blacks Fared:
By passing John Dobler—whose stomach started "behaving in a most disloyal manner," William Pegram won second-place money of $3,392. Edward Williams finished seventh and made $106.

EARLY BLACKS AND BASEBALL

Although blacks had been banned officially from the old amateur baseball association, Moses Fleetwood Walker (1857–1924) and brother Welday (1860–1937) were signed by the Toledo club of the 1884 American Association. Their careers were brief, Fleet appearing in 41 games behind the plate and one in the outfield, which was Welday's position during his entire major-league career of five games.

There can be little doubt that the careers of both men were shortened by racial prejudice. Once in Louisville, Fleet Walker sat in the stands while his team played, one member of the opposition having threatened to walk out if a black took the field. Another time in Richmond, Toledo Manager Charlie Morton received a letter from six local whites, threatening bodily harm to Fleet Walker if he played.

Nor was prejudice confined to the fans. On September 10, 1887, faced with having to play an exhibition game with the Cuban Giants at West Farms, near New York, eight members of the St. Louis Browns drew the color line by sending a letter to President Von der Ahe. After receiving the note at dinner, Von der Ahe got up from the table and confronted the players. When asked the meaning of the letter, none of the men spoke, most staring sullenly at the floor. One would have thought that Von der Ahe could have cowed them into playing, but at that moment he filled the vacuum himself by saying, incredibly, "As it seems to be a matter of principle with you, you need not play tomorrow."

_____

The "Color Line" Letter:
                    Philadelphia, Penn., Sept. 10.
To Chris Von Der Ahe, Esq.:
  "*DEAR SIR: We, the undersigned, members of the St. Louis baseball club, do not agree to play against negroes tomorrow. We will cheerfully play against white people at any time, and think, by refusing to play, we are only doing what is right, taking everything into consideration and the shape the team is in at present.*
  "*W. A. Latham, John Boyle, J. E. O'Neill, R. L. Caruthers, W. E. Gleason, W. H. Robinson, Charles King, Curt Welch.*"
(NOTE: *The W. H. Robinson was not Wilbert Robinson, later a Hall of Fame electee, but William H. [Yank] Robinson.*)

_____

Trouble was brewing in the minor leagues as well. At about the same time, players with the International League adopted a resolution against playing with black players. Their specific targets were second baseman Frank Grant of Buffalo and pitcher George Stovey of Newark.

PETER JACKSON AND OTHERS
Only in the sport of boxing did the black man seem to have a reasonable chance to show his ability before the turn of the century. There were many who disapproved of bouts between whites and blacks, of course, but the fact remains that there were many such contests during the 1890s, when Jim Crowism seemed to grow daily. One of the earliest and most exciting matches took place at Troy,

New York, on March 31, 1891, between George Dixon of Boston—who was black—and Cal McCarthy of Jersey City. Dixon was the favorite, partly because it was rumored that McCarthy had been drinking more heavily than usual before the fight, partly from knowledge that Dixon simply was the better fighter. Nevertheless, bets of eighty and a hundred dollars were common.

The fight began just before ten-thirty. After feeling each other out for one round, Dixon floored McCarthy twice in the second round, but the white man was saved by the bell. After being sent to the canvas one more time in the third, McCarthy seemed to stiffen, forcing the action through the eleventh, when he managed to open a gash under Dixon's left eye with a wild uppercut. Dixon stormed back in the twelfth but the bout was fairly even until the twentieth round, when the black man's better conditioning began to assert itself. Then he started driving McCarthy from one end of the ring to the other. The referee declared Dixon the winner in the twenty-second round.

The same month, another important mixed fight took place in San Francisco, where heavyweight Jake Kilrain met George Godfrey, the "colored heavyweight champion." Kilrain, having lost to John L. Sullivan and Jim Corbett, was generally conceded to be over the hill, but his backers, who were numerous, obviously believed he had one more bout left in him.

Although outweighing Godfrey, 192 pounds to 174 pounds, Kilrain was the favorite only because those who bet on him outnumbered Godfrey's backers. Never a speedy boxer, Kilrain relied primarily on endurance and bull-like rushes to overpower his enemy. The tactic worked only moderately well against the faster Godfrey. Not until the fourteenth round was Kilrain able to land a punch that staggered the black champion, who in the meantime had been unable to penetrate Kilrain's defense. By the sixteenth round, it was obvious that Godfrey could not hurt Kilrain the way Sullivan had; the fight then became a waiting affair to see which man would tire first. Godfrey somehow managed to absorb Kilrain's heavy blows for nearly thirty more rounds, but then his age—thirty-eight—worked against him. Kilrain

_____

Fair Play (Albeit Grudging), 1891:
"*Kilrain in the fifth round got Godfrey's head under his arm for the second time, but cries from the spectators caused him to desist from doing damage.*"
                    Baltimore Sun, *March 18, 1891*

_____

finally landed a succession of punches that sent Godfrey to the canvas for good in the forty-fourth round.

In attendance that night—as Godfrey's "bottleholder"—was twenty-nine-year-old Peter Jackson, a 6-foot, ½-inch, 210-pound Australian black man with tremendous speed and power. Having defeated most of the better fighters in the heavyweight division, including Edward Smith of Denver, Jem Smith, Patsy Cardiff, Joe McAuliffe, "Sailor" Brown, and George Godfrey (in nineteen rounds), Jackson decided to see if he could arrange a bout with either John L. Sullivan, the champion, or James Corbett, the leading challenger.

Sullivan made himself unavailable but Corbett was willing to fight Jackson in order to test his own ability and enhance his national reputation. Despite Jackson's spraining an ankle and losing a week of training, he was installed a 5–1 favorite, the betting centering not on which fighter would win but on how long Corbett could last. They met at the California Athletic Club, San Francisco, Jackson starting with a rush in order to win bets for those who had wagered that Corbett couldn't last ten rounds. But Corbett kept away from the black man and neutralized his rushes by jamming his left shoulder into Jackson's chest. In the sixteenth round, however, Jackson landed a right that was the hardest punch Corbett had ever taken. Gentleman Jim managed to weather that storm and in the twenty-eighth round he nearly knocked Jackson out. The pace slowed down after that until it became apparent that neither man had the power left to put the other down. Yet most of the crowd was surprised when in the sixty-first round the fight was declared a draw. Not so Corbett and Jackson. Neither protested vehemently when the four hours of fine boxing came to a sudden conclusion, and later both men said the other was the finest boxer he had ever met. The only person who affected nonchalance was John L. Sullivan, who when told that Jackson was a remarkable fighter, grunted, "What's that to me? He's colored, isn't he?"

MARSHALL (MAJOR) TAYLOR

The writers of the day dubbed him the "ebony streak" or "black cyclone" out of respect for his speed, and there is small doubt that for a while Major Taylor was undisputed bicycle champion of the United States.

Born in 1878, Taylor early demonstrated ability at nearly every athletic skill, but the sport for which he seemed best adapted was the burgeoning one of bicycle racing. By the early 1890s the highways were crowded with young men and young women, indignation over the antics of "scorchers" on the open road was at an all-time high, and promoters were searching about for ways to turn the national cycling craze into money.

The answer was to bring speed-cycling indoors. New York saw its first six-day bicycle race at Madison Square Garden in 1891, the same year that Major Taylor won his first ten-mile race at age thirteen. Two years later, the young black demonstrated his specialty—blazing speed over a short distance rather than endurance runs—by pedaling a five-lap mile in two minutes, eleven seconds from a standing start.

Scorning the Negro Cyclists' League, the separate-and-unequal group that permitted blacks to race for smaller purses, Taylor set out for the large population centers, determined to win big-time events. The going, as one would expect, was not easy. Once in Boston, a cyclist named W. E. Becker, so incensed that he had been defeated by Taylor, grabbed him at the finish line and nearly choked him unconscious as thousands watched. It was not usually that bad, however, for Taylor soon became a favorite with both the fans and the press; thus public censure held the more obvious prejudice to a minimum.

A clever racer, Taylor seemed always to come from behind when it was apparent that he possessed speed enough to take the lead and hold it. Actually, Taylor enjoyed using his opponents as wind shields, trailing along in their wake until the opportunity arose for him to put his nose close to his front tire, raise his haunches high, and literally jump-sprint his bicycle to victory. Such a bit of showmanship —coupled with frequent wins—made Taylor unpopular with other cyclists, but the little man did not care. As the others cursed or elbowed him during the course of a race, he replied most often with a verse of Scripture and a forbearing smile.

Whatever Happened to Peter Jackson?
Many said he should have won the championship, but Jackson's fortunes declined after his magnificent fight with Corbett in 1891. A year later Jackson was in England, where he defeated Frank Slavin, but it was reported that Jackson contracted tuberculosis while abroad. Taking to drink, he was in poor condition when he was knocked out by Jim Jeffries in three rounds in 1893. Jackson eventually returned to Australia, where he died in 1901, a pauper at age forty.

One of the high points of Taylor's career came in 1898, when a match race—best two out of three paced mile heats—was arranged between the young American black and Jimmy Michael, a Welshman known as the "little rarebit" to his fans. The scene was the Manhattan Beach cycle track, the weather perfect for the event, which began with Michael winning the first heat. But then Taylor showed his determination, opening up such leads in the two remaining heats that Michael quit before the race was over. The announced time—1 minute, 41⅖ seconds—broke French rider Edouard Taylore's time of 1 minute, 43⅗ seconds, the record for a paced mile from a standing start.

A Description of Taylor's Style:

"Taylor skimmed along, swift as the flight of a swallow. On the back stretch in the last lap, Michael sat upright and pedaled leisurely to the tape, as he saw it was useless to attempt to catch his speedy rival. The Welsh rider was pale as a corpse when he jumped off his wheel, and had no excuse to make for his defeat. . . . Taylor's performance undoubtedly stamps him as the premier cycle sprinter of the world. . . ."

So enthusiastic was William A. Brady, Taylor's backer, that he leaped onto the track even before the time was announced and issued a challenge to the effect that his protégé would be happy to race Michael for five thousand dollars or ten thousand dollars, over any distance up to a hundred miles. That, as it turned out, was a mistake, for Taylor's forte was the sprint and Michael's was the middle distances.

The next month, September 1898, more than five thousand spectators were on hand for a twenty-mile race between the two cyclists, each of whom was paced by a team of additional men (Taylor used six, Michael seven). Major Taylor, predictably, started with a blazing first mile of 1 minute 46⅕ seconds, taking a sixty-yard lead. But Michael was a steady performer and as the miles clicked off he continued to narrow the gap until Taylor lost his smooth pace. At the finish, Michael was about two thirds of a mile ahead.

Undeterred by an occasional defeat such as this one, Taylor went abroad, first to Paris in 1901, where he was hailed as the *"sprinter noir"* and *"un diable de négrillon."* Although well aware of the discrimination against blacks in America, Taylor patriotically demanded that his appearances on the track be greeted by a rendition of "The Star-Spangled Banner," and when he defeated the European champion, Edmond Jacquelin, Taylor caused a sensation by waving a small American flag during his cooling-off laps. During the spring of 1906, however, Taylor fared poorly in France, losing to second-rate riders, which caused him to give serious thought to retiring. After making a better showing during the summer of 1907, when he defeated all of the best Europeans except Jacquelin, Taylor returned to Worcester, Massachusetts, with his family, and announced that he intended to retire. He stuck to his decision, making only occasional "old-timer's" appearances after that, but he had provided an example for later blacks to follow.

ISAAC MURPHY

His life was a brief one (1860–96), but during his short career Isaac Murphy set more than his share of records. And when he was elected to the Jockeys' Hall of Fame, he received 432 votes, more than either Johnny Longden or Earl Sande.

Isaac Murphy's Accomplishments:

First jockey to win 3 Kentucky Derbies: 1884—Buchanan   1890—Riley   1891—Kingman

Rode 1,412 races and won 628 of them—44 per cent

In 1879, rode 75 races and won 35—47 per cent

July 4, 1879—rode entire card of winners, Detroit

Born in Kentucky, Isaac Murphy made his debut as a fifteen-year-old ninety-one pounder. That year, 1875, he brought home his first winner, and by the beginning of the 1880s he was so respected as a jockey that noted gambler and horse owner Lucky Baldwin paid Murphy ten thousand dollars just to have first call on his services. Isaac's specialty was the whirlwind finish, for he somehow had the knack of knowing exactly how much stamina each horse had and when was the last possible moment to call for it. Races in which Murphy rode were therefore likely to be thrillers for the spectators and heart-stoppers for owners, some of whom were well aware of the young black man's flair for the dramatic. In contrast to some jockeys who whipped their horses into frenzies as they neared the finish line, Murphy's style was cool, his position upright even at the most exciting moments of a race. British writers, amazed at his ability, called him "Black Archer," thus comparing him favorably

"Colored Jockeys Show the Way"
Conceded the New York Herald *on September 20, 1889, in a highly racist but grudgingly complimentary article dealing with the previous day's racing at Gravesend Race Track, Brooklyn. "If a composite photograph had been made of the jockeys who rode the six winners at Gravesend," it read, "it would have been as black as Erebus. There wouldn't have been a single light line in it, unless the camera had happened to catch Hamilton with his mouth wide open displaying the pearly white teeth which form the only relieving feature of his coal black face."*

Specifically, the article referred to the fact that in every race that afternoon, a black jockey brought his horse in either first or second. The riders were Isaac Murphy, Pike Barnes, Tony Hamilton, Spider Anderson, and Isaac Lewis.

to the greatest British jockey of the early nineteenth century, Fred Archer.

Murphy's greatest moments came during a series of races in 1890 in which he guided Salvator to three victories over Tenny, ridden by Ed (Snapper) Garrison, one of the greatest jockeys of the age. Garrison's neck-hugging riding style and furious whipping attracted more attention from a distance, but the races were won when the inscrutable Murphy gently pressed his knees against Salvator's sides, leaned forward, and whispered something in the big chestnut's ear. History, unfortunately, does not record what the magic syllables were. It does record that Isaac Murphy was buried at Lexington on February 16, 1896, just five years after winning his third Kentucky Derby.

Another Great Black Jockey:
Jimmy Winkfield, who was fourteen years old when Isaac Murphy died, allowed only five years to pass before winning a Kentucky Derby himself. That came in 1901, when he guided His Eminence to victory, then followed in 1902 with a win aboard Alan-a-Dale. By 1930, when he retired at the age of forty-eight, Winkfield had ridden twenty-six hundred winners on tracks in the United States, Poland, Austria, Germany, Russia, Italy, Spain, England, and France.

AND NOW A WORD ABOUT THE OFTEN-NEGLECTED AMERICAN INDIAN

"There is something of pathos in the almost consistent failure of the Carlisle football players to win from their white antagonists," one newspaper editor wrote in 1897, reflecting on the sad state of Indian athletes in that year. "The Indian players are no doubt fine specimens of their tribes. They have strength, courage, and intelligence. . . . But it is only occasionally that they win, and almost never when they face white boys from colleges large enough to give much chance for selection. This has always been the case when the two races have met. . . . The Carlisle boys play good football, the white boys play better; the fathers of these Indians could read the signs of the forest like an open book, but the white man could read that book even more glibly, could follow a fainter trail, could ride a horse more wisely if not more safely, could shoot more accurately, and could fight, not more bravely, perhaps, but certainly with more effect."

Coming at the turn of the century, when white America was seeing its way free to becoming the savior of the entire world, black, yellow, white, and red, such an editorial reflected the self-satisfaction of the majority in the United States. It also seemed to have some basis in fact. Founded in 1879, the Carlisle Indian School had not yet come into its own by the middle 1890s. Nor had Indians distinguished themselves athletically in games other than football and lacrosse. Baseball seemed foreign to them, although in 1897 the career of America's first major-league Indian player, Louis Sockalexis, was about to begin. But if the Carlisle Indians were athletic jokes at mid-decade, they soon began to remedy the situation. By 1899, the football team had developed several stars, the most talented being a strong running back, Isaac Seneca. During the 1899 season, Carlisle lost to Harvard by 22–10 and was shut out by Princeton, 12–0, but in the final game against Columbia, Carlisle put on a grand show for more than eight thousand spectators at Manhattan Field, including a sizable contingent of fans from Carlisle who waved the maroon and gold colors whenever the Indians executed a good play.

The visitors had much to cheer about. Seneca ran for more than two hundred yards, in bursts of thirty, thirty-five, twenty, forty-five, and fifty-five at a time. Most of the yardage was made without the benefit of interference, for the Indians had eliminated the mass play in favor of a naked reverse, Seneca carrying. It worked often enough to turn the game into a rout, Carlisle winning by a score of 45–0. Walter Camp named Seneca to his 1899 All-American team, the first Carlisle Indian so honored.

Sockalexis and the Other Early Chiefs of Summer:

During the late 1890s and early twentieth century, American Indians were permitted to take the diamond with white men, probably because the red man as a group no longer constituted a threat to the white establishment. Some Indians played well, some poorly, a few succumbed to the perils of firewater, and nearly all of them were nicknamed "Chief." They include:

Louis Sockalexis, *a full-blooded Penobscot, had the misfortune to play the outfield for the National League Cleveland Spiders, 1897–99. (The organization was rapidly heading downhill during that period, which might have explained Sockalexis's turning to drink.) His best year was his first, when he batted .338 in 66 games. He also made 16 errors. His productivity declined thereafter, but his lifetime batting average dropped only to .313. He died in 1913.*

Charles Albert Bender (*1883–1954*) *pitched for the Philadelphia Athletics,* Baltimore Terrapins *(Federal League),* Phillies, and White Sox, 1903–25 *(with a long interruption, 1918–24). He won 210 games, lost 128, and is the only American Indian in the Baseball Hall of Fame (1953). His tribe was Chippewa.*

John Tortes Meyers (*1880–1971*) *caught for the New York Giants, Brooklyn Dodgers, and Boston Braves, 1909–17.*

Moses J. Yellowhorse (*1898–1964*), *of the Pawnee tribe, pitched for the Pirates, 1921–22, winning 8 and losing 4. His batting average (6 for 19) was a highly respectable .316.*

George Murphy Johnson (*1887–1922*), *a Winnebago, pitched to a 41–43 record with the Cincinnati Reds and Kansas City Packers (Federal League).*

Austin Ben Tincup, *the only Indian in this list who was not nicknamed "Chief," pitched 1914–16, and 1918 with the Phillies, winning 8 and losing 11. He returned a decade later with the Chicago Cubs, yielding 7 runs and 14 hits in 2 appearances.*

A bit more than a decade later, a Sac and Fox Indian, James Francis Thorpe, appeared on the scene to again put the lie to the 1897 editor's claim that the American Indian seemed to have a penchant for finishing second to white competition. The year 1912 was a triumphant one for Thorpe. At the Olympic Games at Stockholm he won four of the five events in the pentathlon—the 200-meter dash, 1,500-meter run, the long jump, and the discus. He placed third in the javelin throw. In the decathlon, Thorpe won four events—the shot put, the high jump, the high hurdles, and the 1,500-meter run—and placed third in the 100-meter dash, the pole vault, the discus, and the long jump. He also finished fourth in the javelin throw and the 400-meter run. It was probably the greatest display of all-around athletic ability (8,412.96 points out of a possible 10,000).

A Bit of Dialogue at the 1912 Olympics:
GUSTAV V OF SWEDEN: *You, sir, are the greatest athlete in the world.*
JIM THORPE, U.S.A.: *Thanks, King.*

The football season of 1912 also showed Thorpe in fine form. He had been selected for the 1911 All-American team, but was determined to put forth a better effort against Syracuse, which had beaten the Carlisle Indians two years in a row. On October 12, Thorpe led his men through the mud at Syracuse, scoring three touchdowns and kicking three field goals. The final score was 33–0.

At that point, Thorpe's future seemed bright indeed, but a Boston newspaper then revealed that the young Indian had played baseball for the Eastern Carolina League, a minor professional organization, during two summers of college, a not-uncommon practice at the time. Charged with having violated his amateur standing, Thorpe returned the Olympic medals and apologized to the Olympic Committee. His name was stricken from the records and his amateur standing not restored until two decades after his death.

Having turned professional as a result of the Boston paper investigation, Thorpe announced that he wanted to play baseball, an action that started a stampede in his direction. The bidding for Thorpe's services was eventually won by the New York Giants, who paid him five thousand dollars, said to be one of the highest salaries paid a first-year player at that time. As a gate attraction, Thorpe was a success, but he never blossomed into the superstar many predicted he would be on the diamond. His trouble, it was said, was his inability to hit the curve ball. During six seasons as a part-time player for the Giants and Reds, he played in a total of 289 games, hit 7 home runs, and had a lifetime batting average of .252. After baseball came several years of pro football, then the deluge—of firewater.

Jim Thorpe's Real Name:
When asked how he came by the name Thorpe, Jim said he never knew exactly how he got it. His real name, on the Oklahoma reservation, was Drag-his-root.

BACK TO THE BLACK

By the turn of the century, the white establishment's position on black athletes was a solid one. They were permitted to participate in sports but not to the point where they threatened white record-holding. Sometimes, in fact, mixed play was encouraged on the athletic field, as on July 4, 1901, when two white baseball teams engaged a couple of black teams at American League Park, Baltimore. (The games were, of course, exhibitions, which blunted the potentially inflammatory nature.) A crowd of fourteen hundred, the majority of whom were black, was on hand for the games. In the first contest, the white Yanigans played a black club from Norfolk called the Red Stockings. Richard P. (Stub) Brown pitched for the Yanigans, a fact that made the outcome a foregone conclusion. (Brown had pitched for the 1893 and 1894 Baltimore Orioles and the 1897 Cincinnati Reds and was not yet thirty-one. He was thus able to stymie the Norfolk bats to the tune of a 22–2 score.) In two afternoon games, the Baltimore black Giants and white Lafayettes—playing without a former professional on the mound—split a pair. Presumably, everyone went home happy.

Said One White Player:
"Do you see this crowd? If we were playing another white team we would have about thirty-nine paid spectators. . . . I don't know why it is, but people will come to see these games, but not games between white teams."

Sometimes blacks—so long as they were not too numerous—were lauded by the newspapers of the period. On October 18, 1914, the New York *Times* pointed out, with pictures, the feats of some "crack colored athletes of New York," all of whom were repre-

sentatives of the three black athletic clubs—Smart Set AC, Salem-Crescent AC, and St. Christophers Club—then flourishing in the city. At the same time, a bit of nervousness surfaced amid the lines of praise: "The negro's proficiency in athletics has become a source of much speculation and discussion in athletic clubs," the reporter wrote. "Should a corresponding progress be made by them in the next three or four years many laurels now worn by white athletes will pass into the keeping of negroes. This success has been more noticeable during the last month than at any other time, and the fact that four titles were won by colored athletes . . . has caused a flutter of excitement among the registered athletes in the AAU. Nor is the present crop of negro runners likely to suddenly cease, for there are many promising colored boys in the public schools of Greater New York."

Some Outstanding Black Track and Field Athletes of the Period:
Howard P. Drew (USC)
    Ran 100-yard dash in :09⅗ seconds, March 28, 1914
    Ran 220-yard dash in :22⅕ seconds, February 28, 1914
Binga Dismond (University of Chicago)
    Ran 440-yard dash in :47⅖ seconds, June 3, 1916
J. B. Taylor (University of Pennsylvania)
    Ran 440-yard dash in :51 seconds, 1907
J. M. Burwell (University of Pittsburgh)
    Many good times in sprints
H. M. Martin (Smart Set AC)
    Specialty—one-mile walk

Not yet panic, but a sense of impending disaster perhaps. The situation on the track, however, was rosy for the white establishment compared to the chaos taking place in the prize ring. By the turn of the century, it seemed that every white man who ventured inside the ropes with a black came out the loser. Peter Jackson had been kept from the opportunity to win the championship by the simple expedient of denying him a title fight, but it was not possible to keep all of the good blacks out of title contests—unless it could be managed via legislation. And so, following Jack Johnson's defeat of Tommy Burns for the heavyweight title in 1908 and his successful defense against aging Jim Jeffries two years later, it was hardly surprising that bills were offered and passed in several states barring interracial fights. Inevitably the reason for proposing such legislation was that keeping whites and blacks apart in the boxing ring would prevent flare-ups of emotion and perhaps ultimately protect the black population from retaliation by angry whites, who tended to take Jack Johnson's well-earned arrogance and proclivity for white women personally. There was some truth to the comment that the fights inflamed racial tension, but the inflammation seemed to occur only when the blacks won a decisive bout, rather than vice versa. Nevertheless, in February 1913, the New York State Athletic Commission ruled that mixed bouts could not take place. At the same time, a bill was introduced in the California Legislature making it illegal to put on fights between blacks and whites, the convicted party being subject to a fine of five thousand dollars and a prison sentence of three years. The state of Wisconsin also passed a bill barring interracial fights but soon rescinded it. Even more insidious was the action of whites such as Jack Dempsey, who upon winning the heavyweight title from Jess Willard in 1919 announced that he "will pay no attention to negro challengers, but will defend against any white heavyweight as the occasion demands." Surprisingly, there was not a great deal of violent reaction to the drawing of the color line, legislatively and otherwise.

The bans on mixed boxing were not constitutional, of course. Jack Dempsey could make his color line hold, largely because there happened to be few strong black contenders at that time, but boxing clubs found the bans onerous. Nevertheless, New York State did not see another mixed bout until September 26, 1922, when Irish Johnny Curtin won a split decision from black Danny Edwards at the Pioneer Athletic Club. There were no incidents.

Such was not the case at Chicago on March 25, 1929, when Jackie Fields, a white local favorite, tangled with Jack Thompson in a high-ranking welterweight bout. More than ten thousand spectators filled Chicago Coliseum in anticipation of a slugfest, both fighters being crowd pleasers in that respect. The battle was in the eighth round, Fields leading, when suddenly a fight broke out at the rear of the arena between backers of the two men. Apparently a gun was pulled, which sent the crowd in the area into panic. Men rushed toward the ring, bowling over women in their haste; one man was pushed from the balcony, several suffered broken legs; press wires were severed and typewriters trampled; radio listeners got the full story of the stampede from announcers who somehow maintained control of their microphones.

The next day, Sam Luzzo, a member of the Illinois Athletic Commission, stated, "I shall take the matter of prohibiting mixed matches at the Coliseum up with the Board of Directors immediately. . . . In the future either two colored men will fight or two white men will fight together." The edict did not stand, of course, and during the 1930s and 1940s, more and more black-white fights were held in many states and broadcast nationally on television. But some states continued to hold out against the practice. It was not until February 4, 1952, for example, that the state of Florida allowed a bout between Kid Gavilan, welterweight champion, and white Bobby Dykes, a local favorite in Miami. Gavilan won a split decision before a crowd of seventeen thousand.

FOOTBALL AND THE COLOR LINE
All hats off to Robey, men,
All honor to his name!
On the diamond, court, or football field
He's brought old Rutgers fame.
The poetry appeared in the *Scarlet Letter,*

Reaction to One Fight:
On September 3, 1906, at Goldfield, Nevada, black Joe Gans defeated Battling Nelson in one of the most controversial bouts until that time. The day after, six fights broke out in New York City. At Tompkinsville, Staten Island, following a scuffle between a black man and a white man, a mob assembled, grabbed the black man, James Marbine (who reportedly started the battle by declaring "colored gentlemen can always lick po' whites"), and placed a rope around his neck. Only the rapid intervention of police saved him

from being lynched. In another instance a stonecutter who applauded the decision in favor of Gans was assaulted by three men.

And Another:
Four years later, in the wake of the Johnson-Jeffries fight, fifty soldiers from Fort Myer, Virginia, stormed the Alexandria County Jail in an effort to lynch a black prisoner. Meanwhile, in Chicago, a Richard McGuirk, armed with a rifle, tried to force his way into the home of champion Johnson.

Rutgers yearbook, in 1919 when Paul Robeson, singer and gifted athlete, was graduated from the school. The whites who remained behind were truly sorry to see him leave, for during the years Robeson played, he had led the football team—and that was really all that mattered—to a record of twenty wins and four losses.

The First Black Professional Football Players:
They predated the NFL by nearly two decades. One was Charles Follies, who played with the Shelby Blues in 1904. Another was Haiti-born Henry McDonald, who joined the Rochester Jeffersons in 1911 as a 145-pound running back. He spent seven seasons with the team and was nicknamed "The Motorcycle." He also played with a variety of professional teams of the period, including the Lancaster Malleables, the New York Colored Giants, the Pittsburgh Colored All-Stars, and All-Buffalo.

Robeson was the first black player to take the field with a Rutgers squad, and he made it count. Weighing more than two hundred pounds, he was a menacing figure, "a veritable Othello of battle," as he was described by the New York *Herald Tribune*. At linebacker or end, he was equally adept. Against Fort Wadsworth, a World War I service team well populated with former college stars, Robeson caught passes of forty and thirty-seven yards for touchdowns. "Robey would tear you to pieces. Then he'd reach down, pick you up, and ask, 'Did I hurt you?'" recalled Frederick Pollard, an All-American running back at Brown who played against Robeson.

"Fritz" Pollard knew the problems facing Robey, for he too was black and had to play twice as well as his white competitors to earn a spot on the team. The two men became

friends and Pollard was gratified to see Robeson earn All-American honors in 1918. After graduation, Robey also tried his hand at professional football, playing in 1920 with the Hammond Pros, in 1921 with Akron, and in 1922 with the Milwaukee Badgers (a team that had an unprecedented *three* black players that year) before deciding that the stage suited him better.

THE PRE-WORLD WAR II YEARS
During the Depression years, whites still dominated professional and amateur sports, but on the few occasions when blacks were permitted to compete, they usually made exceptional names for themselves. By the time young Jesse Owens graduated from East Technical High School in Cleveland, for example, he had established three national high school records in track. During his career at Ohio State, he broke still more world records. One of his greatest collegiate performances came on May 2, 1935, when Owens got out of a sickbed to compete at the Big Ten conference championships at Ann Arbor, Michigan. The first thing Owens did was run the 100-yard dash in 9.4 seconds, tying the world's record. He then leaped 26 feet, 8¼ inches in the broad jump on his first try to beat the world record. After running the 220-yard hurdles in 22.6 seconds and the 220-yard dash in 20.3 seconds, he had two more world records to his credit as well as the distinction of having shattered or equaled four world marks in a single afternoon—a record in itself.

Some Praise for Blacks, 1932:
"Incidentally, the man that brought the first slaves to this country must have had these Olympic Games in mind, for these Senegambians have just about run the white man ragged. . . ."

Will Rogers

Some Other Early Blacks Who Distinguished Themselves on the Gridiron:
William H. Lewis, *center, Harvard. Was the first black to be selected as All-American when Walter Camp picked him for 1892 and 1893 teams.*
Bobby Marshall, *end, Minnesota. Was second team All-American in 1905 and 1906. His greatest moment came against Chicago in 1906 when he kicked a field goal that gave Minnesota a 4-2 victory*

and knocked Chicago out of contention for conference title.
Fred "Duke" Slater, *tackle, Iowa. Went on to play professionally with the Milwaukee Badgers, Rock Island Independents, and Chicago Cardinals, his career in NFL spanning 1922-31 seasons.*
John Shelbourne, *halfback, Dartmouth. Was good enough to play with Hammond Pros in 1922.*

A year later, Owens was the star of the American Olympic team, winning the 100-meter dash, long jump, 220-meter dash, and kicked off the winning 400-meter relay team—while Adolf Hitler watched and tried to reconcile Owens' performance with his own theories about Aryan racial supremacy.

In addition to Owens, blacks cheered—not too loudly in those days, of course—the performances of several men who distinguished themselves in the prize ring. One was John Henry Lewis, the great-great-nephew of Tom Molineaux, the first of America's great black heavyweights. Born in 1914, John Henry turned professional when he was only fourteen and won the light-heavyweight championship in 1935 by beating Bob Olin on a fifteen-round decision. He then defended the championship successfully five times before running into another Louis, named Joe. John Henry was the first black man to fight Joe Louis professionally, and for John Henry it was the worst mistake of his life. The bout lasted only one round. And John Henry never fought again. He retired in 1939, age twenty-five.

The man who beat John Henry Lewis needs no introduction, of course. Born in Detroit the same year as John Henry Lewis, Joe Louis won the heavyweight championship shortly after his twenty-third birthday by knocking out Jim Braddock in the eighth round. After that, he decided to be a fighting champion, defending his championship twenty times before World War II interrupted his career. "Joe Louis," reported the United Press on one occasion, "was probably the most widely known American black man who ever lived."

Blacks also found satisfaction in the career of a superlative fighter named Henry Armstrong (born Henry Jackson), who learned the art of survival during gang fights in East St. Louis and became one of the fiercest men to step in the ring. Defense was unknown to him. His *modus operandi* was to smother his opponent with blows, taking them in turn on his bullet head and sixteen-inch neck, until one or the other fighter collapsed. So successful was Armstrong that he held three world championship titles at one time—

welterweight, featherweight, and lightweight. After retiring from the ring, Armstrong returned to St. Louis and became a Baptist minister.

GRIDIRON PROBLEMS

Despite the barrier-breaking examples of Paul Robeson and Fritz Pollard on the football field, blacks who earned places on college teams during the Depression years found there was still likely to be trouble when they traveled South for a bowl or intersectional game. One celebrated example of this sort of discrimination occurred in 1940 when New York University was scheduled to play Missouri. NYU had in its backfield a young black named Leonard Bates, but at the beginning of the school year, when it was agreed that Bates' presence could cause embarrassment, he was called into the administration office and told "in a perfectly friendly manner" that he would be unable to make the Missouri trip.

Although Bates seemed content to forget the matter, fellow students held a "Bates Must Play" rally in order to protest. Unfortunately, it rained and only about thirty-five students showed up. A few speeches were delivered by campus leaders and faculty members, but for the most part the NYU staff was quietly in opposition to the protest, claiming that it would "only make for ill feeling." A token rally at the New York Central Railroad station ended the affair, the trains heading South and West without Leonard Bates. Paul Christman passed Missouri to a 33–0 victory.

On the Monday before the United States entered World War II, December 1, 1941, the black sports fan of the New York area had the unique opportunity of seeing how a team of black all-stars could handle themselves against a similar team of whites. The football game, an unusual event for its time, took place at the Polo Grounds and was well attended by residents of Harlem and the old Bedford section of Brooklyn. Many of the blacks had come to see Wilmeth Sidat-Singh, a former college player from Syracuse who also starred at basketball. They were not disappointed, for Sidat-Singh turned in a fine performance.

During the first period, it looked as if the Yankee All-Stars (the name given the white team—the blacks were called "Colored All-Stars") were going to have an easy time of it. Aided by a 15-yard penalty against the black squad, the Yankees marched seventy-two yards for a score. A few minutes later, Fritz Petela, a 230-pound fullback, crashed through center from the one-yard line for a second touchdown.

The black All-Stars came back, however, blocking a Bill De Correvont punt on the

---

"I never understood why we should be the beaten-down race. Certainly, Jesus has said that all men are created in his likeness. But I didn't know much about the Bible as a boy. All I knew was that I had to fight back, or surrender my pride. Boxing, I decided, was the thing."

Henry Armstrong

seven-yard line. Sidat-Singh plunged the final three yards to bring the score to a more respectable 14–7. But a field goal by the whites just before the half ended increased their margin to 17–7.

The second half was an exciting one. It began with Sidat-Singh leading the black All-Stars two thirds the length of the field for a score. Then a pass thrown by De Correvont was batted into the air by black end Charlie Anderson. When it came down, right guard Shaky Stuart was under it. He ran forty-two yards into the end zone to put the black team ahead, 20–17. The whites came back to win in the final minutes, 24–20, but they knew they had been in a ball game.

BASEBALL AND BLACKS AFTER WORLD WAR II

Cubans created problems for those interested in keeping baseball white. It was suspected that they might be black, or part black, trying to sneak into the major leagues via a side door. Therefore white racists were always on particular guard to make sure early Cuban ballplayers were genuine Spanish Caucasians. Vincent Nava (1850–1906), the first Cuban to play in the major leagues, had no particular problems during his stint with the 1882 Providence Grays and the American Association Baltimore Orioles, but by the turn of the century and afterward Americans were more suspicious. Thus, when Cincinnati owner Garry Herrmann decided to bolster his roster in 1911 by adding two Latins, Armando Marsans and Rafael Almeida, it was thought necessary to verify their backgrounds by making a special trip to Cuba or making inquiries with Cuban authorities. Both, he was informed, were "pure Caucasian."

Marsans stayed in the major leagues until 1918, Almeida through the 1913 season. They were followed by others—Jacinto (Jack) Calvo and Merito Acosta in 1913, Angel Aragon, who performed briefly in a total of 33 games for the 1914, 1916, and 1917 Yankees; Emilio Palmero and José Rodriguez with the Giants; Eusebio Gonzalez with the Red Sox; and Oscar Tuero with the St. Louis Cardinals. The most successful of all the pre-World War I imports was Adolfo (The Pride of Havana) Luque, who remained for 20 seasons, winning 194 games for the Red Sox, Reds, Dodgers, and Giants. Catcher Miguel (Mike) Gonzalez spent 17 years in the National League and even managed—but very briefly—the 1938 and 1940 Cardinals.

These importations should have made it easier for blacks to enter the major leagues, but of course they did not. Not until America entered World War II was sufficient pressure applied to force the white establishment to give blacks a chance on the playing field as well as a place on the battlefield. The Pittsburgh Pirates were first to announce that the team would try out black players, followed by a Cleveland Indian statement on September 1, 1942, that three specific players would be tested before the start of the 1943 season. The

---

The Three:
Were third baseman Parnell Woods, pitcher Eugene Bremmer, and outfielder Sam Jethroe of the Cleveland Buckeyes in the Negro-American League. Jethroe made it to the major leagues in 1950 and had three solid years with the Boston Braves. He thus became the first "bandied name" to actually take the big step.

---

war years took their manpower toll on all sports teams, but there was no lack of debate and conversation on the issue. In December 1943, Paul Robeson took time out from his concert tour to appear at the annual baseball meeting and urged Commissioner K. M. Landis to admit blacks to the game as soon as possible. Landis' reply, in the form of a statement to the press, was less than a clarion call against prejudice. "Each club is entirely free to employ Negro players to any extent it pleases," he said, "and the matter is solely for each club's decision without any restrictions whatever."

Such a response presumably did not make Mr. Robeson jump with joy. The following year, however, Congress was given a push toward investigating the problem by Representative Vito Marcantonio, the only member of the American Labor Party in the House of Representatives. "Baseball is America's greatest sport," he said, "and it's silly to pretend that Negroes are not among the best players, when we have a Negro, Joe Louis, as our boxing champion; Jesse Owen was one of our greatest track stars, and Paul Robeson, stage star, and others have been standout football players."

Meanwhile, in the St. Louis Grandstand:
Progress of a meager sort was being made. On May 4, 1944, both St. Louis clubs announced that their old policy of restricting blacks to the bleachers and pavilion at Sportsman's Park would be discontinued.

With Congress hovering in the background and the end of World War II in sight, the baseball powers moved perceptibly faster. In April 1945, Manager Joe Cronin of the Boston Red Sox took a look at three black players —Marvin Williams of Philadelphia, Sam Jethroe (who had won the 1944 batting championship in the Negro-American League), and a twenty-six-year-old former U. S. Army lieutenant and athlete from UCLA named Jackie Robinson.

Although impressed with Robinson, Cronin allowed him to get away and be signed by Branch Rickey and the Brooklyn Dodgers. The rest, as they say, is history. Robinson and John Wright, another black, reported to Montreal for the 1946 season, were subjected to a certain amount of harassment, such as being barred from playing in Jacksonville—but somehow survived. Wright never made it to the major leagues, but on Opening Day 1947, Jackie Robinson was there, the first black man to play American major-league baseball since the 1880s. Obeying Branch Rickey's orders to the letter, Robinson kept a low profile, displaying speed and ability but not too much flamboyance. A total of 26,623 Brooklyn fans attended the historic game.

The Boxscore on Robby's First Day:
The date was April 15, 1947, and Jackie Robinson's debut was surprisingly uneventful. At the plate he went zero for three, hitting into a double play that killed a Brooklyn rally. In the field he played first base flawlessly, making eleven putouts. The Dodgers won the game against the Boston Braves, 5–3.

After Robinson's success, more and more blacks were hired by major-league baseball teams, especially the Dodgers. And on July 17, 1954, the day arrived when, for the first time in major-league baseball, a majority of a team's starting lineup was made up of black players. Three decades after Jackie Robinson played his first National League game, 19 per cent of the ballplayers in both circuits were black. Robinson himself became the first black Most Valuable Player following the 1949 season, when he batted .342, drove in 124 runs, stole 37 bases, and hit 16 home runs for the pennant-winning Dodgers.

THE POSTWAR TURMOIL
After World War II, it became apparent that most blacks would no longer settle for the separate system of sports leagues that had grown up following the Civil War. Many whites were also embarrassed by the segregated facilities. The dissidents began to apply pressure that was barely felt in the beginning, but slowly and surely the old white-only system began to crumble.

BASKETBALL
One of the first black basketball teams was the Renaissance Big Five, an independent team from New York organized in 1922 by Bob Douglas. From 1932 to 1936, the Rens toured the nation, taking on all comers, and soon proved they were the best basketball squad in the country. Despite their ability, the Rens often were forced to sleep in the bus they used for traveling when many hotels refused them accommodations.

Following World War II, however, when many ex-servicemen suddenly found it comparatively simple to obtain a college education, the situation began to change. More and more blacks appeared on college and university courts, thus making it obvious that it would no longer be possible to segregate the best black players into a single traveling group such as the Rens or the Harlem Globetrotters.

Resistance to their presence soon surfaced. When Duquesne University took the court for a scheduled game against the University of Tennessee on December 23, 1946, more than twenty-six hundred fans learned that Coach John Mauer of the Vols refused to play unless assured that Charles Cooper, black freshman at Duquesne, would not play. Coach Chick Davies of Duquesne made a conditional promise, but that was not good enough for Mauer. He and his men left rather than face even the remote possibility that they would have to play against a black athlete. Two weeks later, the University of Miami announced that an outdoor game scheduled to be played in the Orange Bowl against Duquesne on January 15, 1947, was canceled. The city of Miami, it turned out, had a rule against permitting whites and blacks competing in the same athletic contest.

The 1946–47 cancellations aimed at Chuck Cooper were accepted meekly but by early

The First Majority Black Line-up—July 17, 1954:

Brooklyn	Milwaukee
GILLIAM, 2B	BRUTON, CF
Reese, SS	O'Connell, 2B
Snider, CF	Mathews, 3B
Hodges, 1B	AARON, LF
ROBINSON, 3B	Adcock, 1B
AMOROS, LF	Pafko, RF
Furillo, RF	Logan, SS
CAMPANELLA, C	Crandall, C
NEWCOMBE, P	Jolly, P

Chuck Cooper—One of the First Black Pro Basketballers:
The 1950–51 season of the National Basketball Association was the first in which black athletes played side by side with whites. Chuck Cooper spent four seasons with the Boston Celtics, one with Milwaukee, and one with Fort Wayne, scoring a total of 2,725 points (a 6.7-point average per game). Nathaniel (Sweetwater) Clifton was lured from the Harlem Globetrotters by New York. He played seven seasons for the Knicks and one for Detroit, amassing 5,444 points (a 10-point average per game).

1948 some schools had begun to fight back. That year, Kansas City was host for the National Intercollegiate basketball tournament and one of the provisions of the contract to be signed by all participating teams was that no blacks be permitted to play. Manhattan College, which had no blacks, promptly announced its intention to resign from the tourney unless the ban on black players was rescinded. Soon a major controversy developed. Long Island University and Siena College followed Manhattan's lead, turning down their invitations. At that point, the NAIB Executive Committee reversed itself and opened the tournament to blacks.

That was not the end of racial prejudice in basketball, but it was one of the more significant first steps. Within a decade, black stars in college basketball were commonplace. By 1977, nearly 65 per cent of the players on National Basketball Association rosters were black.

BOWLING

In December 1946, the American Bowling Congress received two petitions asking that body to change its membership rules, which permitted "white, male sex" players only. (One petition came from Hawaii, asking that brown persons be allowed to join; the other came from Brooklyn, requesting membership for blacks.)

Moving with all deliberate speed, the ABC erased the 1916 rule from its books—but only after spending forty thousand dollars in litigation and waiting 3½ years. The vote on removing the ban was taken on May 12, 1950, at Columbus, Ohio.

BILLIARDS

During its long history, billiards attracted few blacks. Not until March 6, 1965, was there a black world pocket billiards champion. His name was Cicero Murphy. Competing in his first world tournament at Burbank, California, Murphy compiled a 17–3 record to win the 36-day, $19,500 event.

TENNIS

Although blacks have not been associated with the game of tennis until fairly recently, many played it during the 1890s and later organized tennis clubs in New York City, Philadelphia, Baltimore, Washington, D.C., Boston, Newark, Chicago, Indianapolis, Louisville, St. Louis, Roanoke, Kansas City, and Norfolk, as well as many smaller cities of the East, Midwest, and South.

The First Black Tennis Champs:
Talley Holmes, who won the first men's singles championship at the 1917 tournament in Baltimore, was victorious again in 1918, 1921, and 1924. Other outstanding male blacks included Reginald Weir, singles champion in 1931, 1932, 1933, 1937, and 1942; and James McDaniel, titleholder in 1940, 1941, and 1942.

Some prominent black women include Lucy Slowe, winner of the 1917 women's singles, Isadora Channels, Lulu Ballard, Ora Washington, and Flora Lomax, all of whom won the championship on several occasions. (Ora Washington, in fact, won eight titles in nine years.)

In 1898 an interstate tournament was held in Philadelphia, and in August 1917 the American Tennis Association was formed. That same month, at Baltimore, the first national championships were held under the auspices of the Monumental Tennis Club. While this sort of activity provided a framework for competition and friendship, it did little to break down traditional barriers already raised against all blacks in sports. In 1929, for example, when Reginald Weir, then a student at City College of New York, and Gerald L. Norman, Jr., captain of the Flushing High School team, tried to enter a tournament sponsored by the United States Lawn Tennis Association, they were rejected by the Executive Committee. A protest by the NAACP brought forth only a letter that restated the segregation policy in terms of incredible blandness.

Reginald Weir had to wait nearly two decades before he was allowed to compete in a tournament sponsored by the USLTA. His long-awaited moment came in March 1948, at New York's 7th Regiment Armory. In the first

The USLTA Reply:
*"Answering your letter of December 24,
the policy of the United States Lawn
Tennis Association has been to decline the
entry of colored players in our championships.*

*"In pursuing this policy we make no re-
flection upon the colored race, but we
believe that as a practical matter, the
present method of separate associations for
the administration of the affairs and championships of colored and white players
should be continued."*

round, Weir easily defeated Thomas Lewyn of
Scarsdale, 6–4, 6–2, but in the second he ran
into fifth-ranked Bill Trabert, who eliminated
the talented but past-his-prime Weir, 6–1,
6–1. Nevertheless, new ground had been broken in the struggle to compete with whites on
their own territory.

After Weir, of course, Althea Gibson came
off a Harlem playground to win world ac-
claim as the first black woman to compete at
Wimbledon and in the U.S. national grass
court championships at Forest Hills, New York.
(She won both tournaments twice.) Arthur
Ashe, meanwhile, broke white male domination by winning both amateur and professional championships. Despite rising to the top
of the tennis world, however, Ashe was one of
the few black athletes who warned that excellence in sports was not necessarily a good
thing for blacks to pursue. "We have been on
the same roads—sports and entertainment—
too long," he pointed out in the New York
Times early in 1977. "We need to pull over,
fill up at the library, and speed away to
Congress and the Supreme Court, the unions
and the business world."

GOLF

Before blacks could attain equality on the
links, they had to find ways of using decent
facilities. In Baltimore, for example, blacks in
1948 were required to play on a nine-hole
course at Carroll Park that was not nearly as
good, or as challenging, as the white courses
at Mount Pleasant, Clifton, and Forest Park.
To break up this monopoly, a Baltimore
black, John E. Law, instituted a suit protesting the "present unqualified, prohibitory
regulation" that excluded blacks. On July 13,
1948, he won the case and all of the municipal links were desegregated. Louisville opened
its courses to blacks on January 1952, and the
following decades saw a similar pattern in
other cities.

Some early black golfers included Bill
Spiller and Ted Rhodes, who used California
legislation to earn their way into previously
all-white tournaments. Then, in April 1961,
Charles Sifford became the first black to play in
a PGA tournament in the South when he entered the Greater Greensboro (North Carolina) Open. He won the 1975 World Seniors
Championship in Florida. Lee Elder, meanwhile, broke down doors that had barred
blacks from the Masters tournament in Georgia.

ICE HOCKEY

Of all organized sports, ice hockey is perhaps the least integrated. Not until 1950 did a
black player emerge, Arthur Dorrington, a
Canadian who signed with the Atlantic City
Seagulls of the Eastern Amateur League.

The National Hockey League did not see its
first black until 1958, when the Boston Bruins
called up left wingman Willie O'Ree from its
farm club, the Canadian Aces. O'Ree's first
appearance in the lineup was on January 18,
1958. Boston beat Montreal 3–0, but O'Ree
did not score a goal.

FOOTBALL AGAIN

In much the same manner as basketball,
football teams with black players were forced
to cancel games, or use the threat of cancellation, when they traveled South after the
war. One such imbroglio came on November
4, 1946, the University of Nevada calling off a
scheduled game against Mississippi State when
it was learned that the southern school objected to the presence of blacks Horace Gil-
lom and Bill Bass in the Nevada lineup. The
very next day, for similar reasons, Penn State
canceled a game with the University of
Miami. "The break was very mutual," one
spokesman said.

But if the South seemed to be unrepentant,
there were a few signs of progress. On November 23, 1947, a milestone of sorts in Dixie
was reached when the third annual Piedmont

A Lofty Purpose for the Tobacco Bowl
Game:
*"We arranged this game to show subver-
sive elements in foreign countries—and
particularly in Russia—that the members
of the different races in America can play
together as well as fight a common enemy
together, as we did in the Second World
War."*
*Lewis E. Austin, president,
Piedmont Tobacco Bowl Corporation*

Tobacco Bowl game at Durham, North Carolina, pitted an all-white team against an all-black team. Even more daring, the contest was played before an audience of three thousand who were not segregated. The game, perhaps appropriately, was a 6–6 tie.

Progress seemed to continue as the University of Nevada came South in 1948 and was allowed to use its black players against Tulsa, a situation that might not have been permitted two years before. The visitors showed their gratitude by whipping Tulsa, 65–15, blacks Sherman Howard and Alva Tabor figuring prominently in a pair of touchdowns.

Then, on September 30, 1950, the first black appeared in a Southern Conference game in North Carolina as Flint Greene of the University of Pittsburgh nudged aside another portion of the traditional wall.

Just when it seemed that all was going well, however, ricidivism occurred. Spurred by Ku Klux Klan activity, which had a resurgence in parts of the South following the 1954 Supreme Court decision barring racial discrimination in public schools, some persons who were antiblack decided to make an unofficial test case out of the 1956 Sugar Bowl game. The two teams slated for the game were Georgia Tech and the University of Pittsburgh, which had a black fullback, Bobby Grier. When it was learned that Grier would be the starting fullback, a states' rights group protested that his presence would be a violation of Georgia's "laws, customs, and traditions of racial segregation." The next day, Governor Griffin of Georgia fired off a telegram to Georgia Tech Coach Bobby Dodd, urging him to join the segregationists. That night, students at the university hung the governor in effigy, but he did not withdraw his request.

In response, officials at the University of Pittsburgh made it clear that fullback Grier would "travel, eat, live, play, and practice" with the team.

The next day, December 3, two thousand students gathered in front of the governor's mansion at Atlanta. Signs proclaimed: "Griffin sits on his brains," "Grow up, Marv," and "We play anybody." More than twenty-five police patrol cars and state patrolmen armed with tear-gas bombs stood by to make certain the protest was orderly, but Governor Griffin was not disturbed by the proceedings. "They hooted and sang, and hanged me to a sour apple tree, but it was just a bunch of college boys having a good time, and I never get excited about that."

Fortunately, the Board of Regents of Georgia's university system turned down Governor Griffin's request that the game be canceled.

It Was Not the First Southern Bowl Controversy:
In the 1941 Sugar Bowl, played at New Orleans, Boston College had a black player who did not get into the game. (Boston College beat Tennessee, 19–13.) In the 1948 Cotton Bowl, Pennsylvania used several black players throughout the game as that university and Southern Methodist played a 13–13 tie.

On January 2, 1956, the game was played before a crowd of more than eighty thousand. Bobby Grier started at fullback, but suffered the ignominy of having pass interference called against him, which led to Georgia Tech's score in the 7–0 victory.

That, naturally, was not the end of racial problems in the South. As late as 1963, the Blue and Gray Association advised the National Broadcasting Company that the annual Blue-Gray game at Montgomery, Alabama, would enforce the rule against blacks and whites playing on the same field. The contest was played but NBC refused to telecast it because of the ban.

THE ORIENTALS

Despite a strong nineteenth-century prejudice against Chinese, unofficial bans against Orientals were lifted long before those against blacks. In 1928, the New York Giants announced that the team had signed a Chinese infielder, William T. Lai, who had played four years with Bridgeport in the Eastern League. After he drifted to Brooklyn to play with the semipro Bushwicks, Lai was noticed by John McGraw. He did not play in the major leagues, however.

Rather more successful was Masanori Murakami, a twenty-year-old Japanese left-handed pitcher who was signed in 1964 by the San Francisco Giants. After appearing in nine games and compiling a record of 1–0 at the end of the season, Murakami decided not to report to the Giants the next year but to return to the Nankai Hawks. Unfortunately, Murakami had signed a 1965 contract with San Francisco, a situation that brought Commissioner Ford Frick on the scene. Deciding in favor of the Giants, on February 17, 1965, Frick "severed" U.S.-Japanese relations in baseball until the problem was resolved. Eventually Murakami honored his contract and returned to San Francisco, where he won four games and lost one in 1965. He then returned to Japan.

In boxing, the first Oriental fighter to win a

world championship was Yoshio Shirai, who decisioned Dado Marino on May 19, 1952, to take the flyweight title. He subsequently defended his title four times before losing it in 1954 and retiring one year later.

BACK TO THE BLACKS

But the biggest sports success story of the twentieth century in the United States has been that of black elevation to equality and then domination. By the late 1970s, nearly half of the players in professional football were black, 65 per cent of National Basketball Association players; of the thirty-one medals won by American athletes at the Montreal Olympic Games in 1976, twenty-two were taken by black athletes. Some wondered why. Joe Morgan of the Cincinnati Reds supplied an answer when he said, "I think blacks, for psy-chological reasons, have better speed, quickness, and agility. Baseball, football, and basketball put a premium on those skills." Added O. J. Simpson: "We are built a little differently, built for speed—skinny calves, long legs, high asses are all characteristics of blacks." Whatever the explanation, by the 1970s it was apparent to nearly everyone watching sports that blacks have revolutionized nearly every game. "That is why it isn't difficult to visualize the trend of the conversation when the owners of professional sports teams gather in the 'big house' and talk about what has happened back on the plantation," wrote Sam Lacy, sports editor of the Baltimore *Afro-American* and one-time member of the Hall of Fame selection committee: " 'We shoulda left 'em in the woodpile, dammit!' "

CHAPTER 30—BREAKING THE SEX BARRIER

To most nineteenth-century Americans, the notion that men and women might someday compete on the athletic field was probably as remote as the thought of travel in space. Some even resisted the idea that women participate in sports among themselves, declaring it unladylike and lacking in dignity to move about so briskly as to work up a sweat. Even those young women who played the comparatively sedentary sport of croquet following the Civil War were admonished to display proper feminine "grace in holding and using the mallet."

But the mid-Victorian women of America were more determined and daring than later generations gave them credit for being. They took up tennis and archery almost as soon as these sports began being played by men in the United States. When rowing and pedestrianism grew in popularity, women appeared on the lakes, rivers, and tracks of the nation. Competing against each other at first, they continued to play in ever-increasing numbers until some took the ultimate revolutionary step of challenging the men.

THE LADY SCULLERS

One strenuous sport taken up surprisingly early by women was rowing, an 1870 match near Pittsburgh drawing a crowd that climbed barns and houses in order to get a better view of the Monongahela course. The contestants were a pair of sixteen-year-olds, Lottie McAlice and Maggie Lew, who agreed to race one mile for a considerable prize—a gold watch and chain plus a purse of two thousand dollars. The audience was undeterred by the young women's slow time as Lottie won in eighteen minutes, fifty-four seconds.

"The Fair Feathering the Oar" was the way the New York *Herald* headlined another women's race, which took place on the Harlem River, September 25, 1871, as part of the tenth annual regatta of the Empire City Rowing Club. On this occasion five young women rowed seventeen-foot workboats around a two-mile course that was cluttered with other vessels. "The affair was most disgraceful," one reporter wrote, "and beyond a doubt all of the rowers should have been called back and a fresh start given." Somehow the ladies maneuvered their way through the boats, however, first place going to Amelia Shean in the

Glen. Her winning time was eighteen minutes, thirty-two seconds. Elizabeth Custarce in the *Shoo Fly* came in second. Later, the young women rowed in groups of twos, Miss Custarce and Annie Harris taking that event, for which they won a gold watch.

MARY MARSHALL

No sports encyclopedia mentions Mary Marshall—not even on the hind end of an asterisk —which is strange, because she was the first of her sex to take on a man in a head-to-head (or more precisely, foot-to-foot) professional sports event.

In 1876, Mary Marshall of Chicago was 26 years old, 5 feet, 3 inches tall, weighed 135 pounds, and had been a professional pedestrian for less than a year. The sport of pedestrianism was the fad of the 1870s, and because it called for endurance rather than pure speed, it attracted women. Mary Marshall, following the tradition of the times, raced only against other ladies, one of her more important matches coming early in 1876 against an opponent named Bertha Von Hillern.

As her name suggests, Bertha was a strong Teutonic type. The Baltimore *American* described her as having a "stocky" body with "stalwart" ankles and a face that "is not a handsome one, but is far from being unattractive." A veteran pedestrian, Bertha had walked in Berlin against the clock and most recently had defeated another woman at Peoria. Dressed in somber colors, wearing a black derby and carrying a whip at her side, Bertha Von Hillern presented a formidable appearance on the pedestrian oval.

On the last day of January 1876, Mary Marshall and Bertha began a 6-day competition at Chicago's 2nd Regiment Armory for a purse of $1,000. The women hoped to cover 300 miles during the period, but at the end of the sixth day, Mary Marshall had completed only 234 miles to Bertha's 231. Complaining of unfairness on the part of the referee, Bertha then left town after issuing a challenge for a rematch "anywhere but in Chicago."

The rematch between the two women took place at New York City's Central Park Garden in early November. This time, however, Mary Marshall's feet began to give her trouble after only 75 miles. "She changed her

A Previous Male-female Match, but with a Handicap:

The Marshall-Van Ness match was not the first time man and woman had raced against each other, but it was the first time there was no handicap. In March 1875, at Barnum's Hippodrome, New York, there was a match between William E. Harding and a Mlle. Lola, "a lady pedestrian." The bet was that Harding could complete 50 miles in less time than Mlle. Lola could do 30. Averaging a mile every 13 minutes, Mlle. Lola won the bet by finishing her 30 miles 19 minutes ahead of Harding's time for 50.

shoes twice during the walk," one reporter noted, "her feet having swelled a great deal." Despite obvious discomfort, Mary plodded onward. After 5 days she trailed Bertha, 213 miles to 221, but on one occasion Mary was forced to retire for 3 hours—her left ankle was swollen and a huge blister had developed on the heel of the same foot. Nevertheless, she finished the race, completing 281 miles by the end of the 6 days. Bertha, moving ahead relentlessly, accomplished 323½ miles.

Undaunted by the loss, Mary Marshall issued a challenge to Peter L. Van Ness, a Philadelphia pedestrian who happened to be in New York at the time, to a 3-day race, the winner of any 2 days taking $500 in prize money. Not proud, Van Ness agreed. He was far from the best male pedestrian in New York—he lacked endurance, according to the *Sun*—but he was a strong physical specimen who could walk a mile in less than 10 minutes. Even with his limitations, few doubted that Van Ness could fail to outwalk a mere woman over a 20-mile distance 2 evenings out of 3—especially a woman with a proclivity for sore feet.

The scene of the Van Ness-Marshall contest was a track of packed earth and sawdust 240 feet around and four feet wide, there being 22 revolutions per mile. Interest in the race was high: Central Park Garden was filled with people when the race began at 7:04 P.M., November 17, 1876. Peter Van Ness, as expected, moved quickly into the lead, although "neither appeared desirous of making very good time," according to one reporter. It was soon noticed that Mary Marshall's foot was not completely healed, for she walked with a slight limp. At the end of 8 miles, Peter Van Ness retired "for refreshment" after having turned in a succession of near-10-minute miles. Mary, playing tortoise to his hare,

averaged a mile every 14 minutes, but completed 10 of them without a break.

Van Ness, not noticeably alarmed, appeared on the track as Mary reached the halfway mark and promptly "spurted" his ninth mile in 9 minutes, 45 seconds. During the next 4 miles he cut deeply into Mary's lead, then left the track for a second rest period. Mary plodded ahead in her unspectacular manner until, too late, Van Ness suddenly realized he was nearly out of the race. A determined spurt failed to close the gap, Mary completing her 20 miles about 1⅓ miles before Van Ness.

The next evening, Peter Van Ness adopted a more determined attitude, although it was soon obvious that even at his best he needed more rest than Mary. "He walked rapidly away from her at the start," the New York *Sun* reported, "and made his first 6 miles in 1 hour and 7 minutes, before she had completed her fifth mile. He continued to increase his lead until the end of the tenth mile and then he retired from the track much exhausted, 2¼ miles ahead."

By continuing her steady pace, Mary made Van Ness work hard to win the second night's competition. The stage was set for the deciding match, which began with Van Ness completing 10 miles in 1 hour, 55 minutes. He was more than 2 miles ahead of Mary Marshall, but once again he left the track for a 45-minute rest period. When he reappeared, Mary was ahead, but he caught her at the 13-mile mark and continued to improve until he arrived at 15 miles, at which point Peter Van Ness again ran out of gas. Mary Marshall moved ahead to win the third and deciding match. Some newspapers were inclined to be condescending ("Van Ness on Friday night walked his 20 miles in nearly 2 hours less than

Ada Anderson's Marathons Against the Clock:

A year after the Van Ness-Marshall matches, an English music-hall performer who called herself Mme. Ada Anderson further popularized pedestrianism for women by announcing that she intended to walk 3,000 quarter miles in 3,000 quarter hours. More than 2,000 customers showed up at Brooklyn's Mozart Hall, paying $1.00 each for standing room and $2.00 for a reserved seat. (A bit more than a month later, Mme. Anderson achieved her goal and picked up nearly $10,000 for her efforts. The feat set off a wave of female pedestrian matches from one coast of the nation to the other.

that occupied by Miss Marshall on Saturday night," the *Evening Post* remarked); others were happy for the victorious woman, describing her as "plucky." Thus ended the first sports competition between the sexes in the United States.

Mary Marshall apparently called it quits after that glorious moment. Both Peter Van Ness and Bertha Von Hillern continued walking competitively, but no mention is made of the diminutive Mary Marshall.

It may have been a case of deciding to retire while at the very pinnacle of success. Or it may have been simply a matter of chronic sore feet.

AGNES BECKWITH

One of the first authentic woman athletes of the nineteenth century was young Agnes Beckwith, who thrilled sports fans of both England and America with her ability. Although she did not compete directly against men, she did compete against their common enemies: time and tide.

An expert swimmer for a decade by the time she was fourteen, Agnes created an immediate sensation in 1875 when she decided to swim part of the Thames River from London Bridge to Greenwich, a distance of about six miles. "For a powerful man, the feat may not be an over-difficult one," the London *Times* of September 1, 1875, noted, "but it is a test of some endurance for a slight young girl like the performer of yesterday."

News of Agnes' skill and endurance—along with subsequent attempts to imitate her—soon reached America. In the days and weeks that followed her initial swim, Agnes continued to look for new challenges, for public swimming obviously had become a way of life for her. The distances she traveled grew longer and more difficult and she even developed some tricks to amuse her audiences as she paddled along. On one occasion, according to the London *Echo,* she "passed her body through a hoop—a feat which elicited a special cheer."

Inevitably, promoters found ways of bringing Agnes indoors so as to better exploit her talents. In 1880, she turned up in the whale tank of the Royal Aquarium at Westminster to prove that she could emulate the feat of Matthew Webb by treading water or otherwise stay afloat for thirty hours without stopping. "It was as refreshing as it was interesting," the *Standard* reported, "to witness this graceful young 'naiad' clad in her *costume du bain* trimmed with crimson, disporting herself in her aqueous abode."

Not long afterward, the Beckwith family departed for America, arriving in June 1883. Though not yet twenty-two, Agnes was lionized as a celebrity of the first rank. She was described as "under medium height" with a "pleasing face, with light blue eyes and blond hair, which clings about her head in curls." Along with brother William, who was lauded as "the champion swimmer of the world," Agnes was promoted as "the woman who holds the female championship of the same planet."

The arena in which the Beckwiths performed was called the Forty-fifth Street Natatorium, and through it passed a parade of spectators eager to see the agile Agnes. The act worked up by the Beckwiths was a mixture of athletic skill and hokum, for it had been correctly decided that Americans wanted to see only so much of the endurance display; after that, they wanted to see some action. And so they were given action. William dived beneath the surface and devoured a pair of sponge cakes, then drank a bottle of milk and smoked a pipe with the bowl above the surface. Everyone was quite impressed. "In fact," one reporter wrote, "it would seem that he might as well stay under altogether, for if a man can eat, drink, and smoke underwater during the hot weather New York is at present experiencing, it is folly to come above the surface to be roasted. . . ."

Agnes' part of the act was rather more chic. Clad in "flesh tights and a very decollete bodice," she was described as "walking" in the water "with her hands above her head," then "waltzing in the aqueous fluid" and performing a routine known as "the prayer." The prayer, a reporter for the New York *Times* noted sardonically, "is recommended for steamboat collisions and ocean wrecks, as it gives one an opportunity to pray for help while he or she paddles ashore."

As a grand finale, William imitated a porpoise, while Agnes, accompanied by the music of two pianos, performed a rhythmic ballet on the surface that was compared by the *Sun* to "the gambols of the sea lions in the tank at Central Park."

The Beckwith show at the Natatorium touched off a variety of similar acts, so Agnes decided to return to the open sea. In order to show that women had as much stamina as men, she proposed to swim from Sandy Hook, New Jersey, to the pier at Rockaway Beach, New York, a distance of twenty miles. But three quarters of the way across, frustrated by a vicious tide and high waves, Agnes was forced to give up. In a rather unsporting manner, she preferred to blame the failure not on her own lack of ability but on the pilot's misreading of the tides. "This is a swindle," she said succinctly, and then returned to England.

THE LADY BALLPLAYERS

Because of its popularity with the public at large and comparative lack of physical contact, it was inevitable that baseball extend its appeal to women. The breakthrough came during the 1880s, when a group of daring young women decked themselves out in flowing skirts and played a series of exhibition games at Philadelphia, Newark, and New York City. Most viewed the spectacle as either humorous or erotic, but for some reason the New York *Times* chose to term one 1883 game "a ridiculous exhibition." (Perhaps tampering with the "national game" was more than a sense of outraged patriotism could tolerate.) Despite the criticism and laughter, the women journeyed in September 1883 to New York, where a crowd of about fifteen hundred assembled on the grounds of the Manhattan Athletic Club at Eighty-sixth Street and Eighth Avenue. The game then began, the "blondes" vs. the "brunettes." Their outfits, it was reported, were "bathing dresses of the ancient and honorable order. The loose body had a long flowing skirt, which reached below the knees. Stockings of the regulation style, baseball shoes, and white caps completed the outfit. The dresses were neatly, but not gaudily, trimmed with white braid. The hair was either coiled tightly at the back of the head or worn in long plaits, tied up in ribbon of a color that pleased the wearer's fancy."

Making Fun of the Women:
"All the girls handled the ball in the same way. The right arm was doubled and the hand brought near to the face, then a sudden jerk threw it thirty feet or so. In catching all the girls held their hands out in front of them, with the palms up; and if the ball was well directed, and came at a nice curve they caught it well enough; but if it came straight and fast their courage failed and they got out of the way without delay. . . . It was evident from the start that the diamond of the regulation size was entirely too large for the girls either for running or throwing. A ball thrown from pitcher to second base almost invariably fell short, and was stopped on the roll. The throw from third to first was an utter impossibility. . . ."

A satirical description of the exhibition followed. "When the Blues [blondes] went to bat, Miss P. Darlington, pitcher for the Reds [brunettes], proceeded to tie up her back hair a little tighter. Then she put another hair pin in her hair, seized the ball recklessly, drew back her arm, and let fly viciously. Miss Moore responded gracefully by whacking a lively grounder to first base. The first basewoman made a wild grab, but did not touch the ball, whereupon the runner got around to third, while the other side pegged the ball all over the field. Finally Miss Williams went to bat and hit a daisy cutter to shortstop, who promptly threw it as far as she could into right field. (immense applause) Miss Moore ran home."

And so it went, the score at the end of the first inning being Brunettes 16, Blondes 3. "When five innings had been played," the reporter wrote, "the game was called. The girls heaved long sighs of relief." The final score was Brunettes 54, Blondes 22.

Such satirical treatment could have ended women's participation in baseball, but it did not. Seven years later, the *National Police Gazette* of September 20, 1890, reported the existence of a women's baseball club that was not only competent, but also played men's clubs as well. None of the participants of "Young Ladies' Baseball Club No. 1" ever became famous, but it is likely that all of them found what they were looking for—the chance to compete athletically and have the exhilaration of an occasional victory.

Line-up: Young Ladies' Baseball Club No. 1
W. S. Franklin, manager
May Howard, Pitcher-captain
Nellie Williams, catcher
Kittie Grant, first base
Angie Parker, second base
Edith Mayres, third base
Effie Earl, shortstop
Alice Lee, third base
Rose Mitchell, right field
Annie Grant, center field

ROSE COGHLAN, PIGEON SHOOTER

It is difficult to imagine ladies of the Victorian era pulling off a rifle shot at a pigeon—much less hitting it—but by the 1880s some women had distinguished themselves as expert marksmen, or more properly, markspersons. One of the best was Miss Rose Coghlan of the Philadelphia Gun Club, who on the afternoon of May 6, 1887, made her initial attempt at trap shooting after having succeeded quite well at target shooting with rifle and pistol. After thirty minutes' practice, she agreed to shoot against Messrs. Patterson and Robertson, both of the club. The trap was sprung and a "good strong" pigeon flapped into the air. Miss Coghlan fired and the bird spun to the ground. Suppressing their amazement, the two men downed their birds, then two more each as Miss Coghlan missed. But at the end of ten tries each, the score was tied, 7–7–7. The match was discontinued because of increasing darkness. Miss Coghlan, an actress, expressed delight at having broken the ladies' amateur record. "The party returned to the city in time for the evening performance," one reporter concluded, "but the lady is not apt to embrace very earnestly on the stage for a day or two on account of a rather sore shoulder caused by a kicking gun."

The Mixed Shooting Match—May 6, 1887:

Coghlan	1	0	0	1	1	1	1	0	1	1—7
Patterson	1	1	1	1	1	1	0	1	0	0—7
Robertson	1	1	1	1	1	1	0	1	0	0—7

ANNIE TAYLOR—FIRST OVER THE FALLS IN A BARREL

"I did what no other woman in the world had nerve enough to do, only to die a pauper."

Annie Edson Taylor might have added "no other man" to her last statement to the press, made shortly before her death in 1921, for twenty years earlier no one of either sex had been able to negotiate Niagara Falls in a barrel.

Why anyone wanted to perform such a feat remains something of a mystery. It is not really an athletic accomplishment, although one might conclude that a young and athletic person would have a better chance to survive the fall than an older sedentary daredevil.

Annie Edson Taylor, a forty-three-year-old widow from Bay City, Michigan, was hardly in the prime of life when she suddenly decided in 1901 that she would be first over Niagara. She was teaching grade school at the time, a plump little lady who announced to her students that she intended to "shoot the falls." Her reason was quite simple: "Nobody has ever done that," she said, and off she went.

At 160 pounds, Annie was not in the best physical shape of her life, and that was not her only liability when it came to shooting the Falls at Niagara. She had never tried anything particularly daring before. Nor could she swim. Her motivation, then, must have been to gamble everything in order to escape the gray decades of loneliness ahead of her, to become somebody by performing a feat of derring-do unparalleled in American history.

In any event, not long after making her an-nouncement, she arrived at Niagara Falls, where she gave a barrelmaker named Bocenchia specifications for her vehicle. The barrel, made of Kentucky oak, was to be 4½ feet high, 3 feet in diameter at the top, and tapering to 15 inches at the bottom. Bound by seven iron hoops, it was weighted at the bottom by a 100-pound anvil so that Annie would float upright. Inside, the barrel was lined with leather and had a pair of strong leather loops for her elbows.

Before receiving her barrel, Annie made a test with her own jerry-built barrel with a cat inside as a passenger. Several men who watched her prepare for the test told Annie that her barrel design was faulty, that the vehicle would fall to pieces. They were wrong. The barrel was retrieved in a nearly perfect condition, although the same could not be said of the poor cat.

And so it was that on Thursday, October 24, 1901, Annie Taylor and her specially designed barrel arrived at Port Day, about a mile above the main falls. Downstream a substantial crowd awaited to see if Annie, dressed in a long black dress and large hat, would have the nerve to carry out her stunt. A boatman named Fred Truesdale showed up promptly at two o'clock but another named Fred Robinson was late. After talking with police officers, who informed him that he might be in serious trouble if Miss Taylor were killed, Robinson announced, "I ain't going to be a party to the murder of any woman." Truesdale apparently was not bothered, loading the barrel into his boat and towing it to Grass Island, at which point it was dropped into the water and towed into the center of the stream. Also at that point, the modest Miss Taylor took off her long garments and changed into a short skirt. *"Au revoir,"* she said as she slipped her arms into the leather harness and tried to make herself comfortable in the cushioned barrel. "I'll not say 'good-bye' because I'm coming back."

On Niagara Falls:
"Every American bride is taken there and the sight must be of the earliest, if not the keenest, disappointments in American married life."

Oscar Wilde, 1882

At three-fifty the boat pulled away from Grass Island, seeking a current that would carry Annie over the Falls at the center, which was her only chance for survival.

At four-five, Annie was set adrift. Now, as

one reporter put it, "she was at the mercy of currents in waters that never before have been known to spare a human life once in its grasp." The current was quite swift but Annie floated nicely in an upright position for the greater part of the trip through the rapids above the Falls. About twenty minutes after being cast loose, the barrel was about three hundred feet from the Canadian side when it paused on the very edge of the cataract, caught on a sunken rock. Then it plunged over.

The crowd gasped as the barrel disappeared into the mists, but about one minute later it could be seen at the base of the Falls, still very much intact. Then "the current cast it aside in an eddy and, floating back upstream, it was held between two eddies until captured at four-forty."

As engineer John Ross hooked the barrel and prevented it from moving back into the currents, he could hear no sound from inside. A hush fell over the crowd as he pried off the lid—which was accomplished only with great difficulty. "My God, she's alive!" Ross shouted. Spectators broke into cheers and boat whistles added to the chorus of joy.

Annie's condition, however, was less than perfect. "She has a three-inch cut in her scalp back of the right ear," a reporter noted, "but how or when she got it she does not know. She complains of pain between the shoulders, but this is thought to be from the fact that her shoulders were thrown back during the plunge, as she had her arms in straps, and these undoubtedly saved her neck from breaking."

Although Annie temporarily lost consciousness during the passage over the Falls, she remembered enough of the overall experience to proffer a bit of advice to potential followers. "Nobody ought ever to do that again," she murmured before allowing herself to be led along the shore to a boat and taken to the *Maid of the Mist* dock. Three doctors accompanied her to a nearby hospital, where she was examined more extensively. They pronounced her quite well, although "so severe was the shock that she wanders in her talk. . . ."

Assuming the title "Queen of the Mist," Annie settled back and waited for the riches to roll in, but her career after that one moment of glory was a bitter disappointment. Part of it was Annie's fault. She had little sex appeal and her lectures tended to be boring. Audiences apparently had difficulty associating the squat, homely teacher with her daredevil deed. Thus the fame and fortune Annie expected never materialized after she was released from the hospital. Even more demoralizing, she was later seduced by an opportunist who not only loved her and left, but stole her barrel as well. Shipping it out West, he found himself a dance-hall girl who seemed much more the type who would have shot the Falls and used her and the barrel as a means of living affluently ever after.

A MORE FORTUNATE DAREDEVIL

Mary Myers was not the first American woman to take off in a balloon, but as "Carlotta the Lady Aeronaut" she undoubtedly was the most famous woman balloonist of the late nineteenth century.

Happily for her career, Mary married a young scientist named Carl, who developed an interest in aerial navigation and encouraged his young wife to accompany him and even solo. On July 4, 1880, Mary's maiden voyage took place at Little Falls, New York, where a crowd of fifteen thousand gathered for holiday festivities.

Rising to an altitude of about a mile, Mary and her balloon headed eastward before becoming lost in a cloudbank—"the lonesomest place I was ever in." After breaking into the clear, the young woman released several pigeons to the folks back in Mohawk, New York, telling them how the flight was progressing, then descended after thirty-five minutes aloft. The experience had been invigorating. She decided to continue ballooning as a career.

Soon she was a frequent attraction at fairs and expositions, but her career nearly came to an end on her third flight, in September 1880. In her haste to perform her act before a storm approached and scattered her audience, Mary took off just as dark clouds enveloped the fairgrounds. The turbulence was soon so dense that even the balloon above her was lost to view. Worse, Mary had no control over the vehicle; she let out gas in the hopes it would bring her to the ground, but the balloon continued to be carried high into the clouds. After breaking through the top of the thunderheads, she released even more gas and plunged back into the darkness of the storm clouds. The descent was a harrowing one, Mary having to throw out the balloon's anchor and hook onto a tree. The trip was over, but the vehicle and pilot were eighty feet above the ground. Men with rope and ladders eventually rescued the young woman.

The frightening experience failed to bother Mary Myers. The following year, after giving birth to a daughter—christened Elizabeth Aerial—she returned to the air. By this time she had become so knowledgeable about aerial navigation that she was able to predict approximately where she would land her balloon, a feat that was aided by her development of a basket with a tiltable bottom, which helped guide her descent. In 1886, Mary Myers ascended from Philadelphia to a height of nearly four miles, and two years later, flew her balloon *Zephyr* on a prearranged course around New York City as thousands watched. When she finally gave up her career in 1891, Carl Myers said, "She retires from the field with a record of having made more ascensions than all other women combined throughout the world, and more than any man living in America."

THE "FAIR MOTORISTS"

Not long after the first automobile races and two years before the initial Indianapolis 500, a group of women decided that driving sounded like fun. They proceeded to organize a long-distance (New York to Philadelphia and return) race for a grand prize of a bronze figure valued at about a hundred dollars. The rules stated that no man would be allowed in any car, even as a passenger, but the women were allowed to be followed by men in other cars who could be called upon to "change tires or parts, replenish the supplies of gasoline and water, or do any other of the unpleasant work in connection with handling their cars in the race."

The dozen woman-driven cars left New York on January 11, 1909. First to arrive at the Philadelphia line was Mrs. J. Newton Cuneo, at the wheel of a Lancia, followed by Mrs. A. W. Seaman in a Franklin and Mrs. Alice Ramsey in her Maxwell. Six others followed at ragged intervals. The day's run, over good roads for the time, was an exciting one. "The run from New Brunswick to Trenton," one reporter noted, "a distance of 31.7 miles, was made in an hour flat. . . . The pace was maintained at high speed all the time, and the men drivers of the escorting cars were put to it to keep up with the women."

Burlington, New Jersey, proved to be the undoing of some of the women. Broad Street in that community, known then to many citizens as "muddy hollow," was the only section of road from New York to Philadelphia unpaved at the time. Well bunched when they arrived in the town, the contestants were forced to scatter, a circumstance that did several of them in. One woman attempted to use the sidewalk but it was too narrow and she ended up wedged between two trees. Another car, which collided with hers, was also put out of the race. A third woman, trying to circumvent "muddy hollow" by crossing the railroad tracks, ruptured a tire. A fourth vehicle ran onto a mound of earth and was not worked free until evening.

After arriving in New York, the women, although exhausted, agreed that the race was a wonderful event that should be run at frequent intervals. Prizes were awarded to Mmes. Ramsey, Cuneo, Seaman, Buckman, and Heyes.

BERTHA RAPP, NO BUM AS A WRESTLER

Putting the lie to the later belief that pre-World War I persons were incurable prudes, the committee of the White Star liner *Adriatic* agreed to allow a passenger named Bertha Rapp ("a teacher of calisthenics at a Cincinnati school") take on all comers, men included, in a special Fourth of July wrestling tournament.

The year was 1911, and Miss Rapp, at 5 feet, 9 inches and 150 pounds was certain she could beat anyone on the ship. Arthur Libby, 140 pounds, and George Larmann, 185 pounds, thought otherwise. The first- and second-class passengers who heard of the upcoming matches could hardly believe their ears, but very few of them stayed away.

And so it was that the first midocean mixed wrestling matches were held.

Rapp vs. Libby began soon after Bertha entered the designated area, dressed in a gray sweater, gray skirt, and dark tights. Three minutes into the second five-minute round, Bertha Rapp hurled the lighter man to the mat and pinned him.

The crowd roared its approval as Miss Rapp bowed modestly. After a brief interval for rest, George Larmann entered and soon proved a much more worthy foe. Nevertheless, after twenty minutes, Bertha succeeded in throwing him twice into the air. He, in turn, managed to heave her five feet off the mat, but neither could pin the other. The match was finally declared a draw, although it was conceded that Bertha had made a better showing.

When asked why she had put on such a daring exhibition, Miss Rapp's answer was brief: "Practice," she said.

Athletics, the Love Cure:
"Any athletic girl, American or English, is not as apt to marry as young as the typical society girl. The society girl lives in the atmosphere of dancing, of music, of soft lights, and of flattery. I don't say that society isn't necessary to a girl's development, but I do mean that athletics are the best antidote for the poison of premature love affairs."
May Sutton, November 5, 1909
(later May Sutton Bundy, first woman elected to the Tennis Hall of Fame)

WOMEN AND THE WATER

The best way to prove themselves the equal of male athletes, women knew, was to accomplish feats as dangerous and demanding of energy as those undertaken by men. Inspired by the example of Agnes Beckwith, women swimmers of the late nineteenth and early twentieth centuries were in the forefront of those demanding—and finding ways to prove —their equality.

Some said, a quarter century after Matthew Webb swam the English Channel, that it would never be crossed again by a swimmer, man or woman. Mme. Walburga von Isacescu, an Austrian amateur swimming champion, was determined to disprove that statement when she splashed out of a bathing box outside the Calais Casino, the first woman to make a serious assault on the Channel. It was September 6, 1900, and the weather conditions were perfect.

Accompanied by the steam tug *Jeannette* which carried a group of gentlemen to verify her feat, and a physician, Mme. Isacescu swam quickly into the Channel, alternating breast strokes and side strokes for three hours, at which time she was nearly halfway across the 20.6-mile expanse of water. But there was bad news as well as good. Her progress had been slowed by a strong eastward tide, rather heavier than expected, and as a result she was in sight of the lightship *Walden*. That meant she was too far east to offset the surging tide. The French coast was well out of sight, however, and Mme. Isacescu decided to continue the effort.

She paused first to eat two eggs, several lumps of sugar, and drink a glass of port wine, then forged ahead. But by five-thirty, a heavy mist settled over the water and the sea turned choppy. Almost within sight of the Kentish coast, the woman was forced to give up. She had been in the water for nearly twelve hours.

Eleven years later, Thomas W. Burgess of London, England, became the second to conquer the Channel. The assault continued into the 1920s, but no woman had been able to make a serious effort. Then, in August of 1925, two women seemed strong enough and determined to enter a woman's name alongside those five men who had made the trip.

One was Jeanne Sion of France, the other Gertrude Ederle of New York City, an eighteen-year-old sensation who had burst into prominence three years earlier by winning the 3½-mile International Race for the Day Cups in New York Harbor. She then established new records for the 150-yard and 500-meter swim and represented the United States at the 1924 Olympics. Miss Ederle's only problem seemed to be the cold water of the Channel, which she said reached lower temperatures than anything she had encountered on the American Atlantic Coast. Nevertheless, she was established as a 7–1 favorite by the end of July 1925.

Meanwhile, Jeanne Sion decided to try beating Gertrude to the punch. After Lillian Harrison, another aspirant, failed, Miss Sion entered the water between Boulogne and Calais and headed toward Dover. The first reports of her effort seemed to indicate that she was doing well, that she was only nine miles from the English coast. But once again the treacherous tide became a factor. Cold currents added to the young Frenchwoman's problems as the afternoon faded into dusk and then evening. Thirteen and one-half hours after leaving France, Jeanne Sion gave up, exhausted and numb with cold. She was 1¼ miles from Dover.

On Thursday, August 18, 1925, Gertrude Ederle left Boulogne on a tug for Cape Gris-Nez, the jumping-off point for her own attempt. The calm sea, warm water, and light currents indicated that it was the most favorable time of the year for the strong American. The one disconcerting note was a report that sharks had been captured off the coast near her starting point, which only caused Gertrude to laugh. Preparations to accompany the young woman across the Channel included the use of a Gramophone in a rowboat to play special jazz music, a gift of the Women's Swimming Association of New York.

At 7:12 A.M., Gertrude entered the water, starting as if she would break the Channel swim in record time. For eight hours she continued the strenuous pace, accomplishing 23½ miles and pulling herself to within sight of the British shoreline. But experts later said her pace had been too strong, for she lost control

---

The Male Channel Swimmers:

1. Matthew Web	Eastbourne, England	August 24–25, 1875
2. Thomas W. Burgess	London, England	Sept. 5–6, 1911
3. Henry Sullivan	Lowell, Massachusetts	August 5–6, 1923
4. Enrique Tiraboschi	Buenos Aires, Argentina	August 11–12, 1923
5. Charles Toth	Boston, Massachusetts	Sept. 8–9, 1923

of her stroke all of a sudden and could do little more than flail the water for more than an hour. Shortly before 4:00 P.M. she was in a state of virtual collapse when Ishak Helmy, the Egyptian swimmer and Jabez Wolfe, her trainer, helped her into the boat.

A year later, the women's channel-swimming competition started again when Miss Clare Belle Barrett of Pelham Manor, New York, swam within two miles of Dover before finding herself enveloped in a fog bank. She was also quite exhausted after being in the water twenty-one hours, thirty-five minutes (her trainer, Walter Brickett, estimated that she made 26,400 strokes), so she gave up the struggle.

That was the break Gertrude Ederle needed. Just after seven o'clock on the morning of August 6, 1926, she plunged into the water of the French coastline and headed toward England. Moving with a steady crawl of 28 strokes to the minute, she was admonished by Thomas Burgess—who swam the Channel in 1911 and helped train Miss Ederle—to "take it easy . . . take your time."

A pair of tugs followed the swimmer, who made excellent progress until she reached mid-Channel. There the group of enthusiastic followers paused to sing "The Star-Spangled Banner" and shout words of encouragement to the nineteen-year-old woman. All continued favorably until six o'clock that evening when, with the British shore looming temptingly close, the tide changed against Gertrude. For more than 3 hours she struggled against it, driven by the knowledge that any sudden shift in the tide would be all she needed to become the first woman to conquer the English Channel. Making for Deal instead of Shakespeare Cliff or St. Margaret's Bay, points favored by other swimmers, she finally felt the current flow in a more favorable direction. By nine o'clock she was off Kingsdown. Less than an hour later, happy and smiling, she waded ashore. Her time, 14 hours, 31 minutes, was nearly 2 hours faster than Tiraboschi's best male time.

Bad Timing by the *Daily News*:
Wrote the London Daily News *editorialist on the day Gertrude Ederle crossed the English Channel with the fastest time by man or woman: "Even the most uncompromising champion of the rights and capacities of women must admit that in contests of physical skill, speed, and endurance they must remain forever the weaker sex."*

Americans, overjoyed at the young woman's accomplishment, treated Trudy Ederle to a glorious ticker-tape parade when she returned home. Nor was that the end of English Channel swimming and women's triumphs that summer of 1926. Three weeks after Gertrude Ederle struggled ashore at Kingsdown, Mrs. Clemington Corson of New York rose from the foam beneath the white Shakespeare Cliffs at Dover, having crossed in 15½ hours. Distressed at not being the first woman to make the journey—she had tried and failed in 1923—Mrs. Corson was able to exult that she was the first mother to do so. Her time was better than that of any man.

Will Rogers on the Women Swimmers:
(After Ederle) : *"Immigration authorities are barring any woman that comes from America if she is found to have a bathing suit. Is there any way I can change my sex? I am becoming humiliated."*
(After Corson) : *"Another American woman just now swam in from France. Her husband was carried from the boat suffering from cold and exposure. She has two children, the smallest a girl, who is swimming over tomorrow."*

THE LONG DEBATE

The double crossing of Gertrude Ederle and Mrs. Corson seemed to end speculation that there was no physical activity, save child-bearing, at which women could equal men. Before their accomplishments, a genial debate had been carried on for a quarter century. Victorian women seldom indulged in vigorous athletics, but that situation changed after the turn of the century. By 1913, more than two hundred schools in the New York City area had athletic clubs for seventeen thousand women members, and while few persons were daring enough to suggest that the ladies should compete in the manner of men, hardly anyone railed against the fair sex coming out of its whalebone corsets and stays.

Some men, such as Maurice Daly, even suggested that women possessed great skills in certain areas. Mr. Daly's specialty, of course, was billiards, and in 1915 he was bold enough to claim that women could be the equal of men at that game. He pointed to young May Kaarlus (see "1901"), Mrs. Bertha May King, and a Miss Clearwater as examples of young women who had achieved a high degree of success at billiards. And even as Daly advocated the opening of billiard rooms to women, a new form of entertainment known as the "billiard tea" already had been inaugurated. One of the most celebrated billiard teas had taken place at the White House during the administration of William H. Taft, who invited wives of his Cabinet members to an afternoon of light refreshment and pool playing in the Blue Room. On hand to discuss the fine points of the game was young Willie Hoppe, America's champion billiardist. Mrs. Nicholas Longworth, daughter of former President Teddy Roosevelt, and Miss Helen Taft, daughter of the President, were described as having "much skill in the manipulation of the ivories."

Said Daly on Women Billiard Players:
"It is by all means a woman's game, for, by reason of their sensitive development, they possess a greater delicacy of touch, enabling them to manipulate the more subtle situations that continually arise in position play. They are better equipped with a nervous force for executing the technical nursing play that yields all the large runs. The reason women have not attained the same perfection as men is, owing to a prejudice that has existed for years, namely that the club and billiard rooms are not the places for women to mingle and enjoy themselves."

After the women Channel swimmers showed that it could be done, others ventured into formerly all-male sports. Contact sports were avoided in favor of those in which feminine attributes (less weight, more patience) could be brought into play. Thus women early turned to horseracing as a professional occupation at which they could excel. On October 8, 1925, feminists received a shot in the arm when it was revealed that for the first time since it was inaugurated by King Charles II in 1665, the Newmarket Town four-mile race had been won by a woman jockey. Competing against four other women and three men, eighteen-year-old Eileen Joel brought Hogier home by three lengths in the oldest turf event in history. In France women jockeys quickly became so popular that races in which they participated were advertised as special events. Some men objected, of course. One, Comte de Pourtalis of the French Jockey Club, said, "There is nothing beautiful about the efforts a jockey has to make during a race. Why should any pretty woman want to go through such contortions or such a trial of strength?" The fashionable French riding master, M. de Cornuaud, added that women did not have

sufficient strength in the knees or arms to control a horse, particularly a thoroughbred, from the beginning to the end of a race.

Women Jockeys of the 1920s—Not the First
Before Eileen Joel won the Newmarket Town Plate, there had been two well-established woman jockeys working for several years in England. Even the first of these, a Miss Rickaby, can hardly be considered innovative when one examines the case of Alicia Meynell, who, riding under the name Mrs. Thornton, defeated a leading English jockey of the day, Buckle, in an 1805 race.

Once again, some women were not deterred by the "facts." One was English-born Judy Johnson of Farmingdale, Long Island, who first applied to the Maryland Jockey Club for a license in 1927 but was turned down because no woman had been issued one before that time. She persisted, however, and by the early 1930s was a regular winner against male jockeys on tracks in New Jersey and New York. In October and November 1933 she was at top form, winning three races in a single day on October 7 at Commack, Long Island, another triple on November 12, and a pair the following day. Ten years later, on April 27, 1943, she rode Lone Gallant in a steeplechase race at Pimlico, marking the first time in Maryland history that a woman rode professionally. Unfortunately, the horse selected for Miss Johnson's debut was not the finest (in its previous performance, with a male jockey, it finished four hundred lengths behind the winner), but Judy managed to bring Lone Galant home only thirty lengths behind. She finished tenth in a field of eleven.

Other women, meanwhile, were doing their best to compete with men in other sports, although some famous women athletes, such as tennis star Helen Wills Moody, doubted that top female athletes would ever be able to achieve true equality. Golf champion Maureen Orcutt disagreed, stating that except for Bobby Jones, she could beat any man. Most female athletes, of course, were less concerned about defeating male opposition than they were about being allowed merely to compete. And so they continued to try beating the system. In the case of nineteen-year-old Jackie Mitchell, a left-handed pitcher who once faced Lou Gehrig and Babe Ruth during an exhibition game and struck them out (see "1931"), beating the system meant joining the

63. The 1920 baseball season featured game that remains a record for endurance, the Boston Braves and Brooklyn Dodgers battling to a 1–1 tie in 26 innings. (See "Doing It Till It Hurts.") One of the pitchers who went the route was Boston's Joe Oeschger, who finished season with 15–13 mark.

64. Oeschger's mound opponent in classic 1920 duel was Leon Cadore, then in his sixth year with Brooklyn. His mark at season's end was 15–14, amazingly similar to that of his foe.

65. By the end of the decade, baseball had been transformed from a pitcher's and base-stealer's game into a slugger's game. Some experts claim the 1927 New York Yankees, with Babe Ruth hitting 60 homers and Lou Gehrig 47, was the greatest team of all time. Even some computers agree.

66. The 1920s saw the growth of college football to the point where some claimed it was more popular than baseball. Harold E. (Red) Grange of Illinois, an All-American half-back, 1923–25, did much to promote the sport, then gave professional football a much-needed shot in the arm by turning pro at the end of his college career. Here he is seen turning the corner against Michigan.

67. Notre Dame teams of 1920s had well-deserved air of invincibility about them, especially during 1922, 1923, and 1924 seasons, when the "Four Horsemen" (Don Miller, James Crowley, Elmer Layden, and Harry Stuhldreher) ran out of Notre Dame's backfield. While this team was together, the Irish won 27 games, lost 2, and tied 1.

68. Even more celebrated than his players was Notre Dame coach Knute Rockne, seen here at right. When the "Rock" was temporarily abed in 1929, rather than make that season's All-American selections without him, a committee of William Alexander, Glenn (Pop) Warner, and Tad Jones went to see Rockne. Two years later, Rockne's death in a plane crash was considered a national calamity. (See "1931.")

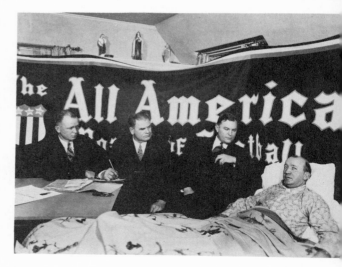

69. Bill Tilden, seen here in 1923 action against Bill Johnson, does not seem to have his eye on the ball, but he was so good he might have beaten some opponents blindfolded. From 1920 through 1930, Tilden's record in Davis Cup competition included 17 matches won against only 5 losses.

70. The 1920s saw professional basketball start to grow as a popular spectator sport. The original Celtics of 1923, seen here, started as a semipro team in 1915. After dominating the American Basketball League during the 1927–28 season by winning 109 out of 120 games, the Celts were ruled out of the league because they were too strong. From left to right: Johnny Beckman, Johnny Whittey, Nat Holman, Jack Barry, Chris Leonard.

71. One of top black fighters of the decade was Louis Phal, alias "Battling Siki," who probably could have been heavyweight champion had he not been so eccentric. After defeating Georges Carpentier for the light-heavyweight title in a disputed battle (see "Flaps"), Siki seemed to lose interest in serious work. He died suddenly in 1925, the victim of an unknown assailant.

72. America's earliest trans-continental motorcyclist was "Cannonball" Baler, who made it from Los Angeles to New York in 8 days, 21 hours, 16 minutes. During his heyday he held most of the endurance records. (See "Doing It Till It Hurts."

73. The 1920s also featured a pair of transcontinental foot races that were dubbed "bunion derbies" by a cynical press. Conceived by C. C. Pyle, the events were not very well managed, with hints that at least one of the two races was rigged. (See "Bad Hypes.") Here runners are seen leaving the New Jersey ferry at the beginning of the 1929 race.

74. Most famous American woman athlete of the 1920s was Gertrude Ederle, who electrified the United States and earned herself a ticker-tape parade when she became the first woman to swim the English Channel, August 6, 1926. Her time was 7 hours better than that of Matthew Webb, the first male to make it. (See "Breaking the Sex Barrier.")

75. Baseball truly reached the end of an era on the final day of the 1933 season when Babe Ruth took the mound for the Yankees against the Boston Red Sox. Although 38 and near the end of his career, the Babe went the full nine innings, yielding 12 hits and 3 bases on balls. He was tough when he had to be, however, and the Yanks won, 6–5. The batter is Mel Almada.

76. The future seemed to belong to Jay Hanna (Dizzy) Dean on October 9, 1934, as the 23-year-old Cardinal pitcher climaxed a 30–7 season by hurling an 11–0 victory in the seventh and deciding game of the World Series against the Detroit Tigers. The future was brief, two productive years followed by an injury in the 1937 All-Star game, then ineffectiveness. But the colorful Dean went on to become one of the more controversial and best-loved radio commentators.

77. Professional football became a serious rival to baseball during the 1930s, with the Chicago Bears, the New York Giants, and the Green Bay Packers emerging as top teams. When the Giants and Bears met in the second NFL title game on December 9, 1934, Chicago was riding the crest of a 13-game winning streak. The Bears, playing well on an icy field in 9-degree temperature, led at halftime, 10–3. But during the intermission, Giant Coach Steve Owen provided the squad with basketball sneakers so they could maneuver better on the frozen turf. The Giants did just that, scoring 27 points in the final period to win, 30–13. Here Ed Danowski, New York quarterback, runs for yardage in that famous "sneaker game."

78. Probably the most versatile athlete among U.S. Presidents, Gerald Ford was No. 48 and center for the University of Michigan during his collegiate days. He is seen here in group picture with 1934 squad. (See "Sports and the Presidents.")

79. Boxing was also quite popular during the 1930s, aided by radio, which gave life to the sport as it did no other. After retirement of Gene Tunney, heavyweight title changed hands several times, the huge Primo Carnera, left, winning the championship in June of 1933. A year later, Carnera granted a title shot to Max Baer, who was much shorter and lighter than the champ. But Baer knocked out the giant in 11 rounds. Note Carnera's garters, socks, and two-tone shoes.

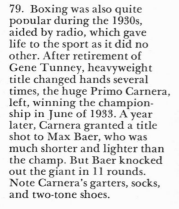

80. Boxing's heavyweight division found a new and worthy champion in 1937 when 23-year-old Joe Louis won the title from James Braddock, then proceeded to defend his crown so many times he was accused of running a "Bum of the Month" club. (See "1941.")

81. Upset team of the decade was the Chicago Black Hawks of the National Hockey League. Having just barely made the playoffs with a poor record, the Hawks were not given much chance to win the Stanley Cup. They managed it, however, and celebrants included, from left to right, Jack Shill, Carl Voss, Cully Dahlstrom, and Mush March.

82. Having shown a penchant for trying to bring all manner of sports indoors or play them under artificial light, it was hardly surprising when the first annual Southland Open ski jump competition at Los Angeles began under the lights on March 1, 1938. Football and baseball had already been played indoors and at night by this time. (See "Doing It Indoors and at Night.")

83. Having won the 1929 U. S. Open was just a prelude to glory for golfer Bobby Jones, right. The following year he astounded sports world by scoring a "grand slam" in golf by winning the British Open and British Amateur, USGA Open and USGA Amateur. The feat had never been accomplished before and has not yet been repeated.

84. Women active in sports included Lottie Schoemmel, center, who regularly engaged in long-distance swimming feats. (See "Doing It Till It Hurts.") Here she is ready to swim from Yonkers to the Battery, a distance of 17 miles, with 12-year-old twins Phylis and Bernice Vitenfield. The trip was made in 6½ hours.

85. The first all-around great American woman athlete was Babe Didrikson, who excelled at everything from hurling the javelin to running to golf. During the 1932 Olympics she won two gold medals, and she once scored 106 points in a basketball game. Here she is warming up on the track in 1932.

86. Badly injured during a fire when he was 8 years old, Glenn Cunningham not only learned how to walk again but also became one of America's top runners of the decade. Although missing all the toes of his left foot, he set a world-record mile of 4:06:8 in 1934 as well as a half-mile mark of 1:49:7 two years later. Here he is seen winning the 1,500-meter run at the AAU track-and-field meet at Palmer Stadium, Princeton, New Jersey, July 4, 1936. In second and third positions behind the Kansas Flier are Archie San Romani of Kansas State Teachers College and Gene Venzke of Pennsylvania.

87. After covering himself with glory during the controversial 1936 Olympic Games in Berlin, American sprinter Jesse Owens had little to do for an encore but challenge a racehorse. The event took place in December 1936 at Tropical Stadium, Havana, Cuba, Owens against a horse known as Julio McCaw. Given a 40-yard handicap, Owens defeated the horse by about 20 yards but the animal was gaining rapidly at the conclusion of the 100-yard dash.
(See "Can a _____ Beat a _____?")

House of David team and pitching for the bearded nine that toured the nation. For Sally Stearns, beating the system meant becoming the first woman coxswain of a male rowing team (Rollins College, 1936); some even attempted to break into football, one of the first to play against male athletes being fourteen-year-old Esther Burnham, who in 1935 turned up as center for the Middlefield (Connecticut) Air Cadets. "I don't see why a girl can't play football just the same as the boys," she said when interviewed.

Meanwhile, on the Bowling Lanes:
Women also broke into the charmed circle of 300-game rollers in 1929 when Mrs. Rose Jacobs turned in a perfect game in a Rainbow League match at Schenectady, New York. On March 4, 1930, Emma (Mrs. Charles) Fahning bowled another perfect game at Buffalo.

Such an attitude seemed simple enough to women, but males resisted the notion that once on the field, sex meant little or nothing. Two years after Esther Burnham had her brief fling on the gridiron, Gus Welch, coach of American University's football team, said he intended to have a young woman—he didn't reveal her name—kick the points after touchdowns at future games. The faculty at that institution quickly voted against the proposal and the idea was dropped, but in September 1943, sixteen-year-old Agnes Risner was allowed to try a pair of extra-point kicks for New Castle (Indiana) High School in a game against Morton Memorial of Knightstown. Her two kicks failed, although New Castle High managed to win, 25–0.

Four years later, another sixteen-year-old

named Frankie Groves made sports history in Texas when she played tackle for Stinnett High School in a game against Groom High. "It was great fun," she said, referring especially to one play in which she knocked down two opposing linemen with a single block. Coach Truman Johnson, while praising the young woman's performance, added that three more ladies were eager to play. Such brief appearances may be considered mere colorful oddities, but there was nothing ephemeral about swimmer Ann Curtis breaking the male monopoly on the James E. Sullivan Memorial Trophy. Established in 1930 and awarded annually to America's outstanding athlete, the Sullivan Trophy was first won by golfer Bobby Jones, followed by thirteen more male athletes. Miss Curtis not only broke the sex barrier, but was the first swimmer to be so honored. The winner of eight National AAU titles in two years of competition, the San Francisco free-style swimmer received 307 votes to 264 for her closest rival in the balloting—ironically, another woman, Pauline Betz, three-time winner of the women's national tennis championship.

After Miss Curtis's triumph, another period of male dominance followed. Then a second woman who could not be ignored arrived in 1956. She was Pat McCormick, a Lakewood (California) mother who became the first Olympic diver to win two gold medals in successive Olympic Games. In addition to winning those prizes in 1952 and 1956, she also won three national AAU diving titles at the outdoor championships in 1956, the platform diving competition at the first Pan-American Games at Buenos Aires in 1951, and was victorious at the second Pan-American Games in 1955. She was also selected as the outstanding woman athlete of the year by the Associated Press in 1956. With such a background, it was

---

Two Women Who Would Make Most Male Athletes Turn Green with Envy Because of Their:
1. Versatility
Babe Didrikson Zaharias first came into national prominence as a basketball player. Though but a teen-ager, she was nominated for three All-America teams and once scored 106 points in a game. Of the 634 track and field events in which she was entered, she won all but 12. She also excelled at golf, winning the U. S. Amateur title in 1946, the British Amateur in 1947 and the Women's professional

titles in 1948, 1950, and 1954. In baseball, she toured the country with a team composed mostly of men and could throw a ball 300 feet on a straight line. (She also threw a third strike past Joe DiMaggio.) In bowling, she rolled a 237 game and averaged 170.
2. Earning Power
Before her death in 1969 at the age of 57, Norwegian-born skater Sonja Henie (winner of figure-skating titles at the 1928, 1932, and 1936 Olympics) had amassed a fortune of $47.5 million.

Sullivan Trophy Winners—1930–44:
1930—Bobby Jones, golf
1931—Barney Berlinger, track
1932—Jim Bausch, track
1933—Glenn Cunningham, track
1934—Bill Bonthron, track
1935—Lawson Little, golf
1936—Glenn Morris, track
1937—Don Budge, tennis
1938—Don Lash, track
1939—Joe Burk, rowing
1940—Greg Rice, track
1941—Leslie MacMitchell, track
1942—Cornelius Warmerdam, field
1943—Gil Dodds, track
1944—Ann Curtis, swimming

hardly surprising—except for the fact that she was a woman—that Mrs. McCormick was awarded the 1956 Sullivan Award. Five years later sprinter Wilma Rudolph added a new dimension to the history of the Sullivan Award by becoming the first black woman to win the trophy.

During the 1950s and 1960s, women continued to improve their skills in a variety of sports, but as in previous decades, competing in "male" sports against male athletes was discouraged. Sometimes, of course, the opportunity arose for an individual woman to demonstrate her superiority—as Louise Suggs did on February 15, 1961, by defeating ten male golfers in the $10,000 Palm Beach par-3 invitational golf tourney. The 54-hole tournament, held on a 2,688-yard course (average distance per hole, just under 150 yards), gave the lighter-hitting women an advantage, but nevertheless substantiated Miss Suggs' contention that women were every bit as good at their short golf games as men. Entering the third and final round trailing Clyde Usina by two strokes and Dub Pagan by a stroke, Miss Suggs went over par only once as she shot a 51, birdieing the fourteenth and fifteenth holes to move ahead. Pagan, meanwhile, shot a 53, and Usina faded all the way to a 57.

BASEBALL, 1952

Although Jackie Mitchell had played organized baseball twenty years before, the odds facing twenty-four-year-old Eleanor Engle were enormous when the Harrisburg Senators of the Interstate League (Class B) announced that she had been signed to a professional contract.

Most men hooted and derided the announcement as a "gag," but Dr. Jay Smith, president of the Senators' Board of Directors, insisted the young woman would play if the league approved the contract. "There is no rule [that] specifically prohibits the signing of women," admitted Robert L. Finch, assistant to minor-leagues president, George M. Trautman. Buck Etchison, manager of the team, meanwhile, sided with those who felt the signing was a publicity gimmick.

The next day, June 22, 1952, Eleanor Engle was at the ball park for the game between Harrisburg and Lancaster. She hit a few grounders and fielded some at shortstop and second base, to the accompaniment of much whistling and applause from the crowd. But when game time arrived, the young woman was banished not only from the field but also all the way to the press box. "I won't have a girl playing for me," said Buck Etchison, who had played briefly with the 1943–44 Boston Braves. Miss Engle, of course, could do or say nothing until Trautman made a decision on the matter.

The ruling was not long in coming. On June 23, Trautman refused to approve the signing, referring to the incident as a "travesty" on baseball.

Mrs. Engle was distraught. "Why should he do this to me?" she asked. "If I can't play baseball, I don't want to do anything."

There were others who felt the decision was a poor one. "She can hit the ball a lot better than some of the fellows on the club," said the Harrisburg general manager, Howard Gordon. But of course there was nothing for the Senators to do but remain in seventh place and nothing for Mrs. Engle to do but return to work as a stenographer with the Pennsylvania Public Utilities Commission.

Louise Suggs' Triumph over the Men—1961:							
Louise Suggs	53	52	51—156	Chick Harbert	53	58	52—163
Dub Pagan	53	51	53—157	Henry Picard	59	53	51—163
Sam Snead	54	53	51—158	Bobby Cruickshank	54	55	54—163
Clyde Usina	53	50	57—160	Shelley Mayfield	57	54	53—164
Gardner Dickinson	57	52	53—162	Dow Finsterwald	53	56	56—165
Lew Worsham	53	56	54—163	Patty Berg	57	55	55—167

BULLFIGHTING, 1952

In Juarez, Mexico, it seems they were a bit more liberal in 1952. On January 20, blond Patricia McCormick (not the swimmer), from Big Spring, Texas, entered the bull ring and became the first North American woman bullfighter.

After a poor showing against her first bull—it battered her with its horns—Miss McCormick killed the second animal on its first charge, a maneuver that was done so well the judges awarded her both ears. Then, dedicating the third bull to her mother, who was seated in a ringside box, the young woman confidently made her second kill and earned the wild applause of the large crowd. It was just the beginning of a career in the bull ring that lasted several years.

THE NEXT QUARTER CENTURY

It seems safe to say that from the early 1950s to the late 1970s, there was more progress in breaking the sex barrier of professional sports than during any other quarter century of American history. And most of the accomplishments were crowded into the last decade of that period, when general ferment regarding minorities of all sorts helped provide courage and inspiration for those who might have otherwise remained silent or inactive.

The women who aspired to becoming jockeys took the lead in early 1969. By January of that year, several women with the ability and determination to ride on pari-mutuel tracks against male jockeys were already in the process of challenging the various racing commissions. The problem was that most tracks required the taking of a test before issuing a license to ride—usually breaking from the starting gate and running in the company of other horses for at least an eighth of a mile. That sounds simple enough—until one considers that it took nineteen-year-old Barbara Jo Rubin two months from the time she first

applied until she was finally permitted to take the test. When she did, on January 13, 1969, the three male stewards judging her promptly issued the approval to ride.

Miss Rubin was, of course, eager to become the first woman to ride in a flat race on a major American track, but two days after taking the test, she ran into trouble. After it was announced that she would ride Stoneland in the fourth race at Tropical Park on January 15, the male jockeys at the track threatened to walk out. Bryan Webb, owner of Stoneland, caved in and announced that Miss Rubin would not ride the horse after all. In addition, a rock was thrown through the window of the trailer used by the young woman as a dressing room.

While both sides of the controversy indulged in threats and legal maneuvering, Barbara Jo Rubin left for Nassau in the Bahamas. There, on January 28, at the Hobby Horse Race Track, she rode heavily favored Fly-Away to a three-length victory and galloped triumphantly into the winner's circle, where she was greeted by her parents and a contingent of Miami supporters.

Meanwhile, in the United States, another young woman was in the process of clearing away obstacles to riding. She was twenty-year-old Diane Crump, a strawberry blonde, who passed her test and received permission to ride shortly after Miss Rubin. On January 31, after it was announced that the striking male jockeys had been fined one hundred dollars each for their action against Miss Rubin, they agreed to ride against women. Diane Crump's first race was on February 7. Six rides later, she became the first woman jockey to guide a winner across the finish line. Apparently not upset at being denied the honor of becoming the first woman jockey in the United States, Barbara Jo Rubin returned from the Bahamas and proceeded to win eleven of her first twenty-two starts. Other young women who

---

Some Women Jockey Firsts:
First to be injured and taken to the hospital:
Diane Crump, after her mount, Misquoia, fell at Gulfstream Park on March 11, 1969
First to ride one hundred winners:
Mary Bacon, on June 30, 1971, by riding California Lassie to victory at Thistledown Race Track, Cleveland.
First to be suspended:
Mrs. Tuesdee Testa, for ten days, careless riding, on August 27, 1969.

First black:
Cheryl White, 17, on June 15, 1971. The horse, Ace Reward, came in last in a field of eleven at Thistledown Race Track, Cleveland.
First to retire:
Barbara Joe Rubin, In January 1970, the result of weak knees (she had contracted polio as a child)
First to ride in Kentucky Derby:
Diane Crump, on May 2, 1970, on Fathom, which finished fifteenth.

followed with victories on the track included Tuesdee Testa, a twenty-seven-year-old mother of two; Robyn Smith, a part-time Hollywood starlet; and Mary Bacon, the lightest of the new breed at a mere ninety-five pounds. Soon, by riding regularly, the women jockeys had built up a small body of statistics and "firsts" which, while not rivaling those of organized baseball, at least proved that the woman jockey was here to stay.

FIRST WOMAN IN PROFESSIONAL FOOTBALL— 1970

Weighing in at 122 pounds, 27-year-old Pat Palinkas had little business in a professional football game, regardless of her sex. But when she expressed the desire to hold the football for her husband, Steve, who place-kicked for the Orlando Panthers of the Atlantic Coast League, permission was granted.

The young woman, who taught school in Tampa, Florida, entered the game with three seconds left in the first half. Orlando had just scored a touchdown, and Steve Palinkas was about to try the extra point. The twelve thousand fans who were on hand cheered at the sudden appearance of the frail-looking player awaiting the snap from center.

Across the line from Pat Palinkas, 235-pound Wally Florence of the Bridgeport Jets stood poised to charge. Later he admitted feeling "up-tight" when he saw the young woman run onto the field. A collegiate football player at Purdue who first broke into professional ball with the 1964 New York Jets, he had knocked around quite a bit in the minor leagues but still regarded football as a serious business. "I'm out here trying to make a living," he thought to himself, "and she's out here prancing around making folly with a man's game. I wanted to show her this is no soft touch. I wanted to smash her back to the kitchen."

Wally Florence got his chance. The snap from Orlando's center was off-target and Pat Palinkas had no choice but to try to run with it. But she was able to take only a step or two before the charging Wally Florence sailed into her, battering her to the turf with the full force of his hurtling body. The crowd moaned, wondering if the young woman would survive the blow. To everyone's surprise, she leaped to her feet almost immediately and ran off the field.

History records that the next pair of extra-point attempts, held by Pat Palinkas on August 15, 1970, were good. History also records that there was no mad rush to sign her to a National Football League contract.

OTHER ASSAULTS ON THE MALE MONOPOLIES

"Some of my women friends think I should stay in the kitchen. My answer to that is I could be in a bar as a topless waitress if I wanted that type of job. . . . I just want to be a part of baseball. . . ."

Forty-year-old Bernice Gera so wanted to be a part of baseball that she took her case to the highest court in the state of New York. Her ambition, to become an umpire, seemed on the way to being fulfilled when the court ruled in her favor on January 13, 1972. The litigation began in 1969 when, after graduating from an umpiring school, Mrs. Gera prepared to make her debut with the New York-Pennsylvania Professional Baseball League. But Philip Piton, then president of the National Association of Professional Baseball Leagues, disapproved the woman's contract, stating that at 5 feet, 2 inches and 129 pounds, she failed to meet the minimum physical requirements of 5 feet, 10 inches and 170 pounds.

After winning her lengthy court battle, Mrs. Gera finally walked onto a baseball diamond as an arbiter in June 1972. The two teams were the Auburn Phillies and the Geneva Rangers, but more players and spectators seemed interested in watching the umpire than the game. Unfortunately, Mrs. Gera, who had been exposed to considerable pre-game harassment in the form of anonymous telephone calls and coolness on the part of league officials, was not long in making a questionable call. In the fourth inning, she forgot that a runner going into second base on an attempted double play did not have to be tagged ("I forgot it was a force play, I had so much on my mind"), so she signaled the Auburn runner safe, then changed her ruling to out. Nolan Campbell, Auburn manager, then stormed onto the field to dispute the change in call. When Mrs. Gera admitted making a mistake, he snapped, "No, that's two mistakes. The first one was putting on a uniform."

Bernice Gera's Predecessor:
Mrs. Gera was not the first woman who aspired to join the ranks of sports officials. On April 30, 1940, the state of California issued Prize Fight Referee License No. 209 to Belle Martell of Van Nuys, California. Miss Martell's first card was on May 2, 1940, when she refereed eight bouts at San Bernardino. But she retired the following month after being assigned to Los Angeles.

After the game was over, Mrs. Gera burst into tears and announced that she was quitting. "In a way they succeeded in getting rid of me," she said. "But in a way, I've succeeded, too. I've broken the barrier. It can be done."

Other women were proving that it could be done in other areas, among them:

Mrs. Helen Gilligan Finn, 53, who became the first woman instructor at a municipal golf course in New York—1971.

Sharon Chambers, 28, first woman in the history of the American Power Boat Association to win a national high point championship in outboard pleasure craft racing—1971.

Mrs. Nina Kuscsik, 33, mother of three who was first woman finisher in 1972 Boston Marathon, beating some 400 men.

Vicky Brown, 18, coxswain of men's varsity at the University of Oregon.

Karen Weiss, who played two games of basketball with men's varsity at Vermont's Wyndham College until sidelined by "men only" rule.

Bonnie Malek, 15, who finished thirty-ninth —and won $16,556—in the 1977 Indianapolis 500.

Yvonne Burch, 13, first girl among 300,000 boys to play in the Babe Ruth Baseball League.

But the young woman who will be most remembered as the David who took on Goliath and proved that sex barriers in sports should be eliminated is, of course, Billie Jean King. A champion at tennis and a tireless fighter for women's rights, Ms. King was the first women sports pro to earn $100,000 a year, the first to admit publicly that she had an abortion, and the holder of more Wimbledon titles than any other player.

But the young woman's greatest moment came on September 20, 1973, when she performed in what was billed "The Tennis Match of the Century" before the largest crowd ever assembled for a tennis match. The competition was 55-year-old Bobby Riggs, "The Happy Hustler" who had defeated another woman champion, Margaret Court Smith, 6–2, 6–1, at Ramona, California.

Mr. Riggs, anticipating the money rolling in, then turned his attention to Ms. King. "She's a great player," he said, "for a gal. But no woman can beat a male player who knows what he's doing. I'm not only interested in glory for my sex, but I also want to set women's lib back twenty years, to get women back into the home, where they belong."

The battle of the sexes packed the Houston Astrodome with a capacity live audience, and additional millions watched on television. Rushing the net frequently and playing to Mr. Riggs' weak backhand, Ms. King hustled "The Happy Hustler" off the court in straight sets, 6–4, 6–3, 6–3.

Could Ms. King have beaten the top male tennis players? Probably not. But it didn't really matter. After September 20, 1973, the sports world would never be quite the same.

CHAPTER 31 — 1931–40

1931

Winners: Baseball: Philadelphia A's, playing in their third consecutive World Series, are defeated in 7 games by the St. Louis Cardinals. . . . *Kentucky Derby:* Twenty Grand. *Preakness:* Mate. *Belmont:* Twenty Grand . . . *Indy 500:* Louis Schneider . . . *Boxing:* Middleweight division in confused state. In August, Gorilla Jones wins decision over Tiger Thomas, is recognized as new champ by National Boxing Association, but in November, Ben Jeby beats Chick Devlin and is dubbed champ by powerful New York State Athletic Commission. Welterweight champion Tommy Freeman yields crown in April to Jack Thompson, who turns it over to Lou Brouillard in October. . . . *Golf: USGA Men's Open:* Billy Burke. *PGA:* Tom Creavy . . . *Hockey:* 1930–31 Stanley Cup winner: Montreal Canadiens . . . *Football: Rose Bowl:* Alabama 24, Washington State 0 . . . *National Football League:* Green Bay leads league with record of 12–2–0, Portsmouth second at 11–3–0. . . . *Basketball:* College champion (selected by Helms Athletic Foundation): Northwestern (16–1).

Other Happenings: National AAU basketball champions of year: for men—Henry Clothiers, Wichita, Kansas; women—Golden Cyclones of Dallas, Texas. . . . First totalisators installed at Hialeah Race Track. . . . Jack Dempsey, attempting a comeback, is booed after close victory over Bearcat Wright. . . . Former lightweight champion Benny Leonard also announces plans to stage a comeback. . . . In November, a letter addressed to University of Georgia end "Catfish" Smith ends up at Georgia Fish Market. . . . Harvard's marching band breaks a halftime record by forming 76 letters. . . . Golfer Bobby Jones begins a series of radio talks and someone suggests that term "golfologist" be used instead of "professional." . . . Tennis champion Bill Tilden, after knocking touring pros for years, announces that he intends to turn professional. . . . Woman star Helen Wills returns from tour of Japan and does little for U.S.-Japanese relations by stating that Orientals are slow. . . . No-hitters are pitched by American League hurlers Wes Ferrell of Cleveland and Bob Burke of Senators. . . . On August 1, Sun Beau passes Gallant Fox as top money-winning racehorse by winning $27,300 Arlington Handicap. . . . On October 28, Edmund Jack Burke of Mississippi returns kickoff 109 yards to score against Alabama, but the Crimson Tide wins, 55–6. . . . Frank Wykoff runs 100-yard dash in 9.5 seconds. . . . Daily double starts at the Reno race track, Reno, Nevada.

1932

Winners: Baseball: Rejuvenated New York Yankees win 107 games during regular season, then embarrass Chicago Cubs by sweeping them in 4 games. . . . *Kentucky Derby:* Burgoo King. *Preakness:* Burgoo King. *Belmont Stakes:* Faireno . . . *Indy 500:* Fred Frame . . . *Boxing:* Jack Sharkey and Max Schmeling meet again on June 21, Sharkey winning the heavyweight championship on 15-round decision. . . . In Paris, Marcel Thil is fouled in eleventh round by Gorilla Jones, is recognized as new middleweight champ by National Boxing Association. Jackie Fields becomes new welterweight king by winning decision from Lou Brouillard, but difference of opinion exists in featherweight division: By beating Johnny Pena, Tommy Paul is recognized as new champ by NBA; Kid Chocolate wins New York State championship by knocking out Lew Feldman in twelfth round. . . . *Golf: USGA Men's Open:* Gene Sarazen. *PGA:* Olin Dutra . . . *Hockey:* 1931–32 Stanley Cup is won by Toronto Maple Leafs. . . . *Football: Rose Bowl:* USC 21, Tulane 12 . . . *National Football League.* Chicago Bears are declared winners with 7–1–6 record (ties are not counted as games, thus making Bears' percentage .875); second are Green Bay Packers, 10–3–1. (.769). . . . *Basketball:* College Champion (selected by Helms Athletic Foundation): Purdue (17–1).

Other Happenings: On July 10, Eddie Rommel, pitching his last of 13 seasons with the Philadelphia A's, enters game against Cleveland in second inning. He proceeds to hurl 17 innings, giving up 29 hits and 14 runs in 18-inning, 18–17 win. . . . Joe McCarthy becomes first baseball manager to win pennants in both leagues (1929 with Cubs, 1932 with Yankees). . . . No no-hitters are pitched in the major leagues, but there is some sharp hitting—namely, Johnny Burnett of Cleveland getting 9 hits in the 18-inning game against Philadelphia . . . Lou Gehrig smashing 4 home runs in a 9-inning game . . . and Johnny Frederick of the Dodgers pinch-hitting 6 homers in a season. . . . The National Football League, meanwhile, begins keeping statistics for the first time: Scoring leader for 1932 season is Earl (Dutch) Clark of Portsmouth with 39 points (4 touchdowns, 6 extra points, 3 field goals). Bob Campiglio of Stapleton is rushing leader with 504 yards in 104 attempts. Arnie Herber of Green Bay leads the passers with 101 attempts and 37 completions for 639 yards and 9 touchdowns. . . . Jack Dempsey hears boos again as he stumbles along comeback trail but on February 8 defeats a pair of opponents before a record crowd of 8,050 at Milwaukee. . . . On November 19, Joe Kershalla of West Liberty State College (West Virginia) scores 71 points as his team defeats Cedarville College, 127–0.

1933

Winners: Baseball: The New York Giants, having ended the John McGraw managerial era, win the National League pennant in their first full year under Bill Terry, then eliminate the Washington Senators, 4 games to 1. . . . *Kentucky Derby:* Brokers Tip. *Preakness:* Head Play. *Belmont Stakes:* Hurryoff . . . *Indy 500:* Louis Meyer . . . *Boxing:* Primo Carnera becomes new heavyweight champion by knocking out Jack Sharkey in sixth round. Lou Brouillard wins New York State championship in middleweight division by beating Ben Jeby, but two months later yields the crown to Vince Dundee in Boston. Young Corbett III begins a three-month reign as welterweight champ by defeating Jackie Fields, then is replaced by Jimmy McLarnin in May. . . . Barney Ross becomes new lightweight king by beating Tony Canzoneri in Chicago, and Freddie Miller takes featherweight crown from Tommy Paul. . . . *Golf: USGA Men's Open:* Johnny Goodman. *PGA:* Gene Sarazen . . . *Hockey:* In NHL, New York Rangers take 1932–33 Stanley Cup. . . . *Football:* In first annual *Orange Bowl,* Miami defeats Manhattan, 7–0. *Rose Bowl:* USC 35, Pittsburgh 0. . . . *National Football League:* For first time, NFL is broken into divisions—Eastern and Western—so as to facilitate a World Series-type championship game. Chicago Bears win first Western Division title, New York Giants first Eastern. In first championship game, Bears win, 23–21. . . . *Basketball:* College champion (selected by Helms Athletic Foundation): Kentucky (20–3).

Other Happenings: National and American League play first All-Star baseball game, July 6 at Chicago. Babe Ruth hits 2-run homer to lead Americans to 4–2 victory. . . . In pro football, a new rule change brings goal posts to the goal line, and forward passing is allowed from any point behind the line of scrimmage (instead of at least 5 yards back). . . . Gil LeFebvre of Cincinnati returns punt 98 yards for a touchdown in December 3 game against Brooklyn. . . . Feeling the pinch of the Depression, baseball's American Association reduces its umpiring staff, the Central League suspends operations, Commissioner Landis cuts his own salary by $10,000, and Kansas City decides to hold spring training at home to save travel expenses. . . . Prohibition having ended, several baseball teams look forward to selling beer in their parks. . . . In one of the first air accidents affecting a sports team, 3 members of the Winnipeg Toilers, a Canadian basketball team, are killed when their plane crashes. . . . On May 31, bizarre incident occurs at Jamaica, New York, when racehorses make false start and go all the way around the track before they can be recalled. Rideaway wins and Clock Tower is second. But when they are sent around for a second time, Clock Tower comes in first and Rideaway is second. . . . Kentucky Derby is one of roughest in history. Don Meade on Brokers Tip and Herb Fisher on Head Play fight through the stretch, but no one claims foul as Brokers Tip wins by a nose. . . . On July 2, first professional midget auto races are held at Sacramento, California. . . . Babe Didrikson makes her first professional basketball appearance, scoring 9 points for the Brooklyn Yankees in a 19–16 victory over the Long Island Ducklings. . . . On October 1, the New York football Giants defeat the Green Bay Packers, 10–7, despite the handicap of making no first downs.

1934

Winners: Baseball: St. Louis Cardinals, led by the pitching Dean brothers—who win all 4 games—defeat Detroit Tigers in World Series, 4 games to 3. . . . *Kentucky Derby:* Cavalcade. *Preakness:* High Quest. *Belmont Stakes:* Peace Chance . . . *Indy 500:* Bill Cummings

. . . *Boxing:* Max Baer ends Primo Carnera's one-year reign as heavyweight champ by dispatching him in the eleventh round. Maxie Rosenbloom loses light-heavyweight crown after 4 years to Bob Olin. Changes occur also in the middleweight and welterweight divisions, Teddy Yarosz decisioning Vince Dundee in the former and Barney Ross beating Jimmy McLarnin in the latter. But Ross yields the crown back to McLarnin four months later. . . . *Golf: USGA Men's Open:* Olin Dutra. *PGA:* Paul Runyan. The first annual *Masters:* Horton Smith . . . *Hockey:* 1933–34 Stanley Cup is won by Chicago Black Hawks, their first championship in NHL. . . . *Football: Orange Bowl:* Duquesne 33, Miami 7. *Rose Bowl:* Columbia 7, Stanford 0 . . . *National Football League:* New York Giants 30, Chicago Bears 13 . . . *Basketball:* College champion (selected by Helms Athletic Foundation): Wyoming (26–1).

Other Happenings: On December 29, 1934, college basketball stages its first doubleheader. NYU defeats Notre Dame, 25–18, and Westminster beats St. John's, 37–33, at Madison Square Garden before 16,188 fans. . . . Professional football stages its first All-Star game at Chicago on August 31. The college players surprise nearly everyone by shutting out the Chicago Bears. The Chicago Bears, on the other hand, also shut out the College All-Stars. . . . In baseball, Goose Goslin of the Detroit Tigers sets a record by hitting into four consecutive double plays on April 28. . . . Football's big college game of the year brings together unbeaten Minnesota and Pittsburgh on October 20. Led by halfback Pug Lund, Minnesota wins, 13–7. . . . In the National League, the Cardinals' Paul Dean hurls a no-hitter to defeat the Dodgers, 3–0, but Bobo Newsom of the Browns manages to pitch 9 hitless innings against the Red Sox, then lose in the tenth. . . . The House of David baseball club, facing competition from another bearded team, asks for and receives an injunction forcing the enemy to either shave or quit playing. . . . Fifteen years after the Black Sox scandal of 1919, Joe Jackson asks Commissioner Landis for reinstatement and is refused. . . . Jack Dempsey gives up any last thoughts of making a comeback and goes into the real-estate business. . . . Fearing loss of gate receipts, the St. Louis Cardinals and Browns forbid radio broadcasts of their baseball games. . . . Babe Ruth's salary is down to $35,000 a year as he ends his last full year as an active player. . . . At the College of the Pacific, football coach A. A. Stagg dismisses a player for smoking. . . . Nazi Germany declares golf the national sport—by official decree, of course. . . . University of

Kansas runner Glenn Cunningham sets a world record by racing a mile in 4.06.7. . . . America's Cup competition sees U.S. entry, *Rainbow,* defeat Britain's *Endeavour,* 4 races to 2. . . . On March 21, Babe Didrikson pitches an inning for the Philadelphia Athletics, setting down the Brooklyn Dodgers on no hits, one walk, and one hit batsman. She is aided, however, by a triple play. . . . NFL championship game is the famous "sneaker" contest in which the New York Giants beat the Bears, 30–13, after putting on basketball shoes to compensate for slippery conditions.

1935

Winners: Baseball: Led by pitcher Lynwood "Schoolboy" Rowe, the Detroit Tigers are in the World Series for the second straight year and this time they win, defeating the Chicago Cubs, 4 games to 2. . . . *Kentucky Derby:* Omaha. *Preakness:* Omaha. *Belmont Stakes:* Omaha . . . *Indy 500:* Kelly Petillo . . . *Boxing:* For the third consecutive year, the heavyweight champion yields his title 12 months after winning it, the winner on this occasion being James J. Braddock; the loser, Max Baer. In the light-heavyweight division, John Henry Lewis begins a 3½-year reign by defeating Bob Olin. Babe Ricko, meanwhile, wins the middleweight crown from Teddy Yarosz, Barney Ross decisions Jimmy McLarnin to take back the welterweight championship, and Tony Canzoneri steps in as lightweight champ by earning a 15-round decision over Lou Ambers. Al Brown's 6-year stint as bantamweight king comes to an end on June 1 at Valencia, Spain, when Baltazar Sangchilli wins the decision. . . . *Golf: USGA Men's Open:* Sam Parks, Jr. *PGA:* Johnny Revolta. *Masters:* Gene Sarazen . . . *Hockey:* Montreal Maroons win 1934–35 NHL championship and take first Stanley Cup since season of 1925–26. . . . *Football: Orange Bowl:* Bucknell 26, Miami 0. *Rose Bowl:* Alabama 29, Stanford 13. First annual *Sugar Bowl:* Tulane 20, Temple 14 . . . *National Football League:* Detroit Lions 26, New York Giants 7 . . . *Basketball:* College champion (selected by Helms Athletic Foundation): NYU (19–1).

Other Happenings: College football game of greatest interest pits TCU and SMU, both with records of 10–0. Despite the passing of TCU's Sammy Baugh, SMU wins, 20–14. . . . On April 16, Babe Ruth, age 40, makes his debut in the National League, hits single and home run off Carl Hubbell as he leads Boston Braves to 4–2 win over New York Giants. . . . In September, a bizarre tragedy occurs when Brooklyn Dodger outfielder Len Koenecke tries to grab the controls of a plane as it flies over Toronto. In order to regain control of the ship, a companion smashes Koenecke on the head with a fire extinguisher, killing him. . . . In American League, Vern Kennedy of the White Sox pitches the only major-league no-hitter, beating the Browns, 5–0. . . . Chicago Cubs' 21-game winning streak is highlight of baseball season. . . . On the boxing scene, Max Baer predicts that 21-year-old Joe Louis will lose June bout with Primo Carnera. He is quite wrong. Louis wins and is touted as logical contender to dethrone Jim Braddock. . . . Max Schmeling, meanwhile, is criticized by hard-core Nazis for having a Jewish manager. . . . On October 18, Vanderbilt football coach Ray Morrison predicts that someday quarterbacks will be able to curve their passes past defenders into the hands of receivers. . . . Hayes Freeland breaks a pair of John Weismuller's swimming records, winning the 60-yard swim in 28.4 seconds and the 80-yard swim in 39 seconds. . . . Frank Bartell establishes a new bicycle record on March 6, covering a mile at Los Angeles at the rate of 80.584 mph.

1936

Winners: Baseball: Lou Gehrig bats .354 and leads the American League with 49 home runs to have one of his best years, taking the New York Yankees into the World Series against the Giants. In the second game, the Yankees set a Series record by scoring 18 runs as every man in lineup gets at least one hit and scores one or more runs. The Giants manage to win 2 games of the Series. . . . *Kentucky Derby:* Bold Venture. *Preakness:* Bold Venture. *Belmont Stakes:* Granville . . . *Indy 500:* Louis Meyer. . . . *Boxing:* Heavyweight champion Jim Braddock manages to avoid Joe Louis, but there is action in other divisions. Middleweight titleholder Babe Risko loses to Freddie Steele, and lightweight champ Tony Canzoneri loses a rematch with Lou Ambers. Petey Sarron becomes the new featherweight champion by winning a 15-round decision over Freddie Miller, and the bantamweight championship changes twice: On June 29, Tony Marino defeats Baltazar Sangchilli, then Marino is knocked out in the thirteenth round two months later by Sixto Escobar. . . . *Golf: USGA Men's Open:* Tony Manero. *PGA:*

Denny Shute. *Masters:* Horton Smith . . . *Hockey:* 1935–36 Stanley Cup is won by Detroit Red Wings. . . . *Football: Orange Bowl:* Catholic University 20, Mississippi 19. *Rose Bowl:* Stanford 7, SMU 0. *Sugar Bowl:* TCU 3, Louisiana State 2 . . . *National Football League:* Green Bay Packers 21, Boston Redskins 6 . . . *Basketball:* College champion (selected by Helms Athletic Foundation): Notre Dame (22–2).

Other Happenings: Professional football holds its first college draft on February 8. Jay Berwanger, an All-American halfback at the University of Chicago, is the first selection, chosen by Philadelphia. He declines to play. . . . On May 24 Tony Lazzeri drives in 11 runs as New York Yankees beat Athletics, 25–2. . . . Walter Alston, meanwhile, plays his first and only game in the major leagues on September 27. Entering the game as a substitute for the Cardinals' John Mize, Alston strikes out in his one time at bat and makes one fielding error in two chances. . . . In December, one of the great early intersectional basketball games is played in Madison Square Garden, Stanford defeating Long Island University, 45–31. . . . New York Giants pitcher Carl Hubbell begins his streak of 24 consecutive victories extending over two seasons. . . . In June, Joe Louis is beaten by Max Schmeling, setting off angry reaction in Harlem and joy in Nazi Germany. Schmeling announces his intention to return to his homeland on the dirigible *Hindenberg*. . . . Another foreigner who makes good, skater Sonja Henie, retains her Olympic title and announces that she will make movies. . . . On January 29, first five members of baseball Hall of Fame are elected: Ty Cobb, Babe Ruth, Honus Wagner, Christy Mathewson, and Walter Johnson.

1937

Winners: Baseball: Joe DiMaggio, now the big gun of the New York Yankees in his second year, leads the league with 46 home runs and helps take the Yanks into the second consecutive subway Series against the New York Giants. Seeking to avenge their 1936 loss, the Giants can win only one game. . . . *Kentucky Derby:* War Admiral. *Preakness:* War Admiral. *Belmont Stakes:* War Admiral . . . *Indy 500:* Wilbur Shaw . . . *Boxing:* Joe Louis begins 12 years as heavyweight champion by knocking out Jim Braddock in the eighth round. Another talented black, Henry Armstrong, wins the featherweight title by

KOing Petey Sarron in 6 rounds, and Harry Jeffra takes over the bantamweight division by defeating Sixto Escobar. . . . *Golf: USGA Men's Open:* Ralph Guldahl. *PGA:* Denny Shute. *Masters:* Byron Nelson . . . *Hockey:* 1936–37 NHL championship and Stanley Cup are won by Detroit Red Wings. . . . *Football:* First annual *Cotton Bowl:* TCU 16, Marquette 6. *Orange Bowl:* Duquesne 13, Mississippi State 12. *Rose Bowl:* Pittsburgh 21, Washington 0. *Sugar Bowl:* Santa Clara 21, Louisiana State 14 . . . *National Football League:* Washington Redskins 28, Chicago Bears 21 . . . *Basketball:* College champion (selected by Helms Athletic Foundation); Stanford (25–2).

Other Happenings: Big college football game is October 16 meeting of Pittsburgh and Fordham, both 3–0. Game ends in 0–0 tie. . . . On May 25, Detroit Tiger catcher-manager Mickey Cochrane, who had homered in previous trip to plate, is beaned by New York Yankee pitcher Bump Hadley. Cochrane survives the concussion but never plays again. . . . On June 25, Chicago Cub outfielder Augie Galan becomes the first switch-hitter to smash a home run from both sides of the plate in the same game. . . . May 27: Carl Hubbell wins his twenty-fourth consecutive game, beating Reds, 3–2. . . . Almost unnoticed is Bill Dietrich's 8–0 no-hitter for the Chicago White Sox. . . . In May, another outstanding pitcher, Bob Feller of the Cleveland Indians, requests a brief leave of absence so that he can graduate from high school. After insuring the 18-year-old for $100,000, the Indians allow him to fly home. . . . In college football, the proliferation of postseason bowls begins, the Ice Bowl, Rhumba Bowl, and Tobacco Bowl coming into existence. . . . In June, ace passer and punter Sam Baugh signs with the Washington Redskins. . . . For the 1937–38 season, basketball makes a sweeping change by eliminating the center jump after each score, an innovation that promises to increase the amount of playing time and lead to more scoring. . . . It is also proposed that a big national postseason tournament be held to determine a college champion of sorts. . . . On March 8, hockey fans are saddened to hear that Howie Morenz, star center of the Montreal Canadiens, is dead of a heart ailment at the age of 34. . . . After a decade of French and British domination of the Davis Cup matches, the United States finally defeats Great Britain, 4–1, at Wimbledon. . . . Britain also loses America's Cup competition, *Endeavour II* bowing to H. S. Vanderbilt's *Ranger,* 4 races to 0.

1938

Winners: Baseball: New York Yankees, in their third consecutive World Series, make it three wins in a row by defeating the Chicago Cubs, 4 games to 0. . . . *Kentucky Derby:* Lawrin. *Preakness:* Dauber. *Belmont Stakes:* Pasteurized . . . *Indy 500:* Floyd Roberts . . . *Boxing:* Among the middleweights, Al Hostrak knocks out Freddie Steele in the first round to become new champ, but his reign comes to an end three months later when he is decisioned by Solly Krieger on November 1. . . . Henry Armstrong, meanwhile, annexes his second title by defeating Barney Ross for the welterweight championship in May. He then becomes new lightweight champion in August by winning a 15-round decision from Lou Ambers. Joey Archibald and Mike Belloise battle for the featherweight crown and Archibald wins. There is action among the bantamweights as well, Sixto Escobar regaining his title from Harry Jeffra in a February bout at San Juan, Puerto Rico. . . . *Golf: USGA Men's Open:* Ralph Guldahl. *PGA:* Paul Runyan. *Masters:* Henry Picard . . . *Hockey:* 1937–38 Stanley Cup winner: Chicago Black Hawks . . . *Football: Cotton Bowl:* Rice 28, Colorado 14. *Orange Bowl:* Auburn 6, Mississippi State 0. *Rose Bowl:* California 13, Alabama 0. *Sugar Bowl:* Santa Clara 6, Louisiana State 0 . . . *National Football League:* New York Giants 23, Green Bay Packers 17 . . . *Basketball:* At the close of the 1937–38 season, the first National Invitational Tournament is held at Madison Square Garden. Temple wins the final contest, defeating Colorado, 60–36.

Other Happenings: Glenn Cunningham runs a 4:04:4 indoor mile, a record that stands for some time. . . . On September 15, brothers Lloyd and Paul Waner of the Pittsburgh Pirates hit back-to-back home runs off Cliff Melton of the Giants. . . . John Donald Budge becomes first tennis player to win four titles in a year (Australian, French, British, American). . . . In basketball, Stanford's Hank Luisetti becomes first to score 50 points, performing the feat in a game against Duquesne. . . . In a dramatic match race on November 1, War Admiral loses to Seabiscuit. . . . Johnny Vander Meer pitches his second no-hitter in a row, beating the Brooklyn Dodgers, 6–0, on June 15. . . . New York Giant Len Grant comes to a bizarre and tragic end when he is struck by lightning. . . . Monty Stratton, Chicago White Sox pitcher, escapes death in a hunting accident, but sees his career ended as his legs are amputated. . . . Joe Louis has return match with Max Schmeling and destroys him in first round. . . . In Germany, Nazis use sports as political tool by forbidding Jews to use bridle paths or bet on races. . . . Fred Plaisted, who rowed against best international oarsmen during the 1880s, celebrates his eighty-second birthday by rowing two miles. . . . Besides Vander Meer's double no-hit feat, other baseball thrills include Monte Pearson's American League no-hitter, the Yankees defeating Cleveland, 13-0. . . . Bob Feller strikes out 18 batters in a 9-inning game, Pinky Higgins of the Red Sox makes 12 consecutive hits, and Lou Gehrig plays his two-thousandth consecutive game. . . . Derby winner Lawrin is ridden by George Edward Arcaro, his first victory in Churchill Downs classic. . . . On February 3, Lou Boudreau, captain of Illinois University basketball team, is suspended for allegedly receiving monthly checks from Cleveland Indians. . . . Battleship, first horse bred in the United States to take the honor, wins the hundredth Grand National Steeplechase at Aintree, England.

1939

Winners: Baseball: By end of 1939 season, Gehrig has retired but New York Yankees continue to win, punishing the Cincinnati Reds in the World Series, 4 games to 0. . . . *Kentucky Derby:* Johnstown. *Preakness:* Challedon. *Belmont Stakes:* Johnstown . . . *Indy 500:* Wilbur Shaw . . . *Boxing:* After John Henry Lewis is beaten by Joe Louis and retires, Melio Bettina knocks out Tiger Jack Fox to become new light heavyweight champion. Seven months later, Billy Conn wins a 15-round decision to dethrone Bettina. In middleweight division, Al Hostak wins back title from Solly Krieger. . . . Lou Ambers earns comeback honors by recapturing lightweight title from Henry Armstrong, but the victory is marred by the charge that low blows were thrown. . . . *Golf: USGA Men's Open:* Byron Nelson, *PGA:* Henry Picard. *Masters:* Ralph Guldahl . . . *Hockey:* 1938-39 Stanley Cup winner is Boston Bruins. . . . *Football: Cotton Bowl:* St. Mary's 20, Texas Tech 13. *Orange Bowl:* Tennessee 17, Oklahoma 0. *Rose Bowl:* USC 7, Duke 3. *Sugar Bowl:* TCU 15, Carnegie Tech 7 . . . *National Football League:* Green Bay Packers 27, New York Giants 0 . . . *Basketball:* Evidence of basketball's growing popularity can be seen in establishment of NCAA postseason tournament, first held on the campus of Northwestern University at Evanston, Illinois. First 1938-39 *NCAA* winner: Oregon 46, Ohio State 33.

1938-39 *NIT:* Long Island University 44, Loyola (Illinois) 32.

Other Happenings: New York Yankee Lou Gehrig plays his last and 2,130th consecutive game on April 30, turns first base over to Babe Dahlgren. . . . On August 26, first televised game emanates from Ebbets Field, where the Brooklyn Dodgers and Cincinnati Reds split a doubleheader. The first televised college baseball game takes place earlier, on May 17, at Baker Field, New York. With Bill Stern calling the plays, Princeton beats Columbia, 2-1, in 10 innings. . . . The first TV prizefight also occurs about this time, on June 1, Lou Nova defeating Max Baer on an eleventh-round TKO. . . . Tennis is first televised on August 9, the Eastern Grass Court Championships at the Westchester Country Club, New York. . . . In football, Frank Filchock of the Washington Redskins connects with Andy Farkas for a 99-yard touchdown pass. . . . At Washington Park, Chicago, the first daily double to pay over $10,000 occurs on August 14, Joy Bet and Merry Caroline paying $10,772.40 to Claude Elkins of Anna, Illinois. . . . In the National Hockey League, Muzz Patrick and Art Coulter become the first bearded players on record . . . but the season ends on a sad note when Montreal Canadiens coach Babe Siebert is drowned. . . . Baseball fans find it ironic that a great former player, Grover Cleveland "Pete" Alexander, earns his living by working with a flea circus. . . . After two years of winning Davis Cup play, the United States loses tennis competition to Australia, 3-2, matches being played at Merion Cricket Club, Haverford, Pennsylvania. . . . On January 3, Don Budge makes his professional tennis debut at Madison Square Garden, New York, before 16,000 fans . . . Kansas miler Glenn Cunningham requests that spectators planning to attend the Pennsylvania AC indoor meet at Philadelphia refrain from smoking in order that he may breathe better and run in better time. . . . On April 15, underwater photo finish is used for first time in national AAU swimming meet at Detroit. . . . Coed drum majorettes at the University of Nevada are ordered to wear skirts that reach as least to the middle of the knee.

1940

Winners: Baseball: The World Series pits Paul Derringer of Cincinnati against Detroit's Bobo Newsom. Both win two games and lose one, but the Reds take the fall classic, 4 games to 3, the first championship for Cincinnati in 21 years. . . . *Kentucky Derby:* Gallahadion. *Preakness:* Bimelech. *Belmont Stakes:* Bimelech . . . *Indy 500:* Wilbur Shaw . . . *Boxing:* Joe Louis has tough fight against Arturo Godoy but retains crown easily. In middleweight division, Tony Zale knocks out Al Hostak in thirteenth round to become champ and Fritzie Zivic strips Henry Armstrong of the welterweight title. Lew Jenkins KOs Lou Ambers in the third to take lightweight championship; Harry Jeffra wins decision over Joey Archibald in featherweight class. . . . *Golf: USGA Men's Open:* Lawson Little. *PGA:* Byron Nelson. *Masters:* Jimmy Demaret . . . *Hockey:* 1939–40 Stanley Cup is taken by New York Rangers. . . . *Football: Cotton Bowl:* Clemson 6, Boston College 3. *Orange Bowl:* Georgia Tech 21, Missouri 7. *Rose Bowl:* USC 14, Tennessee 0. *Sugar Bowl:* Texas A&M 14, Tulane 13 . . . *National Football League:* Chicago Bears 73, Washington Redskins 0 . . . *Basketball:* 1930–40 *NCAA:* Indiana 60, Kansas 42. *NIT:* Colorado 51, Duquesne 40.

Other Happenings: In the battle of the halfbacks, Michigan (5–0) and Tom Harmon meet Minnesota (5–0) and Bruce Smith on November 9. Minnesota comes away with a narrow 7–6 victory. . . . On April 16, Bob Feller pitches Opening Day no-hitter for Indians, defeating White Sox, 1–0. . . . Basketball's first TV game is broadcast on February 28 from Madison Square Garden, Pittsburgh defeating Fordham, 50–37. Five days later, the nineteenth annual AAAA track meet is also televised from the Garden. Twenty-three colleges participate, and NYU wins with 27 points. . . . In NFL, Detroit Lions are fined $5,000 for tampering with Clyde "Bulldog" Turner, center from Hardin-Simmons drafted by the Chicago Bears, and Sam Baugh punts 35 times for an average of 51.4 yards. . . . On July 19, Conn Smythe of Toronto Maple Leafs mails letters to all players on hockey team, urging them to enlist immediately and defend the British Empire. . . . In August, baseball fans are startled and saddened to learn that Cincinnati catcher Willard Hershberger has committed suicide. . . . On April 30, Tex Carleton of Brooklyn Dodgers hurls no-hitter, beating Cincinnati, 3–0. . . . On March 2, Seabiscuit becomes all-time money-winning leader by finishing first in Santa Anita Handicap. . . . Nonstop marathon swim of the Mississippi River from St. Louis to Caruthersville, 292 miles, is made by John Sigmund in 89 hours, 48 minutes.

CHAPTER 32 — 1941

For the United States, it was to be the last year of peace until 1946, but of course few were certain of that as 1941 began. Sixteen months of conquests by Nazi Germany had seen most of Europe fall to Hitler's armies, but America was far away, even out of reach of Nazi bombers that flattened Coventry in November of 1940. There was still time to hope that something would come along to halt or somehow satisfy the warlords of Europe and Asia.

There were inklings, it is true, that all was not right. Selective Service was calling young men from all walks of life, even professional sports. As the new year started, the first to go was Ben Kish, a former football star at the University of Pittsburgh who played for the Brooklyn Dodgers of the National Football League in 1940. Informed that he had been called on December 31, 1940, Kish reacted with a stiff upper lip. "I am used to taking orders from the coach," he said, "so I guess I will be able to bear up under Army discipline." Meanwhile, Charles Gelatka, a member of the 1940 New York Giants, enlisted in the U. S. Army Air Corps. No questioning on the part of these men as to whether the undeclared war into which their country was being drawn was right or not. At least not on the surface.

FOOTBALL

The loss of these two athletes, however, was barely a trickle in the steady stream of inductions taking place in 1941. Sports heroes were still plentiful on January 6, when President Roosevelt declared that the American people "will not acquiesce in an Axis-dictated peace." Ninety thousand fans jammed the Rose Bowl to watch Stanford, led by left-handed quarterback Frankie Albert, beat Nebraska in a thriller, 21–13. In the process, he completed a record number of passes—12.

Teammate Peter Kmetovic was selected by the Helms Athletic Foundation as the game's outstanding player. In the Cotton Bowl, Texas beat Fordham, 13–12, while at Miami, more than thirty-five thousand, an overflow crowd, saw Mississippi State's Billy Jefferson provide the margin of victory over Georgetown by racing sixty-one yards for a touchdown.

It was a year when black stars were permitted to play in a segregated bowl of their own, namely the first annual Steel Bowl at Birmingham, Alabama, to determine the "national Negro title." The colleges in the contest, which was witnessed by a crowd of about 8,000, were Wilberforce, the midwestern champion, and Morris Brown of Atlanta, representing the South.

Wilberforce scored first when Bill Schnebly, a 266-pound tackle, booted a field goal, but from that point on Morris Brown showed its superiority. Fullback John Moody pounded out a series of first downs, taking the ball to the Wilberforce thirty-three-yard line. From there Joe Jenkins, a speedster, swept right end on a double reverse to put Morris Brown ahead, 7–3. Defensive tackles Haywood Settles and William Wysinger continued to stop Wilberforce for the rest of the game, which was won by Morris Brown, 19–3. Everyone agreed that the segregated bowl had been well handled and that the black players should be invited back the next year.

Meanwhile, fans who like all-star games reveled in the sixteenth annual East-West

Who?
January 1, 1941: Meanwhile, in the American Basketball League on this date, the Washington Brewers beat the New York Jewels by a score of 29–26.

Shrine game at San Francisco, which featured stars such as Paul Christman of Missouri for the West and Forest Evashevski and Tom Harmon for the East. Christman's pinpoint passing led the West team to a 20–14 victory.

The rash of bowl games completed, sports fans of January 1941 had time to consider which of their heroes might or might not be called up by the armed forces. Brooklyn Dodger fans received good news on the tenth when it was learned that their dynamic thirty-five-year-old manager, Leo Durocher, had been placed in Group 3, a deferred classification that practically guaranteed that he would not be called for the rest of the year. Detroit Tiger fans had less happy news. On January 15, 1941, began the Hank Greenberg saga, a bittersweet drama that was to continue throughout the year. Despite the fact that "Hammerin' Hank" had hit 41 home runs, batted .340, and been voted the American League's Most Valuable Player in 1940, a Selective Service official declared that he "probably will be in the Army by June 1." Without Greenberg, the pennant-winning Tigers of 1940 would be an ordinary club, said those who felt the thirty-year-old slugger should be deferred. As for Hank himself, reportedly the highest-paid player in baseball, he professed to be resigned to the whole thing. "He indicated he would not ask for deferment," said W. H. Wells, chief clerk of Greenberg's draft board.

The widening war was breaking up sports on both sides of the Atlantic. Fans of former heavyweight champion Max Schmeling—of whom there were only a handful in the United States—received the news that the pride of Germany would not fight in 1941 because of intensive training with the Luftwaffe's parachute corps. Those who hated Schmeling as a prewar representative of Hitler hated him even more now that he was a potential military foe. Even worse was the fact that Schmeling had volunteered rather than waiting to be drafted. (Americans who volunteered were heroes; Germans who volunteered were warmongers, the rationale of 1941 said.)

Elsewhere In Sports, January 1941:

Cycling record established: Starting on April 27, 1940, at New York, cyclist Raymond (Slug) Bryan reached San Francisco on May 24, just twenty-seven days, eleven hours later. The time was recognized as a record by the Amateur Bicycle League of America on January 13, 1941.

BOXING

With or without Max, the fight fan of January 1941 had plenty of action. On the sixteenth, a long-awaited rematch between welterweight champion Fritzie Zivic and Henry Armstrong, former champ, took place at Madison Square Garden. The two had fought on October 4, 1940, Zivic winning, but few thought the twenty-eight-year-old Armstrong, only man to hold three world boxing championships at the same time, was even slightly over the hill. Betting on the fight's outcome was brisk but uncertain. Early in the month Armstrong was installed as a 5–9 favorite, but by the morning of the fight the odds had slipped to 5–7. When the two men entered the ring, it was a matter of 6–5 and pick your own choice, so close was the betting. And financially, the battle was a huge success. More than twenty-three thousand customers jammed the Eighth Avenue arena, the largest crowd ever assembled there. Police had to form a human wall in order to keep an estimated five thousand more from pushing their way inside, but there was no panic or rowdyism.

Henry Armstrong's Glory Days:
October 29, 1937: *Became featherweight champion by knocking out Petey Sarron in the sixth round.*

May 31, 1938: *Became welterweight champion by beating Barney Ross in a fifteen-round decision.*

August 17, 1938: *Won Lightweight crown by beating Lou Ambers in a fifteen-round decision.*

The Fall From Glory:
August 22, 1939: *Lost lightweight championship to Lou Ambers in a fifteen-round decision.*

October 4, 1940: *Lost welterweight championship on fifteen-round decision to Fritzie Zivic.*

1938: *Preferred to fight at higher weights, so resigned featherweight crown. Elimination bout installed Joey Archibald as champion.*

Zivic outweighed Armstrong by five pounds, but the real difference was not one of weight. Armstrong seemed to have slipped greatly from his glory days of three years before, when he was described as a "human windmill." Nor could it have been a matter of age. Zivic was but one year younger and had fought more fights. "The battle was intensely a savage one," a reporter wrote. "Zivic won

Bobo Newsom, The Nomad of Baseball:
During a career that extended from the 1920s to the 1950s, Bobo Newsom (1907–62) was with a total of 17 clubs. After brief stints with the Dodgers and Cubs, 1929–32, he came to the major leagues more or less permanently in 1934. That year and part of the next was spent with the Browns and Senators; in 1937 he was traded to the Red Sox, then back to the Browns again for 1938 and 1939. He also spent part of '39 with the Tigers, the team that housed him longest, through 1941, his glory days when he had seasons of 20–11 and 21–5. In 1942, however he was dealt back to the Senators (time No. 2), then to the Dodgers (time No. 2), Browns (time No. 3), Senators (time No. 3), and finally the A's in 1944. Here he found a second "home," at least until the end of 1946, when he was sent to the Senators (time No. 4). In 1947 he stayed with the Yankees long enough to win seven games, then went to the Giants. After an extensive vacation from the majors from 1949 through 1952, he showed up with the 1952 Senators (time No. 5) and 1953 A's (time No. 2) before retiring at the age of 46. His lifetime record was 211 wins, 222 losses.

nine of the completed eleven rounds by out-boxing and outfighting Armstrong. Disdainful of a once-powerful fighting machine that held no power and no danger this time, Zivic did what he said he would. He knocked out his opponent."

The records indicate that the end came on a technical knockout, however, for the game Armstrong was on his feet at the end. By the eighth round, his face was bruised and swollen, cuts had formed under both eyes, and Zivic consistently hit with such force as to dislodge Armstrong's mouthpiece. At the conclusion of the tenth round, the referee, Arthur Donovan, attempted to have Armstrong retire. When he refused, Donovan said he would give him one more round.

The former champion tried to make the most of the opportunity. At the belt, he leaped forward and pinned Zivic against the ropes. For two minutes he fought like his former self, driving his opponent around the ring, forcing him to do nothing but think of ways to protect himself. But he could not apply the clincher, and during the last minute Zivic started countering the assaults of Armstrong.

A doctor representing the New York State Athletic Commission examined Armstrong's eyes between rounds and consented to let him resume. But after only fifty-two seconds of the twelfth round, when it became apparent that Armstrong was out on his feet, Donovan stopped the fight. For Henry Armstrong, the end of an illustrious career was at hand. His last fight was in 1942.

BASEBALL

Baseball returned to the headlines soon afterward when Bob Feller signed his 1941 contract with the Cleveland Indians. Just 22 years old, Feller already had 82 wins to his credit as well as 973 strikeouts. Even more to the point, he was improving every year. Because Indian officials fully expected this trend to continue, Feller was given a record $30,000

Endangered Species, Early 1941:
According to Selective Service reports of January 1941, the following sports figures were already inducted or in danger of being inducted:
College Football:
Jerry Hines, Coach, New Mexico Aggies
Eddie Schwartzkopf, All-Conference guard, Nebraska
Hugh Gallarneau, halfback, Stanford
Don Scott, quarterback, Ohio State
Pro Football:
Dan Topping, owner, Brooklyn Dodgers
Dave Smukler, fullback, Philadelphia Eagles
Chuck Gelatka, New York Giants
Baseball:
Hank Greenberg, Detroit Tigers
Morrie Arnovich, Cincinnati Reds
Golf:
Ed (Porky) Oliver
Boxing:
Petey Sarron, former featherweight champion
Track and field:
Pete Zagar, NCAA and AAU discus-throwing champion

contract, passing previous highs of $27,500, which had been earned by Lefty Grove and Dazzy Vance. A great deal was made in the papers about the record salary paid the young man, especially in Detroit, where Tiger owner Walter O. Briggs broke a long-standing precedent about keeping salary figures secret to reveal that Feller was not the highest-paid pitcher in baseball. The lucky man for 1941 would be not an Indian, but a Tiger, Norman "Buck" ("Just call me Bobo") Newsom. The hero of the 1940 World Series, Briggs said, had earned $30,000, including his bonuses, in 1940, and would receive $35,000 in 1941. That seemed to settle the issue for the time being, it being a while before anyone again cast doubts on the generosity of Tiger owner Briggs.

On the same day Feller's announcement was made, the Boston Red Sox quietly reported the signing of Robert (Lefty) Grove, no doubt for a considerably smaller figure. Almost 41 years old, Grove had posted a 7–6 record for the Red Sox in 1940, bringing his lifetime victory total to 293. He wanted to enter the charmed circle of 300-game winners, of course, but he was only a pale image of the once-powerful fast-baller who won 31 games a decade before. No one had any illusions that the Red Sox would keep him around for sentimental reasons if he became completely ineffective, but most fans and players were pulling for Lefty to achieve his goal.

No doubt the Red Sox had reasons for signing Grove that were at least partly selfish. Each day the draft situation was changing drastically, and as more young prospects entered the service for indefinite periods, the experienced veterans, even those nearing 41, became more valuable. "From the owner of a National Football League team to the slugging outfielder of a champion softball club, from the former bow man of a Pennsylvania varsity crew to a title-winning discus thrower," the Associated Press wrote on January 25, 1941, "the sports world already is feeling the effects of the Selective Service Act."

In certain specialized cases, the "effect" was considerable. New Mexico State Teachers College, for example, reported early in 1941 that every player on the football and basketball teams had volunteered for service. The University of Pennsylvania also seemed to have been particularly hard-hit, losing two varsity oarsmen and a star football player as well as a half dozen or more athletes who starred in several sports. In contrast, major-league baseball was fairly well off, but no one knew how long the lull would last. Problems had already been created in at least one case —that of outfielder Morrie Arnovich. After hitting .250 with Philadelphia and Cincinnati in 1940, Arnovich had been traded to the Gi-

ants, who welcomed him just about the same time Uncle Sam sent his welcoming questionnaire to the player. Faced with having traded for a man they would soon lose, the Giants were in a quandary. Should they try to void the deal? Or should they appeal for a deferment for Arnovich? Consulted as to the better course of action, National League President Ford Frick, not uncharacteristically, hedged. It depended, he said.

Of course there was always hope that an otherwise perfect athlete might locate a weakness that would disqualify him from Army service. Such a hope bubbled to the surface in the Morrie Arnovich case shortly after Ford Frick's shrewd analysis of the problems facing club owners. Originally classified 1-A, Arnovich telegraphed Giant owner Horace Stoneham that he had just been placed in group 1-B because of "dental deficiencies."

BOXING

One man who did not seem to be worrying about the draft, or anything else, was methodical Joe Louis, heavyweight champion for 3½ years, whose main goal in life seemed to be defending his title as often as possible. Sportswriters quickly dubbed the list of challengers the "bum of the month club," but no one doubted that Louis was the best champion who had come along in quite a while. After winning the title on an eighth-round knockout of James J. Braddock, June 22, 1937, Louis defended his title a dozen times, going an average of six rounds per fight. The thirteenth man to test the twenty-six-year-old champion was Clarence (Red) Burman of Baltimore, whose chance took place on January 31, 1941. Like many others, Burman believed his only hope for winning lay in a violent attack. As soon as the fight started, he therefore rushed forward, hooking furiously. Startling Louis, he opened a cut over the champion's right eye, landed several rights and lefts to his face, and battered him about the body at close quarters.

"Bum of the Month Club"—1937–40
Aug. 30, 1937: Tommy Farr—decision, 15
Feb. 23, 1938: Nathan Mann—KO, 3
Apr. 1, 1938: Harry Thomas—KO, 5
June 22, 1938: Max Schmeling—KO, 1
Jan. 23, 1939: John Henry Lewis—KO, 1
Apr. 17, 1939: Jack Roper—KO, 1
June 28, 1939: Tony Galento—KO, 4
Sept. 30, 1939: Bob Pastor—KO, 11
Feb. 9, 1940: Arturo Godoy—decision, 15
Mar. 29, 1940: Johnny Paychek—KO, 2
June 20, 1940: Arturo Godoy—KO, 8
Dec. 30, 1940: Al McCoy—KO, 6

He kept Louis so off balance that at one point the champion threw a left and slipped through the ropes.

His face betraying no emotion or anger, Louis bided his time, slowly learning the rhythm of Burman's style. Then he began to counterpunch in his expert way, throwing harder and harder lefts and rights split seconds before Burman was ready to defend against them. Moving his attack to the body, Louis found the soft spot he was looking for. Burman could absorb the shots to the head better than those to his midriff. One punch after another dug into the challenger's middle, paralyzing his attack, causing obvious pain. When Burman slipped to the canvas in the fifth round, it would have been possible to count to a hundred over his limp form. The thirteenth "bum of the month" had been dispatched, but Louis was characteristically generous. "That was the only man I've faced lately, except Tony Galento," he said, "who really tried to fight."

Less than three weeks later, Louis was back in the ring with challenger No. 14, Gus Dorazio, a rough-looking Philadelphian, who was determined to please his hometown fans —more than fifteen thousand of whom jammed Convention Hall in the City of Brotherly Love. Joe Louis displayed little affection for the local hero, however, sending him to the floor halfway through the second round with a smashing right to the jaw. Dorazio pitched forward, head first, to the canvas and welcome oblivion. Only the fact that he fought out of a strange crouch, confusing Louis in the first round, saved Dorazio from an earlier knockout.

Also About This Time:
New York Giant Manager Bill Terry announced that his team, which finished sixth in 1940, would improve. (He was right. They finished fifth in 1941). . . . *Frank Leahy signed a five-year contract to coach Notre Dame.* . . . *Babe Dahlgren, the man who replaced Lou Gehrig at first base for the Yankees in 1939, was sold to the Boston Braves, the first of eight moves for Dahlgren until his retirement in 1946.*

HORSERACING

Everything in the sports world was not predictable, naturally. Whirlaway, the horse rated juvenile champion of 1940 by nearly every writer and/or expert, was heavily favored to win the Arcadia Purse at Hialeah on February 18, 1941, especially after winning his three-year-old debut the week before. The Calumet Farms racer was quoted at odds of 3–10, but never could get moving in the seven-furlong race. Carrying 122 pounds to the four other entries, 105½ and 110, Whirlaway was in fourth position at the quarter but moved close behind Agricole and Cadmium going into the stretch. Carrying 12 pounds' less weight over a short distance, the two horses were able to beat off the challenge of Whirlaway, whose advocates promptly started wondering if the much-acclaimed horse was really all that good.

The Hank Greenberg saga continued with rumors that the slugging outfielder had asked for, and received, an occupational deferment until the end of the baseball season. Detroit fans promptly emitted sighs of relief, but official denials from both the American League office and team headquarters confused the situation even more. Meanwhile, British forces occupied Benghazi, German staff officers began to appear in Sofia, Bulgaria, and the U. S. Army Air Force started surveying American golf courses to see which ones would be suitable as emergency landing fields. It was not a world bulging with security.

HOCKEY

Hockey fans could be distracted, however, especially if they happened to be devotees of the Boston Bruins, a team in the process of putting together the longest undefeated streak in the history of the NHL until that time. Unbeaten since December 21, 1940, the Bruins took on the New York Americans at Boston on February 23, having a run of twenty-two consecutive victories behind them. From the game's very beginning, they seemed determined to add to that glittering record, bombarding New York goalie Charlie Raynor with sixty-three shots while scoring three times. The Bruins held New York to a single goal, adding their twenty-third game to the string.

Two days later, the Bruins put the record on the line against the Rangers, who performed in listless fashion until midway into the third period. At that point, however, Bruin captain Dit Clapper was sent to the penalty box and New York came alive. With the scored tied, 0–0, Babe Pratt of the Rangers charged into the Bruin zone and passed to Lynn Patrick following him. Patrick fired at the goal, missed, but New York's Brian Hextall picked up the rebound and drove it past Boston goalie Frankie Brimsek from twenty feet out. A second goal was added later, but that was merely icing on the cake. The Boston streak was halted at twenty-three.

BASEBALL

With the baseball season rapidly approaching, it was disclosed that Hank Greenberg in-

Other Sports-draft News of This Time: *Cambridge, Massachusetts: "An appeal for deferment by pitcher Hugh Mulcahy has been denied and the Phillies' ace right-hander will be subject to induction March 8. . . ."*

Cleveland, Ohio: "Uncle Sam has virtually wrecked the Cleveland Rams' backfield. . . . Ollie Cordill . . . is now awaiting appointment to the Army Air Corps. Quarterback Vic Spadaccini and Dante Manani, Cordill's understudy as halfback, have been placed in Class 1-A by their draft boards. . . ."

Durham, North Carolina: "W. G. Bramham, president of the National Association of Professional Baseball Leagues, said today that induction of players into the national defense program had affected the minor leagues only slightly . . . Since October 1, 1940, and up to and including March 14, 1941, only forty-one players have been accepted into the armed forces of the government and only thirty-nine others have voluntarily retired for any and all purposes." (At that time, there were more than three hundred minor-league clubs, each with about twenty players.)

deed had suggested to his draft board that he be placed in Class 2 rather than Class 1, which would allow him to play the 1941 season and earn the $55,000 Detroit planned to pay him that year instead of the $21 a month the Army had in mind. "My years of earning power are limited," Greenberg wrote in his questionnaire, bringing up a point that athletes have used since time immemorial to justify special treatment and extravagant salaries. "One year out of action will reduce my effectiveness considerably. I shall not be able to resume my present capacity after one year's absence." Greenberg, interviewed while vacationing in Los Angeles, denied that he had "asked" for deferment. In any event, the draft board turned down his suggestion, a development that obviously did not sweeten Greenberg's attitude toward newsmen who continually questioned him about his draft status. "The only way you can get along with news-papermen is to be like Dizzy Dean," he said finally. "Say something one minute and something different the next."

Detroit fans who were inclined to wring their hands at the loss of Greenberg had to wait only a few days before life was restored to their spirits, however. On March 11, another examination of the Tiger outfielder showed that he was afflicted with a condition known as "second-degree bilateral pes planus," or flat feet. Dr. Grover C. Freeman of Lakeland, Florida, made the diagnosis, which brought delight to Tiger partisans. Three days later, Greenberg was reportedly placed in draft category 1-B, a "limited duty" classification. Most important, as no men with 1-B classifications had been drafted in the Detroit area, there were signs of hope that Hammerin' Hank might be available for the entire season.

By spring, it was apparent that the draft situation had changed radically since the beginning of the year. Already among the inducted

were Charles (Chuck) Fenske, one of the nation's greatest milers . . . Hugh (Losing Pitcher) Mulcahy, the "ace" righthander of the Phillies who led the league in 1940 with twenty-two losses . . . Bert Oja, former Minnesota football player who helped bring the Canadian rugby championship to western Canada when he played with the Winnipeg Blue Bombers of 1935. . . . And it seemed that each day brought new changes in players' classifications, especially after President Roosevelt signed bill No. 1776, the Lend-Lease bill, guaranteeing financial assistance to the Allies, as well as increasing the U.S. commitment to one side in the struggle that so many wanted to avoid.

Say Those Teams Again, Please "Chicago, March 19, 1941: *The Detroit Eagles, who earlier had eliminated the 1939 and 1940 tournament champions, defeated the Oshkosk All-Stars, 39–37, to win the 1941 world pro basketball title. . . . Third place went to the New York Renaissance, who defeated the Toledo White Huts, 57–42. . . ."*

There were constant reminders everywhere that things were not normal. On March 21, 1941, Joe Louis knocked out Abe Simon, the fifteenth "bum of the month," in the first round at Detroit. That was a sign of business as usual. But five days later, Melio Bettina, former light-heavyweight champion until decisioned by Billy Conn, was inducted into the U. S. Army.

And there were occasionally strange paradoxes. Just two days after running the fastest two miles in history (8:51.1), Joseph Gregory Rice was declared physically unfit for military service. Selective Service physicians who examined the young man said that he had a triple hernia.

There were stories of mass heroism or mass lunacy—as on April 3, when all eleven first-string players of the Boston University football team filed applications for service in the U. S. Naval Air Corps. In Buffalo, an entire baseball team shuffled off to the war as a unit.

But there was a certain amount of cynicism as well. Writing to the editor of a newspaper, one reader noted that, "Larry MacPhail need not worry about the draft for baseball players. It seems from what I hear that most baseball players are semi-invalids. While the rest of the world works six days a week, disregarding aches and pains, the baseball players ride the rails to and from the Mayo Clinic and Johns Hopkins. . . ."

Eventually a solid decision was made on Hank Greenberg. The news came on April 18, after the season had started, on a day when the slugger went 0 for 3 at the plate. While Cleveland pitcher Jim Bagby was horse-collaring Greenberg, Detroit Draft Board No. 23 declared him 1-A. That meant he would be called into the services as early as May 7.

Did the Indecision Worry Greenberg?
During eight seasons with the Tigers from 1933 to 1940, Greenberg never hit less than .301, with his highest average being .348. His home-run percentage during those years was .0078. During the first month of the 1941 season, while he waited for his future to be decided, Greenberg batted a low figure of .269, and hit 2 home runs in 67 at-bats, a percentage of .003.

BOXING

The month of April 1941 saw Joe Louis meet chunky Tony Musto during the "bum of the month" series, but in many ways Tony turned out to be a disappointment for those who thought Louis was hand-picking the worst challengers he could find in order to bring in purses. The fight, the first ever held in St. Louis for the heavyweight championship, was well attended by Musto partisans, who claimed that the man from Blue Island Illinois, who had never been knocked down in thirty-nine professional fights, would resist the most savage attack Louis could mount.

That record went by the wayside in the third round when Louis flashed a left hook to Musto's jaw, sending him to the canvas, but he bounced immediately to his feet without a count. During the middle rounds of the fight, Musto pressed the action, fighting out of a crouch, leaping out of it only to swing quick series of rights and lefts to any part of Louis's body he could reach with his short arms. The champion seemed content to straighten up Musto with hard jabs, a strategy that seemed ineffective at first but eventually paid off when the challenger's face broke into a series of raw, bleeding cuts. In the ninth round, the referee, Arthur Donovan decided that Musto had more than enough, awarding the decision to Louis on a technical knockout. Musto and his fans were able to claim a moral victory.

HORSERACING

In May the owners of the much-maligned Whirlaway claimed more than a moral victory when the Kentucky colt came into his own before seventy thousand racing fans at Churchill Downs. Despite Whirlaway's penchant for running wide and practically bouncing off both fences, the chestnut was the favorite to win the Kentucky Derby. Having Eddie Arcaro up helped, as did the fact that all eleven horses carried 126 pounds. The track was fast, the weather clear as the horses broke from the starting gate. Dispose took the lead, Whirlaway hanging near the middle of the pack until the mile post. On the final turn, Arcaro burst between two horses and let his horse run. Whirlaway took the lead at the top of the stretch and won going away by a margin of eight lengths. In so doing, a new track record of 2:01⅖ was set, beating the mark of 2:01⅘ established by Twenty Grand a decade earlier.

Kentucky Derby Times, 1931–41:

1931—Twenty Grand	2:01⅘
1932—Burgoo King	2:05⅕
1933—Brokers Tip	2:06⅘
1934—Cavalcade	2:04
1935—Omaha	2:05
1936—Bold Venture	2:03⅗
1937—War Admiral	2:03⅕
1938—Lawrin	2:04⅘
1939—Johnstown	2:03⅖
1940—Gallahadion	2:05
1941—Whirlaway	2:01⅖

BASEBALL

By May, the baseball season was well under way, with few players missing as a result of the draft, but many about to leave. The Cleveland Indians, led by Bob Feller, broke ahead early in the American League, largely as the result of a ten-game winning streak. This was matched by a similar burst in the

National by the St. Louis Cardinals, a team powered by Johnny Mize, Enos Slaughter, Johnny Hopp, and Marty Marion. The Cardinals were a bit thin in the pitching department, but most experts regarded them as the favorite.

The news in May was not good. Great Britain was forced to evacuate her troops from Greece, saw the battle cruiser *Hood* literally detonated by the guns of the German *Bismarck*, and was invaded by a solo peacemaker named Rudolf Hess. In America, President Roosevelt declared an "unlimited state of national emergency," while Joe Louis took care of Buddy Bear in seven rounds and Hank Greenberg prepared to join the U. S. Army. His last game of 1941 was a memorable one, the big slugger going out in style. Until then, Greenberg had not hit a home run for the entire young season, more than three weeks. But in the second inning of his farewell against the Yankees, he smashed his first off Ernie Bonham, then powered another on his next trip to the plate. Before the game he had received a pen and pencil set from the Briggs Stadium ground crew. After the 7–4 victory, Greenberg quietly packed his belongings and left for Fort Custer, Michigan, and an entirely new life. Ever the sport, owner Briggs canceled Greenberg's enormous salary immediately.

HORSERACING

Horseracing continued to grab the headlines during the late spring as Whirlaway and Eddie Arcaro won the second leg of the Triple Crown, Pimlico's Preakness, with ridiculous ease. The first time he passed the grandstand, Whirlaway was five lengths behind the entire field. The next time he passed, he was five lengths ahead. The purse of $69,500 brought the horse's earnings to $194,691. Five days later, at Chicago, a nineteen-year-old jockey named Jim Berger stole the racing limelight by riding five winners in a row at Sportsman's Park. After losing the first race, he booted home five long shots one after the other, none of the horses paying off in less than

double figures. The feat, which had not been accomplished in nearly two years, was not really a rarity, having been performed sixty-five times in the history of American racing until that time, but the young jockey was treated with well-deserved respect.

BASEBALL

That same day, a twenty-six-year-old outfielder for the New York Yankees, Joe DiMaggio, came to the plate against Chicago White Sox pitching and hit safely one time in four at-bats. For the young slugger, who had a .343 batting average for five seasons in the major leagues, May 15, 1941, did not seem like a particularly good day. But it did start something, as DiMaggio and the nation found out later. As it turned out, DiMaggio and the Yankees could do very little wrong in 1941. On May 30, the Yankee Clipper made four errors in two games against the Boston Red Sox, booting a grounder, dropping a fly ball, and twice throwing the ball all the way to the grandstand while trying to cut them down at the plate. But the team continued to win, and Joltin' Joe upped his consecutive-game hitting streak to a modest fifteen games.

Early the next month, on June 2, 1941, the sports world was nearly as stunned as a decade earlier when Knute Rockne had been killed—except that the rapid physical decline of Lou Gehrig had prepared his friends and admirers for the "Iron Horse's" eventual death. Not yet thirty-eight years of age, it seemed impossible that the man who played in 2,130 consecutive games for the New York Yankees had surrendered to the strange paralyzing disease that forced him out of the lineup on May 2, 1939. (His last game was actually played on April 30.) His last days, during which he worked for the New York City Parole Commission, had not been happy ones. The crippling disease continued to sap his strength; in addi-

---

Jim Berger's Big Day—May 15, 1941

Race	Horse	Paid For $2.00 First
2	Killarney Lass	$15.20
3	Millmore	$33.80
4	Patapsco	$12.80
5	Colonel Martis	$11.00
6	Linkville	$31.80
	Total:	$104.60

A $2.00 parlay of the five consecutive winners would have paid $143,770

Was It for Lack of an Aspirin?
Years after Lou Gehrig broke into the New York lineup to stay, the man he replaced at first base, Wally Pipp, said that it happened because he had a headache. In a loud voice, he called down the bench, "Anybody got an aspirin?" But no help was forthcoming. On a hunch, Manager Miller Huggins inserted "the kid," Gehrig, in the lineup. After the 1925 season, Pipp was traded to Cincinnati, where he remained through 1928, retiring at age thirty-five. He died in 1965.

tion, a New York newspaper attributed the extraordinary late-season collapse of the Yankees in 1940 to the fact that several key players had become infected with Gehrig's disease. Gehrig filed a one-million-dollar libel suit against the paper, which quickly apologized, but the mental anguish probably hastened his decline.

In the midst of tragedy such as the death of Gehrig, drama such as DiMaggio's hitting streak, and concern over the international situation, one baseball event was almost totally overlooked. At the beginning of June 1941, Ted Williams, the hawk-eyed twenty-two-year-old slugger with Boston, was batting .429. Of course, such a pace in the spring and early summer could be dismissed easily. Many players over the years had shown a hot bat early in the year but no one had ended the season over .400 since 1930, when Bill Terry edged over the magic line with a .401 average. In the American League, the trick had not been managed for nearly two decades, since Harry Heilmann hit .403 with the 1923 Tigers.

June 1941: Gary Cooper was starring in *Sergeant York,* the story of a pacifist who finds he rather enjoys knocking off people, as long as they're enemy soldiers. . . . Don Ameche and Mary Martin got into the temper of the times with *Kiss the Boys Goodbye.* . . . Bob Hope played the war for laughs with *Caught in the Draft,* featuring a scene in which a reluctant draftee tries to induce flat feet by jumping from a high place onto his outstretched arches. . . . Before a sweltering crowd, Whirlaway won the Belmont Stakes to become the first Triple Crown winner since War Admiral in 1937. . . . Britain, meanwhile, invaded Cyprus, and Germany invaded the Soviet Union. . . . Joe DiMaggio passed the twenty-nine-game hitting streak of Roger Peckinpaugh in 1929 and Earl Combs in 1931, and having become the all-time Yankee leader, started after Willie Keeler's 1897 record of forty-four games. . . . Dom DiMaggio, who batted .301 in 1940, was turned down by the Army because of "poor eyesight" (but they got back to him later). . . . Lefty Grove, struggling desperately, won career game No. 298. . . . London bookmakers, even without the United States as a fully active participant, made the Allies 3–1 odds to win the war before the end of the year.

BOXING

The best fight of the year took place on June 18. At 199½ pounds, Joe Louis outweighed challenger Billy Conn by 25 pounds, but Billy was faster than any of Louis's previous opponents and also smarter—for twelve rounds. No one gave him that much chance at the beginning, but as the fight progressed, it became obvious that Conn had the ability to win on points. Retreating, making Louis miss and look bad, Conn still packed a fair wallop. With his speedy punches, he often forced Louis to hold on. Going into the twelfth round, hardly anyone had Louis ahead in the scoring. "I knew I was losing the fight," Louis said. "My handlers let me know it, even if I didn't know it myself."

In the twelfth round, however, Billy Conn received the gift of something he didn't need at that particular moment—too much success. Until the twelfth, his methodical attack-and-retreat plan had worked to perfection, but in that round he suddenly found that he could hurt the mighty Joe Louis. After hooking two lefts to the head, Conn pounded the champ's body, then staggered Louis with lefts and rights to the face. Joe was holding at the bell.

Between rounds, the idea grew in Conn's mind that he could do something better than win the championship on points. He could knock out Joe Louis. Across the ring, Louis was also thinking. "I was studying Conn all through the fight," he recalled later, "and finally figured I'd nail him when he started to throw a long left hook. . . . I was hoping that he'd lose his head pretty quick, because I knew I was losing the fight."

The fine edge of caution was gone from Conn's style in the thirteenth round. His first punch was a right smash at Louis's head. They continued to trade punches, Conn giving more than he took, until Joe Louis's amazing reflexes told him he had a split-second opening. Conn was staggered by the hard right hand, but continued to fight back instead of retreating. The fighters traded rights to the head, then Louis drilled two rights to Conn's chin. He followed with a couple of fast lefts, then another left and right. Conn sank to the canvas and was counted out at 2:58 in the round. "He knows what it's all about in there," Louis said after the fight, "and if he only could have kept his temper down he might have been the champion."

BASEBALL

Joe DiMaggio, meanwhile, just kept rolling along. Even when a fan stole his favorite bat, he continued to hit, ending the month of June with a streak of forty-two games. The Yankees, meanwhile, were working on a team home-run streak of twenty-five games when the Boston Red Sox came to New York for a doubleheader on July 1. Ted Williams' batting average had dropped from a torrid .429 to a mere .404 by this time, but no one seemed to pay much attention to that. At stake was DiMaggio's chance to tie Willie Keeler's record of forty-four games.

The Yankee Homer Streak—June 1–June 29, 1941:

While Joe DiMaggio continued to extend his consecutive-game hitting streak during that amazing June of 1941, the Yankees as a team put on an impressive show of firepower by playing twenty-five consecutive games in which at least one batter hit a home run. It went like this:

Date	Game No.	H.R. Hit by	Date	Game No.	H.R. Hit by
Jun 1	1	Sturm	Jun 16	12	Gordon
		Selkirk	Jun 17	13	Keller
Jun 2	2	Henrich	Jun 18	14	Keller
		Henrich	Jun 19	15	Keller
Jun 3	3	DiMaggio	Jun 20	16	Henrich
Jun 5	4	Henrich			Keller
Jun 7	5	Keller	Jun 21	17	Rizzuto
Jun 8	6	DiMaggio	Jun 22	18	DiMaggio
		DiMaggio			Rolfe
		Henrich	Jun 24	19	Rolfe
		Rolfe			Henrich
Jun 8	7	Keller			Gordon
		Gordon	Jun 25	20	DiMaggio
		DiMaggio	Jun 26	21	Henrich
Jun 10	8	Crosetti	Jun 27	22	DiMaggio
		Keller	Jun 28	23	Keller
Jun 12	9	Gordon	Jun 29	24	Henrich
		DiMaggio	Jun 29	25	Gordon
Jun 14	10	Henrich			Keller
Jun 15	11	DiMaggio			

DiMaggio did not prolong the agony in either game. In the opener, he contributed a hit in the fourth inning and added another later as the Yankees won, 7–2. But the only home run of the game was hit by DiMaggio—Joe's brother Dom of the Red Sox. The Yankee homer streak ended at twenty-five. In the second game, the Yankees pounced on Boston starter Jack Wilson early, in the first, when an error, singles by DiMaggio and Keller, and a double by Bill Dickey provided three runs. It was a good thing DiMaggio got his only hit early, for at the end of five innings it started to rain and the game was called. Each of the Yankee players received only three turns at bat, although the team won by a score of 9–2. When it was over, DiMaggio had tied the forty-four-game hitting streak of Willie Keeler —after a time lapse of forty-four years.

Year	Player	bats	Hits	2B.	3B.	H.R.	Pct.
1897	Keeler	201	82	11	10	0	.408
1941	DiMaggio	174	66	12	3	12	.379

Ted Williams went three for seven in the doubleheader.

The next day, 8,682 fans watched Joe DiMaggio get just one hit in five times at bat —a home run in the fifth inning off Heber (Dick) Newsome, a rookie who was somehow to survive and win nineteen games for the Red Sox that season.

As the hot summer continued, talk of DiMaggio's fantastic streak mingled with less-happy comments on America's growing involvement in what was already known as World War II—even without the United States. On July 16, at Cleveland, it seemed that DiMaggio could go on forever as he smashed two singles and a double three times at the plate. The next evening the largest crowd ever to see a game of night baseball in the major leagues—67,468—turned out to see if the hometown Indians could somehow stop the streak. Al Smith, thirty-three years old and a former Yankee, was the starting pitcher. Three times he faced DiMaggio, walking him once. Twice DiMaggio lashed the ball down the third-base line, and twice Ken Keltner made excellent plays to deprive Joe of a hit.

The most dramatic moment came in the eighth inning, when, with the bases loaded, relief pitcher Jim Bagby stared down at the plate as DiMaggio stepped into the box for the fourth time. Bagby threw a ball and a strike; then on the third pitch, DiMaggio hit a sharp grounder —into a double play. The streak had ended at fifty-six games.

St. Louis, July 20, 1941: *"In an open letter to Manager Joe McCarthy of the Yankees, J. E. Wray, sports editor of the* Post-Dispatch, *suggested today that Joe DiMaggio's uniform number be changed to 56."*

During the last days of July, Ted Williams' average dipped below .400 for the first time, but another member of the Red Sox, Lefty Grove, struggled to his three-hundredth victory on July 25. He needed a lot of help from his teammates to earn the 10–6 win, but it most assuredly counted. It brought Grove's 1941 record to 7–4. He tried three more times to notch No. 301, but finally settled for an even three hundred, joining the select group of those pitchers winning three hundred or more games. Undoubtedly, Grove could have added many more major-league victories to his record had it not been for Baltimore Oriole owner Jack Dunn, a shrewd minor-league operator who held onto players as long as possible in order to obtain the best deal from big-league clubs. Thus Lefty Grove did not pitch in the majors until he was twenty-five, having lost three or four productive years.

The Select Group, 1941:
Lefty Grove's three-hundredth victory put him in the company of Denton T. (Cy) Young (511 victories), Walter Johnson (416), Grover Alexander (373), Christy Mathewson (373), Charles A. (Kid) Nichols (360), Tim Keefe (344), John Clarkson (327), Eddie Plank (327), Charles Radbourn (310), and Mickey Welch (311). Keefe, Clarkson, Radbourn, and Welch, however, pitched before the distance was increased to 60 feet, 6 inches, and thus had a decided advantage.

TENNIS

Those with a penchant for more genteel spectator sports turned their attention that summer to Seabright, New Jersey, where twenty-year-old Robert L. (Bobby) Riggs was the latest scourge of the American tennis world. The occasion was the fifty-fourth annual invitation tennis tournament of the Seabright Lawn Tennis and Cricket Club, one of the pioneers in U.S. competition. "So convincing was the performance of Riggs," wrote one reporter, "who lost only one set all week, that the crowd . . . capitulated in the end to the player who mastery of the court was beyond question, and certainly beyond Schroeder's physical powers of resistance." Ted Schroeder, the former national champion, lost to Riggs by scores of 6–4, 6–4, and 6–0.

A Four-hour Tennis Match, 1941:
Not long after Riggs subdued Schroeder at Seabright, another match at Brookline, Mass., required a total of 102 games to complete. The players in the national doubles championship were Bryan M. Grant, Jr., and Russell Bobbitt, both of Atlanta, vs. Edwin Amark and Robin Hippinstiel, both of California. The Atlantans won by a score of 14–12, 15–17, 6–4, 4–6, 13–11.

BASEBALL

With the pennant race virtually over in the American League, no team coming close to the Yankees, baseball fans concentrated on the National League, where the Dodgers and Cardinals were fighting out a close one. In August, lean Lon Warneke (nicknamed "The Arkansas Hummingbird") of the Cardinals reached the high point of his career by pitching a no-hitter against the Cincinnati Reds, allowing only three men to reach first base. That was impressive but it didn't throw the Durocher-led Dodgers, who seemed to have a knack for winning the tough games. Early in September, with the Cardinals breathing down their necks, the Dodgers came into Ebbets Field for a series against the Giants, who cherished the thought of cheating their rivals out of their first World Series since 1920. The first game was won by Brooklyn, as was the second, 13–1, but the third and most crucial game started off badly for the Dodgers. In the fifth inning, with the score tied, 0–0, Dolph Camilli was called out by Umpire Tom Dunn on a high, hard pitch. This so enraged Dodger fans that bottles flew from the stands, narrowly missing Dunn's head. Manager Leo Durocher protested so vehemently that Dunn ejected him. Even worse, in the seventh, the Giants pushed across three runs. The Dodgers scored one in the bottom half of the inning, but could not score in the eighth.

In the ninth inning, however, the Dodgers managed to tie the game, the big hit being a two-run single by Joe Medwick. With the sky rapidly darkening, the tenth inning started. The Giants could do nothing against Hugh

Casey, but in the bottom half of the inning, Dodger catcher Mickey Owen led off with a single. Hugh Casey sacrificed him to second base. Dixie Walker flied out and Billy Herman was given an intentional pass. The next batter was Pete Reiser, who promptly singled across the winning run and touched off a storm of celebration. "Seemingly every fan present rose and all began sending a storm of paper onto the field. It came in cascades of torn bits as well as whole newspapers and score cards."

September brought not only the revelation that the Yankees and Dodgers would meet for the first time in the 1941 World Series, but also the resumption of long-dormant football. Could the powerful Chicago Bears repeat? Could the entire league survive the weird schedule the bosses had provided? (It was, for example, staggered in such a way that no two teams opened on the same Sunday as other teams, and the first game to count, between the Cleveland Rams and Pittsburgh Steelers, took place at Akron.)

The latter part of September brought Ted Williams into the final week of his battle with statistics. He was hitting slightly above .400 on the twenty-seventh when he faced Roger Wolff of the Philadelphia Athletics. Wolff, a thirty-year-old rookie, was hardly overpowering. His first time up, Williams walked. He doubled his second time, but after that Wolff retired him three times in a row, once on a strikeout. The Splendid Splinter's average fell from .4009 to .3996 There were only two games remaining on the Red Sox schedule, both against the A's. In the first, Williams found the groove against Dick Fowler, Porter Vaughan, and Tex Shirley, hitting his thirty-seventh home run and three singles to raise his average well above .400. At that point he could have sat down, but Williams played the second game as well, going two for three and finishing the season with a mark of .4057.

Sports News Flash, September 1941:
On September 28, it was reported to a shocked public that Marion Miley, ranked No. 2 among women golfers in 1939 and winner of many national tournaments, had been murdered by an unidentified masked man.

There was a brief respite from baseball while Joe Louis defended his title once again, this time against the possessor of a secret "cosmic punch." Colorful Lou Nova was the Victim of September 29, his end coming with terrifying swiftness in the sixth round. The celebrated "cosmic punch," if thrown, was barely noticed by the efficient Joe Louis.

Then it was back to baseball for the much-anticipated World Series of 1941. The Yankees were favored to win it in six games, but everyone knew an inspired team could defeat even a highly efficient machine in a short series. At least that was what Dodger fans were looking for.

Opening at New York, the Yankees took the first game by a score of 3–2, but not before the Dodgers almost tied it in the seventh inning. Then the Series was one game apiece after the second game, won by Dolph Camilli's single in the sixth. The victory stopped a New York Yankee World Series streak of ten games, going all the way back to the final game of the 1936 classic.

At Ebbets Field, Dodger hopes rose, but in the third game Yankee pitcher Lefty Russo's drive off the leg of Fat Freddie Fitzsimmons knocked the Dodger pitcher out of the box for good. The visitors then went on to score a pair of runs in the next inning to win, 2–1.

"No matter," died-in-the-wool Dodger fans said. And the Brooklyns did seem to retain their aplomb in the fourth game, despite the Yankees' jumping into a 3–0 lead. Battling back in the fourth and fifth innings, the Dodgers moved ahead, 4–3, and hung onto the lead through the eighth inning. Then it was the Yanks' final turn at bat. Hugh Casey was on the mound, and he worked well against Yankee leadoff batter Johnny Sturm, forcing him to ground out. Red Rolfe, Yankee third baseman, bounced the ball right back to Casey and was thrown out with yards to spare.

It was almost over when Tommy Henrich stepped into the box. Hugh Casey worked carefully, not wanting to allow a home run. The count reached three and two, then the Dodger pitcher snapped over a perfect curve ball. Henrich swung and missed. The game was over. Except that the ball skidded out of Dodger catcher Mickey Owen's mitt and rolled toward the backstop; Henrich made it safely to first base. The Yankees had a new life. They immediately took advantage of it, winning the game, World Series, and branding Mickey Owen with the "goat" tag for the rest of his life.

FOOTBALL

Football, fortunately for those who wanted to forget, was already in full swing. The New York Giants and Chicago Bears seemed the teams to beat in the professional variety, Minnesota the top college squad. Against the University of Pittsburgh on October 18, the Gopher captain and running back, Bruce Smith, demonstrated his ability in the second period of a scoreless battle by suddenly bursting forty-nine yards to the Pitt two-yard line. After this led to a score, Smith showed his passing skill by throwing for twenty-two yards, then ran for fourteen more. Another touchdown followed, and before the afternoon was over, Minnesota had beaten a rugged Pittsburgh squad by a score of 39–0. A highly touted All-American, Bruce Smith, was recognized as one of the best all-around backs in the nation. But because he was more liable to be drafted than many other collegians that year, he had to wait until the eleventh round of the professional college draft before being selected by the Green Bay Packers.

Slaughter of the Week, 1941:
Morehead, Kentucky, October 18: "It was billed as a football game—and to a certain extent, played as one—but the score, Morehead State Teachers College 104, Rio Grande College of Ohio 0— looked more like a claim of tank destruction on the battlefields of Russia when weary tally keepers jotted down the last touchdown today. Morehead, Kentucky mountain foothills school, set a new record for its gridiron history in the size of the score and nine Eagle backs contributed touchdowns. . . . Yardage gained: Morehead 686, Rio Grande 94."

It was that kind of a year, the international situation slowly but inexorably imprinting its character on most sports. Even the fifty-sixth National Horse Show in November 1941 departed from usual tradition to become an exhibition battleground for war technology. Instead of opening with a grand parade of horseflesh, the show began with a demonstration of Jeeps, motorcycles, and half-tracks.

Machine guns barked blank ammunition, a 37mm. antitank gun added its sharp voice to the cacophony of violence. It was all just in "fun," of course, rather like the practice blackouts and attempts to ration gasoline earlier in the year.

On top of this there was the news that champion Joe Louis had been classified 1-A, a sure inductee in 1942. But Hank Greenberg, it appeared, had found a way out of the Army. A new Government ruling provided that certain draftees over the age of twenty-eight could be released. Greenberg applied for his release and it was granted. Detroit fans, who felt the 1941 pennant had been stolen from them—the team had slipped to fifth in the standings—as a result of their losing the league's best player now thought there was hope to break the Yankee domination.

There was more baseball news as the year neared its final month. The Cleveland Indians announced the signing of shortstop Lou Boudreau to a player-manager contract, which made the twenty-four-year-old veteran of four seasons baseball's youngest manager. In Philadelphia, one day later, the Phillies announced that their new manager, Hans Lobert, would be the National League's oldest manager at age sixty. (Connie Mack, seventy-nine, manager of the Philadelphia A's was the only older pilot. This left the City of Brotherly Love with two last-place teams looking forward to the 1942 season under the guidance of managers averaging nearly seventy years of age.)

FOOTBALL
On the final day of November, professional football said farewell to Byron (Whizzer) White, twenty-four-year-old ace running back with the Detroit Lions. White, soon to join the Army, made the most of his last chance to play by racing for one touchdown in the first period against the Chicago Cardinals and hurling a twenty-three-yard TD pass to Bill

How Did the Youngest and the Oldest Managers Make Out?
Lou Boudreau took over a fourth-place Indian team with a 75–79 record in 1941 and converted it into a fourth-place team with a 75–79 record in 1942—that is, he won about 48 per cent of the time, and that is just about his lifetime mark as a big-league manager over sixteen seasons with the Indians, Red Sox, Kansas City A's, and Chicago Cubs. Altogether his clubs won 1,162 of 2,404 games, a per- *centage of .483. Only once, in 1948, did Boudreau win a pennant, and some say that was because bouncing Bill Veeck was general manager of the Indians that year.*

Hans Lobert took over a last-place club with a 43–111 record and converted it into a last-place club with a 42–109 record. (Somehow he conspired to play three less games, which is probably his greatest accomplishment.) Lobert didn't last long, being replaced by Bucky Harris in 1943.

Fisk in the third quarter. The Lions won, 21–3. On the same Sunday in Washington, Green Bay's superlative end Don Hutson did his best to lead his team past the Redskins and toward the Western Division title. Washington and Sam Baugh, of course, had other ideas, piling up a 17–0 lead at halftime. The largest crowd of the year for Washington, 35,594, sat back to enjoy the rout in the second half, but saw only an aerial circus, Cecil Isbell pitching and Don Hutson catching. Early in the third period, Green Bay took over on its own thirty-five. Isbell threw three times to Hutson, and the ball was on the Skin 30. Another pass for fifteen yards followed, then the TD pass, which was caught by Hutson over his shoulder.

Don Hutson's Record-breaking Day, November 30, 1941:
By scoring three touchdowns and kicking two extra points, Don Hutson set the following records:
1. *Most points in a season (95), bettering record of 79 set by "Automatic Jack" Manders of the Chicago Bears.*
2. *Most lifetime points (395), also beating Manders' record of 385.*
3. *Most TDs in a season (12), which was one better than the Redskins' Andy Farkas' 1939 mark.*

A few minutes later, big George Svendsen, Green Bay center, intercepted a pass by Baugh and took it twenty yards to the Washington fifteen. Clarke Hinkle, a nine-year vet-

eran running back, made eight yards up the center, setting the stage for the second Isbell–Hutson touchdown pass. At the start of the final period they continued their act, three completions in a row moving the Packers from their thirty-five to Washington's forty-six. Fading back from there, while everyone in the stadium knew he was looking for Hutson, Isbell waited, then fired the ball all the way to the goal line. Although covered by two men, Hutson snagged the ball and trotted into the end zone.

Nothing seemed to be going right for the Redskins. On the very next play, Ray Hare allowed the kickoff to trickle into the end zone and had to accept a safety. Green Bay went ahead, 22–17, and that was the way the game ended. The Packers still had an excellent chance to win their division title—if they could handle the Bears two weeks later. During those two weeks, the world of most Americans changed drastically. One of the most poignant stories was the Hank Greenberg saga. After fighting Army red tape for seven months, losing nearly fifty thousand dollars in salary, and finally earning his release, Hammerin' Hank returned to civilian life—on Saturday, December 6.

The next day, the Japanese attack on Pearl Harbor threw everyone into the same boat and created more than a bit of panic. Plans were immediately made to play the Rose Bowl not at Pasadena, which could be hit by Japanese forces, but at Durham, North Carolina. A rumor that golf balls and tennis balls would be in short supply set off a wave of hoarding. Colleges made plans to compress their courses into three-year programs so that men could be rushed through faster. Football took the lead in announcing that because of

---

The World War II "Line-up"
Shortly after the United States joined the Allies in December 1941, papers published "lineups" of the opposing "teams." It was probably not intentional, but it seemed more like a sports contest than a holocaust. The "lineups" were as follows (December 12):

The Allies

Australia	*Costa Rica*		
Belgium†	*Czechoslovakia†*		
Canada	*Dominican Republic*		
China	*El Salvador**		

*At war with Japan only
†At war with Germany only

Free France
Great Britain
Greece†
Guatemala
Haiti
*Honduras**
Netherlands Indies
New Zealand

Nicaragua
Norway†
*Panama**
Poland†
South Africa
Soviet Union†
United States
Yugoslavia

The Axis

Finland	Japan
Germany	*Manchukuo*
Hungary	*Rumania*
Italy	*Slovakia*

likely manpower shortages, unlimited substitutions would be allowed in the future. Constant pleas to refrain from war hysteria were issued, often in frantically strident tones. A survey showed that most major sports favored an "on with the show" policy. (Why shouldn't they favor continued profits? No one bothered to ask.) Some even felt it was a national obligation to stay open. Operators of race tracks at Santa Anita, Hialeah, Tropical Park, and the Fair Grounds held that "racing is recreation, and recreation helps morale."

FOOTBALL

Two major sports events, both concerning football, still had to be played in the hectic atmosphere at the end of the year. On December 14, the Green Bay Packers journeyed to Chicago for a climactic game with the Bears. Because the two teams had finished in a tie at the end of the regular season, the game would be the first divisional playoff in the history of the league. Packer players should have enjoyed the weather, which was clear, with temperatures about nineteen degrees. On the very opening kickoff, in fact, the Bears' Hugh Gallarneau fumbled the ball, and Green Bay tackle Charlie Schultz recovered on the Bears' nineteen-yard line. Five plays later, the Packers led, 7–0, and the game was only one minute, fifty-seven seconds old.

Gallarneau fumbled the next kickoff, but recovered himself. Then Norm Standlee, hard-driving fullback of the Bears, also lost the ball, and the Packers recovered. But the second time, the Bears held, blocking Hinkle's field-goal attempt. Not long afterward, Hugh Gallarneau grabbed a punt on his own eight-een-yard line and carried it eighty-two yards for a TD. The extra point was missed but Chicago was back in the game.

By the second quarter, the momentum had shifted completely. The Bears started to beat the Packers off the ball time and again. Then Green Bay developed a bad case of fumbleitis, losing the ball twice. Norm Standlee found the hard footing to his liking and rolled off gains that were short but consistent. By the end of the period, the score was 30 for the Bears, 7 for Green Bay.

The second half, happily for Bears' fans, provided no Isbell–Hutson heroics. The Bears were simply too tough. Hutson caught but one pass all afternoon. The final score: Bears 33, Packers 14.

The following Sunday, the Bears had it even easier, molesting the New York Giants to the tune of 37–9. The Bears were once again champions of the NFL, truly deserving of their nickname, "Monsters of the Midway."

The next day, moguls of the league sat down to draft college players. Because of the international situation, nineteen-year-old Bill Dudley of the University of Virginia was the first player taken, by the lowly Pittsburgh Steelers. Bruce Smith, 1-A by December 22, 1941, was the 119th player chosen, despite his acquisition of the year's Heisman Trophy. Merle Hapes—later famous in a pro football scandal—and Frankie Albert were also high choices. There was, everyone agreed, a great deal of talent available, but in view of the situation on planet Earth, the college draft that year must have seemed like an exercise in pure futility.

CHAPTER 33—BEING A PLAYER
ISN'T ALWAYS EASY

"Peters, who attempted to rescue the ball from his fallen companion, got a John L. Sullivan thwack between the eyes. . . . Another slugging match occurred at this point and the ball was given a brief respite. Ronaldo of Yale was stoned square in the mouth by somebody. . . . At the expiration of the intermission there was a rough-and-tumble fight, and the game was delayed while Ferry's breeches could be sewed up. . . ."

Above, just a few excerpts from the Thanksgiving Day football game between Yale and Princeton in 1884, attesting to the fact that playing the game isn't necessarily all glory and fun. Participation in sports, especially those involving bodily contact, inevitably entails risk of injury and even death. The athlete has traditionally accepted this risk, sometimes with almost happy anticipation; so too has the spectator gone along with the element of danger. In fact, some say that the games just wouldn't be the same for those in the stands or along the sidelines if the possibility of maiming or death were completely removed.

Therefore, going along with what the public seems to want, the athlete has seldom complained about the dangers inherent in his game or even hesitated to "fling himself into the fray"—which is why, inevitably, some have not come back, or have come back in a severely altered condition. Following is a very brief casualty list of some plucky but unlucky sports figures of the distant and recent past.

HIGH DIVING: SAM PATCH

Probably the first sports casualty in America whose death was seen by a large audience was Sam Patch, who was born in Massachusetts early in the nineteenth century. When he was barely a teen-ager he discovered that a crowd of admiring people inevitably gathered whenever he or one of his cohorts jumped into the river from the bridge near Sam Slater's cotton mill. And so Sam Patch and his hardier friends performed the trick over and over, sometimes leaping from the top railing of the bridge, occasionally from the roof of an adjoining mill.

Sam's friends eventually gave up sports-show business and worked their farms or went into some form of commercial enterprise, and

for a time Sam himself even had a fling at cotton manufacturing. But when a partner skipped town with the firm's profits, Sam migrated to Passaic, New Jersey, taking a job in a cotton mill. It was there that he first made the local newspapers, on September 30, 1827, by leaping from a covered bridge over Passaic Falls. Raw courage aside, making the leap was no easy matter, for the bridge was still under construction and guarded by constables. Sam had to perform some expert footwork to dodge them before going over the edge.

His reputation made by that one burst of publicity, Sam searched about for encores, one of his most sensational being a dive into the Hudson River from the masthead of a sloop ninety feet above the water. A crowd of about five hundred watched.

"Sam's Song"—Part 1:
Sam Patch achieved the ultimate honor of being "immortalized" in song and story, and even had a race horse named after him long after he was gone. Forty years after his death, he was still so celebrated that a poem about him appeared in a children's book:
"Come and hear the story told of the feats of Sam the Bold.
All the heroes ever seen—heroes fat and heroes lean;
Heroes short and heroes tall! Heroes heavy, heroes light,
Heroes black and heroes white, Up from General Thumb the plucky
To the Giant of Kentucky,
Were not fit to hold a match to our hero, Sammy Patch!"

Before long, Sam was in demand throughout the East, and in 1829 he was invited by a group of Buffalo citizens to add spice to the blasting of Table Rock at Niagara by leaping over the Falls. Sam replied with alacrity via a poster that read: "I shall, ladies and gentlemen, on Saturday next, October 17, precisely at 3:00 P.M., leap at the Falls of Niagara, from a height of 120 to 130 feet (being 40 to

50 feet higher than I leapt before), into the eddy below. On my way down from Buffalo, on the morning of that day, in the steamboat *Niagara*, I shall, for the amusement of the ladies, doff my coat and spring from the mast-head into the Niagara River."

"Sam's Song"—Part 2:
"See his genius budding wild, even as a little child,
When he turned a bold 'flip-flap' from his frightened mother's lap,
And she thought her darling boy had ended there her hope and joy.
Soon of courage he gave proof, jumping from the hen-house roof;
Frightened hens cried 'Cluck! Cluck! Cluck!' 'Quack! Quack! Quack!' screamed goose and duck.
'Stop! Stop! Stop!' his mother cried. ''Tis too late!' Bold Sam replied.
Down he jumped, with deadly whack, on the screaming gander's back.
'Safe!' the mother cried with joy;
'Goose for dinner!' said the boy."

On Saturday morning of the appointed day it was raining, but the crowd was there along with a platform that had been constructed for Sam. Waving nonchalantly to the audience, Patch climbed the ladder and spent considerable time testing the platform and kissing the American flag, waiting for the right psychological moment to descend. Finally it came. Sam Patch moved forward and jumped straightaway into the swirling waters. For what seemed a long while after he struck the surface, he remained hidden from view. Then, just as some began to shout that Patch was dead, he popped his head above the waves and started swimming toward shore. When he arrived there he supposedly greeted the first well-wisher with the line, "There's no mistake in Sam Patch!"

After being feted, admired, and interviewed, Sam decided to tackle the Genesee Falls at Rochester, which were only a hundred feet high. He rectified that situation by adding a twenty-five-foot tower. The event drew considerable attention prior to November 13, 1829. It was Friday, but Sam selected the unlucky omen to show his disdain for the whims of fate.

It would have been better, as it turned out, if Sam had chosen another day, for his condition on the appointed date was a bit erratic, to say the least. Some said later he appeared quite drunk; others contradicted this. Everyone did agree that his dive lacked its normal precision, being replaced by a flappy-armed, almost limp descent into the water. This led some to speculate that Sam had lost his nerve and substituted an especially fashioned dummy for himself. That seems unlikely, considering the courage he displayed on so many occasions. In any event, the eccentric dive was followed by a pair of significant departures from the normal format. The first was that Sam's head did not appear above the plane of cold, gray water as he swam, waving, toward the shoreline. The second was that the body of a man was found frozen in the ice at the mouth of the Genesee in March 1830, when a farmer broke it to water his horses.

"Sam's Song"—Versa Ultima:
"The moment comes—the people cheer—and call for Sam. "Sam Patch is here!"
But why that cloud upon his brow? Sam never looked so strange as now.
He gazes down with visage pale, as if he'd pierced the future's veil;
He looks around on earth and sky, as though he bade the world good-bye,
He takes his 'kerchief from his neck, and barely can emotion check.
'Here, Tom!' he said, 'you bear on this, to my poor mother, Sam's last kiss.'
He jumps! He sinks! The waters roar above him and he's seen no more;
And as their breath the people catch, they sigh, 'Alas! Brave, foolish Patch!'"

PRIZEFIGHTING: WEEDEN-WALKER

The report from Philadelphia started out in casual fashion. "A steamer left this city last night, having on board the pugilists Weeden and Walker and their friends. A landing was effected on the New-Jersey shore, where a ring was formed near Pennsville, and the fight commenced." The "great battle" of 1876 was eagerly viewed by an audience of from seven hundred to one thousand, many of whom followed the men all the way from Philadelphia, down the Delaware River via the *Creedmoor Cutter* (a glorified barge) to the small Salem County town of Pennsville, New Jersey.

Despite precautionary measures designed to throw the police off the scent—the match was held a day later than announced—the "secret" battle was seen by quite a few prominent Philadelphia citizens in disguise and was nearly halted by a vigilant Sheriff Heins of Salem County, who arrived on the scene shortly after the men started fighting. The large crowd intimidated Heins into allowing the bout to continue while he rounded up additional deputies.

Both participants were from the Southwark district of Philadelphia and had fought once before. On that occasion, Jimmy Weeden displayed greater skill, beating Billy Walker (whose real name was Phil Koster) and then continued to badger him for a second match. Finally, Walker accepted, and both men went into training.

Walker was assisted by Sam Collyer, one of the more celebrated professionals of the time, but that did not close the ferocity gap very much. According to the New York *Herald,* both men were in excellent condition but "the face of Weeden was much harder than his opponent. It was like a gun barrel, and seemingly as difficult to mark with the knuckles."

The bout was a crowd-pleaser in the classical bare-knuckle style. Both men explored each other's defenses, and Walker seemed to be doing rather well during the opening rounds, although by the twelfth round both of Billy's eyes had been damaged. Weeden pressed his advantage while partisans of both fighters shouted encouragement from ringside, yelling at their man, "Blow holes in him!" or words to that effect. After forty-eight minutes, the two had completed fifteen rounds and Walker's nose was bleeding. But they continued to battle for more than an hour, Weeden gradually wearing down Walker's ability to fight to the point where he was little more than a punching bag. At the end of the seventy-fifth round, Weeden came out of a

---

The Final Round:
"Walker had not recovered from the fall and punishment of the last round, and he came up staggering. To show his bewildered state, his hands were open and hanging by his side, though instinctively he clutched them for an instant but did not bring them into position. . . . Weeden, perceiving his plight, rushed at him with his whole might, smashed him with his right and left with the force of cannon balls and, then catching him, flung him down and again fell on him with his full weight. A cry went up to Heaven from the more tenderhearted at the cruel exhibition, while Weeden's friends cheered him until they were hoarse. Referee Gormley called 'time' for the next round and Weeden responded, but poor Walker still lay on the ground and was insensible. . . ."

---

clinch by staggering Walker with the heel of his right hand, then clamped hold of the weaker man and threw him to the ground, landing solidly on top of him.

After the brief rest period, Walker staggered out for the seventy-sixth round, obviously in a state of semiconscious helplessness. His hands were at his side, but that did not deter Jimmy Weeden from whaling away at the defenseless man until he collapsed. When Walker could not rise, Sam Collyer threw in the sponge and the fight was over. Walker was taken aside and laid on a pile of brushwood, the presumption being that after ten or fifteen minutes' rest he would be up and walking again.

Walker was still lying there when news arrived that Sheriff Heins and his deputies had taken command of the *Creedmoor Cutter* and were heavily armed and in the process of rounding up everyone connected with the fight. Jimmy Weeden and his seconds made a hasty exit, heading in the direction of Chester. Others scattered in every direction as confusion reigned. The next morning, Billy Walker's body was found at the Salt Wharf at Greenwich Point, several miles south of the fight scene.

A warrant was issued for the arrest of Weeden and his backers. Some said that Arthur Chambers, another famous fighter of the time, should be arrested because he had been instrumental in bringing the men together. That advice was never taken, but Detectives Allaire and Wade of the Fourteenth Precinct, Philadelphia, did manage to round up Weeden and Richard Goodwin, one of his seconds, on September 3, 1876, three days after the bloody battle. Weeden was charged with murder, and Goodwin was charged with being an accessory to murder, both being held in the Philadelphia jail.

Not the First Boxing Fatality in America:
The death of Phil Koster was preceded by at least one similar tragedy in the United States, following a bare-knuckle bout of September 13, 1849, at Hastings, New York. On that occasion, Chris Lilly knocked out Tom McCoy, who died of the injuries a short time later.

While they awaited the trial, several thousand persons, many doubtlessly inspired by morbid curiosity, attended the funeral ceremony of the late Phil Koster. The Reverend W. B. Erven of the Protestant Episcopal Church, Philadelphia, took the opportunity to attack "those who from secure positions use these victims as instruments whereby to further their own ends."

Two months later, on November 2, 1876, trial concluded in the Salem (New Jersey) County Court. By that time the list of defendants had grown to five, Sam Collyer and two of Weeden's backers having been tracked down and arrested. All five were found guilty of manslaughter.

The others were all back on the street in very little time, but one year later James Weeden, still imprisoned at Trenton, was serving out the ten-year sentence he had received. On November 7, 1877, he died, probably of pneumonia. "He had been ailing for some time," the newspapers wrote, "but his death was not looked for."

SWIMMING: CAPTAIN MATTHEW WEBB

From 1875 on, he was simply the most famous swimmer in the entire world. No one had crossed the English Channel before without the aid of a life jacket until twenty-seven-year-old Matthew Webb, the master of an English sailing vessel, performed the trick on August 25. It had taken him almost twenty-two hours to swim the fifty-mile zigzag course, but when he awakened the next day, Webb was famous.

He made money as a result, but not as much as one might imagine. Nor did he invest it wisely. And so he returned to the water, treading it in a London aquarium, he raced other swimmers, toured the world, and ended up in the United States in 1883, newly married but almost destitute. He knew that the public had grown weary of seeing swimmers perform endurance contests or engage in unimaginative long-distance races. What Webb needed in order to make a second financial strike was something sensational, a swimming feat as daring as his English Channel jaunt.

Inevitably he was drawn to Niagara Falls,

with its rapids that had been conquered by no swimmer. Accompanied by his manager, Fred Kyle, Webb inspected the section of water about two miles below the main falls. There, the walls of the river come together, forcing the water to fairly burst along in a glorious boiling torrent of thirty-foot-high waves. Below these Whirlpool Rapids is the whirlpool itself, a coiled weapon of nature ready to destroy any human foolish or unfortunate enough to come within its grasp.

Although he must have known that no one stood a chance of getting through the rapids and whirlpool, Captain Webb announced that he intended to perform the stunt in late July 1883. In a way, he was hampered by his own audacity, for many people simply did not believe anyone would attempt such a suicidal swim. Thus one reporter wrote, "At noon today he went to Niagara Falls with the avowed intention of swimming the Whirlpool Rapids. The announcement that he would undertake so perilous a feat was not credited, and very few persons paid any attention to it. There were no more visitors at the Falls than on ordinary days."

Nevertheless, there seemed to be approximately five hundred gathered on the suspension bridge, along the cliffs and banks of the river when the noted captain, accompanied by John McCloy, a veteran ferryman, moved slowly down to the starting point. Webb then stripped down to a breechcloth and dived into the green water shortly after four o'clock. He kept to the middle of the stream as it narrowed and became increasingly violent. Occasionally he disappeared below the surface but bobbed to the top almost immediately, his arms moving smoothly, with apparent ease.

Approaching the first bridge, he was hurtled along so rapidly that nearly everyone lost sight of him until he suddenly reappeared at the edge of the first wave of rapids. Once again he disappeared, then was seen briefly

---

Captain Matthew Webb's Greater Accomplishments:

July 3, 1875: *Swam 20 miles of the Thames River in 4 hours, 53 minutes.*

July 20, 1875: *Swam from Dover to Ramsgate, England, a distance of 20 miles, in 8 hours, 45 minutes.*

August 24, 1875: *Swam English Channel (20 miles straight distance) from Dover to Calais in 21 hours, 45 minutes.*

August 13, 1879: *Swam from Sandy Hook, New Jersey, to Manhattan Beach, Coney Island, a distance of 10 miles, in 8 hours (high tides and the fact that he was not allowed to land at Coney Island until 5 P.M. added to Webb's time).*

July 1, 1882: *Defeated swimmer George Wade, of Brooklyn, by 40 yards and 1 minute over a 5-mile course off Brighton Beach.*

October 16, 1882: *Remained in a tank of water for 128¼ hours, treading water.*

before dropping from sight. This time he remained from view as "the excited spectators watched in breathless suspense. They looked below, to the sides, and all about, but could see no sign of him. They rushed down the riverbank as far as they could go, but saw nothing of the strong swimmer. They looked at each other and said, "The man is lost."

At four-nineteen, just seventeen minutes after he had plunged into the river, Captain Webb was given up for dead. Fred Kyle waited as the crowd drifted away bit by bit, then left for Nantasket to comfort Webb's widow. In the meantime, searching parties combed the river looking for some sign of the captain, living or dead. The newspapers cautioned that it might be some time before his body was found because of the fact that objects caught by the whirlpool sometimes remained in a state of suspension for days. Four days later, a search party finally located Webb's body near Lewiston, New York. It lay face downward in the water, arms and legs outstretched, with no bones broken and no internal injury sufficient to cause his death. The doctor's verdict was that the power of the water had simply forced the life out of him.

BICYCLING: FRANK LENZ

It was as if the scorched earth had swallowed him whole that fateful day in May. For a long time, no trace of his cycle could be found, much less the adventurous young man's body. And as the mysterious silence continued, hope gradually gave way to resignation that he would never be seen alive again.

His name was Frank G. Lenz; his hobby, photography; his mission, "to travel around the world with wheel and camera," was hardly original, even in the year 1892. In fact, the trick had already been performed by solo cyclists Thomas Stevens and Thomas Beelen, as well as the team of William Sachtleben and T. C. Allen. But the sport of bicycling was still relatively new, and Americans were eager for vicarious adventure. Thus when Lenz quit his bookkeeping job in May 1892 and announced his plan, he became a national celebrity overnight.

Even he was amazed at the enthusiastic sendoff given him by New Yorkers on June 4. "No knight of the olden days," he wrote for the magazine Outing, "ever set out in search of adventures or donned his armor for foreign lands and deeds of high emprise with more fervid acclamations than those which have cheered my outward path." He then added modestly, "I am aware that I owe these attentions not so much to any personal reason as to the fact that my venture is, in a certain sense, typical of my country's energy."

There were a couple of differences between Lenz's chosen mode of operation and those of his predecessors. He was, first of all, to be traveling westward rather than eastward. He was also using pneumatic tires rather than the "ordinary" ones of solid rubber cemented to the rim. If these changes do not seem particularly significant, they were sufficient to inspire many Americans of the 1890s. In fact, Broadway was so jammed with people, according to Lenz, "that I found it impossible to mount my wheel, much less make the start. The police, seeing my predicament, cleared the way for my escorts and myself, and amid the cheers from thousands of throats, I mounted precisely at three o'clock and . . . rode up busy Broadway."

Although only twenty-five years old at the time, Frank Lenz had been cycling long distances for nearly a decade. His cross-country triumphs included a trip with a friend from his hometown, Pittsburgh, to New York. The first three thousand miles, then, were no problem. He was heading North, to Buffalo, generally following the line of the Erie Canal "up the valley of the Mohawk, the cradle of the military forces of the Revolution and the grave of the military hopes of the British," as the patriotic young man put it. From Buffalo to Minneapolis he traveled across Canada, then traced the track of the Northern Pacific Railroad to Spokane Falls and the telegraph route to San Francisco, which he reached on October 20, 1892. Along the way delegates of every cycling club within twenty miles of his route turned out to wine and dine him.

Boarding the steamer Oceanic, Lenz sailed on October 25 for Yokohama to become, by Christmas Day 1892, the "first cyclist ever to invade northern China." Although he was basically a genial young man, he displayed a benevolent contempt for Orientals and was especially scornful of those Chinese who visited opium shops to smoke a pipeful of pleasure. "The Chinese women as well as men are frequenters of these vile places," he wrote sternly in January 1893. "Some of the men were pitiful-looking beings, dirty and unwashed for weeks, their clothing in tatters, their once raven-black hair fallen out, but still every 'cash' they get goes for this deadly drug. In every hamlet or village, ever so remote, and in road inns they sell opium."

In turn, Lenz was called "foreign devil" and was frequently pestered by surly crowds who were not impressed by his round-the-world marathon. His antipathy to the Chinese was further increased when he discovered that his tool bag, which had contained a monkey wrench, screwdriver, and oil can, had been rifled. "Almost distractedly, I pointed to the empty tool-pouch," he wrote. "But the following crowds shook their heads 'no,' insisted that

I should ride, and began throwing stones at a distance. Presently they became bolder and came on closer and one stone struck me on the leg. Things were getting uncomfortable; my wheel clogged up with mud and snow . . . and I could not get away. Drawing my revolver, I flourished it about, but they only gave fiendish yells and came closer. Dropping the wheel in the snow I gave chase and fired three times in the air. The crowd of thirty or forty ran as fast as their legs could carry them. . . ."

For the next fifteen months Frank Lenz continued his slow journey across Asia on the muddy roads of Burma, India, Baluchistan, and Persia. Finding the natives in these countries generally more agreeable, he dutifully described the architecture, countryside, and culture in the manner of the typical nineteenth-century travel writer—with his own mixture of condescension, textbook erudition, and a smattering of weak humor. By the time he reached Teheran, however, a certain poignancy had crept into his prose. "I must confess to a feeling of homesickness," he wrote. "I am tired, very tired of being a stranger. I long for the day which will see me again on my native hearthstone and my wanderings at an end."

On May 2, 1894, his last piece of correspondence was dispatched from Tabriz, Persia. "I leave today," he wrote, "on my way to Constantinople, now only nine hundred miles distant." And with those words, Frank Lenz disappeared for all time.

Because his accounts had been appearing in print on a considerably delayed basis, the general public did not know for some time that no news had been received from Lenz after May 2, 1894. Gradually word leaked out that something was wrong, that he had "been delayed," or "obstructed near the Persian-Turkish border." Finally, veteran cyclist William Sachtleben made an alarming pronouncement: "I think Lenz must have been murdered," he told reporters. "As near as I can learn, he disappeared in the Delibaba Pass between Erzurum and Bayezid. . . . This Delibaba Pass is one of the worst places in Asiatic Turkey, and it is my belief that Lenz was murdered."

Unfortunately, Sachtleben was almost assuredly correct. A detailed investigation proved that Lenz had spent the night of May 9 at the Turkish village of Tchelkani and then headed North toward the hamlets of Muserstie and Shamian—an area, according to R. W. Graves, British consul at Erzurum, that was "infested with brigands." Another story suggested that Lenz had been killed out of a certain fear rather than because of greed. "An argument arose as to whether he was a man or a devil," recounted one native who had never seen a bicycle and referred to it as a "two-wheeled carriage." In order to settle the controversy, he explained, several shots had been fired at the strangely moving creature, who was killed immediately.

At any rate, in May of 1894 a body was found in the River Sherian, about 1½ miles from Tchelkani, improbably equipped with a large hand mirror. At about the same time a particularly ferocious Kurdish tribesman began sporting narrow saddle girths on his horse which suspiciously resembled flattened bicycle tires.

It Wasn't the Last Time:
Almost to the day eighty years later, American motorcyclist Fred Mundy roared into the sandy wasteland of Baja California, one of the participants in a unique motorcycle race of 1974. He was never seen again, despite a thorough search of the area. Some said the trail markers were so obscure that a cyclist could have taken a wrong turning and become marooned fifty miles off course before realizing his error.

Convinced at last that some explanation had to be given the public, the publishers of *Outing* admitted that something had gone amiss. But because the magazine had an ample supply of Lenz's columns still on hand, his words continued to appear in *Outing* just as if he were still alive and well, until the issue of July 1896.

They had paid for the columns, after all, so why not use them?

PARACHUTING: ANNIE HARKESS, BEATRICE VON DRESSDEN, MAY ALLISON
"Suddenly there was a dreadful hush. The parachute had closed and its human burden was falling with frightful velocity. Then the silence was broken by the shrieks of fainting women, of children wailing and crying, and men turned away their faces to shut out the awful sight. Faster and faster descended the parachute and a life had gone out amid pleasure. Quickly a sympathetic crowd gathered about the lifeless, mangled form of the poor girl as she lay in a crushed mass upon the ground. Annie Harkess had made her last parachute descent."

It was the Gay Nineties and the latest spectator sport was parachuting. Annie Harkess was one of the first liberated women to take up the sport and may have been **the** first female fatality when she fell to earth at Cincinnati on August 15, 1891.

The parachute, like most sports and sports devices, started out as the exclusive province of men, having been invented and first tested by Jacques Garnerin, who successfully floated to earth on October 22, 1797. The dubious honor of being the first parachute fatality also went to a man, a Mr. Cocking, who plunged thirty-five hundred feet in a minute and a half when his chute failed to open in 1837. But the courageous Madame Blanchard, wife of early aeronaut Pierre Blanchard, ended an illustrious career in 1819 when her balloon caught fire over Paris and descended like a shot.

Women had taken to the air rather early, and like the male of the species, had run into occasional trouble. One early adventuress was named Lizzie Ihling, the niece of John Wise, America's premier balloonist of the Civil War era. It wasn't long before Lizzie talked her uncle into allowing her to go aloft on a solo flight. On July 5, 1875, she was drifting along a mile above the ground when she noticed the skin of the balloon bag starting to rip. It somehow dropped to the ground without injuring the young woman, who became one of the first ladies who ever lived to tell about such a dangerous flight.

By this time, aeronauts had "perfected" the parachute and started using it as a vehicle for a new spectator sport: aerial acrobatics. During the 1880s, Thomas S. Baldwin regularly astounded visitors to Coney Island and other parks with his parachute leaps into nearby bodies of water.

But the chutes of that time were often cumbersome and prone to malfunctioning. There were, as a result, many early fatalities. A Belgian named DeGroof, for example, fell into a London churchyard in 1874, and six years later August Navarre, who specialized in aerial twists and turns, fell eighteen hundred feet to the streets of Paris when he missed his hold.

When women joined the business of aerial acrobatics and parachuting, there was little public outcry to protect the "fair sex" from the mutilating effects of miscalculation at such heights. Even the death of Annie Harkess apparently failed to frighten Beatrice Von Dressden, who in 1891 was a fourteen-year-old native of Buffalo who had already taken up the new sport of parachuting. Between 1891 and 1894, in fact, Beatrice made twenty ascensions and drops without mishap, touring the eastern part of the United States. Described as "pretty and vivacious," she was a favorite of fairground visitors, who loved watching her descend to earth from an altitude of about a half mile.

Saturday, October 6, 1894, was a sort of homecoming for Beatrice, the site of her performance that day being Buffalo's Franklinville fairgrounds. It was windy, however, which caused Beatrice's parents to advise her not to go aloft. The young woman replied that she simply could not disappoint the hundreds of friends who had made special trips so they could see her. She promised to be especially careful, reminding her folks that she had a reputation as a "safe" aeronaut rather than a reckless showoff. With that, she stepped into the basket of the balloon. Pulled upward by a brisk breeze, it was only a matter of minutes before she was a quarter mile above the fairgrounds, waving cheerfully to the crowd below.

Arriving at an altitude of fifteen hundred feet, Beatrice was seen to move to the side of the basket as if trying to unfasten the parachute that was attached to the side of the balloon. This act was normal, but for some reason on this occasion the usually calm young woman seemed distressed. The audience below stood hushed, wondering if something had gone wrong, if the parachute were stuck. Then, with startling suddenness, Beatrice tumbled over the side. "In some way not clear to those below," one reporter wrote, "she lost her hold of both the balloon and the parachute, and her body came whirling to the ground. The body struck within the fairgrounds, and was imbedded nearly a foot in the ground."

That ended the brief career of Beatrice Von Dressden, who had just celebrated her seventeenth birthday.

During the same year, twenty-year-old May Allison made her first balloon ascension and parachute jump at Urbana, Ohio, and having enjoyed the experience, the brown-haired Sunday school teacher decided to make a career of aerial acrobatics. She married William H. "Kid" Hanner, thirty-three, a veteran parachutist, and together they toured the country. By the time she was twenty-two, May herself was a veteran of more than four hundred leaps.

In addition, she perfected a series of high-wire acrobatics, which included holding a man by a wire held in her teeth, and she often appeared under aliases such as Mlle. Levoy, Louisa, or Lillie Lewis in order to make the troupe's company seem larger than it actually was. But the real highlight of her act came when she donned her special red tights for the parachute jump. On the afternoon of May 26, 1896, May Hanner was at Fairy Grove Amusement Park, Baltimore. After her high-wire act, she received a bouquet of flowers from a little girl and was putting them in her hair just as someone asked if she had finished for the day.

"No," May replied. "I have to go to Heaven yet."

Those who overheard the remark commented later in hushed tones on its strangely prophetic quality.

May's balloon ascension went smoothly, however, at least during the initial stages. It was late in the afternoon and the amusement park had started to fill with those who had just gotten off work. One trolley car after another emptied customers eager to see the young lady jump from the basket and float safely to earth. The parachute that was to break her fall was made of heavy silk fastened to a thick hickory ring by thirty-seven ropes and an equal number of large bolts. It was more dependable than most chutes of the time but was much too heavy to float on water. Thus May had to either descend over land or prepare to cut herself free from the parachute as it neared water.

She had done this many times, of course, so there was little cause for worry. As May reached a height of about a half mile, she was ready for her leap, but the wind had pulled the balloon over the Back River. Then it was buffeted downward, nearing the farther shore. May waited as her husband and several friends launched a rowboat, they having reasoned it might be necessary to pull her from the water unless the wind shifted dramatically.

They were correct. Descending to about a thousand feet, the balloon still refused to reach the shoreline. May decided to jump while there was still time for the parachute to open. As she did so, the Fairy Grove crowd cheered, caught its breath, then cheered again as the colorful umbrella blossomed outward only seconds before it and May struck the surface of the water. But May was having trouble freeing herself from the chute. She and the tangled mass of heavy wood and iron met the water in a solid ball, then promptly disappeared below the surface. Everyone stood silently, waiting for the red-clad figure to appear, shaking the water from her hair and waving happily.

But such was not to be. In the words of a reporter for the Baltimore *Herald,* May Hanner "sank beneath the placid surface of the river and met her fate." By paddling furiously, the men in the rowboat were able to arrive at the scene just as May slipped from sight. George H. Erick, a native Baltimorean, made a desperate reach for her hair and actually caught several strands in his hand. But "they snapped in twain in his fingers and the victim disappeared from view."

Distraught, Kid Hanner made dive after dive into the water until stopped only by sheer exhaustion. For the rest of the night the river was illuminated by the lamps of rescue vessels combing the bottom for the unfortunate young woman. They found her the next day, the flower given her by the little girl still entwined in her hair.

Thus ended the brief and exciting career of yet another daring woman aeronaut of the Gay Nineties. Perhaps the most amazing thing about all of them is that in those days of such straitlaced clothes and morals, they ever got off the ground.

FOOTBALL: WILSON, CHRISTIAN, BYRNE, ET AL.

The fall of 1909 was a grim one for football fans, especially those who were disturbed about injuries. (Some were not overly disturbed, saying that football was a true test of manhood as well as a good bit of training for war.) During the 1890s furor over the "flying wedge" and the "momentum pass play" led to some reforms and rule changes, but the game still relied on mass formations as primary means of moving the ball and "sacrificed" bodies as the primary means of slowing down the charge.

The Momentum Pass Play—It worked like this:

Its secret was having several men in motion before the ball was snapped. Usually linemen moved back, grouped themselves together tightly, then started rushing forward along with the other backs. The quarterback received the snap from center, threw it to one back, who was already running behind the linemen. The opposition could do little except hurl their bodies at the charging linemen in hopes of slowing down the herd.

In Mid-October 1909, Navy took on Villanova at Annapolis, and the game featured the usual type of play at that time. Midshipman Earl D. Wilson was an especially daring tackler that day, breaking through one wall of interference after another to bring down the ball carrier. One individual effort stood out particularly. The play was a long end run by halfback Kelly of Villanova. Behind a wall of blockers, he started across the field, looking for a gap in the defense through which he could dart. But Earl Wilson fought off one lineman after another, then flung himself at Kelly in the manner of a flying missile. Both men went down. Kelly got to his feet and trudged back to the huddle. Wilson was unconscious.

Taken to the Naval Hospital, Wilson was diagnosed as having a fracture of the fifth cervical vertebra, causing complete paralysis from the neck down.

Two weeks later, West Point, in preparation for its upcoming game with the Naval Academy, took the field against Harvard. Left tackle Eugene A. Byrne, hurling himself against the mass formations of Harvard, was no different from the other brave players on the field that afternoon—except that he failed to get up after one particularly violent collision. The force of impact had crushed his first and second cervical vertebrae, severing the nerve centers governing his breathing. Paralyzed from the neck down, Byrne spent an agonizing night in the West Point hospital as two officers took turns artificially inducing respiration. Once during the night he gasped, "I can't breathe. . . . Don't stop that. . . . I'm sleepy but don't stop that. . . ."

It was, of course, an exercise in futility. By six-thirty the next morning, Byrne was dead.

Reaction to the tragedy was immediate, but not by any means consistent. At least two college coaches expressed dismay and anger at the way the game was played. Said one: "I believe that the new rules did little or nothing toward making the game clean. I think that Byrne's death and Wilson's . . . injury will prove the undoing of the game unless further modified." Added another: "This accident is the last straw. Football, to my mind, is henceforth a doomed sport."

Others were more philosophical about the unfortunate events. Fred W. Marvel, supervisor of athletics at Brown University, said, "Such an accident is likely to occur in any sport." Professor George W. Patterson of Michigan added, "In my opinion, canoeing and rowing are more dangerous than football." Bishop Lawrence of Harvard dedicated part of his sermon the Sunday following the game to the value of intercollegiate sports. President A. B. Storms of Iowa State College said, "I like the game of football and cannot see that many permanent injuries are received in it when the number of participants is considered."

Notwithstanding this stiff-upper-lip attitude of those named above, officials at the Naval Academy and West Point decided that to continue the football season of 1909 would be inappropriate. Colonel H. L. Scott, on learning that Byrne had succumbed, sent a telegram to Captain Bowyer at Annapolis. "On account of the sorrow over the loss of a member of our football team," it read, "and out of respect to his memory, West Point desires to cease playing football for the remainder of this season."

On the same day, Roy Spybuck and Ogie Seagraves, players representing the states of Missouri and Indiana, respectively, suffered severe head injuries in pile-ups, dying shortly afterward.

Two weeks later, on October 13, 1909, halfback Archie Christian of the University of Virginia took the ball near the end of the game with his team leading Georgetown, 21–0. The run was a typical "mass play," with Christian having interference in front of him and actual physical assistance (since outlawed) from men in his own backfield. "Georgetown's secondary defense was playing five yards behind the line," one reporter wrote, "and when Christian had been dragged over the first defense the backfield players made a rush for the Virginia halfback. Just as the Georgetown secondary defense reached a point two yards from where the line had failed to hold the onslaught of the Virginians, Christian stumbled and fell to the ground. . . . Just as [he] was getting on his feet, three Georgetown players hit him at one time, knocking him to the ground again. When he fell, he landed on his back, both feet staying in the air. It seemed as if none of the members of the Virginia or Georgetown teams realized that Christian was on the ground, and twenty players piled on the youth."

Taken unconscious from the field, Christian was rushed to Georgetown University Hospital, where he died the next day.

That was the last straw for some persons. A week later, at a scheduled game between Montclair (New Jersey) Military Academy and Montclair High School, fans were disappointed to see a lone man walk onto the field instead of the host team. "You can go back to your homes," he said simply. "There will be no game today."

Subsequent investigation revealed that the mothers of every Montclair High player had visited Principal H. W. Dutsch in a body and informed him that he would be held personally responsible for any injuries that might occur.

Most people did not take the football risks of 1909 quite so seriously. But the rash of publicity did cause rules against piling on, assisting the ball carrier by dragging him, and illegal forward motion to be more strictly enforced after that. And so the most lethal era in football since the day of the flying wedge passed. No amount of public outcry could help young Earl Wilson, however. After lying in a state of paralysis for five months, he finally died on April 16, 1910, the last casualty of that grim season of 1909.

AVIATION: JULIA CLARK

She did not have the flair of Harriet Quimby, the first famous woman of American stunt flying, but she was determined to overtake that young lady's head start as rapidly as possible. Julia Clark of Chicago became interested in flying when she attended the International Aviation Meet in her hometown during August 1911. She left almost immediately for San Diego, where she learned to fly a biplane so quickly that she was only the third American woman to obtain an international pilot's license. Soon afterward, she turned to stunt flying as a means of earning money and polishing her skills.

The planes she flew were not always safe. In early June 1912, for example, officials at a meet in Milwaukee prevented her from flying after inspecting the plane and determining that it was a death trap. Julia spent the next week having it overhauled so that she would be able to fly at Springfield, Illinois, on June 17.

She did fly at Springfield, for a brief while. Soon after takeoff, however, she lost control of her ship and crashed into a tree. She thus became only the third woman aviator to perish, and the first American.

The Women Who Preceded Her:
Deniz Moore, *July 1911: Fell while making a flight at Étampes, France*
Suzanne Bernard, *March 1912: Also crashed at Étampes, France*

Scarcely a month later, Harriet Quimby, the woman Julia Clark admired and emulated, also added her name to the list of aviation casualties.

AUTO RACING: FRANK DEARBORN, HAROLD MC-CARTHY
The machines of 1914 were not infernally fast, averaging only a mile a minute, but the lack of speed was offset by the inconsistency of pneumatic tire manufacturing. A blow-out was possible anytime then.

The two darlings of the meet crowd at Brighton Beach, Coney Island, were Frank Dearborn and Ralph DePalma, a pair of reckless but skillful drivers challenging each other on a hot September afternoon. Early in the competition, DePalma set a new record for the 25-mile run, lowering his August 1913 mark of 24:35⅗ to 24:08⅖. As the crowd cheered him on, Dearborn then made a new time for 10 miles—9:02⅖. The major event of the day, a 50-mile race, thus became a fitting finale to determine which of the two drivers was the more skillful.

Pushing his Peugeot to the limit at the very outset, Dearborn roared into the lead, leaving DePalma and the six other entrants far to the rear. In fact, Dearborn was driving out of control, for he was on only the second lap when his car skidded on the upper turn, swung wildly across the track and stalled directly in the path of the oncoming drivers. DePalma, leading the pack, swung wide and was able to dart through an opening between Dearborn and the stands with so little room to spare that the crowd gasped, paused to take a breath, and then broke into applause and cheers. Dearborn whirled back into the thick of the race and was soon moving even with DePalma.

Going into the forty-first mile, the two rivals continued to set a record pace. Just as they reached the grandstand turn, however, the familiar crack of a tire could be heard above the chugging and pounding of the engines. The Peugeot swerved close to the rail in front of the judges' stand, but Dearborn seemed to get the car under control quickly. No sooner did the machine straighten out than another crack was heard and Dearborn was seen to shoot forward toward the fence. "There was a cry of horror from the grandstand," a reporter wrote, "for all the crowd could plainly see both driver and mechanician thrown high into the air and come down in a wreckage of the fence and a cloud of dust, while the car rolled over on its side against a big tree, which it struck. Dearborn was under the wreckage of the fence and his mechanician was pinned under the car."

Both Dearborn and Harold McCarthy, his mechanic, were rushed to Coney Island Hospital, "unconscious and bleeding." In order to prevent panic, the crowd was told that neither man was seriously hurt.

On Tuesday, September 8, 1914, three days later, Frank Dearborn died at the age of thirty-two. Harold McCarthy survived.

BASEBALL: RAY CHAPMAN
The Cleveland Indians of 1920 were having an excellent year, and so was twenty-nine-year-old shortstop Ray Chapman. On August 16 he was batting .303 with forty-nine runs batted in, and the Indians led the Yankees, 3–0, when he stepped into the batter's box to lead off the fifth inning.

On the mound for New York was Carl Mays, a submarine-balling righthander who had won more than a hundred games in the past five seasons. To a right-handed batter such as Chapman, Mays' best pitches seemed to be coming from somewhere in the neighborhood of third base, yet there was nothing to do but wait until the last second before deciding if the pitch was a strike or a ball.

If Chapman found Mays hard to fathom, the feeling was mutual. "Chapman was one of the hardest men to pitch to in the league,"

Mays said of the Indian shortstop. "He was plucky, crouched over the plate, and the only way to get a ball over was to pitch it so low that there was a risk of it being called a ball. In the fifth inning on Monday I pitched him a straight ball inside, just above the waist. I expected that he would drop as Ruth does when the pitchers swing them in close to the big fellow to drive him away from the plate. . . ."

In other words, Mays had thrown a knockdown pitch. Chapman ducked his head—into the path of the ball. The sound of impact could be heard from one end of the Polo Grounds to the other. Silence gripped the crowd as Chapman was lifted to his feet. He tried to walk by himself but his legs soon doubled under him and he was carried, unconscious, to St. Lawrence Hospital. An emergency operation was performed at midnight when it was discovered that Chapman's skull had been fractured on the left side. It was unsuccessful. Early on the morning of August 17, 1920, Ray Chapman died. As flags were lowered to half mast in Cleveland, fans, writers, and players joined to express their shock and, occasionally, anger. For a time there was talk of barring Carl Mays, and players with Detroit, St. Louis, Boston, and Washington met to discuss a strike against the pitcher. Donie Bush, Tiger shortstop, gallantly offered his services to the Indians (a move that would have sent him from a seventh-place team to possible pennant money). The need for providing players with headgear was discussed but nothing was done, of course. Most newspapers shrugged off the affair, as did the Troy *Record* when it noted, "Swimming on a pleasant Sunday or holiday has more fatalities than big-league baseball has in years. Compared with automobiling, baseball is as safe as a game of parlor croquet." Others pointed out that while the death of Ray Chapman was regrettable, he was actually the first major-league baseball player to die as the result of a beaning. And in a rare note of overt cynicism, one reporter concluded, "The present fatality probably will have been erased from the memory of fandom before another occurs."

FOOTBALL: RICHARD BRINSLEY SHERIDAN

At the U. S. Military Academy's Flirtation Walk there is a statue with the inscription, "Life is the greatest game of all. Play it with courage, wisdom, and loyalty." The Sheridan memorial was erected in memory of a young man who lost his life playing a game of football.

The date was October 24, 1931; the place, New Haven, Connecticut, where a rugged Army team was supposed to score almost at will against a much weaker Yale squad. Happily for the seventy-five thousand spectators gathered at the Yale Bowl, it didn't turn out that way. Three periods passed, in fact, without a score. Eli fans were pleading for their team to hold the line as the final quarter began, but two plays later, Army led, 6–0.

Yale was not upset by the score. When the ball floated down to Bud Parker on the twelve-yard line, he took it, burst through a hole in the West Point defensive charge, and went all the way for an eighty-eight-yard tying touchdown. The Yale Bowl rocked with excitement.

Following the missed extra-point attempt, Army elected to kick off, a surprising bit of strategy in view of Parker's heroics. But instead of allowing that dangerous man to have the ball, West Point kicked the ball to Bob Lassiter, who caught it on his two-yard line and moved upfield with high-knee action. Army end Richard B. Sheridan broke through the protective wedge, making the tackle headon. Both men tumbled to the turf at the twenty-two-yard line. Sheridan did not get up, having suffered a broken neck.

After he was taken from the field, Sheridan was rushed to New Haven Hospital, where Dr. Harvey Cushman, the famous brain and nerve specialist, took charge of the case. After diagnosing a fracture of the fourth cervical vertebra, Cushing ordered Sheridan placed in an artificial respirator, cautioning that although the young man might live for some time, it was a virtual certainty that he would be paralyzed for the rest of his life.

Sheridan's remaining life was less than three days. A military funeral was held later that week. The usual regrets poured in to the cadet's mother, along with some concrete suggestions as to how football might benefit as a result of the tragedy. Primarily, some said,

---

Chapman Was the First on a Major-league Diamond, but—

Former major-league third baseman Johnny Dodge, who played with the Phillies, 1912–13, and the Reds in 1913, was the first man with his name in the record book to die as the result of being hit by a pitched ball. On June 19, 1916, while playing in the Southern League, Dodge took a fast ball on the temple from Nashville's Johnny Rodgers and was killed instantly.

Rodgers went on to win five consecutive shutout games after that, doing his best pitching of the year.

Sheridan's death proved that the kickoff was a dangerous play, one that should be eliminated. But officials responsible for making a decision about the play were hostile to change. "Doing away with the kickoff would not stop injuries in football," said Amos Alonzo Stagg, veteran coach at the University of Chicago, adding that the same logic "would also ban a punt." M. J. Ahearn, director of athletics at Kansas State Agricultural College, described the kickoff as "a beautiful and thrilling play."

By December, however, when it became apparent that 1931 would be the worst year in football as far as fatalities and injuries were concerned (see "1931"), fresh impetus was given to proposals that the kickoff be abolished. A meeting of Southwest Conference coaches produced agreement that the wedge formation to protect the ball carrier on kickoff returns should be banned. Fred Young, an official with the Big Ten Conference, also asserted that the wedge was "a distinct danger." Tommy Mills, Georgetown coach, came out against the kickoff as a whole if rules could not be formulated to abolish the mass formations. Jimmy Crowley of Michigan State, Dr. Marvin Stevens of Yale, and Harvey Harman of Pennsylvania, however, took the opposing view, refusing to believe that doing away with the kickoff would reduce injuries.

There was a compromise group, headed by official Tom Thorp, which proposed that a kicking tee be allowed so that the ball would assume a loftier trajectory, thus forcing the ball carrier and his protective convoy to wait longer before getting up a full head of steam.

In mid-December, however, a poll of college football players themselves killed any hope for reform. Of twenty players interviewed, nineteen declared that the kickoff should be retained. Marchy Schwartz, Notre Dame All-American, was among the most adamant. "The kickoff . . . is the most spectacular and finest of all plays," he said. "Its abolition or change would rob spectators of football's greatest play. Any real fan would rather see the kickoff than a long run or a long pass. Personally, I have never been hurt in running back a kickoff, and I believe those who do get hurt are not in the best physical shape in most cases." Clarence Munn, Minnesota's All-American guard, added that many injuries on kickoffs came because at the beginning of the game some players were not sufficiently warmed up. Only Joe Moran, Syracuse halfback, thought it "might be a good idea if the kickoff were abolished, the team that wins the toss getting the ball on its own twenty-yard line."

And so the kickoff, closest thing to a Japa-

nese *kamikaze* mission yet devised on a sports field, remains. But all was not for naught. West Point did get a very attractive memorial.

Even Ping-Pong?

In 1932, it was banned for members of the St. John's College (Annapolis, Maryland) boxing team. On February 10, Vernon Novicki went after a serve by an opponent so violently that he struck his head against the wall and could not box later that day. The boxing coach, Joe Novak, then barred the rest of his team from the Ping-Pong room on the grounds that it was too strenuous.

POWERBOAT RACING: JOHN COBB

By September 1952 it could be said with little fear of contradiction that powerboat racer John Rhodes Cobb, a taciturn 200-pound London broker, had traveled faster on land than any man alive. At the Bonneville Salt Flats, Utah, for example, he drove a special racing automobile over a mile course at the rate of 403.135 miles per hour. That was on September 16, 1947, but the records established by Cobb went much farther back. In 1939, he covered a mile at the rate of 368.9 mph, a mark that held up for eight years. He also sped over a 5-mile course that same year, averaging 326.7 mph, and he covered 10 miles at the rate of 270.4 mph.

Cobb also enjoyed powerboating and in September 1952 decided to have a shot at breaking the existing record of 178.497 mph set by Stanley Sayres on July 7 with *Slo-Mo-Shun IV* on Lake Washington, Seattle. To be accepted as an official time, the mile course had to be covered twice—once in each direction—and the results averaged. Cobb was confident that he could shatter the mark if he could find a time when the waters of Loch Ness, Scotland, were so smooth that the full power of his jet-propelled *Crusader* could be applied without submitting the 31-foot aluminum and plywood craft to unbearable strain.

On September 29, at high noon, he thought the right moment had arrived. The 52-year-old sportsman entered his craft and roared down the first mile in just 17.4 seconds—a rate of 206.89 mph. With any kind of luck at all, it was apparent that Cobb would shatter the speed record easily.

No sooner had Cobb finished the first mile, however, than the *Crusader* was seen to bounce slightly. It bounced twice more, then flew out of the water and disintegrated. In a matter of seconds, the debris created by the shattered boat settled onto the surface of the lake, smoke and mist rising from the whirlpool of destruction. Cobb was taken from the water quickly but his neck had been broken and he was dead before he reached shore.

One theory was that the bumps were caused by ripples in the otherwise perfectly smooth surface of the lake. Some spectators thought the engine exploded. Still others felt that when he completed the first mile, Cobb throttled down too rapidly, causing the *Crusader's* bow to dip, throwing the odd-shaped projectile out of line.

BASEBALL: BARRY BABCOCK

On May 18, 1961, at Temple City, California, the pitcher burned the ball toward the plate; the batter, Barry Babcock, could not get out of the way before he was struck in the chest. Dropping his bat in a slow-motion fall, he slipped to the ground and shortly afterward died in the umpire's arms.

Barry was just nine years old, a Little Leaguer. Despite the fact that some twelve-year-old pitchers can throw the ball as fast as seventy miles per hour, Barry's death was only the fifth in the twenty-one-year history of Little League baseball. And his father was philosophical enough to comfort young Michael Hanes, the pitcher, who collapsed in hysterics after learning that Barry was dead. "It could have happened anyway," said Mr. Babcock. "It could have been a bike accident just as well."

BOXING: BENNY (KID) PARET

"I wanted to keep punching and punching," Emile Griffith said on March 24, 1962, moments after beating Benny Paret into a state of insensibility. "My manager told me to keep hitting when I saw I had him hurt. So that's why I did."

The two men had been in the ring together before. On April 1, 1961, at Miami Beach, Griffith knocked out Paret in the thirteenth round to win the welterweight title. Six months later, Paret came back to decision Griffith in fifteen rounds. Then, in the twelfth round of their third meeting for the championship, Griffith got his chance. Forcing Paret against the ropes so that he could not go down, the twenty-three-year old challenger, started a two-handed flurry that culminated with ten consecutive right uppercuts to the chin. Sagging like a rag doll, Paret offered no defense. More than twenty-five blows were landed on his exposed face and head, and even the ringside crowd, which usually calls for blood, began to shout to referee Ruby Goldstein, begging him to intervene.

Finally he made his move but had difficulty pulling the enraged Griffith away from the boxer, who slowly slid down the ropes and to the canvas. Eight minutes passed while ringside physicians worked on Paret, but he was still unconscious when he was carted to his dressing room. On the way to Roosevelt Hospital near Madison Square Garden, the last rites of the Roman Catholic Church were administered.

Three days later, following emergency brain surgery, there were some indications that Benny Paret might emerge from his coma. A cautious bulletin was issued by the hospital: "There has been some very slight improvement in his condition," it read. "He has made some purposeful movement with his arms. His condition still remains critical."

While the twenty-four-year-old ex-champion hovered close to death, officials such as Senator Estes Kefauver charged that boxing needed regulation if not outright elimination. Governor Edmund Brown of California attacked the sport as "dirty, rotten, brutalizing" and threatened to introduce legislation in California outlawing it. Other critics were less certain that the sport had to be banned; they

---

Also About This Time:

seemed to feel that voluntary regulation was the answer. And, like the football players of 1931 who favored retention of the kickoff play, most boxers themselves defended the sport. In a radio interview about a year after Benny Paret was carried from the ring, featherweight Davey Moore termed boxing "a good sport" and charged that people who wanted to outlaw it were "sick." The next day, Moore himself was beaten so severely by challenger Sugar Ramos that he died as a result.

On the other hand, Gene Tunney, one of the few to leave the ring while he was at his peak, described a three-day bout of amnesia he had suffered following a sparring mishap. "After returning to normal," he said, "I decided that any sport in which such accidents could occur was dangerous. The first seed of retirement was sown then. The possibility of becoming 'punch drunk' haunted me for weeks."

The debate, of course, solved very little, proposals to outlaw the sport or make boxers wear "safe" headgear and thicker gloves soon getting lost in the shuffle. The only concrete development was that Emile Griffith was the new welterweight champion as of March 24, 1962, and that Benny (Kid) Paret was quite dead as of 1:55 A.M., April 2.

HOCKEY: BILL MASTERTON

Hockey players, especially the professional variety, have long prided themselves on their ability to absorb punishment and return to action with little or no protective gear. As late as the 1968 season, Clarence Campbell, president of the National Hockey League, spoke almost with scorn of headgear. "They are available," he said, pointing out that the league did not require the wearing of helmets and had no intention of doing so. In fact, only about a dozen players put them on.

Bill Masterton, twenty-nine, a center with the Minnesota North Stars, did not wear a helmet; had he done so, it might have saved his life. The end came suddenly. On January 15, 1968, in a game against the Oakland Seals at Bloomington, Minnesota, Masterton skated into the Seals' zone with the puck in the first period, then backhanded a pass to teammate Wayne Connelly. Somehow, about twenty-five feet in front of the goal, a mixup occurred and Masterton was flipped violently backward. He landed on his head, full force. Bleeding profusely, he was taken from the rink on a stretcher and rushed to the hospital, where he died shortly afterward.

Although hockey officials expressed shock at the tragedy, they seemed more preoccupied with pointing out how safe hockey was compared to football and certain other contact sports. Lynn Patrick, general Manager of the St. Louis Blues, said immediately after the incident, "I never believed in helmets and I still don't. The game's been played without them and no one ever got killed before."

But the height of callousness came from league President Campbell, who when asked if there might be a benefit game for the family of the late Bill Masterton, replied in the negative. "A benefit is asking the public to pay for something that is our responsibility," he said shortly.

AUTO RACING: JIM CLARK

In 1963, his third season of auto racing, dark-haired and boyish-faced Jim Clark piled up the best record ever established by one so young. Although only twenty-seven, he had won the Grand Prix races of Belgium, the Netherlands, France, Great Britain, Italy, Mexico, and South Africa. In the German Grand Prix he came in second. In all, he had won nineteen of thirty racing contests he entered.

"I never want to see a racing car again." Jim Clark, immediately following the Monza disaster, 1961

They called him a "most skillful driver," a "smoothie." In 1966 at Indianapolis, while driving a poor-handling car, he twice went into spins on the fourth corner of the 2½-mile oval. Both times he maneuvered so expertly that he was able to get off without a scratch to himself or his machine. He went on to finish behind Graham Hill, and no one could recall a driver doing so well after spinning twice. Yet Jim Clark almost gave up racing before he achieved his great fame. In 1961, at Monza, Italy, he was driving during one of the worst accidents in the history of auto racing. The pile-up started when one car made a sudden swerve into its pit area, forcing a smaller car to swing wide and starting a deadly chain reaction of driver reflexes. Clark, in a Lotus, nicked the wheels of the Ferrari driven by Count Wolfgang Von Trips. The German lost control, he and his vehicle hurtling off the track into the spectator area. Thirteen persons were killed but Von Trips

---

The First Professional Hockey Fatality: *In 1909, Bud McCord, playing at Cornwall, Ontario, in a league that predated the NHL, was injured in a game and died as a result.*

survived. So did Clark, and for a brief time he considered giving up the dangerous sport. He recalled that the year before, he had witnessed the death of Alan Stacey, a friend and fellow driver who died in a new Lotus, but he had gotten over that traumatic experience. "I don't think I'm callous, but I have been blessed with a bad memory for such things," he said.

And so he returned to auto racing, winning the 500 at Indianapolis in 1965 and becoming an undisputable world champion. After that he continued to win his share of races for the next three years. On April 7, 1968, he was at Hockenheim, West Germany, competing in a European champion Formula Two race. He came out of a treacherous "Shrimps Head" curve and was blasting down the straightaway at 175 miles per hour. "Suddenly Jim's car broke out," recalled Chris Irwin of Great Britain, who was trailing Clark by about 250 yards. "It looked like something mechanical," he noted. Others noted that the track was wet, either from oil or water. In any case, no one believed that the spinout was Clark's fault.

"Not everyone kills himself with a rope or gun. Auto drivers at high speed are committing suicide, but how long it takes them is up to them and chance . . ."

Dr. Karl Menninger,
Man Against Himself

Whatever the cause, human or mechanical, Clark's Lotus-Ford suddenly somersaulted off the track and shattered against a tree. He died instantly of a broken neck and multiple skull fractures. "Just where the poor man sat strapped in the cockpit," a policeman at the scene reported, "the front and rear flew off in opposite directions. The midsection crumpled off the tree."

"If one believes that life is beautiful and fine, auto racing is irrational. If one is full of despair, cynicism, or apathy to life, then racing need not be viewed as irrational."

Dr. Karl Menninger,
Man Against Himself

Officials at the track, after examining the wreckage, said the car was so thoroughly smashed that the cause of the accident would probably never be known for sure. So ended

the thirty-two-year life of the first foreign driver to win the Indianapolis 500. Shortly before the fatal event, friends had been urging him to retire. "You can't," he replied when they asked why he could not be satisfied with the success he had already earned. "Racing is like smoking. It gets into your blood and you have to carry on."

FOOTBALL: CHUCK HUGHES

A clue was provided during a preseason game played by the Detroit Lions on September 4, 1971. After taking a pass, twenty-eight-year-old Chuck Hughes, a back-up wide receiver to Larry Walton, was tackled hard. He immediately experienced pains in his stomach and chest. Team physicians allowed him to sit out the remaining exhibition games and the season opener. But the young man's problems continued. Before a game against the New England Patriots on September 26, he said, "I don't know what's wrong. I've had sharp pains in my stomach and my chest and they've made all sorts of tests, but nobody seems to be able to figure them out. I want to play, though. They aren't that bad."

Hughes, a fourth-year player from El Paso, Texas, got his chance to play. In the final quarter of a game against the Chicago Bears on October 23, 1971, Larry Walton was injured. Hughes entered the contest and immediately caught a pass for a short gain. Three more plays were run in which he was not directly involved. After the third, he trotted back to the huddle and collapsed. Mouth-to-mouth resuscitation and external heart massage were tried on the playing field, but except for a brief moment when he gasped for air and his heart seemed to start beating again, he never regained consciousness.

Deaths on the Pro Gridiron (or as a Result of Football Contact):
1948—Stan Mauldin, Chicago Cardinals
1960—Howard Glenn, New York Titans
1963—Stone Johnson, Kansas City Chiefs
1964—Dave Sparks, Washington Redskins
1965—Mack Lee Hill, Kansas City Chiefs (during surgery)

Subsequently an autopsy performed on Hughes revealed, according to Dr. Edwin R. Guise, that the young man had suffered an attack of arteriosclerosis. "Arteriosclerosis heart disease had been coming on for some time, with no visible signs," Guise explained. "Playing football contributed in that it was a stressful situation." Added Dr. Richard A. Thompson, one of the Lions' physicians, "It was something that was bound to happen. It could have happened yesterday, the day before, or tomorrow."

The doctors were careful to point out that Hughes had not been using amphetamines, or pep pills, either as a result of prescription or his own choice.

HORSERACING: RUFFIAN

All she did in her brief racing career was win seven out of her first ten races by at least six lengths, equal eight stakes records in eight attempts, and earn $438,429. Ruffian, one of the fastest fillies to capture the admiration of horseracing fans, began her competitive career on May 22, 1974, and ended it less than fourteen months later.

Her one failing, if it could be termed that, was her high-spiritedness. She may also have been a bit brittle as racehorses go, having suffered a hairline fracture of a bone in her right hind leg, which sidelined her for much of 1974. But she was back in April 1975, setting records in the seven-furlong Comely Stakes, the mile Acorn, and the mile-and-an-eighth Mother Goose.

It seemed almost inevitable in an age that had pitted tennis champion Billie Jean King against male rival Bobby Riggs that a head-to-head confrontation be arranged between Ruffian and a top colt. That colt turned out to be Foolish Pleasure, winner of the Kentucky Derby; it was a natural choice, as was the selection of Belmont as the track for their encounter. The stakes were $350,000.

Before the race was run, jockey Jacinto Vasquez made an inspection on foot of the course the two horses would travel. He noted two places on the track that smart jockeys at Belmont tried to avoid. One was a small hump of ground near the railing where the chute crosses the training track about a sixteenth of a mile from the starting gate. The other was the intersection of the chute and the main track a couple of furlongs beyond, where the texture of the track gets harder. He made mental notes in his mind to avoid the two

spots, even if it meant taking Ruffian slightly wide.

Sunday, July 6, 1975, was the day of the mile-and-a-quarter race. The weather was fair, the track hard and fast—perhaps too hard. Prior to the match race, a number of records had been set on the surface, startling the clockers, but more than the average number of horses had broken down on the track, too.

When the endless preliminaries for television had finally been carried out, Ruffian and Foolish Pleasure, Braulio Baeza up, burst from the gate. Running close together but not bumping, the two horses moved out of the chute and joined the main track, going from a firm base to one nearly rock-hard. The change seemed not to bother either horse. Ruffian, ahead by three quarters of a length, was easing ahead almost effortlessly. "Then I decided I'd better save something and tried to hold her back," jockey Vasquez recalled later, "You can't go a mile and a quarter pumping away, it's too fast, and I took a chance that Baeza would do the same thing. But just after joining the main track, she broke her leg. It sounded like a shot."

As Foolish Pleasure romped home to win, Ruffian and Vasquez edged off the track. Both sesamoid bones in her right foreleg shattered, her racing career was over, but equine surgeons made an attempt to save the horse's life. Ruffian was anesthetized, the bones set, and a cast applied. If she had been a human being, capable of lying in bed until the break healed, the story would have had a happier ending. But Ruffian wanted to move. That was what made her such a splendid piece of horseflesh. Thus when the drugs wore off, there was nothing that could be done to hold her down. "Nobody realizes the tremendous strength of a horse coming out of anesthesia," said Dr. Alex Harthill, one of the surgeons present. "We tried our best but she just fought so hard she smashed the cast we'd put on her leg. She never got up."

She was subsequently destroyed and buried in the infield of Belmont Track, to the right of the toteboard about a sixteenth of a mile past the finish line.

CHAPTER 34—BEING A SPECTATOR
ISN'T ALWAYS EASY

Then, as now, you took your chances.

A ball park or rink or grandstand after the Civil War wasn't necessarily the safest place in the United States, and the law courts didn't make it any easier for the average viewer. For example, when James E. Dolen sued the Metropolitan Exhibition Company in 1888 for twenty-five thousand dollars after a foul ball at the Polo Grounds cost him the loss of an eye, the result was hardly satisfying to him. "Judge Donohue dismissed the complaint," reported the New York Sun of March 22. "He said that the company appeared to have taken all the necessary precautions to prevent accidents, and when a ticket to the grandstand was sold it was a mutual contract between the company and the purchaser that a seat should be provided and a game of ball played. That ended the contract and the spectator must take all risks of accident."

With that landmark decision in mind, there follows a brief compendium of anxiety in the arena, panic in the park, and stampeding in the stands—proving that while life for the sports spectator may not have improved all that much, at least the malfunctioning technology has become more sophisticated. Sometimes.

NOVEMBER 1890

One of the more memorable grandstand collapses occurred at Brooklyn's Eastern Park while twenty-five thousand people were watching Yale and Princeton slug it out on the football field. The wooden bleachers, as was the custom, were temporary and rented, having been brought from Philadelphia early that week. When the workers arrived, however, they discovered that they were minus a few missing parts—nonessentials such as supporting struts, etc.—so they looked about for spare wood and made do with what was lying about the grounds. Sometimes the piece may not have exactly fit, but it was usually close enough.

During the game, it was this section of temporary stands that "fell with a crashing, roaring noise a little after twelve o'clock, precipitating," as one reporter described it, "nearly two thousand persons in a confused and terrified mass to the ground, under and upon the splintered ruins of the stands. About fifty of them injured—two of the victims likely to die . . . ."

The falling section, about 150 feet long and composed of 30 tiers, was only 20 feet above the ground at its highest point. Thus a large percentage of the audience was not seriously injured. There were many flesh wounds and abrasions, but most of the victims "disdained surgical attention, and tied handkerchiefs around their wounded limbs and sought new perches on the ruins of the fallen stands from which to view the great contest." Which proves that American sports spectators have always been either hardy souls or gluttons for punishment, depending on one's point of view.

There was an investigation, naturally, perhaps the most startling aspect of it being that the Eastern Park management placed the blame for the accident on the fans. "The trouble was that the people would not keep still," the company spokesman said. "It was cold, I suppose, and the people got up on their feet and began dancing like a lot of wild Indians." One got the definite impression that he was being kind by not suing the fans for malicious destruction of the rented grandstand.

The newspapers, in turn, blamed the park management. "All was done for gain," one charged. "Those who had it in charge seemed anxious only to make money and cared not a whit how the public fared." There was also a modicum of blame for the police. "The Brooklyn police were absurdly incompetent. . . . They stood around like so many dummies." And the Philadelphia renting firm took its share of journalistic wrath. "There was not a piece of wood about the structure deserving the name of timber."

In the end, of course, the brouhaha faded away, no damages were awarded, cheap rented grandstands continued to spring up whenever the situation called for them, and the fans kept making their way to the tops of the creaking structures with almost masochistic regularity.

AUGUST 1894

The year 1894 was not a particularly good one in which to walk into a baseball park. After a May blaze in Boston, two occurred within a twenty-four-hour period at other National League parks.

It was nearly five o'clock at Chicago during the bottom of the sixth inning when someone in the stands noticed smoke coming up through the cracks of the fifty-cent seat flooring. Cap Anson was at bat for Chicago when someone yelled "Fire!" The inevitable panic followed as people near the smoke tried to elbow and wrestle their way to a safer spot. Others in the park concluded that a fight was taking place, but once the thin stream of smoke became visible to all, a genuine stampede began. Anson, meanwhile, was concentrating on the pitcher so hard that he didn't move a muscle.

One complicating factor was that four strands of barbed wire had been placed at the edge of the grandstand in order to prevent people from moving onto the field after or during the game. With the narrow stairways jammed, many people tried to escape through the barbed wire or pushed others in that direction. Soon the smoke turned into a geyser of flame. Desperate, some customers ripped up the cheap planks of the bleachers and threw them across the barbed wire. "A perfect Niagara" of humanity poured onto the field. "Men and women were trampled under foot and jumped upon, and several hundred people received injuries of a more or less serious character. At least one man, E. W. Bartlett, suffered a broken leg and internal injuries."

Even with the barbed wire bridged at several spots, the crowd continued to buck against the strands of pointed steel. The injury list might have been even longer had not Jimmy Ryan and Walt Wilmot of the White Stockings rushed over with baseball bats and clubbed more openings for the fans.

When firemen arrived, they were hampered by the milling crowd, and by the time the firemen were in position to fight the blaze a considerable section of the park was already beyond saving. A special call for more help brought additional engines but not before 450 feet of the stands had gone up in flames. "The origin of the fire is not positively known," the New York *Herald* reported. "The most plausible theory advanced, however, is that someone dropped a lighted cigar through a crack in the floor and that it fell on a small tool house directly beneath. . . . The park janitor was the first man to reach the point where the fire started, and he turned a hose on the flames, but they had gained too great headway, and he was forced to abandon his position and turn in a general alarm."

The next day, at Philadelphia, a cigarette thrown away by a small boy in the pavilion of the ball club at Broadway and Huntingdon Street started a fire that completely destroyed the grandstands and bleachers. Those structures, fortunately, were not occupied by paying customers, as it was ten-thirty in the morning.

NOVEMBER 1900

One of the grisliest fates to befall fans took place on November 29 at San Francisco during a football game between Stanford and California. The contest attracted about twenty thousand paying customers, as well as several hundred fans who decided not to bother going to the park. Instead, they somehow managed to work their way onto the roof of the Pacific Glass Works Factory on Fifteenth Street, which happened to overlook the stadium and provide an excellent free view.

Unfortunately, the roof, which was made of sheet-iron incapable of holding all that weight, gave way about twenty minutes after the football game started. "There was a crash," one reporter wrote, "plainly audible on the football grounds, and a portion of the crowd on the roof went down." More specifically, the unlucky ones who couldn't find a way of hanging on were pitched into the factory itself. The fires of the furnaces had been started and liquid glass glistened and bubbled in huge open vats. "Some were killed instantly and others were slowly roasted to death," the report said of the one hundred who fell into the inferno.

Immediately ushers raced through the grandstands calling for doctors. The beds and hallways of the Southern Pacific Railway Hospital two blocks from the glass factory were quickly filled. Police Department and Fire Department vehicles as well as private carriages and express wagons were recruited to rush the victims there, but before the game was over, thirteen had died and eighty were seriously injured. The more fortunate ones, as it turned out, had been those who fell directly from the roof to the floor, breaking bones in the process.

NOVEMBER 1902

Another sensational grandstand collapse occurred in Chicago during the 1902 football game between Michigan and Wisconsin. Thirty-two were injured as the grandstand gave way "with a crash that could be heard for blocks." Fortunately, no one was killed; no injury even befell the building inspectors who had pronounced the structure safe and sound and were standing close to it when it descended about their ears.

AUGUST 1903

Philadelphia's baseball park was back in the news nine years after the fire of 1894. It had been reconstructed with a wooden walkway at the top of the left-field section so that people could leave without obstructing others' view of the playing area. The walkway was only three feet wide, however, and projected over the traffic of Fifteenth Street. Ironically it was action in the street, rather than on the field, that caused the accident of August 8.

Ten thousand persons were present at 5:40 P.M. when Boston came to bat in the fourth inning. At that same moment, a scuffle broke out on Fifteenth Street, and several patrons at the top of the grandstand leaned out over the walkway railing to get a better view. More and more followed them until hundreds pressed against each other and the flimsy wooden braces.

When the railing gave way, a two hundred-foot section of it was hurled into the road along with a swirling mass of bodies. "For an entire block," one paper reported, "men were lying . . . some as far out as the car tracks." To make matters worse, the roar made by the structure giving way and subsequent shouts created panic in other sections of the park. Fans rushed onto the field, trampling each other in the narrow aisleways.

Ambulances soon arrived, and when it was noted that a huge transit company car barn was directly opposite the park, a highly appropriate wrecking car was quickly filled with the wounded and driven to St. Joseph's Hospital.

Subsequent investigation of the stands showed that the wooden railing supports were rotten.

AUGUST–SEPTEMBER 1911

The year 1911 was a good one for enthusiasts of auto racing. Meets were taking place all across the nation, bringing with them excitement and a relentless smashing of endurance and time records. The craving for the sport also brought increased dangers to fans in the form of cheap grandstands and out-of-control cars, and 1911 was a banner year for that too.

The scene was Elgin, Illinois; the time, 11:00 A.M., August 26. The race was in its very first lap when a thousand people seated in the flimsy grandstands felt a shiver run beneath their feet. The stringers supporting the structure had given way, at which point the boards of the grandstand "spread out like a pack of cards carefully thrown on a table, and the spectators were shunted into a heap at the bottom." Four persons, including the daughter of a prominent senator, were seriously injured, the wounded being cared for at the field hospital. That ruined the auto races for many others, who drifted away during the course of the afternoon. For the rest of the day, warnings were shouted through megaphones, urging the spectators not to jump to their feet

during moments of excitement. This also carried the implication that it wasn't management's fault if people became so restless or demonstrative that they destroyed perfectly good grandstands.

Three weeks later, one of the worst accidents in the brief history of auto racing occurred at Syracuse, where sixty-five thousand persons had gathered at the state fairgrounds. One of the guests was President Taft, who took the opportunity to circle the racing oval in a car and wave to the crowd. Fair officials, worried that the President would be bothered by choking dust from the track, ordered the section on which Taft rode to be heavily watered down.

When some of the better drivers examined the track, they noted that its condition was poor and that taking the unbanked curves would be dangerous. Officials agreed to a slight delay so that the road would have a chance to dry out, but as the crowd for the advertised fifty-mile event continued to increase and become restive, it was decided to start the race with the track still wet and slippery.

The three major drivers were Ralph DePalma, Bob Burman, and Lee Oldfield, brother of the famous racer, Barney. Early in the race, DePalma developed tire troubles, but once he started to move, he opened a one-lap lead over Oldfield and maintained it for half the contest. At the twenty-fifth mile, however, Oldfield began to creep up on DePalma, causing a crescendo of excitement to roll out of the crowd. Although acknowledged to be "lacking in the daredevil spirit of his brother," Lee Oldfield was skillful and apparently willing to take chances. He had tire troubles on his own car—a right front tire had thrown part of the shoe—but he continued to increase his speed. Even worse, he began not slowing down as he approached the wet section of track, now made even more slippery by the addition of leaking oil and constant use. As he circled the course at a pace rapidly changing from merely daring to reckless, the tire could be seen beating the track at an unusual angle. Efforts were made to have him stop and replace the bad tire, but he continued to move after DePalma.

Gaining bit by bit, Oldfield soon pulled almost abreast of DePalma. "The broken shoe could be seen plainly by the spectators," one reporter wrote. "Apparently intent upon gaining on DePalma, he evidently decided to make speed at the expense of caution." At 5:30 P.M., as the two drivers rounded the turn into the forty-third mile, Oldfield's car was inches behind DePalma's. Suddenly there was a loud report, Oldfield's vehicle leaped into the air, settled back onto the track on four

Some Other Racing Incidents of the Period Which Were Dangerous to Spectators:

1902: *During road races on Staten Island, electric car driven by W. C. Baker dashed into crowd, tossing a dozen persons into the air and killing two.*

1906: *Vanderbilt Cup Race. Car driven by Elliot Shepard killed K. L. Gruner, who had strayed onto road. As a result, no Vanderbilt Cup race was run in 1907.*

1908: *Long Island Motor Parkway Races: Flying piece of metal from car struck spectator and fractured his skull.*

1909: *Dense fog during running of Lowell Cup races prevented Driver Joe Matson from seeing Henry Otis, whom he struck and killed.*

1909: *At Indianapolis, driver Charley Merz blew a tire and plunged into crowd, killing two spectators as well as his "mechanician."*

---

wheels, then roared toward the fence separating the dense crowd from the track. Sputtering and smoking, the car tore through the flimsy barrier and pounded into the midst of a panicked crowd. "So sudden was the tragedy enacted that those in the path of the onrushing machine hardly had time to move an inch before it was upon them. The six who were killed outright were hurled in all directions, their bodies terribly mangled. The three others who died, two on the way to the hospital and a third soon after arrival there, were badly mangled." Doctors from all points of the fairgrounds ran to the scene but there was little they could do except treat minor injuries and help control the panic.

Ralph DePalma, meanwhile, unaware of what had happened, continued to speed around the oval. Oldfield, thrown free of the car, landed some distance away, unconscious. Before coming to a halt, the smoking vehicle tore a twenty-foot opening in the solid wall of spectators. The worst fate befell a young boy, who was decapitated. Many in the crowd broke through the fence and crossed the track even as DePalma raced toward the fiftieth mile. Officials, who seemed paralyzed by the accident, did nothing to stop him from completing the necessary laps to win. Luckily, no one was injured as DePalma zigzagged his way through a maze of crazed pedestrians.

Lee Oldfield, regaining consciousness, said: "I don't know how it happened. I heard my tire blow up, then I went through the fence. After that, everything was a blank. When I came to I was being lifted from the top of another man on whom I had landed."

Two hours later, the track was cleared. "It is the general impression," one newspaper noted a bit sadly, "that to-day's disaster sounds the knell of motor car racing on the State Fair tracks."

Saturday, September 16, 1911—the day Oldfield's car struck the crowd—produced yet another accident. Not far away, on the Niagara River near Buffalo, Frederick Burnham guided his speedy hydroplane *Dixie IV* over a tricky course. Earlier, Burnham had successfully defended the Harmsworth Cup at Huntington, Long Island, and just the day before won the speedboat-racing championship of the United States on the same Niagara River course. Fitted with two 250-horsepower engines and a capacity of developing 1,000 revolutions per minute, *Dixie IV* was widely acclaimed as the finest racing craft in the nation. Just under 40 feet in length with a beam of 7 feet, she was sleek and dramatic in appearance, nearly half of her forward hull projecting from the surface of the water when running at top speed.

After winning the U.S. championship, Burnham entered the Great Lakes race in the hopes of scoring back-to-back victories. Familiar with the currents and geography of the Niagara River, he was able to move his craft ahead to the full limit of her power, reaching 89 miles per hour on the straight sections of the course.

Most of the shoreline near Riverside Park was lined with spectators, who whistled and shouted amazement at the speed of *Dixie IV*. All went well until the boat rounded a stake just above the crowd; then it seemed that she was rudderless. After careening downriver, *Dixie* swerved directly toward the shore and the thousands standing on the banks. Burnham had only seconds to act after he realized something was wrong. Grabbing the wheel in a desperate attempt to bring the boat about, he shouted a warning to the two-man crew.

The crowd, meanwhile, made little effort to scatter, not realizing the boat was totally out of control. When they did understand the situation, it was too late—just as it was too late for Fred Burnham to cut his power and bring *Dixie* to a gradual stop.

Twenty feet from the shoreline, the two members of Burnham's crew leaped over the side into the water. *Dixie* continued dead toward the crowd.

When the collision occurred, Burnham was tossed free, landing in the water and escaping without a scratch. Three members of the crowd were not so fortunate. One, a thirteen-year-old boy named Harold Bell, was crushed beneath the vessel's flip-flopping hull. His mother was struck on the head but not seriously. John Daniels, another spectator who could not get out of the way in time, had his leg severed just above the ankle. The hull and engine of the speedboat were shattered to pieces.

A hearing held a month later indicated that the accident had been caused by the propellers revolving at different speeds, making *Dixie* impossible to steer. Nevertheless, several suits charging Burnham with "criminal negligence and cowardice" were filed, the first on the grounds that he should have acted quickly the moment he realized there was trouble, the second because he "had deserted his post at the steering wheel, jumping overboard when the boat was within three hundred feet of the shore and might have been brought under control."

The second charge, of course, was not true, and the first was not upheld. As a result, none of the victims of the accident received a penny of compensation.

APRIL 1912
Sometimes, of course, the fan's agony is more mental than physical—as when he purchases a ticket to a baseball game and then cannot see what's going on.

Such a situation occurred on Opening Day 1912 at Brooklyn's Washington Park. The game was a natural spectator attraction in that it pitted the lowly Trolley-Dodgers against their crosstown rivals, the Giants, who had won the pennant the year before. The folks in Brooklyn wanted nothing more than to watch their team spoil the first game of the season for McGraw's bullies. Two hours before the game was to begin, they started drifting into the park.

Washington Park's ticket sellers happily took in the money until about a half hour too late, when they suddenly realized that the tiny park was jammed with twenty-five thousand people, about eight thousand more than capacity. At this point no more admissions were sold, but of course there was no way to rectify the situation inside the park. And at first there really seemed to be no major problem. The crowd was in a good-natured mood.

Long before game time, the crowd had filled every seat in the park and spilled onto the field along both sidelines. Then, as even more citizens were allowed to enter, the crowd oozed across the foul lines into fair territory. In right and left field the customers were within a dozen yards of the bases; even in center field a solid bank of humanity defied

efforts of the park police to clear the playing area.

At this point, the holders of box seats started arriving, unaware that they were going to get anything less than the best treatment. Some were refused admission; others couldn't squeeze their way through the angry wall of rejected bleacherites; and many who did manage to identify themselves and gain entrance to the park soon discovered that their boxes were already occupied by gangs of spectators who refused to move. In some cases the chairs in the boxes had been taken onto the field for either sitting or standing purposes.

With every passing minute, the crowd grew surlier. Outside, where trains continued to drop passengers from Manhattan, it was even worse. About three-thirty Mayor Gaynor and Deputy Police Commissioner Walsh arrived, and assisted by a squad of special guards gained entrance to the park. They were appalled at the situation.

Someone suggested that Gaynor call the reserves, but the mayor turned down the idea in favor of using the special police. Assisted by players of both teams, each of whom was armed with a baseball bat, the force charged the crowd, trying to shove them back of the foul lines. Usually the people gave way, only to squirt back in the area just vacated by the officers and players. Occasionally a particularly belligerent fan would attempt to fight back. In any event, the Pinkertons were simultaneously helpless and heartless. Losing their tempers, they began shoving men and small boys as hard as they could. Hats were crushed and coats nearly torn from the backs of their owners.

Sensing disaster, Mayor Gaynor summoned the reserves. When they arrived, resplendent in their blue uniforms, the crowd was sufficiently awed by the dramatic entrance to calm down a bit. Umpire Bill Klem ordered the game started.

Only when the players took the field did a large majority of the crowd realize one thing: it was nearly impossible to see what was happening. People standing along the sidelines totally obscured the playing area except for the far reaches of the outfield. Even worse, when the fans along the sidelines realized *they* couldn't see unless they were in the front row, they rushed the boxes and grabbed every available chair so as to stand on it. This, of course, made the situation even more intolerable for those behind them. Some of the more volatile customers started rolling up newspapers and throwing them at the miscreants who were in their line of sight.

"The game, as it appeared from the press box," one reporter wrote, "was a beautiful exhibition of English tweed, derby, and fedora hats, to say nothing of a broad expanse of wide and narrow manly backs." Occasionally the fans would be treated to the sight of a ball springing from the crowd, hanging in the air for a moment, and then descending once again into the sea of human heads and shoulders. This might or might not be followed by a cheer of some sort, for only a few lucky persons could see any given play from beginnng to end.

Eventually a couple of bright fellows decided to perform a public service and enlighten themselves in the process. Shimmying their way up the side poles of the backstop, they soon attained a vantage point from which they could relay news to all those within sound of their voices.

Because it was Opening Day, of course, both teams started their ace pitchers—the Giants' Rube Marquard, who had won twenty-four games in 1911, the Trolley-Dodgers' Nap Rucker, a twenty-two-game winner the year before. Both probably wished they were somewhere else, for the game soon degenerated into a fiasco.

After a scoreless first inning, the Giant batters discovered that it was relatively easy to pop the ball into the crowds in fair territory behind first and third base and earn a cheap ground-rule double. They performed this ritual so well and so often that at the end of five innings the score stood Giants 14, Brooklyn 3. When the Trolley-Dodgers tried the same maneuver, Marquard outfoxed them. A better low-ball pitcher than Rucker, he forced Brooklyn batters to beat the ball into the ground rather than loft it into the automatic double area.

At this point, Umpire Klem began to realize the game was hardly worth continuing. For one thing, they were likely to run out of balls, as few among the surly sideliners bothered to return either fouls or the balls that went for two-base hits. The field was littered with rolled-up paper and whatever else angry fans deemed worthy of throwing at their neighbors.

Finally, in an unprecedented move, Nap Rucker decided he had had enough of the Giants' fattening their averages with "a lot of punk pop flies into the mob," and removed himself from the ball game. Manager Bill Dahlen sent in twenty-four-year-old Eddie Dent, and may have so traumatized him that his major-league career was irreparably damaged. The record book shows that Dent's statistics for 1912 include one inning pitched, four hits yielded (ground-rule doubles, one suspects), and an ERA of 36.00 Even more significantly, Dent's name disappears from the ranks of major-league pitchers after that. He probably considered himself lucky to return to the industrial smog of his hometown, Baltimore.

With the score 18–3 at the end of six innings, Umpire Klem called the game because of "darkness." He was, of course, absolutely right. Never have so few seen so little through so many.

SEPTEMBER 1912

It was, as the newspapers said without exaggeration, the worst disaster recorded in the history of motorcycling.

The Valisburg Motordrome Stadium in Newark was barely two months old, having been opened in gala ceremonies on the Fourth of July in 1912. Its construction, ironically, was brought about because of the need for greater safety in the comparatively new sport of motorcycle racing. Too many accidents on public thoroughfares had occurred in recent years, threatening to turn people against all cyclists, racers or otherwise. Moving under controlled conditions on specially constructed tracks, the riders at Motordrome Stadium would be not only safer but also more accessible to their fans.

Greater accessibility, naturally, meant better gate receipts, and in that respect the events of September 8, 1912, promised much. A capacity crowd was on hand to see one of their favorites, nineteen-year-old Eddie Hasha from Waco, Texas, race his genial rival, Ray Seymour of Los Angeles. "Hasha, who came East with conquest in his eye," one paper wrote, "was one of the lightest riders in the world and was already accounted its greatest cyclist. They always called him the champion, although the sport is not sufficiently organized for anyone to earn that title definitely and beyond dispute." Others addressed Hasha as "Tod Sloan," the famous jockey who originated the extreme forward riding position. Since arriving in the East, the Texan had beaten every important motorcyclist in the area.

The main event of the night was a four-mile race around the quarter-mile track, Hasha's competition besides Seymour being John Albright of Denver, Ray Peck of Los Angeles, Johnny King of Newark, and Frank King of Denver. As the six men lined up their cycles for the start, young and pretty Mrs. Hasha, whom Eddie had married the year before, quietly got up and slipped out of the arena, for "closely as she always followed the sport she never would stay to see her husband in actual races."

The start was smooth. Hasha and Seymour moving into a slight lead. As they sped around the huge saucer, it was estimated that Hasha quickly hit a speed of ninety-two miles per hour, but Seymour managed to creep up on him. As they were on the second lap, Seymour passed, and just as they reached the spot where bleachers joined grandstand, Hasha lost control of his handlebars. The cycle swerved above the danger line, marked in heavy black paint six feet below the upper edge of the track. "It all happened then so swiftly and in so few seconds that few even of those whose eyes were glued horrified upon Hasha could tell afterward precisely what had happened. Up the dangerous incline to the top the machine shot, tore its way through the wire netting stretched perpendicularly to keep the eager spectators from falling to the track and into the crowded end of the bleachers."

With Hasha still frozen to the handlebars, the motorcycle first struck a small boy, killing him instantly, then hit a ten-inch beam, which caused the vehicle to spin like a top among the crowd, its engine roaring and its wheels spinning. Hasha was thrown into the grandstand, his arms, legs, ribs, and neck broken. Two other boys and a man were also struck down by the wildly careening machine as the crowd, "screaming, cursing, whimpering . . . fought and trampled one another under foot in the frantic struggle to get out of the path of the machine. . . ."

As if that were not enough, the cycle then pivoted back through the torn netting onto the track, directly in the path of John Albright, the last rider in the race. There was a violent impact as the driver was hurled through the air to the top of the inclined track, where he lay completely still. Albright's wife, seated in the grandstand, fainted. By the time an ambulance arrived, however, she was in good enough condition to accompany him to the hospital.

Officials halted the race at this point and the stadium was soon filled with frantic physicians, nurses, and police officers. Twenty persons were seriously injured, and counting Hasha and Albright, six were killed.

Shortly afterward, representatives of the motordrome, which was owned by a syndicate of prominent Newark businessmen, were invited to a hearing in order to determine who or what was responsible for the accident. That seemed to be merely a formality, however, for as one reporter noted, "It is the disposition of the police to believe that the accident was unavoidable."

NOVEMBER 1922

Police investigating the collapse of a grandstand section in Melrose, Massachusetts, on November 30, 1922, also absolved the management of any negligence. Melrose High School had just scored a touchdown in the game, it was reported, and "the dancing about of the cheering girls was too much for the temporary structure. Police who investigated the accident said that the solid packing of the stand saved the lives of many. The girls were all standing and came down feet first." (In other words, the management was to be congratulated on having the foresight to jam as many people into the temporary structure as possible.)

MAY 1927

Philadelphia's antiquated stadium at Broad and Huntingdon streets was back in the news for a third time in 1927. A large holiday crowd of eighteen thousand was on hand for a game between the Phillies and Cardinals when, during the third inning, it started to rain. The bleacher customers made an immediate rush for the protected sections of the left- and right-field stands.

The rain let up enough for the game to continue, but the fans remained huddled beneath the grandstand roof. Shortly after the Phillies scored six runs in the sixth inning, the section of grandstand behind first base split right at the aisleway, forming a huge V into which more than seven thousand tumbled, fell or slid.

Seeing what had happened, fans in the upper pavilion immediately assumed that the entire grandstand was collapsing and began a mad rush toward the iron steps back of the press box. One man was trampled to death in the stampede that followed, another had a brand-new suit torn off his back and was cut about the scalp. Two dozen others were treated for injuries at nearby hospitals.

Secretary Jerry Nugent of the Philadelphia club expressed surprise at what had happpened, stating that the stands had been inspected only two months before by the city and found to be perfectly safe. "I think there is no doubt, however," he added, "that the crash may have been caused by the section in the stands being taxed by the additional seven thousand fans who entered it from the bleachers when rain fell in the third inning."

The Phillies won the game, 12–3.

MAY 1929

Almost two years to the day, a nearly identical accident befell fans at Yankee Stadium, where fifty thousand had gathered for an exciting Sunday afternoon of baseball. More than nine thousand of the fans sat in the bleachers, many wearing straw hats and dressed in summer clothes, for at the beginning of the game, the sun shone brightly.

The third inning was particularly happy in that section of the right-field bleachers known as "Ruthville." That was when the Babe deposited a ball there, followed a few seconds later by Lou Gehrig's shot to left field. At the end of the fourth inning, however, it began to grow dark, and by the time the Yankees came to bat in the fifth, a soft drizzle was settling down on the Stadium. Some bleacherites got up and left but most remained, obviously hoping that the second scheduled batter, Ruth, would hit another their way.

Those fans who did leave congregated at the exit, a vertical drop of fourteen steps and eight feet leading to a dirt passageway thirty feet long. This tunnel was lined on the sides with a chicken-wire partition supported by two-by-four timbers.

Yankee shortstop Mark Koenig grounded out, but any disappointment was drowned in the cheers that greeted Babe Ruth. The idol of countless New York youngsters also went out, and just as Lou Gehrig stepped to the plate, the deluge began, a solid sheet of water so dense it obscured objects only a few feet away. At that, every person in the bleachers headed for the exit tunnel. They ran en masse into the knot of fans who had gathered in the shelter near the ramp, many of whom were still facing the field as the collision took place. Most were able to turn and start down the stairs but because they were not moving as fast as the wet bleacher fans, pressure from the rear became overpowering. Someone tripped, causing others to fall. The area at the foot of the steps, a space about ten feet wide, became a seething receptacle of falling, struggling people. The thin chicken wire at the sides gave way, the struggling persons on the top of the heap thrown into the dirt under either side of the bleachers. One of those caught in the human maelstrom was thirteen-year-old Isidore Simon of the Bronx, who was attending his first professional baseball game. As soon as the heavy rain started, young Simon leaped from his seat and rushed toward the exit ramp. But so strong was the force of those behind him that when the pile-up started, he was lifted into the air and tossed backward, then sideways and through the netting. He escaped with minor bruises, minus his right shoe and hat.

A John Keane, who brought his son to the game, later said: "I never saw such a mad rush before. . . . There must have been a half-dozen people under me, all shouting and screaming. Clothing was being torn from people's bodies. I saw one girl there with all her outer clothing stripped off. My son was torn from my grasp, but later I found him. A couple of policemen and some negro boys were trying to calm the crowd and they managed to rescue a lot of men and boys from the jam. When we were leaving they were laying the injured persons out in rows."

Two spectators were not so fortunate. One fatality, a Hunter College student named Eleanor Price, was just seventeen. The other was a sixty-year-old man named John T. Carter. More than sixty suffered varying degrees of injury.

At least two of those who were injured blamed Yankee Stadium management's "greed for money." Louis Rosenberg, a druggist, claimed that the game had been prolonged

until the fifth inning so that rain checks would not have to be honored. Others said that an exit gate that could have eased the pressure if it had been open was closed. Colonel Jacob Ruppert, owner of the Yankees, later denied that any gates had been closed or anything not done that would have saved lives. "It is just one of those unfortunate things that cannot be helped," he said blandly.

Unlike other instances in the past, that did not close the matter. Two and a half years later, some cases were still in court, thirty-two plaintiffs having filed suits for $30,000 damages each, a total of $960,000.

The Yankees, naturally, argued for dismissal of the cases, holding that there were sufficient exits and the company could not be held responsible, especially for such things as spring showers and crowd panic, the real causes of the tragedy. The plaintiffs charged that the Stadium did not have enough exits or guards to handle an emergency situation.

A verdict was rendered on February 16, 1932, by a jury that was hardly noteworthy for its decisiveness. After deliberating for ten hours, it found both the defendant and the plaintiffs guilty of negligence. Justice Edward Gavegan set aside the verdict until December. At that time, the Yankees announced that the club would pay a total of $45,000, following the decision of an appellate court that because it was the natural instinct of a crowd to seek shelter in a downpour, the plaintiffs could not be held even partly responsible.

NOVEMBER 1938

A most unusual form of fan discomfort occurred on November 12, 1938, when Rita McDonald, a student of Watertown High School, Watertown, New York, opened her mouth to cheer a team touchdown and couldn't get it closed.

She had to be taken to Mercy Hospital nearby where her jaw was snapped back into place.

MARCH 1952

The scene was Baltimore's 5th Regiment Armory, a stone-and-masonry creation of the early twentieth century that was somehow more depressing inside than outside. On the evening of March 6, 1952, the cavernous building had somewhat of a festive air about it, however, because Sonja Henie's ice show was making its initial appearance there.

Baltimore's largest indoor arena, the armory could handle only about seven thousand people even with the addition of temporary seats. When it became obvious that the ice show would be a sellout, every effort was made to cram as many people as possible into the limited area. At the last minute extra temporary stands were rented and a permit requested to erect them. When the city officials responsible for issuing the permit arrived in the afternoon, workmen were still in the process of installing the seats. "They were of temporary construction," said a building inspections engineer, "and not even nailed down. We would not have given a permit for that."

Having done their duty—that is, not issued the permit—the inspectors left and the show went on without the formality of the stands being approved.

That is, it almost went on. Evening came and the armory was soon packed with ticket holders. Those assigned to the six sections of rented seats discovered that even as they made their way up the flimsy iron-and-wooden stands, workmen were hammering away in an effort to complete their job. Soon the temporary structure was filled and the audience settled back to await the beginning of the show.

Seated in her dressing room, actress and thrice-crowned Olympic figure skater Henie, thirty-nine, suddenly heard a roar, which she thought was "a train going under the building."

In the main hall of the armory it sounded more like the rumblings of an earthquake. "We had just reached our seats in O Section when that terrible noise and crash came," one woman recalled later, "and then we hit bottom. Beams and chairs and people started falling down on top of us."

Another described it as "a rumbling noise . . . like an avalanche . . . there was a loud crack before it gave way. . . . Then it began to go . . . it seemed to be moving forward. . . . Then down . . . down . . . down . . . ." Seen from above, the scene resembled a giant's game of jackstraws, beams jutting upward at awkward angles, heavy planks falling into the well of shifting bodies.

Within a few minutes, the shrieks of pain and surprise changed to low moans and cries for help. Here and there could be seen a woman kneeling in prayer or clutching a rosary. Then National Guardsmen appeared, followed by police, firemen, and emergency units. About two hundred nurses who were attending an association meeting at a nearby school arrived.

Meanwhile, in the armory's backstage area, Sonja Henie peeped through an opening at the crowd and muttered, "What shall I do? What shall I do?" The show had cost $500,000 to produce and she was naturally reluctant to cancel it immediately. Nor did she know then the extent of injury wrought by the seats' collapsing.

"If you go on, everybody's going to be nervous," offered Ken Stevens, the stage manager.

"But I'm not responsible," the skater replied. "I contracted with a man to have these bleachers set up. He's been doing it for over twenty years and I certainly thought he knew what he was doing."

Someone else suggested that Miss Henie go out and ask the audience whether they would like to see the show or not. At which point she asked, "But what if another section goes down?"

That seemed to settle the matter. A minute later, Ken Stevens went to a microphone and explained. "I am speaking in behalf of Miss Henie," he said. "She feels terrible about this. Due to the condition we will not give a performance tonight." He added that money would be refunded if a special performance could not be arranged at a later date.

The rest of the crowd filed out without panic, some staying to watch rescue teams work frantically to remove debris and injured people. When it was all over, nearly three hundred people had been treated for injuries on the spot or taken to four hospitals in the area. "It's an outrage," one woman concluded. "For $2.40 they want to kill us."

By the time the "Sonja Henie Ice Revue" of 1952 arrived at New York less than two weeks later, damage suits for $5,175,000 in 230 actions had been filed against the star, her husband, and the contractor who built the bleachers, Edwin P. Coronati of Westfield, New Jersey. Even more to the point, officials in New York, where the show was to begin a two-week run, would not allow it to open unless Sonja Henie Enterprises could post a $1,000,000 bond. The skating star decided to cancel the show.

"We'll be back another time," she said simply.

MAY 1960

Dr. Roy B. Storm, Marion County coroner, had one brief comment on the seating arrangements at Indianapolis. "I have said for years that the Speedway should not permit those towers to be erected," he said shortly after the accident.

The "towers" were joined sections of metal tubing about three inches in diameter, erected in a framework on which board platforms were placed on tiers. The same type of scaffold was often used by painters working alongside buildings. Spectators had to climb a ladder to reach their seats, or perches, upper-tier space selling for $10.

As the race began on May 30, more than a hundred people were in the section of scaffolding when it suddenly collapsed. During the parade lap, spectators leaned forward, causing the structure to fall slowly off its truck base. "It went down in slow-motion," reported one man. Another, a photographer standing on the ground, was directly in front of the scaffold when it began moving toward him. "I turned around and the whole scaffold, people and all, fell right toward me," he recalled later. "I ran away from it. Either the scaffold or somebody falling brushed the back of my leg."

Striking the ground with a metallic roar, the mass of iron and people flung some of its occupants across a fence onto a broad strip of grass bordering the track. The majority fell on top of each other in a tangled web of bodies and planking.

"We went right back in and tried to lift up the scaffold," reported the photographer who was almost struck. "A man had the ashen look of death on his face." Two men, Fred H. Linder of Indianapolis and William C. Craig of Zionsville, Indiana, were killed, and more than seventy were injured. It raised the total number of persons killed from all causes at the Speedway to fifty-two—twenty-nine drivers, fourteen mechanics, and nine spectators in a half century, an average of one person a year.

While scores of people attempted to rescue moaning victims of the fall from beneath fallen timbers, other spectators not ten yards away continued to drink beer and munch fried chicken, their main concern the forty-fourth running of the Indianapolis 500.

MAY 1964

New technology solves some problems, but it can also create new ones. Officials at Baltimore's Memorial Stadium discovered that fact on May 2, 1964, when more than twenty thousand children were admitted free to the Orioles-Indians baseball game. Shortly before the beginning of the contest, many youngsters scorned the sloping ramps leading to the upper deck in favor of taking the escalator.

Thirty-five feet long and about five feet wide, the moving stairway was capable of handling a large number of patient riders, but the children were anxious to get to their seats. A portable gate at the top of the escalator, however, permitted only one youngster at a time to pass through. Some good-natured pushing and shoving began almost immediately, then became more persistent, causing a jam-up at the gate. Children fell to the concrete at the top of the stairs. Meanwhile, more continued to be flung off the escalator.

Panic followed. The escalator, which was supposed to shut itself off automatically at the slightest indication of pressure, continued to operate, piling body on top of body, pressing children against the moving stairway edges or flinging them into the mobile barricade. Mrs. Julia Moran, who was in charge of a busload of children, was at the bottom of the escalator when it happened. "I heard the children

screaming and saw them piling up and I hollered for someone to shut off the moving stairway," she said.

One sixty-five-year-old guard, Melville Gibson, somehow managed to fight his way through the human pile-up at the top of the stairs and reach a button stopping the escalator. But by that time, the crush had continued for thirty seconds. Injured youngsters thrashed about amid shredded programs, soda cups, and cracker jacks. "I've seen accidents, but when it comes to kids this is the worst I've seen," said one policeman who arrived at the scene moments after it happened.

Another officer reported, "It looked like someone had gone through there with a hatchet. I can see them maybe being bruised and scratched, but they were chewed up."

"When they didn't clear, they began to panic and it looked like a cattle stampede," Mr. Gibson added.

One victim of the pileup, fourteen-year-old Nancy Cole, said, "A lot of people fell on top of me and many of the girls were hysterical and screaming." Young Miss Cole was one of the lucky ones, suffering only an abrasion of her right foot. Found crumpled at the top of the stairway was fourteen-year-old Annette Costantini. She was pronounced dead before an ambulance crew could arrive. More than fifty others were treated for injuries at nearby hospitals.

The occasion for the free admission of so many children: It was Safety Patrol Day.

A similar escalator accident occurred on June 23, 1973, at Kansas City, but on this occasion the equipment stopped suddenly rather than refusing to shut itself off.

After speeding up briefly, the moving stairway suddenly lurched to a halt, injuring thirty-one persons and sending six to the hospital. One of the latter was a boy who was taken away on a stretcher, the imprint of the escalator on his chest and forehead.

It was, by the way, Cub Scouts day.

FEBRUARY 1971

Spiro Agnew, former Baltimore County executive who also served from 1969 to 1973 as United States Vice President, probably played golf on every course in the world. His most spectacular round, however, came at Palm Springs, California, on February 13, 1971, when he smashed his first two shots and managed to hit three spectators.

The first blast, off the toe of his club, struck sixty-six-year-old G. L. Decker of Salem, Oregon, on the forearm, then hit Decker's wife, also on the arm. Agnew apologized profusely, kissed the woman's arm to make it well, and then returned to the tee.

His next shot smashed into the left ankle of Mrs. Jacqueline Woods of Chatsworth, California. She was taken to a first-aid station for X rays without the benefit of a vice-presidential kiss, and released in satisfactory condition about an hour later.

After shanking his second shot, Agnew dropped his driver in disgust and ignored the gallery's pleas to try it again. (The fans were obviously in a suicidal mood that day.) Comedian Bob Hope, one of the foursome with Agnew, later remarked that it might be a good idea to send the VP to Laos, scene of international problems, with a No. 3 wood.

A year before, Agnew hit professional golfer Doug Sanders in the back of the head with an errant shot.

DECEMBER 1974

Of course, it's not always a major or a minor problem being a dedicated sportswatcher. Sometimes, in fact, an addiction to spectatorism can even be a distinct advantage. A case in point was when Representative William G. Bray, Republican from Indiana, decided in December 1974 not to return home for the weekend, but remain in Philadelphia so he could see the Army-Navy game.

The plane on which he would have returned to Washington, TWA Flight 514 from Indianapolis, crashed on an approach to Dulles International Airport, killing everyone aboard.

CHAPTER 35 — 1941–50

1941

Winners: Baseball: The New York Yankees go into the World Series with a Series winning streak of 9 games, going back to the final contest of 1937. They extend the streak to 10 games by beating the Brooklyn Dodgers, 3–2, but lose the second. The Yanks then wrap up the 1941 Series by winning the next 3 games. . . . *Kentucky Derby:* Whirlaway. *Preakness:* Whirlaway. *Belmont Stakes:* Whirlaway . . . *Indy 500:* Floyd Davis-Mauri Rose . . . *Boxing:* Billy Conn having vacated the light-heavyweight crown for an unsuccessful shot at Joe Louis, Anton Christoforidis, Melio Bettina, and Gus Lesnevich battle for the division title. Lesnevich wins. Tony Zale emerges as undisputed champion of the middleweights by beating Georgie Abrams in Newark. Freddie Cochrane takes the welterweight crown from Fritzie Zivic, and Sammy Angott defeats Lew Jenkins to become new lightweight champion. The featherweight division is in disarray, Chalky Wright recognized as New York champion and Jackie Wilson as National Boxing Association titleholder. The bantamweight title, meanwhile, changes hands when Lou Salica defeats Tommy Forte. . . . *Golf: USGA Men's Open:* Craig Wood. *PGA:* Vic Ghezzi. *Masters:* Craig Wood . . . *Hockey*: 1940–41 Stanley Cup winner: Boston Bruins . . . *Football: Cotton Bowl:* Texas A&M 13, Fordham 12. *Orange Bowl:* Mississippi State 14, Georgetown 7. *Rose Bowl:* Stanford 21, Nebraska 13. *Sugar Bowl:* Boston College 19, Tennessee 13 . . . *National Football League:* Chicago Bears 37, New York Giants 9 . . . *Basketball:* 1940–41 *NCAA:* Wisconsin 39, Washington State 34. 1940–41 *NIT:* Long Island University 56, Ohio University 42.

Other Happenings: The first Vulcan Bowl, also known as the Steel Bowl, is held at Birmingham, Alabama, bringing together the top black college teams; Morris Brown tops Wilberforce, 19–3. . . . Lou Gehrig dies. . . . After Joe DiMaggio's 56-game hitting streak, it is suggested that his uniform number be changed to 56. . . . The National Basketball League (professional) is in operation, although not yet a "major" league; the Detroit Eagles win 1940–41 championship. . . . Bruce Smith, Minnesota halfback, wins Heisman trophy. . . . News in late December that tennis and golf balls may be rationed causes an outbreak of hoarding. . . . Lon Warneke of St. Louis Cardinals pitches only major-league no-hitter, downing Cincinnati, 2–0, on August 30. . . . Torger Tokle ski-jumps 273 feet at Leavenworth, Washington, then makes 288 feet at Hyak, Washington. . . . On October 4, Bill Hearne of Union College returns a kickoff 109 yards for a touchdown against Transylvania. . . . Bill Dudley of Virginia leads nation's collegiate football scorers with 134 points. . . . On February 26, boxing world is enlivened by double technical knockout, Referee Clarence Rosen stopping fight between Pat Carroll and Sammy Secreet because both are too battered to continue. . . . Larry MacPhail, general manager of the Brooklyn Dodgers, says that Dodger players will begin wearing batting helmets and that before long all major-league teams will do the same. . . . Al Blozis, Georgetown track-and-field star, sets a world indoor 16-pound shotput record of 56 feet 4½ inches on March 16.

1942

Winners: Baseball: The world is at war but the New York Yankees continue to represent the American League in the World Series. They are ambushed by the St. Louis Cardinals, however, who drop the first game and then go on to win the next 4. . . . *Kentucky Derby:* Shut Out. *Preakness:* Alsab. *Belmont Stakes:* Shut Out . . . *Indy 500:* No race because of war . . . *Boxing:* Concern with war results in lack of activity as far as championship fights, only two being held in 1942. Willie Pep is recognized as featherweight champ by winning 15-round decision over Chalky Wright; Manuel Ortiz becomes new bantamweight titleholder by beating Lou Salica. . . . *Golf: USGA Men's Open:* No tournament because of war. *PGA:* Sam Snead. *Masters:* Byron Nelson . . . *Hockey*: 1941–42 National Hockey League champion and Stanley Cup winner: Toronto Maple Leafs . . . *Football: Cotton Bowl:* Alabama 29, Texas A&M 21. *Orange Bowl:* Georgia 40, TCU 26. *Rose Bowl:* Oregon State 20, Duke 16. *Sugar Bowl:* Fordham 2, Missouri 0 . . . *National Football League:* Washington Redskins 14,

Chicago Bears 6 . . . *Basketball:* 1941–42 *NCAA:* Stanford 53, Dartmouth 38. 1941–42 *NIT:* West Virginia 47, Western Kentucky 45.

Other Happenings: One of last drop-kick field goals decides football game when Bill Garness of Minnesota boots one from 11-yard line to defeat Michigan, 16–14. . . . "Dream" football game brings together Georgia (6–0) and Alabama (5–0) on October 31, Frank Sinkwich leading the former to a 21–10 win. . . . During the year, the first full one of war, the National Football League raises $680,384 and change for war relief charities. . . . Colin P. Kelly, a young man who inspires the nation by flying his plane into a Japanese warship, is given a posthumous award as the most valorous athlete of 1941. . . . Other athletes, meanwhile, donate some of their trophies to various scrap-metal drives. Scrap metal is said to be in such short supply, in fact, that in September fans are admitted free to baseball game in Boston if they bring along scrap metal. Chicago also admits fans who bring 2 pounds or more. But in Brooklyn, the metal tariff is higher, fans being required to haul in 10 pounds for a free ticket. . . . Jack Dempsey, who sat out World War I, tries to enlist and is turned down because he is nearly 50. . . . Football officials cancel the Corn Bowl. . . . The American Hockey Association, a minor league, suspends operations for the duration because of player shortage. . . . New York City and other places change skating flag because of its resemblance to the "rising sun" of the Japanese Empire. . . . On April 26, Al Montgomery, promising young Boston Brave catcher, is killed in an automobile accident. Also carried away prematurely is flyweight boxer Victor Perez, who reportedly dies in a Nazi prison camp. . . . On July 15, Whirlaway passes Seabiscuit as top money-winning racehorse by winning Massachusetts Handicap at Suffolk Downs. . . . Army-Navy football game of 1942 is played at Annapolis, Maryland, before a crowd of less than 12,000 because of an order that tickets may be sold only to those within a 10-mile radius of the Naval Academy. . . . In a match race held at Narragansett Park, Pawtucket, Rhode Island, Alsab defeats Whirlaway. . . . Cornelius Warmerdam pole-vaults 15 feet, 7¼ inches on February 14.

1943

Winners: Baseball: Although depleted by the loss of DiMaggio and Rizzuto, the New York Yankees make it to the World Series once again and are able to defeat the repeating National League champion Cardinals, 4 games to 1. . . . *Kentucky Derby:* Count Fleet. *Preakness:* Count Fleet. *Belmont Stakes:* Count Fleet . . . *Indy 500:* No race because of war . . . *Boxing:* Confused state in middleweight division finds Beau Jack, New York State champion, finally defeating Bob Montgomery in November to emerge as fairly clear-cut titleholder. Flyweight division has its first recognized champion when Jackie Paterson knocks out Peter Kane in the first round on June 19 at Glasgow. . . . *Golf: USGA Men's Open:* No tournament because of war. *PGA:* No tournament because of war. *Masters:* No tournament because of war . . . *Hockey:* 1942–43 Stanley Cup winner: Detroit Red Wings . . . *Football: Cotton Bowl:* Texas 14, Georgia Tech 7. *Orange Bowl:* Alabama 37, Boston College 21. *Rose Bowl:* Georgia 9, UCLA 0. *Sugar Bowl:* Tennessee 14, Tulsa 7 . . . *National Football League:* Chicago Bears 41, Washington Redskins 21 . . . *Basketball:* 1942–43 *NCAA:* Wyoming 46, Georgetown 34. . . . 1942–43 *NIT:* St. John's 48, Toledo 27.

Other Happenings: Most sports are feeling the pinch of manpower shortage and take steps to combat it. College basketball teams allow freshmen to participate. National Football League allows free substitution for the duration. . . . Meanwhile, a debate continues over whether sports should be curtailed or continued. Many, including President Franklin Roosevelt, feel that abandoning baseball in particular would be interpreted as a sign of panic. . . . Babe Ruth doubts that 1943 season will be completed, but it is, and overseas Japanese are reported to take steps to jam World Series broadcasts. . . . In the International League, a one-armed outfielder named Pete Gray plays baseball briefly with Toronto, then is released. . . . Brooklyn Dodger fans are admitted free to games in July and August when they bring one-half pound of kitchen fat. . . . Many college football teams drop the sport, including Ursinus, which sees not only many of its players but also its coach drafted into the armed forces. . . . Army-Navy football tickets are restricted to those within a 10-mile radius of the stadium. . . . In March, a tennis expert named Pierre Etchebaster plays singly against a doubles team and wins, 6–2, 6–4. . . . In Augusta, Georgia, golf course usually used for national tournament is turned over to grazing cattle in order to help the war effort. . . . College football teams curtailing action for 1943 season include Alabama, Auburn, Arizona, Florida, Kentucky, Michigan State, Mississippi, Oregon, Syracuse, Tennessee, and Wyoming. . . . Most famous athlete killed in World War II action is Ensign Nile Kinnick, All-American halfback at the University of Iowa, who is lost in the Caribbean when his plane fails to return to its carrier. . . . For single season, NFL Pittsburgh Steelers and Philadelphia Eagles combine franchises, resulting in a player known as a "Steagle." . . . Quarterback Sid Luckman of Chicago Bears becomes first to throw 7 touchdown passes in a game, on November 14.

1944

Winners: Baseball: St. Louis goes wild as both home teams, the Cardinals and Browns, win pennants, thus making St. Louis the third city with two baseball teams to have an intramural World Series (the others: New York and Chicago. Boston and Philadelphia never make it). The Series goes 6 games, the Cardinals winning it. . . . *Kentucky Derby:* Pensive. *Preakness:* Pensive. *Belmont Stakes:* Bounding Home . . . *Indy 500:* No race because of war . . . *Boxing:* Championship title changes occur only in the lightweight and featherweight divisions: Bob Montgomery and Juan Zurita are recognized as New York and National Boxing Association champs in the former division; Sal Bartolo wins decision over Phil Terranova to earn NBA recognition as featherweight king. . . . *Golf: USGA Men's Open:* No tournament because of war . . . *PGA:* Bob Hamilton. *Masters:* No tournament because of war . . . *Hockey:* 1943–44 Stanley Cup winner: Montreal Canadiens . . . *Football: Cotton Bowl:* Texas 7, Randolph Field 7. *Orange Bowl:* Louisiana State 19, Texas A&M 14. *Rose Bowl:* USC 29, Washington 0. *Sugar Bowl:* Georgia Tech 20, Tulsa 18 . . . *National Football League:* Green Bay Packers 14, New York Giants 7 . . . *Basketball:* 1943–44 *NCAA:* Utah 42, Dartmouth 40. 1943–44 *NIT:* St. John's 47, DePaul 39.

Other Happenings: No-hitters are authored in National League by Clyde "Hardrock" Shoun of Cincinnati, who beats Braves 1–0 on August 15, and Jim Tobin of Boston, who turns the trick on Brooklyn, 2–0 on April 27. One-armed Peter J. Wyshner, also known as Pete Gray, is purchased by the St. Louis Browns as more athletes are called to the colors. . . . Baseball's record book is not published for 1944 because of paper shortage. . . . In Brooklyn, children are admitted free to games if they bring waste paper. . . . Jimmy Bivens, boxer, shows the right spirit by refusing to fight for $22,500 because doing so will interfere with his war job. . . . A bill to allow 17-year-olds into the ring is de-

feated. . . . Members of U.S. armed forces play football overseas, inaugurating "Spaghetti Bowl" in Rome following its liberation and "Tea Bowl" in London. . . . Anticipating a sports boom after the war, American businessmen announce plans for establishing new major professional football leagues. They are to be called the All-American Football Conference and the Trans-America League. . . . Despite a lack of players, professional hockey provides many thrills for fans during the 1943–44 season. On January 8, Babe Pratt of Toronto Maple Leafs comes up with 6 assists as Leafs beat Boston, 12–3. Then on February 3, Syd Howe of the Detroit Red Wings scores 6 goals in a 12–2 upending of New York Rangers. . . . War casualties include Alex Santilli, Fordham football great, Elmer Gedeon of the Washington Senators, swimmer Stephen Stavers, and National Football Leaguers Charles Behan, Chet Wetterlund, J. W. Hinton, and Jim Mooney—to name just a few. . . . On the minor-league baseball scene, Baltimore surprises everyone by attracting 52,833 fans to a Little World Series game with Louisville of the American Association, the largest crowd ever assembled for a minor-league contest. . . . List of colleges giving up football teams for the duration expands to include a total of 190 of 250 small schools.

1945

Winners: Baseball: Two dandy pennant races of three teams per league conclude with the Detroit Tigers and Chicago Cubs at the top of their respective heaps. The Tigers, led by baseball's best pitcher during the war year of 1945, Hal Newhouser, take the Cubs in the World Series, 4 games to 3. . . . *Kentucky Derby:* Hoop, Jr. *Preakness:* Polynesian. *Belmont Stakes:* Pavot . . . *Indy 500:* No race because of war . . . *Boxing:* The only championship fight of significance takes place in Mexico City, where Ike Williams knocks out Juan Zurita in the second round and thereby earns National Boxing Association recognition as lightweight champion. . . . *Golf: USGA Men's Open:* No tournament because of war. *PGA:* Byron Nelson. *Masters:* No tournament because of war . . . *Hockey:* 1944–45 NHL winner: Toronto Maple Leafs . . . *Football: Cotton Bowl:* Oklahoma A&M 34, TCU 0. *Orange Bowl:* Tulsa 26, Georgia Tech 12. *Rose Bowl:* USC 25, Tennessee 0. *Sugar Bowl:* Duke 29, Alabama 26 . . . *National Football League:* Cleveland Rams 15, Washington Redskins 14 . . . *Basketball:*

1944–45 *NCAA:* Oklahoma A&M 49, NYU 45. 1944–45 *NIT:* DePaul 71, Bowling Green 54.

Other Happenings: Dick Fowler of Philadelphia A's pitches 1–0 no-hitter over Browns on September 9. . . . Shortstop Tommy Brown of Brooklyn Dodgers hits home run off Preacher Roe of Pittsburgh Pirates on August 20. Just 17 years old, Brown is youngest to hit major-league homer. . . . On September 7, first baseman Joe Kuhel hits only home run by Washington Senators in their home park, Griffith Stadium, during 1945. Kuhel ends season with 2. Harlond Clift leads club with 8 but Senators somehow manage to finish season in second place. . . . In a game against the Detroit Lions, Green Bay's Don Hutson scores 29 points in a single quarter by catching 4 touchdown passes and kicking 5 PATs. . . . Bettors at Belmont on September 22, some 46,614 strong, wager $5,016,745 on the races, first time more than $5,000,000 is bet in a day. . . . Killed in the war: Al Blozis, New York football Giant tackle; Smiley Johnson, Green Bay guard; Waddy Young, Brooklyn end, in the first B-29 raid on Tokyo; and Eddie Kahn, Boston guard. Total of NFL players lost in war comes to 21. . . . Other athletes include Lou Zamperini, star miler, Tommy Hitchcock of polo fame, professional golfers Ben Loving, Bill Harmon, and John Shimkonis . . . also Joseph Garber, senior national singles handball champion, and Torger Tolke, holder of 24 ski records, including the North American jump of 289 feet. . . . Winter of 1944–45 is worst of war as far as manpower shortage goes. St. Louis Browns call up one-armed Pete Gray for 1945 season. He appears in 77 games, collects 51 hits in 234 at-bats for .218 average. . . . Bert Shepard, a returning war veteran with an artificial leg, signs with Washington as coach, hoping to pitch. He does manage to hurl 5⅓ innings during his brief major-league career, allowing one run and three hits. . . . Bowling officials consider reducing the age of pinboys. . . . On April 8, National Football League decrees that wearing of socks will be mandatory.

1946

Winners: Baseball: After National League season ends in tie for first time in history, St. Louis Cardinals defeat Brooklyn Dodgers, then take World Series from Boston Red Sox, 4 games to 3. . . . *Kentucky Derby:* Assault. *Preakness:* Assault. *Belmont Stakes:* Assault

. . . *Indy 500:* George Robson . . . *Boxing:* Sugar Ray Robinson decisions Tommy Bell in fifteen rounds to win welterweight crown, at least according to New York, five other states, Mexico, and South America. (World Boxing Association, meanwhile, insists on conducting its own elimination tournament.) . . . *Golf: USGA Men's Open:* Lloyd Mangrum. *PGA:* Ben Hogan. *Masters:* Herman Keiser . . . *USGA Women's Open:* (match play): Patty Berg beats Betty Jameson, 5 and 4. . . . *Hockey:* 1945–46 Stanley Cup won by Montreal Canadiens. . . . *Football: Cotton Bowl:* Texas 40, Missouri 27. *Orange Bowl:* Miami 13, Holy Cross 6. *Rose Bowl:* Alabama 34, USC 14. *Sugar Bowl:* Oklahoma A&M 33, St. Mary's 13 . . . *National Football League:* Chicago Bears defeat New York Giants in title game, 24–14. *All-America Football Conference:* Cleveland Browns beat New York Yanks, 14–9, for championship. . . . *Basketball:* 1945–46 *NCAA* Championship won by Oklahoma, defeating North Carolina, 43–40, in finals. *NIT:* Kentucky 46, Rhode Island 45.

Other Happenings: On November 9, Notre Dame and Army meet in climactic football struggle, Johnny Lujack vs. Blanchard and Davis. The game ends in 0–0 tie. . . . First heavyweight title fight is televised over WNBT, New York, on June 19. Joe Louis wins dull 8-round knockout of Billy Conn. . . . Bob Feller of Cleveland Indians pitches no-hitter, 1–0 over Yankees on April 30. On April 23, Ed Head of Brooklyn no-hits Boston, 5–0, then vanishes into obscurity. . . . Babe Didrikson and Glenn Davis voted outstanding athletes of the year. . . . Indy 500 attendance hits record 175,000. . . . In July, Chicago White Sox are kicked out of game for heckling umpire. . . . United States and Mexico angry at each other because of Mexican baseball league's raid on U.S. players. . . . On June 25, a chartered bus carrying Spokane's International League baseball team plunges down a 500-foot mountainside in the Cascades, killing 8. . . . In November, the Basketball Association of America plays its first games. . . . Davis Cup tennis competition is resumed after 6 years' interruption because of war. The United States team defeats Australia, 5–0, at Melbourne. . . . In a football game between East Texas State and Sam Houston on November 2, there are 63 punts by the two teams. . . . The Little Brown Jug, pacing race for 3-year-olds, is first run and won by Ensign Hanover. . . . Quarterfinals of NIT basketball tournament feature Ernie Caverley's 55-foot desperation shot that ties game between underdog Rhode Island and Bowling Green, allowing Caverley's teammates to win contest in overtime and go all the way to the finals. . . . New York Yankees become first baseball team to travel entirely by air when they sign a contract with United Air Lines for the 1946 season. . . . On June 16, Byron Nelson loses United States Open golf title when his caddie accidentally kicks his ball. . . . First boxing match at which tickets sell for $100 is the Louis-Conn fight at Yankee Stadium. . . . On August 9, all 8 American and National League baseball games are played at night, the first time in history. . . . Army-Navy football game is so closely followed that 2 million ticket requests are turned down.

1947

Winners: Baseball: New York Yankees defeat Brooklyn Dodgers in World Series, 4 games to 3. Sixth game, won by Brooklyn, features Al Gionfriddo's circus catch of DiMaggio's 415-foot drive. . . . *Kentucky Derby:* Jet Pilot. *Preakness:* Faultless. *Belmont Stakes:* Phalanx . . . *Indy 500:* Mauri Rose . . . *Boxing:* Rocky Graziano KOs Tony Zale in 6 rounds for middleweight crown. Ike Williams becomes new lightweight champ by knocking out Bob Montgomery in 6. In January Harold Dade wins bantamweight crown from Manuel Ortiz, who wins it back in March. . . . *Golf: USGA Men's Open:* Lew Worsham. *PGA:* Jim Ferrier. *Masters:* Jimmy Demaret . . . *USGA Women's Open:* Betty Jameson . . . *Hockey:* 1946–47 Stanley Cup won by Toronto Maple Leafs. . . . *Football: Cotton Bowl:* Louisiana State 0, Arkansas 0. *Orange Bowl:* Rice 8, Tennessee 0. *Rose Bowl:* Illinois 45, UCLA 14. Sugar Bowl: Georgia 20, North Carolina 10 . . . *National Football League:* Chicago Cardinals defeat Philadelphia Eagles, 28–21, for title. *All-America Football Conference:* Cleveland Browns beat New York Yanks, 14–3. . . . *Basketball:* 1946–47 *NCAA:* Holy Cross 58, Oklahoma 47. *NIT:* Utah 49, Kentucky 45. *Basketball Association of America:* 1946–47 champ: Philadelphia defeats Chicago, 4 games to 1.

Other Happenings: Football's annual "game of the decade" pits Texas (6–0) and SMU, led respectively by Bobby Layne and Doak Walker. SMU wins, 14–13. . . . In baseball, Leo Durocher, manager of Brooklyn Dodgers, is suspended for season for "incidents detrimental to baseball"—that is, associating with gangsters. . . . On June 22, Cincinnati pitcher Ewell Blackwell comes within two outs of pitching his second consecutive no-hit-

ter. His first comes on June 18, a 6–0 win over Boston. . . . Jackie Robinson, meanwhile, becomes first black player to step on major-league diamond in twentieth century. . . . Ralph Kiner of Pirates hits 8 home runs in 4 games. . . . In American League, Larry Doby, first black in junior circuit, fans in debut on July 5. . . . Champion race horse, Man o' War, age 30, dies and is embalmed. . . . January 1: One of many bowls spawned by football boom is Raisin Bowl, in which San Jose State defeats Utah State, 20–0. . . . Americans see first TV World Series, September 30–October 6. . . . Sponsors are Gillette and Ford, which get rights for $65,000. Most exciting moment comes during fourth game, when Floyd Bevens, within one out of Series no-hitter, yields double to Cookie Lavagetto. Dodgers also win game, 3–2. . . . Football's Chicago Cardinals are saddened when Jeff Burkett, end from LSU, is killed in plane crash. . . . In Japan, Emperor Hirohito takes his wife to see her first baseball game. . . . In American League, no-hitters are pitched by Don Black of Cleveland and Bill McCahan of the A's (McCahan's career mark will be 16 wins and 14 losses when he leaves the major leagues in 1949). . . . On June 21, Assault becomes top money-winning racehorse by winning Brooklyn Handicap. . . . On July 5, Stymie quickly surpasses Assault by winning Sussex Handicap at Delaware Park, bringing his earnings to $595,510. . . . One week later, Assault moves ahead by winning Butler Handicap at Jamaica; then Stymie takes the lead on July 19, bringing his earnings to $678,510 by winning the Empire Gold Cup. . . . On October 9, Armed takes the lead by taking the Sysonby Mile at Belmont, but Stymie again forges in front on October 25 by winning the Gallant Fox Handicap at Jamaica. His earnings: $816,060. . . . Claude "Buddy" Young of Illinois is first black football player to score a touchdown in Rose Bowl history.

1948

Winners: Baseball: Cleveland Indians, led by pitcher Gene Bearden, defeat Boston Braves in World Series, 4 games to 2. . . . *Kentucky Derby:* Citation. *Preakness:* Citation. *Belmont Stakes:* Citation . . . *Indy 500:* Mauri Rose . . . *Boxing:* Joe Louis still heavyweight champ after 11 years. After defeating Jersey Joe Walcott, Louis retires in June, then unretires in October. Freddie Mills of London, England, becomes new light-heavyweight champion by winning 15-round decision over Gus Lesnevich. In flashy middleweight division, Tony Zale knocks out Rocky Graziano in third round on June 10, then is KOd in 12 by Marcel Cerdan 3 months later. In October, Sandy Saddler knocks out Willie Pep to become featherweight champ. Rinty Monaghan knocks out Jackie Paterson in seventh to become new flyweight champion. . . . *Golf: USGA Men's Open:* Ben Hogan. *PGA:* Ben Hogan. *Masters:* Claude Harmon. *USGA Women's Open:* Babe Zaharias . . . *Hockey:* 1947–48 Stanley Cup won by Toronto Maple Leafs (second year in row). . . . *Football: Cotton Bowl:* Penn State 13, SMU 13 (second tie in a row). *Orange Bowl:* Georgia Tech 20, Kansas 14. *Rose Bowl:* Michigan 49, USC 0. *Sugar Bowl:* Texas 27, Alabama 7. . . . *National Football League:* Philadelphia Eagles beat Chicago Cardinals, 7–0. *All-America Football Conference:* Cleveland Browns win third consecutive championship, beating Buffalo Bills in title game, 49–7. . . . *Basketball:* 1947–48 *NCAA:* Kentucky 58, Baylor 42. 1947–48 *NIT:* St. Louis 65, NYU 52. *Basketball Association of America:* 1947–48 champion: Baltimore Bullets, defeating Philadelphia Warriors, 4 games to 2.

Other Happenings: Bob Lemon, Cleveland Indians, pitches only no-hitter in major leagues, beating Detroit, 2–0. . . . Babe Ruth dies and stadia are promptly named after him in Baltimore; York, Pennsylvania; and White Plains, New York. . . . New York Giants retire Mel Ott's No. 4. . . . Bobo Newsom, baseball's most widely traveled pitcher, signs to pitch for team in Warsaw, Virginia. . . . Jockey Eddie Arcaro becomes first to ride two Triple Crown winners, having accomplished feat in 1941 with Whirlaway. . . . Leo Durocher quits Dodgers in midseason to manage Giants. . . . Pat Seerey of Chicago White Sox hits 4 home runs in an 11-inning game. He ends season with total of 19 and is out of major leagues next year at age 26. . . . On September 24, Chicago football Cardinal tackle Stan Mauldin collapses and dies. The team later retires his jersey No. 77. . . . Bandleader Guy Lombardo, meanwhile, is hurt in speedboat accident. . . . Satchel Paige, age 42, signs to pitch for the Cleveland Indians as the Mexican baseball league announces plans to disband. . . . Peace talks continue between the Basketball Association of America and the National Basketball League, and the All-America Football Conference and the National Football League. . . . Gil Dodds runs a mile in 4 minutes, 5.3 seconds at the Milrose Games in New York City on January 31.

1949

Winners: Baseball: New York Yankees defeat Brooklyn Dodgers, 4 games to 1. . . . *Kentucky Derby:* Ponder. *Preakness:* Capot. *Belmont Stakes:* Capot . . . *Indy 500:* Bill Holland . . . *Boxing:* Joe Louis retires, and on twelfth anniversary of Louis beating Jim Braddock for heavyweight championship, Ezzard Charles decisions Jersey Joe Walcott to become new champ. Jake LaMotta knocks out Marcel Cerdan to become middleweight titleholder. While flying back for return match, Cerdan is killed in plane crash. . . . Willie Pep regains his featherweight crown by winning 15-round decision over Sandy Saddler on February 11. . . . *Golf: USGA Men's Open:* Cary Middlecoff. *PGA:* Sam Snead. *Masters:* Sam Snead. *USGA Women's Open:* Louise Suggs . . . *Hockey:* 1948–49 Stanley Cup won by Toronto Maple Leafs (third consecutive year) . . . *Football: Cotton Bowl:* SMU 21, Oregon 13. *Orange Bowl:* Texas 41, Georgia 28. *Rose Bowl:* Northwestern 20, California 14. *Sugar Bowl:* Oklahoma 14, North Carolina 6 . . . *National Football League:* Philadelphia Eagles 14, Los Angeles Rams 0. *All-America Football Conference:* Cleveland Browns win fourth consecutive championship by beating San Francisco, 21–7. . . . At end of season, NFL and AAC agree to merge, Baltimore, Cleveland, and San Francisco of AAC joining NFL. . . . *Basketball:* 1948–49 *NCAA:* Kentucky 46, Oklahoma A&M 36. 1948–49 *NIT:* San Francisco 48, Loyola 47 . . . *Basketball Association of America:* Minneapolis defeats Washington, 4 games to 2. Also, agreement is reached between *NBL* and *BAA,* which merge to become the *National Basketball Association (NBA).*

Other Happenings: Jackie Robinson becomes first black Most Valuable Player in baseball. . . . At age 61, Willie Hoppe wins his fifth world 3-cushion billiard title. . . . Ernie (Tiny) Bonham, 36, pitcher for New York Giants and Pittsburgh Pirates, dies following an appendectomy. . . . Branch Rickey, baseball mogul, defends reserve clause by saying that those who oppose it "lean to communism." . . . The U.S.S.R., meanwhile, charges that U.S. sports programs really train youth for war-making. . . . In an off-the-field scandal, Philadelphia Phillie first baseman Eddie Waitkus is shot by an angry woman. . . . Babe Ruth's and Lou Gehrig's lockers are moved to the Hall of Fame for permanent enshrinement. . . . Baseball's minor leagues reach high-water mark, the total of 59 circuits being the highest in game's history. But insidious effect of television is just about to begin. . . . Albert "Red" Schoendienst sets National League record for second basemen by handling the ball 320 consecutive times without an error. . . . On July 12, major-league club owners agree to establish safety warning tracks in outfield for 1950 season. . . . Woman jockey Wantha Davis, riding Northeast, defeats Johnny Longden on Grey Spook in a match race at Tijuana, Mexico.

1950

Winners: Baseball: New York Yankees zip the Philadelphia Phillie "Whiz Kids," taking World Series in 4 games. . . . *Kentucky Derby:* Middleground. *Preakness:* Hill Prince. *Belmont Stakes:* Middleground . . . *Indy 500:* Johnny Parsons . . . *Boxing:* Joe Louis tries comeback but Ezzard Charles continues as heavyweight champion. Joey Maxim becomes new light-heavyweight titleholder by knocking out Freddie Mills in tenth round at London. . . . Sandy Saddler rebounds to win the featherweight title once again, dispatching Willie Pep in 8 rounds. Vic Toweel wins decision over Manuel Ortiz to become new bantamweight champ, and in flyweight division, Terry Allen decisions Honore Pratesi to become champion, then loses crown to Dado Marino three months later. . . . *Golf: USGA Men's Open:* Ben Hogan. *PGA:* Chandler Harper. *Masters:* Jimmy Demaret. *USGA Women's Open:* Babe Zaharias . . . *Hockey:* 1949–50 Stanley Cup won by Detroit Red Wings. . . . *Football: Cotton Bowl:* Rice 27, North Carolina 13. *Orange Bowl:* Santa Clara 21, Kentucky 13. *Rose Bowl:* Ohio State 17, California 14. *Sugar Bowl:* Oklahoma 35, Louisiana State 0 . . . *National Football League:* Cleveland Browns, after finishing season with 10–2 record, defeat Los Angeles Rams on field goal by Lou Groza, 30–28. . . .

Basketball: 1949–50 NCAA: CCNY 71, Bradley 68. 1949–50 *NIT:* CCNY 69, Bradley 61 . . . *National Basketball Association:* 1949–50 season: Minneapolis defeats Syracuse, 4 games to 2.

Other Happenings: Gil Hodges of Brooklyn Dodgers hits 4 home runs during a 9-inning game. . . . On August 11, Vern Bickford of the Boston Braves pitches 7–0 no-hitter against Dodgers. . . . Connie Mack retires after a half century managing the Philadelphia Athletics. . . . On the international scene, West Germany and Japan are admitted to the 1952 Olympics, a sign that all is forgiven for their part in World War II. . . . Dick Button wins his third consecutive skating championship, and golfer Ben Hogan hits the comeback trail after an automobile accident. . . . Curt Simmons of the Philadelphia Phillies becomes the first major leaguer to be called to military duty for the Korean War. . . . On the West Coast, players with the Hollywood club open the 1950 season clad in shorts and rayon shirts. . . . Anti-communist feeling is so strong in the United States that basketball players for CCNY withdraw from a game because it is sponsored by the *Daily Worker.* . . . In an effort to improve their skills on the ice, the New York Rangers hire a team hypnotist, but the club loses its thirteenth straight game on the very day he reports for work. . . . On June 3, Citation becomes the top money-winning race horse by finishing first in the Golden Gate Mile, bringing his earnings to $924,630. . . . After 4 years of success in Davis Cup tennis play, United States bows to Australia, 4–1, at Forest Hills. . . . Famous race caller Clem McCarthy, after confusing winner of Preakness in 1947, calls Kentucky Derby winner "Middleburg." . . . On July 27, wrestler-exhibitionist Gorgeous George misses a flying tackle against his opponent and lands outside the ring on a reporter's typewriter. . . . Babe Didrikson Zaharias sets a 1-year money-winning record for women golfers by earning $14,800. . . . Jack Walsh of Trenton sets a new world record by lifting 4,235 pounds on his back.

Section IX
The 1950s

CHAPTER 36 — 1951

It was a year characterized by more than its share of disillusionment. Barely a half decade after the ending of World War II, the United States was in the process of rearming, planning air-raid drills, mounting psychological offenses against enemies trying to destroy the nation from within. Approximately three million Koreans were dead, and American casualties stood at fifteen thousand dead and five times that number wounded. The peace and promised cleansing of the second war to end all wars had not been realized.

The sports world reflected this unfulfilled dream. On January 8, 1951, word was received from Des Moines, Iowa, that Lieutenant John Trent, the captain of 1949's West Point football team, had been named 1950 Man of the Year by the Football Writers Association of America. But Trent was not around to enjoy the award. He had been killed in the bloody stalemate of Korea late in 1950.

Three days later, Princeton football fans were told that two of that team's prospective backfield stars would not be around for the 1951 season. Harry Patterson and Bob Unger, both of whom saw plenty of football action during 1950, planned to leave Princeton to enlist in the Navy.

Baseball enthusiasts got the message when star players such as Dr. Bobby Brown, third baseman for the New York Yankees, and Don Newcombe, a nineteen-game winning pitcher for the Brooklyn Dodgers the year before, were waiting for word from their draft boards in order to see how much of the 1951 season they would be able to salvage. Thirteen-game winner Erv Palica was also among the many young men facing call-up by the ever-expanding war machine.

BASKETBALL

Then came the bombshell of disillusionment. On January 18, 1951, sports fans awoke to the news that college basketball players had been fixing games and shaving points so long and so often that hardly a contest in the past four years could be counted as genuine. The principals on this occasion were two Manhattan College players, Henry Poppe and John Byrnes, who were charged with cooperating with gamblers, three of whom also had been arrested and charged by Edward Breslin, chief assistant district attorney in the Bronx. According to Breslin, Poppe confessed to fixing three games during the 1949–50 season—on December 3, 1949, when Manhattan lost to Siena College of Loudonville, New York, 48–33; three weeks later, when his team lost to Santa Clara College of California, 73–64; and on January 12, 1950, when Manhattan bowed to Bradley College of Peoria, Illinois, 89–67.

The only bright spot of the widening scandal was that it had been reported by an honest basketball player, Junius Kellogg, center of the Manhattan squad. Several days before, Kellogg had been approached by gamblers who offered him a thousand dollars to throw the game against DePaul University. Instead of taking the bribe—or turning it down highhandedly—Kellogg pretended to be interested. He informed Coach Ken Norton and helped trap Poppe and Byrnes along with the gamblers. Manhattan also won the game, 62–59, but not because of Kellogg's ability. As a matter of fact, the young center was so unnerved by the situation that he was definitely off his game. After four minutes, Coach Norton replaced him with Charles Jennerich, the substitute center, who took advantage of the opportunity to score eight baskets in eight tries. DePaul, favored to win by more than six points, lost by three.

The betting revelations upset more than the average fan. Arthur Daley, veteran sportswriter, wrote, "The breath of suspicion had never so much as touched the Jaspers be-

How It All Began:
Gamblers introduced the point betting system in college basketball about 1940. Before that time, bets were made on the straight odds system, much as in horse-racing. But when gamblers discovered that they could make more money by "giving" points (while at the same time knowing which teams were going to win by narrow margins as a result of point-shaving payoffs), the more sophisticated point system began.

fore. . . . Manhattan, like Caesar's wife, had been beyond reproach. . . . That's the lowest and most contemptible punch below the belt yet."

Depression on another level struck Baltimore football fans when owner Abe Watner of the professional Colts took his money and ran, dumping the franchise in January 1951. Claiming the team had lost $760,000 in four years of operation, Watner threw 28 Colt players into the NFL draft pool, earning a pretty penny for himself while enriching other teams with the likes of quarterback Y. A. Tittle, halfbacks Billy Stone, Chet Mutryn, and Jim Spavital, and first-round draft choice Bobby Williams, a hometown product at Loyola of Baltimore who had made it big at Notre Dame.

As the Korean War became more serious with the entry of the Chinese Communists, General of the Army George Marshall announced that he did not intend to repeat the draft policies of World War II, which sometimes provided physical deferments for professional athletes. He even went on record as listing some of the more prominent ballplayers who could reasonably expect to be called into the armed forces if the war continued to expand as it had since June 1950. The players and fans may have cringed at the prospect of wholesale call-ups, but most overage general managers and owners were highly enthusiastic about organized sports supporting the mili-

The Endangered Species List:
Ralph Branca, Dodger pitcher
Cass Michaels, Senator second baseman
Herman Wehmeier, Reds pitcher
Mickey McDermott, Red Sox pitcher
Billy Pierce, White Sox pitcher

tary. "That makes plenty of sense to me," said Walter O'Malley, president of the Dodgers. "That's the way the players would like it and that's the way the owners would like it."

BASEBALL

Despite the war talk and basketball scandal, some aspects of sports continued about as usual. On January 29, 1951, 32-year-old Bob Feller signed a contract with the Cleveland Indians for $45,000–$50,000, the same figure he received in 1950, when he was 16–11 for a fourth-place club. On the same day, the Chicago White Sox paid a reported $40,000 bonus to Floyd Penfold, a 6-foot, 4-inch, 185-pound right-handed pitcher from a high school in Southgate, California. Penfold, White Sox scouts said proudly, was rated a much better prospect than Paul Pettit, a similar phenomenon of 1950.

How They Turned Out:
Paul Pettit, the highly touted youngster signed in 1950 by the Pittsburgh Pirates, pitched a total of 30⅔ innings in the major leagues, winning 1 game and losing 2. He had an ERA of 7.34, yielding 33 hits and 20 walks. Even so, he was luckier than poor Floyd Penfold, who never pitched an inning in the big leagues.

BOXING

The first major sports conflict of the year, not counting the usual football bowl games (which featured the Ice Bowl, Refrigerator Bowl, and Salad Bowl, among other now-forgotten titles), was a middleweight title fight between Sugar Ray Robinson and the Bronx Bull, Jake LaMotta, whose main claims to fame were having beaten Robinson once long before and exercising an uncanny knack for absorbing punishment and remaining on his feet. The scene was Chicago, where more than 14,000 fans paid gross receipts of $180,619 to see if LaMotta could defend his title against the man who was acclaimed as the best fighter, pound for pound, that the twentieth century had produced.

The fight started predictably, LaMotta rushing Robinson in his usual bull-like manner, Sugar Ray stepping aside and scoring points almost at will, not only outboxing the champion but also outpunching him. After building up a substantial lead through the fourth round, Robinson allowed LaMotta to chase him for the next three rounds, giving the illusion that he was tiring, ready to succumb to LaMotta's savage charges. In the eighth, Robinson started hitting again, forcing LaMotta not only to cease his frantic rushes but also to retreat. Then in the eleventh, Robinson cut loose as if angered, hammering LaMotta from one end of the ring to the other. He buckled Jake's knees with a vicious left hook, straightened him out of his crouch with a slashing uppercut, hit him with everything he had. The Bronx Bull began to totter. The pummeling continued until the thirteenth when Referee Frank Sikora stepped between the men and declared Robinson the new champion.

BASKETBALL

Unfortunately for those who liked their sports wholesome and untainted, the basketball fixing scandals did not stay off the front pages very long. Occasionally the story might be uplifting—in late January, for example, it was announced that as a result of his courage in reporting the bribe offer, Junius Kellogg would receive the Chicago Catholic Youth Organization Club of Champions medal, an award previously won by Babe Ruth, Jackie Robinson, and Dwight D. Eisenhower. Two weeks later, the twenty-three-old center was given a scroll of honor by New York Police Commissioner Thomas F. Murphy. Only a few days later, however, more names were released in connection with game-fixing. These included Sherman White, probably one of the best players in the nation, Adolph (Al) Bigos, and LeRoy Smith, all members of the Long Island University squad. Together they admitted accepting bribes amounting to $18,500 as payment for fixing seven games. The payoff man, they said, was Salvatore T. Sollazzo, an ex-convict who used Eddie Gard, LIU senior, as a recruiting agent and intermediary. As a result of the revelations, the Board of Trustees of LIU held an emergency meeting on the evening of February 20 and voted to end all participation in intercollegiate sports, including two basketball games to be played in Madison Square Garden. Quick to react to mounting public concern, New York legislators, with the backing of Governor Thomas Dewey, introduced bills that would double the maximum sentence of game fixers to 10 years in prison. Dewey described those who would bribe players as "evil and corrupting criminals."

BOXING

Against this background, the often-maligned sport of boxing seemed almost scrupulous when heavyweight champion Ezzard Charles stepped into a Detroit ring to defend his title against thirty-seven-year-old challenger Jersey Joe Walcott on March 7, 1951. In 1949, Charles and Walcott had met to determine who would take over Joe Louis's resigned title. Charles had decisioned Walcott in fifteen rounds, but Jersey Joe was clearly the favorite of the people, having fought as a colorful journeyman for twenty-one years, coming close to defeating Joe Louis in their first meeting. Now he seemed over the hill, the odds favoring Charles by 4–1.

Walcott's best chance lay in scoring an early knockout, and he put that strategy into effect immediately, pursuing Charles with a wild assortment of punches. Most of them failed to land, the champion countering with smashes to the body. For three rounds the fight followed that pattern, until the fourth, when Walcott went into his familiar routine of dropping his hands and walking away. When Charles pursued, Jersey Joe suddenly let fly with a long right to the head. The tactic irritated Charles more than it hurt him physically, causing the crowd to shout and cheer for the challenger.

Through the tenth round, Charles bored in on Walcott, fighting a solid, unspectacular style designed to wear down the older man. The problem was that Walcott, despite taking many shots to the head and body, somehow became stronger as the fight progressed. In the eleventh, Ezzard Charles' ear began to swell, but Jersey Joe could not put the champion down. Both men were on their feet at the final bell.

The decision—which went to Charles—was probably earned in the ninth round when Charles landed a right and a left in quick succession to Walcott's chin, sending him to the canvas for a count of nine. But the crowd of nearly fourteen thousand had forgotten that single knockdown by the time the fight was over, loudly booing the decision when it was announced. In the dressing room afterward, Jersey Joe was disconsolate. "I don't think I won the fight," he said to reporters and friends, "I know I did."

BASEBALL

Baseball made news in mid-March when it became apparent that baseball Commissioner A. B. (Happy) Chandler was on the way out. On November 1, 1945, the square-jawed little man with the broad grin had given up his position as a United States senator from Kentucky to take over baseball's top job. Since that time, he had been involved in a number of controversial decisions, a major battle with the newly formed Mexican league, and pressure for increased security for the players. By not acting as a puppet for the owners 100 per cent of the time, Chandler assured himself of inevitable lack of support. That moment came

Why Was Chandler Squeezed Out? Probably Because He Did Things:

1. *Suspended Leo Durocher, manager of the Brooklyn Dodgers, for the entire 1947 season ("conduct detrimental to baseball" was the reason).*
2. *Fined Leslie O'Connor of the Chicago White Sox for signing a player still in high school.*
3. *Fined the New York Yankees and deprived them of a player for signing high-school athletes.*
4. *Ordered Fred Saigh, owner of the St. Louis Cardinals, to cancel a Sunday night baseball game.*
5. *Announced adoption of baseball's first major-league pension plan, with annuity and life-insurance benefits, on April 4, 1947. (This move made him popular with the players, but it was management that held the key to Chandler's job.)*

early in 1951, when even his staunchest associate, Cincinnati Reds' General Manager Warren Giles, felt obliged to propose that a search be started for a successor to Chandler. The list of eighteen men that was eventually drawn up included such luminaries and nonentities (reader's choice) as James J. Farley, former Postmaster General; William O. Douglas, associate justice of the U. S. Supreme Court; J. Edgar Hoover, head of the FBI; Grantland Rice, sportswriter; Bob Carpenter, owner of the Philadelphia Phillies, and Ford Frick, president of the National League.

With spring training in full bloom, new names made the headlines almost daily, followed by glowing accounts of just what the athlete could do for the club he seemed certain to make. The choice of the New York Giants, then in training at Sanford, Florida, was a strapping Cuban catching prospect named Rafael (Ray) Noble. Sportswriters inevitably compared him—not unfavorably—to Roy Campanella, then the top catcher in baseball. Meanwhile, at Fort Worth, the spring headquarters of the St. Louis Cardinals, glowing reports were written concerning Lloyd and Bobby Moore, a brother battery from Texas Christian University who hopefully would rival the Cardinals' wartime brother battery of Mort and Walker Cooper. Lloyd, a nineteen-year-old right-handed pitcher, and eighteen-year-old Bobby were both assigned to Albany of the Georgia-Florida League.

Ray Noble: *Actually played in 107 games for the Giants in 1951, 1952, and 1953. He batted .218 with 9 home runs and 40 RBI.*

Lloyd and Bobby Moore: *Neither played an inning of major-league baseball.*

There were experiments with some other new men. The Pittsburgh Pirates, for example, had a rookie first baseman-outfielder named Dale Long who also caught. The problem was that Pittsburgh's outfield was a good one, with Wally Westlake, Ralph Kiner, and rookie Gus Bell all doing good jobs in 1950. At first base was Johnny Hopp, with young Jack Phillips

Why Not a Left-handed Catcher?
On the one (right) hand . . .
   In the old days, the vast majority of batters were right-handed. It was felt that the hitter's presence on that side of the plate would interfere with the left-handed catcher's ability to throw.
On the other (left) hand . . .
   By 1951, there were nearly as many left-handed as right-handed batters.
On the one (right) hand . . .
   The right-handed catcher is in better position to take a throw from the outfield and tag a runner coming home.
On the other (left) hand . . .
   A left-handed catcher is in better position to field balls hit in front of the plate, not having to turn before making a throw to first base.
On the one (right) hand . . .
   There is a tradition in baseball that says catchers should be right-handed, which explains why all of them are.

available. That left the catching spot, handled in 1950 by ten-year veteran Clyde McCullough, who surely did not have many years left—or so thought Pirates' General Manager Branch Rickey. (Actually, McCullough hung around until 1956, when he finally quit at age thirty-nine.) The best place for twenty-five-year old Dale Long, obviously, was behind the plate.

Dale Long: *The rookie catching prospect of 1951 managed to work in the major leagues for ten seasons with Pittsburgh, St. Louis (A.), Pittsburgh again, Chicago (N.), San Francisco, New York (A), Washington, and the Yankees again. His greatest moment came in 1956 when he hit home runs in eight consecutive games while with the Pirates. His second and third greatest moments came in 1958, when he actually caught two games for the Chicago Cubs.*

At this point, a major problem surfaced. Long was left-handed. In baseball, then as now, it was traditional for all catchers to be right-handed. Despite this prejudice, Branch Rickey made news by announcing—the story hit the major newspapers on April 1, 1951, which may or may not be a clue to its seriousness—that he intended to break the time-honored rule by trying Long as a catcher. After all, it was pointed out that Babe Ruth had been discovered while playing as a left-handed catcher (using a right-handed mitt). Why not Dale Long?

It was food for thought, but only during spring training. When the regular season opened a few days later, rookie Long was used at first base and in the outfield for a total of ten games. After batting .167, he was traded to the St. Louis Browns. Even with that rela-tively unhappy ending, Dale Long's fate was much brighter than the majority of spring training phenoma, both before and since.

It was a spring filled with significant events. Julius and Ethel Rosenberg were put on trial for stealing and selling atomic-bomb information to the Soviet Union. . . . General of the Army Douglas MacArthur and President Harry Truman collided over United Nations policy in Korea. . . . Eddie Collins died. . . . And most significant for America's athletes, the Wage Stabilization Board slapped a freeze on players' salaries, limiting them to token raises above their 1950 salaries. To many players, this national move to fight inflation was academic, they having received only token raises from the benevolent owners in any event. Several stars, however, regarded the ruling with horror. Stan Musial, who had negotiated his salary from $50,000 to $85,000 following a season during which he hit .346 and 28 home runs, was most affected. Others would lose raises of $5,000 or $10,000. What it all meant, of course, was that the Korean War, although referred to as a "police action," was having nearly as much impact on sports of 1951 as the international conflict a decade earlier.

Even worse, the nation seemed to be polarized into those who favored the action of President Truman in trying to limit the Asian war and those who agreed with General of the Army Douglas MacArthur that nothing short of all-out war could convince the Chinese and the Soviets that the United States meant business. The situation was hardly helped when MacArthur appeared before Congress to deliver an emotional attack on President Truman, filled with half truths and appeals to patriotism. Someone immediately suggested, of course, that MacArthur be offered the Chandler vacancy as baseball commissioner.

TRACK AND FIELD

While the nation waited for the Truman-MacArthur problem to resolve itself and the

---

Highest-paid Baseball Players, 1950:
American League:
Boston—Ted Williams
New York—Joe DiMaggio
Detroit—Hal Newhouser
Cleveland—Bob Feller
St. Louis—Ned Garver
Philadelphia—Bob Dillinger
Chicago—Luke Appling
Washington—Mickey Vernon

National League:
Brooklyn—Jackie Robinson
Pee Wee Reese
New York—Larry Jansen
St. Louis—Stan Musial
Philadelphia—Del Ennis
Pittsburgh—Ralph Kiner
Chicago—Andy Pafko
Boston—Johnny Sain
Cincinnati—Ewell Blackwell

baseball season to produce some early leaders, track-and-field fans turned their attention to the running of the fifty-ninth annual Boston Marathon. The event, which drew more than three hundred thousand onlookers along the winding road from Newton, Massachusetts, to Boston, was truly international in scope. Featured were runners such as Yoshitaka Uchikawa, Hiromi Haigo, Shigeki Tanaka, and Shunji Koyanagi of Japan, Anthanassios Ragazos of Greece, Gerald Cote of Canada, S. Koru of Turkey, and a large assortment of American athletes, including John Lafferty. Clarence DeMar, sixty-three, was also on hand, running in his thirty-first Boston Marathon.

In recent years, Koreans had performed quite well in the event, finishing one-two-three in 1950. In addition, the course record of two hours, 25 minutes, and 39 seconds had been set in 1947 by Yun Bok Suh, and still stood four years later. A light splatter of rain marred the early stages of the 1951 race, during which the bespectacled Koyanagi took a quick lead, but conditions on the whole were not bad. Running well ahead of Ellison M. (Tarzan) Brown's 1936 pace at Woodland Park (16.8 miles) and Lake Street (21.2 miles), he held the lead with less than 5 miles to go. The grueling climb between these two stations robbed Koyanagi of much energy, however, and he was soon passed by Shigeki Tanaka, who thrived on uphill work. Not far behind was Lafferty. Sensing a close finish, the crowd along the route began to cheer the American on, but he was too far behind to close the gap. The 19-year-old Tanaka, just out of high school, turned on the speed to win in 2 hours, 27 minutes, 45 seconds, the third-fastest time in the history of the event and barely 2 minutes slower than the best time, in 1947.

BASEBALL

Baseball fans, meanwhile, saw the 1951 season get off to a rather unusual beginning. The New York Giants, who had been picked by the United Press sportswriters poll to win the National League pennant, won two games out of three, then proceeded to lose ten games in a row. As a result, they stood dead last on April 29. In the American League, the Boston Red Sox, choice of the writers, had fallen behind Cleveland, Washington, and the Yankees. The season was still young, naturally, but it was not too soon for those who were inclined to worry to begin crying the blues.

The very next day, however, the Giants broke their dismal streak against Brooklyn, spoiling the major-league debut of twenty-five-year-old Earl Mossor. Fresh from the Class B Piedmont League, Mossor walked Wes Westrum, Alvin Dark, and Don Mueller to force across a run and also force himself back to the minor leagues, never to return.

The last day of April 1951 also saw the beginning of a new attack on the legality of baseball's reserve clause by Jim Prendergast and Jack Corbett, two minor-league players who claimed the clause had deprived them of bargaining power. Most high-ranking officials were confident, however, that the courts would rule that baseball was a sport rather than a business and therefore exempt from regular antitrust laws.

Good fortune seemed to be following nineteen-year-old Mickey Mantle of the Yankees that spring. In April, his draft board classified him 4-F because of an infection in the bone of one leg; on May 1, he smashed the first of 536 career home runs in the American League. Willie Mays, in the meantime, began to stand out as the other top-quality rookie of 1951.

Before the season was three weeks old, the first no-hitter of the year had been thrown. Its author was twenty-nine-year-old Cliff Chambers of the Pittsburgh Pirates; the victims, the Boston Braves. Chambers, who said that only Warren Spahn and Howie Pollet ranked ahead of him as left-handed pitchers, was the first Pirate to throw a no-hitter since Frank Allen, then in the Federal League, performed the feat on April 24, 1915.

Every week seemed to bring news of high bonuses being awarded teen-agers with baseball ability. On May 29, 1951, Cleveland announced the signing of seventeen-year-old pitcher Billy Joe Davidson, "the best prospect since Bob Feller," for $150,000. Three days later, it was the Boston Red Sox giving a nineteen-year-old infielder named Dick Pedrotti a three-year contract for $75,000. Neither youngster played a day in the major leagues.

BOXING

But it was not only the baseball owners who were paying. In June 1951, boxing took the first step in making its fans pay for what they had once gotten for free. With increased interest in Joe Louis's comeback, it had been decided to make the June 13 fight between the former champion and Lee Savold a blacked-out theater-TV venture. The first major experiment in theater TV, eight motion-picture houses across the nation had been engaged for the closed-circuit showing. A total of 22,000 people paid a top price of $1.30—at Shea's Fulton Theater in Pittsburgh—for the right to see the contest, and there were thousands turned away.

Although recognized as champion by the British Boxing Board of Control, Lee Savold at thirty-five was only two years younger than Louis, and with a great deal less talent. Louis,

The Theaters for Boxing's First Closed-circuit Fight:

City	Name of Theater	Regular Price	Price For Fight
Cleveland	Palace	$.75	$.90
Washington	Lincoln	$.50	$.74
Washington	RKO Keith	*	*
Albany	Palace	$.75	$.75
Baltimore	Loew's Century	$.65	$.65
Chicago	State-Lake	*	*
Chicago	Tivoli	*	*
Pittsburgh	Shea's Fulton	*	$1.30

* Not known.

flashing occasional glimpses of his old explosive power, had Savold's face bleeding by the second round, blinding him with snappy, jarring left jabs. In the sixth round, Louis saw an opening and drove home a hard right to Savold's jaw that made his knees buckle. Following it up with short lefts, he knocked Savold to the canvas and nearly out of the ring. That was the end of the contest and the successful experiment. Perhaps not dreaming that they would be someday paying five or ten times the regular theater price for the privilege of watching a bout once televised free, those who went to the theaters acclaimed the theater TV as "wonderful."

TENNIS, BASEBALL

June 1951 was a hopeful month in that peace talks between the United Nations and Communist forces in Korea seemed to become a reality for the first time. Also for the first time, a black American—Althea Gibson—arrived in Great Britain to represent the United States and blacks everywhere at the Mecca of tennis, Wimbledon. The month provided still more hope for sports fans when it was learned that master baseball showman Bill Veeck was returning to the game via the St. Louis Browns. The franchise, it was admitted, was

not the best, but Veeck's followers were certain he would provide more than a modicum of excitement. Little did they realize how much.

The Happy Chandler resignation official, baseball's moguls began that month to select a successor. There was much talk of naming someone with "outstanding" qualities. The average fan, of course, did not understand that "outstanding" really meant "manageable, uninspired, dull" to baseball's hierarchy.

July began with Cleveland's Bob Feller hurling his third lifetime no-hitter, beating the Tigers, 2–1. Feller, who started poorly and had to talk Coach Mel Harder into allowing him to pitch past the third inning, became what the newspapers called the first "modern" pitcher to earn three no-hitters. The Feller victory was the first since 1925 that a pitcher had allowed the opposition to score a run and win his no-hitter. (Detroit scored on two errors, one of them by Feller.) It was also the thirteenth time that Rapid Robert had held the opposition to one hit or less.

BOXING

Boxing returned with a vengeance in July 1951—within a ten-day period three important matches shook up the rankings of the two

Feller's Near-misses (One-hitters)

Date	Opposition	Score	Strikeouts	Spoiler
Apr. 20, 1938	St. Louis	9–0	6	Billy Sullivan
May 25, 1939	Boston	11–0	10	Bobby Doerr
June 27, 1939	Detroit	5–0	13	Earl Averill
July 12, 1940	Philadelphia	1–0	13	Dick Siebert
Sept. 26, 1941	St. Louis	3–2	6	Rick Ferrell
Sept. 19, 1945	Detroit	2–0	7	Jimmy Outlaw
July 31, 1946	Boston	4–1	9	Bobby Doerr
Aug. 8, 1946	Chicago	5–0	5	Frankie Hayes
Apr. 22, 1947	St. Louis	5–0	10	Al Zarilla
May 2, 1947	Boston	2–0	10	Johnny Pesky

All of the hits were singles.

most popular divisions, middleweight and heavyweight. On July 10, word was received that America's premier fighter, Sugar Ray Robinson, had been defeated for only the second time in his entire career of 133 bouts in 11 years. The unlikely victor was Randy Turpin, a 23-year-old British black who had never fought a bout longer than 8 rounds.

The Englishman could have been inspired by native supporters, eighteen thousand strong, who jammed London's Earl's Court Arena to watch the title fight, little suspecting that their hero could administer a solid beating to believers when Randy opened a deep gash under Sugar Ray's left eye in the seventh round, drew blood from his nose in the twelfth, and had him on the verge of a knockout in the fourteenth. Many who watched the fight called it the greatest upset since Gene Tunney outpointed Jack Dempsey on September 23, 1926, for the heavyweight crown.

Just three days later, heavyweight Rex Layne entered the ring a 2–1 favorite to beat an impressive but untested slugger from Brockton, Massachusetts, Rocky Marciano, winner of thirty-five consecutive fights during his career. For two rounds, it seemed that the oddsmakers had been correct in making Layne the favorite, for he was able to attack Marciano's body while the younger man tried without much success to deliver knockout blows to the head. In the third round, Marciano shifted his attack to Layne's body, gradually weakening him to the point where Layne was more concerned with self-protection than pursuing his own plan of destruction. When the end came, it was sudden. A right from Marciano landed flush on Layne's chin. Sinking slowly in a bent position, Layne's head hit the floor as he descended, knees drawn up beneath his chin. After the count of ten, Layne had to be assisted to his corner.

On July 18, at Pittsburgh's Forbes Field, the much-heralded rematch between heavyweight champion Ezzard Charles and Jersey Joe Walcott was held. Once again Charles was the favorite, this time by a margin of 6–1; Walcott, after trying and failing on four previous occasions to win the heavyweight championship, had been branded a loser despite establishing a record for most times challenging. A throwback to the recent days of free fighting on TV, the bout was watched by more than sixty million. At 194 pounds, a bit heavy, Walcott got off to a slow start, then opened a cut beneath Charles' eye in the third round. Walcott racked up points for the next three rounds; then in the seventh he lured the champion into a trap. Feinting a punch to the

body, Walcott released a short, crisp left hook to the point of Charles' chin. The champion fell, tried to rise, then fell back again. Walcott, at age thirty-seven, was the oldest man ever to win the world heavyweight title.

The Second Oldest: *Bob Fitzsimmons, thirty-five, when he defeated Jim Corbett at Carson City, Nevada, March 17, 1897.*

Late in July 1951, more reports on the basketball scandal were made public, these dealing with confessions by eight Bradley University players that thousands of dollars had been taken in exchange for fixing games. The players were Gene (Squeaky) Melchiorre, the diminutive All-American guard who led his team to national recognition, William Mann, Charles (Bud) Grover, Aaron Peerce, and James Kelly. The revelations marked the first time that a school outside the New York area had been involved, and the number of implicated players rose to fourteen. Only a day later, the list grew even longer when it was discovered that players from the University of Toledo had been named as well. All of them, ironically, were veterans of World War II.

Early August brought even more discouraging news. On the second, ninety cadets at West Point were abruptly discharged for breaking the sacrosanct "honor code" of the U. S. Military Academy. The reason, it was learned, was that they had cheated on examinations. Even worse, many of the guilty cadets were members of the football team, which had rolled up twenty-eight victories in a row before being upset by Navy, 14–2, late in 1950. Initially, the names of the guilty cadets were withheld, but rumors leaked that one of the fallen knights was star halfback Al Pollard.

One unfortunate revelation seemed to lead to another. A week later, an eighteen-year-old quarterback candidate for West Point named Duncan MacDonald told the Chicago *Tribune* of a special six-week cram course and "entertainment" that was provided those about to enter West Point. Colonel Earl H. Blaik, director of athletics at the Military Academy, though on the defensive, pointed out that nothing dishonest was involved in such a procedure. But the idea of special tutors for promising athletes seemed to strike many Americans as skirting the moral issue. In any event, on August 9, President Truman ordered an investigation to see if West Point was "overemphasizing" football and other competitive sports.

SOCCER

Faced with such depressing items on the local sports scenes, Americans could hardly be blamed if they looked elsewhere for assurance that athletics could be a source of pride and enjoyment. One unexpected bit of good news came from London, England, where Gil Heron, a black native of Detroit, became the first American to play with a big-league Scottish football (soccer) team. Appearing at center forward, on August 18 Heron led the attack for the Celtics of Glasgow against Morton, drawing applause from the critical Scots audience. A few minutes before halftime, he took a pass and from sixteen yards out, drove the ball at Morton goalie Jimmy Cowan with sufficient force to score a deflected goal. The Celtics won, 2–0.

BASEBALL

A second source of balm was the St. Louis Browns team. On August 18, the cellar dwellers scored twenty runs against Detroit, the most ever tallied by a Browns team. That, however, was not the main cause of merriment. One day later, during the second game of a doubleheader against the same Detroit Tigers, General Manager Bill Veeck sent twenty-six-year-old, forty-three-inch-tall Edward Gaedel to the plate to pinch-hit for Brown center fielder Frank Saucier. Thus poor Frank became the only major-league ballplayer to be taken out for a midget, a fate that is probably a lot worse than it sounds. Anticipating opposition on the part of umpire Ed Hurley, Veeck sent Manager Zack Taylor to home plate with a copy of the midget's contract. The umpire examined it and found it to be genuine. Meanwhile, President Will Harridge of the American League was on the telephone in a desperate attempt to keep Gaedel from batting, but Veeck had anticipated that also, taking the phone off the hook and shutting down the teletype machine.

The result was that Eddie Gaedel dug in at the plate while the crowd roared with delight. Swinging his bat back and forth, Gaedel looked out toward Detroit pitcher Bob Cain. "Let's go," he yelled in a high-pitched voice, "Throw it in there, fat, and I'll murder it."

After a delay of some fifteen minutes, Cain delivered the first pitch to catcher Bob Swift. It was high and away. Three more lobs were thrown, none of which came near the shrunken strike zone. Tossing his bat aside scornfully, Eddie Gaedel trotted down the first-base line, kicked the bag, and waited to be relieved by pinch-runner Jim Delsing.

The idea worked as a delightful promotion for Veeck—and, as some said, a symbolic blow for the little man or the underprivileged in all walks of life—but it did not produce the desired run. Delsing died on the bases and St. Louis lost the game, 6–2. There were some reverberations, naturally. Sportswriter Arthur Daley noted, "Veeck's madcap antics have never before violated good taste. But this one is positively indecent, an ignoble burlesque of a noble sport. Eddie Gaedel's name has appeared in a major-league box score and he now is an official part of baseball history along with Ty Cobb, Honus Wagner, and Babe Ruth." Presumably Mr. Daley was serious when he wrote this treatise suggesting that baseball's record book was a form of holy writ, its characters historical-religious figures. In any event, President Will Harridge, speaking from on high, forbade the use of Eddie Gaedel for eternity, which caused the little man to complain, "Now that somebody has finally taken a step to help us short guys, Harridge is ruining my baseball career." On June 18, 1961—just a month before Ty Cobb, as a matter of fact—Eddie Gaedel died at age thirty-six.

Some Other Veeckaries:
While at Milwaukee, Bill Veeck gave away lots of unusual door prizes as a means of attracting fans—not to win the door prizes but to watch the winners. Some of these included a sway-backed horse; a two hundred-pound cake of ice, which melted in the lucky person's lap; and three live pigeons. Veeck also was the father of the exploding scoreboard.

Criticism of Bill Veeck's antics did not stop him, however. Less than a week later, on August 24, 1951, he was back in operation with what was probably a better stunt than using Eddie Gaedel—better because it gave baseball fans a chance to stop complaining and do something. Using a special section of grandstand populated with 1,115 people, Veeck allowed them to pick the day's lineup as well as vote "Yes" or "No" by holding up cards at a decisive point in the game. Fortunately, the opposition was provided by the Philadelphia A's, a team only slightly better than the Browns. After Gus Zernial put the A's ahead with a three-run homer in the first, the grandstand managers swung into action. Pete Suder of Philadelphia came to bat with only one out, first and third bases occupied. Polled on whether to play in close to try to cut off the run at the plate or play back and go for the double play, the grandstand managers chose the latter. And Suder hit into the needed double play.

In the Browns' half of the first, with Sherm

Lollar on first base and the count 3–2 on Cliff Mapes, the fans were asked whether Lollar should "take off" on the next pitch. They voted against this move. Again they were right. Cliff Mapes struck out instead of making contact with the ball. Lollar, a slow runner, would have been caught at second ·base had he started to run.

After St. Louis tied the score at 3–3, the grandstand managers did make one mistake. With two out and Hank Arft on first base, Veeck's brain trust called for a steal. Arft was thrown out by a good margin. The game was eventually won by the Browns, 4–3, and no one could deny that at least 1,115 fans had had a much better time.

In the meantime, what turned out to be one of baseball's best seasons was moving into its last six weeks. In the American League, the New York Yankees were battling neck-and-neck with the Cleveland Indians and the Boston Red Sox. The National League pennant seemed firmly in the grasp of Brooklyn. Philadelphia's Whiz Kids of 1950 were blowing too many opportunities, and on August 11 the favored New York Giants dropped 13½ games off the pace. All the Dodgers had to do, it appeared, was win more than their share and the flag would fly in Brooklyn once again.

They did win their share, but something ominous for Dodger fans started happening after that. Between August 12 and 27, the New York Giants did not lose a game, including three against the Brooklyn club. The result was that a Dodger fan who went on vacation at the beginning of the two-week period, when his team was safely ahead by 13½ games, returned to find them only 5 games in front. Howie Pollet of the Pirates finally shut

---

The Giant Streak—August 1951:

Aug.	12:	Giants	3,	Phillies	2
		Giants	2,	Phillies	1
Aug.	13:	Giants	5,	Phillies	2
Aug.	14:	Giants	4,	Dodgers	2
Aug.	15:	Giants	3,	Dodgers	1
Aug.	16:	Giants	2,	Dodgers	1
Aug.	17:	Giants	8,	Dodgers	5
Aug.	18:	Giants	2,	Phillies	0
Aug.	19:	Giants	5,	Phillies	4
Aug.	21:	Giants	7,	Reds	4
Aug.	22:	Giants	4,	Reds	3
Aug.	24:	Giants	6,	Cardinals	5
Aug.	26:	Giants	5,	Cubs	4
		Giants	5,	Cubs	1
Aug.	27:	Giants	5,	Cubs	4
		Giants	6,	Cubs	3

---

out the Giants on August 28, 2–0, while the Dodgers beat Cincinnati. The margin crept to 6 games, better but still not nearly as comfortable as 13½.

BOXING

On August 30, boxing recaptured public attention, but not in the way its promoters would have preferred. In the eighth round of a Madison Square Garden bout between George Flores and Roger Donoghue, a sharp left hook to the jaw sent Flores to the canvas. Landing on his back with a heavy sound, Flores lay still. After he was counted out, Dr. Vincent Nardiello, sitting at ringside, leaped through the ropes to assist the young man. After a moment during which he seemed to revive, Flores went into a coma and had to be rushed to the hospital. Three days later, he died without regaining consciousness. The death reminded critics of boxing that in 1950 Lavern Roach of Plainview, Texas, and Sonny Boy West of Washington, D.C., also had been killed in the ring.

FOOTBALL

August produced more information on the West Point cheating scandal, including confirmation that two hundred-pound halfback Al Pollard was among those expelled from the Academy. Because Pollard's original class had already graduated, he was the first athlete eligible to play pro football, a prospect he greeted enthusiastically. Having already been drafted by the New York Yanks, Pollard discussed the possibility of playing with that team, but said little about the cribbing mess.

Both collegiate and professional sports were under attack. At West Point, it was learned that Bob Blaik, son of Army's football coach, Red Blaik, was one of the players dismissed for cheating. By the end of August, disaffection with college football had reached such proportions that thirty-three schools had dropped the sport. Most of them were small colleges, it is true, but few doubted that a strong undercurrent of adverse public opinion was present.

Even Hollywood got into the act. In September appeared Saturday's Hero, a rare sports film in that it treated college football with distinct cynicism rather than the time-tested rah-rah spirit. Starring John Derek, the tale showed a fictional exploitation of athletic talent that seemed believable and compelling. Subsequently a "Late Show" rerun on TV, the film eventually lost much of its impact, but in 1951 audiences were impressed by the bittersweet story of what overemphasis on sports could do to a young man. Saturday's Hero, nurtured by a variety of sports scandals, became a successful movie, touching

88. It started out as a rather ordinary NFL championship game, with the Chicago Bears' Bill Osmanski (9) scoring the opening touchdown on a 68-yard run. But from that point on the 1940 title contest developed into a classic grid massacre with a score that most fans remember: Bears 73, Washington Redskins 0. (See "Losing Big and in Bunches.")

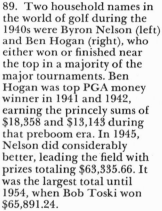

89. Two household names in the world of golf during the 1940s were Byron Nelson (left) and Ben Hogan (right), who either won or finished near the top in a majority of the major tournaments. Ben Hogan was top PGA money winner in 1941 and 1942, earning the princely sums of $18,358 and $13,143 during that preboom era. In 1945, Nelson did considerably better, leading the field with prizes totaling $63,335.66. It was the largest total until 1954, when Bob Toski won $65,891.24.

90. During the 1940s, the number of football bowl games proliferated wildly, with everything from the Poi Bowl to the Finger Bowl receiving its share of publicity. (See "Bad Hypes.") Obviously, except for those who played in it and some who saw it, the January 1, 1947, classic known as the Pepper Pot Bowl has been long forgotten. It was performed at Philadelphia between teams known as the Shamrocks and the Kaskade AA. The Shamrocks won, 14–0.

91. The final pre-World War II baseball season was one of the most exciting in U.S. history, containing Ted Williams' .406 batting mark, and in many ways even more amazing, Joe DiMaggio's 56-game hitting streak. (See "1941.") In the National League, the Brooklyn Dodgers barely nosed out the Cardinals for the privilege of losing to the Yankees in the World Series. Here DiMaggio displays his concentration and batting form during the streak.

92. During the war years, public interest in baseball was so high that President Franklin Roosevelt declared the game a national asset. But as more and more able-bodied players joined the armed forces, the quality of play deteriorated and some teams were forced to plug roster openings with teen-agers or older players. In 1945 the St. Louis Browns made big-league history by using one-armed outfielder Pete Gray (born Wyshner). He batted .218 in 77 games.

93. The war tended to shake up the dynasties of baseball so that teams such as the Cleveland Indians in 1948 were able to win their first American League pennant in 28 years. They played the Boston Braves, who had not won since 1914. The Boston Red Sox also joined the list of the suddenly rich by winning the 1946 flag, their first since 1918. Cleveland's victory in a dramatic playoff sent the city into a wild celebration.

CLEVELAND PLAIN DEALER FINAL

CLEVELAND, TUESDAY MORNING, OCTOBER 5, 1948

INDIANS WIN FIRST PENNANT IN 28 YEARS; BEARDEN VICTOR, 8-3

BOUDREAU'S 2 HOMERS LEAD 13-HIT ASSAULT THAT REPELS RED SOX

94. Immediately following the war, a battle started to recruit American players for the new Mexican League. (See "Other Leagues.") One of the first to yield to the temptation of big money was Brooklyn Dodger player Mickey Owen, seen here in his first game with Vera Cruz in 1946. All of the players who jumped to the Mexican League were banned from American organized ball but the bans were eventually lifted. Owen returned to the States in 1949, finishing his career with the Chicago Cubs and the Boston Red Sox.

95. As a result of a "gentlemen's agreement" made during the war, blacks were given the right to play in the major leagues when the war was over. Jackie Robinson started the trend in 1947 and was so successful that his life story was being made into a Hollywood film as early as 1950. Robinson played himself and Minor Watson (right) acted the part of Brooklyn's Branch Rickey, who gave Robinson his chance.

96. The new All-America Football Conference provided competition for the NFL following the war and also freely employed blacks. One of the most dangerous runners of the AAFC was Cleveland fullback Marion Motley, a 6-foot, 1-inch, 232-pounder, seen here with Claude (Buddy) Young, a 5-foot, 5-inch, 170-pound scatback with the New York Yankees. After four seasons, the two pro football leagues merged (See "Other Leagues.")

97. Professional football, gaining in popularity during the entire decade, reached a high point on December 28, 1958, when the first sudden-death overtime game was played at Yankee Stadium between the Baltimore Colts and the New York Giants. Both teams kicked away leads, the Colts one of 14–3, before the contest was resolved in the fifth period on Colt fullback Alan Ameche's short plunge into the Giant end zone. Here Ameche is tackled in earlier action by Sam Huff and Jim Patton.

98. Scandals involving "point shaving" also eroded public confidence in college basketball, but in 1948, when Kentucky Coach Adolph Rupp discussed plays with players Alex Groza, Jim Jordan, Jack Parkinson, and Ralph Beard, the worst was still to come. (See "Fixes.")

99. Ann Curtis broke a previous all-male barrier in 1944 by winning the James E. Sullivan Trophy, awarded every year since 1930 to the nation's outstanding amateur athlete. (See "Breaking the Sex Barrier.")

100. The years following World War II reminded some of the post-World War I era in that scandals broke out almost immediately. Pro football's imbroglio involved two New York Giants, Merle Hapes and Frank Filchock, who were suspended when it was revealed that they failed to report bribe offers right away. (See "Fixes.") Here Filchock (40) gains five yards in 1946 game against Pittsburgh Steelers.

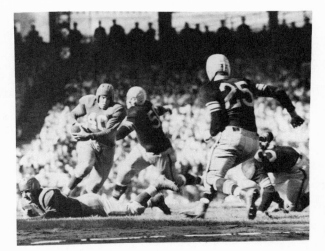

101. America's Olympic Games hero of the late 1940s and early 1950s was Bob Mathias, who was only 17 when he participated in his first Olympic Games in 1948. Shortly before entering the decathlon, he had never touched a javelin or pole-vaulted, but he soon mastered the skills and amassed a total of 7,129 points in the event to win it. The next time he participated, in Helsinki in 1952, he won again, with 7,887 points. As a result, Mathias had a movie made of his life while barely out of his teens, America's sincerest tribute.

102. "Next year" finally arrived in 1955 as Brooklyn Dodgers, perennial losers in World Series, defeated Yankees in seven games. Insult was added to injury in fourth game when foul ball off the bat of Don Larson hit Dell Webb, co-owner of the Yankees, in the head. Brooklyn catcher Roy Campanella does his best to grab ball as notables in boxes duck.

103. Unusual ending to a play occurred in second game of 1959 World Series when Chicago White Sox outfielder Al Smith received cup of beer on his head as climax to Charley Neal's home run. The Los Angeles Dodgers won the game as well as the six-game Series.

104. Professional football continued to challenge baseball as the most popular sport in the United States, with crowds growing larger every year. Popularity took great leap forward in 1958 when Baltimore Colts defeated New York Giants in thrilling overtime title game. Art Donovan, participant in that contest, was nearing the end of his 12-year career at the time. He was elected to the Pro Football Hall of Fame in 1968.

105. First black player to be elected to the Pro Football Hall of Fame was defensive back Emlen Tunnell, who also played in 1958 title game for New York Giants. (See "Breaking the Color Barrier.") Here he is seen in 1952 action, intercepting a third-quarter pass intended for end Billy Wilson (84) of the San Francisco 49ers.

106. For a brief while until television overexposure severely damaged it, boxing in the 1950s nearly became America's most popular spectator sport. "Friday Night Fights" featured crowd-pleasing boxers such as Rocky Graziano, seen here moments after knocking Johnny Greco down for the count in the third round of a 1951 fight. By that time, however, Graziano was past his prime and was most remembered for his battles royal with Tony Zale as well as his involvement in a fixed-fight charge. (See "Fixes.")

107. When he defeated Ezzard Charles in 1951, Jersey Joe Walcott(left) was the oldest man to become heavyweight champion of the world. A year later, however, he seemed a decade older as he attempted to defend his crown against young whirlwind Rocky Marciano. The Rock won on a KO in the thirteenth round and retired four years later undefeated.

108. Fifty-three years after Professor Hinton patented his baseball cannon major league teams began using mechanical pitchers to save wear and tear on the arms of regulars. Here a crowd gathers at the Vero Beach training camp of the 1950 Brooklyn Dodgers to watch the new devices.

109. Sports tragedy of the 1950s took place at Baltimore's 5th Regiment Armory in 1952 when a large section of hastily erected bleachers collapsed just before the start of skater Sonja Henie's ice show. At least 277 people were injured, 32 of them seriously. Shortly afterward, a downcast Henie inspects the ruins. (See "Being a Spectator Isn't Always Easy.")

110. Another tragedy involved racing driver J. E. (Skimp) Hershey of St. Augustine, Florida, whose stock car burst into flames on a curve of the eighty-first lap of a scheduled 100-mile race at Lakewood. Rescue workers arrived too late to save Hershey, who died later in the hospital. (See "Being a Player Isn't Always Easy.")

111. Women continue to make their own brand of sports history, Florence Chadwick, a 32-year-old California typist, becoming the first woman to swim the English Channel in both directions. In 1950 she swam from France to England. Here she wades ashore at Sangatte, France, on September 12, 1951, 16 hours, 22 minutes after leaving England. (See "Breaking the Sex Barrier.")

America's collective conscience, asking questions that needed to be asked.

TENNIS

The soul-searching, of course, was only temporary. Attention returned quickly to sports activities of late summer and early fall, including tennis, which provided a couple of relatively new stars. One was twenty-three-year-old Frank Sedgman, a personable Australian who defeated Vic Seixas in three straight sets to become the first player from overseas to win the United States Nationals tennis championship since Fred Perry of Great Britain beat Don Dudge in 1936. At the same time, a sixteen-year-old girl from California, Maureen Connolly, put on a brilliant display of hitting power to defeat Shirley Fry of Akron, Ohio, becoming what many thought was the youngest women's champion of all time. Actually, she was not, but that hardly tarnished her victory.

Youngest Women's U.S. Tennis Champion:
Having attained the ripe age of 16 years, 11 months, Maureen Connolly missed by 60 days being the youngest ladies' champion to that time. In 1904, May Sutton won the title at 16 years, nine months.

BOXING

The main attraction of mid-September, however, was not a tennis match. Sensing that it was a seller's market, the promoters of the Ray Robinson-Randy Turpin rematch at the Polo Grounds put the attraction in fourteen theaters in eleven cities and jacked prices to $2.60. One Philadelphia movie house, Warner Brothers Stanley Theater, was sold out by Labor Day.

In Chicago, seats for the fight were so much in demand that when fans were denied entrance to the State-Lake Theater in the Loop, they broke down the front doors and windows, injuring themselves in a shower of glass and splintered wood. Meanwhile, others attacked an exit door on the north side. Between seven hundred and a thousand persons, only a few with tickets, battered their way inside the theater. Similar scenes took place at two other theaters in the Windy City where the closed-circuit telecast was presented.

At the Polo Grounds, fans arriving late had to battle their way through a struggling mass that blocked the Eighth Avenue entrance. Inside, they encountered still another jam as they tried to get to the field. Some solved this by leaping from the top of a baseball dugout,

which set off a chain reaction of jumping by fans who thought this was an excellent method of improving their view. Special police had to be summoned to restore order.

As for the fight itself, it was a crowd-pleaser in that neither boxer seemed inclined to delay matters with unnecessary strategy. Both came out swinging at the bell, Robinson carrying the early rounds. But by the sixth, Turpin appeared the stronger. He won the fifth on all three cards, took the eighth by a similar margin, and was doing well in the ninth when a head-on collision between the fighters opened an old wound over Ray Robinson's left eye. This should have been an advantage for Turpin; actually, it served only to infuriate Robinson. Charging forward, he staggered Turpin with a hard right, drove him to the ropes with a variety of punches, then floored him with a right to the jaw. On his feet at the count of nine, Randy Turpin could do little but absorb punishment. At 2:52, referee Ruby Goldstein stepped in and ended the bout. He was later criticized because with only eight seconds left in the round, Turpin could not have been knocked out, and would have had a full minute to recuperate. "I do not think this fight would have been stopped in Britain," wrote Peter Wilson, sports columnist for the London *Daily Express,* "but in Britain we have not had a tragedy like the one which cost twenty-year-old George Flores his life."

In any event, Ray Robinson was richer by a quarter-million dollars and had become only the third middleweight to lose his crown and regain it.

The Others Who Regained the Middleweight Title:
In 1908, Stanley Ketchel became the first dethroned middleweight to regain his crown when he defeated Billy Parke. The second ex-champ to win a second time was Tony Zale, who stopped Rocky Graziano in 1948.

BASEBALL

Another British sportswriter, George Whiting, took in the September 2 baseball game between the Giants and Dodgers at the Polo Grounds and came away shaking his head in both admiration and dismay. While expressing considerable appreciation for the "pitching, catching, and swift accuracy of throwing," he described the game as "a battle unto death in bedlam," and "three hours of hilarious insult and near murder." He was probably right, as

The Other Pitchers to Throw Two No-
hitters in a Season: *Johnny Vander Meer,
Cincinnati (consecutive games) (1938);
Virgil Trucks, Detroit (1952); Jim
Maloney, Cincinnati (1965); Nolan Ryan,
California (1973).*

the Giants won, 11–2, thereby sending their
fans into paroxysms of delight.

On September 12, 1951, the Dodgers seemed
to have stabilized the New York Giant climb toward the National League pennant, winning
while the Giants were rained out, to increase
their lead to six games. Despite the torrid streak
of August, the Giants had gained nothing in the
subsequent two weeks.

After playing the Giants about even until
the middle of September, the Dodgers ran
into more than their fair share of bad luck on
the seventeenth. On that day, Roy Campanella was struck on the head by a pitch
thrown by the Cubs' Turk Lown, young Erv
Palica of the Dodger pitching staff was inducted into the U. S. Army, and the lowly
Chicago Cubs came from behind to win a
ball game that reduced the Brooklyn lead to
just four games, the lowest since June 3.

The game of organized baseball also was
dealt a nasty blow when the voting powers
selected Ford Frick as new commissioner.
Frick, who offended no one and did little but
maintain the status quo during his long reign,
was the perfect sports embodiment of the Eisenhower years.

In the American League the pennant race
was actually closer than in the National. The
Yankees held a small lead over Cleveland and
Boston but had the added advantage of playing nearly all their remaining games at home
while the Indians and Red Sox played theirs
on the road. Lacking in the American League
was the sense of drama and impending
doom that seemed to be stalking the Dodgers.
Allie Reynolds seemed to save his best pitching for when the Yankees needed it most. In
July he beat the Indians with a 1–0 no-hitter,
then came back in September to beat the Red
Sox, 8–0, becoming one of the few pitchers to
hurl a pair of no-hitters in a single season. In
contrast, the Dodger pitching staff, thin but
generally good, often faltered in the clutch.
On September 27, for example, Brooklyn led
the Giants by one game. The Giants had two
days off while the Dodgers had games against
the Braves and the Phillies. Winning both
could increase the Brooklyn lead to two full
games. Even more important, it would mean
that even if the Giants won their two remaining
games against Boston, all the Dodgers would
need was a single victory to win the pennant.

The game against Boston went into the
eighth inning tied at 3–3. Preacher Roe, pride
of the Dodger staff at 22–2, was having his
best year in the major leagues. But at this
point he faltered, allowed singles by Bob Addis
and Sam Jethroe with none out. With the
Dodger infield drawn in tight to catch the run
at the plate, Specs Torgeson grounded to
Jackie Robinson. Robinson threw to Campanella, who tagged the sliding Addis. Umpire Frank Dascoli spread his arms in the
"safe" sign, causing the Dodgers to erupt with
rage. Campanella was ejected from the game,
and on the way back to the locker room
Jackie Robinson kicked a panel loose in the
door of the umpires' locker room.

The next day, as Robinson and Campanella

"It" Being:
Situation: *Don Newcombe, right-hander, on the mound.
Dodgers 4, Giants 1. None out.
Alvin Dark singles.
Don Mueller singles.
Monte Irvin pops up.
Whitey Lockman doubles, scoring Dark.*
Situation: *Dodgers 4, Giants 2
One out. Men on second and third, Bobby Thomson, right-handed
batter, at plate. (Thomson has thirty-one home runs for year.)*
Questions: *Should relief pitcher Branca be brought in? If so, should he pitch to
Thomson, who has six home runs off him, or should the winning run be
put on base? (The next scheduled hitter is Willie Mays, a rookie with a
.274 batting average and twenty home runs.)*
Situation: *Branca pitches to Thomson, who hits home run to give Giants 5–4
victory.*

learned they had been fined a hundred dollars each, the Dodgers took the field against the Phillies determined to gain back the ground they had lost to New York. But after building a 3–0 lead over 1950's fallen champions, the Dodgers' Carl Erskine yielded a home run to Andy Seminick in the eighth, which tied the score. After blanking Brooklyn in the top of the ninth, the Phillies continued their assault on Erksine. Richie Ashburn singled, was sacrificed to second by Dick Sisler, and after Bill Nicholson was purposely passed, Willie (Puddin' Head) Jones slashed a grass-cutter that went just under Billy Cox's glove, scoring Ashburn as 18,895 Philadelphia fans went wild.

The season concluded with the Giants and Dodgers tied, necessitating a three-game playoff that excited the nation as much as the World Series. The Giants won the first game but the Dodgers bounced back to take the second. Going into the bottom of the ninth inning of the deciding game, Brooklyn led 4–1. Then, as all students of baseball know "it" happened.

FOOTBALL

Football fans of 1951 who wondered how a top team would fare if it lost a large portion of its squad as a result of disaster (in this case, the cribbing scandal), found out when Army took the field for its opening game, against Villanova. Populated by freshmen and sophomores, West Point dropped its first season opener since 1893, losing, 21–7. A few weeks later, racism reared its head when a football game between Florida State University and Bradley was canceled because the latter team had a black player. Despite the fact that the Orange Bowl of 1950 "allowed" the University of Iowa, with a black player, to meet the University of Miami, the Florida State Athletic Commission thought it best to cancel the game. The rumblings of discontent over interracial play would continue through the decade and well into the 1960s.

BASKETBALL

On October 20, 1951, the basketball fixing scandal grew to include the University of Kentucky, the seventh college to be involved. Two All-Americans, Ralph Beard and Alex Groza, added fuel to the fire by admitting that for fifteen hundred dollars they had helped throw the first round of the 1949 National Invitation Tournament championship to Loyola University of Chicago. Although heavily favored to win, Kentucky had gone down to a 67–56 defeat. By the end of October, a total of twelve gamblers and twenty-six players had been indicted.

BOXING

The month of October ended on a sad note as former champion Joe Louis, trying desperately to recapture the heavyweight boxing title, ran into a much younger and stronger Rocky Marciano. From the very beginning, it was obvious to the Madison Square Garden crowd that Louis lacked the snap to destroy Marciano, as he had done with so many other good tough men. Nor could Louis's legs carry him the distance. In the eighth round, he slowed to the point where Marciano was able to land a quick left hook. The former champion went down, got to his feet, but was then knocked through the ropes by a flurry of punches. Referee Goldstein signaled the end at 2:36 of the eighth round. That was the end of Joe Louis's ill-advised comeback.

Early in November, baseball management received good news when Federal Judge Ben Harrison upheld the 1917 Supreme Court ruling that baseball was not subject to the Sherman Antitrust Law. For a while at least the men who ran the game would be able to continue their benevolent dictatorship.

FOOTBALL

With the New York Yankees having turned the Giants' impossible dream into a nightmarish World Series defeat in six games, public attention returned to football. Surprisingly, a great deal of attention was given to the Ivy League, largely because of a Princeton running back named Dick Kazmaier. Rolling to its twentieth victory in a row on November 10, Princeton defeated Harvard by a score of 54–13, breaking a win record set in 1897. Kazmaier, a double-threat player running or passing, led the attack along with teammate Dick Pivirotto. Eventually Princeton claimed its second straight eastern and Ivy League titles. Kazmaier went on to win the Heisman trophy with a record plurality of votes, his

The Runners-up: Heisman Trophy, 1951 In second place, Hank Lauricella of Tennessee, often referred to as "the Kazmaier of the South," with 424 points; then Babe Parilli, Kentucky quarterback; Bill McColl, Stanford end; Johnny Bright, Drake halfback; Johnny Karras, Illinois halfback; Larry Isbell, Baylor quarterback; Hugh McIlhenny, Washington fullback; Ollie Matson, San Francisco halfback; Don Coleman, Michigan State tackle; Bob Ward, Maryland guard; and Jim Weatherall, Oklahoma tackle.

The Two-Platoon Controversy

Reasons Given for:

"Allows the coaches to concentrate on the younger players' best potentials."

"Rallies team spirit."

"Spectators like it better."

"Cuts down on fatigue and injuries."

Reasons Given Against:

"Specialists are developed instead of all-around football players."

"It breaks up team unity."

"Large schools have an advantage."

1,277 points nearly tripling the score of his nearest competitor.

Aside from de-emphasis, the major controversy in college football that fall was whether the two-platoon system should be allowed. Most players, coaches, fans, and sportswriters had their own ideas on the subject. A poll taken in late 1951 showed that 80 per cent of the players favored using offensive and defensive units.

The last important sports event of the year was the professional football championship, the perennially powerful Cleveland Browns having won eleven of twelve games to qualify for the Eastern Conference NFL crown. The Los Angeles Rams, meanwhile, edged Detroit and San Francisco by the barest of margins and thus went into the championship game as distinct underdogs. Playing before a hometown crowd, however, the Rams moved into a 7–0 lead after a fifty-five-yard drive was climaxed by fullback Dick Hoerner's one-yard plunge. Cleveland's Lou Groza then set a new distance record for championship games by booting a fifty-two-yard field goal, and quarterback Otto Graham engineered a touchdown drive to put the champions on top, 10–7, at halftime.

In the third quarter, Graham gave it back, fumbling when hit by LA's Larry Brink. The Rams took the lead briefly but the game was tied, 17–17, with eight minutes to go in the final quarter. At this point, Ram quarterback Bob Waterfield wound up and threw a pass that was gathered in by end Tom Fears, who raced seventy-three yards to give his team a 24–17 lead. The Browns continued to threaten until the closing seconds, but Los Angeles held on to win and break Brown domination of their league.

The basketball scandals at least temporarily quiescent, the year 1951 ended on a less depressing note. The University of Pennsylvania announced that its football team had elected the first black captain in the history of the school and only the second black to receive such an honor at a major eastern university. The talented man was Bob Evans, 20, a 6-foot, 2-inch tackle and junior in premedicine. (The first was Levi Jackson of Yale in 1948.) On the same day, Hosea Richardson, a 16-year-old, 105-pound jockey, became the first black rider to be admitted to Florida racing tracks. Joe DiMaggio, meanwhile announced his retirement from baseball and eventually became one of the first sports figures to say such a thing and really mean it.

A year with that sort of landmark obviously can't be all bad.

Cleveland Brown Championship Game Record:

All-America Conference:

1946—Cleveland 14, New York Yanks 9

1947—Cleveland 14, New York Yanks 3

1948—Cleveland 49, Buffalo Bills 7

1949—Cleveland 21, San Francisco 49ers 7

National Football League:

1950—Cleveland 30, Los Angeles Rams 28

CHAPTER 37—SPORTS SUPERSTITIONS

Before the metric system took over, the cliché told us it was a game of inches, "it" being anything from pocket pool to hydroplaning. No doubt the difference between winning and losing a close contest is a very slim margin, especially in the mind of the loser, which is probably why all but the most sophisticated athletes have given in to the power of superstition—the feeling that a slight advantage can be gained as a result of doing something unusual or ritualistic, thereby paying obeisance to some force "up there" or "over there," which in turn will help you win.

Lefty O'Doul: Not that I think if I stepped on the foul line it would really lose the game, but it's just become part of the game for me . . .
Leo Durocher (after wearing same clothes during 1951 pennant drive): I'm wearing the same socks, shirt, and underwear, too!

Perhaps baseball abounds with more superstitions than any other spectator sport because it is such a truly mental game. Batting is a matter of fierce concentration. Ted Williams used to stare at the pitcher facing him from the moment he entered the on-deck circle, searching for some clue as to style or manner of delivery that he could use to advantage. Pitchers often get themselves into a similar state. Robin Roberts, for example, claimed he concentrated so hard, "I would not even see the batter. I would only see the bat as he swung. When I was pitching well I saw only the catcher." Warren Spahn made a similar statement. "I knew I was going to be good," he said, "because I didn't see anything but the bat early in the game."

Baseball's superstitions go back quite far. "Ever since I broke into professional baseball," wrote Frank Chance in 1913, "I insisted upon occupying lower berth No. 13 when traveling, and strangely, I have never been in any serious train wrecks." He added that sometimes when it was impossible to obtain the lower No. 13, he would take a stateroom and mark a "13" on the door.

Chance claimed that the Chicago Cubs of 1898–1912 were the most superstitious players he could imagine. Harry Steinfeldt, for example, invariably wore a soiled undershirt as a result of refusing to change underwear during a winning streak. Another belief held by the Cubs was that solid hits during batting practice were wasted, leading Chance to remark, "In many cases I have seen players drive two or three balls hard and on a line and then go to the bench and refuse to bat any more, asserting that they 'wanted to save the blows for the game.'"

While traveling from the hotel to the ball park before a game, some considered it a bad sign to see a funeral procession or a person who was handicapped. The spell could be broken, however, if you were in a position to toss the unfortunate a coin.

Frank "Wildfire" Schulte, Cubs' outfielder, had a superstition about hairpins. "Find a hairpin," he said, "and you're sure to get a base hit that day. Find two of them and you will get two base hits. Never knew it to fail."

"Suppose you found a dozen and came to bat only four times?" he was asked.

"Then they'll hold good for the next day and the day after that," he replied.

Frank Chance recalled that once during a close pennant race, Schulte came up to him and announced in a stage whisper, "I found two hairpins today. Watch me hit that old pill."

The game was a tight one—naturally. For seven innings neither team could score. Then each got a single run and the game went into extra innings. By the thirteenth, Frank Schulte had one hit, on his first trip to the plate, and had popped up or beat the ball into the ground every time after that. He was scheduled to bat in the thirteenth—if the Cubs could get a man on base. That happened when the first batter singled. He was sacrificed to second, then watched helplessly as the next batter popped out. As Frank Schulte walked confidently to the plate, Chance yelled, "You better get a hit or never mention hairpins in my presence again."

The first pitch was a ball, very wide, but Schulte swung and missed. The next was down the center but he took called strike two with the bat on his shoulder. By this time, Chance and the rest of the team were exasperated. "Hit it, hit it!" they yelled.

The next pitch was also a wide one but Schulte swung. He hit it on the end of his bat, the ball streaking into right-center field for the game-deciding hit. With that, Schulte called back at Chance: "I guess that old hair-pin didn't have nothing to do with that one, eh?"

Shortstop Joe Tinker's superstition was bar-rels. He believed that if he saw a truck or wagonload of barrels it was bad luck. Once in Pittsburgh, he spotted a wagon full of the things, which caused him to rush immediately back to the hotel. Finally, he was convinced that the only thing to do was to double-cross the jinx by returning again by the same route without seeing barrels. Tinker did that and got three hits during the game.

One man's meat is another's potatoes, of course, which explains why Mike Donlin, New York Giant outfielder, thrived on barrels. On the day Donlin first saw a truckload of barrels before a game—and attached any significance to it—he happened to get three hits during the afternoon. The next day he couldn't buy a hit, which caused him to moan something like, "If only I could see some barrels." The prayer was promptly answered. For a considerable time after that, Donlin "happened" to see a truckload of barrels before every game. He went into a hitting streak that led the Giants to a pennant. Manager John McGraw, naturally, had helped things along by hiring a truck driver to circle the stadium every day during the streak.

McGraw's belief in the power of positive su-perstition was so strong that he even hired a totally untalented player and kept him on the roster for years because he believed the man had something mystical to do with the team's winning. The story was told by Fred Snod-grass in Lawrence S. Ritter's *The Glory of Their Times.* Said Snodgrass:

"Early in the 1911 season we were playing in St. Louis, and in those days neither team had a dugout in that park. We had a bench under an awning, about halfway between the grandstand and the foul line. We—the Giants —were having batting practice, when out of the grandstand walked a tall, lanky individual in a dark suit, wearing a black derby hat. He walked across the grass to the grandstand to the bench, and said he wanted to talk to Mr. McGraw. So some of us pointed Mr. McGraw out, and he went over to him.

"'Mr. McGraw,' he said, 'my name is Charles Victory Faust. I live over in Kansas, and a few weeks ago I went to a fortune-teller who told me that if I would join the New York Giants and pitch for them that they would win the pennant.'

"McGraw looked at him, being super-stitious, as most ballplayers were—and are. 'Well, that's interesting,' he said. 'Take off your hat and coat, and here's a glove. I'll get a catcher's mitt and warm you up, and we'll see what you have.'

"They got up in front of the bench and tossed a few balls back and forth. 'I'd better give you my signals,' Charles Victory Faust said. So they got their heads together, and he gave McGraw five or six signals. Mr. McGraw would give him a signal, and he would pro-ceed to wind up. His windup was like a wind-mill. Both arms went around in circles for quite a little while, before Charlie finally let go of the ball. Well, regardless of the sign that McGraw would give, the ball would come up just the same. There was no difference in his pitches whatsoever. And there was no speed— probably enough to break a pane of glass, but that was about all. So McGraw finally threw his glove away and caught him bare-handed, thinking to himself that this guy must be a nut and he'd have a little fun with him.

"'How's your hitting?' McGraw asked him.

"'Oh,' he said, 'pretty good.'

"'Well,' McGraw said, 'we're having bat-ting practice now, so get a bat and go up there. I want to see you run, too, so run it out and see if you can score.'

"Word was quickly passed around to the fellows who were shagging balls in the infield. Charlie Faust dribbled one down to the short-stop, who juggled it a minute as Charlie was turning first, and then they deliberately slid him into second, slid him into third, and slid him into home, all in his best Sunday suit—to the obvious enjoyment of everyone.

"Well, that night we left for Chicago, and when we got down to the train and into our private pullman car, who was there but Charles Victory Faust. Everybody looked at him in amazement.

"'We're taking Charlie along to help us win the pennant,' the superstitious Mr. McGraw announced.

"So, believe it or not, every day from that day on, Charles Victory Faust was in uniform and he warmed up sincerely to pitch that game. He thought he was going to pitch that *particular* game. Every day this happened. To make a long story shorter, this was 1911, and although Charlie warmed up every day to pitch, he never pitched a game.

"He wasn't signed to a contract, but John J. McGraw gave him all the money that was necessary. He went to the barbershop almost every day for a massage and a haircut, he had plenty of money to tip the waiters—in the small amounts that we tipped in those days— and we *did* win the pennant.

"Spring came around the next year and Charles Victory Faust appeared in the train-ing camp. He warmed up every day in 1912, and *again* we won the pennant.

"In 1913 he was again in the spring-training camp, and during the season he continued to warm up every day to pitch. By that time he had become a tremendous drawing card with the fans, who would clamor for McGraw to actually put him in to pitch. Finally, one day against Cincinnati they clamored so hard and so loud for McGraw to put him in to pitch that in a late inning McGraw *did* send him to the mound. He pitched one full inning, without being under contract to the Giants, and he didn't have enough stuff to hit. They didn't score on him. One of those nothing-ball pitchers, you know.

"Well, it was Charlie Faust's turn to come to bat when three outs were made, but the Cincinnati team stayed in the field for the *fourth* out to let Charlie come to bat. And the same thing happened then that happened the very first time that Charlie ever came on the field in St. Louis in his Sunday clothes: they slid him into second, third, and home.

"He was such a drawing card at this point that a theatrical firm gave him a contract on Broadway in one of those six-a-day shows, starting in the afternoon and running through the evening, and he got four hundred dollars a week for it. He dressed in a baseball uniform and imitated Ty Cobb, Christy Mathewson, and Honus Wagner. In a very ridiculous way, of course, but *seriously* as far as Charlie was concerned. And the fans loved it and went to see Charlie on the stage. He was gone four days, and we lost four ball games!

"The fifth day Charlie showed up in the dressing room at the Polo Grounds, and we all said to him, 'Charlie, what are you doing here? What about your theatrical contract?'

"'Oh,' he said, 'I've got to pitch today. You fellows need me.'

"So he went out there and warmed up, with that windmill warm-up he had that just tickled the fans so, and we won the game. And in 1913 we won the pennant *again*.

"That fall I joined a group of Big Leaguers and we made a barnstorming trip, starting in Chicago and going through the Northwest and down the Coast and over to Honolulu. In Seattle, who came down to the hotel to see me but Charlie Faust.

"'Snow,' he said to me, 'I'm not very well. But I think if you could prevail on Mr. McGraw to send me to Hot Springs a month before spring training, I could get into shape and help the Giants win another pennant.'

"But, unfortunately, that never came to pass. Because Charlie Faust died that winter, and we did not win the pennant the next year. Believe it or not, that's the way it happened. It's a true story, from beginning to end."

Players who are superstitious invariably try to re-create the circumstances that led to their winning or breaking a losing streak. One interesting story concerns Al Simmons, a famous slugger of the A's, who went into a terrible batting slump one season. Eventually he became so disturbed he walked around in a sort of daze, wondering how he could bat his way out of it. After a particularly disastrous day, he wandered out of the shower and stood in front of his locker, dripping wet. Slowly he reached into the locker and put on his cap. One by one, his teammates noticed him, and a trickle of laughter soon became a roar. Embarrassed, Simmons stalked out of the dressing room without a word.

Some General Baseball Superstitions:
Place a piece of black cloth in the dugout of the opposing team and it will bring good luck to your team.

If a baseball player sees a cross-eyed woman in the grandstand, he will not get a hit during the game.

It is good luck to spit in the beer of a cross-eyed woman.

It is good luck to pass a wagon loaded with hay as you go to the ball park.

The next day, however, he broke loose from the slump, getting four hits, and sure enough, after the game was over, he went through the same ritual of taking a shower and standing in front of his locker completely naked except for a cap. When he continued to hit the ball well, the habit continued and even spread to some of his teammates.

Another martyr to superstition was George Stallings, manager of the Boston Braves. His routine was to freeze himself in whatever position he happened to be in when a player got a hit, absolutely refusing to move until the rally died. Under normal circumstances this ritual was not too inconvenient, except for the time he squatted to pick up a peanut shell. At that moment, a Brave batter hit safely. Stalling froze like a statue. Another Brave hit the ball hard, then another. It was the beginning of a huge rally. By the time it was over, the team nearly had to carry Stallings to the clubhouse.

The penchant for continuity during good times led Al Lopez, Pittsburgh Pirate catcher, to eat exactly the same food as the day before, so long as happy times continued—which is why he breakfasted on kippered herring and eggs seventeen days in a row on one occasion.

Some Personalized Baseball Superstitions:

Jackie Robinson: *Never stepped into batter's box until the catcher was in position, then walked in front of him rather than behind.*

Carl Hubbell: *Never stepped on foul lines.*

Willie Mays: *Always kicked second base on way in from outfield.*

Phil Rizzuto: *Put wad of gum on button of cap, removing it only when team lost.*

Leo Durocher (as coach): *Always made sure to wipe out chalk line enclosing him.*

Jim Palmer, three-time Cy Young award-winning pitcher, also had a "food superstition" for a number of years. "It started back in 1966," he said. "During the middle of that season, I won four games in a row after eating pancakes for breakfast. Then we came to Los Angeles and I slept late or couldn't have breakfast for one reason or another. Well, I lost that game, then went into a good streak, winning five games after that, again with breakfast that happened to include blueberry pancakes. When I realized what had happened, I mentioned it to Curt Blefary and he turned right around and told some newsmen. That's how it became a big thing. Every day when I was scheduled to pitch, people wanted to make sure I had eaten pancakes for breakfast. And naturally I did eat them—because I enjoy them and also because when you're going to expend a lot of energy you need carbohydrates as well as protein."

And did superstition have anything to do with it?

"Well," Palmer hedged, "I went something like 17–2 during that streak, so why take a chance?"

According to Palmer and some of his teammates, one of the most superstitious Orioles during the late 1960s and early 1970s was pitcher Mike Cuellar. "One thing Mike did," he recalled, "was to never look at home plate when he went out to warm up. He would just pick up the ball and throw it. Once I remember the catcher stopped to talk to the umpire and Mike heaved the ball all the way to the backstop with nobody standing behind the plate. I guess the fans thought he was crazy or something."

"Another thing about Cuellar," added Clay Dalrymple, one of the men who caught the Cuban for a number of years, "was that he never allowed anyone else to warm him up

except the regular catcher. Most pitchers are warmed up by somebody who's not playing that day or a coach. Not Mike. You had to be ready with your gear on as soon as the inning ended. It was inconvenient sometimes—say if you were the last batter, you had to rush back and get into your shinguards and chest protector in a hurry—but I understood the guy and if that made him feel better, I was going to do it."

Dalrymple had superstitions similar to those of most other ballplayers. "Nearly everyone had some superstitions," he said. "It's not something that's talked about very much, I guess because the superstitions do seem a little ridiculous, even to the men themselves. As for myself, I'd get superstitious if, say, I'd get on a hot batting streak—that would be maybe one for four during the week. Well, when that happened, I'd get in the habit of trying to remember which way I drove to the park and keep doing it until the good luck broke—you know, I'd go by the same route, turn the same way, try to get the same lights, keep going at the same speed. Sometimes the ritual became so hard to follow that you were almost glad when your good streak ended."

Despite the quasisilliness of some superstitions, Dalrymple explained that their existence is completely natural. "What it boils down to is this," he said. "Here you have a lot of people who are under tremendous pressure. They know they have to do well, fast, and their mind is completely occupied with that. They know that if they don't do well, they'll be written up in the next day's newspapers or taken to task by the TV people or whatever. So you need a good mental state. It's something to hang onto. That's why I've felt that fringe players ought to be more superstitious than the superstar."

This was certainly true in the case of fringe player Eddie Grant and his lucky domino: The date was about 1910 when Grant, third baseman for the Phillies, showed up at the Polo Grounds for a doubleheader with the Giants. The pitchers facing Grant, a lifetime .249 hitter, were Marquard and Mathewson, a terrible combination for even a superb batter to think about facing during a single afternoon.

As he was walking along the sidelines, however, Grant spotted something in the grass and reached down to pick it up. It was a domino with seven white spots on it. "See this?" Grant said happily. "This means four hits in one game for me and three in the other."

Everyone within hearing distance laughed at the remark, for Eddie Grant's batting record against the two pitchers in question was even lower than his lifetime average.

Of course, the story has a happy ending—it

Hockey's Superstitions:

Just a few of the individual and team rituals practiced by the superstitious of professional hockey:

For years Gerry Desjardins drank a pregame cup of coffee for luck—until one game when he forgot but played well anyway. He continued to take the same route to the arena before each game, however, doing so even when blizzards made it prudent to try other routes.

Ken Dryden invariably averted his eyes when referees made their pregame inspection to see if the red lights of the goal were working.

Gilles Meloche changed his headband between periods, unless he had a particularly good previous period.

The Philadelphia Flyers invited Kate Smith to sing "God Bless America" instead of the National Anthem on one occasion and the team won. She was therefore asked back for important contests. By the end of the 1973–74 season, when the Flyers won it all, Kate's record was thirty-seven wins, three losses, and one tie.

Gary Innes always took in a movie the night before a game followed by a chocolate sundae at Howard Johnson's.

Joe Daley always started getting dressed exactly thirty minutes before game time, then waited precisely fifteen minutes after donning socks, leg pads, and pants before completing the process.

Wayne Thomas insisted that his stick be wrapped with tape from a brand-new roll.

Bernie Wolfe would not step onto the ice until a stick boy struck him solidly across the back with a stick.

---

would have been forgotten if Eddie Grant had popped up and struck out all day. In fact, he hit four times safely against Marquard in the opener, and picked up three more hits off Mathewson in the second game.

The lucky domino was obviously a one-time charm, for Eddie Grant went back to his mediocre hitting after that.

A few other general and specific baseball superstitions might include the following:

It is bad luck to mention a pitcher's having a no-hitter going until the game is over.

The team that is in first place on the Fourth of July will win the pennant.

It is bad luck to change bats after the second strike.

A bat contains only so many hits (rather like the number of shots in a bottle of whiskey). Therefore you are giving away your own hits if you lend a bat to another player and he happens to do well with it.

BOXING

Prizefighters are superstitious, also. Even a champion with as much ability as Bob Fitzsimmons believed that it would be bad luck for him to follow a defeated boxer into a dressing room. "At's bad stuff, followin' a losin' fighter," he remarked on several occasions. Gene Tunney, after his first fight, always refused to enter the ring before his opponent. Even when he was the challenger going against champion Harry Greb, Tunney sat in his dressing room until he was sure Greb was ready. Apparently the later he entered behind his opponent, the better, for Tunney made Jack Dempsey wait twenty minutes before their first match.

Johnny Dundee, another champion of the golden era of the twenties, wore a "good luck" robe so long that by midcareer the pockets were hanging loose and patches made it resemble a frayed crazy quilt. Kid Williams,

Some Old-style Golf Superstitions:

It is bad luck:

• to enter the clubhouse and find a black cat sleeping on your golf bag.
• to stumble on the steps leading from the fourth tee.
• to discover that your caddie is cross-eyed.
• to discover that your caddie is missing the third joint of the little finger on his left hand.
• to find a ladybug perched on the upper edge of your putter as you address the ball on the eighteenth green.
• to have a robin alight on the iron marker of the hole you are approaching.
• to leave your own pencil in the locker room and have to use your opponent's writing implement.

bantamweight champion, put his faith in a small skullcap, as did Willie Jackson, who wore a checkered one.

Lew Tendler said that he felt secure only after shaking the hand of his manager, Phil Glassman. Accordingly, a moment before the gong sounded, the two men would come together for a tight handclasp. On one occasion, Glassman was confined to bed, and Tendler wanted to cancel the bout. Glassman refused to let him do so, and the fighter was noticeably nervous before the fight. At the last moment, just as one might see it in the movies, a feverish Glassman could be seen moving unsteadily down the aisle. He reached the ring in time to bestow a handshake on Tendler. In the best tradition of superstitious folklore, Tendler won the fight.

Stanley Ketchel, middleweight champion, would not fight unless provided with gloves made by a special California manufacturer.

Battling Levinsky said that he believed in starting off right—which is why he would religiously dress himself starting from the right side, carefully putting right foot into trouser leg before left, and the same procedure with the sleeves.

Kid McFadden issued an order in his training camp that no one was to cross a street or pathway diagonally. One day one of his handlers forgot and McFadden spotted him. After losing the fight, he refused to walk with that particular handler during the rest of the time they worked together.

Between rounds of a fight, welterweight Johnny Summers used to kneel on his corner clutching an old rag doll belonging to his daughter. Once an opponent in Paris protested the kneeling action, claiming that Summers was using the superstition as a means of smearing resin on his gloves. The referee warned Summers, but rather than give up his ritual, Summers allowed himself to be disqualified.

Kid Chocolate, lightweight, used to fight with the lace of his right shoe tied in the front, the left tied in back.

Kid McCoy would allow no one to see him tape his hands. Opponents were allowed to inspect the bandages afterward, but McCoy insisted on performing the actual task in complete privacy.

Packey McFarland believed in the charm of green socks. Once he arrived in London only to discover that his beloved green silk socks were missing. He ran out of the hotel and searched for three hours in the suburbs before he located a store with a pair that suited him.

HARNESS RACING

The primary good-luck charm of horse racing, of course, is the horseshoe itself, a superstition that dates back to medieval times. A horse tooth carried in a person's pocket was thought by some to prevent toothaches.

As for trackmen themselves, superstitions in America go back to Budd Doble (1843–1926), who traveled with a veterinarian named Dr. Hollenbeck. Hollenbeck had a strange belief that graveyards were bad luck. So every time the Doble horse car passed a cemetery, everyone, according to Hollenbeck's instructions, would have to get out, clap their hands, and yell "Get away, devil!" three times.

Another famous driver of the nineteenth century, John Murphy, wore one green cap all the time as a good-luck charm. When various parts of it, such as the peak, wore out, he had new sections restitched around the original material.

Some drivers such as Billy Ewing slipped horseshoes in their pockets during a race; others carried a rabbit's foot.

One story deals with the black cat that happened to wander into the stall of Star Pointer (1889–1910), the first horse to pace a two-minute mile. At the time, however, the champion had lost two races in a row, which caused the groom to treat the black cat with rather more kindness than he would have if the animal had walked in during a winning streak. As luck would have it, Star Pointer won a race that very day, and the black cat was welcomed as a mascot. Star Pointer won every race that season, but the next year, when a mare from Canada named Nelly Bruce joined the stable, the black cat left. The departure didn't affect Star Pointer's record, but Nelly Bruce, who had won fifteen straight the year before, promptly ran into a streak of miserable races.

FOOTBALL

"Long after I had stopped believing in the church, I continued to go to the Catholic mass for the team because I didn't want to do anything different that might change my luck."

David Kopay, running back,
National Football League (1964–72)

Regarding football, there is less superstitious folklore, perhaps because the game depends more on concerted team action than golf, boxing, or even baseball. That did not prevent coaches such as Weeb Ewbank from wearing the same baggy suit every Sunday while his teams were winning; nor could any logic force New York Giant running back Alex Webster to shave before a game.

There are other examples. In 1921, the

Penn State team, rated No. 1 by most sportswriters, admitted to a few collective superstitions:

• No player would take No. 13.
• Everyone took the same route to and from the practice field every night.
• Everyone wore good-luck neckties.
• Everyone took the same number berth on the train to each game.
• One player always wore his stockings inside out.
• Another player always changed his headgear immediately following the fifth play of the game.

Carnegie Tech followers had a collective superstition regarding derby hats. The story was that during Carnegie's great years, coach Wally Steffen always wore a derby. Then came the lean years—with no Steffen, no derby, and few victories. Some blamed this on a lack of derbies. Thus when a new coach, Howard Harpster, was hired in 1933, a group of students took up a collection and bought derbies for him and his assistant coaches. The next game was with archrival Temple, and Carnegie won by a score of 25–0.

On November 25, 1922, the United States Naval Academy football team announced that they would not take the field against Army if a single player on the Navy team was wearing an even number on his back. During the two previous games played by Navy at Franklin Field, first against Penn State and then against the University of Pennsylvania, the Middies wore both even and odd numbers and lost. The decision was therefore made to try and break the jinx by using only numbers ending with 1, 3, 5, 7, or 9.

But the jinx of Franklin Field proved too powerful for Navy. Even wearing odd numbers, they bowed to Army, 17–14.

CHAPTER 38—LOSING BIG AND IN BUNCHES

Because the average sports enthusiast expects his team to win every time it takes the field or court and wonders "what went wrong" with an individual player when his performance is less than perfect, it is difficult for most athletes to shrug off a loss or repeated losses. A CPA, brain surgeon, or store manager receives life's victories or setbacks in relative obscurity. Applause for a sterling job is minimal. On the other hand, the brain surgeon who does his best and fails does not have to leave the operating room to the accompaniment of jeers and boos.

The athlete, conversely, must learn to live with public fickleness from Little League days onward and upward. Many are able to handle it. Some never adjust. And because the victory or the defeat takes place in broad, or simulated, daylight, there is no hiding a run of bad luck or mediocre performances from a press and a public devoted both to winning and the compilation of statistics. For better or worse, nearly every facet of the player's performance is fodder for the record books. If he performs well, he is soon subjected to pressure because he is closing in on someone's victory streak or other record; if he does poorly, the tables are reversed and pressure is applied because a mark for futility looms on the horizon. The more cynical athlete, of course, knows that just as many people are rooting for him to smash the current record for losing as would pull for him to break some meritorious mark of long standing.

A great deal of material has been written about the winners in American sports, those who scored an upset or made a comeback against heavy odds. Much less has been written about those who set records for losing or for being consistently humiliated in the face of mediocre competition. Thus it seems appropriate to include this compendium of losing performances, keeping in mind, of course, that many "losers" were simply good players having an off day or an off week, or occasionally, an off month. It also may be added that without losers there could be no winners. Therefore, our debt to the losers is greater than we might think.

BASEBALL

MOST DISMAL FIRST INNING, PITCHER

Anthony John Mullane was well over the hill when he took the hill on Bunker Hill Day in 1894. At thirty-five, he was performing for his next-to-last major-league club, the Baltimore Orioles. During twelve seasons of baseball he had won 276 games and lost 204, but Manager Ned Hanlon was not happy with the way Count Tony was throwing. Maybe he thought Mullane needed the work. Or perhaps he was punishing him. In any event, Boston batters had a feast. When Tony was not walking them, his pitches were ludicrously easy to hit.

Twenty-two Beaneaters went to the plate. Pitcher Jack Stivetts, shortstop Herman Long, and second baseman Bobby Lowe each had two hits, and eight runs scored before an out was made. Mullane did his part for the Boston cause by walking seven batters. After twenty men had gone to bat, Captain Wilbert Robinson of the Orioles "said that he did not propose to remain there for a week," calling Boileryard Clarke to take his place behind the plate.

The inning ended with Boston ahead, 16–0. Even then, Ned Hanlon did not spare Tony, leaving him in the game through the sixth inning, at which point the Beaneaters led, 22–4. The final score was 24–7. Mullane was traded to Cleveland soon after, where he won 1 game, lost 2, and then retired.

MOST DISMAL COMPLETE GAME—PITCHER

Dave Rowe (1856–1918) spent parts of four seasons in the major leagues with Chicago, Baltimore, and St. Louis, but his most memorable turn on the mound came on July 24, 1882, with the Cleveland Nationals. On that date, Manager Ford Evans allowed young Rowe to complete the contest despite Chicago's leading, 18–3, at the end of four innings. Rowe repaid the manager's confidence by allowing the White Stockings to score twice in the fifth, four times in the sixth, once in the seventh, seven times in the eighth, and three times in the ninth. The final score was Chicago 35, Cleveland 4. Rowe's totals included yielding twenty-nine hits and seven bases on balls. He had no strikeouts.

Two years later, Dave started and completed his second game, winning it for the St. Louis Maroons of the Union Association. That was his final year in big league baseball, his lifetime record being one win and two losses.

WORST INNING—TEAM (MAJOR LEAGUE)

The dubious honor of permitting the most runs in a single inning of a big-league game belongs to the Detroit Wolverines, who finished seventh in the eight-team National League of 1883. The date was September 6 and the scene Chicago's lakefront ballpark, where the White Stockings had taken an 8–3 lead after 6½ innings. At that point the game was reasonably respectable—until Detroit came unglued in the bottom of the seventh inning.

Chicago's Ned Williamson started the fun with a double. Tom Burns did the same to produce the first run. After ten men batted, Detroit Manager Jack Chapman yanked pitcher Stump Weidman and inserted Dick Burns.

Burns was greeted by a home run off the bat of another Burns, Tom of Chicago. Eleven runs had scored in the inning and the end was not in sight. With the score 19–3, there was still nobody out. After two more runs scored, pitcher Burns got hot, retiring Abner Dalrymple on a fly ball and George Gore on a grounder. But hits by Kelly, Anson, Williamson, Burns, and Pfeffer made the score 26–3. Chicago had scored eighteen times in a single inning. Billy Sunday fouled out to end it all.

The best threat to Detroit's generosity of 1883 came on June 18, 1953, when another Detroit team went into the bottom of the seventh inning, losing, 5–3, to the Boston Red Sox. Fourteen hits, six walks, and two outs later, Detroit was behind, 22–3. Seventeen runs had crossed the plate to put the Tigers within one run of tying the old Wolverine mark for ineptitude. But with the bases full, George Kell of Boston struck out to end the inning. The Detroit pitchers who contributed to the Boston avalanche of scoring were Ned Garver, Steve Gromek—who gave up nine runs—Dick Weik, and Earl Harrist. By getting three hits in a single inning, Vern Stephens of the Red Sox set a modern major-league mark. The final score of the game was 23–3.

WORST INNING—TEAM (ORGANIZED BASEBALL)

On Friday, August 8, 1941, the Miami Wahoos of the Florida East Coast League (Class D) seemed to have things well in hand as they went into the sixth inning of their game against the Miami Beach Flamingos at Flamingo Park. Pitcher Darden Archer had held Miami Beach's batters hitless while Johnny Douglas, slugging Wahoo first baseman, drove in a run in the fourth. But in the bottom half of the sixth, the Flamingos erupted for twenty runs on thirteen hits, each player in the lineup scoring at least once as Miami Manager Archie Martin sent in five pitchers in a futile effort to halt the scoring spree. The game's final score was 21–1.

Sitting on the bench for the Miami Beach Flamingos that evening was a twenty-year-old pitcher-outfielder named Gene Bearden, who seven years later would become the American League's Rookie of the Year.

WORST TEAM—SEASON

There are many candidates for the distinction of being worst team in the history of American major-league baseball. In the National Association, for example, there were the Brooklyn Atlantics, who during the 1875 season managed to win only 2 of 44 games for a percentage of .04545. That is indeed ineffectual, but the Atlantics were not permitted to prove their lack of skill over the long run and may therefore be discounted.

The next likely candidate is the 1889 Louisville club in the American Association, which had a record of 27 wins and 111 losses during the course of a long and dreary season. Even more to the point, early that year the Louisvilles set a mark that is still unbroken by dropping 26 games in a row.

But for the greatest show of incompetence, it seems unlikely that any team will ever equal the depths of despair reached by the 1899 Cleveland Spiders of the National League. By the end of the season the Spiders had played so poorly that they were 35 games out of contention. Not out of contention for the pennant, it should be noted. The Spiders were 35 games out of eleventh place in a 12-team league.

How did they accomplish this? One reason is that both the Spiders and the St. Louis Cardinals were owned by the same people, who raided their own Cleveland team in order to stock the St. Louis franchise, which had been purchased from G. A. Gruner in 1898. The thieves were Frank DeHaas Robison and his brother Stanley, who had made quite a profit from the Spiders in Cleveland. In 1899, hoping to quickly build a competitive team in St. Louis, which finished last in 1898 with a mark of 39–111, the Robisons shifted Jesse Burkett and Cy Young to St. Louis, leaving Cleveland with a crew of inexperienced and largely untalented players.

The ranks of the Spiders included no one

who went on to greater heights, with the possible exception of a 24-year-old pitcher, Wee Willie Sudhoff, who was fortunate enough to leave the sinking ship in midseason, as well as Manager Lave Cross, who also departed early, presumably with a smile on his face. Otherwise, the Spider roster was populated with people named Highball Wilson, Still Bill Hill, Crazy Schmidt, and Harry Colliflower, a pitcher whose 1–11 year was his first and last in the majors.

The disastrous season of 1899 began in appropriate fashion, the Spiders absorbing a 10–0 pasting at the hands of whom else but the St. Louis Cardinals. The next day, former Spider Bobby Wallace hit the first of his 12 home runs that year to deal his old club its second loss, 6–5. The Spiders were off and crawling as they dropped a pair of shutouts to Louisville before actually winning a game.

Nine games into the season, the Spiders had two victories, a .222 pace that was obviously well over their heads. They promptly started an 11-game losing streak the next day, then returned home to crowds of approximately 200. Even worse, the newspapers had started referring to them as the "castoffs," "wanderers," or "exiles."

June of 1899 featured a pair of modest losing streaks for the Spiders, 7 and 11 games, separated by Still Bill Hill's 6–2 win over Pittsburgh. During this protracted period the team played with such overall ineptitude that the New York *Tribune* gave them a quasi-compliment following an 8–2 loss by remarking that "the Misfits played a trifle better than usual."

As the hot summer continued, there were only a few good moments for the Spiders. On July 1, they somehow scored seven runs in the ninth inning against Boston, then went on to win, 10–9, in the eleventh inning. Harry Colliflower's sole major-league victory, another landmark of sorts, came against Washington on July 21. But that was approximately the sum total of rejoicing. In one contest, Cleveland executed a triple play but still lost. Crowds at home shrank to 100. And then on August 26, with their record standing stagnantly at 19–94, the Spiders got down to the really serious work of losing. Not until the first game of a doubleheader with Washington on September 18 did it end—a 24-game losing streak.

After the victory, the Spiders closed out the season with another losing streak of 16 games, thus dropping a total of 40 games out of a possible 41. The team's final mark was 20–134 (.1299). Cleveland pitchers graciously yielded 1,246 runs along the way, an average of slightly more than 8 per game. The hitters, complementing them nicely, scored about 3

runs per contest. The big winner of the pitching staff was Jim Hughey, who was victorious in 4 games. Unfortunately, he also led the league with 30 losses.

SOME OTHER TERRIBLE TEAMS

When the National League trimmed itself to 8 clubs in 1900, the Cleveland Spiders were among the first to go. Students of baseball even then must have speculated that losing 40 of 41 games and compiling 134 losses during a 154-game season were records for putrescence that would last forever.

They were right, although several clubs made serious runs at establishing themselves as rightful heirs to the Spider basement throne. In 1906, the Boston Braves put together 19 consecutive losses before suffering a victory; this was matched by the Cincinnati Reds in 1914 and surpassed by the 1906 Boston Red Sox, 1916 Athletics, and 1943 Athletics, all of whom dropped 20 games in a row.

No other group of major leaguers came within striking-out distance of the 1899 Spiders and 1889 Louisville club for some time. Then the 1961 Philadelphia Phillies happened along to continue the tradition of that National League franchise, which knew something about bulk losing, having dropped 117 games in 1916, 109 in 1928, and 111 in 1941. The Phillie streaks were rather more modest, 14 straight losses in 1883 and 1936. On their way to the National League basement with a mark of 47–107, Gene Mauch's 1961 Phillies surged past the twentieth century loss streaks, raising the record to 23 before beating the Milwaukee Braves.

Yet few believed the 1961 Phils were in the same league of despair as the Cleveland Spiders. The very next year, however, a team came along that set new standards for incompetence, at least among modern fans of the national game. These were the 1962 New York Mets, which started the season with 9 straight losses, at once equaling the National League mark for losing from a prone start. They managed to win a game in their tenth start by beating Pittsburgh, 9–1, but the remainder of the season was a model of losing consistency. Without putting together an impressive defeat streak, the Mets tied the Phila-

Other Miserable Starts:
National League
1918—Brooklyn Dodgers (9 losses in row)
1919—Boston Braves (9 losses in row)
American League
1904—Washington Senators (13 losses in row)

delphia Phillie mark for 117 losses during a season as early as September 25, thus assuring themselves of becoming one of the worst teams since the American and National leagues ushered in the twentieth century.

Three days later, the New Yorkers lost their 119th before a crowd of only 595 loyal but masochistic fans. (The scene was Wrigley Field, Chicago, where the Cubs were also on their way to a terrible year, 59–103.) On October 1, the season ended as the Mets racked up their 120th defeat against only 40 wins. "Imagine, 40 games," said Manager Casey Stengel, former pilot of the powerful Yankee teams of the 1950s. "I won with this club what I used to lose."

Reaction to a Losing Baseball Team, Newark Style:

On June 24, 1949, the Newark Star-Ledger became so miffed at the poor play of the International League Newark Bears that it announced that the team was being omitted from the standings "because they obviously do not belong in Triple-A competition." At the time, the team had a record of 20 wins and 41 losses but was already 18½ games out of first place. The Bears finished the season with a mark of 55–98, which was bad enough for last place. It was also bad enough to destroy the franchise, for the 1950 season was played without Newark. Thus the omission from the International League standings became permanent.

WORST LOSING STREAK—SEASON (PITCHER)

Losing baseball teams have a way of dragging down individual records; thus it is hardly a surprise that the two longest losing streaks among major-league pitchers belong to two men who toiled for miserable clubs. The first was Jack Nabors, who started his career with the 1915 Philadelphia Athletics, an American League team that amassed a 43–109 mark. The 27-year-old Nabors contributed 5 losses and 0 wins to this season, then began the new year of 1916 with a win. He followed this with 19 consecutive losses, setting a modern baseball record for pitching winlessness.

Nabors' record was virtually unchallenged until 1963, when Roger Craig, an 8-year veteran who had led the league with 24 losses during the 1962 New York Met disaster, suddenly found he could not stop losing. Before he knew what was happening, he had dropped 17

consecutive games, bringing himself within one of the National League mark of 18, set in 1910 by Cliff Curtis of the Boston Braves.

On August 4, 1963, Craig led the Mets onto the field against the Braves in Milwaukee. In the first inning, he threw a home-run ball to Eddie Mathews, then committed a throwing error himself in the 6th inning that permitted the Braves to take a 2–0 lead. The Mets scored a single run in the eighth but that was all they could manage. Roger Craig had tied the National League record for consecutive losses and was but one away from Jack Nabors' 1916 mark.

Five days later, the Chicago Cubs came to the Polo Grounds, and Craig once again took the mound in the quest for his first victory since April 29. The game was a thriller by any standard. Through eight innings, Craig battled the Cubs' Mel Toth, each pitcher yielding a home run and several other hits, but somehow managing to hang in until the ninth inning, when the Mets came to bat with the score tied, 3–3. Frank Thomas flied to left to start the inning but Joe Hicks followed with a single. Met fans groaned as Clarence "Choo Choo" Coleman fanned, then cheered wildly when Al Moran lined a double into the left-field corner. Tom Harkness, pinch-hitting for Roger Craig, walked, bringing Jim Hickman to the plate. With the count full at three and two, Hickman brought the crowd to its feet by driving a shot to the left-field scoreboard for a home run. "The Ballad of Roger Craig," one reporter wrote, "a woeful tale of one of the great right-handed tragic heroes of modern times, came to a glorious end last night as the New York Mets ended his losing streak. . . ."

The record for consecutive pitching losses remained at 19 with the long-deceased Jack Nabors. As for Roger Craig, he led the National League in 1963 with his 22 losses against 5 victories and was traded to the Cardinals the following year. He retired after the 1966 season, his lifetime statistics, thanks largely to the Mets, being a less than sparkling 74 wins and 98 losses.

BASEBALL'S HIGHEST ERA'S

In baseball the ERA, or earned-run average, is the standard gauge used to determine a pitcher's effectiveness. Those with low ERAs use the magic figure to demand sizable raises in pay; those with high ERAs point out that figures can be misleading, and quickly change the subject.

Like other statistics, the ERA can be overemphasized, but it is a fairly accurate indicator of how many runs would have crossed the plate during a nine-inning game if the pitcher had continued to throw—and the batters connect—the same way over the long haul as over the short. In order to have a computable ERA, however, the pitcher must have retired at least one batter. Otherwise the ERA becomes infinity, which is not only completely inaccurate but also totally unusable for getting a raise in pay.

If a good seasonal ERA is about 3.00 and an excellent one in the neighborhood of 2.00, what constitutes an atrocious ERA? So far no pitcher has come through a major-league season with one as high as 200.00, but several have approached that. Below, the ten highest ERA-owners in the history of American baseball:

189.00

The highest ERA in major-league statistical history, 189.00, is owned by two men, Joe Cleary and John Scheible, names that are hardly the household variety. In 1893, Scheible pitched to a 1–1 record with the Cleveland Spiders, then was traded to the Philadelphia Nationals, where he issued two bases on balls and six hits in one-third inning. Seven of those eight base runners scored, which means that according to the laws of mathematics, poor John would have yielded 189 runs if he, the batters, managers, and fans could have lasted nine innings at that rate. More or less the same fate befell Joe Cleary, who tried and failed with Washington's 1945 Senators.

162.00

Tom Qualters, who pitched in the majors for three years to a less-than-brilliant record of 0–0, and Andy Sommerville of the 1894 Brooklyn Bridegrooms share the second-highest ERA, 162.00. Andy's trouble was control. He gave up only one hit during his entire big-league career, but he passed five men, and all six scored. Qualters' problem was just the opposite of Andy's. Tom gave up four hits and one pass while retiring a single batter, then was farmed out by the Phillies after the 1953 season.

135.00

The third-highest ERA, 135.00, is also shared by a pair of obscure young men. One was Clise Dudley, who toiled for the 1933 Pittsburgh Pirates. The other was a gentleman with a literary-sounding name, Pembroke Finlayson. Pembroke gave his all, which apparently was not all that much, for the 1908 Brooklyn Superbas, pitching a no-hitter for a third of an inning before the roof fell in. Clise Dudley's bad year came after four years in the big leagues during which he won 17 games with Brooklyn and Philadelphia of the National League. Unfortunately, he lost thirty-three before giving it one last try with the

1933 Pirates. In one appearance, he could get only one man out while walking another and yielding six hits.

108.00

Clarence Mitchell, Fritz Fisher, Frantz Wurm, and Harry Heitman share the fourth-highest ERA, 108.00, and thus close out the record book on the total of ten men who have attained—or been afflicted with—triple-digit ERAs.

Of the four, Clarence Mitchell is the most celebrated, having served in the major leagues from 1911 to 1932, during which time he won 125 games and lost 139 for six clubs. For trivia fans, it should be noted that Mitchell has the distinction of hitting into five outs in two times at bat during a World Series game, which is surely a record of some sort. In 1920, he hit the ball that Cleveland second baseman Bill Wambsganss turned into an unassisted triple play; the next time at the plate, Mitchell lined into a double play. Mitchell's usual ERA was about 4.00, except for a disastrous 1918 stint with the Brooklyn Robins, as they were called then in honor of manager Wilbert Robinson. During that year, Mitchell started but one game and could retire only a single batter while allowing four runs. The next season, he managed to win seven and lose five.

Henry Heitman, born in 1897, also had a shot with the Robins during that war year of 1918. He grooved the ball to four batters, earned his 108.00 ERA, and promptly went back to Manhattan. The presence of Heitman and Mitchell on the same team during the same year with the identically high ERA adds another bit of trivia to baseball lore.

It is doubtful that most baseball fans have heard of Fritz Fisher and Frantz Wurm, although both are still around. Fisher, born in Adrian, Michigan, had a brief career in 1964 with his local heroes, the Detroit Tigers. He allowed two walks, two hits, and four runs in his one-third inning. Wurm, a native of Cambridge, New York, was just twenty when he toed the rubber for about ten minutes in 1944 with the Brooklyn Dodgers. He issued five free passes and left quickly.

FUTILITY IN HITTING

Because hitting depends on so many things, not the least of which is what pitcher is throwing the ball, it seems unreasonable to brand a batter as "futile" without the benefit of at least a hundred attempts at the plate. In addition, a truly representative batting average does not emerge for a while. Willis Windle is a perfect example of this fact. In 1928, Windle had a perfect year with the Pittsburgh Pirates, coming to the plate one time and stroking a double. But his perfect average of

Name	Club and Year		At-bats	Hits	Average
Vincent Nava	Providence (N.L.)	1884	116	11	.095
Mike Jordan	Pittsburgh (N.L.)	1890	125	12	.096
Red Faber	Chicago (A.L.)	1920	104	11	.106
John Humphries	New York (N.L.)	1883	107	12	.112
Gracie Pearce	Col. (A.A.) N.Y. (N.L.)	1883	103	12	.117
Otto Hess	Cleveland (A.L.)	1904	100	12	.120
Dwain Anderson	St.L. (N.L.) S.D. (N.L.)	1973	124	15	.121
George Baker	St. Louis (N.L.)	1885	131	16	.122
Frank O'Rourke	Boston (N.L.)	1912	196	24	.122
Norm Schlueter	Cleveland (A.L.)	1944	122	15	.123

1.000 dropped to .000 in 1929 when he also came to the plate just one time but struck out. That, incidentally, ended Windle's career, his lifetime average stabilizing at .500.

There have been several players who went through disastrously cold streaks. Lou Camilli, for example, was 0 for 29 during two seasons (1969–70) with the Cleveland Indians. Skeeter Shelton's entire career was with the 1915 New York Yankees, with whom he went 1 for 40 for an average of .025. Haywood Sullivan, Boston Red Sox and Kansas City catcher, had to go through three years until he got his first major-league hit. Brought up for parts of the 1955, 1957, and 1959 seasons, he was 0 for 9 before making the big leagues for good in 1960.

There have also been batters who, for one reason or another, displayed temporary futility during the World Series. One such impressive display was Dal Maxvill's 0 for 22 for the St. Louis Cardinals in 1968. Gil Hodges posted a pathetic 0 for 21 for the 1952 Dodgers and over a two-year stretch, Detroit Tiger third baseman Marv Owen displayed total ineptness 31 consecutive times starting with the fifth game of the 1934 Series and lasting until the final game of the 1935 meeting. He was 3 for 49 during the two Series.

As for batters who went through an entire season and registered at least 100 at-bats, above are the ten worst: (None of the batters, it should be added, was a pitcher.)

THE MOST CONSISTENTLY BAD BATTER WHO SOMEHOW MANAGED TO STAY IN THE MAJOR LEAGUES A LONG TIME

He was William Aloysius Bergen, who

Lest the Above Seem Too Depressing and Negative, It Might Be Added That:
• *In 1916, the New York Giants won 26 consecutive games (one tie played during the streak).*
• *In 1977, Reggie Jackson of the New York Yankees hit three home runs during a single World Series game, becoming only the second player to accomplish that feat. (Babe Ruth did it in 1926 and 1928.)*
• *In 1888, pitcher Tim Keefe won 18 consecutive games.*
• *In 1912, pitcher Rube Marquard of the New York Giants won 20 games in a row.*
• *In 1936–37, Carl Hubbell of the New York Giants won 24 games in a row spanning two seasons.*
• *In 1906, the Chicago Cubs won a record 116 games during the season.*
• *In 1908, Ed Reulbach of the Chicago Cubs won both ends of a doubleheader, shutting out the Brooklyn Superbas, 5–0 and 3–0, the only time a double shutout has been registered.*
• *In 1903, during the month of August, Joe McGinnity of the New York Giants pitched three doubleheader victories against the Braves, Superbas, and Phils.*
• *In 1894, Hugh Duffy of Boston hit .438.*
• *From 1891 through 1904, Cy Young won at least 21 games a season, and five times more than 30.*
• *Not to mention Joe DiMaggio's 56-game hitting streak in 1941 or Whitey Ford's record 32 consecutive scoreless innings in World Series play or a multitude of additional baseball records for excellence.*

played with Cincinnati and Brooklyn in the National League for more than a decade, 1901–11. Going to bat 3,028 times during this span, Bergen hit 2 home runs and 514 other hits for a lifetime average of .170. His high was .227 in 1903 (the year before the Reds traded him) to a low of .132 in 1911 (the year the Superbas ushered him out of baseball for good). Obviously, Bergen was an excellent defensive catcher and handler of pitchers or he could not have lasted that long in the big leagues.

The only other interesting bit of information concerning Bill Bergen is that he was the brother of Marty Bergen, who caught for the Boston Nationals until one day early in 1900 when he suddenly went berserk, killing his family with an ax and then shooting himself. Bill died a natural death in 1943.

BASKETBALL

LONGEST LOSING STREAK—TEAM
(PROFESSIONAL)

In 1973, the Philadelphia 76ers of the National Basketball Association were hardly setting the Atlantic Division on fire. The team had won just 3 games against 38 losses when they managed to edge Seattle, 85–82. That brought the 76er record to 4–38. Optimists of the extreme variety might have felt that better

days were on the way, but such was not the case. Immediately after beating Seattle, the 76ers took on the Chicago Bulls. Led by Chet Walker, who used the opportunity to become the eighteenth NBA player to score 15,000 points, the Bulls defeated the 76ers, 126–110.

January 9, 1973, was just the beginning. For the rest of the month, the 76ers could not win. A new coach, Kevin Loughery, took over, but the losing pattern continued. On February 10, Philadelphia set a new record for futility in the NBA by dropping a 126–121 game to Portland, their nineteenth consecutive loss. Two days later, the team lost still another game, to the Los Angeles Lakers, 108–90.

Then, with 20 losses in a row to their discredit, the 76ers finally ran into the law of averages. Against the Milwaukee Bucks, the 76ers went into the last few seconds of the game with the score close. It was tied, 104–104, when a Philadelphia rookie, Fred Boyd, took a short jump shot in front of the basket that was interfered with by Dick Cunningham. Taking a 106–104 lead, the 76ers held the Bucks to one desperate shot as the clock ran out.

LONGEST LOSING STREAK—TEAM
(NONPROFESSIONAL)

After defeating Illinois Tech on December 6, 1941, the University of Chicago basketball

---

On the Other Hand:

There have been many notable basketball records for winning or outstanding individual performances over the decades, such as:

- *In 1954 Clarence "Bevo" Francis of Rio Grande College (Ohio) scored 113 points in a single game against Hillsdale (Michigan).*
- *In 1954 Frank Selvy of Furman scored 100 points in a game against Newberry.*
- *In 1962, Wilt Chamberlain of the Philadelphia Warriors of the NBA scored 100 points in 169–147 win over New York Knickerbockers.*
- *In 1974, UCLA lost to Notre Dame, 71–70, its first defeat in 89 consecutive games.*
- *During the 1971–72 NBA season, the Los Angeles Lakers won 33 games in a row, then went on to post a season high of 69 wins against only 13 defeats.*
- *On February 25, 1961, St. Bonaventure lost to Niagara, 87–77, snapping a streak of 99 straight home victories.*

- *From the 1958–59 season through the 1965–66 season, the Boston Celtics were champions of the NBA eight times in a row.*
- *From 1954–55 to 1956–57, the University of San Francisco won 60 straight games without a defeat.*
- *Oddity: In December 1933, John Tarleton College (Texas) lost to San Angelo Junior College, 27–26. Tarleton then proceeded to win 86 games in a row before losing on February 2, 1938. The opponent on that occasion was San Angelo Junior College, and the score was 27–26.*
- *From 1919–20 to February 6, 1925, the Passaic High School team won 159 consecutive victories, outscoring the opposition, 9,435–3,236. The streak was finally snapped by Hackensack High, 39–35.*
- *On January 8, 1955, Kentucky lost to Georgia Tech, 59–58, its first defeat at home since January 2, 1943, a total of 130 games.*

team proceeded to lose the remaining 20 games of its season. They then lost all 19 contests on the 1942–43 schedule, bringing the loss streak to 39. Finally, after losing the first 6 games of the 1943–44 season, the Maroon ended the 45-game mark by beating Chicago Technical College, 65–27.

In 1966, Rice University laid claim to the longest major-college losing streak by dropping 28 games, a mark that ended on February 18 when the Owls defeated Baylor, 89–70.

On the high-school level, Rewey High School of Rewey, Wisconsin, in 1949 finally won a basketball game after 92 consecutive losses, believed to be the longest streak in the nation. The victim was Avoca High School, the historic score of November 15, 31–20.

MOST HUMILIATING BASKETBALL DEFEAT

This was inflicted by the Magnolia A and M School (female) team of Arkansas on the Jonesboro Baptist squad on January 10, 1931. The final score was 143–1.

FOOTBALL

Perhaps more than any other spectator sport, American-style football lends itself to the creation of embarrassment for the loser. Once things begin going wrong in football, it seems inevitable that the landslide will continue. Steps taken in desperation to bring the trailing team back into competition often produce even worse situations, and sometimes there is virtually no way to prevent the score from rising higher and higher.

Another factor: Because football is a game of "controlled violence," there is considerable emphasis placed on the need to physically intimidate the opposition. Intimidation sometimes leads to what some have termed "rolling up the score," a phrase that embarrasses nearly everyone, with the possible exception of college alumni.

THE AGE OF EMBARRASSMENT—1910–20

After the turn of the century, when college football became America's national sport in the fall of the year, more than one team gave in to the temptation to see how high the score

could go. In fact, during this 11-year span, there were no less than 39 college games in which the winner averaged 121 points, the loser less than a single point.

With an aggregate score for these 39 games of winners 4,724, losers 12, it was obvious that someone was being severely outclassed.

THE ULTIMATE RIVALRY: YALE-WESLEYAN, 1883–1913

There have been many college football rivalries during the past century, but none in which the loser was so hideously mortified as Wesleyan of Connecticut was during the three decades of grid combat with Yale University, one of the early powers of American football.

The teams first met in 1883, twice, and Yale rolled up scores of 60–0 and 94–0. The following year the Elis triumphed by 31–0, 63–0, and 46–0. It went like that for quite a while. Highlights for Yale included wins of 136–0 in 1886, 106–0 in 1887, and 105–0 in 1888. Highlights for Wesleyan appeared in 1890, when the losers held Yale to a score of 8–0, and in 1912, when Wesleyan actually scored a field goal.

Final tally in the 44-game series was Yale 1,989, Wesleyan 3. The average score was Yale 45.2, Wesleyan .07.

COLLEGE FOOTBALL'S GREATEST SLAUGHTER

According to tradition, football's most lopsided score came about partly because Georgia Tech's coach, John Heisman, felt that undue emphasis was being placed on the margin of victory in college football games. "Finding folks are determined to take the crazy thing into consideration," he said in 1917, "we at Tech determined last year, at the start of the season, to show folks it was no difficult thing to run up a score in one easy game, from which it might perhaps be seen that it could also be done in other easy games as well."

The object of Heisman's unpleasant experiment was Cumberland College of Lebanon, Tennessee, a school for which football held only a passing interest for its undergraduates and one-year law students. The Cumberland squad was handicapped by the war, according

---

Some Sample Scores—1910–20:

1910:	Nebraska 119, Haskell 0	1916:	Rice 143, SMU 0
1911:	Nebraska 117, Kearney Normal 0	1917:	Oklahoma 179, Kingfisher 0
1912:	Notre Dame 116, St. Viator 7	1918:	Georgia Tech 128, North Carolina State 0
1913:	Creighton 128, Omaha 0	1919:	Nevada 134, College of the Pacific 0
1914:	Oklahoma A&M 134, Phillips 0	1920:	VMI 136, Hampden-Sydney 0
1915:	Oklahoma 102, Alva Normal 0		

to one old graduate, although when the team took the field against Georgia Tech, on October 7, 1916, the United States was still six months out of World War I. In any event, Cumberland was low on players, so low that coach Butch McQueen decided to make a stop at Vanderbilt to see if he could pick up some spare athletes for the game.

The answer turned out to be negative, and even worse, three Cumberland players missed the train at Nashville after the layover. As a result, the Cumberland team numbered only thirteen strong when it arrived at Atlanta.

Only about a thousand spectators were on hand for the contest, which began with Tech's kicking off and stopping Cumberland's receiver on the twenty-five-yard line. The first play from scrimmage, a gain of three yards, turned out to be Cumberland's biggest rushing advance of the afternoon.

A punt followed, then an eighty-yard end sweep that put Georgia Tech in the lead, 7–0. Cumberland fumbled on the first play after the kickoff and Tech ran it in for the second TD. Before long, Cumberland was behind, 28–0. At this point, the men from Tennessee attempted a new strategy, that of kicking off to Tech following a touchdown so that the Georgians would be deep in their own territory.

On the first use of this strategy, Tech returned the kickoff seventy yards to the Cumberland ten-yard line. Two plays later the score was 35–0. Two more touchdowns followed, then Cumberland returned to receiving the kickoff. But nothing worked. Georgia Tech returned a punt forty-five yards for still another score. Minutes later the score was 63–0. That ended the first quarter.

During the second quarter, Cumberland took to receiving the kickoff again in the hope that they could use up some time in futile dives into the formidable Tech line. Whatever time was used was hardly enough, for soon the score was Georgia Tech 105, Cumberland 0. By halftime, the count had risen to 126–0.

During the early part of the third period, Tech played it for laughs, at one point handing the ball to J. C. Alexander, a huge and plodding tackle, then standing aside and refusing to block for him. (Alexander made only seven yards under these adverse circumstances.) Nevertheless, the score rose to 154–0 before Cumberland completed a pass good for ten yards, their biggest gain of the afternoon. But the pass did not lead to a first down, Cumberland having lost eighteen yards on two previous running plays.

Surprisingly, Georgia Tech's statistics, which included no passes thrown, were not overly impressive, including 528 yards rushing from scrimmage. The big factor was return yardage, Tech amassing 220 yards on kickoffs and 220 on punts. The final score, one well known to most football buffs, was 222–0.

ANOTHER NEAR-RECORD GAME JUST TWO WEEKS LATER:
In the age of embarrassment, it was hardly surprising that just a few weeks after Georgia Tech destroyed Cumberland, St. Viator College was given credit for a world's record by piling up 205 points versus Lane Technical School. "If it is assumed that quarters of ten minutes each were contested," wrote the New York Times, *"St. Viator backs accounted for a fraction more than five points a minute for the entire progress of the game."*

The total of 222 points has never been matched, although on October 21, 1922, King College defeated Lenoir at Bristol, Tennessee, by 206–0, the second-highest in college noncompetition. "Spectators said the score might have been higher," one newsman wrote, "but the King College backs became exhausted from sprinting."

THE HIGHEST SCORE THAT WASN'T
Some sports encyclopedias list a 1900 game in which Dickinson College of Carlisle, Pennsylvania, overran Haverford, 227–0, but the listing is erroneous. The actual score was 27–0, a careless telegrapher having added an extra digit at the time.

Reaction to a Losing College Football Team—I:
After suffering through 10 consecutive losses, coeds at Boston College in 1931 sent a letter to members of the squad, informing the gentlemen that they would not speak to or make dates with any member of the team until a victory was achieved. The next Saturday, October 24, Boston was leading DePauw in the final period, 9–7, until the very last minute, when halfback Don Wheaton ran thirty-two yards for the score that put DePauw ahead, 14–9. But the next week, against Rhode Island, Boston College won, 25–7. That was a fortunate occurrence, as it turned out, for the next time BC won was midway in the 1932 season.

NOTRE DAME'S LONGEST AFTERNOON

By the early 1920s, the Fighting Irish of Notre Dame were considered one of the top college grid powers in the nation, a dominance that continued long after Coach Knute Rockne's early demise in 1931. In 1900, Wisconsin hammered Notre Dame, 54–0, and beat them 58–0 in 1904, but after that the Irish were never really humiliated in a football game.

Then came the terrible afternoon of November 11, 1944, when West Point, powered by speedsters Glenn Davis and Max Minor as well as Felix "Doc" Blanchard, attempted to compensate for a long string of defeats at the hands of the maddeningly efficient Irish. In the process the Cadets scored more points in a single game than they had in the previous fifteen meetings between the teams.

The first three times it handled the ball, Army scored, building a lead of 20–0 at the end of the first quarter. Scoring twice in each of the next three periods, West Point trotted off the field at the conclusion of the game ahead, 59–0. It was Notre Dame's worst football defeat.

Reaction to a Losing College Football Team—II:

In October 1934, coeds at the University of California, unhappy at their team's 1–4 record at midseason, vowed to swear off dates, cigarettes, manicures, hair waves, and haircuts until the team won by a margin of 7 points or more. The effect was not immediately apparent. On the following Saturday, California dropped its next game, to Washington 13–7. A week later, Santa Clara rolled to a 20–0 victory. On November 11, the situation improved. California won, but USC reduced the margin of victory to 7–2 by scoring a safety. The next week, however, the team laced the University of Idaho, 45–13. No statistics exist as to how many of the school's coeds stuck to their vow until the end.

AN ASSORTMENT OF LOSING AND/OR NON-WINNING STREAKS

1928–31: Hobart: It was a great day for students at Hobart College of Geneva, New York, on November 21, 1931. After twenty-seven consecutive losses extending over parts of four seasons, Hobart finally defeated the University of Rochester, 13–7.

1931–34: Knox: "Old Siwash," otherwise known as Knox College, tied the Hobart mark

for twenty-seven losses on November 29, 1934, losing to Monmouth College, 39–0. The shutout was nothing new. In eight contests the men of Galesburg, Illinois, failed to score a point.

1931–35: Albany: The record loss streak of Hobart and Knox was erased by Albany College (Oregon), which lost its twenty-eighth straight in 1935. By tying Pacific University 7–7, in the next game, the team ended the loss skein on October 27. Two weeks later, Albany actually won a game, the first in nearly four years.

1939—The last days of Chicago: In 1935, the University of Chicago produced Jay Berwanger, first Heisman Trophy winner, but with four years the quality of play by the school's football team had degenerated severely. The crisis atmosphere deepened on October 21, when the University of Michigan scored an 85–0 victory over Chicago, despite using second- and third-string players as early as the first quarter. Tornado Tom Harmon, the Wolverines' sensational halfback, scored 18 points in what was Michigan's biggest margin of victory since it beat West Virginia, 130–0, in 1904.

With the grandstands nearly empty at every game, trustees of the school decided to eliminate football from the schedule. Students and alumni were understandably shocked. One old grad shot off a telegram in which he stated that the decision to drop intercollegiate football "ignores the Bill of Rights and sincerely flatters both Stalin and Hitler."

While the controversy bubbled and boiled, the remainder of the season continued to be played. Harvard, Michigan, Virginia, and Ohio State scored a total of thirty-seven touchdowns while defeating Chicago by an aggregate score of 254–0. The nadir of humiliation came on November 26, when the Delta Kappa Epsilon fraternity football team at Colgate University formally challenged the University of Chicago squad to a postseason contest. The *Daily Maroon,* student paper at Chicago, bemoaned the gridiron events but saw no hope in sight. "Our school has become a benevolent institution furnishing material on which newspaper writers from all over the country may practice cleverness," the editor

---

Reaction to a Losing College Football Team—III:

In 1941, students at Carnegie Tech became so unhappy with their losing football team that they held a rally and contributed lunch money in order to start a scholarship fund for bigger and better players. A total of $537.35 was collected.

---

wrote. "For the football team, however, the matter isn't such a big joke. . . . This might be good moral training for martyrs but football players are human beings, too."

Finally, on November 18, the University of Chicago defeated Oberlin College, 25–0, to end the disaster streak. But by then it was too late. The decision to eliminate intercollegiate football had been made, and the school that gave America its first Heisman Trophy winner never suited up a football team again.

1940–53: St. Paul's Poly: Starting in 1940, St. Paul's Poly of Lawrenceville, Virginia, lost forty-one games in a row, including a string of twenty-two contests in which they were outscored, 890–0. After tying a game, the school then proceeded to lose twenty-one additional games before winning, stretching its nonwinning streak to sixty-three games.

THE PROFESSIONALS

Professional football teams are supposed to be sufficiently close in the quality of their talent so that slaughters or track meets do not happen on the field. Naturally, because the human element is involved, there have been notable cases of near-total collapse, both in single games and entire seasons. While the margin of defeat has been less than in college ranks, spectators with a sadistic bent will be happy to know that the embarrassment to the losers probably has been just as great.

PRO FOOTBALL'S GREATEST SLAUGHTER

The unusual thing was that during the regular season, the 1940 Washington Redskins defeated the Chicago Bears, 7–3. But as NFL Commissioner Pete Rozelle has said many times, "on any given Sunday any team; etc. . . ." and on Sunday, December 8, 1940, the unexpected certainly did happen. On the second play of the 1940 championship game, the Bears' Bill Osmanski ran around left end for sixty-eight yards and a touchdown. That

started it. Before the contest was thirteen minutes old, the Bears led, 21–0.

Yet the Redskins had Sam Baugh, the sensational passer. They could have come back had they not been plagued with fumbles and interceptions. Conversely, Chicago's execution on nearly every play was perfect. By the end of the third quarter, with Bear quarterback Sid Luckman sitting on the bench, the score had risen to 54–0. Nothing, it seemed, could stop the avalanche except time itself, which finally intervened with the Redskins behind, 73–0. The band at Griffith Stadium played "Should auld acquaintance be forgot?" as the hometown crowd, or what was left of it, hooted.

A SELECTION OF OTHER PROFESSIONAL LOSING LANDMARKS

Seventy-two points a game: The highest regular-season scoring total is seventy-two points, which was inflicted by the Washington Redskins on the New York Giants, November 27, 1966. The primary factor in the game's high score was young Giant quarterback Tom Kennedy's inability to deal with the Redskin tactic of blitzing. Three times during the first half, Kennedy threw hurriedly and three times the Redskins converted the mistakes into scores. At the intermission, Washington led, 34–14. Kennedy had been replaced by Gary Wood, who managed to generate some offense. But the Giant defensive squad simply could not stop the Skins. By the time it was over, Washington had a 72–41 victory and the Giants their ninth loss in the season that would see them go 1–12–1.

Seventy points for the winners: Only 16,026 were on hand to see the Los Angeles Rams take on the hapless Baltimore Colts on October 22, 1950. Earlier in the year, the Rams had buried the Colts, 70–21, in an exhibition game, but few thought such a rout would reoccur so soon.

Actually, the Colts did somewhat better,

Some Other Losing and Nonwinning Streaks:		
Losing:	Losses	Years
Northland (Wisconsin) College	31	1940–49
Kansas State	28	1945–48
Virginia	28	1958–60
Olivet College (Michigan)	28	1955–58
Trenton State (New Jersey)	27	1938–47
Hardin Simmons	27	1959–62
Nonwinning:	Losses-Ties	
Montana Mines	42–2	1953–62
Trenton State (New Jersey)	40–3	1938–49
Elmhurst (Indiana)	32–2	1957–61

managing to score twenty-seven points. They fell behind after only twenty-two seconds, however, a Norm Van Brocklin to Elroy Hirsch pass of fifty-eight yards and a TD delighting the hometown audience. The Colts tied the game on a fifty-five-yard aerial, Adrian Burk to Billy Stone, but the lead lasted merely seconds as the Rams' Vitamin Smith raced ninety-five yards with the ensuing kickoff.

By halftime the Colts were behind, 35–13, but the Rams continued to roll. The final score was 70–27.

PRO FOOTBALL'S BIGGEST QUARTER

Just one week after demolishing the Baltimore Colts, the 1950 Rams entertained the Detroit Lions at Los Angeles Memorial Coliseum. For a while the game was somewhat close, Los Angeles taking a 7–3 edge at the quarter mark and 24–10 at the half. But the Rams exploded in the third quarter for forty-one points, one touchdown coming on a ninety-three-yard kickoff return by Vitamin Smith. Before it was over, the Rams had a 65–17 lead. The Lions scored once in the final period as the Rams made no attempt to score additional points. In any event, the two-game total of 135 points ranks highest in the NFL.

The forty-one-point quarter was not a record, however, only tying the second-period output generated by the Green Bay Packers against the Detroit Lions on October 7, 1945. The final score in that noncontest was Green Bay 57, Detroit 21.

FUTILITY ON OFFENSE

Most professional football fans can tolerate their team yielding a lot of points so long as their own offense can manage enough of an attack to keep the game interesting. Much more infuriating for the spectator is having to watch a succession of plays that go nowhere followed by a punt, which is probably why quarterbacks receive more boos when things are going wrong than defensive linemen.

In honor of those sputtering attacks that extinguished themselves by displaying an uncanny ability to go backward rather than forward, the following selected list is offered:

Minus 36 yards rushing: The tired football axiom goes: Establish the running game or you cannot win. It may or may not be true, but Philadelphia quarterback Davey O'Brien probably became a believer on November 19, 1939. On that day he completed twenty-one passes against the powerful Chicago Bears but lost the game, 27–14. Part of the reason lay with the Eagle running game, which simply could not penetrate the Bear line. While Chicago rained 246 yards on the ground, the Eagles were pushed back 36.

Minus 33 yards rushing: The second most futile day on the ground was that suffered by the 1943 Brooklyn Dodgers, who managed to lose 33 yards from scrimmage as they were trounced by the Pittsburgh-Philadelphia Steagles, 17–0.

Minus 29 yards rushing: The Cleveland Rams of October 11, 1942, were nearly as helpless in the air as on the ground against the Washington Redskins, although they did manage to complete 10 passes. The rushing attack went backward 29 yards as the Skins romped to an easy 33–14 victory.

Zero yards rushing: Just to prove the axiom isn't always trustworthy, it should be mentioned that the Kansas City Chiefs pulled off a 45–35 win over the Denver Broncos on December 19, 1965, despite being completely stymied on the ground. Quarterback Len Dawson made up the difference, throwing to Curtis McClinton, in a game that was dedicated to the memory of Mack Lee Hill, Chief running back who died of complications following a knee operation the previous Tuesday.

Minus 53 yards passing: The record for passing helplessness belongs to the 1967 Denver Broncos, who were quarterbacked by Scotty Glacken, Steve Tensi, and Jim LeClair. The Broncos could manage only two first downs against the Oakland Raiders. With minus 53 yards in the air and only 48 rushing, the team's total yardage from scrimmage was minus 5 yards. Not unexpectedly, Denver was shut out, 51–0.

Minus 52 yards passing: Thanks to nine quarterback sacks totaling 68 yards, the Cincinnati Bengals managed to generate minus 52 yards passing, a decisive factor in the team's 10–6 loss to the Houston Oilers on October 31, 1971.

Minus 29 yards passing: And just to prove that you don't necessarily need even a mediocre passing attack to win any given game, the Washington Redskins on November 27, 1955, completed none of eight passing attempts and minus 29 yards in that department but still managed to defeat the Pittsburgh Steelers, 23–14. Leo Elter, a Steeler castoff, was the difference, running 20 yards in the first quarter and 33 yards in the second for Washington touchdowns.

Eleven fumbles: Can a professional football team fumble ten times during a game and hope for anything short of disaster? Frankly, yes. On November 12, 1967, the Detroit Lions fumbled eleven times and lost possession five times. That was a NFL mark, but somehow the Lions were able to overcome a 10–0 deficit and tie the Minnesota Vikings, 10–10. The player who made the record-setting eleventh bobble was Detroit fullback Tom Nowatzke.

Zero first downs: Another axiom of professional football is that ball control, ability to get a string of first downs, is a key to victory. The axiom seemed to hold up on September 3, 1966, when the Houston Oilers trounced the Denver Broncos, 45–7, in the process not permitting a single first down. In fact, the Broncos were able to advance the ball only as far as their own 40-yard line. Goldie Sellers' 88-yard kickoff return was all that kept Denver from being shut out.

On the other hand, the New York Giants did not get a single first down on October 1, 1933, yet managed to defeat the Green Bay Packers, 10–7. The Giant scores came on a fumble recovery followed by a field goal, and

an intercepted pass followed by a 25-yard TD pass.

Nine years later, on September 27, 1942, the Giants performed the trick again. This time the victims were the Washington Redskins, who amassed 120 yards rushing, 113 passing, and 15 first downs, yet lost to the Giants, who completed a single pass (for 50 yards and a touchdown) and a total of a single yard rushing. New York won 14–7, the second touchdown coming on a 65-yard run by O'Neale Adams with an intercepted pass

THE WORST TEAM IN PROFESSIONAL FOOTBALL

It really depends. When Tampa Bay lost all fourteen games on its schedule in 1976 and

---

On the Other Hand:

Football is not all embarrassment, the college and professional record books being full of magnificent achievements. On a team level, some of these include:

Winning Streaks (College) Since 1900:

Team	Wins	Years
Oklahoma	47	1953–57
Missouri Valley*	41	1941–48
Washington	39	1908–14
Hillsdale	34	1954–58
Pittsburgh	31	1914–18
Oklahoma	31	1948–50

Undefeated Streaks (College) Since 1900:

Team	Wins	Ties	Years
Washington†	59	4	1907–17
Michigan	55	1	1901–5
Morgan State	48	6	1932–38
California	46	4	1920–25
Tuskegee	42	4	1923–28
Yale	39	3	1904–8
Notre Dame	37	2	1946–50

* Team lost several games during World War II that were disavowed by school officials.

† University of Missouri record indicates 26–3 victory over Washington in 1914, but game is not included in Washington record.

Winning Streaks (Professional), Regular Season:

Team	Wins	Years
Chicago Bears	17	1933–34
Chicago Bears	16	1941–42
Miami Dolphins	16	1971–73
Los Angeles Chargers, San Diego Chargers	15	1960–61

Undefeated Streaks (Professional), Regular Season:

Team	Wins	Ties	Years
Canton Bulldogs	21	3	1922–23
Chicago Bears	23	1	1941–43
Green Bay Packers	21	2	1928–30

Winning Streaks (Professional), Regular and Postseason:

Team	Wins	Years
Chicago Bears	18	1933–34
Chicago Bears	18	1941–42
Miami Dolphins	18	1972–73

then proceeded to take up in 1977 where it left off, losing 12 more to bring its total loss string to 26, many concluded that the Buccaneers were the worst team in professional football. While it is true that the Bucs performed poorly over that period, it is also a fact that the team was more often than not in the game and was seldom completely embarrassed. Moreover, as an expansion team, it could be expected to have a bad record, as did the 1960 Dallas Cowboys (0–11–1) in their first year with the NFL.

For sheer ineptitude, it must be admitted that several other teams in pro football's history rival the Tampa Bay Buccaneers. High on the list are the Chicago Cardinals of 1942–45. On October 25, 1942, the Cards went into their game with the Cleveland Rams with a seasonal record of 3 wins and 2 losses. Three hours later, a 7–3 loss put them at 3–3, and the following week they dropped another game, to the Green Bay Packers, 55–24. For the rest of the 1942 season, the Cardinals continued to lose; they lost all 10 games in 1943, another 10 in 1944 (as the Card-Pitt compressed entry), then 3 more games of the 1945 season before defeating the Chicago Bears, 16–7, on October 14, 1945. They then proceeded to lose the remaining 6 contests, thus establishing a record of 29 straight losses and but a single victory in 36 games.

To illustrate that a high number of consecutive losses is not necessarily the criterion by which to gauge a team's ineffectiveness, consider the 1950 Baltimore Colts. That squad actually won a game, defeating Green Bay, 41–21, in the seventh game of its season. But by nearly every other standard, the 1950 Colts were just terrible.

They began the season with a 38–14 loss to the Washington Redskins, who finished last in the American Conference, then bowed to the Browns, 31–0, and the Cards, 55–13. In the latter game, the Colts made a hero of Bob Shaw, who caught five passes for touchdowns. Other mismatches during the season included that 70–27 loss to Los Angeles, another to the Giants by a score of 55–20, one to the Detroit Lions in which the Colts allowed the immortal Cloyce Box to score four touchdowns, and finally a 51–14 beating at the hands of the New York Yanks. In all, the Colts gave up 462 points, third highest in NFL history, and 2,857 yards rushing, a record that remained on the books until the 1976 Seattle Seahawks wiped it out by a mere 19 yards. But the Seahawks had 14 games in which to yield all that ground while the Colts had only 12; thus a Ford Frickian asterisk seems in order to properly preserve the magnitude of the 1950 Colts' misery.

Some Other Candidates for Worst Pro Team:		
Team	Year	Record
Detroit Lions	1942	0–11
Oakland Raiders	1962	1–13
New York Giants	1966	1–12–1
Chicago Bears	1969	1–13
Buffalo Bills	1971	1–13
Houston Oilers	1973	1–13

It should be added that there have been several other teams that staggered through the season with but a single win or went completely winless, but none (except possibly the 1966 Giants, who yielded 501 points) went into the record book as a loss leader in the manner of the 1950 Baltimore Colts. Even more amazing is the fact that the Colts were quarterbacked by Y. A. Tittle, then in his third year of professional football.

But even Tittle couldn't help. The final loss for the 1950 Baltimore Colts came early in 1951 when the league voted to disband the franchise—symbolically, the thirteenth in the NFL—and distribute the unemployed Colts to other teams. By grabbing Tittle and Hardy Brown, the San Francisco 49ers did well in this impromptu draft, as did the New York Yanks, who took Don Colo, Sisto Averno, and Art Donovan. Some of the other clubs, surveying the 1950 Colt roster and seeing names such as Ken Cooper, Gino Mazzanti, Ed King, Oliver Fletcher, and Achille Maggioli, decided not to bother.

HOCKEY

THE MOST DISASTROUS GAME

Long after he retired from professional hockey, former New York Ranger goalie Ken McAuley looked back on the evening of January 23, 1944, and said: "I ask people when they remind of that night, 'Where would the Detroit Red Wings have been without me? I gave them the confidence to become big stars.'"

Those seeking an excuse could have pointed to the war as one of the major reasons for the Rangers' miserable record of six wins, twenty-two losses, and one tie as they skated onto the Detroit ice that evening. Two of the team's finest skaters, Dutch Hiller and Phil Watson, were not with the Rangers because Canadians were not allowed to leave their country to play with an American team.

Nevertheless, the war had hit everyone hard, and the Rangers were determined to make the best of a bad situation. And at the very outset it seemed that things were going

New York's way. Brian Hextall, one of the few top players still on the Ranger roster, got a breakaway in the opening moments and lined a shot past Red Wing goalie Connie Dion. The red light did not go on, however, and Referee Norm Lamport had no choice but to rule the shot no good, despite violent Ranger argument.

That threat, as it turned out, was the high point of the evening for New York and just the beginning of the fun for 12,293 Detroit partisans. At 2:48, Murray Armstrong flipped the first goal past Ken McAuley, making the score 1–0. The Rangers then got a break as Red Wing defenseman Cully Simon was sent to the penalty box for two minutes, but could not take advantage of the player advantage. After Simon returned, Detroit's Bill Quackenbush poured a ten-footer past McAuley to make it 2–0.

The first period ended with that respectable score, but the Red Wings roared back to score five times in the second period and eight more goals in the third. Every player except Cully Simon and Detroit goalie Connie Dion either tallied a goal or got an assist. Syd Howe scored three goals in the final period to bring his career total to 149, one more than Herbie Lewis amassed for Detroit. Not until Gordie Howe came along later did the record fall.

With the final score Detroit 15, New York 0, rinkside statisticians reckoned that the Rangers had just been handed the worst drubbing in the history of the National Hockey League. They were right.

After the game was over, someone took out the scoring light and gave it to New York goalie McAuley. Bucko McDonald, Ranger defenseman, offered the consoling thought that no goalie had ever set a record such as that just accomplished by McAuley. "They never even had to clear off the other end of the ice," the goalie said later. "It wasn't even marked."

SOME SELECTED HOCKEY LOSING STREAKS

The Philadelphia Quakers (1930–31): With the 1930–31 NHL season six games old, the Philadelphia Quakers had managed to win just one game and tie another. The team was already in last place in the American group, but Philly fans were hopeful the Quakers could begin putting something together.

In fact, they did, but it wasn't exactly what their supporters had in mind. On November 29, 1930, the Quakers skated onto their home ice and dropped a 6–3 game to the New York Rangers, bringing their record to 1–5–1. After that, the pattern continued through the month of December and into January. Not until January 10, 1931, when the Quakers finally defeated the Montreal Maroons, 4–3, in overtime, did

the Philadelphia team win a game. Total number of consecutive losses: fifteen.

The New York Rangers (1943–44): Having lost the infamous 15–0 game on January 23, 1944—which brought their seasonal record to 6–23–1 and a modest losing streak of one game—the New York Rangers' fortunes grew even worse. They had no place to go but up, but didn't head in that direction. Instead, they continued to lose, or occasionally tie, as January gave way to February and then March. On March 18, goalie McAuley allowed the Montreal Canadiens six consecutive scores leading off the third period as the Rangers lost, 11–2. The next evening, it was all over. "The sorriest season in the history of the New York Rangers hockey team came to an end at Madison Square Garden last night," the New York *Times* remarked, "and in concluding their schedule in the National League, the blue-jerseyed skaters performed just as impotently as they had through virtually the entire campaign."

The Canadiens won the contest, 6–1, bringing the Rangers' record for the 1943–44 season to 6–39–5. Twenty-one games had been played without a Ranger victory. Nor was that all. When the 1944–45 season began, the New Yorkers dropped four more games before winning.

The Washington Capitals (1974–75): Thirty-one years after the New York Rangers established new dimensions of futility, the Washington Caps proved that records are made to be broken. After fifty-seven games of the 1974–75 season, the Caps had won five and tied five. Then on February 17, they took on the Kansas City Scouts and not only won but also earned a 3–0 shutout.

That, as it turned out, was the last glimmer of light before complete darkness enveloped Capital fortunes. The next night, a 6–1 loss to Los Angeles was the beginning of a dismal slide that carried the Caps past several NHL losing records. First, they surpassed the record of having lost sixty games in a single season, which had been set by the New York Islanders in the 1972–73 campaign. This was accomplished on March 20, 1975, via a 5–1 loss to the Minnesota North Stars.

Having dropped sixty-one games, the Caps had also extended their consecutive-defeat streak to fourteen, just a game behind that established in 1930–31 by the Philadelphia Quakers.

The next day, an 8–2 beating at the hands of the Boston Bruins brought the Caps even with the old Quakers. It also brought about the resignation of Coach George "Red" Sullivan, who said he was doing so for reasons of health.

General Manager Milt Schmidt took over

the club, but it didn't help. On March 23, the Caps extended their loss streak to sixteen and their overall mark to 6–63–5. An insurance loss to Los Angeles was added before the team finally broke through to defeat California 5–3. That ended the defeat streak at seventeen, but did not signal the end of Washington's losing ways. Before the season was over, the Caps had dropped sixty-seven of eighty games, easily an NHL record that could stand for some time.

The Kansas City Scouts (1975–76): Although not nearly as futile a team as the Washington Capitals the year previously, the Kansas City Scouts of 1975–76 demonstrated that it was possible to go even longer without winning a game. Beginning on February 13, 1976, when they were last in the Smythe Division with a mark of 12–35–6, the Scouts started out modestly enough by tying the New York Islanders, 2–2. Then the Scouts played through March and into April, logging twenty-one losses and six ties before managing a win. The streak of twenty-seven winless games was a new NHL record.

AND FINALLY, THE LONGEST LOSING—AND WINNING—STREAK IN MODERN SPECTATOR SPORTS:

Which is the America's Cup yacht race, which began in 1851, the schooner *America* winning a sixty-mile race around the Isle of Wight as Queen Victoria, then a young woman in her thirties, watched.

Since that day, British, Canadian, and Australian sailors have tried more than a score of times to recapture the cup, an unattractive baroque silver pitcher that is worth only about $500. The most avid Briton was Sir Thomas Lipton, a tea merchant, who spent approximately $1 million on each of five challenges made between 1899 and 1930 with his five *Shamrocks*. In the end, Lipton failed, but Americans felt such sympathy for his plight

On the Other Hand:
- *The fewest losses during a season were suffered by the 1972–73 Montreal Canadiens, who dropped only 10 of 78 games.*
- *The longest winning streak in NHL history is 14 games, established from December 3, 1929, to January 9, 1930, by the Boston Bruins.*
- *The longest undefeated streak, set during the 1940–41 season when the Boston Bruins went 23 games without a setback was finally equalled by the Philadelphia Flyers during the 1975–76 season and then surpassed by the 1977–78 Montreal Canadiens, who went 28 games without a loss.*

and admiration for his determination that Will Rogers was able to raise $16,000 for a solid gold consolation cup.

During the series, perhaps the closest race was on October 13, 1893, when the British yacht *Valkyrie II*, after rounding the outer mark nearly two minutes ahead of America's *Vigilant*, had its spinnaker ripped into shreds by a reefing breeze that turned into a gale. The *Vigilant* was able to win by forty seconds.

The 1970 series was highlighted by the Australian yacht *Gretel II*'s coming from behind to win by three boat-lengths in the fourth race, but America's *Intrepid* finally won the series, 4–1, after the deciding race had been postponed because of heavy fog.

Thus the longest streak continues after more than a century and a quarter. Whether it is a succession of defeats or victories, of course, depends on which side of the ocean one happens to live.

CHAPTER 39—A CENTURY OF UPSETS

Pulling for the underdog is an old American tradition—unless the underdog happens to be one's immediate foe on the field of sport or battle. Thus the upset has become an element without which spectator sports could hardly survive. Even the vague threat of the unexpected happening—"on any given Sunday any team, etc."—has been enough to keep the National Football League in excellent shape over the decades.

In fact, the upset is an upset because it usually does not happen. In the vast majority of sports confrontations, the odds-on favorite wins, and when he or she does not, it is often because the supposedly weaker opposition has produced an intangible element that some call "will," others "being fired up."

Because we all enjoy seeing the big kid on the block get knocked off by a smaller opponent, most sports fans have a special place in their hearts for a certain game or contest that was won by their favorite despite overwhelming odds. In memory of the little guys, then, there follows a list of selected upsets from the past century of American spectator sports.

1870—After winning 101 games without a defeat, the Cincinnati Red Stockings, baseball's first professional team, lose in eleven innings to the Brooklyn Atlantics, 8–7. Highlight of the game is Brooklyn fan tackling Cincy player while game is in progress.

1882—The great pugilist John L. Sullivan, who boasts that no man can stay in the ring with him for three three-minute rounds, is "defeated" by Tug Wilson, who manages to be on his feet at the finish. Wilson's strategy is simple: As soon as Sullivan touches him he falls to the floor and takes a nine count.

1892—James J. Corbett, 1–4 underdog, knocks out John L. Sullivan in the twenty-first round on September 7 to become the second world heavyweight champion.

1894—After finishing eighth in the National League in 1893, the Baltimore Orioles create baseball excitement by romping to 1894 pennant, defeating Monte Ward's New York Giants by three games.

1898—Although no longer champion, Jim Corbett is favored to defeat Tom Sharkey and challenge Bob Fitzsimmons for heavyweight crown. But Sharkey wins bout with Corbett via a foul.

1903—In the first World Series of the twentieth century, Pittsburgh of the established National League romps in the opening game, defeating Boston of the upstart American League, 7–3. But when it is all over, Boston wins the fall classic, five games to three.

1910—In seventh World Series, American League Philadelphia Athletics are given little chance against Tinker–Evers–Chance Chicago Cubs, winners of series in 1907 and 1908. The A's, however, take the first three games and coast to Series victory in five.

1913—Looking about for opponent to fill open spot on its schedule, West Point football team selects small midwestern college called Notre Dame. The Irish spot Cadets 13–7 lead, then go on to win by score of 35–13, thanks to Gus Dorais–Knute Rockne passing combination.

1913—Francis Ouimet becomes the first native American to win the U. S. Open golf championship by defeating British aces Harry Vardon and Ted Ray at the Country Club, Brookline, Massachusetts.

1914—Many baseball fans are impressed by the amazing pennant drive put on by the Boston Braves, but most experts put their money on the American League Athletics. Paced by slugging catcher Hank Gowdy, the Braves sweep the A's in four games.

1919—Young Jack Dempsey is not given much chance against giant heavyweight champion Jess Willard, who is considered invincible since defeating Jack Johnson in 1915. Dempsey proves he's the better man by destroying Willard in three rounds.

1919—The Chicago White Sox are heavily favored in the World Series but for some reason the Cincinnati Reds of the National League have little trouble winning, five games to three. Many wonder why, in loud voices, but the fixing scandal does not become public until 1920.

1919—The great two-year-old thoroughbred, Man o' War, is established as an 11–20 favorite to win the Sanford Stakes of August 13 at Saratoga, but an aptly named horse, Upset, manages to beat "Big Red" by a nose and give him his only career defeat.

1921—Sporting a twenty-five-game streak during which its football team has gone undefeated, Harvard University is not supposed to have a great deal of trouble with Centre College of Danville, Kentucky. Led by quarterback A. N. "Bo" McMillan, however, Centre scores a stunning 6–0 victory.

1922—An upset of sorts occurs on January 2, when Pacific Coast Conference champion University of California, undefeated since 1919, plays host to unranked Washington & Jefferson. Coach "Greasy" Neale of W. & J. gains 0–0 tie.

1926—The University of Alabama, first southern team to play in the Rose Bowl, scores twenty points in third period to defeat favored University of Washington squad, 20–19. Johnny Mack Brown scores pair of touchdowns for Alabama and looks forward to career in Hollywood.

1926—Heavyweight champion Jack Dempsey is 11–5 favorite to defend his crown successfully against reciter of Shakespeare named Gene Tunney. But on September 23, Tunney dances and jabs his way to a victory on points.

1926—Notre Dame's football team, nearing end of eight-game undefeated season, is not supposed to have much trouble with Carnegie Tech, losers to Washington & Jefferson and New York. But the engineers not only beat Notre Dame, they also shut them out, 19–0.

1929—As a surprise move in World Series opener against the Chicago Cubs, manager Connie Mack of the Philadelphia A's starts pitcher Howard Ehmke, thirty-five, whose 7–2 record for year cannot match those of Lefty Grove (20–6), Rube Walberg (18–11), or George Earnshaw (24–8). Ehmke responds to press amazement by striking out thirteen Cubs for new Series record and A's go on to defeat Chicago, four games to one.

1930—Jim Dandy, relatively obscure thoroughbred, defeats Triple Crown winner Gallant Fox.

1931—St. Louis Cardinals "Gashouse Gang" is not regarded in same league as Connie Mack's 1931 Athletics, going for third consecutive World Series win. But the Cards battle every inch of the way to win in seven games.

1931—Trailing mighty Notre Dame, 14–7, the Trojans of USC rally for a touchdown, then kick the field goal that enables them to take 16–14 victory back to California.

1932—At Olympic Games held in Los Angeles, Japan's swim team amazes the experts by taking many important contests, thus destroying the myth that the Japanese are not good swimmers.

1934—Lou Little's Columbia Lions upset the dope by scoring 7–0 victory over powerful Stanford in Rose Bowl classic.

1935—Jim Braddock is established as a 1–10 underdog for the heavyweight championship bout with Max Baer, who floored Primo Carnera eleven times the year before. But Braddock the journeyman fighter has his finest night, winning the match and the championship via a fifteen-round decision.

1936—Winner of twenty-seven straight bouts, twenty-three of them by knockout, young Joe Louis is regarded as heir apparent to Jim Braddock's heavyweight title when he steps into the ring on June 19 to battle Max Schmeling, former champ looked upon as washed up. But Schmeling punishes and surprises Louis, then finishes him with a twelfth-round knockout.

1938—Chicago Cubs stage great comeback to win National League pennant on Gabby Hartnett's controversial "homer in the gloamin'" that seals Pittsburgh Pirates' fate. Cubs thus earn the right to be destroyed in a four-game World Series by the New York Yankees.

1938—During the regular National Hockey League season the Chicago Black Hawks win only fourteen games while losing twenty-nine and tying nine. But they finish in third place because the other teams are even worse, thus qualifying for the playoffs. In postseason battle for Stanley Cup, however, Black Hawks come to life, eliminating Toronto Maple Leafs to win it all.

1939—Duke University is considered too powerful for USC in Rose Bowl matchup, but Trojans hold Blue Devils to a fourth-quarter field goal to take narrow 7–3 victory.

1940—Detroit Tigers, who finish fifth in 1939, suddenly get the spirit to defeat Cleveland for American League pennant by one-game margin.

1940—Unranked Iowa stuns undefeated Notre Dame with 7–0 gridiron victory.

1940—On October 4, welterweight Fritzie Zivic is considered no match for dynamic and classy Henry Armstrong, but Zivic manages to eke out a fifteen-round decision to win title.

1940—Unimpressive Dartmouth shows unexpected determination as they hold unbeaten Cornell scoreless while kicking field goal. Cornell pushes across touchdown on last play of game for apparent 7–3 victory, but subsequent investigation shows the score came on a "fifth down." Dartmouth is awarded the game.

1941—Billy Conn is regarded as just another "Bum of the Month" for heavyweight champion Joe Louis, but he gives Louis a lesson in fancy boxing for twelve rounds, then gets careless in thirteenth and is knocked out.

1942—Boston College's football team wins eight games during the season, outscoring opposition, 249–19, before they meet undistinguished Holy Cross Crusaders. Boston College is rated 4–1 favorite, but Holy Cross embarrasses them, 55–12.

1942—St. Louis Cardinals not only furnish competition for mighty New York Yankees in World Series, they also win in five games, completely upsetting the odds.

1943—Despite World War II, Notre Dame is still a power on the gridiron, and is a top-heavy favorite to defeat the Great Lakes Naval Training Station team. But the group of all-stars culled from various colleges holds the Irish nearly even, then Steve Lach throws forty-six-yard pass to Paul Anderson in final twenty-five seconds for 19–14 win.

1944—Disruption caused by war allows St. Louis Browns, sixth in American League in 1943, to rise to the top of the heap in 1944, thus bringing about first all-St. Louis World Series.

1944—The University of Utah basketball team, defeated in the opening round of the National Invitation Tournament at Madison Square Garden, is asked to replace Arkansas in the regional finals of the NCAA competition. The NIT losers respond by defeating Dartmouth, 42–40, to win the tournament, then edge NIT winner St. John's in a Red Cross benefit game.

1945—Batting in the lead-off spot against the New York Yankees, one-armed outfielder Pete Gray of St. Louis gets four hits, drives in two runs, scores twice, and handles nine chances in a doubleheader won by the Browns.

1946—Slugging Boston Red Sox are highly favored in World Series but the inspired St. Louis Cardinals, led by Red Schoendienst and Harry Brecheen, win it all after being behind, three games to two.

1946—In season immediately following World War II supremacy, West Point football team is still powerful and working on undefeated streak. But Navy nearly pushes the Cadets off the gridiron in their annual meeting. With score Army 21, Navy 18, the Middies are on the Army three-yard line as time runs out.

1948—Navy again rises to the occasion to hold strong Army football team to 21–21 tie.

1949—Surprisingly, the New York Yankees are not given much chance against the Brooklyn Dodgers in the 1949 World Series, but the Yankees roll to a five-game sweep.

1950—Notre Dame football team is working on a thirty-nine-game undefeated streak when unheralded Purdue stuns the Irish and the nation with a 28–14 victory.

1950—Philadelphia Phillies are not supposed to give Cardinals and Dodgers much competition for National League pennant, but the "Whiz Kids" hang on to win the pennant on the last day of the season.

1950—United States soccer team stuns the world by defeating England in qualifying round of World Cup competition with narrow 1–0 victory.

1950—Navy football squad ends Army's three-year undefeated streak of twenty-eight games by scoring 14–2 victory.

1951—Middleweight champion Sugar Ray Robinson is regarded as nearly invincible until British challenger Randy Turpin takes crown via fifteen-round decision in London.

1951—Joe Walcott, a 1–6 underdog in heavyweight championship fight against Ezzard Charles, proves he still has it by becoming the oldest—thirty-seven—heavyweight challenger to win the title.

1953—In seventy-ninth running of Kentucky Derby, Native Dancer is compared to Man o' War and Whirlaway because of his eleven straight victories leading up to the event. The race is won, however, by a 25–1 long shot named Dark Star.

1954—After winning an American League record of 111 games, the Cleveland Indians are heavily favored to defeat the New York Giants in the World Series. Instead, they are embarrassed as the Giants, led by pinch-hitting Dusty Rhodes, take four games in a row.

1955—Journeyman golfer Jack Fleck is not given much chance in U. S. Open, which seems in the pocket of Ben Hogan, first man who will win the event five times. Fleck manages to tie Hogan during regulation play, then wins playoff by three strokes.

1955—After losing all six World Series in which Brooklyn has participated—five since 1941—the 1955 edition of the Dodgers finally comes through with seven-game win over Yankees, thus destroying the myth of Brooklyn's total vincibility.

1958—In opening Davis Cup singles match, oddsmakers install America's Alex Olmedo as a 1–10 underdog against Australia's Mal Anderson. Olmedo startles the tennis world by winning 8–6, 2–6, 9–7, 8–6 victory that leads to United States Davis Cup win.

1959—Sweden's Ingemar Johansson steps into ring as 1–4 underdog in heavyweight title contest against Floyd Patterson on June 26, then proceeds to show that Patterson has a glass jaw by winning third-round KO.

1960—Upsetting the odds that name Canada and the Soviet Union as the top ice hockey teams in the 1960 Winter Olympic Games at Squaw Valley, California, the United

States team defeats the Canadians, 2–1, and the Russians, 3–2, to win the gold medal.

1961—In inaugural game in National Football League, the expansion Minnesota Vikings, led by rookie quarterback Fran Tarkenton, surprise the veteran Chicago Bears with 37–13 victory.

1962—On May 18, harness racer Thor Hanover is given no better than a 1–70 chance to win the Messenger Stakes. Even worse, the horse draws No. 10 position, on the second tier. But Thor Hanover catches favorite Adora's Dream in the stretch and wins by half a length, paying $144 for a $2.00 ticket.

1963—New York Yankees are 8–5 favorites to defeat Los Angeles Dodgers in World Series, and odds that Yankees will fall in four-game sweep are astronomical. Led by fireballing Sandy Koufax, however, the Dodgers win all four games, their superior pitching limiting Yanks to a grand total of four runs.

1963—College All-Stars have not won a game since 1958 when they take on the NFL champion Green Bay Packers on August 2. But quarterback Ron Vanderkelen, who later has undistinguished career as a pro, throws pass to Pat Richter that gives All-Stars 20–17 win. It is to be the last All-Star victory in the series.

1964—Sonny Liston is looked upon as unbeatable when he walks into ring as 7–1 favorite against young Cassius Clay on February 25. Surviving temporary blurred vision after the fourth round, Clay batters Liston so that he cannot answer the bell for the seventh round.

1965—Baltimore Colts lose both quarterbacks near end of season, leaving team with only Tom Matte, a running back who played quarterback at college. In NFL Western Division playoff against powerful Green Bay Packers, Matte has plays taped to his wrist so that he can remember them and performs so well he captures the imagination of the nation as the "instant quarterback." Only questionable field-goal call gives Green Bay narrow 13–10 overtime win. In the Playoff Bowl against Dallas, Matte leads Colts to 35–3 victory. Tape used by Matte is preserved in Pro Football Hall of Fame at Canton, Ohio.

1966—American League Orioles are ticketed to fall before the one-two pitching punch of Dodgers' Don Drysdale and Sandy Koufax, but it is the Oriole staff that shines in four-game World Series sweep during which Los Angeles is held scoreless for thirty-three consecutive innings.

1967—"The impossible dream" comes true as Boston Red Sox, who finished ninth in American League in 1966 and are rated 1–100 underdogs to win the pennant, edge Detroit by a single game.

1969—In one of greatest turnabouts in modern sports history, the New York Jets of the National Football League beat the older league and the Baltimore Colts in Super Bowl III, 16–7.

1969—"The Miracle Mets" of National League seem to confirm the odds against them when they drop the first World Series game to the American League Orioles. The Mets then come to life and take the next four games.

1973—George Foreman is 1–3 underdog in world heavyweight championship bout against Joe Frazier, but he knocks out champ in second round to take title.

1977—Portland Trail Blazers upset the dope during the 1976–77 National Basketball Association season by roaring through playoffs to become new pro champion.

1978—On February 15, heavyweight challenger Leon Spinks, such an underdog that few professional gamblers take bets on the fight, wins a split 15-round decision over Muhammad Ali to become new champion at age of 24.

1951

Winners: Baseball: After winning dramatic seasonal playoff against the Brooklyn Dodgers, the New York Giants succumb meekly in World Series to the New York Yankees, 4 games to 2. . . . *Kentucky Derby:* Count Turf. *Preakness:* Bold. *Belmont Stakes:* Counterpoint . . . *Indy 500:* Lee Wallard . . . *Boxing:* Jersey Joe Walcott knocks out Ezzard Charles in seventh round to become new heavyweight champ. The middleweight title, meanwhile, changes gloved hands three times during year: In February, Ray Robinson defeats Jake LaMotta on a 13-round KO; in July, Robinson is beaten by Randy Turpin in London; two months later, Robinson knocks out Turpin in the tenth round to regain the championship. . . . Having vacated the welterweight title, Robinson turns the division over to Johnny Bratton, who decisions Charlie Fusari on March 14. Kid Gavilan then wins the crown on May 18. . . . In the lightweight division, Jimmy Carter ends Ike Williams' 4-year reign by knocking him out in 14 rounds. . . . *Golf: USGA Men's Open:* Ben Hogan. *PGA:* Sam Snead. *Masters:* Ben Hogan. *USGA Women's Open:* Betsy Rawls . . . *Hockey:* Winner of 1950–51 Stanley Cup is Toronto Maple Leaf team, their fourth in 5 years. . . . *Football: Cotton Bowl:* Tennessee 20, Texas 14. *Orange Bowl:* Clemson 15, Miami 14. *Rose Bowl:* Michigan 14, California 6. *Sugar Bowl:* Kentucky 13, Oklahoma 7 . . . *National Football League:* Los Angeles Rams 24, Cleveland Browns 17 . . . *Basketball:* 1950–51 *NCAA:* Kentucky 68, Kansas State 58. 1950–51 *NIT:* Brigham Young 62, Dayton 43 . . . *National Basketball Association:* 1950–51 winner: Rochester, 4 games to 3 over New York.

Other Happenings: On September 14, outfielder Bob Nieman of the St. Louis Browns hits home runs in his first two at-bats in the American League. The Browns still manage to lose to the Boston Red Sox, 9–6. . . . The first color television game is broadcast from Ebbets Field, Brooklyn, on August 11. The Dodgers and Braves split a doubleheader. . . . The first coast-to-coast telecast of a sports event features a Chicago boxing match between Carl "Bobo" Olson and Dave Sands. Sands wins a 10-round deci-

sion. . . . The first sports event to be broadcast in color occurs on July 14 at Oceanport, New Jersey. It is the $15,000 Molly Pitcher Handicap, won by Marta, Conn McCreary up. . . . In professional football, the Chicago Bears are penalized 1,107 yards during the season (92 yards per game average) and finish fourth in the National Conference. . . . In one game against the New York Yanks, the champion Los Angeles Rams gain 735 yards (181 rushing, 554 passing). . . . In July, Bob Feller hurls the third no-hitter of his career, but Allie Reynolds pitches two, on July 12 and September 28. . . . In the National League, Cliff Chambers of the Pirates no-hits the Braves, 3–0. . . . In December, Army's football team is battered by Navy, 42–7, the worst defeat in the history of the series. . . . Joe DiMaggio retires as a player. . . . On July 14, Citation becomes the first racehorse to win $1,000,000 when he takes Hollywood Gold Cup, bringing his earnings to $1,085,760. . . . On August 22, the Harlem Globetrotters perform before a nonpaying crowd of 75,052 at Berlin, Germany, the largest number to attend a basketball game. . . . Eddie Gaedel, midget, makes a brief appearance as a pinch-hitter for the St. Louis Browns.

1952

Winners: Baseball: Yankees and Dodgers renew their rivalry in the World Series, Yanks winning, 4 games to 3. . . . *Kentucky Derby:* Hill Gail. *Preakness:* Blue Man. *Belmont Stakes:* One Count . . . *Indy 500:* Troy Ruttman . . . *Boxing:* On September 23, Rocky Marciano knocks out Jersey Joe Walcott to become heavyweight champion. Communist newspapers charge that cheers for Marciano are inspired by American racial bias. But Americans also cheer Archie Moore as he defeats Joey Maxim to win the light-heavyweight crown. Ray Robinson rules the middleweight division, but the lightweight crown is taken from Jimmy Carter by Lauro Salas in May. Carter wins it back five months later. Jimmy Carruthers knocks out Vic Toweel in the first round of their bantamweight title fight, and Yoshio Shirai becomes the first Oriental to rule a boxing division when he beats Dado Marino for the flyweight title. (Marino, 36, at the same time becomes the first certified grandfather to lose a championship.) . . . *Golf: USGA Men's Open:* Julius Boros. *PGA:* Jim Turnesa. *Masters:* Sam Snead. *USGA Women's Open:* Louise Suggs . . . *Hockey:* 1951–52 Stanley Cup winner: Detroit Red Wings . . . *Football: Cotton Bowl:* Kentucky 20, Texas Christian 7. *Orange Bowl:* Georgia Tech 17, Baylor 14. *Rose Bowl:* Illinois 40, Stanford 7. *Sugar Bowl:* Maryland 28, Tennessee 13 . . . *National Football League:* Detroit 17, Cleveland Browns 7 . . . *Basketball:* 1951–52 *NCAA:* Kansas 80, St. John's 63. 1951–52 *NIT:* LaSalle 75, Dayton 64 . . . *National Basketball Association:* 1951–52 championship to Minneapolis, which defeats New York, 4 games to 3.

Other Happenings: On May 21, Brooklyn Dodgers score 15 runs in first inning to beat Reds, 19–1. . . . Robert Eugene Bryan, 22-year-old Stanford football player and track man, is found dead in a campus fraternity house. . . . Jockey Eddie Arcaro wins his three thousandth horse race on June 24, riding Ascent across the finish line in the third race at Arlington Park, Chicago. . . . On June 25, Sugar Ray Robinson attempts to win the light-heavyweight crown by taking on Joey Maxim at Yankee Stadium. But it is so unbearably hot—the mercury reaches 104 degrees—that Robinson cannot come out for the fourteenth round. Even Referee Ruby Goldstein has to be replaced by Ray Miller at the beginning of the eleventh round. Technically, it is a knockout, the first of Robinson's long career. . . . Football's Heisman Trophy winner is halfback Dick Kazmaier of Princeton, who declines to play professional ball. . . . Ted Williams of the Boston Red Sox returns to war in January. . . . Johnny Vander Meer, 37 years old and cast out by the major leagues, tosses a no-hitter for Tulsa against Beaumont in the Texas League. . . . Meanwhile, back in the majors, Walt Dropo of the Red Sox makes 12 consecutive hits and Warren Spahn of the Boston Braves strikes out 18 batters in a 15-inning game. Spahn's work is overshadowed by Virgil Trucks of the Detroit Tigers, who throws no-hitters on May 15 and August 25. Also, Carl Erskine of the Dodgers no-hits the Cubs on June 19. . . . In boxing, Joe Louis again retires, and this time he means it. . . . So does billiard champion Willie Hoppe, after winning 51 world 3-cushion titles. . . . On January 12, ice-skating champion Terry Browne sets a world jumping record by clearing 15 barrels (28 feet, 3 inches) at Grossinger, New York. . . . Don Grate, outfielder with Chat-

tanooga of the Southern Association, also breaks distance record by throwing ball 434 feet, 1 inch, on September 7. . . . Hockey star Maurice Richard tallies his 325th goal, an NHL mark, and the puck is sent to Queen Elizabeth.

1953

Winners: Baseball: Once again the New York Yankees take on the Brooklyn Dodgers in the World Series, and once again the Yankees win, this time 4 games to 2. . . . *Kentucky Derby:* Dark Star. *Preakness:* Native Dancer. *Belmont Stakes:* Native Dancer . . . *Indy 500:* Bill Vukovich . . . *Boxing:* On June 19, Carl "Bobo" Olson wins a 15-round decision over Paddy Young to win the middleweight championship temporarily vacated by Sugar Ray Robinson. . . . *Golf: USGA Men's Open:* Ben Hogan. *PGA:* Walter Burkemo. *Masters:* Ben Hogan . . . *USGA Women's Open:* Betsy Rawls . . . *Hockey:* Winner of 1952–53 Stanley Cup: Montreal Canadiens . . . *Football: Cotton Bowl:* Texas 16, Tennessee 0. *Orange Bowl:* Alabama 61, Syracuse 6. *Rose Bowl:* USC 7, Wisconsin 0. *Sugar Bowl:* Georgia Tech 24, Mississippi 7 . . . *National Football League:* Detroit Lions make it two in a row by defeating Cleveland Browns in title game, 17–16. . . . *Basketball:* 1952–53 *NCAA:* Indiana 69, Kansas 68. 1952–53 *NIT:* Seton Hall 58, St. John's 46 . . . *National Basketball Association:* 1952–53 winner: Minneapolis, 4 games, New York, 1.

Other Happenings: On May 6, Bobo Holloman pitches a no-hitter in his first major-league start as St. Louis Browns win over Philadelphia A's, 6–0. Holloman wins only 2 more games, loses 7 in 1953, his only year in big leagues. . . . On April 13, for the first time in 50 years, there is a new city in U.S. baseball—Milwaukee. The new team taking over the Boston Braves franchise in the National League loses its first game, at Cincinnati, 2–0. . . . Four days later, Mickey Mantle, new strong boy of the bully Yankees, hits a 565-foot home run, clearing the bleachers at Griffith Stadium in New York win over Senators. . . . On June 18 the Boston Red Sox score 17 runs in the seventh inning as they beat Detroit, 23–3. Gene Stephens has three hits in the inning. . . . Tenley Albright, a 17-year-old girl from Newton Center, Massachusetts, wins world figure-skating championship for the United States. . . . Jockey Willie Shoemaker ends the year by riding his 485th winner, Mercenary, at Santa Anita, thus becoming the first **jockey to win** more than 400 races in a single year. . . . The year also ends for Satchel Paige, age 47, who is put on waivers by St. Louis Browns and is not claimed. . . . During early days of October, Massachusetts State Prison convicts threaten to riot unless they are allowed to watch World Series on television. Wish is granted. . . . Baltimore Colts, by selling 15,000 season tickets, are allowed to return to National Football League after two-year absence. . . . Big Bill Tilden, tennis giant of the 1920s, dies in June.

1954

Winners: Baseball: After rolling up a record 111 victories in regular season play, the Cleveland Indians fall to the New York Giants in the World Series, 4 games to 0. . . . *Kentucky Derby:* Determine. *Preakness:* Hasty Road. *Belmont Stakes:* High Gun . . . *Indy 500:* Bill Vukovich . . . *Boxing:* Rocky Marciano continues as heavyweight champion, as does Archie Moore in the light-heavyweight division, but Kid Gavilan loses his welterweight crown on October 20 to Johnny Saxton. A new lightweight champ is crowned as Paddy DeMarco defeats Jimmy Carter, but the reign lasts only eight months, Carter knocking out DeMarco in the fifteenth round on November 17. Robert Cohen becomes bantamweight champ via a 15-round decision over Chamrern Songkitrat on September 19, and flyweight titleholder Yoshio Shirai is decisioned by Pasqual Perez in Tokyo. . . . *Golf: USGA Men's Open:* Ed Furgol. *PGA:* Chick Harbert. *Masters:* Sam Snead . . . *USGA Women's Open:* Babe Zaharias . . . *Hockey:* Winner of 1953–54 Stanley Cup: Detroit Red Wings. . . . *Football: Cotton Bowl:* Rice 28, Alabama 6. *Orange Bowl:* Oklahoma 7, Maryland 0. *Rose Bowl:* Michigan State 28, UCLA 20. *Sugar Bowl:* Georgia Tech 42, West Virginia 19 . . . *National Football League:* Detroit and Cleveland meet for third consecutive time, the Browns winning by a score of 56–10. . . . *Basketball:* 1953–54 *NCAA:* LaSalle 92, Bradley 76. 1953–54 *NIT:* Holy Cross 71, Duquesne 62 . . . *National Basketball Association:* 1953–54 season champion: Minneapolis, 4 games to 3 over Syracuse.
Other Happenings: On June 12, Jim Wilson of Milwaukee pitches 2–0 no-hitter over Phillies. . . . Stan Musial of Cardinals hits 5 home runs in a doubleheader and Braves' Joe Adcock hits four homers and a double in a 9-inning game. . . . On April 13, Henry Aaron makes his debut in left field and goes

0–5 at the plate in 9–8 loss to Cincinnati. . . . Frank Selvy, crack Furman basketballer, scores 100 points in a game against Newberry. . . . Ted Williams, of the Boston Red Sox, returns from the Korean War and promptly breaks his collarbone in his first workout with the club. . . . Owner Bob Carpenter of the Philadelphia Phillies is discovered to have hired private detectives to shadow his players. . . . Cleveland's baseball team draws 84,587 to a regular-season game, and Los Angeles' football team attracts 78,945 to see a 24–24 tie with San Francisco. . . . Karl Spooner, a sensational rookie pitcher for the Brooklyn Dodgers, strikes out 15 men in his first game, 27 in his first two contests, then fades away, washed up in the big leagues at 24. . . . In basketball, Baltimore University defeats Catholic University, 146–121, a new collegiate high-score mark. . . . Satchel Paige joins the Harlem Globetrotters and George Mikan, considered by many the best basketball player of the twentieth century, retires. . . . Pat McCormick, America's premier lady bullfighter, is gored in early September, but returns to fight another day. . . . Boxer Johnny Greco is killed in an automobile accident. . . . Through the efforts of Danny Biasone, owner of the Syracuse Nets, the National Basketball Association adopts the 24-second rule, which revolutionizes the game. . . . The United States breaks Australian domination of Davis Cup by winning, 3–2, at Sydney. . . . Baltimore baseball fans, looking forward to first major-league team since 1901—in the dead-ball era—eagerly anticipate which of the modern Orioles will beat Joe Kelley's high of 10 home runs, a Baltimore mark made in 1895. But to everyone's embarrassment, the best any 1954 Oriole can do is hit 8, by Vern Stephens. . . . On August 16, *Sports Illustrated* publishes its first issue. . . . By gaining 1,000 yards during 1954 season, Joe the Jet Perry becomes first runner in NFL to put back-to-back 1,000-yard seasons together. . . . Joe DiMaggio marries Marilyn Monroe on January 14.

1955

Winners: Baseball: "Next year" comes to Brooklyn as the Dodgers finally beat the Yankees, 4 games to 3, in the World Series. . . . *Kentucky Derby:* Swaps. *Preakness:* Nashua. *Belmont Stakes:* Nashua . . . *Indy 500:* Bob Sweikert . . . *Boxing:* Sugar Ray Robinson, returning to his natural fighting weight, knocks out Carl "Bobo" Olson in the second round to take middleweight title for third time. In welterweight division, Tony DeMarco knocks out Johnny Saxton in the fourteenth round but he holds the crown barely two months before being KO'd himself in the twelfth round by Carmen Basilio. Lightweight champ Jimmy Carter is also dethroned in June by Wallace "Bud" Smith. . . . *Golf: USGA Men's Open:* Jack Fleck. *PGA:* Doug Ford. *Masters:* Cary Middlecoff . . . *USGA Women's Open:* Fay Crocker . . . *Hockey:* 1954–55 Stanley Cup winner: Detroit Red Wings. . . . *Football: Cotton Bowl:* Georgia Tech 14, Arkansas 6. *Orange Bowl:* Duke 34, Nebraska 7. *Rose Bowl:* Ohio State 20, USC 7 . . . *Sugar Bowl:* Navy 21, Mississippi 0 . . . *National Football League:* Cleveland, participating in its sixth consecutive title game since joining the NFL, beats Los Angeles, 38–14. . . . *Basketball:* 1954–55 *NCAA:* San Francisco 77, LaSalle 63. *NIT:* Duquesne 70, Dayton 58. . . . *National Basketball Association:* 1954–55 winner Syracuse defeats Fort Wayne, 4 games to 3.

Other Happenings: Sam Jones pitches 4–0 no-hitter as Cubs defeat Pirates on May 12. . . . On June 24, 18-year-old Harmon Killebrew of the Washington Senators hits his first major-league home run, off Billy Hoeft of Detroit, but Senators lose, 18–7. . . . First color telecast of Davis Cup tennis match made by WNBT at West Side Tennis Club, Forest Hills, New York, on August 26. Australia beats the United States, 5–0. . . . Ted Williams "retires," then hits 28 homers. . . . Elston Howard, black catcher for New York Yankees, announces that he stays at all hotels white members of the team use while on the road except at Baltimore. . . . Some officials attribute 10-year low in crime during early October to extreme excitement of World Series. . . . Slump of New York Stock Exchange also credited to World Series involvement. . . . Three umpires are fined for using abusive language in Longhorn League. . . . Furman basketball team scores a record 154 points in January. . . . Boxer Harold Johnson, losing fight in May, attributes his poor performance to "poisoned orange" given him before fight. Police test pieces of rind and find nothing. . . . Boston Red Sox first baseman Harry "The Golden Greek" Agganis dies on June 27 of "massive pulmonary embolism." . . . Football's Cigar Bowl is dropped, but few notice. . . . Bill Vukovich, seeking a third consecutive win in the Indy 500, is killed in a pileup while leading the field in the fifty-seventh lap. . . . On November 12, Jockey Hall of Fame at Pimlico, Maryland, elects its first three members: Earl Sande, Eddie Arcaro, and George Woolf. . . . *Damn Yankees* opens on Broadway on May 5.

1956

Winners: Baseball: It's business as usual in 1956, the New York Yankees again dominating the Brooklyn Dodgers, 4 games to 3. Highlight of the World Series comes in the fifth game, when Don Larsen pitches a perfect game for the Yankees. . . . *Kentucky Derby:* Needles. *Preakness.* Fabius. *Belmont Stakes:* Needles . . . *Indy 500:* Pat Flaherty . . . *Boxing:* Rocky Marciano retires undefeated and Floyd Patterson knocks out Archie Moore in fifth round to become new champion in heavyweight division. Welterweight champion Carmen Basilio succumbs to Johnny Saxton in March decision, then returns in September to knock out Saxton in ninth and regain title. Lightweight Joe Brown dethrones Wallace "Bud" Smith in New Orleans, and in Rome bantamweight champ Robert Cohen is knocked out in the sixth round by Mario D'Agata. . . . *Golf: USGA Men's Open:* Cary Middlecoff. *PGA:* Jack Burke. *Masters:* Jack Burke . . . *USGA Women's Open:* Kathy Cornelius . . . *Hockey:* 1955–56 winner of Stanley Cup: Montreal Canadiens. . . . *Football: Cotton Bowl:* Mississippi 14, Texas Christian 13. *Orange Bowl:* Oklahoma 20, Maryland 6. *Rose Bowl:* Michigan State 17, UCLA 14. *Sugar Bowl:* Georgia Tech 7, Pittsburgh 0 . . . *National Football League:* New York Giants 47, Chicago Bears 7 . . . *Basketball:* 1955–56 *NCAA:* San Francisco 83, Iowa 71. 1955–56 *NIT:* Louisville 93, Dayton 80 . . . *National Basketball Association:* 1955–56 winner: Philadelphia, 4 games to 1 over Fort Wayne.

Other Happenings: Important college football game pits Tennessee against Georgia Tech, both squads with 6–0 records. Tennessee wins by a score of 6–0. . . . John Unitas, rookie quarterback for the Baltimore Colts, catches his own deflected pass and makes 1-yard gain. . . . Dale Long, Pittsburgh Pirate slugger, hits home runs in each of 8 consecutive games. . . . Rookie Frank Robinson of Cincinnati Reds hits 38 home runs. . . . No-hitters are pitched by Carl Erskine and Sal Maglie of the Brooklyn Dodgers. Mel Parnell of the Boston Red Sox performs the trick in the American League. . . . In May, announcement is made that comedians Abbott and Costello's "Who's on first?" baseball routine will be enshrined in Baseball Hall of Fame. . . . Ted Williams, meanwhile, is fined for spitting at fans, but Massachusetts Legislature leaps to Ted's defense by introducing bill that will punish fans for shouting profanity at players. . . . U.S. lady matador Pat McCormick is gored again. . . . Wilson Sporting Goods announces in September that fumble-resistant football has been developed. . . . On

May 19, Nashua becomes top money-winning racehorse by winning Jockey Club Gold Cup, boosting earnings to $1,100,365. . . . Late in July, a certain Wesley Struble paddles 12½ miles across Lake Erie on his back, wearing trunks, a thick coat of grease, and a pair of handcuffs. . . . First runner to cover a mile in less than 4 minutes in the United States is Jim Bailey, who races distance in 3:58.6 at Los Angeles on May 5. . . . At Hawthorne Race Track in Chicago, Jockey Johnny Heckmann has 7 winners in a single day, October 1.

1957

Winners: Baseball: Milwaukee Braves beat out Dodgers and Cardinals for right to meet Yankees in World Series, then defeat Yanks, 4 games to 3. . . . Highlight of Series comes in fourth game when a smudge of shoe polish on ball convinces umpires that Braves' Nippy Jones has been hit by pitch. Milwaukee goes on to rally and win game in 10 innings. . . . *Kentucky Derby:* Iron Liege. *Preakness:* Bold Ruler. *Belmont Stakes:* Gallant Man . . . *Indy 500:* Sam Hanks . . . *Boxing:* Middleweight division is particularly active as Gene Fullmer wins decision from champion Ray Robinson in January, then loses title back to Robinson in May. In September Carmen Basilio defeats Robinson on 15-round decision. After holding the featherweight title for seven years, Sandy Saddler steps aside and Hogan "Kid" Bassey knocks out Cherif Hamia to become new champ. Robert Cohen's 10-month reign as bantamweight titleholder comes to an end when Alphonse Halimi celebrates April in Paris with a 6-round KO. . . . *Golf: USGA Men's Open:* Dick Mayer. *PGA:* Lionel Hebert. *Masters:* Doug Ford . . . *USGA Women's Open:* Betsy Rawls . . . *Hockey:* Montreal Canadiens win their second consecutive championship of NHL. . . . *Football: Cotton Bowl:* Texas Christian 28, Syracuse 27. *Orange Bowl:* Colorado 27, Clemson 20. *Rose Bowl:* Iowa 35, Oregon State 19. *Sugar Bowl:* Baylor 13, Tennessee 7 . . . *National Football League:* Detroit Lions maul Cleveland Browns, 59–14. . . . *Basketball:* 1956–57 *NCAA:* North Carolina 54, Kansas 53. 1956–57 *NIT:* Bradley 84, Memphis State 83 . . . *National Basketball Association:* 1956–57 winner: Boston, 4 games to 3 over St. Louis.

Other Happenings: Bob Keegan of Chicago White Sox pitches only no-hitter in major leagues, a 6–0 defeat of Washington on August 20. . . . On June 21, Von McDaniel, brother of pitcher Lindy McDaniel, hurls 2-hit shutout in his first start, beating the Dodgers, 2–0. But after winning 7 games and losing 5, he leaves the major leagues in 1958 at age 19. . . . Ted Williams and Mickey Mantle, meanwhile, are fined for throwing bats. Another defeat for the "Splendid Splinter" comes when the Massachusetts Legislature, after considerable debate, defeats the bill that would fine fans for swearing at ballplayers. . . . On June 12, strongman Paul Anderson places a steel safe filled with lead on a specially made table and lifts all 6,270 pounds. . . . Spalding announces that ball No. 10 million has been produced for organized baseball. . . . The Women's Christian Temperance Union attacks the sale of alcoholic beverages in ball parks by calling the national game "beer-ball." . . . More than 11,000 signatures are obtained to keep Dodgers from moving to Los Angeles, but National League approval for shift comes on May 28. . . . In June the New York State Athletic Commission gives approval for French boxer G. Ballarin's wearing a mustache. . . . Willie Shoemaker stands up in his irons at sixteenth pole of Kentucky Derby, thinking race is over, possibly costing Gallant Man a victory over Iron Liege. . . . On February 28, jockey Johnny Longden rides the five thousandth winner of his career, at Santa Anita.

1958

Winners: Baseball: New York Yankees avenge their loss in 1957 by beating Milwaukee Braves in World Series, 4 games to 3. The Yankees are the first team since 1925 to win the Series after being down, 3 games to 1. . . . *Kentucky Derby:* Tim Tam. *Preakness:* Tim Tam. *Belmont Stakes:* Cavan . . . *Indy 500:* Jimmy Bryan . . . *Boxing:* Sugar Ray Robinson wins middleweight championship for fifth time by defeating Carmen Basilio in 15-round decision. In welterweight division, Virgil Akins becomes the new champion by knocking out Vince Martinez in the fourth round, but he is then dispatched by Don Jordan in December. . . . *Golf: USGA Men's Open:* Tommy Bolt. *PGA:* Dow Finsterwald. *Masters:* Arnold Palmer. *USGA Women's Open:* Mickey Wright . . . *Hockey:* Montreal Canadiens win third consecutive NHL title. . . . *Football: Cotton Bowl:* Navy 20, Rice 7. *Orange Bowl:* Oklahoma 48, Duke 21. *Rose Bowl:* Ohio State 10, Oregon 7. *Sugar Bowl:* Mississippi 39, Texas 7. . . . *National Football League:* Baltimore 23, New York Giants 17—first overtime title game in NFL history. . . . *Basketball:* 1957–58 *NCAA:* Kentucky 84, Seattle 72. 1957–58 *NIT:* Xavier (Ohio) 78, Dayton

74 . . . *National Basketball Association:* 1957–58 championship playoff: St. Louis defeats Boston, 4 games to 2.

Other Happenings: Jim Brown of Syracuse sets a college football rushing record by reeling off 1,527 yards. . . . Baseball moves to California on April 15, when transplanted Giants defeat transplanted Dodgers, 8–0. . . . On July 20, Jim Bunning of the Detroit Tigers throws 3–0 no-hitter at Boston, and on September 2, Baltimore's Hoyt Wilhelm no-hits the New York Yankees, 1–0. . . . Vice President Richard Nixon, meanwhile, urges baseball franchises be awarded to Havana, Mexico City, Caracas, and Canada. . . . Ted Williams spits at fan and hurls bat into stands. . . . Army's football team tries out "lonesome end" formation and Pete Dawkins wins Heisman Trophy. . . . Perennial long-distance runner Clarence De Mar dies. . . . On October 11, Round Table becomes top money-winning horse by winning Hawthorne Gold Cup and boosting earnings to $1,336,364. . . . After hiatus of 21 years, America's Cup competition is held, but result is the same, U.S. entry *Columbia* defeating the British *Sceptre.* . . . United States team wins Davis Cup tennis championship, defeating Australians, 3–2, at Brisbane, ending 3-year Aussie domination. . . . On May 5, San Francisco Giants set record by using 6 pinch-hitters in a single half inning. . . . Vic Power of the Cleveland Indians steals home twice in one game on August 14. . . . Eddie Arcaro rides the four thousandth winner of his career, at Santa Anita on February 20. . . . On January 28, Roy Campanella, star catcher of the Brooklyn Dodgers, is seriously injured in a car accident and his career is destroyed.

1959

Winners: Baseball: For the first time since 1954, the New York Yankees are absent from the World Series as the Los Angeles Dodgers defeat the Chicago White Sox, 4 games to 2. . . . *Kentucky Derby:* Tomy Lee. *Preakness:* Royal Orbit. *Belmont Stakes:* Sword Dancer . . . *Indy 500:* Rodger Ward . . . *Boxing:* One of the prize ring's greatest upsets occurs when 1–4 underdog Ingemar Johansson not only knocks out heavyweight champ Floyd Patterson in third round, but nearly wipes up the ring with him. In the middleweight division, Sugar Ray Robinson retires long enough for Gene Fullmer to knock out Carmen Basilio in 14 rounds and become the new champion. Featherweight Davey Moore becomes the new champion of that division by knocking out Kid

Bassey in the thirteenth round, and Joe Becerra takes over the bantamweight championship by dispatching Alphonse Halimi in the third round. . . . *Golf: USGA Men's Open:* Bill Casper. *PGA:* Bob Rosburg. *Masters:* Art Wall . . . *USGA Women's Open:* Mickey Wright . . . *Hockey:* Montreal Canadiens win fourth consecutive NHL title. . . . *Football: Cotton Bowl:* Air Force 0, Texas Christian 0. *Orange Bowl:* Oklahoma 21, Syracuse 6. *Rose Bowl:* Iowa 38, California 12. *Sugar Bowl:* Louisiana State 7, Clemson 0 . . . *National Football League:* Baltimore Colts 31, New York Giants 16 . . . *Basketball:* 1958–59 *NCAA:* California 71, West Virginia 70. 1958–59 *NIT:* St. John's 76, Bradley 71 . . . *National Basketball Association:* 1958–59 champions: Boston, 4 games to 0 over Minneapolis.

Other Happenings: Big football clash of the season pits Mississippi (6–0) with Jake Gibbs at quarterback against LSU (6–0) with halfback Billy Cannon. LSU ekes out a 7–3 victory. . . . Pro season features pair of quarterback receptions of their own passes—Y. A. Tittle of San Francisco 49ers for gain of 4 yards, Milt Plum of Cleveland Browns for 20. . . . In American League baseball, the New York Yankees are in seventh place after 19 games, their lowest ranking since 1940. Two weeks later, they sink to the basement, but finish the season in third place with record of 79–75. . . . The White Sox pennant is the first since they were the Black Sox in 1919. . . . Pirate hurler Harvey Haddix pitches 12 perfect innings and loses. . . . Oriole catcher Gus Triandos, trying desperately to hang onto Hoyt Wilhelm's knuckler, allows four passed balls in a single game. . . . In August a new rival to the NFL, the American Football League, is formed. . . . Army football Coach Red Blaik resigns in January and Navy football coach Eddie Erdelatz resigns in April. Navy beats Army, 43–12, in November. . . . Sandy Koufax of the Los Angeles Dodgers strikes out 18 men in a 9-inning game, and Rocky Colavito of Cleveland smashes 4 homers in a regulation contest. . . . On March 18, Bill Sharman of the Boston Celtics begins a string of 56 consecutive free throws, which does not end until April 9. He finishes season with 93.2 per cent successful shots from the line.

1960

Winners: Baseball: The New York Yankees return to the World Series cast but the Pittsburgh Pirates are not impressed, winning 4 games to 3. Bill Mazeroski's home run in the final inning of play caps the Series. . . . *Kentucky Derby:* Venetian Way. *Preakness:* Bally Ache. *Belmont Stakes:* Celtic Ash . . . *Indy 500:* Jim Rathmann . . . *Boxing:* Stung by a year of criticism concerning his glass jaw, Floyd Patterson storms back to knock out Ingemar Johansson and regain heavyweight crown—the first to do so. . . . Paul Pender decisions Sugar Ray Robinson to become the new middleweight champion, and Benny "Kid" Paret wins the welterweight title from Don Jordan. Among the flyweights, Kone Kingpetch ends the five-year reign of Pasqual Perez by winning a 15-round decision. . . . *Golf: USGA Men's Open:* Arnold Palmer. *PGA:* Jay Hebert. *Masters:* Arnold Palmer . . . *USGA Women's Open:* Betsy Rawls . . . *Hockey:* Montreal Canadiens are tops in 1959–60 season, win fifth consecutive Stanley Cup. . . . *Football: Cotton Bowl:* Syracuse 23, Texas 14. *Orange Bowl:* Georgia 14, Missouri 0. *Rose Bowl:* Washington 44, Wisconsin 8. *Sugar Bowl:* Mississippi 21, Louisiana State 0 . . . *National Football League:* Philadelphia Eagles 17, Green Bay Packers 13 . . . *American Football League:* Houston Oilers 24, Los Angeles Chargers 16 . . . *Basketball:* 1959–60 *NCAA:* Ohio State 75, California 55. 1959–60 *NIT:* Bradley 88, Providence 72 . . . *National Basketball Association:* 1959–60 championship won by Boston, 4 games to 3 over St. Louis.

Other Happenings: In his last at-bat before retiring on September 28, Ted Williams hits home run and Red Sox beat Orioles, 5–4. Williams ends career with 521 homers, despite loss of five prime years for World War II and Korean conflict. . . . Dolph Schayes of Syracuse becomes the first NBA player to score 15,000 points. The exact moment comes on January 12 as Schayes gets 34 points against Philadelphia to bring his total to 15,013. . . . In NFL, Eddie LeBaron and Dick Bielski of Dallas team up for a 2-inch touchdown pass. . . . No-hitters are pitched in National League by Don Cardwell of Cubs, Lew Burdette of Milwaukee, and Warren Spahn, also of Braves; none in American League. . . . It is, unfortunately, a big year for untimely deaths for still-active athletes: On June 5 Rudell Stitch, third-ranking welterweight contender, dies while trying to save a friend from drowning; automobile crashes claim the lives of Olympic ice skater Ross Zucco, 26, Bob Gutowski, holder of the world's outdoor pole vault record, and Billy Woods, 18, a member of the American Alpine ski team; in addition, 16 members of the California State Polytechnic College football team are killed in a plane crash. . . . In baseball, the Chicago White Sox are the first team to wear their names on their uniforms, and Jim Piersall is thrown out of games 6 times during the season. . . . Billy Martin charges out to the mound and sends Cubs pitcher Jim Brewer to the hospital. . . . Joe Bellino leads Navy to a 17–12 victory over Army as banners drape the usually sedate Pentagon in anticipation. . . . On February 17, Mamie Rollins sets new mark for women's 70-yard low hurdles, 8.7 seconds. . . . In February, demolition of Ebbets Field in Brooklyn begins. . . . Italy defeats United States Davis Cup team, the first time that the United States has not reached the finals in 24 years. . . . In a bizarre move, Detroit and Cleveland in American League trade managers, Jimmy Dykes moving from the Tigers to the Indians and Joe Gordon from the Indians to the Tigers.

Section X
The 1960s

CHAPTER 41 — 1961

Charles Dickens might have characterized it as a year of comfort and a year of ferment; a year of despair and a year of opportunity. The United States, as a world power, was on the ropes, to use an apt sports metaphor—or was it? Pessimists pointed to Soviet superiority in space, spreading Communist influence in Cuba and Asia, and indecisive leadership at home as examples of America's slippage. Even the world's fastest miler, Herb Elliott, jumped off the United States bandwagon that year, denouncing the nation and its people as "weak, soft, and synthetic." Many shrugged aside the criticism, but for most Americans the blast from the twenty-three-year-old Australian record-holder (3:54.5) was disheartening. If the same words had come from a foreign diplomat, they might not have hurt so much. That they came from a famous athlete —and therefore a subject of automatic respect —gave the words increased credibility.

Herb Elliott's Blast:
"A people who so thoroughly mollycoddle themselves must become weaker, spiritually and physically. . . . On the whole, Americans are not temperamentally suited to any race beyond 880 yards. . . ."

The Golden Mile

Optimists, on the other hand, pointed out that the battle for space supremacy had just started. America had been behind at the beginning of other races and won them. Moreover, for the first time since Woodrow Wilson's administration, the White House was occupied by a man seemingly as intellectual as political: John F. Kennedy, who played soft-ball and touch football despite an occasionally ailing back, who seemed as vibrant and self-assured as Dwight Eisenhower had seemed lethargic and dull.

As for Elliott's criticism of American athletic prowess, the sports pages of January 1961 put the lie to that. The top athlete of 1960, the winner of the Sullivan Award, was Rafer Johnson, Olympic champion in the decathlon, a test of endurance and all-around ability far beyond that of Mr. Elliott. Johnson, overcoming a serious leg injury, not only set a world record in the decathlon with 8,683 points, he also won the event at the Rome Olympics after an uphill battle against C. K. Yang of Taiwan. A graduate of UCLA, Johnson was selected to carry the United States flag during the parade of athletes.

There were many heroes in purely American sports as well—for example, the Naval Academy's elusive halfback, Joe Bellino. Could a nation that sent such a splendid athlete into the armed services as a lowly ensign be all that soft? And didn't the existence of baseball pitcher Vernon Law, a Mormon elder beating the New York Yankees twice on an injured ankle in the World Series, also prove that the nation had more grit than Herb Elliott imagined?

FOOTBALL

Best not to worry about it. There were too many pleasant distractions in spectator sports as the year began—not only a variety of college bowl games but also the very first championship contest played by the American Football League. That game turned out to be a good one. Even more important to the league, whose woes in 1960 were more fiscal than physical, the highest paid crowd in the short history of the AFL—32,183—was on hand. A mixture of National League castoffs and rookies, the contending Houston Oilers and Los Angeles Chargers were evenly matched. Leading Houston was twelve-year veteran quarterback George Blanda; Jack Kemp of the Chargers was less heady but a better runner who had led the league in passing in 1960. Another weapon in the Charger arsenal was placekicker Ben Agajanian, a veteran playing in his third professional circuit, having started in the All-America Football Conference.

In the beginning, Agajanian seemed to be the difference, kicking a pair of field goals in the first period to put Los Angeles ahead, 6–0. George Blanda then started connecting with passes, two of his sixteen completions during the game leading to touchdowns of seventeen and seven yards. With Houston ahead, 17–16, early in the fourth period, with third down on his own twelve-yard line, Blanda faked a rush into the line, calmly waited for Billy Cannon to gain a step on Charger safety man Jim Sears, and hung the ball neatly for a pass-and-run touchdown of eighty-eight yards. That was the end of the scoring, although the game ended with the Chargers threatening on the Houston twenty-two-yard line. "On the basis of this game," one writer noted, "it may be said that the AFL is on its way." Despite inept pass defenses that could often be exploited by the better quarterbacks in ludicrous fashion, the new league did seem to make a good impression with the American public.

"He fights oil-well fires during the off-season."

If the early television announcers said that about him once, they said it at least a hundred times during the early days of the AFL. Perhaps it was the only thing interesting about Houston fullback Charlie Tolar, except that he was built like a fireplug. They said that a few times, too.

One highlight of the college football season was the Orange Bowl battle between Missouri and Navy, a contest witnessed by Navy veteran and President-elect John F. Kennedy. The game featured the longest run in Orange Bowl history until that time, a ninety-six-yard scamper with an intercepted lateral by Navy's Greg Mather, as well as a sensational twenty-seven-yard touchdown pass by Joe Bellino. Navy scored first and last but lost the game as Missouri contained the Middies' ground game and used its superior speed to push across three scores, enough to win, 21–14.

HOCKEY

Meanwhile, in early January, as Cuba and the United States traded acid comments after a break in diplomatic relations, international politics entered the sports arena in the form of a Soviet hockey team. Visiting the United States as part of an official Soviet-U.S. cultural exchange program, the Soviet squad wended its way from New York to Colorado, beating teams from the Universities of North Dakota (4–3) and Minnesota (10–2) as well as knocking off an all-star team of best United States amateur players. The Soviets arrived at Madison Square Garden on January 7 for still another contest with the American squad, confident that they could beat the best the United States had to offer. Some spectators were upset at the Soviet victories, especially one customer who threw a piece of pizza at the visitors, but most restricted their unhappiness to bits of sarcasm. For a while it even seemed that the unusual pattern would be broken. The U.S. squad outhustled the Soviets in the first period, scoring twice, but in the second period the Soviets turned it on, dazzling everyone on and off the ice with a succession of slap shots, drop passes, behind-the-back passes, crisp checking, and perfect maneuvering. Soon they led by 5–2. A relaxed final period in which each team scored once saved the United States from further humiliation. Maybe it was true, some said. Maybe the United States was slipping. Or perhaps their amateurs were just more professional than our professional amateurs.

Some Sardonic Comments in the Wake of U.S. Hockey Losses:

Following the impressive playing of "The Star-Spangled Banner" while a stream of air kept a flag flapping in an artificial breeze: "Well, anyway, we've out-anthemed them."

Following the U.S. loss: "When we win, it's a great international hockey match. When we lose, it's the cultural exchange program."

Best not to worry about it. Natives of New York could amuse themselves that month by trying to think of a nickname for the brand-new baseball team coming to Gotham for the 1962 season. Mrs. Charles Shipman Payson, one of the principal owners of the franchise, had decided it would be nice to have the public pick a name for the team that had grown out of the threat to create a third major league known as the Continental League. Accordingly, sobriquets of all manner and degree of seriousness came forth, including some, such as the York-Brooks, which were designed to join the old lost franchises of Brooklyn and the Giants. Others thought the team should be called the "Continentals" in honor of the league that spawned them. But when it was pointed out that this title would inevitably be shortened to "Cons," with former members of the teams becoming "ex-Cons," the idea was quickly dropped.

A Sampling of Pre-Met Suggestions:
New York Pacesetters
New York Bankers
New York Farmers
New York Troopers
New York Gold Sox

BOXING

Boxing, having crested in popularity with the Friday night fights of the 1950s, was still reasonably popular, and January 1961 featured one bout designed to partially clear up the middleweight muddle. Paul Pender, champion of New York, Massachusetts, and Europe, attempted to add to his stature by taking on Terry Downes in Boston. Downes, a brawler without a great deal of style, was made to order for Pender, who kept jabbing away until he turned Downes' face a cheerless red, then sent him sprawling with a right hook. That constituted the first round. In the second round, Pender nicked Downe's right eye. In the fourth, he cut a ragged, vertical gash in Downes' nose. Referee Bill Connelly asked Downes if he wished to continue. The challenger said that he did. Swallowing his own blood, Downes ceased to advance in a crouch, which had been his only defense, in order to reach Pender's head and there-

by gain a quick knockout. By the end of the sixth round, house physicians told Referee Connelly to stop the fight if the cuts opened again in the following rounds. They did open, mercifully, and the fight was stopped.

FOOTBALL

Meanwhile, as Sam Snead defeated Harry Weetman of England in a match that introduced golf to Israel, professional football returned briefly to the spotlight. Publication of the first-year losses by American League clubs showed that while the public seemed to enjoy watching the new teams on television, not enough fans were going to the parks. In New York, the Titans showed an average attendance of only nineteen thousand, and the organization had lost $450,000 on the year. Even at that, New York's deficit was average. Los Angeles, fighting competition for the sports dollar from the football Rams, baseball Dodgers, and a new American League baseball club starting in 1961, the Angels, was the AFL disaster area, having lost $900,000. As a result, a transfer of the Los Angeles franchise to San Diego was reportedly under serious consideration by league officials. Not long after the less-than-rosy AFL picture was revealed—a picture that precluded any expansion—the rival NFL moved formally into its second expansion area, Minnesota. On January 26, the Vikings joined Dallas as the newest organization to experience the dubious pleasure of putting together a team via the process of paying top prices for aging veterans and marginal rookies, most of whom would be released at the end of training camp in any event. But without blanching, new Viking coach Norm Van Brocklin checked off a list of has-beens and nonentities and proclaimed that Minnesota would have a representative team in 1961. Actually, Minnesota did field a fair club, but it was largely as a result of

---

Boxing Human-interest Stories, January 1961:
Whatever happened to—
1. Ezzard Charles
The former heavyweight champion, it was reported on January 1, was penniless. After having earned more than two million dollars in the ring, the thirty-nine-year-old Charles was living in Cincinnati. The phone in his home had just been disconnected.
2. Yvon Durelle
In 1958, light-heavyweight Durelle floored

champion Archie Moore several times and came within seconds of winning the title. In January 1961, after having sold his sports car, fishing boat, and other worldly goods, he was reported subsisting (barely) on an eight-dollar-a-day job with the New Brunswick Department of Lands and Mines.
3. Primo Carnera
At the age of fifty-four, the former heavyweight champion was reported to be making fifty thousand dollars a year as a wrestler.

shrewd drafting from the colleges rather than getting top production from the overstocked warehouses of the member teams.

Have You Ever Heard of These Men? The Viking Draft List, 1961:
Fred Murphy, offensive end
Bill Roehneit, linebacker
Gene Johnson, defensive halfback
Byron Beams, tackle
Bill Kimber, offensive end
Dick Mostardo, defensive halfback
Gene Selawski, offensive tackle
Zeke Smith, linebacker
Jack Morris, running back
Don Ellersick, defensive back

Track-and-field watchers of 1961 received a double barrel of record news on January 29 when word arrived from Boston that high jumper John Thomas had cleared 7 feet, 3 inches at the Athletic Association games. But on the same day Tass, the Russian news agency, reported from Leningrad that Valeri Brumel had leaped 7 feet 4½ inches, the highest distance indoors or out. In February, the two would have a direct competition at Madison Square Garden.

That month came in like a lion, snow covering much of the eastern United States, playing havoc with sports attendance. Racing at Maryland's Bowie was canceled early in the month, and on the fourth, New York's slump-

---

SOME MORE PRE-MET SUGGESTIONS:
New York Diamonds
New York Leopards
New York Traders
New York Trojans
New York Avengers
New York Meadowlarks
New York Bats
New York Sparrows
New York Comets
New York Pioneers
New York Muskets
New York Spartans
New York Knights
New York Lancers
New York Rifles
New York Moles
("because they'll be down around the bottom anyway")

---

ing basketball Knickerbockers played a game with the St. Louis Hawks while 943 folks looked on. The weather was so bad, in fact, that even an outdoor winter carnival was postponed. About the only sports activity that continued full blast was dreaming up names for the 1962 National League baseball club in New York. The longer the contest continued, of course, the sillier the names became, as Mrs. Payson would learn later.

ICE SKATING
Interest in ice skating was much in evidence during February 1961. The good news was that the most exciting new star in a generation had come along, hopefully to bring glory to the United States and herself. Just sixteen years old, Laurence Owen, a young woman with a man's name, captured the national singles and pairs championships with her brother, Dudley, while executing programs far removed from the usually tedious arrangements of jumps and spins of obligation. In the February 13, 1961, issue of *Sports Illustrated,* deserved tribute was paid to the Owen family —forty-nine-year-old Maribel, the mother and former skating champion, as well as Dudley and the two daughters, Laurence and sister Maribel. Two days later, Mrs. Owen and her daughters boarded a Sabena Airlines Boeing 707 jet en route to a world figure-skating championship at Prague. Near Brussels, Belgium, the plane circled the landing strip preparatory to descending, then inexplicably plunged to earth, killing seventy-three persons. Eighteen members of the U.S. skating team died, including Mrs. Owen and her two talented daughters. The tragedy caused many Americans over the age of forty-five to recall the national shock of three decades before when Knute Rockne had been among the first victims of airline disasters. "Our country has sustained a great loss of talent and grace which had brought pleasure to people all over the world," America's new President Kennedy announced.

TRACK AND FIELD
Three days later, Valeri Brumel did little to break the gray mood of the times. Arriving in New York, he promptly set out to prove that his outjumping John Thomas at the 1960 Olympics had been no accident. More than sixteen thousand spectators jammed Madison Square Garden hoping to see Thomas restore American supremacy, but the pride of U.S. jumpers failed to clear the bar at seven feet, two inches. Brumel succeeded, then waited patiently as the bar was moved an inch higher. Once, twice, he raced toward it, displaying his best form, one arm extended, the other tucked snugly to his chest. And twice he

failed. Waiting for his third try, he kicked his legs high in the air, loosening the long, compact muscles. Then, standing still, he raised his left hand in near-salute to the crowd and threw himself almost violently toward the pit. His left foot slammed hard against the boards and his body hurtled upward. Suddenly he was clear and falling, the bar untouched. He had matched Thomas's indoor record. No matter that he tried and failed to clear seven feet, five inches three times after that. By then, the gallery cry of "Come on, Valeri, bay—bee!" told everyone that Americans were not as provincial as some liked to think.

BASEBALL

The last snow having fallen in early 1961, thoughts of baseball's spring training warmed the hearts of many. But spring training of 1961 was different than many previous ones. For the first time, racial discrimination became a major issue on a national level. Many clubs had arrived at the point where it was no longer practical to house blacks and whites in separate facilities in the still-segregated South. "Our hotels are almost like private clubs this time of the year," said the manager of one Florida establishment in explaining its policy. "If we opened our dining rooms and other facilities to just anyone, you can see what would happen."

Dan Topping of the New York Yankees made a special plea to the owners of the Soreno Hotel at St. Petersburg to allow all players, including Elston Howard, Hector Lopez, and Jesse Gonder, to be housed under one roof. He received a polite "No." The controversy touched off a variety of emotions in both North and South. "We can't upset the traditions of generations in a single year," said E. C. Robison, Chairman of St. Petersburg's Governor's Baseball Committee. "But we are all apprehensive. Baseball is the lifeblood of some of our communities." Another hotel owner said, "You can't fight it—it's got to come. When it does, I think everybody will greet the change with acceptance rather than repulsion. Hotels will find the Negroes very acceptable patrons."

Even among club owners, there were varying degrees of commitment. Dan Topping openly stated that the New York club would begin searching for other accommodations, but General Manager Frank Lane of the Kansas City Athletics, a team with only one black, responded, "We are not spearheading any political movement."

BASKETBALL

As the baseball teams looked for a way out of the problem, basketball moved inexorably toward the end of its long season, with result-

AND MORE
New York Addicts
New York Beatniks
New York Broads
New York Cousins
New York Dancers
New York Hearts
New York Heroes
New York Humbles
New York Juveniles
New York Keepers
New York Midgets
New York Mothers-in-law
New York Muggers
New York Pets
New York Slumlords

ant fan interest. One sideline included a story about a 13-year-old grammar school student who had attained the height of a 6 feet 7½ inches and was able to outreach star NBA player Richie Guerin by 3 inches. A picture was taken of the youth deftly controlling the ball. The odds were that no one would ever hear of the young man again, but it was pictorially interesting to see eighth-grade Lewis Alcindor in the same shot with an accredited basketball star. Few who saw the picture imagined that Alcindor would ever challenge Wilt Chamberlain, who just a few days later established an NBA individual-season record by scoring 2,734 points in 72 games. The mark was 27 points more than Chamberlain racked up as a rookie in 1960, when he scored 2,707. Wilt also broke his own record for rebounds during a season by grabbing 31 in the February 28 game against Los Angeles, bringing his 1960–61 total to 1,974.

March 1961 saw the revival of national idealism when President Kennedy announced the establishment of a "Peace Corps" of dedicated volunteers to help foreign governments meet their urgent needs for skilled manpower. The response to the program was highly favorable, one of the first to step forward from the ranks of organized athletics being Rafer Johnson.

BOXING

March was also a controversy month in the fight ring, the first flap involving forty-year-old Sugar Ray Robinson and Gene Fullmer. On March 4, the two were scheduled to fight for the title at Las Vegas, but the day before, Robinson suddenly announced that he intended to pull out unless the promoters provided a ring larger than the "sixteen-foot telephone booth they're trying to put me in." Fullmer, in response, threatened to pull out of the fight if the ring were enlarged. At the last minute, however, Fullmer allowed a seventeen-foot ring to be used, despite its greater size impeding his bull-like rushes and allowing the swifter Robinson more room to backtrack and maneuver. The fight, the fourth between the two men—each had won one and there had been a draw—was a "messy but unanimous decision" for Fullmer, who plodded after Robinson relentlessly during the fifteen rounds of sporadic action. The judges and Referee Frank Carter agreed that the champion had earned the decision as a result of his aggressiveness. For those who had been following Ray Robinson for two decades, the ineffectual performance of that great fighter marked the end of a boxing era.

The second controversy came at the end of the third Patterson-Johansson title fight at Miami Beach. Loggy at the beginning, Patterson immediately ran into one of Johansson's roundhouse rights and, by way of providing ammunition for those who claimed he had a glass jaw, promptly fell to the canvas. He was up at the count of two, took an eight count, then received another right and went down again. With remarkable resiliency, Patterson climbed to his feet, beat off an attack by the challenger, and proceeded to floor Johansson with a right and a left hook. The round drew prolonged applause at its conclusion.

There were no more such outbursts during the next four rounds, the fight moving along lackadaisically, both men seeming weak and confused, unable to fill their missions. Thus the end, when it came, was almost dreamlike, Patterson's two clubbing rights sending Ingemar in slow-motion fashion to the canvas. The challenger's attempts to rise by the count of ten were equally lethargic. In fact, he seemed to have beaten the count by a split second, but Referee Billy Regan indicated that Patterson had won by a sixth-round knockout. "I thought I was up in time," Johansson protested later. "I heard the count all the way. I heard nine and he say ten when I was up."

Subsequent review of the count on film indicated that Patterson had won, that Johansson had not received a short count. That ended the Patterson-Johansson series, happily for those who felt it important to have an American as heavyweight champion. But Patterson's qualifications as a true champion were suspect, especially in view of the *bête noire* named Sonny Liston who lurked on the boxing horizon.

BASKETBALL

Also lurking on the horizon at the end of the month was the threat of a new basketball fixing scandal that would dwarf even that of 1951. At the core of the problem was a New York gambler named Aaron Wagman, who had enlisted two Seton Hall players in order to rig a Madison Square Garden contest between Dayton and Seton Hall. During the decade following basketball's premier scandal, a certain amount of sophistication had been injected into the game-fixing racket. Now it was not merely a matter of paying the better team's players to keep the score close. In many cases, bribes were given to the weaker team's men so that the slightly favored opponent would win big. On March 20, 1961, it was revealed that just such a situation had occurred during the February 9 contest between Dayton and Seton Hall. Gamblers had gotten to Hank Gunter and Art Hicks, of Seton Hall, the two stars helping turn the game into a 112–77 runaway for Dayton. Regarding the growing scandal, the New York *Times* lamented, "In its widespread repercussions, it could be compared to the Chicago 'Black Sox' scandal that shook major-league baseball in 1919."

Most assuredly it was better not to think too much about that. There was happier news in jockey Johnny Longden's winning the 5,500th race of his career—not bad for a grandfather. . . . The city of Cincinnati, meanwhile, rocked with a two-hour parade of happiness in honor of the underdog University of Cincinnati Bearcats' whipping Ohio State for the NCAA basketball championship. . . . There was a certain amount of wry amusement in reading about the new system of baseball management that was to be put into operation by the Chicago Cubs in 1961. Instead of having one manager with several assistants, the clubs would eliminate the manager position per se and rotate four coaches in the head coaching position. All told, the team would have eight "associate managers," but only four would be with the squad during the entire season. The others would spend a lot of time in the minor leagues, developing young talent. Because of their diversified backgrounds, it was reasoned that eight baseball

The Cub Coaches of 1961 and How They Fared:

Name	W.	L.
Vedie Himsl	10	21
Harry Craft	7	9
Elvin Tappe	42	53
Lou Klein	5	7
Chicago Cubs		
Total	64	90

men would be able to supply more information and help to new players than one man who might have a detailed knowledge of pitching, for example, but little real understanding of playing the outfield. It sounded good, but the Cubs finished the season in seventh place, the same as in 1960. After an even worse showing in 1962, Chicago went back to the one-manager system the following year, winning 82 and losing 80 under Bob Kennedy.

GOLF

Spring brought with it an exciting Masters golf championship tournament at Augusta, Georgia. It was the heyday of "Arnie's Army" of fairway followers who had developed an affinity of Arnold Palmer's come-from-behind victories. Entered in the Masters of April 1961 was a young amateur named Jack Nicklaus, but Palmer's principal competition would come from fellow professionals Gary Player (the man who usually dressed in black despite being one of the best-known sports representatives of white South Africa) as well as Don January, Billy Casper, and Tommy Bolt.

The first day of the tournament was drizzly and gray, but a good one on which to score. On dry days the greens at Augusta were normally skiddy; when slightly moist, they allowed the ball to stick where the golfer put it. Using the weather to his advantage, Arnold Palmer rushed to the head of the class with a 68, 4 under par. Player scored a 69 and Nicklaus a 70. At the end of 36 holes, Player and Palmer were even at 137, but on the third round Palmer fired a disappointing 73 while Player continued the subpar pace with a 69. Going into the final 18 holes, Player led, 206–210.

As it turned out, the South African had saved his worst round for last. After turning in a good 34 for the first 9 holes, he bogeyed the tenth, double-bogeyed the thirteenth, missed a short putt on the fifteenth for another bogey, and had to scramble to make par on the last 3 holes. As he signed his scorecard and walked off the course, Player, with a 74 for the round and a total of 280, was almost in tears. To win, Arnold Palmer had only to score a 69.

The opportunity seemed to lift Palmer. His game steadied and the gap narrowed. When he stood on the tee of the eighteenth hole, he needed merely a par-4 to win, a bogey-5 to tie. When he sent a perfect drive whistling down the fairway, it seemed as if the biggest single paycheck in gold belonged to Palmer. But the seven-iron shot that followed strayed into a bunker and lodged in a slight depression. Palmer's wedge was too strong, sending the ball over the green, past a crowd of spectators, and down the slope toward a TV tower. Now Palmer knew he needed a miracle to win, a near-miracle to tie. His approach shot landed 15 feet from the pin. Putting for the tie, Arnie missed by inches. "I thought 6's only happened to other people," he said, shaking the hand of Player, the first foreigner to win the Masters title.

BASEBALL

Opening Day of the 1961 baseball season began with a couple of new twists. The American League, for the first time since its inauguration in 1901, would have 10 teams instead of 8. Two new franchises had been added, in Minnesota and Los Angeles, necessitating an increase in the number of games played from 154 to 162 (a decision that would create a great deal of controversy later). Both new clubs started the season with victories, Minnesota beating the powerful Yankees and Los Angeles startling the young and talented Baltimore Orioles. After that, it was mostly downhill, the Twins and Angels finishing the season in seventh and eighth positions, respectively.

HOCKEY, BASKETBALL

Because baseball had started did not necessarily mean that hockey and basketball were over. As the teams took the field for the American League's sixty-first season, Bill Russell had just finished leading the Boston Celtics to another pro basketball championship. Playing the part of Christians in the uneven combat were the St. Louis Hawks, who could not prevent Russell from scoring thirty points and grabbing thirty-eight rebounds in the 121–112 victory. That result, of course, was predictable. The Stanley Cup hockey championship series provided more excitement in that it pitted the Chicago Black Hawks, a team that had finished in third place, against the favored Detroit Red Wings. By defeating Detroit, four games to two, the Black Hawks not only won their first Stanley Cup in twenty-three years but also became the first team since 1945 to finish the season in third place and go on to win the Cup.

April 1961 brought with it an attempt to "liberate" Cuba by landing fifteen hundred CIA-trained Cuban refugees on Castro's Communist colony. When all were killed or captured after failure of United States forces to "intervene," the international situation became sufficiently tense to distract many from sports watching. The rebel landings in Cuba even temporarily halted a basketball tour of the Soviet Union by thirty-one American men and women. It was delayed on April 18, following anti-American demonstrations in Moscow. Tension in this area of international relations as well as the situation in Berlin led to the fear that many athletes and other members of U. S. Reserve units might be called up.

BASEBALL

The first bit of excitement emanating from the new baseball season came on April 28, when forty-year-old Warren Spahn pitched the second no-hitter of his career and his 290th career win. Putting the San Francisco Giants down one-two-three in all but two innings, he permitted only two men to reach second base in the 1–0 victory.

Two days later, Willie Mays became only the ninth major leaguer to hit four home runs in a single game as he almost single-handedly led the Giants to a 14–4 win over Milwaukee. Connecting in the first, third, sixth, and eighth innings, Willie got as far as the on-deck circle in the ninth, but Jim Davenport, who preceded him to the plate, ended the suspense by grounding into the third out. (The home runs, incidentally, were not hit in succession. In the fifth inning, Moe Drabowsky forced Mays to line out to center.)

Not to be outdone, the Baltimore Orioles also tied a major-league mark when three batters hit home runs in a row the same day Mays struck his four. Speculation continued to grow that the ball had gotten livelier, but there were so many conflicting opinions and bits of evidence that no one could be sure. There did seem to be evidence that more batters were swinging for the fences rather than merely trying to meet the ball.

If there was any doubt that it was the year of the home run, a comparative unknown named Jim Gentile, playing first base for the Orioles, proved otherwise. By May 8, the twenty-six-year-old left-handed swinger with a penchant for kicking water coolers had one third as many home runs—seven—as he had collected the entire year before. Coming to bat in the first inning of a game against Minnesota, he hit No. 8 with the bases loaded; in the second inning the bases were again filled with Orioles and once again he homered. He thus joined the select group of Tony Lazzeri, Jim Tabor, and Rudy York, each of whom had hit a pair of bases-loaded home runs in a single game.

HORSERACING

Players circling the bases were temporarily replaced by horses in May as Carry Back came from eleventh position to win the eighty-seventh Kentucky Derby. Two weeks later—just a day after jockey Willie Shoemaker won his four thousandth race at Inglewood, California—Carry Back carried off the eighty-fifth Preakness. The great stretch-runner seemed a definite threat to win the

Triple Crown, which had not been accomplished since Citation in 1948.

While waiting the outcome of the Belmont Stakes, sports enthusiasts noted that on the last Saturday in May, a slender black man named Ralph Boston hurled his body 27 feet, ½ inch, the first broad-jumper to accomplish this equivalent of the 7-foot high jump or the 4-minute mile. . . . The fiftieth anniversary of the Indianapolis 500 was also celebrated without a fatality (although Tony Bettenhausen had been killed two weeks before while testing his car on the speedway). . . . Six more players were accused of accepting bribes in the basketball fixing scandal . . . and the American League set a record on May 27 when 27 home runs were hit in 7 games.

June brought the ninety-third running of the Belmont Stakes, attended by former President Dwight D. Eisenhower and more than fifty thousand customers eager to see if Carry Back could engineer another of his electrifying stretch runs, which had brought him home first not only in the Preakness and Kentucky Derby, but in the Florida Derby and the Flamingo as well. "I want the Belmont more than any other race in the world," said Katherine Price, Carry Back's owner. So did General Eisenhower, backing up his desire to see a Triple Crown winner with a bet on the favorite.

When Globemaster broke in front at the start of the race, there seemed little cause for alarm. Carry Back was far back as usual, but jockey Sellers felt that he was being watched more carefully than usual by the other riders. "It was rough, to put it mildly," he said later. "There was a lot of jostling going on, and all I can say is that when I asked for racing room, I did a lot of asking but didn't get much."

With a half mile to go, Carry Back was only seven lengths off the pace, closer than he had been during the Preakness. Sherluck and Globemaster continued to lead. Finally, Sellers moved Carry Back wide, and the crowd started to scream. But just as the serious move began, it ended. "I don't know what it was," Sellers said, "but after all that jostling in the early part of it, maybe he just got tired of the whole thing and gave up—for the first time this year." Added Mrs. Price sadly after the 65–1 Sherluck won the race, "It can't be helped. If Carry Back finally ran a bad race he was entitled to it."

The summer of 1961 was a warm one in many respects. In the South, "Freedom Riders" tested segregation of public facilities by deliberately inviting arrest as a means of pricking the nation's conscience on racial discrimination. On the international scene, Soviet Premier Khrushchev told the United States to sign a German peace treaty by the end of the year or the U.S.S.R. would sign one with East Germany that would not recognize Western occupation of West Berlin. To demonstrate the schism, East Germans began to construct the Berlin Wall, closing access from one sector of the city to another. President Kennedy hinted strongly that Americans might do well to have atomic shelters ready just in case. To add to the feeling of insecurity, some Reserve units were alerted and called. More than one major-league baseball team, inspecting its roster, discovered that there was a distinct possibility that some teams would lose valuable players if the international situation worsened.

But the summer passed without disaster. Ancient Archie Moore, either 44 or 47 years of age, fought 26-year-old Italian light-heavyweight Giulio Rinaldi and won easily, Moore's only fear that of losing his trunks because he had lost so much weight. . . . The basketball scandal grew to include 12 colleges and universities with players on the take. . . . Frank Budd of Villanova, "the fastest man alive," ran 100 yards in a world-record time of 9.2 seconds. . . . Jim Gentile hit his fourth grand-slam home run of the season, tying the record held by Babe Ruth, Lou Gehrig, Rudy York, Tommy Henrich, Al Rosen, and Ray Boone. . . . Meanwhile, someone somewhere preparing for halftime ceremonies for the coming football season discovered that 1961 looked the same upside-down and rightside-up, a happy coincidence for bands marching downfield that would not occur again until the season of 6009. . . . Sonny Liston was suspended by the state of Pennsylvania for as-sociating with gamblers. . . . Ralph Boston bettered his own world-record broad jump by leaping 27 feet, 1¾ inches. . . . Baseball Commissioner Ford Frick, panicked by the intimidating tactics of Babe Ruth fans throughout the nation, decreed that in the event Roger Maris hit 61 home runs, he would have to do it in 154 games or have an asterisk placed by his name to denote a 162-game season. (Frick did not specify what would be the disposition of other records such as base-stealing, lifetime victories for pitchers, etc., which might also benefit by the added games.)

BASEBALL

The baseball season broke twice in 1961 for All-Star games, that being the era (1959–62) when greed overpowered good judgment in order to fill the pension coffers. The first contest, at San Francisco, was won by the National League, 5–4, but the second, on July 31 at Boston, turned out to be a moral victory for the American League. At the end of nine innings, with the score deadlocked at 1–1, the rains came, causing a thirty-minute delay and then postponement. It was the first tie in the history of the series. (The following year, in one of the last double All-Star games, the American League actually won. It was to be the last time in nearly two decades.)

Early in August, baseball continued to dominate the news as Warren Spahn won his three hundredth game on the eleventh, thus becoming only the third left-hander to enter the exclusive club. (The others, Lefty Grove, with 300 wins; Eddie Plank, with 327.) Another baseball record of sorts came about a day later when Maury Wills, after 1,167 times

---

The Reservist Athletes, Summer 1961:

New York Yankees—*Tony Kubek, Bill Stafford, Ralph Terry*

Detroit Tigers—*Steve Boros, Dick McAuliffe*

Baltimore Orioles—*Brooks Robinson, Ron Hansen, Steve Barber, Chuck Estrada*

Cincinnati Reds—*Gordon Coleman, Jerry Zimmerman, John Edwards, Sherman Jones, Howie Nunn*

Los Angeles Dodgers—*Don Drysdale, Sandy Koufax, Willie Davis, Ron Fairly, Bob Aspromonte, Doug Camilli*

San Francisco Giants—*John Orsino*

Milwaukee Braves—*Bob Hendley, Bob Taylor*

St. Louis Cardinals—*Curt Flood, Bob Miller, Craig Anderson*

Chicago Cubs—*Gerry Kindall, Ron Santo, Billy Williams, Jim Brewer, Dick Ellsworth*

Kansas City A's—*Jerry Walker, Ed Rakow, Billy Kunkel, Norman Bass, Wayne Causey, Dick Howser, Deron Johnson, Lou Klimchock, Jay Hankins*

Los Angeles Angels—*Jim Donohue, Eli Grba, Johnny James, Ron Moeller, Ken Hunt, George Thomas*

Cleveland Indians—*Dick Stigman, Wynn Hawkins, Jim Grant, Jim Perry, Frank Funk, Don Dillard*

Boston Red Sox—*Bill Monbouquette, Chuck Schilling, Gary Geiger*

at bat, hit his first major-league home run, off Jack Curtis, a Chicago Cub left-hander. (During his remaining 11 years in the National League, Maury would clout 19 more.)

No one mentioned it specifically, but Wills' home run, more than anything else, may have resurrected the "lively baseball" controversy during August 1961, for it was in that month that extensive tests were made on the standard sphere with, as one may imagine, mixed conclusions. One test, sponsored by the New York *Times,* used balls from 1927, 1936, and 1961, and failed to show that a home run was easier to hit in one period than any other. Another test, made by *Sports Illustrated,* concluded that the average 1961 ball bounced higher, was firmer, but weighed more. The conclusion was that "the 1961 baseball has more potential to be hit farther than its counterparts in either 1952 or 1953."

Regardless of any changes that may or may not have been made in the ball's construction, losing was no easier in 1961 than previously, and the Philadelphia Phillies put on a grand show of that. On August 8, their losing streak reached modest proportions when the Pittsburgh Pirates handed them 10–2 and 3–2 backhandings in a doubleheader. That made it 12 straight down the drain for the Phillies. They then proceeded to put together 27 consecutive scoreless innings in the next four games, running the consecutive-defeats streak to 16 and passing the club record of 14 straight losses in 1883 and 1936. The next futility mark in sight was a string of 19 losses, set by Boston in 1906 and Cincinnati in 1914.

On August 15, it seemed that the Phils might break out of it. Although in the process of losing their 18th straight, to Chicago, 6–5, they loaded the bases in the 9th inning on a walk, a single, and a hit batter. But Pancho

Herrera came through to strike out and end the threat. The next day, bowing to Warren Spahn, who picked up his 301st victory, the Phillies tied the existing record for defeat, then poured it on by losing to Boston in 11 innings, added insurance the very next day, and having lost 21 straight, reduced the 1906 Red Sox, 1916 Philadelphia A's, and 1943 A's to also-rans.

The next record in sight was the 24 straight losses by the 1899 Cleveland Spiders, a team so bad it ended the season with a mark of 20 wins, 134 losses. Dropping No. 22 was not quite so simple a matter, however. The game seemed to be safely out of reach by a 4–2 score as the Phils came to bat in the top of the 9th. But at that point the Braves' Tony Cloninger weakened, giving singles to Bobby Gene Smith and Tony Taylor. Relief pitcher Don McMahon walked Bob Callison, loading the bases. Tony Gonzalez then grounded into a fielder's choice, scoring Smith and bringing the score to a dangerously close 4–3. Even more ominous, there was only one out. But Tony Taylor came through by being trapped in a rundown by Brave catcher Joe Torre, and Ken Walters lined to Henry Aaron for the third out.

Loss No. 23 presented no particular problem, Spahn earning his 302nd victory at the Phils' expense. For the second game of the August 20 doubleheader, the Phillies started John Buzhardt, who had been the last pitcher to win a game for them, back on July 28. That proved their undoing, for Buzhardt pitched much better than Carlton Willey, Bob Hendley, and Don Nottebart for the hometown Braves. Before the Phils had a chance to recover, they looked at the scoreboard and saw that they led by a score of 7–2 in the 8th inning. Was it too great a lead to throw away? It was. The best that the Phillies could do was yield single runs to the Braves in the bottom of the 3th and the 9th. The string of consecutive losses died at 23, one short of the old Spiders' mark.

Despite this brief flurry of interest in the losers of the baseball world, it was apparent that the summer of 1961 belonged to the M & M boys. While Soviet Premier Khrushchev ranted in the United Nations, ordinary citizens as far away as Japan debated the Frick asterisk decision. The majority of fans polled felt that their hero, Ruth, should be allowed to keep the record if Maris did not hit 61 in 154 games. There were occasional dissenters, however, who recognized the fallacy of trying to establish a "standard" season for the posthumous benefit of the Babe. Said one Japanese who was interviewed near the end of September, "Maris, though he has more games than Ruth, faces many difficulties Ruth did not. There's been improvement in technique, heavier competition, night games, and more travel. One day he has to play on the East Coast and the next he may have to play on the West Coast. Ruth did not have the physical burdens imposed on Maris today."

Casey Stengel, the 71-year-old pixie of baseball, stole the spotlight three days after Maris hit home run No. 60 of Baltimore's Jack Fisher in game No. 158, when it was announced that he had been signed to manage the new National League Mets in their first season. In characteristic style, Stengel referred to the team as the "Knickerbockers."

Roger Maris, subjected to enormous strain from the press and fans at ball parks, struck only one home run during the month of October. That came on the 1st, in game No. 162, off Boston's Tracy Stallard. The Babe's record for a season was broken.

September Home Runs—Roger Maris

No.	Game No.	Date	Pitcher,	Club
52	134	2	Larry,	Detroit
53	134	2	Aquirre,	Detroit
54	139	6	Cheney,	Washington
55	140	7	Stigman,	Cleveland
56	142	9	Grant,	Cleveland
57	150	16	Larry,	Detroit
58	151	17	Fox,	Detroit
59	154	20	Pappas,	Baltimore
60	158	26	Fisher,	Baltimore

As the Yankees and Cincinnati Reds prepared for the 1961 World Series, sports fans noted that Kelso was obviously the horse of the year when the product of the Bohemia Stable won the $109,600 Woodward Stakes by eight lengths. With veteran jockey Eddie Arcaro up, Kelso sprinted the mile and one quarter in two minutes flat. Sports fans also noted that 1961 was going to be one of the most injury- and death-ridden in a great while. On September 28, Midshipman Donald Foley was killed while carrying the football in practice at the Naval Academy; Four days later John Zola, a twenty-year-old Lebanon Valley halfback, collapsed during a football game with Drexel and shortly afterward died without regaining consciousness. He was the third player in the area to die within a week, leading some to call for more protective devices.

The world Series proved that it was a bad year all around for Babe Ruth. As a pitcher in the World Series for the 1916 and 1918 Red Sox, the Bambino had put together a string of 29⅔ scoreless innings, a record that was hardly challenged until Whitey Ford pitched 9-inning shutouts against the 1960 Pittsburgh Pirates in the third and sixth games. Then, in the opening game of the 1961 Series, he added another shutout, bringing his total of scoreless World Series innings to 27. The Babe's record went by the boards in game No. 4 at the end of the third inning. In the sixth inning, however, Ford fouled a ball off his own right foot and had to be removed from the game. His mark of 32 consecutive scoreless innings went into the record book, *sans* asterisk, because this time there was no possible way to protect the Babe.

A dull series, the Yankees won it in five games, making Manager Ralph Houk only the third manager in major-league history to win a World Series in his first year. As for the New York Yankees, the team had been in the fall classic nineteen of the past twenty-six years and had won fifteen of the nineteen World Series. Those who loathed the Bronx Bombers because of their almost mechanical success felt that the Yankee dynasty would never end, and there was good reason for despair. Mantle and Maris, at thirty and twenty-seven, respectively, were still in their prime, and the Yankee front office seemed to have a penchant for obtaining aging veterans with one or two good years left in them. So great was the frustration of the rest of baseball society that a book and a musical based on an imaginary decline of the dynasty found instant empathy with casual and fervid fans all across the nation.

Following the World Series, the National League held a special draft meeting at which the Houston Colts and New York Mets were permitted to resuscitate 45 cast-off players at the bargain-basement price of about $80,000 apiece. (Before the meeting, General Manager Paul Richards of the Colts charged that the players would be of such marginal value that it would be better if the Mets and Colts simply refused to pay the money—since most of the players offered would be cut in the spring. George Weiss, the Mets' president, refused to go along with this perfectly sound strategy, probably because it would have offended the money-hungry National League owners.)

Forced to go along with the draft, Paul Richards selected as his first pick shortstop Eddie Bressoud, then made second baseman Joe Amalfitano his "premium" selection. The Mets picked pitcher Bob Miller and catcher Hobie Landrith as their first and "premium" players. Ironically, one player who was passed over in the draft was 35-year-old Robin Roberts. His age was against him, of course, but he managed to stick around the major leagues for another five years and win 52 more games.

A Miserable Draft

The Four Top Selections *appeared in a total of 173 games for New York and Houston during 1962, an average of 43 games each. Ed Bressoud was traded to the Boston Red Sox before the season started, and Joe Amalfitano was sent to San Francisco the following year. Hobie Landrith appeared in only 23 games with the Mets before going to Baltimore and was through with baseball by the end of 1963. Bob Miller won 1 game, lost 12 for the 1962 Mets, then was traded to the Dodgers in 1963; 59 wins and 60 losses later, he ended his major-league career in 1974.*

FOOTBALL

The 1961 football season brought with it several surprises, including the San Francisco 49ers' "shotgun" offense—not a new formation but one not seen in many years. Using a spread formation with a direct snap to a running quarterback five or six yards behind the center, San Francisco was able to exploit the capabilities of Bill Kilmer and Bob Waters to perfection. Eventually the rest of the NFL was able to blunt the shotgun's effectiveness, but not before the 49ers ran up an impressive string of victories.

A second surprise of the season was the calling up of Green Bay Packer running back Paul Hornung by the U. S. Army Reserve, a move that many thought would be delayed until after the 1961 schedule had been played. Not since Hank Greenberg had been called two decades before (see "1941") had a star player been taken from a contending team while a ball season was in progress. Some charged that Hornung's being sent to Fort

Riley, Kansas, in midseason was a political move to demonstrate to the Soviet Union that the United States was serious about defending West Berlin if the Communists attacked. In any event, Green Bay partisans were disturbed that the move would destroy Packer chances of repeating as Western Division champions. (They need not have worried. Green Bay had an easy time winning the title, and the Army graciously allowed Hornung to leave camp every Sunday so that he could carry and kick the ball for Green Bay.)

HORSERACING

There was a major surprise in the racing world on November 10, 1961, when Kelso lost the prestigious Washington, D.C., International to TV Lark by three quarters of a length. The winner of $722,255 as a four-year-old, Kelso's loss was only the fifth in twenty-five races. Worse, by racing for the first time on grass and overstriding as a result, 1960's Horse of the Year came out of the race with sprains of both front and hind legs. Although the X rays showed no fractures, Kelso was shipped immediately to the DuPont farm in Chesapeake City, Maryland, through with racing for the remainder of the year. There was some speculation that the gelding might be finished on the track for good.

As It Turned Out:

Kelso survived the International loss and sprains quite well, eventually retiring with a grand total of $1,977,896 in earnings.

The remainder of the sports year was a mixture of high- and lowlights. In order to beat the NFL to the negotiating punch with graduating college football players, the American Football League held a secret draft, was discovered, and then backed off in a flurry of conflicting partial truths and outright lies. . . . Washington Redskin owner George P. Marshall decided to do something for blacks by drafting Ernie Davis as the first Redskin with a black skin. . . . After the act was completed, a rumor made the rounds that Marshall intended to trade the rights to Davis to Cleveland. Officials of both teams vociferously denied that there was any validity to the rumor. The rights to Ernie Davis were then traded from Washington to Cleveland. . . . On the baseball front, the deep thinkers of the big leagues succumbed to the spirit of self-sacrifice by going to Florida in order to discuss a variety of questions of major and minor importance—most of them minor. (One actual decision that was made came in response to a proposal that the spitball be legalized. That was defeated by a vote of 8–1. Commissioner Ford Frick came out in favor of spit.) . . . The best that baseball could manage as 1961's Rookie of the Year, meanwhile, was twenty-five-year-old Don Schwall, a pitcher with the Boston Red Sox who won fifteen games, lost seven, and never won more than nine games a season for the rest of his seven-year career. . . . On the college gridiron, Navy startled Army and 101,000 spectators by fielding a team with receivers who wore different-colored helmets than the rest of its players. . . . Frankie Carbo, underworld boxing boss, was sentenced to twenty-five years in prison for trying to cut himself in on the earnings of former welterweight boxing champion Don Jordan. . . . Floyd Patterson defended his title against a nonentity named Tom McNeeley, and Archie Moore flattened a less-than-nonentity named Albert Westphal. . . . Bob Cousy of the Boston Celtics reached the fifteen-thousand-point mark for his career by scoring twenty-two points against the Knicks on November 25. . . . Two weeks later, Wilt Chamberlain scored seventy-eight points in a triple-overtime game against the Los Angeles Lakers, beating by seven the previous career record of Elgin Baylor. (Would Ford Frick as commissioner of basketball have ordered an asterisk because Chamberlain had more opportunity?) . . . Then, as if to demonstrate that records are made to be broken, on the same night that Chamberlain shattered Baylor's mark, Larry Costello of Syracuse broke a record held jointly by Chamberlain and George Yardley by connecting on his first thirteen field-goal attempts. . . . In going over the baseball records for the year 1961, someone noted that Jim Gentile of the Baltimore Orioles had hit his fifth grand-slam home run of the season, thereby tying the 1955 feat of Ernie Banks. But—Gentile had struck his blow in the Orioles' 156th game. Since Commissioner Ford Frick had decreed that Maris had to receive an asterisk because he had hit his last two homers after 154 games were played, did this not also mean that Gentile

would get asterisked? Mr. Frick maintained a discreet silence.

FOOTBALL

The year came to a close in a blaze of pro football predictability. After holding off the Philadelphia Eagles to win the Eastern Conference championship of the NFL, the New York Giants traveled to the icebox known as Green Bay for the title game with the Packers. The result was a massacre on the rocks as the thoroughly intimidated Giants completely collapsed in the second quarter, allowing the Packers to push across twenty-four points and win the game then and there. The result, a 37–0 victory for the Packers, was the fifth most one-sided game in NFL championship history.

The American League, meanwhile, staged an uncharacteristic defensive struggle before a crowd of 29,556 at San Diego. George Blanda of the Houston Oilers began the year as he had ended it, passing his team to its second title. He also added a forty-six-yard field goal to provide the margin of victory by a score of 10–7.

With the Berlin crisis still unsettled as the year 1961 came to a close, the people of America looked for words of encouragement from new President John F. Kennedy, words that would convince the nation that it was as virile and adventurous as in days past. Kennedy did not provide the instant encouragement that was needed, instead expressing the opinion that America had changed into a sort of sedentary giant. Was it, in fact, true that the United States of 1961 had become a nation of spectators instead of performers? Some persons agreed with the criticism; others charged that it was not true, simply that the nation had more leisure time.

"The sad fact is that it looks more and more as if our national sport is not playing at all—but watching. We have become more and more, not a nation of athletes, but a nation of spectators. . . ."
John F. Kennedy, December 5, 1961

An Unusual Basketball Line Score, December 8, 1961:

Los Angeles	25	28	32	24	12	12	18—151
Philadelphia	34	28	21	26	12	12	14—147

The vast majority of Americans, of course, did not know precisely if or how much the character of the nation had changed. So they decided to sit back and watch to see how it turned out.

CHAPTER 42—REFUSING TO DO IT

The strike is essentially a nineteenth-century weapon of organized labor, having become fairly commonplace by the nineties, but the only spectator sport sufficiently professionalized and organized by that time was baseball. Many ballplayers shared discontent with steel workers, factory hands, railway workers, and other laborers of the period, knew they were being treated like cattle by management, but could not find a way out of the dilemma. Disturbed by the reserve system, arbitrary fines, salary limits, the blacklist, and other grievances, the players of the 1880s and 1890s ran into a stone wall when trying to negotiate with hardened owners.

Nevertheless, the players did what they could to organize, the first successful act coming on October 22, 1885, when nine members of the New York Giants rallied around John Montgomery Ward, who was as brilliant a leader as a pitcher (he won forty-seven games in 1879). Together the men formed the Brotherhood of Professional Base Ball Players, a weak union that eventually led, via a series of interruptions and confrontations, to the strong bargaining position of the 1970s. Before that time, there were a few abortive strikes and at least one major one, if the formation of the Players' League is counted.

1889—YANK ROBINSON'S DIRTY-PANTS TALE

The St. Louis *Globe-Democrat* described the affair as "the most serious revolt ever known in a ball club," adding, "the time has come when ballplayers will, if pressed too far, assert their independence."

Looking back on the "revolt" of Yank Robinson, it is difficult to see any great revolutionary spirit lurking beneath the surface, but the incident did illustrate that players and owners didn't always get along.

William H. (Yank) Robinson was a journeyman athlete, versatile in that he played the outfield, every infield position, caught, and even had a lifetime record of three wins, four losses as a pitcher by 1889. One day during that season he showed up at the ball park of the St. Louis Browns of the American Association wearing a pair of dirty pants. When he was ordered to change them, Robinson sent a boy across the street for a clean pair, but when the lad returned he was refused admit-

tance by the gatekeeper. Robinson unleashed a string of profanity, which was heard by owner Chris Von der Ahe in the stands.

Incensed, Von der Ahe fined Robinson twenty-five dollars and ordered him to apologize for his breaches of good conduct. Robinson replied that he would do so only if the fine were lifted. To that the owner replied, "I am still the boss of the club and I intend to run it in my own way."

Robinson's teammates at first vowed that if the fine stood, they would refuse to take the field against Kansas City in the next series. They were finally persuaded to go, but when they dropped three straight games in a listless fashion, it was asserted that they had dumped the series as a means of teaching their boss who the real bosses were. Charlie Comiskey, the Browns' manager, denied any letdown on the part of his players, but he did urge Robinson's reinstatement. The rest of the season passed without further incident, but the next year, when the Players' League challenged the other two circuits, Yank Robinson promptly jumped to Pittsburgh.

1912—TY COBB'S REVOLT

The first genuine strike in the history of baseball came not as a result of discontent with pay or working conditions, but as a kind of reflex action following the bizarre antics of one of the game's most colorful characters, Ty Cobb.

In 1911, the Detroit Tigers, under manager Hughie Jennings, had finished second to Connie Mack's Athletics, and feeling was high that the Tigers could go all the way in 1912. Cobb, recognized as the sparkplug of the team, got off to a slow start that spring—along with the rest of the Tigers—but so did the A's. With a mark of 12–14 on May 15, Cobb and his teammates were in the mood to get a streak started when they invaded the old Highlander Park at 168th Street and Broadway for a game with the lowly New Yorkers.

In the stands that day was Claude Leuker, a one-armed pressman with a foul mouth, a penetrating voice, and a violent hatred of Ty Cobb. That was hardly unusual, for ball parks all across the country had legions of Cobb-haters and -baiters. What was different was Leuker's unique ability to infuriate Cobb. By the second inning, the Detroit outfielder was so angry that he stayed in the field along the sidelines, knowing he would not come to bat and not trusting himself to pass that section of bleachers where Leuker awaited the opportunity to unleash a torrent of abuse from point-blank range.

Two innings later, Cobb sat on the Tiger bench next to Sam Crawford. Cobb was smoldering as one line of obscenity after another rained down on him. "You going to let that bum call you names?" Crawford finally asked.

Cobb replied, "I don't know how much more I can take." But he remained seated even as the abuse continued.

After the Tigers finished batting, Cobb started out toward his position. At that moment, Leuker obviously outdid himself in vituperation, for Cobb suddenly whirled around and charged the stands. In an instant, he vaulted the railing and found his target. Sportswriters of the period had a field day describing what happened. "Everything was very pleasant . . . until Ty Cobb Johnnykilbaned a spectator right on the place where he talks, started the claret, and stopped the flow of profane and vulgar words," the *Times'* writer noted. "Cobb led with a left jab and countered with a right kick to Mr. Spectator's left Weisbach, which made his peeper look as if someone had drawn a curtain over it. . . . Jabs bounded off the spectator's face like a golf ball from a rock. . . ." Leuker's description to police was shorter. "He hit me in the face with his fists, knocked me down, jumped on me, and kicked me in the ear," he said.

Cobb, of course, was banished from the game by Umpire Fred Westervelt. American League President Ban Johnson went even further, ordering an indefinite suspension for Cobb without any sort of preliminary hearing. That sort of high-handed treatment angered Cobb nearly as much as Leuker's barbs. "I should at least have had the opportunity to state my case," he said. "I feel that a great injustice has been done."

The rest of the Tigers agreed. The next day, May 17, a message was dispatched to the league office that stated, ". . . We, the undersigned, refuse to play in another game after today, until such action is adjusted to our satisfaction. [Cobb] was fully justified in his action, as no one could stand such personal abuse from anyone. We want him reinstated for tomorrow's game, May 18, or there will be no game. If the players cannot have protection we must protect ourselves."

Manager Jennings sent off a wire to Detroit owner Frank Navin, saying that he was sure the players were not bluffing, and asking what to do to avoid incurring a five-thousand-dollar fine for every game forfeited. The next day, Jennings' question ceased to be academic, for when the rest of the team heard that Cobb's suspension had not been lifted, the players took off their uniforms and left the Philadelphia ball park.

Frantic and angry, Frank Navin ordered Jennings to put some sort of team together, just to have players on the field, a command that sent Hughie racing to the local sandlots. Some students from nearby St. Joseph's College were recruited, including a pitcher named Al Travers, whose only offering, by his own admission, was a roundhouse curve. "Any ballplayer who could stop a grapefruit from rolling uphill or hit a bull in the pants with a bass fiddle was given a chance," said Arthur (Bugs) Baer, one young man who was picked as stand-in for Cobb and company.

Saturday, May 18, 1912, was a great day for some twenty thousand Philadelphians who filled Shibe Park to see either a reinstated Cobb or a team of misfits. Meanwhile, in the visitors' locker room, Al Travers and his cohorts fought off waves of nervousness as they climbed into Detroit Tiger uniforms. Travers found that pitcher George Mullin's flannels fit him quite well, which caused the striking Mullin to say, "Now listen, kid, you can steal everything but don't steal the glove."

Travers went out to take on the Philadelphia Athletics' Eddie Collins, Home Run Baker, and Herb Pennock, backed up by people named Jack Smith, Hap Ward, and Ed Irvin. Manager Hughie Jennings had beefed up his sandlot lineup with a couple of Detroit scouts, Joe Sugden—whose last game in the major leagues had been played in 1905—and Deacon McGuire, two years out of retirement.

Connie Mack, who loved victory as much as any manager, had his team play with as much vigor as if they had been facing the real Tigers. At the end of four innings, the score stood at 6–0 in favor of the A's, but then it was discovered that Al Travers had no concept of fielding his position. One bunt after another trickled down the third- and first-base lines until the A's scored eight runs. Led by Sugden and McGuire, the "Tigers" actually scored a couple of runs in their half of the fifth, but by then it was too late.

The fans, meanwhile, had a joyous time watching the pickup team try to get the A's out. At one point, the third baseman of Travers' team was struck in the mouth by a ground ball and lost two teeth. "This isn't baseball," he said, running over to Travers, "this is war."

Another time, Jack Leinhauser, stationed in the outfield, stood pounding his glove waiting for a fly ball that eventually landed on his head. Nevertheless, he remained in the game.

"I played nine innings," he recalled, "and did nothing but chase balls all over the place. Jennings finally came out and told me to forget about trying to catch them. 'Just play them off the walls,' he told me."

Al Travers, beleaguered by bunts and screaming liners, decided after a while to try something other than his slow curve. With Frank Baker at the plate, he "put everything I had behind it. He smashed the ball over the right-field fence—foul by a couple of inches." At this point, Deacon McGuire raced from his catching position and threw his arm about the young man's shoulder. "Son," he said, "if you value your life, no more of them fast balls. Stay with the slow stuff."

Finally, after one hour, forty-five minutes, the contest was over. Al Travers had pitched a full eight innings, yielded twenty-six hits, seven bases on balls, and had struck out a batter. The game, a 24–2 victory for the Athletics, counted in the standings.

That did it for Frank Navin, who decided to cancel the remaining games until the strike could be settled. When Ban Johnson fined practically every player on the Detroit team a hundred dollars, Ty Cobb decided he had played the role of martyr long enough. "Forget about me and go back to work," he told his teammates. "You've made our point. With the publicity we've received, the facts are now on record with the public. I don't want you paying any more fines. . . . Johnson will lift my suspension soon."

After the players returned to the field, Johnson did just that, fining Cobb fifty dollars and allowing him to play after a ten-day suspension. Baseball's first strike ended then. Many felt that nothing had been proven, but others disagreed. Baseball players, they said, had shown they were crazy enough to do just about anything.

1918—BASEBALL'S HOUR STRIKE

The 1918 season was an unusually turbulent one for both fan and player. The United States had declared war on Germany in April 1917, but the full effect of the manpower drain wasn't felt until the following year. By mid-1918, amid a rash of transportation foul-ups, work-or-fight orders, and player enlistments, some doubted that the baseball season would be completed or the World Series played. Everyone knew that a massive offensive was being mounted in France, that fall would be a decisive time for both the United States and Germany. Some even felt that finishing the baseball season was unpatriotic in that it diverted attention from war preparations.

Baseball officials and members of government finally agreed that the best compromise would be a shortening of the season to about 126 games, then playing the World Series in early September instead of early October. Led by pitchers Carl Mays and Babe Ruth, the Red Sox won the abbreviated season in the American League. The Chicago Cubs, led by Hippo Vaughn's 22 wins and 1.74 earned-run average, walked away from John McGraw's Giants in the National.

As the World Series began, however, trouble developed over how much the players would receive. By a previous agreement it had been determined that each winning player would get two thousand dollars and each losing player fourteen hundred dollars, but after the Series' receipts started to be tallied, it became obvious that there would not be enough to go around. With four games completed and Boston leading, 3–1, the players decided to strike until they were guaranteed the original amount of money. A meeting among player representatives Bill Killifer, Les Mann, Harry Hooper, Dave Shean, and a National Commission to resolve the issue produced only renewed animosity. "While the Commission has taken no action on the matter, it is pretty certain now that the winners' share will be chopped to twelve hundred dollars and the losers' to eight hundred dollars," one reporter wrote. "If this is done the echo of the kick from the ballplayers will be heard all across the continent."

Before the fifth game, rumors spread that the players would stick to their strike threat. Nevertheless, a capacity crowd showed up at Boston, eager to see the Red Sox finish off the Cubs. Even as the fans made their way to the park, angry negotiations continued. Some of the proposals were niggardly, others grandiose. For example, Harry Hooper, slugging outfielder for the Red Sox, argued that players on the teams that finished second, third, and fourth should give up the small share of the Series money they would receive in order that the winners get their full amount.

While the discussions continued, game time came and passed. Patrolmen and mounted policemen quietly stationed themselves at strategic points around the field in the event there should be no game and a resultant demonstration. A band, meanwhile, kept up a rapid fire of lively tunes in the hopes of soothing the crowd, but an air of general malaise spread as a half hour passed with no players in sight.

A welcome diversion was provided when a contingent of soldiers and sailors who had been wounded in action arrived at the park. "Most of them were on crutches and bandaged," it was reported, "and someone started three vociferous cheers for them, which brought a smiling light into their eyes."

Behind the scenes, a new actor arrived, none other than the former mayor of Boston, "Honey Fitz" Fitzgerald. A semimiraculous transformation followed as he pleaded with the athletes to go on with the show and settle their differences later. The players must have been intelligent enough to realize that as soon as the World Series was over, they had virtually no bargaining power. Nevertheless, they agreed to play the game and, in a spirit of blooming generosity and patriotism, players Mann, Killifer, Hooper, and Scott actually offered to give their share of Series money to some war charity if everyone else involved in the dispute, including members of the Commission, would do likewise. "There has been no evidence of the spirit of these players becoming general," one reporter noted sarcastically.

The impasse over, the Red Sox and the Cubs took the field for the fifth game. Despite the hour delay, the crowd was enthusiastically inclined toward forgiveness, cheering with minimal traces of anger or sarcasm. Fred Merkle, a "goat" of the 1912 World Series while with the Giants, singled to drive in the Cubs' first run in the third inning, and that was enough for pitcher Hippo Vaughn. Limiting the Red Sox to but four hits and no runs, he presided over a 3–0 Chicago victory. That was the Cubs' last gasp, however, as Boston wrapped up the Series the next day.

As for the money and its distribution, the players earned less than their worst fears. Boston's winning share came to only $1108.45 per player. A sliding scale provided significantly less for the other first-division clubs in both leagues, the low amount being about $135 for members of the fourth-place teams.

1925—SITTING ON THE ICE

In the spring of 1925, the Hamilton Tigers of the National Hockey League enjoyed the best record of any team in the league. They were scheduled to meet the winner of the Toronto-Montreal series in the playoffs, but Redvers Green of Hamilton claimed that his team had performed in more games than called for in the contract. The Hamilton players therefore voted not to take part in the playoffs unless they received additional money.

League President Frank Calder promptly suspended and fined the players, declaring that the winner of the Montreal-Toronto series would be NHL champion. Taking still another step, he then announced that the Hamilton franchise would be sold to New York interests. In this respect, it can hardly be said that hockey's first strike was a great success.

1935—CADDIES' STRIKE

In the days before motorized golf carts, the caddie was a very important commodity. Realizing that their presence on the fairways was often the difference between recreation and manual labor for their customers, early caddies were not hesitant to strike as a means of earning higher wages.

One of the first caddie strikes occurred in 1899, at the Harbor Hill Golf Club, New Brighton, Staten Island. In August of that year, when refused a $.10 increase per round, the caddies walked off the course en masse. Worse, they remained on the periphery of the golf club, where they "hooted and yelled like Indians," in the words of the New York *Times,* at the few golfers who decided to carry their own clubs and bags.

Although attendance dropped after the strike started, partly because of intimidation and partly because of laziness on the part of members, the caddies went even farther by sneaking on the course in order to steal direction flags, discs, balls, and hole cups. This brought Captain Otto Hockmeyer of the local police onto the scene: he promptly ordered nine youngsters arrested. "Where the matter will end is not known," one reporter wrote, "but it is thought that with the ringleaders arrested the other boys will abandon the fight and come to terms."

Not long afterward, the dispute was settled, but the caddies were still paid less than they thought they deserved. Fees for caddies increased so gradually, in fact, that by 1935 those who might have been sons of the 1899 strikers earned only $.75 cents for an 18-hole round of golf. Because it was the height of America's Depression, many of the caddies at Brooklyn's Dyker Beach course were married men with children. Work was hard to get anywhere, but in July of 1935 the 225 registered caddies decided to go on strike. One of their grievances was the $.75 fee, which had not been increased from the year before, even though the length of the course had been nearly doubled, to a hefty 6,539 yards. The caddies were also required to buy their own uniforms of brown trousers, white golfing cap, and white shirt with the green maple leaf of the Parks Department on the front and an identifying number on the back. The cost was about $4.50. Another problem was that veteran caddies wanted to be able to work for regular golfers, which was prohibited. In order to circumvent the rule, some caddies took to what they called "hillbillying." One caddie explained the system: "If we wanna work for a steady," he said, "there's a hill at the first tee and we signal the man to tee off and drop his bag just over the hill. Then we back off the line and go out and caddy for him; and if we get caught we get suspended. That's 'hillbilling.' "

Before going on strike, leaders of the caddie group met with park and city officials, presenting them with a petition of demands. When no agreement could be reached, the walkout began. The next day, July 16, about 400 golfers showed up at the Dyker Beach course only to be informed that they would have to carry their own bags. About 300 did so, but officials at the golf club tried to bargain with the caddies. It was agreed that veteran caddies would be allowed to work with "steadies" and that no reprisals would be taken against the strikers; increasing the fee from $.75 to $1.00, however, was out of the question. Unimpressed by management's generosity, the caddies voted to stay out.

Two days later, Parks Commissioner Robert Moses entered the picture in characteristic fashion. A blunt and determined man who would rise rapidly in the New York planning area, Moses issued an order that negotiations with the striking caddies were to be halted and "The permits of all caddies refusing to abide by the rules and regulations of the Department of Parks will be revoked at noon, Friday, July 19."

The caddies, now 215 in number, met that afternoon on a vacant lot near the golf course and voted to remain out until all their demands had been granted.

When noon of July 19 arrived with no caddies reporting, Commissioner Moses proved he was not bluffing. News of a lockout spread, panicking about a third of the strikers. When they went to the club, however, they were bluntly informed that it was too late. Their jobs were gone. Next day the Parks Department began trucking in caddies from other parts of the city. Thirty policemen also had been moved onto the course to make sure there were no disturbances, as the striking caddies began to move angrily near the clubhouse following the announcement that their jobs had been taken away from them.

All was not lost, however. When he saw what was happening, Alderman Donald L. O'Toole filed a protest with Mayor LaGuardia, charging that the use of city equipment to break a strike was illegal and against the interest of organized labor. O'Toole visited the course, talked with the strike-breaking caddies, and when he discovered that many were inexperienced, not wearing uniforms, and were receiving extra benefits such as free lunch and transportation, he professed anger and amazement.

That brought organized labor into the picture. "The striking caddies have the whole-hearted support of all union men in this city,"

said Joseph P. Ryan, president of the Central Trades and Labor Council. Alderman O'Toole suggested that a meeting be held with Mayor LaGuardia. The offer was accepted and on July 21, leaders of the caddies' group waited outside the mayor's office while O'Toole presented their case. In the meantime, golfing continued at the Dyker Beach course, but more than 200 players carried their own clubs, saying they "would rather caddy for themselves than entrust the job to inexperienced boys."

Alderman O'Toole's clout turned out to be less than the optimistic caddies hoped for, however. When he emerged from the mayor's office, all he could offer the strikers were their jobs—no pay increase, no agreement to work with steady golfers, not even permission to discard the heavy Parks Department sweatshirt during very hot weather. It was, he said sadly, a case of take it or leave it.

Remembering that it was the Depression, the unhappy but wiser caddies took it.

1937—SITTING ON THE ICE AGAIN

It was the night of February 14, 1937, when members of the New York Rovers hockey team decided to stage a sit-down strike against the tyranny of management.

The cause of the players' grief was neither playing conditions nor money. After having been on the free-ticket list all season, the Rovers were shocked to learn that they would receive no more complimentary ducats for friends and relatives. They promptly perched themselves on benches, rubbing tables, and the floor of their dressing room, steadfastly refusing to put on their uniforms for a scheduled game with Hershey until assured the free tickets would be returned.

For a half hour coach Frank Nighbor pleaded with his players while Madison Square Garden filled with a near-capacity crowd of 15,277 fans. Finally, on the promise that they would be able to receive the tickets after the game, the Rovers changed into their uniforms. They then went onto the ice and beat Hershey, 6–3, scoring five goals in the final period.

1970—FOOTBALL'S ABORTIVE STRIKE

"This is to inform you that the National Football League Players' Association is now officially on strike, and we believe it would be in the best interest of the fans and pro football to quickly conclude this dispute."

The telegram was delivered in late July 1970 to Commissioner Pete Rozelle, just as the professional football training camps were about to open.

Its timing and wording point up two

axioms that work well for both player and management when a strike is concerned:

1. Always base your case on its being "in the interest of the fans," as this will blunt the force of your greed, be you member of team or management.
2. Always stage your strike just before training camp begins. If you are a player, this means you will get out of some hard work. If you are management, this means you will be able to save some training-camp expenses.

There is one dangerous aspect of the arrangement, however, especially for management: The impending strike must be settled before the beginning of the lucrative exhibition (or "preseason") schedule.

Just such a delicate balance was achieved in July 1970. After dawdling over the pros and cons of increased player pension funds—the athletes demanded $26 million over four years while the owners were willing to give "only" $18 million—management finally lost its collective temper. Until the strike was settled, they said, only rookies would be allowed in training camps, the exception being the camp of the Kansas City Chiefs, who were scheduled to play the 1970 College All-Stars in Chicago's annual charity game.

When the talks continued to fail, the owners then tried another tactic, deciding to open the training camps to any veteran players who wished to come. A trickle did break the ranks, including All-Pro linebacker Mike Curtis of the Baltimore Colts. When he entered the training camp at Westminster, Maryland, he was greeted by applause from the rookies. "Spell my name right," he advised newspapermen. "It probably will be the last time you use it until I'm busted out of the league."

Other reporting veterans included Tim McCann, a New York Giant defensive back, and Bobby Walden and Curt Gentry of the Pittsburgh Steelers. This led to barely veiled hints of reprisal. "I'm not making any threats," said six-seven Ben Davidson of the Oakland Raiders, "but you know how bitter some of these labor disputes get. There are bombings and everything. Football is a rough game and it's conceivable that a team that went against us and all the other teams in the dispute might find itself suffering an unusual number of injuries."

Finally Commissioner Pete Rozelle entered the picture in an effort to break the deadlock. The owners, panicked at the thought of losing an estimated $1 million if the players did not show up for the ten exhibition games Friday and Saturday nights, August 7 and 8, agreed to raise their pension-fund contribution to $19.1 million. A hectic 22-hour bargaining session followed at the National Football League office at 410 Park Avenue, New York. As the debate dragged on, some owners flopped on the couch of Commissioner Rozelle's office; others slept on the beige carpet; Sid Gillman, general manager of the San Diego Chargers, was generally conceded to be the champion snorer.

Dressed in blue suit and tie, Rozelle kept cool long after the air conditioning was turned off at midnight, and he emerged as the hero of the dilemma by bringing the players and management together. When the session ended, the players had an $11 million increase in their pension fund; the owners had a four-year agreement that would guarantee them a semblance of labor peace until 1974.

1970—UMPIRES' STRIKE

The anger had been building in major-league umpires for several months, it seemed. Traditional objects of scorn, baseball's arbiters had received only minimal pay increases at the same time players' salaries skyrocketed; they had been second-guessed by television announcers equipped with instant-replay facilities; then, in September 1970, pitcher Dick Selma of the Phillies charged that the umpires had "fixed" a game between Philadelphia and the New York Mets. The $500 fine assessed Selma hardly seemed sufficient punishment to the long-suffering men in blue.

Finally, at the end of the month, the umpires' union asked that the pay for playoff and World Series games be raised. When management offered what were considered "token" increases of $500, the umpires regarded it as a slap in the face. "You got to believe if the money wasn't there, we wouldn't ask for it," said one umpire who wished to remain anonymous, "but look at the gate this year. Look at what the players got for themselves. . . . You start to think, is that all they think about us—$500?"

When management refused to increase the offer, the forty-eight-member umpires' union voted to strike just as the playoff series were

What the Umpires Got		What They Asked for	What Mgt. Offered
Playoffs	$4,000	$5,000	$3,000
Series	$8,000	$10,000	$7,000

beginning in Pittsburgh and Bloomington, Minnesota. At Three Rivers Stadium, the umps established picket lines outside the park, carrying signs that read, "Major-league umpires on strike for wages." Management, meanwhile, hastily sent off messages to several minor-league umpires and retired umpires Charlie Berry and John Stevens.

As the playoffs started with the patchwork crews, Marvin Miller, executive director of the Player Association, expressed dismay at the situation. "For many, many years," he said, the umpires "were unorganized, and like many unorganized people, they were vastly underpaid. I think a problem like this should have been resolved long ago." As to the substitute umpires, he added, "Scabs are scabs."

The playoff games of October 3, 1970, were without incident. But before the start of the second playoff contests, employees of Pittsburgh's Three Rivers Stadium, who were represented by two labor unions, refused to cross the picket line established by the umpires. A new round of negotiations started, and agreement was finally reached. The umpires signed a four-year contract calling for a fee of $4,000 for the playoffs and $8,000 for the World Series beginning in 1972. It wasn't perfect, they admitted, but at least it gave the men in blue a measure of respect.

1967—Tempest in an Integrated Teapot

When it was discovered that only one of six cheerleaders at Madison High School, Madison, Illinois, was black, seventeen black athletes at the school went on strike, refusing to play.

When the seventeen black athletes were suspended for striking, most of the thirteen hundred black students at the school boycotted classes.

When the school board reversed itself and reinstated the seventeen striking athletes, most of the sixteen hundred white students of the school boycotted classes.

When everyone got tired of boycotting and arguing after nearly a month, and half of the cheerleading corps was black and half white, things returned to normal.

1972—BASEBALL'S REAL STRIKE

"Obviously the losers in the strike action taken tonight are the sports fans of America."

With that bit of original thought from Commissioner Bowie Kuhn, the baseball strike of 1972 began. Previously to March 31 of that year, talks had dragged on endlessly concerning the players' pension fund. Then both sides refused to budge and the players' representatives voted by a margin of 47–0, with a single abstention, to strike until the pension-fund dilemma was settled.

With the spring-training camps already opened, the decision to strike caused some

---

What the Players Got	What They Asked for
$5,400,000 per year from management for pension fund	$6,200,000

---

problems. Six hundred players scattered around the country were simply told to remove their equipment from lockers in the clubhouses. Daily expense accounts for food and lodging ended, although some clubs gave their players one-way nonrefundable plane tickets to wherever the men wanted to go. Most participants on both sides of the fence were certain the impasse would last quite a while. Said Jim Toomey, assistant general manager of the St. Louis Cardinals: "There will be no more games in Florida and there may not be any more games for months."

Contrary to the occasionally optimistic statements that everything would be settled in time for Opening Day, the scheduled date for the 1972 season openers passed with not a ball being thrown in anger. And as the days passed still another issue was created: Would the striking players be paid for an entire season or lose salary proportional to the unplayed games? Both sides, of course, maintained they were in the right and would hold firm to their positions.

The situation seemed truly desperate, with another truly ominous cloud on the horizon. Suppose, someone suggested, fans across the nation discovered they didn't really miss baseball all that much? It was, after all, a possibility. For more than a century the sport dominated the summer season. Given the opportunity to pursue other avenues of recreation, baseball addicts might develop new tastes, never to return to their old one. It was a disquieting thought.

Fortunately for the owners, players, agents, and other hangers-on, the nation's Number 1 Spectator threw his weight into the battle. Richard M. Nixon was so concerned he took time out from planning legal and illegal strategy to secure himself a second term of office as United States President to suggest that both sides reconsider their positions in order to arrive at a prompt settlement. It was suspected that the Chief Executive leaned heavier on the owners than the athletes, for the baseball executives soon increased their offer to the players. Thirteen days after the strike began, after a total of eighty-six games had been missed from the regular season, an agreement was reached to start playing immediately. The owners raised their offer from $400,000 to $500,000 and it was agreed that the missed games would not be replayed. But the players would be paid on the basis of a 155- or 156-game season, meaning that for some in higher brackets, the week's strike was costly.

Some Comments on the 1972 Baseball Strike:
"The greedy bastards. How could they do it?"

> Reading, Pennsylvania,
> beer distributor

"Maybe the average fan couldn't sympathize with us. But we thought it was important. The important thing is, we stuck together."

> Frank Robinson,
> Los Angeles Dodgers

"The first four hundred readers to send in ballots say the strike was not justified."

> The Sporting News

"Money is not the issue. The real issue is the owners' attempt to punish the players for having the audacity not to crawl."

> Marvin Miller,
> players' attorney

1974—FOOTBALL'S REAL STRIKE
In 1970, players of the National Football League struck primarily for money, pension payments, and other benefits. Four years later, although many financial issues were involved, the players were more concerned about "freedom" issues—elimination of the reserve system, options, waivers, and the Rozelle Rule restricting movement of players from one team to another even after they had fulfilled their contracts and played out their options.

When the contract signed in 1970 ran out in January 1974, there was plenty of time to hammer out a new agreement; but once again the owners dragged their feet, refusing to believe that the athletes would strike again.

By early July, however, when a new contract had not been drawn up, rumors of a new walkout started to circulate. Picket lines formed at most of the training camps, including that of the champion Miami Dolphins, who were scheduled to play the traditional

game against the College All-Stars on Friday, July 26. Perhaps the owners counted on the fact that the All-Star game was a worthy, charitable contest as a means of breaking the strike's momentum. Once that game was played, they reasoned, members of the Dolphins as well as several score top rookies would have become committed to the season's beginning. The rest of the teams would then fall into line.

Members of the NFL Players' Association were wise to this line of reasoning, however, and they made plans to influence the College All-Stars against playing, even if this meant public disfavor. Most of the rookies had already reported to the All-Star training camp, but established veterans made every effort to contact them and have them join the strikers.

On July 8, following a meeting that was marked by heated arguments and shouting, Dave Casper of Notre Dame, spokesman for the collegians, issued a brief statement. "We, in light of a difficult situation," he said, "will honor the picket lines. We have signed an agreement to that effect."

The two sentences spelled an end to the 1974 Chicago *Tribune* charities game, which had raised $3.2 million since it was inaugurated four decades before. Few really regretted that the annual fiasco—which the collegians had not won since 1963—had been canceled, except that it did provide funds for needy children. As an artistic event, however, it had become an inconvenience for rookies and coaches as well as a crashing bore for spectators.

In the wake of blame-placing for the charitable loss, Bill Curry, president of the NFL Players' Association, tried to smooth things over by announcing that the union would donate half the receipts of the 1973 game—about $100,000—to Chicago *Tribune* charities. He did not say where the union would get the money.

Having won the opening battle, the players continued to walk their picket lines while the owners and coaching staffs of the various

---

Public Opinion—Did It Matter?
On July 15, the Milwaukee Journal *took a straw vote that produced the conclusion that 88.7 per cent of those answering the ballots favored the owners, only 4 per cent the players. On the same day, another poll completed by Worcester (Massachusetts) radio station WTAG, showed that 83 per cent of the fans who participated sided with owners.*

clubs made preparations to begin the 1974 season with a lineup of rookies and free agents. In the meantime, the World Football League swung into action, filling a void for spectators who wanted to watch professional football regardless of the quality of play. By mid-July, with the strike heading into its third week, the players were still united, although several players had crossed the picket lines to begin workouts with the rookies in various camps. Federal mediator W. J. Usery, Jr., continued to work with both sides for another three weeks while it became obvious that the 1974 season would be either canceled or played with talent that would make the WFL shine by comparison. Then, on August 11, an announcement was made that the players had agreed to a fourteen-day "cooling off" period, during which they would report to training camp.

No one knew exactly what the cooling-off period really meant. Some hinted it was a capitulation on the part of the players; others said the owners had given in. In any event, nearly everyone realized that the fourteen days would assure that the season began while negotiations continued. If that was the object of the decision, it worked. The 1974 season was played, and the painful, often acrimonious, working out of the freedom issues continued.

Four months later, the Chicago *Tribune* charities announced that the NFL Players' Association had contributed $20,000 and the owners sent $106,000 as compensation for the All-Star game's cancellation.

1977—BASKETBALL REFEREES DO IT, TOO

With the average salary of 1977 basketball players $109,000 a year, it was unlikely that any member of that group would consider anything so outlandish as a strike.

With the officials, however, it was another matter. Their base pay was $18,000, with the average salary being $26,000 plus $27 a day for all expenses except air fare. A number of referees claimed this forced them to stay at second-class hotels or share rooms with fellow officials. Richie Phillips, the Philadelphia lawyer representing the twenty-six men calling games for the NBA, said, "These men are the best in the world at their profession. They

have a great deal of influence on a game in which everything else has gone up. . . . The commissioner makes $350,000. Three years ago his salary was $100,000. CBS is paying more for TV rights. Ratings are good. So why not strike for better wages while the time is ripe?"

On the last day of the regular season of 1976–77, just before the start of the playoffs, twenty-four of the twenty-six regular referees did just that. The league responded by recruiting officials from minor leagues, including Vince McKelvey, a Trenton insurance adjustor who worked part-time with the Eastern Basketball League, and Mike Eggers, a twenty-six-year-old CPA with the Pacific Eight Conference. The playoffs continued while Phillips fulminated about the "scabs" who had replaced the regular officials. "How are you going to replace twenty-four men at the pinnacle of their profession with JV referees?" he demanded.

Although most coaches and players greeted the substitute officials warmly—perhaps in response to league policy—at least one coach, Denver's Larry Brown, quickly abandoned the party line. "I've gotten tired of people . . . saying the officiating by these new people is great," he said. "It's not."

A near-riot at a game between Detroit and Golden Gate, which might have been averted by more experienced officials, added substance to the contention that the NBA was being penny-wise and pound-foolish in refusing to negotiate seriously with the striking officials. On April 25, with the playoffs not yet completed, the NBA agreed to give the strikers an across-the-board increase of $150 per game. In addition, it was agreed that the National Association of Basketball Referees would be recognized as the exclusive bargaining agent for the officials.

"They did not get the whole loaf and we did not get the whole loaf," said lawyer Richie Phillips after the sixteen-day strike had been terminated. "We are pleased the strike is over. We consider it a victory for everyone concerned—the league, players, referees, and the fans."

And the fans.

Now there was a phrase with a very familiar ring.

CHAPTER 43—DISSENTERS

Although most American newspapers of the late twentieth century give more space to sports than to art, books, education, music, or the theater, the unbridled love for sports and the availability of sports information were not always facts of American life.

In colonial days, religion—as defined by the Puritans—tended to suppress the spread of sports. Despite Sunday being a day of recreation before the Reformation, the Puritans ordered the burning of the *Book of Sports,* in which King James I recommended the playing of games after Sunday services. Americans in general were intimidated by early moralists who equated all forms of amusement with sin and, by extension, eternal damnation.

In addition to those who objected to sports on religious grounds, there were those—often well intentioned—who regarded the exertions of some athletics as detrimental to health. Still others were simply scornful because they looked upon sporting activity as a waste of time compared to reading, contemplation, or bird watching.

Nevertheless, after the Revolutionary War, horseracing steadily increased in popularity to the point where a match race held in 1823 between a horse named Henry and one named Eclipse drew sixty thousand spectators. Boxing, although illegal, drew large crowds who braved police harassment to follow their favorites from one county or state to another. And baseball, of course, not only attracted

---

Dissenter for Health Reasons: Do Velocipedes Cause Rupture?
In 1869, at the height of the velocipede-riding mania, a physician from West Farm, New York, speculated on whether such exercise brought on hernias. "All those muscles which, when the body is in one straight line, were tense, now become relaxed," he wrote. "The hernial rings and canals are somewhat open, and while thus open, the viscera powerfully pressed upon. . . ." In other words, yes, the doctor thought bicycle riding could lead to the wearing of a truss.

---

larger and larger crowds but also soon reached the point where it was able to charge admission to its games.

THE AGONY OF SUNDAY BASEBALL—PART ONE

By the end of the nineteenth century, exorcising the demon of Sunday baseball seemed a clear and absolute necessity to many people. The nation, they said, stood at a moral crossroads. If the young United States did not draw the line at Sunday baseball, the country's future would be downhill all the way, the same as Rome and numerous other hedonistic societies.

Not everyone agreed. One minister described baseball on Sunday as a form of "moral leprosy," but others were in favor of it. "The game of baseball is not in itself immoral or demoralizing," another cleric wrote, then showed his ignorance of professional players' habits by adding: "It cannot be successfully played except by temperate men."

The Voices of Doom—Baseball Denounced from the Pulpit:
"It can be shown by God's word that a man who breaks the Sabbath is a ruin to society . . . because no nation can prosper that does not respect it."
"Baseball . . . is a traveling contagion that should be quarantined for the public good. The pleasure-seeking spirit weakens and destroys the nobler traits of character. It turns men into dudes and women into dudines."

The difficulty arose not because of rampant hedonism sweeping the nation, but simply because the game was growing in popularity during an era when Sunday was the only day of leisure for most workingmen. Thoroughly aware of this vast untapped source of attendance, many enterprising owners decided during the 1880s to risk eternal perdition for larger crowds. The Union Association was founded on Sunday baseball and beer sales, but lasted only one year. The more successful American Association was also dedicated to beer and Sunday, where allowed; implementing that dedication in the face of organized opposition was another matter.

In Baltimore, an AA city in 1890, it was decided to test the "blue laws" of the city by scheduling some games against Washington clubs. The first was played in Anne Arundel Park on June 8, 1890, and from the very outset, it was possible to smell money. The park gates did not open until one-thirty, but well before then thousands of fans were waiting to go inside. The first of many Baltimore and Ohio excursion trains arrived at two-twenty, disgorging streams of spectators. Nearly nine thousand fans—a huge crowd for the time— filled the wooden bleachers by game time, and nearly as many youngsters clustered around the twelve-foot-high fence that separated the "unholy" event from the rest of Anne Arundel County.

Two hours later, the game ended in a 5–4 victory for Washington. No one had been struck by lightning, but the next day the Sabbath Association of Maryland swung into action. Their instrument was James Armiger, the genial, methodical sheriff of Anne Arundel County. During the next week, Armiger consulted with Maryland States Attorney J. M. Munroe to see if arresting the Sunday ballplayers was legal. It was, the statute book said. And so, armed with the terrible swift sword of Article 27, Section 247, Sheriff Armiger sallied forth on June 15, 1890. All eyes were on him as he entered the ball park, but to everyone's surprise, Armiger sat quietly in the press box from the beginning of the contest until the end. Only then did he rise and approach Baltimore Manager Bill Barnie with news that he was under arrest.

The Law (at Least in Maryland):
"No persons whatsoever shall work or do any bodily labor on the Lord's Day, commonly known as Sunday . . . works of charity and necessity always excepted . . . and any person transgressing this section and being thereof convicted before a justice of the peace shall forfeit $5.00. . . ."

Released on $300 bail shortly afterward, Barnie announced that he had no intention of giving up Sunday baseball. He based his decision on the contention that baseball was entertainment, not work. The opposition was not impressed with this argument. More warrants were drawn up the next week as ministers railed against everyone connected with the Sabbath games.

The following Sunday, the drama continued as James Armiger once again strolled into the ball park. This time, however, he did not wait until the game was over to act. After the first inning, he walked onto the field and served papers on Manager Barnie. He then arrested a different Baltimore player after each inning. Simultaneously, D.C. policemen moved against the Washington club by arresting the secretary and levying a fine of $2.00 per player, and court costs (the entire Washington bill came to $47.50). Farther north, twelve members of the Law and Order League of Irondequoit (New York) interrupted a game between Brooklyn and Rochester, trying to serve warrants. Blows were exchanged until the reformers, seeing they were getting the worse of it, agreed to allow the game to continue under the condition that "the players considered themselves under arrest at the expiration of play."

The following season, as city councils and state legislatures across the nation debated the issue, attacks on the moral leprosy continued, a climax of sorts being reached on May 24, 1891, during a game between Cincinnati and Philadelphia. The Cincinnati chief of police marched onto the field with sixty officers, arrested the entire team, and carted them off to the station, where they were held for a bond of $5,400.

Those opposing the playing of Sunday baseball seemed to have won. But as any fan knew, the game wasn't over until the final out.

THE CHAMPIONSHIP FIGHT NOBODY WANTED

In effect, the 1849 battle between Yankee Sullivan and Tom Hyer was the first heavyweight championship fight in the United States. Promoters should have fought each other for the privilege of staging it; instead, it seemed no one wanted the participants around.

Boxing—or "prizefighting"—was illegal then, of course, which may have had a lot to do with the Keystone Kops atmosphere surrounding the contest. Yet there were many who were willing to brave official censure to watch the bareknuckle boys go at it until one or the other could no longer continue.

The prefight ballyhoo started well before that landmark date of February 7, 1849. Months before, Sullivan, infuriated by the suggestion that he was afraid of Hyer, had stormed into a New York saloon and challenged the champion then and there. Hyer responded by pounding Sullivan into submission within three minutes, an act of commercial naïveté that could have ruined the real fight. It helped, naturally, when a boxing cohort of Hyer's was murdered, all of which made the match between the two something of a grudge affair.

About Yankee Sullivan:

Born in Ireland, Sullivan—who earned the nickname "Yankee" because he entered the ring once with an American flag draped around him—came to the United States after he was thirty. He opened a saloon in New York known as the "Sawdust House" during the early 1840s, all the while continuing to box. One of his best fights was against Vincent Hammond on September 2, 1841, at Philadelphia. Sullivan won in seven rounds. When Tom Hyer defeated Country McCluskey, Sullivan was regarded as the logical challenger.

It was decided that the fight would be held in Maryland on a deserted piece of real estate known as Pool's Island in the middle of Chesapeake Bay. As soon as they heard of it, Maryland officials responded with the warning that the "disgusting exhibition" would not be allowed. Two companies of officers were activated, the Independent Blues and Independent Grays, and a steamer, the *Boston,* chartered as the state's assault craft.

Stimulated rather than deterred by the police activity, fight fans, gamblers, and other amateur and professional patrons of the pugilistic art began pouring into Baltimore during the week before the fight. On February 6, Hyer arrived at Carroll's Island, just south of the city, while the Sullivan group settled into one of the two buildings on Pool's Island. A crew of workmen began clearing an area within which the fight would take place. Simultaneously the steamer *Cumberland* left Philadelphia with about a hundred fans, and two schooners each carrying forty fans left Baltimore.

Just before midnight, the *Boston,* loaded with more than a hundred officers and towing a scow for the transporting of prisoners, pulled out of Baltimore Harbor. Two hours later the expedition arrived at Carroll's Island and the men eagerly swarmed ashore to see who could be the first to lay arresting hands on Hyer.

To their dismay, Carroll's Island was deserted. Forewarned, the Hyer party had left early that evening. In the meantime, Hyer and his friends had arrived at Pool's Island and gone to sleep in the second building. A careful watch was maintained to prevent their being surrounded, for the police outnumbered the fighters' parties, 10–1.

Weather and police incompetence improved the odds considerably. By the time Captain Gifford's men arrived at Pool's Island the scow was barely afloat and the bay so rough that only ten men were able to reach shore. Tired and discouraged, the landing force trundled up to the buildings with a maximum of noise and assaulted frontally.

Neither fighter's party was surprised. At the sound of tramping feet, Hyer crept downstairs and hid himself on the first floor. When the police charged into the house, they went right by him and upstairs to the room where Hyer's trainer, George Thompson, was sleeping. Assuming him to be the champion, they placed him under arrest while Hyer slipped out a ground-floor window and into a small boat.

The operation against Yankee Sullivan was even more inept. Barging into the second structure, the police found themselves facing Sullivan and Tom O'Donnell, his large sparring partner, without knowing who was who. Sullivan solved the mystery for them by putting his hand on O'Donnell's shoulder, shoving and yelling: "Run, Sullivan! Run!" O'Donnell ran and, incredibly, every last one of the police officers took off in hot pursuit. Sullivan strolled calmly out of the building and waded to a nearby schooner.

It was not until an hour later that the police discovered their mistake. In the meantime, the two schooners and the steamer had scattered. The police wondered which boat the fighters had taken, and finally agreed that they must be on the larger *Cumberland.* Under a heavy press of steam, they managed

---

The End of Yankee Sullivan:

Seven years later, while still in his forties, Yankee Sullivan came to a sad end. In 1853, he fought young John Morrissey at Boston Corners, a brutal battle that ended in the thirty-seventh round when the audience became so involved a brawl started that was more interesting than the fight in the ring. Sullivan drifted West after that, settling in San Francisco, where he engaged in stuffing ballot boxes and handling pugilistic chores for local politicians. Eventually he got in trouble with the vigilantes and was thrown in jail. While in prison, he severed the main artery of his left arm and was found dead in his cell on May 31, 1856.

---

to overhaul the ship, brought her to, and thoroughly searched for the pugilists, who were not there. Later, Captain Gifford and his men ran the *Boston* onto a sandbar, remaining there until evening, when they had to be rescued by a second police boat.

One Baltimore paper tried to salvage a modicum of state pride by pointing out that the police action had prevented Maryland's soil "from being desecrated by so foul and brutal an exhibition."

Such was not the case, however. Pulling ashore at Maryland's Kent County, on the eastern shore of the bay, the fighters performed before a meager audience, which had managed to survive the official harassment. Hyer won in the sixteenth round, earning a purse of $10,000. Sullivan suffered a "slightly fractured skull." By all accounts, it must have been an anticlimax.

THOSE AGAINST FOOTBALL—PART ONE

College football was still in its infancy when the first critics started hammering away at the desensitizing effects of the game. In November 1883, Charles Eliot Norton, chairman of the Athletic Committee of the Harvard College faculty, took the unpopular step of recommending that the school discontinue the game because of the high number of accidents on the playing field. In a letter to the team captain, R. M. Appleton, he wrote, "The committee believe that the games hotly played under these rules have already begun to degenerate from a manly, if rough, sport into brutal and dangerous contests." Norton added that arrangements should be made to call off games scheduled to be played in the future.

The decision created shock waves not only on the Harvard campus but also on those of rivals Yale and Princeton. Yale's chief complaint was that the 1882 Thanksgiving Day game between Yale and Harvard had raised a sum of $1,200, which went to Harvard. Calling the 1883 game at such a late date, the Yalemen protested, would deprive their school of the opportunity to raise a similar amount.

Peace talks were held late in the month and eventually Norton and other members of the Harvard Committee relented. Yale and Harvard played their 1883 game, which was won by Yale, 23–2. The 1884 season was played as well, but discontent with the way the game was played continued to grow, especially at Harvard. By a vote of 25–4, the Committee agreed to ban games during 1885, and this time the ruling stuck. Football was restored the following year, but many remained fervent in their belief that the game was a demoralizing and evil influence on the colleges.

THE HALL-FITZSIMMONS FIGHT

Seeking to bring a major sporting attraction to St. Paul, the Minnesota Athletic Club in 1891 managed to sign Bob Fitzsimmons and Jim Hall, who agreed to fight on Wednesday, July 23, in that city. More than $15,000 was pledged for the purse and various expenses, and fight fans looked forward to the bout.

Unfortunately, the enthusiasts had not anticipated that quite so many clergymen of St. Paul would be able to mount such a strong protest against the coming bout. As the date neared, pulpit wrath tumbled forth in ever-increasing volume, and private citizens, urged on by their ministers, petitioned legislators and editors. On July 19, Bishop Gilbert and Archbishop Ireland announced that a mass meeting would be held to denounce the "brutal exhibition." Seven St. Paul Church leaders devoted their Sunday sermons to the evils of pugilism, and one influential newspaper, the *Pioneer Press,* joined the antifight forces the week before Fitzsimmons and Hall were scheduled to enter the ring. Daniel R. Noyes, a member of the St. Paul Chamber of Commerce, made a personal appeal to Mayor Smith, who promptly passed the buck upstairs to Governor Merriam. The governor, it turned out, was caught in a mild conflict of interest, being president of the Merchants' National Bank, which had advanced the money for the boxers' purses. In addition, Merriam was a personal friend and associate of the Minnesota Athletic Club treasurer, H. M. Seymour, who also happened to be cashier at the bank. It was hardly surprising then that Governor Merriam favored the fight, despite the fact that the Minnesota law clearly stated that anyone engaging in a prizefight, issuing a challenge for one, or trying to stage a bout would be guilty of a misdemeanor and subject to thirty-to-ninety-days' imprisonment.

"To witness such exhibitions of skill and endurance is the appropriate amusement of the fast set, the toughs, the rowdies, and the gamblers, and they cannot be lifted to the plane of respectability except by lowering respectability at least halfway to the level of these natural and ordinary associations."

Pioneer Press

When it became apparent that the governor was going to let things slide, a crowd of approximately five thousand started for the state Capitol. On the morning of July 21, about five hundred of the more violent antifight people swarmed over the lawns and trampled flowers as they tried to present their case against violence. Confronted by what one newspaper called "a panting crowd of men and women," the governor turned to Attorney General Clapp for an opinion. Clapp suggested that a proclamation could be issued calling the attention of local authorities to the illegality of the boxing exhibition. The implication was that St. Paul officials would then be free to either ignore or to follow the proclamation.

The crowd, which filled the lobbies of the State House and included some three hundred women with babies in their arms, did not see through the proclamation ploy, greeting it with cheers when the announcement was made. The leaders filed out quietly and went immediately to the office of St. Paul Mayor Smith. His Honor could not be located, however. Rumors circulated that he had gone fishing.

It appeared then that the Hall-Fitzsimmons bout would be held after all. But sometime between noon of the twenty-first and the next day, cases of cold feet broke out in the ranks of those who favored the fight. T. Z. Cowles, president of the Minnesota Athletic Club, stated that he was fearful that a riot would ensue if the bout were held. Bob Fitzsimmons' manager agreed, and Governor Merriam, sensing which way the wind was blowing, decreed that state militia would be used to assist the local sheriff in preventing the bout. Twenty-four hours before they were to enter the ring, Jim Hall and Bob Fitzsimmons learned there would be no fight.

Throwing in the sponge, the Minnesota Athletic Club lost its deposit of $3,000 as a forfeit to protect the contestants, $9,000 for construction of a fighting pavilion, and additional funds for promotion. Such was the power of the Church during the 1890s.

THE SUNDAY GOLF DEBATE

During the 1890s the popularity of golf grew enormously, bringing with it the dilemma of whether or not to play the comparatively quiet sport on the Sabbath. Blue laws could be ignored or interpreted strictly, as they were on October 11, 1897, when nine Harvard students were arrested, booked, and held until bail was provided. Their crime was that they had ventured onto a golf course near the Waverly district, whose residents complained to the police.

Two years later, an attempt to hold a Staten Island golf tournament on Sunday drew forth the sentiment that while most club members agreed it was all right to play on the Sabbath for fun, it was not morally correct to do so when something was at stake—that is, a cup or a medal. As a result, the first attempt to hold a tournament met with failure, only a dozen players showing up when twenty-five or thirty were expected.

The issue was such a warm one in the Boston area that some golf courses were posted with signs stating that players who used the links on Sunday did so at their own risk. Other suburban courses simply discontinued Sunday play until several test cases before the Supreme Court were settled. New York City, on the other hand, made no attempt to discourage use of the public links at Van Cortlandt Park, which were so crowded every Sunday that players were often forced to wait two hours before teeing off.

By 1900, however, so many golfers had given in to temptation that the Women's Sabbath Alliance felt justified in starting a serious crusade against the spreading evil. Mrs. Darwin R. James, president of the WSA, confidently predicted that once golfers knew how wrong it was to abuse the Sabbath with their clubs, they would swear off. Mrs. James' opposition to the Sunday game was based on the fundamental premise that any kind of activity on the Sabbath tended to debase all connected with it. She was involved not only in a campaign against golf at the time; another pet cause was to have the nation's newspapers discontinue their Sunday editions, as their presence caused newsboys to work on the Sabbath, thereby exposing themselves at a tender age to sin and assorted degradation.

Does Sunday Golf Start Caddies on a Life of Sin?
Said Mrs. James: "It isn't so bad for the golfers themselves as for the caddies, who are forced to begin doing wrong by working on Sunday at the very outset of their lives. All criminals start on the downward path by working on Sunday. If golfers only considered that they were starting their caddies in a life of sin by making them work on Sunday, they would soon give up their Sabbath day games. . . . Crime is increasing here a great deal faster than the population. Great Britain is the only country in the world where crime is on the decrease. That is because it is the only country in the world where the Sabbath is observed."

Those Against Other Sports—a Potpourri
"*A large number of our female bicyclists wear shorter dresses than the laws of morality and decency permit, thereby inviting the improper conversations and remarks of the depraved and immoral. I most certainly consider the adoption of the bicycle by women as detrimental to the advancement of morality. . . .*"
Rev. W. W. Reynolds,
Indianapolis (1899)
Basketball . . . should be admitted only tentatively, and under professional supervision, to a place among the sports open to women of a new age. . . . The

chances of permanent injury to beauty and health, the evil influence of such excitement upon the emotional and nervous feminine nature, and the tendency to unsex the player, is not womanly. . . ."
Lucille Eaton Hill,
Wellesley College (1903)
"*Football, as played now, is a sport which induces professionalism, encourages real battle rather than open manliness, is too expensive, and breeds loafing, gaming, and drinking. . . .*"
Dr. Andrew S. Draper,
superintendent of public instruction,
New York City (1904)

Another influential person who was violently against the playing of Sunday golf was the Reverend W. J. Ancient, who was even more specific than Mrs. James. Golf degraded women, the Reverend Ancient said in an address at St. Luke's Cathedral, Halifax, Nova Scotia, on July 23, 1903. It not only caused them to swear "like a trooper," he asserted; there were indications that golfing encouraged women to smoke. Where it would all end, the Reverend Ancient dared not say.

THE AGONY OF SUNDAY BASEBALL—PART TWO
By the first decade of the twentieth century, most major-league cities had made either a legal or an illegal accommodation with Sabbath laws prohibiting games on what was rapidly turning out to be the most profitable day of the week. On April 17, 1904, for example, nearly one hundred thousand fans turned out to see seven games of the National and American League teams. At least one of the contests was against the law—that played at Brooklyn's Washington Park, where twelve thousand turned out to see the first Sunday game ever played in Brooklyn. The law that prohibited Sunday games by professional teams was still on the books, but Brooklyn officials had decided to take a chance that it would not be enforced. The risk paid off, no one bothering to try stopping the game, which was won by the Superbas by the score of 9–0, Boston being the victim.
That the game was allowed to be played did not mean that those who opposed Sunday sports had softened their stands, however. Many were still quite violent and outspoken in their opposition. Not only did they want professional games halted, many also wanted amateur contests prohibited, especially when programs were sold as a means of defraying the costs of uniforms, etc. By 1905, New York

police allowed the major-league teams to play on Sunday, but dealt with the semipros in a severe manner.
On May 28, 1905, for example, local police took to the ball parks in a co-ordinated attack on the ballplayers. At Equitable Park, they arrested one of the team's managers and held him on $500 bail; another game was prevented between the Cedars, champions of the Bronx, and a Cuban team. At Bronx Oval and Ontario Field, games were stopped. Even a game at the Catholic Prefectory grounds was halted. Only at Olympia Field were the police thwarted. There a game between a Manhattan team and a strong black team from Philadelphia was permitted to be played because the participants had fortified themselves with a New York State Supreme Court injunction and served it to New York Police Commissioner McAdoo on Saturday.
Generally speaking, the day was a mag-

The First Sunday Game in Brooklyn: Was the Lord Trying to Say Something?
Although the first man to pitch a Sunday ball game in Brooklyn, Oscar "Flip-Flap" Jones, defeated his opponent, Vic Willis (somebody had to lose), both men had disastrous seasons in 1904. Jones' record was 17–25, the twenty-five losses tying him for league leadership in this sad department with, of all people, Vic Willis, who finished 1904 with a mark of 18–25. Brooklyn and Boston finished sixth and seventh, respectively, in an eight-team circuit, which also indicates something of a black cloud hanging over the principals and their teams.

nificent one for those who opposed Sunday baseball, one game arrest netting a total of sixty-seven participants. The overall number of arrests ran well over two hundred.

The police action infuriated many players and fans, quite naturally, and suits were brought charging that constitutional rights were being violated by the arrests. On July 3, 1905, however, Judge Blanchard of the New York State Supreme Court ruled that Sunday baseball, although not illegal, "may become illegal by attendant circumstances, such as charging an admission fee or inviting the public to the game by advertisement."

Having tasted victory on the amateur ball grounds, the opponents of Sunday baseball returned their attention to the big leagues. By 1906, Brooklyn officials, who thought they were over the hump in 1904, were once again worried as to whether games scheduled for the Sabbath would be continued. The matter came to a head on June 17, when Charlie Ebbets vowed to play a Sunday game in the face of threats that the police would interfere. A crowd of ten thousand was in attendance when Brooklyn and Cincinnati began the game, which was followed a moment later by the appearance of two plainclothes policemen on the field. They walked directly to starting pitchers Mal Eason of Brooklyn and Chick Fraser of the Reds, who meekly left with the police officers.

Arrested also were Brooklyn owner Charles Ebbets; his manager, Patsy Donovan; and the Cincinnati manager, Ned Hanlon. That formality out of the way, the two teams continued to play ball for the amusement of the fans. The entire procedure, of course, was a bizarre charade acted out for the benefit of the anti-Sunday ball militants, providing harassment without actually disturbing the game.

More severely affected were the amateur ball clubs, who often had to resort to the subterfuge of holding a band concert as a front for discarding the instruments and taking up bat and ball. In fact, most amateur organizations relied heavily on the $.50 admission charged for their games, and could not see why they should not be allowed to collect it. Instead, they were dogged by a small army of plainclothesmen with the power to arrest players and halt play.

In 1907, Assemblyman William Mooney of the New York legislature drafted a bill that would permit amateur teams to play Sunday baseball. A meeting was held in the Nassau Theater, Brooklyn, on March 11, prior to sending a delegation to Albany. Every seat was taken, and the sentiment of the crowd was unmistakably in favor of the bill.

Two days later, Albany was visited by a horde of ministers, who stormed the Assembly library, protesting that part of the Mooney Bill that permitted the collection of an admissions fee. A later age might regard such an action as incomprehensible, but there they were, reading a letter from Archbishop Farley describing the evils of ball-playing on the Sabbath.

That was not the end. In October, clergymen of Philadelphia were so upset by Sunday ball games that they carried their protest all the way to President Theodore Roosevelt, demanding that he prohibit a sport that was "harmful to the city."

Eventually, of course, it became nationally permissible to play ball on Sunday, but before that sports utopia arrived, nearly every community had to fight its own battle and make its own decision. As late as 1909, a bill was introduced in the Texas legislature to prohibit games on the Sabbath, which would have virtually killed professional baseball in the entire state. Just two years later, after an absence of twenty-five years, a Sunday baseball game was played in Nashville, despite the serving of warrants on players of both teams. And on May 19, 1918, Sunday baseball was inaugurated in the nation's capital with a twelve-inning game in which the Senators defeated Cleveland, 1–0, before fifteen thousand, one

---

Against Football and "Rooting"

"*Football is the most brutal game that ever was invented. If I had my way, I would abolish it entirely as a game officially sanctioned by the Chicago school authorities. I have two boys. One of them had water on the knee and the other has a twisted thumb. They are not playing football any more.*"

Otto C. Schneider, president
Chicago Board of Education (1907)

"*Partisan cheering is a singular example of mental perversion, an absurd and immoral custom. From every aspect it is bad. It robs the athlete of his due meed of honest praise. Morally, it is on the level with the 'jimmy,' and the 'toe hold,' the stuffed ballot box or the campaign canard. . . .*"

Dr. George E. Howard,
University of Nebraska (1912)

of the largest crowds ever gathered at the Washington park.

Having lost decisive battles in both the Bible Belt and the nation's capital, those favoring the old blue laws faded into the background, never to be heard from again. Except possibly in Baltimore or Philadelphia.

WOMEN AT THE FIGHTS

Should women be allowed to view the nearly naked, perspiring bodies of prize-fighters? It was a question that to some persons of the early twentieth century was almost too vile to pose. The answer, of course, was certainly not.

And yet there were occasional brave souls such as the young Baltimore lady who disguised herself as a man in order to watch Joe Gans—a black man, yet—fight Martin Flaherty in April 1901. She was then one of the rarest of exceptions, but by the outset of World War I, a sufficient number of women had evinced interest in boxing matches to draw out the local and national clergy, who unanimously denounced them and the product they wished to view as prime examples of moral rot.

It began in Paris and in London, where a bout in July 1914 between heavyweights Bombardier Wells and Colin Bell was viewed by a number of society women, including Mrs. E. Temple Thurston, who described the fight for the *Daily Mail*. One writer at the contest wrote, "There were women in every section of the immense audience, but seemed to be more in seats costing from one guinea to five guineas than in those costing five shillings. They drove up in evening dress in their motor cars and they walked across the sanded floor of the great arena as calmly as if they were walking into the opera and just held their skirts and evening cloaks up so as not to sweep the sand. . . . The women seemed to enjoy it about as much as they usually enjoy the Royal Academy."

The United States was not far behind, naturally. On March 25, 1916, Madison Square Garden was filled with a capacity audience for the Jess Willard-Frank Moran fight, and in the crowd were at least two hundred women. A few were dressed in evening clothes; the majority wore the smart new suits that were the rage at the time. Their appearance was not accidental. In fact, promoter Tex Rickard had encouraged ladies to attend the match, hoping to upgrade his clientele and find new sources of revenue.

The fight, a ten-round decision won by Willard, was rather tame, but various members of the clergy attacked it as "an example of doghood" and lambasted the authorities for allowing such exhibitions to be given. Not a great deal was said about the presence of women at the time, but once it became apparent that more and more young ladies were curious and interested in seeing a fight, attacks by clergy and officials followed. One of the more outspoken opponents of women fight fans was the Reverend Dr. John Roach Straton of the Calvary Baptist Church, Fifty-seventh Street and Sixth Avenue, New York City, who regularly took up arms against the rapidly growing practice of mixing ladies into hitherto all-male fight crowds. Dr. Straton had at least one ally in Mayor Fred Kohler of Cleveland, who on January 20, 1922, ruled that boxing clubs that permitted women to buy tickets would have their licenses revoked. Then in November 1933, no less a personage than Pope Pius XI himself issued a statement condemning women who attended fights. Referring to the growing tendency of modern women to "admire spectacles of brutal violence," he stated that it was not possible at a boxing match to preserve "the dignity and grace peculiar to women."

By that time, of course, the issue had been decided. Which was probably just as well.

Dr. Straton on Ladies Who Went to Fights:

"To my mind, it is a terrible thing that our young women could find it in their hearts to attend a prize fight. . . . How could they sit at that ringside and look upon the spectacle of two practically naked men, battering and bruising each other and struggling in sweat and blood for mere animal mastery? And how could these young women come out in the public prints and glorify and exalt such disgraceful exhibitions by their praise?"

THOSE AGAINST FOOTBALL—PART TWO

Just as the golfers of Staten Island's first Sunday tournament set up a double standard that separated playing for fun and playing for a cup or profit, so did many Americans of the early twentieth century insist on a solid dividing line between amateur and professional athletes. Many were convinced that the amateur was noble and the professional base, that somehow the future of America was tied in with our ability to maintain a kind of sports purity. "Whenever the professional element forges to the front, that sport immediately goes to the rear," the New York *Times* stated on July 25, 1900. "By encouraging professionalism, the colleges will kill the goose that is now laying for so many of them eggs indeed golden. . . ."

Football, it was generally agreed, was the worst offender. During the 1880s and 1890s, colleges accused one another of using players who were hired athletes rather than students, and whenever a case was proved, the prophets of doom moved in to repeat their charge that the nation, aided by its fascination with sports, was fast going to hell in a handbasket.

The dissenters had a field day during the first part of 1922, for it was then that massive amounts of truth emerged to substantiate their beliefs that college football was the worst sort of moral cancer corrupting the nation's youth.

It all began in 1920 when two small towns in Illinois—Carlinville and Taylorville—played a football game with local athletes. Carlinville won, 10–7, but citizens of Taylorville vowed that the next year's result would be different. As the months passed, the importance of the rematch seemed to grow rather than diminish, until at some point a group of Carlinville backers decided to clean out their rivals. Several Notre Dame athletes were contacted and hired at the rate of two hundred dollars each plus expenses. With no less than eight Fighting Irish players wearing Carlinville uniforms, victory in 1921 seemed certain.

The persons who arranged the situation quietly passed the word to their friends, urging them to bet the limit. As a result, the hiring of the Notre Dame players soon became common knowledge that reached the ears of Taylorville coach-manager Dick Simpson. Retaliation followed. Simpson contacted some athletes at the University of Illinois and soon had nine of them pledged to play for Taylorville. Confident that they now had the upper hand, Taylorville backers covered all bets, some saying that close to fifty thousand dollars was wagered on the game.

The actual contest, of course, resembled an impromptu Illinois-Notre Dame game, the players so unrecognizable to the average fan that when the Carlinville team ran onto the field they were booed by their own backers, who thought they were Taylorville players. Led by the plunges of Jack Crangle, Joe Sternaman's end runs, and Larry Walquist's passing, Illinois (Taylorville) defeated Notre Dame (Carlinville), 16–0.

The poorly kept secret leaked out about two months after the game, at the end of January 1922. Nine Illinois athletes were disqualified from further play at the school on January 27. The very next day, Notre Dame's involvement was revealed, and on January 30, eight confessed. Two stars suspected of taking part in the game—Gus Desch and John Mohardt—were exonerated, but there was much breast-beating and moralizing about the evils of a system that placed undue emphasis on victory at the expense of sportsmanship. From Notre Dame and Illinois, the spirit of reform spread to other colleges such as Purdue, California, Nebraska, and Princeton, where athletes who had engaged in outside professional sports were quickly suspended. The Illinois-Notre Dame scandal rocked the nation to the point where some wanted to do away with intercollegiate sports, but, of course, the point of no return had been reached long before. During the years immediately following World War I, many colleges, sensing the economic importance of big-time football, committed themselves to the construction of new stadia. Thus the early 1920s saw new facilities at Denver, Northwestern, Pittsburgh, Minnesota, Chicago, Purdue, and many other schools.

Some, such as Coach A. A. Stagg, felt that overhauling the entire national sports system was not necessary. The main problem, according to Stagg, was professionalism. "It seems a matter of little consequence for one to attend the Sunday professional football games," he said, "but it has a deeper meaning than you realize. . . . To co-operate with Sunday professional football games is to co-operate with forces which are destructive of the finest elements of interscholastic and intercollegiate football. . . ." The pros, he added, were a "serious menace."

Fielding H. Yost placed the blame not only on growing professionalism but also on the tendency to play more games than necessary, especially bowl contests, which invariably were viewed with exaggerated importance. He also assailed the attempt to determine a national championship among college teams. Others, such as President Ernest Martin Hopkins of Dartmouth, simply felt that athletics assumed too much importance in the American picture of life. Referring to a 1926 incident in which Captain George Fried of the U. S. Navy risked his life to save the crew of a sinking British freighter, he said: "In New York Captain Fried and his men were given a tremendous ovation, but Captain Fried draws for a year's salary less than Red Grange gets for one single game. Do you want your sons to believe that the contribution made by the professional athlete in ninety minutes rendered a greater service to the world than Captain Fried?"

As for the concern of some during the 1920s that Americans overlavished their sports heroes with praise, one can only hope that the Reverend Straton was wrong when he said, "The weaker we become as a people, the more we will point with pride to our 'strong' men. . . ."

The Rose Bowl Was Only the Beginning:

By the 1920s, money-conscious schools realized that bowl games meant opportunity. And so the number of postseason contests grew until they included the following bowls:

Alamo	Coconut	Gold	Optimist	Rice
Aloha	Corn	Great Lakes	Oyster	Rhumba
Azalea	Cotton-Tobacco	Harbor	Papoose	Salad
Bamboo	Delta	Health	Peach	Snow
Bean	Dixie	Ice	Peach Blossom	Smoke
Boys Ranch	Elks	Lily	Peanut	Steel
Brain	Emancipation	Little Rose	Pearl	
Burley	Finger	Missouri-Kansas	Pineapple	
Camellia	Fish	Olympic	Poi	
Cattle	Flower	Orange Blossom	Poinsettia	
Celery	Fruit	Orchid	Pythian	
Cigar	Glass	Oil	Raisin	

Not to mention Vulcan, Yam, Youth, or the various bowls that are still around . . .

THE DE-EMPHASIS OF 1951

Most organized sports, from college football to professional baseball, emerged from World War II in top shape. Those who looked upon athletics as the work of the devil were clearly in the smallest of minorities; the G. I. Bill sent an avalanche of well-conditioned athletes directly from the war to college or the baseball leagues or boxing rings. Having been deprived of high-quality competition during the last years of the war, most Americans eagerly awaited the new seasons, creating a climate of success for the All-America Conference in football, the National Basketball League, and its rival, the Basketball Association of America. Against this background, the voice of the dissenter was barely heard.

Then something went wrong. From 1946 to 1951, Americans heard one horror story after another of boxers fixing fights, of basketball players shaving points, of colleges using vicious recruiting tactics and treating players like animals. Perhaps, some suggested, those who criticized the growing professionalism and lust for victory in past decades had been right.

The re-evaluation of 1951 resulted in a number of schools deciding it might be better to drop big-time football or big-time basketball and concentrate on improving academic programs rather than athletics. One of the first schools to go public with its thoughts in this area was the College of William and Mary, which published a report in September 1951 stating that overambitious athletic programs had been detrimental to the morale of the student body, the staff, and the players themselves.

The William and Mary report produced a heavy groundswell of agreement. A week later, the Southern Conference, the largest football conference in the East, voted to prohibit bowl games and ban transfer students from athletics. Only Clemson voted against the proposed reforms.

In addition, many smaller schools eliminated football from future schedules during the early 1950s, a strong reflection of the malaise growing out of the scandals at that time. Organized sports eventually made a strong comeback during the 1960s; but those who lived through it never forgot the disillusionment and cynicism generated by the scandals and revelations of the 1950s.

The William and Mary Report (Some Excerpts):

"For over a decade the college . . . has been laboring under conditions imposed by an increasingly ambitious intercollegiate athletic program. . . . The athletic program has . . . steadily snapped the academic standards of the college . . . usurped a dominating position in the college. Instead of a healthy and indispensable extracurricular activity, it has become a commercial enterprise demanding winning teams at any cost, even at a cost of dishonest academic practice. . . . It has weakened the moral fiber of the college and its students and alumni. . . ."

UNHAPPINESS AMID AFFLUENCE

During the late 1960s and early 1970s professional team sports became a multibillion-dollar business, spectators spending more than five hundred million dollars each year for tickets to pro baseball, hockey, basketball, and football. Television contributed several hundred million dollars more, team franchises were being sold for twenty million dollars apiece, and superstars endorsed contracts calling for two hundred thousand dollars a year and up.

In the midst of all this plenty, however, there seemed to be more than enough unhappiness for everyone—owner, fan, and player.

Owners, used to having things their way, suddenly found that players were more than animals who could be bought, sold, traded, or abused without complaining. Arming themselves with knowledge of the law and the skills of agents, the athletes of the sixties showed new moves at the bargaining table. They struck out at the reserve clause— a time-honored tradition that allowed owners to own a player virtually for life—and demonstrated unity when a strike seemed necessary. Faced with skyrocketing salaries as well as inflation in the areas of travel, food, and equipment cost, owners complained that they were fortunate to break even. No one believed it, although it was certain that the era of unlimited profits was definitely over.

The players, although richer, continued to complain of racism, that owners did not care what happened to them after they were injured or forced to retire because of age, and that they were exploited generally. Some, such as Dave Meggyesy, a linebacker for the St. Louis Cardinals, charged that sports was "a circus for the increasingly chaotic American empire." In an extremely articulate book published in 1970, Meggyesy used *Out of Their League* as a vehicle to describe the brutalizing effect of football from his earliest high school days through college and into the ranks of the professionals. The book, written after Meggyesy and several other professional players such as Raider linebacker Chip Oliver had given up the game, contradicted the heroic mystique of sports generated by Vince Lombardi and others who equated winning with good and losing with evil.

But if the players and owners were unhappy, the fans of the 1970s were absolutely miserable. Worse, they were virtually powerless to do anything about rising ticket prices; poor traffic management at games; slow and arrogant concessionaires serving them poor-quality, overpriced food; the selection and retention of play-by-play broadcasters, etc. Several attempts were made to bring fans together into something resembling a union or pressure group, the most successful being Sports Fans of America, which was organized during the summer of 1970 by a Baltimore high-school assistant principal named Dominick Piledggi. A lawyer was retained by the group and a newsletter sent to fans all over the country who expressed an interest in improving the lot of the forgotten man at the ball park.

Unfortunately, the bulk of America's fandom remained sufficiently apathetic to doom the work of Piledggi to a reasonably early demise. "It was strictly a volunteer operation," said Piledggi. "If I had fifty thousand dollars to put in this thing, it could have taken off. If we could have gotten a membership of about fifty thousand, that would have meant something. But it just didn't happen. Maybe the climate will be better at some later time."

Thus after a century of organized sports in the United States, it appeared that what once would have been considered a utopia—lots of attractions for fans, lots of money for players, plentiful revenue for owners—had produced a bumper crop of dissenters as well. Which may tell us more about the species' low threshold of pain than we really want to know.

CHAPTER 44—1961–70

1961

Winners: Baseball: With Roger Maris hitting 61 homers and Mickey Mantle 54 in the American League's first 162-game season, the New York Yankees win the pennant by a comfortable 8 games, then walk over Cincinnati in the World Series, 4 games to 1. . . . *Kentucky Derby:* Carry Back. *Preakness:* Carry Back. *Belmont Stakes:* Sherluck . . . *Indy 500:* A. J. Foyt . . . *Boxing:* In July, Terry Downes knocks out Paul Pender in 9 rounds to become middleweight champion. Emile Griffith dispatches Benny "Kid" Paret to become welterweight champ on April 1. But Paret wins decision from Griffith in September, setting up the fatal—for Paret—third meeting in March 1962. . . . Bantamweight Eder Jofre KOs Piero Rollo to become new champion in that division. . . . *Golf: USGA Men's Open:* Gene Littler. *PGA:* Jerry Barber. *Masters:* Gary Player . . . *USGA Women's Open:* Mickey Wright . . . *Hockey:* Winner of 1960–61 Stanley Cup: Chicago Black Hawks . . . *Football: Cotton Bowl:* Duke 7, Arkansas 6. *Orange Bowl:* Missouri 21, Navy 14. *Rose Bowl:* Washington 17, Minnesota 7. *Sugar Bowl:* Mississippi 14, Rice 6 . . . *National Football League:* Green Bay Packers 37, New York Giants 0. *American Football League:* Houston Oilers 10, San Diego Chargers 3 . . . *Basketball:* 1960–61 *NCAA:* Cincinnati 70, Ohio State 65. 1960–61 *NIT:* Providence 62, St. Louis 59 . . . *National Basketball Association:* 1960–61 winner: Boston Celtics.

Other Happenings: National Basketball Association follows baseball's lead, moving Minneapolis franchise to Los Angeles. . . . On April 28, just 5 days after his fortieth birthday, Warren Spahn of Milwaukee pitches 1–0 no-hitter against St. Louis Cardinals. . . . Willie Mays of Giants hits 4 home runs in a 9-inning game. . . . In May, a patent is issued for a baseball bat with a checkered handle. . . . Ernie Davis, superb halfback of Syracuse University, is awarded the Heisman Trophy, picked by Washington Redskins in pro football draft, then traded to Cleveland Browns. Ron Hatcher, Michigan State back, becomes first black to play with Redskins, but his stay is brief. . . . The Hall of Fame of the Trotter at Goshen, New York, a museum dedicated to preserving the heritage of harness racing, opens an "immortals room" in 1961. It features sculptured likeness of Greyhound as well as those of former pacing champions Billy Direct, Adios Butler, and Bret Hanover. . . . One of worst fights in history of pro hockey takes place in March when Black Hawks and Maple Leafs clear the benches at Toronto. Referee Udvari levies $725 in fines. Then, in third game of Stanley Cup semifinals between Chicago and Montreal, Coach Toe Blake of Canadiens takes swing at referee Dalt McArthur that costs Blake $2,000. . . . In September, cancer takes the life of Ed "Porky" Oliver, forty-five-year-old golfer with the reputation of being the perennial runner-up in big tournaments. But Oliver proves his class by working the last six months of his life for the benefit of cancer research. . . . Bob Cousy joins Dolph Schayes as 15,000-point scorer of National Basketball Association, reaching that plateau on November 25. . . . Jockey Willie Shoemaker wins the four thousandth race of his career at Hollywood Park on May 19.

1962

Winners: Baseball: For the third consecutive year, the New York Yankees are in the World Series, opposed by a powerful San Francisco squad that wins the pennant only after a three-game playoff with the Los Angeles Dodgers. Some predict the "impetus" will inspire the Giants in the World Series, but the Yankees win the fall classic in 7 games. . . . *Kentucky Derby:* Decidedly. *Preakness:* Greek Money. *Belmont Stakes:* Jaipur . . . *Indy 500:* Rodger Ward . . . *Boxing:* Sonny Liston knocks out Floyd Patterson in first round at Chicago to become new heavyweight champion. Harold Johnson and Doug Jones fight for lightweight championship vacated by Archie Moore, who has fought as heavyweight for several years. Johnson wins 15-round decision. On April 7, middleweight Paul Pender decisions Terry Downes to regain title, but Dick Tiger, on the strength of a win over

112. Another star woman athlete of the 1950s was Tenley Albright, of Newton Center, Massachusetts. The undisputed champion at her skill from 1953 to 1956, Miss Albright captured two world titles and the 1956 Olympics. She is seen here practicing in 1954.

113. The biggest baseball story of the 1960s was Roger Maris' assault on Babe Ruth's 60 homers in a single season and controversy over validity of "record" because Maris had more games than the Babe. Yielding to pressure from old-timers, Commissioner Ford Frick decreed that an asterisk would be placed in record books next to Roger Maris' 1961 total of 61 home runs. Here Roger is in the act of hitting the historic No. 61. (See "1961.")

114. The decade began with a bang for baseball fans and Chicago Cub pitcher Jim Brewer when feisty Billy Martin decked the hurler in 1960 following a close pitch. Brewer was taken to the hospital where he was treated for a broken orbit bone in his right eye. Martin's next major title defense came in 1969, when as manager of the Minnesota Twins, he slugged his own pitcher, Dave Boswell.

115. In a decade that was unusually filled with deaths of young athletes, the first tragedy occurred in 1961 when 18 members of the U.S. figure-skating team, seen here, met death when their plane crashed while trying to land in Brussels. Holding sign is 16-year-old Laurence Owen of Winchester, Massachusetts, known as America's "Queen of the Ice." (See "1961.")

116. The 1960s saw golf grow in popularity as a spectator sport, thanks largely to the mystique of Arnold Palmer and his "army" of fans who followed him religiously. In 1963, Palmer became the first PGA player to earn more than $100,000 a year on the tournament trail by taking $128,230. By the end of the decade he was considering purchasing the entire golf course he played on as a youngster.

117. In 1966 the Boston Celtics of the National League put together the longest pennant-winning streak in American sports by taking their eighth straight NBA title. Seen here in 1962 action are the Celtics' "Satch" Sanders (16) and Bill Russell (6), whose right elbow is about to deter Chicago's Walt Bellamy (8) from making a rebound.

118. Although sports of all kinds had been played indoors prior to the 1960s, the construction of the Astrodome at Houston was the real beginning of the end for those who insisted on watching their favorite game in the arms of Mother Nature. (See "Doing It Indoors and at Night.") Aerial view taken in 1964 shows dome of stadium nearly completed.

119. Unlike many other spectator sports, horseracing remained outdoors and "mudders" continued to maintain their occasional advantage. Seen here is Woodlawn Vase and Kauai King, winner of ninetieth running of Preakness Stakes at Pimlico in 1966.

120. Controversy struck the sport of kings in 1968 when Dancer's Image, winner of Kentucky Derby, was disqualified because he had been injected with butazolidin, a pain-killing drug, prior to the race. Nearly two years of trials and appeals followed. In the meantime, Dancer's Image was removed from its honored place on the clubhouse tote board at Churchill Downs. (See "Flaps.")

121. Like every decade, the 1960s had its share of football heroes. In the college ranks, it was Roger (the Dodger) Staubach of the Naval Academy, winner of the Heisman Trophy in 1963. Here he scrambles for the Middies during that outstanding season.

122. The complete opposite of Staubach in life-style, swinging Joe Namath of the New York Jets captured the imagination of sports fans by leading underdog team to victory in Super Bowl III against Baltimore Colts. No. 23, Emerson Boozer, is about to accept Namath's handoff as Colts' Fred Miller tries to make up his mind which man to tackle.

123. For those with a taste for unusual contests, archer George Mann revived the mixed-media sport of archery-golf, which pitted golfer against bowman. Instead of trying to put the arrow in the hole, Mann's object is to hit the small target at far left. (See "Can a ———— Beat a ————?")

124. The 1960s ended with women demanding equal rights with men in competitive sports, much to the chagrin of traditionalists. In 1967 Boston Marathon, trainer Jock Semple became so angry at woman entry (No. 261, K. Switzer) that he tried to force her bodily off the course. Male runners moved in to convoy the woman, however, and she was allowed to finish. (See "Breaking the Sex Barrier.")

126. Biggest baseball story of the 1970s was Henry Aaron's assault on Babe Ruth's career record of 714 home runs. Once again controversy swirled about the validity of Aaron's feat compared with that of Ruth. (The Babe had less times at bat, his followers argued.) But this time there was no Commissioner Ford Frick to belittle Aaron's record with talk of asterisks. Aaron retired with 755 homers. Here he is seen swatting the climactic No. 715 off Los Angeles' Al Downing.

125. Just 97 years after Mary Marchall defeated an American male at his own game (see "Breaking the Sex Barrier"), Billie Jean King, reigning queen of U.S. tennis, proved chauvinist challenger Bobby Riggs was over the hill by defeating him in straight sets at the Houston Astrodome. The purse was for $100,000, but for many the amount of money seemed unimportant. Male supremacists would never be able to sleep soundly again.

127. Jim Bunning of the Philadelphia Phillies also went into the record books in 1970 by becoming the first pitcher since Cy Young to win 100 games in each league. Previously he pitched no-hitters in each league as well.

128. During the 1970s organized baseball tried to cope with the demands of women for equal opportunity in sports. In 1972 Mrs. Bernice Gera achieved her dream of umpiring a professional baseball game, but becoming the first woman umpire was more like a nightmare for her. After weathering three years of litigation, she found Manager Nolan Campbell of the Auburn (New York) Phillies too abusive. She resigned at the end of the contest. (See "Breaking the Sex Barrier.")

129. The decade became that of the strike, with both football and baseball players forsaking the battle lines for picket lines. In 1972, major-league baseball players staged a 13-day strike, the first in history, and 2 years later, National Football League players went out. Here Houston Oilers (left to right) Dan Pastorini, Willie Alexander, Guy Roberts, Bill Curry, Al Jenkins, Fred Willis, and Alvin Haymond picket the training camp. (See "Refusing to Do It.")

130. The 1970s saw the expansion of professional football and the rise of new "dynasties" such as that of the Miami Dolphins and the Pittsburgh Steelers, but it was not possible for a team to win the Super Bowl three times in a row. The Dolphins came the closest, losing to Dallas in 1971, winning the next two years, then dropping a dramatic playoff game to Oakland in 1974. Here Larry Csonka (39) barrels over the goal line in a 1972 game against the New York Jets. The Dolphin fullback fumbled but a teammate recovered.

131. After regaining his heavyweight title, Muhammad Ali was so clearly the best in his field that he was often forced to fight mediocre competition. Tiring of this in 1976, he decided to take on the world's best wrestler, Antonio Inoki, at Tokyo. The battle turned out to be a dreadful fiasco, Inoki spending most of the time on his back, kicking at Ali's face. The bout was declared a draw. (See "Bad Hypes.")

132. European-style football or soccer made slow but steady growth in the United States during the 1970s with the North American Soccer League putting itself on solid ground despite a plethora of franchise switches. Although few soccer enthusiasts maintained that the sport was "major league" in the same sense as that of professional baseball and football, there could be little doubt that soccer was growing wildly, especially at the grass-roots level. Here Denny Harezlak of Rockford (Illinois) College accidentally kicks teammate Wayne Gartner while losing to Trinity, 6–1.

133. Time seemed to roll back a century as a match race was run in 1973 between a bicycle and a harness racer. (See "Can a ——— Beat a ———?")

134. Another race that might have taken place in the nineteenth century was the 1977 America's Cup, which ended as all previous encounters had —with American victory. Here *Courageous,* the U.S. entry, top, drives toward the starting line with the Australian challenger in the fourth race of the event. Leading at that time, 3–0, *Courageous* won again to take the series.

135. After a period of relative quiet dating back to the 1940s, tennis grew in popularity during the 1970s, with new heroes and new villains. Among the women, Billie Jean King and Chris Evert became household names; among the men, Jimmy Connors and archbadman Ilie Nastase, seen clowning here at Wimbledon in 1976.

Gene Fullmer, also claims middleweight crown. On March 24, Emile Griffith knocks out Benny "Kid" Paret to regain welterweight crown. Paret dies shortly afterward of injuries. Joe Brown loses lightweight title to Carlos Ortiz on 15-round decision at Las Vegas, and Fighting Harada becomes new flyweight champ by knocking out Pone Kingpetch in 11 rounds. . . . *Golf: USGA Men's Open:* Jack Nicklaus. *PGA:* Gary Player. *Masters:* Arnold Palmer. *USGA Women's Open:* Murle Lindstrom . . . *Hockey:* 1961–62 Stanley Cup winner: Toronto Maple Leafs . . . *Football: Cotton Bowl:* Texas 12, Mississippi 7 . . . *Orange Bowl:* LSU 25, Colorado 7. *Rose Bowl:* Minnesota 21, UCLA 3. *Sugar Bowl:* Alabama 10, Arkansas 3 . . . *National Football League:* Green Bay Packers 16, New York Giants 7. *American Football League:* Dallas 20, Houston 17 (2 overtime periods) . . . *Basketball:* 1961–62 *NCAA:* Cincinnati, 71, Ohio State 59. *NIT:* Dayton 73, St. John's 67 . . . *National Basketball Association:* 1961–62 winner: Boston Celtics (fourth consecutive season).

Other Happenings: On April 10, first major-league baseball is played in Texas as the expansion Houston Colt 45s defeat Chicago Cubs, 11–2, before 25,000 fans. . . . Expansion Mets play first game April 11 and lose to Cardinals, 11–4. . . . On June 24, Yankees and Tigers are locked in 22-inning game that is broken up by Yankee outfielder Jack Reed's home run. It is the only homer Reed ever hits in his entire major-league career. . . . the year 1962 is the year of the pitcher. Sandy Koufax pitches a no-hitter and also strikes out 18 batters in a 9-inning game. Tom Cheney of the Washington Senators strikes out 21 men in a 16-inning game, and Bill Fischer of Kansas City pitches 84⅓ consecutive innings without allowing a base on balls. American League no-hitters are pitched by Bo Belinsky of Los Angeles, Earle Wilson of the Red Sox, Bill Monbouquette, also of Boston, and Jack Kralick of Minnesota. Maury Wills beats Ty Cobb's 1915 record of 96 stolen bases in a season by swiping 104 in 162-game season. No one mentions placing an asterisk after the feat. . . . Arnold Palmer's $109,100 purse is highest in sports history. . . . Jockey Eddie Arcaro retires after riding since 1932. . . . On November 8, California Tech and California Western play highest-scoring football game to end in a tie, 42–42. . . . America's Cup yacht race competition is held September 15–24, the U.S. entry, *Weatherly,* winning 4 races to 1 for *Gretel* of Australia. . . . Ken Hubbs of Chicago Cubs sets record for second basemen by handling 416 consecutive chances without an error. . . . On March 2, Wilt Chamberlain sets a record for most successful free throws,

28, and most points, 100, in a basketball game played between Philadelphia and New York at Hershey, Pennsylvania.

1963

Winners: Baseball: New York Yankees win American League pennant by 10½ games but are demolished in the World Series by the Los Angeles Dodgers, 4 games to 0. In first game, Sandy Koufax strikes out 15 batters to set a new Series record. . . . *Kentucky Derby:* Chateaugay. *Preakness:* Candy Spots. *Belmont Stakes:* Chateaugay . . . *Indy 500:* Parnelli Jones . . . *Boxing:* In return match at Las Vegas, Charles "Sonny" Liston again knocks out Floyd Patterson in first round, but it takes him 4 seconds longer than in 1962 (2:10 to 2:06). . . . In light-heavyweight division, Willie Pastrano outpoints Harold Johnson to become champion. Following Paul Pender's retirement, Joey Giardello wins a 15-round decision over Dick Tiger to become middleweight champion. Welterweight crown shifts when Luis Rodriguez decisions Emile Griffith on March 21, then loses rematch on June 8. . . . Sugar Ramos knocks out Davey Moore to win featherweight title and Pone Kingpetch regains flyweight crown by winning 15-round decision over Fighting Harada. Kingpetch is then dethroned via a 1-round knockout at the hands of Hiroyuki Ebihara. . . . *Golf: USGA Men's Open:* Julius Boros. *PGA:* Jack Nicklaus. *Masters:* Jack Nicklaus . . . *USGA Women's Open:* Mary Wills . . . *Hockey:* 1962–63 Stanley Cup champion: Toronto Maple Leafs . . . *Football: Cotton Bowl:* LSU 13, Texas 0. *Orange Bowl:* Alabama 17, Oklahoma 0. *Rose Bowl:* USC 42, Wisconsin 37. *Sugar Bowl:* Mississippi 17, Arkansas 13 . . . *National Football League:* Chicago Bears 14, New York Giants 10 . . . *American Football League:* San Diego 51, Boston 10 . . . *Basketball:* 1962–63 *NCAA:* Loyola (Illinois) 60, Cincinnati 58. *NIT:* Providence 81, Canisius 66 . . . *National Basketball Association:* Boston Celtics (fifth consecutive season).

Other Happenings: Jim Clark becomes first racing driver to win 7 major races in a year. . . . Elston Howard, meanwhile, becomes first black player to be voted Most Valuable Player in American League. . . . Last pitcher to win 300 games is Early Wynn, 43, of Cleveland Indians, who accomplishes feat on July 13. . . . Untimely sports death during 1963 claims Ernie Davis, Heisman Trophy winner, who never plays a game for Cleveland Browns but has jersey No. 45 permanently retired. Browns also lose 25-year-old Don Fleming, and Pittsburgh Steelers lose Gene "Big Daddy" Lipscomb, a victim of narcotics overdose. . . . Boxing is attacked by Pope John XXIII following ring death of Davey Moore. . . . Sports figures publishing books are coach Vince (*Run for Daylight*) Lombardi and quarterback Lee (*Fourth and One*) Grosscup. . . . On May 11, Sandy Koufax pitches his second no-hitter. . . . Don Nottebart of Houston and Juan Marichal of San Francisco also pitch no-hitters in National League. None is pitched in American League. . . . Alex Karras of Detroit Lions and Paul Hornung of Green Bay Packers are suspended for 1963 season as a result of investigation revealing gambling on football games. . . . Baseball statistics mania reaches its zenith when commentator Lindsey Nelson proclaims that slugger Duke Snider is the first player "to hit his four hundredth career home run on color television. . . ." U. S. Davis Cup team defeats Australia, 3–2, ending Australia's 4-year domination of tennis championship. . . . On December 7, "instant replay" is used by CBS for first time during televising of the Army-Navy football game. . . . Bob Hayes sets a world record for the 100-yard dash, 9.1 seconds. . . . At $100,000 a year, Willie Mays of San Francisco Giants becomes baseball's highest-paid player. . . . Don Schollander becomes the first swimmer to accomplish the 200-meter freestyle in less than 2 minutes, swimming it in 1:58.4 at Osaka, Japan, on August 24.

1964

Winners: Baseball: New York Yankees win pennant for fifth year in a row but lose second consecutive World Series. St. Louis pitcher Bob Gibson is the hero as the Cardinals defeat the Yanks, 4 games to 3. . . . *Kentucky Derby:* Northern Dancer. *Preakness:* Northern Dancer. *Belmont Stakes:* Quadrangle . . . *Indy 500:* A. J. Foyt . . . *Boxing:* In a startling development for most fight fans, Cassius Clay (Muhammad Ali) wins heavyweight title when Sonny Liston can't answer the bell for the seventh round. . . . In featherweight division, Sugar Ramos loses title to Vicente Saldivar in 12 rounds at Mexico City. Kone Kingpetch wins back flyweight championship by decisioning Hiroyuki Ebihara in Bangkok. . . . *Golf: USGA Men's Open:* Ken Venturi. *PGA:* Bobby Nichols. *Masters:* Arnold Palmer . . . *USGA Women's Open:* Mickey Wright . . . *Hockey:* 1963–64 Stanley

Cup winner: Toronto Maple Leafs (third consecutive year). . . . *Football: Cotton Bowl:* Texas 28, Navy 6. *Orange Bowl:* Nebraska 13, Auburn 7. *Rose Bowl:* Illinois 17, Washington 7. *Sugar Bowl:* Alabama 12, Mississippi 7 . . . *National Football League:* Cleveland 27, Baltimore 0 . . . *American Football League:* Buffalo 20, San Diego 7 . . . *Basketball:* 1963–64 *NCAA:* UCLA 98, Duke 83. 1963–64 *NIT:* Bradley 86, New Mexico 54 . . . *National Basketball Association:* 1963–64 winner: Boston Celtics (sixth consecutive season).

Other Happenings: Boston Celtics' sixth consecutive championship is rated tops of any sports team. . . . Kansas City owner Charlie Finley builds "Pennant Porch" to get cheap home runs similar to those in Yankee Stadium but commissioner vetoes the idea. . . . Another iconoclast is pitcher Bo Belinsky, who slugs newspaperman and refuses to report to Hawaii when Los Angeles Angels try to farm him out. . . . The Yankees are sold to CBS, and the Soviets comment that such is the corruption of American sports. . . . Pitcher Ken Johnson of Colt 45s becomes first to hurl 9-inning no-hitter and lose. . . . Other no-hitters are pitched by Sandy Koufax (his third), Jim Bunning (perfect game), and, once again, none in American League. . . . The New York Mets and San Francisco Giants play a 7-hour, 23-minute game that Frisco wins, 8–6, in 23 innings. . . . After losing World Series to Cardinals, Yankees fire Yogi Berra and replace him with St. Louis Manager Johnny Keane. . . . Untimely deaths in sports world: Ken Hubbs, 22, Chicago Cubs second baseman, whose plane crashes in Utah; Willie Galimore and John Farrington of the Chicago Bears (automobile accident); Jim Umbricht, Houston pitcher (cancer); Lucien Reeberg, Cleveland Browns tackle (uremic poisoning); and Alejandro Lavorante, 27, Argentine heavyweight who finally succumbs after spending 18 months in a coma following a bout with Johnny Riggins. . . . After serving year's suspension for gambling on games, Alex Karras of Detroit Lions and Paul Hornung of Green Bay Packers return to their clubs. . . . America's Cup competition sees United States entry, *Constellation,* win 4 races to none for England's *Sovereign.* . . . Australian tennis squad defeats United States, 3–2, at Cleveland, to regain Davis Cup. On April 4, Dallas Long breaks his own shot-put record with a 65-foot, 11½-inch heave at Pasadena, California. . . . On February 29, Frank Rugani drives a shuttlecock 79 feet, 8½ inches. . . . At $85,000, lefty Warren Spahn of the Milwaukee Braves is the highest-paid pitcher in major-league baseball. . . .

1965

Winners: Baseball: Minnesota Twins compile excellent 102–60 season mark to win American League pennant, but lose World Series to Los Angeles Dodgers, 4 games to 3. . . . *Kentucky Derby:* Lucky Debonair, *Preakness:* Tom Rolph. *Belmont Stakes:* Hail to All . . . *Indy 500:* Jim Clark . . . *Boxing:* José Torres becomes new light-heavyweight champion by knocking out Willie Pastrano in 9 rounds at New York City. . . . Dick Tiger regains middleweight crown by winning 15-round decision over Joey Giardello. . . . Lightweight champ Carlos Ortiz loses decision to Ismael Laguna on April 10 but regains title on November 13, also by decision. . . . Fighting Harada enters bantamweight division, defeating Eder Jofre to become champion. . . . Flyweight Kone Kingpetch loses his title for third time, on 15-round decision to Salvatore Burruni. . . . *Golf: USGA Men's Open:* Gary Player. *PGA:* Dave Marr. *Masters:* Jack Nicklaus . . . *USGA Women's Open:* Carol Mann . . . *Hockey:* 1964–65 Stanley Cup winner: Montreal Canadiens. . . . *Football: Cotton Bowl:* Arkansas 10, Nebraska 7. *Orange Bowl:* Texas 21, Alabama 17. *Rose Bowl:* Michigan 34, Oregon State 7. *Sugar Bowl:* LSU 13, Syracuse 10 . . . *National Football League:* Green Bay 23, Cleveland 12. *American Football League:* Buffalo 23, San Diego 0 . . . *Basketball:* 1964–65 *NCAA:* UCLA 91, Michigan 80. 1964–65 *NIT:* St. John's 55, Villanova 51. . . . *National Basketball Association:* 1964–65 winner: Boston Celtics (seventh consecutive season).

Other Happenings: Swimming star Don Schollander, 18, becomes youngest athlete to win the Sullivan Award, given since 1930 to amateur doing most to "advance the cause of good sportsmanship during the year." . . . Jackie Robinson becomes the first black athlete to serve as commentator on Sports broadcasts. . . . Baseball Commissioner Ford Frick is succeeded by no-name named Eckert. . . . Juan Marichal strikes John Roseboro with a baseball bat in August and in September, Sandy Koufax becomes first pitcher to hurl 4 no-hitters. . . . Jim Maloney of Cincinnati pitches 2 no-hitters during the season. He loses the first when the New York Mets make a hit and score in the tenth inning, but he wins the second, beating Chicago, 1–0, in 10 innings. In the American League, Dave Morehead of the Boston Red Sox no-hits Cleveland on September 16. . . . Willie Mays hits 17 home runs in a month, ends year with league-leading 52. . . . On April 9, an exhibition game is held between the New York Yankees and the Houston Colt 45s (now called the Astros) in the brand-new Houston Astrodome. Houston wins, 2–1. . . . On May 16, 19-year-old Jim Palmer hits his first major-league home run and pitches his first win as the Baltimore Orioles beat the Yankees, 7–5. . . . On September 8, all-around athlete Bert Campaneris plays all 9 positions for Kansas City A's but has to retire following a ninth-inning collision with Ed Kirkpatrick of the Angels. As a pitcher, Campaneris allows a hit, 2 bases on balls, and a run, striking out a batter during his inning on the mound. The Angels win, however, 5–3, in 13 innings. . . . Casey Stengel, 75, retires, and so does Sugar Ray Robinson. . . . Joe Namath signs with New York Jets for $400,000 and Gale Sayers scores 6 touchdowns in a single game. . . . Untimely deaths: Wayne Estes, 21, basketball star (electrocuted when he accidentally touches power line); Jay Dahl, 19, Houston pitcher (auto accident); Murray Balfour, 28, hockey star with Chicago Black Hawks (cancer); Dick Wantz, 25, Los Angeles Angels pitcher (brain tumor); and Mack Lee Hill of the Kansas City Chiefs, following surgery to correct a football injury.

1966

Winners: Baseball: Los Angeles Dodgers repeat in National League and Baltimore Orioles win first pennant since 1896, when team was in National League. Orioles celebrate with 4-game sweep of World Series. . . . *Kentucky Derby:* Kauai King. *Preakness:* Kauai King. *Belmont Stakes:* Amberoid . . . *Indy 500:* Graham Hill . . . *Boxing:* Dick Tiger wins light-heavyweight crown by taking 15-round decision from José Torres, December 16. Eight months previously, Tiger had lost middleweight crown to Emile Griffith. . . . In welterweight division, Griffith is forced to give up his title after winning middleweight crown. Curtis Cokes and Jean Josselin battle for vacant championship, Cokes winning a 15-round decision. . . . Flyweight division title passes from Salvatore Burruni to Walter McGowan via decision, then is taken by Chartchai Chionoi, who knocks out McGowan in 9 rounds. . . . *Golf: USGA Men's Open:* Billy Casper. *PGA:* Al Geiberger. *Masters:* Jack Nicklaus . . . *USGA Women's Open:* Sandra Spuzich . . . *Hockey:* 1965–66 Stanley Cup champions: Montreal Canadiens. . . . *Football: Cotton Bowl:* LSU 14, Arkansas 7. *Orange Bowl:* Alabama 39, Nebraska 28. *Rose Bowl:* UCLA 14, Michigan State 12. *Sugar Bowl:* Missouri 20, Florida 18

. . . *National Football League:* Green Bay 34, Dallas 27 . . . *American Football League:* Kansas City 31, Buffalo 7 . . . *Super Bowl:* Green Bay 35, Kansas City 10 . . . *Basketball:* 1965–66 *NCAA:* Texas Western 72, Kentucky 65. *NIT:* Brigham Young 97, NYU 84 . . . *National Basketball Association:* 1965–66 winner: Boston Celtics (eighth consecutive season).

Other Happenings: In contrast to other wars, Vietnam conflict sees few athletes volunteering or being drafted for duty—only 2 of 960 professional athletes serving, according to one published report. . . . Bill Russell becomes first black basketball coach when he takes over Boston Celtics. . . . Big football story takes place on November 19, when Ara Parseghian, coach of Notre Dame, settles for 10–10 tie with Michigan State instead of gambling for victory. . . . Enshrinement of professional athletes reaches a high point when Lou Groza's toe is cast in bronze for Pro Football Hall of Fame. . . . The American Football League rules in January that all players must be clean-shaven except for mustaches. . . . The Milwaukee Braves are moved to Atlanta, first major-league baseball team in Deep Southeast. Fifty thousand are on hand for first game, with Pittsburgh, which is won by Pirates, 3–2. . . . October 6 is a bittersweet day for devotees of excellent pitching. On that date, Jim Palmer of Orioles becomes youngest (twenty) to pitch World Series shutout, but Sandy Koufax, losing pitcher in that game, retires at age thirty and never again makes a game appearance. . . . Kelso runs last race, at Hialeah. He finishes fourth and picks up $500 to bring earnings to $1,977,896, tops among flat racers. He is retired soon afterward. . . . Only no-hitter during major-league season comes on June 10, when Sonny Siebert of Cleveland tops Washington, 2–0. . . . Bret Hanover, champion pacer, covers a mile in 1:53⅗ in a time trial at Lexington, Kentucky, the fastest mile ever recorded by a harness horse. . . . Untimely deaths in sports world come to Tony Lema, 32-year-old golfer (plane crash); 37-year-old 3-cushion billiards champion Harold Worst (cancer); and Greatest Crawford, 28-year-old light-heavyweight boxer, one day after being knocked out by Marion Conner in Canton, Ohio. . . . On December 11, Al Nelson of Philadelphia Eagles races 100 yards with a missed field-goal attempt by the Cleveland Browns. . . . Bobby Hull becomes the first hockey player to score more than 50 goals in a season. . . . Wilt Chamberlain sets basketball point-scoring record with 20,884 during 7 seasons of play.

1967

Winners: Baseball: The St. Louis Cardinals win National League pennant and Bob Gibson does an encore of 1964, winning 3 games as the Cards defeat the Boston Red Sox in the World Series, 4 games to 3. . . . *Kentucky Derby:* Proud Clarion. *Preakness:* Damascus. *Belmont Stakes:* Damascus . . . *Indy 500:* A. J. Foyt . . . *Boxing:* Muhammad Ali is stripped of heavyweight title for refusing to allow himself to be drafted into the U. S. Armed Forces. . . . In April, Nino Benevenuti defeats Emile Griffith to become middleweight champion, but 5 months later Griffith regains title via 15-round decision. . . . After successfully defending his championship by defeating Mitsunori Seki and Howard Winstone, featherweight champ Vicente Saldivar retires. . . . *Golf: USGA Men's Open:* Jack Nicklaus. *PGA:* Don January. *Masters:* Gay Brewer . . . *USGA Women's Open:* Catherine Lacoste . . . *Hockey:* 1966–67 Stanley Cup winner: Toronto Maple Leafs. . . . *Football: Cotton Bowl:* Georgia 24, SMU 9. *Orange Bowl:* Florida 27, Georgia Tech 12. *Rose Bowl:* Purdue 14, USC 13. *Sugar Bowl:* Alabama 34, Nebraska 7 . . . *National Football League:* Green Bay 21, Dallas 17 . . . *American Football League:* Oakland 40, Houston 7 . . . *Super Bowl II:* Green Bay 33, Oakland 14 . . . *Basketball:* 1966–67 *NCAA:* UCLA 79, Dayton 64 . . . 1966–67 *NIT:* Southern Illinois 71, Marquette 56 . . . *National Basketball Association:* 1966–67 champion: Philadelphia 76ers.

Other Happenings: America's Cup competition is renewed September 12–18, but result is same as every other series since 1851—U.S. entry, *Intrepid,* wins 4 races to 0 for Australia's *Dame Pattie.* . . . Formed: American Basketball Association, rival to NBA . . . Notre Dame football team becomes only second non-Ivy League school to win 500 games (the other is Michigan). . . . Professional soccer comes to the United States and is sponsored on CBS television. Game proves difficult to adapt to commercial needs of TV, leading to rumor that players are told to fake injuries in order to break for commercial messages. . . . Big college football game of year takes place on November 18, when UCLA, led by quarterback Gary Beban, meets USC, led by O. J. Simpson. USC wins, 21–20. . . . Emlen Tunnel becomes first black player elected to Pro Football Hall of Fame. . . . No-hitter is pitched in National League on June 18 by Don Wilson of Houston. In American League, Steve Barber and Stu Miller of the Baltimore Orioles combine to pitch 9 no-hit innings but lose to Detroit, 2–1. Dean

Chance of Minnesota and Joel Horlen of Chicago White Sox also pitch no-hitters. . . . Death claims Walter Bond, 29, former major-league first baseman who succumbs to leukemia, and Mike McKeever, USC football star, who is killed in an automobile accident. . . . On June 23, Jim Ryun sets a new world record by running the mile in 3:51.1 at Bakersfield, California, track meet. . . . Daredevil Evel Knievel clears 16 automobiles in a row in a stunt motorcycle jump at Ascot Speedway, Gardena, California, on May 30. . . . On May 14, Mickey Mantle of Yankees hits his five hundredth career home run, only the sixth man in baseball to reach that mark.

1968

Winners: Baseball: The St. Louis Cardinals repeat in the National League, and Bob Gibson sets a World Series record by striking out 35 batters. But the Detroit Tigers manage to win the key game, winning the Series in 7. . . . *Kentucky Derby:* Forward Pass. *Preakness:* Forward Pass. *Belmont Stakes:* Stage Door Johnny . . . *Indy 500:* Bobby Unser . . . *Boxing:* In scramble to fill vacancy created by Muhammad Ali's defeat by officialdom, Joe Frazier KO's Buster Mathis and is recognized as champ in New York and 5 other states, Mexico, and South America; Jimmy Ellis, by defeating Jerry Quarry, is recognized as World Boxing association champion. . . . In light-heavyweight division, Bob Foster knocks out Dick Tiger to become champion. Nino Benevenuti returns to win decision from Emile Griffith and take middleweight title once again. In lightweight division, Carlos Cruz wins 15-round decision from Carlos Ortiz to become new champion, and bantamweight titleholder Fighting Harada loses decision to Lionel Rose. . . . *Golf: USGA Men's Open:* Lee Trevino. *PGA:* Julius Boros. *Masters:* Bob Goalby . . . *USGA Women's Open:* Susie Berning . . . *Hockey:* 1967–68 Stanley Cup champ: Montreal Canadiens. . . *Football: Cotton Bowl:* Texas A&M 20, Alabama 16. *Orange Bowl:* Oklahoma 26, Tennessee 24. *Rose Bowl:* USC 14, Indiana 3. *Sugar Bowl:* LSU 20, Wyoming 13 . . . *National Football League:* Baltimore 34, Cleveland 0 . . . *American Football League:* New York 27, Oakland 23 . . . *Super Bowl III:* New York 16, Baltimore 7 . . . *Basketball:* 1967–68 *NCAA:* UCLA 78, North Carolina 55 . . . 1967–68 *NIT:* Dayton 61, Kansas 48 . . . *National Basketball Association:* 1967–68 winner: Boston Celtics.

Other Happenings: In May, massive Frank Howard of Washington Senators hits 10 home runs in 6 games. He is finally stopped on May 19 by Detroit's Earl Wilson, but leads league with 44 for season. . . . On September 22, Cesar Tovar of Minnesota plays one inning at each position. As pitcher, he strikes out a batter, yields a base on balls, and retires side without a run. . . . Back-to-back no-hitters are pitched in same ball park, Gaylord Perry of San Francisco blanking Cardinals at Candlestick Park on September 17, followed by the Cardinals' Ray Washburn no-hitting the Giants on September 18. . . . Other no-hitters are pitched by George Culver of Cincinnati and, in American League, by Tom Phoebus of Orioles and Jim "Catfish" Hunter of Oakland (perfect game). . . . On June 25, 22-year-old Bobby Bonds of Giants hits home run in first at-bat in major leagues. . . . Big flap of year occurs on November 17, when exciting pro football game between New York Jets and Oakland Raiders is replaced on tube by *Heidi.* TV station switchboards light up as Oakland scores two quick touchdowns that are never seen by home audience. . . . Second biggest flap of year concerns winner of Kentucky Derby, Kentucky Racing Commission taking first place from Dancer's Image when it is revealed that the horse received a shot of butazolidin, a pain killer, prior to race. . . . Cardigan Bay, the first harness racer to win more than $1 million, is retired on September 14, age 12. . . . On October 8, Mark Spitz sets world 200-meter butterfly mark of 2 minutes, 5.7 seconds at Berlin, Germany. . . . Chicago White Sox set American League frustration mark on September 3 . . . by losing thirty-ninth game by a single run. The United Soccer Association and the National Professional Soccer League merge on January 4 in a two-division Professional Soccer League. . . . Baseball moguls drop height of pitching mound from 15 to 10 inches in hopes it will help hitters during 1969.

1969

Winners: Baseball: Baltimore Orioles defeat Minnesota Twins, 3 games to 0, to take American League title while New York Mets handle Atlanta Braves, 3 games to 0 for National League championship. In World Series, Mets defeat Orioles, 4 games to 1. . . . *Kentucky Derby:* Majestic Prince. *Preakness:* Majestic Prince. *Belmont Stakes:* Arts and Letters . . . *Indy 500:* Mario Andretti . . . *Boxing:* Heavyweight division still in confusion. . . .

On April 17, José Napoles knocks out Curtis Cokes in 13 rounds to take welterweight crown. Carlos Cruz' brief reign as lightweight champ comes to an end when he is KO'd in 11 rounds by Mando Ramos. . . . Following retirement of Vicente Saldivar, Johnny Famechon wins 15-round decision from José Legra to become featherweight titleholder. . . . Ruben Olivares knocks out Lionel Rose to become bantamweight champ, and Efren Torres stops Chartchai Chionoi in 8 rounds to take flyweight championship. . . . *Golf: USGA Men's Open:* Orville Moody. *PGA:* Ray Floyd. *Masters:* George Archer . . . *USGA Women's Open:* Donna Caponi . . . *Hockey:* 1968–69 Stanley Cup winner: Montreal Canadiens. . . . *Football: Cotton Bowl:* Texas 36, Tennessee 13. *Orange Bowl:* Penn State 15, Kansas 14. *Rose Bowl:* Ohio State 27, USC 16. *Sugar Bowl:* Arkansas 16, Georgia 2 . . . *National Football League:* Minnesota 27, Cleveland 7 . . . *American Football League:* Kansas City 17, Oakland 7 . . . *Super Bowl IV:* Kansas City 23, Minnesota 7 . . . *Basketball:* 1968–69 *NCAA:* UCLA 92, Purdue 72 . . . 1968–69 *NIT:* Temple 89, Boston College 76 . . . *National Basketball Association:* 1968–69 champion: Boston Celtics.

Other Happenings: First divisional baseball playoffs are held in American and National leagues and first regular-season game is played outside the United States on April 14 when Expos, expansion team, beat St. Louis, 8–7, at Montreal. . . . Evidence of sports boom can be seen in deal in which Philadelphia Eagles are sold for a record $16,155,000. In 1968, Eagles finished with mark of 2–12–0 in NFL. . . . Bowie Kuhn is named new baseball commissioner, and Billy Martin, Minnesota manager, teaches pitcher Dave Boswell discipline by slugging him. In October Martin is relieved of command. . . . Jim Brewer, meanwhile, another pitcher who was clobbered by Martin in 1960, is awarded $10,000 damages in January, so it is not a good year for violent Billy. . . . Lew Alcindor becomes first basketball player to be voted Most Valuable Player of NIT tournament 3 years in row. . . . Rocky Marciano is killed in a plane crash, and Joe Frazier knocks out someone named Zyglewicz. . . . Super Bowl commercials sell for $135,000 a minute, and O. J. Simpson becomes the highest-paid rookie since the two leagues cut salaries by merging. . . . Tennis star Rafael Osuna is killed in a plane crash at age 31. . . . Steve Carlton of St. Louis strikes out 19 batters in a 9-inning game, breaking record of 18 set by Bob Feller in 1938 and tied by Sandy Koufax in 1959. . . . No-hitters are recorded by Jim Palmer, Baltimore, in American League, and by National Leaguers Bill Stoneman of Montreal, Jim Maloney of Cincinnati, Don Wilson of Houston (his second), Ken Holtzman of Chicago, and Bob Moose of the Pirates. . . . On June 29, Jim Northrup of Detroit Tigers hits his third grand-slam home run in a week, a baseball record. . . . At age 17, Ruth White becomes youngest national fencing champion and first black to win a major U.S. title, by defeating Harriet King at Van Nuys, California. . . . In a track-and-field meet at Los Angeles, Bill Toomey sets a record 8,417 points in the decathlon.

1970

Winners: Baseball: Cincinnati defeats Pittsburgh, 3 games to 0, to take National League title while Baltimore wins 3 straight from Minnesota. In World Series, Orioles roll over the Reds, 4 games to 1. . . . *Kentucky Derby:* Dust Commander. *Preakness:* Personality. *Belmont Stakes:* High Echelon . . . *Indy 500:* Al Unser . . . *Boxing:* Joe Frazier knocks out Jimmy Ellis in 5 rounds, is recognized as heavyweight champion. . . . In middleweight division, Carlos Monzon KOs Nino Benevenuti in 12 rounds to take championship. José Napoles loses welterweight crown on 4-round KO to Billy Backus. . . . Lightweight championship also changes hands, Ismael Laguna regaining title by knocking out Mando Ramos, then losing decision to Ken Buchanan. . . . Former featherweight champion Vicente Saldivar comes out of retirement to win 15-round decision over Johnny Famechon and regain title. But he loses it 6 months later to Kuniaki Shibata on 13-round KO. . . . Bantamweight champ Ruben Olivares loses title to Chu Chu Castillo, and Chartchai Chionoi regains flyweight crown from Efron Torres, only to lose it later in year to Erbito Salvarria. . . . *Golf: USGA Men's Open:* Tony Jacklin. *PGA:* Dave Stockton. *Masters:* Billy Casper . . . *USGA Women's Open:* Donna Caponi . . . *Hockey:* 1969–70 Stanley Cup champion: Boston Bruins . . . *Football: Cotton Bowl:* Texas 21, Notre Dame 17. *Orange Bowl:* Penn State 10, Missouri 3. *Rose Bowl:* USC 10, Michigan 3. *Sugar Bowl:* Mississippi 27, Arkansas 22 . . . *National Football League: NFC:* Dallas 17, San Francisco 10. *AFC:* Baltimore 27, Oakland 17. *Super Bowl V:* Baltimore 16, Dallas 13 . . . *Basketball:* 1969–70 *NCAA:* UCLA 80, Jacksonville 69 . . . *NIT:* Marquette 65, St. John's 53. . . . *National Basketball Association:* 1969–70 champion: New York Knickerbockers.

Other Happenings: Biggest sports book of

year is Jim Bouton's *Ball Four,* which infuriates many by treating baseball players as human beings rather than athletic idols. . . . America's Cup yacht race is longest in history of competition as a result of 20-knot northeast breezes and fog, but twenty-first defense of Cup is successfully made by the United States, *Intrepid* defeating the Australian entry, *Gretel II,* 4 races to 1. . . . Computer fights are invented and data fed into machines "prove" that Rocky Marciano in his prime could beat Muhammad Ali. Few believe it, however, and British Broadcasting Corporation version of fight shows Ali winning. . . . Ali returns to ring following court settlement of draft problems and beats Jerry Quarry; it's the first U.S. prizefight to be carried on Soviet television. . . . Tragedy strikes the Marshall University football team, a plane crash killing 38 players and 6 coaches. Brian Piccolo, 26, running back for the Chicago Bears, dies of cancer, and Bob Kulsu, Buffalo Bills' guard in 1968, is killed in Vietnam. . . . Dave Meggyesy writes *Out of Their League* and John Sample *Confessions of a Dirty Ballplayer,*

while Lance Rentzel exposes himself, and some wonder if anything is sacred. . . . To make matters worse, Vince Lombardi, a bulwark of discipline, dies. . . . "Monday Night Football" comes to television and quickly captures one third of the viewing audience. . . . Cesar Gutierrez, Detroit shortstop, becomes first player since Wilbert Robinson in 1892 to go 7 for 7 in a single game, and Jim Bunning becomes first pitcher since Cy Young to win 100 games in each league. . . . No-hitters are pitched in National League by Dock Ellis of Pirates and Bill Singer of Los Angeles, and in American by Clyde Wright of California and Vida Blue of Oakland. . . . On November 8, Tom Dempsey of New Orleans Saints in NFL, who was born without a right hand and only a partial right foot, kicks a record 63-yard field goal to defeat Detroit Lions, 19–17. . . . Hoyt Wilhelm, 47, of Atlanta Braves, appears in his 1,000th game, a record for pitchers. . . . Willie Shoemaker becomes winningest jockey by riding his 6,033rd winner at Del Mar race track in California, breaking Johnny Longden's record.

Section XI
The 1970s

CHAPTER 45—1971

"I believe that sport, all sport, is one of the few bits of glue that hold our society together, one of the few activities where young people can proceed along traditional avenues, where objectives are clear, where the desire to win is not only permissible but encouraged. . . ."

Vice President Spiro T. Agnew

"I think the values of football as it is now played reflect a segment of thought . . . that is pretty prevalent in our society. The way to do anything in the world, the way to get ahead, is to aggress against somebody, compete against somebody, try to dominate, try to overcome. . . ."

George Sauer, Jr.

The pair of quotes from 1971 gave an inkling to the kind of topsy-turvy year it might be, in sports and many other phases of life. For, ironically, the praise of sport came from a political figure without noticeable athletic ability; the quotation downgrading sports were the words of a superbly gifted professional athlete.

The previous year, which had given American sports enthusiasts Jim Bouton's *Ball Four,* had been bad enough for those who were happy with the status quo. For some—including many major-league baseball players—reading the first sports book to treat the "national game" and its participants in a light-hearted, irreverent manner was a traumatic experience. That had been the year of the football strike, a previously unthinkable situation. And also in 1970, for the first time fans had gotten together to form an organization that had as its express purpose the protection of the average fan. Instead of expressing gratitude for the wonderful recreation provided them by the athletes and owners, the group known as Sports Fans of America promulgated the heretical view that both management and labor in the sports world were money-hungry and insensitive to the feelings of their supporters. The fan, caught in the middle, had no recourse but to boycott events if he thought he was being manipulated.

"Sports fans take the brunt of the suffering because inevitably any increase is passed along to them in the form of higher ticket prices. Fans have got to have a voice. . . . We're tired of paying forty or forty-five cents for a cold hot dog and forty or fifty cents for a warm beer. . . . The fan is everybody's sucker."

Dom Piledggi, Founder,
Sports Fans of America

Player disaffection . . . fan disaffection . . . Where would it all end? Some pondered the issue, but most Americans sat back and enjoyed the year 1971, for it was a memorable one. Before the year was over, Americans would be playing golf on the moon, Ping-Pong (make that table tennis) in Red China, and volleyball in Red Cuba. The longest professional football game would be played, the world's best boxer would be defeated in the ring and upheld in the courts, women would take giant steps into previously all-male corners of the sports world, and off-track betting, which the prestigious New York *Times* had battled since the Gay Nineties, would become a legal reality.

The year got off to a flying start at Dallas's Cotton Bowl, where the University of Texas, owners of a thirty-game winning streak, threw their wishbone atack at underdog Notre Dame. A capacity crowd of seventy-three thousand watched and cheered as Texas' Happy Feller kicked a twenty-three-yard field goal as a climax to the Longhorns' first series to put his team ahead, 3–0. The Irish came right back, however, scoring three touchdowns in the next thirteen minutes on a pair of darting runs by quarterback Joe Theismann and a Theismann-to-Tom Gatewood pass. Texas scored again, but at halftime Notre Dame led, 24–11. The second half was a scoreless defensive battle, Texas' highly touted wishbone attack being totally blunted by Coach Ara Parseghian's defensive maneuvers. A total of nine fumbles by the Longhorns also contributed to the winning streak's demise.

The Irish Had Been Spoilers Before:
On November 16, 1957, at Norman, Oklahoma, Notre Dame ended the University of Oklahoma's record forty-seven-game winning streak by eking out a 7–0 victory. With four minutes left in the game, quarterback Bobby Williams faked a handoff to Nick Pietrosante and tossed a pitchout to Dick Lynch for the score. Excited Associated Press reporters, shattered by the result, wired the story beginning: "Notre Dame, November 16 (AP): Notre Dame defeated Oklahoma, 7–0, today. . . ."

The event was an exciting one, but not everybody joined in the cheering. On January 2, a Gallup Poll report showed that attendance at athletic contests at a number of schools had dropped and that general interest in sports was also on the decline. In addition to apathy, the report noted several more specific and tangible signs of student disaffection. One was a vote by students at the University of California at Berkeley in December 1970, recommending that the $310,000 used annually to make up the athletic department's deficit be "reallocated in a manner more broadly representative of all students." Even at the University of Notre Dame, where football interest was definitely on the rebound, more than seven hundred undergraduates gave up tickets to a

game against Georgia Tech so that underprivileged children from South Bend, Indiana, could attend. It seemed to be an era of more sophisticated priorities, a re-examination of traditional values in the reflection of a highly controversial Vietnam war. As one critic, Jay Brown of the Brown *Alumni Monthly,* put it, "This is the era of the antihero. . . . If a coach tried to pull the old 'win one for the Gipper' routine in the scintillating seventies his players would probably reply: 'Get serious.'"

The Antisports Poll:
Of 1,061 students interviewed at 60 colleges:
Interest declining in sports 43%
Interest not declining in sports 47%
No opinion 10%

The college students may have been losing interest in big-time athletics but the average citizen continued to display a lively love for pro football. The year began with thirty-seven-year-old John Unitas leading the Baltimore Colts to a 27–17 victory over the Oakland Raiders in the AFC, earning the right to meet Dallas in Super Bowl V.

While waiting for that epic contest to take place at Miami, sports fans noted the death of Sonny Liston, the man considered unbeatable in the boxing ring until the myth was shattered by young Cassius Clay. . . . Bill Austin, interim coach of the Washington Redskins following the death of Vince Lombardi, was fired, as was Charlie Winner of the St. Louis Football Cardinals. . . . Baseball's hot-stove league discussed the possibility of Babe Ruth's career home-run record being broken in the next few years by either Henry Aaron or Willie Mays, the two active players with chances to do so. . . . In what could only be termed preretaliation, advocates of the Babe promptly turned to their statistics and slide rules in order to show that Ruth came to bat only 8,399 times, not counting 2,056 bases on balls. Because both Mays and Aaron had surpassed that figure by the end of the 1970 season, it was argued that even if they hit more career homers, it shouldn't count. . . . Meanwhile, 26-year-old Chi Cheng, was

---

Chasing the Babe, 1971:

	Age	H.R.	Avg. H.R./Yr.
Henry Aaron	37	592	34.8
Willie Mays	40	628	33.0

named Female Athlete of 1970 by the Associated Press, largely on the basis of her world record of 10 seconds for the 100-yard dash. Other candidates for the honor included Debbie Meyer, the swimmer, and tennis player Margaret Court.

FOOTBALL

On January 17, 1971, Super Bowl V was played—or misplayed, as some charged—a total of 11 turnovers occurring in the controversial 16–13 victory by the Baltimore Colts (see "Flaps"). But while some writers insisted on deriding the game because of its seemingly sloppy quality, few thought to point out that Super Bowl V was the first of the postseason clashes to be even vaguely interesting—or, for that matter, to even have a lead change hands. Fewer still brought up the fact that fumbles are frequently the result of hard hitting and interceptions the result of heads-up playing. And so Super Bowl V earned the title "Blooper Bowl" and the Dallas Cowboys left with the equally undeserved reputation as "losers."

A week and a half later, representatives of the NFL teams gathered at New York's Belmont Plaza Hotel for the annual college-player draft. It was a particularly good year for quarterbacks, according to the co-operative scouting combine known as Blesto VIII, and the first three clubs took advantage of the opportunity to draft strong-armed saviors hoping they would lead them to future Super Bowls.

First Pick: *Quarterback Jim Plunkett, Stanford (Boston)*
Second Pick: *Quarterback Archie Manning, University of Mississippi (New Orleans)*
Third Pick: *Quarterback Dan Pastorini, Santa Clara (Houston)*

BASEBALL

Early in February, 1971, baseball crept back into the headlines when it was decided to admit black stars of the pre-integration days into baseball's Hall of Fame. "The Hall of Fame is not segregated," said Commissioner Bowie Kuhn a trifle sanctimoniously. "In addition to being a brick building, it's a state of mind. The two greatest Negro stars eligible are already there [Jackie Robinson and Roy Campanella] and they will soon be joined by the Willie Mayses, Henry Aarons, Ernie Bankses, and other major leaguers. Now we're trying to give recognition to the significant

contribution made to baseball by the Negro leagues." To do so, the commissioner announced that the new black stars would be enshrined in a separate exhibit.

Note the Sportswriterese Language Used by Kuhn:
Willie Mayses, Henry Aarons, Ernie Bankses . . . How many of each player were there? Would Marv Throneberry pluralized be Marv Throneberrys or Marv Throneberries? Would Ollie Welf pluralized be Ollie Welfs or Ollie Welves? Johnny Peskys or Johnny Peskies? Joe DiMaggios or Joe Dimaggii? Edwin Newmans or Edwin Newmen?

The first week of February 1971 marked a meeting of technology and sports when American astronaut Alan B. Shepard, Jr., stepped out of the recently landed lunar module and placed a special heat-resistant golf ball on a tee, wiggled a six-iron at it, swung, and missed (his backpack apparently shortened his swing). Remaining calm after the "mulligan," Shepard then swung again, and as millions of Americans watched on television, connected solidly, driving the ball nearly a thousand yards along the surface of the light-gravity Moon.

Meanwhile, back on Earth, another golfer named Jack Nicklaus achieved what no other player had done before. By shooting a final round of 73 on February 28, the thirty-one-year-old won the Professional Golfers' Association championship for the second time. Although "Arnie's Army" and similar partisan groups still existed, no one doubted that Jack

---

The Others:
Of the eight unfortunate "Black Sox," who were driven out of organized baseball despite being acquitted at their trial, only Swede Risberg remained. He died on October 13, 1975, having lived exactly eighty-one years. Before Gandil, the others were:
Shoeless Joe Jackson (1887–1951)
Fred McMullin (1891–1952)
Buck Weaver (1890–1956)
Lefty Williams (1893–1959)
Happy Felsch (1891–1964)
Eddie Cicotte (1884–1969)

Nicklaus was the world's best golfer. By winning the tournament, he completed the cycle of having captured each major title at least twice—the Masters, British Open, United States Open, and PGA. He also picked up forty-thousand dollars for his trouble.

Later that month, a memory of the past was recalled with the death of Arnold (Chick) Gandil, the next-to-last surviving member of the 1919 Black Sox. Actually, Gandil had passed away on December 13, 1970, at the age of eighty-two, but his occupation at the time the obituary appeared was listed as "retired plumber." (For additional information, see "1921" and "Fixes.")

HOCKEY, BASKETBALL

With the coming of March—too late for football and a bit too early for baseball— hockey and basketball reigned supreme on American sports pages and television. On the second of that month, Wayne Carleton of the Boston Bruins whistled a shot past Minnesota North Star goalie Cesare Maniago at 2:10 of the second period to set a team record of 304 goals, a mark that lasted only until later in the game when teammates Ed Westfall and Derek Sanderson increased the figure to 306. The Bruins also won the game by a score of 6–0.

In basketball, the Milwaukee Bucks, led by Kareem Abdul-Jabbar (then known as Lew Alcindor) and Oscar Robertson, also established a new National Basketball Association record by winning nineteen games in a row, which was the team's sixty-fourth season victory, only four short of the record high set by the 1966–67 Philadelphia 76ers. Earlier in the year, the Bucks had threatened the record by winning sixteen games in a row, and few doubted that they were the best squad in professional basketball. Some of the doubters were members of the New York Knicks, who felt that the short duration of their own consecutive-win record meant little or nothing. They argued that records were made to be broken, that the playoffs were the true test of a team's ability. Eventually the Milwaukee Bucks won twenty games in a row. The mark seemed unbeatable, but it lasted only until January of 1972, when the Los Angeles Lakers made a twenty-game streak seem like the work of children (see "Losing Big and in Bunches").

BOXING

The major event of March 1971, however, was the world championship heavyweight title fight between Muhammad Ali (once known as Cassius Clay) and a fighter who actually seemed to be a worthy challenger, Joe Frazier. It was the classic struggle between a brawler and a quick-reflexed boxer who had the ability to hit hard when necessary. Writers likened the two fighters to Ezzard Charles and Rocky Marciano, Joe Louis and Billy Conn, Tunney and Dempsey, even Achilles and Hector. The promoters loved every comparison, for it soon became apparent that the Ali-Frazier fight, as seen on closed-circuit television, would be the greatest money-maker of all time. The site of the fight was New York's Madison Square Garden, but that arena was small compared to some of the places where closed-circuit television screens had been set up. At Pittsburgh's Three Rivers Stadium, for example, more than fifteen thousand seats went on sale for prices ranging from ten dollars to fifteen dollars. In Los Angeles, a late rush of three thousand fans filled the Los Angeles Sports Arena, and two thousand more were turned away. In eleven Ohio cities, fifty-four thousand of sixty-one thousand seats were sold for a gross of six hundred thousand dollars. Only in the Midwest did Americans seem to bridle at paying such extravagant fees for what they used to receive free on television. Jim Journigan, a promoter who laid out two hundred thousand dollars for rights to the territory around Kansas City, Topeka, and Wichita, Kansas, Iowa, and South Dakota, ended up losing more than seventy-five thousand dollars. But in most of the nation, it was standing-room only for the fight of the century.

Other Million-dollar Gates
1921—Dempsey-Carpentier
1923—Dempsey-Firpo
1926—Dempsey-Tunney
1927—Dempsey-Sharkey
1927—Dempsey-Tunney
1935—Louis-Baer
1938—Louis-Schmeling
1946—Louis-Conn
1955—Marciano-Moore
1960—Patterson-Johansson
1962—Patterson-Liston
1963—Ali-Patterson
1965—Ali-Liston
1965—Ali-Patterson
1966—Ali-Cooper
1970—Frazier-Ellis

It turned out to be worth the money, most agreed. Ali and Frazier put on a splendid show. Even Arthur Mercante, the referee, was impressed. "The way they were hitting each other," he said, "I was surprised that it went fifteen. I thought it would be more wide open on Ali's part. I was surprised to see him in close so much, slugging toe to toe. But it was a beautifully fought fight, and they threw some of the best punches I've ever seen."

A financial and artistic success, the fight was the high point of Joe Frazier's life. He never fought better (and would never fight that well again) as he achieved his lifelong dream of winning undisputed claim to the heavyweight title. Punching with savage power, he stunned Ali in the eleventh round with a smashing right hand, then knocked the former champ to the canvas with a left hook in the fifteenth and final round. His boxing philosophy was hardly original—"Kill the body and the head will fall"—but it worked. No one before Frazier had tried to beat Ali by attacking his body rather than the head that bobbed and weaved like a spastic waterbug. Despite the convincing victory, Frazier emerged from the fight with a face that was lumpy on both sides. The record gate of $1,352,951 plus an estimated three hundred million fans who saw the fight on closed-circuit television and via satellite, however, soothed whatever physical ills the finally recognized champion had experienced.

FOOTBALL

In April 1971, football returned briefly to the headlines when it was learned that John Unitas, leader of the Super Bowl Colts, had torn an Achilles tendon while playing paddleball with running back Tom Matte. Although the football season was months away, many Colt fans realized that the Achilles tendon had been the key to permanent retirement for many ballplayers. It was recalled, for example, that Baltimore fullback Alan Ameche had been forced to give up the game following a similar accident. After surgery, Unitas and his fans could do little but hope that a quarter-back would not be hampered by the injury as much as a running back.

BASKETBALL

In basketball, Baltimore was also in the spotlight as the Bullets and Knicks entered the final phase of the playoffs to determine which of the teams would earn the right to be annihilated by the Milwaukee Bucks for the 1970–71 championship. Playing a best-of-seven semifinal series, the Knicks delighted a Madison Square Garden crowd of 19,500 in the opening game by defeating the Bullets, 112–111. Last-second heroics were provided by Willis Reed, who executed a perfect jump shot to put the Knicks in front with only six seconds remaining in the game.

HOCKEY

While waiting for game No. 2, 17,250 hockey fans took over the Garden for the Stanley Cup playoff series between the New York Rangers and the Toronto Maple Leafs. This contest did not go very well for natives of Gotham. By the middle of the second period, Toronto led, 3–0, and by the third period, with the score 4–1, it was apparent that the series was about to be tied at one game apiece. With four minutes and forty-two seconds remaining, a fight broke out between two players, and Toronto goalie Bernie Parent violated a cardinal hockey rule by leaving the net. Vic Hadfield took advantage of the situation to lift Parent's face mask from the spot where it had fallen on the ice and toss it into the crowd. When the smoke cleared and play was about to resume, Parent decided he didn't want to play without a mask. "Don't give it back!" fans shouted as Garden security police circulated through the crowd searching for the missing face guard. Eventually forty-two-year-old Jacques Plante took Parent's place. The

---

A Slight Mix-up:

The Baltimore Sun *was in the throes of a computerized type-setting dilemma when fans turned to the April 7, 1971, edition of the paper to find out what would be the fate of the 1971 Colts. Hoping to receive some clarification of the situation, here is what they read:*

"'It wasa severe shocktous . . . but we hope he's back. In fact, we expect him back. It's suptotheindividual.' If Unitas is able toreturnafter six months he will doso just as a new ceason is about to begin and thus will miss the entiretrainingcamp period. The Colts naturally are sorry to lose *him, but they are not strapped forquarterbacks . . . and George Mira, a taxisquadmenber who formerly saw backup duty with San Francisco and Philadelphia . . . Sam Havrilak, who was a quarterback at Buckness, and the club's No. 3 draft choice during the winter washighly toutde KarlDouglas ofTexasA.andwi. Havrilakgot a chance to runa handful of plays late in the 1970 campaign and McCafferty already has had Sam in for a number of visitsto absorb some of the mental gymnastics that go withthe job."*

game ended with a free-for-all as Maple Leaf players held up first four fingers, then one finger, to the crowd; fans responded by shouting epithets, and one youngster even waved a rubber chicken at the Toronto team.

April 8, 1971, was a red-letter day in New York history, marking the legalization of off-track betting as a means of earning revenue for local government and, hopefully, providing competition for illegal numbers operations. To inaugurate the event, Mayor John Lindsay placed a bet in the main concourse of Grand Central Terminal. Others followed his example—so many, in fact, that the city's Offtrack Betting Corporation eventually had to limit tickets to five per customer. By the end of the first day's operation, $66,098 had been bet on nine races, despite a slow manual system that obviously discouraged some from playing. OTB officials promised that a more efficient computerized system would speed up the entire operation.

Lindsay's Choice: Money Wise, a pacer (4–1) in the seventh race at Roosevelt Raceway. The horse finished fourth.

As the Baltimore Bullets and the New York Knicks took to the boards for the second game of their playoff series, Clarence Campbell, president of the National Hockey League, announced that a total of $14,600 had been assessed the Toronto Maple Leaf and the New York Ranger clubs and the players who participated in the riot two days before. The Maple Leafs promptly announced that a bill for $150 would be sent to the Rangers in order to compensate for the loss of goalie Bernie Parent's face mask, which had been tossed into the crowd.

New York Knick fans began to anticipate their team's coming series with Milwaukee when Cazzie Russell and Dick Barnett led a second-game rout of the Baltimore Bullets, 107–88. Both Gus Johnson and Earl Monroe, stars of the Bullets, were rendered ineffective because of knee problems, but diehard Knickerbocker fans had seen their team beat Baltimore too often to believe a healthy Johnson and a healthy Monroe would have made much difference.

SPORTS IN COURT

With the hockey and basketball playoffs far from completed, the 1971 baseball season opened and organized sports promptly moved from the playing field into the courtroom. Soon after the New York Mets insisted on playing 4½ rain-swept innings rather than

call off their well-attended opener, three angry fans brought suit against the club, charging that the game should not have been played. Meanwhile, outfielder Curt Flood, after a year of litigation, took his antitrust suit against baseball to the U. S. Supreme Court while having still another book published debunking the "national game." In the book, Flood explained why he sat out the 1970 season rather than allow the St. Louis Cardinals to trade him to Philadelphia after twelve years. "It violated the logic and integrity of my existence," he wrote, "I was not a consignment of goods. I was a man, the rightful proprietor of my own person and my own talents." While awaiting for the final disposition of the court case, some—especially officials of the Washington Senators, who had acquired the rights to Flood—hoped the young man would return to baseball. Finally, April of 1971 also saw a final court ruling in the case of Lance Rentzel, the Dallas Cowboy flanker, who pleaded guilty to indecently exposing himself in November 1970. Although the judge could have sentenced the football star to fifteen years in prison for what was obviously an open-and-shut case, he placed Rentzel on five years' probation. The former Oklahoma star also agreed to undergo psychiatric and medical treatment during the initial part of the probationary period.

Rentzel *had run his post pattern for the Cowboys, however. He played the 1971 and 1972 seasons with Los Angeles, then retired from the game. (He may have decided he wasn't getting open enough.)*

Having spread to the moon, sports took what for many was an even greater step—from the United States to Red China. On Sunday, April 11, 1971, fifteen members of the U.S. table-tennis team arrived at Peking and were greeted with a breakfast of bacon and eggs. Even more significant, for the first time since 1949, full-time news correspondents with U.S. citizenship and no particular pro-Communist bias were allowed in mainland China. The decision to raise part of the Bamboo Curtain came only after a decade of negotiations, charges, and countercharges.

BASKETBALL

The end of April saw Curt Flood report to the Washington Senators, and the Baltimore Bullets rebound from the 0–2 playoff record to defeat the New York Knicks by scores of 114–88 and 101–80, thereby evening the series at two games apiece. Back in Gotham, the Bullets faltered, however, losing, 89–84, and it seemed the Knickerbockers were back in the driver's seat. New Yorkers celebrated that along with the Rangers' eliminating Toronto and moving into the semifinal hockey playoff against the Chicago Black Hawks. But when the Baltimore Bullets returned to their home territory, they responded once again with an easy 113–96 victory, setting the stage for the final showdown at Madison Square Garden.

Television Announcer at Halftime of the Second Bullet Win:
"They rose like Lazarus from the ashes!"

With a capacity crowd of 19,500 looking on, the Knicks took a first-quarter lead of 21–19, then methodically increased the pressure with a 26–24 second period. But following intermission, the Bullets put together a 30-point third period to take a lead of 73–68. Then it was the Knicks' turn to rally, and they did, moving ahead, 88–87, with 2:44 seconds remaining on the clock. Madison Square Garden was a madhouse as Earl Monroe put Baltimore ahead and Fred Carter dropped in a 19-footer with 1:08 remaining. Despite the frenzied shouts of encouragement, the Knicks couldn't overtake the Bullets, who held on to win by a margin of 93–91. The game and the series probably took the last ounce of emotional strength from the Bullets, for they promptly lost to Milwaukee in the finals, bowing weakly in four games. The powerful Bucks thus became only the second team in NBA history to sweep the championship round in four straight games.

HOCKEY

It was, it turned out, the era of brief dynasties. After nearly rewriting the record book of the National Hockey League during the 1970–71 regular season of 78 games, the Boston Bruins, winners of the previous year's Stanley Cup, were described as an "unbeatable team."

In the Boston area, automobile bumper stickers proclaimed "God Bless ORR Country," as the Bruins awaited the Montreal Canadiens and the playoffs. Beaten by Boston in five of six regular-season games, the Canadiens had a rookie goalie, Ken Dryden, only recently graduated from Cornell, a veteran of but six NHL contests. Defeat for Montreal seemed imminent, especially after the Bruins won the first game, 3–1, and proceeded to shell Dryden with five more goals in the beginning of game No. 2. But then something startling happened. Instead of lying down and hoping for better luck back in Montreal, the Canadiens came to life right before the wide eyes of Boston's rabid fans. In rapid succession, Henri Richard and Jean Beliveau tied the score at 5–5; then Jean Lemaire broke through the Boston defense and sent the Canadiens into the lead. To rub it in, Frank Mahovlich added another to give Montreal a 7–5 victory.

After that, the series seesawed into the seventh and final game, which would be played at Boston Garden. "There's no way the Canadiens are going to beat us in Boston," promised Phil Esposito. "No way. Believe me!"

He turned out to be wrong. Before 14,994 suffering Boston Garden spectators and a national television audience, the Mahovlich brothers and goalie Dryden led Montreal to an impressive 4–2 victory that, as the aphorism goes, was not as close as the score seemed to indicate.

BASEBALL

It was the year of the dissident player, no doubt about that. Late in April, after amassing an unimpressive record in thirteen games with the Washington Senators, Curt Flood repaid owner Bob Short's faith in him by failing to show up for a game with the Minnesota Twins. He also sent a telegram from John F. Kennedy International Airport in New York before taking a plane believed bound for Barcelona, Spain. "I tried," he said in the message, "a year and a half is too much. Very serious personal problems mounting every day. Thank you for your kindness and understanding." And with that the tor-

---

Some Records Set by the 1970–71 Bruins:

Most goals, one season, team	399
Most goals, one season, player (Phil Esposito)	76
Most Assists, one season, player (Bobby Orr)	102
Most points, one season, player (Phil Esposito)	152
Most points, one season, defenseman (Bobby Orr)	139
Most goals, one season, by a line (center Phil Esposito [76], right wing Ken Hodge [43], left wing Wayne Cashman [21])	140

tured soul of Curtis Charles Flood flew off into the beyond. At about the same time, a much more prosaic exit from baseball was taken by Kansas City Royal outfielder Carl Taylor. While playing at Baltimore, the twenty-seven-year-old Taylor walked off the field between innings and announced to Manager Bob Lemon that he was through. "You'll have to get a new left fielder," he said moments after making a fine running catch of a liner by Boog Powell. "I'm quitting." He was, as it developed, completely serious. After the game, when the Royals entered the dressing room, they smelled smoke. Taylor had methodically piled everything in his locker—including his sweaty uniform—and set fire to it.

Carl Taylor's Comeback:
Leaving the Kansas City Royals in 1971 was not the end of Carl Taylor's major-league career, although it might as well have been (except for pension purposes). Late in 1971 he returned to play in seven games with the Pittsburgh Pirates, batting .167. He was then shipped back to the Royals for 1972 and 1973, batting .265 and .228, respectively, before retiring for good. In the majority of his post-1971 games he was used as a catcher.

There was some good news, of course. On the day Curt Flood exited, Henry Aaron hit his six hundredth home run, becoming the third-highest homer hitter of all time. A colt named Canonero II added spice to the ninety-seventh running of the Kentucky Derby, confounding the experts and winning by 3¾ lengths. And Communist China's table-tennis squad showed remarkable kindness by defeating the United States team with a minimum of humiliation.

May of 1971 brought with it the end of hockey season—Montreal defeated Chicago

Also in May 1971: A Broadway musical entitled Frank Merriwell, based on the Mythical Yale athletic hero, c. 1900, closed after one performance. Good field, no hit.

for the Stanley Cup—part two of racing's Triple Crown, the Preakness—also won by Canonero II—and an Indianapolis 500 in which a pace car crashed into some portable bleachers, injuring about 20 occupants. . . . Then, on the 30th of the month, Willie Mays moved into the limelight by hitting his 638th home run and scoring his 1,950th career run. The latter put him one ahead of Stan Musial's career record of 1,949 which was tops in the National League. Mays also was only the 10th man in baseball history to collect more than 3,000 hits.

HORSERACING
"The horse shouldn't have run. It was only 75 per cent fit. But he told me he wanted to run." Thus spake Juan Arias, trainer of Canonero II, late on June 6, 1971, after Pass Catcher, an unheralded colt, surprised a record crowd of 81,036 at Belmont Park by winning the $162,850 Belmont Stakes. The outcome of the event's 103rd running brought a great deal of disappointment to most of the crowd, which anticipated seeing the first Triple Crown winner since Citation turned that trick in 1948. A strong betting favorite among the field of 13 entries, Canonero II went off at 3–5, while Pass Catcher, a definite long shot, paid $71, $21, and $10.80 for a $2.00 wager. Even worse for those who came to see an exciting race, Canonero II finished in fourth place and never seriously threatened for the lead. A fungus growth in the horse's right rear foot was blamed for interrupting the rigorous training so necessary to carry off the Triple Crown. Later in the month, the horse—which had been purchased for $1,200 as a yearling—was sold for a sum in excess of $1 million.

Since 1948, It Had Happened Six Times: *Great horses had won the Kentucky Derby and Preakness only to falter in the Belmont Stakes. The unlucky ones:*

Year	Kentucky Derby	Preakness	Belmont Stakes
1958	Tim Tam	Tin Tam	Cavan
1961	Carry Back	Carry Back	Sherluck
1964	Native Dancer	Native Dancer	Quadrangle
1966	Kauai King	Kauai King	Amberoid
1968	Forward Pass	Forward Pass	Stage Door Johnny
1969	Majestic Prince	Majestic Prince	Arts and Letters

The summer of '71 had other surprises in addition to the unfortunate and unexpected failure of Canonero II. For one thing, Muhammad Ali won his court case appealing the government's calling him for Army induction despite his being a minister of the Muslim faith. Four years after being convicted by a court in Houston, stripped of his heavyweight championship title, and sentenced to five years in prison, the world's finest fighter—Joe Frazier notwithstanding—was vindicated. The vote of the U. S. Supreme Court was 8–0 in Ali's favor, with Justice Thurgood Marshall abstaining. An even greater upset took place on July 13, at Detroit, where the American League somehow managed to win its first All-Star baseball game since 1962 (when two a year were played and they had the laws of inevitability if not probability on their side). Heroes of the contest were Reggie Jackson of Oakland, Frank Robinson of Baltimore, and Minnesota's Harmon Killebrew, all of whom donated home runs to the 6–4 victory. The game also featured a home run by the National League's Henry Aaron—incredibly, his first in All-Star competition.

Among the Notably Missing at the '71 All-Star Game:
Denny McLain, *who pitched in the 1968 and 1969 games and won 31 regular-season contests in '68. In July 1971, McLain was again making a strong bid for 30—but this time 30 losses, with the Washington Senators. On July 4, his 1971 record stood at 5 wins, 14 losses. At that rate of progress (or regress) he would have ended the season with 30 or more losses, but fortunately he developed arm trouble and was put on the injured list. Thus he completed the season with a record of 10 wins and only 22 defeats.*

FOOTBALL
With the passing of the baseball midseason classic, it was obvious that professional football was already standing in the wings, waiting to entertain Americans (for a slightly higher price than last year in most cities). Summer training camps opened—unmarred by the threat of a strike similar to that of 1970. But that did not mean individual players couldn't strike on their own, and one who did was the New England Patriots' tempestuous quarterback Joe Kapp. After being signed as a free agent when he played out his option with Minnesota, Kapp refused to sign the standard player's contract for 1971, on the advice of his lawyer. The Patriots, even though they had recently drafted Jim Plunkett, were quite upset.

That was just the beginning of a quarterback shortage that had started in April with John Unitas' tearing an Achilles tendon. During an exhibition game between the Detroit Lions and the New York Jets at Tampa, Joe Namath was in the process of picking the Lion defense to pieces, hitting on seven of 13 tosses for 116 yards and a touchdown. Hoping to score again, Namath handed off to Matt Snell, who lost the ball to Detroit linebacker Mike Lucci. Instead of allowing the hefty Lucci a reasonable amount of space, Namath threw himself at the Lion with all his might. Namath's knee collapsed when he missed and was himself pounced on by Paul Naumoff. Orthopedic surgeons were optimistic but refused to predict if Namath would play during the 1971 season.

The next day, quarterback Fran Tarkenton of the Giants decided he didn't like his contract and promptly walked out of the training camp immediately before an exhibition game. Without him, the Giants were demolished by the Houston Oilers, 35–6. And if that were not enough, the second-string quarterback, Dick Shiner, aggravated a groin injury in the game, and regular punter Phil Johnson walked out of camp after kicking poorly. "I'm discouraged," said Coach Alex Webster, not one usually given to such masterful understatement.

Even Inanimate Objects Conspired Against Them:
When the New York Giants received the game films of the miserable effort against Houston, they weren't even allowed to benefit from seeing their mistakes. The film turned out to be blank.

What Webster did not know was that somehow Dick Shiner had gotten word that the Giants had asked waivers on him immediately before the exhibition game. No doubt Shiner felt betrayed, for it wasn't long before he was seen packing his gear prior to a quick exit. Eventually the Giants patched things up with Tarkenton in time for the 1971 season, but for a while the situation seemed desperate.

Nor was that all. In Green Bay star offensive tackle Francis Peay, miffed at the coaching staff, walked out of camp just five days before it was learned that Packer quarterback Bart Starr would have to undergo surgery to correct a bleeding artery in his arm.

Meanwhile, back in New York, Giant offensive tackle Joe Taffoni left camp without an explanation, and in Washington, regular quarterback Sonny Jurgensen suffered a broken shoulder, also in a game against the Detroit Lions. These events coincided with the publication of still another book by an ex-player attacking the establishment. Entitled *They Call It a Game,* the book, written by a former defensive back named Bernie Parrish, did more than make fun of the game, as Jim Bouton had, even did more than attack the sports establishment as a group of despots carrying on a form of slave-trading, as Curt Flood had charged. What Parrish said was most upsetting of all—that professional football games were often rigged in order to make a killing for bettors or organized crime. According to the former Cleveland player, the greatest fixed game of them all was the 1969 Super Bowl in which the New York Jets surprised the Baltimore Colts, 16–7. (Many Baltimoreans probably agreed with Parrish, especially those with anguished memories of Colt receiver Jimmy Orr standing in the Jet end zone, practically sending signal flares to quarterback Earl Morrall, who somehow managed to throw an interception in the direction of an alternate receiver.) As might be expected, Parrish had a few ideas on how football's ills could be cured, which included making the clubs municipally owned corporations with federal regulation and profit-sharing for the players.

Wrote Parrish:
"I have played in NFL and AFL games that left me with an uneasy feeling that something was wrong. . . . with what I have learned as a player, no one will convince me that NFL games aren't fixed. . . ."

BOXING
Having vindicated himself in the courts, Muhammad Ali returned to the boxing ring in July 1971 to work himself into shape for a rematch with Joe Frazier. Ali's opponent was Jimmy Ellis, an old sparring partner, and during the fight Ellis resembled nothing more than an old sparring partner. Although it was apparent to many that Ali could have put Ellis away several times, the former champion obviously used the bout to relearn his skills and condition himself to going more than thirty minutes in the ring at top speed. In the twelfth round he had Ellis groggy against the ropes but declined to land more punches against the defenseless fighter's head. Instead

he stepped back and allowed the referee to end it. "Ain't no reason for me to kill nobody in the ring," said Ali simply when it was over.

VOLLEYBALL
Having gone to the moon and China, Americans next set their sights on Communist Cuba. In 1969, a team of U.S. fencers competed in the world championships there, but no Americans had returned since. On August 11, 1971, the United States State Department received final approval for clearance of a men's volleyball team to go to Havana in order to decided which team would represent the North American Zone at the 1972 Olympics in Munich. "It should be an interesting trip," said U.S. Head Coach Allen Scates. "Our players think they can win and they want to make the best showing possible."
The Cubans were rightfully confident that they would win, having seen their athletes emerge victorious in the politically charged Pan-American Games at Cali, Colombia, in July, taking a gold medal with a dramatic three-game sweep of the United States. In anticipation of seeing another Yankee defeat, 16,500 partisan Cubans jammed the Sports Coliseum to hear Fidel Castro first lambaste the United States, then turn abruptly generous. "We shouldn't consider those athletes as representatives of imperialism," he said. "Rather we should look upon them as representatives of the United States."
At the beginning of the match, it seemed that the Yankees would cause Fidel considerable anxiety. Getting strong blocking from Duncan McFarland and Smitty Duke, the U.S. team took just nineteen minutes to win the opening game, 15–8. But the Cubans swept the next three games, 15–10, 15–6, and 15–8, to take the best-of-five series. The Cuban audience, to its credit, gave the Americans generous applause at the conclusion rather than derision.

Things were not going well for the United States, no doubt about it. Late in August, even the OTB computer system broke down, de-

---

Meanwhile, on the Track, A Human Triumph:
On September 2, 1971, seventeen-year-old Cheryl White became the first black woman jockey in American thoroughbred history to win a horse race. At Waterford Park, Chester, West Virginia, she rode Jetolara, owned and trained by her father, to victory in the third race.

---

priving many horseplayers of their daily wager for four days running. Hardly were the computers put back in action than they broke down again, three of the OTB shops having to shut down completely and eleven reverting to manual operation. The situation became so frustrating after a time that, in sharp contrast to most situations, where officials blame humans rather than computers for breakdowns, Charles B. Chriss, vice president of the OTB operations, said, "We made the original human error, but the computer made a stupid, catastrophic response to a very simple mistake. There's no reason it should respond that way to such a ridiculous error." (The human mistake: an OTB employee entered a number starting with 80 into the central computer as the next available account number. Since all accounts at the beginning stage start with 00, the computer assumed it would have to find space in its memory banks for 800,000 new accounts.) "Apparently it just flipped its lid trying to generate 800,000 new accounts to fill up the space," Mr. Chriss said. History does not record whether or not he actually kicked the machines at the height of the crisis.

TENNIS

Meanwhile, as New York Jet fans wondered if the season would really open with a quarterback named Chris Farasopoulos, a new name entered the world of tennis at Forest Hills. Just 16 years old, Chris Evert trailed one of America's better grass-court players, Mary Ann Eisel, by love–40 in the twelfth game of the second round of U. S. Open championship play. More than 10,000 spectators were on hand to watch the teen-ager stage a dramatic victory over the more experienced player. Chris Evert immediately became the underdog popular favorite. But when she took the court against Billie Jean King on September 10, 1971, the happy summer came to a halt for Chris Evert. Only $25,000 away from becoming the first woman in American tennis to win $100,000 in a single year, the 27-year-old King did away with her teen-aged opponent in two sets, 6–3, 6–2. The poker-faced teen-ager with a two-fisted backhand won many fans, however, and gave the U. S. Open tournament a badly needed flash of life.

September was a traditionally confusing month for casual sports-watchers, the seasons overlapping at that point, plus the added complication of there being more divisions with more teams. The dramatic year came in 1969 for baseball, the two ten-team leagues being replaced by two leagues of two divisions each, six teams per division. In football, the change came in 1970, when the NFL broke itself into the National Conference and the

Meanwhile, Another Youngster Wins Applause:

On September 11, 1971, 9-year-old Priscilla Hill of Lexington, Massachusetts, in winning a gold medal at Lake Placid's ice- and figure-skating tests, became the youngest figure skater to reach the coveted rank of gold medalist. Barbara Ann Scott previously achieved the distinction at the age of 10 and went on to become a world champion.

American Conference, each with three divisions of four (or five) teams apiece. By 1971, some people still had trouble keeping the systems straight.

And to add just a bit to the team proliferation, in September 1971 announcement was made that a new hockey league was in the process of being formed, fourteen groups from as many cities standing in line for franchises.

BASEBALL

The baseball races that month had settled down into the playing out of the string in three of the four divisions—Baltimore, Oakland, and Pittsburgh were well ahead. But the Western Division of the National League had one good battle going. On August 24, the San Francisco Giants enjoyed a 7½-game lead over the Los Angeles Dodgers; by mid-September, the Giants clung to a single-game edge and seemed to be fading fast. On September 15, San Francisco hoped to add to that lead, playing at home against Jim McGlothlin of Cincinnati, who was having a terrible year, with 7 wins and 12 losses, having won only 1 of his last 8 starts. As luck would have it, however, McGlothlin chose that game to emerge briefly from his slump, recording a 6-hit, 4–2 victory that reduced the Giants' lead briefly to ½ game. But Los Angeles lost the opportunity to tie by dropping a 2–1 game to the lowly San Diego Padres.

Not that it counted in the standings, but Philadelphia Phillie ace right-hander Rick Wise was having one of his best years on the

Wise's Feat:

Was good but not quite close enough for a record. The major-league mark for retiring consecutive batters was established in 1959 when Harvey Haddix of Pittsburgh set down 38 in a row while somehow managing to lose the game.

mound. After pitching a no-hitter on June 23 against Cincinnati, he came back in September to retire 32 consecutive Chicago Cubs between the second and eleventh innings. Ron Santo's two-out single broke the string, but in the bottom half of the twelfth, Wise himself singled home the run that sent 7,740 Phillie fans to their own homes happy.

On the same day, President Richard Nixon, the nation's No. 1 sports watcher who seldom participated in sports, actually pushed himself away from the television set and the telephone long enough to roll a ceremonial ball on the White House executive bowling alley. The occasion was a visit to the White House by Edwin Luther and Aida Gonzalez, who won the World International Tournament at Milwaukee in August. The first ball thrown by Mr. Nixon went straight down the gutter.

That was the lighter side of the sports news for that month. The heavier concerned retirement of thirteen-year defensive tackle and raconteur Alex Karras of the Detroit Lions. The thirty-six-year-old athlete, who played without glasses despite being able to see very little without them, was offered a job with the Washington Redskins after being cut by the Lions. In a sarcastic reference to the fact that Detroit had never had a top quarterback and that Sonny Jurgensen of the Redskins was laid up with a broken left shoulder, Karras said, "No thanks, I've played long enough without a quarterback."

The Players to Whom Karras Referred: *Milt Plum, with the Lions 1962–67, Jim Ninowsky, 1960–61, Greg Landry, and Bill Munson, all of whom tried to lead the Lions to a title. The last to succeed had been Bobby Layne (1957).*

Four days after rolling his gutter ball, President Nixon was back in the sports news, this time deploring a 10–2 vote in favor of moving the Washington Senators to a town in Texas known as Arlington. As if it really mattered, Nixon then added that if the Senators did actually leave town, he would switch his allegiance to the California Angels, the team closest to his western home at San Clemente, California. At the same time, Senator Sam Ervin, Jr., of North Carolina, chairing hearings before the Senate Judiciary Committee's antitrust and monopoly subcommittee, voiced strong words against a proposed merger between the National Basketball Association and the American Basketball Association. The situation seemed to be the same as earlier in the

year, when more sports news was taking place off the field than on it.

BASEBALL

Not that the field was devoid of life. As a matter of fact, late in September, the division race between the San Francisco Giants and the Los Angeles Dodgers flared into a beanball war as the Giants lost eleven of twelve games and held onto a one-game lead. As the two teams began their final confrontation of the season, tempers were understandably short. Adding to the emotional heat, the weather at San Francisco rose above a hundred degrees, the hottest September since 1901.

Hoping to double their lead at the outset, the Giants led with ace Juan Marichal, who had beaten the Dodgers twenty-one of twenty-two times at Candlestick Park. Los Angeles got two runs off him in the very first inning, however, when Richie Allen homered with a man on base, and it seemed that the divisional race might go down to the last game of the season. In the bottom of the same first inning, Los Angeles pitcher Bill Singer nicked Willie Mays on the arm with a pitch, causing the outfielder to writhe on the ground as the crowd booed. Three innings later, Singer added fuel to the fire by hitting Giant shortstop Chris Speier, causing the partisan crowd to scream "Out! Out! Out!" They screamed other things when Singer came to bat in the top of the fifth, then shrieked with delight as Marichal's first pitch—a high, inside fast ball —drove Singer back from the plate. When Marichal's second pitch was in the same area, Umpire Shag Crawford issued a warning, which carried an automatic $150 fine.

Other Home-run Milestones in September 1971:

September 13: Frank Robinson hit home run No. 500
September 21: Ron Santo hit home run No. 300

Marichal proceeded to retire Singer on a fly ball, then hit Bill Buckner on the elbow. Bat still in hand, the volatile Buckner started toward the pitching mound; a general melee started, and Umpire Crawford banished Marichal. Jerry Johnson of the Giants then attacked Crawford, had to be wrestled to the ground, and Willie Mays was punched on the head. Buckner was also sent to the showers, but with Marichal out of the game, the Dodgers' chances looked better than ever.

Some Other Races that Went Down to the Wire:

1908: (N.L.) *McGraw's Giants and Frank Chance's Chicago Cubs fought it out until the last day, Cubs winning by 1-game margin (single-game playoff).*

1908: (A.L.) *Detroit Tigers edged Cleveland by ½ game.*

1922: (A.L.) *Yankees and St. Louis Browns battled until final day, Yanks winning by 1 game.*

1940: (A.L.) *Detroit Tigers finished in front of Cleveland Indians by single game.*

1944: (A.L.) *St. Louis Browns won their only American League pennant, edged Detroit Tigers by single-game margin.*

1946: (N.L.) *Dodgers and Cardinals tied, Cardinals won playoff in 2 games.*

1949: (N.L.) *Dodgers won by beating Phillies in 10 innings, thereby holding off Cardinals, 1 game back.*

1949: (A.L.) *Yankees defeated Boston Red Sox, 5–3, to win pennant by 1 game.*

1950: (N.L.) *Phillies beat Dodgers, who could have tied them, in 10 innings at Ebbets Field.*

1951: (N.L.) *Giants and Dodgers tied on final day, and Giants won playoff on Bobby Thomson's home run.*

1956: (N.L.) *Dodgers won by beating Pittsburgh, thereby edging Braves (now in Milwaukee), who also won.*

1959: (N.L.) *Dodgers (now in Los Angeles) and Braves tied, Dodgers winning playoff, 2 games to 1.*

1962: (N.L.) *Giants (now in San Francisco) and Dodgers finished in a tie. Giants won 3-game playoff.*

1964: (N.L.) *St. Louis won by beating the Mets while Cincinnati Reds, tied before final game, lost to Phillies.*

1967: (A.L.) *Boston Red Sox won final game while Detroit split a doubleheader.*

1972: (A.L.) *Detroit Tigers hung on to edge Red Sox by ½ game (Eastern Division).*

They won the game and left San Francisco three days later in good shape. But then, after outdrawing Bob Hope on television as a result of the exciting pennant battle, the Dodgers blew a pair of contests with the San Diego Padres, destined to finish last in the Western Division, two more to Atlanta, and found themselves in the position of blowing the pennant before they actually won it. Finally, as the season came down to the final few games, the Dodgers got their act together, beating the Houston Astros, 2–1, on the last day, but by then the Giants had steadied themselves and managed to win the division title by a single-game margin.

The other races were less spectacular. Baltimore walked away in the American League East, becoming only the second team in major-league history to have four 20-game winners on its roster as a result of Jim Palmer's September twenty-sixth victory, over Cleveland. (But the game was played during a 162-game season! Would this mean that because of former Commissioner Ford Frick's declaration that a "Babe Ruth" 154-game season was the standard, the record would not count? By this time, of course, no one even bothered to ask.)

As baseball's four winners began their postseason, pre-Series playoffs, a record was established in the world of tennis when Billie

Jean King won the Virginia Slims–Thunderbird tourney at Phoenix, thus becoming the first woman professional—and first woman athlete in history—to win $100,000 during a single competitive year. Hardly had the young woman completed the task, of course, than a phone call from Mr. Spectator himself, Richard Nixon, was put through to her. She accepted the President's congratulations graciously.

The First Roster With Four Twenty-Game Winners:

The 1920 Chicago White Sox (soon to be the Black Sox), whose roster included Lefty Williams (22–14), Eddie Cicotte (21–10), Red Faber (23–13), and Dickie Kerr (21–9). Ironically, the White Sox failed to win a pennant that year, losing to Cleveland by a 2-game margin. Williams and Cicotte were subsequently suspended from organized baseball as a result of the Black Sox scandal.

Baltimore's four 20-game winners included Jim Palmer (20–9), Dave McNally (21–5), Pat Dobson (20–8), and Mike Cuellar (20–9).

BASEBALL

Mr. Spectator then turned his attention to the National Football League season, already in full swing by early October, and, naturally, the baseball playoffs and the World Series. Baltimore, which had beaten Minnesota, 3 games to 0, in both the 1969 and 1970 playoffs, continued its mastery of the post-season elimination by downing Oakland, 5–3, 5–1, and 5–3. Pittsburgh, meanwhile, handled the Giants, 3 games to 1, setting up what many felt would be a super Series. After Baltimore won the first two contests, however, the old "dynasty" talk began to be heard. But like the Boston Bruins earlier in the year, the Orioles rediscovered the truth of the old axiom about anything happening during a short series. After breezing through the opening pair of games at Baltimore, the Orioles ran into excellent Pirate pitching during the next three games (losing the first night World Series game in the process). Leading by a margin of 3 games to 2, the Pirates returned to Baltimore on the verge of becoming only the sixth team in World Series history to win the championship after losing the first 2 games. But the sixth game, a 10-inning thriller, was won by the Orioles, 3–2, when Frank Robinson scored on a sacrifice fly by Brooks Robinson.

The Other Five Who Came from Behind:
1921—*New York Giants beat Yankees, 5 games to 3.*
1955—*Brooklyn Dodgers over New York Yankees, 4 games to 3.*
1956—*New York Yankees turn tables on Dodgers, 4 games to 3.*
1958—*New York Yankees beat Milwaukee Braves, 4 games to 3.*
1965—*Los Angeles Dodgers defeat Minnesota Twins, 4 games to 3.*

The final game featured a pair of heroes for Pittsburgh—Steve Blass, who limited the Orioles to four hits and a single run, and Roberto Clemente, who climaxed his .414 World Series hitting spree with a home run in the seventh game. As soon as the Pirates applied the finishing touches to their 2–1 win, Manager Danny Murtaugh received a telephone call.

The dramatic Pittsburgh victory was somewhat marred, however, by a triumphant homeward journey that degenerated into a riot involving 100,000 persons. Instead of merely cheering their heroes, Pirate fans went on a bottle-throwing, stone-hurling rampage, over-turning cars, setting bonfires, engaging in nude dancing in the streets, and ripping telephone booths from their emplacements. Police reported a dozen or so rapes as well. Apologists for the rioters—or celebrants—pointed out that the rowdyism was a natural expression of joy at the Pirates' winning their first World Series since 1960. Skeptics remarked that it was a good thing the Washington franchise had not won the Series or the nation's capital might be a mass of rubble.

FOOTBALL

The baseball season having run its lengthy course, Americans turned their attention to the battle leading up to professional football's Super Bowl VI. Meanwhile, college football was more popular than ever, the great debate of 1971 centering around the relative power of Nebraska vs. Oklahoma. Nebraska pounded out its eighteenth straight win on October 30, beating Colorado, 31–7. Oklahoma, which beat Iowa State on the same Saturday, had already whipped Colorado by a score of 45–17. The debate, however, was hardly necessary, for unlike most college situations in which the best teams do not meet each other, the Oklahoma-Nebraska controversy would be settled on the field on Thanksgiving Day. Dedicated fans looked forward to the clash eagerly.

Other highlights included the rushing of Ed Marinaro of Cornell, who had averaged 209

A Funny Thing Happened on the Way to the Heisman Award Ceremony:
Unaccountably, Ed Marinaro did not win the 1971 Heisman Trophy, which shocked and angered many sports fans nearly as much as it did Marinaro. The winner turned out to be Pat Sullivan, Auburn quarterback. Both players turned professional, of course, but did not blossom into immediate stars, as did O. J. Simpson (1968), Steve Owens (1969), or Jim Plunkett (1970), previous winners of the award. Sullivan was probably the most disappointing Heisman Trophy winner as a pro since Gary Beban (1967), who played two seasons with the Redskins before calling it quits. Marinaro, playing alongside but mostly behind Minnesota Viking star Chuck Foreman, found it equally difficult to set the sports world on fire.

---

yards per game since 1969 and seemed destined to win the coveted Heisman Trophy for 1971. Not far behind Marinaro was Penn State's Lydell Mitchell, a bread-and-butter runner; Howard Stevens of Louisville; Greg Pruitt of Oklahoma; and Robert Newhouse of Houston. But because he led in all three categories—rushing yardage, scoring, and total number of yards per game, including pass receiving and punt returns—Marinaro was regarded as the best football player in the college ranks of 1971.

Football was on the TV tube in every conceivable fashion as the college and professional seasons moved to their conclusions. On Tuesday, November 30, 1971, The American Broadcasting Company presented its movie of the week, entitled *Brian's Song*, the true story of Chicago Bear running back Gale Sayers and Brian Piccolo, who died in 1970 of cancer at the age of twenty-six. The film, while marred with occasional bits of bathos such as the two players running in slow motion through glades in the manner of young men and women peddling deodorants, worked on an emotional level and provided game sequences that mixed stock footage and location film with great effectiveness. Not since *Pride of the Yankees* (when Gary Cooper broke American hearts as Lou Gehrig by saying what a "lucky man" he was just prior to his screen death) had sports fans been so thoroughly but wonderfully depressed.

Wrote One Columnist:
"The film left no possible manipulation of the emotions unmanipulated. One report had it that even the TV technicians at ABC broke down and wept, something that hadn't happened since the last time they had to compromise on a labor contract."

John J. O'Connor

The year concluded with a pair of sensational football contests—one college, the other professional. The first took place on Thanksgiving Day, a traditional holiday on which football is played; the second occurred on Christmas, a holiday traditionally "unmarred" by trivia such as an NFL playoff game. But in order to have a full two weeks in which to promote Super Bowl VI, Commissioner Pete Rozelle (who had ordered NFL games played on the weekend following John F. Kennedy's assassination) tackled Christmas—although many thought it closer to a clip—by allowing playoff games on that hitherto-sacred day. Oklahoma and Nebraska aroused less emo-

tion when they played just four weeks before the NFL playoffs. The game, however, needed no artificial stimulus, for it was one of the rare "game of the decade" meetings that lived up to its promise. The scene was Norman, Oklahoma, which should have provided an inspirational lift to the Sooner squad—and probably did just that—but the Nebraska Cornhuskers quickly moved to a 14–3 lead in the second quarter. Nearing the end of the third period, Nebraska had another 11-point lead, 28–17, at which point Oklahoma quarterback Jack Mildren thrilled the hometown crowd of 63,385 by engineering 2 touchdowns. For the first time in the game, Oklahoma led, 31–28. There was still 7:10 left in the game, however, enough time for Nebraska quarterback Jerry Tagge to drive his team down the field, handing off to Johnny Rodgers or Jeff Kinney, until there were only 2 minutes of time left and 2 yards of ground to cover. It was third down, goal. After consulting with Coach Bob Devaney, Tagge decided to go with Nebraska's most effective play, an off-tackle slant, Jeff Kinney following All-American guard Larry Rupert.

Meanwhile, Between the Holidays:
Tennis: *Rod Laver became the first tennis millionaire, winning runner-up money of $20,000 in the Dallas "World Championship of Tennis," thus bringing his 1971 winnings to $292,717 and his career money to $1,006,947. Ken Rosewall won the tourney.*
Baseball: *The Senators, lately of Washington, having moved to Dallas-Fort Worth, announced that the new name of the team would be the Texas Rangers.*
Golf: *Jack Nicklaus set a single-season money-winning mark of $244,490.50 by winning the $150,000 Disney World Open tournament at Orlando, Florida.*
Football: *Willie Ellison of the Los Angeles Rams set an NFL single-game rushing record by gaining 247 yards in the Rams' 45–28 win over the New Orleans Saints on December 5.*

The well-coached Oklahoma team no doubt sensed that the play was coming, but Nebraska's execution was simply too good. Kinney burst into the end zone to give the Cornhuskers a tenuous but satisfying 35–31 victory.

The second excellent contest of late 1971 took place on Christmas at Kansas City, where the Chiefs and the Miami Dolphins fought it out in the first round of the NFL playoffs. At the end of regulation play, the score was tied, 24–24, so the teams began a fifth quarter. When that had expired without a score, a sixth quarter of play started. Long-time football buffs with good memories recalled that the Dallas Texans, which had been moved to Kansas City for the 1963 American Football League season, had been involved in the only other professional game to require more than five quarters of action. Dallas won that game, 20–17, but their counterparts known as the Chiefs finally bowed to the kicking skill of Miami's Garo Yepremian, losing 27–24 in the longest football game ever played, 82 minutes, 40 seconds. (For further details, see "Doing It Till It Hurts.")

Meanwhile, at San Francisco, the Washington Redskins lost a heartbreaker to San Francisco, 24–20, thus losing their opportunity to go to the Super Bowl and disappointing their Number 1 fan, who watched them, as usual, on television. As soon as the game was over, a long-distance call from the White House to the Redskin locker room brought words of consolation for the team that had made a good fight of it despite losing its regular quarterback.

History does nor record the exact extent to which the players were uplifted by the presidential words of wisdom.

CHAPTER 46—AMERICANS ABROAD AND VICE VERSA

No sooner had spectator sports become popular in America than the urge arose to import and export. The breeding of local champions created controversy over whether they could defeat the best of other nations, and as means of communication improved, so did the ability to test America's stars against foreign athletes.

In addition, many Americans felt that if other nations could see not only our stars but also our games, they would be indeed envious of the New World's progress. Thus baseball was only four seasons old, professionally, in 1874 when two teams representing Boston and Philadelphia toured England, playing a total of fourteen games for the edification of the British sports fan. The viewers were amused but not converted.

More serious international competition took place in sports that were common to America and other nations. In 1851, Queen Victoria watched as a schooner named *America* won the first America's Cup as the reward for a sixty-mile race around the Isle of Wight. That event inaugurated the series of yacht races that continues until this day. It was also a harbinger of additional sports competition between the United States and Great Britain, an involvement that led to contact with other parts of the world.

HARVARD ON THE THAMES

In 1869, having established itself as the best rowing team in the United States, Harvard issued a challenge to crews from Oxford and Cambridge, England. Although amateurs, the Harvard men had defeated several professional teams in six- and three-mile races and had given the famous Ward brothers a close match. It seemed possible, with that kind of experience, that Harvard could beat the British at their own game.

Enthusiasm for such an international match was high but the English declined at first because the Americans rowed without a coxswain, an indispensable man in the British system. When Harvard agreed to carry a coxswain in a four-oared race, Oxford accepted the challenge, but Cambridge declined. Since Oxford was the best university crew in England, the stage was set for a true battle of champions from the Old and the New worlds.

Build-up for the August race began as early as May 1869, when Harvard announced that it had selected the crew members who would make the trip. William H. Simmons, a senior, was the strongest man, at nearly six feet and 170 pounds. "He is safely a 15 per cent stronger oarsman than any other who ever rowed in the Harvard boat," one reporter noted, "and is a man of most manly carriage and fine presence." With such credentials and praise, it was not surprising that Simmons was selected as stroke for the team.

When the Americans arrived in London, they were graciously received by the British, who made them guests of the London Rowing Club and extended invitations to all manner of pleasure parties. To their credit, the Yanks turned down most of the diversions in order to learn as much as possible about the convoluted Putney-to-Mortlake course of 4½ miles. Rowing experts, meanwhile, criticized the American style of stroke, which they considered choppier and more dependent on sheer strength than the even and smooth British style. Subjected to Super Bowl scrutiny for weeks before the event, the teams' eating habits were duly reported to the public and analyzed. (The British stuck to beef and mutton washed down with beer and claret, it was reported; the Americans preferred softer foods such as rice, eggs, and fruit. "When I heard the Harvards were training on soft food," one Englishman remarked, "I knew it was all up with 'em. There's no muscle in it.")

The British Press Sneered Ever So Politely:

"The Oxfords will defeat their gallant adversaries without difficulty. If otherwise, the Harvards must have an ovation to show that we are not ashamed to be beaten by our excellent cousins."

London Telegraph

"The Americans are individually more powerful than the Oxfords, but it is thought their training is not according to the English notion of strictness."

London Star

On August 27, 1869, the day of the race, it was reported that nearly a million people crowded the banks of the Thames to watch the two crews in action. During the morning the roads in the vicinity of Putney, Hammersmith, Chiswick, Barnes, and Mortlake were choked with spectators on their way to the river. The railway companies soon gave up trying to provide trains to carry those waiting at the depots; London, meanwhile, languished in the manner of a ghost town, the streets of its business district deserted, shops neglected.

At five o'clock, the Harvard crew won the toss for position and chose the Middlesex side of the river (the outside of the semicircle), feeling this would give them better maneuverability. A quarter hour later the race began, the Americans moving into a quick lead with a stroke of 45 per minute to the English crew's 40. At Craven Point, three quarters of a mile from the start, Harvard led by nearly a boat length; a half mile farther, they were ahead by two lengths. That, as it turned out, was the high point of the visitors' glory. Arriving at the Hammersmith Bridge, the crews were obliged to swing sharply to port, and here the relative inexperience of Harvard coxswain Burnham sent the Americans too wide. Oxford reduced the lead significantly without having to "spurt." Gaining better water, the Englishmen moved ahead at the third mile and won by a half length. The time for their 4½-mile run was 22 minutes, 40 seconds.

Both sides agreed the race had been a great success. The British accepted the victory with a noticeable lack of gloating, one reporter commenting, "We are sure that the Harvards would sooner be beaten by us than by any other nation on the globe." The Pall Mall *Gazette* called it a race with "peculiar honor to the victor without humiliation for the vanquished." And in New York, a businessman erected a sign that read, "Though they are beaten, the Harvards forever!"

No one, happily, even bothered to mention the possible adverse effects of all that soft food.

1884—CRICKET AND LACROSSE

During the spring of 1884, a flurry of activity led to a pair of American squads touring Great Britain. One was a team of top Lacrosse players led by R. J. Aspinwall Hodge, Jr., former captain of the Princeton squad. The other players for the most part were graduates of other colleges who had maintained their amateur standing by joining various athletic clubs on the Eastern Seaboard.

Arriving in England in May, the Americans played their first match game at Rock Ferry, the Cheshire team furnishing the opposition.

Cheshire scored the first goal, but it soon became apparent that the American team was more nimble. The equalizing goal was scored soon afterward, and the Yanks went on to win, 4–1. For the remainder of the tour, Hodge's club scored well against the British, although the hosts did obtain a bit of revenge on June 15 when an all-star team representing the United Kingdom defeated the Americans, 5–3, at Belfast. The game was unique in that play was stopped at halftime and lunch served to the participants. With some good British food under their belts, each team scored three goals in the second half.

That same month, a team of cricketers from Philadelphia, a hotbed of cricket enthusiasm in the United States, landed in Britain for a series of matches beginning on June 2. Led by Captain Robert S. Newhall, who scored a total of 801 runs, including 126 in a single inning, the Americans won eight games, lost five, and drew four.

1886—THE FIRST INTERNATIONAL POLO MATCH

Two years after American cricket and lacrosse clubs toured Great Britain, it was the United Kingdom's turn to visit the United States. Polo was still in its infancy in America, the game having been imported after millionaire publisher James Gordon Bennett saw it played on a visit to England in the early 1870s and was impressed. Arrangements for an international match were made when Griswold Lorillard, the American tobacco magnate, mentioned that polo was played rather well in the United States while he was a dinner guest at the Hurlingham clubhouse in Fulham, near London. The British responded with scorn, not realizing that the game had spread much beyond the boundaries of the Empire. Before long, a match was arranged between the Hurlingham club and the Westchester Polo Club, which was considered one of America's best.

The setting for the event was Newport, Rhode Island, an exclusive town furnishing just the right regal background for the English. Thomas Hitchcock, the most experienced of America's poloists, was named captain of the home team; other players included Raymond Belmont, Foxhall Keene, Edwin Morgan, and William K. Thorn, Jr. The British players were all officers in Her Majesty's Army with the exception of the team captain, John Watson, and a substitute named T. Shaw Safe.

The first game, played on the afternoon of Wednesday, August 25, 1886, began in auspicious fashion for the underdog Americans. With the ball placed in the center of the field, Captain Malcolm Little of the Hurlingham team started from one end of the playing area and Foxhall Keene from the other. Keene reached the ball first, hit it three times, and before the English had touched it a single time, knocked home a goal for the United States in just twenty-four seconds. Immediately a band struck up "Yankee Doodle" and the spectators "applauded as freely as polite society is capable of doing" by way of celebration.

The lead did not stand up long. The ball was faced and again taken by Keene but was captured by Captain Lawley of Hurlingham, who moved it toward the Westchester goal, where it was taken by Little. Forty-five seconds after the start of the second "game," the British scored, and the band struck up "God Save the Queen." The Americans seemed to come apart after that, going on the defensive, knocking the ball out of bounds in order to compensate for the better horsemanship of the British squad. At one point the dashing Captain Watson broke his mallet but continued to use it minus the wood on the end, a bit of pluck that electrified the crowd.

Pulling themselves together, the Westchester riders scored two quick goals to take a 3–1 lead and cause some to think that the daring but disorganized Americans actually had a chance. The visitors rallied, however, then ran away with the contest by a score of 10–4. Explaining that their trip over had been extremely rough, the Englishmen apologized for their shoddy style of play.

Three days later, the second of the best-of-three series was held, and this time the results were even worse for the Americans. By the time the score was 13–2, a dense fog had settled over the grounds and many persons had drifted away from the sorry exhibition. At that unlikely moment, the Americans suddenly stiffened, holding the British scoreless for sev-

enteen minutes before losing, 14–2. It was, of course, too little too late. Hurlingham took home the thousand-dollar cup emblematic of the international polo championship, and the United States had to "wait until next year" for victory in the series.

Unfortunately for American polo enthusiasts, "next year" did not occur until 1909.

THE SECOND GREAT BASEBALL TOUR

It was in 1889, fifteen years after the Boston and Philadelphia squads of the National Association toured Great Britain, that Americans again took baseball overseas to entertain and enlighten the rest of the world. The tour was the brainchild of Al Spalding of the Chicago White Stockings, who suggested that his team be pitted against a squad of all-stars captained by John Montgomery Ward. Starting for Australia, the teams visited thirteen countries, playing in Honolulu, Sydney, Colombo, Rome, Paris, and Cairo before making their final stops in Great Britain. Their mission was a simple one. According to one player quoted in the Melbourne *Telegraph,* "We are here to show you a game which has evoked more enthusiasm in our hemisphere than all the games of the ancients and moderns combined." Australians no doubt regarded such a statement as typical Yankee bragging and were more than willing to give the visitors a grand welcome. Even when the Americans criticized English cricket, calling it slow and dull, the hosts accepted the comments with good-natured smiles.

In March 1889 the teams arrived in London, visited the House of Commons, and played several games at Kennington Oval before large crowds, including the Prince of Wales. "The spectators appeared to take only a lukewarm interest in the play itself," reported the London *Times.* "To those unac-

---

A Look at the "All-Star" Team:

While the majority of the second-place Chicago White Stockings made the trip, led by .344-hitting Cap Anson, the "American" team that furnished the opposition had less than glittering statistics.

Name of Player	1888 Major-league Team	1888 Bat Avg./Pitch Record
Cannonball Crane	New York Giants	Won 5, lost 6
Ned Hanlon	Detroit Wolverines	.266
Monte Ward	New York Giants	.251
Billy Earle	No team; signed by Cin. for 1889 season	—
Willard Brown	New York Giants	.271
Fred Carroll	Pittsburgh Alleghenys	.249
George Wood	Philadelphia Phillies	.229
Jim Fogarty	Philadelphia Phillies	.236
John Healy	Indianapolis Hoosiers	Won 12, lost 24
Jimmy Manning	No team; Detroit in 1887	.192 (1887)

quainted with the rules, the frequent changes from batting to fielding were distinctly puzzling, while the indifferent light made it difficult at the football end of the ground to follow the ball."

The next day, with better weather, British interest in the game seemed to perk up. Predictably, the London writers witnessing their first baseball contests were awkward in their play-by-play descriptions, but for the most part told the story in an understandable manner (although phrases such as "First-class fielding dismissed America pointless," might have caused United States readers to wonder a moment). Perhaps the strangest habit the foreign writers had was that of referring to the team at bat as the one "on defense." For the most part, Britons were polite if not wildly enthusiastic. One writer agreed that baseball had its merits, one of which "is that it is not spun out over two or three days. . . . As for the essentials of the game, it would be singular if they did not strike some chords of sympathy in the English breast, considering that they are the same as those of 'rounders.'" A. G. Spalding, naturally, dismissed the notion that America's national game had any roots in the older British game of rounders, one of his favorite self-delusions being that baseball was a "pure" product of Yankee ingenuity.

In April the players bade farewell to England and returned home on the steamer *Adriatic,* a huge crowd awaiting them in New York. But though the players were welcomed as heroes, some were put out that neither New York Mayor Hugh J. Grant nor President Benjamin Harrison was on hand to greet them. Later, however, the entourage was treated to a grand banquet at Delmonico's Restaurant, which smoothed any ruffled feathers. Theodore Roosevelt, Chauncey M. Depew, Brooklyn Mayor Alfred C. Chapin, and Mark Twain paid their respects to the men who had glorified America abroad, the champagne flowing freely.

Only later did most of the players learn that while they were out of the country, baseball's owners—not having to worry about strong union supporter Monte Ward—had passed the Brush Classification Plan, which grouped players according to skill so that their salary demands could not get out of hand.

1895—THE FIRST GREAT INTERNATIONAL TRACK MEET

Although Americans had met other nations in track-and-field meets prior to 1895—four years earlier a team from the Manhattan Athletic Club carried off numerous prizes against British and French athletes on the Continent—the contest of September 21, 1895, was regarded as "the greatest international athletic meeting ever held in this country" according to the New York *Herald,* which added: "It was a fight of heels and toes, and of lungs, arms, and legs. It was an argument of muscle and of methods."

Even allowing for hyperbole, there could be no doubt that New York and America were excited at the prospect of England's best amateurs and those of the United States competing. More than ten thousand spectators jammed Manhattan Field, despite temperatures that reached ninety-eight degrees. Many young women were in the crowd as the tanned and well-muscled Englishmen trotted onto the field at two o'clock. "It was red-hot American weather, and the Englishmen were not supposed to be used to it," one reporter noted. "You cannot tell, however, just what an Englishman will do in any kind of weather. They have managed to endure the jungles of India and Africa, and have won almost everything worth winning in those places."

The half-mile run was the first event of the day, America represented by Charles H. Kilpatrick and Henry S. Lyons, England by Frederick S. Horan and Charles H. Lewin. (The Americans ran bare-headed while the Britishers wore straw hats.) "Set!" cried starter A. A. Jordan, and a moment later, at

---

British Reporting of the Game of Baseball:

"Chicago now began their eighth venture," one account went, *"which produced the most runs of the day. Pettit and Sullivan reached numbers one and two bases respectively, and then there was a vigorous hit by Anson towards the right among the spectators. This enabled Pettit and Sullivan to reach home, while afterwards Anson and Pfeffer both scored.*

Then Tener, Burns, and Baldwin were ousted. . . . When America went in again the pitcher was altered, Baldwin superseding Tener. . . . Chicago began their last innings against the majority of a single. Daly reached the first base, but Ryan was cleverly caught and Pettit run out. Sullivan was quickly disposed of and the match ended. All America thus won by seven runs to six after an exciting finish."

the crack of his revolver, "away sprang the flyers like four gaunt stags." Lyons and Lewin led briefly but at the quarter-mile pole Kilpatrick swung ahead and was never threatened, winning by 20 feet in 1:53⅖, a new world record.

The crowd cheered wildly as the band blared "Oh Mrs. O'Flaherty, What Do You Think of That?" after which everyone settled down to watch the 100-yard dash. In this event, Bernie Wefers and "Johnnie" Crum, who was known as the "pride of the West," represented the United States, and Charles A. Bradley and H. G. Steavenson the visitors. Bradley was considered the favorite.

All four athletes got off to a good start. For nearly 50 yards there was barely an inch of space between them. Then the lanky Wefers burst ahead to break the yarn at 9.8 seconds. By tying the world record for the 100-yard dash, he had set the stage for an afternoon of glory for the United States and misery for the United Kingdom. Thomas Conneff followed immediately by winning the mile run in the excellent time of 4:18½; Wefers next took the 200-yard dash in 21⅘ seconds, still another record.

The Start Graphically Described in Nineties Prose:
"As the four human greyhounds froze into position they looked like white and crouching statues. . . . Then the four white statues sprang into delirious life. Down the chute they came like catapults, four abreast and with their arms swaying like the wings of windmills. . . ."

While these events were taking place on the track, a chunky Irish American named Michael F. Sweeney, holder of the world high-jump mark of 6 feet, 5⅛ inches, fought for the honor of defeating Britain's A. B. Johnston. The latter proved only scant competition, however, missing the bar at 5 feet, 10 inches, and the other American, S. A. W. Baltazzi, failed at 6 feet. Sweeney ordered the bar set at 6 feet, 5½ inches to try for a new record. He stepped off 10 paces very carefully, walked back 5 yards more, then "approached the bar with a little mincing jump, like a lady in a minuet." But his trousers caught the bar and it fell. The crowd groaned and groaned again as his second attempt also failed. But on his final try he went over with an inch to spare and the audience erupted with cheers. Even the two beaten Englishmen clapped

their hands with the rest of the excited Americans.

By the time the afternoon was over, the U.S. athletes had won all eleven events and broken or tied four world records. The British magazine *Punch* responded to the loss by depicting John Bull as grossly overweight and embarrassed as he glared at his younger cousin Jonathan. His chest well decorated with medals, Jonathan—the British version of Uncle Sam—said: "Say, John! You'd better go into training again!"

It was truly a great day for the United States. And the first modern Olympics were less than a year in the future.

1896—MODERN OLYMPIAD I

One might suspect from the amount of enthusiasm engendered by the 1895 meet with Great Britain that Americans would mount a great effort to win the first modern Olympics a year later. Actually, the effort was lukewarm at best, only eight athletes making the trip to Athens in March. Where were all the daring young men from the many amateur clubs in the nation as well as the universities and colleges? No one could say for sure. The absence led one zealot seeing the men off to shout to a reporter: "There go eight men instead of eighty. Where are all the vaunted clubs that live on their amateur sporting reputations?"

The American team consisted of four men from Princeton and another four from the Boston Athletic Association. All were gifted athletes, although the distance man, Arthur Blake, had never run the marathon, and no one had thrown the discus in competition. But they made up for their lack of experience by training hard, running and jumping on the decks of the *Fulda* during the overseas crossing. As a result, they were in good shape when the contests began on the afternoon of April 5,

---

Origin of the Modern Olympics:
It was not necessarily to promote international goodwill and understanding. The initiative for reviving the games was provided by a young Frenchman named Baron Pierre de Coubertin, who felt his country had lost the Franco-Prussian War of 1870 because physical education was not taught in French schools and the youth were getting soft. His actual motive, then, was to awaken his nation to the benefits of athletics so that France would do better during the next war —hardly a noble purpose.

1896. W. F. Lane of Princeton won the first heat of the 100-meter dash in 12⅕ seconds; T. P. Curtis of the BAA took the second heat; and T. E. Burke of the BAA won the third in 11⅘ seconds. The Greeks were astonished at the way America's runners started in the crouch position, which would later lead to the introduction of starting blocks.

Along the way to winning nine out of twelve track-and-field events, the U.S. team produced more than its share of heroes. One was Jim Connolly, who threw down his hat a meter beyond the hop, step, and jump effort of his nearest rival, then thrilled the crowd by leaping just where the hat was. Another was Robert Garrett, who had paid his own way to Athens and whose only experience with the discus had been with a homemade model on the Princeton campus. But fortunately, Garrett's model was heavier than the standard discus and he was able to win a gold medal by defeating the Greek champion, Panagiotis Paraskevopoulos, by more than seven inches. Until the final day of the meet, in fact, the only non-American winner of an event was Edwin Flack, a runner from Australia representing the British Empire. The Greeks salvaged a measure of pride, however, when America's Arthur Blake collapsed in the marathon and Spiridon Loues raced home the winner. So excited was George Averoff, a wealthy Greek merchant who had financed the stadium, that he left his seat to run the final lap with Loues. As a prize for winning the event, Spiridon was given 365 free meals and free shoe polishing for life.

Winner: United States, with ten gold medals, most of which were in the important track-and-field events.

1900—THE DAVIS CUP

The spirit of international sports received another boost in 1900 when a twenty-one-

---

Davis Cup Winners, 1900–76*

1900—United States	1950—Australia
1903—British Isles	1954—United States
1907—Australia	1955—Australia
1912—British Isles	1958—United States
1913—United States	1959—Australia
1914—Australia	1963—United States
1920—United States	1964—Australia
1927—France	1968—United States
1933—Great Britain	1973—Australia
1937—United States	1974—South Africa
1939—Australia	1975—Sweden
1946—United States	1976—Italy

* Champion retained title in years not mentioned, except 1901, 1910, 1915–18, and 1940–45, when no competition was held.

---

year-old graduate of Harvard and president of the U. S. Lawn Tennis Association, Dwight Filley Davis, donated a cup as a world tennis trophy. After a meeting of the Council of the English Lawn Tennis Association in London on March 7, 1900, it was agreed that the United States and Great Britain would hold a series of matches soon after the Wimbledon championships. The site of the first Davis Cup competition was announced as Hoboken, New Jersey, the date July 31, but both time and place were changed.

Instead of Hoboken, the teams met at more prestigious Boston on August 8, 9, and 10, 1900. To the surprise of many experts, the U.S. team won easily, and after a year without competition, defeated the British again, 3–2, in 1902 at the Crescent Athletic Club in Brooklyn. In 1903, however, the British team defeated the United States, 4–1, at Boston, to begin a four-year championship reign. By that time, his cup already well established, Dwight Davis had started a public career as commissioner of the St. Louis Public Baths. After serving as Secretary of War in the Coolidge administration, he died in 1945, much esteemed.

1900—MODERN OLYMPIAD II

Unlike the well-handled 1896 Games, the second Olympics were tied to the 1900 International Exposition at Paris, the events spread out over a five-month period, with confusion so rampant that Baron Pierre de Coubertin resigned from the organizing committee. Two years after the events were completed, some of the winning athletes had not received their medals.

A major controversy in the competition came in July when the French insisted on holding important events on Sunday. Their view was that this was a perfect day for large numbers of working people to enjoy the games; some American athletes, however, preferred not to compete rather than sully the Sabbath. Despite this handicap, U.S. athletes won seventeen of the twenty-three track-and-field events, Alvin Kraenzlein winning four gold medals in sprinting and Ray Ewry of the New York Athletic Club taking three in jumping. Although he won one less medal than Kraenzlein, Ewry's feat was more remarkable in that he was twenty-seven years old and a former invalid who had been doomed to an early death before a doctor recommended simple exercises.

The Games, as usual, produced some interesting quirks of fate. In the pole-vault competition, for example, the favorite, Bascom Johnson of the New York Athletic Club, left the field early after a French official incorrectly informed him that the event had been postponed. A teammate of Johnson's, Irving Baxter, took his place at the last moment and won with a jump of 10′ 9⅞″. Another bit of irony occurred when Michel Theato, a Paris bread delivery man, won the marathon in such good time that some of the losers said he knew the course so well he had taken several shortcuts through the back alleys.

Winner: United States, with eighteen gold medals to France's sixteen and Great Britain's twelve. But the French claimed victory on the basis that they had outscored all other nations with second- and third-place finishers.

tenth. One of them said he would have won had he not been chased nearly a mile off course by a vicious dog.

Other American stars included New York City policeman John Flanagan, winner of the hammer throw; Martin Sheridan, another New York City cop who finished first in the discus throw; Ray Ewry, who added four gold medals in jumping events; and Myer Prinstein, who took the running triple jump and running broad jump.

Winner: United States, with seventy-six gold medals to six each for Cuba and Germany.

1904—MODERN OLYMPIAD III

The 1904 Olympic Games were once again tied to an exposition, this time at St. Louis, which was celebrating the centennial of the Louisiana Purchase with a World's Fair. Because the site was so far removed from Europe, only eight nations sent athletes. France was among the absent.

Stretched out from May through November, the Olympics were once more a side show, with the largest crowd at any single event numbering only two thousand. Promoters of the Exposition added a garish note to the athletic Games by putting together a freak show that was billed as "Olympic Anthropology Days."

The marathon was undoubtedly the high point of the Games, largely because of two men named Carvajal and Lorz. Felix Carvajal was a Cuban postman who predicted he would win the event. He had not been picked for the Cuban team so he raised money for his passage by running around Havana's public square and soliciting coins from the crowd. In New Orleans, he lost the money in a dice game and had to hitchhike to St. Louis. During the race, Carvajal stopped to talk with spectators and wandered off into apple orchards, where he gorged himself and earned a bad case of stomach cramps. But the colorful postman somehow managed to finish fourth in the event.

Fred Lorz of the United States added controversy to the marathon by quitting in mid-race and accepting a ride in a passing truck. About five miles from the finish line, the truck broke down and Lorz hopped out, deciding to jog the rest of the way in order to loosen his muscles. The crowd along the way, however, thought he was the leader and encouraged him all the way to the finish line. Lorz went along with the joke until he was about to be presented with the winner's trophy. He then confessed that it was all a hoax. Thomas Hicks, another American, was the bona fide winner. Finally, in that maddest of marathons, two Kaffirs working at a concession stand decided to enter the race, finishing ninth and

1905—THE UNITED STATES FLEXES ITS SPORTS MUSCLES

"The year 1905 has made history in the world of international sport, and is conspicuous by its brilliancy," wrote the New York *Times* on the last day of that year. "The year's record shows that America more than held her own in international contests, and in many branches proved to be so overwhelmingly superior that she is almost invincible."

The chauvinistic pronouncement was very nearly unassailable. There had been a bit of a sports disaster three months before, when a British soccer team, the Pilgrims, came to the United States in order to create interest in football, non-American style. "Of course we play to win," said Fred Milnes, captain of the Pilgrim club, when he was interviewed on October 21, 1905, "but that is not our principal purpose. What we particularly desire to accomplish is to impress Americans with the manner in which we play the game. I think and hope they will like, approve, and . . . find it to their advantage and to their pleasure to play the game as we do."

The big game of the British team tour took place at the Polo Grounds the following day, but only three thousand spectators paid their way into the park. Those who were taken by the new game of "socker" enjoyed the contest; those who came to root for the home team were disappointed, for the British played rings around the New York club, winning, 7–1. Little mention was made after that of having America's soccer teams engage in international competition. The Pilgrim club left North America after taking twenty-two of twenty-four matches from U.S. and Canadian teams.

Foreign-style football, however, was an embarrassment that was easily forgotten among the positive accomplishments of Americans abroad. Tennis enthusiasts were especially delighted at the success of young May Sutton, eighteen, who in 1905 became the first American woman to capture the women's singles tennis championship of England. The United States' top male player, Charles Sandes, also beat Great Britain's best on a regular basis. Other sports figures upheld the honor of the new nation, although there were losers as well. These included the Davis Cup squad, which defeated Belgium by default in the opening round of the 1905 competition, went on to beat France, 5–0, and then lose to the British Isles by the same score. An American crew from the Vesper Boat Club attempted to win the Henley Regatta but lost to the Leander Boat Club of London. And Tom Jenkins, America's champion wrestler, was beaten by the "Russian Lion," George Hackenschmidt.

Some Notable American Winners of 1905:
Bicycling—*Frank Kramer of Newark won the international Grand Prix at Paris, losing only three of twenty races abroad. Americans Eddie Root and Joseph Fogler took a six-day race at Madison Square Garden, besting a field of thirty-two foreign and U.S. riders.*
Boxing—*Lightweight Jim Britt of California defeated Jabez White of London.*
Horseracing—*Jockey Danny Maher won 101 races in England while William K. Vanderbilt became the most successful owner on the Continent.*
Swimming—*Charles Daniels of the New York Athletic Club won several important races in England.*
Yachtracing—*Wilson Marshall's schooner* Atlantic *won the cup offered by Kaiser Wilhelm for an ocean race.*

Most American sports enthusiasts who assessed the situation must have agreed, despite the occasional losses, that the United States was in excellent shape as it awaited the next Olympiad.

1908—MODERN OLYMPIAD IV
Originally scheduled for Rome, the 1908 Olympics were moved to London when it was learned that the Italian Government could not finance the project. In contrast to the spirit of the Games, controversy and antagonism emerged almost immediately. In the 400-meter run, for example, British officials disqualified U.S. runner J. C. Carpenter when he took a wide turn and cut in front of England's Wyndham Halswelle during the last 100 yards of the race. Incensed at the decision, the other Americans refused to participate in the ordered rerun. Halswelle thus be-

came the first and only Olympic athlete to win a gold medal by running a race all alone.

In the marathon, it was Italy's turn to burn when Dorando Pietri staggered into the stadium ahead of all the other runners but obviously out on his feet. After running in the wrong direction when he reached the track, he collapsed. Two doctors propped him up and other officials pointed him in the direction of the finish line. Thirty seconds before Johnny Hayes of the United States entered the stadium, Pietri was literally dragged across the finish line and declared the winner. As British officials ran up the Italian flag, fights broke out among the fans. Nearly an hour passed before the judges reversed their decision, giving the race to Hayes, and almost 2½ hours before it was known that Dorando Pietri would survive. The Italian lived to become a legend in his homeland and the subject of an Irving Berlin song, "Run, Run, You Son-of-a-gun, Dorando."

Criticism of the 1908 Olympics:
"The Olympiad leaves minor heart-burnings with the representatives of other nations, and altogether, while an athletic success, as a means of promoting international friendship it has been a deplorable failure."
New York Times, *July 26, 1908*

Still another controversy was generated when the British tug-of-war team, a group of Liverpool policemen who had been practicing together for months while wearing heavy boots, pulled the American squad across the line on the word, "heave." Angry at the quick decision, the United States protested that the boots gave the British an unfair advantage. The protest, predictably, was denied. And finally, to add insult to injury, the gold medal won by the American rifle team was stolen from the hotel room of General James A. Drain, president of the National Rifle Association, who made the trip with the team.

American heroes of the games included Martin Sheridan, who won the discus throw; Ray Ewry, who picked up his ninth and tenth Olympic gold medals; and John Flanagan, who won the hammer throw for the third time.

Winner: Great Britain, with fifty-seven gold medals to twenty-two for the United States. Some claimed victory for the United States, however, pointing out that in the all-important track-and-field contests, Americans had taken fifteen gold medals, ten silver, and eight bronze compared to Britain's eight gold, six silver, and three bronze. The British victory, they added, was achieved by winning less-significant contests, such as those in yachting, aquatics, and wrestling.

1912—MODERN OLYMPIAD V

The 1912 Olympic Games were most famous as those in which Jim Thorpe established records in the pentathlon and decathlon, only to have them erased because of "professionalism" charges. But it was also the year when electric timing devices and photofinish cameras were first used to help eliminate controversies. Held in Stockholm, Sweden, the 1912 Olympics were courteous and genial compared to those of 1908.

American heroes included eighteen-year-old Ted Meredith, winner of the 800-meter race; Ralph Craig, who took gold medals in the 100- and 200-meter dashes; shot-put champion Pat McDonald; and Duke Kahanamoku, who made his Olympic debut by winning the 100-meter free-style swim in 1:03.4. Kahanamoku later became Hollywood's most famous Polynesian, playing a native prince in countless movies before his death in 1968.

One disappointment for the United States included two-time champion shot-putter Ralph Rose, who reportedly lost to McDonald because the event was held in the morning before he was completely awake. There was also George Patton, later a famous general, who was favored to win the modern pentathlon after winning the cross-country race, but did so poorly in target shooting that he wound up fifth in the pentathlon.

Americans responded to their team's fine showing by holding a parade in New York City at which 250,000 persons and 15,000 troops turned out to cheer the athletes and escort them through town.

Winner: United States, with a narrow margin of twenty-four first-place finishes to twenty-three for Sweden, but a much larger total overall.

1914—BASEBALL AND THE SPHINX

After the 1913 baseball season, the New York Giants and the Chicago White Sox celebrated their first- and fifth-place finishes, respectively, by embarking on a world tour to promote the national game and pick up some money.

John McGraw, manager of the Giants, sent back accounts of the games and byplay, which overshadowed the exhibitions themselves and gave the fans the opportunity to revel in the zanier side of their diamond heroes. One favorite clown was Germany Schaefer—then a Washington Senator—who had a penchant for getting into trouble, which was duly reported by McGraw. In Hong Kong, for example, Schaefer was nearly taken off the barnstormers' steamer because he was suspected of stealing a billiard ball from a local pool establishment; later, at Paris, he came to bat in the sixth inning of a game wearing a false nose and a gray mustache. He struck out.

The world tour, which started on October 18, 1913, at Cincinnati and proceeded westward, consisted of fifty games, including four against foreign clubs. The Giants won twenty and the White Sox twenty-four of the remainder, two contests ending in ties. One of the notable ties came on February 1, 1914, at Cairo, where the teams played "in the shadow of the Pyramids," then had their pictures taken alongside the Sphinx.

Other highlights included a visit to the Pope in Rome and King George V in London, where a game was staged before thirty thousand spectators. Some in the crowd were curious about baseball customs, of course. One Britisher was heard to ask, "Why does the catcher wear an armor?" Another inquired, "Why does the pitcher kiss the ball all the time?" referring to the spitball habits of the Giant and Sox hurlers. Still others thought it too bad that foul balls didn't count. "Twas a shame when the ball goes so far," they lamented. King George, a personal fan of Jim Thorpe, looked mystified when someone yelled "There's a hole in the bat" as Thorpe swung mightily and missed. Perhaps it was summed up best by a London writer who said, "I'm not going to another game until I have taken the Berlitz course in baseball language."

Weary but happy, the teams returned to America on the *Lusitania* six months before World War I engulfed Europe and only fourteen months before that ship was sent to the bottom by a German torpedo.

The Olympic Pennies That Never Made It:
In anticipation of the 1916 Olympic Games, scheduled for Berlin, Germany, some patriotic children in Chicago collected pennies at playgrounds to help train America's athletes. The 41 pounds they donated to the AAU came to $60.69.

1916—MODERN OLYMPIAD VI
Canceled because of war.

1920—BOBBY MCLEAN GOES TO NORWAY
Even before the 1920 Olympics got under way, an ambitious young speed skater named Bobby McLean claimed the American championship and embarked for Christiania, Nor-

way, to challenge Oscar Mathisen for the world speed-skating title.

Upsetting the Norwegian would be no easy task, for Mathisen had been establishing world records for better than a decade. In 1908, he led all others in the 1,500-, 5,000-, and 10,000-meter races, a superiority he held on and off until 1914, when World War I put an end to international competition. Nevertheless, McLean felt that time had caught up with Mathisen and was confident when he sailed on January 16, 1920.

Arriving in Norway ten days later, McLean met Mathisen on February 7. The weather was excellent, the ice firm and clear for the series of races, which were attended by the King and the crown prince of Norway along with several thousand spectators.

The first event, 500 meters, proved that Mathisen had lost little speed since he set a world mark of 44.2 seconds in 1912. Bobby McLean was in fine form, flashing the distance in 43.7 seconds—but Mathisen was even faster, at 43.4. The crowd roared as a new record was established in the two men's first encounter. McLean then went on to win the 5,000-meter race in 8:53.7. Mathisen was far behind, at 9:06.0.

Twenty-four hours later, under a cloudy sky, the two met again in the 1,500-meter event, McLean taking an early lead. But Mathisen caught him at the last turn and won by .4 second at 2:27.8, seven seconds slower than his world mark of 1912. McLean's only hope at that point was to win the 10,000-meter race, which he started well. One lap through, however, he seemed to become confused, taking the wrong turn on the course and having to back up. Mathisen won the event by more than 30 seconds in the slow time of 18:28.1.

That seemed to put an end to Bobby McLean's claim to the world speed-skating championship. After blaming a Norwegian official for his wrong turn in the final event with Mathisen, McLean continued to tour Europe until spring. At that time he returned to the United States with a tidy profit of $51,000, presumably more than enough to compensate for any embarrassment suffered at Christiania, Norway.

1920—MODERN OLYMPIAD VII

Barely twenty months after the last guns were fired in World War I, Coubertin's dream resumed at Antwerp, Belgium (the decision having been made to designate the nonevents of 1916 "Olympiad VI"). Germany and Austria were not invited to the Games, and the Russians continued their practice of not coming.

America's heroes included Charlie Paddock,

a sprinter who literally threw himself across the finish line; Norman Ross, who won both the 400- and 1,500-meter swimming events; defending champion Duke Kahanamoku, who won the 100-meter swim; and the entire women's swim team, who lost only one event.

Some color was provided by the mechanical nature of Paavo Nurmi of Finland's debut (he ignored other runners in the long-distance races, concentrating only on a stopwatch); in addition, pedestrian Ugo Frigerio of Italy won the 3,000-meter and 10,000-meter events only after giving the band a selection of tunes he wanted played during the race. When the group was not playing loudly enough, Frigerio paused and told the conductor to increase the volume.

Winner: United States, followed by Finland, Sweden, and Great Britain.

1924—MODERN OLYMPIAD VIII

Held at Paris, the 1924 Olympic Games pitted the United States against Finland in track and field, the latter winning ten gold medals to twelve for the United States. Once again Paavo Nurmi starred, taking four gold medals while setting Olympic records for both the 1,500- and 5,000-meter runs, despite having little more than an hour's rest between the two events. Additional excitement was provided when the cross-country race was held in such a heat wave that only fifteen of thirty-nine starters were able to finish. One of the losers ran into a concrete wall and collapsed in a pool of blood. Apparently undeterred by the heat, Nurmi won by two minutes.

1924—The First Winter Olympics:
Site: *Chamonix, France*
Winner: *Norway, followed by Finland, with the United States a distant fourth*

Americans managed to win the 400- and 1,600-meter relays, setting world records, and Johnny Weissmuller established swimming marks in the 100- and 400-meter freestyle. Yale's boat crew won the eight-oar competition with Benjamin Spock in the No.7 seat.

The most unusual winner of Olympiad VIII was probably Harold Abrahams of Great Britain, who continued drinking beer and smoking cigars during training but managed to win the 100-meter dash in 10.6 seconds. Charlie Paddock finished fifth.

The 1924 Games saw the end of lawn tennis as an Olympic sport, the United States sweeping all five titles thanks to Vincent Richards and Helen Wills.

1925–26—INVASION OF THE FOREIGN RUNNERS

The 1920s saw track and field become a truly major spectator sport in the United States, and the near-invincibility of Finland's Pavvo Nurmi spurred promoters to arrange a U.S.-Finnish track meet the year after the Paris Olympics. Madison Square Garden was the scene of the 1925 match, and every seat was sold well in advance of Nurmi's appearance in New York City. Many Americans looked to Joie Ray as the distance runner most likely to make a strong showing against the mechanical Finn.

America got its first look at Nurmi on January 6 when he thrilled 9,000 fans by dashing 1,500 meters in 3 minutes, 56 seconds, beating the Madison Square Garden mark of 4:01.6 set in 1924 by Joie Ray. Nurmi also won the mile run in 4:13.6, 3 yards ahead of Ray, who had set a mark of 4:14.6 in April 1919. "He raced a rejuvenated Ray into the ground," an American reporter was forced to admit. Ninety minutes later, Nurmi added the 5,000-meter run to his victories.

The natives were convinced, but Nurmi continued to tour the country, winning as regularly as clockwork. Not until March 17, when he returned to New York, did he have trouble in a race. After running thirty laps in the Knights of Columbus indoor meet at Madison Square Garden, Nurmi and his archrival, Ville Ritola of the Finnish-American AC, matched strides. Then Nurmi moved ahead until there were only four laps to go. With Ritola a half lap to his rear, the race seemed won, but at that point Nurmi clutched his stomach and staggered off the track to his dressing room. Physicians blamed the problem on distension of the stomach caused by eating too much veal. The powerful Finn was up and about in a day or two, ready to resume a highly successful tour.

Less successful was Hubert Houben, a German sprint star who pointed to victories over Americans Charlie Paddock and Loren Murchison as proof that he was the world's fastest man. Amid much fanfare, Houben arrived in America in January 1926. He was given a fine reception at Boston, where his debut was marked by the playing of "Watch on the Rhine." Houben then proceeded to win his first event, the 40-yard dash. But in the final heats he was beaten by Al Miller of Harvard. "I'll do better on these boards in another week," the German star said philosophically.

That statement was made on January 30. On February 5, at Madison Square Garden, Houben lost to Loren Murchison in the 40-yard dash, finishing third. Several minutes later, at the beginning of the 60-yard sprint, he was patently nervous, leaping over the line

in a false start. Murchison won again, Houben finishing fourth. A week later, Hubert Houben, German sprint star, sailed for home on the liner *Westphalia*.

1928—MODERN OLYMPIAD IX

After winning the past two Olympics, America's track-and-field athletes of 1928 tended, some said, to be overconfident. During the trip to Amsterdam, they indulged in cracker-eating contests, played poker, and did very little training. And when the competition started, the lack of effort and concentration showed. Canadians did well, especially 19-year-old Percy Williams, who won the 100- and 200-meter dashes. The only U.S. runner to win a gold medal was Ray Barbuti, who defeated James Ball of Canada by .2 second in the 400 meters by lunging at the tape *à la* Charlie Paddock. Back home, sports enthusiasts wondered why Americans were doing so poorly. Perhaps with tongue only partly in cheek, Will Rogers hinted that the national love affair with the automobile was making everyone soft. He also noted, as did others, that the United States had been first to specialize in one event with expert trainers, a situation that created a temporary victory gap now being closed. "Now they have all learned and are doing that," Rogers wrote, "so we are no better than any other nation, after they get on to our tricks. Same way with our mass production and buying on credit. They are getting on to that now. So it looks like Prohibition is about all we have on 'em."

Will Rogers on the Disappointing Americans:

"About the only way the United States can ever win a race at the Olympic Games is to annex Canada. The fact of every fourth person in the United States owning an automobile is having its effect."

Another disappointment at the 1928 Games was Paavo Nurmi, now 32, who managed to win the 10,000 meters but lost the 5,000 meters to Ville Ritola and finished second in the 3,000-meter steeplechase behind another Finn, Toivo Loukola.

A measure of consolation was provided by American shot-putter John Kuck's setting a world record distance of 52 feet, 13⁄16 inch. Hollywood movie star Bruce Bennett, competing under his real name, Herman Brix, was third in the event. And Johnny Weissmuller won the 100-meter freestyle in swimming and anchored the American victory in the 800-meter relay, while Peter Desjardins of the United States won both diving competitions. For the first time, American women competed in track-and-field events, Elizabeth Robinson setting a world record of 12.2 seconds for the 100-meter dash.

The 1928 Winter Olympics:
Site: *St. Moritz, Switzerland*
Winner: *Norway, with the United States in second place*
Highlight: *Sonja Henie won her first Olympic gold medal, at age 15.*

Winner: The United States, with twenty-four gold medals to ten each for Finland and Germany. But because of the U.S. failure in track and field, the margin of victory was not as lopsided as it appears.

1929—THEY PLAY OUR KIND OF FOOTBALL
American college football grew enormously in popularity during the 1920s, so much so that the University of Mexico took up the game in the hopes of competing with its northern neighbors. One of Mexico's prime movers in the field was Reginald Root, a 1926 graduate of Yale, who agreed to coach the new team. Bringing his men along slowly, Root scheduled an informal game with a group of Americans in Mexico who had played for prep schools or colleges in the United States. The contest ended in a scoreless tie, but Root's players had learned some fundamentals. He was more certain of this when his team defeated another Mexican squad, the Club Deportivo Internacional, 19–6.

The real test came in October 1929, with the first game against an American college. True, Louisiana College of Alexandria was hardly a big name on the gridiron, but its players were reportedly fast and well coached. In anticipation of a close game that would spur international competition, officials from both sides of the border gathered at Mexico City for the kickoff on October 4. About twelve thousand spectators looked on as the first clash of college football teams from the United States and Mexico began. Unfortunately, the game turned out to be a rout. The Mexicans simply could not find a way of breaking the well-co-ordinated interference of the Louisiana squad, and time and again backs tore off forty and fifty yards around the ends. At halftime the score was Louisiana 45, the University of Mexico 0.

Some South-of-the-border Terminology:
patada—*to punt* señales—*signals* block-ear—*to block*
And the Home-team Cheer:
Urah, urah, urah
*Cachin, cachin—
  Urah, cachin, cachin—
¡ Urah!
¡ Universidad de Mexico!
*"*Cachin,*" like "*Siss, boom, bah,*" *has no real meaning in Spanish, but was obviously selected for its sound quality.*

Whether the Louisiana players decided to do their bit for Latin-American relations during the second half or were simply tired is not known. They scored only twice while holding the Mexican team scoreless, but on several occasions it seemed that the home team might actually make it into the end zone. The game ended at 59–0.

In November, the University of Mexico tried again, playing Mississippi College. During the first quarter, the Americans scored three times to lead, 21–0, but at that point the Mexicans stiffened. For the remaining three periods they played Mississippi nearly even while completing twenty-three of twenty-eight passes. Just before the game ended, Mississippi managed to score one more touchdown to win, 28–0.

Despite the improved showing of their team in its second game against competition from the United States, American-style football never became very popular in Mexico.

1932—MODERN OLYMPIAD X
Despite the worldwide Depression, the 1932 Olympic Games were held in lavish style on 250 acres in a suburb of Los Angeles, attracting record crowds. But there were problems, of course. A group of 69 athletes from Brazil had to utilize a banana boat for transportation, and when the International Amateur Athletic Federation ruled that 36-year-old Paavo Nurmi could not compete because he had padded his expense account during a European tour and thereby violated his amateur status, the rest of the Finnish team threatened to withdraw. They did not carry out their threat but thousands of demonstrators marched to Olympic headquarters.

Besides Nurmi, there were other familiar faces missing from the Games, most notably Johnny Weissmuller, who had defected to Hollywood and a long career in films as Tarzan and Jungle Jim. But among the newcomers was Mildred "Babe" Didrikson, who set three Olympic records, although one was not allowed because of a technicality. The latter involved Babe's high-jump mark of 5 feet, 4$^{15}/_{16}$ inches—a tie with Jean Shiley—the officials ruling that because her head had gone over the bar before her feet, Babe was guilty of "diving."

The 1932 Winter Olympics:
Site: *Lake Placid, New York*
Winner: *The United States, followed by Norway and Canada*
Highlight: *The victory of Eddie Eagan in a bobsled event, which, combined with his 1920 gold medal as a light-heavyweight boxer, made him the first to win in both winter and summer Olympics.*

Some of Babe's methods were unusual, but she managed to get the job done. Her javelin-throwing technique, for example, resembled a catcher pegging the ball to second base in order to nab a base stealer; the javelin never got higher than 10 feet from the ground, but it landed at a distance of 143 feet, 3$^{11}/_{16}$ inches to beat the world's record by 11 feet.

Another American star was Clarence "Buster" Crabbe—later to follow Johnny Weissmuller to Hollywood—who managed to give the United States its only gold medal in swimming. The Japanese surprised most of the experts by dominating the water events. Eddie Tolan also won a pair of gold medals for America in the 100- and 200-meter dashes.

Some reverse highlights of the 1932 Games included the disqualification of Brazil's water polo team when three members attacked the referee, and the disruption of a swimming event when a German sportswriter leaped into the pool in order to collect a $100 bet.
Winner: The United States, followed at a great distance by Italy and Germany.

1934—THE INVASION OF JAPAN
By the early 1930s, Japan had started to show her strength, not only in the Olympics but also as a first-rate military power. This situation generated renewed respect, especially among Americans who admired the Japanese because of their interest in baseball. American professionals seemed to have little trouble beating their Japanese counterparts during the 1930s, but the question arose as to how amateur Japanese baseball players would fare against amateur Americans.

Early in 1934, an agreement was worked out that enabled the Harvard University nine to tour Japan playing Japanese college teams. On July 19, the players sailed on the *Tatsuta Maru* for Honolulu, confident that they could not only promote international goodwill but also show the Orientals how skillful American college players were. A month later, the first game was held at Tokyo, Minister of Education Genji Matsuda throwing out the first ball to. U. S. Ambassador Joseph C. Grew, Harvard, 1902. Grew's alma mater then proceeded to defeat the Imperial University team, 4–2. It seemed as if the Westerners were superior in all departments as far as baseball was concerned.

The very next day, however, Harvard dropped an 8–6 contest, then was mauled on August 26 by Hosei University, 12–3. Next on the schedule was Rikkyo University, which limited the Crimson to five hits while winning, 9–3. Twenty-four hours later, it was Meiji University that added still another loss, this time by the score of 10–8, to the Harvard embarrassment.

That was not all. Early in September Waseda University topped the Americans by 17–2 and Keio added a 6–5 upset. A few days later, Harvard managed to beat Kwansai and Keio in a second game, but by the time the tour was completed, no one spoke anymore about showing the Japanese ballplayers how it was done in America.

1936—MODERN OLYMPIAD XI
Most heads of state praise the Olympic Games as regularly as all politicians praise motherhood. Adolf Hitler was different. Shortly after coming to power, he denounced the Games, already awarded to Berlin, as "an infamous festival dominated by Jews." As a result, the Games were nearly canceled in 1934—but were saved when Hitler decided it would be better to use the international festival as a propaganda platform. He set about ordering the construction of a $25 million Olympic Village and even established precise standards and prices for items such as hot dogs so that visitors would not be overcharged.

The political atmosphere assured that the 1936 Games were well watched and well attended. American athletes found themselves uncomfortable when confronted with a raised arm and shout of "Heil Hitler!" and the Nazi fervor was equally intimidating. But the anti-Semitic feeling also resulted in America's removing its two Jewish athletes, Martin Glickman and Sam Stoller, and replacing them with black runners Jesse Owens and Ralph Metcalfe. Owens turned out to be the star of the 1936 Olympics, winning the

100-meter dash in the world-record time (10.3 seconds) as well as the 200-meter dash, the 400-meter relay anchor, and the broad jump. Those who felt that Adolf Hitler was less angry at losing to blacks than to Jews were mistaken, for his hatred for what he termed America's "black auxiliaries" was almost as strong as his anti-Jewish bias.

The 1936 Winter Olympics:
Site: *Partenkirchen, Germany*
Winner: *Norway, followed by Germany, with the United States in faraway fifth place*

Despite the showing of Americans such as Owens, Metcalfe, and Cornelius Carpenter, the Germans picked up an astonishing number of medals, each accompanied by a deafening roar from the capacity crowd of 110,000. Outside of track and field, the Germans dominated in rowing, gymnastics, equestrian sports, and handball.

Winner: Germany, with 33 gold medals and a total of 628 points to 24 gold medals and 451 points for the United States.

1938—FOOTBALL AND FRANCE
According to Jim Crowley, one of Notre Dame's "Four Horsemen" and coach of Fordham in 1938, the idea began when Kurt Reiss, American representative of the Paris newspaper *Le Soir,* thought that the French people would enjoy and perhaps adopt American-style football. He approached Crowley and suggested that a series of exhibitions be arranged between U.S. college players and French rugbymen, who could be instructed on the subtleties of American football in a short time. Crowley liked the idea, and the trip was made official in November 1938.

Unfortunately, when Crowley and his players arrived on December 7, he discovered that the rugby team that was supposed to face them was nonexistent. (Teaching the basics of American football, it turned out, was not so easy a matter.) Fortunately, Crowley had brought twenty-four young men, enough to divide into two squads. If some were ill adapted to the positions they would have to play in the new arrangement, it seemed unlikely the French would know. Newspapers added excitement to the event by showing the players in their pads, helmets, fierce expressions, stiff-arming one another in ways that promised delight to the fan who appreciated mayhem. The French were enchanted, so much so that more than twenty-five thousand turned

out—in a driving rain—to see the first American football game, on December 10. In fact, the press of the crowd was so furious that the turnstiles could not work quickly enough at Parc des Princes stadium in Paris. The result was more than two thousand impatient fans who resolutely crashed the gate when it seemed they would miss the opening kickoff.

Crowley had dubbed his teams the "All-Stars" and "New York Selection," although the Parisians could hardly have cared less which squad won. They cheered, though, as the players slashed at each other and raced through the mud. The newspapers described the contest, which was won by the All-Stars 25–14, as a combination of rugby, soccer, and basketball, with a touch of wrestling and bullfighting thrown in for good measure.

The football tour, most of which was held in bad weather, continued at Lyon, Marseilles, Toulouse, and Bordeaux, the games drawing a total of seventy-five thousand spectators. Many were bewildered by the action, but Jim Crowley was sufficiently pleased by the French reaction to talk about a second tour the following year as well as taking an American coach to France in order to instruct the locals. The American players were in agreement that the French liked the "Statue of Liberty" play the best and the "huddle" the least.

By the following year, of course, Europe was involved in World War II and no one had the time or the inclination to learn American-style football. Had that catastrophe not intervened, the possibility exists that the NFL even now might be considering expansion that would include a team in Paris.

1940—MODERN OLYMPIAD XII
Canceled because of war.

1944—MODERN OLYMPIAD XIII
Canceled because of war.

1948—MODERN OLYMPIAD XIV
Having fought its second "war to end all wars" in a bit more than a quarter century, the world resumed peaceful competition via the Olympic Games at London. The British were still hampered by rationing, which gave the 1948 Games a Spartan flavor, and international politics in the form of Israel vs. Arab nations detracted from the professed Olympic spirit. Nevertheless, nearly everyone welcomed the spectacle and the opportunity to see new heroes in action. (The twelve-year hiatus assured that there would be few if any athletes returning from the last series of competitions.)

New heroes included Czechoslovakia's Emil Zatopek, a 27-year-old long-distance runner whose debut had been delayed by the war; 30-

year-old Fanny Blankers-Koen of the Netherlands, who became the first woman to win four gold medals, in the dashes, hurdles, and a relay; and 17-year-old Bob Mathias of the United States, who had never pole-vaulted or touched a discus until only months before the Games. But during the time he started practicing and the outset of the 1948 Olympics, he won the U.S. decathlon championship. At Wembley Stadium, London, he ran the 100 meters in 11.2 seconds; the 400 in 51.7; the 1,500 in 5 minutes, 11 seconds; the 110-meter hurdles in 15.7; he broad-jumped 21 feet, 8 inches; high-jumped 6 feet, 1¼ inches; pole-vaulted 11 feet, 5½ inches; threw the javelin 165 feet, 1 inch; shot-put 42 feet, 9 inches; and hurled the discus 144 feet, 4 inches. In all, he earned 7,139 points to lead the field and take home a gold medal. Asked what he would do to celebrate, Mathias replied: "Start shaving, I guess."

The 1948 Winter Olympics:
Site: *St. Moritz, Switzerland*
Winner: *Sweden, followed by Switzerland and the United States*
Highlight: *Dick Button, 18, making his figure-skating debut for the U.S. and Gretchen Fraser winning first U.S. gold medal in skiing.*

Another highlight of the 1948 Games occurred during the 400-meter relay, when the U.S. team of Barney Ewell, Harrison Dillard, Mel Patton, and Lorenzo Wright was disqualified for illegally passing the baton. The gold medal that the American squad would have won was awarded to runner-up Great Britain, with Italy second and Hungary third. But nearly two weeks later, after the Games were over, a rerun of the event on film showed that the officials were in error. Belatedly the United States was declared the winner and the medals were reshuffled. *Winner: The United States, followed by Sweden and France.*

1949—FURUHASHI COMES TO THE UNITED STATES

Just four years after the conclusion of World War II, the first Japanese athletes since before Pearl Harbor came to the United States to compete. They made up a six-man swimming team led by Hironoshin Furuhashi, a young man who had unofficially broken six world records.

The National AAU swimming meet, featuring the best swimmers of the United States, Canada, and Mexico, soon turned into a showcase for the visiting Japanese, especially Furuhashi. On the first day, he won the 1,500-meter free-style by four yards over teammate Shiro Hashizume in 18:29.9, nearly 30 seconds better than the previous world record of 18:58.8, set by T. Amano of Japan in 1938, and almost 1 minute better than the 19:23.1, the best time of America's James McLane. A day later, Furuhashi won the 400-meter free-style in 4:33.0 to set another world record. Then on August 19 he swam the 800-meter free-style in 9:35.5 for his third world record in three days.

Although Furuhashi made a shambles of the AAU meet as far as the United States was concerned, Americans reacted to "the Nippon flash" with something close to idolatry, calling him a swimming immortal. Meanwhile, in Japan, as news of the team's victory spread and touched off near-riots of pleasure, the Japanese Communist Party condemned the public happiness and branded the swimming meet as a "plot of the ruling masses . . . commercial articles to make people forget about the hardships of their daily life."

When Furuhashi and the rest of the Japanese team returned home, they were appropriately greeted as heroes.

1950—MIRACLE AT BRAZIL

The United States soccer team was given little chance to make a creditable showing, much less win a game, as it prepared for the 1950 World Cup competition at Brazil. True, there were several promising players such as Walter Bahr, halfback of the Philadelphia Nationals club, but it was generally conceded that American players simply could not match those of the rest of the world.

The opening game at Brazil seemed to substantiate U.S. weakness, Spain earning a 3–1 victory over the Americans. Next on the agenda was powerful England, heavily favored to breeze past the U.S. squad and make a serious run for the World Cup. The game started slowly, the play of the English forwards obviously superior to that of the Americans, but their aiming for goals was uncertain. Time and again opportunities were spoiled or turned back. And then, after thirty-nine minutes of play, center forward Larry Gaetjens headed a goal to give the United States a 1–0 lead.

In the second half the English team stormed back, mounting fifteen attacks to the American goal and gaining six corner kicks. But the Yanks held on to turn them back and win. Immediately Brazilian fans swarmed onto the field and took the Americans on their shoulders. An American embassy official said that the soccer victory had done more for U.S.-Brazilian relations than anything else in years. The ball was autographed and plans made to have it sent back to the United States, where it would be kept in a museum as a perpetual memory of the victory.

Some British Reaction to the 1950 "Catastrophe":

"It marks the lowest ever for British sport."

London Daily Express

"A fitter, faster, fighting team of the United States have done the unbelievable. This is the biggest soccer upset of all time."

London Daily Mail

"It was pathetic to see the cream of English players beaten by a side most amateur players at home would have beaten, and there was no fluke about it."

London Daily Graphic

Of course, what goes up must come down. In the very next match, the Americans suffered the rude awakening of losing to Chile, 5–2, and were thereby eliminated from the tournament. The victory over England, as it turned out, was the high-water mark of U.S. soccer greatness, few teams after that being able to throw even a slight scare into World Cup competition.

1951—THE PAN-AMERICAN GAMES

Not satisfied with having to wait four years

between international Olympiads, the nations of the Western Hemisphere in 1951 began a series of athletic events known as the Pan-American Games. (They were scheduled originally to begin in 1942 but were postponed by the war.)

The first were held in March 1951, at Buenos Aires, Argentina, an opening ceremony complete with torch-bearing athlete tying the Games symbolically to the older Olympics. Also like the Olympics, the Pan-American Games are held every four years.

1952—MODERN OLYMPIAD XV

It was the Olympiad that saw the U.S.S.R. finally decide its athletes were good enough to compete, the last Russians having given their all in 1912 for the Czar rather than the proletariat. Held at Helsinki, Finland, the opening ceremonies were highlighted by the sudden appearance of Paavo Nurmi bearing the Olympic torch, an event that threw the hometown crowd into a frenzy of adulation. After running one lap, the fifty-six-year-old Nurmi handed the torch to another Finnish hero, Hannes Kolehmainen, who won three gold medals in 1912. The nostalgic exchange, of course, was very touching. Only later was it revealed that Nurmi almost failed to show up because he could not identify himself to a stadium guard.

The fifteenth competition soon developed into a nip-and-tuck battle between the United States and the Soviet Union. Bob Mathias repeated his decathlon victory with 7,887 points, becoming the first man to win two Olympic decathlon titles; pole vaulter Bob Richards earned a gold medal; Parry O'Brien repeated as shot-put champion; Pat McCormick won in platform diving. But the Soviets

Pan-American Games Rundown:

Year	No. of Events	Winner (No. of Events Won)	Runner-up (No. of Events Won)	Standouts for U.S.A
1951	141	Argentina (67)	United States (45)	Bob Richards—pole vault
				Pat McCormick—diving
1955	147	United States (87)	Argentina (23)	Rafer Johnson—decathlon
				Parry O'Brien—shot put
1959	165	United States (123)	Argentina (8)	Ray Norton—sprints
			Brazil (8)	Althea Gibson—tennis
1963	167	United States (115)	Brazil (14)	Ralph Boston—broad jump
				Eleanor Montgomery—high jump
1967	175	United States (124)	Canada (11)	Bob Seagren—pole vault
				Don Schollander, Mark Spitz—swimming
1971	166	United States (92)	Cuba (24)	Frank Shorter—distance runs
				Rick Wanamaker—decathlon
1975	196	United States (113)	Cuba (44)	Ray Leonard—boxing
				Bruce Jenner—decathlon

did extremely well in wrestling, gymnastics, and women's events. In unofficial scoring, the U.S.S.R. led the United States as the 1952 Olympics went into the final day.

At that point, five American boxers emerged to win gold medals. One of them was 16-year-old Floyd Patterson, fighting as a middleweight.

Winner: The United States, with 40 gold medals, 19 silver, and 17 bronze to the Soviet Union's 22, 30, and 17. In points, the U.S. victory was 614 to 553½.

The 1952 Winter Olympics:
Site: *Oslo, Norway*
Winner: *Norway, with the United States second*

1953—GOOD SOCCER COMES TO THE
UNITED STATES

Like those Americans who tried to indocrinate other peoples in the charm of baseball and football, Europeans continued from time to time to promote soccer here. The game was hardly unknown in America, naturally, but was less than major-league until the 1960s or even the early 1970s, when the acquisition of a fading Pélé gave the sport new life with American spectators.

In 1946 and 1948, the Liverpool club of Great Britain toured the United States, scoring an impressive string of victories against local teams. Five years later, it was felt the time was right for a repeat visit, and the Liverpool team made preparations to embark.

As it turned out, others had the same idea. Before the Liverpool club landed, a team from Nuremberg, Germany, had already arrived in New York, and another from Switzerland was on the way. *Aficionados* of good soccer licked their chops in anticipation. Others with a more practical frame of mind may have hoped that the visitors were not overwhelmingly good, for a concentrated show of American soccer weakness could have a dampening effect on those who hoped that one day the United States would embrace the game as a major-league sport.

On May 10, 1953, more than twenty-two thousand fans crowded Triborough Stadium on Randalls Island, New York City, for the first game between Nuremberg and a squad of American All-Stars. As it turned out, the pregame pageantry, which included gymnastics and fencing events, was the highlight of the day. The German team from the toy and criminal-trial center of the world played with the American All-Stars for a while, then sen-

tenced them to a 9–1 lambasting. It was hardly exciting soccer.

Eight days later, the British landed and promptly registered victory No. 23 against American teams by defeating another group of "All-Stars" from the American Soccer League, 4–1. The game was not as close as the score seemed to indicate. The day before, to make matters worse, the Nuremberg team had moved inland, shattering the American team known as the Milwaukee Brewers, 12–1.

The Swiss arrived in early June and promptly treated a crowd of 3,517 at Yankee Stadium to an evening of masochistic entertainment by battering the local All-Stars, 9–0. Four days later, word from the West was that the touring team from Liverpool had won its seventh straight of the tour by defeating a team of Chicago All-Stars, 4–2.

As the three clubs moved about the country, winning at will, an amateur club from England arrived at New York and swept to a 6–3 victory over still another American club of All-Stars.

With the coming of summer and departure of the various touring clubs, it must have become apparent to some that the United States, despite its upset victory in the early round of the 1950 World Cup competition, was still a terribly inept nation as far as European-style football was concerned. Whether this set back the development of soccer as a spectator sport in the United States is difficult to say with accuracy. But it is probably safe to say it didn't help very much.

1956—MODERN OLYMPIAD XVI
"Keep out Russia and her barbaric goon squads."
       Senator John Marshall Butler
       (Republican, Maryland)

There were many who felt, as the 1956 Olympics approached, that the Soviet Union had come too close for comfort in 1952, a proximity caused by a dedication to training and subsidization that violated the amateur spirit of the Olympic Games.

Of course, the United States was not without its subtle forms of subsidization. In April 1956, for example, the Colgate-Palmolive Company, manufacturer of soap, toiletries, and detergents, announced that for every box top or wrapper of a C-P product sent in, the company would donate ten cents for the expenses of American Olympic athletes at the summer Games to be held in November at Melbourne, Australia. In the absence of government support, it was said, private industry would have to do its part. And so it was that the Colgate-Palmolive Company was able to contribute one hundred thousand dollars to the U. S. Olympic team—all the while making a nice profit on the million or so items sold. Unfortunately, the world was unusually tense as the 1956 Olympics began. A revolt in Hungary had been brutally crushed by the Soviet Union, and a combined British-French-Israeli strike closed the Suez Canal. A rash of withdrawals afflicted the sports competitions—Spain, the Netherlands, and Switzerland protesting the Soviet rape of Hungary, and Egypt, Iraq, and Lebanon protesting the Israeli invasion. The Soviets, meanwhile, accused the United States of trying to weaken its athletes by getting them in compromising situations with young women. Communist China, which had a group of athletes ready to participate, also withdrew when it was learned that the Olympic Committee had accepted a team from Nationalist China.

The 1956 Winter Olympics:
Site: *Cortina d'Ampezzo, Italy*
Winner: *The Soviet Union, with 121 points, to 78½ for Austria; the United States a distant sixth*

Although it seemed that the Games would be destroyed by politics, somehow the athletes managed to carry on. Not without incident, however: In a water polo game, the Soviet Union's Valentin Propkopov butted Hungary's Ervin Zador so hard Zador had to be dragged from the pool. And, naturally, everyone kept his eye on the scoreboard to see how the U.S.A.-U.S.S.R. rivalry was doing. The United States did well in track and field, Bob Richards again winning the pole vault and Parry O'Brien repeating in the shot put. Tom Courtney won the 800-meter dash with a finish that was so exhausting to him that the medal-awarding ceremony had to be delayed a full hour while he rested. Bobby Joe Morrow won a pair of gold medals in the 100- and 200-meter dashes—the first to score a double since Jess Owens in 1936—and then added a third as a member of the U.S. 400-meter relay team. But the Soviets persisted, Vladimir Kuts becoming the first Soviet to win a gold medal in track with his 10,000-meter victory. Harold Connolly of Boston won the hammer throw, beating Mikhail Krivonosov of Minsk, but the Soviets scored heavily in gymnastics and wrestling.

Some said Soviet officials also aided by giving low scores to U.S. diver Gary Tobian—even though the winner of the event, Juan Capilla of Mexico, agreed with the majority of viewers that Tobian was the best.

Winner: The Soviet Union, with 37 gold medals, 29 silver, and 33 bronze to the United States' 32, 25, and 17.

1958—THE FIRST SOVIET VISIT

Despite the warnings of some congressmen and senators who wanted as little as possible to do with Soviets, the sports competition created by the 1956 Olympics resulted in the first visit of Soviet athletes to the United States two years later.

The Soviet pioneers were eight members of the U.S.S.R. wrestling team, a courteous and well-behaved group ranging in size from 114½-pound Meriyan Tsalkalamanidze to 6-foot, 3-inch, 219-pound heavyweight Otar Kandelaki. Arriving in New York, the team followed a curious itinerary—New York to Tulsa to Norman, Oklahoma, to Stillwater to Tulsa and back to New York—because the trip was dependent on financing from American wrestlers. Several Oklahomans, it turned out, were interested in bringing the Soviet athletes to their state, so that is where the bulk of their visit took place.

Although there was more than a normal amount of curiosity about the men, a crowd of only three thousand showed up at the six-thousand-capacity University of Oklahoma field house to see the first Soviet-American athletic match on U.S. soil. For a while, all went well. America's flyweight Dick Delgado took the offensive against Tsalkalamanidze and earned a draw at the six-minute bell. In the second period Delgado was pinned by the Soviet, but Terry McCann retaliated by handling Vladimir Arsenyan with ease in the 125½-pound-class match.

That was it for the United States, however, as the Soviets went on to win the rest of the matches. A measure of consolation for the home crowd was that only a single match was lost by a fall, the rest by hard-fought decisions.

A week later, after winning the vast majority of their matches, the Soviets gave their farewell performance at New York (where the recording of the Soviet national anthem was played at the wrong speed, making the somber song sound like a jig), before the largest crowd—fourteen hundred—assembled in the gymnasium of the New York Athletic Club. Everyone agreed that the visit had been a success for both nations. The Soviets, contrary to the stereotype that preceded them, even displayed a sense of humor. When the weather was continuously bad during the trip to Oklahoma, Mikhail Peslyak said, "I have seen stars in the American flag, but not in the American sky." And when Meriyan Tsalkalamanidze was asked how to pronounce his name, he replied, "Just say it the way it's spelled."

1960—MODERN OLYMPIAD XVII

"If you win, you'll be as good as the tenth-ranked pro. It can open the door to fame and wealth."

With those words, Kentucky patrolman Joe Martin persuaded eighteen-year-old Cassius Clay that he should cast aside thoughts of turning professional until after he had boxed with the U.S. Olympic squad. Clay agreed, and the rest, as they say, is history.

Rafer Johnson also made history at the 1960 Games in Rome, Italy, by becoming the first black U.S. athlete to carry the torch. And for some unfathomable reason, the Olympic Committee provided athletes with a questionnaire that asked, among other things, whether the participant had been breast- or bottle-fed. As a final bow to international understanding, the Olympic Committee somehow managed to have the Association of Roman Thieves refrain from pickpocketing and purse-snatching while the Games were in progress. And miraculously, street crime dropped to a record low during the eighteen days of sports competition.

The most-heralded athlete in Rome was twenty-year-old Wilma Rudolph, the first American woman to win both Olympic spring gold medals. In the broad jump, Ralph Boston smashed Jess Owens' 1936 record of 26 feet, 5¼ inches with a leap of 26 feet, 7¾ inches, but teammate John Thomas, considered the favorite in the high jump, failed to clear 7 feet, 1 inch, losing to Soviets, Robert Shavlakadze and Valery Brumel. The Soviets scored heavily in weight-lifting, gymnastics, and women's events.

The 1960 Winter Olympics:
Site: *Squaw Valley, California, U.S.A.*
Winner: *The Soviet Union, with 165½ points to 71½ for Sweden and 71 for the United States*
Highlight: *The U.S. ice hockey team's upsets of Canada and the U.S.S.R. for the championship*

Tragedy and scandal occurred when twenty-three-year-old Danish bicyclist Knud Enemark Jensen collapsed in the 100-kilometer race and died soon afterward. A later investigation revealed that Jensen had been given a shot of Ronicol before the race to intensify blood circulation. In the summer heat,

the stimulant helped bring on a massive brain hemorrhage.

Winner: The Soviet Union, with 43 gold medals and 807½ points to the United States 34 gold medals and 564¼ points.

1961–62—AMERICANS SHOW POORLY ABROAD

From the end of 1961 and throughout 1962, U.S. athletes touring Europe ran into one defeat after another, a situation that seemed to give credence to Australian miler Herb Elliott's assertion that Americans were getting soft.

In November 1961, for starters, a team of American amateur boxers took on the British at Wembley Pool, a London auditorium, and managed to lose ten out of ten bouts. Six U.S. fighters failed to go the distance, two were badly enough injured to drop out of the tour, and three of the ten losers ended up in the hospital. Manager Red Taylor blamed the losses on a poor training program necessitated by lack of funds. The team's trunks and robes, for example, had been donated by Taylor's friends.

A month later, a crack U.S. ski team led by Bud Werner and Chuck Ferries arrived in France for a series of world-championship races. In the first race, Werner and Ferries were third and fourth. But each fell in the next race, and the much-heralded American ski team never came close to winning.

In addition, Whitney Ford, who was ranked No. 1 in U.S. amateur tennis, toured Europe and was thoroughly beaten by unknowns in nearly every tournament. Dan Gurney, one of America's best auto racers, won the Grand Prix de France, but all the rest of his countrymen finished out of the money. Jim Beatty, a long-distance runner, also set out for Europe to establish some new marks but was forced to come home without them. Even U.S. horseflesh seemed to be affected by the rash of loserism as Carry Back, winner of the 1961 Kentucky Derby and Preakness Stakes, finished tenth in the Prix de l'Arc de Triomphe.

For the American sports chauvinist, it had been a bad year indeed.

1964—MODERN OLYMPIAD XVIII

To celebrate the first Olympic Games held in Japan, a young athlete named Yashinori Sakai was selected to ignite the Olympic flame at Tokyo. Born on August 6, 1945, within sight of the first atomic bomb explosion at Hiroshima, Sakai was a living symbol of Japan's special horror of nuclear warfare.

After a lackluster performance in 1960, U.S. athletes bounced back at Tokyo, winning so many track-and-field medals that a Japanese band began playing an abbreviated version of "The Star-Spangled Banner" in order to speed things up. Bob Hayes, later of the Dallas Cowboys, won a gold medal in the 100-meter dash, and two relatively unknown Americans, Bob Schull and Billy Mills, won the 5,000- and 10,000-meter races, the first time U.S. athletes ever won these events. (The sardonic joke said that in distances over 1,500 meters, Americans preferred to drive.)

The swimmers dominated, however, Donna de Varona winning a gold medal in the 400-meter individual medley, and Don Schollander winning four, something no other swimmer had ever accomplished. All told, U.S. athletes took 16 firsts in 22 events. Heavyweight boxer Joe Frazier also won a gold medal.

The 1964 Winter Olympics:
Site: *Innsbruck, Austria*
Winner: *The Soviet Union, with 11 gold medals in 34 events, followed by Norway in second place and the United States in eighth position*

Oddities of the 1964 Games included Soviet women's defending discus champion Nina Ponomaryeva cutting her hair off because she finished fifth and 22-year-old Reginald Spiers of Australia having himself sent home in a COD crate when he failed to make the team and ran out of money.

Winner: It depends. The United States won 36 gold medals, 26 silver, and 28 bronze for a total of 90. The Soviet Union earned 30 gold, 31 silver, and 35 bronze for a total of 96. The U.S.S.R. magazine *Sport* calculated that the Soviets won by a point total of 608.3 to 581.8 but did not say on what it based its figures. Americans held to the tradition that "Fort Knox" or gold was all that mattered. As for the International Olympic Committee, it wasn't saying.

1965—THE GREAT KIEV TRACK MEET
By 1965, the U.S.A. and the U.S.S.R. were accustomed to meeting in their own private track meets, six previous meetings having produced a perfect split in men's and women's competitions. Invariably the U.S. men defeated the Soviet men and the Soviet women overpowered their American counterparts.

In 1965, however, it turned out differently —which was really too bad for the United States.

The disaster probably started with the selection of a site, for after glamorous Los Angeles in 1964, the industrial city of Kiev could

hardly be regarded as a vacation spot. Soon afterward, Hal Connolly, world record-holder in the hammer throw, was forced to withdraw from the trip because of back spasms. After the team arrived in Kiev, Billy Mills, the Olympic 10,000-meter champion, was scratched because of infected tonsils, and Gerry Lindgren came down with a bad cold. To make matters worse, Darel Newman pulled up lame after winning the 100-meter dash in 10.1 seconds, a record for the meet, which necessitated a patchwork lineup in the 400-meter relay.

The end result was the first overall victory for the Soviets in the series dating back to 1958. Led by Tamara and Irina Press, the Soviet women defeated the American women, 63½–43½, while the Soviet men won, 118–112. Bill Easton, president of the U. S. Track Coaches Association, promptly charged that the Amateur Athletic Union was responsible for the double loss. He said that the AAU was directly to blame for "the hours without sleep; the obvious lack of advance planning and arrangements, which resulted in inexcusable delays; the fatigue and general rundown condition of all our competitors." But Brutus Hamilton, the U.S. coach, had another reason for the Soviet victory. "With us," he said, "it's just a track meet. With them, it's war."

1968—MODERN OLYMPIAD XIX
It was the Olympic Games where political and social protest stole the show.

The site was appropriate—Mexico City, where just a few weeks before the Games, hundreds of demonstrating students had been shot by policemen. As for the sports, before they could get under way, some problems had to be resolved: a threatened boycott of U.S. black athletes; the question of whether South Africa should be allowed to participate; a controversy over whether women participants should be subjected to sex tests. And as a climax to the atmosphere of dissension, a Mexican spectator shot himself at the start of a cycling event, protesting the government treatment of students.

Eventually the problems were resolved and the Games proceeded. To the chagrin of the Soviet Union, for it was the Americans' show. Once again the swimmers pulled more than their share, although Mark Spitz, who boasted he would win a half dozen gold medals, did not win any. Debbie Meyer became the first swimmer to win three individual gold medals, taking the 200-, 400-, and 800-meter free-style events. Heavyweight boxer George Foreman won a gold medal, as did Randy Matson in the shot put and Bob Seagren in the pole vault. Jim Hines raced the 100-meter dash in

9.9 seconds, an Olympic record; Bill Toomey piled up 8,193 points in the decathlon; and Tommie Smith ran the 200-meter dash in a record time of 19.8 seconds. Then, just to prove that protest had not been forgotten amid the wealth of U.S. victories, Smith and teammate John Carlos raised their hands in the black-power salute during the awards ceremony. The action was infuriating to some persons but was certainly in better taste than shooting oneself before a bicycle race.

The 1968 Winter Olympics:
Site: *Grenoble, France*
Winner: *Norway, followed by the U.S.S.R. The United States was a distant eighth.*

Winner: The United States, with 45 gold medals to 29 for the Soviet Union.

1972—MODERN OLYMPIAD XX
The 1972 Games will probably be remembered most for the skillful feats of Mark Spitz and the insane tactics of Arab terrorists. Held at Munich, Germany, the city in which Adolf Hitler first became a world figure, the Olympics were transformed from a symbol of international brotherhood to a background for murder when a group of Arabs attacked the Israeli compound. After killing two and taking nine hostages, the terrorists blew up a helicopter and, with most of the world watching on television, demanded the release of two hundred Arabs being held in Israeli jails. Fighting broke out when this demand was refused. Eleven Israeli athletes, five Arabs, and a German police officer were killed before the tragedy ended. Some participants left and others requested that the Games be stopped, but Avery Brundage insisted that the competition continue. "The greater and more important the Olympic Games become," he said, "the more they are open to commercial, political, and now, criminal pressure."

America's Mark Spitz, more subdued after his failures at Mexico City in 1968, soon proved himself the best swimmer since Johnny Weissmuller by winning not six, but seven gold medals. According to some reporters, he immediately began to look around for ways to capitalize financially on his success.

Another American swimmer, Rick DeMont, sixteen, won the 400-meter free-style but was disqualified when traces of Ephedrine were found in his urine. DeMont claimed he had been taking the drug to curb an asthmatic condition.

In contrast to 1968, U.S. athletes did not perform well in track-and-field events. Frank Shorter won the marathon, the first American winner in this event since 1908, and twenty-two-year-old Dave Wottle was a surprise in the 800-meter race. But Finland and the two Germanys took many events that the United States might have won in the past.

The 1972 Winter Olympics:
Site: *Sapporo, Japan*
Winner: *The Soviet Union, followed by East Germany, with the United States in eighth place*

Winner: The Soviet Union, with 50 gold medals to 33 for the United States, the most disastrous being that taken in basketball, an Olympic event won by the United States since 1936.

1973—FEEBLE REVENGE FOR 1972
Most Americans who saw the 1972 basketball finals on television agreed that the Soviet Union's last-second win had been one of the worst swindles ever perpetrated in Olympic history. Therefore the thirst for revenge was strong the following year when the U.S.S.R. basketball team arrived in America for a six-game series.

Led by Bill Walton, the U.S. squad tore into the Soviets at Inglewood, California, winning by 83–65. But the victory was costly. Walton injured his knee and had to sit out the second game at San Diego. The Russians edged out a narrow 78–76 win to even the series.

The Americans came back to win strongly at Albuquerque, 83–67, holding the infamous Alexander Belov—the Soviet hero of the 1972 Olympics—to just five points. Several days later, Ernie DiGregorio scored twenty points at Indianapolis, the United States winning its third game, 83–75. The fifth game of the series took place on May 8, 1973, at Madison Square Garden before a crowd of 15,734. With the U.S. team behind by 73–69 with only fifty-five seconds remaining, DiGregorio scored a pair of baskets to send the contest into overtime. Inspired, the American team ran away from the Soviets in the extra period as the crowd displayed bad sportsmanship by shouting "We're No. 1" throughout. When the final score of 89–80 was posted, a youngster ran out on the court waving an American flag.

The Soviets salvaged their second win of the series at Baltimore, but the 4–2 victory by the U.S. squad was poetic justice for many sports fans. It did not make up for the bitter Olympic defeat, but as someone pointed out, revengewise, it was the only game in town.

1976—MODERN OLYMPIAD XXI

The 1976 Games at Montreal were tame, politically and socially, compared to those at Munich, but there were plenty of thrills for sports watchers and even some hope for those who had fretted at the American skid of 1972. American swimming, for example, was still in excellent shape, records being established by Jim Montgomery, Bruce Furniss, Brian Goodell, and John Naber. Bruce Jenner, with 8,618 points in the decathlon, also set a new mark, as did Mac Wilkins, with a 221-foot, 4-inch discus throw, and Edwin Moses, with a time of 47.64 seconds for the 400-meter hurdles. In boxing, gold medals were won by Ray Leonard in the light-welterweight division and by Leon Spinks, later dethroner of Muhammad Ali, in the light-heavyweight class. Even more important for some, the U.S. basketball team came back to reclaim the Olympic title it had held for thirty-six years. But despite these high moments, the Soviet Union once again demonstrated its overall superiority in the Games.

The 1976 Winter Olympics:
Site: *Innsbruck, Austria*
Winner: *The Soviet Union, with 13 gold medals to East Germany's 7 and third-place United States' 3*

Winner: the Soviet Union, with 47 gold medals, 43 silver, and 35 bronze to the United States' 34, 35, and 25.

CHAPTER 47—ODDMENTS

Being an assortment of items that do not fit into any of the categories or years described earlier.

1. Computed on the basis of one minute per rendition, during Willie Mays' career, he spent a total of more than two days standing at attention listening to "The Star-Spangled Banner."

Some other players with longevity in the major leagues, such as Honus Wagner or Ty Cobb, played before the National Anthem was performed before each and every game. Not until World War II did it become customary to make "The Star-Spangled Banner" a prelude to the words, "Play ball!"

2. Where do all the lost golf balls go? Some frustrated players swear the balls have learned a secret technique of burrowing into the ground, or that like a chameleon, they can change color so as to blend into the background. These assertions are open to debate, as is the charge that there may be a larger conspiracy afoot. This "conspiracy" involves a variety of dumb animals who have been taking golf balls into their nests or stomachs or holes just about as long as man has been driving them off tees. One philosopher, who wishes to remain anonymous because the idea sounds so bizarre, has suggested that certain very sensitive animals feel that the golf balls, like themselves, are victims of man's takeover of planet Earth. Pitying the swatted orbs, they have on occasion attempted to "rescue" them. That, of course, is just one man's theory.

At any rate, the balls have been doing more than hiding in America's grass since the game became popular during the late nineteenth century. In 1923, for example, a squirrel living near the Senneville Course of Montreal was spotted carrying a golf ball out of the rough. A player, Mrs. Archie McLean, followed the little devil who—obviously not very surveillance-conscious—led her to a nest filled with sixty-eight other balls. The gracious woman replaced them with an equal number of nuts.

Four years later, an operation was performed on a terrier named Zip of Nyack, New York, after the dog suffered a violent attack of indigestion. When Zip was unzipped, not one but two brand-new golf balls were found in his stomach. That was chicken feed, however, compared to a blackbird that set up shop in 1928 at Paris' St. Germain Club course. The bird's base of operations was the seventh green, where a bunker provided the necessary concealment for his acts of piracy. When a ball landed in the trap, the blackbird swooped down, picked it up in one swift motion, and flew off to its secret hiding place. Eventually a cache of thirty balls was located and a sentence of death officially mandated against the bird. History does not record the final fate of this modern Robin Hood of the fairways.

Winged creatures are particularly adept at ball stealing, as one might imagine, and crows seem to be better than the average bird. In September 1929, the Gedney Farm course at White Plains was visited by a crow that plucked Eugene McKinley's third-hole shot right off the fairway and disappeared. That may have been the same crow that started a flying larceny band of his own five years later, when Taconic Club Superintendent Richard Baxter saw ten crows fly away from the fourth and fifteenth greens, each with a ball in its mouth. The tournament that began a week later undoubtedly was one of the few in the history of golf at which the entrants were allowed to carry shotguns.

Sometimes birds have cost a golfer more than the price of a ball. In 1930, a cheeky seagull plucked the green shot of Austin Green from its ideal location twenty feet from the pin. Forced to shoot again, Green lost the match.

Even crustaceans have learned the knack of ball stealing. In 1935, the culprits responsible for a rash of disappearances turned out to be a family of land crabs living in the mangroves along the fairways of Australia's Darwin Club. An observant caddy, racing after a ball sliced into the rough, arrived just in time to see a crab ambling away with it. A new rule was immediately put into effect whereby a player could rescue his shot from a crabhole without penalty.

There are other examples—such as the case of a Jersey cow that gobbled twenty-nine balls in 1929—but not all of the instances are so circumstantial in nature. There was, that same year, a mysterious epidemic of missing golf balls at the Van Cortlandt Park course in New York. For a month anguished players had been executing perfect drives only to arrive at the spot on the fairway where the ball should have been and finding nothing. Eventually the percentage of lost balls became so high that the police at Kingsbridge station were informed and an inspector assigned to the case.

The officer, Joseph Cleary, took his work seriously. Disguising himself as a golfer by donning plus fours and borrowing a set of clubs, he set out with two assistants, whom he instructed to hide in a clump of trees down the fairway. Cleary then teed up a marked ball and drove it away. When it rolled to a stop, a bulldog suddenly bounded from the underbrush, picked up the ball with its teeth, and raced back to cover. Cleary drove a second ball, then a third, and the same thing happened. Convinced that the three incidents were somehow related, Cleary and his men converged on the underbrush and located twenty-four-year-old Frank Conroy, who happened to have seven golf balls in his pockets, all with sharp teethmarks. Conroy explained that he was a nurse from San Francisco who was earning extra money by searching for lost balls.

Two days later, after finding that Conroy had a history of dog training and ball stealing, Magistrate Delagi of West Farms Court sentenced the young man to ten days in the workhouse. The search for Conroy's canine confederate continued, even as the New York *Times* editorialized, "One cannot but ponder the career that would be open to such an animal if he were shown the evil of his ways and induced to lead an honest life."

3. On December 18, 1937, two Eskimo football teams of King Island, Alaska, were preparing for the New Year's Day Ice Bowl game when their practice field floated away. They had decided to use a huge ice floe near their village because of its convenient shape and flatness, but a gale-force wind blew the floe completely out of sight.

4. In the eighth inning of the first game of a doubleheader between the New York Giants and the Pittsburgh Pirates on June 9, 1946, Manager Mel Ott of the Giants was ejected by Umpire Tom Dunn. During the fifth inning of the second game, Ott protested a decision by Umpire George Magerkurth and was again thumbed from the game, thus becoming the first major-league manager or player to be thrown out of both ends of a doubleheader.

5. The shortest reign as a boxing champion, although not officially noted in the record books, is that of Young Stribling, who held the light-heavyweight crown for approximately three hours on October 4, 1923.

The situation was peculiar, as one might imagine. Held in Columbus, Georgia, the home state of nineteen-year-old ring sensation Willie Stribling, the bout was agreed to by Joe Jacobs, manager of Mike McTigue, as a genuine title fight. One suspects that McTigue, thirty-one, was looking for an easy chance to pick up some money following his recent decision over Battling Siki, which earned him the title in March. In any event, he could hardly have appreciated the true fighting ability of Young Stribling, but it still did not pay to take unnecessary risks, especially when fighting in a local hero's own backyard. So just to make certain everything went well, Jacobs imported his own referee, Harry Ertle. When he discovered that Young Stribling was as good as the locals said, Jacobs tried to have the bout canceled. When that failed, he attempted to remove the "world title" label from it, but that didn't work very well either. Jacobs then looked to Ertle as his savior, although he realized that the referee was not a man of particularly strong character.

The fight was a disaster for Jacobs and McTigue, who managed to stay off the canvas because of his experience. Otherwise, most of the writers at ringside agreed that Stribling had been the aggressor and deserved to win. The highly vocal crowd thought so, too, which posed a terrible dilemma for Harry Ertle as he stood in the ring at the end of the fight, pretending to mark his scorecard. Finally, unable to bring himself to declare McTigue the winner and equally afraid to cross Jacobs by awarding the bout to Stribling, Ertle meandered over to the fight's promoter, a fellow named John Paul Jones, in the hope that Jones would announce the decision, which was a draw. Jones, a tough bird, yelled, "If that's your decision, get back out there and tell it to the folks."

Ertle went back to the center of the ring, took one look at the angry crowd, and did the only thing possible under the circumstances: He raised Young Stribling's hand in triumph. The arena shook with cheers and applause, the only shouts of rage coming from Joe Jacobs as the happy crowd streamed into the open air. Ertle flung himself under the ropes and left as quickly as possible.

Joe Jacobs caught up with him, however, and three hours later, after the crowd had dispersed and he was immune from hometown wrath, Ertle nullified his verdict and declared the fight a draw.

That ended the brief reign of Young Stribling, who might have become a true champion, had he not died in a motorcycle accident at the age of twenty-eight.

6. During a 1935 football game played at Welasco, Texas, three players carried the ball nearly three hundred yards for a single touchdown. With the ball on Welasco Junior High's fifteen-yard line, Torres carried all the way for a score, but the play was called back. Mattar then ran the length of the field but once again there was an infraction. Finally, Porter took the ball all the way across the goal line and the play counted.

7. Was there a real Casey at the bat?

Most people love a mystery. The exception seems to be the hard-core baseball fan, who venerates statistics that establish beyond the shadow of a doubt that such-and-such happened at such-and-such a time and you can look it up.

Thus it irritates some baseball buffs that the most famous piece of baseball literature has a hero who cannot readily be identified. The immortal fifty-two-line poem *Casey at the Bat,* first published in the San Francisco *Examiner* on June 3, 1888, is a work known to nearly everyone, although the author's name, Ernest Lawrence Thayer, is hardly a household phrase.

The situation described in the poem is also familiar. There in the bottom of the ninth inning, his team behind, 4–2, stands mighty Casey at the plate. With the tying runs on the bases, Casey sniffs disdainfully at two pitches, then unlooses his powerful swing, which will produce the necessary RBIs and victory for the hometown Mudville multitudes. But the mighty swing produces only a deadly letdown:

"But there is no joy in Mudville—
mighty Casey has struck out."

The poem was an immediate success, a fact attested to by a couple of facts. The first was that numerous authors—or would-be authors—came forward to assert that "Phin" (the byline used by Thayer) was none other than themselves. The second evidence of popularity can be found in the forty-seven-year "run" given the poem by actor DeWolf Hopper, who latched onto it soon after it was written, reciting the crowd-pleasing epic at least ten thousand times before his death in 1935.

As for E. L. Thayer, the author asserted several times before his demise in 1940 that he based the poem on no particular character or athlete. That may or may not be true, for we cannot discount the subconscious in these matters. Even more to the point is that several "Caseys" have been thrust forward—either by themselves or their champions—over the years. Thus it seems appropriate to re-examine the evidence in the manner of baseball statisticians who even now are probably culling pertinent data on Napoleon Lajoie's 1901 stats for the umpteenth time to see if he really did bat .422.

Prior to 1888, there were four real Caseys in the major leagues and at least one player who possessed both the physical and geographical attributes to be Casey in disguise. Naturally, Thayer could have based his poem on a minor-league Casey, but that can be discounted by a shred of evidence in the poem itself—namely, that a crowd of five thousand Mudvillians was on hand for the crucial game. No tank town could have provided such an audience in the 1880s. "Mudville" was clearly a major-league city.

The most easily discounted of the real Caseys is undoubtedly one William Casey, who played in one game for the Philadelphia Nationals of 1887. A pitcher, Bill Casey hardly qualifies as the cool and powerful slugger Thayer depicted. As a matter of fact, he wasn't even much of a pitcher—his record being a tepid 0–0 and his ERA a gargantuan 18.00. His having appeared in but one game also reduces the chance of Thayer knowing his name, much less his deeds, to practically zero.

A second easily discounted Casey is third baseman Bob Casey, who represented Detroit during the year 1882. Hardly a slugger, Bob Casey hit one home run during his brief career and went overall 9 for 39 at the plate (.231).

The third Casey was Daniel Maurice Casey, who hung around the major leagues with Milwaukee (Union League), Detroit, and Philadelphia for seven years before retiring to Syracuse in 1890. Forty-eight years later, Daniel Casey began promulgating the story that he was the fallen hero of Thayer's poem. He even told his story to national publications and appeared at various ball parks, graciously acknowledging the applause with a wave of his seventy-three-year-old hands. Five years later, old Danny died, having convinced some of the people some of the time. Sadly, his story doesn't hold up very well, for Daniel Casey was a pitcher whose lifetime batting average was a pitiful .162, including a single home run. One must write off his assertion as the last hurrah of an elderly warrior.

Danny did have a brother, however, and the older brother definitely qualifies, at least compared to the other Caseys. Born in 1858, Dennis Patrick Casey worked for a time on a farm near Binghamton, New York, before turning to baseball as a means of support. He was twenty-six when he broke into the major leagues with Baltimore of the American Association. A left-handed-hitting outfielder, Dennis Casey hit for power on more than one occasion. "The fine batting and fielding of Casey alone aroused any particular enthusiasm, he making two three-base hits and six fine fly catches," the Baltimore papers noted soon after he joined the club. And on another occasion, "Clinton and Burns hit safely, and Casey brought them home on a terrific drive to center, and scored himself before the drive could be brought in."

There was even one instance where Dennis Casey struck out in the ninth inning with two men on base, losing the game. That whiff did bring forth a shout of joy, however, for the contest was played not in hometown Mudville, but in New York.

Dennis Casey's slugging, while considerable, was not prodigious. He departed the major leagues in 1887 with a grand total of six career home runs. Settling down back home in Binghamton, he married, reared seven children, and died in 1909 before anyone thought to ask him whether he was the Casey of Thayer's poem. One of his children who survived him, Mrs. J. Henry Hipskind of Fort Wayne, Indiana, did express a view a half century after her father's death. "It was my father about whom the poem was written," she asserted. "I feel sure of it."

Others are less positive, especially those who belong to the Mike "King" Kelly school. That gentleman, they say, was the Casey in disguise Thayer was writing about. A strapping figure of a man, King Kelly broke into the majors in 1878. Six years later he hit the astronomical figure of thirteen homers with Chicago before coming to Boston in 1887, where he clobbered a total of twenty-six home runs during a three-season spree. He had a lifetime batting average of .307, thus qualifying even more than Dennis Casey as the superhero whose failure came as such a disappointment and shock to his myriad fans.

Even more to the point, Kellyites say, Ernest Thayer himself was from the Boston area. He was, in fact, editor in chief of the Harvard Lampoon and Ivy orator of the class of 1885. This means he certainly would have been aware of Kelly's exploits. He, like many other Bostonians of that era, may even have regarded Kelly as something of a messiah capable of "saving" the team (Boston had fallen from first place in 1883 to fifth in 1886), and we all know what happens to messiahs who do not produce immediate results. They are hissed and booed, made the butt of satiric jabs, even the subject of humorous poetry.

A prodigious base-stealer who once stole eighty-four in a season (1887), Kelly was already the subject of one song by the time Casey at the Bat was written. That was "Slide, Kelly, Slide," by monologuist John W. Kelly, which made the ballplayer's name familiar even to those who had never set foot in the park. The phrase was supposed to have been one of the last uttered by King Kelly himself when he succumbed to high living and pneumonia in 1894, aged thirty-six. While on the way to the hospital, he slipped from the stretcher onto the floor, an accident that inspired him to smile and say, "I think, me lads, this is me last slide."

One final point on the side of those pushing King Kelly as Thayer's hero: Boston during the nineteenth century had a curious nickname: "Beantown." It sounds a little like "Mudville" when you think about it—sarcastic on the surface but with a hint of affection beneath it all.

At any rate, if we must have an answer to the Casey riddle, it will have to be a three-pronged one. If Thayer based his poem on a real Casey, it was undoubtedly Dennis Casey of the Baltimore Orioles. If he based the work on the exploits of the best batter in his geographical area, the hero must have been King Kelly of Boston. More likely, however, is that Thayer touched a universal chord by basing his Casey on the Charlie Brown in all of us who have felt the despair of striking out with the winning runs on base.

For Baltimoreans, however, there is this bit of consolation: If Casey cannot be claimed as the genuine article, at least when someone says "Kilroy was here," the baseball honors definitely belong to the Queen City of the Chesapeake. There were but two Kilroys in the major leagues, brothers Matt and Mike, and both played for the Baltimore Orioles.

8. In the 1935 Notre Dame-Northwestern game, the Irish had a star player named William Shakespeare. Northwestern, meanwhile, had a right end named Henry Wadsworth Longfellow. Early in this battle of the bards, Shakespeare was instrumental in the Irish taking a 7–0 lead. But in the fourth quarter, Longfellow made a sensational catch of a fourteen-yard scoring pass to tie the game. Not long afterward, Northwestern went ahead and won, 14–7.

Some other literary figures on the gridiron include West Point's Richard Brinsley Sheridan, who was killed in 1931 during a kickoff play, and Edgar Allan Poe, All-American quarterback for Princeton in 1889.

9. Occasionally one of the casualties of a sports contest is the ball itself. In 1929, Frank Andresko, one of the players in a basketball

game played at Oshkosh, Wisconsin, was thrown against the wall and had his jersey torn when the basketball suddenly exploded. Ten years later, a football was reported to have exploded and split in half just as it was kicked for an extra-point attempt. The kick was ruled good because one section of the ball passed over the crossbar.

10. Charles Abner Powell spent only two seasons in the major leagues, but made several real contributions to baseball. In 1887, while at New Orleans, in a rainy climate, he noted that the standard practice for a rainout was to distribute new tickets to the fans as they left the park.

This system had problems, however, for not only was it time-consuming, many freeloaders would find ways of entering the park in the confusion and take gratis tickets for the next day's game. This worried Powell, who felt a proprietary interest in the club, until one June morning at three o'clock, he got the inspiration for what is now known as the "rain check." The next morning he began working on the split-ticket design that is now used everywhere.

Powell also came up with the idea for ladies' day, a revolutionary concept for its time (although there were already "ladies' days" at racetracks and regattas by that year). At first the idea was resisted, largely because there were many brawls and a great deal of profanity at baseball games during the 1880s. (Abner Powell's own mother, as a matter of fact, once forbade him to play the game because it wasn't "respectable," despite the fact that she herself ran a bar and smoked a pipe.)

Powell advertised the first ladies' day on April 29, 1887, but only nine women showed up at the park. The idea caught on after that, however, and before long, crowds of five thousand and ten thousand were not uncommon.

Powell was also first to cover the infield with a tarpaulin, and he organized a knothole gang, or free-admission day for kids. He died in 1953 at the age of ninety-two.

11. The Green Bay Packers started the 1948 season in fine style, winning three straight exhibition games, then beating the Boston Yanks, 31–0, in the league opener. They were then trounced by the Chicago Bears, 45–7, turned in a weak performance against Detroit, and lost to the Chicago Cardinals. When the Packers dropped to fourth place in the five-team division, Coach Curly Lambeau took the drastic step of fining the entire squad.

It didn't help, obviously, the Packers finishing the season with a mark of 3–9, barely a game ahead of the Detroit Lions.

12. Baseball's yearly schedule was first set in Braille for the 1956 season, appearing in the May 7 issue of the *Weekly News,* the only newspaper in the English-speaking world at that time for blind people.

13. Certainly one of the most interesting characters in modern professional football—often criticized for turning its players into unimaginative robots—was Joe Don Looney, who lived up to his name during a five-year career that promised much but delivered little.

Unless one happened to enjoy unusual behavior, that is, because Looney was totally unpredictable. A powerful and speedy running back from Oklahoma who could lift 450 pounds from a squat and run 100 yards in 9.5 seconds, Looney was regarded as a player who could not miss when drafted No. 1 by the New York Giants in 1963. In fact, he did not make even training camp, refusing to learn the plays on the grounds that "a good back makes his own holes. Anybody can run where the holes are."

Traded to Baltimore, Looney ran out of his shoes for a fifty-eight-yard touchdown run against the Chicago Bears, but that was more or less the highlight of his pro career. Soon afterward, he was arrested for breaking down a door and slugging a man while searching for a nurse he had met the previous evening. His next ring encounter came during a Baltimore wrestling match when he came to the rescue of Bruno Sammartino, who was being attacked by fans.

In addition to having considerable talent as a runner, Looney also punted. Once, during a Colt practice session, he kicked a sixty-yard skyscraper. While everyone stood and admired the tremendous kick, Looney said in a loud voice, "How'd you like that one, God?"

Another time, he announced his intention of sleeping in a nearby cemetery, "because it's nice and peaceful down there." According to Looney mythology, he actually performed the act and returned the following day quite pleased as a result of the experience. "I had a nice talk with a guy about death down there," he said.

Traded to Detroit by strict disciplinarian Don Shula, Looney often showed up at the Lion training table wearing Denver Bronco T-shirts. But he finally aroused the ire of Coach Harry Gilmer when he refused to deliver a play to quarterback Milt Plum. "If you want a messenger," Looney said, "call Western Union."

Looney's reaction to being traded from Detroit to Washington was typical of his bizarre outlook on life. "You know, I'm glad I'm not a building," he said as he strolled down the street with a bartender friend. "It would be awfully hard on you moving from town to town."

After the Redskins finally gave up on Looney following the 1967 season, Joe Don spent nearly a year in Vietnam before giving pro football one last fling with the New Orleans Saints. But a knee injury sidelined him and he soon quit the game for good. Retiring to his Texas ranch, he gave that up too because he decided it would be nice to go to India. And by 1976, that was where he was, about forty miles outside Bombay, helping the natives develop their agricultural skills. Hopefully, that's where he found a measure of inner contentment. If not, he could always go back to sleeping in cemeteries.

14. Then there was the case of the missing Preaknesses.

Inaugurated in 1873, the prestigious stakes race for three-year-old horses was run on a regular basis through 1889, when it suddenly disappeared from the record books until 1909. Most people assumed that the nineteen-year hiatus was brought about by a series of problems involving the Maryland Jockey Club and Pimlico Race Track, that the events had simply been canceled.

Not true. During the midtwentieth century, a researcher going through the records of Gravesend Race Track in Brooklyn—long since made into a housing development by then—discovered that the Preakness Stakes was actually held there during the years 1894 through 1908, the year before returning to its native Pimlico.

That left four Preaknesses unaccounted for, which was how the situation remained until 1965, when still more research turned up the fact that the 1890 event had been run at Norris Park, New York.

Not only that. Not only was the 1890 Preakness run on June 10 of that year—so was the Belmont Stakes! The Preakness was the second race of the day, and was won by Montague before a sizable crowd of fifteen thousand. The fourth race of the same day was the Belmont Stakes, which meant that if Montague had entertained any notions about becoming a Triple Crown winner, he had about an hour to get ready for the Belmont. Suffice it to say Montague was not entered in the 1890 running of the Belmont Stakes.

15. Did an auto race change the future of the United States?

Even more specifically, is it possible that a gully on a beach in 1907 drastically influenced American foreign policy and quality of life more than a half century later?

If the question seems farfetched, consider the situation on January 25, 1907. On that date the American people were still in a state of collective indecision as to what kind of automobile was best for them. The automotive industry was still in its formative stages then, with literally thousands of models on the market—cars driven by gasoline, by steam, and by electric power. From the very outset, the limitations of the electric automobile were realized, namely short range and low power.

Advocates of steam and gasoline, however, were in much better positions as they genially, and sometimes angrily, debated the merits and demerits of their respective models.

Both types of engine had pluses and minuses. The steamer, as perfected by twin brothers F. E. and F. O. Stanley, was a quiet, smooth-running vehicle. It was also capable of extraordinary speed and greased-lightning acceleration compared to other cars of the day. On October 11, 1901, for example, at a meet held in Detroit, a white steamer hit a top speed of 30 miles per hour, which was astonishing to a large crowd. The car, not unexpectedly, was victorious in both the 5- and the 10-mile races. Thereafter, steamers won races so regularly that they were often informally banned from meets with gasoline cars despite the fact that competition was open to all automobiles in the same price range.

After establishing several speed records with their ordinary machines, the Stanley brothers designed and built a car especially for racing. Shaped like an inverted canoe, painted a garish red, and promptly dubbed "Wogglebug" by the press, the racer made history in January 1906 by speeding a mile in 28⅕ seconds, the equivalent of 127.6 mph.

In addition to being fast, the steamer was basically a very simple machine. "Our present car is composed of but thirty-two moving parts," the Stanleys pointed out in their 1916 catalogue, "which number includes front and rear wheels, steering gear, and everything moving on the car, as well as the power plant. This is about the number of parts contained in a first-class self-starter. We use no clutch, nor gear shifts, not fly wheels, nor carburetors, not magnetos, nor spark plugs, nor timers, nor distributors, nor self-starters, nor any of the marvelously ingenious complications that inventors have added in order to overcome the difficulties inherent in the internal-explosive engine and adapt it to a use for which it is not normally fitted."

What the Stanleys could have stressed even more was the nonpolluting nature of their vehicle. For not only did it refrain from befouling the atmosphere with burned hydrocarbons, it also added little or no noise to the environment. It was also capable of using fuels that were not only much cheaper than gasoline but also were more readily available—kerosene, alcohol, coal gas, and even coal.

On the other hand, operation of the steamer did cause considerable trouble for many persons, especially before the installation of a condenser that permitted the vehicle to reuse its water supply. Until that innovative development became a reality, it was necessary for steamer owners and operators to carry a hose with them in order to raid horse troughs every forty or fifty miles.

But the biggest problem facing steamer manufacturers and their sales representatives was fear itself. Americans at the turn of the century had been through three generations of steam boiler explosions on riverboats and locomotives and were extremely nervous when it came to high-pressure boiler systems. The fact that early steamers trailed a light vapor as they moved along, giving the impression that the car was already on fire or smoldering preparatory to a massive explosion, added little to public confidence.

Despite these drawbacks, by January 1907 the steamer had become a favorite of President Teddy Roosevelt, who advocated its properties openly, and progress was being made in overcoming public fears concerning safety. Few dared predict that the steamer's end was near, so close was it to winning the battle for American minds, and some even stated that it would be the vehicle of this nation's future.

Then came the international speed trials at Ormond Beach, Florida, on January 25. Expecting a new world's record, an unusually large crowd turned out to view such items as the first Rolls-Royce entered in a U.S. meet, and, of course, the new Wogglebug with ace racing driver Fred Marriott at the tiller.

Gradually warming himself and his vehicle to the task, Marriott made two runs along the mile section of beach, the first at 32⅖ seconds, the next at 29⅗, just about 1½ seconds slower than his previous best time.

For his third attempt, Marriott hit the starting line at full throttle and shot up the beach. Although running against the wind, the steamer's speed was approaching 200 mph when the accident occurred. "He was almost out of sight," one reporter wrote, "being almost at the end of the mile, when the machine upset."

At the time, no one knew exactly what happened. Those nearest the car agreed that the hood appeared to come loose "seemingly lifted by the wind, while the front wheels were so tilted upward that they did not strike the sand of the beach by several inches. . . .

The tubing broke and the car was enveloped in a cloud of steam. . . ."

By the time the crowd raced up the beach to the scene of the accident, a Rolls-Royce had arrived and Marriott had been picked up, "his face covered with blood and lying insensible across the laps of two men in the rear seat. . . . He was found well up on the beach, while the round boiler, four or five times the size of a cheese box, was rescued rolling around in the ocean. When the car broke in two it dropped the boiler as it did Marriott. . . . The debris was thrown into two piles, over which hundreds of amateur photographers hovered like seagulls and many souvenirs were carried away. . . ."

Interviewed later, the Stanleys agreed that a gully in the sandy beach caused the racer to rise, but they accepted blame for their flat-bottomed design, which contributed greatly to the steamer's becoming airborne.

Although Fred Marriott survived the accident by more than a half century, both the American public and the Stanley brothers were severely depressed by the incident. For their part, the Stanleys never again used the automobiles for racing. The public, retreating into its former shell of fear concerning steam propulsion, leaned more and more to the gasoline engine, a preference that was clearly established by the advent of World War I.

Yet who knows what might have happened if Fred Marriott's racer had not struck that uneven sand at Ormond Beach? If his run had been successful and no other accidents occurred, perhaps the United States might have adopted the steamer as its kind of car, a car relatively free of noise and air pollution as well as having no need for foreign oil. And who is to say the United States would not be a vastly different society without those three liabilities?

16. On March 16, 1937, during a basketball game between seniors and sophs at St. Peter's High School, Fairmount, Virginia, all of the players on his team except Pat McGee fouled out. The score was 32–32, with four minutes still to play.

On his own, McGee scored a goal and a foul shot, then prevented the other team from scoring, winning single-handedly, 35–32.

17. After computing that Willie Mays (the player with the longest career totally encompassed by baseball games preceded by "The Star-Spangled Banner") spent slightly more than two days of his life listening to F. S. Key's immortal but syntactically cryptic lyrics, it seems almost logical to break down the career of Babe Ruth into similar statistical

modules. Suppose, for example, that the Babe had been able to cram all of his hits, walks, strikeouts, etc., into blocks? How long would he—and his followers—have had to wait for the endless bases on balls to end? How long would the rain of homers have continued?

To arrive at an answer, it is necessary to twist the framework of Ruth's career. During 22 seasons, he came to bat 10,455 times, counting bases on balls, but this average of 475 trips to the plate per season ranged all the way from 10 (1914, his first year) to 540 (1927, his greatest season) and then back down to 72 (in 1935, the Babe's final year). In some seasons, he appeared in as few as 5 games, and in as many as 154. Thus, in order to do a statistical breakdown on his accomplishments, we must spread his appearances evenly. This can be done by imagining that Ruth appeared in 22 seasons, each of which was 154 games long, the first game being played on April 15, the last on September 25. By never missing a game and coming to bat an average of 3.08 times per contest, the Babe's career spreads neatly over the 1914–35 period.

Let us suppose that he fell on hard times at the very beginning of his career, getting his 1,330 strikeouts out of the way first. If he had done that, Ruth would have struck out his first time at bat on April 15, 1914, and continued to strike out until the last week of August 1916. (The world would have plunged from peace to war during the interim and experienced two years of trench warfare.) If, turning cagey, Ruth had then learned the strike zone and started his skein of bases on balls, he would have earned his first pass that last week in August 1916 and continued trotting to first base until the first week of May 1920. (The world, meanwhile, would have found its way out of the Great War while Russia turned to revolution and America to Prohibition.)

Finally, after more than seven years, Ruth would at last make solid contact with the ball in early May 1920. But he would continue to fly out, pop up, and ground out until mid-September 1929. He would then be well into his thirties—0 for 5,526—and wondering if it was ever going to end. (The world, that same month, would be taking its last happy breath before the stock market collapse and the onset of the Great Depression.)

But sometime shortly after the middle of September in the sixteenth season of the Babe's career, the hits would start to come. He would single until early May 1933, while Hoover gave way to FDR, then pound out doubles and triples until the second week of June 1934. He would ice the whole grand gooey cake by smashing home run after home run until the final day of the 1935 season.

If this statistical breakdown seems to indicate that the greatest hitter of all time would have had to wait an inordinately long time before experiencing the fruits of his ability, that may not be such an unreal message after all. Even the most dedicated optimist needs to be reminded occasionally that going 1 for 3 over the long haul is a lot better than most get out of life.

18. In 1958, 53-year-old Robert F. Legge, a U. S. Navy physician, swam the Panama Canal, a distance of 28½ miles, in 21 hours, 54 minutes. A boa constrictor and an iguana were the only live creatures he encountered, he said, but swells from heavy ship traffic made progress difficult at times. Upon arriving at Balboa, he was greeted by a crowd of several hundred well-wishers and a toll collector, who charged him $.72, the minimum fee for a 1-ton vessel in ballast.

19. Football, an emotional game for both player and fan, has seen many examples of "twelfth men" suddenly appearing on the field to dumfound officials, athletes, and other spectators.

One celebrated incident occurred in 1915, when Jim Thorpe was playing for Canton against Massillon. More than eight thousand fans were on hand at Canton's League Park, with many more crowded onto the field and the end zones. So thick was the crowd that the two teams decided on a special ground rule—namely, that any player crossing the goal line into the mass of fans had to emerge with the ball for the score to count.

After Thorpe drop-kicked two goals, the home team led, 6–0. For three quarters the lead held up. Then Massillon's passing game started to work, culminating in an end named Briggs catching a pass, sprinting fifteen yards to the end zone, and disappearing in the crowd. Gideon Smith, the first black player on Canton's team, rushed into the crowd in hot pursuit of Briggs and was on the verge of overtaking him when a Canton streetcar conductor knocked the ball out of the Massillon player's hands. Smith pounced on it and raced back onto the field. Canton was awarded a safety and won the game, 8–0, at which point Massillon fans poured on the field to protest the decision.

The protest continued until it was decided that an official ruling would be made later that evening, the decision to be placed in a sealed envelope and delivered to the Massillon team manager thirty minutes after midnight. A tense crowd of both Canton and Massillon supporters was on hand when the ruling was read aloud. It upheld Canton's tarnished victory.

Another famous "twelfth man" was Tommy Lewis, a member of Alabama's squad playing Rice in the 1954 Cotton Bowl. Dicky Moegle, an elusive back for Rice, was running wild during the early part of the game, Alabama being completely unable to contain him. At one point, Moegle was given the ball on his own five-yard line, squirted through the line, and darted free of his nearest pursuers. It was apparent to everyone in the crowd that he was off on a ninety-five-yard TD romp. As Moegle ran near the Alabama bench, however, the frustrated and fired-up Tommy Lewis suddenly leaped up, raced onto the field, and tackled the Rice speedster forty-two yards away from the goal line. The officials awarded the touchdown to Rice, which won the game, 28–6, and the embarrassed Lewis was treated with admiration rather than scorn. Hailed as a "great competitor," he spent the next few days opening letters and congratulatory telegrams.

Another "twelfth man" tackle that did not come to light until two days after the game was over took place in the 1949 Washington and Lee-Virginia contest. It was late in the day, with only seconds left in the game. Bob Smith, a substitute left tackle for Washington and Lee, was slowly trudging down the sideline toward the dressing room when Virginia end Ed Bessell grabbed a pass and headed for the goal line. Smith ran onto the field just in time to tackle Bessell inches short of the touchdown. Bessell fumbled the ball into the end zone and a teammate fell on it. The touchdown counted, but no one knew that Smith was an extra man until the films were processed two days later. Virginia won the game, 27–7.

Occasionally, the desire to participate has reached the stands. One instance occurred in the 1935 Princeton-Dartmouth game, which was played in a raging snowstorm. Dartmouth was being pushed around rather handily by the Tigers and obviously needed help. Late in the game, with the ball near the Dartmouth goal once again, that help came. As Princeton's quarterback called signals for the third-down play, a spectator leaped from the stands, raced across the end zone, and took a place on the Dartmouth line before the officials could stop him or the play. The Tigers, somewhat confused by it all, executed their line smash timidly and failed to score, at which point the twelfth man was led off the field.

That same year, during the Susquehanna-Pennsylvania Military College game, Susquehanna's quarterback noticed that he had twelve men in the huddle but the fact was apparently unnoticed by the officials. Rather than take a time-out, he cleverly called an end run toward the side of the field with the Susquehanna bench. The play was run, and the still-unnoticed extra man casually walked off the playing area and took his seat.

Another case of extra assistance came in a 1947 contest between Richmond and Washington and Lee. On a kick-off, Washington and Lee back Brian Bell took the ball at his six-yard line. He broke free for a moment, racing to his own forty-yard line with a single blocker in front of him. As two Richmond defenders closed in on him, a newspaper photographer shot off a flash bulb for an action picture. The sudden burst of light apparently blinded or confused the Richmond players, for they both tackled the blocker, leaving Bell free to race ninety-four yards for a touchdown. Washington and Lee subsequently awarded a monogram to the photographer as the "star" of the game.

More recently, in 1977, a sixty-five-year-old "twelfth man" named Jim Johnson turned up during a contest between East Carolina University and William and Mary at Norfolk, Virginia. With East Carolina in the lead by 17–14, William and Mary quarterback Tom Rozantz bootlegged the ball and started around his end toward the goal line.

Johnson, a former East Carolina coach, was walking up and down the sideline as the play developed. "I was wondering what I would do if the play came my way," he said later. "Then I was standing near the five and here he comes. I had to make a quick decision."

Johnson's decision was to rush onto the field and make the tackle. Just as Rozantz neared the goal line, the young man and the older man collided. "It was a good hit," Rozantz said good-naturedly. "He read the play perfectly and I never saw him coming." The quarterback's momentum carried him into the end zone, however, and Jim Johnson was led quietly from the field, muttering, "I'm getting too old for this" to himself as the crowd applauded his nerve.

The extra man who bolts from the blue does not always get off that easily, though. A case in point occurred during a 1971 game at Baltimore between the Colts and the Miami Dolphins. The teams were just breaking from their defensive and offensive huddles when a fan from Rochester named Donald W. Ennis raced onto the field and made an effort to scoop up the ball. Colt linebacker Mike Curtis, well known for his aggressive disposition while on the field, quickly threw out an arm that sent Ennis down for the count. The "twelfth man" that day ended his brief moment of glory with a bill from both the hospital and the local police.

20. During the first official baseball game played in the United States, between the "New York nine" and the Knickerbockers on June 19, 1846, a New York player named Davis was fined for swearing at the umpire. The fine was six cents.

21. The Army-Fordham football game of 1949 provided Cadet place-kicker Jack Mackmull with the opportunity to prove that he was a man of determination. After an Army touchdown, Mackmull kicked the extra point, but roughness was called, and the ball was moved back to the seventeen-yard line. Mackmull kicked again, successfully, but once again Army was penalized fifteen yards. From the thirty-nine-yard line, Mackmull booted a third time. The kick was wide, but a Fordham player was charged with an infraction. Mackmull had a fourth chance. He missed, but Fordham was offside. Mackmull's fifth attempt, from the eighteen-yard line, was good and finally counted.

22. Many star athletes have had their uniform numbers retired. The New York Yankees, for example, have retired, among others, Babe Ruth's No. 3 and Lou Gehrig's No. 4, but the Detroit Tigers have not retired the number of their greatest player, Ty Cobb.

The reason? Ty Cobb did not have a number, having broken in during the days before numbering became prevalent.

The New York Yankees used to assign uniform numbers according to the player's position in the batting order. Thus, after the great Babe left New York, outfielder George Selkirk took the field wearing No. 3 on his back. Fans protested so much that Selkirk switched numerals and soon the Yankees made Ruth's No. 3 retirement official.

In recent decades the practice of retiring a famous player's number has grown. After a touching ceremony, the uniform is immortalized (or at least the top half, pants seeming peculiarly inappropriate to immortalization) by being placed in a glass cage or otherwise displayed. Thereafter, if an athlete happened along who wanted that number, he presumably would be told, "We're sorry, but that number has been retired. It belonged to the great————. No one else may use it."

One wonders if that goes far enough, however. Suppose a young and talented player showed up at Yankee training camp with the name Henry Louis Gehrig? Wouldn't it make sense to inform him as soon as it became evident he was going to make the team that the name "Gehrig" had already been used by the Yankees, that it wouldn't be right for someone else to use it, especially someone with the Christian names Henry Louis?

In a nation that goes out of its way to honor its outstanding athletes, it seems obvious that before such a ticklish situation develops, some thought should be given to the possibility of retiring a great star's name as well as the number. It is true that a young man who comes along later might object to changing his name, or at least part of it, but in the long run that might be preferable to spending the remainder of his career as a living asterisk.

23. Is winning the only thing in football?

No doubt most fans and players agree with that Vince Lombardi dictum, but in 1951 a noble experiment was made in an effort to emphasize other aspects of the game. During a contest between Swarthmore and Haverford, the teams and fans of both sides were graded according to competitive spirit, appearance, respect for authority, and mental poise under pressure. The system was inaugurated as a result of frequent complaints of rowdyism at games, the object being to place more emphasis on self-control and good sportsmanship.

Two members of the Philadelphia Northeast Junior Chamber of Commerce, along with the regular-game officials, acted as judges, watching both players and fans and grading them accordingly. At one point in the contest Haverford fans loudly criticized the officials when they thought a bad call had been made. That was probably what cost them the "Courtesy Bowl," for Swarthmore won the complicated scoring, 45–43. Swarthmore also won on the field, 19–7.

Another game was subjected to the same experiment, on November 24, 1951, between the University of Maryland and West Virginia. Judges gave the Terp fans 45 points for "alertness and perfection," and also awarded the West Virginians 45 points for "character and will to compete."

On the field there was no tie, though, Maryland winning easily by a score of 54–7.

24. There are 336 dimples on a golf ball.

25. One of the longest times-out in football history occurred in October 1941 at Eldorado, Illinois, during a game between Eldorado and Metropolis high schools. With the home team leading, 12–0, and slightly more than two minutes to go in the first half, the lights went out. The game could not be resumed until nearly three days later, the time-out lasting 65 hours, 50 minutes. Eldorado won, 18–6.

26. On June 4, 1923, a jockey named Hayes won the first race of his career and then immediately dropped dead.

27. Those wondering how high a basketball could bounce had their question answered on April 30, 1958, when the United States Navy dropped a ball from a blimp from a height of 1,472 feet. Before the blimp took off, Commander John Hannigan of the Naval Air Reserve Training Unit at Lakehurst, New Jersey, said, "This is no frivolous stunt. Continual developments of our bombing accuracy for antisubmarine missions demand constant practice in dropping missiles with varying ballistic characteristics."

Loaded with twelve basketballs, the blimp took off, the object being to drop the "missiles" as near as possible to a ten-foot cross marked in the runway. None of the twelve came anywhere near the target, one scattering a group of photographers, others landing in the woods or sand far off the runway.

The maximum bounce, determined by Navy cameras, was twenty-two feet, nine inches.

28. There have been many fights during sporting events, but the vast majority do not happen until after the game starts. One notable exception took place on May 23, 1946, when the Brooklyn Dodgers and Chicago Cubs engaged in a free-for-all during batting practice. The brawl, which was witnessed by only a handful of fans, was precipitated by remarks left over from a fight the day before.

29. There have been, of course, many hoaxes in the world of sports. One turned up in October 1929 when authorities discovered that a certain "Salem Trade School," which everyone believed existed because it fielded a football team, was actually mythical. In fact, the school was made up by a group of husky fellows who wanted to earn some comparatively easy money. Booking games with other high-school teams around the commonwealth of Massachusetts and dividing their share of the gate among them, the men who played for the "Salem Trade School" were much in demand for a period of six years. This was probably because they usually made sure they lost, thus causing the host instant gratification.

Another hoax took place during the 1941 football season, when a team known as Plainfield State Teachers College rolled to four victories in a row. During those games, according to school press releases, fullback John Chung, a Chinese American, received special attention. Writing in the New York *Post,* Herbert Allan reported, "John Chung has accounted for fifty-seven of the ninety-eight points scored by his unbeaten and untied team in four starts. If the Jerseyans don't watch out, he may pop up in Chiang Kai-shek's offensive department one of these days."

After Plainfield scored two more victories it came out that there was no such school as Plainfield State Teachers and no Chinese American fullback named John Chung. The chief instigator of the hoax was Morris Newburger, a stockbroker at Newburger, Loeb, and Company, Wall Street, who, with a group of cronies, spent Saturday afternoons calling sportswriters and writing press releases.

30. A 1930 hockey game produced an unusual casualty when the puck lined at goalie Abie Goldberry struck a pack of matches in the young man's pocket, setting fire to his uniform. He was badly burned before players and spectators could put him out. His team also lost the Quebec junior amateur game.

31. Modern swimmers may regard the "good old days" as truly idyllic. Coney Island, for example, during the late nineteenth century evokes an image of polite, simple, and comfortable days unmarred by the crass vulgarities of later times. How pleasant it must have been before pollution, overpopulation, and neglect converted white sand and clear water to mottled minefields of thrown-away throwaways and putrid petrochemicals.

Unless, of course, the good old days at Coney Island and adjacent beaches never really existed. Is that possible?

It is. For one thing, even then there was pollution. Three miles offshore a garbage buoy was anchored. But occasionally a scow pilot would shorten his trip considerably. The results of one abbreviated journey became apparent on an August Sunday in 1886. That day a huge island of decaying vegetation appeared twenty yards offshore. "There were layers of stuff, like a big raft," a reporter wrote. "The substratum seemed to be of straw, hay, and weeds. This was cemented with mud, ashes, and sewage. . . . It carried a miscellaneous cargo . . . cut melons, decayed fruit, grease-coated barrel staves, old bottles, and an assortment of cats and dogs in various post-mortem stages. . . . The breakers came up and lapped this mass, but could not get over, under, or around it. They served, however, to push it up on the beach. . . ."

Of course, this wasn't an everyday occurrence at Coney Island. What was were the discomforts of the transportation systems, which crushed visitors together on steamers and in railroad cars and frequently left hundreds stranded at dockside.

Those who made it to Coney had to contend with the basic problem of the 1870s and 1880s swimwear. Anxiety attacks among women of all ages must have been common when they faced the prospect of donning the traditional loose flannel bathing gowns that apparently were designed to make the wearers appear as ugly as possible.

"In this respect the flannel gown was a complete success, since had Venus herself risen from the ocean arrayed in a bathing gown, she would have been mistaken for the grandmother of the gods," wrote the New York *Times*. "Nevertheless, it had one conspicuous facet. When in the water it had a way of expanding and floating to the surface, whereby the wearer was made to resemble a blue cotton umbrella. . . . For this reason it gradually fell into disrepute and is now met only on remote New England beaches where it is worn by angular schoolteachers who desire to strike terror into casual sharks."

The one-piece gown was succeeded by a blouse-and-trousers outfit, of which the *Times* wrote, "At rare intervals beauty actually triumphed over the bathing-dress and at every sea-beach legends yet survive of some miraculous woman who was beautiful in spite of flannel blouse and trousers." Less fortunate women had someone meet them at water's edge with a large shawl.

32. In 1931, the University of Tennessee football team claimed a record for near-errorless ball. During that season, Tennessee battled Vanderbilt through an entire game without drawing a penalty. Games with NYU, Alabama, and Kentucky followed, in which the Vols drew a single 5-yard penalty each. Being assessed an average of 3.75 yards a game may not be a record, but it certainly helped the Vols win three games and tie the other.

33. The slowest time for a winning racehorse was set in 1945 when during a steeplechase, Never Mind II refused a jump and his jockey gave up and returned to the paddock. Upon arriving there, he was told that all the other horses had been disqualified or fallen. So back on the track he went with Never Mind II. The total time was 11 minutes 28 seconds for the two-mile race, which is normally completed in 4 minutes.

34. Although no one can say why it seemed necessary—other than for publicity—Charles C. Peterson of St. Louis played a game of aerial billiards 4,000 feet above that city on August 16, 1930. Flying at a speed of 100 miles an hour in a Curtiss-Wright Condor airplane, he made 100 points in 28½ seconds, only 2½ seconds slower than his record time on an earthbound table.

35. It had to happen eventually, of course, that an ambidextrous pitcher would meet a switch-hitting batter, with both bound and determined to preserve the advantage. (According to baseball's rules of probability, a left-handed pitcher does better against a left-handed batter, a right-handed pitcher better against a right-handed batter.) Thus when ambidextrous Paul Richards of the Muskogee Western Association club met left-handed batting Art Wilson of Topeka on July 23, 1928, he immediately prepared to throw left-handed. Wilson quickly jumped to the right-handed side of the plate. Richards then prepared to throw right-handed, but again Wilson switched positions. This happened several times until Richards finally started a unique wind-up with both hands in the air. Wilson won the battle, however, waiting until he received a base on balls.

36. The longest count in a fight was not in the fourteen-to-sixteen-second respite given Jim Tunney against Jack Dempsey in 1927. On March 12, 1948, Marcel Cerdan sent his opponent, Lavern Roach, to the canvas with a punch that was so hard it caused Cerdan to lose his feet as well. The referee and the timekeeper were confused over whether the two fighters were legitimate knockdowns or had fallen. In the meantime, while they discussed it, Cerdan leaped to his feet and Roach remained dazed on the canvas. By the time he arose—before the official count of ten—Roach had been down more than thirty seconds. Cerdan eventually won on an eight-round knockout.

37. In 1924, the French Boxing Federation issued an official ban against fighters kissing each other at the end of bouts.

38. The 1890 postseason best-of-seven-games series between New York of the National League and St. Louis of the American Association remained tied at three games apiece. After winning their third game, the Browns spent all night celebrating and professed to being "too tuckered out" to take the field. So the final game was canceled.

39. Notre Dame Coach Knute Rockne announced in 1923 that every player on his football team would be required to take dancing lessons—"to develop a sense of rhythm essential in the timing of shift plays." Rockne also proclaimed, in 1922, that athletics could cure the "male effeminate." In an article published for *The Sportsman Magazine*, Rockne wrote: "For every woman who smokes we see the male lizard who wears complexion dope . . . for every woman who apes man in dress we

have the sissie who wears corsets or pinch-back coat . . . for every woman who drinks we have the lowest form of male degeneracy, the shimmy hound." Rockne's antidote: compulsory boxing and football for every male in America's colleges.

40. In 1865, billiard champion Louis Fox was playing John Deery for a thousand dollars at Rochester, New York, and was far in the lead when a fly suddenly landed on the cue ball and refused efforts to shoo it away without moving the ball. Fox became so unnerved that he miscued, lost the match, and rushed angrily out of the hall. Several days later his body was found floating in the river near the hall. It was assumed that he had committed suicide as a result of the unsettling incident.

41. A unique football game for charity was played on December 12, 1931, at Washington, D.C., when the University of Alabama took on three different teams for twenty minutes each. In the first "game" against George Washington, neither team scored, but against the second opponent, Catholic University, Alabama scored and won, 7–0. Showing signs of fatigue during the third match, against Georgetown, Alabama was shoved all the way back to its one-foot line, then put on a great goal-line stand, forcing Georgetown to attempt a field goal. It went beneath the crossbar, however, thus preserving Alabama's feat of not being scored on during the football triple-header.

42. Baseball trivia item: "Most games won, one club, by two bespectacled pitchers, National League"—41, Pittsburgh, 1927. Carmen P. Hill, 22; H. Lee Meadows, 19.

43. In 1908, a 58-year-old oarsman named George W. Johnson made a racing shell out of newspapers he had collected during a 1,200-mile trip from St. Augustine, Florida, to New York City. The boat was 20 feet long, 20 inches beam, 6 inches deep, had 3 inches draft, and 3 inches freeboard. It weighed 150 pounds.

44. The slowest time for the Indy 500 was in 1912 when Ralph Mulford, driving a Knox, developed clutch trouble 100 miles from the finish line. Nine cars had already finished the race and the other entrants had withdrawn, which meant that Mulford could earn tenth-prize money if he could somehow finish. Easing his car to 60 mph, he circled the track until he had only 17 laps to go, then stopped for supper. Nearly 9 hours after he started the race, Mulford chugged across the finish line and picked up the $1,200 prize money.

45. When a sports contest is postponed or canceled because of weather, it is usually the weather outdoors that causes the problem. But on January 28, 1961, a basketball game between McAdoo High School and West Hazelton, played at the McAdoo gymnasium, was called because of weather inside the arena. The problem began when someone opened a window to offset the gym's becoming overheated as a result of 600 fans jamming their way into space for 300. When the cold air from the outside met the hot air inside, the court became slick and small puddles of condensation formed, causing the players to slide all over the place. With the score West Hazelton 31, McAdoo 29, the contest was postponed until a later date.

46. On October 25, 1951, six consecutive horses listed as No. 1 on the program at Sportsman's Park, Chicago, finished first. A $2.00 parlay on the six horses would have paid $10,114.

47. Sometimes athletes go bananas.

One early example was a pedestrian named Gowan, who was representing the Salvation Army in an endurance walk at Madison Square Garden on March 19, 1891. Suddenly he burst from the track, still clad in his satin jumper and tights, and raced out of the hall, pursued by policemen. When he was brought back and locked in his hut, he proceeded to take a drink of kerosene, mistaking it for whiskey.

That same year, another athlete named Harry Martin, twenty-nine, somehow worked his way past the White House guard and burst into the dining room where President Benjamin Harrison and Mrs. Harrison were at the table with guests. Clad only in shoes, undershirt, and trousers, Martin leaped through a window as a means of gaining his entrance. But once inside, all he did was scream loudly until taken away by special officers.

48. For a while there, man-bear wrestling was rather popular in the United States.

The contests were probably by-products of public interest in Greco-Roman wrestling, which belies its name by having little similarity to classical wrestling. It was developed in France and became popular on the Continent about 1860 and in America a decade or so later, and persists in modified form as an Olympic sport. In order to score a fall, a wrestler had to throw his opponent so that his two shoulders touched the floor simultaneously. Neither tripping nor any holds below the hips were allowed; as a result, the bouts tended to be hideously long, and more often than not, boring. But if Greco-Roman was not exactly ideal for men, the style seemed made to order for bears.

That fact caught the attention of Emil Regnier, a businessman-athlete who opened a beer shop at 104 Prince Street, New York City, during the 1870s. Described by the New York *Times* as the "protean wrestler of the Western Hemisphere" and "the greatest Greco-Roman wrestler of them all, with one or two exceptions," Regnier decided to increase trade at his establishment by holding wrestling matches in a tiny adjacent building known as Athletic Hall. It was in this three hundred-seat auditorium on December 11, 1877, that bear wrestling had its debut in America.

Eager spectators began to fill the hall at 8:15 P.M. and spent half an hour smoking and talking before watching a pair of young men wrestle for another thirty minutes as a preliminary to the main event. This bout was followed by a musical interlude supplied by three Italians (a harpist and two violinists). Then Regnier, resplendent in blue trunks and white tights with medals prominently displayed, leaped upon the main platform and "flung fifty-pound weights about his head with alarming rapidity." Newspapermen described him as "comely and muscular."

A few minutes later two bears from the circus and their handlers made their way through the crowd. Upon arriving at the platform, one of the animals proceeded to sit up on its haunches while, according to one writer, "the other, a tall, brown fellow, for whom music had charms, waltzed with irresistible drollness to the tune played by the sunny Italians." Finally, the fourth participant, a wrestler named William Heyster, made his entrance. After acknowledging the cheers of the crowd, Heyster—nicknamed the "Oak of the Rhine"—prepared to square off against the larger of the two bears.

Certain precautions had been taken to protect the men. Both bears wore iron muzzles and their foreclaws had been rounded off with a file. This did not diminish their enormous strength, which soon became apparent when Heyster was unable to throw his opponent to the ground. "The bear did not understand the fun of the thing," the *Times* noted satirically. "He did not want to be thrown, but he exhibited no desire to throw his opponent." The match was therefore declared a draw.

Regnier fared much better. After considerable grappling, he managed to throw his bear, but was dragged down with it. As the crowd cheered and the sawdust from the stage filled the air, Regnier finally rolled the animal over on its back and pinned its shoulders to the platform.

A bit more than a week later, bear wrestling graduated to the respectability of the Théâtre Français. Regnier was back, of course, and according to one newspaper report, his opponent was a "most sagacious brute" named Lena who "poked her iron muzzle in his face . . . put unlawful crooks upon his legs . . . was evidently disposed to pull his hair and used every artifice within the range of her sagacity to defeat him." Despite the three-hundred-pound bear's tactics, Regnier eventually managed to secure a good grip under her forelegs, threw her to the canvas, and was declared the winner.

The second match featured a wrestler named Theobald Bauer, who happened to be Regnier's partner in the beer shop but was well known in the eastern United States as a wrestler, against a large bear known as Martin. Although introduced as "unvanquished," Martin was not a very willing fighter. Backing away all the time, he soon had Bauer "swearing audibly" in his efforts to get a grip. After many minutes Bauer finally succeeded in flinging Martin to the ground.

Lena and Regnier then went at it again, this time with a different result. Having learned something, no doubt, Lena grasped Regnier around the hips, got a crook on his leg, and brought him down with a loud thump. Despite the illegal tripping, Referee Fred Englehardt declared Lena the winner.

On Christmas Day 1877, the sport had become sufficiently popular to entice a sizable audience of "sporting gentlemen" to Central Park Garden for a series of bouts. Regnier and Lena, obviously the best of both species, were cheered as they came onto the stage. They held each other tightly for two minutes before Lena forced Regnier to the floor "on one point, with a thud." The bear then pressed its advantage, "clawed him, squeezed him, and poked . . . about his shoulders as if . . . eating the Frenchman's ears." But eventually Regnier regained his feet and won the match.

A short time later, after Regnier and Bauer had closed their saloon, Referee-entrepreneur Englehardt formed a troupe, which consisted of Lena, Martin, and a third bear named Marian, to tour the States and promote the sport. At first all went well. Then Lena, perhaps smarting at the string of losses to Regnier, grabbed another wrestler named Jean Francis Borne and squeezed him until he nearly collapsed. Borne was taken to New York Hospital, where an examination showed internal injuries. On April 14, 1878, Borne died, and bear wrestling went into a severe decline. New York Deputy Coroner Miller may have tried to save the sport by reporting after the autopsy that Borne's system was "in a very bad condition, caused by fast living, and that he was also suffering from pyaemia as a result of a disease contracted in his youth," but according to legend the real cause of Borne's demise was Lena's revenge, and so far it has lasted a hundred years.

49. It is hardly unusual for a major league baseball player to have his name emblazoned on the back of his uniform, but only one man has the date of his birth as well. That player is Carlos May, whose number is 17 and who was born on May 17.

50. When Johnny Vander Meer broke into semi-professional baseball, he pitched on a fee-per-inning basis. For every three batters retired, he received $.30.

CHAPTER 48—1971-77

1971

Winners: Baseball: Baltimore wins its third straight American League pennant by defeating the Oakland A's, then meets Pittsburgh Pirates, who beat San Francisco for NL crown. Pirates then become only the sixth team in World Series history to win after dropping the first two games. Decisive seventh game is won by Roberto Clemente home run. . . . *Kentucky Derby:* Canonero II . . . *Preakness:* Canonero II . . . *Belmont Stakes:* Pass Catcher . . . *Indy 500:* Al Unser . . . *Boxing:* In heavyweight division, Joe Frazier defeats Muhammad Ali to retain crown. . . . In June, welterweight José Napoles knocks out Billy Backus in eighth round to regain the title. . . . Bantamweights ChuChu Castillo and Ruben Olivares fight again, Olivares winning title on 15-round decision. . . . *Golf: USGA Men's Open:* Lee Trevino. *PGA:* Jack Nicklaus. *Masters:* Charles Coody . . . *USGA Women's Open:* Joanne Carner . . . *Hockey:* 1970–71 Stanley Cup champion: Boston Bruins . . . *Football: Cotton Bowl:* Notre Dame 24, Texas 11. *Orange Bowl:* Nebraska 17, LSU 12. *Rose Bowl:* Stanford 27, Ohio State 17. *Sugar Bowl:* Tennessee 34, Air Force 13 . . . *National Football League: AFC:* Miami 21, Baltimore 0. *NFC:* Dallas 14, San Francisco 3. *Super Bowl VI:* Dallas 24, Miami 3 . . . *Basketball:* 1970–71 *NCAA:* UCLA 68, Villanova 62. 1970–71 *NIT:* North Carolina 84, Georgia Tech 66 . . . *National Basketball Association:* 1970–71 champion: Milwaukee Bucks.

Other Happenings: It is the last Opening Day for baseball in Washington, D.C., on April 5. Senators beat Oakland, 8–0, behind Dick Bosman. A crowd of 45,000 attends. . . . On February 21, Ruth Jensen wins the $60,000 Sears Women's World Classic, richest event on women's professional golf tour. . . . On August 14, the Cardinals' Bob Gibson pitches an 11–0 no-hitter against the Pirates, first no-hit game pitched at Forbes Field. Other no-hitters are hurled by Ken Holtzman of the Chicago Cubs and Rick Wise of the Phils. . . .On May 27, a team of British golfers defeats a U.S. team to give Great Britain its first Walker Cup defeat of Americans since 1938 and only second victory in the 50-year-old event. . . . On September 13, World Hockey Association is formed, to begin play in 1972. . . . Fred Steinmark, 22, defensive back on Texas' 1969 national champions, dies of cancer, and Michel Briere, 21, rookie star of the Pittsburgh Penguins of the National Hockey League, dies of injuries suffered in 1970 car accident. . . . On May 18, Hedley Woodhouse and his son, Robert, are jockeys in a daily double win at Aqueduct. . . . On April 3, hockey great Gordie Howe retires, having scored 786 goals during his career. He later unretires to play in WHA. . . . Houston Astro Cesar Cedeno hits 200-foot fly ball against Los Angeles Dodgers on September 2, scores inside-the-park home run as Jim Lefebvre and Bill Buckner collide. . . . On November 28, Hale Irwin wins the Heritage Golf Classic at Hilton Head Island, South Carolina, despite a tee shot that hits a woman on the head and then becomes lodged in her blouse. . . . Playing a doubleheader against the Yankees on September 7, the Boston Red Sox start nine different players in each game but lose both. . . . Harness racing driver Hervé Filion rides more than 500 winners in single year. . . . Jackie Stewart is world champion auto-racing driver for second time. . . . Tennis star Rod Laver picks up record earnings of $292,717. . . . On March 12, an airline stewardess sues Boston Red Sox third baseman Rico Petrocelli because he grabbed her during flight. . . . Super Bowl contest in 1971 is unique in that Chuck Howley, linebacker for Dallas Cowboys, is selected as Most Valuable Player. It is the first time since 1958 that a member of the losing team is picked in final championship game. . . . Fans complain about NFL playoff games scheduled for Christmas, but to no avail, of course. . . . North American Soccer League, still struggling, adds franchises in New York, Montreal, and Toronto, but Kansas City drops out. . . . In tidy 9–4 win over the California Angels on September 17, each of the nine Chicago White Sox players knocks in one run.

1972

Winners: Baseball: Cincinnati Reds defeat Pittsburgh Pirates for National League pennant, and Oakland A's take Detroit for American. Then in thrilling seven-game series, A's win first World Series since 1930, when the franchise was in Philadelphia. . . . *Kentucky Derby:* Riva Ridge. *Preakness:* Bee Bee Bee. *Belmont Stakes:* Riva Ridge . . . *Indy 500:* Mark Donohue . . . *Boxing:* In light-heavyweight division, Bob Fostor KOs V. Rondon in second round to become champion. . . . Carlos Monzon, middleweight champ, is voted Boxer of the Year. . . . Lightweight division has three claimants for World Boxing Association version of title: Ruben Duran, Mando Ramos (World Boxing Council champion), and Ken Buchanan. On June 26, Duran scores 13-round KO over Buchanan. . . . In featherweight division, Clemente Sanchez knocks out Kuniaki Shibata on May 19 to become champion. Sanchez is then defeated on 10-round KO by José Legra, who is recognized by WBC as champion. WBA champion is Ernesto Marcel. . . . On March 19, Rafael Herrera knocks out Ruben Olivares in 8 rounds to become bantamweight champion, then is defeated by Enrique Pinder on July 30. . . . Recognized champions in flyweight class are Masao Ohba (by WBA) and Venice Borkorsor (by WBC). . . . *Golf:* USGA Men's Open: Jack Nicklaus. *PGA:* Gary Player. *Masters:* Jack Nicklaus. *USGA Women's Open:* Susan Berning . . . *Hockey:* 1971–72 NHL champion: Boston Bruins. . . . *Football: Cotton Bowl:* Penn State 30, Texas 6. *Orange Bowl:* Nebraska 38, Alabama 6. *Rose Bowl:* Stanford 13, Michigan 12. *Sugar Bowl:* Oklahoma 40, Auburn 22 . . . *National Football League: AFC:* Miami 21, Pittsburgh 17. *NFC:* Washington 26, Dallas 3. *Super Bowl* VII: Miami 14, Washington 7 . . . *Basketball:* 1971–72 *NCAA:* UCLA 81, Florida State 76. 1971–72 *NIT:* Maryland 100, Niagara 69 . . . *National Basketball Association:* 1971–72 champion: Los Angeles Lakers.

Other Happenings: On February 16, Wilt Chamberlain of the Los Angeles Lakers becomes the first NBA player to score 30,000 points. His total is 30,003 following a game against Phoenix Suns, his 940th regular-season contest. . . . For first time, there is no regular opening to the baseball season, baseball's players on April 6 starting a strike that is to last 9 days. . . . Boston Marathon features first woman, Mrs. Nina Kuscik, who finishes ahead of 800 male runners and is only one of 9 women to break the tape. . . . Bobby Hull of NHL scores his 600th goal on March 25, becoming only second player in hockey history

to reach that mark. . . . On August 1, Nate Colbert of San Diego becomes one-man gang, batting in 13 runs with 5 home runs and 2 singles as Padres defeat Atlanta in doubleheader, 9–0 and 11–7. . . . Roberto Clemente hits a double in the 4th inning of a game against the Mets on September 30, his 3000th career hit. It is to be his last, for he is killed in a plane crash on the last day of the year 1972. . . . On December 16, the Miami Dolphins defeat the Baltimore Colts, 16–0, to become the first team in National Football League history to be undefeated and untied in a 14-game regular-season schedule. . . . On October 3, while pitching for Baltimore in the second game of a double-header vs. Cleveland, pitcher Roric Harrison connects for a home run off the Indians' Ray Lamb, helping Orioles to 4–3 victory. The home run is last hit by a pitcher in the American League. (The designated hitter rule goes into effect in 1973.) . . . Baseball season features three no-hitters, all in National League. Burt Hooten of Cubs beats Cincinnati, 1–0, on June 3; Milt Pappas, also of Cubs, silences San Diego, 8–0, on September 2; and Montreal's Bill Stoneman beats Mets, 7–0, on October 2. . . . Jim Barr of San Francisco retires 41 batters in a row while pitching consecutive shutouts, breaking previous record of 38 set by Harvey Haddix in 1959. . . . On August 7, a baseball game at Midland, Texas, is called on account of grasshoppers, literally millions of them suddenly appearing between games of a doubleheader. . . . In October, Baltimore Colt defensive back Jim Duncan, 26, commits suicide. . . . On July 26 there is a new major-league first when Bill Haller is scheduled as umpire behind plate while brother Tom catches for Detroit Tigers. . . . Another first in basketball takes place when Bob Douglas, owner and coach of the Renaissance Five, is first black honored for individual achievements off the court to be elected to Basketball Hall of Fame. . . . In New York a service known as "phone time" is created to provide sports fans with scores on a 24-hour basis.

1973

Winners: Baseball: Oakland A's repeat as American League champions by defeating Baltimore, and New York Mets beat Cincinnati Reds for NL title. For 3rd consecutive year, World Series goes to final game, Oakland winning on home runs by Reggie Jackson and Bert Campaneris. . . . *Kentucky Derby:* Secretariat. *Preakness:* Secretariat. *Bel-*

mont Stakes: Secretariat. (Secretariat is first Triple Crown winner since Citation in 1948.) . . . *Indy 500:* Gordon Johncock . . . *Boxing:* In heavyweight division, George Foreman knocks out Joe Frazier in 2nd round to become champion. In featherweight class, Eder Jofre scores 15-round decision over José Legra and wins WBC recognition as champion. Ernesto Marcel is still recognized by WBA. Romero Anaya knocks out Enrique Pinder in 3rd round to become bantamweight champion, then is KO'd in 13 by Arnold Taylor later in year. . . . Flyweight champion recognized by WBA, Masao Ohba, is killed in car accident on January 25. His crown is taken by Chartchai Chionoi, who defeats S. Hanagata on October 27. Venice Borkorsor retains WBC title. . . . *Golf: USGA Men's Open:* Johnny Miller. *PGA:* Jack Nicklaus. *Masters:* Tommy Aaron. *USGA Women's Open:* Susan Berning . . . *Hockey:* 1972–73 NHL Stanley Cup winner: Montreal Canadiens. *World Hockey Association:* New England Whalers . . . *Football: Cotton Bowl:* Texas 17, Alabama 13. *Orange Bowl:* Nebraska 40, Notre Dame 6. *Rose Bowl:* USC 42, Ohio State 17 . . . *National Football League: AFC:* Miami 27, Oakland 10. *NFC:* Minnesota 27, Dallas 10. *Super Bowl VIII:* Miami 24, Minnesota 7 . . . *Basketball:* 1972–73 *NCAA:* UCLA 87, Memphis State 66. 1972–73 *NIT:* Virginia Tech 92, Notre Dame 91 . . . *National Basketball Association:* New York Knickerbockers. *American Basketball Association:* Indiana Pacers.

Other Happenings: In surprise for boxing world, Ken Norton defeats Muhammad Ali in a 12-round split decision, breaking the former champion's jaw in the process. . . . Ron Blomberg of the New York Yankees becomes baseball's first official designated hitter. With the bases loaded in a game against the Red Sox, he draws a base on balls, but Boston wins, 15–5. . . . On October 27, Alabama's football team sets a total-offense record of 828 yards, defeating Virginia Tech, 77–6, at Tuscaloosa. Mark surpasses old NCAA offense of 789 yards, set by Davidson against Vanderbilt in 1969. . . . On May 15 and July 15, California Angel pitcher Nolan Ryan pitches no-hitters against Kansas City and Detroit, only the 5th time a pitcher has thrown two no-hitters in a single season. Others are Johnny Vander Meer, Allie Reynolds, Virgil Trucks, and Jim Maloney. Other no-hitters during 1973 season are thrown by Steve Busby of Kansas City, Jim Bibby of Texas, and Phil Niekro of Atlanta Braves. . . . On December 16, O. J. Simpson becomes the 1st 2,000-yard rusher in NFL history, breaking Jim Brown's 1963 mark of 1,863. . . . By riding his 500th,

501st, 502nd, and 503rd winners of the year on December 15 at Laurel, Maryland, jockey Sandy Hawley becomes first to bring home more than 500 in a year. . . . On June 19, Pete Rose of Reds and Willie Davis of Dodgers both collect their 2,000th career hit. . . . On August 29, Nolan Ryan of Angels loses potential third no-hitter in season when two infielders call for Thurman Munson's pop fly and let ball drop between them. Angels defeat Yankees, 5–0. . . . On November 4, the Chicago Bears hold the Green Bay Packers to minus 12 yards passing and win 21–0 in NFL game. . . . In North American Soccer League, Philadelphia Atoms become new franchise and become immediate success. Atoms are first club to have an American head coach, Al Miller, win the championship. . . . By winning the Walt Disney Open, golfer Jack Nicklaus becomes the first player in history to win more than $2 million in his career. . . . On January 26, Diane Werley, 26, who has sights set on becoming top professional woman jockey, slips and falls in bathtub at her home and is killed. . . . Kathy Whitworth, winner of 7 events during the year, is top woman golfer with earnings of $82,864. . . . On July 3, brothers Jim Perry of Detroit and Gaylord Perry of Cleveland face each other for first time as opposing pitchers. Neither finishes the game but Gaylord is charged with the 5–4 loss.

1974

Winners: Baseball: Oakland's A's again beat Baltimore in playoff to take American League pennant while Los Angeles Dodgers triumph over Pittsburgh. World Series goes only 5 games, Oakland easily handling the Dodgers, who win only the second game. . . . *Kentucky Derby:* Cannonade. *Preakness:* Little Current. *Belmont Stakes:* Little Current . . . *Indy 500:* Johnny Rutherford. *Boxing:* By knocking out George Foreman in eighth round in Zaire, Muhammad Ali becomes second ex-heavyweight champion to regain title. Lightheavyweight champion Bob Foster retires after 14 successful defenses of his crown, citing WBA-WBC problems. John Conteh wins 15-round decision over Jorge Ahumada for WBC recognition, Victor Galindez taking WBA version via 13-round TKO of Len Hutchins. . . . In lightweight division, Roberto Duran retains WBA version of title while Suzuki Ishimatsu KOs Rodolfo Gonzalez in eighth round to earn WBC recognition. WBC withdraws recognition of featherweight champion Eder Jofre for refusing to defend his crown. Bobby Chacon KOs Alfredo Marcano in thirteenth round to fill vacancy, and Alexis Arguello defeats Ruben Olivares for WBA recognition. In bantamweight class, Soon Hwan wins decision from Arnold Taylor to win title. Flyweight Chartchai Chionoi retains WBA title, while Shoji Oguma wins decision from Betulio Gonzales for WBC recognition. . . . *Golf: USGA Men's Open:* Hale Irwin. *PGA:* Lee Trevino. *Masters:* Gary Player. *USGA Women's Open:* Sandra Haynie . . . *Hockey: 1973–74 NHL* champion: Philadelphia Flyers. *WHA:* Houston Aeros . . . *Football: Cotton Bowl:* Nebraska 19, Texas 3. *Orange Bowl:* Penn State 16, LSU 9. *Rose Bowl:* Ohio State 42, USC 21. *Sugar Bowl:* Notre Dame 24, Alabama 23 . . . *National Football League: AFC:* Pittsburgh 24, Oakland 13. *NFC:* Minnesota 14, Los Angeles 10. *Super Bowl IX:* Pittsburgh 16, Minnesota 6 . . . *Basketball: 1973–74 NCAA:* North Carolina State 76, Marquette 64. *1973–74 NIT:* Purdue 87, Utah 81 . . . *National Basketball Association: 1973–74* champ: Boston Celtics. *American Basketball Association:* New York Nets.

Other Happenings: In earliest opening in major-league history, April 4, Cincinnati Reds defeat Atlanta, 7–6, in 11 innings at Riverfront Stadium. Highlight of game is Henry Aaron's home run No. 714, off Jack Billingham. . . . Skippered by Ted Hood, the U.S. entry *Courageous* wins twenty-second defense of America's Cup yachting classic, 4–0, over Australia's *Southern Cross.* . . . In September, Colonial Charm sets world record for trotting mares (1:56⅗) while winning Transylvania Stakes at Red Mile Race Track, Lexington, Kentucky. . . . Roosevelt Raceway, meanwhile, prohibits brothers or father and son from riding in same race. . . . After attacking Referee Malcolm Ashford and inflicting him with broken nose on February 20, Connie Forey of Western Hockey League's Denver Spurs is fined $10,000, heaviest penalty in history of professional hockey. He is also suspended for remainder of 1973–74 season and all of 1974–75. . . . For first time since 1966, there are no no-hitters pitched in National League, but American League features three, by Kansas City's Steve Busby, Cleveland's Dick Bosman, and California's Nolan Ryan. . . . On January 13, WBC lightweight bout between Rodolfo Gonzales and Ishimatsu Suzuki is postponed when Gonzales is stung by a spider. . . . Professional hockey mourns loss of Tim Horton, 44, the oldest regular in NHL history, who is killed in an auto accident, and Wayne Maki, 28, wing for the Black Hawks, Blues and Canucks, who dies of a brain tumor. . . . On December 14, NHL game between the St. Louis Blues and the New York Rangers produces a record 246 penalty minutes. During the third period 180 are issued, which leaves a total of only 8 players available to finish the game, which is won by the Blues, 6–2. . . . During 1974 baseball season, Lou Brock steals 118 bases, shattering Maury Wills' mark of 104 set in 1962. . . . Year reveals growing prominence of women in U.S. sports. Some winners include Jean Balukas, 15-year-old native of Brooklyn who wins U.S. pocket billiards championship for second year in a row; Leah Poulos of Illinois, world champion spring speed skater; and Chris Evert of Fort Lauderdale, Florida, winner of Wimbledon's women's tennis title.

1975

Winners: Baseball: The Boston Red Sox bring Oakland's quest for fourth consecutive World Series victory to sudden halt by defeating A's in playoff. Cincinnati, winner over Pittsburgh in National League, then goes on to beat Boston in Series, 4 games to 3. . . . *Kentucky Derby:* Foolish Pleasure. *Preakness:* Master Derby. *Belmont Stakes:* Avatar . . . *Indy 500:* Bobby Unser is declared winner at 435-mile mark, race being halted because of a downpour. . . . *Boxing:* Muhammad Ali defends heavyweight title by defeating Chuck Wepner, Ron Lyle, Joe Bugner, and Joe Frazier on 14-round TKO. . . . In welterweight division, John Stracey defeats José Napoles in sixth for WBC share of title. Angel Espada wins WBA recognition by taking 15-round decision from Clyde Gray. Ruben Olivares wins WBC nod as featherweight champ by knocking out Bobby Chacon in 2 rounds, then loses decision to David Kotey of Ghana. . . . In bantamweight class, Alfonso Zamora KOs Soon Hwan in fourth round to become new WBA champ. Flyweight Miguel Canto takes decision from Shoji Oguma for WBC recognition as champion while Erbito Salavarria earns WBA share with decision over Susuma Hanagata. . . . *Golf: USGA Men's Open:* John Mahaffey. *PGA:* Jack Nicklaus. *Masters:* Jack Nicklaus. *USGA Women's Open:* Sandra Palmer . . . *Hockey: 1974–75 NHL:* Philadelphia Flyers. *WHA:* Houston Aeros. . . . *Football: Cotton Bowl:* Penn State 41, Baylor 20. *Orange Bowl:* Notre Dame 13, Alabama 11. *Rose Bowl:* USC 18, Ohio State 17. *Sugar Bowl X:* Nebraska 13, Florida 10 . . . *National Football League: AFC:* Pittsburgh 16. Oakland 10: *NFC:* Dallas 37, Los Angeles 7. *Super Bowl X:* Pittsburgh 21, Dallas 17 . . . *Basketball: 1974–75*

NCAA: UCLA 92, Kentucky 85. *NIT:* Princeton 80, Providence 69 . . . *National Basketball Association:* 1974–75 champ: Golden State Warriors. *American Basketball Association:* Kentucky Colonels.

Other Happenings: On April 8, Frank Robinson makes debut as first black manager in major-league baseball. As designated hitter for Indians, he hits home run in first at-bat and Cleveland goes on to beat Yankees, 5–3. . . . In world of soccer, Pélé unretires to play the New York Cosmos and provide great boost for sport in the United States. . . . On June 1, California Angels' Nolan Ryan pitches the fourth no-hitter of his career and also his hundredth victory, a 1–0 whitewash of Orioles. On September 28, Vida Blue pitches 5 innings of hitless ball for Oakland against Angels, then is followed on the mound by Glen Abbott, Paul Lindblad, and Rollie Fingers, who also deny Angels a hit in A's 5–0 win. . . . In National League, Ed Halicki of Giants no-hits Mets, 6–0, on August 24. . . . Chris Evert wins U. S. Open tennis title and total of $362,227 in prize money, and Billie Jean King wins her sixth singles crown at Wimbledon. . . . Jean Balukas retains her U.S. pocket billiards title. . . . On September 16, the Pittsburgh Pirates annihilate the Chicago Cubs, 22–0, the most one-sided shutout since 1900. . . . Death claims 29-year-old Houston Astro pitcher Don Wilson, who dies of carbon monoxide inhalation. Alvaro Pinedo, also 29, is killed when his mount rears and throws him against the rail at Santa Anita. . . . Gary Sanders, 25, touring golf professional, dies of a massive cerebral hemorrhage. . . . On July 21, Joe Torre of New York Mets grounds into 4 double plays in a 6–2 loss to the Houston Astros.

1976

Winners: Baseball: Cincinnati Reds defeat Philadelphia Phillies in National League playoff and New York Yankees beat Kansas City Royals for American League pennant. Reds then proceed to destroy Yankees in World Series, 4 games to 0. . . . *Kentucky Derby:* Bold Forbes. *Preakness:* Elocutionist. *Belmont Stakes:* Bold Forbes . . . *Indy 500:* Johnny Rutherford is declared winner after 255 miles, the race being halted by rain for second year in a row. . . . *Boxing:* In heavyweight division, Muhammad Ali announces yearly retirement but finishes 1976 with Jean-Pierre Coopman, Richard Dunn, and Ken Norton as his victims. . . . Welterweight Carlos Palomino TKOs John Stracey in 12 rounds to become WBC champ. José Napoles

retires, and José Cuevas defeats Angel Espada on 2-round TKO to earn WBA recognition. . . . In flyweight division, Alfonso Lopez wins WBA recognition by defeating Erbito Salavarria on 15-round TKO. . . . *Golf: USGA Men's Open:* Jerry Pate. *PGA:* Dave Stockton. *Masters:* Ray Floyd. *USGA Women's Open:* Joanne Carner . . . *Hockey:* 1975–76 *NHL* champ: Montreal Canadiens . . . *WHA:* Winnipeg Jets . . . *Football: Cotton Bowl:* Arkansas 31, Georgia 10. *Orange Bowl:* Oklahoma 14, Michigan 6. *Rose Bowl:* UCLA 23, Ohio State 10. *Sugar Bowl:* Alabama 13, Penn State 6 . . . *National Football League: AFC:* Oakland 24, Pittsburgh 7. *NFC:* Minnesota 24, Los Angeles 13. *Super Bowl XI:* Oakland 32, Minnesota 14 . . . *Basketball:* 1975–76 *NCAA:* Indiana 86, Michigan 68. *NIT:* Kentucky 71, North Carolina-Charlotte 67 . . . *National Basketball Association:* 1975–76 champ: Boston Celtics. *American Basketball Association:* New York Nets.

Other Happenings: On June 18, National Basketball Association and ABA agree to merge for 1976–77 season. The Denver Nuggets, Indiana Pacers, New York Nets, and San Antonio Spurs become part of the new expanded NBA. . . . During Stanley Cup playoffs, Guy Lafleur of Canadiens is put under police guard because of kidnap plot. . . . Pélé is voted Most Valuable Player of North American Soccer League. . . . John Havlicek of Boston Celtics sets NBA record by scoring more than 1,000 points for 14 consecutive years. . . . Rebuilt Yankee Stadium opens April 16. Priced at $24 million when reconstruction started, the final price tag is $70 million. . . . Janet Guthrie is first woman driver to enter Indy 500. She is approved by U. S. Auto Club and makes debut on track, but is forced out by mechanical difficulties. . . . Charlie Finley makes sensational baseball deals by selling Vida Blue to Yankees for $1.5 million and Rollie Fingers and Joe Rudi to Red Sox for $1 million each, but Commissioner Bowie Kuhn nullifies deals. . . . On October 22, the New York Nets sell "Dr. J.," Julius Erving, to the Philadelphia 76ers. . . . Jim Palmer becomes first American League pitcher to win Cy Young Award three times. On August 10, John Candelaria of Pittsburgh Pirates hurls 2–0 no-hit victory over Los Angeles Dodgers. Other no-hitters are pitched by Larry Dierker, who leads Houston to 6–0 defeat of Montreal Expos; by John Montefusco of San Francisco Giants; and by Blue Moon Odom and John Barrios, who combine to win 2–1 no-hitter for Chicago against Oakland A's. . . . Tragic death claims young sports figures Bob Moose of Pittsburgh Pirates, boxer Oscar Bonavena, and shortstop Danny Thompson of Minnesota Twins. . . . Only minutes after completion of AFC playoff game between Colts and Steelers at Baltimore, light plane crashes into upper deck of Memorial Stadium. . . . North American Soccer League expands to 20 teams with addition of franchises in Chicago, Hartford, Portland (Ore.), San Antonio, and Tampa Bay. . . . On November 25, Buffalo's O. J. Simpson rushes for record 273 yards against Detroit Lions.

1977

Winners: Baseball: New York Yankees, nicknamed "the millionaires," again defeat Kansas City Royals for American League pennant while Los Angeles Dodgers take Philadelphia in National. Yankees, led by slugging Reggie Jackson, who becomes only second player to hit three home runs in World Series game, roll over Dodgers, 4 games to 2. . . . *Kentucky Derby:* Seattle Slew. *Preakness:* Seattle Slew. *Belmont Stakes:* Seattle Slew (first undefeated Triple Crown winner) . . . *Indy 500:* A. J. Foyt, first racing driver to win race four times . . . *Boxing:* In light-heavyweight division, Miguel Cuello knocks out Jesse Burnett in ninth round to win vacant WBC title. . . . *Golf: USGA Men's Open:* Hubert Green. *PGA:* Lanny Wadkins. *Masters:* Tom Watson . . . *USGA Women's Open:* Hollis Stacy, 23, youngest to win the event . . . *Hockey: NHL champion:* Montreal Canadiens . . . *WHA:* Quebec Nordiques . . . *Football: Cotton Bowl:* Houston 30, Maryland 21. *Orange Bowl:* Ohio State 27, Colorado 10. *Rose Bowl:* USC 14, Michigan 6. *Sugar Bowl:* Pittsburgh 27, Georgia 3 . . . *National Football League: AFC:* Denver 20, Oakland 17. *NFC:* Dallas 23, Minnesota 6. *Super Bowl XII:* Dallas 27, Denver 10. *Basketball:* 1976–77 *NCAA:* Marquette 67, North Carolina 59. 1976–77 *NIT:* St. Bonaventure 94, Houston 91 . . . *National Basketball Association:* 1976–77 champ: Portland Trail Blazers.
Other Happenings: On January 4, Chicago White Sox hire Mary Shane as TV play-by-play announcer, the first woman in major-league baseball. . . . *Sport* magazine names "Dr. J.," Julius Erving, Athlete of the Year. . . . Ken Stabler, quarterback of Oakland Raiders, wins Hickok Award. . . . On

January 24, American League owners meet to discuss proposal to split baseball circuit into three divisions, but of course no decision is made. . . . Adelphi University cancels basketball games following mysterious death of player Marshall Williams. . . . America's Cup is successfully defended for twenty-third consecutive time, the U.S. ship *Courageous* defeating *Australia*, 4–0. . . . On October 16, Buffalo running back O. J. Simpson gains 138 yards against Atlanta to push his career mark to 10,062, only 2,250 yards behind Jim Brown. The next month, however, Simpson's single-game mark of 273 yards is eclipsed by Walter Payton of Chicago Bears, who gains 275. . . . For the third consecutive year, Earl Anthony is selected as Bowler of the Year by the Bowling Writers of America. . . . In his first professional fight, Olympic champion Howard Davis defeats Joe Resto. . . . Bing Crosby golf tournament features first women entrants since Babe Didrikson competed in 1939. . . . Derek Sanderson, former terror of National Hockey League now with Kansas City Blues of Central Hockey League, writes article on his life as a minor-leaguer. . . . Scandal develops when it is revealed that many athletes are taking bee pollen as a food supplement. . . . In soccer world, the St. Louis Stars are moved for the fourth time in 5 years. . . . Another bit of unfortunate news is revelation that New York Yankees did not vote World Series share of money for their batboys after '76 Series. Concerning bats, a 101-foot steel bat created by sculptor Claes Oldenburg is commissioned to stand in front of Social Security Administration Building in Chicago as monument to U.S. sports. . . . Fidel Castro invites the New York Yankees to play exhibitions in Cuba. . . . The New York Jets finally give up on single-miracle man Joe Namath, after waiting 8 years for him to produce encore to Super Bowl III, placing him on waivers. . . . New York Mets also banish a local hero, trading pitcher Tom Seaver to Cincinnati for 4 players. . . . Danny Frisella, a relief pitcher for the Mets, dies in a dune buggy accident on January 3. The following month, former University of California quarterback Joe Roth, 21, succumbs to cancer. . . . Charlie Finley trades Paul Lindblad to Rangers for $400,000. . . . No-hitters are pitched by Dennis Eckersley of Indians, Jim Colborn of Kansas City Royals, and Bert Blyleven of Texas Rangers.

Index